Visions for Change

Crime and Justice
in the Twenty-First Century

FIFTH EDITION

ROSLYN MURASKIN
and
ALBERT R. ROBERTS

PEARSON

Prentice
Hall

Upper Saddle River, New Jersey 07458

Library of Congress Cataloging-in-Publication Data

Muraskin, Roslyn.
 Visions for change : crime and justice in the twenty-first century / Roslyn Muraskin and Albert R.
 Roberts.— 5th ed.
  p. cm.
 Includes bibliographical references and index.
 ISBN-13: 978-0-13-613939-3
 ISBN-10: 0-13-613939-6
  1. Criminal justice, Administration of—United States—Forecasting. 2. Crime forecasting—United States.
 I. Roberts, Albert R. II. Title.

HV9950.M87 2009
364.973—dc22

                                                                                    2008007795

Vice President and Executive Publisher: Vernon Anthony
Senior Acquisitions Editor: Tim Peyton
Editorial Assistant: Alicia Kelly
Director of Marketing: David Gesell
Marketing Manager: Adam Kloza
Marketing Coordinator: Alicia Dysert
Production Manager: Kathy Sleys
Creative Director: Jayne Conte
Cover Design: Studio Indigo
Cover Illustration/Photo: SuperStock/Photodisc
Full-Service Project Management/Composition: Chitra Ganesan/GGS Book Services
Printer/Binder: R.R. Donnelley & Sons, Inc.

Credits and acknowledgments borrowed from other sources and reproduced, with permission, in this
textbook appear on appropriate page within text.

Pearson Education Ltd., London
Pearson Education Singapore, Pte. Ltd
Pearson Education Canada, Inc.
Pearson Education–Japan
Pearson Education Australia PTY, Limited

Pearson Education North Asia, Ltd., Hong Kong
Pearson Educación de Mexico, S.A. de C.V.
Pearson Education Malaysia, Pte. Ltd.
Pearson Education Upper Saddle River, New Jersey

10 9 8 7 6 5 4 3 2 1
    ISBN-(10):   0-13-613939-6
    ISBN-(13): 978-0-13-613939-3

Dedications

Dedicated to all my children and grandchildren: Seth/Stacy, Lindsay & Sloane: Craig/Savet, Nickia & Zachary: Tracy/Ted, Benjamin & Sydney, and to my husband, Matthew with love! And my deepest thanks to all who have contributed to this fifth edition and have made it the most complete text in the field.

Roslyn Muraskin

The fifth edition is dedicated to my wife, Beverly Jean Roberts, and our son, Herbert Seth Roberts, and all of the diligent chapter authors and their families. This comprehensive volume is a result of the united efforts of our prominent chapter team.

Albert R. Roberts

Contents

PART II
TECHNOLOGY IN THE CRIMINAL JUSTICE SYSTEM

CHAPTER 11
The Past, Present and Future of Waivers in Juvenile Courts   188
Michael P. Brown

CHAPTER 12
The Situation of Crime Victims in the Early Decades of
the Twenty-First Century   200
Andrew Karmen

CHAPTER 18
The Influence of Community in Community Policing
in the Twenty-First Century   301
Michael J. Palmiotto

CHAPTER 19
Contemporary Policewomen: A Working Typology   314
Mark Lanier and Kelly Jockin

CHAPTER 20
Current and Future Practices and Strategies for Managing
Police Corruption and Integrity   328
Vincent E. Henry and Charles V. Campisi

CHAPTER 28

Prisoner Reentry: Moving Beyond the Identification of Inmate Needs
Upon Release   529

Martha Henderson and Dena Hanley

CHAPTER 29

The Current Status of Inmates Living with HIV/AIDS   542

Mark M. Lanier and Roberto Hugh Potter

Foreword

Richard R. Bennett
Professor of Justice
American University

Criminal justice faces the continuously shifting challenge of dealing with new forms of criminal behavior based upon new technologies, the rapid shrinking of our globe, and the weakening of sovereign boundaries that once protected nations. *Visions for Change* directly addresses these issues by underscoring the need to move from our traditional responses to crime and justice to innovative approaches that mirror the rapidly changing landscape of our society and world. The overriding theme of the 37 chapters is the call for a broad and conscious movement in the criminal justice system from a reactive to a proactive stance in dealing with the twenty-first century issues in crime and criminal justice. This fifth edition includes in-depth discussions of innovation and proactiveness in the areas of technology, crime/gangs, policing, the law/prosecution, corrections, terrorism, and gender/diversity.

Rather than discuss specific contributions to this edited work, I would like to discuss five themes that run throughout the book and are important to understanding criminal justice visions for the twenty-first century. The first theme centers around what was alluded to in the first paragraph of this forward: movement from the traditional to innovative solutions and from a reactive to a proactive posture. This theme is best illustrated by the works of Hoang and Meadows (Chapter 6), Palmiotto (Chapter 18), Henry and Campisi (Chapter 20) and Nugent-Borakove and Rainville (Chapter 25). In each chapter, whether dealing with violent, cross-national gangs, community policing, police corruption, or community prosecution, the authors demonstrate that traditional means of handling these long standing issues are no longer effective and that new approaches and tools must be employed in the twenty-first century. The authors call for the development and use of new strategies, such as encouraging productive partnerships among communities, the police, and prosecutors to address crime problems, the use of computer tracking to tackle police corruption, and the enhancement of cross-national cooperation to address transnational gangs, crime, and terrorism. Based upon the substance of these sections, the call for change in the twenty-first century will require unique partnerships, new levels and types of cooperation among agencies both nationally and internationally, and the novel use of technology. However, as Welch (Chapter 33) so convincingly argues, there is a potential dark side to innovation and proactiveness which can operate to deny human rights and citizens' freedom.

The second theme that I see emerging from the book's chapters is the growing need for more basic, applied, and evaluation research to generate answers to the questions already arising in our understanding crime and criminal justice in the twenty-first century. As the editors note in Chapter 1, "Do we have all the answers? No. But we have given the problems considerable thought and hope that this fifth edition will motivate us to take that next needed step," which will involve a rigorous and far-reaching research agenda.

Several of the chapters' authors directly call for additional research while others imply that further research is needed to expand our understanding of a specific crime and justice issue. As an example, Slosarik (Chapter 9) states in the introduction to her chapter on identity theft that it " . . . establishes a literature review on which future, and much-needed research can be based." Although agreeing that the concept of community policing is here to stay, Palmiotto (Chapter 18) laments that we currently don't know if " . . . community policing is successful." He calls for both applied and evaluative research to determine whether community policing works and the best practices in the field. I also see the need for basic research on the related topic of how to build trust in segments of our society that have traditionally been leery of the motivations of the police. Benekos and Merlo (Chapter 10) present an eloquent review of the research in juvenile justice and show the reader how important both applied and evaluative research are to attacking our juvenile crime problem. Their chapter illustrates how research guides policy and how academics and practitioners alike can benefit from research into best practices. Finally, Hoang and Meadows (Chapter 6) highlight the need for evaluation research into prevention and intervention programs to stem the rise in violent predatory gang crime. In short, these authors stress the place and need for basic, applied, and evaluative research in their visions of crime and justice in the twenty-first century.

The third theme is an adjunct to the second theme: Even more so today, there is a pressing need to refocus governmental funding agencies on supporting basic, applied, and evaluation research into the causes and prevention of crime as well as the advancement of all aspects of the criminal justice system. The current federal administration has, over the past eight years, shifted research funding away from social issues to refinements in technology and hardware in the fight against crime. In addition, the funding of the "war on terror" has shifted what little research funding was originally targeted for criminal justice into intelligence gathering and analysis activities. Although none of the authors directly addressed this issue, the future research on terrorism called for by contributors such as Welch (Chapter 33) and DuPont Morales and Asthappan (Chapter 32) can only be accomplished if governmental funding agencies dramatically shift from their current emphasis on hardware to an emphasis on social science research and an understanding of how crime and terrorism can be prevented or controlled. In another funding area, Hallett (Chapter 15) argues that the shift in funding priorities has changed the face of enforcement and punishment by shifting spending from social welfare to security programs which was only intensified by the September 11 attacks and our involvement in Iraq and Afghanistan.

The fourth theme that emerges from this collection involves our criminal justice agencies' tendency to "stove pipe" information and thus inhibit the prevention, apprehension, prosecution and correction of crime, criminals and terrorists—all activities that require coordination and shared resources. This theme resonates throughout the collection but is addressed directly in the chapters by DuPont Morales and Asthappan (Chapter 32) and Hoang and Meadows (Chapter 6). The argument for addressing the lack of communication among the agencies of criminal justice has both national and transnational implications. The 9/11 Commission's report places partial blame for the terrorist attacks squarely on the shoulders of the intelligence and law enforcement communities and their refusal or inability to share critical information that might have prevented the attacks. Hoang and Meadows (Chapter 6) document the need for transnational collaboration in the fight against gang crime. Although such crime takes place on the streets of our large cities and victimizes people on American soil, the answer to its control lies not just within our borders but also across national boundaries. As crime becomes more transnational and global in the twenty-first century, so must our criminal justice efforts. To do this, there must be a sea change in the way criminal justice and intelligence agencies cooperate and exchange information. The change must take place not only in the United States at the local, state and federal levels but also transnationally.

The fifth and final theme running throughout the book is that crime and justice issues and organizations in the twenty-first century must reflect the changing values of the greater society in which they are housed. Lanier and Jockin (Chapter 19) exemplify this need in discussing the changing role of women in policing and how policing is changing to accommodate women. Hallett (Chapter 15) relates how shifts in society are mirrored in shifts in punishment. Welch (Chapter 33) shows how shifts in society's values concerning security have resulted in shifts on how we address human rights in our country. In each of the preceding examples, the justice system has adapted to the prevailing values of our society, both good and bad. The relationship between society and the criminal justice system should be no different in the twenty-first century. It is the job of the academic and practitioner to monitor social changes in our and other nations' social structures and processes so as to anticipate and meet the challenges of an ever-changing crime picture and to fashion a criminal justice system that is more adept, flexible, and responsive. Finally, and this is a proclivity of my own, we need to be more comparative in our analysis of crime and justice issues. We can increase our understanding of the challenges we are and will face in the twenty-first century if we look beyond our borders and learn from the mistakes and accomplishments in other countries.

Visions for Change assembles the works of serious scholars in various fields of study and asks them to look into the future and see how crime and justice issues might or must be addressed. I think Roslyn Muraskin and Albert Roberts have compiled a thoughtful selection of issues that will help the reader envision the challenges we will face as we move more into the twenty-first century.

Preface by Roslyn Muraskin

When we wrote the first edition of this book, it was still the twentieth century, and who could have imagined the destruction that would come about as we were attacked on our own land in 2001. Now in its fifth edition, this work examines our criminal justice system with a very critical eye. We have attempted to forecast what the future holds for our constantly changing criminal justice system. We do not present the system in a pessimistic light, but rather examine all policies and practices by linking the past with the present, and looking to the future, we present a system that demonstrates how globalization is so much an integral part of our current system. Debates continue to rage regarding the benefits of incarceration, the use of the death penalty, alternatives to incarceration, the use of forensics, the future of gangs, the rights of victims as opposed to defendants, the use of newer and better technology, the role of the police, the roles of both the defense and prosecuting attorneys, how to protect against acts of terrorism, yet still protect the rights of those incarcerated, and gender issues that are still part of the ongoing battle in criminal justice.

The rhetoric of justice and fairness is still evident. It is an accepted fact that in the field of criminal justice, the courts dispense justice. The crime challenges that face us in the twenty-first century appear to be more serious than in previous centuries because of the advanced technology that has turned our world into a global village. The dimensions of the crime scene have changed. It is vital to blend research with creativity to shape a vision for the future, a vision that moves well beyond the status quo. This fifth edition of *Visions for Change: Crime and Justice in the Twenty-First Century* is a representation of all changes reflective in this new century.

We have added many new chapters and updated all other chapters. Each chapter examines the most promising and reform-oriented policies, programs, and technological advances necessary for this new century. The text reads as a "who's who" in criminal justice. We review contemporary issues, including that of terrorism that has touched us since September 11, 2001, as well as advanced uses of technology. Technological innovation has prompted the development of new means to "capture the bad guy" while improving our system. Workforce investment has become a major economic development theme in this global world. The crises are so dire in today's world that we as a civilized nation cannot afford to simply stand by and watch. The field of law has had to adapt to the changes in this new world while reducing the rights of citizens to a certain extent. All issues, including gender and race, which continue to be a serious problem within the criminal justice system, are examined with the most up-to-date research available.

The development of juvenile justice laws has grown in the last 100 years; gangs continue to be an ever-growing population, not yet controlled; and the media continue to misrepresent the criminal justice system, forever giving us headlines meant to terrorize rather than represent the true picture. The problem of drugs continues to haunt us, and we look to alternatives in treatment. The new crime of identity theft has evolved; an identity thief needs only a social security number to decimate a victim's life and credit. Deterioration of the family and other social control institutions always a part of keeping our families together and now no longer there does not help as we examine the laws regarding obscenity and pornography. The current state of justice administration continues to pose very fundamental challenges as examined in this work.

Terrorism, a word that once was unthinkable in this country, is very much on the minds of all Americans. The war on terror began in the wake September 11, 2001; what was to be a regular working day for nearly 3,000 people has assumed a new timbre not only in our homeland but also around the world. The types of antiterrorism legislation that have been and are currently being adopted not only in our country but in nations around the world are similar to legislation that was once thought to be useful in repressive states, including the criminalization of peaceful demonstrations; security with a new focus on asylum seekers; and the detainment of individuals without a trial, reminiscent of the incarceration of Japanese Americans in concentration-like camps at the start of World War II. What of corporate security, and how are we dealing with this type of activity? The fact that we have theft of intellectual property, identity theft, and threats to our corporate world is all new to us, yet we must be prepared to act quickly. The role of the prosecuting attorney is changing to adapt to the current modes of our present criminal justice system.

Law enforcement still faces problems today. We recognize that community policing as envisioned may not be the solution we once thought. We still deal with problems of domestic violence as well as managing the corruption in our own police departments. There is a cry for organizational changes; the use of excessive force is noted in many a police department.

The death penalty still exists, although the former governor of Illinois declared the death penalty to be null and void, finding that nearly 100 persons on death row were innocent of their crimes or were not as "guilty" as believed. The prediction is that by 2050, there will no longer be a death penalty because Americans and the courts themselves will find that through the proper use of technology, not all inmates believed to be guilty will actually be found guilty. As the only Western civilization that executes its citizens, the United States will find itself once again declaring the death penalty void. The death penalty is nothing but an arbitrary discriminatory punishment against an occasional victim. It is not necessarily the guilty who suffer, but rather the friendless and poor convict.

Our civil liberties have been attacked since the start of this new century, and all relevant cases since our last edition have been added. These new cases indicate challenges to our Bill of Rights. Additionally, the passage of the U.S. Patriot Act has impacted our civil rights through denying rights originally guaranteed by our founding fathers. We compare the cyclical effect of the loss of civil liberties to the red scare and McCarthyism in the U.S. of the 1950s. Funding for representation of the indigent is slowly being eroded, leaving us with a biased system that appear to help only those who have the necessary means.

Corrections continue to pose problems in this country. According to the Bureau of Justice Studies, the U.S. prison population continues to grow in the twenty-first century despite declines in crime rates. The cost to the federal government and states is estimated at $40 billion a year. The United States incarcerates close to three million individuals in its local, state, and federal facilities. Children of incarcerated parents have become a hidden population. The cost of housing, feeding, and caring for a prison inmate is more than $30,000 a year, or minimally $40 billion nationwide. Construction of new prison facilities are about $100,000 a cell. Bells and alarms should be ringing with this cost of incarcerating the "guilty." Are there advantages to alternatives to incarceration, and how do we handle the guilty once released back into society?

The use of technology is prevalent in our twenty-first century criminal justice system. Prisons can and are being run with advanced technology, which is evident in all criminal justice organizations. During this first decade of the twenty-first century, criminal justice professionals are encountering gargantuan challenges and organizational changes. Technological and social developments as well as policy changes may hold the key to the future of our criminal justice system.

It would be great to believe that equality exists for all, including women and minorities, but that is not yet the case. We cannot at this juncture state that equality is present. Using the words of Richard Rorty, philosopher (as quoted by Catherine MacKinnon), a woman "is not yet the name of the way of being human." *Diversity* is a word used but not practiced. Discrimination exists, and there appears to be no end in sight. It is evident that men are still in power in the field of policing. Women who have had a proactive role since the start of the twentieth century are still in many instances relegated to second-class status. Diversity is so very important in this new world of ours, yet we continue to struggle with it. The issues facing our criminal justice system in the decades to come will continue to challenge our institutional effectiveness. Meaningful reforms must be implemented if we are not to fall apart.

It is vital to blend research with creativity to shape a vision for the future, a vision that moves us well beyond the status quo. When the first edition of this work was published, it was expected that positive change would take place. Each chapter examines the most promising and reform-oriented policies, programs, and technological advances necessary for this century. Rhetoric alone will not change the system; new polices and plans of action are needed to renew today's visions for tomorrow.

Tremendous thanks to Tim Peyton for having the "vision" to publish a fifth edition of this vital text. He has been there when we needed him and has shown much patience as he guided us through this awesome project. It is a pleasure to work with all the people at Prentice Hall. I would be remiss if I did not thank our editor, Chitra Ganesan who I have been working along doing all the proofing. It has made my job that much easier. Thank you. To all of our contributors, thank you for your dedication, love, and meeting all the deadlines to make this book a work of love.

To our families, thank you for sharing us with Prentice Hall.

Roslyn Muraskin, Ph.D.

REFERENCE

MACKINNON, C.A. (2001) Sex Equaltiy. New York, N.Y.: Foundation Press

About the Authors and Contributors

ABOUT THE AUTHORS/EDITORS

Roslyn Muraskin, Ph.D., is a Full Tenured Professor of Criminal Justice at the C. W. Post Campus of Long Island University. She received her doctorate in criminal justice from the Graduate Center of the City University of New York. She holds a master's degree in political science from New York University and a bachelor of arts degree from Queens College. She served as Trustee for the northeast region for the Academy of Criminal Justice Sciences (ACJS). Dr. Muraskin received the Becky Tatum Excellence Award for Outstanding Scholarship in Criminal Justice and Contributions to Women and Minorities by the *Minority and Women's Section of the Academy of Criminal Justice Sciences (2007)* as well as recognized as Outstanding Civic Leader of the Year (2007). She has been honored for her work with AIDS education by the Long Island Association for AIDS Care, and received Woman of the Year by Women on the Job as well as the Fellow Award from the Northeastern Association of Criminal Justice Sciences.

Muraskin is a past president of the Northeastern Association of Criminal Justice Sciences and past vice president of the Criminal Justice Educators of New York State. Professional organizations include the Academy of Criminal Justice Sciences, where she chairs the committee on Affirmative Action, American Society of Criminology (where she served as vice president of the Women's Division and remains an active member), American Society of Public Administration, American Academy of Political and Social Science, and she has served on the Fund for Modern Courts advisory board. These are among some of her academic and community activities.

Dr. Muraskin is the editor of the refereed journal, *A Critical Journal of Crime, Law and Society,* published quarterly by Routledge, Taylor & Francis Group, as well as the Editor of the Women's Series for Prentice Hall. To date the topics of these latter publications include "The Female Homicide Offender," "The Incarcerated Woman," and "Justice for All: Minorities and Women in Criminal Justice." Forthcoming works are "Women and White Collar Crime"and "Women and Issues of Mental Health in

Criminal Justice." She is the author/editor of *Key Correctional Issues* for Prentice Hall (2004) and is currently working on the second edition; author/editor of *It's a Crime: Women and Justice* (4th ed., Prentice Hall 2007); coauthor of *Crime and the Media: Headlines vs Reality* (Prentice Hall, 2007); and *Women and Justice: Development of International Policy* for Gordon and Breach. Dr. Muraskin has a forthcoming article in the *Encyclopedia of Criminology* entitled "Abortion and the Rights to Privacy," and has prepared three chapters for the *Encyclopedia of Women and Crime* (2008) "Rosa Parks," "Jean Harris," and "Dolree Mapp". Her article "Ethics for Correctional Officers: Corrections/Punishment–Ethical Behavior of Correctional Officers" was published in *Forum* (Illinois Law Enforcement Forum, V 2 No 3, July 2002). Other works for the Prentice Hall Women's Series include *The Incarcerated Woman: Rehabilitative Programming in Women's Prisons* and *With Justice for All: Minorities and Women in Criminal Justice; Morality and the Law* (2001), and she served as editor of *The Justice Professional*. Other publications include *Women and Justice: International Policy Implications: A Comparative Study* for Gordon and Breach as well as "Disparate Treatment in Jails: Development of a Measurement Instrument" for *The Magazine of the American Jails Association*. She is the author of many major papers, including "Accrediting Criminal Justice Programs," "The Role of Criminal Justice Education in the Twenty-First Century," "Women and the Death Penalty," "Correctional Philosophy/Changes in the Twenty-First Century," and other articles, and is often quoted in the media as an expert in women's issues and issues of criminal justice.

At Long Island University, Dr. Muraskin served as Associate Dean of the College of Management as well as Director of the School of Public Service. As Associate Dean she was involved in promotion and tenure decisions, budget planning, oversaw program and curriculum development, etc. She was elected to Faculty Council and has and does currently serve on the Committee for Promotion and Tenure having been reelected to this position for 2007–2009, and she still serves on the Honors Committee. Her current responsibilities include that of Executive Director of the Alumni Chapter for the College of Management as well as Director of the Long Island Women's Institute. She serves as the institutional representative for the American Association of University Women, as well as for the Justice Semester at American University Prior to her administrative responsibilities at the University she served as Chair of the Department of Criminal Justice. Her grant activities include funding for the Center for Drug Education, New York State Legislative Grant and a grant from the New York State Department of Corrections.

Dr. Muraskin was previously with the Vera Institute of Justice and was the Assistant Director of the Manhattan Bail Bond Project and then was appointed to the New York City Department of Probation as the head of its Bail Project.

Albert R. Roberts, **Ph.D., B.C.E.T.S., D.A.C.F.E.,** is Professor of Criminal Justice, Faculty of Arts and Sciences, Livingston College Campus at Rutgers, the State University of New Jersey in Piscataway. (He has been a tenured professor at Rutgers since 1989.) He served as Director of Faculty and Curriculum Development for the Interdisciplinary Program in Criminal Justice from 2001 to 2004 and Chair for

Administration of Justice Department from 1990 to 1993. Dr. Roberts has over 21 years administrative experience as department chairperson, program director, project director, and director of social work field placements. During the 1970s and 1980s, he taught at Indiana University, the University of New Haven, Seton Hall University, and Brooklyn College of C.U.N.Y. Dr. Roberts has 35 years of full-time university teaching experience at the undergraduate and graduate level in both criminal justice and social work. His doctorate is in Social Work from the University of Maryland School of Social Work and Community Planning (1978), with a double specialization in Advanced Criminology and Research Methods. In 2002, he was the recipient of The Richard W. Laity Academic Leadership Award of the Rutgers Council of AAUP (American Association of University Professors). In addition, Dr. Roberts was the recipient of the Teaching Excellence Award by the Sigma Alpha Kappa chapter of the National Criminal Justice Honor Society in both 1997 and 1998. He is a charter member of the Gamma Epsilon Chapter of Alpha Delta Mu National Social Work Honor Society at Indiana University (1985–present). He has over 240 publications to his credit including 36 books. Most recent books are:

- *Correctional Counseling and Treatment* (2008), Prentice Hall;
- *Battered Women and Their Families* (January, 2007), 3rd ed., Springer Publishing Company;
- *Handbook of Forensic Mental Health* (January, 2007, David W. Springer, coeditor), Springer Publishing Company;
- *Social Work in Juvenile and Criminal Justice Settings* (November, 2006), 3rd ed., David W. Springer, coeditor, Charles C. Thomas, Publisher;
- *Evidence-Based Practice Manual: Research and Outcome Measures in Health and Human Services* (2004, Kenneth R. Yeager, coeditor, Oxford University Press,)

Professor Roberts is the Editor-in-Chief of *Brief Treatment and Crisis Intervention* journal, published by Oxford University Press. He is also the Editor-in-Chief of the peer-reviewed journal *Victims and Offenders: A Journal of Evidence-Based Practice and Policies* (Routledge/Taylor & Francis). He currently serves on the editorial board of 10 different scholarly journals. Dr. Roberts is a member of The Board of Scientific and Professional Advisors, a diplomate in forensic traumatology as well as domestic violence, and a Board Certified Expert in Traumatic Stress for The American Academy of Experts in Traumatic Stress (AAETS). He serves as a member of the editorial advisory board for *Encyclopedia Americana* (2002–Present). Dr. Roberts has been the project director or principal investigator on eight different national studies including crisis intervention, suicide prevention, and victim/witness assistance. Juvenile offender treatment and domestic violence emergency services in the past 25 years.

Dr. Roberts is currently working on three books: *Victimology: Past, Present, and Future* which is coauthored by Ann W. Burgess and Cheryl Regehr (Prentice Hall); *Critical Issues in Crime and Justice* (3rd ed., nearing completion), Sage Publications; and *The Social Workers' Desk Reference* (2002; Oxford University Press, 146 original chapters), which has received three prestigious library reference awards, and the second edition is currently in preparation. Dr. Roberts is also the founder of the Crisis Intervention Network Website (2001–Present), which focuses on crisis intervention, suicide prevention, disaster mental health, domestic violence, and criminal justice: www.crisisinterventionnetwork.com

CONTRIBUTORS

JAY ALBANESE, Ph.D., is Professor in the Department of Criminal Justice at Virginia Commonwealth University.

ELIZABETH L. MAYFIELD ARNOLD, Ph.D., is Assistant Professor of Social Work at the University of North Carolina.

JIBEY A. ASTHAPPAN, M.S., is at Pennsylvania State University, Capital College.

DAVID V. BAKER, Ph.D., is Associate Professor of Sociology and Chair of the Department of Behavioral Sciences at Riverside Community College, Riverside, California.

PETER J. BENEKOS, Ph.D., is Professor of Criminal Justice and Sociology and Director of the Center for Justice and Policy Research at Mercyhurst College in Erie, Pennsylvania.

PIA BISWAS former research assistant at Rutgers and is now attending law school.

DALE J. BROOKER, Ph.D., is a faculty member at Saint Joseph's College of Maine.

MICHAEL BROWN, Ph.D., is an Associate Professor of Criminal Justice at Ball State University, Muncie, Indiana.

BRUCE BULLINGTON, Ph.D., is Professor of Criminology at Florida State University.

ANN BURGESS is a senior Lecturer at the University of Wisconsin-Madison.

CHARLES V. CAMPISI is Chief of Police of Internal Affairs for the New York Police Department.

M. A. DUPONT-MORALES, Ph.D., is Professor of Criminal Justice at the Pennsylvania State University, Capital College.

CHARLES B. FIELDS, Ph.D., is Professor and Chair of the Department of Correctional Services at Eastern Kentucky University.

ROSEMARY L. GIDO, Ph. D., is Associate Professor of Criminology at the Indiana University of Pennsylvania. She served as the Director of the Office of Program and Policy Analysis for the New York State Department of Correction.

KENNETH C. HAAS, Ph.D., is Professor in the Department of Sociology and Criminal Justice at the University of Delaware.

MICHAEL HALLET, Ph.D., is Associate Professor of Criminal Justice at the University of North Florida.

DENA HANLEY, Ph.D., is Assistant Professor at the University of Akron.

MARTHA HENDERSON, Ph.D., is a faculty member in the Department of Political Science and Criminal Justice at The Citadel.

VINCENT E. HENRY, Ph.D., is Director of the Homeland Security Program at the Long Island University Campus in Riverhead, New York.

HACO HOANG, Ph.D., is at the Faculty of California Lutheran University, in Thousand Oaks, California.

SILVINA ITUARTE, Ph.D., is Assistant Professor of Criminal Justice at the Department of Criminal Justice Administration at California State University, East Bay.

ROBERT A. JERIN, Ph.D., is Associate Professor and Chair of the Law and Justice Department at Endicott College.

KELLY JOCKIN is an associate of Mark Lanier, Ph.D., at the University of Central Florida.

JANICE JOSEPH, Ph.D., is Professor of Criminal Justice at the Richard Stockton College of New Jersey.

ANDREW KARMEN, Ph.D., is a Professor in the Sociology Department at John Jay College of Criminal Justice. He earned his doctorate from Columbia University.

DOUGLAS KING received his DDS degree from New York University and has served as Chief Dental Surgeon for a number of police and fire departments in the New York area and is a recognized expert in forensic odontology.

KAREL KURST-SWANGER, Ph.D., is an Assistant Professor in the Department of Public Justice at the State University of New York at Oswego.

MARK M. LANIER, Ph.D., is Associate Professor and Chair of the Law and Justice Department at Endicott College.

C. AARON MCNEECE, Ph.D., is Professor of Social Work and Director of the Institute for Health and Human Services Research at Florida State University.

ROBERT MEADOWS, Ph.D., is a faculty member of the Criminal Justice and Legal Studies Department at California Lutheran University in Thousand Oaks, California.

ALIDA V. MERLO, Ph.D., is Professor of Criminology at Indiana State University of Pennsylvania.

OLIVER MILLER, III, is with the Reno, Nevada Department of Police.

ETTA F. MORGAN, Ph.D., is Assistant Professor of Criminal Justice in the School of Public Affairs at the Pennsylvania State University Capital Campus.

MATTHEW MURASKIN, J.D., is the former Attorney-in-Chief of the Nassau County Legal Aid Society and is currently in private practice.

BAHIYYAH M. MUHAMMAD is a doctoral student in the School of Criminal Justice at Rutgers University, Newark, New Jersey.

M. ELAINE NUGENT-BORAKOVE is the Director of Reserach and Evaluation at the Natonal District Attorneys Assocaiton's American Prosecutor Reserach Institutue.

COLLEEN O'BRIEN is a doctoral student at Rutgers University in Newark, New Jersey.

MARTIN L. O'CONNOR, J.D., is Associate Professor of Criminal Justice at the C. W. Post Campus of Long Island University.

MICHAEL PALMIOTTO, Ph.D., is Professor of Criminal Justice in the School of Community Affairs at Wichita State University.

KENNETH J. PEAK, Ph.D., is Professor at the University of Nevada, Reno.

HARRIET POLLACK, Ph.D., is Professor Emerita of Constitutional Law at the John Jay College of Criminal Justice.

ROBERTO HUGH POTTER, Ph.D., is with the State University of West Georgia.

GERARD RAINVILLE is NDAA/APRI's Senior Associate, is chiefly interested in the application of quantitative and qualitative methods for the purposes of theory testing and the evaluation of emerging justice approaches.

SAMANTHA A. SHEEHAN is from the University of South Florida.

ROBERT SIGLER, Ph.D., is a faculty member at the University of Alabama.

KATHERINE SLOSARIK, Ph.D., is at the University of Akron, Ohio.

ALEXANDER B. SMITH, Ph.D., J.D., (deceased) was Professor Emeritus of Social Psychology at John Jay College of Criminal Justice.

DAVID W. SPRINGER, Ph.D., is Assistant Professor at the School of Social Work, the University of Texas at Austin.

MICHAEL WELCH, Ph.D., is Associate Professor of Criminal Justice at Rutgers University, New Brunswick, New Jersey

PART I

Overview

Chapter 1

The Future of Criminal Justice

Today and Tomorrow

Roslyn Muraskin, Ph.D., and Albert R. Roberts, Ph.D.

This is the fifth edition of *Visions for Change: Crime and Justice in the Twenty-First Century.* What continues to change? Terrorism and the use of technology are certainly in the forefront, and criminal justice continues to remain an integral concern of all human beings and societies worldwide. In the early years of the twenty-first century, emerging changes have been demanding more accountability while offering challenges that we never thought we would face. With the public and legislators calling for accountability and the protection of public safety, a growing number of police departments have implemented COMPSTAT—computer-aided police management systems—as well as specialized police units such as domestic violence crisis response units and driving under the influence (DUI) enforcement units. Police departments of what was once considered the future are now becoming more accountable to the community, more involved in strategic planning, more community oriented, and more technologically advanced in terms of computer management and rapid deployment systems. With more and more people being incarcerated and crime rates being lower than previously, the argument persists that it is not enough to simply lock inmates up. Instead, we must do something to reduce the likelihood that after incarceration they will continue to commit crimes. Public sentiment is divided as to whether offenders should be rehabilitated or prison sentences should be longer and more punitive. We still remain the only Western civilization that metes out long sentences and still supports capital punishment in many of our states.

Predictions and visions of the future are marked by challenges, expectations, advanced preparedness, and technological developments. During this, the first decade of the twenty-first century, criminal justice professionals are encountering enormous challenges and organizational changes. Whether or not the technologically advanced changes in criminal justice investigations and crime control will continue to significantly reduce violent crime rates remains to be seen. Technological and social developments as well as policy changes offer much promise for the future. Some of the most promising strategies include the following:

- Increased use of biosensors, lasers, and thermal neutron analysis equipment assisting investigators searching for missing persons and toxic wastes;
- Electronic tracking devices such as subdural implants, bracelets, and anklets hopefully saving states millions of dollars for home detention and electronic monitoring instead of incarceration;
- Cellular phones, electronic pendants, and geo-satellite tracking devices helping to protect chronically battered women and those in life-threatening situations;
- Increased development and use of digital technology, artificial intelligence systems, data-based court management systems, and computer-based tracking systems are being used to solve crimes of today;
- Increased development of nonlethal weapons such as laser guns, rubber bullets, and chemical sprays are being looked upon as saving thousands of lives each year;
- The use of bionic eyes and eardrums providing a major aid to police surveillance activities;
- Behavior-altering drugs implanted in the back of a sex offender or an alcoholic can be activated automatically, for example, when an offender approaches an elementary school or a tavern;
- Microprocessors implanted in persons could relay physiological reactions to a central monitoring station, which would trigger the release of a small amount of tranquilizer or a fast-acting sleep inducer as situations warrant;
- Day reporting, day fines, intensive probation supervision, and restitution could save states and counties millions of dollars while dealing with nonviolent offenders provided that each jurisdiction has an adequate accounting and monitoring staff;
- With the emergence of bioterrorism and other weapons of mass destruction, federally sponsored crime laboratories are rapidly developing vaccines and other protective measures.

TECHNOLOGY IN THE CRIMINAL JUSTICE SYSTEM

What are the crime challenges facing us in the twenty-first century? One of the most technological legal issues that causes controversy to our criminal justice system is the use of technology while attempting to reaffirm the rights of privacy. Technological devices such as the use of the retina and iris, as well as hand geometry biometrics, can all be invasive while having the ability to capture information about not only a person's health but also his or her medical history. Many of these new technological devices such as biometric scanning, finger scanning, eye scanning, hand scanning and hand geometry, and facial recognition among others are all being utilized to detect illegal drugs and concealed weapons and to prevent overall illegal activities in the correctional system.

As an example of the new technology, Australia is the first country to use smart card technology as an integral part of a prison, providing greater security, efficiency, and flexibility. What is involved from a constitutional point is the protection of the right of privacy in the United States. One of the questions to be determined is the effect that technology has on the relationship, for example, between correctional officers and inmates. The use of technology alone in the prison systems demonstrates how technology has become part of the landscape of the criminal justice system.

In our system of justice, each person is promised his "day in court." Etta Morgan in Chapter 3 "Criminal Justice and Forensic Science: Partners in Solving Crimes" writes about how the forensic scientist can provide to counsel information about cases in order to make a determination if a trial is warranted. Today we have forensic anthropologists, as well as forensic biologists who help in the identification process of defendants. Additional advances include tele-forensics and cyclovision. The admissibility of scientific evidence is having an impact in criminal cases. We have entered uncharted territory in the twenty-first century as we explore the use of different kinds of technology that enable us to identify evidence in cases.

The economy of the United States is being reshaped by a technoeconomic revolution comparable to the Industrial Revolution in terms of its impact on the definition of work, organization, and worker. The integration of information technologies in the twenty-first century requires dynamic organizational structures as well as employee participation. The criminal justice organizations need to change. The challenges facing us today are the degree to which income disparity and job displacement can be translated into high-value jobs and "informed" workplaces. Specifically we need to reallocate necessary resources to support new technical competencies and high quality workplaces. According to Gido, "the alternative is a future where criminal justice agencies and agents continue to function as reactive forces to crime and violence as enacted by those permanently displaced from the labor market."

CRIME CHALLENGES IN THE TWENTY-FIRST CENTURY

Benekos and Merlo look at how to balance the juvenile court's initial mission with those challenges facing us today. They describe the ongoing challenges faced by the juvenile court system. One problem we examine is that as more and more juveniles are transferred to the adult court system, greater demands will be placed on correctional institutions and their staff. There is a need for policy makers to focus on the antecedents of delinquent behaviors while evaluating ways to reduce acts of delinquency as we know them.

Globalization has helped to transform domestic problems into transnational challenges. According to Hoang and Meadows, "porous borders, technological innovations and global communications networks have allowed gangs such as MS-13 to evolve into transnational crime syndicates that extend beyond national borders." In predicting the future, we understand that without viable alternatives for youth, the deteriorating social as well as economic conditions that exist in the United States make gang membership all that more glamorous in today's world.

In looking at the crime challenges that face us in the twenty-first century, Peak and Miller look to forecast what is in store for society, especially as we look at gangs and the problems they are posing today. Is there for example a relationship between gangs and acts of terrorism? There are predictions that "urban terrorism," where aggressive gangs are dominating the social lives of some American neighborhoods, is more of a threat than the foreign terrorist. In the post-September 11, 2001 world, law enforcement and national security professionals can ill afford to ignore potential links between terrorism and other criminal activities. There are groups that share with terrorists the ability as well as the inclination to use violence to achieve whatever political and economic ends they desire. There are those who predict that terrorism with its violent gang activity may be the tangible threat to societal safety.

In looking at crime victims in the early years of the twenty-first century, Karmen indicates that a number of existing developments are going to increase the varied courses of action and options facing today's victims. Professional advocates on behalf of the victims will be present more so in the twenty-first century than ever before, as well as private prosecutors who may become a necessity if public prosecutors do not do their job. There will also need to be victim–offender reconciliation programs to handle the many cases of victims. By projecting emerging social trends, "it becomes possible to paint plausible scenarios about likely developments over the next several decades." The question posed is whether crime victims in the twenty-first century will be looked upon with more favor by officials than in previous years.

We review the role of the media as it impacts the perception of crime and criminality by the public. The question posed is whether or not the public's views are distorted by what is printed in the newspapers as well as what is viewed on television. According to Jerin and Fields, the reporting of news events across this country follows previous patterns that are found in regional newspapers as well as other reporting sources. The reporting of crime may not be based on actual crime statistics. The media tend to over sensationalize cases out of proportion to reality, which translates into the overreporting of crime news, particularly in the low-crime-rate states. There needs to be a conscious decision by the public to inform the public in a format that presents the truth, thereby reporting the news as it truly is, not as it makes the headlines.

The large use of illegal drugs in this country and the incarceration of those who are convicted of using them make it very clear that incarceration does not break the cycle of illegal drug use and related crimes, that offenders who are incarcerated tend to recidivate once released, and that drug treatment programs can be effective in reducing both drug abuse and drug-related crimes. McNeece, Bullington, Arnold, and Springer propose the decriminalization of drug use if not outright legalization. Between 2001 and 2002, the estimated number of persons age 12 and older needing treatment for a problem with illegal drugs increased from 4.7 million to 6.1 million, so current programs addressing these problems must be doing something wrong. During the same period, the number of persons needing—but not receiving—treatment increased from 3.9 million to 5.0 million. Presently, there are over 2,100,000 persons incarcerated in the nation's prisons and jails. These facts indicate that these increases were fueled by the war on drugs, as those convicted of using illegal substances experienced mandatory sentences and the consequences of lengthier sentences. The drug court whose mission is to eliminate substance abuse and the resulting criminalization of substance abuse is discussed.

Identity theft is a problem that has grown and is still growing in this new century. Law enforcement, faced with jurisdictional and technological issues, according to Slosarik, is ill equipped to deal with this problem. In the United States, it is estimated that one in four citizens has become a victim of identity theft. We know that unscrupulous people will misuse information. What we have failed to understand is the extent to which someone's identity can be readily stolen, meaning that information once private is no longer private. There continues to be legislation passed, but the passage of such laws has failed to stop the problem. The fact that identity theft is viewed as a nontraditional crime is in and of itself a problem. This area has been ignored. Victims of identity theft need better tools to repair their identity problem.

Albanese indicates that when it comes to the future of obscenity and pornography, the latest of concerns is the Internet and the easy access that one has to the depiction of sex and violence. There continues to be concern over the kinds of songs sung, movies shown, cable television, talk radio, chat rooms, and what their impact is having on young people. The concerns are that individuals such as Ted Bundy admitted prior to being executed that he was addicted to pornography. We see evidence that police are arresting more suspects who download child pornography from the Internet. The mere fact that television, movies, and the recording industry have been forced in this century to provide warnings to consumers is an indication of the impact of this widespread industry. There are growing complaints over the use of young teenagers and children in advertisements depicting suggestive poses. This is an old problem with new technology that needs to be addressed in this century.

In Chapter 15, "Militarism and Global Punishment" Michael Hallett looks at and addresses the factor of research on punishment being in full-fledged renaissance of late. He indicates that "a transnational 'reinvention of the prison with a focus on incapacitation and punishment' has arguably positioned the United States as the global archetype for contemporary imprisonment and its practices, industries, and rhetoric of justification." There is a renewed body of criminological work that has been built on scholarship that views punishment as a social process that is evolving independently of crime and criminality. The study of punishment is more important today than ever before.

Another challenge in the twenty-first century is that the disposition of offenders at the sentencing stage has gone from extreme punishment to extreme treatment. According to Morgan and Sigler, we are at the climax of the punishment cycle. As we have followed the credo of "get tough on crime," the prison system has grown by leaps and bounds with minorities being at an increased representation in the correctional facilities. As we continue into the twenty-first century, the prediction is that we will move away from strictly punishment toward treatment. The prediction is that mandatory sentence enhancements will be softened.

ISSUES IN POLICING

Every 9 seconds a woman is battered by her current or former intimate partner somewhere in the United States. According to Roberts, Kurst-Swanger, and O'Brien, the latest statistics on domestic violence indicate that 8.7 million women are abused each year, and serious injuries include head and traumatic brain injuries, neck and back injuries, knife wounds, attempted homicides, homicides, and murder-suicides. Many large and small city police departments have developed specialized domestic violence units, restraining orders and orders of protection have become available in some jurisdictions on a 24-hour, 7-day-a-week basis, and criminal court divisions have developed much needed specialized domestic violence courts.

Community policing has also evolved in the twenty-first century according to Palmiotto. There are facets of community policing concepts that will survive during the twenty-first century, and it will continue to grow. It has become an acceptable philosophy of policing. The driving force behind the concept of community policing comes from the desire to maintain within the neighborhoods a high standard of living for all residents. Community policing is oriented toward problem solving and uses the input of citizens. We live in a changing world in the twenty-first century, and with community policing, we find that there is an emphasis on listening to the citizens while understanding that citizens know what is best for their own communities. Since September 11, we find as well that community policing is playing a role in keeping communities safer from terrorists.

What is the status of women officers in the twenty-first century? As viewed by Lanier and Jockin, policing as a profession has changed. There are more concerns regarding security, there are more educational requirements for officers, there is more antidiscrimination legislation impacting the field of policing. Women are now on the move from being reactive crime-fighters to proactive, more service-oriented police persons. The research on women officers proves that women play a vital role in the field of policing and will do even more so as we continue to progress in this twenty-first century.

LAW

The government is the only institution in society that has a legitimate right to exert physical force over us. Since the beginning of the twenty-first century there has been evidence of a shift in the Court and its movement away from restrictions placed on the police, the conduct of trials, and the concerns regarding sentencing and punishment. This is pointed out by the late Alexander Smith, and by Pollack and Muraskin. The composition of the U.S. Supreme Court, which has shifted during the first part of this century, and is bound to continue to shift still, will play a major role in determining both the thrust and focus of the first ten amendments to the Constitution, known as the Bill of Rights. The function of the Bill of Rights in this century, as in the eighteenth century, is to protect the rights of minorities against majorities. Presently there appears to be little likelihood that there will be a sweeping denial of those rights that are basic to all "mankind," but with an increase in crime, and the different crimes facing us, our social fabric is likely to be strained. The success of dealing with this strain will make a determination of the criminal justice system in the twenty-first century. There is a specific movement away from the death penalty in this country. Both Baker and Haas in their analysis of the death penalty predict when the death penalty will cease to exist. Looking at both the international and domestic movements away from the use of capital punishment, we recognize that it is not by happenstance that defendants who are convicted and sentenced to death are indigent and that those who receive such sentences are basically in the minority, that is, gays and lesbians, individuals with mental problems, and those who are subjects of racism. The United States has not followed suit with the rest of the world by moving away from the use of the death penalty. A full examination is made by both authors who write about the death penalty, its problems, and why it is used in an arbitrary manner. It will be interesting to see when and if the use of the death penalty will disappear in this new century.

Juvenile justice started in the late nineteenth century. The idea was that juveniles would not face the same system as adults. The juvenile courts were to act as surrogate parents. It appears that the juvenile justice system is about to be dismantled. Michael Brown, considers how to revitalize the system as we understand the differences between the handling of adolescents and adults by the criminal justice system. The law may have to make changes regarding the handling of all juvenile cases.

There are recognized bias-motivated offenses that extend across a continuum of behaviors ranging from harassment to murder, but we find that both researchers and practitioners agree that the majority of bias-motivated events involve lower-level offenses often overlooked by the criminal justice system. Prosecutorial investigations are studied by Silvina Ituarte in order to examine how the process of categorizing bias-motivated events effects how defendants go through the criminal justice system. Though bias-motivated offenders may begin with minute incidences of bias, an examination of the multiagencies and their role is needed during this century.

Great attention has been paid over the years to the community prosecution movement, which is generally thought to represent a new way of thinking in problem solving. Developments in this century in the area of prosecution as suggested by Nugent-Borakove and Rainville demonstrate that community prosecution as we have defined it is not a mere adjunct of community policing but something that has happened since colonial days. The prosecutor's role that has evolved has not necessarily produced a brand of justice that has been seen to benefit communities. Chapter 24 explains the evolutionary path of the American prosecutor with the proposed thesis that in the development of community prosecution, prosecutors provide direct services to the citizenry. Is this workable today?

CORRECTIONS

The American correctional system has faced tremendous challenges in recent years to deal with overcrowded prisons, much longer prison sentences due to "Three Strikes and You're Out" laws, and a dearth of rehabilitation and reentry programs. In recent years, incarcerated individuals have faced momentous social, psychological, and legal barriers as they have sought to reenter society. Such barriers have always included lack of motivation and social skills, housing, vocational skills and employment, public assistance, and licensing prohibitions. Roberts and Biswas present the latest information on individual and group treatment programs, substance abuse treatment, sex offender treatment, academic education, vocational training programs, and prisoner reentry programs in Chapter 26. They document the fact that several hundred million dollars is now being spent on developing and supporting prisoner reentry programs nationwide. Chapter 27 by Brooker examines whether the legal needs of those who were formerly incarcerated are being met. There was a time when we had mass incarceration. As huge numbers of inmates reenter society, we need to meet their needs upon reentry or allow the cycle of violence and recidivism to continue unabated.

The criminal justice system during the twenty-first century is already viewing a larger number of prisoners reentering society than ever before. What problems exist for these prisoners and how does the criminal justice system meet their needs is discussed further. There are complex issues involved with the reentry and reintegration process, and we explore how such a phenomenon influences community life, family life, and what the inferences are for the criminal justice system in the future. In order to understand fully the problems implicit in the reentry process, the past, present, and future of prisoner reentry is reviewed by Henderson and Hanley as it exists in the United States. Today, we find that the biggest problem lies not in putting forth programs but in their implementation. Future directions for the reentry movement are suggested in Chapter 28.

Obstacles and challenges continue to face inmates who are HIV positive. Over the past decade, tremendous strides have been taken with regard to providing those who are incarcerated and who are HIV positive with programs and treatment. According to Lanier, Potter, and Sheehan in Chapter 29, "[m]uch like leper colonies of the 18th century today's 'correctional' facilities segregate the disempowered, the poor, drug users and the violent from the rest of society." Today's inmates are not trusted with the responsibility of controlling their own medications. During the twenty-first century, there will be more and more cases of those incarcerated with HIV and with full-fledged AIDS. The complexity of treatment will be a burden on correctional systems. Medical models are suggested in order to meet the demands of these incarcerated inmates.

The care of children left behind by their incarcerated parents (mother and/or father) is also a problem in the criminal justice system (see Chapter 30 by Muhammad). These children are considered a hidden population, primarily because there are no reliable data available to measure such a factor. By estimating the number of children left behind, we can infer what impact parental incarceration has on them. If this population continues to be overlooked, the continual growth in the use of imprisonment will pose major problems for society in the future. Muhammad suggests recommendations for where to look and how to deal with these "hidden" children.

TERRORISM

Prior to the twenty-first century, many Americans would never have thought that they would be attacked on their land and that they would see some 3,000 lives lost in a few moments of terror. According to Perlstein, September 11, 2001 was probably the most devastating day in the bloody history of terrorism for all Americans. Terrorism and other forms of political violence have always been part of America's heritage, but the destruction on 9/11 was almost unthinkable. There had existed the myth that America was somehow a unique society where parties settled their disputes in a peaceful manner, but history demonstrates otherwise. Historically, America has always been a victim. But the terrorism that hit American soil in 2001 was none ever experienced by any citizen living in this country.

Violent serial predation and terrorism share common factors, all of which need further examination according to Asthappan and DuPont Morales. We learn that a terrorist frames his self-interest as indistinguishable from community or state goals. Can terrorism actually be eradicated? Is Congress, the military strategists, and law enforcement officials who work to prevent acts of terrorism limited by their perspective of apprehension and punishment? What are the future policies of the United States? It is suggested that moderation is a first step.

As suggested, the war on terror has taken on a new resonance. While we deal with terrorism, we deal also with the rights of all our citizens. With the issue of profiling members of certain ethnic and religious groups are being typecast as possible terrorists. In the twenty-first century, we must be concerned with the potentiality of terrorism but concerned as well with ethnicity and human rights. According to Welch, "the war on terror, even in its early stages, is strikingly similar to another major criminal justice movement, namely the war on drugs. Both strategies are intricately linked to race/ethnicity and produce an array of civil liberties violations compounded by unnecessary incarceration." We are locking up an unprecedented number of those who are ethnics who may be small fries rather than big fish. The fight against terrorism as it continues in this century has to be one of a long-term commitment, but the criminal justice system has to curb its tendency to look at minorities only.

GENDER, DIVERSITY, AND THE LAW

The twenty-first century is here, yet the struggles continue with equality for both females and minorities as viewed by Muraskin. Historically, women have been classified as second-class citizens, individuals who may be citizens but without rights. Women today are being arrested at higher rates than ever before. Women are also victims of crimes at a rate higher than that of past decades. Women as well as minorities have been victimized by policies designed to protect them. There still exists the attitude that women and minorities, though infusing any aspect of social and political thought, are still being treated differently. There is no way to guarantee both men and women equal protection of the law unless there is a commitment made to eliminate all gender discrimination. There are cases of domestic violence, sexual abuse, rape, and sexual harassment that continue to be spoken about and dealt with by the criminal justice system. Although we do not have a federal equal rights amendment, there are states that recognize its potential worth. There is a tendency to use gender-neutral terms. In this new century, more has to be done to insure the equality of all humans. The rhetoric is there but not the practice.

To date, the issue of sexual harassment still pervades the legal system as viewed by O'Connor. Sexual harassment cases have their genesis in statues created by Congress. There exists little legislative history to guide the courts as to the exact meaning of sexual harassment. But in the cases of sexual harassment, some business interests have complained that "anti-bias laws are creating a more hostile environment for employers." There is not the expectation, even in the twenty-first century, that this country will be free of envy, jealousy, personal grudges, and the like, but the issues of sexual harassment no longer lies on the back burner. To reduce the harassment in our society, there must be a change in the gender power balances in our society. There also has to exist an internalization of values that speak against such harassment.

According to Morgan, "gender and race have been identified as perhaps the most consistent extralegal factors that impact the criminal justice system of today." We examine the influences of race and gender on decisions within the criminal justice system from initial contact with law enforcement to sentencing in the twenty-first century. The laws of our society must represent those boundaries as recognized by social contracts that are inherent in our society. Here we scrutinize the influence of race and gender on decisions with the criminal justice system from first contact with law enforcement to sentencing in the twenty-first century. Most studies suggest that our criminal justice system continues to be weighed down by discriminatory practices. In order to establish a fair and efficient system of justice from beginning to end, we must be willing to go that extra step.

Understanding there is gender discrimination in our system of justice, and understanding that such discrimination is amplified because of the race and gender of our inmates, there is a topic of concern that is not easily recognizable, let alone spoken about in our criminal justice system. The topic of concern is transgender prisoners, who appear to be dehumanized and rendered invisible in prison because of the discriminatory rules against them. Joseph, who examines issues of gender discrimination, looks at the issue of transgender prisoners and the discrimination regarding their gender identity. Over these many years, the number of transgender people incarcerated in the prisons has increased tremendously. Prisons now and in the future will have to be more inclusive of transgender prisoners. The challenge faced by the criminal justice system in this century is the need to make major reforms to accommodate the diverse prison population of today. Transgender prisoners face many different kinds of problems, and there exists the need for special policies for this very diverse population.

"Thinking about crime and justice in the twenty-first century conjures up an enormously ambitious agenda" (Finckenauer 2005:xxi).[1] Criminal justice change must be evident in the twenty-first century. The time to *reshape* the system is now. Its character and method of operation have already been somewhat redefined in view of the terrorist attacks on our soil. A revisiting of the facilitation, planning, coordination, and implementation of the criminal justice system is in order now. Improved legislation and procedures are in order, just as a commitment to additional human and financial resources is necessary to

---

[1]MURASKIN, R., and ROBERTS, A. R. (2005). *Visions for Change: Crime and Justice in the Twenty-First Century*. 4th ed. Upper Saddle River, NJ: Prentice Hall.

focus on immediate problems. Both short range and long-term range planning is an absolute necessity. We need for now and the future national policies for crime prevention, improved criminal justice strategies, and the availability of sophisticated technology to guarantee the preservation of democracy and justice based on the role of law.

Programs must be implemented in order to give us the capability to plan, implement, and evaluate crime prevention and criminal justice projects to sustain national developments and enhance justice in furtherance of gaining human rights without the possibility of putting our own lives in jeopardy. Efficiency, fairness, and improvement in the management and the administration of criminal justice and related systems *must* be the theme for this millennium.

As before, there continues to exist the need for an understanding of compatible information technology to facilitate the administration of justice while strengthening practical cooperation on crime control throughout this country. This important text was written by persons who have the needed expertise in those areas that are of major concern to all our citizenry. The future has unfolded, and our visions for the next several decades must continue to grow and to be realized. Do we have all the answers? No. But we have given the problems considerable thought and hope that this fifth edition will motivate us to take that next needed step.

PART II

Technology in the Criminal Justice System

Chapter 2

Technoprison

Technology and Prisons

Janice Joseph

INTRODUCTION

The great technological advances in the last 25 years are having an impact on prisons. Combined with the ever-present need to reduce prison cost and increase security, the use of technology is becoming prevalent in the penal system. Less than 15 years ago, there were perhaps very few computers, technology review committees, or technology products of any kind in prisons. However today, technology has emerged as a critical issue in prisons and is used in many aspects of prison life. Technological innovations have occurred in internal security with the use of advanced X-ray devices, closed-circuit monitoring, magnetic "friskers," and officer tracking/alerting systems. Drug and alcohol abuse testing packages, telemedicine, and videoconferencing all are products of advances in technology used in prison. This chapter examines several types of technological devices used in prisons and the issues surrounding their use. The chapter focuses primarily on biometrics, technology to detect illegal activities in prison, smart cards, electroshock devices, monitoring and surveillance technology, and teleconferencing technology.

BIOMETRIC SCANNING

Biometrics, which means "life measurement," is based on the principle that everyone has unique physical attributes that a computer can be programmed to recognize. It is a science of using a particular biological aspect of the human body (National Law

Enforcement and Corrections Technology Center 2000) and uses mathematical representations of those unique physical characteristics to identify an individual (Desmarais 2000; Wood 2001). Biometric technologies automate the process of identifying people based on their unique physical or behavioral characteristics such as the finger, hand, eye, face, and voice.

Biometric scanning is used for identification and verification of individuals. *Identification* is defined as the ability to recognize a person from among all those enrolled (all those whose biometric measurements have been collected in the database) and seeks to answer the question: Do I know who you are? It involves a one-compared-to-many match (or what is referred to as a "cold search"). Biometrics is also used for *verification,* which involves the authentication of a person's claimed identity from his previously enrolled pattern. Verification seeks to answer the question: Are you who you claim to be? and involves a one-to-one match (see Campbell, Alyea, and Dunn 1996; Miller 1996). In order to accomplish this, the system has to (1) receive biometric samples from a candidate/user; (2) extract biometric features from the sample; (3) compare the sample from the candidate with stored template(s) from known individual(s); and (4) indicate identification or verification results (Idex 2000).

There are two phases in the system; one is the enrollment phase, and the other is the verification phase. During the enrollment phase, individuals submit a "live sample" of their biometric information (e.g., the eyes, face, or fingerprints), which is scanned and stored in a database along with the subject's name and any other identification information. During the verification phase, individuals present their biometric information, and the recognition system compares the current scan with the sample stored in the database. While biometric technologies come in many forms, the procedure for storing and retrieving biometric information is uniform (Isaacs 2002a). Biometric scanning involves the scanning of the fingers, eye, hand, and face.

Finger Scanning

Finger-scan technology is the oldest and most prominent biometric authentication technology used by millions of people worldwide. It measures the unique, complex swirls on a person's fingertip. The swirls are characterized and produced as a template requiring from 250 to 1,000 bytes. What is stored is not a full fingerprint but a small amount of data derived from the fingerprint's unique patterns (Chandrasekaran 1997). Finger-scanning extracts certain characteristics of the image into templates known as "minutiae" that are unique to each finger. Optical, silicon, and ultrasound are mechanisms that are currently used to capture the fingerprint image with sufficient detail and resolution (Finger-Scan.com 1999). After the fingerprints are scanned by the reader, templates are recorded and compared with the templates that are stored on the databases (ZDNet 1999). The County of Los Angeles and Middlesex County in Massachusetts use finger scanning (Esser 2000). The Pierce County Sheriff's Department uses finger-scanning identification systems made by Tacoma, Washington-based Sagem Morpho to verify inmates upon release (Issac 2002b). Overall, the biometric industry made $196 million in 2000, with finger imaging being the most popular tool (Pries 2001).

Eye Scanning

Eye scanning is probably the fastest growing area of biometric research because of its promise for high scan accuracy. There are two types of eye scanning: retinal scanning and iris scanning.

Retinal scans examine the blood vessel patterns of the retina, the nerve tissue lining the inside of the eye that is sensitive to light. An infrared light source is used to illuminate the retina of the eye. The image of the enhanced blood vessel pattern of the retina is analyzed for characteristic points. A retinal scan can produce almost the same volume of data as a fingerprint image analysis. By emitting a beam of incandescent light that bounces off the person's retina and returns to the scanner, a retinal scanning system quickly maps the eye's blood vessel pattern and records it into an easily retrievable digitized database (Ritter 1999; Tierney 1995).

While retinal scanning uses lasers that focus on the back of the eye, iris scanning zooms in on the front. Iris scans digitally process, record, and compare the light and dark patterns in the iris's flecks and rings, something akin to a human bar code. Iris scanning works by capturing the image of a person's iris; using a video conferencing camera; and establishing a 512-byte code of the image's unique characteristics (McManus 1996). Iris recognition stands out as perhaps the most "hygienic" of the biometric technologies in that no part of the user's body has to touch anything to operate the system. A retinal scan can produce almost the same volume of data as a fingerprint image analysis. Along with iris recognition technology, iris scan is perhaps the most accurate and reliable biometric technology (Woodward 1997).

Iris recognition gives prison officials absolute assurance that the right inmate is being released and eliminates the risk of human error in matching a face with photograph identification. In addition, the iris recognition system lets the prison administration determine if a new inmate was previously incarcerated there under a different name. The Sarasota County Detention Center in Florida uses iris scanning to prevent former prisoners from visiting former inmate friends (National Law Enforcement and Corrections Technology Center 2000). The Lancaster County Prison and the York County Prison in Pennsylvania also use iris scanning to verify prisoners before they are released from prison for routine events such as court appearances and medical visits. There are currently 30 county prisons and 10 state prisons using iris scanning. Inmates are verified by iris recognition before they are released from prison at the end of their sentences and for routine events such as court appearances and medical visits (Center for Criminal Justice Technology Newsletter 2001; Pries 2001).

Hand Scanning/Hand Geometry

With hand geometry, the biometric hand unit employs a miniaturized camera to capture a digital template of the back of the individual's hand. These photographs analyze the size, shape, width, thickness, and surface of the hand. In effect, a digital map of the outline of a person's hand is created. The biometric hand readers simultaneously analyze over 31,000 points and instantaneously record over 90 separate measurements of an individual's hand. The results are converted into a less than 10-byte code and are stored in the system's memory for future comparisons (Chandrasekaran 1997; Zunkel 1998).

Hand scanning/geometry has been used to identify inmates, employees, and visitors to correctional facilities. The Federal Bureau of Prisons, for example, uses hand geometry to verify the identity of visitors and staff members in order to avoid mistaken identifications. Inmates use it for access to the cafeteria, recreation, lounge, and hospital. In San Antonio, Texas, hand geometry helps to prevent escape attempts. The Florida Department of Corrections currently also utilizes hand scanning in 19 of its facilities (The Corrections Connection 2001).

Facial Recognition

The facial recognition technique is one of the fastest growing areas. It measures the peaks and valleys of the face, such as the tip of the nose and the depth of the eye sockets, which are known as nodal points—the human face has 80 nodal points, only 14–22 are needed for recognition—concentrating on the inner region, which runs from temple to temple and just over the lip. The scan also reads the heat pattern around the eyes and cheeks; and the ability to scan the dimensions of an individual's head. It then comes up with a face print (National Law Enforcement and Corrections Technology Center 2000). It also measures such characteristics as the distance between facial features (from pupil to pupil, for instance) or the dimensions of the features themselves (such as the width of the mouth). Facial recognition software uses a camera attached to personal computer to capture and map key identifying features (ZDNet 1999). In addition to photographs, the system records other identifying attributes such as scars, tattoos, and gang insignia. Identification cards are produced for department employees, inmates, and offenders, and face-recognition technology is utilized for positive identification. The advantage of the facial recognition system is that it can work with people still at a distance. As one approaches, the system could recognize the face and activate the system, such as turning on a computer or unlocking a door stages (Desmarais 2000).

The Facial Recognition Vendor 2000 (FRVT 2000) was tested at a correctional facility in Prince George's County, Maryland, to assist correctional officers in their decision to unlock an electronically controlled door providing access to the facility (Bone and Crumbacker 2001). In 1998, the Wisconsin department of corrections awarded Viisage Technology, Incorporated, a $1.4 million contract to develop a biometric facial identification system for the State's prison system. The facial recognition system is used in more than 44 locations throughout the State (Colatosti 1998). The Ohio Department of Rehabilitation and Corrections also uses facial recognition to identify inmates (Prison Talk Online, 2004).

ILLEGAL ACTIVITIES DETECTION TECHNOLOGY

To prevent illegal activities in prisons, manufacturers have developed new detection technologies. These include technologies to detect illegal drugs, concealed weapons, pulse radar, and the number of heartbeats in vehicles.

Illegal Drugs

Attempts to control the influx of drugs entering prison facilities have ranged from closed-circuit television in visiting areas to an increased use of drug dogs and pat- or rub-down searches of visitors. Unfortunately, a large amount of controlled substances continue to penetrate many prisons. So today, scanners such as Ion Track Instruments' ITEMISER and VaporTracer are used to detect traces of microscopic particles associated with 40 different types of drugs. Generally, drug detection systems are categorized as trace detectors or bulk detectors. Bulk detectors are typically much larger, less mobile, and less sensitive than trace detectors. Most trace detection systems in use today are based on ion mobility spectrometry (IMS), which is a highly portable equipment and with capabilities that, until recently, were confined to the laboratory. Originally developed for medical imaging and diagnosis, trace detectors can determine if items have been in the presence of drugs or touched by people who have been using, handling, or hiding drugs. Another use for trace detection is in the nonintrusive inspection of cargo and containers. Drug residue on the exterior or vapors seeping from the interior can be detected to signal inspectors that an enclosure needs further scrutiny. Trace detectors operate in two basic modes: vapor detection and particle detection and can use a "wipe and spray" method to detect drug residue (Wright and Butler 2001).

Drug detection systems are used on both prisoners and visitors. In most situations, the scanner is positioned at the security checkpoint where the visitors' access into the prison is located. Before entry into visiting rooms is permitted, visitors can be screened for controlled substances. Typically, if traces of drugs are found on the visitor, either entry is refused into the visiting area or the visitor is subjected to further search procedures before being permitted entry (Ion Track 2002). Some prisons have chosen to use trace detection technology for searching inmates' cells for drugs. Individual cells can be checked and analyzed on location with the portable, battery-operated VaporTracer or by running the ITEMISER from a portable power supply, and personal items, such as furniture and virtually any surface, can be checked for drugs. Because some drugs can easily be hidden in or on a letter or envelope, contraband screening of all incoming mail is essential. The prisons also scan multiple letters and parcels for drugs in just seconds. If a detection is made, the letter or parcel is opened and searched according to that prison's standard procedures. The machine can also search for particles that are gathered on paper used to wipe hands or clothing or through a special vacuum (Bucsko 2001).

The Department of Corrections in Pennsylvania purchased 3 ion scanners and 15 ITEMISERS for the prisons. In 1998, 22,074 visitors were scanned, and 734 were found to be carrying drugs (Caramanis 1999). The Federal Bureau of Prison uses the explosive/drug detectors, from IonTrack Instruments, which can change from detecting narcotics to explosives in 10 seconds (Gaseau 1999). California, a leader in particle-sniffing technologies, has a system that requires inmates and visitors to wipe their hands on a tissue, which is then inserted into an analyzer sensitive to trace amounts of narcotics in parts per trillion. The machine can not only indicate what narcotic the inmate has but also the quantity of that narcotic. California has also been using the Rapidscan 500 in its prisons to detect contraband in packages. It breaks down the molecular structure of what is inside a package and when it finds the drug, it circles it on the monitor and tells the operator it has found the preprogrammed substance (Wired News 1997).

Concealed Weapons

Inmates can easily hide metallic objects such as tweezers, lighters, safety pins, needles, and other items in orifices on their bodies, but the "Big BOSS" (Body Orifice Scanning System), which is a chair that scans and detects metallic objects hidden on or in the body, has been improving security in Arizona's prisons. The chair, which costs $6,500, scans an inmate's head, lower digestive tract, groin, rectum area, and feet, and sounds an alarm if any foreign objects are detected. Arizona purchased five 5 of these chairs and with this system Arizona caught 17 inmates hiding weapons on their bodies. The problem is that the machine cannot be used for extended periods of time so it has to be shut down and be allowed to cool off before resuming operation. Physical contact, however, is still required to find nonmetallic foreign objects that inmates hide from officers (*Directions* 2001; Lau 2001).

Heartbeat Detectors

Perhaps one of the weakest security links in any prison has always been the sally port where trucks unload their supplies and where trash and laundry are taken out of the facility. Over the years inmates have hidden in loads of trash, old produce, laundry—any possible container that might be exiting the facility. Oak Ridge National Laboratory has produced sound detectors or seismometers that count the number of heartbeats in service vehicles as they leave the prison, reducing the need for routine searches. Likewise the Springfield, Virginia Ensco Incorporation and Houston's Geo Vox Security have also developed sensors that can detect the heartbeats of those hiding inside cars or trucks at prisons and which use magnets and tiny weights to sense minute vibrations. The Advanced Vehicle Interrogation and Notification System (AVIAN)—being marketed by Geo Vox Security—also works by identifying the shock wave generated by the beating heart, which couples to any surface the body touches. A potential escapee can be identified in less than 2 minutes after two specialized AVIAN sensors are placed on the vehicle. Prisons can buy the system for $50,000 or lease it for $1,000 per month. The average cost of locating and capturing an escaped inmate is estimated at $750,000 (deGroot 1997). About 6 of the 25 state prisons in Pennsylvania use the Geovox system to detect escapees before vehicles leave the prison, and one state prison in New Jersey has installed the system developed by Ensco. These devices are also now in use at other facilities, most notably at Riverbend Maximum Security Institution in Nashville, Tennessee, where four inmates escaped in a hidden compartment in a flatbed truck several years ago (Weed 2001).

Pulsed Radar

Special Technologies Laboratories has created a new technological device, GPR-X— with GPR standing for ground penetrating radar, and X indicating the new generation of technology that GPR represents. The device transmits energy into the ground, and by measuring the time it takes for that energy to be reflected, it can detect changes in ground material. GPR can, therefore, detect contraband buried in the recreation yard, for instance, or a tunnel being built under the prison (deGroot 1997).

Contraband Cellular Phones

Cellular phones have become the latest epidemic in prison contraband, posing a danger that extends beyond prison walls. Cellular phones have become more valuable in prison than drugs or other contraband. They have become the new prison cash because the inmates can sell minutes or cellular phone use to other inmates. As cellular phones become smaller, it has become very easy to smuggle them inside correctional facilities and easier for inmates to continue their criminal activities, harass victims, or transmit photographs of information. Prisoners are willing to pay between $350 and $600 to have a phone smuggled into prison. The cellular phones are smuggled into the prison inside mayonnaise jars, hidden in compost piles, shoved into the soles of shoes, and slipped inside hollowed-out blocks of cheese. More importantly, corrupt correctional officers sometimes smuggle cellular phones into the prison for the inmates. In Texas, for example, a correctional officer was charged with trying to smuggle a cell phone and drugs into a prison. In Philadelphia, a sweep of three city jails in 2002 netted more than 60 phones. New Jersey, Maryland, and Tennessee are having similar problems with cellular phones in prison. At least three states—Texas, Pennsylvania, and Iowa—have made it a crime for inmates to possess cell phones (Cellular-news 2006; Demsky 2005; Sullivan 2006).

Equipment that would jam or intercept cell phones also would interfere with the signals needed by prison personnel, so prison officials are using a technological device that can pinpoint cell phone activity within a small area, like a single pod inside a prison. The GEO Group Inc., the second largest private prison management company in the United States has created a high-tech equipment for detecting and locating hidden contraband cellular phones (even if the phone is not transmitting or even turned off). The equipment, the ORION Non-Linear Junction Detector (NLJD) can respond to electronic components, allowing the user to detect and locate electronic items (such as hidden cellular phones). Previously correction institutions were limited to physical searches and this technology makes detection of contraband easy. Florida and Pennsylvania have been using this system (Cellular-news 2006).

Smart Card

A smart card is a standard-sized plastic card with an embedded computer microchip containing a central processing unit (CPU) and up to 8K bytes of electronic, updatable memory. It is a photo identification card containing embedded computer chips that electronically store inmates' personal identification and medical information. Smart card technology has been emerging over the past two decades and there are now millions in circulation. The card stores all types of information about an inmate, including his or her movement, medical care, commissary purchases, treatment needs and meals eaten. They can also provide access to restricted areas and some are service-related, like telephone calling cards or those that deduct purchases from a holder's account. Some can be used for identification purposes only, while others enable remote payment, money access, and information exchange via computer, telephone, or television "set-top boxes" (Jackson 1998a).

Australia is believed to be the first country in the world to use smart card technology as an integral part of the operation of a prison—providing greater security, efficiency and flexibility. Fujitsu Australia's SmartCity smart card system has been incorporated throughout Western Australia's new Acacia Prison, the most advanced medium security prison in the world. The smart cards allow prison officers to monitor the movements of individual prisoners within the jail and also replace cash inside the institution. The cards are used to keep two prisoners from having any contact by restricting them from moving into the same area of the prison at the same time. Smart card also increases security considerably during prisoner transfers. Money that prisoners earn by working is credited to their smart card, and they use the card to purchase snacks, cigarettes, toiletries, magazines, or pay for telephone calls, and so forth (Fujitsu Australia Limited 2001).

Smart-card technology is still in its infancy and they are used in prison primarily to dispense medication in United States. When an inmate's smart card is inserted into a reader, that inmate's medication history is displayed on a computer screen. Any administration of medicine is entered into the record electronically, including the date and time of the dispensation—information that can be retrieved at any time by the institution's medical staff (Gaseau 1999).

The Ohio Department of Rehabilitation and Correction (ODRC) has conducted a project which was funded by the National Institute of Justice to manage inmate information with a "smart card." Initially, the cards were used to track the medication activity of 2,300 inmates in a medium-security men's facility. In this system, the inmate's photo is electronically stored, indicating who the inmate is and what his inmate number is. When an inmate needs service, such as the library, he/she puts the card into a reader that scans the information on the microchip contained in the card. These smart cards will be integrated with the ODRC's electronic photo-imaging system, so that when the card is used, it will automatically bring up a picture of the inmate on a computer screen. In the future, the smart card will be a multiuse card that will be used in prison to control many aspects of prison life. Inmate classification, medical and mental health information, education status and parole information will be stored on the microchip (Justice Technology Information Network 1998).

ELECTRO-SHOCK DEVICES

Stun Belt

The stun belt is an electronic shocking device secured to a person's waist and is available in two styles: a one-size-fits-all minimal-security belt (a slim version designed for low visibility in courts) and the high-security transport belt, complete with wrist restraints. Both come attached to a 9-volt battery. When activated, the stun belt shocks its wearer for 8 seconds, with 3–4 milliamps and 50,000 volts of stun power. Guards like it because they do not have to get near prisoners who wear the belt. They can set off the 8-second, 50,000-volt stun from as far away as 300 feet. It shocks the left kidney, blood channels, and nerve pathways.

Stun Tech, manufacturer of the stun belt, recommends the belt as a psychological tool, an effective deterrent for potentially unruly inmates, and a humane alternative to guns or nightsticks. More than 100 county agencies have employed the belt for prisoner transport, courtroom appearances, and medical appointments (Schulz 1999; Yeoman 2000).

In 1995, the use of stun belts was reported to be illegal in Illinois, Hawaii, New Jersey, New York, Michigan, Massachusetts, and Rhode Island and some municipalities. However, these shock devices have been adopted by at least 19 state prison systems including Oklahoma, Arizona, Florida, Wisconsin, and Iowa, as well as by the federal government. They are currently used in both medium- and high-security prisons; on chain gangs, during prisoner transport including transport to and from medical facilities; and on prisoners deemed a "security risk" during court appearances. At Red Onion State Prison in Virginia, 10 inmates were required to wear the belts while meeting with an attorney investigating charges of human rights violations; one prisoner who refused to wear the device was barred from speaking to the lawyer. There have been few tests run to determine the safety of stun belts; and these tests that have been conducted have led to highly suspect and vague results (Schulz 1999; Yeoman 2000).

Electric-Stun/Lethal Fences

Perhaps the largest contributor to keeping inmates locked up has been the introduction of electric fences, also known as *lethal fences*. These fences are erected around the perimeter of the facility and often carry about 10,000 volts of electricity, more than enough to take a human life. They are usually positioned between double perimeter fences and the electrified fence serves as an unmanned lethal barriers or deterrents. The fences usually consist of galvanized posts spaced approximately 30 feet apart supporting wires powered with high voltage and are located approximately 10 feet from the outer perimeter fence and approximately 15 feet from the inner perimeter field. Any movement of the wire or variation in the current will trigger an alarm and a lethal jolt. These fences would shock would-be escapees with a lethal dose of 5,000 volts, or more than double the jolt of an electric chair. Guards in the command center can watch a graphic representation of the fenced perimeter that instantly pinpoints any change in current; the same system also sends a message to the watch commander's beeper in the event of an incident (Jackson 1998a).

In 1992, California began installing the first electric fences around its prisons. At the time, skeptical industry observers said the system would never work and would never be widely accepted in the field. Today, all of California's 33 prisons are surrounded by electric fencing, and several other states have installed them as well (deGroot 1997). Nevada, Colorado, Missouri, Wisconsin, Arkansas, Alabama, Arizona, Pennsylvania, Illinois, and the federal government use this type of fencing (Brustad 2001; Scolforo 2005).

Verichip

A company in Florida called Applied Digital Systems has marketed the "Verichip," which is the size of a grain of rice and can be embedded beneath a person's skin. The information on this chip could include a person's medical records, banking records, how much the person owes on his or her mortgage, credit cards, and other personal loans. It could also be used to track your activities anywhere in the world. It would replace all of a person's present forms of identification such as passport, driver's license, social security, and credit/debit cards. The chip would also include data on your family history, address, occupation, criminal record, income tax information, and so forth. The chip is powered electromagnetically through muscle movement or can be activated by an outside monitoring facility. One will not be able to withdraw money from the bank without it, receive benefits from the government without it, buy or sell anything without it. This is one of the dangers of the chip; once a person has it, the person can be controlled by someone else. The technology is used in some U.S. prisons where prisoners have a chip implanted in their bodies; when they become violent, the guard simply pushes a button on a remote control and paralyses the prisoner (The Ultimate Scam 2002).

MONITORING AND SURVEILLANCE TECHNOLOGY

Perimeter Security Control Devices

A prison is only as secure as its perimeter. The basic role of a perimeter security system is fourfold: deter, detect, document, and deny/delay any intrusion of the protected area or facility. Six factors affect the probability of detection of most surveillance sensors, although to varying degrees. These are (1) the amount and pattern of emitted energy, (2) the size of the object, (3) distance to the object, (4) speed of the object, (5) direction of movement, and (6) reflection and absorption characteristics of the energy waves by the intruder and the environment (e.g., open or wooded area, or shrubbery) (Jackson 1998b). Electronic sensors monitor the tension in barbed-wire barricades, seismometers detect any suspicious shaking of chain-link fences, and microwave beams pick up motion in the deserted areas between fences. A positive signal from any of the systems sounds an alarm, swings surveillance cameras to the appropriate spot, and sets off warnings in a guard booth and the perimeter patrol car. A few of the newest prisons, including the Toledo Correctional Institution in Ohio, use "smart" perimeters that can eliminate the need for staffed watchtowers (Weed 2001).

Control of Inmate Movement Inside Prison

The number of inmates in the United States has doubled over the past decade to nearly 2 million, so it has become difficult to monitor prisoners. Prisoners can be fitted with tamper-proof transmitter wristbands that broadcast a unique serial number via radio frequency every 2 seconds. Antennas throughout the prison pick up the signals and pass the data via a local area network to a computer. This system can alert a monitor when a prisoner gets dangerously close to the perimeter fence or when an inmate does not return from a furlough on time; it can even tag gang members and notify guards when rival gang members get too close to each other (prison employees also carry transmitters with panic buttons) (Roberti 2002). Prisons in Arizona and Texas have tested a similar system developed by Motorola in which prisoners and officers wear bracelets that transmit personal radio IDs (PRI). Correctional facilities in California, Michigan, Illinois, and Ohio have implemented the Alanco's TSI PRISM(TM) RFID officer safety and inmate management system. Under this system, every inmate is issued a bracelet when he or she is processed. The bracelet, which is approximately the size of a divers' watch, includes an active RFID tag as well as a bar code if the correctional system.

With RFID tags worn by inmates and RFID readers deployed throughout the prison. This allows correctional officers to continuously monitor and track the location and movement of approximately inmates. Receivers pick up the signals and relay them to a computer that displays everyone's exact location in the prison. The TSI's wristbands for inmates transmit signals every two seconds to a battery of antennas mounted in the prison facility. With this PRI, each prisoner can be seen on a map of the prison as a red dot, and each officer as a blue dot. A single officer monitoring the display can keep track of thousands of prisoners. The computer can alert a guard if a dangerous prisoner comes into his area, or raise an alarm if someone is out of place. It can also track two prisoners who hate each other and selectively block access through certain checkpoints to make sure they never come in contact. The computer can also keep a log of everyone's movements, aiding investigations of assaults or other crimes. The device also has a sensor that is designed to set off an alarm in 15 seconds if it loses contact to skin (Swedberg 2005).

VIDEO TELECONFERENCING

The uses of teleconferencing and videoconferencing have become common in prison. The individuals can see and talk to one another from any place around the world with picture and audio as clear as if we were having a face-to-face conversation. This tool is now readily available to all criminal justice agencies. Teleconferencing allows prisoners more virtual contact with the outside world and can be used in court hearings, prison visits, and telemedicine.

Video Court Appearances/Video Arraignment

Videoconferencing is used in prisons for routine court hearings, thus reducing the number of inmates transferred out for their hearing. This basically enables prisoners to be arraigned without physically being present in a courtroom or allows witnesses from across the country to testify electronically, thus completing cases faster. Also, with the video technology, an inmate with an open warrant from a surrounding community is placed on the videoconferencing list. The judge can recall or resolve the warrant, appoint counsel, schedule a trial date, or resolve the case all in one day. States like Montana and Wisconsin have recently begun videoconferencing initial court appearances for inmates (The Associated Press State & Local Wire 2002; Miller 2002). The use of videoconferencing in prisoner civil rights proceedings was authorized by Congress in the Prison Litigation Reform Act. The Judicial Conference also has encouraged courts to use videoconferencing in certain proceedings, and currently 100 federal court sites make use of the technology (The Third Branch 2001).

The cost for commercial packages for video teleconferencing can run as high as $90,000 (Gaseau 1999). However, the Hampden County, Massachusetts, Correctional Center bought its own equipment and used existing fiber optics to run the technology at a cost between $7,000 and $10,000 per site. The Eastern District of Texas and the Central District of Illinois were among the first courts to receive funding for videoconferencing for court hearings for prisoners (The Third Branch 2001).

The Conference Court Administration and Case Management Committee reviewed the merits of using videoconferencing in court proceedings and found that a potential for savings in personnel time and travel costs existed and this can outweigh the cost of purchase and operation of videoconferencing systems when used in prisoner civil rights proceedings. In support of this observation, the Committee, in collaboration with the Conference Automation and Technology Committee, established the Prisoner Civil Rights Videoconferencing Project, which analyzed courts' use of videoconferencing technology for prisoner proceedings. Between 1996 and 2001, approximately 58 video-conferencing sites within the district courts were funded under this project (The Third Branch 2001).

Prison Visits/Video Visiting

Inmate visitation is required in all correctional agencies but it can be difficult to manage. One facility in Colorado, however, is working on a way to automate and simplify the process. The automated visitation system, created by the Arapahoe County, Colorado, Detention Facility and AMA Technologies, allows visitors to call and schedule dates and times for visits, using an identification (ID) number (the last four digits of the photo ID that will be presented upon arrival). This system is integrated with a television system at the facility. When the visitor arrives at the facility at the scheduled time, he or she enters by a separate entrance into a visitor reception center and sits at a 27-inch interactive screen to visit with the inmate, who will sit at one of 80 video stations throughout the facility. Inmates in the infirmary who once had to be transported to booking for a visitation can sit in their beds and have visitation directly from the infirmary (Gaseau 1999). A similar situation exists in Arizona, where inmates can remain in their housing units and visit their relatives and friends who are located in the visiting room (Villa 2005). Friends and family can avoid standing in line by scheduling videoconferences with inmates. Because inmates remain in their housing units, this form of video visitation cuts down on movement in the prison, thereby reducing the number of assaults and eliminating the opportunities for contraband to be smuggled into prison.

Telemedicine

Telemedicine is one of the newest and most exciting advances in medicine. The process allows a doctor in the prison to examine the patient with a stethoscope or performs an electrocardiogram, and the results are then relayed over the Internet to a remote medical specialist who sends back a diagnosis. It could provide prisoners with adequate, cost-effective health care in the future. Taking a prisoner to a specialist outside the prison can pose a danger to the correctional officers and the community by giving the prisoner an opportunity to escape. Telemedicine allows physicians to consult with on-site medical personnel through videoconferencing and compatible medical devices such as medical microcameras. Telemedicine also helps prisons comply with a court order mandating standardized and uniform health care for inmates. Georgia, Michigan, Ohio, Arizona, and Texas are the major states that are providing telemedicine in the field of corrections (The Third Branch 2001).

According to a report prepared by Abt Associates (1999) and funded by the National Institute of Justice (NIJ), prisons that use telemedicine systems instead of conventional care could save approximately $102 per specialist encounter. In addition, telemedicine can improve the quality of care available to prisoners by reducing the waiting time between referral and consultation with specialists and by increasing access to distant physicians who specialize in prison health care (Weed 2001).

ISSUES REGARDING THE USE OF TECHNOLOGY

Usefulness

Many of these technological devices are very useful to the operation of the prison system. They save time and money. The smart card system, for example, can be used to manage to process inmate data at a fast rate to dispense medication. While it could take one minute per patient to dispense medication to patients, the smart card can reduce the time for this process to a few seconds. Electric perimeter fences in California eliminated the need for 24-hour watchtower surveillance, thus saving about $32 million per year, about $1 million per prison. Heartbeat sensors used to detect inmates can be cost effective and can identify an escapee in less than two minutes after two specialized AVIAN sensors are placed on the vehicle. Prisons can buy the system for $50,000 or lease it for $1,000 per month. This may seem high, but the average cost of locating and capturing an escaped inmate is estimated at $750,000 (deGroot 1997). Pennsylvania's Luzerne County has saved $120,000 in six months on court transportation, manpower, and cost on local correctional facility because of their innovative use of teleconferencing (Weiss 2003). The benefits of telemedicine are obvious: (1) travel costs are reduced dramatically because the number of vans needed to transport inmates is substantially reduced and (2) through telemedicine, dozens of medical specialists serve several inmates right into a prison (Weed 2001).

Many of these technological devices used in prison can enhance the effectiveness and efficiency of institutional security. Explosive/drug detectors from Ion Track Instruments can reduce contraband, and field-monitoring devices can prevent inmates from entering restricted areas in the prison. According to Stewart (2000) "we are beginning to see the application of technology widely influencing virtually every aspect of institutional security. In some respects, this influence can be described as a revolution in security innovation" (p. 8). Telemedicine's most valuable asset may be its ability to minimize security risks associated with taking inmates outside of a corrections facility for health care (Weed 2001).

Despite the usefulness of technological devices in prisons, there are some serious problems with their use. These include constitutional issues, reliability, cost, and the inhumane nature of these devices.

CONSTITUTIONAL ISSUES

One of the most controversial legal issues regarding technology and prisons is the right to privacy. Some of these technological devices, for example, retina and iris and hand geometry biometrics can be invasive and may capture information about a person's health and medical history. Recent scientific research suggests that finger imaging might also disclose sensitive medical information about a person. There is a relationship between an uncommon fingerprint pattern, known as a digital arch, and a medical disorder called chronic, intestinal pseudo-obstruction (CIP) that affects 50,000 people nationwide. In addition, Turner syndrome, Klinefelter syndrome, and certain nonchromosomal disorders, such as leukemia, breast cancer, and Rubella syndrome, may cause certain unusual fingerprint patterns (see Chen 1988).

The availability of medical and other types of personal information on individuals whether they are inmates, employees, or visitors who are subjected to biometrics raises concern about the right to privacy. It is quite possible that personal information on individuals stored in correctional databases for the purposes of identification and verification could be disseminated to other sources, since a biometric system in one correctional facility may be connected with other databases in the correctional system. Once in use, therefore, a biometric system in a prison may not be confined to its original purpose. The more people have access to a database, the less likely that this information will remain private.

The right to privacy becomes a bigger issue when biometrics is used in conjunction with smart cards. Smart cards, which may contain data, such as medical, financial, health history, and criminal record, can be stolen or lost. Unauthorized individuals who possess lost or stolen smart cards and have means to decrypt the biometric data could discover information that are very personal to the card owners (Esser 2000).

Another constitutional issue relates to the Eighth Amendment, concerning cruel and unusual punishment. There is a great deal of criticism of the use of electroshock devices in prisons as their use in prison is viewed as a violation of the Eighth Amendment. Stun belts, which have two metal prongs positioned just above the left kidney, leave welts that can take up to six months to heal, and the belt could cause fatalities. Like the stun belt, the taser, and the stun gun, the shield is an electronic shocking device. Guards frequently use the shield when removing prisoners from their cells, but the death of a Texas corrections officer who suffered a heart attack shortly after receiving a shock from an electric shield similar in design to the stun belt raises serious questions about the belt's safety. As part of the training, Officer Landis was required to endure two 45,000-volt shocks, but on December 1, 1995, something went terribly wrong. Shortly after the second shock, Landis collapsed and died. Although the maker of the shield denied that it had killed

Landis, the Coryell County justice of the peace who conducted an inquiry into Landis's death reported that Landis's autopsy showed that he died as a result of cardiac dirhythmia due to coronary blockage following electric shock by an electronic stun shield. The electric shock threw his heart into a different rhythmic beat, causing him to die. The Texas Department of Criminal Justice, which had used the shields to subdue prisoners since September 1995 immediately suspended their use (Cusac 1996; Roberti 2002). In another incident in Virginia, the state used a stun gun repeatedly to shock a 50-year-old prisoner, Lawrence James Frazier, who was already in the infirmary because of his diabetes. Frazier lapsed into a coma and died five days later. Although the Virginia Department of Corrections later claimed that a "medical study" proved that the use of the stun gun did not cause Frazier's death, the study was actually only a review of policies and procedures and did not include an examination of the body or forensic reports (Amnesty International 2000).

The electric/lethal fence has been criticized for its cruelty. At Calipatria prison (California), the electric fence has caused the deaths of wild and endangered birds that came in contact with the fence. This outraged bird lovers and after the "death fence" (as it became known as) had become an international environmental scandal, the state was forced to create a birdproof fence (the only one in the world) by using vertical mesh netting that envelops both sides of the electrified fence, thus making it an ecologically sensitive death fence. It also now consists of a warning wire for curious rodents, antiperching deflectors for wildfowl, and tiny passageways for burrowing owls. It has also built an attractive pond for visiting geese and ducks (Davis 1995).

One of the greatest concerns over the user of electroshock devices is their abuse by the officers and the institution. In a prison, operators of these devices could use them (and the threats of their use) for simply sadistic purposes or to coerce prisoners to do whatever the operator wants. This would allow these guards to take retribution on the prison population. Amnesty International has criticized the use of high-tech weapons in prisons as torture, especially the stun belt. It has argued that there is something frightening about them. Since there is no independent medical testing, Amnesty International found it outrageous that prison officials use the stun belt on inmates with HIV/AIDS in Old Parish Prison in New Orleans. At Parish Prison, inmates must sign a release form granting prison officials authorization to fit them with the belt for transportation to health facilities for life-saving medical treatment. What was especially disturbing to Amnesty International was that if an HIV-positive inmate refuses to sign the release, he or she would be denied transportation and thus denied urgent medical care (Schulz 1999). Amnesty International has recommended that federal, state, and local authorities (1) ban the use of remote control electroshock stun belts by law enforcement and correctional agencies and (2) prohibit the manufacture, promotion, distribution, and transfer (both within and from the United States) of stun belts and all other electroshock weapons, such as stun guns, stun shields, and tasers pending the outcome of a rigorous, independent, and impartial inquiry into the use and effects of the equipment. The organization also suggested that American companies should cease production of the remote control stun belt and suspend all manufacture, promotion, and transfers of all other stun weapons, pending the aforementioned inquiry (Schulz 1999).

Reliability and Accuracy

One of the major issues regarding technological devices is their reliability and accuracy. Automated biometric systems, for example, are not 100 percent foolproof. Although fingerprints, the face, and the voice, for example, remain constant from day to day, small fluctuations, such as cold or moist hands, different degree of lighting for face recognition, and background noise for voice authentication can confuse the devices. Setting the sensitivity too low increases the odds of an imposter's logon being accepted (false positive). High-sensitivity setting means greater security, but it also means that an authorized user may be erroneously rejected (false negative) (Gunnerson 1999).

Recently, a scanner that registers traces of microscopic particles associated with 40 different types of drugs at the State Correctional Institution in Woods Run, Pittsburgh, Pennsylvania, gave several false positive results, including one for a prison guard's shift commander (Bucsko 2001). Also on January 20, 2001, six inmates escaped by circumventing a 5,000-volt malfunctioning electric fence in Alabama by using a broomstick to pry up the electric fence and slide under it. The alarms of the electric fence did not go off (*News Tribune Online Edition* 2001).

The geophone-based detector for detecting heartbeats of inmates trying to escape in a vehicle is not without shortcomings as well. The main problem is that it can be used only on a vehicle that is cushioned from the ground—for instance, by shock absorbers, springs, and rubber tires. If the vehicle is not cushioned from the ground, the earth itself serves as a kind of vibrational damper. That is, the vehicle and the earth virtually become one solid body. Vibrations from heartbeats are strong enough to move a truck but not strong enough to move the earth. This means that ships, which are essentially one with the water they rest in, and railroad cars, whose rigid steel wheels ride on steel tracks, will not vibrate strongly enough for heartbeats to be detected by the geophones (Strauss 1997).

High Cost

Although technology has reduced prison cost in many instances, start-up cost can be high. The cost for technological devices in prison is too high for some states. Although high-tech solutions may ultimately reduce staffing demands, they require funds for construction, installation, and training (Weed 2001). The price tag attached to implementing telemedicine can be high. In Ohio, for example, the largest investment in its telemedicine program was the video hardware, which includes video codecs (coder/decoder), cameras, and monitors. The initial cost of hardware per site was approximately $87,000 and there is the possibility the equipment will not be usable beyond five years (NASCIO 2001). Likewise, in Texas, telemedicine units alone cost $50,000. The total package, including the unit, communications system, equipment on the receiving end, and software, adds up to a cost per facility of $100,000–$300,000 (Proctor 2000). Smart cards could be expensive; each card can cost $8.88; readers, $59; and handheld readers, $8,000. Hardware and software can cost $125,000; systems engineering, $175,000; conversion, $50,000; and support, another $50,000 (Guseau 1999). The installation of

Arizona's lethal fence will cost $1.2 million (Tugan 2000) and the chair in Arizona's prison that scans inmates for weapons costs $6,500 (Lau 2001).

Apart from the specific problems discussed above, there are still some general issues and questions regarding the use of technology. One is the effect that technology will have on the relationship between inmates and correctional officers. One wonders whether the increased isolation (because of technology) between inmates and officers will increase the hostilities of the inmates for officers. After years of being this coercive environment of technological devices, how would the inmates adapt to society on the outside once they are released? What are the physical and psychological effects of years of exposure to technological devices on inmates? What are the goals of all this technological gadgetry and are these goals being achieved? Finally what types of prisoners are being created with this extensive use of technology; will inmates be turned into robots? These are some of the unanswered questions that have not been addressed as society continues to create prisons with the prison system using the "Big Brother is Watching You" strategy.

RECOMMENDATIONS

Although technological devices are beginning to revolutionalize the prison system, they are subjected to manipulation. More needs to be done to prevent abuses. The following are some recommendations designed to improve the use of technological devices:

1. To curtail the unauthorized use of technology by prison personnel, Congress should pass legislation regulating the use of the technology. The legislation should clearly stipulate that the use of technological devices should be limited to its original purpose. Violation of the legislation should result in criminal sanctions.

2. State and federal governments should ensure that technological databases in prison are physically secured. Any physical documents pertaining to the database should be kept in a secured area, which could be protected by security personnel, alarm systems, video surveillance, and other related security devices to prevent unauthorized access to the information (see Woodward 1997).

3. To prevent constitution challenges to the use of technology in prisons, manufacturers should work closely with legal scholars to ensure that their systems are secure and free from constitutional challenges.

4. To maximize the use of technology, all states should establish technology review committees in prison to evaluate various technologies before purchased or used. The benefit of such committees is that the prison agency becomes more knowledgeable about technological needs and requirements.

5. State and federal governments should force manufacturers of these devices conduct comprehensive tests to determine their reliability, accuracy, and safety of these technological devices.

SUMMARY

Over the last decade, technological innovation has spurred the development of new devices to improve supervision in prisons. Technological advances have occurred in virtually every aspect of prison life and have led to changing roles for prison officials. Management information systems and smart cards have been introduced as a more affordable and comprehensive means of tracking inmate activities. Perimeter detectors, biometrics, and electroshock devices can prevent prison escapes. Drug and alcohol abuse testing packages, telemedicine, and videoconferencing all are products of advances in technology in prisons.

The extensive use of technology in prison has created images of an Orwellian nightmare "Big Brother" society since these technological devices are being used to watch, detect, secure, and contain inmates all across the United States. It is expected that technology will increase its appeal to prison administrators and politicians because of its versatility. Consequently, future prisons will become more and more technologically sophisticated.

It is undeniably true that through the use of these technological gadgetry, a large number of inmates can be supervised. However, as the prisons continue to be an integral part of the technological revolution, there are challenges ahead. Administrators should be cautious not to rely on technology to the point where safety is compromised. It is also important for prison officials to remember that technologies are devices that require well-trained staff to operate them. It is also perhaps too early to evaluate whether high-tech supervision will, in the long run, be the cost-effective, cost-efficient, and safer way to operate prisons. All new technology has it pitfalls and problems, and only time will tell how effective they really are. What is quite clear is that prisons have become part of the technological landscape and technology will continue to affect the way prisons are operated in the United States.

REFERENCES

ABT ASSOCIATES (1999, July 9). Abt Associates Finds Use of Telemedicine Can Reduce Health Care Costs in Prisons. [Retrieved February 15, 2003, from http://www.abtassoc.com/html/newsroom/press-releases/pr-telemedicine.html]

AMNESTY INTERNATIONAL (2000, July 11). After Prison Stun Gun Death, Virginia Refuses Amnesty International Visit: Amnesty International demands VA Suspend Electro-Shock Stun Gun Use. Washington, DC: Amnesty International (Author). [Retrieved February 14, 2003, from http://www.amnestyusa.org/news/2000/usa07112000.html]

BUCSKO, M. (2001). Scanning of prison visitors under fire: Inaccurate drug detector prompts unfair penalties. *Pittsburgh Post-Gazette:* B5

BONE, J. M. and C. L. CRUMBACKER. (2001, July). Facial Recognition—Assessing its Viability in the Corrections Environment. *Corrections Today*, 62–64.

CAMPBELL, J. P., L. A. ALYEA, and J. DUNN. (1996). *Biometric Security: Government Applications and Operations.* At 1 in CardTech/SecurTech (CTST). Government Conference Proceedings. [Retrieved March 15, 2003, from http://www.biometrics.org/REPORTS/CTSTG961]

CARAMANIS, C. B. (1999). Detection and monitoring technologies help DOC become virtually drug-free. *The Corrections Connection.* (February). [Retrieved February 15, 2003, from http://www.corrections.com/news/technology/detection.html *Post* (March 30): H1.

CELLULAR-NEWS. (2006). Locating Cell Phones Inside Prisons. [Retrieved April 13, 2007 from http://www.cellular-news.com/story/18558.php]

CENTER FOR CRIMINAL JUSTICE TECHNOLOGY NEWSLETTER. (2001, June 18). Biometrics at York County (Pa) prison. [Retrieved February 11, 2003, from http://www.mitretek.org/business_areas/justice/cjiti/ccjtnews/weekly/vol5-4.html]

CHANDRASEKARAN, R. (1997). Brave new whorl: ID systems using the human body are here, but privacy issues persist, *Washington Post* (March 30): H1.

CHEN, H, (1988). *Medical Genetics Handbook*. St. Louis, MO: W.H. Green.

COLATOSTI, T. (1998, November 18). *Wisconsin Department of Corrections Chooses Viisage*. Viisage Technology, Inc. [Retrieved February 15, 2003, from http//www.viisage.com]

CRUELTY IN CONTROL? The stun belt and other electroshock weapons in law enforcement.

CUSAC, A. (1996). Stunning technology. *Progressive* 60(7): 18–22.

DAVIS, M. (1995, February 20). Hell factories in the field: A prison-industrial complex. *Nation*. 260(7): 229–234.

dEGROOT, G. (1997). Hot new technologies. *Corrections Today* 59(4): 60–62.

DEMSKY, I. (2005). Prisons combat contraband cellular phones. Tennessean.com. [Retrieved March14, 2007 from http://tennessean.com/government/archives/05/03/67493825.shtml?Element_ID=67493825]

DESMARAIS, N. (2000). Biometrics and network security. *Information Technology Interest Group, New England Chapter* (November/December). [Retrieved February 15, 2003, from http://abacus.bates.edu/acrlnec/sigs/itig/tc_nov_dec2000.htm]

DIRECTIONS. (2001). ADC brings in the boss: 1, 8. [Retrieved February 20, 2003, from www.adc.state.az.us/Directions/2001/julydirections2001]. Publications of Arizona Department of Corrections.

ESSER, M. (2000). *Biometric Authentication* [Retrieved February 6, 2003, from http://faculty.ed.umuc.edu/-meinkej/inss690/messer/Paper]

FINGER-SCAN.COM. (1999). Finger scan technology [Retrieved February 16, 2003 http://au.fujitsu.com/FAL/CDA/Articles/0,1029,305~1063,00.htm]

FUJITSU AUSTRALIA. (2001). Fujitsu smart card solution for Australia's 21st Century prison. [Retrieved February 16, 2003, from http://www.au.fujitsu.com/FAL/CDA/Articles/0,1029,305~1063,00.htm]

GAILIUN, M. (1997). Telemedicine. *Corrections Today* 59(4): 68–70.

GASEAU, M. (1999). Corrections technology options are expanding. *Corrections Today* 61(6), 22–25.

GEO GROUP INC. (2006, July 26). GEO Group Inc. implements leading technology to combat hidden contraband cellular phones in correctional facilities. [Retrieved February 16, 2003, from http://www.reiusa.net/downloads/REI_GEO_July_06.pdf]

GUNNERSON, G. (1999). *Are you ready for biometrics?* [Retrieved February 16, 2003, from http://www.zdnet.com/products/stories/reviews/0,4161,386987-2,00.html]

ION TRACK. (2002). Prisons. [Retrieved *January 19, 2003*, from http://www.iontrack.com/applications/prisons/notes.html]

IOSOFTWARE. (2000). *Biometrics explained.* [Retrieved February 14, 2003, from http://www.iosoftware.com/biometrics/explained.htm]

ISAACS, L. (2002a). Emerging technologies use physical characteristics to verify identities of residents and employees. *American City and County* 117 (3): 22–27.

ISAACS, L. (2002b). Body language. *American City and County* 117(3): 22–27.

JACKSON, K. (1998a). Evaluating correctional technology. *Corrections Today* 60(4,): 58–67.

JACKSON, K. (1998b). The application of security measures. *Corrections Today* 60(4): 58–67.

JUSTICE TECHNOLOGY INFORMATION NETWORK. (1998). Ohio inmates get "carded". [Retrieved March 2, 2003 from http://www.nlectc.org/virlib/InfoDetail.asp?intInfoID=293]

KELLEY, D., and K. OIEN (2000, May 3). Implementing biometric technology to enhance correctional safety and security. [Retrieved February 12, 2003, from http://tunxis.commnet.edu/ccjci/futures/classviii/kelley_oien.html]

LAU, J. (2001, August 16). Inmates hide assortment of metallic items. 08/16/2001—NLECTC News Summary. [Retrieved February 11, 2003, from http://www.mail-archive.com/justnetnews@nlectc.org/msg00068.html]

McMANUS, K. (May 6, 1996). At banks of future, an eye for an ID. *Washington Post*, p. A3

MILLER, B. (1996). Everything you need to know about automated biometric identification. CardTech/SecurTech (CTST) Government Conference Proceedings: 1.

MILLER; M. (2002, March 20). Live video used in court case; keeps dangerous criminals in jail. *The Capital Times* (Madison, WI) (March 20): 3A.

NASCIO (2001). Ohio-telemedicine-innovative use of technology. [Retrieved February 16, 2003, from https://www.nascio.org/awards/1998awards/Innovative/ohio.cfm]

NATIONAL LAW ENFORCEMENT AND CORRECTIONS TECHNOLOGY CENTER (2000). *TechBeat Fall 2000.* [Retrieved January 25, 2003 from http://www.nlectc.org/txtfiles/tbfall2000.html]

NEWS TRIBUTE ONLINE EDITION (2001). 5 of 6 Alabama escapees caught in Tennessee. [http://www.newstribune.com/stories/020101/wor 0201010013.asphttp://www.new]

PRIES, A. (2001). Looking into the future; Iris recognition: Could replace pins and passwords. *Bergen Record* (August 6): L6.

Prison Talk Online (2004, November 9). Ohio Prisons Pilot Facial Recognition Technology. Retrieved January 28, 2008 from http://prisontalk.com/forums/showthread.php?t=92796

REID, K. (2001). Detection devices squelch escape tries in just a heartbeat: Prisons screen vehicles at gate. *Chicago Tribune* (September 10): B7.

RITTER, J. (1999). Eye scans help sheriff keep suspects in sight. *Chicago Sun-Times* (June 22): 18.

ROBERTI, M. (2002). Big brother goes behind bars. *Fortune* (September 30): 44.

SCHULZ, W. (1999). *Cruelty in Control? The Stun Belt and Other Electroshock Weapons in Law Enforcement.* Washington, DC: Amnesty International USA. [Retrieved February 9, 2003, from http://www.amnestyusa.org/rights forall/stun/press-schulz.html]

SCOLFORO, M. (2005, July 1). Federal prisons install killer fences. *Associated Press.* [Retrieved April 10, 2007 from http://www.unknownnews.org/0507050701prisons.html]

SWEDBERG, C. (2005, May 15). L.A. County Jail to Track Inmates. [Retrieved April 10, 2007 from http://www.tsilink.com/assets/media/rfid journal_la.pdf]

STEWART, T. L. (2000). *Technology* and Security—Opportunities and Challenges. *Corrections Today* 62 (4): 8–9.

STRAUSS, S. (1997). Detecting stowaways. *Technology Review* 100(1): 14–15.

SULLIVAN, L. (2006, October 12). Inmates smuggle in cell phones with ease. NPR. [Retrieved April 13, 2007, from http://www.npr.org/templates/story/story.php?storyId=6248833]

THE ASSOCIATED PRESS STATE & LOCAL WIRE (2002, April 15). Prison inmates now make court appearances via TV. Retrieved February 16, 2003 from http://www.cor.state.mt.us/css/news/NewsRelease.asp

THE CORRECTIONS CONNECTION (2001). Florida DOC increases security with identification technology. [Retrieved March 2, 2003, from http://www.corrections.com/technetwork/thtml]

THE THIRD BRANCH (2001, November 12). Video-conferencing in courts shows potential and possible problems. Vol. 33 (12). [Retrieved December 15, 2002, from http://www.uscourts.gov/ttb/dec01ttb/videoconferencing.html]

THE ULTIMATE SCAM (2002). Smart card 'n Micro-chips. [Retrieved February 16, 2003, http://www.members.shaw.ca/theultimatescam/Smart%20Card.htm]

TIERNEY, T. (1995). Eyes have it in future of law enforcement: Technology expands to identify suspects. *Chicago Tribrune* (June 27): 1.

TUGAN, B. (2000). $100 million prison to open September 8. *Las Vegas Sun* (Nov. 12, 2001). [Retrieved February 13, 2003, from http://www.ndoc.state.nv.us/news/display.php?article_id=8]

VILLA, J. (2005, October 31). Video screens edge out face-to-face visits in jail. *The Arizona Republic.* [Retrieved February 10, 2003, from http://www.azcentral.com/arizonarepublic/news/articles/1031videovisitation31.html]

WEED, W. S. (2001). Future tech: Iron bars, silicon chips: High-tech prison reform comes to America's state and federal inmates. Discover 22(5). [Retrieved February 20, 2003, from http://www.discover.com/may_01/feattech.html]

WEISS, D. (2003, May 2). Court teleconferencing a big money saver. *Times Leader.* [Retrieved February 20, 2003, from http://www.timesleader.com/mld/timesleader/news/5898553.htm]

WIRED NEWS (1997). Prisons aim to keep, and keep ahead of, convicts. [Retrieved February 23, 2003, from http://www.wired.com/news/technology/0,1282,8583,00.html]

WOOD, M. (2000). Overview of biometric encryption. *Information Security Reading Room.* [Retrieved February 23, 2003, from http://rr.sans.org/authentic/biometric3.php]

WOODWARD, J. D. (1997). Biometric scanning, law and policy: Identifying the concerns—Drafting the biometric blueprint. *University of Pittsburgh Law Review* 59: 97

WRIGHT. S, and R. F. BUTLER, (2001). Can drug detection technology stop drugs from entering prisons? *Corrections Today* 63(4): 66–69.

YEOMAN, B. (2000, March/April). Shocking discipline. *Mother Jones* 25(2): 17–18.

ZDNET. (1999). *How biometrics works.* [Retrieved February 23, 2003, from http:// www.zdnet.com/products/stories/reviews/0,4161,2199371,00.html]

ZUNKEL, R. (1998). Hand geometry based verification. In *Biometrics: Personal Identification in Networked Society,* eds A. Jain, R. Bolle, and S. Pankanti, 87–102. Norwell, MA: Kluwer Academic Publishers.

Chapter 3

Criminal Justice and Forensic Science

Partners in Solving Crimes

Etta Morgan

The American system of criminal justice is believed to be a fair and impartial system. This belief may be due in part to the Pledge of Allegiance's assurance that each individual is entitled to justice. How do we define the term justice? According to Black (1979), justice is the "proper administration of laws. In jurisprudence, the constant and perpetual disposition of legal matters or disputes to render every man his due" (p. 776). The administration of justice seems to be an easy task to accomplish, yet, there have been numerous cases in which the administration of justice had been obscured due to one or a combination of the following: (a) prosecutorial misconduct, (b) ineffective assistance of counsel, (c) judicial overrides, (d) mis-identification, (e) improper police investigations, (f) plea bargains, and (g) perjuried testimony. What actually takes place is a miscarriage of justice. The administration of justice should focus on the truth about a case and not on nonlegal matters.

In criminal cases, the evidence is crucial not only to the prosecution but also to the defense. According to Coleman and Swenson (1994), "evidence in a criminal trial concerns the intent, motive, means, and opportunity to commit a crime." The attorneys rely on the forensic scientist to interpret the physical evidence found at the scene of a crime to provide information such as specifics about a possible suspect, the events leading up to the crime, an approximation of the time of death, and additional information about the victim(s) from a medical perspective. Working with the evidence, the forensic scientist is able to provide attorneys with information about a case in order to determine if the facts warrant a trial (American Academy of Forensic Sciences 2007). If it is determined that the facts justify a trial, the district attorney's office prepares the case for trial. Based on the facts of the case he/she may require the expert testimony of various forensic scientists and others who are deemed experts in a particular area.

There has been impressive growth in the tools that are available to the criminalist. Science has advanced greatly in the past 50 years due in part to military research. Much of this research as well as advanced medical research has generated a long list of scientific tools and analytical tools that can be used to seek evidence at the crime scene. These new skills are highlighted in television programs, such as *Forensic Files*, *Medical Detectives*, *the System*, and the new CSI series. These new tools have had a mixed impact on the administration of justice. New tools such as deoxyribonucleic acid (DNA) analysis both help identify offenders and open the doors of the prison for men and women wrongly accused and convicted. They also permit the development of sophisticated evidence that can build a circumstantial case that impresses juries putting additional innocent people in prison. New technology gathers information to prosecute sophisticated offenders but can also be used to greatly reduce the freedom and liberty of all of us.

Although new technology provides excellent crime fighting tools, they are not without cost to the privacy of ordinary citizens. New legislation permits the use of eavesdropping of certain citizens in an attempt to fight terrorism. Additionally, the increased use of cameras in public places will allow the government to establish a face recognition database and ordinary citizens cannot choose to be omitted from the database. These and other measures are being implemented as national security measures and therefore do not require citizenry approval.

The use of forensic science in criminal or civil cases is an attempt to provide scientific support in the determination of facts (American Academy of Forensic Sciences 2007). Forensic science is most often associated with criminal justice, but, in fact it also plays a vital role in civil cases. For the purposes of this chapter the focus will be on criminal cases. The importance of forensic science to criminal investigations is not a new role; instead, it is a role that has been popularized in recent years because of some high profile criminal cases. In fact, the Chinese solved a criminal case in 1248 using forensic science to determine the cause of death. Again in 1784 in England, physical evidence was linked to a suspect using the principles of matching (New York State Troopers 2003a).

Further research in forensic science by Edmond Locard led to what is known as the Locard's Exchange Principles that suggests that there is an exchange of particles, fibers, hairs, and other physical evidence when an individual makes contact with an individual or object. These minute items may be microscopically examined and chemically tested to determine a match. It is on the premise of Locard's Exchange Principles that forensic science continues to advance our understanding that evidence has no particular size or shape, but that all evidence has particular properties that can be identified as having either a class or individual characteristic (Saferstein 2007).

HISTORY OF FORENSIC SCIENCE

The earliest known recordings documenting scientific methods as investigative tools have been credited to the Chinese who "used fingerprints to establish the identity of documents and clay sculptures" (New York State Troopers 2003:1a) during the 700s.

King Richard I was the first to establish an Office of the Coroner whose duties included not only documenting criminal matters but also investigating suspicious deaths. Because of the complexities of unnatural deaths, coroners soon realized that they needed the assistance of physicians to assist in determining the cause of death and that attending physicians required specific training in determination of death. Noting the need for specialization in death determination in order to assist the office of the coroner, a department of legal medicine was established at the University of Edinburgh in 1807 (Forensic Science 2003).

As with many imported ideas, the coroner system was also a product of England. The colonies experienced an increase in the use of physicians in death determinations and, as a result, there was a demand for changes in the processing of unnatural death investigations. This led to the establishment of the Office of the Medical Examiner in Massachusetts in 1877, headed by a physician, whose duties were to investigate unnatural deaths (Forensic Science 2003). Throughout the 1800s there were many advancements in forensic science such as Marthieu Orfila's treatise on forensic toxicology, Francis Galton's fingerprint analysis and classification system, a refined method of bullet comparison, the use of photography as an investigative tool, and the development of tests for blood identification. Perhaps one of the most interesting events during this period in forensic science was trying to identify wound patterns in the victims of Jack the Ripper (Saferstein 2007; New York State Troopers 2003a).

Prior to 1902, there was no formal training in forensic science and the first university course offering did not occur until 1930. By 1950, "the University of California at Berkley established one of the first academic departments of criminology/criminalistics" (New York State Troopers 2003a). Some of the advancements in forensic science during the 1900s have included voice print identification, the use of the comparison microscope as a vital instrument in studying bullets, development of procedures for determining blood group identification from a dried bloodstain, the first text identifying the principles of document examination, and the use of DNA in court proceedings. As a result of challenges to some DNA evidence, several changes occurred in the forensic science community. There was a movement to establish accreditation, standardization, and certification criteria along with specific procedures to ensure quality not only in DNA laboratories but also within the forensic science community (New York State Troopers 2003a).

In some instances, the challenge to the DNA evidence was the push that was needed to cause some professionals to form professional organizations identifying their purposes and goals, but there were also some organizations already established. For example, The American Society of Questioned Document Examiners (ASQDE) was officially established in 1942, although Albert Osborn conducted the first meeting in 1913 with meetings continuing yearly until its formal inception. The purpose of ASQDE was and remains "to foster education, sponsor scientific research, establish standards, exchange experience and provide instruction in the field of questioned document examination, and to promote justice in matters that involve questions about documents (American Society of Questioned Document Examiners 2007)."

SPECIALTY AREAS OF FORENSIC SCIENCE

Perhaps the best known individual involved in a forensic investigation is the Medical Examiner (ME). The ME is responsible for determining the extent of injuries present, the cause and time of these injuries, and the cause of death. If after an external examination of the body, the cause of death cannot be determined, or it appears suspicious an autopsy will be performed (Saferstein 2007). If an autopsy is performed, the ME will call upon other forensic experts to assist in determining the cause of death.

Forensic toxicologists examine body fluids, organs, and tissue to determine what chemicals are present in the body. If the body has not been identified, the ME forwards the fingerprints of the individual to a fingerprint unit. Local and state agencies may request the services of the Federal Bureau of Investigation's Integrated Automated Fingerprint Identification System (IAFIS), which is capable of searching a database of more than 35 billion known fingerprints (Federal Bureau of Investigation 2007b) if there are no matching fingerprints in either the local or Statewide Automated Fingerprint Identification System (SAFIS) databases. In the event the ME is unable to collect fingerprints to use as a method of identification, a forensic odontologist must assist in the identification by examining the teeth of the individual and comparing them to dental charts of known missing individuals. The forensic odontologist can also assist in the identification of a perpetrator in instances where the victim and/or the perpetrator left bite marks. Photographs taken of the bite marks can be matched to an individual after a suspect has been identified and plaster impressions are made of the suspect's teeth. Teeth are similar to fingerprints in that no two sets are alike.

The ME is sometimes faced with only the bones of an individual that need to be identified. In cases of this nature, a forensic anthropologist must assist in the identification process. According to Byers (2008), the forensic anthropologist has specific objectives: (1) determine ancestry of the individual, (2) identify the type of trauma the individual has experienced, (3) assist in determining the approximate time of death, (4) assist in recovering forensic evidence from the scene where the remains were found, and (5) "using the unique features present in virtually all skeletons . . . provide information useful in obtaining positive identification of deceased persons" (p.1). Using information such as race, sex, and thickness of the facial skin, the forensic anthropologist can reconstruct a facial likeness of an individual that law enforcement personnel can present to the media in an attempt to solicit public information that could assist in identifying an individual.

In addition to the forensic anthropologist, the forensic biologist can assist in identification by using bone tissue from the individual. Forensic biologists use DNA extracted from bone tissue to create a DNA profile. This profile can be compared to known family members of missing persons in hopes of establishing an identity. "Even without a DNA match to conclusively identify the body, a profile is useful because it can provide important clues about the victim, such as his or her sex and race" (O'Connell 2003). The use of DNA can also help to identify a suspect in a criminal case. Local and state laboratories participate in the Combined DNA Index System (CODIS). DNA that has been collected from convicted offenders, unsolved crime scenes, and missing persons is maintained in databases in each participating laboratory. When DNA is present, but there is no suspect, a profile is established and transmitted electronically to all CODIS databases within a state in search of a match. In 1998, the DNA search capabilities were expanded with the establishment of The National DNA Index System (NDIS) operated by the FBI. This new system allows DNA profiles to be shared nationwide; previously, only 24 states and the FBI participated in this system. The use of DNA evidence is such an important factor in criminal cases that every state now authorizes the collection of DNA samples from convicted offenders along with the establishment of CODIS databases where they currently do not exist on the state level (Federal Bureau of Investigation 2007b). Other areas of forensic science can also contribute to establishing facts in criminal and civil cases.

According to Byrd (2007a), "Forensic Entomology is the use of the insects and their arthropod relatives that inhabit decomposing remains to aid in legal investigations" (www.forensicentomology.com/definition.htm). Using insect evidence, the forensic entomologist can provide valuable information such as establishing a time of death, known as the *postmortem interval (PMI)* as well as determining the likelihood of whether or not a body has been moved from one location to another (American Board of Forensic Entomology 2007; Byrd 2007b). The forensic entomologist can also assist in an investigation by noting any signs that insects might have transported blood during their normal activities that could cause a misinterpretation of the blood evidence. Because of their living and feeding habits, insects are able to provide information that may be able to assist investigators in reconstructing the crime. Additionally, insects may be analyzed by a forensic toxicologist in order to yield information about drugs and toxins that were in the human remains (Byrd 2007b).

Another aspect of forensic science is forensic serology. O'Connor (2002) states, "determination of the type and characteristics of blood, blood testing, bloodstain examination, and preparation of testimony or presentations at trial are the main job functions of a forensic serologist, who also analyzes semen, saliva, other body fluids and may or may not be involved with DNA testing." Blood evidence can assist a forensic serologist in reconstructing a crime scene. Based on its location and amount, blood evidence can tell body position of the victim and the perpetrator during various stages of the crime, movement through the crime scene, and the direction of the blows that caused the splatter or drops of blood (O'Connor 2002). In some instances, blood may not be visible, yet traces may remain on surfaces for years. If investigators suspect that blood has been "cleaned up" at a crime scene, they may use luminol to expose it. Harris (2003) notes that "the basic idea of luminol is to reveal these traces with a light-producing chemical reaction between several chemicals and hemoglobin, an oxygen-carrying protein in the blood." In order to be sure that blood has been located, the item(s) containing the suspected blood must be tested. Although luminol is a valuable asset in criminal investigations, it is used with caution since it can also destroy other crime scene evidence.

Forensic imaging is also a vital component in criminal investigations whether it is in the field or laboratory. Forensic imaging provides services such as suspect drawings, age progression photographs of individuals, courtroom presentations, and "enhancing blurred or distorted photographs" (New York State Troopers 2003c). Photographic comparisons can be conducted using videotapes, surveillance films, and photographs once a suspect has been identified and a known photograph is obtained. Additionally, mathematical formulas can be applied to photographic images in order to determine various dimensions of specific items or persons in videotapes, surveillance film, and ordinary photographs (Federal Bureau of Investigation 1999).

The photographic unit of a crime laboratory can also establish the location, date, and time of a photograph and its authenticity. Most manufactured material possesses characteristics that are unique to its particular processes, such as materials used in composition, date and batch numbers or codes, and location of manufacturing plant. Using this information, the photographic unit is able to provide a specific window of time related to the taking of the photograph. Cameras, like guns, produce their own markings on film. According to the FBI, "cameras can be examined and compared with negatives to determine whether a specific camera exposed a specific image [and] black and white and color photographic images can be produced from video images for enlargements and courtroom presentations" (Federal Bureau of Investigation 1999). Videos that contain suspected automobile images can be identified using the National Automotive Image File to establish a make and model of the vehicle to assist in the investigations. The FBI's photographic unit also maintains the Child Exploitation and Obscenity Reference File. Law enforcement personnel are able to request a comparison of known photographs in this database to current child pornography photos to determine their origin (Federal Bureau of Investigation 1999) in an attempt to identify a suspect.

With the advances in technology, crime scene photographers can now use tele-forensics and cyclovision. According to the New York State Troopers (2003c) tele-forensics has the following benefits:

> [It] brings a crime scene to the experts rather than the experts to the crime scene, reduces traffic, contamination and unauthorized personnel at a crime scene, and increases the quality and the number of items admitted to court and opportunities for expert review. . . . The photographer records the images of the scene with a digital video camera, sending the images directly to a remote trailer, located anywhere within a radius of 2.5 miles. . . . Cyclovision creates new capabilities for digital photography . . . enabling the videographer to capture a 360-degree image of the entire crime scene; the digital is then converted into a panoramic image on a computer. An entire room can be photographed in a single shot.

Other evidence collected at a crime scene related to toolmarks and firearms are referred to a forensic firearm and toolmarks unit of a crime laboratory. During an examination of a firearm, information is collected that will tell the investigator, the overall condition of a weapon, whether or not the casings found at the scene were fired from the weapon that was recovered, the amount of pressure required to fire a particular weapon, and information regarding the rifling characteristics of fired bullets which helps to identify the weapon used in the crime. Once a weapon has been identified, the firearms unit can conduct gunshot residue examinations that will establish the distance between the target and the muzzle when it was fired. Also, if a weapon has been identified, the firearms unit can conduct a shot pattern examination. "Shot pattern examinations can determine the approximate distance at which a shotgun was fired by testing a specific firearm and ammunition combination at known distances" (Federal Bureau of Investigation 2003a).

Identification of a weapon or ammunition manufacturer can also be determined from cartridge cases and wadding. When there is limited information available to identify a weapon, "the images of questioned cartridge cases and shotshell casings can be scanned into DRUGFIRE to compare evidence from other shooting incidents" (Federal Bureau of Investigation 2003a). DRUGFIRE is a nationwide computerized database that can match firings with specific weapons that have been recovered from other crime scenes.

The firearms and toolmarks unit is also responsible for matching impressions left by various tools used in a crime. For example, if a window was forced open with a crowbar, the crowbar will leave an impression that is unique to the suspect crowbar. Once the unit has identified the type of tool used, the investigators can request a search warrant of the suspect's home and car in an attempt to find the tool identified. Toolmark impressions may be left on almost any surface including human bone and cartilage (Federal Bureau of Investigation 2003b). As with all evidence collection, care must be taken to preserve the impressions in the condition in which they were found even it requires removing a door.

There are several other forensic science specialties available to criminal investigators to assist in the apprehending and conviction of offenders. The above list is not exclusive and should only be used as a guide to more detailed information.

ADMISSIBILITY AND USE OF FORENSIC EVIDENCE IN COURT

In *United States v. Frye* (1923), the U.S. Supreme Court established what is known as the "general acceptance test" to determine if scientific evidence is admissible in court. At the time of the *Frye* ruling, the deception test was in its infancy and not established in its field; therefore the Court ruled that the lie detector evidence was inadmissible because the design from which it evolved was not yet accepted as scientific. *Frye* identified two keys elements to scientific identification: (1) an identifiable scientific community in which the principle is compatible and (2) the procedures related to the principle accepted by the scientific community of which it is a part. The *Frye* standard has been the guiding standard for many years regarding the admissibility of scientific evidence. In 1976, California adopted an additional component to be used with the Frye standard. This component required that when scientific evidence was being introduced, the scientist presenting the evidence must demonstrate to the court that the correct scientific procedures were applied to the case in question.

Prior to the enactment of the Federal Rules of Evidence, the *Frye* and California standards served as the ruling authority on the admissibility of scientific evidence. As such, DNA evidence was successfully challenged and excluded using the *Frye* and California standard in a New York court. With the passage of the Federal Rules of Evidence governing the admissibility of evidence in federal cases, some jurisdictions revised their evidence codes to reflect the requirements of the Federal Rules of Evidence. In *Daubert v. Merrell Dow Pharmaceuticals Inc* (1993), the Court stated that Rule 402 establishes the baseline for evidence noting:

> All relevant evidence is admissible, except as otherwise provided by the Constitution of the United States, by Act of Congress, by these rules, or other rules prescribed by the Supreme Court pursuant to statutory authority. Evidence that is not relevant is not admissible.

RULE 401 "Relevant evidence" is defined as that which has "any tendency to make the existence of any fact that is of consequence to the determination of the action more probable or less probable than it would be without the evidence".

In the Court's opinion, the standard of relevance is rather liberal in these rules; however, the problem is addressed in Federal Rules of Evidence Rule 702 in that "the Rule's requirement that the testimony 'assist the trier of fact to understand the evidence or to determine a fact in issue'" goes primarily to relevance by demanding a valid scientific connection to the pertinent inquiry as a precondition to admissibility (*Daubert* 1993; Federal Rules of Evidence 2003). The admissibility of scientific evidence will continue to face challenges under the auspices of the *Frye*, California, and Federal Rules of Evidence standards as we increase our scientific knowledge base and make it applicable to criminal investigations. In the meantime, the Court should be asked to rule on standards of admissibility of evidence to eliminate the ambiguity that exists between the current Federal Rules of Evidence and the *Frye* standard that is being used in some jurisdictions.

The admissibility of scientific evidence is just the beginning of the impact of this evidence in a criminal case. While the experts might feel comfortable explaining the evidence, there is no way to determine the extent of understanding experienced by the jury. In a case that uses a substantial amount of scientific evidence, some jurors may tend to dismiss the evidence rather than openly admit a lack of understanding. Additionally, when there is conflicting information given regarding the same evidence by experts in the field, jurors are left possibly confused regarding the evidence. As stated earlier, scientific evidence might develop into an impressive circumstantial case against a defendant, and a confused jury might render a verdict of guilty when in fact the defendant is innocent. This may happen when some traditional forms of scientific evidence is presented and passes the *Frye* standard, yet the evidence is erroneous and should be subjected to more rigorous scientific testing (Connors et al. 1996).

If scientific evidence is to be used to identify or link a suspect to a crime, it is best to use DNA testing to decrease the probability of error that may be associated with blood typing evidence. Connors et al. (1996) examined 28 cases that failed to use DNA testing during the trial. "DNA tests results obtained subsequent to trial proved that, on the basis of DNA evidence, the convicted persons could not have committed the crimes for which they were incarcerated" (Connors et al. 1996:20).

The use of forensic evidence to establish an individual's identity is more reliable than eyewitness identification. In *United States v. Wade* (1967), Justice Brennan states, "the vagaries of eyewitness identification are well-known; the annals of criminal law are rife with instances of mistaken identification. Mr. Justice Frankfurter once said: 'what is the worth of identification testimony even when uncontradicted? The identification of strangers is proverbially untrustworthy. The hazards of such testimony are established by a formidable number of instances in the records of English and American trials.'" Since eyewitness testimony may be unreliable, the criminal justice system should seek to insure that the most reliable method of identification is used in order to decrease the number of appeals that are filed in response to mistakes in identification that could have been cleared with scientific evidence once a suspect had been identified. Forensic evidence can indirectly assist in the efficient operation of investigations by possibly eliminating suspects early in investigations thus allowing investigators to focus on finding the true perpetrator(s) of a crime and also in court systems by reducing the number of cases going to trial as well as the number of appeals filed because of erroneous convictions.

SOME ADDITIONAL FORENSIC ORGANIZATIONS

The American Academy of Forensic Sciences (AAFS) was established in 1948. In its professional capacity, AAFS is "dedicated to the application of science to the law, the AAFS is committed to the promotion of education and the elevation of accuracy, precision, and specificity in the forensic sciences (American Academy of Forensic Sciences 2007)." In 1969, The Forensic Sciences Foundation, Inc. (FSF) was established as "a nonprofit organization studying the application of science to the resolution of social and legal issues" (The Forensic Sciences Foundation 2007) and became associated with AAFS in 1973. Today, as a vital component of AASF, FSF represents the "educational, scientific, and research arm of the Academy" (The Forensic Sciences Foundation 2007).

The American College of Forensic Examiners Institute of Forensic Science (ACFEI) has adopted a set of principles of professional practice that states in part,

> ACFEI and its members are to remain completely objective and use their ability to serve justice by the accurate determination of the facts involved. ACFEI members are not advocates for one side or the other. Members should not intentionally withhold or omit any findings or opinions discovered during a forensic examination which would cause the facts to be misinterpreted or distorted

> *(American College of Forensic Examiners Institute of Forensic Science 2007).*

Included in the principles of professional practice is the creed of the forensic examiner that identifies in further detail what is expected of a member of ACFEI in regards to professional performance. These are just a few examples of the organizations that exist to promote standards and development certification criteria for the discipline of forensic science as well as to provide input for boards of crime laboratories.

The American Society of Crime Laboratory Directors (ASCLD) is an organization that is committed to

A- Accuracy and Quality

S- Standards and Ethics

C- Communications and Education

L- Leadership and Vision

D- Development and Technology (American Society of Crime Laboratory Directors 2007)

Using these principles as a foundation, ASCLD focuses on improving management practices in the various labs by proposing suggestions that directly affect the delivery of services provided by the crime lab. Additionally, ASCLD has established The Crime Laboratory Accreditation Program of the American Society of Crime Laboratory Directors/Laboratory Accreditation Board (ASCLD/LAB) whose duties include accrediting crime labs, examining various components of the crime labs for deficiencies in areas of management, equipment, procedures, and so on. Participation in the accreditation program is strictly on a voluntary basis (American Society of Crime Laboratory Directors 2007). For those jurisdictions without a crime laboratory, the Federal Bureau of Investigation Laboratory is available for forensic and technical services at no cost (Federal Bureau of Investigation 2007a).

CONCLUSION

The criminal justice system, like society, continues to evolve. In the process of that evolution, we should embrace ideologies and methods that assist in clarifying information that will lead to the truth as supported by the evidence. The advances in forensic science have assisted in and will continue to assist in the search for the truth during and after prosecution. Using forensic science in the courtroom is not without its problems. First, there have been times when experts have reached totally different conclusions regarding the same scientific evidence and this conflicting information may confuse jurors. Second, the technical explanation used by forensic scientists may be too complex for some jurors to understand and this lack of understanding may lead to a misinterpretation of the evidence during jury deliberation. While these problems should be addressed, they do not possess such a threat to justice to suggest discontinuing its use. The resources required to employ forensic scientists should be available to both the prosecution and defense attorneys in criminal cases.

The professional standards established by various forensic organizations suggest that persons wishing to serve the criminal justice community as experts in their respective fields must adhere to the standards and certification requirements of the organization. These organizations will continue to develop as technological advances open doors to new methods and procedures to examine "uncharted territory" of evidence that in the past was not considered evidence at all. It is because of these advances that the real essence of justice will be achieved in our society.

REFERENCES

AMERICAN ACADEMY OF FORENSIC SCIENCES (2007). About Us. [Retrieved April 4, 2007, from http://www.aafs.org]

AMERICAN BOARD OF FORENSIC ENTOMOLOGY (2007). More about the Science. [Retrieved April 10, 2007, from http://research.missouri.edu/entomology/.]

AMERICAN COLLEGE OF FORENSIC EXAMINERS INSTITUTE OF FORENSIC SCIENCE (2007). About ACFEI—Principles of professional practice. [Retrieved April 5, 2007, from http://www.acfei.com.]

AMERICAN SOCIETY OF CRIME LABORATORY DIRECTORS (2007a). About ASCLD. [Retrieved April 4, 2007, from http://www.asqde.org/about_purpose.htm.]

AMERICAN SOCIETY OF CRIME LABORATORY DIRECTORS (2007b). About ASCLD/LAB-History. [Retrieved April 4, 2007, from http://www.ascld-lab.org/dual/aslabdualhistory.html.]

AMERICAN SOCIETY OF QUESTIONED DOCUMENT EXAMINERS (2007). Stated Purpose of the ASQDE. [Retrieved April 5, 2007, from http://www.asqde.org.]

BLACK, H. (1979). *Black's Law Dictionary,* 5th ed. St. Paul, MN: West.

BYERS, S. (2008). *Introduction to Forensic Anthropology: A Textbook,* 3rd ed. Boston: Allyn and Bacon.

BYRD, J. (2007a). What is forensic entomology? [Retrieved April 10, 2007, from http://www.forensicentomology.com/definition.htm]

BYRD, J. (2007b). What information can a forensic entomologist provide at the death scene? [Retrieved April 10, 2007, from http://www.forensicentomology.com/info.htm]

COLEMAN, H. AND E. SWENSON, (1994). *DNA in the courtroom: A trial watcher's guide.* Seattle, WA: GeneLex Press. [Retrieved April 4, 2007, from http://www.genelex.com/paternitytesting/paternitybook5.html]

CONNORS, E. T., LUNDREGAN, N., MILLER, AND T. MCEWEN, (1996). *Convicted by Juries, Exonerated by Science: Case Studies in the Use of DNA Evidence to Establish Innocence After Trial.* Washington, DC: National Institute of Justice (NCJ 161258).

Daubert v. Merrell Dow Pharmaceuticals, Inc. 509 U.S. 579 (1993).

FEDERAL BUREAU OF INVESTIGATION (1999). Evidence examinations—photographic. [Retrieved April 17, 2003, from http://www.fbi.gov/hq/lab/handbook/examphot.htm]

FEDERAL BUREAU OF INVESTIGATION (2003). Firearms examinations. [Retrieved April 11, 2007, from http://www.fbi.gov/hq/lab/handbook/intro7.htm#firearms].

FEDERAL BUREAU OF INVESTIGATION (2003). FBI laboratory: Firearms-toolmarks unit. [Retrieved April 17, 2003, from http://www.fbi.gov/hq/lab/org/ftu.htm]

FEDERAL BUREAU OF INVESTIGATION (2007a). FBI laboratory. [Retrieved March 28, 2007, from http://www.fbi.gov/hq/lab/labhome.htm]

FEDERAL BUREAU OF INVESTIGATION (2007b). Forensic systems. [Retrieved March 28, 2007, from http://www.fbi.gov/hq/lab/org/systems.htm]

FEDERAL RULES OF EVIDENCE (2003). Article VII opinions and expert testimony. [Retrieved April 5, 2003, from http://www2.law.cornell.edu/cgi-bin/foliocgi.exe/Fre/query=[jump!3A27rule702!27]/doc/{...]

"Forensic Science," Microsoft® Encarta® Online Encyclopedia 2003. [Retrieved April 3, 2003, from http://encarta.msn.com © 1997–2003 Microsoft Corporation.

HARRIS, T. (2003). How luminol works. [Retrieved April 17, 2003, from http://science.howstuffworks.com/luminol.htm]

MEEKER-O'CONNELL, A. (2003). How DNA evidence works." [Retrieved April 4, 2003, from http://science.howstuffworks.com/dna-evidence.htm]

NEW YORK STATE TROOPERS (2003a). Forensic science history. [Retrieved April 2, 2003, from http://www.troopers.state.ny.us/ForSc/ForScHist/ForScHistindex.html]

NEW YORK STATE TROOPERS (2003b). Forensic imaging. [Retrieved April 2, 2003, from http://www.troopers.state.ny.us/ForSc/LabSect/Imaging.html]

NEW YORK STATE TROOPERS. (2003c). Mobile crime scene trailer: Tele-forensics/Cyclovision. [Retrieved April 4, 2003, from http://www.troopers.state.ny.us/ForSc/ModFor/CrimeSceneTeleforensic.html]

O'CONNOR, T. (2002). *Part of web cited.* MegaLinks in Criminal Justice. [Retrieved April 18, 2003, from http://faculty.ncwc.edu/toconnor/]

SAFERSTEIN, R. (2007). *Criminalistics: An Introduction to Forensic Science,* 9th ed. Upper Saddle River, NJ: Prentice Hall.

THE FORENSIC SCIENCES FOUNDATION (2007). Profile. [Retrieved April 11, 2007, from http://www.forensicsciencesfoundation.org.]

United States v. Frye 54 App. D.C. 46 (1923).

United States v. Wade 388 U.S. 218 (1967).

Chapter 4

"The World Is Flat"

Globalization and Criminal Justice Organizations and Workplaces in the Twenty-First Century

Rosemary L. Gido, Ph.D.

ABSTRACT

In the shadow of 9/11 and the Iraq War, the United States economy has grown an average of 3 percent annually since 2001. Yet, in the last 15 years, the "New Economy," an intense knowledge-based, digital technology-driven global competition, has policy makers focused on the American workforce—one seen as lacking in learning and skills in today's "flatter" world. Key issues include a growing labor market divide between the highly educated and less educated, outsourcing of jobs to developing countries, the growing shortage of skilled workers, and poor performance of U.S. education systems at all levels. What this means for the criminal justice workplace of the future are challenges of attracting a high-quality workforce in the face of increased competition, affording opportunities to an increasingly diverse workforce, and embracing new organizational work models. The integration of information technologies will require dynamic organizational structures and employee participation inputs. The traditional reactivity and inertia of criminal justice organizations and workplaces will need to change. Elements of community policing recruitment and implementation are reviewed as a model for criminal justice organization and workplace change.

INTRODUCTION

"The World is Flat" according to Thomas Friedman (2007) who has written the best-selling book on the recent acceleration in the "technoeconomic revolution" (Gido 2005). Friedman defines economic "flatness" as connectivity—a global phenomenon whose pace has been fueled most recently by frenetic advances in and access to digital technology, as well as the lowering of trade and political barriers. The major result is that the United States can no longer assume its position of economic dominance in the world, as labor, products, and services are cheaper with global entrepreneurs and workers are on a more equal footing. The "New Economy" is here (*New Economy* Task Force Report 2000).

While the United States post-9/11 and War on Iraq economy "has grown at an average of 3 percent annually since the bottom of the 2001 recession," (*Innovation America: A Final Report* 2007:1), there is still a concern for the growing inequality between higher-educated and lower-educated workers, the outsourcing of high-tech work to countries like China and India, and the failure of U.S. educational systems to prepare students for international competition (p.1).

WORKFORCE ISSUES FOR THE DECADE

The transformation of the U.S. economy from a manufacturing base to a "Knowledge Economy" has been widely documented (Schaffner and Van Horn 2003). The need to direct federal and state workforce development policy to attract "knowledge workers" has become a priority issue. Most recently, the 99th Annual Meeting of the National Governors' Association focused on innovation and technology diversity by aligning higher education (postsecondary) and state economic needs (National Governors' Association 2007). Such initiatives are based on some startling demographic facts and trends that document the growing shortage of skilled workers (*Perfect Labor Storm Indicators: Where Have All the Skilled Workers Gone* 2007):

> By 2008, the number of young adult workers, 25 to 40 years old, will DECLINE by 1.7 million. This is 1.7 million less workers to replace the nearly 77 million baby boomers eligible for retirement.
>
> The 50 and older population from 2000 to 2050 will grow at a rate 68 times faster than the rate of growth for the total population.
>
> The annual growth rate in the working population (those between 20 and 64) is projected to average just 0.3 percent per year over the next 75 years.
>
> Nearly one in five Americans speaks a language other than English at home, a surge of nearly 50 percent during the past decade (Spanish being the predominant other language).
>
> 50 percent of the U.S. population ages 16 to 65 are functionally illiterate.
>
> 52 percent of high school graduates lack the basic skills required to do their jobs adequately.
>
> In the future, 80 percent of jobs will require some sort of postsecondary education.

As technology and knowledge emerge as the critical factors of U.S. economic productivity, is the American workforce prepared for the knowledge economy? One of the most critical reports calling for a top-to-bottom transformation of all levels of U.S. education is *Tough Choices or Tough Times* (National Center on Education and the Economy 2007). Acknowledging global economic competitiveness for skilled workers, the report finds the core problem in the United States to be outdated education and training systems. The need for high levels of preparation in reading, writing, speaking, mathematics, history, and the arts is recommended as the key foundation for worker preparation (p.xix).

An even more dramatic assessment of workforce skills deficiencies comes from The Partnership for Twenty-First-Century Skills' Report, *Are They Ready to Work? Employers' Perspectives on the Basic Knowledge and Skills of New Entrants to the 21st Century Workforce* (2006). The report is based on a detailed survey of 431 human resource officials to examine employers' views on the readiness of the workforce entrants. Most notably, the report finds the following:

> Too many new entrants to the workforce are not prepared in applied functional skills like teamwork, critical thinking, and communication. Both high school and college graduates should master basic academic skills as well as a complement of applied skills.
>
> Nearly 70 percent of the survey participants found deficiencies in high school students in "applied" skills, such as professionalism and work ethic. More than 40 percent found incoming high school graduates to be deficiently prepared for entry-level jobs, lacking basic skills in writing, reading comprehension, and math.
>
> Knowledge of foreign languages, cultures, and global markets will become increasingly important to future workforce entrants. New entrants to the U.S. workforce are not demonstrating the levels of excellence to compete successfully in the face of rising global labor market challenges.

Overall, in the last decade, the "boom" and "bust" economy has not addressed the endemic problems of unskilled workers and the skills gap. *The Skills Gap 2001* report of the National Association of Manufacturers identified a persistent skills gap in the workforce "despite an economic downturn and billions of dollars spent on education and training initiatives in the past decade" (The Skills Gap 2001). This report echoed an earlier analysis based on the Hudson Institute's Workforce 2000 study (Gido 1996:273):

> The stagnation of earnings among the young and less educated raises more critical long-term issues. High level jobs resulting from technological change are not likely to go to those most disadvantaged by lack of education, discrimination, or language barrier. To what degree will such patterns of uneven economic growth and opportunity and change in the structure of jobs erode communities and increase the risk of crime and violence (Currie, 1987)? . . . Will our nation continue to rely on expansion of the criminal justice system as a response to those displaced from the labor market who turn to crime?

The degree to which there is public commitment to these labor market strategies will directly affect the role of the criminal justice system in the twenty-first century. At the same time, the criminal justice workplace will face similar dilemmas to that of the private sector: managing an increasingly diverse workforce; affording opportunities to

women; retaining and retraining seasoned and new employees; and embracing new organizational models that permit flexibility, employee participation, and proactive human
resource strategies.

Information Technology and Workplace Organization

The most dramatic changes in the workplace are unfolding as information technology
(IT) reframes the structure and content of work environments. *Distributed workforces* are
becoming the norm as electronic technology has made it possible to link workers and
functions at various locations (Barner 1996). Corporate and public employment downsizing has actually increased reliance on such virtual organizations and has resulted in
reengineering workplaces that support group decision-making, teamwork, and employee
empowerment (Gido 1996:275).

The integration of IT into work organizations supports a more flexible and dynamic
organizational structure. The term *learning organization* refers to a more flexible and
adaptable work setting, with the emphasis on continuous improvement and work defined
more fluidly as projects are managed in teams (Garvin 1993; Barner 1996).

The need to produce both technically trained employees and those capable of adaptability, self-direction, motivation, and team communication points to a "mismatch between
higher education and economic conditions and trends" (Jury and D'Amico 1997:139).
What is more, "it has been argued that the accelerating pace of technological change may
lead to a widening of the gap between rich and poor . . ." (Anton et al. 2001:2).

TWENTY-FIRST-CENTURY WORKFORCE TRENDS: PERSONNEL DILEMMAS FOR CRIMINAL JUSTICE ORGANIZATIONS AND WORKPLACES

The workforce trends outlined above will present significant personnel-related dilemmas
for criminal justice administrators in the future. Specifically (Gido 1996):

- The creation of higher-paying, higher-skill jobs in the private sector will make it more difficult to attract such talent to the traditional criminal justice work environment. The
  smaller size of the labor pool will increase competition for such qualified workers, driving
  up salaries that will be impossible to match by police and corrections agencies.

- The remaining worker pool will be largely semiskilled and unskilled. Even more qualified
  workers displaced by reengineering may not be available to the criminal justice workplace,
  as they are likely to be quickly absorbed by the private sector, given the smaller labor pool.
  As entry level jobs decline and reengineering or a slowing of economic growth stalls new
  job creation, will the criminal justice system have to recruit from a less qualified labor pool?

- Women, minorities, and immigrants represent a potential source for recruitment to the
  criminal justice workplace. Women are now more likely than men to graduate from high
  school and complete college (Mishel and Teixeira 1991). Will criminal justice administrators attract these groups as affirmative action policies are being dismantled?

• The implementation of virtual organizations and learning organizations are advancing in today's public and private sector workplaces. To what degree will such criminal justice innovations as community policing and unit management go forward if more qualified employees cannot be attracted and retained? Similar to the private sector, will reengineering and the introduction of computer-based and other technologies into the criminal justice workplace enhance productivity with fewer workers (Archambeault 1996)?

The effects of the technoeconomic revolution on the criminal justice work environment of the future are directly related to present criminal justice management and personnel practices. It is clear that criminal justice agencies need to address both organizational structures and human resource policies that are resistant to internal and external change. These structural and cultural barriers are obstacles to the reengineering of proactive human resource policies, flexible organizational models, and employee decision-making—all essential elements to high-quality criminal justice workplaces in the future.

BARRIERS TO CRIMINAL JUSTICE ORGANIZATIONAL CHANGE

Reactivity and Inertia

Foremost among the impediments to change across criminal justice agencies is the reactive nature of the criminal justice business. Unlike private sector employers, the public sector serves the public, and public safety dictates often preclude long-term fiscal planning and personnel training. With current state and local budgetary constraints, prison building has even been impacted—and funding for employee development is clearly a lower priority. Even with "homeland security" a priority, large cities like New York have experienced high turnover in law enforcement ranks. The War in Iraq has also drawn out large numbers of criminal justice system employees for military and national guard assignments.

Organizational inertia is often cited as the enemy of change and innovation. Despite integration of the concepts and language of "emerging and new organizational paradigms" in publications for police (DeParis 1997), the extent to which policing has changed in the United States is a subject of debate (Buerger 2000). And research has documented that implementing management strategies based on empowerment and participation alone will not solve resistance to the implementation of community policing (Mastrofski 2006; Alaird 1999; Gaines and Swanson 1997). Indeed, only one "workforce planning report" (*Future Force* 2006) was identified in the literature addressing the need to assess the twenty-first-century criminal justice workforce requirements (in the community corrections workforce)!

Gender and Racial Barriers

Assessments of the status of women and minorities in police work indicate that most of the blatant discrimination practices of the past have been eliminated (Martin 1989). There are, however, still obstacles in the formal and informal structures of police work organizations related to gender and race (Strandberg 2000; Van Wormer and Bartollas 2000:162). Hale and Wyland (1993), for example, find that despite evaluation studies, which indicate that women are successful as patrol officers, the organizational culture of policing has resisted women's integration into this role over the last 20 years. They cite three types of organizational resistance to blocking the recruitment and retention of female patrol officers. *Technical resistance* includes both the failure to adapt police uniforms and equipment adequately for women and the continued emphasis on physical testing and firearms during training. *Political and cultural resistance* is evidenced in the failure to develop child care programs, flexible and gender-neural shifts, and maternity–paternity policies (Hale and Wyland 1993:5).

Zupan (1992) has also documented cultural and structural roadblocks to women correctional officers in all-male prisons. Tokenism, differential treatment, and discrimination by first-line officers in the assignment of women officers and continued opposition to women by male co-workers still exist (Van Wormer and Bartollas 2000:222–225).

While some researchers have noted the dramatic effects on police agencies of the assimilation of African-Americans and other minorities into law enforcement (Maghan 1992), the recruitment, promotion, and retention of minority officers, particularly female officers of color, is still at issue (Greene 2000; Osborn 1992; Wood 1998). Continued reliance on written examinations and the negative image of policing as an occupation for people of color hinder recruitment efforts. The underrepresentation of minority officers above the patrol level as well as lack of access to informal "white-power networks" within police departments represent obstacles to promotion.

Despite these major obstacles to organizational change and workplace quality, there are some positive models of change that have been developed and implemented in contemporary criminal justice agencies. These innovations represent the basic change agents that will enable criminal justice organizations to become more flexible, respond to employee needs, and attract and retain qualified personnel.

EMERGING MODELS OF CRIMINAL JUSTICE ORGANIZATIONAL CHANGE

Community Policing

Despite the intransigence of law enforcement resistance to change, problem-oriented and community policing hold the best hope for institutional change. Program complexity, variation in scope, and limitations in research design have been cited as barriers to comprehensive evaluations of community policing efforts (Cordner 1995:7). While many observers of police organizations call for a "complete overhaul of screening, hiring and training of employees . . ." (Buerger 2000:459), others locate the chances of long-term success for strategic policing in (1) the qualitative changes that are taking place in police recruitment and training and (2) implementation strategies that are aimed at long-term comprehensive organizational change.

Research on community police officers' job satisfaction and community perceptions and attitudes has found beneficial effects, particularly for those who are volunteers or members of special units (Cordner 1995:7). Clearly, recruitment efforts must be focused on candidates who match skill and motivation profiles that include problem solving, decision making, critical thinking, and creativity. Support for the empowerment of officers comes from changes in recruitment standards and training (Bradford and Pines 1999), new guidelines for the exercise of discretion, and the inculcation of values to guide decision making (Goldstein 1993).

Changes in the work environment beyond the development of new management styles are critical to the success of community policing. The major obstacle to achieving full implementation of community policing has been the failure to "engage and elicit a commitment from those having management and supervisory responsibilities" (Goldstein 1993).

The implementation of organization-wide change to effect community policing, as opposed to a narrower focus on "new" management strategies such as empowerment and participative management, has been proposed (Cordner 1995). Such a comprehensive change strategy includes (Gaines and Swanson 1997:5–6):

1. *Goals and strategy.* Drawing on the key building blocks of community partnership and problem solving, administrators must develop new policies at all department levels to ensure diffusion and commitment to the new philosophy and focus.

2. *People.* Complete restructuring of human resource systems to attract appropriate personnel as outlined above is necessary, as well as training and policies that are specific to the program and community.

3. *Services.* Replacement of the traditional reactive service model with a citizen "client-based" system is the key. This includes citizen input into problem solving and forming police goals and objectives.

4. *Technology.* Police information systems are utilized to scan the environment as a routine part of proactive problem solving and a basis for developing police tactics to address the problem.

CONCLUSIONS

Workforce investment is a major economic development theme as the U.S. economy competes globally. Critical to this transition is the degree to which income disparity and job displacement can be translated into high-value jobs and "informated" workplaces. The challenge for this society is to allocate the resources to support citizen access to higher education and training, technical competencies, and high-quality workplaces. The alternative is a future where criminal justice agencies and agents continue to function as reactive forces to crime and violence as enacted by those permanently displaced from the labor market.

REFERENCES

ALARID, L. F. (1999). Law enforcement departments as learning organizations: Argyris' theory as a framework for implementing community-oriented policing. *Police Quarterly* 2(3): 321–337.

ANTON, P. S., R. SILBERGLITT, and J. SCHNEIDER (2001). *The Global Technology Revolution.* Arlington, VA: Rand National Defense Research Institute.

ARCHAMBEAULT, W. G. (1996). Impact of computer based technologies on criminal justice: Transition to the 21st century. In *Visions for Change*, eds. R. Muraskin and A. R. Roberts. Upper Saddle River, NJ: Prentice Hall.

Are They Ready to Work? Employers' Perspectives on the Basic Knowledge and Skills *of New Entrants to the 21st Century Workforce (2006)*. [Retrieved January 23, 2008, from http://www .21stcenturyskills.org/ index.php?option=com content&task=view&id=250&Itemid=64]

BARNER, R. (1996). Seven changes that will challenge managers—and workers. *Futurist* (March–April): 14–18.

BAYLEY, D. (1994). *Police for the Future*. New York: Oxford University Press.

BITTNER, E. (1990). Some reflections on staffing problem-oriented policing. *American Journal of Police* 9(3): 189–196.

BOLMAN, L. G., and T. E. DEAL (1991). *Reframing Organizations: Artistry, Choice and Leadership*. San Francisco: Jossey-Bass.

BRADFORD, D., and J. E. PYNES (1999). Police academy training: Why hasn't it kept up with practice? *Police Quarterly* 2(3): 283–301.

BRIGGS, V. M. (1996). Immigration policy and the U.S. economy: An institutional perspective. *Journal of Economic Issues* 30(2): 371–387.

BUERGER, M. E. (2000). Re-envisioning police, re-invigorating policing: A response to Thomas Cowper. *Police Quarterly* 3(4): 451–464.

CORDNER, G. W. (1995). Community policing: Elements and effects. *Police Forum* 5(3): 1–8.

CURRIE, E. (1987). *What Kind of Future? Violence and Public Safety in the Year 2000*. San Francisco: National Council on Crime and Delinquency.

DEPARIS, R. J. (1997). Situational leadership: Problem-solving leadership for problem-solving policing. *Police Chief* (October): 74–86.

FRIEDMAN, T. L. (2007). *The World Is Flat: A Brief History of the 21st Century*. New York: Farrar, Straus, and Giroux.

Future Force: A Guide to Building the 21st Century Corrections Workforce (2006). Washington, DC: National Institute of Corrections.

GARVIN, D. A. (1993). Building a learning organization. *Harvard Business Review* July–August: 78–91 (Reprint 93402).

GIDO, R. L. (1996). Organizational change and workforce planning: Dilemmas for criminal justice organizations for the year 2000. In *Visions for Change*, eds. R. Muraskin and A. R. Roberts. Upper Saddle River, NJ: Prentice-Hall.

GIDO, R. L. (2005). The technoeconomic revolution: Reengineering criminal justice organizations and workplaces. In *Visions for Change*, 4th ed, eds. R. Muraskin and A. R. Roberts. Upper Saddle River, NJ: Prentice-Hall.

GOLDSTEIN, H. (1993). *The New Policing: Confronting Complexity*. Research in Brief. Washington, DC: U.S. Department of Justice.

GREENE, H. T. (2000). Black females in law enforcement. *Journal of Contemporary Criminal Justice* 16(2): 200–239.

HALE, D. C., and S. M. WYLAND (1993). Dragons and dinosaurs: The plight of patrol women. *Police Forum* 3(2): 1–6.

Innovation America: A Final Report (2007). National Governors' Association for Best Practices. [Retrieved January 23, 2008, from http:// www.nga.org/Files/pdf/0707INNOVATION FINAL.PDF]

JOHNSON, J. J., R. BALDWIN, and B. DIVERTY (1996). The implications of innovation for human resource strategies. *Futures* 28(2): 103–119.

JOHNSTON, W. (1987). *Workforce 2000*. Prepared for the U.S. Department of Labor. Indianapolis, IN: Hudson Institute.

JURY, R. W., and C. D'AMICO (1997). *Workforce 2020: Work and Workers in the 21st Century* (sequel to *Workforce 2000*). Indianapolis, IN: Hudson Institute.

MAGHAN, J. (1992). Black police officer recruits: Aspects of becoming blue. *Police Forum* 2(1): 8–11.

MARTIN, S. (1989). Female officers on the move? A status report on women in policing. In *Critical Issues in Policing*, eds. R. G. Dunham and G. P. Alpert. Prospect Heights, IL: Waveland Press.

MASTROFSKI, S. (November 28-19, 2006). Police organization and management issues for the next decade. Washington, DC: National Institute of Justice Police Research Planning Workshop.

MISHEL, L., and R. A. TEIXEIRA (1991). *The Myth of the Coming Labor Shortage: Jobs, Skills and Income of America's Workforce 2000*. Washington, DC: Economic Policy Institute.

NATIONAL ASSOCIATION OF MANUFACTURING (NAMONLINE) 2001. *The Skills Gap 2001*. [Retrieved from http://www.nam.org/tertiary.asp?TrackID=&CategoryID=958&DocumentID=24443]

NATIONAL CENTER ON EDUCATION AND THE ECONOMY (2007). *Tough Choices or Tough Times*: *The Report of the New Commission on the Skills of the American Workforce*. Washington DC: National Center on Education and the Economy.

NATIONAL GOVERNORS ASSOCIATION (July 21, 2007). News release. [Retrieved from http://www.ngaorg/portal/site/nga/menuitem]

OSBORN, R. S. (1992). Police recruitment: Today's standard—tomorrow's challenge. *FBI Law Enforcement Bulletin* 61(6): 21–25.

SCHAFFNER, H., and C. E. VAN HORN (EDS) (2003). *A Nation at Work: The Heldrich Guide to the American Workforce*. Newark, NJ: Rutgers University Press.

SCHWANDT, D. R., and M. J. MARQUARDT (2000). *Organizational Learning: From World-Class Theories to Global Best Practices*. Boca Raton, FL: CRC Press.

SCHWARTZ, J. E. (1997). *The American Dream in Question*. New York: W. W. Norton.

SENGE, P. M. (1990). *The Fifth Discipline: The Art and Practice of Learning Organizations*. New York: Doubleday.

SNYDER, D. P. (1996). The revolution in the workplace: What's happening to our jobs? *Futurist* (March–April): 8–13.

STRANDBERG, K (2000). Breaking through the "brass" ceiling. *Law Enforcement Technology* 27(6): 76–82.

The New Economy Task Force Report: Making the New Economy Grow (2000). Progressive Policy Institute. [Retrieved from http://www.ppionline.org/ppi?ci.cfm?knlgAreaID=123&contented=1490]

The Perfect Labor Storm: Workforce Indicators, Statistics, Facts and Trends (2007). [Retrieved from http://perfectlaborstorm.com/facts]

UCHITELLE, L. (2002). After pausing, income gap is growing again. *New York Times* June 23: B4.

UCHITELLE, L. (2003) Red ink in states beginning to hurt economic recovery. *New York Times* (July 27): A1, A10.

VAN WORMER, K. S., and C. BARTOLLAS (2000). *Women and the Criminal Justice System*. Boston: Allyn and Bacon.

WOOD, R. (1998). *College Educational Requirements and the Impact on the Recruitment of Minority Officers*. Sacramento, CA: CA Commission on Peace Officer Standards and Training, Center for Executive Development.

ZUPAN, L. (1992). The progress of women correctional officers in all-male prisons. In *The Changing Role of Women in the Criminal Justice System*, ed. I. Moyer. Prospect Heights, IL: Waveland Press.

PART III

Crime Challenges in the Twenty-First Century

Chapter 5

Gangs: Etiology, Composition, Responses, and Police Implications

Kenneth J. Peak and Oliver Miller, III

ABSTRACT

As futurists, criminal justice academicians, and lay persons "peek over the rim" and attempt to forecast what is in store for our society, certainly today's expanding fear of gang behaviors will rank high on their lists of causes for future trepidation. In this chapter we examine gangs—their etiology, composition, characteristics, police and societal responses, outlook, and policy implications. Related problems such as graffiti and terrorism are also considered, as well as several examples of activities and programs that have been undertaken to minimize their debilitating effects. In the latter sense, emphasis is placed on problem analysis and responses, in this era of community-oriented policing and problem solving.

INTRODUCTION

Street gangs pose a significantly damaging problem in a given community. Gangs play a role in firearms transactions and violence, drug sales and use, home invasions, car theft, homicide, graffiti (discussed below), and a number of other crime problems.

Moreover, reported levels of gang activity have increased dramatically in the past three decades (National Youth Gang Center 2006). During this period of time, in American communities large and small, the fear wrought by teen gangs has increasingly become a source of victimization and fear. In communities where gang-related crimes and

55

victimizations occur almost daily, people might feel as though they have become virtual prisoners in their own homes; the fear caused by gang "drive-by" shootings is palpable and can lead parents to huddle in their darkened homes afraid to let their children go outdoors.

This chapter examines gangs in terms of their etiology, composition, characteristics, police and societal responses, outlook, and policy implications. Related problems such as graffiti and terrorism are also considered, and several examples are provided of activities and programs that have been undertaken to minimize their debilitating effects. In the latter sense, emphasis is placed on problem analysis and responses, in this era of community oriented policing and problem solving.

ETIOLOGY, COMPOSITION, AND CHARACTERISTICS

Early Development

Researchers have traditionally been unable to agree on a single definition of gang (Esbensen et al. 2001). However, the idea of addressing gangs as a social problem implies some level of threat. Therefore, for this discussion, a definition of "gang" will be as provided by Sanders (1994:20):

> Any transpersonal group of youths that shows a willingness to use deadly violence to claim and defend territory, and attack rival gangs, extort or rob money, or engage in other criminal behavior as an activity associated with its group, and is recognized by itself and its immediate community as a distinct dangerous entity. The basic structure of gangs is one of age and gender differentiation, and leadership is informal and multiple.

Although gangs seem to be a recent problem, they have existed for many decades. Indeed, they were present in many American cities in the nineteenth century (Hyman 1984); it has been estimated that in 1855, New York City alone had over 30,000 gang members (Asbury 1971). The 2002 film *Gangs of New York* provided a dramatic illustration of these predominantly Irish immigrant gangs and their influence in the social and political evolution of New York City.

It has also been estimated that some of the Hispanic gang members in Los Angeles are now fifth-generation gang members (Donovan 1988), and that some of the Los Angeles gangs' names date back 80 years (Pitchess 1979). Hispanic youth gang activity was first recognized in the early 1900s in the Southern California area. Thrasher's seminal study of 1,313 gangs in 1927 found that most gangs were small (6–20 members) and formed spontaneously in poor and socially disorganized neighborhoods by:

> . . . disintegration of family life, inefficiency of schools, formalism and externality of religion, corruption and indifference in local politics, low wages and monotony in occupational activities, unemployment, and lack of opportunity for wholesome recreation. Such underlying conditions . . . must be considered together as a situation complex which forms the matrix of gang development. *Among the groups within which the boy delinquent finds expression, the gang is one of the most vital to the development of his personality* [emphasis his] (Thrasher 1927:33, 339, 346).

Thrasher also observed that the gang functions with reference to these conditions in two ways: "It offers a substitute for what society fails to give; and it provides a relief from suppression and distasteful behavior. It fills a gap and affords an escape" (Thrasher 1927:33).

Cloward and Ohlin (1960) later asserted that gangs emerged from "blocked opportunity" for legitimate success, resulting in one of three outcomes: juveniles becoming organized or career criminals, wanton violence in search of status, or a retreat into drug use and dropping out. This typology of gangs has been substantially confirmed by a number of subsequent studies in several different cities (see, e.g., Fagan 1990; Huff 1989; Taylor 1990; Yablonsky 1962).

After this flurry of interest in gangs during the 1950s and 1960s, gang studies and investigations virtually ended. There is little evidence of serious concern about gangs from police or scholars from the mid-1960s to the mid-1970s. In fact, the National Advisory Commission on Criminal Justice Standards and Goals reported in 1973 that "Youth gang violence is not a major problem in the United States" (p. 33). Since then, the concern with gangs has experienced a rebirth, and it continues today at a high level. Immigration patterns, economic conditions, and increased violence have been identified as contributing factors to the reemergence of gangs (Albanese 1993).

If gangs are a product of socioeconomic conditions, then they tend to develop and expand during periods of rapid social change and instability. However, it should not be assumed that juveniles join gangs solely because of poverty or for the pursuit of wealth. There have been a number of studies indicating that large numbers of gang members come from the middle- and lower-middle classes (Spergal 1990). Deterioration of the family and other social control institutions also tend to cause an increase in gang activity. When social conditions deteriorate, the gang tends to serve as an extended family for many juveniles.

Members usually join the gang either by committing a crime or by undergoing an initiation procedure. Gang members use automatic weapons and sawed-off shotguns in violent drive-by shootings while becoming more sophisticated and prosperous in their criminal activities. Methamphetamine, crack cocaine, and other illegal enterprises have provided gang members a level of wealth and a lifestyle that they would probably otherwise not have attained.

Gangs and Their Members: Status and Types

Alarmingly, the age range of gang members is broadening and becoming younger. The typical age range of gang members is about 14–24; youngsters generally begin hanging out with gangs at 12 or 13 years of age, join the gang at 13 or 14, and are first arrested at 14 (Huff 1998). Furthermore, gangs have also spread into rural areas. Also, the line between prison and street gangs is becoming muddled as gang members flow in and out of the correctional system (McGloin 2005).

Gangs proliferate as well. According to estimates by the National Young Gang Center, there are now more than 24,000 gangs, with more than 760,000 gang members in the United States, in more than 2,900 jurisdictions (U.S. Department of Justice, Office of Juvenile Justice and Delinquency Prevention 2006). Nearly half (49 percent) of all gang members are Hispanic/Latino, 34 percent are African American/black, 10 percent are Caucasian/white,

6 percent are Asian, and the remainder are of some other race/ethnicity. However, the racial composition of gangs varies considerably by locality (National Youth Gang Center 2006).

Gangs are comprised of three types of members: hardcore (those who commit violent acts and defend the reputation of the gang); associates (members who frequently affiliate with known gang members for status and recognition, but who move in and out on the basis of interest in gang functions); and peripherals, who are not gang members, but associate or identify with gang members for protection—usually the dominant gang in their neighborhood. Most females fall into this latter category (Witkin 1991). Next we discuss some, but certainly not all, of the gangs now operating in the United States.

Two very notorious and entrenched gangs, the Crips and the Bloods, began in Southern California over 40 years ago. Although predominately a black gang, many other ethnic groups have adopted the Crips name because of its notoriety. Crips usually identify with the color blue and usually wear a blue rag or handkerchief as well as selected athletic clothing. They have an intricate communication system that involves not only graffiti to mark territory but also the use of hand signals (flashing) and displaying their colors; they seldom wear tattoos. The initials BK represent "Blood Killers." Crips gangs are found in nearly every city in the United States and are in several foreign countries. The most prominent traits of Crips are individualism and maintaining a commitment to foster violence upon other gangs. If Crips were more structured, they would present an even greater problem. For a short time, some members claimed that the word Crip was an acronym for "Community Revolution in Progress." This was an attempt to gain public sympathy. Despite this temporary claim of being a peaceful organization, the gang is still heavily involved in urban warfare, drug sales, robberies, and warehouse burglaries (Know Gangs 2006).

Although the majority of Bloods gangs identify with the color red, members may not always wear gang identifiers when engaged in criminal activity. On the West Coast, members are more likely to use a bandana for identification, while some Bloods sets on the East Coast will use a colored beaded necklace. Although Bloods gangs share the same name, there is no formal leadership structure that controls all Bloods gangs. For example, a Bloods gang member in Utah may be very active in the gangster lifestyle, yet have no connection to Bloods gangs in the West or East Coast. Bloods will align themselves with other gangs to engage in criminal activity, including their rival Crips, although most alliances quickly fade away. The Bloods are known to be involved in all forms of criminal activity, but are mostly known for drug sales (Know Gangs 2006).

Asian gangs include Chinese, Cambodian, Vietnamese, and Filipino youths. Chinese gangs can be traced back to the latter part of the nineteenth century with the influx of Chinese immigrants. In 1965, the first Chinese gang was formed in Southern California; it is believed that they have continued to flourish because of the exploitation of migrant workers, which led to a breakdown in traditional family ties and crime (Toy 1992). Research suggests that Chinese gangs in New York routinely participate in extortion rackets among Chinese business, although they rarely resort to the use of violence in enforcing their demands. Asian gangs can present unique challenges to law enforcement agencies, since there are often language and cultural barriers that must be overcome for successful prevention and outreach (Kudlobov 1996). Yet, Asian gangs in the United

States have made recent advances in international drug and gun markets and other criminal activities, and must be accorded due attention from law enforcement in the future

Hispanic gangs often name their gangs after a geographical area or "turf" that they feel is worth defending. Hispanic gang activity often becomes a family affair, with young males (10–13) being the "pee wees," the 14–22 year old being the hardcore, and those living beyond age 22 becoming a "vetrano," or veteran. Two predominant Hispanic gangs originated in California correctional facilities and are very active in prisons. They identify themselves as being Nortenos, from the northern part of California, or Surenos, from the south (the dividing line being approximately Bakersfield) before they go to prison. The Mexican Mafia originated in the mid-1950s at a vocational institute in Tracy, California, and soon became the gang of many Mexican-Americans from neighborhoods in East Lost Angeles. They patterned their organization after the Italian Mafia and soon took hold in the California prison system. While in prison, members are expected to engage in drug trafficking, extortion, and any activity to acquire money and control over other inmates. *The Nuestra Familia* (Our Family) was organized in the Folsom (California) State Prison in 1968. Inmates were tired of the abuse and victimization at the hand of the Mexican Mafia. Both are heavily involved in drug sales and murder, and are bitter enemies (Know Gangs 2006).

Some have argued that hate groups should be included in the definition of gang for research and law enforcement purposes, as the predictors of participation and strategies for remedy might often be the same (Anderson, Mangels, and Dyson 2001). Gangs are also expanding among whites; a growing number of "White Power"-oriented youths and neo-Nazi Skinheads are linking up with old-line hate groups in the United States. This unity has bolstered the morale and criminal activity of the Ku Klux Klan and other white supremacist organizations. Numerous skinhead groups have aligned with the White Aryan Resistance, which tends to encourage violence for "self-defense." Skinheads have shaved heads and may sport Nazi and/or Satanic insignia or tattoos. They preach violence against African Americans, Hispanics, Asians, and homosexuals. They range in age from 13 to 25, associate with "white power" music, and prefer military-like dress.

But perhaps the most violent and aggressive street gang in the United States today is a combination of the above racial and ethnic groups: the 18th Street Gang, which is heavily populated with illegal immigrants from both Mexico and El Salvador, but also has numerous Asian, African American, and Caucasian members. The 18th Street Gang was created in the late 1960s in Los Angeles. As with most gangs, 18th Street Gang members can be easily identified by their tattoos, especially the number 18, which is usually represented in the Roman numeral (XVIII). Members engage in graffiti vandalism to mark their territory. Although 18th Street maintains a stronghold in several Southern California cities, members have continued to migrate across the nation and are involved in all areas of criminal activity, ranging from producing fraudulent identification cards and food stamps to murder and involvement with Mexican and Columbian drug cartels (Know Gangs 2006).

Another particularly violent gang in the United States is Mara Salvatrucha, also known as MS-13. In the early 1980s, a civil war erupted in El Salvador, killing an estimated 100,000 people; between 1 and 2 million people immigrated to the United States as a result of the unstable environment—many of whom settled in Los Angeles in areas plagued with gangs and crime. They created a group called MS-13 to protect themselves from other gangs, and were soon engaged in violent acts. Some members were arrested and deported, but many other MS-13 members illegally immigrated to the United States, where law enforcement efforts and prisons seem tame when compared to their homeland. They have committed many high-profile murders and assaults with firearms and machetes. The federal government has increased efforts to locate and deport illegal MS-13 members, but MS-13 remains problematical (Know Gangs 2006).

A RELATED PROBLEM: GRAFFITI

In addition to the aforementioned array of problems caused by gangs, another debilitating problem that is inextricably tied to, and flows from, gang activities is graffiti. In addition to its unsightliness and general source of irritation, graffiti can incite gang violence, depreciate property values, add to the deterioration of neighborhoods, and contribute to economic and urban blight.

In the United States, the annual cost of graffiti is estimated to be between $10 and $12 billion. In New York City alone, the average cost of removing graffiti has increased from $300,000 to about $10 million. In a ten-year period, Los Angeles removed 162 million square feet of graffiti. A graffiti-removal worker painting over a wall was fatally shot in Los Angeles in June 2004 by a man who police believe was angry because his gang's tags were being covered (Page 2005).

Like New York and Los Angeles, most cities fight graffiti by quickly dispatching work crews with their paint brushes to put on a fresh coat of paint over tagger or gang scribblings. Some experts, however, advocate photographing and filing graffiti markings, however, because they represent actual communication and can be a valuable source of intelligence.

Five types of graffiti communication have been identified by researchers:

1. *Publicity graffiti (47 percent):* the most frequently found form of graffiti contains the name or abbreviation of the gang, but does not include a threat or mark territory.

2. *Roll call graffiti (26 percent):* this form identifies the gang name and a list of gang monikers (member nicknames).

3. *Territorial graffiti (17 percent):* this type is identified by some sort of marking of a gang's territory, often in the form of an arrow pointing down.

4. *Threatening graffiti (9 percent):* these contain some sort of threatening message aimed at a rival gang or perhaps toward the police. It can appear as a gang crossing out another gang's graffiti.

5. *Sympathetic graffiti (1 percent):* the least observed form of graffiti, this type is used to honor a slain gang member, usually in the form of an RIP (rest in peace) (Page 2005).

To combat the problem, some cities have enacted ordinances that require property owners to remove graffiti within a specified period of time. For example, in St. Petersburg,

Florida, business owners are required to remove graffiti within 48 hours; in other areas the city will paint over the graffiti for a set fee, usually $50–$75. Exhibit 5.1 below shows an example of a graffiti ordinance.

EXHIBIT 5.1

EXAMPLE OF A MUNICIPAL ANTIGRAFFITI ORDINANCE

WHEREAS, property defaced by gang members is an act of vandalism and is against the law; and

WHEREAS, gang graffiti constitutes a public nuisance causes depreciation of the value of the defaced property, the surrounding property, and contributes to the deterioration of the neighborhood and the City in general; and

WHEREAS, depreciation of property values and deterioration of neighborhoods leads to economic blight, an increase in criminal activity, and is injurious to the public health, safety, morals, and general welfare,

NOW, THEREFORE, BE IT ORDAINED BY THE CITY COUNCIL OF THE CITY OF LAKEWOOD, COLORADO, THAT:

9.85.060 NOTIFICATION OF NUISANCE. (a) The owner of any property defaced by gang graffiti shall be given written notice to abate the public nuisance on his property by removal within five (5) days after service of the notice. Such notice shall be by personal service to the owner, or by posting the notice on the defaced property together with written notice mailed to the owner by first-class mail. The notice to the property owner shall contain:

1. The location of and a description of the violation;

2. A demand that the owner remove or eradicate the gang graffiti from the property within five (5) days after service of the notice;

3. A statement that the owner's failure or refusal to remove or eradicate the gang graffiti may result in abatement by the City;

4. A statement that if the costs of abatement plus the $75 fee for inspection and incidental costs not paid to the City within 30 days after notice, an additional $75 will be assessed for administrative and other incidental costs.

Source: Adapted from the Antigraffiti Ordinance of Lakewood, Colorado, 0-91-29, Title 9, Article 85, Chapter 9.85.

The police must endeavor to eradicate the graffiti problem in order to diminish the gangs' sense of territory, improve the appearance of the neighborhoods, and make a community statement that gang-type activities will not be tolerated. Following are some means by which the police and the public can attempt to reduce the rewards for, and increase the detection of, those who spread graffiti.

- Detect graffiti rapidly and routinely (by monitoring graffiti-prone locations and increasing reporting).
- Remove graffiti rapidly.
- Increase natural observation of graffiti-prone locations, through use of police, security personnel, and citizens.
- Conduct publicity campaigns, combined with beautification efforts and cleanup days.

- Control access to, and vandal-proof prone locations (using dark or textured surfaces and special products that are resistant to graffiti and are easy to clean).
- Focus on chronic offenders (Weisel 2002).

GANG MEMBERS AS TERRORISTS?

While the relationship between gangs and terrorism has been little studied and understood, there are links between the two that demand further investigation. First, some gangs share with terrorists the inclination toward the use of violence to achieve political and economic ends. Some have even suggested that "urban terrorism," in which aggressive gangs dominate the social lives of some American neighborhoods, is a more tangible and daily threat to societal safety than the specter of foreign terrorism. In this sense, then, gang activity could be regarded as a subset of terrorist threats that should be addressed. Furthermore, there might be physical links between street gangs. For example, there is evidence that Sri Lankan ethnic gangs in Toronto might be funneling funds toward terrorist operations (High Commission of Sri Lanka 2002). Second, for some time there has been evidence of an intersection among drug and terror operations, such as in Latin America and the Middle East. Traffickers might benefit from terror organizations security assurances, while the terrorists can funnel drug money for operations (Pollard 1996).

Finally, gang members and terrorists might be drawn from similar ranks of disaffected youths who are either subconsciously or ideologically convinced that the existing social order has betrayed or exploited them, and who could see participation in deviant groups as a means to lash out against it. Najee Ali, a Muslim minister and community activist in Chicago and Los Angeles, warned of the potential parallels between the causes of gang and terrorist activity:

> You can just recruit gang members, the disenfranchised in the inner cities, because most of the converts don't fully understand the different sects of Islam. It's easy to be misguided and misled by those misusing the religion of Islam for their own, evil purposes. (Christian Science Monitor 2002)
>
>   It is still too early to assume a definitive link between gangs and terrorist groups. The most sophisticated terror networks, such as al-Qaeda, might not yet find marginalized Westerners to be promising recruits. At this point, it seems best that the gangs/terrorism connection is one that not be ignored, but is evaluated and addressed with caution (Peak and Griffin 2005).

POLICE RESPONSES

Outreach and Enforcement

Today about half of all police departments serving cities with a population of 50,000 or more operate a specialized unit with at least two officers assigned to handle gang-related matters (U.S. Department of Justice, Bureau of Justice Assistance 2006). Police agencies should first attempt a problem analysis of the involved street gangs. First, why are the gangs a problem, and what are their harmful behaviors? Not all gang members are criminals, therefore it is important to examine the gang's behaviors and determine which behaviors are harmful (e.g., wearing "colors," to school to create fear among students and teachers, which may result in fights between rival gang members; spreading graffiti; being involved in drug use and sales; engaging in drive-by shootings and other forms of violence; having a threatening presence; and so on), and then design responses appropriate to deal with those behaviors. Those behaviors that pose a threat to the community should be the focus of police problem-solving efforts. Identifying harmful behaviors helps to take a huge, nondescriptive term/problem—gangs—and break it down into smaller, more manageable problems to identify the underlying causes or related conditions that contribute to illegal gang activity and become the basis for officers' responses. Eliminating the harmful behaviors (graffiti, drug sales, and so on) is a sensible and realistic strategy for reducing the impact of gang behaviors. Therefore, it makes sense to address a large problem at a level where there can be a reasonable expectation of success (see Exhibits 5.2 and 5.3).

This is also essential because no "cookie-cutter" approach will work; gangs are unique phenomena, particular to time and place. Failing to undertake a problem analysis of the crime problems and the general gang landscape will likely result in a futile response strategy.

The options available to the police when attempting to address a street gang problem(s) exist on a large spectrum with regard to both goals and tactics. Following are four programs that represent the range of activities that exist for this purpose: prevention, intervention, suppression, and comprehensive strategies (McGloin 2005):

1. *Prevention* programs have the broadest audience of interest and are typically aimed at groups that pose some risk, or more broadly, at general populations. For example, a prevention program may focus on preschool children who reside in gang neighborhoods before they show any symptoms of having joined the gang life. Perhaps the best known of these programs is Gang Resistance Education and Training (GREAT), discussed below.

2. *Intervention* strategies typically address individuals or places that have manifested some problems. In most cases, such programs attempt to persuade gang members or gang-affiliated youth to abandon their current lifestyle or to reduce gang-related crime. At this stage, defining the type of gang of interest, the level of individual involvement in the gang, as well as the specific problem of focus becomes extremely important and integral to any success. Interventions may include a gang truce or the use of nonmembers to persuade gang member to leave gang life.

3. Third, *suppression* programs also have the aim of reducing gang activities, but they typically rely on the law as a guide and on criminal justice agencies as the primary, and often only, partners. Deterrence principles often include law enforcement task forces or units and sentencing enhancements. Their success hinges on developing a plan based on a problem analysis, noted above, to understand the gang problem in the jurisdiction. When operating alone, however, suppression tactics are rarely successful in the long term. Even if a program appears successful in the short term, gangs tend to endure because the police can rarely

eradicate them completely, nor do the police have the resources to sustain such an intensive focus over time and across all gangs and gang members.

4. In addition, crime may simply be displaced. Suppression tactics are important but appear to provide the most benefit when part of a larger, comprehensive program.

5. Exhibit 5.2 shows an example of a suppression tactic.

EXHIBIT 5.2

"DESIGNING OUT" GANGS

"Designing out" gang homicides and street assaults has been successful in Los Angeles. When a systematic pattern of opportunity was found—that the majority of drive-by shootings and violent gang encounters occurred in clusters on the periphery of neighborhoods linked to major thoroughfares—police closed all major roads leading to and from the identified hot spots by placing cement freeway dividers at the end of streets that led directly to these roads. An evaluation determined that blocking opportunities reduced homicides and street assaults significantly, and that crime was not displaced to other areas.

Source: James Lasley, *"Designing Out" Gang Homicides and Street Assaults* (Washington, DC: U.S. Department of Justice, National Institute of Justice Research in Brief, November 1998), pp. 1–4.

EXHIBIT 5.3

BOSTON'S OPERATION CEASEFIRE

An innovative and successful gun project, Boston's Operation Ceasefire began as an attempt to address a dramatic increase in local youth violence, from 22 victims in 1987 to 73 victims in 1990. The partnerships that formed the base of this strategy included the local, state, and federal criminal justice agencies (police, prosecution, probation) as well as social service agencies, academic researchers, and community groups. After an in-depth analysis of data, the project selected a strategy of focused deterrence that combined suppressive and social intervention techniques. In combination with a focus on shutting down the city's illegal firearms trafficking, a tactic of "pulling levers" was used. When a gang used violence, the relevant partners would pull every potential criminal justice sanction "lever" for that particular gang. At the same time, social services were made available to gang members to support an alternative to life in the gang. The operation resulted in declines in youth homicides, firearm assaults, and shots-fired calls for service. Specifically, the gangs' drug market was disrupted, arrests were made for outstanding warrants, strict enforcement of probation, and federal sanctions were used. These penalties were borne by the whole gang, not just the shooter, and would be deployed within days of a violent event. Communicating regularly to the gangs served a number of purposes: to ensure that members knew of the new policy and to tell other gangs; to make cause and effect clear—that a particular drug raid, for example, was but a means to an end and was not about drugs but a penalty for violence; and to allow the creation of a fundamental balance of power between the authorities.

Source: David Kennedy, *Pulling the Levers: Getting Deterrence Right* (Washington, DC: National Institute of Justice Journal, July 1998), p. 6.

6. Finally, *collaborative, comprehensive* programs typically include prevention, intervention, and suppression techniques and hinge on the collective work of a variety of agencies, from criminal justice to social service, to mental health, to faith-based groups. Though they often require intensive resources and time, such programs appear to have the most promise in areas that have an array of problems surrounding a gang problem and fit well within an existing COPPS philosophy. In addition, should a particular gang pose numerous problems, such as intense gang recruitment in schools, drug sales, and gang-related homicides, it may require a variety of techniques and partners to address the issues. Perhaps the best example of a comprehensive program is the Boston Gun Project, described in Exhibit 5.3.

Gang Resistance Education and Training Program

Another police response to gangs is the GREAT program. In 1991, GREAT was developed through a combined effort of the U.S. Bureau of Alcohol, Tobacco, Firearms, and Explosives and the Phoenix, Arizona, Police Department. GREAT emphasizes the acquisition of information and skills needed by students to resist peer pressure and gang influences

The program began as an eight-lesson middle school curriculum. In early 1992, the first GREAT Officer Training was held, and in 1993, the program was expanded nationwide. In 1998, the program added four additional law enforcement agencies to assist in administering the program: La Crosse, Wisconsin, Police Department; Orange County, Florida, Sheriff's Office; Philadelphia, Pennsylvania, Police Department; and Portland, Oregon, Police Bureau.

In 1995, a five-year longitudinal evaluation was initiated, which showed the following positive results for students who had completed the training: lower levels of victimization, more negative views about gangs, more favorable attitudes about police, reduction in risk-seeking behaviors, and increased association with peers involved in pro-social activities. During 1999–2000, the program underwent an extensive program and curriculum review. The objective was to ensure program adherence to the latest scientifically supported data regarding prevention and educational research and theory. This review enhanced the original program to 13 lessons, placed more emphasis on active learning, and increased teacher involvement. The new curriculum was successfully piloted in 14 cities nationwide in 2001 and implemented nationally in 2003. Currently, the GREAT Program consists of a 13-week middle school curriculum, an elementary curriculum, a summer program, and families training.

In 2004, Congress directed that overall program administration be transferred to the Office of Justice Programs, Bureau of Justice Assistance (BJA). In October 2004, a grant was awarded by BJA to the Institute for Intergovernmental Research® (IIR) to provide national training coordination services and related tasks.

Since its inception in 1991, over 8,000 law enforcement officers have been certified as GREAT instructors and more than 4 million students have graduated from the GREAT Program (U.S. Department of Justice, Bureau of Justice Assistance 2006).

Mediating a Peace Agreement

Another innovative approach to gang behavior was developed in San Mateo, California. There, when gang violence spread because of seven-year warfare between two opposing gangs—involving shootings, stabbings, car bombings, and murder—a detective enlisted the support of a local volunteer mediation agency as well as that of the probation department, due to its court-ordered guardianship over many of the seasoned gang members. The detective also requested a juvenile court judge to waive the non-association clause that was a term of most of the gang members' probation, so that they could meet without fear of court-ordered sanctions. The mediation service arranged for separate meetings with the two rival gangs, to be held in a neutral place. Three mediators, two probation officers, and the detective also attended. The groups talked about respect, community racism, and the police; the idea of a truce was raised but the two gangs' leaders scoffed at the idea. The mediators met individually with each gang four more times; both sides seemed tired of the ongoing violence, and finally agreed to meet together. Each gang selected five members as spokesmen who brought a list of items to be addressed; respect was at the top of both lists. An agreement for peace was eventually reached and handshakes were exchanged; all agreed to a follow-up meeting, where 41 gang members agreed to a truce and that there would be no more violence. They agreed to respect each other; and if a confrontation arose, they would try to talk through it as opposed to using weapons. In the four years following implementation of the program, there were no reports of violence between the two gangs (Sampson and Scott 2000).

WHICH IS BEST: PROGRAMS OR CRACKDOWNS?

Determining the best course of action for dealing with street gangs is not easy. A number of questions about the origin, activities, and future of gangs are still unanswered; several common sense approaches have been offered for addressing the problem. Most experts describe programs in communities with gangs that would include some combination of the following:

- *Fundamental changes in the way schools operate.* Schools should broaden their scope of services and act as community centers involved in teaching, providing services, and serving as locations for activities before and after the school day.

- *Job skills development for youths and young adults accompanied by improvements in the labor market.* Many youths have dropped out of school and do not have the skills to find employment. Attention needs to be focused on ways to expand the labor market, including the development of indigenous businesses in these communities and provide job skills for those in and out of school.

- *Assistance to families.* A range of family services including parent training, child care, health care, and crisis intervention must be made available in communities with gangs.

- *Changes in the way the criminal justice system—particularly policing— responds generally to problems in these communities and specifically to gang problems.* Police agencies need to increase their commitment to understanding the communities they serve and to solving problems. This may require a shift from a strict calls-for-service approach to a proactive community policing and problem-solving approach.

- *Intervention and control of known gang members.* Illegal gang activity must be controlled by diverting peripheral members from gang involvement and criminal activity. Achieving control may mean making a clear statement—by arresting and incapacitating hard-core gang members—that communities will not tolerate intimidating, violent, and/or criminal gang activity (Conly et al. 1993:65–66).

Support for such a strategy has by no means been unanimous. Observers like Walter Miller (1990), who studied gangs for decades, maintain that gang programs have not worked when based on the notion that the solution lies with changing the characteristics of lower-class life (e.g., community conditions). The major assumption that gangs arise out of lower-class life is confounded by the fact that there are lower-class communities with no gangs. Miller advocated programs narrowly focused on gang members and those at immediate risk of membership, organized at the community level, and to involve the provision of educational and employment support to these individuals.

Clearly, the police understand that enforcement alone provides little relief or solution to the underlying problem, which is vested in social, political, and economic factors. A fundamental question to ask is this: How do we as a society replace the gang's social importance and financial benefits (with children "earning" literally hundreds of dollars a day in drug-related activities) with education or work programs that pay minimum wage? This is a complex issue, with no simple answers.

SUMMARY AND POLICY IMPLICATIONS

This chapter has discussed the state of America's gangs, specifically their origins and contemporary composition and characteristics, police and community responses, and possible future strategies for addressing the problem. Clearly, gangs are not going to disappear. Where poverty and hopelessness are at their worst, and people live in violent surroundings and seek protection in numbers, gangs will thrive as they have for nearly 100 years. There is room for hope, however. If the advice of experts is heeded and communities take the initiative toward developing policy, programs, and necessary resources, we may be able to stem the growing tide of illegal gang activities.

There are several policy implications for the future. First, while support must be unflagging for police anti-gang activities, the community policing and problem-solving strategy hold promise for addressing this problem. Intervention strategies to reduce violence must be built on a foundation of current information about the types of street gangs and their activities in each neighborhood where gangs flourish. Initiatives for reducing gang violence must also recognize the difference between turf protection and drug trafficking. A strategy to reduce gang involvement in drugs in a community in which gang members are most concerned with defense of turf will have little chance of success (Block and Block 1993). Another focus of control over gang violence should be on reducing the availability of the most dangerous weapons (e.g., large caliber, automatic, or semiautomatic).

Finally, street gang membership, violence, and other illegal gang activity must be understood in light of both long-term and chronic social patterns. We must also attempt to understand rapidly changing street-gang problems stemming from the existing economic conditions, weapons availability, drug markets, and the spatial arrangement of street gang territories across a city. The ultimate solution rests on a coordinated criminal justice response, changes in educational opportunities, racial and ethnic attitudes, and job structure.

It is also important that criminal justice practitioners who work to address gang problems in their communities are cautious to avoid simplistic or draconian responses to perceived gang activity. While gangs have historically posed a very real, and often inadequately addressed, threat to public safety, at times the opposite has also been the case. McCorkle and Meithe (1998) showed that a media-driven and overstated belief in a "gang problem" in the large urban areas of Nevada resulted in an unjustified "moral panic," which in turn can lead to controversial gang-prevention strategies, such as aggressive police stoppage tactics and more punitive prosecution of "gang-affiliated" youth. Citing a striking disparity between police perceptions of gang-related crime in Nevada and the actual levels of gang activity, McCorkle and Meithe (1998) caution that criminal justice practitioners must discern between real crime threats and those which are merely "social constructions" based on popular and/or mass media imagery.

This highlights a consideration that both students of gangs and criminal justice agencies need to consider—the unique contextual bases of local gang problems. While evidence and examples from other jurisdictions can serve as models and resources for police, courts, and juvenile justice agencies in addressing gang problems in their communities, they cannot be treated as either absolute descriptions of the "gang problem" or exhaustive representations of their solution (Boerman 2001). The best advice for local criminal justice agencies, then, is to try to understand *their* gang problem, rather than trying to understand *the* gang problem.

REFERENCES

ALBANESE, J. S. (1993). *Dealing with Delinquency: The Future of Juvenile Justice,* 2nd ed. Chicago: Nelson-Hall.

ANDERSON, J. F., J. MANGELS, and L. DYSON (2001). A gang by any other name is just a gang: Towards an expanded definition of gangs. *Journal of Gang Research* 8 (4):19–34.

ASBURY, H. (1971). *Gangs of New York: An Informal History of the Underworld.* (Originally published in 1927) New York: Putnam.

BLOCK, C. R., and R. BLOCK (1993). *Street Gang Crime in Chicago.* Washington, DC: National Institute of Justice, Research in Brief.

BOERMAN, T. (2001). Ecological assessment. Establishing ecological validity in gang intervention strategies: A call for ecologically sensitive assessment of gang-affected youth. *Journal of Gang Research* 8 (2): 35–48

CHRISTIAN SCIENCE MONITOR (2002). June 14th.

CLOWARD, R. A., and L. E. OHLIN (1960). *Delinquency and Opportunity: A Theory of Delinquent Gangs.* New York: The Free Press.

CONLY, C. H., P. KELLY, P. MAHANNA, and L. WARNER (1993). *Street Gangs: Current Knowledge and Strategies.* Washington, DC: U.S. Department of Justice, National Institute of Justice.

DONOVAN, J. (1988). *An Introduction to Street Gangs.* Paper prepared for Senator J. Garamendi, Sacramento, CA.

ESBENSEN, F., D. W. OSGOOD, T. J. TAYLOR, D. PETERSON, and A. FRENG. (2001). How great is G.R.E.A.T.? Results from a longitudinal quasi-experimental design. *Criminology and Public Policy* 1 (1): 87–118.

FAGAN, J. A. (1990). Treatment and reintegration of violent juvenile offenders: Experimental results. *Justice Quarterly* 7 (June): 233–263.

HIGH COMMISSION OF SRI LANKA (2002). Press release: Street gangs in Toronto fund terrorism in Sri Lanka. [Retrieved November 27, 2007, from http://203.115.21.154/news/press/27th march 2000.html]

HUFF, C. R. (1989). Youth gangs and public policy. *Crime and Delinquency* 35: 525–537.

HUFF, C. R. (1998). *Comparing the Criminal Behavior of Youth Gangs and At-Risk Youths.* Washington, DC: National Institute of Justice Research in Brief, pp. 1–2.

HYMAN, I. A. (1984). Testimony before the Subcommittee on Elementary, Secondary, and Vocational Education of the Committee on Education and Labor, U.S. House of Representatives.

KNOW GANGS. (2006). 18th Street. [Retrieved December 7, 2007, from http://www.knowgangs .com/gang resources/profiles/18th/]

KUDLOBOV, D. (1996). *Asian Youth Gangs: Basic Issues for Educators.* Washington, DC: National School Safety Center.

McCORKLE, R. C., and M. TERANCE D. (1998). The political and organizational response to gangs: An examination of a "Moral Panic" in Nevada. *Justice Ouarterlv* 15: 41–64.

McGLOIN, J. (2005). *Street Gangs and Interventions: Innovative Problem Solving with Network Analysis.* Washington, DC: U.S. Department of Justice, Office of Community Oriented Policing Services, p. 1.

MILLER, W. (1990). Why has the U.S. failed to solve its youth gang problem? In *Gangs in America,* ed, C. Ronald Huff, pp. 263–287. Newbury Park, Calif.: Sage.

NATIONAL YOUTH GANG CENTER (2006). Frequently ssked questions about gangs. [Retrieved December 6, 2007, from http://www.iir.com/ nygc/faq.htm#q11]

PAGE, D. (2005). Taggers beware: The writing is on the wall. *Law Enforcement Technology* (September): 194, 196.

PEAK, K. J., and G. TIMOTHY. (2005). Gangs: Origin, status, community responses, and policy implications." In *Visions for Change: Crime and Justice in the Twenty-First Century,* 4th ed., eds. Roslyn A. Muraskin and Albert R. Roberts, p. 49. Upper Saddle River, N.J.: Prentice Hall.

PITCHESS, P. J. (1979). *Street Gangs.* Los Angeles: Human Services Bureau, Los Angeles Sheriff's Office.

POLLARD, N. A. (1996). *Terrorism and Transnational Organized Crime: Implications of Convergence.* Terrorism Research Center.

SAMPSON, RANA, and M. S. SCOTT. (2000). *Tackling Crime and Other Public Safety Problems: Case Studies in Problem Solving.* Washington, DC: U.S. Department of Justice, Office of Community Oriented Policing Services, p. 67.

SANDERS, W. B. (1994). *Gangbangs and Drivebys: Grounded Culture and Juvenile Gang Violence.* New York: Aldine De Gruyter.

SPERGAL, I. A. (1990). Youth gangs: Continuity and change. In *Crime and Justice: A Review of Research,* Volume 12, eds. Michael Tonry and Norval Morris, pp. 171–275. Chicago: University of Chicago Press.

TAYLOR, C. S. (1990). Gang imperialism. In, *Gangs in America,* ed. C. Ronald Huff, pp. 103–115. Newbury Park, Calif.: Sage.

THRASHER, F. (1927). *The Gang*. Chicago: University of Chicago Press.

TOY, C. (1992). A short history of Asian gangs in San Francisco. *Justice Quarterly* 9 (December): 647–665.

U.S. DEPARTMENT OF JUSTICE, Bureau of Justice Assistance (2006). History of the G.R.E.A.T. Program. [Retrieved December 6, 2007, from http://www.great-online.org/history.htm]

U.S. DEPARTMENT OF JUSTICE, Office of Juvenile Justice and Delinquency Prevention (2006).

Highlights of the 2004 National Youth Gang Survey. Washington, DC: Author, pp. 1–2.

WEISEL, D. L. (2002). *Graffiti*. Washington, DC: U.S. Department of Justice, Office of Community Oriented Policing Services.

WITKIN, G. (1991). Kids who kill. *Newsweek* (April 8): 26–32.

YABLONSKY, L. (1962). *The Violent Gang*. Baltimore: Penguin Books.

Chapter 6

A Multilateral Approach to the Globalization of Gangs

Targeting MS-13 and Transnational Gangs

Haco Hoang, Ph.D., and Robert J. Meadows, Ph.D.

ABSTRACT

Globalization has helped to transform domestic problems into transnational challenges. The problem of gangs is a case in point. Porous borders, technological innovations, and global communication networks have allowed gangs such as MS-13 to evolve into transnational crime syndicates that extend beyond national borders. The transnational nature of gangs requires a multilateral and multifaceted approach that coordinates gang reduction activities of local, state, and federal agencies in the United States and vis-à-vis foreign governments. Los Angeles, as one example, has adopted comprehensive policies incorporating law enforcement and preventive approaches with various domestic agencies in the United States and foreign governments in Central America to tackle the growing threat posed by the globalization of gangs.

INTRODUCTION

MS-13 has two characteristics that give us great concern and have drawn our attention. One is that they are extremely violent, and they're proliferating around the country. Two is they're an international criminal organization. They're not confined in the United States. You can find them in five countries, and now even in Europe. FBI, Assistant Director Chris Swecker.

The emergence of violent street gangs in our American cities normally follows a pattern of rapid population shifts combined with perceived social inequalities by disenfranchised youth. Historically, gang members were immigrants who formed social groups for protection. In the early nineteenth century, Irish immigrants formed the first street gangs in New York City. By the 1920s, the city of Chicago is reported to have had over 1,300 gangs. About the same time period, gangs began to form in Los Angeles, resulting from immigration patterns from Mexico and Central America. As industrialization and population demographic changes continued, these gangs flourished in many of our larger cities (Finestone 1976; Sheldon 1998).

In recent years, street gangs have become increasingly violent, influenced by increased mobility, access to more lethal weapons, and a steady flow of angry recruits from dysfunctional homes. And their ranks are growing. The Department of Justice estimated in 2005 that there were approximately 30,000 gangs, with 800,000 members, impacting 2,500 communities across the United States. These gangs are comprised of violent street gangs, motorcycle gangs, and prison gangs. It was reported during a gang conference of mayors and police chiefs from across the country that street gangs like MS-13 are far more violent than the Mafia. The Mafia killed 1,111 persons from 1919 to 2004, but street gangs killed 1,276 persons from 2000 to 2004 (Ward 2005).

This chapter addresses one of the most violent gangs confronting American communities. Known as MS-13 or Mara Salvatrucha, the gang is responsible for a number of murders, sexual assaults, illegal drug smuggling, and weapons trafficking. Unlike other gangs, MS-13 is more transnational and diversified in their criminal enterprises, making them more dangerous and unpredictable. An overview of the gang and its background is presented followed by recommended policy responses in thwarting this menacing threat to our nation's security. Our discussion will address strategies to combat MS-13 with specific reference to policies adopted in Los Angeles.

THE PROBLEM

> Gangs like MS-13 have evolved into coordinated and well-financed criminal organizations . . . an international problem . . . the territorial expansion of these criminal organizations is the principle menace we are facing from gangs like MS-13. El Salvador President Antonio Saca, 2006

The concerns raised by the President of El Salvador are real because MS-13 is not the typical organized street gang. The gang is more transnational and structured than traditional black, Hispanic, or Asian street gangs roaming many of our cities. Law enforcement officials report that MS-13 gang members from across the country have come together to unite affiliated groups up and down the East Coast of the United States. The leadership for these cliques is now coming from as far away as California and even from El Salvador (Domash 2005).

MS-13 originated in Los Angeles in the 1980s following a mass migration from a civil war in El Salvador, in which reportedly more than 100,000 people were killed. Many of the original refugees participated in the war, either as soldiers or guerillas, or witnessed the explosive violence in their communities. Thus, a form of desensitization and justification to violence may partly explain the callous violence perpetrated by MS-13. Reportedly, more than 1 million people who fled the violence of their country headed to major population centers such as Washington, D.C., Boston, New York, and Los Angeles (see generally Know Gangs 2007).

While many immigrated for better lives and jobs, some gravitated toward the gang lifestyle. According to the Gang Threat Assessment conducted by the National Alliance of Gang Investigators Association, MS-13 members and associates now have a presence in more than 33 states and the District of Columbia. MS-13 has a significant presence in Northern Virginia, New York, California, Texas, as well as Oregon, Idaho, and Nebraska. The gang is active in Canadian cities, including Vancouver, Montreal, Toronto, and reportedly in Edmonton and Calgary as well.

In Los Angeles, the gang's primary purpose was to defend Salvadoran immigrants from other Los Angeles street gangs. But like any other street gang that was created to defend a particular ethnic group, MS-13 began to prey upon its own community, and diversify their criminal activities. The gang violently defends their turf against any other gang that might infringe upon its territory. And like other criminal gangs, MS-13 members sometimes wear distinct clothing, which are often blue and white, representing colors taken from the national flag of El Salvador.

Members are marked with numerous body and facial tattoos, which represent their cliques or violent accomplishments. In short, MS-13 members are easily recognized because most are heavily tattooed, mainly on their arms and face, with MS-13 lettering done in Gothic style. A shaved head with a goatee beard is also popular. Enforcement pressure in Los Angeles forced many gangs such as MS-13 to move to other cities. The MS-13 presence in the Northern Virginia area, for example, began in 1993 when three of its members traveled from Los Angeles to begin a new sect of the gang.

These three MS-13 members had the goal of uniting all Latino gangs in Northern Virginia. Over the years, Mara Salvatrucha has become the dominant Latino gang in Northern Virginia through recruitment and the absorption of many smaller Latino gangs in the area (Saywer 2004).

Due to the lack of a national database and standard reporting criteria for the identification of gang members, the frequent use of aliases by gang members, and the transient nature of gang members, the actual number of MS-13 members in the United States is difficult to determine. The National Drug Intelligence Center estimates there to be between 8,000 and 10,000 hard-core members in MS-13 (Swecker 2005). Los Angeles is the major population center for MS-13 members, with Washington, D.C., the next largest center. There are reportedly between 3,000 and 4,000 in Fairfax County, Virginia (Kim 2004).

The violent methods of MS-13 surpass those of other gangs because of

- their willingness to use overt violence to punctuate their activities;
- their paramilitary type structure and order that comes from years of civil wars and insurgencies in Central America;
- the concern that MS-13 could form an alliance with terrorists or other violent gangs.

Law enforcement in 28 states have reported that MS-13 members are engaged in international retail drug trafficking, primarily trafficking in powdered cocaine, crack cocaine, and marijuana, and, to a lesser extent, in methamphetamine and heroin. The drug proceeds are then laundered through seemingly legitimate businesses in those communities. MS-13 members are also involved in a variety of other types of criminal activity, including rape, murder, extortion, auto theft, alien smuggling, and robbery (Swecker 2005). And, it is not uncommon for a deported gang member, having benefited from newly established links to the drugs, weapons, and other criminal networks in Central America, to return to the United States within a matter of months (Reisman 2006). In other words, deportation of gang members may have an opposite effect in curtailing gang violence.

International response to the violence of the MS-13 gang has forced Honduras to adopt strict antigang laws. The country passed a law making it illegal and subjecting one to arrest if they look like a gang member. In 2004, El Salvador adopted a similar law. A suspect in violation of these laws could find themselves facing a 12-year prison sentence even if no crime had been committed. Gang tattoos are sufficient evidence for conviction of gang crimes. Due to increasing violent crime by MS-13, Mexico initiated a campaign in 2004 to eradicate MS-13 when it arrested 300 members, calling them a "threat to National security" (Know Gangs 2007).

POLICY RESPONSES

It is recognized that the MS-13 gang has grown into a transnational criminal syndicate with roots in Los Angeles, extending its reach into Central America, Canada, and the East Coast cities of the United States, including Virginia and Washington, D.C. How do we respond to the threats posed by transnational gangs such as MS-13? Should there be more crime legislation and deportation? Do we invest in more early intervention social programs? Responding to the dangers of MS-13 requires a comprehensive multilevel policy response composed of a variety of strategies and partnerships.

Since MS-13 represents a new trend: the globalization of gangs. Eliminating or reducing the threat posed by MS-13 and other transnational gangs will not only require coordination of all levels of government in the United States, but a regional effort on the part of the United States and Central American countries. Thus, an effective strategy for dealing with transnational gangs such as MS-13 must be multi-pronged and multilateral.

Los Angeles has taken steps to address MS-13 and other gang members who are also illegal immigrants. On April 5, 2007, Los Angeles City Attorney Rocky Delgadillo and Los Angeles County District Attorney Steve Cooley agreed to partner more closely with federal immigration officials and attorneys to prosecute and depart gang members for immigration violations. The announcement was significant for Los Angeles because it is a place that has historically "kept federal immigration authorities at arm's length and largely prohibits its police officers from asking the immigration status of either crime victims or suspects" (McGreevy and Winton 2007).

The partnership allows local law enforcement officials to check the immigration status of all suspected gang members who commit violent and nonviolent or petty crimes including violating gang injunctions, graffiti, and loitering. This agreement represents a realization on the part of local, state, and federal officials that gangs may have local origins but eradicating or reducing gang crimes and violence cannot be addressed without harnessing the resources of all levels of government. However, there is also a growing awareness that gang activities extend beyond national borders and are proliferating throughout the Western Hemisphere, especially in Central American countries.

A comprehensive approach must be multipronged because it must address both the causes and the symptoms of gang-related activities through the creation of prevention and intervention programs. Furthermore, a comprehensive approach to transnational gangs must also entail a multilateral strategy of coordinated suppression and law enforcement policies between the United States and its regional neighbors, especially in Central America.

In essence, the globalization has transformed gang violence into a transnational problem that can only be addressed through the coordination of domestic and foreign policies.

A Multilateral Approach to Gang Suppression and Law Enforcement

As for a law enforcement response, confronting the Central American gangs at home and abroad has become a top priority within U.S. law enforcement circles, with the Federal Bureau of Investigation (FBI) going so far as to set up an MS-13 task force in 2005 as part of its attempt to address this problem. While deportation has shown to have mixed results as an effective strategy in combating illegal immigration, the Department of Homeland Security (DHS) and more specifically Immigration and Customs Enforcement (ICE) employ deportation as a tool for antigang law enforcement.

As a result of this comprehensive program, ICE field offices are responsible for identifying gangs that pose a serious threat of violent criminal activity. Field offices have reported that most major metropolitan areas were experiencing a surge in gang activity. Membership in violent transnational gangs is comprised largely of foreign-born nationals, with MS-13 gang among the largest and most violent of street gangs in the United States (ICE 2007). Gang suppression and law enforcement efforts in the United States and Central America must be consistent in terms of police training, information sharing, and immigration policies.

Since its inception in 1992, U.S. Justice Department's International Criminal Investigative Training Assistance Program (ICITAP) has provided technical assistance and training in the areas of police management, police accountability, criminal investigations, and police academy enhancements to the civilian police forces in El Salvador. ICITAP-El Salvador has also helped the police forces develop a comprehensive and long-term strategy on gang violence prevention, intervention, and suppression as well as a centralized police records system for tracking suspected and convicted gang members (DOJ 2007). ICITAP also provides training and criminal investigative assistance to Guatemala's police forces. However, the focus of ICITAP-Guatemala has been on police reform, recruitment, and deployment, given the widespread corruption throughout government institutions. ICITAP should replicate its efforts in El Salvador and extend its antigang training assistance and resources to law enforcement officials in Guatemala and Honduras.

Transnational gangs in Central America like MS-13 often seek refuge by fleeing across borders into neighboring countries with lax border security. Fostering professionalism among all Central American police forces will also reduce the corruption and bribery that have diverted attention and resources from the enforcement of local antigang laws in the region.

In February 2007, U.S. Attorney General Alberto Gonzales announced the establishment of a new Transnational Anti-Gang (TAG) Unit to enhance collaborative efforts between the United States and El Salvador on gang enforcement, fugitive apprehension, international coordination, information sharing, law enforcement training, and prevention. The FBI will provide training, gang intelligence, and other support to enhance the capacity of Salvadoran police forces to identify and prosecute the most violent gang members. The FBI will also expedite the implementation of the Central American Fingerprinting Exploitation (CAFE) Initiative that allows law enforcement officials in the region to acquire digital fingerprints of gang members (DOJ 2007).

Similar to expanding the scope of ICITAP initiatives to other Central American countries, the TAG Unit and CAFE Initiatives should be expanded to include Honduras and Guatemala in order to establish a regional rather than bilateral approach to combating MS-13 and other transnational gangs. A multilateral effort must also include intelligence collection and sharing between U.S. antigang officials and their counterparts in the region. In 2005, the FBI announced that it would "integrate the gang intelligence assets of the FBI and other federal, state and local law enforcement entities to serve as a centralized intelligence resource for gang information and analytical support" (FBI 2005). The National Gang Intelligence Center (NGIC) focuses on the "growth, migration, criminal activity and association of gangs that pose a threat to communities throughout the United States" (FBI 2005).

A national gang database allows law enforcement officials at all levels of the U.S. government to receive and share timely and accurate information about gangs in the country. However, the activities of MS-13 and other transnational gangs extend beyond the borders of the United States. Therefore, it is essential for the United States to work with its Central American neighbors to establish a regional database on gang intelligence. Starting in the 1990s, many gang members residing in the United States were deported to their country of origin in Latin America. However, Central American police forces were unaware that the deportees were suspected and/or convicted gang members.

A region-wide gang intelligence database could provide Central American officials with important information about the criminal backgrounds of the repatriated gang members especially since most of the deportees resumed their criminal activities in their home countries. As gang members move across borders throughout the region, it is difficult to track their activities. A gang database that can be accessed by police forces in Central America would facilitate law enforcement efforts. Since the 1990s, flawed immigration policies have exacerbated the gang problem in both the United States and Central America. When the United States repatriated gang members back to their countries of origin in Central America, they were sending them back to nations that were politically, socially, and economically unstable.

These underlying conditions coupled with law enforcement's underestimation of MS-13's organizational capacity have allowed transnational gangs to flourish. U.S. law enforcement officials have recognized that there is a link between immigration policies and gang proliferation. In February 2005, U.S. Immigration and Customs Enforcement (ICE) established Operation Community Shield to partner with other federal, state, and local law enforcement agencies to target gangs by

1. identifying violent gangs and developing intelligence on their membership, associates, and organizations;

2. deterring, disrupting, and dismantling gang operations by tracing and seizing their cash, weapons, and other assets;

3. criminally prosecuting or removing gangs from the United States;

4. partnering with law enforcement agencies in the United States and abroad against gangs;

5. conducting outreach efforts to boost public awareness about the fight against violent gangs (ICE 2007).

ICE inaugurated Operation Community Shield by targeting MS-13 in a nationwide sweep to arrest its members but has now expanded its efforts to include all criminal street and prison gangs. Using intelligence provided by local, state, and federal agencies in the United States and abroad, ICE operations have led to nearly 1,000 criminal arrests and more than 3,000 immigration-related arrests (ICE 2007).

Similar to the policies of the 1990s, ICE is using immigration violations to deport gang members but the difference today is that Central American countries are aware of ICE's efforts and are cooperating with U.S. law enforcement officials to enforce immigration policies. Cities such as Los Angeles have also used immigration status as a means for detaining gang members. Special Order 40, which prohibited L.A. police officers from investigating the immigration status of crime victims or suspected criminals, was recently revised so that L.A.P.D. officers could hold in custody suspected or convicted gang members based on immigration violations until ICE officials arrived to investigate and process them for deportation (LAPD 2007).

Operation Community Shield has yielded some success. In the months that followed, ICE agents nationwide joined ranks and continued targeting MS-13 members in their jurisdictions. In this first phase of Operation Community Shield, ICE arrested 359 MS-13 members and associates, including 10 clique leaders (ICU 2007). Deporting gang members to Mexico and Central America may reduce U.S. gang activities in the short-term but this strategy poses long-term problems. The U.S. gang problem is being deported to our regional neighbors while deteriorating socioeconomic and political conditions in Central America and ineffective border security allow gang members to return to the United States. It is estimated that 90 percent of the gang members repatriated back to El Salvador return to the United States (Johnson 2005).

Immigration reform in the United States is vital to combat the problem of transnational gangs. One idea is to build a 700-mile fence to stem the flow of immigrants crossing the deserts of Mexico into the United States. A more extreme proposal is to completely seal off the U.S.–Mexico border. Neither measure would address the real threat to U.S. border security: the migration of gang members into the United States.

Transnational gangs like MS-13 are transporting their members across borders by engaging in human smuggling and trafficking activities that include bribery of immigration officials and controlling transportation networks along the U.S.–Mexican border. MS-13 is "present all along the highways and railroads that run from the U.S. southwest border through Mexico to Guatemala" (Johnson 2005). A 700-mile fence may stop illegal border crossings for those traveling on foot, but not for those who are being smuggled into the country via covert underground tunnels and poorly monitored highways and roads. It is logical to assume that gang members are using human smuggling networks to enter or return to the United States rather than making the perilous journey through the arid deserts of Arizona, Nevada, Texas, or California. Sealing off the U.S.–Mexico border would also be an ineffective strategy to stem the flow of gangs across borders given the U.S. economy's reliance on undocumented labor and the infeasibility of constructing a barrier that could stop the flow of all migrations.

A more pragmatic approach to dealing with the security issues at the southern border of the United States is to focus law enforcement resources on the human smuggling activities of criminal organizations. Gangs are in the human trafficking business to make money and move their gang members across borders. Given the limited resources available and width of the U.S.–Mexico border, it seems wiser to focus immigration efforts on targeting the human smuggling networks and the illegal entry of gang members rather than engaging in broad sweeps of all illegal immigrants. The flow of non-gang members across the border is better addressed through common sense immigration reforms such as guest worker programs, amnesty options, earned citizenship requirements, and/or a combination of these initiatives. Most undocumented immigrants are not violent criminals, and treating them as such diverts the attention and resources of immigration officials away from those who directly threaten U.S. national security along the southern border: violent gang members.

A multilateral approach to fighting cross-border gangs must also include coordination with local law enforcement. Deference to local officials in the assessment of threats and needs is essential because gangs operate differently across communities. For instance, MS-13 and other gangs are deeply entrenched in Los Angeles communities that span generations while other cities have only recently experienced violent gang activity.

Los Angeles is a good example of how local law enforcement officials are working with officials at the state, federal, and foreign government levels to harness resources in their fight against gangs. As previously mentioned, the City Attorney's Office in Los Angeles collaborates with federal prosecutors to deport violent gang members for immigration violations.

In the past, Los Angeles has also used federal racketeering, nuisance abatement, and gang injunction laws to incarcerate gang members. Los Angeles officials have also directly collaborated with Central American countries to combat gangs. During his trip to El Salvador in May of 2007, Mayor Antonio Villaraigosa signed an antigang accord with Salvadoran officials. The accord includes an exchange training program for their respective law enforcement forces and assistance in developing intervention programs that help former gang members transition into Salvadoran society (Reuters May 3, 2007). The accord was the culmination of discussions that began at an international summit of police chiefs on cross-border gangs that was hosted by Los Angeles in February. Effective gang suppression requires an integrated and comprehensive strategy that coordinates the resources and personnel of law enforcement officials from local, state, and federal agencies in the United States and Central America. A comprehensive strategy against transnational gangs must be multilateral to promote the domestic and international coordination of gang databases, police training, and immigration policies while allowing local law enforcement to identify the specific threats and needs posed by gangs in their communities.

Domestic and Regional Strategies for Gang Prevention and Intervention

Suppression or law enforcement strategies are a necessary strategy for dealing with gang members, but its effectiveness has limits based on practical grounds. The sheer number of gang members in the United States and Central America make incarceration impractical due to prison capacity issues. The National Gang Youth Center estimates that there are over 700,000 gang members in the United States (DOJ 2005).

In the City of Los Angeles, there are an estimated 39,000 gang members (LAPD 2007). MS-13 membership in the United States and Central America alone is estimated as 70,000–100,000 (Arana 2005). In essence, there are not enough jails in the United States or Central America to house the hundreds of thousands of gang members. Furthermore, Los Angeles Police Chief William Bratton contends that "prison is like going to finishing school . . . and reinforce . . . loyalty to gangs" (Arana 2005). In order to survive incarceration, gang members often rely on gang ties for protection especially if they have committed offenses against rival gang members. Prisons have also become fertile recruitment grounds because non-gang members also seek the security provided by gangs to survive their incarceration.

The overwhelming number of gang members requires that officials target suppression toward the most dangerous gangs and their leaders. Arresting gang leaders, that is, shooters and shot callers who are primarily responsible for the violence and organized criminal activity, should be the focus of suppression efforts. But suppression alone will not reduce gang appeal or membership.

Efforts should be made to outreach to peripheral gang members or associates through prevention and intervention programs. Los Angeles again serves as a useful example of a multipronged approach to the gang problem. In 2006, the city commissioned a study assessing the effectiveness of its gang reduction programs and policies. In response to the report, Mayor Villaraigosa issued a comprehensive plan that targets the most gang-infested communities and calls for collaborative efforts by public agencies at all government levels and community-based organizations to provide gang reduction services.

The targeted zones are based on gang-related crime statistics and will receive "saturated prevention, intervention, and re-entry resources coupled with integrated law enforcement suppression strategies" (City of Los Angeles 2007). Los Angeles and other cities with endemic gang problems have an existing infrastructure and network of community and social-based gang prevention and intervention programming that Central

American countries should adopt to complement its tough antigang laws known as Mano Dura. Nongovernmental organizations in the region, which have traditionally focused on community development issues, have started to establish programs focused on gang reduction. Alliance for the Prevention of Crime in Guatemala, Jovenes Hondurenos Adelante in Honduras, and Homies Unidos in El Salvador are just a few examples of community-based organizations in Central America that have established initiatives to prevent youth violence and gangs.

U.S. anti-gang officials and agencies, especially at the local level, should offer technical and programmatic assistance to help Central American countries expand the number of gang prevention and intervention programs. The recent accord between Los Angeles and El Salvador is a good example of how local officials in the United States can assist Central American countries with this effort.

CONCLUSION

Globalization has helped to transform domestic problems into transnational challenges. The problem of gangs is a case in point. Porous borders, technological innovations, and global communications networks have allowed gangs such as MS-13 to evolve into transnational crime syndicates that extend beyond national borders. The transnational nature of gangs requires a multilateral and multifaceted approach that coordinates gang reduction activities of local, state, and federal agencies in the United States and vis-à-vis foreign governments. Los Angeles, as one example, has adopted comprehensive policies incorporating law enforcement and preventive approaches with various domestic agencies in the United States and foreign governments in Central America to tackle the growing threat posed by the globalization of gangs. Officials in the United States and abroad must integrate their foreign and domestic efforts at eradicating gangs and their criminal activities. Coordination of law enforcement and immigration officials at home and abroad is essential to the task of curbing the flow of gang members across borders and suppressing gang activities. However, suppression must be complemented by gang prevention and intervention programs. Without viable alternatives for youth and resources that address the deteriorating social and economic conditions in the United States and Central America, gang membership and violence will increase.

REFERENCES

ARANA, A. (2005). How the street gangs took Central America. *Foreign Affairs* 84(3): 98–110.

CITY OF LOS ANGELES. (2007). *Gang Reduction Strategy.*

DOMASH, S. (2005). America's most dangerous gang. *Police Magazine,* .8–12

FINESTONE, H. (1976). *Victims of Change.* Westport: Greenwood.

JOHNSON, S. C. (2005). *Testimony before the Subcommittee on the Western Hemisphere, U.S. House of Representatives.* Washington, D.C.

KIM, T. (2004). *Youth Gangs Fact Sheet.* Southern California Center of Excellence on Youth Violence Prevention, p. 1.

KNOW GANGS. [Retrieved May 4, 2007, from http://www.knowgangs.com] *Los Angeles to*

Help El Salvador Fight Crime Gangs. [Retrieved May 3, 2007, from http://www .reuters.com]

Los Angeles Police Department. (2007). *Gang Statistics.*

McGreevy and Richard Winton (2007, April 5). Feds Bolster War on Gangs, *Los Angeles Times*. [Retrieved April 5, 2007 from http:// www.latimes.com]

Reisman, L. (2006). Breaking the vicious cycle: Responding to Central American youth gang violence. *SAIS Review* 26.2 (2006): 147–152.

Saywer, D. (2004). *The Use of Mapping to Analyze Gang Activity in Fairfax County Virginia.* Washington DC: Police Foundation, 6(3).

Sheldon, H. D. (1998). The institutional activities of American children. *The American Journal of Psychology* 9: 424–448.

Swecker, C. (2005). *Congressional testimony provided to the Subcommittee on the Western Hemisphere, U.S. House of Representatives.* Washington, D.C.

United States Department of Homeland Security, Immigration and Customs Enforcement, Operation Community Shield, 2007.

United States Department of Justice, International Criminal Investigative Training Assistance Program, 2007.

United States Department of Justice, National Youth Gang Survey, 2005.

United States Department of Justice, Transnational Anti-Gang Unit, 2007.

Violent Hispanic gang spreading in Canada. [Retrieved May 30, 2007, from http://www .canada.com/globaltv/national/story.html]

Ward, J. (2005). Gang follows illegal aliens. *Washington Times.*

Chapter 7

Homicide Victims, Their Families, and the Community[*]

Albert R. Roberts and Ann W. Burgess

CASE ILLUSTRATIONS

Case 1 (NEWARK, NEW JERSEY)

On August 5, 2007, four young adults were shot in the head at close range in a school parking lot, killing all but one. The victims were shot overnight after they were lined up against a back wall execution style near a set of bleachers at the K-8 Mount Vernon School, the prosecutor's office spokesman said. The shootings happened just a few weeks before these four young college students would be starting their Fall semester at Delaware State University in Dover, Delaware.

A woman, Ofemi Hightower, and two men, Terrance Aeriel and Deshawn Harvey, were killed. Aeriel's 19-year-old sister, Natasha, was in fair condition at a hospital Sunday afternoon. The victims were friends from Newark who had gone to the school to hang out and listen to music, said Essex County pros-

ecutor Paula Dow. "They were good kids," she said. "A motive has not been determined, and no suspects have been identified," Dow said. "Some of the victims' belongings had been stolen," she said.

The fourth and fifth alleged perpetrators in this horrific triple homicide were apprehended by Newark homicide detectives on August 19th, 2007 in Oxen Hill, Maryland and the Woodbridge section of Northern Virginia. The detectives had received a tip, the source of which was an FBI informant, that the perpetrators were heading to Mexico, and then El Salvador, the birthplace of the MS-13 violent gang. The suspects were members of the Central American gang that has a strong presence in Washington, DC, Prince George's County Maryland, and Newark, New Jersey.

---

[*]The study of homicide victims and offenders, and homicide typologies that are discussed in this chapter are adapted and condensed from the forthcoming book: ROBERTS, A. R., A. W. BURGESS, and C. REGEHR (2009). *Victimology: Past, Present, and Future*. Upper Saddle River, NJ: Prentice-Hall.

Case 2   (WEYMOUTH, MASSACHUSETTS)

Six-year-old Joanna Mullin died of strangulation by homicide, according to the state's medical examiner. Police have charged Joanna's 20-year-old cousin Ryan Bois with murder. He is being held without bail at Bridgewater State Hospital for evaluation.

"The preliminary medical results name the cause of death as strangulation," said David Traub, a spokesman for Norfolk County District Attorney William R. Keating. Prosecutors are trying to determine if Joanna was sexually assaulted by Bois before he allegedly murdered her late in the evening of August 4 or early in the morning of August 5 at her grandmother's home on Randall Avenue. Detectives are trying to determine if Joanna's bedding has evidence of a sexual assault.

"We do not have any comment on that at this point," Traub said. Bois must return to court on August 24 for a status hearing on his Bridgewater State evaluation. "The judge will be checking in on the status of his evaluation," Traub said.

Police have charged Bois, a 2004 Weymouth High School graduate, with first-degree murder, possession of heroin, and various motor vehicle charges in connection with Joanna's death. He was led into Quincy District Court shackled and in a nightgown during his August 6 arraignment.

Police from Quincy and Weymouth arrested Bois at 1:30 A.M. on August 5, after he allegedly tried to flee in a white SUV. Bois reportedly took the child from her 64-year-old grandmother's home where she was sleeping overnight. Investigators found an aluminum ladder perched against the side of the house, leading to an open window on the second story, but authorities now say that Bois allegedly gained entry to the house from the roof of the SUV. Police allege that Bois drove the SUV at a high speed down Route 53 through Weymouth and Braintree.

He was arrested after his vehicle struck a Braintree Best Taxi cab at the corner of East Howard Street and Quincy Avenue in Quincy. Bois allegedly brandished a knife at officers while trying to outrun them near the former General Dynamics Shipyard. Officers apprehended Bois after he was bitten on the arm by a police dog. Bois was taken to South Shore Medical Center for treatment of the bite marks.

Bois reportedly asked police to kill him right before they found Joanna's bruised and battered body in the back seat of the stolen SUV he'd just crashed. "Just kill me, just kill me. It's over, it's over," he reportedly bellowed.

Prior to his arraignment, Bois spat at reporters while entering the courthouse, and a Patriot Ledger reporter was taken to South Shore Hospital for evaluation as a precaution because Bois is reported to have Hepatitis C.

Case 3   (CHESHIRE, CONNECTICUT)

On July 24, 2007, two men were charged with burglary, arson, and sexual assault for allegedly breaking into a doctor's home, forcing a hostage to withdraw cash at a bank, burning the house several hours later, and killing the doctor's wife and two daughters.

William Petit Jr., a prominent endocrinologist, was severely injured and was the sole survivor of Monday's attack. The suspects were caught fleeing the burning home, which they apparently set on fire to cover their tracks, authorities said.

Joshua Komisarjevky, 26, of Cheshire, and Steven Hayes, 44, of Winsted, were due in court Tuesday on charges of assault, sexual assault, kidnapping, burglary, robbery, and arson. State police said additional charges were likely. Both men had extensive criminal records, and were on parole for burglary.

Bank employees contacted police when one of the suspects accompanied a female hostage, who was not identified, to make a withdrawal around 9:30 A.M. Monday.

Petit's wife, Jennifer Hawke-Petit, 48, and daughters Hayley, 17, and Michaela, 11, were found dead in the home, a law enforcement official with knowledge of the investigation said.

The attack rocked Cheshire, an upper-middle-class community of 29,000 full of colonial-style homes just east of Waterbury and about 15 miles north of New Haven. "In Cheshire we're not used to this type of event," town Police Chief Michael Cruess said. "It's a very unfortunate, tragic event that's probably going to reach right down to the core of the community."

Hayley Hawke-Petit had received an early acceptance to Dartmouth, her father's alma mater. She was a fundraiser for multiple sclerosis and captain of the basketball and crew teams. She was also devoted to her school, so much so that even while she was recovering from a collapsed lung, she attended commencement. Jennifer Hawke-Petit was a nurse and codirector of the health center at Cheshire Academy, a private boarding school.

"They're just a lovely family," said the Rev. Ronald A. Rising, a neighbor for more than a decade. "It's just awful to think it would happen to a family like that in this community. You don't think about those things happening."

This chapter on homicide provides a history of the classifications and typologies used to determine motive. Motive is not necessary to prove in a criminal court case, but it helps a jury in its deliberations.

These three homicide cases call into question the motive of the killers. Additional information is needed to determine motive in these three cases. However, Case 1 suggests a gang-related motive since five suspects were identified, two of whom were juveniles and all were members of MS-13 violent gang. Case 2 suggests a sexual motive for the murder of the child and the dimension of a domestic situation wherein the victim and offender were cousins. Case 3 suggests robbery as an initial motive with an added sexual dimension.

Case Study

Darlene Allen, age 53, began working at Food King in 1975 and married Bill Allen, owner of the store, in 1978. She started as an office manager and eventually became a vice president working in all parts of the store, including public relations and customer relations. Darlene and Bill raised three children.

In the fall of 1996, Darlene was recuperating from neck surgery. In part to celebrate their 16th wedding anniversary and to visit their daughter Terry who was enlisted in the military at Keesler air base, the Allens decided to travel to Gulfport over the weekend of October 25, 1996. Reservations were made at a Comfort Inn.

DESCRIPTION OF THE ARMED ROBBERY AND MURDER

The couple checked into the Comfort Inn on Thursday, October 24, 1996. Their daughter joined them for dinner and then left to return to her quarters to study. Darlene and Bill went sightseeing, ending up visiting a Food World store and then to a casino. They returned later that evening to the Comfort Inn. Bill wanted ice, took an ice bucket and prepared to leave the room to go to the ice machine. Following several loud knocks to the door, the door burst open, a man dragged Bill out of the room and gun shots were heard. A gun was placed to Darlene's head with the threat of death if she didn't stop screaming. She turned around and was hit over the top of her head. More shots were fired and the gunmen left. Darlene screamed for help, called on the room telephone and eventually the police arrived. Bill was pronounced dead at the scene.

Crime Classification

William Allen was the victim of a situational felony murder, 108.02. Situational felony murder is unplanned prior to commission of the felony. The homicide is committed out of panic, confusion, or impulse. The Crime Classification Manual (Douglas et al. 2006) states: "The victim is one of opportunity. The offender perceives the victim as a threat or impediment to a successful robbery."

Criminal Trial Testimony

One of the three offenders testified as follows.

Lanier's testimony (pp. 1467–1473): In Montgomery, Alabama, McCall and Wilson asked me if I wanted to go for a ride. Picked up some more marijuana and two six-packs. McCall said we were going to rob some people from out of town that usually go to Mississippi casinos. Came into Gulfport. Rode around checking out different casinos. Saw a van and we followed. Made a left into the Comfort Inn. We got out; earlier had seen guns (had a 9 mm Taurus; McCall had a .380 and another man had a .38 snub-nose, like a police backup gun).

We walked through the breezeway; a soda machine on my right and an ice machine. They sat there trying to come up with a plot on how to get into the room. So Wilson just walked down there and knocked on the door. Gentleman came to the door; they were conversating through the door. Wilson like banged his way into the door and McCall took off running toward the door. The man backs out; it looked like he had Wilson around the neck. I heard one shot and then couple seconds later another shot. I looked around the corner and saw Wilson yelling at the man to give him the wallet, give up the money.

Then got in car and headed back on highway to Montgomery . . . "What I was saying is they really didn't have a plan or strategy or anything like that. It was pretty much a spur of the moment. When they got to the hotel they pretty much came up to the stuff off the top of their head. The only thing was that really set was they wanted to rob someone out of town. They didn't want to rob anyone that stayed in Mississippi (p. 1480).

The aftermath response of Darlene is reported in the section under family member response.

———=o/o/o=———

INTRODUCTION

Homicide can be operationally defined as the intentional and sometimes unintentional or accidental killing of another person. It has been a tragic phenomenon that has aroused great public and professional concern for decades. Homicide is clearly one of the most violent forms of crime, and it is probably one of the oldest puzzles in criminology and criminal justice (Everitt 1993; Nash 1993). We have come a long way since Marvin Wolfgang's doctoral dissertation and the book that he completed at the University of Pennsylvania in the 1950s. For those criminologists such as the authors studying offender typologies based on the victim–offender relationship, we owe a great debt to Wolfgang's classic study. Dr. Wolfgang provided the first sociological and statistical analysis of 588 homicide victims and 621 homicide offenders in the city of Philadelphia between 1948 and 1952 (Wolfgang 1958). The Roberts et al. (2007) typology of homicide offenders and recidivism builds on the early classification of homicide by Wolfgang. Wolfgang conceptualized the term "victim-precipitated homicide" since the majority of the homicide offenders in his study were acquaintances or close relatives of the victims. The Roberts et al. typology emphasizes that while there is no excuse or rational reason for almost all homicides, the interaction and distorted perceptions of many of the homicide offenders do result in lethal outcomes.

Despite the unique characteristics, circumstances, and criminal history of each of the 336 homicide offenders, as a result of longitudinal analysis, four patterns and types of homicide were documented: stranger to stranger/felony homicide; domestic violence; accidental (usually DWI [driving while intoxicated] related); and altercation/argument precipitated.

Despite a great deal of information on various types of offenders, there is only limited longitudinal research on the offending patterns, typologies, and recidivism of different types of homicide perpetrators. There is also limited knowledge of the under-class and lower socioeconomic class type of homicide offenders included in this study compared to notorious middle-class serial killers. A random sample of 336 homicide offenders who were released between the years 1990 and 2000 from the New Jersey Department of Corrections were identified and followed for a minimum of five years. These offenders were tracked to determine if incarcerated homicide offenders who have no criminal histories prior to their current homicide conviction recidivated less, and which specific variables correlated with recidivism. As a result of our analysis, we were able to conceptualize a new four-fold typology of homicide offenders: (1) offenders who committed a homicide that was precipitated by a general altercation or argument, (2) offenders who committed a homicide during the commission of a felony, (3) offenders who committed a domestic violence-related homicide, and (4) offenders who were charged with a degree of homicide after an accident. Statistical analysis was completed to determine which variables correlated with the different types of recidivism and which of the four types of homicide offenders recidivated. In conclusion, none of the 336 homicide offenders committed another murder. However, we found that the highest risk of recidi-vism for new violent or drug crimes were the felony homicide group (slightly over one-third), followed by the altercation precipitated homicide offenders (27%), which was in sharp contrast to the domestic violence homicide offenders with less than 10% recidivism due to a new violent or drug offense, and the accidental homicides with 17% recidivism due to a new violent or drug offense. This exploratory study shows that a homicide typol-ogy can be a good indicator of homicide offender recidivism if it is structurally grounded to examine the complex articulation of relations between offender characteristics and their post-incarceration behavior.

SCOPE OF THE PROBLEM

The Uniform Crime Reports (UCR) of the Federal Bureau of Investigation (FBI) defines homicide to include murder and nonnegligent manslaughter, which is the willful killing of one human being by another. In 2005, according to the UCR, approximately 16,692 peo-ple were murdered in the United States, an increase of 2.4% from the 2004 figure of 16,148. In 2005, there were an estimated 5.6 murders per 100,000 inhabitants. The U.S. homicide rate steadily decreased throughout the decade of the 1990s. In 1991, the homi-cide rate was 9.8 per 100,000 inhabitants. In 2000, it was reduced to 5.5 per 100,000 inhabitants. But it started increasing again from the beginning of the year 2001. In 2001, the nation's homicide rate was 5.6, and it remained at 5.6% in 2005 (Federal Bureau of Investigation 2006). Between 2004 and 2005, homicide in the United States increased at a rate of 2.4% (Federal Bureau of Investigation 2005). The rate of increase, however, was much higher in many states, such as Alabama (+46.0), Rhode Island (+31.2), Delaware (+30.0), Wyoming (+26.6), Wisconsin (+25.2), Tennessee (4−19.3), Utah (+19.3), West Virginia (+17.4), Virginia (+16.9), Pennsylvania (+16.0), Ohio (+15.5), Missouri (+12.8), South Carolina (+8.7), and New Jersey (+6.0).

The FBI's Supplementary Homicide Reports 1980–2004 estimated that there were 13,137 known homicide offenders in the United States in 2004. Out of them, 8,390 offenders (63.7%) acted alone and 4,741 offenders (36.13%) acted with others. In 2002, there were estimated 624,900 offenders who were in state prisons for committing violent crimes. Out of them, 165,200 inmates (about 13.4%) were sentenced for committing murder and manslaughter (Bureau of Justice Statistics 2005).

These homicide offenders, in comparison to other forms of violent crime, serve longer prison terms. One study by the Bureau of Justice Statistics (1998) on prison sentencing in 1994 shows that the average sentencing for homicide offenders in the United States was 266.4 months (slightly over 22 years) in comparison to 123 months for rape, 88.8 months for robbery, and 47.8 months for assault. After the enactment of the Violent Offenders Incarceration and Truth-in-Sentencing Act of 1994, the average length of sentencing given to and average prison time served by homicide offenders further increased in almost all states (Bureau of Justice Statistics 1995; Illinois Department of Corrections 2002; Washington Institute For Public Policy 2004). In Iowa (Iowa Legislative Services Agency 2003), for example, between 1996 and 2003—after the enactment of new states statutes on Violent Offenders Incarceration and Truth-in-Sentencing Act—the average length of stay for second-degree homicide offenders increased from 190 months to 510 months (168%), for attempted homicide from 85 months to 255 months (200%), and homicide by vehicle—Class B from 85 months to 255 months (200%). Between 1986 and 2003, the average length of stay in prison by homicide offenders in the state of Washington increased by about 116% (Washington Institute for Public Policy 2004). These trends of growth in sentencing and time served by homicide offenders in recent years have significantly impacted, not just state correctional budgets and population, but also on issues related to their reentry and reintegration to society.

It is estimated that every year, more than 600,000 sentenced prisoners are released from state and federal prisons (Bureau of Justice Statistics 2004). In 2000, state and federal prisons released 604,858 inmates. In 2002, the number of prisoners released by federal and state prisons was 632,183—an increase of 4.5% (Bureau of Justice Statistics 2004). The percentage of released prisoners from 2000 to 2002, however, was much higher in many states including Montana (47.2), West Virginia (43.3), South Dakota (35.4), Iowa (31.3), North Dakota (28.8), Oregon (28.7), Oklahoma (26.4), Illinois (25.2), Nebraska (22.4), Arkansas (21.1), and Indiana (20.7). It is this increased growth in released prisoners every year from the beginning of the late 1990s that has led to the growth of recent initiatives for prison reentry by most of the states. In 2004, President Bush initiated a four-year $300 million prisoner reentry initiative. The 1990s began with strategies and initiatives for more incarceration and more expansion of prisons. The 2000s seemed to have begun with new thoughts and ideas for prison reentry and social reintegration (La Vigne and Mamalian 2004; NGA Center for Best Practices 2004a,b,c; Travis, Keegan, and Cadora 2003; Travis and Visher 2005).

One of the significant challenges for prison reentry is the high rate of recidivism and re-incarceration. Out of the more than 650,000 released prisoners from federal and state prisons every year, about 67% (435,500) are rearrested and 50% (325,000) are reincarcerated within three years (NGA Center For Best Practices 2006). One of the major studies done on recidivism by the Bureau of Justice Statistics, that tracked 272,111 prisoners for three years after their release from prisons in 15 States in 1994, found that the rate of recidivism among homicide offenders was about 40.7%. Out of 19,268 homicide offenders released, 3,051 committed homicides again within three years. The study also finds that the released homicide offenders accounted for about 7.7% of other crimes committed between 1994 and 1997. The homicide offenders committed 10% of other crimes within a year after their release (Bureau of Justice Statistics 2002).

The National Governors Association's Best Practices is currently running seven Prisoner Reentry Academies in six states—Georgia, Idaho, Massachusetts, Michigan, Rhode Island, and Virginia. Predicting recidivism and understanding the social ecology of the returning prisoners is one of the major issues being raised and studied in these academies. The present study is concerned with this problem of recidivism among homicide offenders. Is homicide typology a good predictor of assessing the risk of repeat offending by homicide offenders? Do we know what configuration of offender characteristics can predict whether a particular homicide offender will re-offend? In other words, do we have a homicide typology that can make reasonably valid predictions about the nature of re-offending by homicide offenders? These and other related questions have been explored and examined on the basis of the study of 336 homicide offenders released from 14 correctional institutions between 1990 and 2000 in New Jersey. The major objective of this research is to determine which offender characteristics correlate with recidivism versus non-recidivism among a diverse group of homicide offenders released throughout the state of New Jersey.

HOMICIDE TYPOLOGY AND RECIDIVISM: REVIEW OF LITERATURE

Criminal profiling and typifying criminal personalities is one of the enduring scientific passions in criminology and criminal justice, a passion that goes back to the study of Cesare Lombroso's *Criminal Man* published in 1876. Very few criminologists today lend scientific credence to Lombroso's physiognomic approach to the understanding of criminality, but the search for a typology of criminal offenders, particularly homicide offenders, has remained as a genuine curiosity. During the last decades, particularly after the formation of the Homicide Research Working Group (HRWG) in 1991, a considerable amount of literature has emerged on issues of understanding the social and demographic characteristics of homicide offenders and their behavioral peculiarities, motivational contexts, crime scene behavior, and typology (Canter 2004; Douglas, Burgess, and Ressler 1992; Fox and Levin 2005; Hickey 2002; Holmes 2002; Holmes and Holmes 1998; Holmes, Salfati, and Grey 2002; Owen 2004; Petherick 2005; Salfati 2001).

DEMOGRAPHIC CORRELATES AND HOMICIDE OFFENDING

The demographic variables most consistently examined in homicide research are race, ethnic origin, gender, social class, age, and victim–offender relationship (Fowles and Merva 1996; Fox and Zawitz 2004; Gottredson and Hirschi 1990; Neapolitan 1998; Pridemore 2002; Zimring and Hawkins 1997). The FBI's Supplementary Homicide Reports 1980–2004 show that blacks represented 48.38% of the homicide offenders in 1980. This high representation of blacks among homicide offenders remained consistent through the last 24 years. In 2004, blacks, who constitute about 13% of the U.S. population, represented 49.42% of the homicide offenders. Between 1980 and 2004, blacks committed 50.50% of all total homicides reported to law enforcement as opposed to 46.29% by whites, 1.24% by Asians, and less than 1% by Native Americans.

Homicide offending also shows a consistent pattern of variations in terms of gender, age, victim–offender relationship, and weapons used in the commission of homicide. Homicide is primarily a male crime. According to the FBI's Supplementary Homicide Reports 1980–2004, males in the year 1980 represented 86.10% of the homicide offenders. In 2004, males accounted for 90.20% of the homicides, and females accounted for 9.80% of the homicides. Between 1980 and 2004, males accounted for a total of 88.81% of the homicides. In terms of age, most homicide offenders are relatively young, but are not juveniles. In 2004, juveniles between 12 and 17 accounted for only 8.42% of homicides. Adults between 18 and 34 were responsible for 44.44% and those between 25 and 59 accounted for 42.09% of the homicides. In most highly populated cities, acquaintance homicide is consistently the most frequent, with stranger homicide a close second, followed by family-related homicides. The FBI's Supplementary Report indicates that in 2004, 43.75% were acquaintance homicides, 18.96% were stranger homicides, and 14.89% were family-related homicides. Additionally, the firearm is the weapon used in most homicide cases. In 2004, firearms were used in 62.77% of homicide cases. This has remained consistent since the 1980s. In 1980, firearms were used in 63.62% of cases.

A large amount of literature in recent years has empirically substantiated these variations in homicides in terms of race (LaFree and Drass 1996; Sampson and Wilson 1997), gender, age (Blumstein 1995), victim–offender relationship (Zahn and Mccall 1999), and the use of weapons (Zimring and Hawkins 1997). LaFree and Drass (1996) indicated that race combined with social class has a strong correlation to homicide. They found that disadvantaged minority group members were overrepresented as both perpetrators and victims of homicide. Rogers et al. (2001) examined black–white differentials in adult homicide mortality and found that blacks living in the inner city had a 6.3 times higher risk of homicide compared to whites living in the inner city, despite controlling for age and gender. Much of the racial gap seems to be highly correlated with socioeconomic status, especially low marriage rates, low educational attainment, and high unemployment rates (Murphy 2000; Parker and Pruitt 2000). Disadvantaged communities with large amounts of social disorganization, economic and social distress, drug use, and street gang membership have a large number of homicides (Loftin and Hill 1974; Sampson and Wilson 1997).

HOMICIDE TYPOLOGIES

In recent years, in addition to their strident efforts to understand the nature of homicide offender characteristics and the socio-demographic contexts of homicide offending, criminologists have also developed a number of homicide typologies or classificatory schemas in order to profile and explain the personality and the inner motivations of homicide offenders. One of the oldest and widely known typologies is between organized and disorganized homicides used by the FBI. The typology was created by John Douglas, Patrick Mullany, Howard Teten, Robert K. Ressler, Ann Burgess, and others associated with the FBI's Behavioral Science Unit in Quantico, Virginia, and the FBI's National Center for the Analysis of Violent Crime (NCAVC) in the 1970s. The typology was derived from the understanding of crime scene behavior. The logic of the typology is that disorganized crime scenes represent those homicide offenders who lack social competence and a stable family, and who are emotionally abused and/or withdrawn. They are most likely to be high school dropouts with a below-average IQ. Organized crime scenes, on the other hand, suggest the presence of those offenders who have all the hallmarks of a psychopathic personality—above-average IQ, socially skillful, educated, urban, mobile, and sexually promiscuous. Disorganized homicide offenders leave a chaotic crime scene, and they depersonalize their victims. In sharp contrast, organized homicide offenders leave a controlled crime scene and attempt to develop more personal relationship with their victims.

The FBI's NCAVC developed a four-fold typology of homicide motivations. This typology is also primarily based on crime scene indicators. The four types are (1) criminal enterprise homicides (contract murders, gang-motivated murders, insurance/inheritance-related killings, and felony murders), (2) personal cause homicides (domestic violence-related murders, political and religious murders, or mercy killing), (3) sexual homicide (rape and murder, child rape, and child serial killing), and (4) group cause homicides (cult-related homicides and homicides related to extremism and terrorism). The Crime Classification Manual (CCM; Douglas et al. 1992, 2006) used by the FBI classifies homicides into six categories: single homicide, double homicide, triple homicide, mass murder, spree murder, and serial murder.

Later, Holmes and Holmes (1998, 2001) classified homicide offenders, particularly serial killers, in terms of four categories: visionary killer, mission killer, hedonistic killer, and power or control killer. The visionary killers kill in the name of god, a devil, or an angel. They think that they are commanded by some supernatural powers to kill. The mission killers are driven by earthly missions to establish a just regime or a group. They are driven by their own constructed rationality of removing the ills of society. The hedonistic killers, on the other hand, kill for thrills, lust, and pleasure. For them, killing is the expression of their pleasure principle. The power killers kill to symbolize their power and control on the victims. For them, killing is a way of regaining the control of their fractured mind and personality.

Several homicide studies have been generated in recent years on the basis of a model developed by C. Gabrielle Salfati of the Center for Investigating Psychology of the University of Liverpool, England. Salfati (2002, 2001) classified homicides into two categories on the basis of 36 crime scene indicators: expressive homicide and instrumental homicide. Expressive homicides are anger-induced and linked to rape, arson, or physical attack. Extreme violence; multiple wounds; and the use of multiple weapons, suffocation, and dismemberment of victims' bodies characterize expressive crime scenes. Instrumental homicides are linked to violence, theft, robbery, and burglary where the offenders are motivated by some ulterior aims for money or sex. In instrumental crime scenes, bodies are not hidden, and the offenders leave traces of weapons, blood, clothes, semen, and shame and guilt.

Fox and Levin (1996, 2005, 2006) have been studying the issue of homicide typology for more than a decade. They divided homicide into three main categories: serial murders, mass murders, and spree killing. On the basis of these three categories, they developed a five-fold motivational typology: power-based homicides, revenge-based homicides, loyalty-based homicides, profit-based homicides, and terror-based homicides.

These typologies, used as tools in much empirical analysis, have considerably improved our knowledge of the nature of homicide offending and homicide offenders (Table 7.1). What is missing in most of these typologies, however, is an analysis of how and whether they can predict homicide recidivism. The core concern in most of these

TABLE 7.1   Samples of Existing Homicide Typologies

Author/Origin	Nature	Homicide Categories	Core Focus
Behavioral Science Unit, FBI (1971)	Two-fold typology	Disorganized homicides Organized homicides	Homicide motivations
NCAVC, FBI (1978)	Four-fold typology	Criminal enterprise homicides Personal cause homicides Sexual homicides Group cause homicides	Homicide motivations
Holmes and Holmes (1998, 2001)	Four-fold typology	Visionary killers Mission killers Hedonistic killers Power killers	Homicide motivations
Salfati (2001)	Two-fold typology	Expressive homicides Instrumental homicides	Homicide motivations
Fox and Levin (2005)	Five-fold typology	Power-based homicides Revenge-based homicides Loyalty-based homicides Profit-based homicides Terror-based homicides	Homicide motivations

typologies is to be able to grapple the inner mind of the homicide offenders—the complex trajectories of motivations for homicide. The search for homicide motivation is a genuine intellectual challenge in criminology and criminal justice. But the extent to which motivational understanding can help us develop an understanding of the social trajectory where the offenders live and commit the crime, and the degree to which the complex nature of homicide motivations are amenable to empirical analysis are open to questions (Goodwin 1998, 2002; Canter and Wentink 2004). Most typologies based on motivational understanding are drawn from the Freudian theory of psychodynamics—the theory that is based on assumptions that most homicide offenders are driven by the unconscious, and their psychopathic personalities are the by-products of childhood trauma and victimization. It seems that to use homicide typology as predictors of recidivism and to develop evidence-based reentry policies, we need a typology that is based on a more structural (Sampson and Wilson) understanding of the social ecology within which the offenders live and where offender will return after they are released. A typology is needed that can provide a more empirically grounded analysis of the offender characteristics and their complex relations with homicide offending and recidivism. The present empirical analysis of 336 homicide offenders drawn from New Jersey aims to contribute to this end through the development of a new typology and an analysis of its application and relevance to homicide reentry and recidivism.

TOWARD A NEW HOMICIDE TYPOLOGY

Homicide research is disproportionately dominated by intellectual passion and scientific curiosity to understand the mind of the serial and brutal killers—"the high class of the murderers"—who make headlines, create tenors, and generate a collective sense of national traumas (Fox and Levin 2005). Many even believe that the classification of serial killers is a misleading venture (Hickey 2002). Over the past three decades, there have been hundreds of thousands of homicide offenders who do not make headlines and who do not raise any collective sense of terror and tragedies. They commit the crime, serve the time, and get back to the community only to return to prison for committing new crimes or violating parole. The understanding of the nature and peculiarities of this "underclass" of homicide offenders is far more significant from the point of view of increased stress and strains on criminal justice. In this study, we have sampled 336 homicide offenders who fall largely within this group of "underclass" homicide offenders. They commit violence and kill people for small amounts of money, and over few stretches of arguments. They come from a fragile social ecology, fragmented families, or failed communities; they come from communities where some even glorify and justify a culture of violence (Sampson, Raudenbush, and Earls 1997; Sampson and Wilson 1995).

After examining the statistical findings of our longitudinal retrospective study and after a comprehensive and open-ended analysis of the circumstances surrounding each of the homicide cases, it became apparent that there are usually four types of incarcerated homicide offenders (Table 7.2).

TABLE 7.2   A New Four-Fold Homicide Typology and Its Characteristics

Homicide Types	Nature and Characteristics	Case-Based Data and Homicide Circumstances
1. Altercation/ argument precipitated homicides	Magnified perception of money or property loss; argument over money or property; dispute over relatively small amount of money or possessions; verbal disputes escalates into fight, and fight into stabbing and shooting. In this category, homicides are driven by what Salfati (2001) called instrumental expressions	#282 "Argument and fight over $4.00. Victim died of beating." #347 "Defendant hit victim in the head with a 2X4 because they were fighting over a bike." #142 "Shot victim over argument over dog." #361 "Victim was shot after an argument over money." #348 "Beat victim with a bat and dumped his body in the woods. Argued over drugs." #366 "Defendant shot victim after some altercation they had earlier in the day." #358 "Beat victim with baseball bat over money."
2. Felony homicides	Perpetrators kill their victims during the commission of a felony crime. Homicides are committed in the way of or as means to committing other crimes. Most felony offenders have records of past criminal histories	Robbery, burglary, grand theft, kidnapping, and other felony crimes induce homicides
3. Domestic violence or intimate partner violence-induced homicides	Perpetrators are family members, current or ex-spouses, cohabiting intimate partners, or girl-friends or boyfriends. This category of homicidesis mostly precipitated, not because of intentions to commit a felony crime or achieve any instrumental goals, but because of complexities and fragilities in relations involving sex, love, and emotion	#22 "Shot victim. He believed she was unfaithful." #44 "Shot wife after she left him." #64 "Stabbed his wife to death because he thought she was cheating him." #151 "Defendant used car to run over and kill husband who had beaten her badly in the car." #214 "Shot and killed victim after years of emotional abuse." #222 "Stabbed victim in back twice. Claimed unable to take abuse any longer. Defendant stabbed boyfriend in chest with kitchen knife after argument."
4. Accident homicides	Perpetrators cause death of victims usually by automobiles	Driving under the influence of alcohol or drugs; driving after binge drinking

Based on Homicide Offenders and Offending Data from New Jersey.

ASSESSMENT MEASURES

Homicide Crime Scene Assessment and Classification by Motive

Crime scene analysis of a homicide is critical to directing investigators to a possible suspect. This section reports on a sample of 100 homicides of solved and unsolved cases that were analyzed to field test a crime scene checklist instrument on homicide classification. The HCSCL is a 268-item instrument designed to elicit information about a homicide in the following areas: victim demographics, possible victim relationship to offender, victim characteristics, crime scenes (initial contact scene, assault scene, death scene, and body location scene), other evidence or crime-related information, forensic findings (cause of death, weapons used, victim forensic findings, evidence of multiple offenders, and other forensic information), probable motives, primary and secondary homicide classification code, and whether or not the case was solved.

The HCSCL requires the following information for completion of the form: crime scene photographs, forensic reports, on-site police reports, and investigative reports.

RESULTS

Victimology

Victimology is critical to a crime investigation as a first step in determining motive. This sample was predominately white and unmarried, with fairly equal distribution of males and females. Fifty percent of victims were single, 27 percent married, 15 percent divorced or separated, 4 percent widowed, and 4 percent with no data. The majority (89%) were Caucasian, 9% were black, 4% were from a minority ethnic group, and 4% were not identified by race.

Close to half of the victims (47%) were employed primarily in blue collar occupations including accountant, aide, analyst, baker, barmaid, clerical, clerk, courier, sales, factory worker, insurance sales, laborer, mechanic, nurse, railroad worker, roofer, secretary, and waiter. Employment was unknown in 21%, 13% were students, 7% were housewives, 5% were self-employed, 4% were prostitutes, 2% were retired, and 1% were drug dealers.

There was an 80-year age range of the 53 female victims and 47 male victims with a mean age of 27. The youngest victim, a one-day-old boy, was found suffocated in a plastic bag in a garbage dumpster. The oldest victim, an 80-year-old white, married, self-employed tavern owner, was killed in his workplace. He had opened his bar for business, apparently left the bar area and went into the bathroom. An unknown subject, entering the bar and seeing no one present, went to the cash register and removed the paper money. The suspect was then confronted by the victim; a brief struggle ensued at which time the victim was struck in the head. The blow did not contain the victim and he was then shot in the head with a small caliber weapon. The victim was found by a patron who later came into the tavern. Victimology noted that the victim lived in an apartment above the tavern, in a rural coaltown with limited businesses and primarily residences. He was described as having an abusive, argumentive personality.

Victims are assessed as to their risk level in terms of lifestyle and situation. Lifestyle risk level is a function of age, physical size, race, marital status, living situation, location of residence, and occupation. In this victim sample, 38% were assessed as having a low to moderate risk, 35% had a moderate to high risk, and 24% had a high risk level. There were no data on three cases.

Situational risk level assesses the victim's location and activities at the time of the crime, and interacts with lifestyle risk. For example, the situational risk of a person remains the same inside a residence unless the doors are unlocked. Traveling to a social site, workplace, or residence may increase a person's situational risk level. Situational risk level varies from day to day depending on a person's routine. In this victim sample, 41% were assessed to have a low to moderate risk, 25% had a moderate to high risk level, and 31% had a high risk level. There were no data for three cases.

An example of an individual with a high lifestyle risk who increased his situational risk (from 3–5) was a 15-year-old white male runaway from a youth residential shelter. He had been removed from his residence for truancy and being incorrigible. He was last seen near a housing project. The victim was found on a little-traveled rural road, dead of massive thermal burn, in the ashes of a cardboard barrel, the metal rings of which were in the debris. Paint thinner was used as the accelerant, and the victim was identified through dental records. Victimology noted the victim to be a trouble maker, streetwise, and involved in all types of street activity.

The very young and the elderly may be high-risk victims under certain situations. Children walking home from school or alone at home may be targeted or stalked. Five child victims under the age of 12 were abducted from either their residence or walking home from school. One 10-year-old white girl arrived home from school on the school bus. She entered her residence to await the arrival of other family members. She disappeared from the residence and a search was conducted as a missing person. After a two-day search of the area, the victim's body was found in a wooded area covered with scrub branches. The victim had a fractured larynx, abrasions, and contusions of the body and genitalia. She had been raped and strangled with an unknown ligature.

Elderly living alone may be targeted because of their situation and fraility. A 73-year-old white widow was beaten with fists about the head and face by several offenders who entered her house on New Year's Eve. There were no signs of forced entry. The victim was tied at the wrists using her nylon hose. The next day she was found in her backyard covered with a piece of sheet metal and boards thrown over her. She had been hit with a blunt instrument, possibly a brick found at the scene. The victim's skull was struck many more times than necessary to kill the victim. Some watches and coins were known to be taken from the home. It was not known why the victim was taken outside as she had been beaten while in the house. Victimology noted that the widow lived alone in a small town residential area, and it was rumored that she had money in the house.

There were two interesting findings from the victim characteristics of this sample. First, the majority of victims knew their murderer. Forty-nine victims had a close relationship (family member, business associate, boyfriend, girlfriend, etc.) with the offender; 24 of them were in a common-law relationship; one victim was a caregiver of the offender; in four cases, the offender was the victim's supervisor.

Second, almost half of the victims were known to use either drugs (46%) or alcohol (47%). Forensic results of drug screens indicated the victim positive for drug use at the time of death in 9% of 78 cases and positive for alcohol use in 21% of 74 cases. This finding suggests that the use of drugs and/or alcohol may have increased the risk of victimization in 30% of the cases.

There were four multiple-victim cases in which there were surviving victims. In one case, a 17-year-old white male was shot in the left side of the head with a small caliber handgun while sitting in a parked car with his 15-year-old girlfriend. An unknown assailant approached the vehicle and shot the homicide victim through the driver's side window. The assailant then demanded sex from the female companion. When she refused, he shot her and left the scene. She survived.

Crime Scene Locations

The crime scene assessment is divided into four distinct scenes. The initial contact scene is where the victim has the first contact with the offender. The assault scene is where the assault—physical or sexual—occurs. The death scene is where the death of the victim takes place. The body location scene is where the body is discovered. These four scenes can be the same physical location, multiple locations within a single building, physically separated locations, or any combinations of the above. In this sample, there were multiple crime scene locations in 45 cases.

For each crime scene location, a risk-level assessment is made of the risk level of the victim and the offender. The initial contact scene risk is a function of location, time of day, number of people at the location, and the routine of the victim as to the location. In cases with data, 47% of the initial contact locations were low to moderate, 24% were moderate to high, and 19% were high. Nine cases were not ranked.

The risk level of location for offender is a function of the offender's risk at being recognized/identified, apprehended at the site, time of day, and probability of executing the crime. In this sample, 39% were low to moderate risk, 27% were moderate to high, and 16% were high. Nine cases were not ranked.

Examining the four crime locations, more than half of the murderers' risk level by location was low to moderate, and less than 20% selected an area of high risk. Similarly, the victims' risk level of location was low to moderate. This finding suggests the difficulty that the detectives had in their investigation and apprehension of a suspect. Minimal evidence or witnesses were available.

Crime Scene Matrix

The Crime Scene Checklist assesses steps taken by the offender in commissioning a homicide. It is interesting to note that while half of the initial contacts were made inside a building, about two-thirds of the final body location were outside in a public place. One-third of the cases originated and ended inside a residence. About 20% of the cases initiated where the location was a source of cash (e.g., convenience store, bank). Over half of the victims were specifically targeted or preselected by the offender, with one-third being a victim of circumstance. Six victims were believed to have been randomly selected with over one-third being victims of a quick, brutal blitz style attack that immediately incapacitates the victim. Three victims were stalked. While over half of the victims were well controlled with no signs of a struggle, 15 initial contact scenes indicated signs of a struggle such as knocked over furniture, broken items, blood splattered. In one-third of the cases, evidence was noted to be removed from the initial contact scene. The scene was noted to be consistently altered across crime locations in about 25% of the cases, and 39% of the cases indicated preplanning.

Weapons accompanied the offender in about half of the cases. In 23 additional cases, weapons of opportunity were found near or at the crime scene. Seventeen of the weapons were left at the scene. In only three cases was excess ammunition found at the crime scene.

Other evidence of crime-related information included hidden weapons (2), victim's personal items missing (41), symbolic items (3), syringes/medical vials (3), unexplained articles (5), fingerprints on weapon (6), shell casings (20), witnesses (14), careful disposal of evidence (24), careless disposal of evidence (10), and indication of multiple offenders (15).

The most common cause of death was gunshot (49) followed by stabbing (13); strangulation (8); blunt force (6); asphyxia (4); overdose (2); head fracture (4); and one each of burns, chest compression, drowning, and exposure. In nine cases, the cause was unknown.

A variety of weapons (63) were used by offenders in this group, including handguns (28), small caliber weapon (20), cutting or stabbing instrument (14), semiautomatics (10), rifles (7), and shotguns (8). Asphyxiation was by ligature (10) or manual (5). Blunt force trauma occurred to the head (25), torso (7), limbs (4), and sex organs (1). The number of gunshot wounds to victims ranged from 1 to 8. Contact gunshot wounds occurred in 9 cases, close range wounds in 36 cases, intermediate wounds in 4 cases, long-range gunshot wounds in 1 case. Defensive wounds were noted in seven cases. Facial battery was noted in 13 cases, and there was a focused area of injury in 48 cases. Overkill was noted in 21 cases, and postmortem mutilation occurred in three cases. There was evidence of sexual assault in 10 cases, and the sex organs were cut in three cases.

Multiple offenders were indicated by multiple fibers found in one case, multiple hairs in two cases, multiple fingerprints in four cases, and multiple shoe prints in two cases.

In 27 cases, the victim was initially reported as a missing person; in seven cases, the homicide was initially reported as another crime, accident (3), natural cause death (2), suicide (3), and emergency (1). In 34 cases there was evidence of secondary crime. In 13 cases the offender was wounded.

Homicide Classification

The CCM classifies homicides by motive. There were multiple motives in this sample of homicides. Over half of the homicides were believed to be motivated by argument/ conflict with a little over 20% believed to be motivated by revenge, domestic conflict, material/financial gain, and forced sex.

Assessing motives is a critical step in determining a homicide classification. Out of 43 homicide classifications in the CCM, this sample classified 17 types. A brief case example will illustrate a case from each category.

101: Contract (Third-Party) Killing (1 case)

A contract killer murders by surprise or by secret assault; the person may be hired or appointed murderer, who makes a contract to take the life of another person for financial gain (e.g., a hit man).

A male subject entered the main front doors of a gymnastic center, stepped inside and fired three shots from a 12-guage shotgun striking the 63-year-old white married male in the back as he stood at a counter purchasing merchandise. The assailant walked from the building and fled the area. The victim had taken his daughter to the gymnastic center for lessons and was waiting to take her home. The victim was the target of a major crime figure hit.

106: Drug Murder (8 cases)

A drug murder is death resulting from a victim's involvement in the sale/purchase of illegal drugs.

Two suspects arrived in town two days prior to the shooting. The suspects began dealing drugs out of different units in a housing project and hired residents, including the victim, as runners in delivering drugs to prospective buyers. These runners were alleged to have planned on robbing the suspects, and at one point all went to the unit where the suspects were staying but were unsuccessful in their attempt. The suspects then stopped dealing and left the area. During the early morning hours, the victim and two others were talking through the housing project when the suspects pulled up in a car without lights. The suspects got out and ran up to the victim, ordered the others out of the way, and then began to fire point blank eight times at the 21-year-old black single male's body. He was transported unconscious to the hospital where he died 16 days later. During the autopsy, five .22 caliber bullets were removed from his body. No casings were found at the scene. Victimology noted that the victim lived in a high drug, low income, high unemployment, single parent area. Victim was described as a drug dealer, user, and enforcer known to be combative and argumentive.

107.01: Insurance/Inheritance-Related Death (2 cases)

In an insurance/inheritance-related death, the victim is murdered for insurance or inheritance purposes.

An 18-year-old white single male mechanic was found dead of multiple traumatic chest injuries inside his garage. The death was reported as a medical emergency and accident. There was evidence of multiple offenders. One of the suspects had taken out an insurance policy on the victim two weeks prior to the murder. The murder scene was staged in the garage to make the incident appear as an accident.

108: Felony Murder (11 cases)

In a felony murder, property crime is the primary motivation, with murder a secondary motivation. In the commission of violent crime (burglary and robbery), a person is murdered.

A 76-year-old white widow with an estate valued at $1.1 million was found dead in her home from a gunshot wound to her heart. She lived alone, was disabled, and needed a cane. She was in her kitchen when she was shot in the right wrist. As she stood at the sink tending her wounds, she was shot again in the right shoulder. The bullet deflected and struck her heart. A third shot was fired and found in the wall. All shots were fired from outside the house. Suspects entered forcibly and stole the keys to her car and drove the car to a large city bus stop where it was abandoned and later towed. Her house was not burglarized. Investigators believed it might have been a professional hit. Victimology noted that she lived just outside a highly populated area in the county, that she was a private person who had many friends but did not visit with them at her house. She had two daughters living in California.

120: Personal Cause Homicide (3 cases)

Personal cause homicide is motivated by an underlying emotional conflict.

The victim's mother, in a very depressed state and using a .22 caliber handgun, shot her 2-year-old daughter four times in the back before shooting herself once in the upper left chest, committing suicide.

122: Domestic Homicide (19 cases)

A domestic homicide involves a victim and offender who have a familial or common-law relationship. Of the 19 cases of domestic homicide, 11 were homicide–suicide, where a male partner killed his female partner and then turned the gun on himself.

A 25-year-old single white woman left her residence taking items to wash her car. The woman was later found at 5:06 A.M. by the local police in her car in the parking area of a self-service car wash. The victim was lying face up in the right front seat with her upper portion of torso between the bucket seats toward the rear of the vehicle. There were signs of a struggle. The cause of death was asphyxiation due to ligature strangulation using her sweatshirt. She had contusions on her neck and left face, right foot, and left hand. There were defensive wounds to hand. Investigation was greatly hampered due to entire group of victim's friends and associates being involved in drugs and making initial false statements. Victimology noted that she was a fast-food clerk in a restaurant, living with her boyfriend (also the boyfriend's brother and her brother). She had many friends, used drugs, and was sexually active with other partners. Her boyfriend had recently learned of her sexual activity with his brother.

123: Argument/Conflict (15 cases)

This murder occurs as a result of argument or conflict. It can also be classified as argument murder (123.01) and conflict murder (123.02).

The 23-year-old single black male, self-employed hairdresser, was discovered shot 12 times while sitting in the driver's seat of his vehicle. The motor of the vehicle was running, the transmission was in the park position, the headlights were on, and the right front window was down. The victim was slumped over to the right and was later found to have seven entrance wounds to the right side of his torso and five shots to the head, all fired from close range. It appeared that the victim was shot either by a passenger sitting in the right front seat or by someone leaning in the right front window.

Police responded to the scene as a result of a prowler/burglary complaint from a neighbor whose residence adjoins the alleyway; the neighbor complained of hearing noises coming from the alley. Response by the officers was within a 1–2-minute-time frame. The smell of gunpowder was still in the vehicle, and the victim was still in an upright position. A witness looking from a window from a nearby residence reported seeing a dark figure running from the area of the scene but could offer no description due to darkness.

The victim had $100 in his possession. He apparently feared for his life as a result of a previous threat approximately two weeks prior. The threat was due to a several thousand dollars being borrowed from a drug dealer to help set up the victim's business. Victimology noted that he lived on the fringes of drug activity with a common-law wife and several children.

125: Revenge (4 cases)

Revenge killing is in retaliation for a perceived wrong, real or imagined, committed against offender or offender's significant other.

A 41-year-old separated white woman was found dead in her home. There was no sign of forced entry. The victim was clad in a short nightgown covering to the waist. The assault began at the entry (kitchen) door, with the assailant stabbing and slashing at the victim, pursuing her from the kitchen area back to the victim's daughter's bedroom and back to the hallway where she died. The victim put up a fight and suffered numerous defensive wounds along with indications that she did grab the blade of the knife at some point in time with both hands. Her hands were severely cut. In the bedroom area, the victim apparently fell back onto the bed and kicked at the assailant who at this time slashed out and cut the legs. The victim was able to get to her feet and then in a short distance, in the bedroom doorway, collapsed from a previous wound that struck the heart. At this time, the victim's throat was severely slashed and the victim fell into the hallway where she was found. The throat slashing was post mortem. The victim's daughter was not home and had stayed at a friend's house for the night. The daughter found her mother upon her return the next morning. The victim suffered approximately 50 wounds to the body, both defensive and as a result of the assault. There was no evidence of sexual assault. Victimology noted the victim, who maintained a low social profile, to be employed as a telephone sales representative, living in a single family house on a rural farm with her teenage daughter.

126: Non-specific (9 cases)

The motive for the nonspecific homicide is unknown.

Ten days after being last seen in a bar, a 22-year-old single white woman was found with her body anchored in a small stream, inside a drain pipe. The cause of death was asphyxiation by unknown means. All personal items were missing except her shirt, which was tied loosely around her neck and used to secure the body. Victimology noted that she was unemployed, associated with a bike gang, and used drugs and alcohol.

130: Sexual Homicide (9 cases)

Sexual homicide involves sexual element (activity) as a basis in the sequence of acts leading to death. Performance and meaning of sexual element varies with offender. Act may range from actual rape involving penetration (either before death or postmortem) to symbolic sexual assault, such as insertion of foreign objects into victim's body orifices.

A 15-year-old white female, a 9th-grade student, left her residence to purchase cigarettes for her mother at a nearby convenience store. The victim never returned and was reported as a missing person. Two months after her disappearance, the body was found in the basement of a vacant building in the neighborhood by a fireman who was checking the building. When the body was found, the victim was lying face down in a prone position. Her jeans were lying next to the body with the inseam completely ripped apart. Her underwear and socks were found near her feet. The victim's head was laying on her blue jean jacket. The lower portion of her body was nude. The victim's blouse was partially on the body and the bra had been pulled up over the breasts. The victim died from strangulation by some type of ligature, probably some type of rope. It appears that she was killed and assaulted at another unknown location and the body placed in the basement of the vacant abandoned building for disposal. Victimology noted that the neighborhood was low-income family and that the victim was described as streetwise, an occasional drug user and was known to trade sex for favors.

SPECIAL ISSUES

Response to Family Member Homicide

Sadly, the murder of a family member leaves more than just bodies behind. Murder leaves survivors to struggle and cope with sudden, unpredictable, and violent loss of life. The impact of violence on families, especially those in inner-city areas, remains a complex issue (Buka et al. 2001). Statistics tell that youth exposure to violence peaked in 1993 and since that time has been on a somewhat optimistic linear decline (Cole 1999). Nevertheless, the degree to which children and adolescents are affected by it remains "unacceptably high" (Centers for Disease Control and Prevention [CDC] 2000).

There are the mental health consequences for those exposed to traumatic bereavement following family member homicide. In the flurry of the investigative activity following a homicide and the grief and bereavement process, children may be overlooked. While they are diminutive in stature, they are not limited in their emotional capacity. What may be different in comparison to the adult survivor, however, are the ways in which children think about the victim, feel about the murder, and express their grief.

Forensic Issues

A number of agencies swing into action when a homicide is reported. There is a flurry of media coverage and a police investigation ensues at the crime scene. Emotions run high with fear and disbelief, with the focus usually on the deceased and the assailant. And then there are the additional victims of the crime: the co-victims or those left with the emotional aftermath of the traumatic loss (Spungen 1997). For children of all ages, family homicide is an extremely painful experience with which to contend. It may be the biggest challenge that they may face in their entire lives.

Death Notification

Law enforcement usually has the responsibility of ringing the doorbell and announcing to the family that one of their members had been murdered. News of a homicide is inherently sudden and traumatic in nature.

Death notification begins a range of internal thoughts and questions for the child. What are the facts? Who did it; who is the murderer? Death notification requires reality issues the family must complete. Homicide includes all the activities that are part of the grieving process, including viewing the victim and attending to funeral activities. Someone has to identify the body; this can place an added psychological burden on a family member to whom the task falls.

Funeral Activities

One of the duties that occupies the family's time in the first week following a homicide is attending to the funeral details and arrangements. Such decisions as to whether to have an open casket must be made. This may depend on the physical appearance of the body and can be a difficult decision for the family. Families must take into account how newspaper reporting has handled the situation in terms of what peoples' fantasies might be of the injuries to the deceased. Families must also consider the wishes, if they are known, of the victim regarding an open casket.

Police Investigation

It is the role of the police officer to initiate an investigation toward clarifying the circumstances surrounding the death. Just as the police are searching for answers surrounding the murder, so too are the family members.

Medical Examiner's Office

The Medical Examiner's Office (MEO) plays a critical role in the aftermath of a homicide. Although the work of this agency is of upmost importance, it is intertwined with an association to death. The MEO is the final voice of the victim, in that he or she makes a final determination of the cause and manner of death from the information gleaned from the forensic autopsy.

Media

Murder is newsworthy and as a crime it becomes an act against the community. There is no confidentiality. Murder victims are named and family members are thrown into the public's view. Privacy for grief and stabilization of the family system is lost.

Aftermath

After the crisis of the death notification and funeral activities, friends and relatives typically must return to the daily routines from which they came prior to the death. The house, which may have been suddenly burgeoning with love, support, and numerous shoulders to cry upon, may now seem like an empty shell, filled with haunting reminders and echoes of the person who is now dead. Returning to work, school, or church can be quite an ominous event.

The immediate time period following the death notification and funeral is one of shock and disbelief for the family and the children. Families are numb and confused, and generally have a number of physical concerns. Insomnia, sleep pattern disturbance, headaches, and gastrointestinal upsets are common.

Return to Work or School

Since the return to work or school may occur within a time frame of less than a week after the murder, the reentry into this subcommunity has been described as pivotal in dealing with trauma.

It can be distressing in this phase. Family members may feel misunderstood by coworkers, teachers, and peers. There may be little validation of the homicide of the family member. People may not know what to say.

Children may be unable to concentrate and complete certain school tasks. They can become defiant, verbally aggressive, and in some cases, physically violent. They may skip class, refuse to do their work, and succeed in being sent home.

Grief

Grief and mourning are part of the bereavement process. Grief is the subjective experience and behavior noted after a significant loss, while mourning refers to the process of the attenuation of grief as an adaptation to loss (Horowitz et al. 1981). Family members feel sad, depressed, guilty, preoccupied, lonely, and angry, and struggle to adjust to their environment, including home, school, and peers.

Grief-stricken children differ in some respects from adult family members. Developmentally, they have a shorter attention span, and the capacity to sustain sadness over time increases with maturity. Children's grief and pain may go unnoticed by their adult caretakers or teachers. Children also seek to maintain the attachment to the deceased despite their conscious knowledge of the permanence of death. Thus, one may note a complex series of defensive maneuvers aimed at denying the significance of the loss.

Grief work is the psychological process that moves the person from being preoccupied with thoughts of the lost person, through painful recollections of the loss experience, to the final step of settling the loss as an integrative experience (Parkes 1972). Successful mourning allows for the slow withdrawal of the attachment to the deceased and the increased availability of psychic energy to forge new or stronger relationships (Green 1985).

Pathological grief occurs when the grief becomes so intense that the child is overwhelmed, resorts to maladaptive behavior and does not complete the mourning process. This type of grief is seen in children who show severe behavior problems and marked impairment of social function (Green 1985).

Guilt and Blame

Murder undermines one's faith in the world as an ordered and secure place. Studies show that untimely natural deaths shake confidence in this sense of security. Blaming someone for a tragedy is a less disturbing alternative than facing the fact that life is uncertain. It allows people to control by putting the responsibility onto another person. Not to be able to explain a situation makes people feel helpless.

People look for a target to project their feelings. A main target, of course, is the assailant. Families want justice and the assailant prosecuted. Another target is the criminal justice system. Families can become angry at the police for being unsuccessful in finding the assailant, and not infrequently the victim may be blamed. This concept holds that no victim is entirely innocent but rather participates to some degree in the crime.

Family members may have thoughts of how he or she could have prevented the death. This phenomenon is known as survivor's guilt; it is not uncommon and is extremely disturbing (Henry-Jenkins 1993).

Stigma

Homicides are often sensationalized in the media and thus, violent death can damage the victim's family and social network. There are cases where people deliberately avoid the family and consequently are not supportive. Such cases may involve drugs in which the victim "squealed" to federal agents. Thus, the victim was not seen as worthy of grieving, and the family member receives no support. And there are situations where people unwittingly avoid the family and thus no support is offered. Such cases usually involve horrific situations that overwhelm the social network to the point that they do not know what to say to the family.

Family members may feel "different" and embarrassed, especially if the death evolved around a crime such as drug trafficking and this was on the news.

Fears and Phobias

As with crime victims, fears and phobic reactions are common and develop according to the specific circumstances surrounding the events of the crime. Families become very aware of the potential for a crime occurring and cope by adding protective measures. Adults will obtain permits to carry guns or will put burglar alarms in their homes.

Mental Health Effects

Post-Traumatic Stress Disorder (PTSD) and related symptoms have been the focus of most studies investigating the effects of family member's exposure to violence (Buka et al. 2001). Murder is a crime of human design, and grief counseling is always advised in an attempt to prevent PTSD.

Darlene Allen's Response to the Murder of Her Husband

Wife's post-trauma response Darlene, a witness to the murder of her husband and a victim of a head-and-neck assault, suffered traumatic bereavement and symptoms of chronic posttraumatic stress.

Immediately after the murder, Darlene's daughter and sister arrived to help. She was taken to the military base and provided room in the officer's quarters. Armed guards were placed outside her room. She felt safe and, to this day, only feels safe (outside her home) when staying on a military base.

She stayed in a state of shock for months. She described how she has lost time and has no memory of those months. Her friends became so concerned about her that they made arrangements for her to seek a doctor. But she had problems remembering appointments and would just stay at home. She developed severe headaches and neck pain from the assault on her head. She sought help with pain management and medication. She had injections in her neck. Nothing relieved the headaches and the pain which she has to this day.

Darlene had continual flashbacks of the murder and recurring nightmares. She needed sleeping medication but then would be exhausted all day. She felt she was losing her mind. She refused to see her friends or be with people she knew. She felt paranoid. She didn't want to talk with anyone. She was irritable and cried constantly. She missed her husband. She could not take care of the stores and had to sell them. This made her feel like a failure, saying not only had she lost her husband but also the stores. She did not feel she could manage without him. She would not answer the telephone because she did not want to talk to people.

Two years after the murder, she felt she was making some progress but had a set back after her deposition for a civil suit. All the traumatic memories came back. She withdraws by sleeping as much as she can. She felt she lost several years. She cannot remember many events in 1997–1999. She does remember grandchildren being born. But when reminded of something she said, she often has no memory; her mind is blank. She used to be very social, managing public relations for the store but now she can hardly get through a dinner with friends. She hyperventilates in social settings.

She is suspicious of people, a new behavior. She cannot stay in a hotel. She is chronically fatigued having little interest in current events. She watches reruns of television shows from the 1970s and 1980s, like the Andy Griffin show. On the radio, she listens to the oldies but goodies music. She reads a little but stops if there is any violence. When she went to a movie with her sister, she became ill while watching a scene where someone was shot; she vomited and had to leave the movie. Then she felt guilty. She has mood dysregulation, still having many crying spells. Her weight fluctuates. She is 5'5" and weighs about 180 pounds.

Case: Recovery from Attempted Homicide

Many victims of attempted murder survive when emergency medical care is provided quickly. Such was the situation in the following case of three college roommates.

Kerri had been to class and returned home about 6:45 P.M. She was enjoying the quiet of the apartment, doing homework and typing on her computer. She looked at the clock around 9:30 P.M., and because she wanted to watch ice skating at 10 P.M., she thought it would be a good time to take a break. She put her books away in the bookcase by the front door and then heard keys in the front door. She knew it would be Tiffanie returning from cheerleading.

The door was always kept locked so she flipped the lock and turned away but heard Tiffanie startle a bit. The door opened fast and an armed man pushed Tiffanie into the room. The women were put into a back bedroom with Tiffanie forced face down on the bed. Kerri initially refused the assailant's instructions to "give him head" and "lick it hard" until she felt the gun pressed against her head. He then issued the same order to Tiffanie who refused saying she was a virgin. The assailant demanded oral and vaginal penetration to Tiffanie; he then returned to Kerri and sexually assaulted her again. He then left the room, came back, and isolated Kerri in the bathroom.

Kerri heard the assailant struggling with Tiffanie; she tried to think of an escape but after hearing Tiffanie cry out her name, she knew she could not leave her. Then Kerri heard a gunshot. Next the assailant opened the door, turned on the light, and shot Kerri through a pillow into her chest. As he watched, Kerri slid down the wall and he left. She held herself together, saw blood drop on her leg, and heard him russling through the apartment. Next, the front door opened and Laura, the third roommate, called out for Kerri. The assailant came up behind Laura and forced her into another section of the bathroom. He then returned to Tiffanie who was successful in grabbing the gun and shooting. Shortly after that, the assailant fled the apartment with his gun.

Tiffanie locked the door, hit the panic button, and collapsed. Laura called 911 and the police and emergency medical team arrived.

The aftermath All three roommates survived but each had separate post-trauma symptoms.

Kerri was hospitalized for gunshot wounds to the chest; a chest tube was inserted for several days. She stayed with her brother and parents for a time following her hospitalization. She withdrew from her campus activities and classes for second semester. She was physically uncomfortable, could not sleep, had flashbacks where she would see a dark bathroom. She could not stand dark rooms. She could hear Tiffanie calling her name and could smell the assailant. She worried about Tiffanie; she missed her favorite pillow made by her mother that was used in the crime.

She could not lie on her side because of the discomfort from the lodged bullet. She had little appetite and lost 7–8 pounds. She went to a few classes just to "let people see she was still alive." She went home for spring break but did not feel any safer at home than at school. The victim advocates found her a new apartment and her friends moved with her. Months later she had surgery to remove the lodged bullet that was causing her great physical and psychological discomfort.

In the weeks and months that followed, she was tormented by many thoughts of the crime. It was on her mind constantly. She could not concentrate; walking alone made her nervous. She armed her new apartment with alarms and panic buttons. She sought counseling to help her "get over the jumpies." She continued to have mood swings with many unprovoked crying spells. The counselor taught her relaxation techniques to help her sleep at night. She found it distressing to attend counseling since it was a reminder of what happened.

The assailant was apprehended and at the trial Kerri said she was at least 20 minutes into her testimony before she was able to look over at the assailant. She was shocked and unnerved to see how different he looked in a suit and tie compared to the night of the shooting.

Kerri's mother observed the following changes in her daughter. Kerri is afraid to be alone; will freeze and stare at a man who resembles the assailant; continues to have nightmares; talks of her inadequacy ("Who will want to date me now?"); does not freely socialize as before; feels men are staring at her breasts; has difficulty talking about the ordeal; threw up at night during the trial; has great fatigue; is restless at night; is very private about her body; avoids wearing certain clothes that may expose her scars; was very anxious returning to school this fall and called home crying that she did not think she could make it at school; and has difficulty making decisions.

REFERENCES

BUKA, S. L., T. L. STICHNICK, I. BIRDTHISTLE, and F. J. EARLS. (2001). Youth exposure to violence: Prevalence, risks and consequences. *American Journal of Orthopsychiatry*, 71(3): 298–310.

BUREAU OF JUSTICE STATISTICS (1995). Violent offenders in state prison: Sentences and time served (by A. J. Beck & L. A. Greenfield). Washington, D.C.: Department of Justice, Office of Justice Programs.

BUREAU OF JUSTICE STATISTICS. (1998). Justice in the United States and in England and Wales. Washington, D.C.: Department of Justice, Office of Justice Programs.

BUREAU OF JUSTICE STATISTICS. (2002). Recidivism of prisoners released in 1994 (Special Report by P. A. Langan and D. J. Levin). Washington, D.C.: Department of Justice, Office of Justice Programs.

BUREAU OF JUSTICE STATISTICS. (2004). Prison and jail inmates at midyear 2003. Washington, D.C.: Department of Justice, Office of Justice Programs.

BUREAU OF JUSTICE STATISTICS. (2005). Prisoners in 2004 (By P. M. Harrison and A. J. Beck). Washington, D.C.: Department of Justice, Office of Justice Programs.

CANTER, D. (2004). Offender profiling and investigative psychology. *Journal of Investigative Psychology and Offender Profiling*, 1, 1–15.

CANTER, D. V. and WENTINK, N. (2004). An empirical test of Holmes and Holmes's Serial Murder Typology. *Criminal Justice and Behavior*, 31(4), 488–515.

Manual (2nd Ed.) San Francisco, CA: Jossey-Bass.

DOUGLAS, J., BURGESS, A. W., BURGESS, A., and RESSLER, R. (1992). *Crime Classification Manual*. Lexington: Lexington Books.

EVERITT, D. (1993). *Human Monsters: An Illustrated Encyclopedia of the World's Most Vicious Murderers*. NY: Contemporary Books.

FEDERAL BUREAU OF INVESTIGATION. (2005). *Supplementary Homicide Reports 1980–2004*. Washington, D.C: Department of Justice.

FEDERAL BUREAU OF INVESTIGATION. (2006). *Uniform Crime Report–Crime in the United States*. Washington, D.C.: Department of Justice.

FOX, J. A. and LEVIN, J. (1996). *Over Kill: Mass Murder and Serial Killing Exposed*. NY: Bantam Books.

FOX, J. A. and LEVIN, J. (2005). *Extreme Killing: Understanding Serial Murder*. Thousand Oaks: Sage Publications.

FOX, J. A. and LEVIN, J. (2006). *Will to Kill: Explaining Senseless Murder*. Boston: Allyn and Bacon.

GOODWIN, M. (1998). Reliability, validity and utility of extant serial murder classifications. *The Criminologist*, 22, 194–210.

GOODWIN, M. (2002). Reliability, validity and utility of criminal profiling typologies. *Journal of Police and Criminal Psychology*, 17, 1–18.

GOTTFREDSON, M. and HIRSCHI, T. (1990). *A General Theory of Crime*. Stanford, CA: Stanford University Press.

GREEN, A. H. (1985). Children traumatized by physical abuse. In *Post-Traumatic Stress Disorder in Children,* ed. S. Eth and R. S. Pynoos, 135–154. Washington, DC: American Psychiatric Press.

HICKEY, E. (2002). *Serial murderers and their victims* (3rd Ed.). Belmont, CA: Wadsworth.

HOLMES, R. M. and S. T. HOLMES, (1998). *Serial Murder* (2nd Ed.). Thousand Oaks, CA: Sage Publications.

HOLMES, R. M. and S. T. HOLMES, (2001). *Mass Murder in the United States*. Upper Saddle River, NJ: Prentice-Hall.

HOLMES, R. M. and S. T. HOLMES, (2002). *Profiling Violent Crime: An Investigative Tool* (3rd Ed.). Thousand Oaks, CA: Sage Publications.

HOROWITZ, M. J., J. KRUPNICK, N. KALTREIDER, N. WILNER, A. LEONG, and C. MARMAR. (1981). Initial psychological response to parental death. *Archives of General Psychiatry*, 137: 316–323.

ILLINOIS DEPARTMENT OF CORRECTIONS. (2002). *Statistical Presentation, 2001: Part II: Length of Stay*. Illinois: Springfield.

IOWA LEGISLATIVE SERVICES AGENCY. (2003). *Review of Iowa's 85.0% Sentencing Laws*. Des Moines, Iowa: State Capitol.

LA VIGNE, N. G. and C. A. MAMALIAN, (2004). *Prison Reentry in Georgia*. Washington, D. C. Urban Institute, Justice Policy Center.

LYONS, J. (1987). Post-traumatic stress disorder in children and adolescents: A review of the literature. In *Annual Progress in Child Psychiatry and Development,* ed. S. Chess and A. Thomas, 451–457. New York: Brunner Mazel.

NASH, J. R. (1993). *World Encyclopedia of 20th Century Murder*. NY: Marlowe & Company.

NGA CENTER FOR BEST PRACTICES. (2004). *The Challenges and Impacts of Prison Reentry*.

Washington, D.C.: National Governors' Association.

NGA CENTER FOR BEST PRACTICES. (2004). *Prison Reentry: Massachusetts*. Washington, D.C.: National Governors' Association.

NGA CENTER FOR BEST PRACTICES. (2004). *Prison Reentry: Virginia*. Washington, D.C.: National Governors' Association.

NGA CENTER FOR BEST PRACTICES. (2006). *Prison Reentry*. Washington, D.C.: National Governors' Association.

PETHERICK, W. (2005). *The Science of Criminal Profiling*. NY: Barnes and Noble.

RKES, C. M. (1972). *Bereavement: Studies of Grief in Adult Life*. New York: International Universities Press.

ROBERTS, A. R., K. ZGOBA, and S. M. SHAHIDULLAH. (2007). Recidivism among four types of homicide offenders: An exploratory analysis of 336 homicide offenders in New Jersey. *Aggression and Violent Behavior*, 12(5): 493–507.

SALFATI, C. G. (2001). The Nature of Expressiveness and Instrumentality in Homicide, and its Implication for Offender Profiling. Paper presented at the 6th Investigating Psychology Conference, Liverpool, England.

SALFATI, C. G. and GREY, J. (2002). Profiling U.S. Homicide. Paper presented at the Annual Meeting of the American Society of Criminology, November, Chicago.

SAMPSON, R. J., RAUDENBUSH, S. W. and EARLS, F. (1997). Neighborhoods and violent crime: A multilevel study of collective efficacy. *Science*, 277, 918–924.

SAMPSON, R. J. and WILSON, W. J. (1995). Towards a theory of race, crime and urban inequality. In J. Hagan and R.D. Peterson (Eds.), *Crime and Inequality*. Stanford, CA: Stanford University Press, pp. 37–52.

TRAVIS, J., KEEGAN, S., and CADORA, E. (2003). *A Portrait of Prison Reentry in New Jersey*. Washington, D.C.: Urban Institute.

TRAVIS, J. and VISHER, C. (2005). *Prison Reentry and Crime in America*. NY: Cambridge University Press.

WASHINGTON INSTITUTE FOR PUBLIC POLICY. (2004). *Sentencing for Adult Felons in Washington (Part I – Historical Trends)*. Washington: Olympia.

WOLFGANG, M. E. (1958). *Patterns of Criminal Homicide*. Philadelphia: University of Pennsylvania Press.

Chapter 8

The War on Drugs

Treatment, Research, and Substance Abuse Intervention in the Twenty-First Century

C. Aaron McNeece, Bruce Bullington, Elizabeth Mayfield Arnold, and David W. Springer

ABSTRACT

This chapter provides an overview of justice system interventions with drug users, reviews a number of harm reduction approaches, and suggests a different strategy allowing the medical use of marijuana. It concludes by suggesting that there is a need for a paradigm shift from the prohibitionist policies associated with the war on drugs. Overall, a strong argument is made for the decriminalization of drug use if not for outright legalization.

INTRODUCTION

Three facts have become increasingly clear from the U.S. experience with the war on drugs: (1) incarceration alone does little to break the cycle of illegal drug use and crime, (2) offenders sentenced to incarceration for substance-related offenses exhibit a high rate of recidivism once they are released (Drug Court Clearinghouse and Technical Assistance Project 1996:8), and (3) drug abuse treatment has been shown to be demonstrably effective in reducing both drug abuse and drug-related crime (National Institute on Drug Abuse 1999:18–19).

Although the cost of the war on drugs has grown astronomically, there is no evidence that the ever-increasing expenditures have brought the United States any closer to victory (Orenstein 2002:36).

> Consider: The federal government spends about two-thirds of its $19.2 billion drug budget on law enforcement and interdiction. A result has been a skyrocketing prison population—it

has tripled in the last two decades with at least 60 percent of inmates reporting a history of substance abuse. The cost of warehousing nonviolent drug offenders is more than twice as great as treating them. Meanwhile, a study by the RAND Corporation's drug-policy center found that for every dollar spent on treatment, taxpayers save more than seven in other services, largely through reduced crime and medical fees and increased productivity. A visit to the emergency room, for instance, costs as much as a month in rehab, and more than 70,000 heroin addicts are admitted to E.R.s annually.

Treatment for substance abuse addiction is seen as a key component in preventing reoffenses, but treatment is frequently not available. Between 2000 and 2001, the estimated number of persons age 12 or older needing treatment for an illicit drug problem increased from 4.7 million to 6.1 million. During the same period, the number of persons needing but not receiving treatment increased from 3.9 million to 5.0 million. The majority of people receiving treatment for either alcohol or drug abuse received it only from a self-help group (Samsha 2002).

In the war on drugs, three-fourths of the expenditures went for domestic enforcement of drug laws, and only 7 percent was used for treatment (RAND 1994). Since the early 1980s, the criminal justice system has felt the impact of the substance abuse problem as the number of offenders arrested on drug-related charges has increased dramatically and prisons throughout the nation have become inundated with drug offenders. There were more than 723,637 marijuana arrests in the United States in 2001 (Federal Bureau of Investigation 2002). Since 1992, approximately 6 million Americans have been arrested on marijuana charges, more than the entire populations of Alaska, Delaware, the District of Columbia, Montana, North Dakota, South Dakota, Vermont, and Wyoming combined. Annual marijuana arrests have more than *doubled* in that time (NORML 2002).

JUSTICE SYSTEM INTERVENTIONS WITH DRUG USERS

There is little doubt that drug users will continue to provide much of the fodder for our rapidly expanding correctional system well into this century. During the last few decades, there have been record increases in the numbers of persons brought under some form of correctional control in the United States. During the early 1990s, the nation easily surpassed Russia and South Africa in incarceration rates, making the United States the standout leader among industrialized nations in the imprisonment of its citizens. At the end of 2006, 2,258,983 persons were incarcerated in the nation's prisons and jails (Bureau of Justice Statistics 2006).

It is also clear that these increases were fueled largely by the war on drugs as consequences of lengthier sentences and mandatory sentencing for those caught with these illicit substances. By the mid-1990s for example, more than 52 percent of federal inmates were drug offenders. Drug violators accounted for nearly 30 percent of prisoners in state facilities (Irwin and Austin 1994).

The results of these changes in incarceration rates were often not what had been anticipated by those who fostered them. For example, in Florida it was discovered that various new penal provisions for drug offenders that were passed in the 1980s resulted in serious criminal offenders actually serving less time than they had before, with many violent offenders being released prematurely to increase the availability of prison beds for nonviolent drug offenders who had been incarcerated under mandatory sentencing provisions (Rasmussen and Benson 1994). Although these trends were eventually halted in the 1990s, they had a marked effect on prison and non-prison correctional populations at the time and will continue to influence the Florida system for some time to come.

Whenever correctional concerns are mentioned, people often think only in terms of prison, although these total institutions have never handled more than a small proportion of those who are serving a correctional sentence. At the present time, about 20 percent of sentenced persons are actually serving time in prisons or jails; the remaining 80 percent are involved in some alternative sanction provided for under both federal and state justice systems (Clear 1995). For those not imprisoned, probation is generally thought of as the only available option. Despite this perception, there exists a wide variety of programs that provide alternatives to institutionalization and probation. Recently, these approaches have been labeled *intermediate sanctions* by scholars and researchers in the field, who see them as located between the two extremes of incarceration and probation.

The forms that intermediate sanctions take include a rich diversity of options. Clear (1995) has identified nine distinct methods of intermediate sanction methods. One of these is *intensive supervision*, an approach that is coupled with either probation or parole. It involves very frequent contacts between those being observed and their supervision agents. In a second method, *house arrest*, the offender is confined to his or her residence either continually or during non-work hours. A third strategy, *electronic monitoring,* requires that the offender wear a bracelet that signals a homing device when the person has gone beyond an acceptable range. *Urine screening* is a fourth tactic that is used to detect illicit drug or alcohol use by the offender. The fifth method includes *fines,* which are generally used in conjunction with several other approaches. A sixth program type, *community service,* calls for the offender to work for a specified number of hours in a community service project. *Halfway houses and work release centers* compose the seventh strategy. These provide living facilities for offenders, who are usually required to maintain regular employment during the day. An eighth form of intermediate sanction, *shock probation,* provides a brief period of confinement designed to alert offenders to the seriousness of their behavior followed by intensive supervision on probation. Finally, *treatment programs* can be prescribed for offenders who are ordered to participate in substance abuse programs and related activities. These can include both inpatient and outpatient methods, depending on the person involved and the nature of their chemical dependency problem.

Several different goals may be established for these programs. Most can be classified as being principally concerned with controlling offenders or with changing them through some therapeutic intervention. Given these distinct goals, the various programs identified may be utilized in several combinations. Offenders are likely to be concurrently assigned to several of these intermediate sanction conditions simultaneously based on the judge's perception of the nature of their problem, life circumstances, and amenability to specific types of intervention. It has long been believed that the probability of producing favorable outcomes with these populations may be enhanced by careful selection and matching of conditions to individual needs. Of course, the problem remains as to how we are to accomplish this, especially given the relatively primitive state of our current knowledge.

Supporters see intermediate sanctions as being much less expensive than incarceration and as more effective at producing desirable outcomes. If such claims are proven to be accurate, these methods should expand considerably in the years to come. While the pressures brought about by the extreme incarceration rates generated during the 1990s are subsiding somewhat, there remains considerable interest in lowering the costs of corrections. If intermediate sanctions can produce positive results and at a cost that is but a small fraction of those associated with institutionalization, it seems likely that these programs will receive a great deal of attention.

CURRENT PRACTICES IN DRUG OFFENDER INTERVENTION

Although substance abuse treatment for offenders varies across programs, facilities, and locations, the National Task Force on Correctional Substance Abuse Strategies (1991) notes that effective programs have common characteristics: clearly defined missions, goals, admission criteria, and assessment strategies for those seeking treatment; support and understanding of key agency administrators and staff; consistent intervention strategies supported by links with other agencies as the offender moves through the system; well-trained staff who have opportunities for continuing education; and ongoing evaluation and development based on outcome and process data. One of the main issues of contention among researchers and substance abuse providers has been an operational definition of the term *effective treatment.* The Treatment Outcome Working Group, a meeting of treatment and evaluation experts sponsored by the Office of National Drug Control Policy (ONDCP), established some results and outcomes that define effective treatment (ONDCP 1996):

1. Reduced use of the primary drug;

2. Improved functioning of drug users in terms of employment;

3. Improved educational status;

4. Improved interpersonal relationships;

5. Improved medical status and general improvement in health;

6. Improved legal status;

7. Improved mental health status;

8. Improved noncriminal public safety factors.

Though some of these desired outcomes are not pertinent to incarcerated offenders receiving treatment, they are appropriate long-term goals following release. Failure to accomplish these goals is likely to lead to continued involvement in future drug use and criminal activity, and possibly, incarceration.

In addition to these criteria, the National Institute on Drug Abuse (NIDA) (1999:i) believes that effective treatment attends to multiple needs of the individual, not just his or her drug use. To be effective, treatment must address the user's medical, psychological, social, vocational, and legal problems.

One problem in evaluating drug treatment methods and programs for criminal offenders is that recidivism tends to be defined solely in terms of re-arrest rates, yet a number of offenders who successfully complete treatment may continue to use drugs and not be rearrested. Thus, if recidivism is defined only as re-arrest, an unknown percentage of subjects may continue to have substance abuse problems even though they have been defined as successful. Another problem is that offenders may be rearrested for non-drug offenses, resulting in a type of false positive in the recidivism statistics.

Considering data on re-arrests may lead us to either underestimate or overestimate the actual rate of continued substance abuse among offenders. One alternative in gaining a better estimate of continued drug use is to examine the substance-use level and productivity after treatment completion (Van Stelle, Mauser, and Moberg 1994). However, monitoring post-treatment offender behavior is difficult unless the offender is mandated to have follow-up through probation or parole and urine drug testing. These methods of monitoring are discussed later in this chapter.

We now turn our attention to a discussion of the most common types of intervention and treatment programs. These programs and models are included either because they represent a prevalent model or because they have shown unusual promise in assisting substance-abusing offenders.

Self-Help Programs

Alcoholics Anonymous (AA), founded by William (Bill W.) Wilson and Robert (Dr. Bob) Holbrook Smith, is an abstinence-based 12-step program maintaining that alcoholism is a disease that can be coped with but not cured. Thus, according to the AA philosophy, there are recovering alcoholics but not cured or ex-alcoholics. Other self-help 12-step programs, such as Narcotics Anonymous (NA), follow the conceptual framework as that used in Alcoholics Anonymous. AA and NA meetings are held in both adult- and juvenile-secured correctional settings. Additional self-help groups include Rationale Recovery and Women for Sobriety.

As noted earlier, self-help is the most common type of treatment for alcohol or substance abuse problems. Self-help groups, such as AA and NA, also are the most commonly used (64 percent) substance abuse programs provided in jail settings (Bureau of Justice Statistics 2000). Studies on the effectiveness of AA have generally focused on middle- and upper-class populations with rather stable lives prior to the onset of a drinking problem (Alexander 1990), and much of the evidence regarding the effectiveness of self-help groups is based on anecdotal reports (Miller and Hester 1986).

Individual, Family, and Group Counseling

Individual Counseling

Individual counseling might address areas such as depression, faulty cognitions (often referred to in the field as *stinking thinking*), and using behaviors. This modality usually entails talk therapy between a client and psychologist, social worker, or substance abuse counselor. Regardless of a practitioner's theoretical orientation, non-possessive warmth and empathic understanding should serve as the foundation for the therapeutic relationship but must be coupled with more directive interventions to realize positive treatment effects with substance-abusing offenders (Springer, McNeece, and Arnold 2003). Indeed, motivational interviewing, a client-centered, directive method for enhancing intrinsic motivation to change by exploring and resolving ambivalence (Miller and Rollnick 2002:25), has been used effectively with substance-abusing clients (Harper and Hardy 2000). The most comprehensive application of motivational interviewing with substance-abusing offenders is a group program Graves and Rotgers developed called *motivational enhancement treatment* (Jamieson, Beals, Lalonde, and Associates 2000). It is rare that individual treatment is the sole modality used with substance-abusing offenders. Rather, it is usually combined with group or family treatment as well.

Family Counseling

A truism in substance abuse treatment is that the family is a critical factor to consider when developing a treatment plan for the client (Springer 2005). The relationship between adolescent substance abuse and family system characteristics or parental behaviors is supported in the literature (Anderson and Henry 1994; Denton and Kampfe 1994), revealing that family drug use, family conflict, lack of parental monitoring, and rigid family rules are all correlated with an increased risk of adolescent substance abuse. While logistical constraints may prevent incarcerated offenders from including their family members in treatment, many community-based programs for offenders offer opportunities for family participation.

A commonly used family treatment approach with substance-abusing adolescents is structural-strategic family therapy (Springer 2005; Todd and Selekman 1994). Developed by Salvador Minuchin and his associates (Minuchin 1974; Minuchin and Fishman 1981), this approach incorporates family development and a family systems conceptual framework. Other family therapy approaches that have demonstrated effectiveness with substance-abusing adolescents include functional family therapy (Alexander and Parsons 1973) and brief strategic family therapy (Szapocznik, Murray, Scopetea, Hervis, Rio, Cohen, Rivas-Vazques, and Posada 1989). In the past decade, considerable advances have been made in researching the effectiveness of family interventions for alcohol- and substance-use problems in general and adolescent substance abuse in particular (Waldron 1997:199). There are several recent reviews and meta-analyses of well-controlled family therapy outcome studies (Liddle and Dakoff 1995; Stanton and Shadish 1997; Waldron 1997), demonstrating that family therapy leads to decreased substance use and, when compared to alternative, nonfamily interventions, family therapy appears to emerge as the superior treatment (Waldron 1997:229).

One of the newer community-based family preservation approaches, multisystemic therapy (MST), was developed by Scott Henggeler and colleagues (Henggeler and Borduin 1990; Henggeler et al. 1998). MST is one of the few scientifically based approaches for adolescent substance abuse treatment recommended by the National Institute on Drug Abuse (1999) and the Center for Substance Abuse Treatment (2000). According to Henggeler (1999), MST utilizes treatment approaches that are pragmatic, problem focused, and have some empirical support including, but not limited to, strategic family therapy (Haley 1976), structural family therapy (Minuchin 1974), behavioral parent training (Munger 1993), and cognitive-behavior therapy (Kendall and Braswell 1993). According to Brown (2001:458),

> To date, MST is the only treatment for serious delinquent behavior that has demonstrated both short-term and long-term treatment effects in randomized, controlled clinical trials with violent and chronic juvenile offenders and their families from various cultural and ethnic backgrounds.

MST is currently being used in approximately 25 sites across the United States and Canada (Schoenwald and Rowland 2002).

Group Counseling

Group counseling, often the treatment of choice among chemical dependency counselors, can take the form of support groups, psychoeducational groups, and interactional thera-peutic groups. These groups may be conducted in outpatient and inpatient settings, including settings within the criminal justice system.

Working with groups in the criminal justice system has a different connotation than working with groups in the community because of issues of confidentiality, control, and safety. Nevertheless, the primary objective remains the same. The worker should focus on the strengths of the individual, consider group exercises that will emphasize these strengths, and foster therapeutic factors (Yalom 1995) within the group (Springer et al. 2003). These principles also apply to support groups that are often made available for parents, spouses, siblings, and other family members. Scott (1993) reported generally positive group therapy results with mentally and emotionally disturbed adult prisoners, and Ferrara (1992) has written a useful guide to conducting effective group work with juvenile delinquents.

Group work with juvenile substance abusers in therapeutic community and juvenile justice settings is also often delivered using a form of Positive Peer Culture (PPC; Vorrath and Brendtro 1985), which is a holistic approach aimed at changing the culture in a ther-apeutic setting. PPC does not seek to enforce a set of specific rules but to teach basic val-ues. The essence of PPC is captured in this statement: "If there were one rule, it would be that people must care for one another" (Vorrath and Brendtro 1985:xxi). A key assump-tion of this approach is that youths feel positive about themselves when two conditions are met: The youth feels (1) accepted by others and (2) deserving of this acceptance. EQUIP (Equipping Youth to Help One Another; Gibbs, Potter, and Goldstein 1995), a comprehensive treatment approach to help youths with antisocial behavior problems, incorporates into the PPC approach a multicomponent psychoeducational program called *aggression replacement training* (ART). The research on both EQUIP (Leeman, Gibbs, and Fuller 1993) and ART (Goldstein and Glick 1987) is generally positive and encour-aging, and it appears that the psychoeducational component enhances the effects of PPC.

Psychoeducational Approaches

In many corrections settings, both adult and juvenile offenders are required to complete educational classes as a part of their treatment plan. About 30 percent of substance abuse programs provided in jails offer education or awareness programs (Bureau of Justice

Statistics 2000). In the justice system, two major types of educational programs for offenders exist: didactic educational programs and psychoeducational methods.

Didactic educational programs closely resemble a seminar or class. In these programs, offenders are presented information about substance abuse and its effects. Offenders may learn about topics such as the physical effects of drug and alcohol abuse or the impact of substance abuse on family members, or they may be provided information about substance abuse treatment. In didactic educational programs, offenders are expected to listen to the information provided, and although there may be some interaction, the presenter is the focus of the program and interaction is generally minimal.

Psychoeducational educational methods combine the presentation of didactic information to increase knowledge with a variety of other techniques to help clients make desired changes and to provide support (McNeece and DiNitto 1994:117). In these programs, the emphasis is not solely on the facilitator, and group interaction is encouraged. Structured exercises such as role-play, group discussion on specific topics, and homework assignments are generally a part of psychoeducational programs.

The major objectives of psychoeducational approaches include development of motivation and commitment to treatment through recognition of the addiction history, stages of recovery, and the impact of drug use on physical health and vocational and social functioning; the enhancement of life skills (e.g., managing a checkbook, time management) and communication skills; AIDS education and prevention activities; relapse prevention skills, including recognition of signs and symptoms of relapse, avoidance of active drug users, identification of high-risk situations, and strategies for managing a lapse or relapse; and development of an aftercare plan that incorporates the use of community treatment resources (Peters 1993:53).

Pomeroy, Kiam, and Green (2000) examined the effectiveness of an HIV/AIDS psychoeducational approach with male inmates, with findings revealing that the intervention had small-to-moderate effects on depression (0.37) and anxiety (0.59), and a greater impact on trauma symptoms (0.71) and HIV/AIDS-related knowledge (1.13). Overall, however, the literature examining the effectiveness of psychoeducational approaches with offenders is scant (Springer et al. 2003).

Case Management

Case management activities originated in early-twentieth-century social work practice that provided services to disadvantaged clients. Most descriptions of case management include at least six primary functions: (1) identification and outreach to people in need of services, (2) assessment of specific needs, (3) planning for services, (4) linkage to services, (5) monitoring and evaluation, and (6) advocacy for the client system (Ridgely et al. 1996). Workers are increasingly engaging in case management activities in their work with substance-abusing offenders.

The importance of workers providing case management services for substance-abusing clients in the criminal justice setting has been supported by Martin and Inciardi (1993:89), who state that "[d]rug-involved criminal justice clients often face a wider spectrum of problems than other populations targeted by case management, including the life disruptions associated with police and court processing, the perceived stigma of a criminal record, the possibility of lost freedom through incarceration, and the disruptions caused in work, school, and family activities." Others also support the use of case management services because they have been shown to encourage substance abusers to remain in treatment and reach their treatment goals (Koeofed et al. 1986; Springer, McNeece, and Arnold 2003).

Treatment Alternatives to Street Crime

In the attempt to combat substance abuse in communities, a number of alternatives other than incarceration have been tried in recent years. One of the most widely known of these alternatives is treatment alternatives to street crime (TASC), a specially designed form of case management initially funded in 1972 with federal monies but now operated by states and communities. TASC targets offenders who appear to have the potential to benefit from treatment and who do not pose significant safety risks to their communities with supervision (Lipton 1995). The purpose of TASC is to identify, assess, refer for treatment, and conduct follow-up on drug offenders. Offenders in TASC programs are not incarcerated but are treated outside the court system in community-based programs. Each offender is assigned a case manager who assists in gaining access to treatment, provides linkages to other needed community services, and reports back to the appropriate court officials about the offender's progress. The monitoring function of the case manager is one of the hallmarks of TASC.

Acupuncture

Acupuncture is a form of ancient Chinese medicine that has been used for the last 20 years to treat addictions. The first substance abuse facility known to use acupuncture with substance abusers was Lincoln Hospital Substance Abuse Center in South Bronx, New York. The use of acupuncture involves inserting four or five needles into a person's ear for approximately 45 minutes. It is believed that acupuncture can cause headaches, nausea, sweating, and muscle cramping. (The exact mechanisms through which these improvements are supposed to occur have never been clearly identified.) Supporters of acupuncture also claim that it relieves depression, anxiety, and insomnia (Turnabout ASAP 1997). The needles are believed to produce a powerful response that helps decrease the desire for drugs and/or alcohol, thus helping the brain retain its chemical balance. Once this crucial balance is restored, the abuser will hopefully become more introspective and receptive to therapy (Edwards 1993). Recent data presented at a National Institute on Drug Abuse conference on acupuncture services in an outpatient methadone maintenance program indicate that those receiving acupuncture believe it has been effective for them, report that it has decreased their cravings, and indicate that they would recommend it to other patients (McLaughlin 2000).

Initial enthusiasm for acupuncture was based on anecdotal reports of success, but in recent years acupuncture has been subject to empirical examination. The outcome literature on the use of acupuncture to treat cocaine addiction has been mixed, with some studies reporting modest positive outcomes in short-term abstinence (Margolin et al. 1995) and self-reported drug use that was not consistent with urinalysis findings (Brewington, Smith, and Lipton 1994). Similarly, there is some support from one study for the use of acupuncture to treat opiate addiction (Newmeyer, Johnson, and Klot 1984). Few studies, however, have examined the impact of acupuncture with offenders. One study (Brumbaugh 1993) of female offenders documented lower rates of re-incarceration among those who received acupuncture as compared to controls.

The lack of research on the impact of acupuncture on offenders may be due in part to the fact that the use of acupuncture to treat offenders is a fairly new phenomenon. While it has become increasingly popular among drug court programs, all areas of the country and treatment facilities do not have access to acupuncture services. Furthermore, given that acupuncture is categorized as an experimental procedure, offenders cannot be ordered by the courts to receive this form of treatment (Brumbaugh 1993). Substance-abusing offenders must voluntarily agree to acupuncture treatment. The combination of these factors has led to a dearth of studies on the use of this method of intervention with offenders. Thus, while the general outcome of research on acupuncture with substance abusers suggests some positive effects in some studies, one cannot definitively conclude that acupuncture is an effective form of treatment for drug addiction.

Urine Drug Testing

Urine drug testing is a common method of testing offenders for substance use. The need for testing is generally based on the assumption that offenders tend to underreport drug use because of the consequences of such use. During the 1960s, these methods were used for the first time to detect the presence of banned substances in the blood and urine of parolees and probationers. At that time, urine-testing programs were costly, however, and few reliable laboratories could be counted on to minimize the number of faulty readings (both false positives and false negatives). In the late 1970s and early 1980s, the use of drug testing expanded, based in part on two developments: changes in drug-testing technology that allowed agencies to establish their own testing programs and evidence of the link between drug use and crime that led to zero tolerance of drug use (Bureau of Justice Assistance 1999).

In recent years, urine drug testing has become more sophisticated. Initially, thin layer chromatography was the main testing method, but in the last few decades, the immunoassay methods of testing were developed and have become increasingly popular (Bureau of Justice Assistance 1999). In addition, analyzer-based methods and handheld urine-testing devices that allow for more options in the use of testing offenders have developed (Bureau of Justice Assistance 1999). Offenders are now being tested in a variety of settings with the enhanced flexibility of testing methods.

Urine drug testing has also become increasingly commonplace in correctional settings. In 1998, 54 percent of offenders in jail were in facilities that test for illegal drug use (Bureau of Justice Statistics 2000). Inmates were most commonly tested on indication of use or at random (69 percent and 49 percent of jurisdictions, respectively) (Bureau of Justice Statistics 2000). Similarly, for offenders confined in state or federal prisons, most facilities test on indication of use (75.8 percent) or at random (62.7 percent) (Bureau of Justice Statistics 1992). The National Institute of Justice Drug Use Forecasting (DUF) program calculates the percentage of offenders arrested in certain cities throughout the country who have positive urine drug screens at the time of arrest. Recent DUF data show that the percentage of male inmates testing positive for any drug ranged from 51 to 83 percent (ONDCP 1997). As described by Fraser and Zamecnik (2002), the Correctional Service of Canada has an established drug-testing program for both incarcerated offenders and offenders on conditional release in the community. In 2000, among conditional release offenders, 27.2 percent tested positive for drugs, most commonly for cannabinoids (43.3 percent of positive tests) (Fraser and Zamecnik 2002). To address the issue of diluted specimens, a specific dilution protocol was established that uses different confirmation cutoff values for specimens as compared to non-diluted specimens (Fraser and Zamecnik 2002).

Urine drug testing is used in the criminal justice system with offenders in three main ways: (1) as an adjunct to community supervision, (2) as an assessment tool for offenders entering the system, and (3) as an assessment of drug use during mandated drug treatment. The utilization of drug testing serves several purposes in the criminal justice system: to inform judges of an offender's current drug use as a consideration for bail setting or sentencing; to indicate whether an offender is complying with a mandate to be drug-free; and to identify those offenders who need treatment (Timrots 1992).

Drug testing appears to serve a useful purpose in monitoring offenders with substance problems. However, drug testing alone is not sufficient to keep offenders from using drugs and re-offending. The best approach may be to combine random drug testing with forms of rehabilitative drug treatment to treat the addiction. However, not all offenders who test positive will receive treatment. Decisions about whether offenders who test positive for drugs will be mandated to treatment vary depending on the setting, jurisdiction, and access to treatment services.

While urine drug testing is used with both adult and juvenile offenders in a variety of correctional settings, it is not without criticism. Del Carmen and Barnhill (1999) note that drug testing for offenders can potentially violate six constitutional rights: (1) the right against unreasonable searches and seizures, (2) the right against self-incrimination, (3) the right to due process (when challenging the accuracy of testing), (4) the right to confrontation and cross-examination (if the person who does the testing is not in court), (5) the right to privacy (related to monitoring of the offender when providing the urine specimen), and (6) the right to equal protection (when the offender must pay for confirmation of a test but cannot afford to do so). To enhance the legal defensibility of testing, Del Carmen and Barnhill assert that agencies should have proper authorization to do testing, establish and adhere to procedural guidelines, and provide proper training to staff.

It is undeniably true that the existence of this technology considerably enhances the power of the state over citizens. We are now able to tap into their very body chemistry to determine whether they have consumed any illegal substance. Whether the benefits of extending this level of social control over a group of people are really desirable in a democratic society, however, needs to be resolved. Critics have repeatedly argued that a whole wave of new control techniques has been developed since the 1960s when *diversion* became the catchword for the latest innovation in U.S. corrections and that these techniques have often not had the intended results. Instead of playing a supporting role as alternatives to incarceration, many of these strategies have simply allowed for and encouraged a net-widening effect (Blomberg, Bales, and Reek 1993; Blomberg and Lucken 1993). Populations that had never before been reached by criminal justice correctional services are now fair game, and many of those sanctioned under these diversion programs appear to be persons who previously would not have been dealt with officially at all. For example, many juvenile courts have implemented juvenile delinquency diversion programs with perfectly good intentions. Many find that rather than diverting the traditional juvenile offender from official court processing, they are recruiting new groups of clients from populations of non-offenders. A teacher hears of a great diversion program and refers a troubled student who has never been in any legal difficulty. Once that juvenile is into the diversion program, he or she is more likely to be identified and labeled as an offender.

A close inspection of anyone's life may lead to the observation of a violation of one of the diversion rules. Ultimately, the rigid enforcement of these very strict conditions of probation and parole can actually lead to a swelling of prison and jail populations, with cells being filled with those who could not muster the rules of diversionary alternatives and who are sent to a total institution for these technical violations. If this occurs, it certainly has defeated the purposes for which these alternative programs were established in the first place.

MILIEU APPROACHES

Inpatient and Residential Programs

Inpatient treatment has changed drastically over recent years. The era of 28-day treatment programs is almost extinct. The cost of such programs is too high for most people to pay for out of pocket, and third-party payers overwhelmingly no longer reimburse for such services. Inpatient programs typically provide respite for family, drug education, group encounters with peers, and individual treatment, which may include a pharmacological component.

Longer inpatient (residential) programs for offenders, such as therapeutic communities (TCs), also exist. Once admitted into such facilities, clients are encouraged to form close emotional ties with other residents. When successful, clients will perceive themselves as part of a group of peers who act as a support network (Obermeier and Henry 1989).

There is no evidence to suggest that inpatient treatment is any more effective than outpatient treatment with most substance abusers (Gerstein and Harwood 1990; McNeece and DiNitto 2005). However, for many families who avail themselves of extended inpatient treatment for their children or spouses, the treatment period acts as a respite. Changes that do occur within an inpatient setting frequently occur within a vacuum; the typical frustrations and challenges that might encourage alcohol and drug use and abuse are absent in an inpatient setting. Thus, improvements seen in the hospital do not necessarily extend to home settings (Joaning, Gawinski, Morris, and Quinn 1986).

One residential model that has been implemented throughout the states is the restitution center, which controls and provides support for residents who must pay victim restitution out of earnings from community work. One such program is the Griffin Diversion Center in Georgia, where residents typically work eight hours a day, maintain the center's operations, complete community work on weekends, attend classes or counseling sessions in the evenings, submit to routine drug testing, and organize food and clothing drives (DiMascio 1995).

Intensive Outpatient Programs

Alternatives to the more expensive and restrictive inpatient and residential care described earlier are intensive outpatient programs (IOPs) and partial hospitalization programs (PHPs), both of which allow clients to return home each night with his or her family rather than live at the facility (McNeece and DiNitto 2005). Generally, a PHP, also referred to as *day treatment,* is more intense than an IOP, with one distinct difference being that a PHP client typically attends treatment Monday through Friday for the entire day, whereas a client in an IOP might attend only three days a week for three hours each day. Otherwise, IOPs and PHPs provide the same services as inpatient or residential treatment at lower costs. These approaches have gained popularity in recent years as goal-oriented and planned short-term treatment is being favored over longer-term treatment approaches (Wells 1994).

Therapeutic Communities

TCs may be considered to fall under the realm of residential programs or jail treatment programs. A therapeutic community is a residential treatment environment that provides an around-the-clock learning experience in which the drug user's changes in conduct, attitudes, values, and emotions are implemented, monitored, and reinforced on a daily basis (DeLeon 1986). Although there is no generally recognized TC model, typically it is a highly structured program, lasting one to three years. However, due to the confrontational nature of the community, it is common for residents to leave within the first three months of the program (Goldapple 1990).

The treatment philosophy is that substance abuse is a disorder of the whole person; the problem lies in the person, not the drug; and the addiction is but a symptom, not the essence, of the disorder (Pan et al. 1993). The primary goal of the TC approach is to lead the client to a responsible, substance-free life. Although individual, family, and group counseling may be components of the TC, the cornerstone of the program is the peer encounter that takes place in the group process (see the earlier brief discussion on positive peer culture, for example). Rules of the community are specific and enforced by the residents themselves. Generally, the TC staff are themselves recovering substance abusers who have successfully completed treatment in a therapeutic community.

Gerstein and Harwood (1990) found that therapeutic community programs, when closely linked to community-based supervision and treatment programs, can significantly reduce re-arrest rates. TCs have been tried in correctional settings, but for obvious reasons, they must be modified substantially (Lipton, Falkin, and Wexler 1992). The implementation of TCs in correctional settings has been hindered at times by a reluctance to provide long-term therapeutic services, by philosophical opposition to the use of staff who themselves are former offenders, by coercive treatment strategies, and by the need for specialized staff training and technical assistance (Peters 1993). A recent evaluation of several TCs in correctional settings produced mixed results (National Institute of Justice 2000). The research on the effectiveness of TCs for adolescents reveals that a longer length of stay in treatment is the largest and most consistent predictor of positive outcomes (Catalano et al. 1991; DeLeon 1986), including reduced criminal activity, reduced alcohol or drug use, and employment (McBride et al. 1999).

Boot Camps

Today's boot camp can be traced back to the first U.S. penitentiaries at the turn of the nineteenth century, which used military-style marches, physical labor, silence, and discipline (Rothman 1990). Elements of today's juvenile boot camps (also known as *shock incarceration*) are based on similar principles, usually handle small groups, and last three to six months. They stress discipline, physical conditioning, and strict authoritarian control (McNeece 1997). Most local and state boot camps are designed for the first-time offender. The Shock Probation and Scared Straight programs are both based on the boot camp approach, which is grounded in the philosophy of breaking down and then building up the offender in a quasimilitary setting (Parent 1989).

Lipsey's (1992) well-known meta-analysis of treatment for juvenile offenders revealed that deterrence programs, such as boot camps, actually had negative treatment effects on delinquent youths. A report conducted by the Florida Department of Juvenile Justice indicates that re-arrest rates at Florida's six boot camps averaged between 63 and 74 percent for the first 60 boot camp graduates. The results were similar to comparison groups in other programs. Similarly, the Florida Juvenile Justice Advisory Board released a study indicating a 45 percent re-arrest rate for all youth ($n = 317$) who went through the state's six boot camps during a six-month period (Kaczor 1997). In general, it appears that juvenile boot camps are not cost-effective and do not deliver positive treatment effects for juvenile offenders when compared to traditional services such as probation or parole (Springer et al. 2003).

Studies of adult boot camps revealed mixed findings (Clark, Aziz, and MacKenzie 1994; MacKenzie and Shaw 1993; MacKenzie et al. 1995). However, as is the case for findings on juvenile boot camps, the outcome research on adult boot camps is not promising (Zhang 1998). A thorough review of the adult boot camp literature by MacKenzie and colleagues revealed that adult boot camp participants fare no better or worse on recidivism rates than offenders in traditional prison or probation programs (MacKenzie as cited in Henggeler and Schoenwald 1994). In sum, it is somewhat puzzling and troubling that boot camps continue to receive support when community-based approaches, such as MST, lead to much more positive outcomes (Springer et al. 2003).

Drug Court

A promising and innovative alternative used to combat the growing substance abuse problem in this country is the establishment of diversionary programs known as *drug courts*. The mission of drug courts is to eliminate substance abuse and the resulting criminal behavior. Drug court is a team effort that focuses on sobriety and accountability as the primary goals (National Association of Drug Court Professionals [NADCP] 1997:8). The team of professionals generally includes the state attorney, public defender, pretrial intervention or probation staff, treatment providers, and the judge, who is considered the central figure on the team. Drug court provides a new role based on a growing realization that active judicial participation and leadership are crucial to the successful organization, design, and implementation of coordinated anti-drug systems (NADCP and Office of Community Oriented Policing Services 1997:5).

Drug courts have generally processed offenders in two ways: (1) through the use of deferred prosecution (herein adjudication is deferred, and the defendant enters treatment) or (2) through a post-adjudication process by which the case is adjudicated but sentencing is withheld while the defendant is in treatment (U.S. General Accounting Office [GAO] 1995). Drug courts tend to be a non-adversarial process (Goldkamp 1998) that focuses on treatment rather than criminal sanctions.

The great expanse of the drug court movement is due, in part, to the federal monies made available by the Attorney General of the United States under Title V of the Violent Control and Law Enforcement Act of 1994. These grants helped to establish drug courts nationwide. As a result, the number of drug courts, the scope of services, and the range of addicted populations served have increased. In June 2000, 508 drug courts were operating in all 50 states, the District of Columbia, Guam, and Puerto Rico. This included 19 tribal drug courts. Another 281 drug courts were being planned (Office of Justice Programs 2000).

Judicial supervision may have beneficial effects on reducing recidivism among drug court participants. In a recent three-year study in Oklahoma, Huddleston (1997) compared 48 graduates and 62 non-graduates of a drug court with 47 program graduates and 41 non-graduates of an alternative sentencing precursor to drug court. Findings suggest that there were beneficial effects of judicial supervision in decreasing recidivism rates. Judicial supervision in drug courts, combined with cognitive therapy, increased the success rate for defendants (96 percent) while decreasing failures (2 percent), compared to 74 and 39 percent, respectively, for the comparison group (Huddleston 1997).

Probation

The main method of monitoring offenders who have not been sentenced to prison is probation. In combination with counseling, support, and surveillance, probation is the most common type of treatment used as an alternative to incarceration (Lipton 1995). With regular probation, an offender lives at home and receives periodic monitoring. Many offenders with substance abuse problems are sentenced to intensive supervision probation (ISP), a more restrictive type of probation than traditional probation and an alternative to incarceration. ISP requires the offender and probation officer to keep in close contact, which generally includes random home visits to ensure compliance with the program's requirements. In addition, the offender may have to perform community service, maintain employment, adhere to a curfew, and submit to urine drug testing. Compared to basic probation, ISP is generally more expensive and requires that probation officers have smaller caseloads to accommodate the increase in supervision of the offender. ISP may, however, be more cost-effective than basic probation in the long run if the alternative for offenders is prison or jail (Edna McConnell Clark Foundation 1995).

PARADIGM SHIFT IN DRUG POLICY

In our view, the United States must experience a paradigm shift in its approach to drug use and abuse if it is ever to make any significant improvements in this area of social policy. Such a paradigm shift would include, at a minimum, a switch from the prohibitionist or zero tolerance concept of drug use to one of harm reeducation and a gradual decriminalization of some currently illicit drugs. On that issue, a possible beginning would be the limited use of marijuana for medical purposes.

Prohibitionist Reduction Approaches

During the 87 years that have elapsed since the passage of the Harrison Act (the landmark federal legislation defining illicit drugs) in December 1914, U.S. drug policy has clearly defined an approach to the drug problem that is prohibitionist by design and dominated by criminal justice agencies, methods, and ideologies. Most often, drug users here have been considered criminals first. Severe sanctions have been applied to violators to discourage their further involvement in illegal enterprises and to deter others from following the same path. Despite these aggressive attempts to control the problem, there is little or no evidence that any of these tactics have had their intended deterrent effects. Indeed, several contemporary observers have remarked that given the degree of our commitment, it is incredible that so little has been accomplished (Currie 1993).

Over time, the financial commitments to fighting a series of drug wars have escalated considerably. For example, when President Richard Nixon first declared war on drugs in 1969, a budget of $600 million was set aside for the effort. In contrast, by 1997, President Clinton had committed more than $16 billion to the fight (ONDCP 1997). Of course, these monies are only a portion of the total amount allocated to the war because state and local governments spend an amount that is at least equal to that committed by the federal government in their efforts to combat drugs. Just during the last 10 years, the federal commitment to the drug war has exceeded $100 billion (on DCP 1997)!

Despite ongoing disagreement among experts, many (Nadelmann 1988; Duke and Gross 1993; Bugliosi 1996; Bullington 1997) have come to the conclusion that the drug wars have not produced their intended results. The evidence that supports this position is easily accessible. For example, the United States continues to have the highest drug use rates of any industrialized, advanced nation (Currie 1993). Although some modest "gains" have been made in terms of reductions in reported use among high school seniors and other vulnerable population groups during the last 15 years or so, the most recent figures show that such use is once again on the rise. It has also been pointed out that the drug wars were not really targeting these groups at all because they are mostly casual, recreational users. Rather, the drug wars have been fought against a much smaller group of "problematic" drug users, and that group has not diminished. In fact, it now appears that the rate of such use has actually gone up, despite the extraordinary efforts made to reduce or eliminate it.

Other indicators of the failure of drug-policy efforts are easily observed. Despite huge increases in police confiscations of drugs, these substances are still available in great supply and in purer form than ever before. For example, the heroin that is currently sold throughout the United States is now said to be as much as 90 percent pure, compared with the 3–5 percent purity that was typically found during the 1960s. (Coomber 1999)

In the face of this compelling evidence, it may be difficult to see how anyone can continue to support the present policies. Of course, many persons do and often vigorously defend the status quo approach to the drug problem. One example of this may be found in recent statements made by Robert L. DuPont (1996:1,942), the nation's first appointed drug czar under the Nixon administration: "After more than a quarter of a century in the field of addiction medicine, I have found that the policy of prohibition remains the bedrock of the modern response to the risks posed by brain-rewarding chemicals. Harm reduction, a compromise between drug prohibition and legalization, is a failed policy since it undermines the clear and powerful message of prohibition."

Other experts disagree. They believe that the drug policies that United States aggressively pursued throughout most of the twentieth century have seemingly failed to accomplish their stated goals. The strong prohibitionist law enforcement and criminal justice orientation favored here has simply not worked. Amazingly, there is very little evidence that the drug wars, whether their most recent iteration or those launched much earlier, have had *any* salutary effects.

Enter Harm Reduction

A strikingly different drug-policy approach is currently being implemented enthusiastically, and with considerable apparent success, in several Western European nations. This strategy, generally labeled *harm reduction,* promotes a public health rather than criminal justice perspective when determining what to do about drug users and drug problems generally. The police role in these countries is largely restricted to attempts to control large-scale trafficking and sales of illegal substances. The Netherlands has been the clear leader in defining this new method for attending to drug problems, although similar approaches are now also being tried in Switzerland, Spain, Italy, Germany, Czech Republic, and several other emerging democracies in central Europe.

The harm reduction philosophy is based on several underlying assumptions about the nature of drug use and related concerns. The first of these is that drug use is in a sense inevitable because we know of no societies, either ancient or contemporary, that have not promoted the use of some substances while opposing the use of others. Thus, the historical record alone provides irrefutable proof that drug use will not go away regardless of what society may choose to do about it. Given this observation, a policy that is based on the notion that a drug-free society can be achieved, such as that which has been doggedly pursued in the United States during this century, is seen as impractical and doomed to failure.

A second defining characteristic of the harm reduction philosophy is that it treats all drug use, whether of "licit" or illicit substances, as potentially problematic. It is thought that the distinctions made between legal and illegal substances are totally artificial and that they have led to a myopic focus solely on the illicit chemicals. Harm reduction advocates suggest that all drugs have the potential to be used either productively or harmfully. Consequently, no distinction is made between these drugs based on their legal classification alone. Rather, differences are identified on the basis of the real damage and harm that these drugs do. Of course, by this standard, the two generally favored social drugs of tobacco products and alcohol must appear at the head of the list of "problem" drugs. Consequently, they also would be included in any drug policy designed by harm reduction proponents.

A third feature of harm reduction notions is that all drug problems must be seen fundamentally as public health rather than criminal justice concerns. In this model, various health agencies and professionals are expected to play key leadership roles in assessing and treating the problematic symptoms associated with the use of these substances. In the harm reduction model, law enforcement continues to play a role in societal efforts to control illegal production, importation, and sales of illicit drugs. The key difference here is that the police are denied the opportunity to pursue users, who are defined here as sick people in need of medical assistance.

Finally, given the obvious reluctance of drug users to volunteer for treatment under the old, police-dominated systems, it is thought that new and very different forms of outreach must be developed to gain their confidence and involve them in therapeutic interventions. Of utmost concern is the establishment of some contact between health authorities and problematic users. Whereas the prohibitionist approach conditions users to hide and resist efforts to get them into treatment, harm reduction is designed to entice them through non-threatening interventions and aggressive social work.

Practically speaking, the harm reduction methods that are currently being tried in the Netherlands and elsewhere include the following specific strategies for dealing with users:

- Street social workers establish initial contacts with users.

- Friendly users are enlisted in the efforts to contact their fellows and to encourage them to come in to obtain health services.

- Low-threshold programs are established to provide methadone in low doses to street addicts who are not yet willing to come in for help and without any contingent conditions, that is, they give up all drug use or submit to urine tests. Several methadone "buses" are used to deliver the drug on a daily basis to these users in their neighborhoods.

- Free needles and needle exchange programs are in place to minimize the potential for HIV infections among injecting users.

- Safe disposal receptacles are provided to individual users, and larger receptacles are placed in the apartments of known sellers.

- Clinics are available for high-dose methadone and regular medical care for those users who are willing to participate.

- Safe houses have been established to allow addicts to come off the streets to fix in a clean, regulated environment.

- There has been a liberal dose of public advertising of the potential hazards of particular drugs, unsafe sex, needle sharing, and the like.

- An extensive variety of treatment programs has been established to appeal to a wide range of users who are ready to undertake their own rehabilitation.

Each of these tactics has been developed to provide a user-friendly environment to bring users back into the mainstream of their societies.

The results of harm reduction methods have been quite impressive thus far. The goal of making treatment an attractive option has resulted in approximately 85 percent of Dutch drug addicts now being in contact with government agencies and helpers. This figure compares favorably with the estimated 10–20 percent of U.S. addicts who are in contact with health officials (Bullington 1995). Users throughout the Netherlands and other countries that have adopted similar methods are more likely to be receiving basic health care and nutritional advice, are experiencing fewer drug-related health problems, such as abscesses, hepatitis, and AIDS, and are better able to live somewhat normal lifestyles, unlike their U.S. counterparts.

In assessing the outcomes of these harm reduction programs, one must keep in mind their goals. It is taken as a given that drug use will continue regardless of social attitudes about it and that the dominant theme of intervention approaches must be based on reducing the harm that drugs do to those who consume them! By this measure, these programs have been very successful, although they did not, and were never intended to, eliminate drug use. None of this is to suggest, however, that the citizens residing in these nations approve of drug use; on the contrary, they often condemn it in the same manner that U.S. citizens do.

Based on the U.S. failures with criminal justice methods and the apparent successes experienced in these other places, there is reason to hope that many of these methods could be adopted here in the near future. The point is that harm reduction can be undertaken anywhere, regardless of the dominant policy orientation (Erickson 1996). Thus, even with a prohibitionist policy, it would be conceptually possible to consider how harm reduction could be implemented to minimize drug-related harms. In fact, there is already evidence that harm reduction efforts have been initiated in various locales throughout the United States. For example, a number of cities now promote needle exchange programs or at least the provision of information regarding the use of sterile equipment and bleach to clean injection equipment. There has been considerable resistance to such programs, however, because they are said to encourage or signal societal approval for injecting drugs. In several cases, the practices have been initiated in direct violation of the state and/or local law that prohibits them. Methadone maintenance has also been available for many years, and well over 100,000 addicts are currently being treated with the substitute narcotic. Although these programs are supposed to reduce the dosage over time and eventually to wean the addict entirely from the drug, most do not attempt or require this.

Of course, harm reduction can also be implemented as a prevention strategy with those who have not yet experimented with drugs. This would require that all drugs, whether legal or illegal, be included in these discussions; there can be no sacred cows. It also necessitates abandoning the "just-say-no" claims for serious discussions of safe and unsafe use practices. To date, Americans have been very reluctant to accept such educational tactics, believing instead that this objective stance would ultimately lead to increased use (Rosenbaum 1996). The evaluations of current primary prevention methods, however, have revealed that these methods do not have their intended consequences; in other words, they do not prevent youth from experimenting with drugs.

Ultimately, the adoption of large-scale harm reduction methods would require a significant shift in the current dominant prohibitionist drug policy and mind-set. For these strategies to be adopted successfully, Americans would first have to jettison their long-held faith and commitment to punitive tactics in fighting wars on drugs against users. A public health strategy calls for an entirely different view of the user as a sick person in need of basic medical assistance rather than as a criminal who is willfully subverting the law.

Although many skeptics might argue that these changes seem highly unlikely, we need to only look back as far as the nineteenth century to find a time when these substances were treated very differently than they are now. Drugs were not then seen as constituting major social problems, and certainly not as posing a serious threat to the very survival of the nation as they are now. These laissez-faire ideas were not a result of being few drug users then, however, for there is a formidable array of data supporting the conclusion that there may have been as many serious or problematic users as there are today (Courtwright 1982). Historian David Musto (1991) reminds us that even in the twentieth century, the drug war hysteria had ebbed and flowed with succeeding generations. He argues that the lessons learned about the dangers of drugs by one generation are slowly replaced by a collective naiveté in later cohorts. One consequence of these fluctuations has been that drug policies have cycled from extreme, often hysterical levels of concern to apathy several generations later. The adoption of harm reduction measures could moderate these national mood swings and provide a much more consistent and enduring set of responses from one generation to another.

MEDICAL MARIJUANA

When the twentieth century drew to a close, the U.S. government and several states were embroiled in a highly visible public debate regarding the usefulness of marijuana as a medicine. There is little question that this issue will not be resolved quickly, for all of the participants remain fiercely committed to maintaining their respective positions, which seem irreconcilable. Moreover, the middle ground, if it exists at all, is a veritable no-man's land at present. In this conflict, the group that opposes medical marijuana typically argues that much more scientific research is needed regarding the drug's actual benefits and liabilities before a reasoned, final judgment can be made. Those approving its medical use contend that sufficient evidence has been available for some time and that the call for more research is just a delaying tactic by opponents. Despite occasional acrimonious interactions between members of the various interest groups involved, the issue itself is fascinating and is likely to continue being discussed well into the twenty-first century.

As is often true of current debates about aspects of various national policies, the contestants in this struggle are an odd lot indeed. Those in favor of changing the laws to allow for marijuana use in medicine have included the following: a majority of the voting citizens of the populous states of California and Arizona, as well as those of a number of other states; cannabis activists such as members of NORML (the National Organization for the Reform of Marijuana Laws), who promote a change in the legal status of marijuana for everyone; patients who have used the drug illegally to relieve their symptoms; a small but determined group of researchers, academics, and professionals who have already investigated the drug's medical uses and found them promising; and political libertarians who are committed to the idea that drug use is an individual choice that the government has no business regulating. These supporters of medical marijuana make strange bedfellows, although their coalition has proven to be a potent force, as their opponents can attest.

A few examples of some of the most prominent participants in this movement may be in order. One interest group is NORML, a small but vocal national organization that has for several decades been calling for the repeal of all laws regulating the drug. In recent years, several other organizations have joined the conflict. One of these is the Marijuana Policy Project (MPP), a grassroots organization working for the reform of marijuana laws. Another group, the Drug Policy Alliance (DPA) has been working to reform all drug laws in the United States. A second major constituency is made up of a wide variety of medical patients. Many of these patients are enduring the terminal stages of an illness or disease such as AIDS or cancer and have found that marijuana seems to help them cope with the severe nausea that often accompanies chemotherapy treatment. They also report that it helps to increase their appetites. Others have glaucoma, the progressive eye disease that eventually results in blindness. These patients smoke the drug to relieve the painful pressure of fluid build-up within the eye itself. A third group of patients with multiple sclerosis has reported that the drug gives them relief from muscle spasms and other chronic symptoms of their illness. Another distinct group of participants is the families and friends of these patients and others who similarly believe that marijuana should be used for these compassionate purposes. A number of scientific notables, such as the late Stephen Jay Gould and Dr. Lester Grinspoon, have freely acknowledged that they or another family member used illegal marijuana to counter severe side effects of their debilitating illnesses (Goldstein and Goldstein 2001).

Those opposing any change in the status of marijuana compose a formidable group of government leaders, including all recent presidents and their drug czars; nearly all national, state, and local politicians; law enforcement leaders and personnel; many government-supported scientists; public prosecutors; a number of grassroots citizen groups; and others. These groups claim either that the drug is neither safe nor effective for the treatment of any medical problems or that it is of limited utility, although there are legal medicines that are more effective in treating these conditions. One favored strategy of these claimants has been to suggest that the other side, especially those who wish to use it recreationally, is merely using the medical marijuana issue as a subterfuge to legalize the drug for all citizens. A review of the supporters of this side of the debate clearly indicates that the weight of the existing law and political machinery is behind them, and as a result, the efforts to bring about any major changes in the drug laws have failed.

It should be noted that for hundreds of years marijuana had been used as a popular medication all over the world. The first modern concerns with it were raised in Great Britain at the end of the nineteenth century, leading to a large-scale investigation and the Indian Hemp Commission Report of 1898. In its findings, the commission suggested that the drug had a number of practical uses in medicine and that many of the stories then being circulated about its dangerousness could not be documented.

A brief review of the modern history of marijuana in this country might prove helpful in understanding the current dispute over its efficacy in medicine. Despite the drug's relatively low toxicity (especially when contrasted with other popular licit and illicit drugs), it has long served as the touchstone for U.S. drug policies. In one early study of the literature, Howard Becker (1963) found that there was little public interest in the drug before about the mid-1930s. That was soon to change. American concerns with marijuana initially focused on its alleged use by members of dangerous classes, in this instance male Mexican immigrants and African-American jazz musicians.

In 1937, the Marijuana Tax Act was passed as an addendum to the Harrison Act, the first comprehensive federal drug law enacted in 1914. This marijuana law, like its parent, was ostensibly a revenue measure calling for dealers to obtain a federal license to legally dispense the drug and requiring them to pay a tax of $100 per ounce on any sales. Of course, no one did this; even if one were to buy the license, state laws at the time forbade marijuana sales and use and criminalized both. Interestingly, there was absolutely no debate over the new law; medical practitioners and other interested parties were not even invited to testify at the hearings.

Following the approval of the Marijuana Tax Act, the federal, state, and local police soon had a field day with the drug's users. When one reviews the drug arrest statistics for this early period, it is clear that marijuana users were the favored targets of law enforcers. For many years, fully two-thirds of all arrests of drug law violators were for marijuana possession and use only. Given the then common beliefs and claims about the drug's capacity to induce crimes of violence and to debauch its users, this result could have been expected. Marijuana addicts were seen as fair game for the drug police, and because there were many more of them than opiate and cocaine users, they were easy prey.

Special state and local laws were passed in the 1960s to target marijuana. At that time, a number of jurisdictions provided for as much as a life sentence for first offense of possession of a small amount of the drug. For example, a 1967 study of these patterns in the state of Texas revealed that 19 persons were serving life sentences for first-offense possession of a small amount of the drug. Things might have continued in this manner for some time had it not been for the massive youthful rebellions of the 1960s. At the time, marijuana use served as another form of resistance to authority for young people who openly disobeyed the law and thereby exposed themselves to the severe sanctions that were then in place. Many white middle-class youth were arrested for these violations and faced heavy penalties in the form of the prescribed prison sentences for these offenses. Their parents were appalled, however, and soon brought intense pressure on government officials to reassess the utility of and justification for U.S. marijuana laws.

Finally, in 1970, President Richard Nixon appointed the Schafer Commission, a distinguished commission that studied the known effects of marijuana to advise officials what to do about the crisis that had been brewing. In 1972, the commission issued its final report, *Marijuana: Signal of Misunderstanding,* the culmination of two years of extensive investigations. In reading this account, it is readily apparent that all of the earlier archetypal claims about the dangers of marijuana use were no longer seen as valid; the drug did not lead to crime and insanity. In fact, very few toxic effects were found, leading the commission to suggest that decriminalization of the drug might be the most appropriate policy for the government to pursue. The president was incensed with this suggestion, however, telling the nation and his own drug czar (who agreed with the report's recommendation) that he would never accept legalization of marijuana.

During the first Reagan administration, the federal office of Health and Human Services produced another government research monograph on the subject. This report, *Marijuana and Health,* was thought to be a comprehensive assessment of what was then known about the drug's medical effects. All claims about the serious health effects attributed to marijuana were again scrutinized by a panel of experts, but this time they came away with a somewhat different set of conclusions than those of the Schafer Commission regarding the health risks the drug presented. They stated that the earlier report had been incorrect in suggesting that marijuana was a harmless substance.

We should note that the nature of the claimed dangers associated with marijuana use had shifted perceptibly over the years. The old horror stories were no longer believed by anyone, or so it seemed. Rather, the drug was now said to cause a motivational syndrome among the young, leading them to inactive, unproductive lives. Damaging health effects were also suggested, such as impotence and breast enlargement among males, short-term memory loss, possible birth defects among children born to mothers who were marijuana smokers, and the permanent loss of brain cells. Although the evidence in support of these claims was weak at best, health concerns had become the most pressing rationale for opposing decriminalization efforts, replacing the crime and degeneracy themes of earlier generations. Barry McCaffrey, President Bill Clinton's drug czar, became the first active spokesperson who promoted a "science-based" drug policy. His many speeches often included calls for more scientific studies and evidence. With regard to marijuana, his stance was that there were many documented harmful health effects caused by the drug, implying that it could never be used in legitimate medicine.

Finally, in 1999 the prestigious Institute of Medicine published a major report on the state of the art of scientific knowledge regarding medicinal marijuana. After being commissioned in 1997 by the Office of National Drug Control Policy to undertake this assignment, the Institute solicited input from participants in scientific workshops, conducted site visits to a variety of cannabis buyers' clubs, reviewed the literature, and interviewed many experts, including persons who had used marijuana illegally to counteract their medical symptoms. The group published its report in *Marijuana and Medicine: Assessing the*

Scientific Base. In that comprehensive document, the workgroup developed six major recommendations. The first of these states, "Research should continue into the physiological effects of synthetic and plant-derived cannabinoids and the natural function of cannabinoids found in the body. Because different cannabinoids appear to have different effects, cannabinoid research should include, but not be restricted to, effects attributable to THC alone." One of the primary concerns raised about smoked marijuana was that it is potentially dangerous. Researchers urged the development of a rapid onset, reliable, and safe delivery system, such as a vaporized form of the drug that could be delivered through an inhaler. Until such a device was made available, however, the group advised that smoked marijuana should be allowed for selected terminal patients as a compassionate measure.

Given these conflicting observations, debate regarding the effects of marijuana smoking has continued almost unabated to the present day. The modern arguments commonly used against any change in its legal status have relied heavily on the belief that the drug does not have any therapeutic value and that it is more dangerous than previously thought. The exact nature of these harmful effects is only partially known, however, because there has been little scientific research of marijuana's effects. Thus, the lack of knowledge about marijuana's actual effects is now being remedied, we are told, as a direct byproduct of new federal commitments to the funding of large-scale marijuana research projects. The outcomes of these investigations will not be known for another decade or so, however. As with any other substance that has not been adequately tested before, the drug must be assumed to be potentially hazardous until proven otherwise.

This brief account of the modern history of marijuana in the United States brings us back to the present. One of the lessons to be learned from these events is that this drug has had tremendous symbolic value in the United States for nearly a century. Earlier it was argued that users were dangerous criminals and that their use of the drug predisposed them to violence and insanity. As evidence accrued that these claims were fallacious, new charges were leveled against the substance focusing on health-related problems and "a motivational syndrome" that was said to be a common result of regular use. These arguments have sustained and bolstered the position firmly held by government officials and their supporters ever since.

Modern campaigns against marijuana use have undoubtedly had some effect on consumption patterns, although exactly what these have been are unknowable. Several national surveys of high school seniors and respondents from other age groups indicate that use has dropped dramatically since about 1979. These trends have proven to be ephemeral and subject to periodic fluctuations, however, and the most recent surveys have reflected some increases in youthful marijuana use. Regardless of the exact number of persons who have used the drug—either recreationally or very regularly—we know with certainty that marijuana is the most popular illicit substance in the United States. At the present time, approximately 72 million Americans report having used the drug at least experimentally, and about 700,000 say they are daily users (Zimmer and Morgan 1997).

These facts may go a long way toward explaining why the government has so strongly resisted any change in its official position with regard to this substance, including the latest medical marijuana proposals. To admit that they may have been wrong all of these years or—worse yet—that they had knowingly distorted the truth—would seemingly open the floodgates to total rejection of the anti-marijuana message and the anti-drug message generally. Thus, the claim that marijuana is a gateway drug has been fostered by government sources, suggesting that those who use it, regardless of its potential harmfulness, are likely to go on to use far more harmful substances. Given what we know about the consumers of this drug, however, this result seems unlikely. Moreover, critics have been quick to point out that the real gateway drugs, if they exist at all, are tobacco and alcohol.

Despite the adamant resistance of those defending the official position on marijuana, large numbers of medical patients have clamored for legal access to the drug. Rather than waiting for a change in the policy, however, many have been willing to risk arrest to procure the substance in the illicit market and self-medicate with it. A substantial number of patients have claimed dramatic improvements in terms of the alleviation of some of the most bothersome symptoms that they suffer directly from their illness or as a secondary result of some treatment they have been receiving (especially from radiation and chemotherapy). Meantime, friends, families, and physicians attending these patients have often become converts based on their own observations of these events and the salutary effects the drug has had.

In 1996, both California and Arizona approved the medical use of marijuana through popular referenda. The specific details of these proposals differed somewhat, but both states intended to allow physicians either to prescribe or to recommend marijuana to patients whenever they thought it appropriate to do so without fear of arrest. The opposition, in this case represented by the federal government, responded by threatening physicians with suspension of their federal prescription-writing privileges if they did in fact recommend marijuana for their patients. The matter continues to be debated, both within and outside the courts.

The struggle over the legal status of marijuana continues. The substance is currently listed federally as a Class I drug, which means that it has no medical utility and a high potential for abuse. This classification also means that the drug cannot be used at all, even experimentally, by medical practitioners. Medical marijuana proponents have been attempting to have it reclassified as a Class II drug, which would mean that it has recognized medical utility and a high potential for abuse. Although the latter claim (that it has high abuse potential) could certainly be contested, especially in light of the known abuse potential and harmful effects associated with legal alcohol and tobacco products, this has not been a prominent issue raised in the most recent attempts to change marijuana laws.

The lines have been clearly drawn between those who support the medical use of marijuana and those who oppose any change in the drug's current status. Many persons are currently illegally self-medicating with the drug, regardless of the potential harmful effects they could suffer in the form of criminal penalties, fines, forfeiture of their possessions, and the like. One may assume that they knowingly take these risks because they are personally convinced that this substance works to alleviate some of the symptoms of their illness/disease and that similar relief cannot be obtained with other legally available medications. On the other side of the issue are large numbers of medical professionals, politicians, and others who insist that the drug has no demonstrated medical or therapeutic application that cannot be assuaged with legal medicines such as Marinol (a synthetic form of THC, the active ingredient in marijuana), Dronabinol, and others. They argue either that much more research must be completed before the drug can be properly judged one way or the other or that no additional research is needed because we already know that marijuana is not an effective medication.

This issue is not likely to be resolved legally, even temporarily, in the immediate future. Although for the first time in recent history, the federal government has committed large sums of money to support marijuana research, it is also actively pushing for the wider use of alternatives. The results of these studies may be pivotal in determining what happens next, at least officially. Unofficially, however, marijuana is currently being used therapeutically by many patients despite its legal status, and such use seems destined to escalate among our nation's aging population.

As we write this at mid-year 2008, the debate continues. At this point, 21 states have medical marijuana laws already in place or approved by state voters. However, only six of these states have actually made any effort to implement these statutes. In 1998 the residents of Washington, D.C., voted to allow the medical provision of marijuana, but Congress blocked the law's approval. The situation in California has still not been resolved either, and the U.S. Supreme Court has not clarified the matter. Federal agents have closed down cannabis buyers' clubs and attempted to prosecute those who are providing the drug to clients.

In the end, this issue will not be resolved on the basis of research results and controlled studies. In truth, medical marijuana is more a political than a scientific issue, and the exigencies of politics are likely to reign over reason in determining the appropriate course of action. We have argued earlier that marijuana has been vilified not because it is so dangerous but because it appears to threaten to undermine the logic of all drug laws. Thus, it is viewed as the hole in the proverbial dike, a weak spot in drug law that, if altered, could give way to all kinds of new problems. So long as that view prevails among the most powerful elements in our society, it seems unlikely that its legal status will be changed, regardless of the scientific evidence about its efficacy.

CONCLUSIONS

The funds that the United States currently spends on drug interdiction, law enforcement, the courts, and incarceration would allow the country to make substantial progress in improving treatment and in making treatment available to those who need it. Reducing the number of people arrested and incarcerated for drug possession and other minor drug offenses would also allow the police to concentrate their efforts on more serious crimes, thus making communities safer.

The decline of inner cities and the consequent deterioration of the quality of life for the poor and minorities are to a large degree responsible for the epidemic of drug abuse. It is foolish to believe, in the face of declining economic opportunities, that either the threat of criminal punishment or the promise of a short-term treatment program will cause teenagers and young adults to avoid lives of crime and involvement with drugs. In the long run, stable families, safe neighborhoods, and economically healthy cities are the keys to controlling both drug use and crime.

REFERENCES

ALEXANDER, B. K. (1990). Alternatives to the war on drugs. *Journal of Drug Issues* 20(1): 1–27.

ALEXANDER, J. F., and B. V. PARSONS (1973). Short-term behavioral intervention with delinquents: Impact on family process and recidivism. *Journal of Abnormal Psychology* 81: 219–225.

ANDERSON, A. R., and C. S. HENRY (1994). Family system characteristics and parental behaviors as predictors of adolescent substance use. *Adolescence* 29(114): 405–420.

BECKER, H. (1963). *Outsiders: Studies in Deviance.*Becker, New York: The Free Press.

BLOMBERG, T., B. BALES, and K. REEK (1993). Intermediate punishment: Redistributing or extending social control? *Crime, Law and Social Change* 19: 187–201.

BLOMBERG, T., and K. LUCKEN (1993). Intermediate punishment and the piling up of sanctions. In *Criminal Justice: Law and Politics,* ed. G. Cole. Belmont, CA: Wadsworth, 470–481.

BREWINGTON, V., M. SMITH, and D. LIPTON (1994). Acupuncture as a detoxification treatment: An analysis of controlled research. *Journal of Substance Abuse Treatment* 11(4): 289–307.

BROWN, A. (2001). *Beyond Work First: How to Help Hard-to-Employ Individuals Get Jobs and Succeed in the Workforce.* New York: Manpower Demonstration Research Corporation.

BRUMBAUGH, A. G. (1993). Acupuncture: New perspectives in chemical dependency treatment. *Journal of Substance Abuse Treatment* 10: 35–43.

BUGLIOSI, V. (1996). *The Phoenix Solution.* Beverly Hills, CA: Dove Books.

BULLINGTON, B. (1995). War and peace: Drug policy in the United States and the Netherlands. *Crime, Law, and Social Change* 22: 213–238.

BULLINGTON, B. (1997). America's drug war: Fact or fiction? In *The Control of Drug Users: Reason or Reaction,* ed. Ross Coomber. London: Harwood Publishers.

BUREAU OF JUSTICE ASSISTANCE (1999). *Pretrial Drug Testing: An Overview of Issues and Practices.* NCJ 176341. Washington, DC: U.S. Department of Justice.

BUREAU OF JUSTICE STATISTICS (1992). *Drug Enforcement and Treatment in Prisons, 1990.* NCJ 134724. Washington, DC: U.S. Department of Justice.

BUREAU OF JUSTICE STATISTICS (2000). *Drug Use, Testing, and Treatment in Jails* (Publication No. 179999). Washington, DC: Author.

BUREAU OF JUSTICE STATISTICS (2006). *Prison and Jail Inmates at December 2006.* Washington, DC: U.S. Department of Justice.

CATALANO, R., J. HAWKINS, E. WELLS, E. MILLER, and D. BREWER (1991). Evaluation of the effectiveness of adolescent drug abuse treatment, assessment of risks for relapse, and promising approaches for relapse prevention. *The International Journal of Addictions* 25(9): 1085–1140.

CENTER FOR SUBSTANCE ABUSE TREATMENT (2000). *Strengthening America's Families: Model Family Programs for Substance Abuse and Delinquency Prevention* (N215 HPER). Salt Lake City, UT: Department of Health Promotion and Education, University of Utah.

CLARK, C. L., D. W. AZIZ, and D. L. MACKENZIE (1994). Shock incarceration in New York: Focus on treatment (NCJ Publication No. 148410). Washington, DC: National Institute of Justice.

CLEAR, T. (1995). Correction beyond prison walls. In *Criminology,* ed. J. F. Sheley. Belmont, CA: Wadsworth, 453–471.

COOMBER, R. (1999). The cutting of heroin in the United States in the 1990s. *Journal of Drug Issues* 29(1): 17–35.

COURTWRIGHT, D. (1982). *Dark Paradise: Opiate Addiction in America before 1940.* Cambridge, MA: Harvard University Press.

CURRIE, E. (1993). *Drugs, the Cities, and the American Future.* New York: Hill & Wang.

DEL CARMEN, R. V., and M. B. BARNHILL (1999). Legal issues in juvenile drug testing. *Federal Probation* 63: 72–77.

DELEON, G. (1986). The therapeutic community for substance abuse: Perspective and approach. In *Therapeutic Communities for Addictions: Readings in Theory, Research and Practice,* ed.

D. DeLeon and J. T. Zeigenfuss. Springfield, IL: Charles C. Thomas, 5–18.

DENTON, R. E., and C. M. KAMPFE (1994). The relationship between family variables and adolescent substance abuse: A literature review. *Adolescence* 29(114): 475–495.

DIMASCIO, W. M. (1995). *Seeking Justice: Crime and Punishment in America.* New York: Edna McConnell Clark Foundation.

DRUG COURT CLEARINGHOUSE AND TECHNICAL ASSISTANCE PROJECT (1996). *Fact Sheet.* Technical Report. Washington, DC: American University.

DUKE, S., and A. GROSS (1993). *America's Longest War.* New York: G.P. Putnam's Sons.

DUPONT, R. (1996). Harm reduction and decriminalization in the United States: A personal perspective. *Substance Use and Misuse* 31(14): 1929–1943.

EDNA MCCONNELL CLARK FOUNDATION (1995). *Seeking Justice: Crime and Punishment in America.* New York: The Foundation.

EDWARDS, B. (1993). Drug court's success rate outstanding. *Tampa Tribune* June: 1–2.

ERICKSON, P. (1996). Comments on harm reduction and decriminalization in the United States: A personal perspective by Robert DuPont. *Substance Use and Misuse* 31(14): 1965–1969.

FEDERAL BUREAU OF INVESTIGATION (2002). *Crime in the United States: 2001.* Uniform Crime Reports. Washington, DC: U.S. Government Printing Office.

FERRARA, M. L. (1992). *Group counseling with juvenile delinquents.* Newbury Park, CA: Sage.

FRASER, A. D., and J. ZAMECNIK (2002). Substance abuse monitoring by the correctional service of Canada. *Therapeutic Drug Monitoring* 24: 187–191.

GERSTEIN, D. R., and H. J. HARWOOD (eds.) (1990). *Treating Drug Problems,* Vol. 1. Washington, DC: National Academy Press.

GIBBS, J. C., G. B. POTTER, and A. P. GOLDSTEIN (1995). *The EQUIP Program: Teaching Youth to Think and Act Responsibly Through a Peer-Helping Approach.* Champaign, IL: Research Press.

GOLDAPPLE, G. (1990). Enhancing retention: A skills-training program for drug dependent therapeutic community clients. Ph.D. dissertation, Florida State University, Tallahassee, FL.

GOLDKAMP, J. S. (1998). Challenges for research and innovation: When is a drug court not a drug court? In *Judicial Change and Drug Treatment Courts: Case Studies in Innovation,* ed. C. Terry. Thousand Oaks, CA: Sage.

GOLDSTEIN, A. P., and B. GLICK (1987). *Aggression Replacement Training: A Comprehensive Intervention for Aggressive Youth.* Champaign, IL: Research Press.

GOLDSTEIN, M. C., and M. A. GOLDSTEIN (2001). *Controversies in Medicine.* Westport, CT: Greenwood Press.

HALEY, J. (1976). *Problem Solving Therapy.* San Francisco, CA: Jossey-Bass.

HARPER, R., and S. HARDY (2000). An evaluation of motivational interviewing as a method of intervention with clients in a probation setting. *British Journal of Social Work* 30: 393–400.

HENGGELER, S. W. (1999). Multisystemic therapy: An overview of clinical procedures, outcomes, and policy implications. *Child Psychology & Psychiatry* 4(1): 2–10.

HENGGELER, S. W., and C. M. BORDUIN (1990). *Family Therapy and Beyond: A Multisystemic Approach to Treating the Behavior Problems of Children and Adolescents.* Pacific Grove, CA: Brooks/Cole.

HENGGELER, S. W., and S. K. SCHOENWALD (1994). Boot camps for juvenile offenders: Just say no. *Journal of Child and Family Studies* 3(3): 243–248.

HENGGELER, S. W., S. K. SCHOENWALD, C. M. BORDUIN, M. D. ROWLAND, and P. B. CUNNINGHAM (1998). *Multisystemic Treatment of Antisocial Behavior in Children and Adolescents.* New York: Guilford Press.

HUDDLESTON, W. (1997). Summary of drug court evaluation: Recidivism study. *Cognitive-Behavioral Treatment Review & CCI News* 6(1–2): 16–17.

IRWIN, J., and J. AUSTIN (1994). *It's About Time: America's Imprisonment Binge.* Belmont, CA: Wadsworth.

JAMIESON, BEALS, LALONDE, & ASSOCIATES (2000). *Motivational Enhancement Treatment (MET) Manual: Theoretical Foundation and Structured Curriculum. Individual and Group Sessions.* Developed for the State of Maine, Department of Mental Health, Mental Retardation and Substance Abuse Services, Office of Substance Abuse. Ottawa, Ontario, Canada: Author.

JOANING, H., B. GAWINSKI, J. MORRIS, and W. QUINN (1986). Organizing a social exology to treat adolescent drug abuse. *Journal of Strategic and Systemic Therapies* 5: 55–66.

JOY, J. E., S. J. WATSON, Jr., and J. A. BENSON, Jr. (eds.) (1999). *Marijuana and Medicine: Assessing the Scientific Base.* Washington, DC: National Academy Press.

KACZOR, B. (1997). Legislators let down by boot camps. *Tallahassee Democrat* June: 3B.

KENDALL, P. C., and L. BRASWELL (1993). *Cognitive-Behavioral Therapy for Impulsive Children,* 2nd ed. New York: Guilford Press.

KOEOFED, L., R. TOLSON, R. ATKINSON, R. TOTH, and J. TURNER (1986). Outpatient treatment of patients with substance abuse and coexisting psychiatric disorders. *American Journal of Psychiatry* 143: 867–872.

LEEMAN, L. W., J. C. GIBBS, and D. FULLER (1993). Evaluation of a multi-component group treatment program for juvenile delinquents *Journal of Aggressive Behavior* 19: 281–292.

LIDDLE, H. A., and G. A. DAKOFF (1995). Efficacy of family therapy for drug abuse: Promising but not definitive. *Journal of Marital and Family Therapy* 21: 511–544.

LIPSEY, M. W. (1992). Juvenile delinquency treatment: A meta-analytic inquiry into the variability of effects. In *Meta-Analysis for Explanation: A Casebook,* eds. T. D. Cook, H. Cooper, D. S. Corday, H. Hartman, L. V. Hedges, R. J. Light, T. A. Louis, and F. Mosteller. New York: Russell Sage Foundation.

LIPTON, D. S. (1995). *The Effectiveness of Treatment for Drug Abusers Under Criminal Justice Supervision.* National Institute of Justice Research Report. Washington, DC: U.S. Department of Justice.

LIPTON, D. S., G. P. FALKIN, and H. K. WEXLER (1992). Correctional drug abuse treatment in the United States: An overview. In *Drug Abuse Treatment in Prisons and Jails,* eds. C. Leukefeld and F. Tims. National Institute on Drug Abuse, Research Monograph Series, No. 118. Washington, DC: U.S. Government Printing Office.

MACKENZIE, D. L. (1991). The parole performance of offenders released from shock incarceration (boot camp prisons): A survival time analysis. *Journal of Quantitative Criminology* 7: 213–236.

MACKENZIE, D., and J. SHAW (1993). The impact of shock incarceration on technical violations and new criminal activities. *Justice Quarterly* 10(3): 463–486.

MACKENZIE, D., R. BRAME, D. McDOWALL, and C. SOURYAL (1995). Boot camp prisons and recidivism in eight states. *Criminology* 33(3): 327–357.

MARGOLIN, A., S. K. AVANTS, P. CHANG, and T. R. KOSTEN (1995). Acupuncture for the treatment of cocaine dependence in methadone-maintained patients. *American Journal on the Addictions* 2(3): 194–201.

MARTIN, S. S., and J. A. INCIARDI (1993). Case management approaches for criminal justice clients. In *Drug Treatment and Criminal Justice,* Vol. 27, ed. J. A. Inciardi. Thousand Oaks, CA: Sage, 81–96.

McBRIDE, D. C., C. J. VANDERWAAL, Y. TERRY, and H. VANBUREN (1999). *Breaking the Cycle of Drug Use Among Juvenile Offenders.* Washington, DC: U.S. Department of Justice. Peer reviewed Web Only Document: http://www.ojp.usdoj.gov/nij/pubs-sum/179273.htm.

McLAUGHLIN, P. (2000). Acupuncture services in an out-patient methadone maintenance program. Paper presented at the National Institute on Drug Abuse Conference, Blending Clinical Practice and Research: Forging Partnerships to Enhance Drug Addiction Treatment. New York.

McNEECE, C. A. (1997). Future directions in justice system policy and practice. In *Policy and Practice in the Justice System,* eds. C. A. McNeece and A. R. Roberts. Chicago: Nelson-Hall, 263–269.

McNeece, C. A., and D. M. DiNitto (2005). *Chemical Dependency: A Systems Approach,* 3rd ed. Upper Saddle River, NJ: Prentice Hall.

Miller, W. R., and R. K. Hester (1986). The effectiveness of alcoholism treatment methods: What research reveals. In *Treating Addictive Behaviors: Processes of Change,* eds. W. R. Miller and N. Heather. New York: Plenum, 175–204.

Miller, W. R., and S. Rollnick (2002). *Motivational Interviewing,* 2nd ed. New York: Guilford Press.

Minuchin, S. (1974). *Families and Family Therapy.* Cambridge, MA: Harvard University Press.

Minuchin, S., and H. C. Fishman (1981). *Family Therapy Techniques.* Cambridge, MA: Harvard University Press.

Munger, R. L. (1993). *Changing Children's Behavior Quickly.* Lanham, MD: Madison Books.

Musto, D. (1991). Opium, cocaine and marijuana in American history. *Scientific American* July: 40–47.

Nadelmann, E. (1988). U.S. drug policy: A bad export. *Foreign Policy* 70: 83–108.

National Association of Drug Court Professionals, Drug Court Standards Committee (1997). *Defining Drug Courts: Key Components.* Washington, DC: NADCP.

National Association of Drug Court Professionals and Office of Community Oriented Policing Services (1997). *Community Policing and Drug Courts/Community Courts: Working Together Within a Unified Court System.* Alexandria, VA: U.S. Department of Justice.

National Institute of Justice (2000). Recent research findings. *NIJ Journal* March.

National Institute on Drug Abuse (1999). *Principles of Drug Addiction Treatment: A Research-Based Approach.* NIH Publication 99-4180. Washington, DC: U.S. Government Printing Office.

National Organization for the Reform of Marijuana Laws (2002). Special release: Marijuana arrests for year 2001 second highest ever despite feds' war on terror, FBI report reveals [Retrieved May 16, 2003, from http://www.norml.org/index.cfm?Group_ID=5444]

National Task Force on Correctional Substance Abuse Strategies (1991). *Intervening with Substance-Abusing Offenders: A Framework for Action.* Washington, DC: U.S. Department of Justice, National Institute of Corrections.

Newmeyer, J. A., G. Johnson, and S. Klot (1984). Acupuncture as a detoxification modality. *Journal of Psychoactive Drugs* 16: 241–261.

Obermeier, G. E., and P. B. Henry (1989). Adolescent inpatient treatment. *Journal of Chemical Dependency* 2(1): 163–182.

Office of Justice Programs (2000). Drug court activity update: Composite summary. [Retrieved May 16, 2003, from http://www.american.edu/academic.depts/spa/justice/publications.html].

Office of National Drug Control Policy (1996). *Treatment Protocol Effectiveness Study.* Washington, DC: U.S. Government Printing Office.

Office of National Drug Control Policy (1997). *The National Drug Control Strategy: 1997.* NCJ Publication 163915. Washington, DC: U.S. Government Printing Office.

Orenstein, P. (2002). Staying clean. *New York Times Magazine* February: 34–75.

Pan, H., F. R. Scarpitti, J. A. Inciardi, and D. Lockwood (1993). Some considerations on therapeutic communities in corrections. In *Drug Treatment and Criminal Justice,* Vol. 27, ed. J. A. Inciardi. Thousand Oaks, CA; Newbury Park, CA: Sage, 30–43.

Parent, D. (1989). *Shock Incarceration: An Overview of Existing Programs.* Washington, DC: U.S. Department of Justice, National Institute of Justice.

Peters, R. H. (1993). Drug treatment in jails and detention settings. In *Drug Treatment and Criminal Justice,* Vol. 27, ed. J. A. Inciardi. Thousand Oaks, CA: Sage, 44–80.

Pomeroy, E. C., R. Kiam, and D. L. Green (2000). Reducing depression, anxiety, and trauma of male inmates: An HIV/AIDS psychoeducational group intervention. *Social Work Research* 24(3): 156–167.

RAND (1994). *Projecting Future Cocaine Use and Evaluating Control Strategies.* Santa Monica, CA: RAND Corporation.

RASMUSSEN, D., and B. BENSON (1994). *The Economic Anatomy of a Drug War.* Lanham, MD: Rowman & Littlefield.

RIDGELY, M. S., J. P. MORRISSEY, R. I. PAULSON, and H. H. GOLDMAN (1996). Characteristics and activities of case managers in the RWJ foundation program on chronic mental illness. *Psychiatric Services* 47(7): 737–743.

ROSENBAUM, M. (1996). *Kids, Drugs, and Drug Education: A Harm Reduction Approach.* National Council of Crime and Delinquency. San Francisco: Lindesmith Center.

ROTHMAN, D. (1990). *The Discovery of the Asylum: Social Order and Disorder in the New Republic.* Boston, MA: Little, Brown.

SCHOENWALD, S. K. and M. D. ROWLAND (2002). Multisystemic therapy. In *Community Treatment for Youth: Evidence-Based Interventions for Severe Emotional and Behavioral Disorders,* eds. B. J. Burns and K. Hoagwood. New York: Oxford University Press, 91–116.

SCOTT, E. M. (1993). Prison group therapy with mentally and emotionally disturbed offenders. *International Journal of Offender Therapy and Comparative Criminology* 37(2): 131–145.

SPRINGER, D. W. (2005). Treating substance-abusing youth. In *Chemical Dependency: A Systems Approach,* 3rd ed., eds. C. A. McNeece and D. M. DiNitto. Boston, MA: Allyn & Bacon.

SPRINGER, D. W., C. A. MCNEECE, and E. M. ARNOLD (2003). *Substance Abuse Treatment for Criminal Offenders: An Evidence Based Guide for Practitioners.* Washington, DC: American Psychological Association.

STANTON, M. D., and W. R. SHADISH (1997). Outcome, attrition, and family/marital treatment for drug abuse: A meta-analysis and review of the controlled, comparative studies. *Psychological Bulletin* 122(2): 170–191.

SUBSTANCE ABUSE AND MENTAL HEALTH SERVICES ADMINISTRATION (2002). National household survey on substance abuse, 2001. [Retrieved May 16, 2003, from http://www.drugabuse statistics.samhsa.gov/oas/nhsda/2k1nhsda/vol1/highlights.html]

SUBSTANCE ABUSE AND MENTAL HEALTH SERVICES ADMINISTRATION (2002). National household surveyon substance abuse, 2001. Retrieved 5/16/03 from http://www.drugabusestatistics.samhsa.gov/oas/nhsda/2k1nhsda/vol1/highlights.html

SZAPOCZNIK, J., E. MURRAY, M. SCOPETEA, O. HERVIS, A. RIO, R. COHEN, A. RIVAS-VAZQUES, and V. POSADA (1989). Structural family versus psychodynamic child therapy for problematic Hispanic boys. *Journal of Consulting and Clinical Psychology* 57: 571–578.

TIMROTS, A. (1992). *Fact Sheet: Drug Testing in the Criminal Justice System.* Rockville, MD: Drugs and Crime Data Center and Clearinghouse.

TODD, T. C., and M. SELEKMAN (1994). A structural-strategic model for treating the adolescent who is abusing alcohol and other drugs. In *Empowering Families, Helping Adolescents: Family-Centered Treatment of Adolescents with Alcohol, Drug Abuse, and Mental Health Problems,* eds. W. Snyder and T. Ooms. Rockville, MD: U.S. Department of Health and Human Services, Center for Substance Abuse Treatment, 79–89.

TURNABOUT ASAP (1997). *Acupuncture Treatment for Substance Abuse.* Santa Monica, CA: Turnabout.

U.S. DEPARTMENT OF HEALTH AND HUMAN SERVICES (1999). Investigating possible medical uses of marijuana. Health and human services fact sheet. [Retrieved May 16, 2003, from http://www.marijuana.org/HHS3-24-99.htm].

U.S. GENERAL ACCOUNTING OFFICE (1995). *Drug Courts: Information on a New Approach to Address Drug-Related Crime.* GAO/GGD Publication 95-159BR. Washington, DC: U.S. Government Printing Office.

VAN STELLE, K. R., E. MAUSER, AND D. P. MOBERG (1994). Recidivism to the criminal justice system of substance-abusing offenders diverted into treatment. *Crime and Delinquency* 40(2): 175–196.

VORRATH, H. H., and L. K. BRENDTRO (1985). *Positive Peer Culture,* 2nd ed. New York: Aldine De Gruyter.

WALDRON, H. B. (1997). Adolescent substance abuse and family therapy outcome: A review of randomized trials. *Advances in Clinical Child Psychology* 19: 199–234.

WELLS, R. A. (1994). *Planned Short-Term Treatment.* New York: Free Press.

YALOM, I. D. (1995). *The Theory and Practice of Group Psychotherapy,* 4th ed. New York: Basic Books.

ZHANG, S. (1998). In search of hopeful glimpses: A critique of research strategies in current boot camp evaluations. *Crime and Delinquency* 44(2): 314–344.

ZIMMER, L., and J. MORGAN (1997). *Marijuana Myths: Marijuana Facts.* New York: Lindesmith Center.

HELPFUL WEBSITES

Center for Medicinal Cannabis Research (University of California)

> http://www.cmcr.ucsd.edu/geninfo/ index.htm

Drug Policy Alliance (DPA)

> http://www.lindesmith.org/library/ bibliography/medicinal/index.cfm

This website currently lists 53 recent books and articles that serve as general references to the medical marijuana subject. It also provides references to 19 HIV/AIDS articles, 27 articles on glaucoma treatment with marijuana, 18 on cancer treatment, and 23 on epilepsy, multiple sclerosis, and spinal cord injury.

Marijuana Policy Project (MPP)

> http://www.mpp.org

National Organization to Reform Marijuana Laws (NORML)

> http://www.norml.org/index.cfm?Group ID=3391

Chapter 9

Identity Theft: An Overview of the Problem[*]

Katherine Slosarik

ABSTRACT

Identity theft has become a prevalent and increasing problem in the United States. An identify thief only needs one thing—a Social Security Number; with it, the thief can decimate a victim's life and credit. Historically, federal laws in place to combat identity theft are weak and ineffective. Law enforcement, faced with jurisdictional and technological issues, is ill equipped to deal with this. State and local law enforcement are forced to look to numerous federal agencies for help in combating this crime. It is difficult to determine the scope of this problem but initial figures show that identity theft has many different types of victims and financial targets. The ways in which identity thieves both victimize and the kind of prevention practices individuals can use to protect themselves are also examined. This chapter establishes a literature review on which future and much-needed research can be based.

INTRODUCTION

Identity theft is not what Hollywood has led us to believe. It is not a James Bond type donning latex and wigs, essentially becoming someone else, in order to infiltrate a super secret organization to gain top secret knowledge. The real identity theft is more subtle

*Reproduced from Roslyn Muraskin (Ed.), *The Justice Professional (2002: 329–343)* with permissions by publisher Routledge, Taylor & Francis Group. ISSN 0888-4135 print; ISSN 1477-2787 online copyright 2002 Taylor & Francis Ltd DO1: 10.1080/08884310220000070458

and far easier to accomplish. The identity thief does not even have to look like his/her victim. Only one thing is needed—a Social Security number (SSN). With it, the thief can assume an identity and begin a reign of unnoticed terror.

Unfortunately, there is little research or figures to show the true scope and trauma associated with identity theft. It is estimated in the United States that one in four is a victim of an identity theft (Rothman 1999:34). Identity theft is splintered among many statutes and covered by almost every federal agency. Because "identity theft is typically not a stand alone crime" (Government Accounting Office 2:3), law enforcement agencies are ill equipped to deal with this crime. It has become one's responsibility to detect fraudulent attempts to steal his/her identity. If there are fraudulent actions, it is up to the victim to sort out and clean up his/her credit record.

Academia has yet to address identity theft. The research presented here demonstrates a literature review and identity theft as a major focus for research.

AN OVERVIEW OF IDENTITY THEFT

Laws, Agencies, and Court Cases

Congress has, over the years, taken into account that unscrupulous people will misuse information. They have dealt with privacy issues and focused on areas to keep certain types of information private. Regrettably, "individuals have no control over what information will become public or remain private" (Hatch 2001:1470).

In an attempt to curb governmental abuses, several pieces of legislation were enacted. The Privacy Act of 1974 made sure that the federal government had regulations in place to oversee the collection and use of personal data. This act specifically limits the government and allows them to only collect "relevant" and "necessary" data. It also limited the types of information available under the Freedom of Information Act (FOIA) (Byers 2001:149). This legislation failed to address information collected by private parties like data collection companies, banks, consumer reporting agencies, or insurance companies. Information contained in lawsuits or court documents also remained unregulated (Buba 2000:646).

Two or more important pieces were designed in 1986. The Computer Fraud and Abuse Act made it a crime to use a computer to commit a crime or cause damage. The Electronic Communications Privacy Act also involved computers. It stated that one could not intercept electronic communications (e-mail or telephone calls). Both pieces were ineffective in controlling identity theft due to the limited scope and application or gaping loopholes (Byers 2001:150–151).

States had a habit of selling driver's license information. The Driver's Privacy Protection Act of 1994 (DPPA) put an end to that. Under this act, states can be fined and/or sued in civil court for failing to adhere to the requirements. The courts found that this act sees the states as "owners of databases" (Byers 2001:150).

Under the Fair Credit Reporting Act (FCRA), personal information collected by credit card and consumer reporting agencies is regulated. Agencies are required to provide "fair and accurate reports" and must provide "procedures by which the states can be fined and/or sued in controlling identity theft due to the limited scope and application or gaping loopholes (Byers 2001:150–151).

It directed consumer reporting agencies to provide a free credit report when credit is denied and to charge no more than $8.50 for a copy when otherwise requested. Some state laws mandate that all or some reports are free or available for a lesser charge (Case of *Stolen* 2000). This act also shields consumer reporting agencies from liability (LoPucki 2001:92):

> No consumer may bring any action or proceeding in the nature of the defamation, invasion or privacy or negligence with respect to the reporting of information against any consumer reporting agency, based on information disclosed except as to false information furnished with malice or willful intent to injure such consumer.

This clause allows consumer reporting agencies to essentially ignore identity theft victim complaints. Their only duty is to investigate the complaint. Only federal or state agencies can file against those agencies and are extremely unlikely to do so on behalf of one individual (LoPucki 2001:92). Thus, the agencies keep in place procedures sufficient enough to keep state agencies at bay. "Consumers have no legal right to stop credit [consumer] reporting agencies from collecting data or reporting on them" (LoPucki 2001:101).

The U.S. Supreme Court, in *TRW, Inc v. Adelaide Andrews* (2001), made it harder for victims of identity theft to seek redress. In a 9-0 decision, they ruled that victims do not get extra time to sue over damaged credit. Consumer advocates filed an amicus curie brief in support of Andrews. They feel that the threat of lawsuits would force consumer and credit agencies to adopt more stringent policies to prevent identity thefts. Currently, there is a two-year limitation on the right to accuse reporting agencies of law violations. Consumer advocates decided that the two years start when the reporting agency discovers the problems, not when the victim does. The Court argued that agencies could not keep records forever in anticipation of consumers discovering problems years later (Holland:1–2) *(Petitioner v. Adelaide Andrews)*.

On a related front, the Fair Credit Billing Act and Electronic Fund Transfer Act mandates limited liability on fraudulent electronic or credit card charges (Federal Trade Commission: 1–2). It also "establishes procedures for resolving billing errors on . . . credit card accounts" (1). The Fair Debt Collection Practices Act maintains that debtors must behave accordingly in the process of trying to collect overdue debt (1). Lastly, the Gramm–Leach Bliley Act of 1999 dictates that all financial institutions have in place safeguards and procedures to deter fraud and protect consumer information (GAO-02-363:12–13).

In 1998, President Clinton signed into law the Identity Theft and Assumption Deterrence Act (ITADA). This Act provided victims with tools to pursue help in repairing his/her credit and closed the loophole that perplexed law enforcement officers for so long. Now identity thieves could be prosecuted more easily. By making it a federal crime, federal law enforcement officers could now become involved and federal penalties could be issued. This was important because identity theft often crosses state lines, making it difficult for state law enforcement to proceed (Provenza 1999:324). However, the ITADA falls short in two areas. Foremost, it lacks regulations standards and addresses identity theft only after a crime has occurred (Buba 2000:657). In other words, it does not create any substantial prevention programs or standards. It also fails to focus on procedures used by thieves to obtain personal information (Provenza 1999:326). It ignores the threat new Internet databases pose to consumer identity.

Under the ITADA (1998), Congress defined identity theft as the following (U.S. Department of Justice 1998:4):

> Knowingly transferring or using, without lawful authority, a means of identification of another person with the intent to commit or to aid or abet any unlawful activity that constitutes a violation of Federal law, or that constitutes a felony under any applicable state or local law.

This act also made it unlawful to "make, possess, use or transfer any means of identification, identification document, false identification document or document-making implementation (Buba 2000:649). It specifically states that means of identification include

> Any name, social security, date of birth, official state or government issued driver's license or identification number, unique biometric data, such as fingerprint, voice print, retina or iris image.

The ITADA imposes stiff federal sentences upon anyone who attempts to misuse any type of identification. These sentences include incarceration of up to 15 years, and/or a fine of up to $250,000 (Buba 2000:649). But the GAO has found that most convictions "do not result in long sentences" (General Accounting Office 2002:18).

Until 1998, identity theft was not named a crime (Moss 2001). Some critics argue that specifically assuming someone's identity is still not a crime. The mere theft of identity is not enough; "it is the fraudulent use of another person's identity that constitutes the crime" (Provenza 1999:322). Besides the laws stated above, numerous statutes covering crimes associated with identity theft like fraud regarding identification documents, mail crimes associated with identity theft like fraud regarding identification documents, mail fraud, credit card fraud, and the misuse of Social Security numbers are used to arrest individuals. These crimes are covered by five different agencies: the Secret Service, the Federal Bureau of Investigation, the Internal Revenue Service, the Social Security Administration, and the Postal Inspection Service (U.S. Department of Justice 1998:4). Each state also has copious statutes covering this or associated crimes. The GAO notes that the Secret Service is leading the pack in creating task forces with local and state agencies to investigate and combat identity theft (General Accounting Office 2002:20–21). They are also developing training tools for the states to use (17). However, "current law does not provide victims of fraud with ready aid from law enforcement agencies" (Provenza 1999:321). The GAO also recommends that law enforcement file reports of identity theft regardless or whether or not they are going to investigate it (General Accounting Office 2002:16).

But this is slowly changing. The Federal Trade Commission Act mandates that the FTC has authority over "unfair or deceptive acts or practices" (Harrington 2001:1). They are able to take civil actions against violators. Under the ITADA, the FTC is required to maintain a clearinghouse database, "Consumer Sentinel," and a consumer complaint and education hotline. The Consumer Sentinel is a consortium of public and private organizations like the Better Business Bureau and over 300 law enforcement organizations (Consumer Sentinel:2). The Sentinel provides a search engine to law enforcement officers, allows them to communicate with other officers using the "alert" function, provides a list of current court orders, and gives a vast amount of rare quantitative data on identity theft. The FTC does charge a fee to use the network, and the user must sign a confidentiality agreement. "As of May 24, 2002, a total of 306 state and local law enforcement agencies [out of 18,000] had entered into such agreements" (General Accounting Office 2002:28–29). The toll-free hotline allows consumers to file complaints against consumer reporting agencies and companies and advises consumers about the steps to take to reclaim one's identity (Harrington 2001:2). They also maintain a consumer booklet (both hard copy and online), *Identity Theft: When Bad Things Happen to Your Good Name,* in an attempt to educate the public about identity theft (Broder 2000:4).

The FTC has the authority to contact consumer reporting agencies on complaints and information about identity theft. They are working to reduce the amount of time a victim needs to spend straightening out his/her credit report (Harwood 2001:7). These ultimate institutions and law enforcement databases develop "standardized fraud declaration for creditors" (Harwood 2001:3; Broder 2000:3). A victim spends, on average, 175 hours and $100.00 (not counting legal fees) to fix his/her credit report (GAO-02-363:9). Some insurance companies are starting to offer identity theft policies. These policies range from $10 to $40 premiums and have a $1,000 deductible. However, the policy covers up to $25,000 in out-of-pocket expenses spent on clearing up one's identity. Critics argue that the policy does nothing to help clear up one's credit; the victim still has to make all the phone calls and do all of the legwork (Spencer 2002:1–2). The FTC is also releasing data to banks and businesses in the hopes that they will set up better detection and prevention practices to further reduce the amount of identity theft and consumer fraud. Furthermore, they hold workshops to keep the government, businesses, and the public informed on identity theft and victim assistance (Harwood 2001:7).

The ITADA set up a Subcommittee on Identity Theft under the Attorney General's Council on White Collar Crime. The subcommittee combines the efforts of the Justice, Treasury, and State Departments. ITADA also seeks aid from several financial and professional organizations and have federal regulatory agencies. Their ultimate purpose is to educate the public. Various task forces have been set up as well. These task forces mostly address interstate frauds that cross multi-jurisdictions (Harrington 2001:12).

It is important to note that the underlying problem is the reliance on Social Security Numbers (SSNs) as a national identifier. As early as 1974, Congress expressed its concerns over the widespread use of SSNs and the privacy issues they raised. Yet SSNs have become so important in day-to-day business and government actions, it is almost impossible to curtail their use (Komuves 1998:535–536). "Characteristic values used in the process of identification . . . must be widely distributed. Once they are widely distributed, they cease to be secret" (LoPucki 2001:109). For example, universities, insurance companies, credit card companies, banks, standardized testing agencies, blood donation entities, tax collecting governments, employers, medical communities, courts, state government agencies, and law enforcement use SSNs as their primary identifier in files. The main source of restrictions upon SSN use is the Privacy Act. However, the courts have found that Section 7 does not apply to private entities like banks and are reluctant to award damages to those cases where states stepped beyond their boundaries (Komuves 1998:553). "Federal law does not bar private actors from requesting SSNs or refusing to do business with someone if they refuse" (569). Because Congress had made so many exemptions, Congress allows states and other entities to decide whether or not to use SSNs. Entities generally opt for their use (569): "Limits on private actors are . . . virtually nonexistent."

COMMISSION OF A CRIME

Identity Theft in Action

Identity thieves can use a variety of methods to steal someone's identity. These methods can range from simple to complex. Technological advances, although benefiting society in numerous ways have made identity theft easier to commit. Essentially, pilfers need only a few of the following: date of birth, SSN, mother's maiden name, and an address (Hermocillo 1998:2). Often victims are not aware of the theft until years later or even how the thief obtained their information (see Table 9.1).

After identity thieves have the information they need, they file change of address forms with bill collectors and credit card issuers. This prevents the victim from ever knowing about the unlawful activity that is being committed in his/her name (Laribee and Stephen 2001:2). Someone's SSN becomes the key that magically unlocks financial doors. Armed with a new SSN, a thief can drain bank accounts, open new credit cards, lease automobiles, obtain loans for new homes or other purchases, and in some extreme cases commit other crimes (3). Table 9.2 illustrates the methods used to obtain information, whereas Table 9.3 indicates the various types of activities committed once an identity thief has a victim's personal information. Credit card fraud is the most prevalent; this may have to do with ease of obtainment.

Traditional thieves "dumpster dive" or dig through the trash to find any type of personal information like bills from credit cards or utilities, bank statements, medical records, employment documents, or anything that may contain some kind of personal

**TABLE 9.1   Identity Theft Complaints the FTC Received
(November 1999 to September 2001)**

Method Used to Obtain Information	Number of Complaints	Percent
Method not known	58,078	61.7
Information not collected (non-FTC data)	16,781	17.8
Method known	19,241	20.5
Total	94,100	100.0

TABLE 9.2   Methods of Obtaining Personal Information

Method Known Cases	Number of Complaints	Percent (based on subtotal)
Access through relationship with victim	10,101	52.5
Wallet or purse stolen	6,615	34.4
Mail theft or fraudulent address change	2,577	13.4
Compromised records	1,322	6.9
Burglary or break-in	686	3.6
Internet	462	2.4
Telephone or mail solicitation or purchase	132	0.7
Other	1,706	8.9
Missing	<u>572</u>	3.0
Subtotal	19,241	

Details and percentages do not add up due to multiple methods of obtaining data as reported by victims.

Source: GAO-02-363:27 http://www.gao.gov/New.item. Stana, R. M., "Identity Theft: Growing Prevalence and Cost". February 14, 2002. Adapted from Identity Theft: Data Indicate Growth in Prevalence and Cost.

information. The U.S. Supreme Court ruled in 1988 that anything left on the curb as trash is public domain (Armstrong 2001:2). Another form used is "shoulder surfing." Thieves obtain key information by looking over a victim's shoulder (at an ATM, for example). Thieves even use technology to obtain information from far away (Buba 2000:638). Yet some rely on a tried and true method—wallet or purse (Ramirez 1998:486). They even steal their victim's mail (Supplemental 2001:2).

Another method of obtaining information is "pretext calling." In this scenario, a thief calls a financial institution like a bank and poses as a "victim." Through a series of techniques and artful questions, the thief attempts to obtain information from the often ill trained, incautious, unsuspecting teller/customer service representative (Bielski 2001:4). This information is either sold or used by the thief in criminal activities (Moss 2001:2).

Even widely distributed publications, like *Forbes Magazine,* can serve as a vehicle to commit identity theft. Abraham Abdallah used the "400 Richest People in America" article to bilk 200 people over the course of six months. Abdallah would contact financial associations like Merrill Lynch and request that large amounts of money be transferred in a Yahoo account held by Abdallah. Abdallah used pretext calling to gain information from companies like TRW, Equifax, and Experian. With this, he was able to gain access to accounts. Couriers were employed to relay any goods ordered. He also used "post office boxes, Web-enabled cell phones and online voice mail services" to avoid discovery (Massive Identity 2001:2). He was finally apprehended when Merrill Lynch noticed that a transaction he requested would have unbalanced an account. The bank contacted the owner of the account only to find he did not request the transfer of funds. The authorities were contacted. By tracing email requests and the Yahoo money

TABLE 9.3   SSA/OIG Hotline Statistics on Allegation of SSN Misuse That
Directly Involve Identity Theft (March to September 2001)

ID Theft Category	Number of Complaints	Percent
Credit card	9,488	36.5
Employment	4,637	17.8
Lost/stolen SSN	3,421	13.2
Bank fraud	2,765	10.6
Utility	2,761	10.6
Tax return	1,032	4.0
Medical care	548	2.1
Driver's license	496	1.9
Housing	224	0.9
Child support	171	0.7
Internet	157	0.6
Government loan	93	0.4
Bankruptcy	83	0.3
INS document	79	0.3
Birth certificate	24	0.1
Passport	12	0.0
Total	25,991	100.0

Source: GAO-02-363:30 Identity Theft: Prevalence and Cost Appear to be Growing www.gao.gov/New
.items/d02363.pdf

accounts, they were able to discover other victims and eventually apprehended Abdallah
(Massive Identity 2001:2).

Technology provides even more variations on a theme. Information can be lifted
through a scanning device. These scanners are sold on the net and can be purchased by
unscrupulous individuals who use this product at their job (e.g., waitressing). This practice is known as "skimming" (Bielski 2001:2). Cameras can be used to zoom in to videotape personal information from a distance (Buba 2000:638).

Computers have only added to the problem. Technology has made information
gathering cheap and easy (Hatch 2001:1473). This is known as "data mining." Data files
can contain "income, marital status, hobbies, medical ailments . . . preferred brand of
antacid tablets, . . . dentures, . . . room deodorizers, sleeping aids, and hemorrhoid remedies" (1473–1474). No information is too personal or too mundane (Hatch 2001:1472).
As a result, data collection has become a staple in targeting consumers. Data collection
agencies can provide this data for fees to anyone who can afford it (Buba 2000:642–643).
This information can be purchased as a whole or in pieces. For example, an SSN can be
purchased for as little as $49 (Hatch 2001:1472). The Medical Marketing Service (MMS)
sells lists of people who suffer from certain medical conditions like diabetes, depression

or Alzheimer's. Businesses argue that these databases benefit the consumer by providing discounts on frequently used products (Hatch 2001:1471, 1475) and that less junk mail is released as a result. Conversely, hackers and interception programs can take advantage of these databases as well (Buba 2000:638). Critics moreover argue that these databases can be used to target certain groups of individuals who are more susceptible (like the elderly) for diabolical purposes (Hatch 2001:1474). Unsecured or bogus web sites provide a hotbed of information for "lurkers," "slurpers," and "snoopers" (Buba 2000:638).

The Internet has proven an indispensable tool for identity crooks. "Many employers use Internet technology to maintain employees' personal records" (Lucey 2001:2). Other information available through Intranets are insurance and retirement data, employee records, and benefit information (2). It took Senator Dianne Feinstein (D-CA) only minutes to locate her SSN on the Internet (Hermocillo 1998:3). This prompted her to propose a new identity theft bill, the Identity Theft Prevention Act of 2000, in Congress. This bill would amend the Social Security Act and make selling an SSN a crime. Alas, this bill died in committee (Byers 2001:153).

Not all identity theft is the result of strangers. As Table 9.4 illustrates, most thieves obtain access through a relationship with the victim (GAO-02-363:27). Other cases are the direct result of thieves obtaining records from work. These thieves are employees of an institution like a university, bank, or hospital who take advantage of the situation. Documents with personal information provide them with the opportunity and means (Mandelblit 2001:2).

Employees can become tempted to use job-related information for their own personal gain. Valerie Shoffner was one such person. Shoffner, who worked for New York State Insurance Fund, "had access to the personal identifying information of thousands of state employees and other citizens" (Office of New York State AG Spitzer 2001). She used this information to go on a spending spree and obtain a plethora of commodities. She also sold this personal information to others for cash. These accomplices also went on shopping sprees. Over $100,000 was stolen by Shoffner and associates. Computer items accounted for the largest portion ($70,000) of the estimated total theft. When

TABLE 9.4   Relationship of Suspect to Victim Reported to FTC
(November 1999 to September 2001)

Relationship of Suspect to Victim	Number of Complaints	Percent (based on 94,100 complaints)
Family member	4,629	4.9
Roommate/cohabitant	1,137	1.2
Neighbor	1,003	1.2
Workplace (employer/employee/coworker)	836	0.9
Other	2,496	2.7
Total	10,101	10.7

Source: GAO-02-363:28

Shoffner's home was searched, the authorities discovered that she had orchestrated a similar scheme at her old place of employment, the Empire State College in New York City. This identity theft ring is an example of the growing prevalence of identity theft. New York's State Inspector General Roslynn R. Mauskopf said that people have an expectation of privacy when they entrust personal information to a government agency (Office of New York State AG Spitzer 2001).

Most of these examples fall under the monetary harm typology set up by the FTC. The other type of harm is non-monetary. Examples of this include being denied credit, being arrested, being unable to get a job, spending time clearing up one's financial credit, difficulty obtaining loans for cars or a home, loss of productivity, evictions, and having to show up in court (GAO-02-363:58–60). Tables 9.5–9.7 illustrate the wide range of costs and harm victims deal with.

TABLE 9.5   Monetary Losses Reported to FTC
             (November 1999 to September 2001)

Monetary Issues	Number of Complaints	Percent
No data	77,063	81.9
Zero	14,404	15.3
1–100	502	0.5
101–500	653	0.7
501–1,000	399	0.4
1,001–5,000	669	0.7
5,001–10,000	207	0.2
Over 10,000	203	0.2
Total	94,100	100.0

At the time, most complaints provided no information regarding out-of-pocket expenses.
Source: GAO-02-363:57

TABLE 9.6   Non-monetary Harm Reported to FTC
             (November 1999 to September 2001)

Was There Monetary Harm	Number of Complaints	Percent
No	63,959	68.0
Yes	13,357	14.2
Non-FTC data	16,784	17.8
Total	94,100	100.0

Non-FTC data was forwarded from the SSA/Org.
Source: GAO-02-363:56

TABLE 9.7   Types of Non-monetary Harm as Reported to FTC
(November 1999 to September 2001)

Types of Nonmonetary Harm	Number of Complaints	Percent Based on Subtotal
Denied credit or other financial services	7,376	55.2
Time lost to resolve problems	3,489	26.1
Harassed by debt collector or creditor	2,968	22.2
Criminal investigation, arrest, conviction	1,281	9.6
Civil suit filed or judgment entered	819	6.1
Denied employment or loss of job	580	4.3
Other	3,780	28.7
Total	20,293	

Details and percentages do not add up due to victim being subject to more than one type of harm.
Source: GAO-02-363:56

These tables demonstrate that most victims do not report non-monetary harm. It is possible that complainants do not realize that being denied credit or financial services is a direct harm associated with identity theft. It is also quite apparent that victims either do not keep track of the monetary amounts spent trying to fix their credit or fail to report these amounts.

Terry Rogan, unfortunately, found out first hand how out of hand identity theft can get. Rogan, a native of Michigan, was arrested for trespassing. The police ran his name through the National Crime Information Center (NCIC) database only to find that Rogan was wanted for two robbery–murder combos in Los Angeles, California. However, the physical description and fingerprints on file did not match with Rogan's. The NCIC information was removed. Two months later the Los Angeles Police Department (LAPD) reentered Rogan's name into the database. When Rogan was stopped for failing to use a turn signal, the sheriff's department again discovered he was wanted for two robbery–murder combos. This pattern continued again later that same year. Each time after being ordered out of his vehicle at gunpoint and detained for hours, the police unraveled his identity and Rogan was released. This process was repeated at least five times. Rogan filed suit with the City of Los Angeles. It was here they discovered that another man, McKandes, who had escaped from prison in Alabama, was using Rogan's name. McKandes had obtained a copy of Rogan's birth certificate. With this, he was able to get a driver's license in California. The LAPD had detained him on suspicion of murder but later released him. Once the LAPD realized that he was the right suspect, they issued an arrest warrant in McKandes' name and placed the corresponding information into the NCIC database (Saunders and Zucker:3, 4).

Although Rogan's story is extreme, it is not as rare as thought. Table 9.8 illustrates the wide range of identity theft crimes and the various harms inflicted upon victims.

TABLE 9.8   Summary of GAO's Interviews of Victims

Victim	Activities Committed in Victim's Name	Nonmonetary Harm	Monetary Harm
1	Opened 12–18 charge accounts Obtained housing Obtained utility services Obtained fraudulent identification Opened cell phone account	Harassed by collection agency Reappearance of charges after they had been removed Time (200 hours over 10 months) to clear name	Out-of-pocket expenses ($100–$200) Lost job and wages ($6,000)
2	Attempted to open charge account Made charges on existing account	Time (400 hours over 4–6 weeks) to clear name	Out-of-pocket expenses (less than $20)
3	Opened charge accounts Obtained housing Purchased car Wrote bad checks Obtained employment and owed back taxes	Time (3–6 months) to clear name Difficulty in obtaining credit Harassed by collection agencies	Out-of-pocket expenses ($20) Could not claim refund ($1,000)
4	Opened charge accounts Attempted to obtain car loan Wrote bad checks Obtained fraudulent identification Opened cell phone account	Time (between 150 and 200 hours over 6 weeks)	Out-of-pocket expenses ($20–$30)
5	Violated traffic laws (3 speeding tickets) Opened charge accounts Wrote bad checks Obtained employment Obtained fraudulent identification Attended college classes	Arrest warrant issued for speeding tickets Time (hundreds of hours over last 6 years) to clear Went to court to contest tickets Difficulty in obtaining credit	Could not claim IRS tax refund ($814)
6	Opened 10 charge accounts Wrote bad checks	Harassed by retailers over bad checks	Purse was stolen Out-of-pocket expenses ($20)

Victim	Activities Committed in Victim's Name	Nonmonetary Harm	Monetary Harm
	Made fraudulent identifications	Time (missed 3 days work in 2 months)	
	Used existing credit accounts	Lower productivity at work	
7	Opened 20 charge accounts	Difficulty obtaining credit	Out of pocket expenses (several hundred dollars)
		Time (48 hours over 2.5 years) to clear name	
		Difficulty purchasing car	
8	Filed for income tax refunds	Time (30 hours over 1.5 years) to clear name	
	Arrested 3 times in victim's name	Car searched for drugs at police station	
9	Obtained fraudulent identification	Difficulty in obtaining credit	Lost job and wages ($2,500)
	Opened bulk account	Difficult in obtaining employment	
	Opened multiple charge accounts	Difficulty in purchasing car	
	Obtained prescription medication	Time (hundreds of hours over 6 years) to clear name	
	Obtained employment and later fired	Used victim's name in auto accident	
	Received unemployment benefits	Arrested twice in victim's name	
	Evicted 3 times from housing		
10	Obtained fraudulent identification	Difficulty obtaining credit time (15–20 hours over 3 years) to clear name	Out-of-pocket expenses ($59)
	Opened multiple charge accounts		
	Traffic violations in victim's name		

The experiences of these 10 victims are not statistically representative of all victims.

Source: GAO-02-363:67, 58–60

Associated with these crimes are the costs to the criminal justice system. Although agencies do not keep track of "average costs," they are aware of variables that affect this figure:

The number of personnel assigned, the use of technical and surveillance assets, transcriptions and translation services, case-related travel (domestic and foreign), task force expenses, expenditures for investigative information and evidence, expenditures associated with undercover activities, and trial preparation (GAO-02-363:65).

Most agencies involved in identity theft note that these crimes operate within a white collar crime program so it is difficult to isolate costs directly associated with identity theft (GAO-020363:65). Table 9.9 provides an example of the number of cases the FBI alone

TABLE 9.9   FBI Accomplishments Under Identity Theft Related Crimes

ID Theft-Related Crime	1996	1997	1998	1999	2000	2001
Identification documents						
Indictments and information*	33	33	22	55	99	49
Arrests	24	17	20	28	40	41
Convictions	33	27	17	21	50	29
Access device						
Indictments and information	90	95	114	96	125	39
Arrests	38	60	78	69	90	35
Convictions	60	80	77	105	74	35
Loan and credit applications						
Indictments and information	311	290	235	189	206	94
Arrests	58	62	72	38	85	38
Convictions	304	242	170	146	121	50
Bank fraud						
Indictments and information	1,225	1,159	1,305	1,492	1,481	626
Arrests	311	468	579	691	645	311
Convictions	1,121	896	983	1,047	1,112	449
SSN misuse						
Indictments and information	85	75	97	119	98	40
Arrests	25	15	40	48	62	22
Convictions	61	50	62	64	68	23
Fraudulent use of credit cards						
Indictments and information	11	1	1	1	1	1
Arrests	2	0	1	0	0	2
Convictions	5	2	2	0	0	1
Total	3,797	3,572	3,875	4,209	4,357	1,887

Fiscal Year 2001 figures are as of April 10.

*An indictment is an accusation presented in writing by a grand jury. An information is presented by a competent public office on his/her oath of office.

Source: GAO-02-363:33

handled in a six-year period. Other agencies like the Social Security Agency, Secret Service, and states are also responsible for some of these crimes. Figures show only the FBI's involvement and do not represent accomplishments of criminal justice as a whole.

SAFEGUARDING IDENTITY

Current Practices and Policies

Most law enforcement agencies lay the burden of preventing identity theft on individuals. They advise individuals to buy a paper shredder and shred all unnecessary documents that contain personal information. This includes ATM receipts, which should not be left at the bank machine or in a trashcan near the ATM machine. They also suggest getting a lockable mailbox or a PO Box to ensure that mail stays private. All outgoing mail should be taken to the post office, especially if it contains personal information. A credit report copy should be ordered every year from one of the three consumer reporting bureaus (Equifax, Experian, or Trans Union). It is also possible to remove one's name from junk mail and telemarketing lists; this will stop preapproved credit card applications (Armstrong 2001:1–3). If one does receive telemarketing calls, never give out personal information, especially an SSN. Legitimate organizations and governmental agencies already have this information (Case of Stolen 2000:2). Websites that also request too much information should be avoided (Francis 2002:2).

Even cleaning out one's wallet or purse can help prevent identity theft. Social Security cards should not be carried in either of these items. It should be kept in a safe and secure place. Rarely used credit cards should either be canceled or kept elsewhere. When it comes to passwords and PINs, one should not use birthdays, phone numbers, anniversaries, addresses, or any other numeric combination that is easily figured out (Armstrong 2001:3).

If one does suspect that he/she has become a victim of identity theft, he/she should "immediately file a police report and send copies of the report to [his/her] bank, credit card companies and insurance companies" (Montgomery 2001:1). Consumer reporting agencies should be contacted so a fraud alert is placed on the victim's account. Any debts incurred by the suspect should not be paid by the victim. Once the victim starts trying to pay off these debts, he/she acknowledges that the debt is his/hers and assumes liability. The FTC has an "ID Theft Affidavit." This helps provide proof that the debt was not created by the victim (Federal Trade Commission 2001:1).

Each consumer reporting agency has its own policy dealing with identity theft. Since 1998, fraud units at these agencies have increased by 84 percent (GAO-02-363:21). Fraud alerts are posted to a consumer's file when he/she suspects fraudulent activity. One agency, referred to by the GAO as Agency A, posts a seven-year fraud alert on consumer files when fraud is suspected (GAO-02-363:24). Agency B has "two types of fraud alerts—a temporary or 90 day security alert and a seven year victim statement" (23). Agency C has a six-month fraud alert, which is then audited to determine if a longer alert is needed; this alert ranges from two to seven years. Each agency noted that the majority of alerts are put on by consumers as a preventative measure even though no actual fraud has occurred. Consumers may also feel this is an added protection against identity theft. Agency A noted that only about 25 percent of the alerts are identity theft based (22). But most of what these agencies do is shrouded in secrecy. The GAO only obtained this information once they agreed not to identify which agency (Trans Union, Equifax, or Experian) used which policy (GAO 21).

The American Bankers Association (ABA) also sets forth recommendations and tools (computer programs or authorization and verification systems) that member banks can use to fight identity fraud. The ABA notes that identity theft is not a major problem at banks because they "have experience in dealing with identity fraud, including using new technology to detect where such fraud may be taking place" (GAO-02-363:44). However, the highest amount (56 percent) of identity fraud occurs at community banks with assets under $500 million (41). These banks provide the least amount of expenses to deal with prevention, detection, or investigation. Larger banks have fraud departments and devote more resources to safeguarding their customer's finances (General Accounting Office 2002:47). Policies vary from bank size to bank size. It is difficult to determine the impact identity theft has on the financial system or what practices are in place to prevent it. Nevertheless, all deposits are federally insured.

CONCLUSION

Future Bound

While restricting SSN use seems like the obvious course of action, this action will be quite costly. While new legislation could restrict use, collection, and circulation, it can do nothing without the destruction of databases already in place that house SSNs (Komuves 1998:575–577). "Information that has essentially been public for decades cannot be made private by passing a law against selling it" (LoPucki 2001:134). Essentially, SSNs are used for matching purposes. If SSNs are no longer allowed to be used this way, what will take its place (LoPucki 2001:135)?

Fingerprints and biometric data (retina scans, photos, height, weight, eye color, DNA, etc.) have been suggested. The FBI already has a vast fingerprint database containing prints of anyone who has been arrested. Thieves, under current technology constraints, would be unable to duplicate records when tested. These tests would have to be done directly and would be costly to consumers and the agencies that employ these methods. Photos are considered too personal, whereas, height, weight, and eye color are too easily mimicked. But the biggest obstacle in the way of these methods is invasion of privacy (LoPucki 2001:111).

Governmental agencies and businesses need to adopt practices that insure identity cannot be proven with a mere SSN and a mother's maiden name (LoPucki 2001:135). Data collection agencies and information brokers need to be restrained in the types of information they collect or sell and to whom they sell (Byers 2001:162). Business owners must restrict the ways personal information is used and stored. Background checks on employees need to become routine if not already, especially if they have contact with personal data. SSN use should be curtailed wherever possible (Laribee and Stephen 2001:4).

Most proposals to reform the current system are met with disdain by both business and privacy advocates (LoPucki 2001:112).

The GAO maintains that most local and state agencies remain unaware of the importance of investigating identity theft. They view it as a "nontraditional crime" with too many venue and jurisdiction problems (General Accounting Office 2002:3). Task forces tend to help with these problems but state and local law enforcement lack the money necessary to properly train and provide equipment to combat identity theft (General Accounting Office 2002:17).

This area of study has been widely ignored. More research into the nature of identity theft needs to be conducted. It would be interesting to discover how much focus is placed on identity theft, the prevalence of the crime, how aware the public really is about identity theft, how much governmental and consumer reporting agencies are to blame, and how effective the current policy at curtailing identity theft is. One thing is certain; the victim needs to have better tools to repair his/her identity problem. The blame needs to be shifted away from the victims; they need to be innocent until proven guilty; currently they are asked to prove a negative.

REFERENCES

ARMSTRONG, L. (2001). Don't let crooks steal your identity. *Business Week* (3758): 134–136. [Retrieved from http://www.proquest.umi.com]

BIELSKI, L. (2001). Identity theft. *American Bankers Association* 93(1): 27–30. [Retrieved from http://www.proquest.umi.com]

BRODER, B. (2000). *Prepared Statement of the Federal Trade Commission on Identity Theft Before the Committee on Banking and Financial Services United States House of Representatives.* [Retrieved from http://www.ftc.gov/os/2000/09/idthefttest.htm]

BUBA, N. M. (2000). Waging war against identity theft: Should the United States borrow from the European Union's battalion? *Suffolk Transnational Law Review* 23: 633. [Retrieved from http://www.lexis-nexis.com]

BYERS, S. (2001). Note: The Internet: Privacy lost identities stolen. *Brandeis Law Journal* 40: 141. [Retrieved from http://www.lexis-nexis.com]

CASE OF STOLEN IDENTITY (2000). *Successful Meetings* 49(13): 28. [Retrieved from http://www.proquest.umi.com]

FEDERAL TRADE COMMISSION. *ID Theft: Federal Laws.* [Retrieved from http://www.consumer.gov/idtheft/fedlaw.htm]

FEDERAL TRADE COMMISSION (2001). *Instructions for Completing the ID Theft Affidavit.* [Retrieved from http://www.consumer/idtheft/affidavit.htm]

FRANCIS, F. (2002). *Protecting Against Identity Theft.* MSNBC.com. [Retrieved from http://www.msnbc.com/news/71562.asp]

GENERAL ACCOUNTING OFFICE (2002a). *Identity Theft: Prevalence and Cost Appear to Be Growing.* GAO-02-363.

GENERAL ACCOUNTING OFFICE (2002b). *Identity Theft: Greater Awareness and Use of Existing Data Are Needed.* GAO-02-766.

HARRINGTON, E. (2001). *Internet Fraud a Prepared Statement of the Federal Trade Commission Before the Subcommittee on Commerce, Trade, and Consumer Protection of the Committee on Energy and Commerce United States of Representatives.* [Retrieved from http://www.ftc/gov/2001/05/internetfraduttmy.htm]

HARWOOD, C. (2001). *Identity Theft: A Prepared Statement Before the Committee on Labor Commerce and Financial Institutions.* [Retrieved from http://www.ftc.gov/be/v010001htm]

HATCH, M. (2001). The privatization of big brother: Protecting sensitive personal information from commercial interests in the 21st century. *William Mitchell Law Review* 27: 1457. [Retrieved from http://www.lexis-nexis.com]

HERMOCILLO, J. (1998). Identity theft: Yet another issue fueling the privacy debate. *Credit World* 86(4): 24–27. [Retrieved from http://www.proquest.umi.com]

HOLLAND, G. *Identity Theft Case Rejected.* ABCNEWS.com [Retrieved from http://www.more.abcnews.go.com/sections/us/dailnews/scotus rep011113.html]

KOMUVES, F. L. (1998). We've got your number: An overview of legislation and decisions to control the use of social security numbers as personal identifiers. *The John Marshall Journal of Computer and Information Law* 16: 529. [Retrieved from http://www.lexis-nexis.com]

LARIBEE, S. F., and D. H. STEPHEN (2001). Identity theft: Will you be the next victim? *The National Public Accountant* 46(4): 8–11. [Retrieved from http://www.proquest.umi.com]

LOPUCKI, L. M. (2001). Human identification theory and the identity theft problem. *Texas Law Review* 80: 89. [Retrieved from http://www.lexis-nexus.com]

LUCEY, J. M. (2001). Identity theft risks: Business beware. *National Underwriter* 105(39): 25–28. [Retrieved from http://www.proquet.umi.com]

MANDELBLIT, B. D. (2001). Identity theft: A new security challenge. *Security* 105(39): 25–28. [Retrieved from http://www.proquest.umi.com]

MASSIVE IDENTITY THEFT BY NY DISH WASHER (2001). *Network Security* 2001(4): 2.

MONTGOMERY, B. D. (2001). *Protect Yourself Against Identity Theft.* [Retrieved from http://www.ag.state.oh.us/consumer/identityfraud.htm]

MOSS, V. (2001). Combating identity theft. *Credit Union Magazine* 67(6), 83–84. [Retrieved from http://www.proquest.umi.com]

OFFICE OF NEW YORK STATE ATTORNEY GENERAL ELLIOT SPITZER. (2001). State worker charged in massive identity theft scam. [Retrieved from http://www.oag.state.ny.us/press/2001/jul/jul17a 01.html]

PROVENZA, K. S. (1999). Identity theft: Prevention and liability. University of North Carolina School of Law Banking Institute. *North Carolina Banking Institute* 3: 319. [Retrieved from http://www.lexis-nexis.com]

RAMIREZ, P. M. (1998). Identity theft on the rise: Will the real John Doe please step forward. *University of the Pacific McGeorge Law Review* 29: 483. [Retrieved from http://www.lexis-nexus.com]

ROTHMAN, S. (1999). Identity theft. *Credit Union Magazine* 65(8): 34–41. [Retrieved from http://www.proquest.umi.com]

SAUNDERS, K. M., and B. ZUCKER (1999). Counteracting identity fraud in the information age: The identity theft and assumption deterrence act. *International Review of Law Computers and Technology* 13(2): 183–192. [Retrieved from http://www.proquest.umi.com]

SPENCER, C. (2002). Policies cover identity theft. *Yahoo! News,* [Retrieved from http://www.story.news.yahoo/com/news?tmpl=story&u=/ap/20020827/ap wo en po/us identity insurance]

STANA, R. M. (2002). *Identity Theft: Growing Prevalence and Cost.* February 14, 2002. Adopted from Identity Theft: Data Indicate Growth in Prevalence and Cost. GAO-02-363.

SUPPLEMENTAL GUIDELINES ON IDENTITY THEFT PRETEXT CALLING ISSUED (2001). *ABA Bank Compliance* 22(5): 2–3. [Retrieved from http://www.proquet.umi.com]

TRW, INC. (2001). *Petitioner v. Adelaide Andrews,* 534 U.S. 19.

U.S. DEPARTMENT OF JUSTICE (1998). What Are Identity Theft and Identity Fraud? [Retrieved from http://www.usdoj.gov/criminal/fraud/idetheft.html]

Chapter 10

Juvenile Justice

Persistent Challenges; Promising Strategies

Peter J. Benekos and Alida V. Merlo

ABSTRACT

The history of juvenile justice and *parens patriae* demonstrates a vision of trying to help youth survive the challenges of adolescent development and the risks of delinquency. The realities of the juvenile justice system, however, demonstrate transformations of that vision into more punitive and restrictive policies. This chapter reviews some of challenges facing juvenile justice as well as some of the promising interventions that demonstrate commitment to the original vision.

INTRODUCTION

In 2007, the public became aware that two administrators working in Texas Youth Commission institutions for delinquents were sexually assaulting youth in their care (Blumenthal 2007a,b). News reports indicated that the abuse had been reported as early as December of 2003; but no official action was taken to address these concerns until 2007 (Blumenthal 2007a,c). Allegations of sexual and physical abuse of girls in youth correctional institutions in New York were also reported in 2006 by Human Rights Watch (Lewis 2006). The report detailed the conditions of confinement in two facilities where girls who had been placed for delinquent behavior were subjected to harsh physical treatment by staff members. There were at least three confirmed reports of sexual abuse by staff members (Lewis 2006).

These abuses illustrate the vulnerability of children and the conundrum the juvenile justice system faces. Although there has been a call for harsher sanctions for delinquent youth, there is also the realization that youth are children who need treatment and protection. Youth who engage in serious delinquent behavior may require institutionalization; however, there is an expectation that the system will ascertain that they are treated in a safe and humane environment. Balancing the juvenile court's original mission in a more conservative era is one of the challenges that the system will address in the future.

In the mid-1990s, in response to the perception that youthful violence was escalating, state legislators swiftly initiated a series of reforms that lowered the age of eligibility for transfer to adult court, mandated the removal of certain kinds of offenses from juvenile court jurisdiction, and authorized blended sentencing (Merlo 2000; Finley and Schindler 1999; Merlo, Benekos, and Cook 1997). These strategies reflect a continuing reaction to sensationalized and dramatized cases of youth violence and explain Shepherd's concern that "the future of the juvenile court is in question" (1999:21).

The census of youth in adult correctional institutions documents the legislative consequences. On June 30, 2004, there were approximately 7,083 young men and women in jail who were under the age of 18 (Snyder and Sickmund 2006:236). In 2002, there were 4,100 young men and women under the age of 18 who were new court commitments to state prison systems for adults in 2002 (Snyder and Sickmund 2006:237). While these data reflect a decrease from the peak of new court commitments to adult prisons that occurred in 1996 (Snyder and Sickmund 2006:237), the incarceration of youth in adult institutions is a significant issue in the history of juvenile justice.

This "adultification" of juvenile offenders was illustrated in the case of Nathaniel Abraham, who was 11 years old when he was charged with first-degree murder in the October 1997 shooting of an 18-year-old stranger, Ronnie Greene, Jr., in Pontiac, Michigan. In November 1999, Abraham was found guilty of second-degree murder, and in January 2000, he was sentenced to serve seven years in a maximum-security juvenile detention center (Bradsher 2000). Abraham was the youngest child in Michigan to be charged, tried, and convicted as an adult for murder. This was possible as the result of a 1996 state law that "allows prosecutors to seek judges' permission to try any juvenile as an adult, no matter how young" (Bradsher 1999:A21).

The sentencing judge, Eugene Arthur Moore, rejected the prosecutors' request for additional time and publicly criticized the state's juvenile laws as "weighted too heavily toward punishment instead of rehabilitation" (Bradsher 2000:A1). The statement made by Judge Moore and his "lenient" sentence contrast sharply with the 111-year sentence (without the possibility of parole) imposed on another juvenile murderer, Kip Kinkel, who killed his parents and two students, and wounded several other students at a school shooting near Portland, Oregon (Bradsher 2000). Both the Kinkel school shooting and the Abraham random shooting are tragic but extreme cases that received intense media attention that served to further distort public understanding and diminish support for juvenile justice.

As critics and supporters look back to the beginning of the juvenile court, both can agree that the founding principles and original intent of a separate court for youth have been severely challenged. Critics would argue that flawed assumptions and failed performance should justify the dismantling of the system. Proponents, however, would see transformations and emerging paradigms as evidence of a system capable of adapting to social and political change and meeting challenges in this century. In contributing to this discussion on the future of juvenile justice, this chapter is organized into four sections: (1) the history and lessons since the juvenile court was first established; (2) the rationale for optimism about juvenile justice; (3) evidence of successful strategies; and (4) issues and models that will persist in shaping (and reshaping) the juvenile justice system.

HISTORY OF JUVENILE JUSTICE

Readers are familiar with the orthodox view that at the end of the nineteenth century–well-intentioned reformers championed the cause of "wayward" children who they believed needed benevolent supervision, guidance, and socialization (Tanenhaus 2004; Albanese 1993). The founding of a juvenile court in 1899 in Illinois signaled a rejection of the prevailing practice of punishing youth as little adults and instituted an informal process to determine the best interests of youth and to seek therapeutic interventions in reforming youthful miscreants. Guided by the doctrine of *parens patriae*, a kind and benevolent judge would rely on "substantive" rationality to order social welfare agencies to divert youth from negative influences and to correct their delinquent tendencies (Bortner 1988).

Since this new jurisprudence was concerned with child-saving and not criminal prosecution, youth did not require due process or protections for their rights. Delinquent acts were not viewed as crimes but as symptoms of problems that needed treatment (Albanese 1993:68). A new lexicon was used to denote the distinction between juvenile and criminal court, and as this separate system was established throughout the country (all but two states had a separate court by 1925), the concept of adolescence as a unique developmental phase gained acceptance (Bilchik 1999a):

> A century ago, the focus of the juvenile justice system was on the juvenile offender—rather than the offense . . . and on the principle that youth are developmentally different from adults and more amenable to intervention.

Transformation

While the intent of this informal, child-centered social welfare approach was recognized, the performance of the system began to raise objections. From 1905 when the Pennsylvania Supreme Court upheld the informal, rehabilitative model of the juvenile courts (*Commonwealth v. Fisher*) until the 1967 landmark decision establishing procedural safeguards (*in re Gault*), critics objected to the mistreatment of youth, the abuse of judicial discretion, and failure of rehabilitative programs (Albanese 1993).

As a result of Court decisions in the 1960s and 1970s that required more formal procedure and due process in the juvenile court, the distinction between the separate courts was diminished and the courts began to converge. In addition, as crime became more politicized and as a more conservative, punitive model of criminal justice emerged in the 1970s, the rehabilitative model was challenged and replaced by crime control as the salient jurisprudence of criminal justice. These developments—increasing crime, politicized crime policy, punitive dispositions, and an ideological shift to the right—also influenced the direction of juvenile justice.

In his critique of these developments, Feld (1993) credits (1) the procedural convergence, (2) the jurisprudential shift to crime control and punishment, and (3) the jurisdictional changes of removing status offenders from the juvenile court and waiving serious youthful offenders to criminal court with transforming the juvenile court into a barely separate but equal system that was no longer needed or justified. With the juvenile court under scrutiny, the confluence of four factors raised doubts about a future for juvenile justice: guns, gangs, drugs, and race.

Beginning in the mid-1980s, and aggravated by the (1) "epidemic" of crack cocaine, (2) growing numbers of youth gangs, and (3) proliferation of guns, policies toward youth have become more politicized and punitive. The images of younger and younger offenders using firearms to kill innocent citizens have precipitated more retributive and get-tough policies that—intended or not—have reinforced a link between race and youth crime that resulted in the "targeting" of young black men (Feld 1999a; Finley and Schindler 1999). In his assessment of the transformation of the juvenile court, Feld noted the importance of race as an impetus for get-tough sentencing and waiver policies (1999a:361):

> The politicization of crime policies and the connection in the public and political minds between race and youth crime provided a powerful political incentive for changes in waiver policies that de-emphasized youths' "amenability to treatment" and instead focused almost exclusively on "public safety."

Juvenile Arrest Data and Minority Representation

Prior to 2002, the Juvenile Justice and Delinquency Prevention Act used the term "disproportionate minority confinement" (DMC) to assess the confinement of minority groups relative to their representation in the population. In 2002, Congress amended the Act to incorporate all stages of the juvenile justice process. Currently, the term *disproportionate minority contact* is used to refer to the representation of minorities from arrest through disposition (Snyder and Sickmund 2006:97).

One salient consequence of this legislative change has been an examination of all the processes to assess *disproportionate minority contact*. In 2004, black youths comprised 17 percent of the juvenile population in the United States. However, the arrest data indicate that black youth accounted for 46 percent of all arrests for violent crimes and 28 percent of all arrests for property crimes. As these data illustrate, black youth were overrepresented in juvenile arrests (Snyder 2006:9).

Using a national Relative Rate Index matrix for 2002 national data, Snyder and Sickmund (2006:189) found evidence of racial disparity for black youth at arrest, at referral to court, at detention, waiver, and out-of-home placement. These data suggest that when there is disparity at the arrest stage, it actually increases as the youth progress through the system. For example, black youth accounted for 28 percent of the arrests in 2002, but 33 percent of the out-of-home placements that year (Snyder and Sickmund 2006:189). When the juveniles are referred for violent offenses, the disparity is even more pronounced. In 2002, black youth comprised 16 percent of the total juvenile population; but accounted for 37 percent of the violent crime referrals and 41 percent of the cases waived to adult court (Kempf-Leonard 2007:73).

Despite this overrepresentation, the disparity that has historically characterized black-to-white arrests for violent crimes has actually declined. In comparing 1980 to 2004, Snyder found that the violent crime arrest rate for blacks was 6.3 times the white rate in 1980. By contrast, in 2004, the black arrest rate for violent crimes was 4.1 times the white rate (Snyder 2006:9). Although the arrest rates for black and white juveniles experienced similar increases between 1980 and 2004, the robbery arrest rates declined 46 percent for white juveniles and 62 percent for black juveniles during the same period. The decline in robbery arrest rates helps explain the decrease in disparity between black-to-white arrests (Snyder 2006:9).

As these data suggest, and as Feld (1999a) concluded, get-tough attitudes and politicized policies have created not only a more punitive juvenile justice system but also one that disproportionately targets black youth. Similarly, a study of school disciplinary practices also found that black students are disproportionately expelled or suspended under "zero tolerance" policies. For example, in Chicago, suspensions in elementary schools increased from 8,870 to 20,312 between 1994 and 2003. According to Kelleher (2004), black youth constituted 84 percent of the suspensions in elementary schools despite the fact that their overall representation in the school system declined from 52 percent to 50 percent.

Expulsion from school is another area where black youth are adversely affected. Using data from the Illinois State Board of Education, Finkel (2004) reported that the number of youth expelled from the Chicago public schools increased from 172 in 1997 to 712 in 2003. Although black youth account for 50 percent of the enrollment in the Chicago public schools, black youth comprised 77 percent of the expulsions (Finkel 2004).

Focusing on these issues of race and minority overrepresentation is crucial to efforts to promote both juvenile justice and social justice. As Finley and Schindler conclude "elected officials must stop using fear and stereotypes to justify an increasingly and unnecessarily punitive juvenile justice system that disproportionately impacts minority youths and communities" (1999:14). Similarly, Kempf-Leonard in recognizing that disproportionate minority contact is both a national and a local problem, recommends that ". . . regional, state, and local communities must also work to overcome structural barriers to opportunity and equity and to understand values among subcultures that preclude success for some minority groups" (2007:84). These kinds of strategies include local policies that are designed to support equality in opportunities (Kempf-Leonard 2007).

Media reports, especially television news, of open drug dealing, drive-by shootings, inner-city gang warfare, and images of young black male gang-bangers created public panics and precipitated a series of legislative reforms that lowered age of exclusion, increased penalties for crimes committed with firearms, and sent large numbers of minority youth to prisons. Even though crime rates have been dropping for 10 years for both adults and juveniles, a lingering suspicion of youth has sustained get-tough attitudes and punitive public policies. And after a series of well-publicized school shootings, the tolerance for youthful offending has been further eroded. Reactionary, punitive crime control policies and a demonized portrayal of youth highlighted the close of the twentieth century. However, it is anticipated that a more balanced approach to juvenile offending will ultimately prevail in the next decade.

Lessons from the History of the Juvenile Court

If a fundamental principle of the juvenile court is that youth are developmentally different and therefore should be separated from adults, then this has been obscured by the tyranny of a small number of young violent offenders. The slogan "adult crime-adult time" and the accompanying legislation that automatically waives 14- and 15-year olds into adult courts and institutions reflect reactionary, emotional, and bankrupt responses to youth. This, however, is consistent with Bernard's thesis that juvenile justice cycles between "get-tough" and do-nothing policies (1992). In contrast to comparatively liberal and lenient policies in the 1960s and 1970s, the juvenile crime problem of the 1980s and 1990s was met with hardened attitudes and tough punishments. By limiting the possibility of leniency, Bernard believes that (1992:155)

> justice officials eventually will reach the point when they have only harsh punishments available for responding to delinquents. They then will be forced to choose between applying those harsh punishments and doing nothing at all.

Bernard predicts that extreme harsh punishments will function "to reintroduce leniency in the responses to juvenile offenders" (p. 155). If his analysis about the softening–hardening–softening cycles is accurate, then a challenge for juvenile justice is to find "balance" in the response to youth. This will be discussed in the Section "Emergent Themes and Trends in Juvenile Justice."

In response to the challenge of defining the juvenile court for the twenty-first century, five encouraging developments suggest optimism in assessing future directions for juvenile justice:

1. Crime is decreasing and the trend is continuing.
2. As a result, issues other than crime are receiving public and political attention.
3. There is increasing evidence of effective prevention programs and intervention strategies.
4. There is public support for prevention and treatment programs.
5. Alternative models of juvenile justice have been developed.

This section briefly reviews these developments and examines some strategies, initiatives, and directions for the future of the juvenile justice system.

EMERGENT THEMES AND TRENDS IN JUVENILE JUSTICE

Good News: Juvenile Crime Continues to Decline

The good news about juveniles is that the arrest rate for juvenile offending continues to decrease. The incidence of arrests for youth under the age of 18 in 2005 was 3.1 percent less than 2004, and considerably less than 1996 (*Uniform Crime Reports* 2006). As reported by Puzzanchera et al. (2006), the rate of juvenile arrests for violent crimes dropped from 330 per 100,000 youth (ages 10–17) in 1999 to 271 per 100,000 youth in 2004, an 18 percent decrease.

Regarding juvenile crime, Snyder determined that juvenile arrests for violent crime (murder, forcible rape, robbery, and aggravated assault) were the lowest since 1987 and represent "about one-third of 1% of all juveniles ages 10–17 living in the U. S." (2005:4). For murder arrests, the long-term decrease is dramatic. In 1996, there were 1,388 youth under the age of 18 arrested for murder in the United States. By contrast, 10 years later in 2005, there were 739 youth under the age of 18 arrested for murder. These data illustrate that there was a 47 percent drop in arrests in the 10-year period (*Uniform Crime Reports* 2006). This precipitous decline in arrests for violent offending is not likely to continue for the next 10 years. In fact, the arrest of youth under the age of 18 for murder in 2005 represented almost a 20 percent increase over the previous year (*Uniform Crime Report* 2006). However, the overall data suggest that the media representation of youthful offenders as increasingly violent is exaggerated and not substantiated by the Federal Bureau of Investigation reports.

In his critical analysis of juvenile crime trends using both Uniform Crime Reports (UCR) and National Crime Victimization Survey (NCVS) data, Bernard concluded that with the exception of increased juvenile arrests for homicide between 1984 and 1993 ("linked to guns"), essentially there has not been a juvenile crime wave in the United States (1999:353). "In fact, nearly 9 out of every 10 counties nationwide did not have a juvenile murderer and 1 out of every 4 juvenile murderers were located in eight counties" (Forum on Child and Family Statistics 1999:1).

These data disspell concerns about a coming generation of "superpredators," and raise questions about the reactionary, counterproductive "reforms" that focus on waiver and punishment, and transformation of the juvenile court (The Sentencing Project 1999). However, as juvenile crime continues a downward trend, intense media coverage of school shootings has contributed to misperceptions and new fears about school dangerousness and new reactionary policies against youth. In the aftermath of the April, 1999, school shootings and 15 deaths at Columbine High School in Littleton, Colorado, and the school shootings in Santee, California in 2001, students faced increased zero-tolerance policies and increased security measures.

Based on these media reports, it is understandable why the public believes that school violence is escalating. This information about school shootings and crime trends presents conflicting images. School shootings like those which were widely publicized in the 1997–1998 academic year continue to garner headlines and to create fear that supports reactive policies. Although the *Indicators of School Crime and Safety* reports that 21 homicides occurred in schools in 2004–2005 compared to 19 in 2003–2004, the trend in school violence has continued to decline (Dinkes et al. 2006).

Safer and more secure schools and a decline in crime present an opportunity to rationally assess the performance of juvenile justice and to consider prevention and intervention strategies, especially in the context of schools, which are effective in reducing delinquency. In addition, since crime is down, other issues are being recognized as national priorities.

Politics, Public Opinion, and National Issues

Although it is too soon to predict all the major issues of the 2008 presidential campaign, issues like the war in Iraq, international conflict with Iran and North Korea, the environment, and the economy appear most likely to continue to be the focus of public attention and political rhetoric. While posturing on crime is integral to presidential politics, the prevailing get-tough ideology has essentially eliminated serious debate on crime policy and centered political platforms on punishment. The result has been a distortion of rational policies and an excessive reliance on punishment versus prevention (Benekos and Merlo 2006; Merlo and Benekos 2000).

However, rather than focusing on punitive reactions to youth crime as in the past, substantive policies addressing these issues have the potential to ameliorate conditions that contribute to crime and delinquency. Essentially, this is about the quality of life (poverty, family, schools) and improving conditions for children, and evidence suggests that these efforts can be effective as delinquency "prevention" strategies (Greenwood 1998, 1999). With attention on these issues, policy debates are more likely to shift away from punitive, retributive juvenile justice legislation that emphasizes statutory waiver and instead begin to focus on assessing strategies that can reduce risks of delinquency and enhance protective factors.

PREVENTION AND EARLY INTERVENTION

As discussed above, the receding "crime wave" offers a respite from a "crisis management" mode of reacting to juvenile crime and creates an opportunity to consider strategies that prevent delinquency, and especially youth violence. Coincidentally, there is a growing literature that presents empirical evidence of the effectiveness of such strategies (Greenwood 1998, 1999; Kumpfer and Alvarado 1998; Ohlin 1998; Sherman et al. 1997; Grossman and Garry 1997; Kracke 1996). Greenwood reports that not only is the tide slowly beginning to turn but also policy makers are "beginning to recognize that wise investments in early prevention are not only effective ways of reducing crime, but reduce the need for future prison cells as well" (1998:137).

As policy makers seek information on promising strategies, reports such as those provided by the National Institute on Drug Abuse (NIDA) have identified several "prevention principles" for drug abuse that generally apply to developing and supporting delinquency prevention programs (1997). The principles include family-focused efforts; media campaigns; community programs; skill development (e.g., peer relationships, assertiveness, communications); age-specific interventions; programs that enhance "protective factors" and reduce known "risk factors"; and collaborative, comprehensive partnerships.

Prevention and early intervention strategies that incorporate these principles can lead to some of the following outcomes (Greenwood 1999): improved parent–child relationships; increased emotional and/or cognitive development for children; improved educational outcomes; and decreased criminal activity. Evidence that these types of strategies and programs can reduce crime and delinquency, and do so with cost savings, provides important support for initiatives to counter or at least contain the "waiver" mania that continues to transform juvenile justice (Feld 1999a,b, 1993; Schiraldi and Ziedenberg 1999). With arguable evidence that legislative exclusion and prosecutorial discretion have not been effective strategies in reducing crime—and most likely may have detrimental consequences for youth and society (Schiraldi and Ziedenberg 1999), the next era of juvenile justice may be better served by focusing on more cost-effective, primary prevention strategies.

Public Support for Prevention

While fear of crime remains a salient public concern, successive surveys indicate that "a clear majority" of citizens still favor "governmental efforts designed to intervene with families and children" (Cullen et al. 1998:197). In their study on public attitudes, Cullen et al. found citizen support for early intervention with youth, and they concluded that "policies that seem harsh toward at-risk children are inconsistent with the public mood" (p. 198). Perhaps even more compelling is the analysis of these data by Moon, Cullen, and Wright, which found that " . . . 80% to more than 90% of the sample favored programs to support at-risk youths, even if it meant raising taxes. This included programs such as preschool interventions, family interventions, drug education and school-based interventions"(2003:42).

In more recent research, Applegate and Davis (2006) found some evidence among Florida respondents of a softening in public attitudes toward sentencing of juvenile offenders. Similarly, Nagin et al. (2006) surveyed 1,500 randomly selected adults in Pennsylvania. Specifically, the researchers were interested in knowing respondents' opinions to various polices designed to address youth crime that included their willingness to pay for rehabilitation versus incarceration strategies. Their findings indicate that the respondents were more willing to pay for rehabilitation than for extended periods of incarceration for youthful offenders (Nagin et al. 2006:642).

In assessing public attitudes toward prosecutorial waiver, Schiraldi and Soler (1998) found that almost twice as many respondents were "strongly opposed" to this practice compared to those who "strongly supported" it (29 percent:16 percent). Just as there is evidence that supports the effectiveness of intervention strategies, there is evidence that get-tough strategies are an "over-reaction" that are not effective. Butts and Harrell (1998a) suggest that looking to the adult criminal justice system for solutions to juvenile crime is counterproductive: the "one-size-fits-all" approach "simply isn't fair" and leads to abuses. In addition, Schiraldi and Ziedenberg (1999) report on the risks youth face in adult institutions and the doubtful effectiveness of waiver on reducing recidivism.

With evidence of public support, as well as support from some policy makers who are receptive to more progressive, cost-effective responses to crime and delinquency, this is a crucial juncture in determining the future of juvenile justice.

Future Models for Juvenile Justice

Based on his critical and provocative analysis of the history of juvenile justice, Feld concluded that it is time to abolish the juvenile court and treat youthful offenders as adults (1993). Essentially, Feld argued that the intent of the juvenile court—to seek the best interests of children through an informal process guided by the doctrine of *parens patriae*—has failed. He identified three reforms that have transformed the juvenile court from an informal, child-centered, welfare-based court into a more formal, rational-legal, and retributive process that parallels the adult criminal justice system. The consequences of these reforms—jurisdictional, jurisprudential, and procedural—are the convergence of juvenile and criminal courts and a juvenile court in which youth receive the "worst of both worlds": incomplete due process protections and ineffective care and treatment.

While dismissing a reaffirmation of the juvenile court, Feld poses two options: Maintain the present practice of parallel but separate courts or abolish the juvenile court and provide due process and punishment to all offenders, with a "youth discount" for age-diminished culpability. Butts and Harrell, however, maintain that this is a "simplistic substitution" of "treating youth as miniature adults" (1998a:2). While many states are lowering the age that youth can be tried as adults (McLaughlin 1999; Merlo, Benekos, and Cook 1997), the performance of the criminal justice system also leaves much to be desired and does not instill optimism for this type of legislative reaction (Schiraldi and Soler 1998).

The confluence of economic prosperity, decreasing crime rates, concern about the quality of schools and education, and empirical evidence of effective intervention strategies suggest that the "cyclic nature of juvenile justice" (Bernard 1992, 1999) is on the edge of an emerging era. Some of the effective strategies in this emerging model are reviewed below.

PROMISING STRATEGIES FOR YOUTH INTERVENTION

Specialty Courts

As an encouraging effort to preserve and strengthen the juvenile court, one alternative to the abolitionist perspective favored by Feld (1993) is the implementation of specialty courts designed to address specific problems and criminogenic factors related to youthful offending (Butts and Harrell 1998b). These courts target offenders who have unique needs that can best be addressed by the agencies and organizations that have staff and treatment programs to serve the identified population.

For example, **teen courts**, which are also referred to as *youth courts* and *peer courts*, have become increasingly popular in juvenile justice. In 1995, 25 states had established teen courts (Godwin 1996:1) and by 2000, there were over 800 teen courts in the United States (NYCC: National Youth Court Center cited in Butts, Buck, and Coggeshall

2002:1). By 2006, the number of teen courts in operation was 1,128 (Heward 2006). Youthful offenders between the ages of 14 and 16, arrested for the first time, and involved in shoplifting, disorderly conduct, and minor vandalism, are the most likely candidates for teen courts (Butts, Buck and Coggeshall 2002).

Most teen courts require the youth to admit to the charges brought against them in order to be eligible for a teen court disposition (Butts, Hoffman, and Buck 1999:1). Youth and their families volunteer to go to the teen court as an alternative to the formal juvenile court. In choosing to go to teen court, youth are likely to face tougher sanctions and more involvement with their peers than traditional juvenile court. In their research, Butts and Buck found that the most frequently used sanction was community service followed by the requirement that the youth write the victim a formal letter of apology (Butts and Buck 2000:5).

There is plenty of anecdotal evidence that teen courts are desirable, but it was not until 2000 that a large-scale evaluation was conducted. The Urban Institute used a quasi-experimental design and studied teen courts in four states, Alaska, Arizona, Maryland, and Missouri (Butts, Buck, and Coggeshall 2002). Their findings indicate a lower recidivism rate for youth processed through teen courts versus traditional juvenile court, although it was only statistically significant in two of the four states. In addition, more than 90 percent of the parents of youth who participated in teen courts indicated that they were happy to have the opportunity to participate in teen court instead of the traditional juvenile court (Butts, Buck, and Coggeshall 2002:37). As a result of these encouraging findings, teen courts are perceived as an appropriate, less costly response to youthful nonviolent offending.

Although **drug courts** are more widely utilized in the adult system (over 1,264 in 2004), there were approximately 357 such courts operating for juveniles in the United States in 2004, up from 140 in 2000 (Huddleston et al. 2005:3; Cooper 2001:1). Typically, the courts require offenders to participate in drug treatment, mental health, counseling, and education programs while receiving strict monitoring. The services offered are intended to reduce the youth's involvement in delinquent activity and drug use (Cooper 2001:1, 13).

In their review of the drug court initiatives, Inciardi, McBride, and Rivers (1996:88) contend that these courts offer great promise, not only as a relevant approach for dealing with the drug offender, but also as an incentive to make system improvements that are necessary in order to develop and implement effective drug court programs (Merlo and Benekos 2000:154). In their study of juvenile offenders and eligibility for drug court, Roberts and Benekos found that a large majority of youth arrested for drug or alcohol-related offenses (77 percent) were eligible for the intensive supervision, comprehensive treatment, and incentives offered by drug court (1999). They concluded that "juvenile drug courts seem to be an encouraging option for providing treatment while still ensuring accountability" (p. 6). Based on their evaluation of the Orange County (Florida) Juvenile Substance Abuse Treatment Court, Applegate and Santana also concluded that "the drug court model shows promise for youthful drug offenders" (2000:297).

Based on the success of the drug courts, **gun courts** operate with a similar orientation. These courts target first-time, nonviolent offenders and require parental education

(Office of Juvenile Justice and Delinquency Prevention 1999:153). Programs require a firearms education course and classroom presentations by experts, victims and/or their survivors who have been affected by firearm violence, and also provide social services for youth and their families (Office of Juvenile Justice and Delinquency Prevention 1999:153).

The gun court program in Birmingham, Alabama, which was established in 1995, is an intense program with strict supervision guidelines and requires parental involvement in a seven-week workshop. Youth who admit their involvement in a gun violation are sent to a boot camp program for short-term incarceration and then placed on maximum supervision probation for 30 days to six months (Office of Juvenile Justice and Delinquency Prevention 1999:161). In addition, while on probation, youth are required to complete the Alabama Substance Abuse Program. Data indicate that youth who complete gun court had a lower recidivism rate than pre-gun court youth and were less likely to return to the juvenile court on offenses related to gun charges (Office of Juvenile Justice and Delinquency Prevention 1999:162).

This research suggests that youth who complete the program tend to have somewhat lower rates of new charges compared to youth who do not complete the program. The new charges are more likely to be status offenses or misdemeanors (88 percent) rather than felonies (12 percent). By contrast, the majority of youth who did not complete the program tended to be referred for felonies (65 percent) rather than misdemeanors (35 percent) (Office of Juvenile Justice and Delinquency Prevention 1999:164).

These specialized courts—teen, drug, and gun—illustrate alternative approaches that can be used to work with youth who are involved in property offenses, drug offenses, and weapon violations. By targeting specific offenders and providing intensive treatment and certain sanctions, there is an opportunity to conduct research and determine which strategies are most effective and which strategies need to be reexamined and perhaps discarded. Such efforts are important in preventing future offending and expanding or revising program initiatives.

In addition to specialty courts, there are a number of interventions that target at-risk youth to provide them with a comprehensive array of programs and services. The most promising strategies to prevent youth from engaging in delinquency or to deter youth who have already been involved in some law violating behavior are collaborative efforts that include the courts, law enforcement, family, school, and the community. Rather than simply focusing on the youth, these programs involve cooperation among agencies and organizations and they can begin at various stages in the child's development.

SHIELD Program

Early intervention efforts are especially appealing because they have the potential to prevent youth from engaging in predelinquent or delinquent activities and thus preclude contact with the juvenile justice system. A promising policy direction for responding to juveniles is the important role that police have in prevention, intervention, and suppression of youth crime. As Lawrence (2007:204) described, police are not only the most "visible" officials in responding to youth, they also have strategic importance in initiating intervention. In this context, police roles include both child protection and delinquency prevention, and suggest the salience of police service in complementing juvenile justice policy.

A recognized example of proactive policing with youth is the SHIELD Program that was developed in 1996 by the Westminster Police Department in Orange County, California (Wyrick 2000a). The objective of this program is "to identify at-risk youth" and refer them to appropriate community programs and resources (Wyrick 2000a:1). As police respond to routine calls (e.g., domestic violence), they encounter youth in home situations that expose them to negative influences of crime, drugs, and violence. Officers use these contacts to identify potential SHIELD youth who are then referred to the SHIELD Resource Officer (SRO) who conducts a risk assessment and determines whether referral is indicated and which agencies or resources are suitable. The case management aspect of SHIELD ensures follow through and reassessment of the referral. In critiquing this police initiative, Wyrick concluded (2000a:6):

> The critical supporting factor for the SHIELD program is not funding—it is the commitment and support of law enforcement administrators and personnel who are dedicated to preventing delinquency.

In developing delinquency prevention efforts, schools are also an arena where police presence and roles have "changed and become more prevalent in recent years" (Lawrence 2007:207).

Project CRAFT

Another type of collaborative effort is the vocational training program sponsored by the Home Builders Institute. Project CRAFT (Community Restitution and Apprenticeship Focused Training Program) began in 1994 (Hamilton and McKinney 1999:1) and has been implemented in North Dakota, Tennessee, Maryland, Florida, and Texas. Utilizing a holistic approach that incorporates career training; community service activities; support services such as social skills training, employability training, and case management, this program demonstrates how private business (the construction industry) can collaborate with the juvenile justice system to assist youth (Hamilton and McKinney 1999:1).

In addition to job training, Project CRAFT is a comprehensive approach to high-risk youth. In partnership with schools, court staff, drug and alcohol counselors and treatment programs, private organizations, mentors, local governments, and juvenile court judges, Project CRAFT demonstrates the importance of addressing youth difficulties through a cooperative and inclusive strategy. An independent evaluation of Project CRAFT illustrates that over a four-year period, graduates of the program had a very high job placement in the home building industry; the recidivism rate for youth who were involved in the program at three of the sites was 26 percent, which was significantly lower than the national average; and the program has been successful in continuing to work with youthful offenders long after they have been placed in jobs, particularly those youth who were in residential facilities (Hamilton and McKinney 1999:2).

Identifying Risk Factors

Project CRAFT successfully demonstrates that agencies and organizations can collaboratively intervene in the lives of troubled youth. However, in order to prevent youth from engaging in delinquent conduct, it is helpful to identify risk factors (Catalano, Loeber, and McKinney 1999:1). The Office of Juvenile Justice and Delinquency Prevention convened 22 researchers for the Study Group on Serious and Violent Juvenile Offenders. They concluded that there are a number of interventions that have demonstrated positive effects in reducing risk and enhancing protection against adolescent antisocial behaviors. Family, school, and community interventions are critical in preventing children from becoming violent (Catalano, Loeber, and McKinney 1999:1).

One of the ten effective intervention programs that the Study Group identified is behavioral monitoring. This program is designed to provide disruptive, low-achieving seventh grade students with close supervision and rewards for positive behavior. For two years, intervention staff and teachers met regularly to assess student tardiness, class preparedness, performance, and behavior (Catalano, Loeber, and McKinney 1999:2). In addition, staff members worked with students in small group sessions and reviewed their school behavior. Staff members continued meeting with teachers and held small review sessions for students every two weeks for one year after the interventions (Catalano, Loeber, and McKinney 1999:2).

The results indicate that the comprehensive intervention strategy was successful. Students who were monitored had significantly higher grades, better attendance, and engaged in far fewer problem behaviors at school than students in a comparison group that received no interventions (Bry and George cited in Catalano, Loeber, and McKinney 1999:2). Even after five years, youth who had received the intervention were far less likely to have a juvenile court record than youth who were not in the program (Bry and George cited in Catalano, Loeber, and McKinney 1999:2).

The Study Group also identified comprehensive community intervention programs. Of particular interest were the collaborative community intervention efforts that were designed to deter youth smoking and alcohol use in Minnesota (Catalano, Loeber, and McKinney 1999:6). Project Northland, an alcohol prevention program, was initiated when children were in the sixth grade and demonstrates another effective collaborative effort. The project included a special curriculum in the school and community-wide task force activities that involved parents and peer leadership. After three years, children who completed the program had lower scores on a tendency-to-use-alcohol scale and showed considerably lower rates of alcohol use. The participants were also less at risk for drug use (Catalano, Loeber, and McKinney 1999:6).

Parenting Programs

Parenting programs are also an integral component of a comprehensive prevention strategy. One of the more successful interventions focuses on parenting skills that identifies youth who are at risk, reduces their risk factors, and attempts to prevent them from becoming involved in delinquent activities by augmenting protective factors. Preparing for the Drug Free Years began in 1987 and is designed for adult learners (i.e., parents) who have children in grades 4 through 7 (Haggertyet al. 1999). The goal of the program is ". . . to empower parents of children ages 8 to 14 to reduce the risks that their children will abuse drugs or alcohol or develop other common adolescent problems" (Haggerty et al. 1999:1).

Preparing for the Drug Free Years is delivered through video presentation and requires a minimum of 10 hours. The program is typically offered by two trained workshop leaders from the community and they are encouraged to increase the number of hours and topic areas as appropriate. There have been over 120,000 families in 30 states who have participated in the program (Haggerty et al. 1999:1,6).

Preliminary evaluations indicate that the program is effective in teaching important parenting concepts to a wide audience. Parents appear to adopt the approaches including family meetings, which are an important part of the curriculum. The utilization of instructors who are community leaders also appears to be effective. In addition, when parents volunteer to participate, they generally attend most of the sessions. Although more evaluation is needed, the Preparing for the Drug Free Years Program is easily disseminated, inclusive, and a successful strategy for parents of children who may be at risk for becoming delinquent (Haggerty et al. 1999:9).

Multisystemic Therapy

Another effective strategy for family preservation that targets youth who are at risk for out of home placement is Multisystemic Therapy (MST). This evidence-based therapeutic intervention focuses on providing parents or primary caregivers with skills to deal with antisocial adolescent behaviors and antecedents of juvenile offending (Swenson 2006:para. 1). The strategy is predicated on the social ecological model and behavioral parent training that includes family systems theories and cognitive behavior therapies (Swenson 2006:para. 4).

The program targets both chronic, violent offenders and their families; and services are provided in the home and include comprehensive approaches that recognize the "multiple determinants of serious antisocial behavior" (Multisystemic Therapy Services 1998:para. 1). MST is described as a "very analytical yet pragmatic and task-oriented treatment," which is time limited (1–5 months) and tailored to meet family dynamics and needs. The treatment plans are "family driven rather than therapist driven" and empower parents to address the problems, to access community resources, and to help youth cope with teen risk factors (Multisystemic Therapy Services 1998:para. 5).

Swenson emphasizes that this Blueprints Model Program has not only been demonstrated to reduce long-term rearrest rates by 25–70 percent but it is also "the most cost-effective of a wide range of intervention programs aimed at serious juvenile offenders" (2006:para. 7). Evaluations find a 47–64 percent reduction in out-of-home placements and "extensive improvements in family functioning" (Swenson 2006:para. 6). (For more information on the Blueprints Model Programs, see www.colorado.edu/cspv).

Multisystemic Therapy is one of three Blueprints programs that has been endorsed and funded in Pennsylvania as being an effective strategy for helping youth in the juvenile justice system (Aryna et al. 2005). (The other two programs are Multidimensional Treatment Foster Care and Functional Family Therapy.) MST is endorsed because it is a risk-focused program that uses effective and developmentally appropriate therapies to keep youth with their families and in their communities. It is also an effective violence prevention program (Aryna et al. 2005:33).

Low-Birth Weight Babies

Recent research suggests the importance of intervention efforts before or shortly after birth. In their longitudinal analysis of low birth weight and its relationship to early onset offending of minority youth in Philadelphia, Tibbetts and Piquero (1999) found that individuals with low birth weight and who were from a low socioeconomic status were more likely to have an early onset of offending (p. 865). Low birth weight is often associated with a number of factors including lack of prenatal care for pregnant women, drugs and/or alcohol use, smoking cigarettes during pregnancy, poor diet, low socioeconomic status, and low educational attainment level (Tibbetts and Piquero 1999:848). The good news is that low birth weight can be prevented through early intervention programs; and these strategies reduce the complications associated with low birth weight (Tibbetts and Piquero 1999:868–869). Effective intervention policies that include good quality prenatal care and Nurse Home Visitation programs can be developed in communities.

Although there are many other successful programs that target youthful offenders, the programs described above provide evidence that successful strategies can be implemented and refined to deliver services to at-risk youth and their families. These programs are more cost-effective and more humane than punishment and long-term incarceration for juvenile offenders. Rather than developing reactive programs, juvenile justice is in an unprecedented position. With sufficient resources, it will be able to expand programs with demonstrable success (Merlo 2000).

ISSUES FOR THE FUTURE

In the early decades of the twenty-first century, the juvenile justice system will devote increasing attention to at least five issues: disproportionate minority contact (DMC), gangs, comparative juvenile justice, juveniles incarcerated in adult institutions, and juveniles sentenced to life without parole (JLWOP). In addition, rather than simply retaining or abolishing the tenets of the original juvenile court, there will be a greater emphasis on balancing and integrating three alternative models for handling juvenile offenders.

Disproportionate Minority Contact

In spite of attention on racial profiling, DMC in the juvenile justice system will persist and strategies to reduce the over-representation of minorities will need to focus on broader social issues. As discussed earlier, minority youth are over-represented in the juvenile justice system in every stage of the process. Snyder and Sickmund contend, however, that there is evidence "that disparity is most pronounced at the beginning stages" of juvenile justice (1999:193). It is arrest, detention, and court intake where the greatest disparity in outcomes occurs, and it is these actions that have profound consequences for youth (Bilchik 1999b:3).

Although a study of seventeen states utilizing the National Incident-Based Reporting System (NIBRS) found no direct evidence that an offender's race affected the police decision to take a youth into custody for a violent offense, other research suggests that minority youth are processed through the system differently than are white youth (Pope and Snyder 2003).

While the effects of race vary at different decision points, as reported by Hsia, Bridges, and McHale (2004:20) "at the detention decision point, minority youth were more likely to be detained than white youth, even after differences between" offenses and youth backgrounds were controlled. They noted the significance of this finding and concluded that "the mere fact of being detained prior to adjudication seemed to affect subsequent stages of case processing" (2004:20).

In a 2007 report, the National Council on Crime and Delinquency (NCCD) cautioned that not only is DMC a problem in the juvenile justice system, "it is also about youth of color being too often subjected to adult court processing and incarceration in adult jail and prison with all of its collateral consequences and obstacles to reentry" (2007:5). In their study using 1997 data, Poe-Yamagata and Jones (2000) found that three of four youth under the age of 18 who were admitted to adult prisons were minority youth. Similarly, in 2002, three of four youth admitted to adult prisons were minority and 58 percent were black (National Council on Crime and Delinquency 2007:3).

Although these findings pertain to confinement in juvenile facilities, Bilchik contends that "disproportionate minority confinement sends a signal that we need to take a closer look at how our society treats minority children, not just those who become offenders" (1999b:1). Even as Feld (1993, 1999b) has advocated for the abolition of the juvenile court, he has recognized the importance of "providing a hopeful future for all young people" which includes "the pursuit of racial and social justice" and "public policies that reduce and reverse the proliferation of guns among the youth population" (1999a:394).

In response to the widespread and cumulative effects of disproportionate minority confinement, the 2002 reauthorization of the Juvenile Justice and Delinquency Prevention Act of 1974 required states to go beyond the problem of disproportionate confinement by targeting disproportionate representation of minority youth at all decision points in the juvenile justice system (Hsia, Bridges, and McHale 2004). To address this mandate, Hsia, Bridges, and McHale acknowledge that additional efforts are needed to develop alternatives to detention and incarceration, to reduce racial stereotyping and cultural insensitivity, and to establish culturally and linguistically appropriate services (2004:12). Feld's analysis of the social structural changes that have contributed to "the disproportionate overrepresentation of minority youth in the juvenile justice system" also underscores the importance of focusing policy on reducing poverty, urban disorder, minority alienation, and violence (1999a:394).

Gangs

In the closing decades of the twentieth century, sensationalized media attention to gangs and gang violence exacerbated public concern about youth crime. Esbensen (2000) noted that the "superpredator" model that was predicted by DiIulio and Fox helped foster the belief that gang members were the forerunners of a coming wave of a new breed of young criminals. Even though their projections regarding violent youth have not been realized, attention has focused on gang crimes as well as female involvement in gangs. While some evidence suggests that females may comprise more than one-third of gang members (Miller and Brunson 2000:422; Esbensen and Winfree 1998), Snyder and Sickmund observe that the number of girls and nonminority males who view themselves as gang members is much greater than the official law enforcement records indicate (1999:78).

Researchers have recognized that girl gang members are not identical to their male counterparts. Miller (2000) studied female gangs in Columbus, Ohio and St. Louis, Missouri. Female gang members engage in violence but are not likely to commit a drive-by shooting. By contrast, when they engage in assault, it is usually fighting with other females who are members of rival gangs.

In their study of 58 male and female gang members (who ranged in age from 12 to 20) in St. Louis, Missouri, in 1997 and 1998, Miller and Brunson (2000) found that when describing their risk of victimization, young girls and young boys perceived different risks. While males verbalized fear of being "lethally victimized" (i.e., killed) by a rival gang, female gang members perceived their greatest risk was being "jumped and beaten up" (2000:442). Miller and Brunson contend that it is important to study variations in gangs to fully understand the risks faced by females. Although many of the gangs' activities are mundane, some of them are quite dangerous (2000:443).

Law enforcement agencies have reported fluctuations in gang problems (Egley and Ritz 2006). For example, in 2002–2004, rural counties experienced a slight decrease in the average percent of law enforcement agencies reporting gang problems (from 13 percent in 1999–2001 to 12 percent in 2002–2004). Smaller cities (2,500–49,999 population) and larger cities (more than 50,000 population), however, experienced increases: from 26 percent to 28 percent of law enforcement agencies reporting gang problems in smaller cities and 78 percent to 80 percent of the agencies reporting problems in larger cities (Egley and Ritz 2006). Incidents of juvenile gang killings increased from 580 in 1999 to 819 in 2003 (National Criminal Justice Reference Service 2007). In addition, there was a 53 percent increase in the number of "gangland killings" from 2002 (75) to 2003 (115) (National Criminal Justice Reference Service 2007).

Gang activity is dependent on the location and size of the community. For example, Chicago and Los Angeles report the highest rates of gang homicide in the late 1990s, but both cities had decreases in gang homicide from 1996 to 1998 (Curry, Maxson, and Howell 2001:1–2). In the 2002 Youth Gang Survey, cities with larger populations (250,000 or more) were more likely to report the presence of gang activity (100 percent) versus cities with smaller populations (2,500–24,999) where only 20 percent reported gang activity (Egley and Major 2003:1). In addition, Egley and Major report that over 60 percent of the gang-problem jurisdictions participating in the survey noted that gang members returning to the community after having been incarcerated were contributing to the gang problems, primarily violent crime and drug trafficking by local gangs (2003:1).

Although gang migration was thought to be responsible for the increasing presence of gangs in various parts of the United States, there is no evidence to substantiate the claim. On the contrary, most gang members are residents of the urban, suburban, or rural area where their gangs exist (Snyder and Sickmund 1999:78). For those offenders who are returning to their home communities after having been incarcerated, Egley and Major found that 34 percent of these communities reported the lack of programs designed to assist offenders reentering the community after incarceration (2003:1).

From available research, it appears that delinquent activity, which typically precedes gang involvement, is enhanced through gang membership (Esbensen 2000:6; Snyder and Sickmund 1999). This suggests that prevention efforts have to target at-risk youth as well as youth who have already joined gangs (Esbensen 2000:6; Wyrick 2000b:2). In an effort to control gangs and gang violence, in 2006 the U.S. Attorney General's office announced a Comprehensive AntiGang Initiative that was designed to provide support to law enforcement (U.S. Department of Justice 2007). The initiative included both prevention programs and "robust" enforcement policies. The first six sites targeted for support were Los Angeles, CA; Tampa, FL; Cleveland, OH; Dallas/Ft. Worth, TX; Milwaukee, WI; and the 222 Corridor-Easton to Lancaster, PA (2007:para 3). In 2007, Oklahoma City, OK, Indianapolis, IN, Raleigh-Durham, NC, and Rochester, NY were also granted funding to combat gang violence (2000:para.1). The grants include S1 million per community for prevention and $1 million per community to support law enforcement programs.

In particular, some important steps to discourage gangs and gang membership include (1) early identification of at-risk youth in rural as well as urban areas; (2) implementation of comprehensive community based programs; (3) programs to reduce truancy and keep youth in school; (4) employment opportunities for youth; (5) increased efforts to remove guns from the street; and (6) community participation in a collaborative strategy designed to deter youth from engaging in delinquent behavior (Howell and Decker 1999:9).

Comparative Juvenile Justice

As the United States grapples with juvenile crime, there has been an increasing emphasis on studying policies in other countries. In examining juvenile justice systems in four countries, Canada, Japan, Russia, and Sweden, there is some evidence of change in attitudes toward youthful offenders. For example, more Swedish youth are being referred to the courts in recent years even though diversion from the court and the use of social welfare services still predominates (National Council for Crime Prevention 2000: 43–45).

Although it is difficult to obtain comparable statistics on youth from all the countries, and the number of youth in the population varies considerably among the four countries compared to the United States, there are signs of treatment and prevention initiatives in the United States and in the four countries. There is an emphasis on restorative justice and the use of victim offender mediation conferences. Some form of restorative justice is found in Canada, Sweden, and the United States. In Japan, there appears to be greater involvement of the community; volunteers patrol the streets, provide counseling to parents and youth, and work to improve the social environment (Yokoyama 1997:14–15). In Russia, more volunteer social service agencies now attempt to deal with drug offenders (Gilinsky 1998).

Other countries have also begun to re-evaluate their ideology and policies toward youth, but none of them appears to have emulated the United States in the area of incarceration of youth for long periods of time in adult correctional institutions. Although youth can be incarcerated with adults, none of these countries has legislation that makes it possible to incarcerate youth for life or for the length of time characteristic of the United States. In short, these countries have taken a more rehabilitative approach to young offenders and do not deem them to be intractable.

There is much to be gained by studying other countries juvenile justice policies. These countries can inform the debate and provide an opportunity to incorporate a more comprehensive and collaborative treatment approach. Comparative research helps to facilitate that process.

Adultification

One consequence of the get tough era of juvenile justice was statutory exclusion of youth from juvenile court. These legislative reforms removed discretion from judges and replaced individualized court proceedings with policies that attempted to standardize the transfer of youthful offenders to criminal court. In a 2007 survey of citizen views on the juvenile justice system, 92 percent of adult respondents agreed that decisions about trying youth in adult court should be made on a case-by-case basis and 72 percent believed that the decision should be made by a juvenile court judge (Krisberg and Marchionna 2007). In spite of these views and how jurisdictional transfer is decided, the transfer of youth to criminal court has implications on what happens to juvenile offenders.

As more juveniles are transferred to adult court, greater demands will be placed on adult correctional institutions and their staff. This will necessitate construction or renovation of jails, construction of new "juvenile prisons" for youthful offenders, and renovation of adult institutions to accommodate the changing demographics of the prison population. For example, Snyder and Sickmund report that in June 2004 there were 7,083 youth (under 18) confined in jails (2006:236). These youth comprised approximately 1 percent of the jail population (p. 236). By contrast, in 1998, Austin, Dedel Johnson, and Gregoriou (2000:x) reported that there were 9,100 youth who were under 18 years old incarcerated in local jails. These recent data suggest that the number of youth in jails has decreased since 2002 when 10,000 inmates under the age of 18 were confined in prisons and jails (Anderson 2003:A-9).

Using data derived from states that reported the number of youth under age 18 in state prisons, Snyder and Sickmund (2006) found that there were approximately 4,100 youth who were new court commitments in 2002 (p. 237). These commitments represented

1.1 percent of all new prison commitments; and most of these youth (79 percent) were 17 years old when they were admitted (Snyder and Sickmund 2006:238).

Prison data suggest a slowdown in the incarceration of youth in adult prisons but it has coincided with an overall decline in violent offending as demonstrated by the number of arrests for violent offenses (Snyder and Sickmund 2006:237). Rather than a halt in sentencing juveniles like adults, these data suggest that juveniles continue to be adversely affected by legislative initiatives that were implemented in the 1990s. In 1985, 18 youth for every 1,000 arrests were incarcerated in an adult prison. By 1997, there were 33 youth incarcerated for every 1,000 juveniles arrested (CNN.com 2000).

Regarding the risks faced by youth imprisoned in adult institutions, inmates in local jails who were under the age of 18 had the highest rate of suicide between 2000 and 2002; their rate was 101 for every 100,000 inmates (Mumola 2005:5). These data contradict the overall trends in jail suicide rates. Typically, it is the oldest inmates, age 55 or older, who have the highest rate of suicide. However, their rate was 58 suicides for every 100,000 jail inmates in the 2000–2002 data (Mumola 2005:5).

The situation is even worse for youth under the age of 18 incarcerated in state prisons. Although the suicide rate of state inmates ranged from 13 to 14 suicides for every 100,000 inmates for all age groups over age 18, "the suicide rate of State prisoners under 18 was 4 times higher (52 per 100,000), but this group accounted for less than 0.3% of State prisoners and had 3 suicides nationwide over 2 years" (Mumola 2005:6). In short, the suicide rate for offenders under 18 incarcerated in jail or prison is high, but the actual number of suicides is low when compared to the other age groups.

These data indicate that adultifying youth has adverse consequences. In the 2007 survey noted above, 67 percent of respondents believed that youth should not be incarcerated with adults in jails and prisons, and 69 percent "does not believe that putting youth in adult facilities is a deterrent to future crime" (Krisberg and Marchionna 2007:5).

Adolescents in adult institutions pose a formidable challenge for administrators. Not only do they face a greater risk of suicide and violent victimization, but they are also less likely to have the insight and maturity of the adult population (Ziedenberg and Schiraldi 1997). As a result, they are more likely to be victims of sexual assault and staff abuse. A youthful offender serving a life sentence with no possibility of parole may also be a particularly difficult inmate to manage.

Life Without Parole

Another issue in juvenile justice that is gaining recognition is the number of offenders sentenced to life without parole for crimes committed when they were juveniles (JLWOP). In a comprehensive study of "child offenders" sentenced to life without parole, Amnesty International and Human Rights Watch (Amnesty International and Human Rights Watch 2005) identified that 2,225 prisoners in the United States "have been sentenced to spend the rest of their lives in prison for the crimes they committed as children" (1).

On average, 98 youth under the age of 18 have been admitted to prison with a sentence of life without possibility of parole in each year from 1990 to 2003 (Hartney

TABLE 10.1   Total Number of Youth Serving Life without Parole by State

State	Youth LWOP Total	State	Youth LWOP Total
Alabama	15	Montana	1
Arizona	30	Nebraska	21
Arkansas	46	Nevada	16
California	180	New Hampshire	3
Colorado	46	New Jersey	0
Connecticut	10	North Carolina	44
Delaware	7	North Dakota	1
Federal	1	Ohio	1
Florida	273	Oklahoma	49
Georgia	8	Pennsylvania	332
Hawaii	4	Rhode Island	2
Idaho	Data missing	South Carolina	26
Illinois	103	South Dakota	9
Indiana	2	Tennessee	4
Iowa	67	Utah	0
Louisiana	317	Vermont	0
Maryland	13	Virginia	48
Massachusetts	60	Washington	23
Michigan	306	Wisconsin	16
Minnesota	2	Wyoming	6
Mississippi	17		
Missouri	116	**Nationwide**	**2225**

Source: Amnesty International/Human Rights Watch (2005). *The Rest of Their Lives: Life without Parole for Children Offenders in the United States*. New York: Human Rights Watch. p. 35.

2006:3). Data in Table 10.1 indicate that four states accounted for over half (55 percent) of the 2,225 LWOP offenders sentenced for crimes committed before they were 18 (p. 35): Pennsylvania (332); Louisiana (317); Michigan (306); and Florida (273). While the *number* of life without parole sentences imposed on "children" peaked in 1996 (50 in 1989, 152 in 1996, 54 in 2002), the *use* of life sentences without parole increased during the 1990s (Amnesty International and Human Rights Watch 2005:2):

> For example, in 1990 there were 2,234 youths convicted of murder in the United States, 2.9 percent of whom were sentenced to life without parole. Ten years later, in 2000, the number of youth murderers had dropped to 1,006, but 9.1 percent were sentenced to life without parole.

In 2003, even though 54 life without parole sentences were imposed, the rate was "three times higher today than it was fifteen years ago" (Amnesty International and Human Rights

Watch 2005:2). Using the rationale of *Roper v. Simmons* (2005) that youth are fundamentally different from adults and lack full cognitive development and therefore should not be eligible for the death penalty, the sentence of life without parole for youth has also been challenged as a violation of evolving standards of decency as well as the Eighth Amendment (Cruel and Unusual Punishment). In the case of *Commonwealth v. Phillips* (2006), the Pennsylvania Supreme Court has been asked to review a Pennsylvania Superior Court ruling that upheld the life sentence of Aaron Phillips who was sentenced for second degree murder that was committed when he was 17 years old. The appeal is based in part on the rationale that a sentence of life without parole is in effect a death sentence and therefore a violation of *Roper*.

Models of Juvenile Justice

In addition to these specific challenges, responses to youthful offenders will continue to reflect competing ideologies and politicized public policies. Rather than adhering to a strict punishment or treatment model, juvenile justice in the twenty-first century will be characterized by a multifaceted approach that will incorporate three models: Prevention, Education and Treatment (PET), Balance and Restorative Justice (BARJ), and Retribution, Adultification, and Punishment (RAP).

The PET model symbolizes the philosophical orientation of the original juvenile court. In this model, there is increasing reliance on prevention/early intervention programs to deter youth from offending. As evidenced by the recent research by Cullen et al. (1998), the public appears to be supportive of early intervention/prevention programs. Child-centered strategies that were once the mainstay of juvenile justice have been expanded to include parenting programs, prenatal care, and preschool programs, along with prevention programs for adolescents. These are comprehensive strategies such as antigang programs for adolescents, special after-school programs for at-risk youth, and counseling programs for youthful offenders.

The BARJ model that emphasizes accountability, public safety, and competency development for juveniles, has been adopted in several jurisdictions (Bazemore and Umbreit 1994, 1995). Rather than focusing solely on youth, this model incorporates community safety and protection along with holding youth accountable, compensating victims, and providing treatment. Programs like teen courts, drug courts, boot camp programs, and victim restitution/community service programs are emblematic of this perspective. With the inclusion of accountability, punishment, and public safety in the purpose clause of juvenile court statutes, it is clear that this perspective has been endorsed and supported (see Bilchik 1999a).

The third model, RAP, rejects earlier perspectives on youth and adolescence, and supports a tough, punitive approach to dealing with youthful offenders. This is the legacy of the get-tough era of the 1980s and 1990s and legislative reforms that politicized youth policies. The manifestations are evident in the number of states that lowered the age for transfer to adult court, the number of youth waived to adult court, the increased number of youth incarcerated in adult institutions (some sentenced to life without possibility of parole), and the number of states that enacted blended sentences (statutes that authorize the courts to utilize juvenile and/or adult correctional sanctions) (Bilchik 1999a:19).

This continuum of "trifurcated" approaches incorporates the themes of early intervention and prevention, accountability and public safety, and punishment and retribution.

The conceptualization more accurately reflects juvenile justice policies that embody both preventive interventions and reactive sanctions. Rather than being limited to one approach, public policies for dealing with delinquent offenders will utilize strategies that reflect these perspectives. Juvenile justice is poised to proceed in this direction. Even though "get tough" political rhetoric and adultification legislation have characterized juvenile justice in the last two decades, the juvenile justice system will continue with its mission to help youthful offenders and reduce delinquency.

CONCLUDING COMMENT

In assessing future efforts to reduce delinquency, policy makers and community leaders would be well-advised to consider strategies that focus on the antecedents of delinquent behaviors. Research has identified that child abuse, neglect, and youth victimization are robust predictors of delinquency, adolescent violence, and substance abuse as well as mental health problems (Kilpatrick, Saunders, and Smith 2003:13). Using data from the National Survey of Adolescents, Kilpatrick, Saunders, and Smith found that 1.8 million adolescents ages 12–17 had been sexually assaulted, 3.9 million had been "severely physically abused," 2.1 million had been punished by physical abuse and 8.8 million "had seen someone else being shot, stabbed, sexually assaulted, physically assaulted, or threatened with a weapon" (2003:1). They concluded (13):

> . . . victimization and its mental health correlates play a role in the development of substance use and delinquency behavior among adolescents. Policies that promote the prevention of child and adolescent victimization also would promote the prevention of youth substance use and delinquency.

In the annual *Child Maltreatment* assessment, the U.S. Department of Health and Human Services (2007) reported that in fiscal year 2005, in addition to the 1,465 children who died as a result of abuse or neglect, of the 3.3 million allegations of abuse (involving over 6 million children) that were reported, over 940,000 cases of abuse involving at least one victim were substantiated (p. 5). About 60 percent of the victims of abuse and neglect received postinvestigation services (p. 84).

The lesson is clear that preventing child abuse is not only a compelling moral imperative but also a salient strategy for reducing delinquency.

REFERENCES

ALBANESE, J. S. (1993). *Dealing with Delinquency: The Future of Juvenile Justice.* Second Edition. Chicago, IL: Nelson-Hall.

AMNESTY INTERNATIONAL/HUMAN RIGHTS WATCH (2005). *The Rest of Their Lives: Life Without Parole for Children Offenders in the United States.* New York: Human Rights Watch.

ANDERSON, C. (2003). "Prison count tops 2 million." *Pittsburgh Post-Gazette,* April 7, A-1, A-9.

APPLEGATE, B. K. and R. K. DAVIS (2006). "Public views on sentencing juvenile murderers: The impact of offender, offense, and perceived mMaturity." *Youth Violence and Juvenile Justice.* 4:55–74.

APPLEGATE, B. K. and S. SANTANA (2000). "Intervening with youthful substance abusers: A preliminary analysis of a juvenile drug court." *The Justice System Journal.* 21(3): 281–300.

ARYNA, N., E. LOTKE, L. RYAN, M. SCHINDLER, D. SHOENBERG, and M. SOLER (2005). *Keystones for Reform: Promising Juvenile Justice Policies and Practices in Pennsylvania.* San Francisco, CA: Youth Law Center.

AUSTIN, J., K. DEDEL JOHNSON, and M. GREGORIOU (2000*). Juveniles in Adult Prisons and Jails: A National Assessment.* Bureau of Justice Assistance. Washington, DC: U.S. Department of Justice.

BAZEMORE, G., and M. UMBREIT (1994). *Balanced and Restorative Justice: Program Summary.* (October). Washington, DC: U.S. Department of Justice, Office of Juvenile Justice and Delinquency Prevention.

BAZEMORE, G., and M. UMBREIT (1995). "Rethinking the sanctioning function in juvenile court: Retributive or restorative responses to youth crime.*" Crime & Delinquency.* 41 (3): 293–316.

BENEKOS, P. J. and A. V. MERLO (2006). *Crime Control, Politics, and Policy, Second Edition.* Cincinnati, OH: Matthew Bender and Company, Inc

BENEKOS, P. J. and A. V. MERLO (2000). "The Future of the Juvenile Court: Reaffirmation or Requiem?" Paper presented at the Annual Meeting of the Academy of Criminal Justice Sciences, March 21, 2000, New Orleans.

BERNARD, T. J. (1992). *The Cycles of Juvenile Justice.* New York, NY: Oxford University Press.

BERNARD, T. J. (1999). "Juvenile crime and the transformation of juvenile justice: Is there a juvenile crime wave?" *Justice Quarterly.* 16(2): 337–356.

BILCHIK, S. (1999a). *Juvenile Justice: A Century of Change.* (December) Washington, DC: U.S. Department of Justice. Office of Juvenile Justice and Delinquency Prevention.

BILCHIK, S. (1999b). *Minorities in the Juvenile Justice System.* (December) Washington, DC: U.S. Department of Justice, Office of Juvenile Justice and Delinquency Prevention.

BLUMENTHAL, R. (2007a). "Texan calls for takeover of State's juvenile schools." *New York Times,* February 28: A11.

BLUMENTHAL, R. (2007b). "Texas, addressing sexual abuse scandal, may free thousands of its jailed youths." *New York Times,* March 24: A8.

BLUMENTHAL, R. (2007c). "2 charged in Texas state school abuse case." *New York Times,* April 11, A14.

BORTNER, M. A. (1988.) *Delinquency and Justice: An Age of Crisis.* New York, NY: McGraw-Hill.

BRADSHER, K. (2000). "Boy who killed gets 7 years; Judge says law is tToo harsh." *New York Times,* January 14, A1, 21.

BRADSHER, K. (1999). "Murder trial of 13-year-old puts focus on Michigan Law." *New York Times,* October 31, A21.

BUTTS, J. A. and A. V. HARRELL (1998a). *One-Size-Fits-All Justice Simply Isn't Fair.* (December 1). Washington, DC: The Urban Institute.

BUTTS, J. A. and A. V. HARRELL (1998b). *Crime Policy Report: Delinquents or Criminals: Policy Options for Young Offenders.* Washington, DC: The Urban Institute.

BUTTS, J. A., D. HOFFMAN, and J. BUCK (1999). *Teen Courts in the United States: A Profile of Current Programs.* (October) Washington DC: U.S. Department of Justice, Office of Juvenile Justice and Delinquency Prevention.

BUTTS, J. A., and J. BUCK (2000). "Teen Courts: A Focus on Research." *Juvenile Justice Bulletin,* Washington D.C.: U.S. Department of Justice (October): 1–16.

BUTTS, J. A., J. BUCK, and M. B. COGGESHALL (2002. *The Impact of Teen Courts on Young Offenders.* Urban Institute. Justice Policy Center, Washington, D.C.: The Urban Institute.

CATALANO, R., F., ROLF LOEBER, and K. C. MCKINNEY (1999). "School and Community Interventions to Prevent Serious and Violent Offending." *Juvenile Justice Bulletin,* Washington, DC: U.S. Department of Justice, Office of Juvenile Justice and Delinquency Prevention. October:1–12.

CNN.com (2000). "Number of juveniles sent to adult prisons skyrocketing, study shows." 28 February. [Retrieved February 15, 2006, from http://archives.cnn.com/2000/US/02/37/juveniles.in.jail/]

COOPER, C. S. (2002). "Juvenile Drug Court Programs." *Juvenile Accountability Incentive Block Grants Program* (JAIBG), Office of Juvenile Justice and Delinquency Prevention. Washington, D.C. May:1–14.

CULLEN, F. T., J. P. WRIGHT, S. BROWN, M. M. MOON, M. B. BLANKENSHIP, and B. K. APPLEGATE (1998). "Public support for early intervention programs: Implications for a progressive policy agenda." *Crime and Delinquency* 44(2):187–204.

CURRY, G. D., C. L. MAXSON, and J. C. HOWELL (2001). "Youth Gang Homicides in the 1990's." *OJJDP Fact Sheet*, Office of Juvenile Justice and Delinquency Prevention. Washington, D.C.: U.S. Department of Justice (March): 1–2.

DINKES, R., E. F. CATALDI, G. KENA, and K. BAUM (2006). *Indicators of School Crime and Safety: 2006* (NCES 2007-003/NCJ 214262). U.S. Departments of Education and Justice. Washington, DC: U.S. Government Printing Office.

EGLEY, A., and A. K. MAJOR (2003). *Highlights of the 2001 National Youth Gang Survey.* Washington, DC: U.S. Department of Justice, Office of Juvenile Justice and Delinquency Prevention.

EGLEY, A., and C. E. RITZ (2006). *Highlights of the 2004 National Youth Gang Survey.* Washington, DC: U.S. Department of Justice, Office of Juvenile Justice and Delinquency Prevention.

ESBENSEN, F.-A. (2000). "Preventing Adolescent Gang Involvement." *Juvenile Justice Bulletin*, Office of Juvenile Justice and Delinquency Prevention. Washington, D.C. September:1–11.

ESBENSEN, F.-A., and L. T. WINFREE, Jr. (1998). "Race and gender differences between gang and non-gang youth: Results from a multisite survey." *Justice Quarterly* 15(3): 505–526.

FELD, B. (1999a). "The transformation of the juvenile court-Part II: Race and the 'crack down' on youth crime." *Minnesota Law Review* 84(2): 327–395.

FELD, B. (1999b). *Bad Kids: Race and the Transformation of the Juvenile Court.* New York, NY: Oxford University Press.

FELD, B. (1993). "Juvenile (In)justice and the criminal court alternative." *Crime and Delinquency* 39: 403–424.

FINKEL, ed. (2004). "700 students kicked out of CPS." *Catalyst* (December): [Retrieved April 15, 2007, from www.catalyst-chicago.org/]

FINLEY, M., and M. SCHINDLER (1999). "Punitive juvenile justice policies and the impact on minority youth." *Federal Probation* LXIII (2): 9–15.

Forum on Child and Family Statistics (1999). *Indicators of Youth Violent Crime and Victimization Show Continuing Declines.* (July 8). [www.childstats.gov]

FUJINO, K. (2002). Personal Correspondence, December 10.

GILINSKY, Y. (1998). "The penal system and other forms of social control in Russia: Problems and perspectives." In *The Baltic Region: Insights in Crime and Crime Control*, ed. K. Aromaa, pp. 197–204. Oslo, Norway: Pax Forlag.

GODWIN, T. M. (1996). "A Guide for Implementing Teen Court Programs". Office of Juvenile Justice and Delinquency Prevention Fact Sheet #45. Office of Juvenile Justice and Delinquency Prevention, Office of Justice Programs, Washington, D.C.: (August):1–2.

GREENWOOD, P. (1999). Costs and Benefits of Early Childhood Intervention. Office of Juvenile Justice and Delinquency Prevention. *Fact Sheet* (February). Washington, DC: Office of Justice Programs.

GREENWOOD, P. (1998). "Investing in prisons or prevention: The state policy makers' dilemma." *Crime and Delinquency* 44(1): 136–142.

GROSSMAN, J. B., and E. M. GARRY (1997). *Mentoring—A Proven Delinquency Prevention Strategy.* (April) Office of Juvenile Justice and Delinquency Prevention. Washington, DC: Office of Justice Programs.

HAGGERTY, K., R. KOSTERMAN, R. F. CATALANO, and J. D. HAWKINS (1999). *Preparing for the Drug Free Years.* Juvenile Justice Bulletin. Office of Juvenile Justice and Delinquency Prevention, Washington, D.C.:July (1–11).

HAMILTON, R., and K. MCKINNEY (1999). *Job Training for Juveniles: Project CRAFT.* Office of Juvenile Justice and Delinquency Prevention Fact Sheet. Office of Juvenile Justice and Delinquency Prevention, Office of Justice Programs, Washington, D.C. (August): 1–2.

HARTNEY, C. (2006). *Youth Under Age 18 in the Adult Criminal Justice System.* OAKLAND, CA: National Council on Crime and Delinquency.

HEWARD, M. E. (2006). *An Update on Teen Court Legislation.* National Youth Court Center. [www.youthcourt.net]

HOWELL, J. C., and S. H. DECKER (1999). *The Youth Gangs, Drugs, and Violence Connection.* Washington, DC: U.S. Department of Justice, Office of Juvenile Justice and Delinquency Prevention.

HSIA, H. M., G. S. BRIDGES, and R. MCHALE (2004). *Disproportionate Minority Confinement 2002 Update.* Washington, DC: U.S. Department of Justice, Office of Juvenile Justice and Delinquency Prevention.

HUDDLESTON, C. W. III, K. FREEMAN-WILSON, D. B. MARLOWE, and A. ROUSSELL (2005). *Painting the Current Picture: A National Report Card on Drug Courts and Other Problem Solving Court Programs in the United States.* Washington, DC: U.S. Department of Justice, Bureau of Justice Assistance.

INCIARDI, J. A., D. C. MCBRIDE, and J. E. RIVERS (1996). *Drug Control and the Courts.* Thousand Oaks, CA: Sage.

KELLEHER, M. (2004)."Suspensions up in CPS." *Catalyst.* (December) [Retrieved April 14, 2007, from www.catalyst-chicago.org/]

KEMPF-LEONARD, K. (2007). "Disproportionate minority contact after nearly 20 years of reform efforts." *Youth Violence and Juvenile Justice* 5(1): 71–87

KILPATRICK, D. G., B. E. SAUNDERS, and D. W. SMITH (2003). *Youth victimization: Prevalence and implications,* Research in Brief. Washington, DC: U.S. Department of Justice, National Institute of Justice. [ncjrs.gov/App/Publications /abstract.aspx?ID=194972]

KRACKE, K. (1996). *SafeFutures: Partnerships to Reduce Youth Violence and Delinquency.* (December) Office of Juvenile Justice and Delinquency Prevention. Washington, DC: Office of Justice Programs.

KRISBERG, B., and S. MARCHIONNA (2007). *Attitudes of US Voters Toward Youth Crime and the Justice System.* Oakland, CA: National Council on Crime and Delinquency.

KUMPFER, KAROL L., and R. ALVARADO (1998). *Effective Family Strengthening Interventions.* (November). Office of Juvenile Justice and Delinquency Prevention. Washington, DC: Office of Justice Programs.

LAWRENCE, R. (2007). *School Crime and Juvenile Justice.* New York, NY: Oxford University Press.

LEWIS, M. (2006). *Custody and Control: Conditions of Confinement in New York's Juvenile Prisons for Girls.* Human Rights Watch.

MCLAUGHLIN, A. (1999). "Easing get-tough approach on juveniles." *Christian Science Monitor.* (August 16):A1.

MERLO, A. V. (2000). "Juvenile Justice at the Crossroads." Presidential Address delivered at the Academy of Criminal Justice Sciences Annual Meeting on March 23, 2000 in New Orleans, Louisiana. *Justice Quarterly.* 17(4):701–723.

MERLO, A. V., and P. J. BENEKOS (2000). *What's Wrong with the Criminal Justice System: Ideology, Politics and the Media.* Cincinnati, OH: Anderson Publishing Co.

MERLO, A. V., P. J. BENEKOS, and W. J. COOK (1997). "'Getting tough' with youth: Legislative waiver as crime control." *Juvenile and Family Court Journal* 48(3): 1–15.

MILLER, J. (2001). *One of the Guys: Girls, Gangs, and Gender.* New York, NY: Oxford University Press.

MILLER, J., and R. K. BRUNSON (2000). "Gender dynamics in youth gangs: A comparison of males' and females' accounts." *Justice Quarterly* 17 (3): 419–448.

MOON, M. M., F. T. CULLEN, and J. P. WRIGHT (2003). "It takes a village: Public willingness to help wayward youths." *Youth Violence and Juvenile Justice* 1(1): 32–45.

MULTISYSTEMIC THERAPY SERVICES (1998). "How Is MST Different?" [mstservices.com]

MUMOLA, C. J. (2005). *Suicide and Homicide in State Prisons and Local Jails*. Washington, DC: Department of Justice, Bureau of Justice Statistics.

NAGIN, D. S., A. R. PIQUERO, E. S. SCOTT, and L. STEINBERG (2006). "Public preferences for rehabilitation versus incarceration of juvenile offenders: Evidence from a contingent valuation survey." *Criminology & Public Policy* 5(4): 627–652.

NATIONAL COUNCIL FOR CRIME PREVENTION (2000). *English Summary: The Sanction System for Young Offenders*. Stockholm, Sweden.

NATIONAL COUNCIL ON CRIME AND DELINQUENCY (2007). *And Justice for Some: Differential Treatment of Youth of Color in the Justice System*. Oakland, CA.

NATIONAL CRIMINAL JUSTICE REFERENCE SERVICE (NCJRS) (2007). *Gang-Facts and Figures*. [www.ncjrs.gov/spotlight/gangs/facts.html]

NATIONAL INSTITUTE ON DRUG ABUSE (1997). *Prevention Principles for Children and Adolescents*. (April 2). [www.nida.nih.gov/]

OFFICE OF JUVENILE JUSTICE AND DELINQUENCY PREVENTION (1999). *Promising Strategies to Reduce Gun Violence*. (February) Office of Justice Programs. Washington, DC: U.S. Department of Justice.

OHLIN, L. E. (1998). "The future of juvenile justice policy and research." *Crime and Delinquency* 44(1): 143–153.

POE-YAMAGATA, E., and M. A. JONES (2000). *And Justice for Some: Differential Treatment of Minority Youth in the Juvenile Justice System*. Washington, DC: Building Blocks for Youth.

POPE, C. E. and H. N. SNYDER (2003). *Race as a Factor in Juvenile Arrests*. Washington, DC: Office of Justice Programs, Office of Juvenile Justice and Delinquency Prevention.

PUZZANCHERA, C. M., B. ADAMS, H. SNYDER, and W. HANG (2006). "Easy Access to FBI Arrest Statistics 1994–2004 Online." [http://ojjdp. ncjrs.gov/ojstatbb/ezaucr/]

ROBERTS, L. M. and P. J. BENEKOS (1999). "Assessing the Feasibility of Drug Courts

for Youthful Offenders." Paper presented at the Annual Meeting of the American Society of Criminology, (November) Toronto, Canada.

SCHIRALDI, V., and J. ZIEDENBERG (1999). *The Florida Experiment: An Analysis of the Impact of Granting Prosecutors Discretion to try Juveniles as Adults*. Washington, DC: Justice Policy Institute.

SCHIRALDI, V., and M. SOLER (1998). "The will of the people: The public's opinion of the Violent and Repeat Juvenile Offender Act of 1997." *Crime and Delinquency* 44(4): 590–602.

SHEPHERD, R. E., Jr. (1999). "The juvenile court at 100 years: A look back." *Juvenile Justice* 6(2) (December): 13–21.

SHERMAN, L. W., D. GOTTFREDSON, D. MACKENZIE, J. ECK, P. REUTER, and S. BUSHWAY (1997). *Preventing Crime: What Works, What Doesn't, What's Promising*. Washington, DC: National Institute of Justice.

SHESTAKOV, D. A., and N. D. SHESTAKOVA (2001). "An overview of juvenile justice and juvenile crime in Russia". In *Juvenile Justice Systems: International Perspectives*, ed. J. A. WINTERDYK, 2nd. ed. Toronto: Canadian Scholars' Press Inc.

SNYDER, H. N. (2006). *Juvenile Arrests 2004*. Washington, DC: U.S. Department of Justice, Office of Juvenile Justice and Delinquency Prevention.

SNYDER, H. N. (2005). *Juvenile Arrests 2003*. Washington, DC: U.S Department of Justice, Office of Juvenile Justice and Delinquency Prevention.

SNYDER, H. N., and M. SICKMUND (2006). *Juvenile Offenders and Victims: 2006 National Report*. (March) National Center for Juvenile Justice. Washington, DC: U.S. Department of Justice, Office of Juvenile Justice and Delinquency Prevention. .

SNYDER, H. N., and M. SICKMUND (1999). *Juvenile Offenders and Victims: 1999 National Report*. (September) National Center for Juvenile Justice. Washington, DC: U.S. Department of Justice, Office of Juvenile Justice and Delinquency Prevention. .

SWENSON, M. (2006). *Multisystemic Therapy*. Blueprints Model Programs Fact Sheet. Boulder,

CO: Center for the Study and Prevention of Violence. [www.colorado.edu/cspv]

TANENHAUS, D. S. (2004). *Juvenile Justice in the Making*. New York, NY: Oxford University Press.

THE SENTENCING PROJECT (1999). *Briefing Paper: Prosecuting Juveniles in Adult Court*. Washington, DC. sentencingproject.org/brief/juveniles.html.

TIBBETTS, S. G,, and A.R. PIQUERO (1999). "The influence of gender, low birth weight, and disadvantaged environment in predicting early onset of offending: A test of Moffitt's Interactional Hypothesis." *Criminology*. 37(4) (November): 843–877.

Uniform Crime Reports (2006). *Crime in the United States 2005*. [www.fbi.gov/]

U.S. DEPARTMENT OF HEALTH AND HUMAN SERVICES, ADMINISTRATION ON CHILDREN, YOUTH AND FAMILIES. (2007). *Child Maltreatment 2005*. Washington, DC: U.S. Government Printing Office.

U.S. DEPARTMENT OF JUSTICE (2007). "Attorney General Gonzales announces expansion of anti-gang initiative." Press Release: April 26, #07-292. [www.usdoj.gov]

WYRICK, P. A. (2000a). *Law Enforcement Referral of At-Risk Youth: The SHIELD Program*. Washington, DC: U.S. Department of Justice, Office of Juvenile Justice and Delinquency Programs.

WYRICK, P. A. (2000b). *Vietnamese Youth Gang Involvement*. Office of Juvenile Justice and Delinquency Prevention. Washington DC: U.S. Department of Justice, Office of Justice Programs (February 1–2).

YOKOYAMA, M. (1997). "Juvenile Justice: An overview of Japan." In *Juvenile Justice Systems: International Perspectives,* ed. J.A. WINTERDYK. Toronto, Canada: Canadian Scholars Press.

ZIEDENBERG, J., and V. SHIRALDI (1997). *The Risks Juveniles Face When They Are Incarcerated with Adults*. Washington, DC: Justice Policy Institute.

CASES

Commonwealth v. Fisher, 213 Pa. 48, Supreme Court of Pennsylvania, (1905).

Commonwealth v. Phillips, Pa. Supreme Court 887 MAL (2006)

In re Gault, 387 U.S. 1; 87 S. Ct. 1428 (1967).

Roper v. Simmons, 543 U.S. 551 (2005).

Chapter 11

The Past, Present, and Future of Waivers in Juvenile Courts

Michael P. Brown

ABSTRACT

Juvenile justice was a progressive and innovative idea that manifested in the first juvenile court in 1899, in Cook County, Illinois. That juvenile court and those that soon followed after it were intended to be a break from the traditional punishment-oriented criminal justice system. Children were considered to be less culpable than adults for their behaviors and therefore needed a substantively different justice system response when they violated the law. Juvenile justice was rooted in the *parens patriae* doctrine, which sought to provide rehabilitation services for children in need of care, protection, and education (Mack 1909). But juvenile justice was supposed to be more than that. Guided by the principles of *parens patriae*, the juvenile court was to act as a surrogate parent concerned with the welfare of its children. That dictate served as the foundation of the first juvenile court and was clearly articulated in the original Illinois Juvenile Court Act of 1899: ". . . the care, custody and discipline of a child shall approximate . . . that which should be given by its parents . . ." (*Illinois Juvenile Court Act of 1899*, §21). Therefore, juvenile court judges were to make decisions they believed were in the "best interests" of the child. And when juvenile justice interventions were considered to be in a child's best interest, the principles of *parens patriae* called for the least restrictive alternative as the sanction, usually taking the form of community-based supervision and treatment (Siegel and Tracy 2007).

    The juvenile court process was to also be different from that found in criminal court. It was thought that the interests of the child were best served through an informal and non-adversarial system. Hence, the juvenile justice process was "decriminalized," even to the point of using different terminology than that used in criminal court (Tanenhaus 2000). The juvenile court was not to find juveniles guilty of crimes and then impose punishments upon them. Rather the juvenile court was to find children to be delinquent, dependent, or neglected and then, exercising vast discretion, juvenile court judges were to fashion sentences that met the needs of troubled youth.

Yet, not all juveniles were considered appropriate for juvenile court intervention. There were provisions in place from the very beginning to transfer (or waive) juveniles who were not amendable to treatment to criminal court (Tanenhaus 2000). Juvenile transfers to criminal court received little attention during the first half of its nearly 110-year history, but that started to change in 1966 when the U.S. Supreme Court turned its attention to the juvenile court for the first time. Since that time, there have been three related areas of change. First, the U.S. Supreme Court has imposed constitutional safeguards to establish procedural regularities by which juveniles are transferred to criminal court. Second, legislation has increased the number of mechanisms by which juveniles are transferred to criminal court. Third, the criminal justice system's influence on the juvenile court has increased because (a) legislation has made younger offenders eligible for transfer to criminal court, (b) many states have expanded the number of offenses for which juveniles may be transferred to criminal court, (c) blended sentences have provided an additional method to impose criminal sanctions on juveniles, and (d) "once an adult, always an adult" legislation retains juveniles in the criminal justice system. This chapter addresses these three areas of change and then offers likely futures of transfers to criminal court.

JUVENILE TRANSFERS TO CRIMINAL COURT

Constitutional Safeguards and Procedural Regularities

At first, juvenile transfers occurred without regard for constitutional safeguards. The juvenile court was not designed to exact retribution, and procedural due process was not considered necessary within a system designed to nurture and care for juveniles instead of punish and deter. The juvenile court's orientation is epitomized by what Jane Addams, an activist involved with the development of the first juvenile court, described as the court's philosophy and process: "The child was brought before the judge with no one to prosecute him and with no one to defend him—the judge and all concerned were merely trying to find out what could be done on his behalf" (1935:137).

In practice, however, these ideals were never achieved and they probably never really had a chance. The number of delinquency cases entering the system exceeded what the juvenile court could handle. Tanenhaus (1997) indicated that the judge and chief probation officer diverted young children away from the juvenile court because of the large volume of cases and low level of seriousness. Older juveniles, those near the age of majority and soon to be under the jurisdiction of the criminal court, were also frequently diverted away from the juvenile court. It would just be a matter of time before they would run afoul with the criminal justice system. It was the serious offenders, especially recidivists, who served as the target population for the new court. If unsuccessful with those offenders, the future of the juvenile court would be in question (Tanenhaus 1997). So, practitioners conserved the finite resources of the court for the cases they believed would be most important in showing the success of the new court system.

State laws standardized who should be transferred to criminal court, but these laws were void of the procedures by which cases were to be transferred. For example, the Illinois juvenile court excluded those aged 16 and older (and later increased the age to 17 and older), unless they recidivated while being supervised on juvenile probation. In such cases, jurisdiction included probation violators up to aged 21 (Tanenhaus 2000). Hart (1910) reported that in 1910, of the 32 states with juvenile courts, most of them set the age limit at either 16 or 17, three states set the age limit at 18, and one state set the limit at 19. Many states, such as Indiana, Michigan, and Kentucky, also allowed for the transfer of cases involving felony charges (Hart 1910). And, most states with juvenile courts provided provisions for the transfer of "serious cases" to the criminal court (Sargent and Gordon 1963). Hence, as Tanenhaus (2000:21) aptly points out, "the limited jurisdiction [of the juvenile court] kept older children out of the juvenile justice system, while offense exclusions and the transfer option made it possible to remove those accused of the most serious crimes."

The lack of uniform standards in the juvenile court transfer process remained unchanged from the court's inception through 1966 when the U.S. Supreme Court heard *Kent v. United States*, its first consideration of a case related to juvenile justice processing. In *Kent v. United States*, the U.S. Supreme Court considered the process by which juveniles were transferred to criminal court for adjudication. In the majority opinion issued by Associate Justice Abe Fortas, the Court concluded that Morris Kent's transfer was invalid because it had been decided without a hearing, without assistance of counsel, and without the presiding judge's reasons for ordering the transfer. In the words of Justice Fortas:

> The Juvenile Court judge . . . held no hearing. He did not confer with petitioner or petitioner's parents or petitioner's counsel. He entered an order reciting that after "full investigation, I do hereby waive" jurisdiction of petitioner and directing that he be "held for trial for [the alleged] offenses under the regular procedure of the U.S. District Court for the District of Columbia." He made no findings. He did not recite any reason for the waiver. He made no reference to the motions filed by petitioner's counsel. We must assume that he denied, *sub silentio,* the motions for a hearing, the recommendation for hospitalization for psychiatric observation, the request for access to the Social Service file, and the offer to prove that petitioner was a fit subject for rehabilitation under the Juvenile Court's jurisdiction.

Kent v. United States is best known for producing procedural regularities to the transfer process. Justice Fortas emphasized the centrality of *parens patriae* to the decision-making process when he stated that the ". . . Juvenile Court should have considerable latitude within which to determine whether it should retain jurisdiction over a child or—subject to the statutory delimitation—should waive jurisdiction." But discretion had it limits; the court's limitations are founded on the ". . . basic requirements of due process and fairness, as well as compliance with the statutory requirement of a "full investigation." In short, ". . . the juvenile court [had] a substantial degree of discretion as to the factual considerations to be evaluated, the weight to be given them, and the conclusion to be reached . . .", but the procedures are not to be arbitrary.

Kent also endorsed judicial waivers as a viable means of integrating the paternalism of the juvenile court with the procedural safeguards that were specified by the U.S. Supreme Court (Tanenhaus 2000) and later written into the legislation in many states and served as guidelines for the transfer process (Feld 1987). But laws are not developed and implemented in a legal vacuum. By the 1970s, the American public had serious reservations about the rehabilitation ideal of the juvenile court. The retribution advocated by the just-deserts approach began to replace rehabilitation as the preferred juvenile justice response. And in 1975, in the midst of this continued change of the juvenile court process came *Breed v. Jones*.

In *Breed v. Jones* the U.S. Supreme Court considered whether the double jeopardy clause of the 5th and 14th amendments to the U.S. Constitution applied to the juvenile court. In the majority opinion issued by Chief Justice Warren Burger described the elements of the case:

> . . . a petition was filed in the Superior Court of California, County of Los Angeles, Juvenile Court, alleging that respondent, then 17 years of age, . . . while armed with a deadly weapon, he had committed acts which, if committed by an adult, would constitute the crime of robbery . . . The jurisdictional or adjudicatory hearing was conducted . . . After taking testimony from two prosecution witnesses and respondent, the Juvenile Court found that the allegations in the petition were true and . . . it sustained the petition. The proceedings were continued for a dispositional hearing, pending which the court ordered that respondent remain detained.
>
> At a [later hearing] the Juvenile Court indicated its intention to find respondent "not . . . amenable to the care, treatment and training program available through the facilities of the juvenile court" . . . Respondent's counsel orally moved "to continue the matter on the ground of surprise," contending that respondent "was not informed that it was going to be a fitness hearing." The court continued the matter for one week, at which time, having considered the report of the probation officer assigned to the case and having heard her testimony, it declared respondent "unfit for treatment as a juvenile," and ordered that he be prosecuted as an adult.

The question put before the Court was whether ". . . by reason of the proceedings in Juvenile Court, respondent was 'twice put in jeopardy.' Chief Justice Burger noted that 'jeopardy' had been traditionally 'associated with a criminal prosecution. . . .' "

He also stated that

> Although the juvenile-court system had its genesis in the desire to provide a distinctive procedure and setting to deal with the problems of youth, including those manifested by antisocial conduct, our decisions in recent years have recognized that there is a gap between the originally benign conception of the system and its realities . . . the Court's response to that perception has been [generally] to make applicable in juvenile proceedings constitutional guarantees associated with traditional criminal prosecutions . . .

Burger continued by asserting that ". . . in terms of potential consequences, there is little to distinguish an adjudicatory hearing such as was held in this case from a traditional criminal prosecution . . . [and] . . . we can find no persuasive distinction in that regard between the proceeding conducted in this case . . . and a criminal prosecution, each of which is designed to vindicate [the] very vital interest in enforcement of criminal laws . . . We therefore conclude that respondent was put in jeopardy at the adjudicatory hearing . . . ." The double jeopardy clause pertains to the risks associated with trials and convictions and not just the punishments imposed as a result of the convictions.

The *Kent* and *Breed* decisions serve as bookends to a series of judicial decisions that transformed juvenile justice by bringing due process provisions to juvenile court processing. While *Kent* and *Breed* addressed the transfer process, *In re Gault* (1967) and *In re Winship* (1970) brought about sweeping changes throughout the juvenile justice process. In the *In re Gault* case, the U.S. Supreme Court denounced juvenile court practices and established sweeping due process provisions. Writing for the majority, Justice Fortas noted that

> The constitutional and theoretical basis for this particular system is—to say the least—debatable. And in practice, as we remarked in the Kent case . . . the results have not been entirely satisfactory. Juvenile court history has again demonstrated that unbridled discretion, however benevolently motivated, is frequently a poor substitute for principle and procedures . . . The absence of substantive standards had not necessarily meant that children received careful, compassionate, individualized treatment. The absence of procedural rules based on constitutional principle has not always produced fair, efficient, and effective procedures. Departures from established principles of due process have frequently resulted not in enlightened procedure, but in arbitrariness . . .
>
> Failure to observe the fundamental requirements of due process has resulted in instances, which might have been avoided, of unfairness to individuals and inadequate or inaccurate findings of facts and unfortunate prescriptions of remedy. Due process of law is the primary and indispensable foundation of individual freedom.

In re Gault established procedural right for the adjudication phase of the juvenile court process. Juveniles involved in delinquency proceedings that could end in institutionalization were granted the (1) right to timely notification of specific charges; (2) right to counsel; (3) right to confront and cross-examine accusers; and (4) right against self-incrimination.

In re Winship also dealt with delinquency proceedings. Specifically, the U.S. Supreme Court ruled that when adjudicating delinquency cases, the juvenile court must use proof beyond a reasonable doubt as the evidentiary standard. Prior to the *Winship* decision, the evidentiary standard was preponderance of the evidence, the same standard used in civil court proceedings. *Winship* extended another essential due process protection to juveniles, one consistent with the protections provided by *Kent*, *Breed,* and *Gault*.

Mechanisms for Transferring Juveniles to Criminal Court

There are several mechanisms by which juveniles may be transferred to criminal court. While judicial transfers have always been available, a number of other methods of transfer were enacted in the 1980s and 1990s. The transfer mechanisms differ in terms of who makes the transfer decision or how the transfer is initiated (Snyder and Sickmund 2006).

Judicial transfers exist in 46 states, including the District of Columbia (Griffin 2006), and it is the first mechanism by which juveniles were transferred to criminal court. Judicial transfers take three forms: discretionary, presumptive, and mandatory. Forty-five states allow for discretionary waivers; Connecticut allows only for mandatory judicial transfers (Griffin 2003). All of the states that have presumptive transfers also have discretionary waivers.

Discretionary judicial transfers conform to the original philosophy of the juvenile court that advocated individualized decision making (Feld 1987). That is, juvenile court judges decide whether or not to waive juvenile court jurisdiction over individual offenders. Discretionary waivers authorize, but do not require, juvenile court judges to decide which cases will be prosecuted in criminal court (Griffin 2003). Discretionary transfers tend to be conducted based on the eight due process principles delineated in *Kent v. United States*. These principles are

- The seriousness of the alleged offense to the community and whether the protection of the community requires waiver.

- Whether the alleged offense was committed in an aggressive, violent, premeditated or willful manner.

- Whether the alleged offense was against persons or against property, great weight being given to offenses against persons especially if personal injury resulted.

- The prosecutive merit of the complaint . . .

- The desirability of trial and disposition of the entire offense in one court when the juvenile's associates in the alleged offense are adults . . .

- The sophistication and maturity of the juvenile as determined by consideration of his home, environmental situation, emotional attitude and pattern of living.

- The record and previous history of the juvenile, including previous contacts with . . . law enforcement agencies, juvenile courts . . ., prior periods of probation . . . or . . . commitments to juvenile institutions.

Most discretionary transfer statutes have criteria that must be met before that court considers the waiver. The criteria include one or more of the following: a minimum age requirement, a specified level of offense seriousness, and serious delinquent history (Dawson 2000). Many states also allow for lesser offenses associated with the crime that initiated the transfer to also be tried in criminal court. Alabama's discretionary transfer law, for example, allows for children of 14 or older accused of any offense to be subject to a transfer hearing. If transferred to criminal court, the offender will be tried not only for the offense associated with the transfer but also for lesser associated crimes (Griffin 2005). Ohio's law is only slightly different: A child of at least 14 who is charged with a felony, after an investigation and hearing by the juvenile court, may transfer the case to criminal court. Furthermore, the criminal court has jurisdiction over all offenses related to the case (Griffin 2005).

Presumptive judicial transfers exist in 16 states (Griffin 2006). Presumptive transfers have statutory triggers—that is, offense seriousness, age, and delinquent history—that require the accused to provide an adequate defense against transfer or else it is presumed that the case will be waived to criminal court. Some states require "preponderance of the evidence" while others require "clear and convincing evidence" against the waiver. Alaska's presumptive transfer law stipulates that a minor (with no minimum age requirement) who commits a class A felony against a person is presumed to not be amenable to treatment in the juvenile court and has the burden of showing otherwise by preponderance of the evidence (Griffin 2005). Minnesota's law, on the other hand, indicates that the child must be at least 16 and accused of an offense resulting in a presumptive prison sentence or accused of committing a felony with a firearm. The child then has the burden of showing by clear and convincing evidence that retaining the case in juvenile court would be in the interest of public safety (Griffin 2005).

Fifteen states have mandatory judicial waivers (Griffin 2006). The juvenile court has a limited role in the mandatory transfer process. Mandatory judicial transfers are similar to statutory exclusion (Griffin 2003), which is discussed later in the chapter. Mandatory judicial transfers require judges to confirm that statutory requirements have been met, at which time the case is transferred to criminal court. These statutory requirements may consist of the offender's age or delinquent history. In the state of Indiana, for example, the juvenile court transfers juveniles to criminal court at any age when the charge is a felony and he/she has a prior delinquent conviction for a felony or nontraffic misdemeanor (Griffin 2005). In Connecticut the accused must be at least 14, charged with a capital crime, class A or B felony, or arson murder to be automatically waived to criminal court. The juvenile court must confirm the age of the accused and, if the child is indigent, appoint counsel. This law goes so far as to indicate that the attorney for the accused is not permitted to file a motion to oppose the transfer (Griffin 2005).

Concerns began to surface over the effectiveness of juvenile court sanctions in the 1950s and 1960s, and by the 1970s state legislatures enacted transfer laws that focused primarily upon the age of the juvenile and the seriousness of the current offense: direct file waivers and exclusionary statutes (Snyder and Sickmund 2006). Excluded from these new transfer mechanisms was the consideration of factors related to the amenability of the child to juvenile court intervention.

Prosecutors may seek direct file transfers to criminal court. Direct file transfers are also known as prosecutorial waivers or concurrent waivers (Snyder and Sickmund 2006). In such cases, prosecutors are authorized to determine whether a case is to be tried in juvenile or criminal court. Direct file transfers are considered analogous to the charging decision in criminal court, and it is therefore considered an executive function of the prosecutor's job and not subject to judicial review (Snyder and Sickmund 2006). There are 15 states (including the District of Columbia) that use direct file transfers (Griffin 2006). All direct-file states also allow for judicial waivers, and 8 of the 15 also allow for transfer to criminal court through statutory exclusion (Griffin 2006).

The state of Arkansas allows for direct file transfers; age and offense seriousness serve as triggers to the transfer. A prosecutor may seek to transfer those who are 16 years of age or older and charged with any felony or at least age 14 and charged with capital murder, first-degree murder, kidnapping, aggravated robbery, rape, first-degree battery, or terrorist activities (Griffin 2005). Any party to the case may file an appeal seeking a reverse waiver. To be successful, the appellant must provide clear and convincing evidence that the juvenile should not be tried as an adult (Griffin 2005).

Florida prosecutors may also use direct file transfers. Like Arkansas, Florida's law uses age and offense triggers, but Florida's law allows for a rather long list of scenarios for which juveniles may be waived to criminal court (Griffin 2005). For example, juveniles who are a minimum of 16 years old may be transferred to criminal court when charged with any felony. Sixteen-year olds may also be directly filed in criminal court when charged with any misdemeanor, if she or he has at least one prior felony conviction. Fourteen-year olds may also have their cases transferred to criminal court for personal crimes including robbery, sexual battery, kidnapping, or aggravated child abuse; property crimes including arson, burglary involving damage to a dwelling or structure, or grand theft; or weapons crimes including carrying, displaying, threatening, or attempting to use a weapon during the commission of a felony. For juveniles facing capital crimes, the prosecutor may present the case to a grand jury and seek an indictment. If the grand jury returns a no bill, the prosecutor must file the case in juvenile court. But if the grand jury returns a true bill, the prosecutor may file charges in criminal court; all offenses related to the capital charge are also tried in criminal court. The state of Oklahoma also uses age and crime triggers, but it has a number of conditions that are not found in the Florida statute (Griffin 2005). For instance, at age 15, juvenile cases may be directly filed in criminal court by the prosecutor if the juvenile is alleged to have discharged a firearm or other weapon from a vehicle; charged with second-degree murder or first-degree manslaughter; charged with such personal crimes as kidnapping for extortion, armed robbery or attempted armed robbery, first-degree or attempted first-degree rape, or lewd molestation; or charged with first-degree or attempted first-degree arson. On the other hand, at the age of 16, the prosecutor may directly file any felony committed with a firearm; personal offenses including aggravated assault and battery on a police officer, witness intimidation, or second-degree rape; property crimes such as first-degree or attempted first-degree burglary, second-degree burglary after two or more delinquency adjudications for first-degree burglary or residential second-degree burglary; or trafficking in or manufacturing illegal drugs. Statutory exclusion, also known as legislative exclusion, is found in 29 states. What make these provisions different from other transfer laws is that the transfer is automatic (Griffin 2006). That is, when the prosecutor files charges the cases originate in criminal court.

The state of Utah uses exclusionary statutes for 16-year olds who are charged with any felony who have also been previously confined in a secure juvenile facility or charged with murder or aggravated murder (Griffin 2005). While California also places murder on the list of offenses that are excluded from juvenile court jurisdiction, it has a lower age requirement (14) and several other personal offenses. These include the crimes of rape, spousal rape, forcible lewd and lascivious acts on a child who is younger than 14, or forcible penetration with a foreign object, or when one or more aggravating circumstances require life imprisonment if found guilty. The state of Mississippi has specified the age of 13 for criminal responsibility when a felony is committed with the use of a shotgun, rifle, or other deadly weapon, or when the charges are capital crimes when the punishment is life imprisonment or death (Griffin 2005). Mississippi also uses exclusionary statutes for all felony charges involving 17-year olds.

Extending the Reach of Criminal Justice Sanctions

The impact of transfer provisions has been considerable and far-reaching since the early 1990s. For example, during the 1990s all states, with the exception of Nebraska, made it easier to transfer juveniles to criminal court (Snyder and Sickmund 2006). More specifically, Snyder and Sickmund (2006) noted that from 1992 to 1995, 41 states (including the District of Columbia) enacted or expanded their transfer laws. Then, from 1998 to 2004, 20 states expanded their laws even further or enacted additional transfer provisions. An analysis of these trends reveals that transfer laws have been traditionally expanded by lowering the age at which children become eligible for criminal sanctions and/or expanding the list of offenses for which juveniles may be transferred to criminal court.

Torbet et al. (1996) reported that adding offenses to the list of crimes for which juveniles become eligible for transfer is the most common approach to extending the criminal justice net into the juvenile justice system. By the mid-1990s, 24 states expanded their transfer laws by adding crimes to the list of offenses that may be transferred. Eighteen states expanded their transfer provisions from 1998 to 2002 (Griffin 2003), adding automatic transfers in California, New Jersey, and Maine, for example. In addition, six states increased the number of juveniles eligible for criminal prosecution by lowering the transfer age to 14 (Torbet et al. 1996). The most recent national survey of transfer laws (including the 2004 legislative sessions) indicates that 23 states do not have a minimum age for one or more transfer provision (i.e., judicial transfer, direct file transfer, or statutory exclusion transfer) (Snyder and Sickmund 2006). The other states and the District of Columbia have set their minimum transfer age as 10 $(n = 2)$, 12 $(n = 2)$, 13 $(n = 7)$, 14 $(n = 16)$, and 15 $(n = 1)$.

Blended sentences and "once an adult, always an adult" legislation have also transformed the juvenile court and extended criminal sentencing into the juvenile justice system. Snyder and Sickmund (2006) reported that there are 34 states with "once an adult, always an adult" provisions. This legislation may stipulate that juveniles who have been convicted in criminal court cannot return to juvenile court when there are subsequent violations of the law. California's "once an adult, always an adult" law states that once a juvenile has been transferred and convicted in criminal court, all subsequent charges should be filed in criminal court. If the juvenile is not convicted, subsequent charges may still be filed in criminal court so long as the minor was at least 16 at the time of the alleged offense, and the offense is one for which transfer to criminal court is allowed (Griffin 2005). Hawaii takes a dramatically different approach from that of California. For the state of Hawaii, the act of transferring a case for criminal prosecution forever terminates the jurisdiction of the juvenile court over cases involving the accused (Griffin 2005).

Blended sentencing schemes are relatively new laws in 15 states (Snyder and Sickmund 2006). Generally speaking, blended sentencing exposes children to criminal sanctions within the juvenile court. Like transfer laws, blended sentencing laws specify certain offenders as eligible for criminal sanctions (Snyder and Sickmund 2006) and regulate the movement of all cases from the juvenile justice system to the criminal justice system (Griffin 2003). While they share these characteristics, Griffin (2003) makes several important distinctions between transfer laws (discussed earlier) and blended sentencing laws. Transfer laws specify—based on age, juvenile record, or seriousness of current charge(s)—who will be waived or, after exercising due discretion, may be waived to criminal court jurisdiction. Hence, transfer laws indicate the conditions upon which cases are heard in a criminal court. Conversely, blended sentencing laws specify whether juveniles will serve out their sanctions in the criminal or juvenile justice system.

For example, some blended sentences (i.e., criminal court blended sentences) allow criminal courts to impose sentences in which the offender serves out his or her sentence in the juvenile court. Criminal court blended sentences exist in 17 states. Six of the seventeen states also have juvenile court blended sentences. Criminal court blended sentences provide juveniles who are convicted in criminal court another chance to serve out a sentence under juvenile court jurisdiction. In effect, criminal court blended sentences provisionally mitigate a criminal sanction so long as the conditions of that sentence are abided by. Other blended sentences (i.e., juvenile court blended sentences) allow juvenile court judges to combine juvenile dispositions with a suspended criminal sentence. The threat of a criminal sanction is intended to serve as a deterrent. In 11 of the 15 states with juvenile court blended sentences, the courts are usually required to impose a combination of juvenile dispositions and criminal sentences (Snyder and Sickmund 2006). This type of blended sentence is also known as an inclusive blend. If no violations occur, juveniles are not required to serve out the criminal sentence. Three of the remaining four states with blended sentences have contiguous models that involve an initial commitment to a juvenile facility until an age specified for transfer to an adult facility. The remaining state has what is referred to as an exclusive blend that authorizes juvenile courts to impose adult sentences.

DISCUSSION AND CONCLUSIONS

The convergence of the U.S. Supreme Court's decisions about the absence of constitutional safeguards in the transfer process of the juvenile court and the publics' perception that the sanctions arising out of the *parens patriae* doctrine were ineffective may have contributed more than any other factors to the transformation of the juvenile justice system. The transformation—as evidenced by the popularity of transfer provisions that primarily rely upon age and offense seriousness, the adoption of blended sentencing legislation by many states, and the widespread enactment of "once an adult, always an adult" legislation—signifies that the juvenile court has reached a defining moment in its history.

On the one hand, there is the process by which the juvenile court is dismantled, and this is done primarily through a process of recriminalizing delinquency. This process is the opposite of what occurred when the juvenile court was established, as juveniles were diverted from criminal to juvenile court. Hence, recriminalization is an "effort to return a part of the juvenile justice system to a period that existed prior to the creation of juvenile courts" (Singer 1996:1). Stevenson et al. (1996:9) state: "The sweeping changes in public policy affecting the juvenile court's delinquency jurisdiction have been the responses to concerns about serious, violent, and chronic offenders and the perceived leniency of juvenile court sanctions toward these juveniles." Consequently, we have witnessed changes in the way juveniles are processed that increase the likelihood that they will come into contact with the criminal justice system.

On the other hand, there is the process by which the juvenile court is revitalized. Revitalization is achieved by restoring legitimacy to juvenile justice, and this approach constitutes a comprehensive strategy to reduce delinquency in general and violent offenses in particular (Bilchik 1998). Bilchik (1998) proposes two fundamental premises upon which legitimacy is restored. First, effective juvenile justice systems hold offenders accountable, help offenders become responsible and productive citizens, and help to make the larger community safe. These objectives help to make the adolescent a part of the larger community and they are consistent with the principles of restorative justice. Second, " . . . effective juvenile justice interventions are swift, certain, consistent and appropriate" (Bilchik 1998:2). This is accomplished with effective prevention programs, early intervention programs, graduated sanctions, and assessments to improve system administration and operation.

The momentum is with the process by which the juvenile court is dismantled. While it is unlikely that the juvenile court would be abolished, it is conceivable that a scaled down, hybrid system of juvenile justice could be devised that targets first-time, nonviolent offenders who are considered malleable. The others would be considered too high a risk to remain outside of the criminal justice net. However, there are signs that the juvenile justice system may be revitalized. The recent *Roper v. Simmons* (2005) 543 U. 551 decision is perhaps the most decisive break from the dismantling of the juvenile court in over a decade and it is an explicit recognition of the developmental differences between adolescents and adults. Research is being conducted on adjudicative competence (see, e.g., Grisso et. al. 2003), which tends to support the revitalization of a separate system of justice for adults and adolescents.

REFERENCES

ADDAMS, J. (1935). *My Friend Julia Lathrup.* New York: MacMillan.

BILCHIK, S. (1989). *A Juvenile Justice System for the 21st Century.* Washington, DC: Office of Juvenile Justice and Delinquency Prevention, U.S. Department of Justice.

DAWSON, R. O. (2000). Judicial Waiver in Theory and Practice. In *The Changing Borders of Juvenile Justice*, ed. J. Fagan and F. Zimring, pp. 45–82, Chicago, IL: University of Chicago Press.

FELD, B. C. (1987). The juvenile court meets the principle of the offense: Legislative changes in juvenile waiver statutes. *Journal of Criminal Law and Criminology* 78: 471–533.

GRIFFIN, P. (2003). *Trying and Sentencing Juveniles as Adults: An Analysis of State Transfer and* Blended Sentencing Laws. Pittsburg, PA: National Center for Juvenile Justice.

GRIFFIN, P. (2005). "*Transfer Provisions.*" State Juvenile Justice Profiles. Pittsburgh, PA: National Center for Juvenile Justice. [Retrieved from http://www.ncjj.org/stateprofiles/]

GRIFFIN, P. (2006). "*National Overviews.*" State Juvenile Justice Profiles. Pittsburgh, PA: National Center for Juvenile Justice. [Retrieved from http://www.ncjj.org/stateprofiles/]

GRISSO, T., L. STEINBERG, J. WOLLARD, J. CAUFMAN, E. SCOTT, S. GAHAM, F. LEXCEN, N. REPUCCI, and R. R. SCHWARTZ. (2003). Juveniles' competence to stand trial: A comparison of adolescents' and adults' capacities as trial defendants. *Law and Human Behavior* 27(4): 333–363.

HART, H. H. (1910). *Juvenile Court Laws in the United States Summarized.* New York: Russell Sage.

ILLINOIS JUVENILE COURTACT (1899) Ill. Laws 131, 131.

MACK, J. (1909). The juvenile court. *Harvard Law Review* 23: 104–120.

SARGENT, D. A., and D. H. GORDON. (1963). Waiver of jurisdiction: An evaluation of the process in the juvenile court. *Crime and Delinquency* 9: 121–128.

SIEGEL, L. J., and P. E. TRACY. (2007). *Juvenile Law: A Collection of Leading U.S. Supreme Court Cases.* Upper Saddle River, NJ: Prentice Hall.

SINGER, S. I. (1996). *Recriminalizing Delinquency: Violent Juvenile Crime and Juvenile Justice Reform.* New York: Cambridge University Press.

SNYDER, H. N., and M. SICKMUND. (2006). *Juvenile Offenders and Victims: 2006 National Report.* Washington, DC: U.S. Department of Justice, Office of Justice Programs, Office of Juvenile Justice and Delinquency Prevention.

STEVENSON, C. S., C. S. LARSON, L. S. CARTER, D. S. GOMBY, D. L. TERMAN, and R. E. BEHRMAN. (1996). The future of children. *The Juvenile Court* 6(3): 4–28.

TANENHAUS, D. S. (1997). *Policing the Child: Juvenile Justice in Chicago 1870–1925,* 2 vols., PhD Dissertation. Chicago, IL: University of Chicago Press.

TANENHAUS, D. S. (2000). The evolution of transfer out of the juvenile court. In *The Changing Borders of Juvenile Justice,* ed. J. Fagan and F. Zimring, pp. 13–44, Chicago, IL: University of Chicago Press.

TORBET, P., R. GABLE, H. HURST IV, I. MONTGOMERY, L. SZYMANSKI, and D. THOMAS. (1996). *State Responses to Serious and Violent Juvenile Crime.* Washington, DC: Office of Juvenile Justice and Delinquency Prevention.

CASES

Breed v. Jones, 421 U.S. 519, 95 S.Ct. 1779 (1975).

In re Gault, 387 U.S. 1, 87 S.Ct. 1428 (1967).

In re Winship, 397 U.S. 358, 90 S.Ct. 1068 (1970).

Kent v. United States, 383 U.S. 541, 86 S.Ct. 1045 (1966).

Chapter 12

The Situation of Crime Victims in the Early Decades of the Twenty-First Century

Andrew Karmen, Ph.D.

ABSTRACT

In the late twentieth century, the basic needs and interests of crime victims were rediscovered after decades of severe neglect. In the early twenty-first century, a number of existing trends will expand the different courses of action and options that victims face. Commercial interests will develop and market a much greater selection of antitheft and personal security devices. Professional advocates will be assigned routinely to help victims to exercise their formal rights within the criminal justice process. Private prosecution will become possible if victims grow dissatisfied with the services of public prosecutors. Victim–offender reconciliation programs will proliferate and handle a wider variety of cases. Also, differential justice will be recognized as a problem, as the gap widens between the way privileged victims as opposed to second-class complainants are handled by criminal justice agencies.

FORECASTING FUTURE DEVELOPMENTS

Several different strategies can be pursued to try to anticipate what the situation facing crime victims will be like in the first few decades of the twenty-first century. Futurologists can generate informed predictions about social and political arrangements in the years ahead by looking back over the developments of the past several decades in order to see how much can change during this amount of time. A second basis for speculations about what lies just beyond the horizon requires identification of the driving forces for change. By projecting emerging social trends, it becomes possible to paint plausible scenarios about likely developments over the next several decades. Such linear extrapolations basically predict "more of the same" but at higher (or lower) levels or to greater (or lesser) degrees. However, this "extrapolation" approach can yield gross inaccuracies if what are actually short-run phenomena are mistaken for long-term trends and are extended too far into the future. Furthermore, oppositional groups leveraging countervailing pressures could arise that might put up enough resistance to hold in check the forces that were bringing about reforms. Still a third way to make predictions is to speculate that completely new and currently unheard-of developments will evolve out of familiar situations. Although exercising the imagination is the foundation for good science fiction, it generates questionable social science.

Of course, when reviewing the past, describing the present, or imagining what the future holds, "what is" must always be distinguished from "what ought to be." Social scientists have to strive for objectivity and be vigilant that subjective interpretations and personal biases don't find their way into the analysis. Applying this principle of impartiality to forecasting means making a distinction between "what is likely to happen" versus "what would be desirable." Wishful thinking about a better future should not be substituted for a realistic assessment of what will probably take place.

THE SITUATION VICTIMS FACED IN THE LATE TWENTIETH CENTURY

When the plight of crime victims in the not-too-distant past is reviewed, it becomes clear that sweeping and profound changes can occur in a relatively short time span of several decades. As recently as the 1970s, victims were still largely written off as an undifferentiated mass of faceless, pitiful "losers" who were the unfortunate "casualties" of a growing and intractable street crime problem. A number of commentators characterized them as the forgotten figures within the criminal justice process, virtually "invisible" (Rieff 1979), systematically overlooked, totally excluded from meaningful participation, and beset by pressing needs that were routinely ignored (see Barkas 1978; Carrington 1975). The plight of crime victims had not yet been rediscovered by the news media, law enforcement officials, political movements, or academic researchers.

Public consciousness of the victims' plight was raised when the women's liberation movement started to expose and criticize the way the men at the helm of the justice system callously disregarded the best interests of sexually assaulted girls and women (see Griffin 1971). But there were no rape crisis centers until feminist activists in the San Francisco Bay area challenged police and hospital practices in 1972 (Largen 1981). In university libraries, students searched in vain for analyses of rape that presented the violated female's point of view (Schwendinger and Schwendinger 1983:10). Similarly, magazine articles rarely addressed the predicament of battered women trapped in romantic relationships that had turned violent. As articles began to appear about "the silent crisis," the *Reader's Guide to Periodical Literature* first introduced the subject heading "wife beating" in 1974 (Loseke 1989). There were no shelters for battered women to flee to until activists set up a hotline and a refuge in an old house in St. Paul, Minnesota in 1974 (Martin 1977).

Inspired by the dramatic power struggles of the 1960s involving African Americans, students, women, gays, soldiers, and even prisoners, victim activists organized self-help and support groups and advocacy organizations during the 1970s. The loose coalition that constituted the victims' rights movement started the process of redressing grievances by publishing newsletters, demonstrating for reforms, monitoring trials, petitioning criminal justice officials, and lobbying lawmakers (see Friedman 1985). But the earliest proponents of victims' rights (see Hook 1972) envisioned these new statutes mostly as weapons in a zero-sum game to counter or even "trump" the expanding rights of "criminals" (suspects, defendants, and prisoners) granted by landmark decisions handed down by the Warren Court. Activists did not yet conceive of victims' rights as a means of empowerment for individuals who deserved input into how "their" cases were resolved by indifferent officials and remote criminal justice bureaucracies.

Prosecutors routinely overlooked the needs of their ostensible clients in criminal court proceedings, according to a survey conducted in the mid-1970s. Many victims never found out if anyone was arrested or convicted in their cases, if their stolen property was ever recovered, or if they were entitled to modest witness fees for missing work when called to testify (Lynch 1976). A short-lived Law Enforcement Assistance Administration began to channel federal funding during the 1970s to county district attorneys to experiment with victim/witness assistance programs to provide support services to people who were needed to testify on behalf of the state (see Schneider and Schneider 1981; Roberts 1990). Also during the 1970s, the potential of civil lawsuits as a means of recovering financial losses was recognized. Soon some legal activists realized that besides suing offenders directly, victims could launch lawsuits against third parties such as businesses, colleges, and psychiatric hospitals whose gross negligence about security matters made it easier for criminals to harm them (Carrington 1977).

By the end of the 1970s, activists talked about amending the U.S. Constitution to guarantee victims legal standing in criminal justice proceedings. That course of action was not taken seriously until the President's Task Force on Victims of Crime (1982) suggested rewording the Sixth Amendment to include a pledge that "[t]he victim, in every criminal prosecution shall have the right to be present and to be heard at all critical stages of judicial proceedings." It took until the mid-1980s before victim advocacy groups realized that they could be much more successful in their drive to secure new rights by organizing campaigns to amend state constitutions, one at a time [National Organization for Victim Assistance (NOVA) 1986]. Activists made considerable progress: By the close of the twentieth century, 49 states had passed a "Victims' Bill of Rights" and 22 states had enacted amendments to their constitutions that required the provision of certain benefits and options (Tomz and McGillis 1997). On the federal level, both the Clinton administration and then the Bush administration endorsed the campaign to amend the Constitution to guarantee that victims can state their views at court proceedings involving bail, sentencing, and parole, and can receive information, restitution, and reasonable protection from further harm. In 2004, the movement to redraft the Sixth Amendment achieved a partial victory when Congress passed the Crime Victims' Rights Act (CVRA), which pledged that these rights to be present and to be heard would be implemented in federal court proceedings.

Only one area of legal reform was already well under way by the early 1970s: compensating innocent, physically injured victims for their out-of-pocket monetary losses. A few states set up their own funds during the 1960s, while members of Congress were debating whether it was an appropriate area of responsibility and jurisdiction for federal aid. Die-hard believers in rugged individualism denounced the possibility of spreading a government-sponsored safety net under wounded victims facing financial ruin as "creeping socialism" (see Meiners 1978.) Congress was unable to muster the majority of members needed to authorize the partial funding of state compensation programs until 1984, when the Victims of Crime Act was passed. But these early, faltering steps toward helping certain unfortunate victims pay off some of their devastating medical bills were largely symbolic political gestures that were grossly underfunded, fiscally inadequate, and personally demeaning (Elias 1983). It took until the 1990s for federal funding to reach modest levels for the Office for Victims of Crime within the Justice Department and for the Crime Victims Fund.

Also on the economic front, few judicial systems (except some juvenile courts) had demonstrated a sustained commitment to revive the ancient practice of compelling offenders to make restitution to the parties they harmed (Galaway and Hudson 1975). Restitution became a real possibility when legislation enacted in the various states authorized judges to impose reimbursement as a court-ordered obligation. But a federal tracking system revealed that this pro-victim feature of a sentence imposed on convicts was failing to realize its full potential at the turn of the century. In state courts, offenders were ordered to repay their victims in about one-quarter of all burglary convictions and in roughly a third of all fraud convictions in 1992 (Langan and Graziadei 1995). But the corresponding figures for 2002 slipped to one-fifth of all burglary convictions and one-quarter of all fraud sentences (Durose 2004). Although restitution is widely viewed as fair and even potentially therapeutic for both parties, it remains underutilized, statistically speaking.

Victimology—the scientific study of crime victims—began to emerge in the 1970s as an area of specialization within criminology. Victimologists from around the world did not hold their first professional conference until 1973 in Jerusalem (Drapkin and Viano 1974). No journal was devoted to publishing studies about crime victims until 1976 (Viano 1976). Only one scholarly work that could serve as a textbook (Schafer 1968) was available for college courses, but it was filled with either historical material about a "Golden Age" in faraway places in the distant past or conjecture about what the future might hold because there were very few actual research findings for the author to cite about the plight of victims in the United States. Police statistics compiled by the Federal Bureau of Investigation since the 1930s in its annual Uniform Crime Report were known to be undercounts of the actual numbers of individuals who were harmed by acts of violence and theft. But no systematic efforts were undertaken on a regular basis to determine the extent and seriousness of crime-inflicted suffering until the first victimization surveys of a cross-section of the public were initiated by the federal government in 1972 and modified in 1973 (now called the National Crime Victimization Survey, or NCVS).

The number of incidents of both violent crimes (aggravated assault, robbery, and forcible rape and other sexual assaults) and property crimes (burglaries, motor vehicle thefts, and other larcenies)—and consequently the number of new victims—dropped sharply during the 1990s, according to the findings of the National Crime Victimization Survey. During the early years of the twenty-first century, victimization rates stabilized at their lowest levels since the surveys were first carried out at the start of the 1970s (Catalano 2006). Unfortunately, no "blue ribbon commission" of experts was ever convened to determine why crime rates fell so dramatically during the 1990s (see Karmen 2000). Therefore, no one knows how long this impressive improvement in public safety that slashed the growth rate of the ranks of crime victims will continue, or whether another crime wave will grip the nation sometime in the next few decades (and if another crime wave does erupt again, how to best quell it).

As the brief historical overview presented above demonstrates, during the past several decades, momentous changes took place in the way victims were responded to and the way they came to grips with their plight. What current trends might provide clues about likely developments during the next few decades?

ANTICIPATING THE SITUATION OF VICTIMS IN THE EARLY TWENTY-FIRST CENTURY BY PROJECTING EXISTING TRENDS

To anticipate what the future holds, the way to proceed is to identify the most important contemporary trends and then to project how they might shape the situation of crime victims in the years to come. Five significant tendencies currently are at work: a trend toward marketing victimization prevention devices and services of unknown usefulness; a trend toward granting victims more formal rights that necessitate the services of knowledgeable advocates; a trend toward privatization of criminal justice functions; a trend toward out-of-court resolution of criminal incidents; and a trend toward differential case handling.

How the Trend Toward Commercialization Is Leading to the Marketing of More Victimization Prevention Devices and Services That Must Be Evaluated for Their Effectiveness

One strong current that emerged during the latter part of the twentieth century was the quest for personal safety, stability, and risk reduction in an otherwise unpredictably dangerous world. Crime prevention programs on a societal level tackle the "social roots" or social conditions that breed lawlessness. But victimization prevention strategies have much more modest goals: to reduce the odds of violence and theft faced by specific individuals, small groups, and communities. Commercial interests have discovered that crime victims constitute a significant group of consumers of goods and services that allegedly will help reduce the risks of being harmed physically, emotionally, or financially, and speed recovery. The market will surely expand for high-tech victimization prevention gadgetry and private security, protection management, and loss prevention services. Already, the ranks of police departments, sheriffs departments, and other local, state, and federal law enforcement agencies are reinforced by a growing number of security consultants, private detectives, and personal bodyguards along with night watchmen, store detectives, hotel detectives, chauffeurs, even doormen. Antitheft devices already abound and will become even more commonplace. Alarm systems are being sold as standard equipment on vehicles, boats, and new homes. Satellite tracking and recovery systems and license plate recognition devices that now help to retrieve stolen vehicles will be used to locate embedded computer chips and to repossess all sorts of valuable goods—and even locate missing persons. Electronic monitoring systems, surveillance cameras, preprogrammed cell phones, and emergency transmitters will protect particularly vulnerable groups, such as battered women, with orders of protection against their estranged mates, along with latchkey children. Insurance companies that have traditionally sold policies that protect customers against losses from violence (life insurance, injury and health coverage, income maintenance) and theft (from homes, automobiles, boats) now promote policies that protect fearful people from the potential costs arising from identity theft, kidnappings for ransom, and even terrorist attacks.

The rising popularity of gated communities epitomizes how commercial interests can package and sell "peace of mind" for economic gain. There is a growing demand for such living arrangements by people who feel the need to withdraw from the seemingly chaotic existence of urban dwellers into exclusive and isolated low-risk environments where the threats posed by burglars, robbers, rapists, and auto thieves can be minimized. In the early 1990s, about 30,000 gated communities across the country housed an estimated 4 million residents, as personal security became one of the highest priorities of home buyers (Anonymous 1994; Blakely and Snyder 1997; Wilson-Duenges 2000). By 2001, a Census Bureau survey projected that about 7 million households, or roughly 6 percent of the nation's total, lived behind walls and fences; 4 million of these residents enjoyed the extra degree of protection afforded by limited access mechanisms, controlled by either guards or key cards or entry codes (El Nasser 2002). The "siege mentality" of "defensible space" against "outsiders who don't belong" will pass for a "sense of community" in the early decades of the twenty-first century.

Similarly, Business Improvement Districts (BIDs) have been set up nationwide by real estate interests, merchants' associations, and community organizations to attract and reassure apprehensive customers that they will be safe and secure while in the presence of uniformed guards in these reclaimed sections of town. When people venture out from their fortified sanctuaries to shop or pursue leisure activities, squads of private security forces and banks of surveillance cameras watch over them. From the early 1970s to the early 1990s, more than 1,000 BIDs sprung up in cities across the country, funded by assessments on property owners within their districts (Lueck 1994). By the end of the century, that number had risen to 1,200 (Liedtke 2000). New York City led the nation with 56 BIDs dispersed within its five boroughs (Small Business Services 2007).

Victimologists can play a more important role in the near future, by conducting consumer-oriented research to evaluate the real-world effectiveness of these high-tech devices and victimization prevention services. In the face of bold claims about foolproof devices and safety-enhancing services issued by various businesses during high-power marketing campaigns, victimologists must insist "Prove It! Show me the evidence!"

Independent assessments are needed in order to protect vulnerable victims and fearful non-victims from commercial exploitation. Product evaluations, real-world track records, and before/after social experiments can determine whether risk reduction services (such as uniformed guards) and antitheft hardware (such as car alarms and store surveillance cameras) actually safeguard customers from harm, and if so, which company's offerings work best. Similarly, victimologists and criminologists can study whether gated communities and business improvement districts are really as safe as they claim to be and whether these victimization prevention measures merely displace criminal activity on to other less-privileged people living, working, and shopping in less-protected environments.

How the Trend Toward Granting Victims Greater Formal Rights Within the Criminal Justice Process Is Leading to the Emergence of Victim Advocates

Despite the marketing of many new goods and services in recent years, one line of work seems to have been largely overlooked. One likely development over the next few decades will be the emergence of a new kind of criminal justice professional: the victim advocate (see Karmen 1995). The provision of an advocate by the government, at no cost, probably will become institutionalized in one jurisdiction after another in the near future. Upon filing a report with the police, a complainant will be offered the services of an advisor familiar with the increasingly complicated rights, opportunities, options, and obligations victims face. Advocates will look after their clients' best interests in their dealings with police officers, detectives, defendants, defense attorneys, prosecutors, judges, probation officers, corrections officials, parole boards, compensation boards, and the news media.

In many jurisdictions, victims are now entitled to know about developments in their cases and to timely notification about optional and required appearances at bail and evidentiary hearings, trials, sentencing hearings, and parole board meetings. Victims are empowered to pursue a number of strategies for reimbursement of their out-of-pocket expenses (restitution from offenders, compensation from government-administered funds, judgments from civil lawsuits, and reimbursement from insurance coverage). In some localities, police chiefs, district attorneys, and judges have granted victims additional privileges above and beyond what procedural law requires as the minimum standard for fair treatment. Special solutions have been devised to address the particular problems burdening abused children, survivors of childhood incest, abused elders, battered women, rape victims, and targets of bias-motivated hate crimes. In some jurisdictions, new practices protect their personal privacy (especially from media exposure in sexual assault cases) (see Karmen 2007).

To date, only a relatively limited number of dedicated volunteers and some overworked and underpaid professionals, both outside the criminal justice system, are available to assist victims. Victim advocates work as counselors for complainants serving as witnesses for the prosecution at district attorneys' Victim–Witness Assistance Programs (VWAPs). Other advocates work or volunteer their time at shelters for battered women and at rape crisis centers. Judges appoint special advocates (guardians ad litem) who attend to the needs of mistreated children in family courts and in criminal court in serious child abuse cases involving parents. But no permanent paid staff of independent professionals is yet at work on a daily basis, looking after the best interests of every complainant who turns to a local police department in the aftermath of a burglary, robbery, rape, assault, auto-theft, and identity theft from start to finish in the justice process. Just like attorneys are made available to all indigent defendants at a public defender's office, advocates someday will be provided by a government agency, or supplied by an independent nonprofit organization. Other advocates will be independent professionals and freelancers who will have their own private practices, such as defense attorneys in law firms specializing in civil lawsuits against offenders or against negligent third parties, and will be retained for a fee by those who can afford their services, or will be hired on a contingency basis to pursue lawsuits.

The emergence of credentialism is a sign that the institutionalization of victim advocacy is underway. Since the early years of the twenty-first century, a national organization that assists victims has been offering training to advocates who seek to become certified and recognized as knowledgeable professionals (NOVA 2003). Victimologists can carry out research to assess the effectiveness of the efforts undertaken by victim advocates in behalf of their clients by comparing how victims who have support and guidance fare when compared to those who must fend for themselves.

How the Trend Toward Privatizing Criminal Justice Functions Might Lead to Private Prosecution

The trend by government to divest itself of certain responsibilities and tasks within the criminal justice process and to hand them over to nonprofit organizations as well as profit-oriented enterprises is likely to accelerate in the next few decades. One impact on victims will be to open up the possibility of private prosecution.

All through history, the inherently public and governmental nature of justice and punishment has been symbolized by the badge of the police officer, the robe of the judge, and the uniform of the corrections guard. However, a number of contemporary developments are undermining the government's monopoly over criminal justice functions. Privatization began by nibbling away at the front and back stages of the criminal justice process. At the front end, privatization took the form of furnishing added protection, above and beyond the minimal degree provided by government from tax revenues (security firms offering guards for hire) and individually financed investigations (carried out for a fee by "private eyes"). At the tail end, privatization took the form of independently operated nonprofit therapeutic communities and profit-oriented residential and outpatient alcohol and drug treatment programs. During the 1960s and early 1970s, a prisoner's rights movement called for a moratorium on new prison construction and for decarceration and deinstitutionalization—symbolically, a call to "tear down the walls." But the ensuing crackdown on crime demanded by the law and order movement instead generated soaring inmate populations, skyrocketing probation and parole caseloads, and escalating expenditures. During the 1980s, proponents of privatization began to "sell the walls," giving companies a chance to profit from incarcerating the government's growing number of prisoners by running detention centers, jails, and prisons (Steinberg 1984; DiIulio 1988).

Now the middle stage of adjudication is undergoing privatization, and a dual court system is emerging: criminal courts handle most cases, but neighborhood justice centers and victim–offender reconciliation programs (VORPS) practicing dispute resolution work on selected cases diverted from the government's system (see the following section for further implications of this development). What remains to be privatized is the function of prosecution itself. It is likely that activists and advocacy groups within the victims' movement eventually will launch campaigns demanding the right to private prosecution (see Cole 1992:718).

When they take up this cause, they will encounter another example of how politics creates strange bedfellows. Self-styled militia and "constitutionalist" groups that portray themselves as the backbone of a "patriot" movement already have begun to agitate around the issue of reviving private prosecution (as part of their larger attack on what they perceive to be a corrupt judicial system and an intrusive federal government) (see Roland 1996).

A branch of the victims' movement might call for private prosecution if frustrations mount with the way that assistant district attorneys handle cases. Victims and the lawyers assigned by the government to "dispose of" their cases can disagree over the goals of the process. A victim might want to press charges, but the prosecutor's office might want to drop some or all charges (or vice versa). A victim might want the offender to admit guilt and to be held responsible for everything in the indictment, by going to trial if necessary, while the prosecutor's office usually will be satisfied with a conviction on a lesser charge, preferably through a timesaving and cost-effective negotiated plea. A victim might want court-ordered restitution from the offender, but the government might not consider reimbursement to be an important priority. Similarly, a victim might want the legal system to compel the offender (perhaps a violence-prone husband or a drug-abusing neighbor) to undergo treatment, but the government might be more intent on securing some other disposition, ranging from a suspended sentence to imprisonment.

The seeds of dissension between victims and "their" lawyers are sown by contradictions within each party's roles. One contradiction revolves around the duality of the victim's role: On one hand, victims are "on the side of the government" in the adversarial system. Specifically they are allied with the police and the prosecution in the quest for conviction. On the other hand, victims are independent actors who might want to pursue what they perceive to be their own best interests. Similarly, prosecutors confront a contradiction in their own role whenever they try to bridge a gap by representing both the interests of the government that hires them and the clients they are assigned to help (see Karmen 1992). The role strain faced by assistant district attorneys was minimal until victims began to exercise their recently granted rights and started to conceive of their personal interests as being separate from those of the bureaucracy that furnished them with a lawyer (assistant district attorney) at no cost to them. Of course, when forced to choose, assistant district attorneys will act in accord with the interests of the agency that employs them rather than in behalf of the injured parties who rely on them.

The underlying philosophy of jurisprudence (which victims are questioning) is that all criminal acts, including interpersonal violence and theft, should be conceptualized as offenses against the state requiring an official response, and are not simply wrongs inflicted on innocent parties that could be righted by individually arranged settlements.

Because the government gets drawn in, to safeguard the public interest, victims are relegated to the role of mere complainants who set the machinery of justice into motion by reporting incidents to the police. If their cases are solved (most are not; clearance rates are low) and an arrest is made, victims bear the obligation of testifying for the prosecution; but even as star witnesses, they just provide dramatic evidence of criminal conduct on the part of the accused but otherwise lack legal standing.

A new philosophy is emerging from the ranks of the victims' movement that challenges the government's monopoly on the exercise of prosecutorial discretion. It proceeds from the assumption that person-against-person crimes such as rape, robbery, assault, and burglary do more than just violate an abstraction known as the criminal law, or threaten the social order, or harm a vague collectivity such as "the People of the State of . . .," as indictments read. The real flesh-and-blood persons who have suffered emotional damage, physical injuries, and financial losses have a rightful claim to exercise some input into the way the system handles "their" cases, especially given the great latitude concerning the range of penalties written into the law and the considerable discretion exercised by prosecutors and judges. If victims are viewed as "consumers" of prosecutorial "services" made available by the government's "public law firm," shouldn't those attorneys be accountable to their "customers"? If their handling of cases cannot be influenced by their clients, shouldn't these disgruntled complainants be allowed to go elsewhere and choose an attorney of their own to prosecute, perhaps for a fee?

In anger and frustration, people holding this personalized outlook about justice have sought to gain some leverage over prosecutorial decision making, in addition to the long-standing negative, self-defeating strategy of simply discontinuing cooperation with the authorities. In most jurisdictions, victims are now informed about the terms of a negotiated plea but cannot exercise the privilege of "veto power" over unacceptable deals. Prosecutors have rejected proposals to permit victims to participate directly in negotiations. Through the vehicles of victim impact statements and allocution (personal appearances), victims have attempted to influence sentencing decisions, but their recommendations are just one of many sources of input influencing judges.

Clearly, the attraction of private prosecution is that it would enable a lawyer hired by the victim to pursue what the victim defines as his or her best interests: some personalized mix of retribution, restitution, rehabilitation (of the offender), and/or reconciliation of the two estranged parties. Victims who did not like the way the government attorney was planning to "dispose of" the case could select their own lawyer to press charges, negotiate a plea, or present the case before a jury.

Crime victims had to bring their own cases to court and pay a lawyer to prosecute them under a common law practice that prevailed when the American system was first set up in 1776 (McDonald 1996; Senate Judiciary Committee Report 2006). As recently as 1955, this "do-it-yourself" option was permitted in at least 28 states. But by the 1970s, only a few jurisdictions allowed private lawyers hired by complainants to join forces with government attorneys (Sigler 1979). Over the years, the Supreme Court has handed down a number of rulings (in 1967, 1973, 1977, 1981, and 1983) establishing that victims cannot compel prosecutors to take action and that judges cannot intervene on behalf of victims in their disagreements with prosecutors. Attorneys general and district attorneys retain sole discretion over whether or not to charge defendants with crimes and over which charges to press or drop (Stark and Goldstein 1985).

Private prosecution is possible in routine criminal matters in Canada, Great Britain, and most European countries (Leigh 2007). If European practices are adopted, what must be worked out is whether the victim will be permitted to go forward only if the government prosecutor fails to press charges and whether private prosecution will be allowed only for certain minor interpersonal offenses such as assault and trespass (see Newman 1986; Sebba 1992). It is likely that federal, state, and county prosecutors will remain convinced that private prosecution poses a threat to their professional stature and job security, and will continue to oppose this trend toward privatization in ways that will retard its acceptance and implementation (Sentencing Commission's Practitioners' Advisory Group 2005).

How the Trend Toward Developing More Alternatives to Both Adjudication and Incarceration Is Bringing About a Greater Reliance on Victim–Offender Reconciliation Programs

During the closing decades of the twentieth century, severely punishing wrongdoers was the dominant theme within criminal justice and within many sectors of the victims' movement. But the fixation on "getting even" that motivates the proponents of "retributive justice" is increasingly being challenged by advocates of "restorative justice" who are exploring and inventing nonpunitive approaches that can peacefully resolve the underlying conflicts that fuel interpersonal violence. Although this theme can be traced back to biblical times, it was not until 1975 that an inspiring, innovative experimental program to enable offenders to repay their victims as part of an effort to resolve their antagonisms and achieve mutual reconciliation was set up by a religious group in Canada (McKnight 1981). Since then, a branch of the victims' movement has been enthusiastically developing restorative justice both in theory (as an alternative paradigm to retributive justice) and in practice (e.g., see Elliott and Gordon 2005).

The first VORP in the United States was established in Indiana in 1978. The initiators were inspired by biblical teachings: that crime symbolized a rupture or wound that afflicted an entire community and had to be healed through reparation rather than retribution. To heal their emotional wounds, both the victim and the offender need to be empowered (authorized to resolve their conflict by themselves). Just as prisons were invented by the Quakers early in the nineteenth century and were then copied by government, the reconciliation model originated by the Mennonites was replicated by nonprofit groups and local agencies throughout the 1980s. The range of cases handled by centers for mediation/restitution/reconciliation quickly expanded. Originally, only quarrels entangling people who knew each other previously or involving property damage or loss (generally, vandalism, burglary, and other forms of thievery) were considered suitable. But within a few years, cases surrounding assaults committed by strangers were being referred for restitution and reconciliation as well (Umbreit 1990). By the late 1990s, the National Institute of Justice was encouraging the spread of restorative justice experiments that promised to involve victims and community activists in the process of repairing the harm caused by lawbreakers (Anonymous 1997). The number of reconciliation programs mushroomed from about 100 at the start of the 1990s to nearly 300 across the United States (and Canada) by the end of that decade (VORP Information and Resource Center 2000). By 2005, more than 300 restorative justice programs operated within the United States (although by then, Canada alone had over 100 programs, and European countries an additional 500) (Prison Fellowship International 2005).

In theory, this particular alternative to incarceration offers advantages to victims, offenders, and crime-plagued neighborhoods. For victims, these evolving programs provide a safe, secure setting to confront their offenders in the presence of trained and skilled intermediaries. When they meet in person, victims get an opportunity to vent pent-up feelings and ask troubling questions. Besides the potential for emotional catharsis, victims ought to be able to leave the negotiations with a satisfactory restitution agreement in hand. For offenders, the encounter offers a rehabilitative opportunity to accept responsibility for wrongdoing, express remorse, and ask for the victim's forgiveness. Most perpetrators get the chance to substitute restitution obligations (through work at regular jobs) for hard time behind bars. For the community, the pragmatic benefit is that negotiated settlements relieve court backlogs as well as jail and prison overcrowding and eliminate the need to build more cells to confine greater numbers of convicts at the public's expense. A less tangible but significant spiritual dividend is that restorative justice nurtures an atmosphere of forgiveness, redemption, acceptance, tolerance, and harmony within the community (Hudson and Galaway 1975; Umbreit 1990; Viano 1990; Wright 1991).

The growth of interest in restorative justice is likely to accelerate because of the need to divert cases out of the formal adversarial system of court adjudication into the informal case-processing track of alternative dispute resolution (ADR). For decades, police officers, prosecutors, judges, and court administrators have been weeding out what they consider to be the "garbage" from the case flow. What they deem to be "junk" cases that don't merit much public attention involve people who had prior relationships (as lovers, family members, coworkers, neighbors, etc.) before they became embroiled in minor disputes in which both parties share responsibility for the outbreak of hostilities (Silberman 1978). After years of neglect, the federal government in the early 1970s provided the seed money to set up several neighborhood justice centers to mediate some of these conflicts diverted from the court system. In 1980, Congress passed the Dispute Resolution Act to further the spread of "storefront justice." Many of these experimental, non-adversarial programs employing mediators and arbitrators to settle cases in which the labels "totally innocent victim" and "completely guilty perpetrator" did not fit the facts, evolved into VORPS.

At the same time that these alternatives to adjudication were developing, a growing chorus of voices and a coalition of diverse interest groups called for the development of new alternatives to incarceration. Jails and prisons have long been indicted for being overcrowded, disease-ridden, explosively violent, and strikingly counterproductive "schools for crime" that churn out hardened convicts prone to recidivate. By the turn of the century, support was building for "downsizing prisons" (see Jacobson 2005) and for discovering constructive, cost-effective ways of handling non-dangerous lawbreakers without removing them from their communities.

The convergence of these two trends—diverting "garbage cases" from an overburdened criminal justice process and searching for effective alternatives to expensive yet ineffective incarceration facilities—will bring about a greater reliance on restorative justice, and in particular on the use of mediation techniques to arrive at out-of-court settlements in which offenders avoid serving time behind bars by making restitution to their victims as a precondition for mutual reconciliation.

How the Trend Toward Differential Justice Might Increase the Gap in the Way Victims Are Handled

Public Service Homicides; Missing Persons of Color

It is likely that in the near future, any obvious "double standards" in the ways in which victims are handled by agencies and officials will become a contentious issue. Whereas in the recent past, just about all victims suffered from neglect, now the potential is developing for some victims to receive first-class, VIP treatment, whereas others continue to be relegated to the status of second-class citizens.

This troubling problem of "double standards" within American society does not have an appropriate, evocative, widely accepted name. It might best be referred to as "differential access" but is also called "class privilege" and "dual systems." The term "differential" is preferable because it is more accurate; "double" or "dual" implies only when two distinct systems operate—in reality, usually there are several systems: a top track, a bottom track, and one or more gradations in between (with people in the middle groupings enjoying some privileges and benefits but not others). The phrase "class privilege" accentuates the importance of wealth and power, but it overlooks stratification and discrimination based on gender, race, disability, and age as well. Differential or dual systems and class privilege in other areas of American society have been studied extensively (e.g., schooling, health care, and housing). The persistent pattern in each of these areas is that the affluent benefit from the best goods and services that modern technology can deliver and money can buy, while the underclass is grudgingly provided with the minimal, lowest-quality services the system can get away with, without fully exposing its false promises of "equality."

Differential access to justice has been the subject of a great deal of interest, research, and debate. Some argue that in the United States, the country is run "by laws, not men [sic]," and that "justice is blind." But others work to expose and put an end to the thinly disguised continuation of the long-standing practice of differential access to justice, which leads to double standards, in which a perpetrator's and a victim's personal characteristics are improperly and unfairly taken into account in the way the system handles their cases (see Karmen 2007) (e.g., opponents of capital punishment argue that the death penalty certainly used to be and apparently still is handed down in a discriminatory manner, depending on the race and class of the victim as well as the murderer).

As noted above, the opportunities, rights, and privileges available to victims have proliferated thanks to the victims' rights movement; as predicted above, victims might secure additional advantages and options in the near future (specifically, assigning victim advocates, purchasing anticrime devices and services, permitting private prosecution; and allowing mediation/restitution/reconciliation). Differential access to justice could become more blatant, in the sense that the way cases will be resolved will depend even more on the victim's status and the offender's place in the social order. The victimization of some people will continue to be taken much more seriously than the harming of others. When "important" members of society turn to the legal system for redress, they will receive a more satisfactory and supportive response than they do now. When the meager possessions of "marginal" members of society are stolen, or when they are beaten, robbed, or raped, the same old uncaring, impersonal assembly-line disposal of their cases will take place.

Pushing these projections still further, a more obviously unjust situation than exists at present could develop in the early decades of the twenty-first century. While more affluent and influential victims might be able to compel the system to deliver satisfactory service, the most underprivileged strata at the bottom of the social class hierarchy might be forced to fend for itself. The current trend toward a high-tech service economy coupled with deindustrialization (the decline of American manufacturing) is bringing about pervasive long-term structural unemployment for those lacking the requisite skills. That could further polarize the population into a prospering upper class, struggling middle class, and growing "surplus population" (what some call the underclass or outclass of marginalized, excluded, demoralized, crushed, defeated, self-destructive, and ineffectively rebellious jobless, homeless, and hungry people). Contained within run-down inner-city neighborhoods and scattered pockets of poverty in outlying districts, these victims of economic dislocations will be viciously preyed upon by even more desperate people who live among them. Their existence will be written off as unimportant, and their life-and-death struggles will be deemed "private matters" not worthy of governmental intervention. If the authorities turn their backs on these victims of "poor-on-poor" crimes, the profoundly alienated residents in these areas will be forced to defend their lives and possessions as best they can. They will be driven routinely to impose their own brands of on-the-spot "street justice," vigilante style.

The stark contrast between the sheltered lives of the privileged classes in gated communities (buttressed by a responsive criminal justice system that tends to their needs and wishes should they become victimized) and the misery endured by the inhabitants of out-of-control "free-fire zones" and "no-man's lands" will serve as an indictment of the gross inequities imposed by the problem of differential access to justice—if this nightmare scenario actually materializes.

Victimologists who conduct research in the future can monitor whether the constitutional pledge of "justice for all" and "equal protection under the law" is actually being carried out, or whether differential access to justice remains a stubborn problem.

THE PERILS OF CRYSTAL-BALL GAZING

Will the situation of victims in the first few decades of the twenty-first century be marked by more favorable treatment by criminal justice officials, by technological breakthroughs that enhance personal safety and protect valued possessions, and by universal access to professional advocates, private prosecutors, and mediation/restitution/reconciliation programs? Or will countervailing forces arise to keep today's tendencies in check? When gazing in a crystal ball, it is necessary to recognize that each action can provoke a reaction and that each reform can stiffen resistance from other interest groups. Pro-victim arguments provoke opposition, competition over limited resources and conflicting priorities lead to stalemates, temporarily favorable conditions fade away, and historical opportunities for meaningful change may be missed. Will profit-oriented enterprises commercially exploit the victims' plight by marketing ineffective devices and services? Will criminal justice officials rally to stop the emergence of dedicated advocates who will force them to live up to their rhetoric about handling victims with dignity and compassion and guaranteeing them notification and participatory rights? Will government attorneys lobby to preserve their virtual monopoly over the exercise of prosecutorial discretion and thereby thwart the revival of private prosecution? Will adherents of the punishment-oriented approach stifle the spread of restorative justice? Will egalitarian-oriented organizations fight against any widening of the gap in the way that disadvantaged victims are treated in comparison to affluent and privileged ones? Only time will tell.

REFERENCES

ANONYMOUS (1994). Circling the wagons: More communities adopt gated-enclave approach. *Law Enforcement News* 15(November): 6.

ANONYMOUS (1997). Events: Restorative justice regional symposiums. *NIJ Journal* 233 (September): 26.

BARKAS, J. (1978). *Victims*. New York: Scribners.

BLAKELY, E., and M. SNYDER (1997). *Fortress America: Gated Communities in the United States*. Washington, DC: Brookings Institution Press.

CARRINGTON, F. (1975). *The Victims*. New Rochelle, NY: Arlington House.

CARRINGTON, F. (1977). Victims' rights litigation: A wave of the future? *University of Richmond Law Review* 11(3): 447–470.

CATALANO, S. (2006). *BJS Bulletin: Criminal Victimization, 2005*. Washington, DC: U.S. Department of Justice.

COLE, G. (1992). *The American System of Criminal Justice*, 6th ed. Pacific Grove, CA: Brooks/Cole.

DIIULIO, J. JR. (1988). What's wrong with private prisons. *The Public Interest* 92(Summer): 66–83.

DRAPKIN, I., and E. VIANO (1974). *Victimology: A New Focus*, Vols. 1–5. Lexington, MA: D.C. Heath.

DUROSE, M. (2004). *BJS Bulletin: Felony Sentencing in State Courts, 2002*. Washington, DC: U.S. Government Printing Office.

EL NASSER, H. (2002). Gated communities more popular, and not just for the rich. *USA Today*, December 15, A2.

ELIAS, R. (1983). *Victims of the System: Crime Victims and Compensation in American Politics and Criminal Justice*. New Brunswick, NJ: Transaction Books.

ELLIOTT, E., and GORDON, R. (2005). *New Directions in Restorative Justice: Issues, Practice, Evaluation*. Devon (UK): Willan Publishing.

FRIEDMAN, L. (1985). The crime victim movement at its first decade. *Public Administration Review* 45(November): 790–794.

GALAWAY, B. and J. HUDSON (1975). Restorative Justice: International Perspectives. New Jersey: Erlbaum.

GRIFFIN, S. (1971). Rape: The all American crime. *Ramparts* September: 25–30.

HOOK, S. (1972). The rights of the victims: Thoughts on crime and compassion. *Encounter* (April): 29–35.

HUDSON, J., and B. GALAWAY (1975). *Considering the Victim: Readings in Restitution and Victim Compensation*. Springfield, IL: Charles C Thomas.

HUDSON, J., and B. GALAWAY (1990). *Criminal Justice: Restitution and Reconciliation.* Monsey, NY: Criminal Justice Press.

JACOBSON, M. (2005). *Downsizing Prisons: How to Reduce Crime and End Mass Incarceration.* New York: New York University Press.

KARMEN, A. (1992). Who's against victim's rights? *St. John's Journal of Legal Commentary*, 8(1): 157–176.

KARMEN, A. (1995). Towards the institutionalization of a new kind of criminal justice professional: The victim advocate. *Justice Professional* 9(1): 1–16.

KARMEN, A. (2000). *New York Murder Mystery: The True Story Behind The Crime Crash of the 1990s.* New York: New York University Press.

KARMEN, A. (2007). *Crime Victims: An Introduction To Victimology*, 6th ed. Belmont, CA: Wadsworth Publishing/Thomson Higher Education.

LANGAN, P., and H. GRAZIADEI (1995). *BJS Bulletin: Felony Sentences in State Courts, 1992.* Washington, DC: U.S. Government Printing Office.

LARGEN, M. (1981). Grassroots centers and national task forces: A history of the anti-rape movement. *Aegis*, 32(Autumn): 46–52.

LEIGH, L. (2007). Private prosecutions and discretionary justice. *The Criminal Law Review* (April): 289.

LIEDTKE, C. (2000). Merchants support cities with business improvement districts. *Nation's Cities Weekly* 23(6): 7.

LOSEKE, D. (1989). "Violence is violence". . . or is it? The social construction of "wife abuse" and public policy. In *Images of Issues: Typifying Contemporary Social Problems*, ed. J. Best, pp. 191–206. New York: Aldine de Gruyter.

LUECK, T. (1994). Business districts grow at price of accountability. *New York Times*, 20 (November): 1, 46.

LYNCH, R. (1976). Improving the treatment of victims: Some guides for action. In *Criminal Justice and the Victim*, ed. W. MacDonald, pp. 165–176, Thousand Oaks, CA: Sage Publications.

MARTIN, D. (1977). *Battered Wives.* New York: Pocket Books.

McDONALD, W. (1996). Toward a bicentennial revolution in criminal justice: The return of the victim. *American Criminal Law Review*, 13: 640–660.

McKNIGHT, D. (1981). The victim–offender reconciliation project. In *Perspectives on Crime Victims,* ed. B. Galaway and J. Hudson, pp. 292–298, St. Louis, MO: Mosby.

MEINERS, R. (1978). *Victim Compensation: Economic, Political, and Legal Aspects.* Lexington, MA: D.C. Heath.

NATIONAL ORGANIZATION FOR VICTIM ASSISTANCE (1986). NOVA sponsors forum on constitutional amendment. *NOVA Newsletter*, March: 1–2, 7.

NATIONAL ORGANIZATION FOR VICTIM ASSISTANCE (2003). *National Advocate Credentialing Program.* [Retrieved June 24, 2007, from http://www.trynova.org]

NEWMAN, D. (1986). *Introduction to Criminal Justice*, 3rd ed. New York: Random House.

PRESIDENT'S TASK FORCE ON VICTIMS OF CRIME (1982). *Final Report.* Washington, DC: U.S. Government Printing Office.

PRISON FELLOWSHIP INTERNATIONAL (2005). *Centre for Justice and Reconciliation Newsletter*, May, p. 4.

RIEFF, R. (1979). *The Invisible Victim: The Criminal Justice System's Forgotten Responsibility.* New York: Basic Books.

ROBERTS, A. (1990). *Helping Crime Victims: Research, Policy, and Practice.* Thousand Oaks, CA: Sage Publications.

ROLAND, J. (1996). Private prosecutions. *Modern Militiaman*, 2(July–August): 3–5 (Internet newsletter).

SCHAFER, S. (1968). *The Victim and His Criminal.* New York: Random House.

SCHNEIDER, A., and P. SCHNEIDER (1981). Victim assistance programs: An overview. In *Perspectives on Crime Victims*, eds. B. Galaway and J. Hudson, pp. 364–373, St. Louis, MO: Mosby.

SCHWENDINGER, J., and H. SCHWENDINGER (1983). *Rape and Inequality.* Thousand Oaks, CA: Sage Publications.

SEBBA, L. (1992). The victim's role in the penal process: A theoretical orientation, in *Toward a*

Critical Victimology, ed. E. Fattah, pp. 195–221, New York: St. Martin's Press.

SENATE JUDICIARY COMMITTEE REPORT (2006). Senate committee report on crime victims' rights amendment. *Federal Sentencing Reporter* 19(1): 58–61.

SENTENCING COMMISSION'S PRACTITIONERS' ADVISORY GROUP (2005). Letter from practitioners' advisory group on victim participation. *Federal Sentencing Reporter* 19, 2(December): 138–139.

SIGLER, J. (1979). The prosecutor: A comparative functional analysis. In *The Prosecutor*, ed. W. McDonald, pp. 53–74, Thousand Oaks, CA: Sage Publications.

SILBERMAN, C. (1978). *Criminal Violence, Criminal Justice*. New York: Random House.

SMALL BUSINESS SERVICES (2007). *Business Improvement Districts*. [Retrieved June 22, 2007, from http://www.nyc.gov]

STARK, J., and H. GOLDSTEIN (1985). *The Rights of Crime Victims*. Chicago, IL: Southern Illinois University Press.

STEINBERG, A. (1984). From private prosecution to plea bargaining: Criminal prosecution, the district attorney, and American legal history. *Crime and Delinquency* 30(4): 568–592.

TOMZ, J., and D. MCGILLIS (1997). *Serving Crime Victims and Witnesses*, 2nd ed. Washington, DC: Office of Justice Programs.

UMBREIT, M. (1990). Victim–offender mediation with violent offenders: Implications for modifications of the VORP model. In *The Victimology Handbook: Research Findings, Treatment, and Public Policy*, ed. E. Viano, pp. 337–352, New York: Garland Publishing.

VIANO, E. (1976). The study of the victim. *Victimology* 1: 1–7.

VIANO, E. (1990). The recognition and implementation of victim's rights in the United States: Developments and achievements. In *The Victimology Handbook: Research Findings, Treatment, and Public Policy*, ed. E. Viano, pp. 319–336, New York: Garland Publishing.

VICTIM–OFFENDER RECONCILIATION PROGRAMS (VORP) Information and Resource Center (2000). *Current News*. [Retrieved April 12, 2000, from http://www.vorp.com]

WILSON-DUENGES, G. (2000). An exploration of sense of community and fear of crime in gated communities. *Environment and Behavior* 32(5): 597–612.

WRIGHT, M. (1991). *Justice for Victims and Offenders*. Philadelphia, PA: Open University Press.

Chapter 13

Murder and Mayhem in the Media

Media Misrepresentation of Crime and Criminality

Robert A. Jerin and Charles B. Fields

ABSTRACT

There are two widely held assumptions concerning the effects of the media on the public's perception of crime and criminality. The first assumes that the mass media (especially television) are the prime sources of our understanding in these areas. The second assumption is that the media present erroneous and distorted information about crime. Are our views distorted by what we read in the newspaper and what we see on television? This chapter addresses the various ways in which crime and related issues are reported, their relationship to the actual crime problem, and influences on public perceptions by the media. Two separate media, television and print, are considered. This chapter also discusses the type and frequency of some of the more popular crime-dramas and reality crime shows. Future trends in these areas are also addressed.

INTRODUCTION

Although the public's perception of crime is influenced by various sources, the media seem to have the greatest influence on the perception of crime and criminality. Crime in the media was brought forth in print during the mid-1600s. Surette (1998) discovered that publications during this time period functioned as entertainment for the public using an informational format, which in turn assembled a relationship between crime and the social counterpart of sin. In one of the first and most important studies examining crime

217

and crime news coverage, Davis (1952) presented evidence that there is no relationship between official crime statistics and crime as reported in the print media. In fact, this study indicated the public perception of crime depends almost entirely on what is read in the newspapers. However, this study was conducted before widespread television viewing. Surette (1998:68) states, "Crime is seen to be the single most popular story element in the history of U.S. commercial television, with crime-related shows regularly accounting for one-fourth to one-third of all prime time shows."

The television market for illustrating crime has significantly increased over the last few decades. The television at one time could be classified into either news or entertainment. It wasn't long until this line became blurred between these two distinctions. *Police Story*, the first police drama aired in 1952 on CBS, was a live, half-hour program that dramatized actual crimes depicted from files of law enforcement agencies around the nation. Between 1973 and 1977 the familiar *Police Story* series aired on NBC. During 1988 four made-for-television movies based on the original script of *Police Story* aired on ABC created by Los Angeles police officer and writer Joseph Wambaugh. This police drama laid the groundwork for future reality-based police programs such as *Law and Order, COPS,* and *CSI.*

Several competing schools of thought provide interesting study when examining the relationship between the media and crime. Ericson (1991) believes that most previous research on mass media and crime has been deficient because it focused too much on the effect of the mass media on the perceptions of crime and criminals. He addressed this "effects" tradition by critiquing several widely held assumptions, two of which deserve further attention.

The first assumption assumes that the mass media (especially television) are the primary sources of public understanding of crime areas. It should be noted that some research (Graber 1979, 1980), however, indicates that the knowledge comes from a variety of sources, the media being but one of several. Nevertheless, most research recognizes the growing influence of the media on public opinion and society's understanding of criminal justice issues (Page, Shapiro, and Dempsey 1987; Newman 1990; Hans and Dee 1991; Schlesinger, Tumber, and Murdock 1991; Lawrence 2000; Fox and Van Sickel 2001). Fienberg (2002) conducted a content analysis of newspaper articles and found that increased coverage of crime produces a significant effect on the size of the police agency and policy making. Dowler (2002:210) found that crime-drama viewers were more likely to "favor eased restrictions on carrying concealed guns" and "are more likely to think that being armed is advantageous." This does not mean that the public is blind to the influence of the media. One particular study conducted by the Center for Media and Public Affairs (1999:7) found "popular culture (television, movies, music, video games, etc.) was the most frequently cited source of blame for the outbreak of violence in our nation's schools," consuming 40 percent of the study's responses.

The second assumption is that the media present erroneous and distorted information about crime. The distortion of the extent of crime and its coverage in the news media is well documented. Studies have focused on the extent of crime as reported in local print media (Cohen 1975; Meyer 1975, 1976; Antunes and Hurley 1977; Graber 1979; Humphries 1981; Windhauser, Seiter, and Winfree 1990; Marsh 1991; Dorfman 2001; Getty 2001), the amount on television news reports (Graber 1979; Surette 1998; Howitt

1998), and on comparison with newspaper coverage of crime in other countries (Marsh 1991; Teece and Makkai 2000). In assessing the literature in the area, Marsh (1991:67) found that "there is an overrepresentation of violent crimes . . . and the percentage of violent crimes does not match official crime statistics." Additionally, the "emphasis on relatively infrequent violent crimes may contribute to a heightened concern of fear" (68). While Ericson (1991:220) admits that discrepancies can be found between the types and amount of crime reported in the media and official reports of crime, why should we expect the "cultural products of mass media to reflect the social reality of crime?"

These are all important areas of inquiry. Here we address the various ways in which crime and related issues are reported, their relationship to the actual crime problem, the influences on public perceptions by the media, and speculation as to what the future may have in store. Both qualitative and quantitative assessments are employed. We also summarize data that examine the amount and type of crime reported in the only national newspaper, *USA Today,* and attempt to discover whether there are differences in the amount, type, or seriousness of the coverage of statewide news in the national daily compared to official crime statistics (Uniform Crime Reports) and whether the state population and crime rates are in any way a determining factor.

Crime Reporting and Public Perceptions

Previous research examining the effect of the media treatment of crime addresses several areas: the study of criminal justice themes in the popular culture media (Newman 1990; Klite, Bardwell, and Salzman 1997; Potter and Kappeler 1998), the use of public information programming (Sacco and Trotman 1990; Bennett 2000), the use of advertising (Eder 1990), the national print media (Jerin and Fields 1994; Hochstetler 2001; Fienberg 2002), television (Schlesinger et al. 1991; Cottle 1993; Miller 1998; Fox and Van Sickel 2001), and combinations of media sources (Sheley and Ashkins 1981; Barak 1994). These studies have all surmised that the true pictures of crime, criminals, and dangerousness are out of proportion to actual crime statistics.

The accuracy of media reports on crime and criminality can have a direct impact on the public's perception of the extent of the crime problem as well as on the operation of the criminal justice system itself. Hans and Dee (1991) correctly recognize that the public's knowledge and views of the law and legal system depend largely on what they read in the newspaper and what they see on television; the vast majority of citizens have little direct experience with the entire criminal justice system. Victimization data establish that over a person's life, the likelihood of victimization is very high; however, fewer than half of such cases are even reported to authorities and from the known crimes, only a very small percentage is related to a conclusion in the justice system (Macguire et al. 1993).

According to a national survey, nearly two-thirds of people get most of their views about crime from television, 20 percent from newspapers, 7 percent from radio, and less than 10 percent from friends, neighbors, coworkers, or personal experience (Morin 1997). The amount of coverage given to crime reporting is significant, but it may not be more than that given to other topics (Graber 1980), it seems, however, that the crimes covered are largely sensational or extraordinary (Surette 1998; Roberts and Doob 1990;

Marsh 1991; Jerin and Fields 1994; Kappeler, Blumberg, and Potter 2000) and do not reflect the reality of the type or amount of victimization that is occurring.

This information does not seem to reach the general public. As an example, in a USA Today/CNN/Gallup Poll (1993), 69 percent of the 1,000 adults polled (plus an over-sample of African Americans) believed that local television news accurately reflected the amount of crime. It should be noted that only 58 percent of African Americans in the sample agreed. The poll additionally found that only 25 percent of those responding believed that TV news exaggerated the amount of crime, and 90 percent believed that crime was worse than it had been a year earlier. These beliefs do not correspond to official data; the actual amount of crime reported to the police actually fell by 5 percent over the previous year (Macguire et al. 1993). The link between the public's misconception concerning the amount of crime and the operation of the criminal justice system and whether this trend will continue in the future is an important area for study.

One of the first inquiries into the public's conception of a crime problem and the media's misrepresentation was an examination of how the press fabricated a "crime wave" in 1919 (Schlesinger et al. 1991). Through the use of increased coverage and a call for government action, the public was erroneously led to believe that the crime problem was becoming much worse even though actual change was only minimal. It seems that over the past century, drug issues are more susceptible to these "crime waves." Phillip Jenkins (1999) highlights the role of the mass media in distributing antidrug hysteria and illustrates how synthetic panics influence popular culture. He points out that in some instances the media have been used to facilitate these crime waves. The first crusade that portrayed a crime wave was associated with the opium dens at the turn of the twentieth century. Soon afterward crusader Harry Anslinger used propaganda such as "Assassin of Youth" and "Reefer Madness" to validate the "evils" of marijuana. A report presented to the State Department by William Howard Taft in 1910 stated "the illicit sale of [cocaine] . . . and the habitual use of it temporarily raises the power of a criminal to a point where in resisting arrest there is no hesitation to murder" (Inciardi and McElrath 2001:101). He reported that these allegations actually forced some police departments in the South to switch from a .32 caliber to a .38 caliber revolver. Additionally, Inciardi reported that Tom Brokaw reported on *NBC Nightly News* in 1986 that crack was "flooding America" and that crack was "America's drug of choice." Reinarman and Levine (1997:28) argued "at the time of these press reports, there were no prevalence statistics at all on crack." Reinarman and Levine (1997) went on to find that the *Washington Post* ran 1,565 stories about the crack crisis during the rise of the crack epidemic in 1989. More recently, there have been the same increased media reports of synthetic or designer drugs such as ecstasy, methamphetamines, and OxyContin (Jenkins 1999) yet the presentation of this information has been transformed. For example many of these "drug scares" are turning up in new formats, such as one-hour shows dedicated to entertain and inform, including *60 Minutes, 20/20, Dateline,* and HBO's *America Undercover*. These formats are designed to be both entertaining and informative.

While misrepresentations of crime information are of serious concern, the accuracy in how the media portray the operations of the criminal justice system is questionable. False depictions of "crime waves" and other crime-related information (e.g., amount of violent crime) reflect poorly on the police, courts, and corrections. The USA

Today/CNN/Gallup Poll (1993) also found that 86 percent of those surveyed believed that the courts were not harsh enough in dealing with criminals. Given the public's lack of personal contact with what the courts do, this perception of the quality of justice being dispensed is being driven by other sources.

Research has found that "the content of network television is shown to account for a high proportion of . . . U.S. citizens' policy references" (Page et al. 1987:23). Extending this information to the criminal justice field, the influence of media sources on the public's view of crime and the criminal justice system is apparent. Because most information reported by the various types of media covers similar types of stories, inaccuracies in the information presented can lead to inaccuracies in the public's perception of crime and the job that the criminal justice system is doing.

A study by the authors of this chapter conducted a content analysis on articles reported in the *USA Today*'s "Across the USA: News from Every State" (Jerin and Fields 1994). *USA Today* claims to be the foremost daily newspaper in the United States and is the only source that reports news from every state every day. Using Graber's (1979) differentiation of news topics to establish four general headings, the analysis established the central theme of each news *byte* in an effort to reduce duplication of recordings. The topics used in the study were (1) crime and justice, (2) government and politics, (3) economics and social issues, and (4) human interest and family.

In the initial analysis of the news, the different types of news and categories were first examined according to Graber's model. In "News from Every State," the crime and justice section received the least amount of coverage. The percentage of stories that fell into the crime category was 16 percent ($n = 4,236$). The percentage of additional news categories was government/politics, 24.4 percent ($n = 6,412$); human interest/family issues, 26.7 percent ($n = 7,015$); and economic/social issues, 32.8 percent ($n = 8,638$). A relatively small number of summaries ($n = 260$) that were difficult or impossible to categorize were excluded from the analysis. This balance of issues is unique compared to Graber's (1979) earlier study in Chicago (see Table 13.1).

TABLE 13.1   Frequency of News Topics (*n*) in *USA Today* (1990) and *Chicago Tribune, Chicago Sun-Times,* and *Chicago Daily News* (1979)[*] (Percent)

Topic	*USA Today* ($n = 26,301$)	*Tribune* ($n = 33,200$)	*Sun-Times* ($n = 581$)	*Daily News* ($n = 506$)
Crime and justice	16.1	21.8	28.0	26.7
Government and politics	24.4	41.4	41.5	43.9
Human interest and family	26.7	10.6	5.5	7.9
Economic and social issues	32.8	26.0	23.5	21.5

[*]With the exception of the *USA Today* figures, which were collected by the present authors, the primary data included in the table come from a year-long content analysis of the *Chicago Tribune*. The other two Chicago daily newspapers were analyzed on a more limited basis. For a more detailed discussion of the methodology, see Graber (1979).

It is perhaps unusual that crime- and justice-related news summaries make up the smallest category of "News from Every State" in *USA Today* while human interest and family summaries constitute the largest. The three papers examined by Graber (1979) report more news in the area of government and politics, while crime and justice, or economic and social issues rank second. Human interest and family news rank last.

The manner in which crime and justice news is reported in the state section of *USA Today* is similar to what was found in earlier research (e.g., Marsh 1991). The amount of violent index crimes reported is almost 42 percent, with murder at 28 percent. Property crimes make up 6 percent of the crime reported, with white-collar/corporate crimes totaling about 10 percent. The level of drug crimes is the third-highest recorded category, with more than 8 percent. The "other" crime category constitutes 29 percent of the recordings.

Because of the brevity of the material reported (i.e., two stories per day) the type of crime story that made the news is unique. The material in *USA Today* followed a pattern found in Roshier's work. Roshier (1973:34–35) identified four sets of factors that seemed to establish why some crimes are selected in preference to others:

1. The seriousness of the offense
2. "Whimsical" circumstances (i.e., humorous, ironic, unusual)
3. Sentimental or dramatic circumstances
4. The involvement of a famous or high-status person in any capacity.

Examples of these factors can be found throughout *USA Today*'s reporting of state events. In many cases a combination of these factors can be observed in the crimes reported.

The differences between the states are somewhat difficult to analyze because of the subjective descriptions of crimes reported in each state. Typically, in a brief sentence or two, routine crime-related summaries list the location of the offense and describe the offense itself (perhaps naming the offender and victim) but little else. It is a little easier, however, to determine a subjective category in which to list the offense.

The total number of crime-related stories by state ranged from 38 in Alaska to 152 in New York. Many crime-related stories, including drugs, rape, and robbery, had no reporting in some states. The population of the state in many cases seems to establish the frequency of the crime reporting more than anything else. An additional concern is the high percentage of crimes fitting into the "Other" category. There was a need to redefine this category because of the number of crimes and the important social issues that some address (e.g., hate crimes).

Crime Reporting and Official Crime Statistics

Many earlier studies have dealt with the relationship between the extent of crime reporting and actual crime rates (see, e.g., Antunes and Hurley 1977; Phillips 1977, 1979; Fedler and Jordan 1982). In an attempt to assess further the differences between crime rates and crime reporting, statistics for selected offenses from the Uniform Crime Reports (UCR) were compared with the same offenses reported in *USA Today*. Using a ranking system, comparisons between states and the UCR offer some interesting information. States were ranked by population, the UCR index crime rate, and the number and percent of news summaries relating to crime and justice reported in *USA Today.* In addition, four offense categories (murder, rape, drug violations, and corporate crime) were examined and ranked according to the reporting rate for each state.

The five most populated states, California, New York, Texas, Florida, and Pennsylvania, are among the states with the highest number of reported crimes (Macguire et al. 1993), but they are not ranked highest in crime- and justice-related reporting in the paper. The inference is that the number of crime and justice summaries is somewhat indirectly related to state population.

A comparison of the five areas with the highest UCR index crime rates—the District of Columbia, Florida, Arizona, Texas, and Georgia—and the reporting of more serious crimes offers additional insight into crime reporting behavior. None of the states with the five highest crime rates are included in the top five rankings of murder and rape. This difference in reporting may be due primarily to the commonality of major crimes in these states so that the newsworthiness of serious crimes in these same states may be minimized, and other factors (see Roshier 1973) may play a larger role.

This comparison is in direct contrast to the five states—West Virginia, South Dakota, North Dakota, Kentucky, and Pennsylvania—with the lowest index crime rates. Three of these states (West Virginia, South Dakota, and Kentucky) are ranked in the top five in rape and rape-related news summaries. This discrepancy may be due to the perception in the media that certain sensational crimes are more "newsworthy" in states with low crime rates.

Even the states with the highest rankings in terms of *USA Today*'s crime-related reporting—Arkansas, New Jersey, Wisconsin, Tennessee, and Missouri—are not states with relatively high crime rates. Only New Jersey is in the top half of the UCR index offenses (ranked twenty-second). The fact that Arkansas is ranked first in terms of total crime- and justice-related reporting, first in murder reporting, and second in drug reporting questions the objective reporting of crime-related stories in *USA Today.* Further analysis of this phenomenon reveals that certain sensational crimes may be responsible for the extensive coverage of serious crime in Arkansas.

Although statistical comparisons between official crime rates and the extent of crime-related reporting in *USA Today* may be problematic, there are at least some preliminary indications of a relationship between the reporting of certain crimes and crime rates (see Table 13.2). When correlations between rape as reported in *USA Today* and the UCR index are examined, it seems that those states with high crime rates were less apt to have rape-related summaries during the year. There is, however, a strong positive correlation between reporting of corporate/white-collar offenses, murder, and drug-related news summaries and total crime-related summaries for small states (in terms of population) than for larger states.

In the future, the media's representation of crime and criminality will probably follow the same course. With the evolution of some 500 television channels and the competition that will be generated by these networks, the use of sensationalism and hyperbole seems unavoidable. The print media could also fall victim to perceived market forces that

TABLE 13.2   Simple Correlations between Uniform Crime Reports (1990) and Crime and Justice Reporting in the *USA Today* (Selected Offenses)

	All offenses	Crime and Justice Reporting		Drugs	Corporate
		Murder	Rape		
UCR					
Index	0.0193	−0.0032	−0.2346[*]	0.3663[**]	0.1742
Violent	0.2313	0.1731	−0.1166	0.3884[**]	0.1830
Murder	0.0743	0.0259	−0.2215	−0.3699[**]	0.1071
Population	−0.6598[***]	−0.1441	−0.2557[*]	−0.4250[**]	−0.0935

[*], $p < 0.05$; [**], $p < 0.01$; [***], $p < 0.001$.

try to increase the public's interest while providing the smallest amount of objective information. The use of sensationalism incidents will continue to distort the true picture of crime.

Notwithstanding the possibility of continued misinformation, the increase in news coverage may also tend to educate the public. The use of cameras in the courtroom, which is occurring in more than 45 states (Verhovek 1991), along with the development of the Courtroom Television Network (Court TV), provides the public coverage of actual trials without a media filter. This should provide the public with a more accurate picture of the criminal justice system. Surette (1998) points out that in 1976, all but two states prohibited cameras in the courtroom but by 1996, all except three *allowed* cameras.

Court TV seems to be preoccupied with coverage of celebrity court trials. Actor Robert Blake has been covered in his court appearances 18 times since his indictment on charges of murder. Court TV's lineup includes the shows *Forensic Files; I, Detective; Body of Evidence;* and *The System.* Court TV has also been changing to succumb to society's entertainment needs. Its well-known series *Forensic Files,* which addresses true-life criminal cases, is merging with CBS's fictional *CSI: Crime Scene Investigation.* Chunovic (2002) reports that this is not the first time Court TV has expanded outside its network, stating that *CSI, ABC News,* and *Dateline* producers often contact Court TV for information. Court TV is also working on a pilot named *The Caper Challenge* (working title), a reality game with a crime twist. In this series, teams of specialists will compete to recreate on-set actual famous crimes. Court TV has also currently extended its broadcasts to Sirius's Satellite Radio.

There is evidence that sensational cases can influence the perception of the general public. A mock trial found that jurors predisposed to sensational cases were more likely to convict. Although sensational crimes have received extensive coverage over the years (e.g., the 1925 Scopes "monkey" trial and the 1935 Lindbergh kidnapping trial), recent sensational cases have provided the public with a greater interest in watching an actual trial unfold. The William Kennedy Smith and Mike Tyson rape trials captured the attention of the public and every media source (Lacayo 1991; Corliss 1992). Athletes are no exception to this type of coverage; other cases that have been followed by the media have included Kobe Bryant, Jayson Williams, and Jason Kidd. Similarly the case of JonBenet Ramsey which started in 1996 still heads the headlines as it is one of the most unsolved crimes and mysteries. The most notorious athlete trial coverage was O.J. Simpson's murder trial. The number of stories related to the Simpson case appearing on ABC, CBS, and NBC evening newscasts during 1995 accounted for 70 percent of all murder news (see Table 13.3). At the time it went so far as to take precedent over President Bill Clinton's State of the Union Address in 1997. All nine national cable networks, including CNN, MSNBC, ESPN, and ESPN2 covered the trial *over* the State of the Union message. ABC held some restraint and altered its schedule to include a two-hour special on the verdict (Fox and Van Sickel 2001). Although coverage of such cases have been characterized as a media "free-for-all" (Pollitt 1991; Nack 1992), the ability of the public to watch actual trials from start to finish allows many people to see this part of the criminal justice process that they would never experience. There also should be an awareness of the rise of programming referred to as *infotaining* (Surette 2002), such as People's Court, Judge Judy, Judge Joe Brown, Judge Hatchett, and Divorce Court. These shows try to bring a type of humor to usually mediocre cases.

This type of coverage is not limited to the courts. Law enforcement also has been the center of attention with television shows such as *COPS, America's Most Wanted*, and

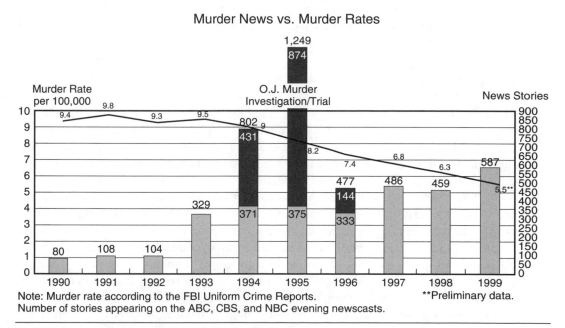

Note: Murder rate according to the FBI Uniform Crime Reports.   **Preliminary data.
Number of stories appearing on the ABC, CBS, and NBC evening newscasts.

TABLE 13.3   Murder News vs. Murder Rates

Source: The Center for Media and Public Affairs, TV News Crime Story Topics January 1 thru August 31, 2000.

Rescue 911. *COPS* follows actual police officers to narrate the action that the audience is watching. *America's Most Wanted* investigates the most wanted criminals and uses the public to assist apprehension. *Rescue 911* reenacts police dramas with the cooperation of the original participants. These programs focus on appealing law enforcement situations rather than an accurate picture of crime and criminals. *Law & Order, CSI, Third Watch, NYPD Blue* represent a more recent hybrid referred to as reality-based crime TV shows. They use actual cases as the foundation for their weekly television scenarios. *Law & Order* is advertised as having "presented the investigation and prosecution of cases ripped straight from today's headlines." For example *Law & Order's* 2003 season finale mirrored two contemporary, highly sensationalized and highly followed cases. The first represented a missing pregnant mother, an extramarital affair, and the husband's defense of boating to represent the disappearance of Laci Peterson. The second scenario focused on a celebrity holding an infant out a window (as Michael Jackson did) and allegations of pedophilia. These dramas provided a false sense of closure regarding the actual cases, which are still pending. TNT airs 8 hours of *NYPD Blue* and 14 hours of *Law & Order* during weekdays. A & E offers programs such as *Cold Case Files*, *American Justice*, and *Third Watch* in primetime slots plus reruns of CSI and Monk can be found on HBO almost on a daily basis.

The use of these and similar programs is certain to increase due to their low costs of production, convenience, and the continued public prurient interest. The accurate portrayal of the crime problem and the criminal justice system will depend on the media's actions coupled with the public's desire for more information regarding crime and criminality. If the public is allowed to view only a "cut-and-paste" version of these events or has access only to sensational cases, a distortion of both the crime problem and operation of the system will continue.

CONCLUSIONS

The reporting of news events across the United States follows previous patterns found in regional newspapers and other media sources. The print media sensationalize certain crimes and ignore many others. Often the media report lesser crimes because of the notoriety of the people involved or the humor that was evoked. However, the breakdown of crime news compared to other areas of interest does not seem out of proportion.

It has been suggested that the reporting of major crimes is not based on official crime statistics. Furthermore, the media reporting of a few sensational crimes in low-crime-rate states can distort the actual amount of crime in those states. The portrayal of a strained criminal justice system accompanied by an overrepresentation of violent crime translates into public policies that often lead to simple solutions to complex problems. This study has also found that a major factor in the media reports of crime is not the crime itself but the circumstances surrounding the crime, the public nature of the offender or victim, and the humorous nature of the incident. This is especially true with minor offenses. It seems that the accuracy of the reporting of criminal acts will always be compromised by the newsworthiness of the incident.

The future may hold more promise for accuracy given the possibility of competing news sources and greater variety that may be available to the general public. Live action reporting, gavel-to-gavel coverage of court proceedings, and innovations in information technologies should provide the public with increased and more accurate information. The conscious decision by the public to use these sources instead of continued reliance on the more traditional "news bits" and fictionalized programs for information can do much to ensure the elimination of the public's misperception of crime and criminality.

REFERENCES

ANTUNES, G. E., and P. A. HURLEY (1977). The representation of criminal events in Houston's two daily newspapers. *Journalism Quarterly* 54: 756–760.

BACON, J. (1992). Personal Communication (February 15).

BARAK, G. (ed.) (1994). Between the waves: Mass-mediated themes of crime and justice. *Social Justice* 21(3): 133–147.

BENNETT, L. (2000). *Globalization, Media Market Deregulation, and the Future of Public Information:* Presented at the UNESCO-EU Conference on *The Global Public Sphere, The Media and the Information Society.* Santiago de Compostela, Spain (November 2000). NA

CENTER FOR MEDIA AND PUBLIC AFFAIRS (1999). *Violence Goes to School: How TV News Has Covered School Shootings* 13(3).

CENTER FOR MEDIA AND PUBLIC AFFAIRS (2000). *TV News Crime Story Topics.*

CHUNOVIC, L. (2002). Court TV promotes "CSI" on local news. *Electronic Media* 21(6): 3.

COHEN, S. (1975). A comparison of crime coverage in Detroit and Atlanta newspapers. *Journalism Quarterly* 52: 726–730.

CORLISS, R. (1992). The bad and the beautiful. *Time* 139(8): 25.

COTTLE, S. (1993). *TV News, Urban Conflict and the Inner City.* London: Leicester University Press.

DAVIS, F. J. (1952). Crime news in Colorado newspapers. *American Journal of Sociology* LVII(June): 325–330.

DEADEN, J., and J. DUFFY (1983). Bias in the newspaper reporting of crime news. *British Journal of Criminology* 23: 159–165.

DORFMAN, L. (2001). *Off Balance: Youth, Race & Crime in the News.* Berkeley Media Studies Group, Public Health Institute, Vincent Schiraldi Justice Policy Institute (April).

DOWLER, K. (2002). Media influence on attitudes toward guns and gun control. *American Journal of Criminal Justice: AJCJ* 26(2).

EDER, P. F. (1990). *The Futurist* 38–41.

ERICSON, R. V. (1991). Mass media, crime, law, and justice. *British Journal of Criminology* 31(3): 219–249.

FEDLER, F., and D. JORDAN (1982). How emphasis on people affects coverage of crime. *Journalism Quarterly* 59: 474–478.

FIENBERG, S. (2002). Media effects: The influence of local newspaper coverage on municipal police size. *American Journal of Criminal Justice* 26(2).

FOX, R., and R. VAN SICKEL (2001). *Tabloid Justice: Criminal Justice in an Age of Media Frenzy.* Boulder, CO: Lynne Rienner.

GETTY, C. (2001). Corrections—Media wise? *Corrections* 63(7): 126–129.

GRABER, D. A. (1979). Is crime news excessive? *Journal of Communication* 29: 81–92.

GRABER, D. A. (1980). *Crime News and the Public.* New York: Praeger.

HANS, V. P., and J. L. DEE (1991). Media coverage of law: Its impact on juries and public. *American Behavioral Scientist* 35(2): 136–149.

HEATH, L. (1984). Impact of newspaper crime reports on fear of crime: Multimethodological investigation. *Journal of Personality and Social Psychology* 47(2): 263–276.

HOCHSTETLER, A. (2001). Reporting of executions in U.S. newspapers. *Journal of Crime and Justice* 24(1): 1–26.

HOWITT, D. (1998). *Crime, the Media and the Law*. New York: John Wiley.

HUMPHRIES, D. (1981). Serious crime, news coverage, and ideology: A content analysis of crime coverage in a metropolitan paper. *Crime and Delinquency* 27: 191–205.

INCIARDI, J., and K. MCELRATH (2001). *The American Drug Scene: An Anthology*, 3rd ed. Cary, NC: Roxbury.

JAEHNIG, W. B., D. H. WEAVER, and F. FICO (1981). Reporting crime and fearing crime in three communities. *Journal of Communication* (Winter): 88–96.

JENKINS, P. (1999). *Synthetic Panics: The Symbolic Politics of Designer Drugs*. New York: New York University Press.

JERIN, R., and C. FIELDS (1994). Murder and mayhem in the *USA Today:* A quantitative analysis the reporting of states' news. In *Media, Process, and the Social Construction of Crime: Studies in Newsmaking Criminology*, ed. G. Barak, New York: Garland Publishing.

JORDAN, D. L. (1993). Newspaper effects on policy preferences. *Public Opinion Quarterly* 57: 191–204.

KAPPELER, V., M. BLUMBERG, and G. POTTER (2000). *The Mythology of Crime and Criminal Justice*, 3rd ed. Long Grove, IL: Waveland Press.

KLITE, P., R. A. BARDWELL, and J. SALZMAN (1997). Local TV news: Getting away with murder. *Press/Politics* 2(2): 102–112.

LACAYO, R. (1991). Trial by television. *Time* 138(24): 30.

LAWRENCE, R. (2000). School violence, the media, and the ACJS. *ACJS Today* 20(2): 4–6.

MACGUIRE, K. (eds.) (1993). *Sourcebook of Criminal Justice Statistics, 1992*. Washington, DC: USGPO.

MARSH, H. L. (1991). A comparative analysis of crime coverage in newspapers in the United States and other countries from 1960–1989: A review of the literature. *Journal of Criminal Justice* 19: 67–79.

MEYER, J. C. JR. (1975). Newspaper reporting of crime and justice: An analysis of an assumed difference. *Journalism Quarterly* 52: 731–734.

MEYER, J. C. JR. (1976). Reporting crime and justice in the press: A comparative inquiry. *Criminology* 14: 277–278.

MILLER, M. C. (1998). *It's a crime: The Economic Impact of the Local TV News in Baltimore: A Study of Attitudes and Economics*. New York: Project in Media Ownership.

MORIN, R. (1997). An airwave of crime: While TV news coverage of murders has soared—feeding public fears—crime is actually down. *The Washington Post National Weekly Edition* (August 18): 34.

NACK, W. (1992). A gruesome account. *Sports Illustrated* 76(5): 24–28.

NEWMAN, G. R. (1990). Popular culture and criminal justice: A preliminary analysis. *Journal of Criminal Justice* 18: 261–274.

PAGE, B. I., R. Y. SHAPIRO, and G. R. DEMPSEY (1987). What moves public opinion? *American Political Science Review* 81(1): 23–43.

PHILLIPS, D. P. (1977). Motor vehicle fatalities increase just after publicized suicide rates. *Science* 196: 1464–1465.

PHILLIPS, D. P. (1979). Suicide, motor vehicle fatalities and the mass media: Evidence toward a theory of suggestion. *American Journal of Sociology* 84: 1150–1174.

POLLITT, K. (1991). Media goes wilding in Palm Beach. *The Nation* 252(24): 833.

POTTER, G., and V. KAPPELER (1998). *Constructing Crime: Perspectives on Making News and Social Problems*. Long Grove, IL: Waveland Press.

REINARMAN, C., and H. LEVINE (1997). *Crack in America: Demon Drugs and Social Justice*. University of California Press.

ROBERTS, J. V., and A. N. DOOB (1990). News media influence on public views of sentencing. *Law and Human Behavior* 14: 451–458.

ROBINSON, M. J., and A. KOHUT (1988). Believability and the press. *Public Opinion Quarterly* 52: 174–189.

ROSHIER, B. (1973). The selection of crime news by the press. In *The Manufacture of News*, eds.

S. Cohen and J. Young, pp. 29–39. Beverly Hills, CA: Sage.

SACCO, V. F., and M. TROTMAN (1990). Public information programming and family violence: Lessons from the mass media crime prevention experience. *Canadian Journal of Criminology* 32(1): 91–105.

SCHLESINGER, P., H. TUMBER, and G. MURDOCK (1991). The media politics of crime and criminal justice. *British Journal of Sociology* 42(3): 397–420.

SHELEY, J. F., and C. D. ASHKINS (1981). Crime, crime news, and crime views. *Public Opinion Quarterly* 45: 492–506.

SHOEMAKER, P. J., and S. D. REESE (1990). Exposure to what? Integrating media content and effects studies. *Journalism Quarterly* 67: 649–652.

SURETTE, R. (1998). *Media, Crime and Criminal Justice: Images and Realities*. Pacific Grove, CA: Brooks/Cole.

SURETTE, R. (2002). A test of a crime and justice infotainment measures. *Journal of Criminal Justice* 30: 443–453.

TEECE, M., and T. MAKKAI (2000). Print media reporting on drugs and crime 1995–1998. *Trends and Issues in Criminal Justice* 158: 1–6.

USA TODAY/CNN/GALLUP POLL (1993). Crime in America (October 28).

VERHOVEK, S. H. (1991). News cameras in courts? New York's law disputed. *New York Times* (May 28): B1, B6.

WINDHAUSER J. W., J. SEITER, and L. T. WINFREE (1990). Crime news in the Louisiana Press, 1980 vs. 1985. *Journalism Quarterly* 67: 72–78.

Chapter 14

Looking for a New Approach to an Old Problem

The Future of Obscenity and Pornography

Jay S. Albanese, Ph.D.

ABSTRACT

Internet access to explicit depictions of sex and violence is the latest manifestation of public concern over unwanted exposure to objectionable material. There is also alarm over songs, movies, cable TV, talk radio, chat rooms, and their impact on young people. Two national commissions investigated these issues during the last 40 years and drew widely different conclusions. A comparison of these investigations is used as a backdrop to propose alternatives for the future in defining and regulating obscenity and pornography. Recent court decisions on new laws to control pornography are also examined. Six major issues are reviewed: (1) what is pornography?, (2) how much obscenity is there?, (3) the effects of pornography on behavior, (4) appropriate action to be taken by private citizens, (5) legislative and law enforcement remedies, and (6) the role of the Internet in the distribution of pornography. A closer examination of the consumers of pornography, and a change in the focus of obscenity from sex to violence, is proposed.

NEW CONCERN FOR AN OLD PROBLEM

- Convicted serial killer Ted Bundy admitted prior to his execution that he was "addicted" to pornography.
- Police make more arrests of suspects who download child pornography from the Internet.

- Following public complaints, the television, movie, and recording industries are forced to provide warnings on their products to warn consumers of their sexual and violent content.

- Growing numbers of library books are being challenged each year for censorship on grounds of offensive descriptions of sex and violence.

- Complaints increase over the use of young teenagers and children in advertisements depicting suggestive poses.

- Bumper stickers, movies, radio announcers, and late-night television proliferate in their references to sexual conduct.

These incidents have combined to create a high level of concern regarding exposure to obscenity and pornography. One indication of this concern is that the last 40 years have produced two national investigations into obscenity and pornography in the United States. These investigations were paralleled by similar governmental investigations in Canada and England (Special Committee on Pornography and Prostitution in Canada 1985). The interest and concern about the effects of obscene and pornographic material are international in scope, especially now that the Internet serves as a primary means of access and distribution of pornographic material.

WHAT IS PORNOGRAPHY?

Every investigation or discussion of pornography necessarily gets bogged down in defining its target. The 1970 U.S. Commission on Obscenity and Pornography commission noted correctly that the term pornography has no legal significance. Pornography is a colloquial expression to describe sexually explicit written or photographic material designed to cause sexual excitement. Obscenity is the legal term that attempts to more clearly circumscribe the allowable limits of such material. The legal standard has evolved over a series of laws and Supreme Court interpretations, which ultimately resulted in the current legal definition of obscenity established by the U.S. Supreme Court in 1973. Obscene material must be "taken as a whole, appeal to the prurient interest in sex," portray sexual conduct in a "patently offensive way," and lack "serious literary, artistic, political or scientific value" (*Miller v. California* 1973). This three-part definition is known as the "Miller test" to determine whether material is obscene.

Determination of how this definition applies in a given situation has been difficult, resulting in a long series of laws, arrests, legal challenges, and court reversals. Some actual cases serve to illustrate the problem. Thirty to forty people at a tavern in Illinois watched as female participants jumped into a kiddie pool filled with mashed potatoes, and wrestled with each other, lifting up one another's shirt exposing their breasts. The tavern owner was charged with obscenity (Arresting Sight 2007). An Ohio couple pled guilty to obscenity charges for running a catalog business that offered sexually explicit DVDs that featured defecation, violence, and sex acts with animals (Recent Federal Obscenity 2005). In Alaska, more than 50 people went to City Hall to protest a chain video store, Movie Gallery, which has an adult video room away from its main selection of movies featuring sex-oriented movies. The city debated whether this activity violated obscenity laws (White 2006). These few examples show the wide range of conduct that is considered under obscenity law, and how the Miller test for obscenity does not lead to easy application in practice.

Some authors have found the definition of pornography offered by the Williams Committee in England to be the most understandable. It stated that "pornographic representation is one that combines two features: it has a certain function or intention, to arouse its audience sexually, and also a certain content, explicit representations of sexual material" (Committee on Obscenity and Film Censorship 1979:104; Hawkins and Zimring 1988:27).

HOW MUCH OBSCENITY IS THERE?

The true extent of obscenity is unknown for two primary reasons: no national count is made, and there is disagreement over what material should be covered under obscenity law.

The two U.S. pornography investigation commissions were formed in response to what was seen as a dramatic increase in the availability of explicit materials. In the 1960s and 1970s it took the form of books, magazines, television, radio, and films. From the 1980s to the present, concern has focused on new forms of distribution that did not heretofore exist: cable TV, video rental and purchases, dial-a-porn, and the Internet. In every instance, the commissions attempted to address the proper balance between free speech, individual privacy, and the public interest.

The 1970 U.S. Commission on Obscenity and Pornography found that there were approximately 14,000 movie theaters in the United States at that time, attended by 20 million people each week. General release films were found to be shown in 90 percent of all theaters, and sexual "exploitation" films were found to be shown in about 6 percent of all theaters. The commission noted the rating system implemented by the motion picture industry in 1968 (i.e., G, PG, R, and X) as a step toward industry self-regulation of sexual content, violence, and suitability for children. The PG-13 and NC-17 ratings were added years later in an effort to make further gradations in scaling objectionable contents.

An attempt was made to discover the number of sex films made each year, but it was found to be "primarily a localized business with no national distribution" that was "extremely disorganized" (U.S. Commission on Obscenity and Pornography 1970:22). The commission found the industry to be small: "There are no great fortunes to be made in stag film production. It is estimated that there are fewer than half a dozen individuals who net more than $10,000 per year in the business" (p. 22). The commission also detailed the size and scope of the "adult" book, magazine, and bookstore markets. It found that 85 percent of men and 70 percent of women have some exposure to pornographic materials during their lifetimes, and 75 percent of adult males have some exposure to explicit sexual materials before age 21, although "the experience seems to be more a social than a sexual one" (p. 25). It was found that American patterns of exposure were similar to those in Denmark and Sweden, where pornography has been decriminalized.

The 1986 U.S. Attorney General's Commission on Pornography did not conduct similar research into the nature and volume of traffic in explicit sexual materials. Therefore, it was unable to assess trends in exposure and availability of this material during the intervening 16 years. The commission drew conclusions anyway, finding that "men's" magazines, sometimes referred to as "male sophisticate" magazines, were objectionable, declaring that "all of the magazines in this category contain at least some material that we would consider 'degrading' " (U.S. Attorney General's Commission on Pornography 1986:281). Concern was also expressed about the sexual content of material on cable TV.

The 1986 commission concluded that approximately 80 percent of all U.S.-produced pornographic films and video tapes are made in and around Los Angeles, California (p. 285). The source of this information was not indicated. Similarly, the commission found that many video retailers sell or rent pornographic films: "Based on the evidence provided to us, it appears as if perhaps as many as half of all the general retailers in the country include within their offerings at least some material that, by itself, would commonly be conceded to be pornographic" (p. 288). The commission also noted that the adult movie theater "is becoming an increasing rarity" (p. 287), and that the growing popularity of videotape also "has hurt the pornographic magazine industry" (p. 289). Unfortunately, no figures were generated to indicate the precise nature of these apparent changes in the pornography industry.

The other aspect of the pornography industry addressed by both commissions was the influence of organized crime in the manufacture and distribution of pornographic materials. The 1970 commission found that "there is insufficient data to warrant any conclusion" about the involvement of organized crime in pornography (p. 23). The commission cited disagreement among both law enforcement officials and researchers in this regard (p. 142). The 1986 Meese Commission came to a different conclusion, stating that "We believe that such a connection does exist" (p. 291). This conclusion was reached despite the fact that the director of the FBI testified that "about three quarters of [FBI field] offices indicated that they have no verifiable information that organized crime was involved either directly or through extortion in the manufacture of pornography" (p. 292).

There exist data on arrests and prosecutions that reflect government activity against obscenity. These are summarized in Table 14.1.

It is shown in Table 14.1 that there have been relatively few federal case referrals over the past decade, averaging 38 per year with only half resulting in an actual prosecution. Overall, less than half of prosecutions results in prison terms, although those sentenced to prison terms received sentences of more than three years (average of 38 months). Regarding case referrals, the FBI is the agency primarily responsible for obscenity investigations. It handles more than half of all federal cases of this type. Agencies in the Department of Homeland Security (usually Customs), together with the U.S. Postal Service, handle about a third of obscenity investigations.

Why are there so few obscenity cases? These cases are not easy to make due to uncertain applicability of the law and its unclear definition (the Miller test), and the difficulty in securing convictions when a case is brought due to tolerant public attitudes about depictions of consensual adult sexual conduct. This leads to the important question of the link between exposure to obscenity and pornography and criminal behavior.

TABLE 14.1   Federal Obscenity Prosecutions

Fiscal Year	Case Referrals from Investigative Agencies	Federal Prosecutions Filed	Convictions	Sentenced to Prison Term	Average Prison Sentence (months)
1996	37	5	6	6	22
1998	47	29	12	4	9
2000	37	11	10	7	72
2002	32	15	17	13	39
2004	40	34	14	11	30
2006	38	21	19	14	57
Average	38	19	13	9	38

Source: Transactional Records Access Clearinghouse/Syracuse University. http//:www.trac.syr.edu

THE PORNOGRAPHY-HARM LINK

Perhaps the most significant question is the possible effects of pornography in causing antisocial or criminal behavior. The 1970 commission conducted a great deal of new research on the subject. The 1986 commission conducted no new research of its own, but relied instead on the results of prior investigations.

In a national opinion poll, the 1970 commission found that there was no nationwide consensus among the public about the effects of pornography. Empirical studies found that both sexes were equally aroused by explicit sexual material and that exposure appeared to have no effect on frequency of masturbation or intercourse. Similarly, four separate research studies indicated "little or no effect" of erotic stimuli on attitudes "regarding either sexuality or sexual morality" (p. 29). Finally, it was found that, similar to adults, delinquents and nondelinquents have similar experiences with explicit sexual material and that there is no evidence of a pornography-crime link (p. 286). "In sum, empirical research designed to clarify the question has found no evidence to date that exposure to explicit sexual materials plays a significant role in the causation of delinquent or criminal behavior among youth or adults. The commission cannot conclude that exposure to erotic materials is a factor in the causation of sex crime or sex delinquency" (1970:32). This conclusion was echoed by national commissions in both Canada and England reporting in 1985 and 1979, respectively. (For a summary of this research, see Malamuth and Donnerstein 1984.)

The 1986 Attorney General's Commission came to a different conclusion on the subject of harm. It admitted that the testimony it received from various offenders and victims of pornography was suspect, and the report offered an extended discussion of the nature of harm, the standards of proof involved, and the problems of valid and reliable evidence of harm (pp. 302–320). Nevertheless, the commission separated sexually oriented materials into four categories that it admitted were arbitrary. That is, the commission noted that "some items within a category might produce no effects, or even the opposite effects from those identified" (p. 321). These four categories were sexually violent material, nonviolent but degrading material, nonviolent and nondegrading material, and nudity. The commission drew different conclusions for each of these categories.

With regard to sexually violent material, the commission recognized that there was no consensus about its effects on behavior in the research literature. This led the commission to make a number of significant assumptions: "Finding a link between aggressive behavior towards women and sexual violence, whether lawful or unlawful, requires assumptions not found exclusively in the experimental evidence. We see no reason, however, not to make these assumptions" (p. 325). The commission ignored a great deal of the empirical evidence and took an ideological approach to the question of harm, concluding that "substantial exposure to sexually violent materials as described here bears a causal relationship to antisocial acts of sexual violence and, for some subgroups, possibly to unlawful acts of sexual violence" (p. 326). The commission also found a deleterious effect of this form of pornography on attitudes as well.

The commission recognized that the empirical evidence is divided concerning the effect of nonviolent but degrading material. Nevertheless, the commission made substantially similar conclusions as it did for the effects of sexually violent material, "although we make them with somewhat less confidence and our making of them requires more in the way of assumption than was the case with respect to violent material" (p. 332).

The conclusions of the 1986 Meese Commission regarding harm were not based on the available research. "The absence of evidence should by no means be taken to deny the existence of a causal link" (p. 332). Therefore, it was concluded that "substantial exposure to materials of this type bears some causal relationship to the level of sexual violence, sexual coercion, or unwanted sexual aggression in the population so exposed" (pp. 333–334). It was also found that this type of material results in attitudinal changes regarding personal responsibility for actions and attitudes toward victims of sexual aggression. These conclusions have been challenged by several of the researchers relied upon by the commission. They claim that the commissioners made "serious errors" of omission and commission in their characterization of the research findings regarding the pornography-harm link (Donnerstein, Linz, and Penrod. 1987).

On the other hand, the Meese Commission found that nonviolent and nondegrading sexual material appears to have no effect on antisocial behavior. It was concluded that there "seems to be no evidence in the social science data of a causal relationship with sexual violence, sexual aggression, or sex discrimination" (1986:378). Nonetheless, it was found that "the material in this category in some settings and when used for some purposes can be harmful" (p. 346).

With regard to nudity, the Meese Commission showed little interest. It found that "by and large we do not find that nudity that does not fit within any of the previous categories to be much cause for concern" (p. 349). The differences in the commissions' conclusions about the harm caused by pornography are perhaps the most significant differences between them.

These mixed conclusions are also reflected in public views that are sharply divided over whether exposure to pornography causes harm to the viewer. The scientific evidence is very weak in showing harm, but it is believed by many that at least some kinds of obscene materials are harmful to those exposed and also to society in general.

LAW AND LAW ENFORCEMENT

Given unclear law, and mixed public views regarding obscenity and pornography, what should the role of law and law enforcement be in addressing it? Both commissions recognized the inability of law to control behavior effectively. The 1970 U.S. Commission on Obscenity and Pornography found that legal regulation "is not the only, or necessarily the most effective, method of dealing with these materials" (p. 32). Similarly, the Meese Commission believed that "to rely entirely or excessively on law is simply a mistake" (U.S. Attorney General's Commission on Pornography 428).

The 1970 commission did not "believe that a sufficient social justification exists for the retention or enactment of broad legislation prohibiting the consensual distribution of sexual materials to adults" (pp. 47–48). In fact, the 1970 commission made only four legislative recommendations.

1. Repeal of laws prohibiting sale of sexual materials to consenting adults. This was based on the commission's finding that exposure to explicit sexual material does not play a "significant role" in causing social or individual harm. Public opinion also supported the availability of sexually explicit materials for consenting adults.

2. Prohibition of distribution of certain sexual materials to young people. The commission believed that public opinion, as well as insufficient research on the particular effects on children, made prohibition desirable. The commission recommended the prohibited materials be limited to pictures, rather than books, and that the prohibited pictures must depict more than mere nudity.

3. Legislation should prohibit public displays of sexually explicit pictorial materials to protect children and nonconsenting adults from exposure they find offensive.

4. Prosecutors should be granted authority to obtain declaratory judgments and seize material to have the courts determine if it was obscene, prior to a complaint being filed. This would provide fair notice to the alleged offenders in such actions.

The 1970 commission's four legislative recommendations were supplemented by nonlegislative alternatives, such as sex education. As the commission declared, "much of the 'problem' regarding materials which depict sexual activity stem from the inability or reluctance of people in our society to be open and direct in dealing with sexual matters" (p. 53).

The 1986 Meese Commission took a different approach in its recommendations for change. It made a total of 86 recommendations, most of which involved calls for new laws and better enforcement of existing laws. The commission's conclusion regarding the existence of a pornography-harm link caused it to reject the adult consensual access approach of the 1970 commission. It also did not like the city zoning approach aimed at grouping or dispersing adult stores or theaters that offer material containing explicit depictions of sex. The courts have found zoning laws to be unconstitutional, when they are used merely as a guise for prohibition. Similarly, the civil rights approach first attempted in Minneapolis (arguing that pornography violates the civil rights of those portrayed) has been found unconstitutional thus far, because the definitions of obscene material have gone beyond the legal standard set by the U.S. Supreme Court in 1973 (see O'Neill 1985:177–187). Like the 1970 commission, the Meese Commission found that there should be preliminary judicial review of material before a complaint is filed. This is necessary to protect publishers and distributors from perpetual civil suits.

Of the Meese Commission's 86 recommendations, many dealt with the use of forfeiture laws in the prosecution of pornographers to allow for seizure of assets as well as criminal penalties. Fifty of the eighty-six recommendations dealt with child pornography in some manner, although the commission made no systematic survey of the size of the problem, finding that "there now appears to be comparatively little domestic commercial production of child pornography" and that most is produced as a "cottage industry" rather than through mass production (1986:409–410).

The emphasis of many of the commission's recommendations was on greater priority to obscenity investigations. It was found that obscenity investigations among law enforcement agencies are not common and that prosecutors rarely take these cases to court. Therefore, many recommendations included suggestions for better training, coordination, and resources for investigations in suspected obscenity cases.

The Meese Commission also recommended that possession of child pornography be a felony and that photo labs should be required to report suspected child pornography. Clearly, the 1986 commission took a regulatory-law enforcement approach to the issue of pornography, whereas the 1970 commission took a deregulation approach, at least with regard to adults.

EXPLAINING THE DIFFERENCES BETWEEN THE 1970 AND 1986 COMMISSIONS

Table 14.2 summarizes the major findings of the two national commission investigations of obscenity and pornography during the last 40 years. Seven significant issues that the commissions addressed continue to lie at the heart of the pornography debate today. As the table indicates, the only significant issue on which the two commissions agreed was the prohibition of public displays of explicit material in order to protect children and non-consenting adults.

The large differences in the findings and recommendations of the two commissions are not difficult to explain. The 1970 commission took an empirical approach to the issue. This was understandable given the presence of three sociologists and two psychiatrists on

TABLE 14.2   Comparisons of Conclusions of Two National Commission Investigations

U.S. Commission on Obscenity and Pornography (1970)	U.S. Attorney General's Commission on Pornography (1986)
No demonstrated link between exposure to pornography and sexual activity or crimes.	A pornography-harm link exists, although there is not yet conclusive evidence.
Sex education in school for children and professional workers.	Warn children about sexual abuse and exploitation rather than sex education in school.
Practical effect of citizen protests against pornography is minimal.	Protests and boycotts of offending establishments useful.
Self-regulation of film, television, and book industry is largely effective.	Greater priority should be given to civil and criminal enforcement.
Sale of sexual material to consenting adults should be permitted.	Greater emphasis on prosecution of producers and distributors of pornographic materials.
Prohibit distribution or display of sexual materials depicting more than mere nudity to juveniles.	Fifty recommendations regarding child pornography, including criminalizing its possession.
Public displays of explicit pictorial materials should be prohibited.	Public displays of explicit pictorial materials should be prohibited (same recommendation).

the commission. Absent a finding of a pornography-harm link in its research, legislation to regulate its distribution to consenting adults appeared unnecessary. The 1986 commission's approach was ideological. Recognizing that the empirical research was imperfect and inconclusive, the commission chose the route to which the commissioners were predisposed. That is, they believed there was some kind of link between pornography and harm, so that is what they concluded (see Albanese 1987). Six of the 1986 commission members had previously established views on the subject and some of the research cited by the commission as supportive of its positions was later challenged by the researchers themselves as misinterpretations of their work (see Donnerstein, Linz, and Penrod. 1987).

It is ironic, but few of the significant recommendations of either commission were enacted into law. The same fate met the Williams Committee report in England (Simpson 1983:57). This is probably due to the fact that there did not exist wide public support in 1970 for decriminalization of sexually explicit materials for consenting adults. Similarly, in 1986, in a more favorable political climate, there did not exist sufficient public interest in the prosecution approach endorsed by the Meese Commission. As the commission recognized, only 71 persons were convicted for violation of federal obscenity laws nationwide from 1978 to 1986 (1986:367). There were no federal prosecutions from 1984 to 1985 in Manhattan or Los Angeles, the two largest reputed centers of pornography manufacturing and distribution in the United States (1986:504). From 1977 to 1984 only one person was convicted for production of child pornography under the Protection of Children from Sexual Exploitation Act of 1977 (Simpson 1983:604). This low level of enforcement actions and/or incidence of obscenity cases continues to the present (as noted in Table 14.1).

SEX EDUCATION AND CITIZEN ACTION

If the law and law enforcement have not been shown to be effective thus far in addressing obscenity and pornography, what about the role of private citizens? Sex education, community organization, and industry self-regulation are ways that citizens can assert themselves without the assistance of government.

The 1970 commission found that parents are frequently "embarrassed or uninformed" about sex, only about half of all medical schools had even elective courses in human sexuality, and that opportunities for training professional workers "are still not widely available" (1970:34). The commission also cited a study which found that girls who had a particular sex education course "were less likely to have illegitimate children" than a comparison group. These facts led the commission to recommend sex education in the schools "because the existing alternatives for communicating about sex with young people are felt by so many people, both adults and young people themselves, to be inadequate or undesirable" (pp. 36, 317).

The 1986 Meese Commission also believed that "education is the real solution to the problem of pornography," but it did not recommend sex education in the schools (p. 426). Rather, it limited its attention to the desirability of warnings to children about sexual abuse and exploitation from a variety of sources.

The 1970 commission noted that an evaluation of two organized citizen action groups found that "their practical effect on the availability of erotica in their respective communities had been quite minimal" (pp. 38, 343). On the other hand, the 1986 commission recommended "protesting near the premises of establishments offering material that some citizens may find dangerous or offensive or immoral" (pp. 421–422). Boycotts of an establishment were also seen as desirable.[1]

The 1970 commission also identified industry self-regulation as an important positive approach to sexual material. It recognized the comic book industry, radio, television, and motion picture industries for their self-imposed standards. Greater than 90 percent compliance with these voluntary standards was seen as an indication of their success within these industries. The 1986 commission did not similarly emphasize the role of industry self-regulation as a positive approach to pornography.

This debate continues today, as citizens remain divided over the desirability and effectiveness of sex education, community organization, and industry self-regulation as ways to address the issues of obscenity and pornography.

THE RISE OF THE INTERNET

The role of the Internet in distributing pornographic text and images led to new concern about the portrayal of minors in pornographic material. This has resulted in legislative efforts that focus specifically on the portrayal of children in pornography and the distribution of that material to minors.

Congress passed in 1996 the Communications Decency Act, which contained two provisions that prohibit "the knowing transmission of obscene or indecent messages to any person under 18 years of age," or sending or displaying "patently offensive messages in a manner available to a person under 18 years of age" (Title V of the Telecommunications Act of 1996, 47 U.S.C.A. Sec. 223). The law was challenged in court immediately after it was passed, and was before the U.S. Supreme Court the following year. The Court held that the terms "indecent transmission" and "patently offensive display" violate the First Amendment's protection of freedom of speech, because the terminology was too vague, imprecise, and would "provoke uncertainty among speakers" regarding its applicability. The Act was held to be unconstitutional (*Reno v. American Civil Liberties Union* 1997). Other Court decisions reflect analogous problems in distinguishing offensive materials from those that are obscene under law, and how to restrict their dissemination to children and non-consenting adults without infringing on protected speech under the First Amendment.

The Supreme Court used the same argument in evaluating dial-a-porn operators who offer sexually suggestive telephone messages for a fee. The Court held there that obscene messages are illegal but that "indecent" ones are not (*Sable Communications v. FCC* 1989). Unlike radio and television, where one can be "taken by surprise by an indecent message," both dial-a-porn and the Internet "require the listener to take affirmative steps to receive the communication" (at 2836–2837). As a result, both indecent and obscene messages are prohibited on television and radio broadcasts, but only obscene messages are prohibited on the Internet or in dial-a-porn (*FCC v. Pacifica Foundation* 1978). The Court concluded that "it is true that we have repeatedly recognized the governmental interest in protecting children from harmful materials. But that interest does not justify an unnecessarily broad suppression of speech addressed to adults" (*Reno v. American Civil Liberties Union* at 2346). Quoting itself from an earlier case, the Court remarked: "The level of discourse reaching a mailbox simply cannot be limited to that which would be suitable for a sandbox" (*Bolger v. Drug Products Corp* 1983).

Public access to pornography in public libraries was the subject of a Supreme Court ruling in 2003. Because libraries routinely provide Internet access, Congress passed the Children's Internet Protection Act in 2000 that requires public libraries (as a condition of receiving federal money for library support) to put electronic "blocks" on their computers to protect against access to pornographic web sites. More than 14 million people use public library computers. The government argued that libraries don't carry X-rated movies or magazines on their shelves, so access to pornography via the Internet should be similarly prohibited. In a 5 to 4 ruling, the U.S. Supreme Court upheld the law admitting that blocking software inadvertently restricts access to some non-pornographic sites, but adult library patrons can have the blocking software disabled by request to the library. The Court held that public funds are spent to help public libraries "fulfill their traditional roles of obtaining materials of requisites and appropriate quality for educational and informational purposes." Access to pornographic web sites on public library computers does not fulfill this purpose (*United States v. American Library Association* 2003).

In another congressional attempt to deal with access to pornography, the 1998 Child Online Protection Act ("COPA" 47 U.S.C. 231) attempted to criminalize web sites making available materials that is harmful to minors, using a variation of the legal definition of obscenity to define "harmful." The problem, of course, is applying this definition of obscenity that relies on "contemporary community standards" to the Internet, which is available in places both inside and outside the United States where community standards differ widely (*Ashcroft v. American Civil Liberties Union* 2002).

The U.S. Supreme Court upheld a temporary injunction to prevent COPA from taking effect, and a federal judge issued a permanent injunction in 2007. The basis for the Court's rejection of the law was that software filters that block access to pornographic sites without proper adult documentation work well and do not pose the free speech problems that COPA does (*ACLU v. Gonzales* 2007; Russo 2006).

ISSUES FOR THE FUTURE: NEW APPROACHES TO AN OLD PROBLEM

Where does this leave the citizen or policy maker who sees crime, violence, and disrespect in the community that appears to correspond with a rise in explicit sex and violence in books, television, movies, and the Internet? Three central issues need to be more directly addressed in the concern about obscenity and pornography: (1) protecting children more effectively, (2) moving from sex to violence in defining obscenity, and (3) identifying causes of the entrenched popularity of pornographic material. These three issues, perhaps more than any others, will chart the course for the future.

Protecting young people from exposure to objectionable material underlies much of the obscenity issue. As laws and court decisions have shown, efforts tend to fail because material inappropriate for children may be suitable for adults. Some recent alternative efforts show promise for the future: industry pressure, targeting child pornography, and creative uses of the law to shield children from unwanted exposure.

A report of the Federal Trade Commission (FTC) found the music recording industry to market violent and sexually explicit material to young people through advertisements on television, magazines, movie trailers, and the Internet. The study by the FTC was requested by the president after the Columbine High School shooting in 1999 and the concerns raised about the exposure of depictions of violence on youth. The FTC study found that 80 percent of R-rated films were targeted to children under age 17. Similarly findings were discovered for violent video games. Of 55 music recordings with "explicit content" labels, industry marketing plans identified teenagers under age 17 as part of the audience (Federal Trade Commission 2000). This study forced the industry to promise to change its marketing practices, or else face more stringent legal regulation of their business. Follow-up reports have monitored industry compliance with their promises. The FTC created a web site in 2003 as a guide to parents regarding accepted standards for television program ratings, appropriate programming, and other information to help parents and children make better entertainment choices (http://www.fcc.gov/parents).

TABLE 14.3   Federal Child Pornography Prosecutions

Fiscal Year	Case Referrals from Investigative Agencies	Federal Prosecutions Filed	Convictions	Sentenced to Prison Term	Average Prison Sentence (months)
1996	558	275	83	64	34
1998	898	366	263	209	38
2000	1,325	621	475	421	44
2002	1,449	866	611	550	50
2004	1,399	1,309	866	836	64
2006	1,366	1,479	1,251	1,200	98

Source: Transactional Records Access Clearinghouse/Syracuse University. http//:www.trac.syr.edu

Making child pornography a higher investigative priority among police agencies is another method to address inappropriate exposure. In recent years there have been significant cases involving police undercover "sting" operations that lured child pornographers and molesters into traps set for them in Internet chat rooms and web sites. Improved police training gives them the technical ability to "seize" the information stored on computer hard drives in child pornography investigations. In one case, 50 persons were arrested in seven countries in a synchronized raid and seizure of dozens of computers, videos, and compact disks containing obscene images of children (Leeman 2002; Jenkins 2003; McNerthney 2007). These widely reported cases are likely to have some deterrent impact. Indeed, the federal government is focusing its efforts more on child pornography than on obscenity cases. Table 14.3 documents this trend.

As shown in Table 14.3, prosecutions and convictions for child pornography are much higher than for obscenity (Table 14.1), and the numbers are increasing significantly. This may be due to the fact that child pornography cases are more "winnable," given that there is significant public consensus against juvenile involvement with obscene materials whether as a participant or a consumer, so convictions are more likely than in obscenity cases that involve consensual conduct between adults.

Washington was the first state to enact a law designed to punish those who rent or sell violent computer games to kids under 17. Passed in 2003, the law fined (up to $500) those who rent games in which the player kills or injures a human form recognizable as a police officer or firefighter. This interesting law aimed to limit the distribution of antisocial depictions to young people, which many believe to be a factor associated with a antisocial behavior (see the next section "Obscenity: From Sex to Violence").

The Washington law, and similar laws in several other states addressing sexually explicit or violent video games have been overturned for overbreadth and vagueness, but legislatures continue to work on more narrowly tailored versions in order to reduce the exposure of young people (Dean 2006; Morse 2005/2006). In related fashion, a New York City zoning law that prohibits strip clubs and other adult sex-related businesses to operate within 500 feet of homes, schools, houses of worship, or each other, was upheld by the U.S. Supreme Court. The impact of the law forced 80 percent of the existing adult businesses to either move to an industrial area of the city or else reduce the adult-oriented portion of their business to less than 40 percent (*Hickerson v. New York City* 1999). The ability of localities to zone adult businesses away from areas frequented by youth can be a significant tool in reducing unwanted exposure.

Obscenity: From Sex to Violence

Definitions and prosecutions for obscene materials always have been directed at depictions of sexual conduct. A case can be made, however, that there is nothing inherently obscene about explicit depictions of sexual conduct. Explicit depictions of sex have long played a role in psychological counseling, physiological education, sex therapy, and art. The terms "patently offensive" and "prurient interest" invariably result in subjective line-drawing in attempting to distinguish gratuitous depictions of sex from those that have "literary, artistic, political, or scientific value." Simply stated, the value of sex is an elusive concept, difficult to determine in an objective way, and is a problem that underlies legislation and court decisions in this area. When sexual conduct is carried out in a tasteless manner, little social interest is involved. This makes it difficult to regulate or prohibit, due to its unclear impact on public health, safety, or welfare.

More objectionable than gratuitous sex are depictions of gratuitous violence. A significant social concern arises when sex is depicted in a way that involves force against an unwilling victim, against children, or even when unjustified violence without sex is depicted. Perhaps the future will witness a move from sex to violence in defining obscenity. Obscenity law might prohibit the depiction of gratuitous violence rather than sex alone. Depictions of violent assaultive behavior exhibited without legal justification could be held objectionable and punishable under law. The legal justifications for the use of force (e.g., self-defense, defense of others) are well defined in existing law, as are the definitions of assault. Such a new definition of obscenity might include photographs or broadcasts depicting assaultive behavior committed by persons without legal justification. The inclusion of sex in these depictions of violence could be a sufficient, but not necessary, element of obscenity. The only exception might be factual accounts of real events that have informational or educational value.

Unlike the inconclusive link between depictions of sex and sex offenses, there is a body of research that reports on the effects of depictions of violence on aggressive behavior (National Institute of Mental Health 1982; Donnerstein, Linz, and Penrod. 1987:108–136). Therefore, it might be argued that descriptions of wanton violence be declared obscene due to their possible effects on behavior. It could also be claimed that violence without justification is something our society sees as more objectionable than sex without social "value."

Before a proposal like this could be considered, changing the focus of obscenity from sex to violence, better answers to at least two important questions are needed:

- How does the effect of depictions of violence on aggressive behavior compare with other possible influences on aggressive attitudes and behavior (such as family and peer groups)?
- If gratuitous violence was determined to be obscene, what deleterious impact would this have on the creative arts, where books, films, and songs portray fictional violence without legal justification?

Why Is Pornography So Popular?

The 1970 commission conducted studies of the consumers of pornography and found that the vast majority of pornography is directed at the male heterosexual audience. Studies conducted by the commission in a number of different cities found men also to account for 90 percent of the consumers of sexually explicit materials (1970:10ff.; U.S. Commission on Obscenity and Pornography 1971–1972, Vol. 4:16ff.).

Other studies carried out for the commission found that "symbolic materials have a noticeably less arousing and erotic effect on women than they do on men." It was found that in both the United States and Sweden (where depictions of sex are more widely available) there is greater "acceptance of pornography" by men than women and that most pornography is produced by men, rather than by women (Kinsey et al. 1953; U.S. Commission on Obscenity and Pornography 1971–1972, Vol. 9:220). The "traditionally more conservative and restrictive attitudes that women have about virtually all sexual matters" reported by the 1970 commission might be changing, however. A Gallup Poll reported by the 1986 commission found that the proportion of young women (18–24 years old) who had rented an X-rated videocassette was two-thirds of the male figure (U.S. Attorney General's Commission on Pornography 1986:920). This apparent trend was not addressed by the Meese Commission, nor was the issue of consumers of pornography in general.

If the availability of sexually explicit materials is identified as a social problem in terms of explicit radio, television, books, films, computer services, and dial-a-porn, it is essential that a better understanding emerge of why those interested in seeing and hearing it are so resilient (see Kipnis 1999). There are at least two questions for which better answers are needed:

- Why are consumers of pornography predominately male, and females increasingly consumers of sexually explicit materials?
- Does sex education promote healthier (i.e., less prurient) attitudes toward sex that, in turn, reduce interest in pornography?

These questions underlie the current debate about the effects of pornography on attitudes toward sex and toward women (Assiter 1989; Downs 1989; Kendrick 1987; Maschke

1997; Saunders 2006). Finding the answers to these questions through research will make future decisions about obscenity and pornography less a matter of taste and more a matter of fact.

ENDNOTE

1. It should be noted that early in 1986, the executive director of the Meese Commission, Alan Sears, notified several corporations that they had been identified as pornography distributors and that unless they proved otherwise within 30 days, they would be described in this way in the commission's final report. This resulted in several chain stores dropping such magazines as *Playboy* and *Penthouse*. Following a suit by Playboy, Penthouse, and the American Booksellers Association, a federal court ordered the commission to retract its letter six days before it issued its final report.

REFERENCES

ALBANESE, J. S. (1987). Review essay: The accusers, the accused, and the victims in the debate over pornography. *American Journal of Criminal Justice*, 11(1).

ARRESTING SIGHT (2007). Bar Maids Wrestle in Pool of Mashed Potatoes. *Nation's Restaurant News*. Vol. 41, January 15, 15.

ASSITER, A. (1989). *Pornography, Feminism, and the Individual*. Winchester, MA: Pluto Press.

CAVAZOS, E. A., and G. MORIN (1994). *Cyberspace and the Law*. Cambridge, MA: MIT Press.

COMMITTEE ON OBSCENITY AND FILM CENSORSHIP (1979). *Report*. London: Her Majesty's Stationery Office.

DEAN, C. (2006). Returning the pig to its pen: A pragmatic approach to regulating minors' access to violent video games. *George Washington University Law Review* 75 (November): 136.

DONNERSTEIN, E. I., D. G. LINZ, and S. PENROD (1987). *The Question of Pornography*. New York: Free Press.

DOWNS, D. A. (1989). *The New Politics of Pornography*. Chicago: University of Chicago Press.

FEDERAL TRADE COMMISSION (2000). Marketing violent entertainment to children: A review of self-regulation and industry practices in the motion picture, music recording and electronic game industries. [Retrieved from http://www .ftc.gov/opa/2001/12/violence.htm]

HAWKINS, G., and F. E. ZIMRING (1988). *Pornography in a Free Society*. Cambridge: Cambridge University Press.

HERTZBERG, H. (1986). Big boobs. *New Republic* (July 14 and 21): 21–24.

JENKINS, P. (2003). *Beyond Tolerance: Child Pornography on the Internet*. New York: New York University Press.

KENDRICK, W. (1987). *The Secret Museum: Pornography in Modern Culture*. New York: Viking Press.

KINSEY, A. C., W. B. POMEROY, C. E. MARTIN, and P. H. GEBHARD (1953). *Sexual Behavior in the Human Female*. Philadelphia: W.B. Saunders.

KIPNIS, L. (1999). *Bound and Gagged: Pornography and the Politics of Fantasy in America*. New York: Grove Press.

LEEMAN, S. (2002). 50 arrested in child porn, abuse ring. *The Boston Globe* (July 3): A13.

MALAMUTH, N. M., and E. DONNERSTEIN (Eds.) (1984). *Pornography and Sexual Aggression*. San Diego, CA: Academic Press.

MASCHKE, K. J. (Ed.) (1997). *Pornography, Sex Work, and Hate Speech*. New York: Garland Publishing.

MCNERTHNEY, C. (2007). Detective tells girls how to stay safe on the Internet. *Seattle Post-Intelligencer*, March 21.

MORSE, R. (2005/2006). If you fail, try, try again: The fate of new legislation curbing minors' access to violent and sexually explicit video games. *Loyola of Las Angeles Entertainment Law Review* 26: 171.

NATIONAL INSTITUTE OF MENTAL HEALTH (1982). *Television and Behavior: Ten Years of Scientific Progress and Implications for the Eighties.* Washington, DC: U.S. Government Printing Office.

O'NEILL, T. (1985). *Censorship: Opposing Viewpoints.* San Diego, CA: Greenhaven Press.

RECENT FEDERAL OBSCENITY LAW CASES (2005). *The Associated Press State & Local Wire*, May 4.

RUSSO, R. (2006). *Ashcroft v. ACLU*: Congress' latest attempt to get COPA passed depends on the effectiveness and restrictiveness of filtering software. *Loyola University New Orleans School of Law: Law and Technology Annual* 6 (Spring): 83.

SAUNDERS, K. (2006). *Saving Our Children from the First Amendment.* New York University Press.

SIMPSON, A. W. B. (1983). *Pornography and Politics: A Look Back to the Williams Committee.* London: Waterlow Publishers.

SPECIAL COMMITTEE ON PORNOGRAPHY AND PROSTITUTION IN CANADA (1985). *Pornography and Prostitution in Canada.* Ottawa: Minister of Supply and Services.

U.S. ATTORNEY GENERAL'S COMMISSION ON PORNOGRAPHY (1986). *Final Report.* Washington, DC: U.S. Government Printing Office.

U.S. COMMISSION ON OBSCENITY AND PORNOGRAPHY (1970). *Report.* Washington, DC: U.S. Government Printing Office.

U.S. COMMISSION ON OBSCENITY AND PORNOGRAPHY (1971–1972). *Technical Reports*, Vols. 1–9. Washington, DC: U.S. Government Printing Office.

WHITE, R. (2006). Obscenity law review is planned for Palmer. *Anchorage Daily News (Alaska)*, March 8, G1.

CASES

ACLU v. Gonzales, 2007 U.S. Dist. Lexis 20008 (2007).

Ashcroft v. American Civil Liberties Union, 122 S. Ct. 1700 (2002).

Bolger v. Drug Products Corp., 103 S.Ct. 2875 (1983).

FCC v. Pacifica Foundation, 98 S.Ct. 3026 (1978).

Hickerson v. New York City, 146 F.2d 99 (Cert. Denied 1999).

Miller v. California, 93 S. Ct. 2607 (1973).

Reno v. American Civil Liberties Union, 117 S. Ct. 2329 (1997).

Sable Communications v. FCC, 109 S. Ct. 2829 (1989).

United States v. American Library Association, 156 L. Ed. 2d 221 (2003).

Chapter 15

Militarism and Global Punishment

Michael Hallett

> *It reflects a new, more "muscular" peacekeeping justified by the idea that the "natives" will not understand anything besides force and that their crises are so dire that no civilized nation can stand by and fail to act. Such projects anticipate grateful natives appreciative of Western military and governance capacity. They operate within a racial hierarchy in which civilized First Worlders discipline and instruct uncivilized Third World peoples in democracy and human rights. . . . Third world peoples are represented as the bearers of "culture," understood as tradition, and thus unable to participate adequately in the modern world.*
>
> —Race, Inequality, and Colonialism in the New World Order,
> SALLY ENGLE MERRY, 2006

> *On this island, indeed and on all the others I have seen, the inhabitants of both sexes always go naked, just as they came into the world. When they perceive that they are safe, putting aside all fear, they are of simple manners and trustworthy and very liberal with everything they have, refusing no one who asks for anything they may possess and even themselves inviting us to ask for things. They show greater love for all others than for themselves. They are very ready and favorably inclined for Christian conversion.*
>
> —Letter from Christopher Columbus to Ferdinand
> and Isabella of Aragon and Castille,
> EPISTOLA CHRISTOFORI COLUM, 1493

FORTRESS AMERICA: A PUNISHMENT RENAISSANCE IN BOTH WORD AND DEED

Research on punishment is in full-fledged renaissance of late, revealed in part by the ubiquitous popularity of David Garland's *The Culture of Control* and *Punishment and Modern Society*—as well as a growing body of work bespeaking dissatisfaction within criminology about its sometimes myopic focus on "hot spots" and "statistical residues," even as global mass imprisonment and military cooptation of penal devices proliferate. A hallmark feature of this renaissance in punishment research, such as may be found in *Cultural Criminology Unleashed* by Jeff Farrrell et al. or the widely adopted *The New Punitiveness*, or Jock Young's *The Exclusive Society*, is a renewed focus on global and cross-cultural "transfers" of policy in an expanding "supranational" carceral regime (Newburn and Sparks 2004:3; Welch 2005a; Zimring 2006).

A transnational "reinvention of the prison with a focus on incapacitation and punishment" has arguably positioned the United States as the global archetype for contemporary imprisonment and its practices, industries, and rhetorics of justification (Christie 1994; Savelsberg 2002:688). "In terms of the topography of contemporary crime control it is undoubtedly the case that the USA is perceived to be the source of the greatest number of exported ideas and practices" (Newburn and Sparks 2004:5). While interestingly much of the renaissance research is focused on England, Wales, and the United States—to the point where "the United States and England continue to hold a near monopoly on scholarly inquiry in the English language academic literature"—a growing body of work also examines rises and falls in the use of imprisonment beyond the Anglo context (Doob and Webster 2006:330; Pakes 2004; Von Hoffer 2003; Weigand 2001).

Thus, while fluctuations in incarceration dot the map of imprisonment worldwide, the beginning point of much recent research is the sentiment that "crime rates alone cannot explain the movements in prison populations" (Doob and Webster 2006:325; Walmsley 2003:71). A renewed body of work in criminology is built on a tradition of scholarship viewing punishment as a social process that evolves, operates, and transforms itself quite independently of crime and criminality (Garland 2001; Sellin 1976).[1] Many other things are going on in the operation and unfolding of punishment—such as political posturing by politicians and social entrepreneurs, confinement and demonization of the "dangerous classes," artificial management of surplus labor and official unemployment, profit-taking, and not least, the assuaging of middle-class anxieties about crime and vulnerability (Scheingold 1998; Shelden 2001).

As "globalization" expands the gaze of social science to incorporate and recognize multinational influences on what appear to be merely localized debates, deeper understandings of "justice" both complicate and enrich agendas for punishment research. Recent research on imprisonment, then, builds on a tradition that seeks a more fully global and "social" accounting of the operations of punishment—but takes it a step further: By exploring particularly how "populist" and "expressive" fervor for harsh punishment among the world's "haves" relates to broader shifts in the geopolitics and citizenship claims of the world's "have-nots," a new focus on globalization has reenergized the critical tradition in penal studies (see Weiss 2001; Welch 2005; Young 1999, 2002, 2004).

Based on an actuarial calculus, protecting some by neutralizing the real and imagined threats of "others," the "New Penology" has arguably gone global (Davis 1998; Ferrell et al. 2004; Young 1999).[2]

What, for example, are the implications of an American county-level government contracting the management of its local jail to a multinational private prison firm in order to expand local capacity for incarcerating illegal immigrants from Mexico, Eastern Europe, and Southeast Asia (Gilbert 2000; Shichor and Gilbert 2000)? In a newly global context of imprisonment, the connections between global versus local penality are of increasingly prominent importance. From Rothman to Foucault, if the history of penality has taught us anything, it is that punishments always involve dynamics larger than the individual offender.

LATE MODERN PUNISHMENTS: THE HAVES AND HAVE-NOTS

This chapter explores some of the enabling preconditions of global mass imprisonment from a historical and theoretical perspective, as chiefly orchestrated, exported, and exemplified internationally through American legal and corporate practices. Driven in part by Western first-world anxieties about economic well-being, declining safety and standard of living, increasing social isolation in a "society of strangers," and the mediated perception of "risk" all around, exploring the rising supranational carceral state and its relation to democratic society is of paramount importance (Garland 1990, 2001; Jones and Newburn 2005; Nelkin 1994; Shichor 2006; Welch 2005). Recent research on punishment problematizes the retrenchment of "security state" methods for establishing social order amidst the global decline of welfare state programming (a condition dubbed "late modernity") but does so through an examination of increasingly global patterns: mass imprisonment of cultural minorities, the reemergence of actuarial for-profit prisons, situational rather than causal crime control strategies, loss of civil liberties—and most importantly of all "a blurring of the nation state's external and internal security functions" (Kraska 1999:205; Western and Beckett 1999).[3] "Late modern" societies are those in which the social engineering ambitions of welfarist governments have fallen into disfavor, in deference to demands for lower taxes and market-based "private" solutions to social problems (Garland 2001).

Amid the glaring dependency and powerlessness of incarcerated populations worldwide, meanwhile, mainstream U.S. criminology bolsters "containment strategy" agendas facilitating expansive police practice, while becoming decidedly ahistorical and less sociological. "Policing's overt political dimension has become sanitized by reattaching itself to policy science, problem solving, and its 'client's desires' rather than being associated with the strong arm of the government or the rule of law as both the source of and limits to its authority" (Kappeler and Kraska 1998:297).[4]

As prison populations increase worldwide, a punitive turn is thus taking place not only amidst crumbling support for welfarist regimes with previously inclusive agendas, it is built upon a renewed denigration of group characteristics that are *unacceptable* as being worthy of democratic inclusion (Young 1999). Put another way, in the global expansion of penal regimes, punishment is built not simply on a platform mindful of declining fortunes, but explicitly focused upon the "incapacitation" of "others" as a social imperative of the haves, by "risk management" and containment of the have-nots (Hallett 2002; Welch 2005). In the switch from "rehabilitation" to harsh punishment and "incapacitation," middle-class "ontological insecurity" has as its new ambition the de facto "disappearing" problematic populations (Davis 1998).

THINK HISTORICALLY, ACT LOCALLY: RACE, NEO-COLONIALISM AND "OTHERNESS"

> It is not overstating the case to suggest that criminal justice has become the institutionalization of militarism in US culture.
> —*Militarism, Feminism and Criminal Justice*, Susan Caulfield 2001

In thinking about the disturbing realities of global imprisonment, it is useful to remember that private commerce with prisoners has been underway for centuries in Anglo societies, dating back to the 1600s and before. Profit-driven mechanisms for punishing adjudicated offenders have long been a routinized form of criminal justice activity. Transportation, a practice developed by private merchant shippers in seventeenth-century-England, literally involved "transporting" convicted criminals to North American and Australian plantations for periods of indentured labor (Hughes 1986). This "privatized" sentencing option cheaply expanded the sanctioning power of the state and exponentially increased the case processing capacity of the criminal justice system (Feeley 2002). Later, free indentured servants (who generally for the cost of passage) would submit "voluntarily" to "transportation" and a period of indenture from four to seven years, after being pardoned for vagrancy (Smith 1965:89–135). According to Malcolm Feeley (2002), to a remarkable degree, this mercantile system of offender punishment was developed not by state officials, but by commercial entrepreneurs *dependent upon criminal adjudication for their profits*.

"Actual shipment of the convicts was performed by merchants trading to the plantations. The merchants made their profit by selling the convicts as indentured servants in the colonies" (Smith 1965:97–98). In the case of "transportation," colonial use of convict laborers was thought a commonsensical solution to the problems of crime and listlessness, as well as an economical means of expanding British influence (Smith 1965). White indentured servants during this period, however, were keenly distinguished from "negro slaves."

In the history of for-profit punishment schemes, racialized caste systems imposed varying degrees of servitude among people subjected to labor, "variously known as indentured servants, redemptioners, or, in order to distinguish them from the Negroes, as Christian or white servants" (Smith 1965:3). From the beginning, then, race, social class, and nationality defined the parameters of so much of punishment, reminding us again that how prisoners are treated locally cannot be thoroughly comprehended without reflection on how punishment operates within a wider matrix of extralegal relations (Hallett 2006). A renewed focus of punishment research is on how race, punishment, and profit have long been bound together in widely construed, multinational capitalistic schemes.

THE PANOPTICON: EARLY ACTUARIALISM

Another imperative reality that often escapes the attention of contemporary (even critical) students of criminology is that Jeremy Bentham, designer of the famed "panopticon," very much viewed himself as a private prison contractor who *"expected to become rich"* from his "prison management" scheme (Feeley 2002:332). The circular Panopticon was intended to be a cost-efficient means of mitigating risk by enabling a small number of guards to supervise a large number of convicts by way of its design. Much of Bentham's writing on the panopticon is actually in the form of a contract proposal for the administration, construction, and management of his "inspection house"—in early drafts he states the following: "To come to the point at once, I would do the whole by contract" (Bozovic 1995:51).

Bentham's self-titled "plan of management" relied upon the use of contractors who would manage the inmates for a profit—with Bentham holding a patent and monopoly on the venture (Bozovic 1995:51). Bentham developed his panoptic model of inspection not just for prisons, but also for "houses of industry," "poor houses," hospitals, manufactories, mad-houses, and schools (Bozovic 1995:51). Each of these schemes relied on, in Bentham's words, "the apparent omnipresence of the inspector combined with the extreme facility of his real presence" (Bozovic 1995:45). Writes Malcolm Feeley: "Only with the American Revolution and the demise of Transportation did the prison 'become synonymous with punishment' in England: 'Within 50 years, the prison was so well inscribed in public imagination and so well established on the landscape, that it was impossible to envision criminal punishment in its absence" (Feeley 2002:330).

In their writing on the "new penology," Malcolm Feeley and Jonathan Simon (1992, 1994) mark an "actuarial" shift as distinctive, between an "old penology"—"rooted in concern for individuals" and anchored by a "habitus of the rehabilitative ideal" (Garland 2001:5) versus the "new penology," which is "actuarial" in nature and "concerned with techniques for identifying, classifying and managing groups assorted by levels of dangerousness" (Feeley and Simon 1994:173). Actuarialism has thus long-driven criminal justice policy—and as David Shichor notes (quoting Ulrich Beck), "the social production of wealth is systematically accompanied by the social production of risk" (2006:77). The roots of corporate and globalized punishment schemes thus run deep in the United States and date to mid-seventeenth century.

SHIFTS IN PUNISHMENT: THE RACIST FOUNDATION OF CONVICT LEASING

> Given the vast over-representation of men and women of color in penal establishments across the world, it is clear that there is a worrying relationship between imprisonment and race. What if ideas of "race" which are historically contingent and constructed are necessary for the prison? Rather than searching for the singular reason for racism, such as in the war on drugs, for example, what if race has simply been written into the entire notion of punishment itself?
>
> —*Race and Punishment*, Mary Bosworth, 2000

The eventual abolition of "transportation" exacerbated the need for and utility of slavery in colonial America, where "society was not democratic and certainly not equalitarian" (Smith 1965:7). Agricultural production mechanisms of the time were labor intensive, requiring large numbers of slaves to till, plant, harvest, process, transport, and refine products. The racist doctrine of "white supremacy" conveniently began to thrive during this period, with the exploitation-derived benefits of the African slave trade quickly surpassing those of white indentured servitude (Smith 1965). Slaves, after all, had no right to ultimate freedom, whereas white indentured servants would eventually achieve it.

It is perhaps astonishing to realize that the very instrument of slavery's abolition in the United States—the Thirteenth Amendment to the U.S. Constitution—also authorized the "involuntary servitude" of prisoners as a punishment for crime. During the operation of the so-called "convict lease system," from 1865 to the 1920s, the Thirteenth Amendment simultaneously enabled the continuation of racialized forced labor in the South at what was supposed to be the start of freedom for African-American slaves.

> Neither slavery nor involuntary servitude, except as a punishment for crime whereof the party shall have been duly convicted, shall exist within the United States, or any place subject to their jurisdiction.
> — Thirteenth Amendment, Constitution of the United States

Upon release from their former owners' captivity, "emancipated" slaves often had nowhere to go—and found themselves designated trespassers, disturbers of the peace, vagrants, or loiterers on their former owners' plantations. Caught between the legal restrictions of abolition and a paramount need for cheap labor, convict leasing emerged as a uniquely Southern solution to the postbellum labor shortage and facilitated a continuation of the ideology of white-supremacy.

Shifts in punishment strategies have long been the focus of academic studies of penality because they often proffer glimpses of the broader forces at work shaping institutions of punishment (Sellin 1976). In this case, the emerging industrial economy brought with it well-documented changes in social organization, concepts of social identity and punishment practices as well. The abolition of slavery in the United States destroyed with it the relations of production necessary for Southern economic survival. After the Civil War, former slaves were no longer legally subject to forced servitude, while many able-bodied white workers had been killed or maimed during the war. White servitude in the form of indenture had ceased to exist as well. This combination of factors created a massive labor shortage. The labor crisis was felt not only by plantation owners facing the prospect of having to pay laborers a wage but also by emerging Southern industrialists desperate for laborers they could afford.

Social and economic elites of the "New South," be they industrial or agrarian, then, needed a mechanism through which they could abide by the legal tenets of abolition while maintaining their exploitative power over a large class of vulnerable and needed workers—namely, the now free but indigent former slaves still populating the South. While in many respects the Civil War was fought over the increasing dominance of an industrialized economy during a time of profound economic and social transition, the convict lease system emerged to serve the interests of both industrial entrepreneurs and the weakened but still-powerful agrarian planter class. The fulcrum of this systematic forced labor for *both* was the ideology of white supremacy.

FOLLOW THE MONEY: CONTEMPORARY GLOBAL SHIFTS IN PUNISHMENT

That the United States is today's world's leader in incarceration is well documented. As noted by the National Council on Crime and Delinquency in November 2006 (see Table 15.1):

- The U.S. incarcerates the largest number of people in the world

- The incarceration rate in the US is four times the world average

- Some individual U.S. states imprison up to six times as many people as do nations of comparable population

- The U.S. imprisons the most women in the world

- Crime rates do not account for incarceration rates

Moreover, U.S. imprisonment rates are driven largely by imprisonment of minority males in the prime of life, mostly for nonviolent drug crime (Hallett 2006). The incarceration rate for black males in the United States is roughly 8 times higher than that of white males in the population. The future of punishment for minorities in the United States is not likely to change in the immediate future. As a 2007 Pew Charitable Trust report titled *Public Safety, Public Spending: Forecasting America's Prison Population 2007–2011*

TABLE 15.1   Countries with the largest number of people held in penal institutions

Country	Prison Population	Date
United States of America	1,962,220	31 December 2001
China	1,428,126[a]	mid-2001
Russia Federation	919,330	1 September 2002
India	281,380	1999
Brazil	233,859	December 2001
Thailand	217,697	mid-2001
Ukraine	198,885	1 September 2001
South Africa	176,893	14 June 2002
Islamic Republic of Iran	163,526	April 2002
Mexico	154,765	30 June 2000

[a]Sentenced prisoners only.

documents, U.S. "state and federal prisons will swell by more than 192,000 inmates over the next five years. This 13-percent jump triples the projected growth of the general US population, and will raise the prison census to a total of more than 1.7 million people" (2007:ii). Moreover, due to a lack of after-release programming and resources for prisoner reentry into the communities in which they must live and work, "more than half of released prisoners are back behind bars within three years" (Pew 2007:v). Consequently, according to the Pew report, "the US may need an additional $27.5 billion over the next five years to accommodate projected prison expansion and operations" (2007:17).

Worldwide, as noted in a report titled *Global Incarceration and Prison Trends,* by Roy Walmsley at the University of London in 2003, "Prison populations grew during the 1990s in many parts of the world. In Europe, they grew by over 20 per cent in almost all countries and by at least 40 per cent in one half of the countries; in the Netherlands, the prison population grew by 89 per cent. . . . The general trend during the 1990s, at least in many developed countries, was for the prison population to increase, often by 40 per cent" (2003:70).

There are thus numerous examples of commerce with the captive marginal around the world today, much of which is undertaken by multinational corrections firms with strong ties to the United States and United Kingdom. In Great Britain, for example, the *London Times* reported, May 15, 2002, that "tens of thousands of destitute asylum seekers will be held in up to 15 large for-profit accommodation centers planned for rural areas of the country" (Ford 2002). Or take, as another example, in South Africa recently (January 2002), "the 3,024-bed Kutama Sinthumule Maximum Prison, one of the largest prisons in the world, was opened by a consortium known as the South African Custodial Services Pty Ltd made up of the U.S.-based Wackenhut Corrections and their South African partners, Kensani Corrections Pty Ltd." lternatively, take for example this recent headline from Australia:

> WACKENHUT DETAINEES SEW LIPS TOGETHER
> At least 58 asylum seekers have sewn their lips together during a hunger strike at the Woomera detention center. The asylum seekers also threw rocks at security guards trying to assist those who had mutilated themselves, seriously injuring one guard. . . . It's understood the detainees are upset at the time being taken to process their visa applications.
>
> *(Hallett 2006:18)*

Private corporations in the areas of policing and corrections have boldly sought to fill state-based gaps in service, in recognition of the fact that consumers (including state and local governments) will seek to devolve governmental criminal justice functions to private vendors. A recent story by Dow Jones News Service reported the private corrections industry a "safe place to lock away investments"; it reported that "Industry watchers predict that the prison population is set to grow due to higher unemployment and tougher law-and-order policies following the September 11 terrorist attacks" (McCarty 2002).

A November 2006 Lehman Brothers analysis reports "we continue to remain positive on the private prison industry, quite simply because the demand that exists for private prisons today is at an all-time high since we started coverage in 2001. There are four fundamental primary factors that we believe should drive the industry's intermediate-term

growth" (Lehman Brothers 2006:253): (1) continued growth in the overall prison population; (2) the Baby Boom Echo Effect (children of the Baby Boom generation are entering
the crime-prone age for 15–24 years of age); (3) the over occupancy issue (state prisons
are at 99 percent and Federal prisons at 140 percent capacity); and (4) "demand for prison
beds is at an all time high" (2006:257).

Most ominously of all, the Lehman Brothers report indicates that the Federal
Bureau of Prisons "could require up to 30,000 beds by 2011," while the Bureau of
Immigration and Customs Enforcement, in cooperation with the Department of
Homeland Security, received its "third consecutive funding increase of $1.4 billion . . .
which basically authorized significant increases in BICE beds for illegal and criminal
aliens" under the auspices of the 2004 Intelligence Reform Bill (Lehman Brothers
2006:258). Finally, Lehman glowingly highlights the "Protecting America's Borders
Initiative," which eliminated such procedures as "catch and release:" "On June 16, 2006
the President signed into law an emergency funding bill to assist DHS in protecting
America's borders. The bill was for $1.948 billion and included procurement of about
4,000 new detention beds" (Lehman Brothers 2006:258). Thus, a new hybrid of global/
local penality has taken root and remains firmly embedded in contemporary punishment
practice. Amidst "virtually no supply from the public sector," Lehman Brothers also
notes that the industry capitalizes on dynamics that leave "prisoner demand unaffected by
economic cycles" (2006:265). In other words, "historically general economic downturns
have not affected industry demand for beds" in what is widely seen as a "recession-
proof" industry (Hallett 2006). As Welch (2007) notes, "Corporate actors in the private
prison industry must make important connections in government so as to tap into the
growing pool of prisoners. Such connections are made possible by considerable lobbying
campaigns that push not only for legislation that calls for lengthier sentences but also to
persuade government officials to transfer a portion of their inmates to private facilities."

GLOBAL SECURITY STATE: THE GROWING MILITARY/CRIMINAL JUSTICE INDUSTRIAL COMPLEX

> There's another bright side to the somewhat dark prospect of owning shares in a
> company that's bread and water, er, butter, is prisons: They have a defensive
> aspect . . . [T]hey're almost counter-cyclical to the broader economy. "When times
> are bad, more people tend to go to jail. It's awful, but it's true."
> —Jamie Cuellar, comanager of the Brazos Micro Cap Fund Report,
> February 2007

In the "civilized West," dispossession affects people of color and "aliens" in far
greater proportion than whites. These same populations of disenfranchised people have
also once again become the targets of private, multinational, corporate entrepreneurship,
where modernist assumptions of free will and self-determination are belied by the corporatist plans of multinational corporations, banking on high crime rates, increasing public
fear, and diminishing economic opportunity.

That consumers (including state and local governments) now widely seek to devolve
governmental criminal justice functions to private vendors, renders the democratic

"common good" a condition of fiscal capacity, not social aspiration. American corrections firms are currently vying for contracts in Iraq and Israel, Ireland and South Africa—within a global market for incarceration and "security" services. British-based SecuriCor, the GeoGroup (formerly Wackenhut), and Corrections Corporation of America are all firms newly profitable in the area of global "security services." Former President of Corrections Corporation of America, Doctor Crants ("Doctor" is his name, not his title) is now president of Homeland Security Corporation (HSC). He is a graduate of West Point. The opening words to his bio on the HSC website reads:

> Doctor R. Crants founded Homeland Security Corporation in 2001 to provide highly specialized security management training to government and commercial entities. Its training division, PPCT Management Systems, Inc., is an internationally recognized authority on use of force and self-defense training for criminal justice agencies, the military, and corporations.

HSC listed contracts in 2003 with the CIA, FBI, the U.S. Secret Service, Department of the Army: John F. Kennedy Special Warfare School, the Department of Defense, and many others. According to HSC's website, "Homeland Security Corporation (HSC) provides highly specialized security management and training services to government and commercial entities" (see http://www.about-hsc.com/).

The trend toward spending more on security and less on social welfare has only been exacerbated by September 11 and the Iraq War, but started well before either of these. The recent reorganization of the federal government to include the former Immigration and Naturalization Service, newly renamed the Bureau of Immigration and Customs Enforcement (euphemistically known as "ICE"), under the umbrella of the Department of Homeland Security, subsumes incarceration and immigration policy into one sphere (see Welch 2002, 2005). The U.S. Federal Bureau of Prisons is one of the fastest growing arms of the federal government. In fact, the U.S. Department of Homeland Security is expanding a national prison system that detains immigrants facing possible deportation. The current population of detainees represents the fastest-growing segment of the federal prison population.

CRIME AND THE NEO-LIBERAL GLOBAL CORPORATE AGENDA

> This age-old strategy of scapegoating the most vulnerable, frightening the most insecure and supporting the most comfortable constitutes a kind of iron law signaling the decline of modern civilizations, as in Tolstoy's Russia and Kafka's central Europe: chaotic and inchoate rebellion from below, withdrawal and retreat from public life from above and a desperate search for authoritarian law and order, at any cost, from the middle.
>
> —Black Strivings in a Twilight Civilization, Cornel West, 1999

In an insightful recent *British Journal of Criminology* piece by Trevor Jones and Tim Newburn, "Comparative Criminal Justice Policymaking in the United States and the United Kingdom," the authors compare and contrast American versus British implementation of prison privatization, suggesting that privatization in Great Britain was adopted in a "u-turn" fashion to accomplish expressive rather than instrumental goals for the conservative government of Margaret Thatcher. "Whilst there were political similarities (in terms of ideology) between the Reagan and Thatcher administrations," they write, "privatization as a national governmental program was far more significant in the United Kingdom than in the United States" (2005:68).

The Jones and Newburn piece, however, curiously underemphasizes one very important commonality regarding privatization in the United States and United Kingdom, mentioning it in reference to the United Kingdom, but not the United States: the use of privatization by conservative parties and their allied interest groups at all levels to weaken organized labor wherever it exists.[5]

In the United States, public employee corrections officer unions have been the primary agents of organized resistance to privatization, in unholy alliance with activists, academics, and religious groups (Hallett 2006). Labor unions have, in fact, orchestrated the few major setbacks to the private prisons industry and certain of its insiders (Geis, Mobley, and Shichor 1999). More broadly, correctional officer and teacher unions are among the last bastions of welfare state economic relations surviving in the United States. Breaking the "public monopoly" of the correctional officer unions in the United States, therefore, involved more than just symbolic importance: It involved opening up growing and previously impervious markets to friendly stakeholders financing major portions of legislative crime control agendas. This vital part of the strategy of both Reagan-allied ALEC and Thatcher-friendly ASI is key to understanding the larger dynamics of the revitalization of privatized punishment schemes. Much of the "opposition" to privatization made reference to but not highlighted by Jones and Newburn (2005) is actually part of a broader characteristically "late–modern" agenda of scaling back the welfare state in favor of unregulated free market structures—the very source of most "private" prison profit in the first place (accomplished through lower wages and benefits for nonunionized prison workers, but still sourced by taxpayer funds). Breaking of the British correctional officers' union, the Prison Officers Association (POA), therefore, may well have been an expressive goal but was also a very definite *instrumental* objective of the progenitors of privatization—and both the corporate and political interests who promoted it—who, as the authors do point out, were all well connected to one another and worked directly in a coalition of like-minded American politicians and businessmen to develop their proposals.

The so-called U-turn for privatization of corrections by Thatcher was therefore both expressive and instrumental, but hardly "radical" (p. 69). A bold and direct privileging of market-based strategies over government ones, wherever they may reside, is very much the bedrock of neo-liberal corporatism worldwide—and is very much part of the story of expansion in global imprisonment. To scale back the power of labor and orchestrate more private access to this enormous sector of the public labor market is part and parcel of the supranational corporatist agenda. Weaker labor unions, massive corporate access to public funds for operating privately held profit enterprises has a long tradition in punishment practice. Looking at it trans-nationally and historically, then, we're arguably not entering a brave new world, but reinventing a brave old one.

CONCLUSION: MILITARISM AND COLONIALISM
IN THE GLOBAL ECONOMY OF PUNISHMENT

> The police and prisons have adopted military tactics such as squads and teams with specialized tasks. While the nineteenth-century transfers were aimed at making criminal justice institutions more acceptable to a public deeply skeptical of governmental power, current transfers are intended to intensify the instrumental capacity of criminal justice institutions to address criminal threats perceived as more invidious and distinct than in the past.
>
> —*Sacrificing Private Ryan: The Military Model and the New Penology*,
> Peter Kraska, 2001

In order to comprehend emergent and global patterns of renewed harsh punishment, Stuart Scheingold utilizes the concept of "political criminology" to describe a research agenda focused on the dynamics of punishment beyond the individual offender:

> Political criminology is defined as the study of forces that determine how, why, and with what consequences societies choose to deal with crime and criminals. At the core of this conception of political criminology is a focus on the nature and distribution of power as it shapes the social and political construction of crime and influences on crime control policies. How, political criminology asks, do the relevant actors—political leaders, criminal process professionals, and multiple publics—make sense out of crime? . . . Whereas most criminological inquiry is focused on what actually causes crime and on how best to control it, political criminology is about the social and political meanings that attach to crime—irrespective of whether those meanings are consistent with what criminologists claim to know about causes and cures.

(1998:859)

Whereas criminology set as its original aspiration the identification of the causes of crime, the renaissance sociology of punishment fixes instead on transformations, expansions, and retrenchments of punishment strategies themselves. The current renaissance, however, only extends and enhances a long-standing tradition exploring punishment's stated versus its latent functions. To borrow a classic statement, "Punishment is neither a simple consequence of crime, nor the reverse side of crime . . . Punishment must be understood as a social phenomenon freed from both its juristic concept and its social ends. We do not deny that punishment has specific ends, but we do deny that it can be understood from its ends alone" (Rusche and Kirchheimer 1968 [1939]).

Many critics of the modern criminal justice system argue that its workings are devoted less to actually reducing crime—and more to providing politicians and other social entrepreneurs suitable targets worthy of "actions" which justify *their* existence (Chambliss 2001; Gusfield 1963). In the case of private prisons—the drug war—as the fountainhead of most private prison revenue in America so far, cannot be understood outside of the context of race (see Christianson 1998; Garland 2001; Miller 1996; Parenti 2000; Rose and Clear 1998; Tonry 1995; West 1999). What better to have a "war on immigrants/terror" to replace the failing drug war? A population of unseen enemies, poorly understood and easily demonized, with no legal rights, will be easy grist in the supranational mill of global punishment anchored in the United States (Christie 1994).

According to Garland, beginning in 1980s America, "changes in demography, in stratification and in political allegiance, led important sections of the working and middle classes to change their attitudes towards many "welfare" policies (excepting "corporate" welfare, of course, to airlines, agricultural firms, the steel industry)—to see them as being at odds with their actuarial interests and as benefiting groups that were undeserving and increasingly dangerous" (Garland 2001:76). In retrospect now, it seems that a much larger turn of history of not so much "modern" but glacial proportions is upon us: the diminishing sovereignty of nation states, weakening traditional economies for an increasingly global labor pool, middle-class fear and corporate profiteering on containment of the unwashed masses. Ultimately relying on a "global" versus "local" dichotomy of penality is thereby increasingly misleading, as revealed through examinations of both historical and contemporary shifts in punishment.

The reemergence of "privatized" prisons in the twenty-first century has thus taken place within an important and dynamic geopolitical context. (1) The traditional power of the nation state is weakening, with economic alliances transcending national borders and ignoring traditional forms of sovereignty and self-determination; (2) the prevailing economy (of industrialized market economy of good jobs and high wages) is following the same path of diffusion; and (3) work itself—the relation of labor to capital—is changing as well. The realities of wages, security, and complex nationalism are all changing rapidly in a global economy and a world newly threatened by terrorism (Frank 2000; Gold 1995; Melman 2001; Welch 2005). During periods of intense social change, "crackdowns" on minority groups are historically quite common (Gusfield 1963).

Swings of the punishment pendulum thus become a subject of interest, as does the fact that locales of varying persuasions in close proximity to one another may simultaneously exhibit contradictory orientations toward punishment. Canada, for example, our nearest neighbor and leading trade partner, has an incarceration rate that "has not changed appreciably since 1960" (Doob and Webster 2006:325), whereas Great Britain—our lead partner in the "war on terror"—has experienced over a doubling of their rate of incarceration since just 1990, with the country now being "the prison capital of Western Europe" (Sim 2004:39). The study of punishment is arguably more important today than ever. A recent *Los Angeles Times* story profiling the link between immigration and incarceration in Colorado offers compelling affirmation of the connection between forms of punishment and the labor market (see also Weiss 2001):

> Ever since passing what its legislature promoted as the nation's toughest laws against illegal immigration last summer, Colorado has struggled with a labor shortage as migrants fled the state. This week, officials announced a novel solution: use convicts as farm workers . . . The inmates will be watched by prison guards, who will be paid by the farms.

(Riccardi 2007)

ENDNOTES

1. As Greenberg & West put it: "Sociological analyses of the history of penality have *taken as their premise* that institutionalized punishment practices are not entirely determined by the functional necessity of preventing crimes" (2001:638)
2. "Cultural Criminology" is arguably so popular among students because the alienating reality of so much of mainstream criminology is that it fails to recognize the disconnectedness and isolation that is the fountain of high crime in the first place.
3. Beckett and Western point out regarding the supposed "success" of welfare reform as it relates to rising incarceration rates that: "Reduced welfare expenditures are not indicative of a shift toward reduced government intervention in social life, but rather a shift toward a more exclusionary and punitive approach to the regulation of social marginality" (2001, pp. 46–47).
4. Kraska laments many criminologists becoming "security specialists" as opposed to social scientists (1999:208).
5. And not just individual Maverick leaders but allied political stakeholders in both England and the US, including the American Legislative Exchange Council [ALEC] in the US and the Adam Smith Institute [ASI] in the UK.

REFERENCES

BOSWORTH, M. (2000). Race and punishment. *Punishment & Society* 2(1): 114–118.

BOZOVIC, M. (1995). The panopticon writings. In *Trans: Miran Bozovic*, ed. J. Bentham, New York: Verso.

CAULFIELD, S. (July/August 2002). Militarism, Feminism and Criminal Justice. *Northeastern University Magazine* 15(7).

CHAMBLISS, W. (2001). *Power, Politics & Crime.* Boulder, CO: Westview Press. Christianson, S. (1998). *With Liberty for Some: 500 Years of Imprisonment in America.* Boston, MA: Northeastern University Press.

CHRISTIE, N. (1994). *Crime Control as Industry: Towards Gulags, Western Style.* New York: Routledge.

CUELLA, J. (February 2007). Brazos Mico Cap Fund Report *Private Corrections Institute (PCI) 1114 Bradtt Dr., Tallahassee Florida 32308*

DAVIS, A. (1998). Reflections on the prison industrial complex. *ColorLines* 1:(2): 1–8.

DOOB, A., and C. M. WEBSTER (2006). Countering punitiveness: Understanding stability in Canada's imprisonment rate. *Law & Society Review* 40((2): 325–367.

ENGLE, S. (March 1, 2006). Race, Inequality and Colonialism in the New World Order *Social Review 343 pages published in Somalia.*

FEELEY, M. M. (2002). Entrepreneurs of punishment: The legacy of privatization. *Punishment & Society* 4(3): 321–344.

FEELEY, M. M., and J. SIMON (1992). The new penology: Notes on the emerging strategy of corrections and its implications. *Criminology* 30: 449–474.

FEELEY, M. M., and J. SIMON (1994). Actuarial justice: The emerging new criminal law. *The Futures of Criminology*, pp. 173–201. London: Sage.

FERRELL, J., K. HAYWARD, W. MORRIS, and M. PRESDEE (2004). *Cultural Criminology Unleashed.* Portland, OR: Cavendish Publishing/ Glasshouse Press.

FORD. (May 15, 2002) London Times.

FRANK, T. (2000). *One Market Under God: Extreme Capitalism, Market Populism, and the End of Economic Democracy.* New York: Doubleday.

GARLAND, D. (1990). *Punishment and Modern Society: A Study in Social Theory.* Chicago, IL: University of Chicago Press.

GARLAND, D. (2001). *The Culture of Control: Crime and Social Order in Contemporary Society.* Chicago, IL: University of Chicago Press.

GEIS, G., A. MOBLEY, and D. SHICHOR (1999). Private prisons, criminological research, and conflict of interest: a case study. *Crime and Delinquency* 372–388.

GILBERT, M. J. (2000) Not a true partner: Local politics and jail privatization in Frio County. In *Privatization in Criminal Justice: Past, Present & Future*, ed. D. Shichor and M. Gilbert, pp. 171–206. Cincinnati, OH: Anderson Publishing.

GOLD, S. D. (1995). *The Fiscal Crisis of the States: Lessons for the Future*. Washington, DC: Georgetown University Press.

GUSFIELD, J. (1963). *Symbolic Crusade: Status Politics and the American Temperance Movement*. Urbana, IL: University of Illinois Press.

HALLETT, M. A. (2002). Race, crime, and for-profit imprisonment: Social disorganization as market opportunity. *Punishment & Society: The International Journal of Penology* 4(3): 369–393.

HALLETT, M. A. (2006). *Private Prisons in America: A Critical Race Perspective*. Urbana, IL: University of Illinois Press.

HUGHES, R. (1986). *The Fatal Shore*. New York: Random House.

JONES, T., and T. NEWBURN (2005). Comparative criminal justice policy-making in the United States and the United Kingdom. *British Journal of Criminology* 45: 58–80.

KAPPELER, V. E., and P. B. KRASKA (1998). A textual critique of community policing: Police adaptation to high modernity. *Policing: An International Journal of Police Strategies & Management* 21(2): 293–313.

KRASKA, P. B. (1999). Militarizing criminal justice: Exploring the possibilities. *Journal of Political and Military Sociology* 27(2): 205–215.

KRASKA, P. B. (ed) (2001). *Militarizing the American Criminal Justice System: The Changing Roles of the Armed Forces and the Police*.

LEHMAN BROTHERS (2006). *2006 Security Report*. New York.

MCCARTY, P. (2002). Corrections industry: Safe place to lock away investments. *Dow Jones Newswires*. June 21, 2002.

MELMAN, S. (2001). *After Capitalism: From Managerialism to Workplace Democracy*. New York: Alfred Knopf.

MERRY, S. E. (2006). Race, inequality, and colonialism in the new world order. *Law & Society Review* 40(1): 235–247.

MILLER, J. (1996). *Search and Destroy: African-American Males in the Criminal Justice System*. Cambridge, MA: Cambridge University Press.

NATIONAL COUNCIL ON CRIME AND DELINQUENCY (2006). *FACT SHEET: US Rates of Incarceration: A Global Perspective*. Washington, DC: NCCD.

NELKIN, D. (1994). *The Futures of Criminology*. Thousand Oaks, CA: Sage.

NEWBURN, T., and R. SPARKS (2004). Criminal justice and political cultures. In *Criminal Justice and Political Cultures: National and International Dimensions of Crime Control*. London: Willan Publishing.

PAKES, F. (2004). The politics of discontent: The emergence of a new criminal justice discourse in the Netherlands. *The Howard Journal* 43: 267–283.

PARENTI, C. (2000). *Lockdown America: Police and Prisons in the Age of Crisis*. New York: Verso Publishing.

PEW CHARITABLE TRUSTS (2007). *Public Safety, Public Spending: Forecasting America's Prison Population, 2007–2011*. Washington, DC: Pew Charitable Trusts.

RICCARDI, N. (2007). Colorado to Use Inmates to Fill Migrant Shortage: Tough Laws Passed Last Year Against Illegal Immigration Have Created a Need for Farmworkers. [Retrieved March 1, 2007, from http://www.latimes.com/news/nationworld/nation/la-na-inmates1mar01,0,7469220.story]

ROSE, D., and T. CLEAR (1998). Incarceration, social capital, and crime: Implications for social disorganization theory. *Criminology* 36(3): 441–479.

RUSCHE, G., and O. KIRCHHEIMER (1968 [1939]). *Punishment and Social Structure*. New York: Columbia University Press.

SAVELSBERG, J. (2002). Cultures of control in contemporary societies. *Law & Social Inquiry* 27: 685.

SCHEINGOLD, S. (1998). Constructing the new political criminology: Power, authority, and the post-liberal state. *Law & Social Inquiry* 23: 857–895.

SELLIN, T. (1976). *Slavery and the Penal System.* New York: Elsevier.

SHELDEN, R. (2001). *Controlling the Dangerous Classes: A Critical Introduction to the History of Criminal Justice.* Boston, MA: Allyn & Bacon.

SHICHOR, D. (2006). *The Meaning and Nature of Punishment.* Long Grove, IL: Waveland Press.

SHICHOR, D., and M. GILBERT (2000). *Privatization in Criminal Justice: Past, Present and Future.* Cincinnati, OH: Anderson Publishing.

SIM, J. (2004). Militarism, criminal justice, and the hybrid prison in England and Wales. *Social Justice* 31(1–2): 39–50.

SMITH, A. E. (1965). *Colonists in Bondage: White Servitude and Convict Labor in America, 1607–1776.* Chapel Hill, NC: University of North Carolina Press.

TONRY, M. (1995). *Malign Neglect: Race, Crime, and Punishment in America.* New York: Oxford University Press.

VON HOFFER, H. (2003). Prison populations as political constructs. The case of Finland, Holland and Sweden. *Journal of Scandinavian Studies in Criminology and Crime Prevention* 4: 21–38.

WALMSLEY, R. (2003). *Global Incarceration and Prison Trends.* London: King's College London, School of Law, International Centre for Prisons Studies.

WEIGAND, T. (2001). Sentencing and punishment in Germany. In *Sentencing and Sanctions in Western Countries*, ed M. Tonry and K. Hatlestad. New York: Oxford University Press.

WEISS, R. P. (2001). "Repatriating" low-wage work: The political economy of prison labor reprivatization in the postindustrial United States. *Criminology* 39(2): 253–291.

WELCH, M. (2005a). Private corrections, financial infrastructure, and transportation: The new geo-economy of shipping prisoners. *Social Justice.*

WELCH, M. (2005b). Immigration lockdown before and after 9/11: Ethnic constructions and their consequences. In *Race, Gender, and Punishment: Theorizing Differences*, ed M. Bosworth and S. Bush-Baskette. Boston, MA: Northeastern University Press.

WELCH, M. The Role of For Profit Prison in the History of Oppression and Legal Discrimination Aimed Primarily at African American Men. In *Private prisons in America: A Critical Race Perspective.* Michael A. Hallet (ed.) University of Illinois Press

WEST, C. (1999). *The Cornel West Reader.* New York: Basic Books.

WESTERN, B., and K. BECKETT (1999).How unregulated is the U.S. labor market? The penal system as a labor market institution. *American Journal of Sociology* 104(4): 1030–1053.

YOUNG, J. (1999). *The Exclusive Society: Social Exclusion, Crime and Difference in Late Modernity.* Thousand Oaks, CA: Sage.

YOUNG, J. (2002). Searching for a new criminology of everyday life: A Review of *The Culture of Control* by David Garland. *British Journal of Criminology* 42: 228–261.

YOUNG, J. (2004). Crime and the dialectics of inclusion/exclusion. *British Journal of Criminology* 44: 550–561.

ZIMRING, F. (2006). "The necessity and value of transnational comparative study: Some preaching from a recent convert" Vollmer Award Address. *Criminology & Public Policy* 5(4): 615–622.

Chapter 16

Getting Tough on Crime, Community Corrections, and Sentencing Philosophy

Etta F. Morgan and Robert Sigler

ABSTRACT

The disposition of offenders at the sentencing stage has cycled from extreme punishment to extreme treatment throughout history. Each peak is characterized by the creation of statutes that enable the increased use of the preferred disposition. We are presently at the peak of a punishment cycle. The "get tough on crime" perspective has caused continuous increases in prison populations that have continued into the twenty-first century. An unintended consequence of "get tough on crime" has been the increased representation of minority groups in the justice system. As the twenty-first century continues to unfold, it is likely that we will move toward a treatment orientation. We anticipate that in the next cycle, community corrections will be enhanced and expanded.

As we move into the new century, the conservative trend that emerged in the 1970s has continued to dominate justice system policy. Prison populations continued to grow throughout the 1990s (Wees 1996), continued to expand in the first years of this century, and are expected to continue to expand in the immediate future. Community corrections programs are being framed in terms of alternative sanctions and continue to be developed and expanded but at a slow pace with emphasis on control, punishment, and retribution potential rather than on treatment or rehabilitation potential.

CYCLES IN ORIENTATION TOWARD THE SENTENCING OF CRIMINAL OFFENDERS

Punishment and treatment represent two extremes on a continuum of approaches for the disposition of offenders who have been found or pled guilty to the offenses they have committed. Punishment stresses the protection of society through the use of incarceration and tends to have elements of retribution, incapacitation, and deterrence. Treatment stresses the protection of society by changing the offender so that he or she stops committing crimes, and it tends to have elements of rehabilitation and reintegration. It is rare in practice to have one extreme to the exclusion of the other, with most systems changing emphasis rather than eliminating programs when public sentiment changes. Orientation toward the punishment or treatment of convicted offenders has vacillated from treating the offender as if he or she had no rights or reason to expect help, to treating the offender as a person who retains his or her rights and who should receive education, training, and psychological services (Smith and Berlin 1988; Steiner et al. 2005).

Bartollas (1980) identifies four waves of treatment reform. During the colonial period in the United States, punishment dominated as the philosophy for disposition of convicted offenders with severe penalties such as the stocks, whipping post, and gallows seen as appropriate dispositions. Treatment-oriented reform emerged after the war for independence, producing the prison. A second wave of reform in the latter part of the nineteenth century produced the reformatory. A third wave of reform in the early twentieth century produced individual treatment, and the medical model emerged during the mid-1900s in a fourth wave of reform. He notes that punishment became dominant in the 1970s but suggests that support for rehabilitation will remerge.

While shifts are not necessarily distinct or universal, clear shifts in orientation can be observed. When punishment dominates, laws are passed making incarceration easier to apply with provisions for longer sentences. The use of prison as a disposition increases, putting pressure on correctional systems. The response of correctional systems combined with factors such as increasing costs, overcrowding, the incarceration of relatively mild offenders for long periods of time, and deterioration of the quality of life in prisons produces a reaction against the use of prisons. Crime rates do not decline, and punishment is projected in the media as an ineffective strategy. Public sentiment changes and treatment-oriented reformers press for a treatment-oriented response to the criminal offender to reduce crime. Laws, policies, and practices are adopted to change the orientation of the correctional system. At the extreme point in the swing to treatment, the system "treats" and releases all offenders. Offenders spend very little time incarcerated, and some of the released and non-detained offenders commit spectacular new crimes. The public comes to believe that crime is not reduced through treatment. Treatment is projected as a failure in the public media. Public sentiment changes and treatment falls into disfavor. Punishment-oriented reformers press for a more restrictive system to provide protection from criminal offenders and to reduce crime.

The rehabilitation ideal is believed to have dominated corrections throughout the nineteenth and twentieth centuries (Allen 1981). Although the treatment/punishment cycle is relatively pervasive, there appears to be a continuous shift toward more humane, if not more treatment-oriented, use of incarceration. That is, with each cycle some treatment-oriented programs tend to remain in place (education, vocational training, and work release) and, with the exception of the death penalty, punishments have tended to become less severe than has historically been the case (corporal punishment, severity of the prison environment).

The alternating preference for punishment or treatment predates the use of the prison as a sentence. Shifts in the cycle from treatment to punishment can be seen in the development of the work house or the development of the English poor laws. The development of the prison as a disposition in the late 1600s was the product of a reform movement that sought to reduce crime through the treatment of criminal offenders and was to replace less humane dispositions, such as corporal punishment and capital punishment. By the early 1700s, sentiment had changed and while the prison was maintained, the colonial assembly reimposed the English criminal code, including capital punishment and whipping (McKelvey 1977).

Clear peaks in the cycles are difficult to identify during the 1800s because of the different rates of development of prison systems in the various states. While some states had well-established systems that progressed through stages of development and reform, other states did not build prisons until the latter part of the century (McKelvey 1977). In states with well-developed systems, pressure for reform began to develop in the early 1800s, with much of the controversy emerging from the debate on the preference for either solitary confinement or congregate confinement. This pressure produced the use of indeterminate sentences, prison societies, probation and parole, and the reformatory movement with firm discipline and education defined as part of the treatment process (McKelvey 1977). For the treatment of children, Houses of Refuge emerged with an emphasis on training and inculcation of proper moral standards (Bernard 1992). By the end of the 1800s, the cycle was shifting, as reflected in statutes providing for longer sentences for minor offenders, the use of some mandatory sentences, habitual offender statutes, restrictions on the use of parole, and statutes criminalizing vagrancy. Overcrowding became common, and operations of reformatories came to resemble those of earlier prisons with increased emphasis on control; the spread of the reformatory philosophy declined. The costs of maintaining prisons became an issue, existing institutions were expanded, and living conditions deteriorated. Contract labor, convict lease systems, and prison industries were developed as legitimate forms of punishment and as a way of reducing the costs of maintaining a prison system as a reaction to charges of the lack of a need for collegiate and hotel prisons (McKelvey 1977). Houses of refuge fell into disrepute, and the focus of these institutions shifted to the control of children (Bernard 1992).

At the turn of the century, reform was emerging in the form of the separation of children from adult offenders, the development of the juvenile court (Bernard 1992), and the reemergence and expansion of the reformatory movement (McKelvey 1977). Growing interest in mental health and its application to criminal offenders led to expanded indeterminate sentencing and defective delinquent statutes. In practice, treatment-oriented reformers sought to replace mark and ratings systems (an earlier treatment innovation) with clinical prognosis as a basis for determining release of imprisoned offenders. The medical model for treating offenders began to emerge. Much of the legislative reform during this period focused on the use of convict labor and was driven as much or more by economic factors as by treatment and punishment philosophies.

In the late 1920s, the focus shifted to the failure of the system to correct offenders, with studies indicating high failure rates on parole and among released offenders. The use of prison as a disposition increased, overcrowding became an issue, and most states undertook construction of expanded prison systems. During the mid-1900s, legislative action and practice produced classification systems that were based on offender risk. Educational and vocational training programs remained but were not adequately supported. Special programs were developed for incorrigible offenders, and prison violence increased. New programs such as movies and organized sports were implemented on the basis of potential for maintaining peace in the institution. Prison disturbances increased and the public became concerned.

In the 1930s and 1940s, the medical model emerged and classification shifted with an emphasis on classifying inmates for treatment and on an upgrading of the status of parole beginning with the federal system and moving to the states (McKelvey 1977). Studies of the impact of prisonization (Clemmer 1958) appearing in the 1940s added to the shift toward treatment as did rapidly emerging therapies such as psychodrama, transactional analysis, and guided group interaction. Legislation and practice emerged, permitting the implementation and expansion of the medical model of treatment, including enabling statutes, modified death penalty statutes, and expanded good time provisions (McKelvey 1977).

By the 1970s, sentiment had shifted away from treatment. Rehabilitation was perceived as a failure with the severity of crime perceived as increasing and the safety of the public decreasing because of the emphasis on treatment in the correctional system (Allen 1981; Fogel 1978). The juvenile court became more legalistic (Bernard 1992). Reformers who advocated punishment as the correct function of sentencing prevailed and incarceration became prominent. Legislative initiatives restored determinate sentences, abolished parole, reestablished or strengthened habitual offender provisions, increased the use of sentence enhancement, and developed sentencing guidelines. As a result, the incarceration rate more than doubled between 1973 and 1983 (Currie 1985). This trend has continued, and, presently, correctional systems are unable to house all of those sentenced to state incarceration, in spite of aggressive construction programs (Wees 1996). Prison populations had grown to 2,193,798 prisoners in the federal prison system, jails, and various state departments of corrections (Bureau of Justice Statistics 2007a) and over 4,162,500 probationers (Bureau of Justice Statistics 2007b) by 2005.

MEDIATING INFLUENCES

A number of factors work to mediate the impact and, to some extent, the visibility of the treatment/punishment cycles. First, the shift is not complete. There is an identifiable group of treatment-oriented reformers that is relatively stable over time. When punishment is dominant, they continue to argue for treatment. There is a similar group of punishment-oriented reformers who continue to argue for punishment when treatment dominates orientation toward the disposition of criminal offenders. While the size of these groups is undetermined, it appears probable that most people are relatively uninformed and uncommitted to punishment or to treatment; thus, the shift from one extreme to the other is likely to reflect a relatively small shift on the part of the uninvolved majority, permitting justice agencies to resist full implementation of reform measures.

Diffusion of concepts, particularly as reflected in legislation and policy development, is slow. Reform will begin in one state and spread to other states over many years. As a result, at any one time, there are likely to be states in which punishment is still dominant, while in others, a treatment orientation prevails. In addition, later adaptations may be less extreme than the original models, whether it be legislation or policy. System resistance to change also moderates the impact of extreme legislation. Judges may choose to avoid judicial notice of sentence enchantment conditions, particularly in plea bargained cases when punishment is dominant, or give longer sentences from a range of sentences when treatment dominates. Correctional institutions may maintain treatment programs with decreased emphasis during punishment peaks and find ways to retain "dangerous" offenders during treatment peaks.

Correctional professionals change the terms and rationales for the programs they want to maintain, expand, or develop. Practitioners speak in terms of risk control, effective correctional intervention, restorative or community justice, and structured sanctioning policy development (Harris 1998) instead of treatment, rehabilitation, supervision and equitable sentencing.

CONTEMPORARY PRACTICES

Punishment presently continues to dominate policy, legislation, and practice regarding convicted offenders. Society is still strongly endorsing the use of punishment to deter criminals from criminal activity as we move into the twenty-first century. The inclination to punish is an emotional reaction that becomes salient with the violation of social sentiments (Garland 1990). The social sentiments that Garland addresses are referred to as the conscience collective by Durkheim (1965).

If punishment is merely an expressive institution that serves to release psychic energy, then it has no objective or intended goal regarding risk reduction either by treatment or by deterrence. If punishment simply occurs without a risk reduction objective to be achieved, then it is not particularly useful other than in the context of retribution. If there is no action against the collective sentiment, then there is no need for a reaction to protect the collective sentiment. If punishment functions to create a community that is harmonious and unified, then the effects of punishment are positive. Punishment should be perceived as a part of the cultural matrix that supports a complex pattern of rules and sentiments (Garland 1990). Punishment can be perceived as a symbolic issue that directly affects the psychological and overall development of individuals in a society. Politically, the extent of punishments in a society represents the definitive authority that is maintained by the political order of that society.

Because all of the facets of a society are interrelated in the social order, punishments, and all other dispositions available to the justice system, like other social factors, are determined by means of inclusion or exclusion in the social group (Garland 1990). It is the preferences of the conscience collective that are implemented by a select few who are elected to office. In most cases, legislators attempt to codify in law what they believe to be the wishes of the public, or at least that portion of the public who elected them to office. Other agencies such as the police and the courts are also sensitive to what is perceived to be the wishes of the public. It should be noted that these wishes generally are not empirically determined but reflect the beliefs of the elected or appointed officials and thus are subject to false consensus. It has been suggested that to some extent, legislation and its implementation tend to reflect the sentiments of those persons with political and personal power rather than those of the general pubic (Headley 1989).

Three types of legislative initiatives reflect a shift in orientation toward punishment: habitual offender statutes, other sentence enhancement alternatives, and determinate sentencing (with a reduction or elimination of the use of parole). These statutes are enacted to control dangerous or serious criminal offenders. An increase in public safety through the use of incarceration to control severe offenders is characteristic of periods in which punishment dominates disposition philosophy.

These initiatives developed in the federal system. Sentencing disparity, particularly insufficiently punishing sentences for some offenders, became an important issue for Congress during the 1970s. Congress charged the United States Parole Commission with the task of developing a plan to address the problems involved in sentencing offenders. The plan that was developed was short lived because of lack of judicial acceptance. The second plan advanced involved rewriting the federal criminal code, but it, too, was not implemented successfully. The third plan focused on sentencing reform and proposed a comprehensive criminal law package, the Comprehensive Crime Control Act of 1984, and included the Sentencing Reform Act (Wilkins, Newton, and Steer 1993).

The purpose of the Sentencing Reform Act was to enhance the ability of the criminal justice system to combat crime through an effective, fair sentencing system. In order to achieve this goal, Congress identified three objectives: (1) the sentence imposed would be the actual sentence served, except for "good-time" credits, and the possibility of parole would not be a factor; (2) there would be uniformity in sentencing practices; and (3) the sentence would be proportional to the defendant and the offense (Wilkins et al. 1993). Several states have followed the federal model by enactment of similar sentencing procedures that provide for sentence enhancements for the career criminal. Common characteristics of sentence enhancement statutes are the imposition of a greater sentence for persons convicted under another statutory provision; the application of procedures for sentence hearings; and the use of titles that classify them as sentence enhancing statutes (Rafaloff 1988:1090).

Two particularly traumatic criminal acts (bombing of the Murrah Federal Office Building in Oklahoma City and the destruction of the World Trade Centers) reinforced the contemporary punishment orientation. As a result, there has been increased movement to limit the rights of some types of offenders including nonrelated threats such as increased pressure for the effective registration of and extension of societal control over sexual offenders and increased efforts to enact "truth in sentencing" legislation.

HABITUAL OFFENDER STATUTES

In an attempt to reduce recidivism, many states have enacted habitual offender acts. This is a direct response to evaluations that question the effectiveness of correctional programs in reducing criminality (Maltz 1984). Maltz concluded that (a) nothing works or is an effective deterrent to reducing recidivism and (b) getting tough works if the intervention is tough enough. States that have enacted habitual offender acts hold the belief that getting tough works.

Much of the research in this area has focused on the career patterns of dangerous and repeat offenders who are the targets of habitual offender legislation. One group of studies focuses on the operation of special programs at the law enforcement and prosecution level and reports mixed results (Blumstein and Moitra 1980; Phillips and Cartwright 1980; Weimer 1980). A number of studies focus on the outcomes of special programs for the treatment of dangerous and career criminals and also tend to report mixed results (Beres and Griffith 1998; Heilbrun, Ogloff, and Piracello 1999; Hoffman and Beck 1984; Tennent and Way 1984; van der Werff 1981).

Habitual offender statutes tend to reflect most clearly the preference for incarceration as a disposition. Forty-three states had adopted legislation providing for mandatory sentencing for offenders who demonstrated repeated violations of felony statutes by 1983 (U.S. Department of Justice 1983). This approach to controlling the crime problem was adopted without the benefit of supporting research and with, at best, limited consideration of the potential consequences. Reservations have been expressed by both correctional professionals and academic researchers who suggest that habitual offender acts may prove to be costly and ineffective, while others suggest that the use of imprisonment would be cost effective.

Attempts to understand the "criminal," the individual who earns his or her livelihood by committing criminal acts, have dominated criminology since its inception. Research indicates that as much as 80 percent (Shinnar and Shinnar 1975) or 85 percent (Wolfgang, Figlio, and Sellin 1972) of serious crimes committed are committed by habitual offenders and that these offenders begin their careers at an early age (DeLisi 2006). Habitual offender acts attempt to control this population by assigning longer sentences to repeat felony offenders.

Concern about repeat offenders is not new. Proposed solutions are varied and have been present since the beginning of the use of prisons. Judges have taken prior criminal history into account when sentencing an offender and they have, and do use, longer sentences to control habitual or career criminals. The indiscriminate use of longer sentences for repeat offenders is not effective because plea bargaining, lack of information, and other factors can and do reduce the judge's freedom in assigning a sentence. The use of automatic sentencing has been present since as early as 1926 (Inciardi 1986) when legislation very similar to current habitual offender legislation was introduced in the

New York legislature, with a mandatory life sentence following a fourth felony conviction. Contemporary proposals for selective incapacitation (Blackmore and Welsh 1983; Janus 1985), which are the product of both a desire to control career offenders and pressure to contain the growth of prison populations, are an updated version of an old response to an enduring problem.

Attempts to develop an effective operational definition for habitual offenders have led to the reduction of this concept to a specific number of felonies, thus creating a condition in which the offenders captured by the statute may not be the career criminals sought. Relatively nondangerous offenders could commit three mild felonies (a popular threshold for many legislatures), plead guilty to all three, and receive a harsh sentence for a fourth mild felony offense. The career criminal or the individual with a criminal orientation would avoid the statute by bargaining for a plea to a reduced charge (a misdemeanor), by leaving the jurisdiction after posting bond and avoiding a conviction, or by moving from jurisdiction to jurisdiction during his or her criminal career.

Habitual offender acts have sentence enhancement provisions (add one or more years to the sentence when two or more prior convictions exist) that mandate the use of a life without parole sentence for some (usually on the fourth felony conviction), regardless of the dangerousness or level of commitment to criminal behavior. Other statutes provide for life without parole sentences because of the severity or offensiveness of the act. These statutes permit the assignment of a life without parole sentence when an offender's behavior is so dangerous that society has an interest in permanent incarceration for public safety or for punishment. If the statutes are effective, there should be two life without parole populations. One is composed of offenders (who may not be career criminals) who have committed extremely offensive and dangerous acts, usually involving an element of physical assault; the other is a group of career criminals who frequently have no personal violence in their offense history. Habitual offenders tend to be the younger, more violent, and more assertive offenders (Flanagan 1982; Irwin 1981). If the habitual offender acts are ineffective, a third group of life without parole inmates is created. This group of offenders exhibits relatively mild levels of criminal activity and is not dangerous.

The growth in prison populations has been attributed to changes in the orientation of the justice system (MacKenzie, Tracy, and Williams 1988). For example, prior to 1980, growth in Louisiana prisons was related to demographic changes in the general population, but the rapid growth of Louisiana's prison population in the early 1980s has been attributed to a number of changes in the law which increased the severity of sentences (MacKenzie et al. 1988). Similar statutes have been adopted in many states.

The cost of maintaining the life without parole population is high. If the use of these recent more severe statutes is heavy, a department of corrections might be required to build a new prison every two or three years just to accommodate new life without parole offenders. These prisons would be expensive, secure facilities requiring more and better-qualified staff. Thus, in addition to adding the cost of staffing and maintaining new institutions to the operating budget of the department of corrections, the cost per inmate would increase as well.

SENTENCE ENHANCEMENT

Legislators in most states have passed sentence enhancement statutes. Legislators failed to realize the impact that sentence enhancements would have on prison populations and prison management. Sentence enhancements have contributed greatly to the problem of prison overcrowding in many states. For this reason, many prison officials have reconstructed their programs to accommodate the increase in population. The overall effects of punitive sentence reforms extend beyond the inmate population increase and prison management to include the management of human and material resources (Luttrell 1990:54).

Many sentence enhancement acts focus on the use of firearms. The federal model is the Armed Career Criminal Act. Criminal justice administrators trying to comply with the requirements of the Armed Career Criminal Act found that its application as a sentence enhancement depended on judicial interpretation. The Armed Career Criminal Act's original objective was to punish habitual or repeat offenders, who are sometimes referred to as career criminals. The statute, however, failed to define the career criminal, thereby leaving the definition of such a person to the sentencing authority.

On the state level, firearm laws have been changed to shift discretionary powers in some states from the judges and parole boards to the prosecutors and police. In some states, there tends to be an overuse of sentence enhancements with those identified as serious repeat offenders, while in others there is a tendency to avoid using these enhancements as the law mandates.

California's gun crime sentence enhancements include a one-year additional sentence if the offender or the accomplice is in possession of a gun during the commission or attempted commission of a felony. Actual use of a gun during a felony mandates an additional two-year sentence. An additional two years is added to the sentence if the perpetrator is armed during a sexual offense; in all cases, using a firearm adds a third year to the sentence (Lizotte and Zatz 1986).

In a study conducted by Lizotte and Zatz (1986) that covered a three-year period, data revealed that use of a firearm does not significantly affect the length of sentence to prison. The sentence enhancer is not used for first convictions of any type, and sentences were influenced more by the length of time required to process the case than by mandatory sentences. The use of firearms did begin to influence the sentence length, with the fourth or later arrest increasing the sentence length by 14 months. For the fifth and subsequent arrests, the sentence length increased by 29 months whether or not the prior arrests involved firearms (Lizotte and Zatz 1986). The firearm sentence enhancer is not used until the fifth and later offenses for rape, although the California Penal Code mandates a three-year add-on sentence to the sentence for rape whenever a firearm is used. Courts in California, like those in many other states, only use the sentence enhancer for the most serious repeat offenders (Lizotte and Zatz 1986).

Massachusetts statutes mandate a sentence of one year for persons illegally carrying a firearm. This enhancer does not establish an add-on sentence in relation to another felony; it is directly associated with possession of a firearm. With this enhancer in place, police officers have been granted unlimited discretion in terms of selective policing. As a means of "protecting" a particular group of citizens, the police decide who will be frisked and whether or not to report when a gun is found (Lizotte and Zatz 1986).

In Michigan, if a person is convicted of possessing a firearm during the commission of a felony, the law mandates a two-year add-on sentence. Michigan officials have responded in two different ways to this law. In some instances, they have chosen to "throw the book" at the defendant if the defendant is considered a serious repeat offender. Michigan officials have also found ways to avoid using or lessening the effect of the Felony Firearm Law, such as (a) adjusting the sentence for the mandatory two-year add-on sentence, (b) adjudicating the defendant as innocent of all charges, (c) adjudicating the defendant as guilty of all charges except the Felony Firearm Law, or (d) adjudicating the defendant guilty of a misdemeanor, at which point the Felony Firearm Law cannot be applied (Lizotte and Zatz 1986).

In addition to firearm sentence enhancers, there are also drug enhancement sentences. In response to citizen outcry for more stringent drug laws, Congress passed the Anti-Drug Abuse Act of 1986. This Act established mandatory provisions concerning the quantity of drugs involved. Mandatory sentences range from a minimum of 10 years without parole for 1 kilogram or more of heroin or 5 kilograms or more of cocaine to a minimum of 5 years for lesser amounts of either drug (Wilkins et al. 1993). If an offender has prior convictions, the mandatory sentence is doubled. In instances in which death or serious bodily injury occurred due to the use of a controlled substance, the mandatory minimum sentence is 20 years. The 1986 Act also provided sentence enhancements for the location of the distribution, the age of purchaser, and pregnancy of the purchaser (Wilkins et al. 1993).

Habitual offender acts are also sentence enhancement acts. In addition to the use of life without parole, habitual offender statutes use sentence enhancements for lower levels of repeat offenses. Thus, a second conviction might call for two to four additional years, while a third conviction might call for five to ten additional years.

RESTRICTED HOUSING

Statutes were enacted that limited the ability of the departments of corrections to house some offenders in specific types of housing. Some of these restrictions are explicit; others are implicit or related to classification restrictions. Explicit statutes identify classes of offenders who cannot be housed in specific types of facilities. For example, Alabama statutes prevent murderers, those who commit manslaughter while driving under the influence of alcohol, drug dealers, and offenders convicted of a sexual offense from receiving community custody status. Thus, they cannot be placed in community corrections facilities such as halfway houses or work release centers. As a result, these offenders are returned to the community from at least a minimum security correctional facility.

Habitual offender statutes, particularly those with life without parole provisions, produce a similar effect. Because a life without parole offender has no reason to avoid escape, he or she must be kept in at least medium security correctional facilities. Sentencing enhancing provisions have a lesser impact but delay the time the offender will spend in secure facilities (most classification schemes consider length of sentence remaining to be served as well as severity in determining classification).

DETERMINATE SENTENCES AND PAROLE

In the middle 1970s, justice-model-based-determinate sentencing began to emerge as an alternative to rehabilitation-based indeterminate sentencing (Cullen and Gilbert 1982). Determinate sentencing was used until the latter part of the nineteenth century. Indeterminate sentencing developed as a product of treatment-oriented reform and was well established by the beginning of the twentieth century. In the 1970s, punishment-oriented reformers pressed for sentences to be suited to the crime. The provisions for shorter sentences were acceptable to many rehabilitation-oriented reformers who perceived the justice system as victimizing the offender, with set sentences reducing the degree of victimization. Programs to help offenders could remain in place but would not be related to release. By the beginning of the 1980s, 12 states and the federal system had adopted some form of determinate sentencing, but the justice model was not fully adopted in any jurisdiction. In many cases, the differences in legislation reflected the outcome of a debate between conservatives and liberals about the severity of the sentencing provisions and the range of offenses that should be addressed with incarceration. Other differences include the amount of discretion permitted, the abolishment or modification of parole, and the use of good time to reduce prison sentences (Cullen and Gilbert 1982).

FINANCIAL CONSIDERATIONS

The justice system frequently is displayed as a funnel representing the reduction in the size of the population as cases flow from arrest to incarceration. The population to be served is largest at the community level and smallest at the institutional level, in spite of the rapid growth of the use of institutional corrections. At the end of 2005, there were 2,193,798 prisoners in the federal prison system, jails, and various state departments of corrections (Bureau of Justice Statistics 2007a) and over 4,162,500 probationers (Bureau of Justice Statistics 2007b). The client population to be served is almost twice the size in the community before prison and treatment is not provided to many incarcerated offenders. While the cost of treatment in the community is less than the cost of treating men and women in prison, the overall cost would be higher because of the larger amenable-to-treatment population in the community. As many of those on probation succeed without treatment, communities are hesitant to initiate even inexpensive programs.

The source of funding is a second financial factor influencing the adoption of community corrections programs. The prison system, in most cases, is funded at the state or federal level. Community corrections programs are usually funded at the local level. Even when federal seed money is available, the local community is responsible for assuming the funding, usually after three years of federal funding. Local political leaders tend to see the management of felons as a state or federal responsibility and are reluctant to spend scarce county or city funds on "state" inmates. As a result, community correction programs are not implemented or are phased out as federal and state subsidies are withdrawn.

Get tough on crime emphasizes punishment. Community corrections programs are often projected as treatment and soft on crime. As elected political leaders have attempted to insure reelection on a get tough on crime platform, they have passed legislation increasing the penalties for many crimes, both increasing the number of crimes for which prison is appropriate and increasing the lengths of the sentences proscribed for other crimes. While prison construction is a growing business, legislators often have not provided sufficient funds for the construction of enough prisons or for hiring and training a sufficient number of correctional officers to adequately hold and supervise this rapidly growing population, creating the overcrowding that we see in today's prison systems.

UNINTENDED CONSEQUENCES

There are at least four unintended consequences of the get tough on crime movement—financial crisis, effective inmate civil suits, early release of serious and career criminals, and increased representation of minority populations in the justice system. As prison populations have increased, most states have responded by building new prisons. These institutions are expensive to build and expensive to maintain. As a result, department of corrections budgets have steadily increased to the point that in some states, such as Alabama, the department of corrections is becoming the largest single category of state funding. The impact of the slowing economy in the late 1990s and early 2000s has aggravated the burden of rapidly increased spending for corrections producing or increasing the fiscal crisis faced by many states.

This growing fiscal pressure has led to an increasing gap between the number of men and women sentenced to prison and the number of prison beds available to house them. A pattern familiar in the 1960s is emerging that includes severe overcrowding in both the prisons themselves and in the county jails that are holding inmates for transfer to state facilities that are too crowded to accept them. We are beginning to see the response to crowded prisons of the 1960s—increased civil suits filed on the behalf of prison inmates alleging inhumane (unconstitutional) conditions. These suits are producing similar results—orders from federal judges to state authorities mandating reform (Shook and Sigler 2001).

In responding to these civil suits, state administrators are resorting to increased use of parole to reduce populations. Parole is granted at the earliest possible time. As a result, relatively high-risk inmates are released from prison to make room for relatively low-risk offenders. In particular, career criminals who make good prison adjustments tend to be released as quickly as possible. When this occurs, get tough on crime increases our risk instead of decreasing our risk. This can be seen in the fact that today's prison populations contain fewer violent offenders than was the case in the 1980s (Gido 2002).

Getting tough on crime has an increased impact on disadvantaged minority groups. Prison populations continue to grow with disadvantaged minority groups growing more rapidly than majority groups (Gido 2002; U.S. Department of Justice 2001). Getting tough on crime places pressure on law enforcement, prosecutors, and judges to capture and incarcerate more offenders. The system has consistently made every effort to capture and incarcerate serious and professional criminals so it cannot reasonably increase productivity in this area. The system response has been a reduction in the use of discretion in the processing of minor offenders. That is, minor offenders who would have been diverted at the law enforcement or prosecutorial level or who would have been given probation as a sentence are processed into the system and into prison. When the offender is affluent or the child of an affluent family, prosecution of the case is less likely to be successful. Political pressure can be brought to bear, influential and effective legal talent can be purchased, investigators and experts can be engaged, and alternative treatment can be arranged. When the increase in processing into the justice system is economically influenced, disadvantaged minorities are more likely to be processed. While these factors have always influenced incarceration, get tough on crime exaggerates this process because the increase occurs at the level where discretion is more likely to occur. All serious and career offenders are processed into the system as much as possible regardless of their financial resources. As the proportion of mild offenders in relation to serious and career criminals processed increases, the differential impact of income increases. More disadvantaged minorities are processed and their proportional representation in the justice system increases because a greater proportion of them are poor.

LOOKING TO THE FUTURE

Currently punishment dominates as the appropriate disposition for convicted offenders. This preference for punishment developed in the 1970s and has influenced legislation, policy, and practice. Legislation enhancing habitual offender statutes, providing for determinate sentencing, restricting the ability of departments of corrections from housing some offenders in some types of housing, and providing longer sentences when specific conditions are present have increased the number of offenders sentenced to prison, have provided for longer sentences, and have made prisons more difficult to administer. The practical consequences of these actions have been to produce overcrowded prisons, to aggravate the present fiscal crisis in many states, and to increase the disproportionate representation of disadvantaged minorities in the justice system.

Punishment tends to become dominant when treatment is perceived as ineffective in curing offenders, and crime and the risk of the public to criminal victimization is seen as increasing. Punishment is perceived to have a deterrent effect, and long incarceration is perceived to have an incapacitation effect. It is anticipated that the combination of deterrence effect and incapacitation effect will reduce victimization by reducing crime. In particular, the identification of severe and persistent offenders and their subsequent incarceration is expected to greatly reduce crime by incarcerating a relatively small number of offenders. It was noted earlier that this strategy as reflected in the application of habitual offender statutes has not effectively removed serious offenders from society.

The ability to sentence severe offenders to prison and to maintain them for long periods of time is effectively prevented by overcrowding that is caused by implementation of the various sentencing reform statutes. Prisons were overcrowded when the shift from treatment to punishment began. A series of judicial decisions in the 1960s established minimal standards for humane living conditions that continued to be reinforced into the 1970s. A central position in many of these decisions addressed population density, forcing many prison systems to reduce the number of inmates housed in existing facilities, thus defining many operating prisons as overcrowded. In many cases court orders prevented, and in some cases still prevent, exceeding specific population limits for specific jails, correctional facilities, and correctional systems. While more recent decisions have modified the earlier rulings, upper population limits are in place for many correctional institutions. The mandatory provisions of many statutes force the placement of specific offenders in prison for minimum periods of time. In order to accept these prisoners, other offenders must be released. When mandatory provisions apply to relatively mild offenders such as shoplifters, more serious offenders are released through a number of compensatory provisions enacted by legislatures at the request of system components. While most correctional systems have responded with rapid expansion, new construction cannot keep up with the flow of new inmates into the system. Prisons and jails are once again becoming severely overcrowded, producing a new wave of civil suits filed on behalf of inmates, many of which are producing judicial orders for reform.

When overcrowding occurs and is capped at the state level, prisoners sentenced to the department of corrections remain in the county jail until a bed becomes available. In most states, the county jails are full. In many instances, they are under a court order capping jail population, and pressure is brought to bear on the court system to reduce the flow of offenders sentenced to incarceration. As a result, more serious offenders with fewer convictions (assault) or career criminals who manage the system effectively are given probation, and first offenders and less serious offenders with longer records (shoplifters) are incarcerated.

As the problems develop, secondary adaptations that avoid some of the statutory provisions emerge. For example, the court might not take judicial notice of the presence of three prior felony convictions when sentencing a specific offender thus avoiding the mandatory prison sentence or the need to enhance the sentence appropriate for the offense. Pressure to use incarceration remains, producing an uneasy balance in the sentencing process that causes some less severe offenders to be incarcerated while more severe offenders are released. When added to the process that causes some more severe offenders to be released rather than some less severe offenders, the degree of risk to which society is exposed increases rather than decrease.

Statutes with mandatory sentence enhancement and mandatory life without parole provisions are vulnerable to court challenge. The mandatory provision in many of these statutes has been included to answer criticism that such acts are discriminatory. If the imposition of a sentence is automatically applied to a set of circumstances related to the offense, it is not discriminatory. The decision to avoid taking judicial notice of conditions requiring the application of a mandatory sanction effectively removes the direct link between the conditions relative to the crime and the sentence. At some point, it is probable that the application of these statutes will be challenged as discriminatory, particularly as their application can differentially impact disadvantaged minority populations.

As we move into the second decade of the twenty-first century, it is probable that there will be a shift in philosophy from a preference for punishment in the disposition of offenders to a preference for treatment as a disposition for criminal offenders. It will be held that punishment is expensive and does not work. The construction costs of new prisons are high; however, the more substantial costs lie in operating budgets. As more prisons are brought on line, the operating budgets of correctional systems increase. This growth mandates either increased taxes or reduction in the budgets of other state government activities. News articles, refereed articles (Beres and Griffith 1998), and books (Jacobson 2005) will begin to focus on the cost issue and ask the questions "What are we receiving for this investment?" and "Is what we receive worth higher taxes or poorer highways?" The belief that offenders who are incarcerated become worse and that all offenders cannot be locked up for life will be advanced along with examples of mild offenders who are serving life without parole sentences. The argument will emerge that it is not enough to lock people up—something must be done to reduce the likelihood that they will continue to commit crimes. As a result, a situation in which public sentiment for treatment will develop, producing a new wave of treatment-oriented reform.

While the exact nature of these reforms cannot be determined, a number of reactions are probable. Community corrections is presently advanced as the next stage in the development of an effective treatment agenda for offenders. Community corrections continue to refer to a variety of programs located in the community, with little attention given to conventional definitions of community corrections or to purpose and function. As a result, community corrections is a relatively vague entity encompassing such a variety of programs that most people can identify a community corrections program that they find acceptable. In essence, many programs defined as community corrections are not treatment-oriented in the pro-offender sense. Home detention, halfway houses, shock probation, and similar programs can be perceived as having punishment elements. Although statutory revision would not be required to implement community corrections as a disposition, it is probable that statutes defining or expanding the scope of various community corrections sentencing alternatives will be enacted. It is also likely that additional enabling legislation and legislation supporting development and dissemination of community corrections will be enacted. The recent popularity of drug courts, alternative sentencing programs, and boot camps is one indication that the process is beginning at the operational level if not at the pubic opinion level.

Contemporary concern with the perceived increase in the amount and severity of violence may moderate the response to pressure to modify sentencing provisions. Recent concern with acts of terrorism, child kidnapping, and child sex offenders has reinforced commitment to the punishment philosophy. If the focus on sentence enhancement and life without parole sentences focuses on the number of relatively mild offenders captured by these statutes, these statutes may be revised such that they apply only to those who commit the most serious assault and weapons linked felonies. It is likely that mandatory sentence enhancements will be softened. Drug-related enhanced sentencing provisions may prevail unless the tendency to identify drug use as a cause of crime moderates. The expansion of the adoption of determinate sentencing will moderate; however, statutes in place are likely to remain in place. While determinate sentences reflect the positivist perspective and are keyed to the crime rather than to the characteristics and needs of the offenders, determinate sentences do not prevent the application of treatment programs, particularly if the next shift to a treatment perspective focuses on community corrections as treatment.

REFERENCES

ALLEN, F. A. (1981). *The Decline of the Rehabilitative Ideal: Penal Policy and Social Purpose.* New Haven, CT: Yale University Press.

BARTOLLAS, J. S. (1980). Practitioner's attitudes toward the career criminal program. *Journal of Criminal Law and Criminology* 71: 113–117.

BATES, R. L. (1981). Search and seizure—the effect of unrecorded misdemeanor corrections on enhancement statutes. *American Journal of Trial Advocacy* 4: 739–760.

BENNETT, R. (1983). A favorable decision for recidivists facing life sentences without parole. *St. Louis University Law Journal* 27: 883–894.

BERES, L. S., and T. D. GRIFFITH (1998). Do three strikes laws make sense? Habitual offender statutes and criminal incapacitation. *Georgetown Law Journal* 87(1): 103–138.

BERNARD, T. J. (1992). *The Cycle of Juvenile Justice.* New York: Oxford University Press.

BLACKMORE, J., and J. WELSH (1983). Selective incapacitation: Sentencing according to risk. *Crime and Delinquency* 29(4): 505–527.

BLUMSTEIN, A., and J. KADANE (1983). An approach to the allocation of scarce imprisonment resources. *Crime and Delinquency* 29(4): 546–559.

BLUMSTEIN, A., and S. MOITRA (1980). The identification of career criminals from chronic offenders in a cohort. *Law and Policy Quarterly* 2: 321–334.

BONTICY, M. K. (1983). Proportionality review of recidivist sentencing. *DU Paul Law Review* 33: 149–182.

BRAUCHI, R. (1983). From the wool sack: Inconsistencies in supreme court decisions on recidivists. *Colorado Law* 12: 1658–1659.

BUREAU OF JUSTICE STATISTICS (2007a). *Prison Statistics.* U.S. Department of Justice. [Retrieved April 20, 2007, from http://www.ojp.usdoj.gov/bjs/prisons.htm]

BUREAU OF JUSTICE STATISTICS (2007b). *Probation and Parole Statistics.* U.S. Department of Justice. [Retrieved April 20, 2007, from http://www.ojp.usdoj.gov/bjs/pandp.htm]

CARNEY, L. (1980). *Corrections: Treatment and Philosophy.* Englewood Cliffs, NJ: Prentice Hall.

CLEMMER, D. (1958). *The Prison Community.* New York: Holt Rinehart and Winston.

CONNOUR, W. F. (1982). Habitual offender issues. *Res Gestae* 26: 86.

CULLEN, F. T., and K. E. GILBERT (1982). *Reaffirming Rehabilitation.* Cincinnati, OH: Anderson Publishing Co.

CURRIE, E. (1985). *Confronting Crime.* New York: Pantheon Books.

DAVIS, W. L. (1982). Recent developments in persistent felony offender cases. *Kentucky Bench & Bar* 46: 10.

DELISI, M. (2006). Zeroing in on early arrest onset: Results from a population of extreme career criminals. *Journal of Criminal Justice* 34(1): 17–26.

DUNFORD, F. W., and D. S. ELLIOTT (1984). Identifying career offenders using self-reported data. *Journal of Research in Crime and Delinquency* 21: 57–86.

DURKHEIM, E. (1965). *The Rules of the Sociological Method.* New York: Free Press.

FELDMAN, S. W. (1984). The habitual offender laws of Tennessee. *Memphis State University Law Review* 14: 293–335.

FLANAGAN, T. (1982). Correctional policy and the long-term prisoner. *Crime and Delinquency* 28(1): 82–95.

FLANAGAN, T. (1985). Sentence planning for long-term inmates. *Federal Probation* 49(3): 23–28.

FOGEL, D. (1978). *We Are the Living Proof,* 2nd ed. Cincinnati, OH: Anderson Press.

FORST, B. (1984). Selective incapacitation. *Judicature* 68: 153–160.

GARLAND, D. (1990). Frameworks of inquiry in the sociology of punishment. *British Journal of Sociology* 41: 1–15.

GIDO, R. L. (2002). *Turnstile Justice: Issues in American Corrections*. Upper Saddle River, NJ: Prentice Hall.

GOTTFREDSON, M., and T. HIRSCHI (1986). The true value of lambda would appear to be zero: An essay on career criminals, criminal careers, selective incapacitation, cohort studies, and related topics. *Criminology* 24(2): 213–233.

GRANT, I. (1985). Dangerous offenders. *Dalhousie Law Journal* 9: 347–382.

GREENWOOD, W. (1980). Career criminals presentation: Potential objectives. *Journal of Criminal Law and Criminology* 71: 85–88.

GREENWOOD, P., J. CHAIKEN, J. PETERSILIA, and M. PETERSON (1978). *The Rand Habitual Offender Project: A Summary*. Santa Monionica, CA: Rand Corporation.

HARRIS, M. K. (1998). Exploring the implications of four sanctioning orientations for community corrections. *Federal Probation* LXII(2): 81–94.

HEADLEY, B. (1989). Introduction: Crime, justice, and powerless racial groups. *Social Justice* 16(4): 1–9.

HEILBRUN, K., J. OGLOFF, and K. PICARELLO (1999). Dangerous offender statutes in the United States and Canada: Implications for risk assessment. *International Journal of Law and Psychiatry* 22(3–4): 393–415.

HOCHBERGER, R. (1980). Justice bar recidivist sentence. *New York Law Journal* 83: 1.

HOFFMAN, P. B., and J. L. BECK (1984). Burmont—age at release from prison and recidivism. *Journal of Criminal Justice* 12: 617–623.

INCIARDI, J. (1986). *Criminal Justice*. New York: Harcourt Brace, Jovanovich.

IRWIN, D. (1981). Sociological studies of the impact of long-term confinement. In *Confinement in Maximum Custody*, ed. D. Ward and K. F. Schoen. Lexington, MA: Lexington Books.

JACKSON, F. (1984). Second-degree burglary held a serious felony. *LA Daily Journal* 97: 2.

JACOBSON, M. (2005). *Downsizing Prisons: How to Reduce Crime and End Mass Incarceration*. New York: New York University Press.

JANUS, M. (1985). Selective incapacitation: Have we tried it? Does it work? *Journal of Criminal Justice* 3: 117–129.

KINDELL, L. R. (1983). Ohio adopts a mandatory sentencing measure. *University of Dayton Law Review* 8: 425–441.

KRAMER, R. C. (1982). From habitual offenders to career offenders: The historical construction and development of criminal categories. *Law and Human Behavior* 6: 273–293.

LANGAN, P., and L. GREENFELD (1983). *Career Patterns in Crime*. Washington, DC: U.S. Department of Justice, Bureau of Statistics.

LIZOTTE, A., and M. ZATZ (1986). The use and abuse of sentence enhancement for firearms offenses in California. *Law and Contemporary Problems* 49(1): 199–221.

LUTTRELL, M. (1990). The impact of the sentencing reform act on prison management. *Federal Probation* 55(4): 54–57.

MACKENZIE, D. L., G. S. TRACY, and G. WILLIAMS (1988). Incarceration rates and demographic change hypothesis. *Journal of Criminal Justice* 16(3): 212–253.

MALTZ, M. (1984). *Recidivism*. Orlando, FL: Academic Press.

MARSHALL, L. (1980). The constitutional infirmities of Indiana's habitual offender statute. *Indiana Law Review* 13: 597–626.

MCKELVEY, B. (1977). *American Prisons: A History of Good Intentions*. Montclair, NJ: Patterson Smith.

MONAHAN, J. (1981). Identifying chronic criminals. In *Confinement in Maximum Custody* (NCJ-77087), ed. D. Ward and K. F. Schoen. Lexington, MA: D. C. Heath and Company.

MORAN, T. J. (1982). Separation of powers and the Illinois habitual offender act: Who sentences the habitual criminals? *Loyola University of Chicago Law Journal* 13: 1033–1053.

MORRIS, N. (1951). *The Habitual Criminal*. Cambridge: Harvard University Press.

MORRIS, W. (1983). Colorado's habitual criminal act: An overview. *Colorado Lawyer* 12: 215.

MUELLER, N. R. (1982). Attacking prior convictions in habitual criminal cases: Avoiding the third strike. *Colorado Lawyer* 11: 1225–1230.

PECK, D., and R. JONES (1981). The high cost of Alabama's habitual felony offender act: A preliminary assessment. *International Journal of Offender Therapy and Comparative Criminology* 29(3): 251–264.

PETERSILIA, J., P. HONIG, and C. HUBOY (1980). *Prison Experience of Career Criminals.* Washington, DC: U.S. Department of Justice.

PHILLIPS, J., and C. CARTWRIGHT (1980). The California career criminal prosecution program one year later. *Journal of Criminal Law & Criminology* 71: 107–112.

PINDUR, W., and S. P. LIPEC (1981). Prosecution of the habitual offender: An evaluation of the Portsmouth commonwealth's attorney major offender program. *University of Detroit Journal of Urban Law* 58: 433–457.

RADZINOWICZ, L., and R. HOOD (1980). Incapacitating the habitual criminal: The English experience. *Michigan Law Review* 78(3): 1305.

RAFALOFF, J. (1988). The armed career criminal act: Sentence enhancement or new offense? *Fordham Law Review* 56: 1085–1099.

SHILTON, M. K. (1995). Community corrections acts may be Rx system needs. *Corrections Today* 32,34–26,66.

SHINNAR, E., and K. SHINNAR (1975). The effects of the criminal justice system on the control of crime: A qualitative approach. *Law and Society Review* 23(4): 547.

SHOOK, C. L., and R. T. SIGLER (2001). *Constitutional Issues in Correctional Administration.* Durham, NC: Carolina Academic Press.

SHORE, J. M. (1984). An evaluation of Canada's dangerous offender legislation. *Les Cahiers Droit* 411–426.

SMITH, A. B., and L. BERLIN (1988) *Treating the Criminal Offender.* New York: Plenum Press.

SORENSON, C. W. (1980). The habitual criminal act. *Nebraska Law Review* 59: 507–537.

STEINER, B., J. WADA, C. HEMMENS, and V. S. BURTON, JR. (2005). The correctional orientation of community corrections: Legislative changes in the legally prescribed functions of community corrections 1992–2002. *American Journal of Criminal Justice* 29(2): 142–159.

SUPREME COURT (1980). Cruel and unusual punishment: Life sentences for repeated nonviolent felonies. *Harvard Law Review* 94: 87–96.

TENNENT, G., and C. WAY (1984). The English special hospital: A 12–17 year followup study. *Medical Science and Law* 24: 81–91.

U.S. DEPARTMENT OF JUSTICE (1983). *Setting Prison Terms.* Washington, DC: Bureau of Justice Statistics.

U.S. DEPARTMENT OF JUSTICE (2001). *Bulletin.* Washington, DC: Bureau of Justice Statistics.

VAN DER WERFF, C. (1981). Recidivism and special deterrence. *British Journal of Criminology* 21: 136–147.

WEES, G. (1996). Inmate population expected to increase 43% by 2002. *Corrections Compendium* April: 1–4.

WEIMER, D. L. (1980). Vertical prosecution and career criminal bureaus: How many and who? *Journal of Criminal Justice* 8: 369–378.

WEST, D. J., and R. S. WRIGHT (1981). A note on long-term criminal careers. *British Journal of Criminology* 21: 375–376.

WILHEIM, M. G. (1982). Recidivist statutes. *Washington Law Review* 57: 573–598.

WILKINS, L. T. (1980). Problems with existing prediction studies and future research needs. *Journal of Criminal Law & Criminology* 71: 98–101.

WILKINS, JR., W., P. NEWTON, and J. STEER (1993). Competing sentencing policies in a "war on drugs" era. *Wake Forest Law Review* 28: 305–327.

WILLIAMS, K. M. (1980). Selection criteria for career criminal programs. *Journal of Criminology Law & Criminology* 71: 89–93.

WOLFGANG, M., M. FIGLIO, and T. SELLIN (1972). *Delinquency in a Birth Cohort.* Chicago, IL: University of Chicago Press.

YOUNG, J. (1980). Constitutional law—Texas habitual offender statute. *American Journal of Criminal Law* 8: 209–216.

PART IV

Issues in Policing

Chapter 17

Advanced Technology, Enhanced Funding, and Specialized Police Domestic Violence Programs in the Twenty-First Century

Albert R. Roberts, Karel Kurst-Swanger, and Colleen O'Brien

INTRODUCTION

Domestic violence is a prevalent criminal justice and public health problem that has enormous consequences for the safety, survival, and health of millions of women and children. Every nine seconds a woman is battered by her current or former husband, boyfriend, or date somewhere in the United States. Each year, it is estimated that 8.7 million women are physically abused by a male partner, and about 2 million of these women are victims of severe violence (Roberts and Roberts 2005). Most of the severe injuries consist of broken bones, head and traumatic brain injuries, neck and face injuries, and/or miscarriages (Roberts and Kim 2005).

The future bodes well in terms of federal funding for advocacy as well as criminal justice and social service intervention programs on behalf of battered women and stalking victims. More specifically, President George W. Bush has been highly committed to reducing domestic violence, and by January, 2006, he had signed the Violence Against Women Act III and increased the five-year appropriation to $3.9 billion for federal fiscal years 2006–2010.

Important progress has been made in the past decade through the use of technological advancements to protect battered women, while holding the batterer accountable.

More specifically, a growing number of communities nationwide have been using the following:

1. Preprogrammed cellular phones, pages, or panic alarms free of charge to the victims. In addition, city and county prosecutors, police departments have begun to offer GPSs with alarms that alert authorities to the battered women's exact location.

2. The Massachusetts Legislature recently authorized court-mandated electronic monitoring devices in order to monitor the batterer's location in proximity to the battered woman. These electronic ankle and wrist bracelets have been found to be effective in notifying police when the batterer has violated an Order of Protection.

3. Improvements in electronic information systems have provided local courts and police with immediate information regarding arrest records, court orders, court records, and criminal history databases. Specific information tracking alerts can be placed on various addresses in order to protect battered women and their children from their ex-abusive partner.

The following statistics reveal the nature, extent, and seriousness of domestic violence:

- Each year an estimated 8.7 million women are abused by their partners (Roberts and Roberts 2005).

- Each year approximately 1.5–2 million women need emergency medical assistance as a result of domestic violence (Roberts 1994; Straus and Gelles 1986).

- Estimates indicate that annually approximately 2,000 battered women are murdered by their abusive partners and 750 batterers are killed by their partners (Roberts and Burman 1998).

- According to the National Violence Against Women survey, 41.5 percent of the women respondents reported that they had sustained injuries as a result of being assaulted by their partners. The injuries included cuts and bruises, broken bones and internal injuries, knife wounds, gunshot wounds, and being knocked unconscious (Tjaden and Thoennes 2000).

- "The lifetime prevalence of intimate partner battering reported by studies of hospital emergency rooms ranged between 11 percent and 54 percent" (Roberts 2002).

- "26 percent of female suicide attempts presented to a hospital seem to be preceded by abuse" (Flitcraft and Stark 1986).

The aftermath of this domestic violence reaches far beyond just the abuser and abused—it affects members of the law enforcement community, the criminal justice system, the legal system, members of the medical profession, psychologists, social workers, mental health counselors, substance abuse counselors, crises hotline specialists, and family members of both the abuser and abused. It is estimated each year that more than 10 million children witness domestic abuse in their own homes (Carlson 1996), and the impact of this often results in an intergenerational cycle of violence. Lieberman Research, Inc. (1995) found that one third of women who are physically abused by a husband or boyfriend grew up in a household where their mother was a victim of domestic violence. What can be done about this cycle of abuse? What types of specialized criminal justice programs and strategies can be implemented to stop it? What types of technology can lessen and eventually eliminate woman battering? The answers to these critical questions constitute the basis for this chapter.

In recent years, multiple agencies have recognized the need to treat domestic violence as what it is: a serious crime and major social problem. These agencies have developed new training and programs to combat domestic violence and create programs to help those who have been abused. Police agencies are increasingly using technology (e.g., cellular phones, electronic monitoring, and use of the web) to protect battered women and deter violent batterers. The courts and advocacy groups are also recognizing the need for technology in the fight against domestic violence. Since the 1990s, the courts have begun to examine and reinvent court processes to improve victim protection and offender accountability. Information regarding domestic violence statistics and prevention programs is now accessible through the web and is available to the courts, police departments, medical personnel, various social service agencies, and victims.

The Mary Kay Ash Charitable Foundation has recognized the need for the use of technology in combating domestic violence. It has teamed up with more than 650,000 Mary Kay Independent Beauty Consultants nationwide to raise $500,000 for the National Network to End Domestic Violence's "National Safe and Strategic Technology Project" (Safety NET) (Statewide California Coalition for Battered Women 2003). The Safety NET project is an initiative to educate victims and their advocates on how to use technology to safely escape abusive relationships. The project also encourages technology innovators to create safety nets for victims, and it works in conjunction with policy makers to create strong guidelines to protect the victims of domestic violence as our society advances into the electronic age. This project has resulted in the training of over 2,100 advocates, police officers, and prosecutors in the use of technology to help victims of domestic violence, and these people are now disseminating that information to others in order to save and transform the lives of victims of domestic violence (National Network to End Domestic Violence 2003).

An anonymous survivor of domestic violence abuse was quoted as saying, "As a survivor, after nine years I still look over my shoulder. I need to know that I am doing everything necessary to ensure my safety. This includes technology" (NNEDV 2003). How are police agencies implementing technology to combat the nationwide problem of domestic violence? What are some of the training and policy changes of these agencies in regard to domestic violence issues? What are some of the initiatives being taken to help prevent domestic violence and protect the victims? This chapter will provide answers to these important questions.

Law Enforcement Model Domestic Violence Training and Intervention Programs: A Prelude to Change

During the past two decades intimate partner violence, also known as domestic violence, has become recognized as a serious crime (i.e., a felony rather than a misdemeanor) in state criminal codes and family court statutes in all 50 states. Specifically, because of the prevalence and potential lethality of women battering, all 50 states have passed civil and/or criminal statutes to protect battered women. In some areas, as many as 50–75 percent of all police calls involve domestic violence (Roberts 2002).

Today society at large has finally recognized that beating women (wives, cohabitants, or companions) is a crime and a major social problem. This recognition of woman abuse as a major social problem grew out of four noteworthy activities. First, the women's movement has reached maturity by consistently drawing public attention to the plight of battered women. Second, two national prevalence studies on the extent of domestic violence in the United States were conducted. The results confirmed our worse fears. Domestic violence occurs with great frequency and should be given top public policy priority (Straus, Steinmetz, and Gelles 1980). Third, a proliferation of research, culminating with books and news articles on battered women brought scholars, professionals, and the public closer to the issue (Fleming 1976; Roberts and Burman 1998; Roy 1982; Walker 1979, 1984). Finally, recent litigation and legal reforms and federal legislation have prompted institutional change (Roberts 2002).

As a result of such social changes, police departments have literally endured a metamorphosis in their customary practices, norms, and formal policies regarding domestic violence. Many police departments now have new policies and procedures specifically addressing how they handle calls regarding domestic violence. Many departments now have protocols regarding how dispatchers, patrol officers, and investigators should handle cases. Many departments have trained volunteers and crisis-response teams to assist battered women in crisis. Many also coordinate their law enforcement roles with local victim service providers and the courts. Departments nationwide have embraced mandatory and proarrest policies as an important intervention strategy and have begun the process of retraining seasoned police officers.

However, the road toward implementing effective policies for batterers has been bumpy and uneven, and research studies on the short-term deterrent effects of arresting batterers vary from one jurisdiction to another. Nevertheless, Americans have come a long way from the time when the use of violence by men to control their partners was condoned. Mandatory and warrantless arrest laws are just one part of the improved police response to victims of battering. In addition, the police in highly populated cities and counties throughout the nation now provide immediate protection to battered women.

The Violence Against Women Act of 1994 authorizes Services, Training, Officers and Prosecution (STOP) grants, with required matching funds from the state, providing dollars for training of law enforcement personnel. The Urban Institute conducted an evaluation of STOP grants and found that states were using their grants to improve training in number of ways: expanding training requirements to be effective statewide; developing or updating training curricula; training process servers on issues related to domestic violence; developing multidisciplinary training for law enforcement, prosecutors, judges, and victim services; and creating specialized seminars, in-service courses, and roll-call packages (The Urban Institute 1998). For more information on model STOP grant programs in different regions of the United States, see the section Model Police Departments in this chapter.

Training for police on domestic violence issues includes a wide array of topics. Training may include dynamics of violent families and impacts on victims, understanding the batterer's use of violence to maintain control over the victim, dispatcher protocol, securing the crime scene, assessment of victim safety, identifying and interviewing victims and witnesses, and the collection of forensic evidence. Since many state legislatures have moved to include proarrest and/or mandatory policies in the cases of domestic violence, training often focuses on the appropriate implementation of state law.

The Violence Against Women's Act also provided funding in 2000 to the Federal Law Enforcement Training Center to implement its newly developed domestic violence train-the-trainer program for law enforcement officials in rural communities. This training, centered on domestic violence issues present in rural communities, provides officers with instruction on training curriculums, copies of training materials, and videos for use in their own jurisdictions.

Contemporary police training has evolved to include topics and issues not typically considered in traditional police training. For example, the New Haven Police Department's Child Development–Community Policing Program in Connecticut is a promising example of multidisciplinary training aimed at increasing the competence of police officer interactions with children and families. The training is centered on the reorientation of police officers to approach their work from a mental health perspective and to learn to work in partnership with local social service providers. Administered by the The Yale Child Study Center and the New Haven Department of Police Service, both new and veteran police officers have the opportunity to complete a ten-week course on child development and community policing. Case conferences, consultation services, and child development fellowships for police supervisors are unique features of this police/mental health collaboration (New Haven Police Department 2001).

Similarly, the International Association of Chiefs of Police (IACP), based on recommendations from a Summit on Family Violence, included the following training recommendations for police departments. Training should be multidisciplinary in nature, including professionals such as law enforcement, fire department, and EMT workers; religious leaders; teachers and other school personnel; child care workers; health care workers; substance abuse providers; child welfare and public assistance workers; prosecutors and judges. Training should be tailored to meet the specific needs of the local community and should include preservice, in-service, and continuing education curricula. The summit work groups also stressed the importance of establishing and maintaining policy initiatives that are multidisciplinary in nature and the fact that agencies should look to pool resources to collaborate for effective intervention strategies (IACP 2001).

Future Training

Another aspect of training that should be considered for future use for law enforcement personnel, health care workers, substance abuse providers, child welfare and public assistance workers, prosecutors, judges, and others is the understanding of the typology of the domestic violence victim. While there has been a great focus on understanding the nature of the perpetrator in crimes of domestic violence, there has been a lack of understanding of the typology of the victims. In his *Handbook of Domestic Violence Intervention Strategies* (2002), Roberts has developed a continuum that describes the duration, severity, and lethality of abuse of women within five levels. In it he describes actual examples of women at each level of the continuum and how their personal and situational characteristics determine their potential for leaving the batterer. He also discusses how the typology or continuum provides a framework that previously did not exist for evaluating battered women and improving risk assessments of dangerousness and the importance for having this tool for assessment purposes.

SPECIALIZED DOMESTIC VIOLENCE UNITS

In addition to changes in arrest policies and customary practices in domestic cases, many police departments have created specialized domestic violence units to follow up on all domestic related complaints. Specialized units have the ability to further investigate domestic crimes, make appropriate referrals and arrests, and ensure victim safety long after the patrol officer has left the scene. In some cases, unit members serve as the first responders to domestic calls for service. Units are generally staffed with police investigators or detectives and are often linked with specialized units in a prosecutor's office. They offer an opportunity for personnel to develop specialized knowledge and expertise regarding the investigation and prosecution of domestic crimes. In theory, units create the infrastructure necessary for aggressive, proactive responses to domestic violence rather than the traditional reactive policing approach.

These units also provide an opportunity to link police services with shelter, victim/witness, and batterer programs. Multidisciplinary approaches that integrate the need for both legal and social service interventions are likely to be the most effective in terms of protecting victim safety and ensuring offender accountability. The following police departments are illustrative of the modern police response to domestic violence.

Ann Arbor Police Department: Domestic Violence Enforcement Team

In Ann Arbor, Michigan, the Domestic Violence Enforcement Team, in partnership with the local battered women's advocacy program, is illustrative of innovative police practice regarding domestic violence. The Enforcement Team was strategically placed in a building adjacent to the SAFE House in an effort to break down the barriers between the police and victim advocacy services and to improve the outcomes for victims. The police unit is able to track the status of cases, cutting through bureaucratic red tape, expediting the serving of bench warrants, and so on. Police attend every defendant arraignment and are able to take all domestic cases seriously. Police link with SAFE house staff after an arrest has been made, bringing immediate in-person services to the victim (Littel et al. 1998).

Austin Police Department: Austin/Travis County Family Violence Protection Team

Travis County, Texas, is another example of a collaborative, community response to family violence providing multiple services in one location. Leading the community in a zero-tolerance policy toward family violence, the team, consisting of members of the

Austin Police Department, Travis County Sheriff's Office, SafePlace (formerly the Center for Battered Women and Rape Crisis Center), Legal Aid of Central Texas, Women's Advocacy Project (attorneys), and the Travis County Attorney's Office, collaborates to investigate, prosecute, and provide legal and social services for victims.

Investigations center around cases of assault, kidnapping, stalking, and protective order violations. Legal services streamline the process for obtaining emergency or long-term protective orders. The majority of cases are processed by the county attorney's office and felonies are handled by the district attorney's office. Victim services are provided by victim service counselors from SafePlace, the Austin Police Department, and the Travis County Sheriff's Department. The Austin Child Guidance Center is also available to provide free counseling for children. The team has been in operation since 1997, funded by the Violence Against Women Grants Office (Austin City Connection 2000).

Longview Police Department: Domestic Violence Impact Unit

In Longview, Washington, a six-member team consists of a sergeant, officer, civilian investigator, legal coordinator, crime analyst, and administrative specialist. The unit works to coordinate law enforcement, prosecution, probation, and victim services in domestic violence cases. The team provides education and training to police officers, advocates, prosecutors, probation, and other community and criminal justice partners. An automated case management system assists the team in tracking offenders and their activities as they are processed through the system.

Not unlike the departments highlighted here, specialized units provide departments the opportunity to thoroughly investigate misdemeanor-level domestic crimes, a function that in the past has been lost to other felony crimes. Following up on high-risk cases is critical to breaking the cycle of violence before it escalates to the felony level. Creating dialogue between police units and victims promotes the protection of victims helps to prevent future acts of violence.

Police departments frequently organize their functions through the creation of specialized departments or units. The division of labor into smaller subunits has been an effective tool for contemporary police departments to manage the variety of tasks required of them. For example, police departments may have investigative units or squads regarding narcotics, sex crimes, juvenile crimes, fraud, special weapons, and arson, among others. Generally organized around specific crime types, specialized units have afforded police departments the opportunity to attend to the specific dynamics of particular crimes.

Although there are inherent challenges in the specialization of police functions, Peak (1998) identifies several advantages to such specialization. Specialized units place the responsibility of certain tasks with specific individuals, ensuring the work is completed. In the case of domestic violence, this is especially true. Historically police investigators only followed up on domestic cases that involved felony-level assaults and/or homicides. Therefore, the majority of battering incidents were addressed only by patrol officers at the scene. Only the most severe cases of abuse would be transferred to an investigative bureau. Specialized units also provide for the development of expertise and training that ultimately leads to increased efficiency, effectiveness, staff cohesion, and improved morale.

Although the potential is great for specialized units, Krumholz (2001) argues that there may be a disjuncture between the image of the domestic violence unit and the reality that some units merely serve a symbolic role. Her research with 169 police departments in Massachusetts revealed a number of issues to cause concern. First, only 8 percent of the police departments with domestic violence units reported being supported from a line item in the department's budget, and 11 percent received partial funding by line item. The majority of departments acknowledge they were funded solely by grant funding. This raises serious questions about the stability of such units after the grant period has ended. She also found that departments with units required on average, only two more hours of training per year than police departments without such units. Additionally, she found the average unit was staffed by two full-time officers, and the majority of units were only in operation during normal business hours.

Further research is needed before we can fully understand the impact of specialized units in the creation of a local community environment where victims can be protected and abusers can be held accountable. Since many police departments find that the majority of their calls for service involve domestic incidents, specialized units may provide the most prudent organizational strategy to taking domestic assault seriously.

THE ROLE OF TECHNOLOGY IN A COORDINATED COMMUNITY RESPONSE

Technology has already begun to revolutionize police work. Advanced photographic techniques, computers, DNA profiling, innovations in fingerprinting and forensic techniques, automated crime analysis, computer-aided investigations, computer-aided dispatch, case management systems, simulated training tools, nonlethal weapons, and surveillance technologies are but a few of the many examples of innovative crime fighting tools. As police departments become more skilled with the uses and advantages of such technologies and communities agree to invest resources in them, police departments are likely to apply such advancements to combat domestic violence in a broad way.

We have already begun to see the potential for technology in protecting battered women from their abusive partners and deterring violent batterers from repeating their abusive and brutal acts. Cellular phones, electronic monitoring systems, and online police services are just a few of the applications of modern technology to policing domestic violence.

Cellular Phones

A national campaign to donate cellular phones for victims of domestic violence is currently underway. Sponsored by the Wireless Foundation, a philanthropic organization dedicated to utilizing wireless communication for the public good, the Call to Protect program to date has received 30,606 donated cellular phones to provide links to emergency services for victims and their advocates. Established by the Cellular Telecommunications Industry Association (CTIA), the Wireless Foundation coordinates the Call to Protect, a national Donate a Phone campaign. CTIA members, Motorola, and Brightpoint, Inc., in partnership with the National Coalition Against Domestic Violence (NCADV), provide free wireless phones and airtime.

The phones are preprogrammed to notify authorities at the push of a button. Victim advocates have also been given donated phones and airtime. This national initiative has involved numerous organizations, clubs, and companies to join the fight against domestic violence. Additionally, the Wireless Foundation coordinates the Communities on Phone Patrol (COPP) program, in partnership with Ericsson and CTIA companies to provide free wireless phone and airtime to volunteer neighborhood watch patrols. On average 52,000 crimes and emergencies are reported each month in the United States by neighborhood watch group using wireless phones (Wireless Foundation 2001).

Electronic Monitoring

Recent developments in electronic monitors, computerized tracking of offenders and victims, and video surveillance have greatly bolstered crime investigations and crime prevention efforts. The goal is to lessen and eventually eliminate violent crime by controlling the physical environment. In most severe cases, the formerly battered woman agrees to maintain an active restraining order, agrees to testify in court and cooperate with any criminal proceedings against the alleged batterer, has a telephone in her residence, and believes that she is in extreme danger of aggravated assault or attempted murder by the defendant. In these cases, a home electronic monitor (e.g., panic alarm or pendant), also known as the abused woman's active emergency response pendant, can deter the batterer from violating his restraining order.

Private security companies recently began donating and marketing electronic security devices called panic alarms to battered women. The main purpose of these portable alarms, which have a range of about 200 feet from the victim's home, is to provide the battered women with an immediate and direct link to their local police in an emergency with just a press of a button. In some jurisdictions in Colorado and New Hampshire, the electronic pendant alarms are coupled with electronic monitoring of batterers through the Juris Monitor ankle bracelet, manufactured by B.I., Inc. If the batterer comes within close proximity of the victim's home, the ankle bracelet sounds a loud alarm in the home and immediately alerts the police. ADT Security has set up electronic pendants for battered women in 30 counties and cities throughout the United States. The women are carefully selected for each program by a screening committee comprised of community leaders, including a prosecutor or deputy prosecutor, a supervisor from the local battered women's shelter, and a police administrator. In all cases, the victim has an active restraining order against the batterer and is willing to fully cooperate with the prosecutor's office. One major drawback of these alarms is that the unit will not work if the telephone line is cut or is not working.

Several companies—including T.L.P. Technologies, Inc., Transcience, and B.I., Inc.—are currently developing other electronic monitors. The alarm system developed by T.L.P

Technologies works even when the phone lines are down and when there is no electric power. In the victim's home, police install the system, which includes a radio transmitter with a battery backup, an antenna, and a remote panic or motion detector device. T.L.P.'s Visibility Plus Radio Data Alarm System integrates both the alarm system and computer-generated data immediately into the police radio channel instead of using a private security company as an intermediary. This system has been used with hundreds of battered women in both Nassau and Suffolk Counties, New York (Roberts 2002).

The most promising device that pinpoints the location of the victim whether she is at home, at work, or in the supermarket was developed by Geo Satellite Positioning Equipment. This advanced technology works by means of a satellite that sends a special signal from a receiver on the ground to the local police computer screen. A street map comes on the screen and sends a burst of data over the network, including the alarm number and the longitude and latitude of the victim's location within 5–10 feet (Roberts 2002).

Because of the growing awareness of the acute injuries sustained by battered women throughout the United States and the millions of dollars spent on health and mental health care for victims of domestic violence, we predict that the electronic monitoring programs will be expanded to thousands of battered women in every state by the year 2010. Unfortunately, as has been the case with other new legislation, a high-profile crisis situation needs to occur before Congress enacts new legislation.

Online Police Information

Police departments nationwide are beginning to use the worldwide web as a tool to communicate with the community regarding crime issues. Through web pages, police departments have created a vehicle through which information about domestic violence issues can be disseminated to the public at large. Police department web pages can provide community members with critical information regarding the dynamics of domestic violence, what to do if you are a victim, and where to access community resources.

For example, the Madison Police Department in Madison, Wisconsin, has a web page dedicated to domestic violence information. Created by Detective Cindy Murphy, the page provides links to topics such as safety issues to consider when leaving an abusive relationship, personal safety plan, state laws regarding domestic violence, the cycle of domestic violence, myths and facts about domestic violence, domestic abuse risk assessment, how to obtain a restraining order, and referral to resources and programs available in the Madison area (Madison Police Department 2000).

Both short-term emergency support and long-term security services are critically needed by battered women and their children. It seems important that emergency services, including electronic pendants and/or cellular phones, be initiated for the thousands of battered women in imminent danger of suffering repeated assaults and being murdered by their abusive former partners. Funding for the new technology should come from both corporate sponsors and government agencies. But first, research needs to be carried out to determine which emergency electronic systems are most effective in protecting battered women. Also, under what conditions does the electronic technology fail to ensure the battered women's safety? Before new electronic technology is purchased by battered women's shelters and law enforcement agencies, it is critical that comprehensive evaluations and outcome studies be planned and carried out.

COMMUNITYWIDE INTERVENTION PROGRAMS

Some populated cities and communities have developed citywide and communitywide task forces to provide a well-coordinated response to family violence from the police, the courts, victim/witness assistance, and social service agencies. Many of these community task forces have followed the model of the programs developed during the 1980s in such areas as Baltimore County, Maryland; Quincy, Massachusetts; Duluth and Minneapolis, Minnesota; Boulder and Denver, Colorado; Memphis, Tennessee; Milwaukee, Wisconsin; Lincoln, Nebraska; and Seattle, Washington. The model police programs noted in this chapter all have strong elements of linking police services with local community efforts.

The era of community- and problem-orientated policing has unleashed a paradigm shift in many police departments across the country. Departments have come to recognize the role of engaging the broader community in solving and preventing crime-related problems. Victim assistance programs, health care workers, schools, child welfare agencies, prosecutors, and judges, have come together in conjunction with changes in state law to initiate prevention and intervention programs.

For coordination to be effective among battered women's shelters, police, prosecutors, victim/witness assistance programs, and batterers' counseling programs, certain policies and practices are required. Agencies must have a mutual respect for the individual role each plays, especially when those roles are in conflict. Coordinated community responses should involve as many of the local system players as possible, with the support and guidance from local businesses, religious leaders, and public policy makers. Central to any communitywide response should be the voice of survivors.

At the same time, community education is an equally important component to reducing the incidents of domestic violence. Coordinated communitywide coalitions and task forces have the opportunity to educate the members of their community about abuse and where to get help early in the process. For example, programs in local middle and high schools can educate young people about battering in dating relationships. Understanding that violence often begins early in dating relationships, educators must recognize that educating young people regarding the dynamics of abusive relationships provides a critical dimension in prevention.

Although the police have a substantial role to play in domestic violence cases, it is fair to say that police departments alone cannot be responsible for reducing incidents of battering. Community efforts that encourage a multidisciplinary approach to violence reduction are likely to be most effective. Schools, businesses, victim assistance programs, offender treatment programs, religious organizations, and so on all play a critical role in reducing violence in the home. Attention to prevention and early intervention are probably key to interrupting the cycle of violence.

MODEL POLICE DEPARTMENTS

The Violence Against Women Act II (VAWA) of 2000 strengthened federal law against domestic violence, sexual assault, and stalking and provided 3.3 billion in grant programs over five years (2000–2005) to assist states and local communities to fight violence against women. For fiscal year 2001, Congress authorized approximately $677 million toward such programs, although only $468 million was finally appropriated.

One of the largest grant programs under VAWA is the STOP grant program, which awards funding to every state and territory in the nation to combat violence against women. The STOP grants program had been authorized at an annual amount of $185 million for fiscal years 2001–2005. The cornerstone of the STOP grant program was to improve law enforcement, prosecution, and victim services. As a result of STOP grant funding, as well as other state and federal funding initiatives, local police departments have been able to develop innovative practices.

In addition to the STOP funding, many police departments have utilized funding through the Violent Crime Control and Law Enforcement Act of 1994. This act created the Office of Community Oriented Policing Services (COPS) of the U.S. Department of Justice and has placed over $6.3 billion in almost 12,000 agencies nationwide. Many police departments have applied for COPS dollars to improve their response to domestic violence.

These grant programs provide the critical resources necessary to initiate new responses to domestic violence. Although it is too early to evaluate the overall effectiveness of such police initiatives and it is unclear how police departments will fund such programs after the STOP and COPS grants are no longer available, police departments have an opportunity to test out innovative practices. As a component to STOP funding, the Violence Against Women's Act Grant Office engaged in a study to identify and develop a comprehensive package of best practices for law enforcement and prosecutors. Although police departments vary in the strategies utilized to respond to battering, the fundamental elements of any law enforcement response should be promoting the safety of women and their families, providing assistance to regain control and autonomy in their lives, and holding officers accountable (Littel et al. 1998). The following police departments have been cited as being model examples of how specific best practice protocols can be achieved in the field (Littel et al. 1998).

Duluth Police Department

In Duluth, Minnesota, the Duluth Police Department is an active partner in a community-wide strategy to develop a comprehensive, victim-sensitive law enforcement response to issues of domestic violence. The police department participates in a program of ongoing evaluation through the Domestic Abuse Intervention Project (DAIP), a not-for-profit organization charged with monitoring the response to domestic violence by all agencies within the city's criminal justice system. The police department serves on the DAIP's emergency response team, which deploys members to problem solve a particular system's issues regarding high-risk cases.

Key elements of the police department's model response to domestic violence includes a system of evidence collection and report writing coordinated with the city attorney's office to improve the rate of successful prosecutions. The department contributes information to the Domestic Abuse Information Network (DAIN) by including data from incident and arrest reports, investigative reports, warrant requests, and 911 watch reports providing information to other partner agencies in the project. The department, committed to responding to every incidence of reported domestic violence, uses a computer-aided dispatching system to provide patrol officers with critical information regarding orders of protection and previous calls for service. Officers have been trained to provide victim-sensitive support and to identify high-risk cases. Central to the success of the law enforcement response has been a mandatory arrest policy coordinated with immediate victim services. After careful review of different arrest policies in Duluth, the DAIP concluded that a mandatory policy produced the most consistent race-neutral arrest results. Officers refer victims to the Women's Coalition and other victim services. Once the abuser has been booked, the jail staff contacts the on-call advocate at the Women's Coalition, who sends an advocate to the victim within a few hours of the abuser's arrest. The advocates provide crisis counseling, referrals, and information about the criminal justice system. Advocates also complete a danger assessment utilized by the courts for sentencing and release decision making.

Appleton Police Department

In Appleton, Wisconsin, the Appleton Police Department demonstrates its commitment to combating domestic violence by applying the fundamental elements of community-based policing to their response. Guided by a proarrest policy, the officers are strongly encouraged to arrest the party considered to be the primary aggressor and in cases in which an arrest is not made, the officer must document the reasons why an arrest was not made. Victims are encouraged to complete a domestic violence victim worksheet, providing an opportunity to document details of the incident, and are offered the services of Habor House (the local shelter) at the scene. Advocates from Habor House will respond to the scene if the victim wishes.

A unique feature of the department's response includes the implementation of officer follow-up to the home even when an arrest cannot be made. Officers remind the abuser of the potential for arrest, emphasizing the seriousness of their behavior. The department has found that officer follow-up visits are most successful if conducted 24–48 hours after the initial incident. The Appleton Habitual Offender program includes targeting the top domestic violence offenders and notifying the patrol of their high-risk status. Calls involving these offenders can then be fast tracked into the criminal justice system.

Seattle Police Department

In Seattle, Washington, the Domestic Violence Unit of the Seattle Police Department operates a specialized unit dedicated to the investigation and prosecution of both misdemeanor and felony domestic crimes. Staffed by eight sworn police officers and two domestic violence court order process servers, the unit investigates an average of 80 cases per month and successfully obtains felony arrests in over 45 percent of its cases.

Guided by a mandatory arrest policy, officers are required to submit a written report of each incident regardless of arrest status. If no arrest is warranted, the officers must document the justification. Required only to arrest the primary aggressor, officers must conduct a rather thorough investigation at the scene, collect appropriate evidence, take photos of injuries, and document all statements made by the victim, offender, and witnesses. The domestic violence unit conducts ongoing training to patrol staff regarding their role as first responders to incidents of domestic violence.

The domestic violence unit coordinates with the Victim Assistance Office (also located in the police department), the city attorney's domestic violence unit, as well as local shelters and community-based services. Victims are given a pamphlet with information regarding the domestic violence unit and the incident number. The department's commitment to combating domestic violence is evidenced by the assignment of two detectives who work exclusively on misdemeanor cases. Interrupting violence early in the battering process is critical in the prevention of felony level assaults.

Nashville Metropolitan Police Department

The Family Violence Division of the Nashville Metropolitan Police Department in Nashville, Tennessee, focuses on measures to stop stalking behavior. Staffed by 29 civilian employees and sworn officers as well as many volunteers from the local domestic violence shelter, the division combines attention to victim safety with an aggressive investigative approach to apprehend stalking suspects. Technology, infused with a commitment to investigate such crimes, is central to the division's counter-stalking tactics. The division employs a six-phase domestic violence counter-stalking plan, which involves the use of technology to increase victim safety, deter pre- and posttrial stalking behavior, prove offender violations, and gather evidence for trial. The division utilizes self-contained phone traps, cellular phones, VCR kits, CPS tracking systems, silent hostage alarms, and phone bugs to capture incriminating evidence against the stalker and to promote victim safety.

Colorado Springs Police Department

The Domestic Violence Enhanced Response Team (DVERT) of the Colorado Springs, Colorado, Police Department combines the philosophies of community policing and problem-oriented policing with its model of effective intervention in domestic violence. The DVERT team, consisting of a multidisciplinary staff of 16, responds to cases in which there is a high risk for lethality. The DVERT team receives referrals from advocates, prosecutors, judges, and citizens. Reviewing referrals on a weekly basis, the team determines whether a case meets the criteria for lethality. Criteria used to determine lethality include the perpetrator's previous history of domestic abuse, incidents of stalking, threats made to kill, access to weapons, recent loss experience (such as a separation or divorce), and numerous prior police interventions. Once a case is determined to warrant the attention of the DVERT team, the team immediately follows up. Departmental communication regarding the perpetrator is improved by the labeling of a hazard alert on the victim's and perpetrator's addresses, adding a red flag concerning the potential for lethality to all members of the police department. When patrol officers are dispatched to an address with a hazard alert, three members of the DVERT team (consisting of a police officer/detective, deputy district attorney, and victim advocate) also arrive on the scene to assist the victim and the patrol officer.

The DVERT team provides the local community the benefits of swift and dedicated attention to domestic violence. DVERT team members receive specialized training across disciplines and promote community dialogue around domestic violence issues.

As evidenced by the model programs described here, initiative coupled with creativity and community partnership can combine to ensure a police response that attends to the needs of victims and the accountability of the offenders. Innovative police practice with attention to the development of protocols, implementation of state mandates, and coordination with prosecutors and victim service programs is likely to prevail as the preferred police response to domestic violence.

This has described the police response to domestic violence, but what happens within the courts? How are the courts responding to the problem of domestic violence?

THE RESPONSE OF THE COURTS TO DOMESTIC VIOLENCE

During the past two decades, responsive prosecutors, judges, and legislators have begun to recognize family violence as a serious crime. All 50 states have passed civil and/or criminal statutes to protect battered women, and prosecutors' offices are beginning to implement efficient systems of screening and prosecuting cases. Police and courts, in a small yet growing number of jurisdictions, have set up an around-the-clock method of issuing temporary restraining orders and providing advocacy as the cases move through court. Batterer treatment programs have been court mandated, although they have been developed on a limited basis, and it is obvious that more are needed. Further research into treatment modalities is needed to provide the courts with more and better alternatives for treating the batterers.

Historically, there has been a lack of consistency in the way domestic violence cases have been handled by the courts. Although court jurisdiction varies from state to state, typically women who were married or had children with the abuser had to utilize the civil court system, often referred to as "family courts." A woman who had been battered by a partner to whom she was not married or with whom she had no children in common could only seek assistance from the criminal courts, thus resulting in a fragmented court response to domestic violence. Just as the police have historically been reluctant to intervene in cases of domestic abuse, family and criminal courts have also been plagued by the same lack of knowledge about the dynamics of domestic violence. Civil courts lacked the power to sanction the abusers, and criminal courts have previously been unresponsive to the needs of victims. Domestic violence cases were rarely regarded seriously in comparison with other "real" crimes the court was responsible for processing. Victims were left feeling frustrated, unheard, and unprotected.

However, institutional reforms regarding domestic violence have led to sweeping changes in statutes and court responses to domestic violence. Recognizing the impact of system fragmentation on the victims of domestic violence, many jurisdictions have moved to a more integrated court response. Since the 1990s, the courts have begun to examine and update court processes to improve victim protection and offender accountability. States continue to revise and improve legislation to enable the courts to respond appropriately to cases of domestic violence. Here we discuss recent trends in domestic violence legislation, protective orders, prosecutor policies, and sentencing options.

Prosecutors have the potential to break the cycle of violence. Many believe that more domestic violence cases should be actively prosecuted, particularly those acts involving alleged abusers with prior criminal histories. Responsive prosecutors have been instituting promising strategies and policies in regard to family violence, which have enhanced the different stages of the prosecution process. Prosecutors must delicately balance the goal of conviction with the goal of guarding victim safety. Today, many prosecutors have embraced mandatory prosecution policies in regard to domestic abuse cases, and a growing number of them sign complaints themselves or file charges based on the arresting officer's signed complaint. They do this in order to prevent batterers from intimidating and pressuring victims to drop charges or restraining orders. When prosecutors take official responsibility by signing and filing charges themselves, they are sending the important message that domestic violence is a serious crime against the state, not a personal family matter.

In some jurisdictions, specialized domestic violence courts have been created to enhance the case management of such cases. In other jurisdictions, prosecutors have partnered with police departments and victim service programs to enhance their ability to protect victims and make offenders accountable. Changes in prosecutor policies have reflected a paradigm shift viewing domestic violence as a crime against the state.

Confidentiality of Identifying Information

Many states have added legislation to further protect victims by enacting laws to prohibit the disclosure of identifying information in such cases where there is reason to believe such information would endanger the safety of the victim(s). For example, Alabama and Tennessee enacted legislation in 1999 creating privileged communication between victims and victim service providers. Florida and California enacted legislation in 1998 that created confidentiality procedures and programs, allowing program participants the ability to vote by absentee ballot. In 1997, Nevada amended a confidentiality statute by allowing a victim of domestic violence to file with the secretary of state to establish a fictitious address. Georgia made it a crime to reveal the location of a domestic violence shelter (Roberts 2002).

During the 2000 legislative session, 12 states passed laws that protect the confidentiality rights of battered women or their children. California enacted a new law that protects battered women's e-mail addresses, and Georgia passed legislation to prevent disclosure of confidential information by insurance companies. Iowa enacted a law to protect domestic violence victims' address. Rhode Island enacted a law to prevent disclosure and shield information in child support actions, and Wisconsin has a new law that shields and keeps confidential voting registers. Missouri enacted a law to establish privileged communication between battered women and domestic violence advocates, and Pennsylvania enacted a similar law to protect communication between sexual assault victims and their counselors. Finally, Louisiana and Kentucky will ensure confidentiality of records in rape crisis centers and specific information related to the backgrounds of victims of sex offenses (National Council of Juvenile and Family Court Judges 2001).

The Violence Against Women Act of 1994 has been instrumental in providing funding for prosecutors and courts to revolutionize the way they handle domestic violence cases, and STOP grants have been awarded to prosecutors' offices to improve their response to domestic violence. Littel et al. (1998) note that appropriate prosecutor responses include the following: assisting the victim with safety planning; coordinating with local victim advocates to communicate effectively with victims throughout the entire criminal justice process; advising victims regarding the collection of evidence, initiating protective orders, calling the police if an order is violated, using vertical prosecution models whenever possible; recognizing the work of victim advocates who have the dual role of advocating for the victim and effecting systemic change; and establishing clear guidelines for decisions not to prosecute a case. One promising approach is included in the following example of a prosecutor program.

Prosecuting Attorney's Office, City of Dover Police Department

In Dover, New Hampshire, the prosecutor's office has collaborated with the city police department to aggressively prosecute stalkers. The prosecutor is able to be involved in cases early on because the office is located within the police department. Key components to the prosecutor's strategy are vertical prosecution, early intervention, and a good working relationship with victims. Victims are assisted with protective orders, safety plans, and information regarding the court process. The prosecutors' approach has also embraced the use of technology to improve victim safety outcomes with the recommendation of the use of the JurisMonitor system. This system enables them to monitor the behavior of stalkers after they have been released from custody on bail or to probation. Prosecutors also provide victims with cellular phones donated by Cellular One that are programmed to dial 911 immediately. Prosecutors also give pendant Alert Link alarms, donated by Elderwatch, to stalking victims.

Policies to Protect Women's Rights

The legal rights of battered women need to be fully protected. Courts need to be sensitive to the unique dynamics of domestic violence by providing specialized training in handling domestic violence cases. This training should be provided to every court clerk, case manager, legal advocate, probation officer, and judge in state and county courts throughout the United States. All courts should provide systematic guidelines, simplified mandatory forms, and step-by-step instructions for processing court orders. Police officers and court clerks should have brochures available to disseminate to all victims of domestic violence. The brochures should provide information on the battered woman's legal rights and options, instructions on how to obtain a court order or restraining order, and a list of local community resources.

The use of technology as an aid in the protection of battered women and the prosecution of batterers should also be explored further. Scholars and practitioners need to continue to come together to plan appropriate courses of continued research and to examine some of the unintended consequences of certain public policy choices.

CONCLUSION

The problem of domestic violence as an issue of national concern for criminal justice theoreticians and practitioners is well illustrated by the degree of attention this subject has recently received in many diverse spheres and by the body of research it has generated. The Violence Against Women Act (VAWA I) of 1995 and the Violence Against Women Act (VAWA II) of 2000 led to millions of dollars in appropriations for improving and expanding law enforcement and social service responses to battered women and their children nationwide. Particularly in the past decade, efforts to define and institutionalize appropriate roles and responsibilities for police and court officers when responding to domestic violence have led to considerable academic research, have generated a significant body of statutory and case law, and have been the subject of an uncommon degree of public and political discourse.

Although substantial progress has been made in strengthening domestic violence laws and improving police training and responses, we must not become complacent. Responsive communities must work toward an integrated response from the police, the courts, health care providers, and social service agencies and focus on innovative prevention strategies. The use of technology is just one critical example of these innovative prevention strategies. Technology has been embraced by the police, the courts, and advocacy groups such as the National Network to End Domestic Violence (NNEDV). The NNEDV, through its partnership with the Mary Kay Ash Foundation, promotes the implementation of current technology to develop strategies to address the overwhelming incidences of domestic violence within the United States. The NNEDV also provides education regarding the use of technology to police agencies, the courts, and other advocacy groups. The development in the mid-1990s, by the security firm ADT of heart-shaped electronic pendant necklaces, also known as panic alarms for battered women in upstate New York, central New Jersey, and throughout Florida has expanded to many other states in the Northeast and Midwest. These and other strategies must be explored further to improve agency response to domestic violence issues.

We must also not forget that intimate partner abuse is one of the most prevalent forms of violence found in U.S. families and is often a co-occurring factor in child abuse, sibling abuse, parental abuse, elder abuse, and so on. We should attempt to explore coordinated community responses that do not continue to fragment systems and family services and recognize the intergenerational nature of domestic violence. Finally, we should continue to make the needs of survivors of domestic violence and their families a priority.

REFERENCES

AUSTIN CITY CONNECTION (2000). *Austin Police Department: Family Violence Protection Team.* Available on line from [http://www.ci.austin.tx.us/police/afvpt]

CARLSON, B. E. (1996). Children of battered women: Research, programs and services. In *Helping Battered Women: New Perspectives and Remedies,* ed. A. R. Roberts. New York: Oxford University Press.

FLEMING, J. B. (1976). *Stopping Wife Abuse.* Garden City, NY: Doubleday.

FLITCRAFT, A., and E. STARK (1986). Woman battering: A prevention oriented approach. In *The Physician Assistant's Guide to Health Promotion and Disease Prevention.* Emory University School of Medicine. [http://www.dvsheltertour.org/fact.html]

INTERNATIONAL ASSOCIATION OF CHIEFS OF POLICE (2001). *Family Violence Summit Recommendations.* [http://www.theiacp.org/pubinfo/Research/FamVio]

KRUMHOLZ, S. T. (2001). Domestic violence units: Effective management or political experience? Paper presented at the annual meeting of the Academy of Criminal Justice Sciences, Washington, DC.

LIEBERMAN RESEARCH, INC. (1995). Domestic violence advertising campaign tracking survey: Wave III. Prepared for The Advertising Council and Family Violence Prevention Fund. [http://www.dvsheltertour.org/fact.html]

LITTEL, K., M. B. MALEFYT, A. WALKER, D. D. TUCKER, and S. M. BUEL (1998). *Assessing Justice System Response to Violence Against Women: A Tool for Law Enforcement, Prosecution and the Courts to Use in Developing Effective Responses.* Washington, DC: Department of Justice, Office of Justice Programs. [http://www.vaw.umn.edu]

MADISON POLICE DEPARTMENT (2000). *Domestic Violence Information.* [http://www.ci.madison.wi.us/police/domestic]

NATIONAL COUNCIL OF JUVENILE AND FAMILY COURT JUDGES (2001). *Family Violence Legislative Update,* Vol. 6. Reno, Nevada: Paper presented at the Annual meeting of the Academy

of Criminal Justice Sciences, June, 2001, Washington, DC.

NATIONAL NETWORK TO END DOMESTIC VIOLENCE (2003). *Technology Safety Project.* [http://www.nnedv.org]

NEW HAVEN POLICE DEPARTMENT (2001). Child development–community policing program. [http://www.cityofnewhaven.com/police/cdcp]

PEAK, K. J. (1998). *Justice Administration: Police, Courts, & Corrections Management,* 2nd ed. Upper Saddle River, NJ: Prentice-Hall.

ROBERTS, A. R. (1984). Police intervention. In *Battered Women and Their Families: Intervention Strategies and Treatment Programs,* ed. A. R. Roberts, 116–128. New York: Springer.

ROBERTS, A. R. (2002). Myths, facts, and realities regarding battered women and their children: An overview. In *Handbook of Domestic Violence Intervention Strategies: Policies, Programs and Legal Remedies,* ed. A. R. Roberts, 3–22. New York: Oxford University Press.

ROBERTS, A. R., and S. BURMAN (1998). Crisis intervention and cognitive problem-solving therapy with battered women: A national survey and practice model. In *Battered Women and Their Families,* ed. A. R. Roberts, 2nd ed., 3–18. New York: Springer.

ROBERTS, A. R., and J. KIM (2005). Exploring the effects of head injuries among battered women. *Journal of Social Service Research* 32(1): 33–47.

ROBERTS, A. R., and K. KURST-SWANGER (2002). *Police Responses to Battered Women: Past, Present, and Future.* 101–125. New York: Oxford University Press.

ROBERTS, A. R., and B. S. ROBERTS (2005). *Ending Intimate Abuse: Practical Guidance and Survival Strategies.* New York: Oxford University Press.

ROBERTS, A. R. and S. BURMAN (1998). Crisis intervention and cognitive problem-solving therapy with battered women: A national survey and practice model. In *Battered Women and Their Families,* 2nd ed., A. R. Roberts, 3–18. New York: Springer Publishing Company.

ROY, M. (1982). *The Abusive Partner.* New York: Van Nostrand.

STATEWIDE CALIFORNIA COALITION FOR BATTERED WOMEN (2003). Mary Kay Ash Charitable Foundation raises funds for national campaign to help victims of domestic violence use technology to prevent further abuse. [http://www.SSCBW.org]

STRAUS, M. A., and R. GELLES (1986). Medical care costs of intrafamily assault and homicide. *Bulletin of New York Academy of Medicine* 6(5): 556–561.

STRAUSS, M. A., R. J. GELLES, and S. K. STEINMETZ (1980). *Behind Closed Doors: Violence in American Families*. Garden City, NY: Doubleday.

TJADEN, P., and N. THOENNES (2000). *Extent, Nature, and Consequences of Intimate Partner Violence*. Washington, DC: U.S. Department of Justice.

THE URBAN INSTITUTE (1998). *Evaluation of the STOP Formula Grants Under the Violence Against Women Act of 1994*. Washington, DC.

WALKER, L. E. (1979). *The Battered Woman*. New York: Harper & Row.

WALKER, L. E. (1984). *The Battered Woman Syndrome*. New York: Springer.

WIRELESS FOUNDATION (2001). *Donate a Wireless Phone and Save Lives*. [http://www.wirelessfoundation.org or http://www.donateaphone.com]

Chapter 18

The Influence of Community in Community Policing in the Twenty-First Century

Michael J. Palmiotto, Ph.D.

ABSTRACT

What influence will the community have in community policing in the twenty-first century? The difficulty of projecting the influence of the community on community policing lies with the fact that there exist limited concrete data that community policing is successful. Although community policing is in its infancy, it has evolved in the first decade of the twenty-first century. It is anticipated that community policing will continue evolving well into the twenty-first century. Although gazing into a crystal ball of the future is nebulous, certain facets of the community-policing concept will survive and have an impact on policing and crime control. The impact and influence of the community on policing should grow and be greater than it was in the last decades of the twentieth century. The influence of the community on policing in the twenty-first century is reviewed in this chapter.

INTRODUCTION

Community policing in the first decade of the twenty-first century has received creditability and has become an acceptable philosophy of policing. In the last quarter of the twentieth century, police practitioners came to the realization that the traditional reactive approach to crimes already committed was not working and that development of a new police strategy was imperative. This new policing concept became known as *community policing*. The philosophy of community-oriented policing grew out of police strategies known as *team policing* and *ministations*, which were established in many of our cities during the 1960s and 1970s. In the first decade of the new century, most police practitioners and an informed public have accepted community policing as a workable alternative to traditional policing.

A driving force behind community policing was the desire by citizens to maintain the quality of their neighborhoods and the police who had the legal authority to maintain social order in the neighborhoods. Former California Governor Pat Brown had this to say: "As I see it, the single greatest problem over the next twenty years will be keeping the quality of life in the state from deteriorating any further than it already has" (Brown 1990:8). Citizens' concern about their quality of life has influenced the police to examine the service orientation philosophy of community policing at the expense of the traditional law enforcement model. The average citizen has indicated his or her concern about incivilities that can often devastate a neighborhood.

Herman Goldstein, a noted police scholar of the late twentieth century, developed the concept of *problem-oriented policing*, which compelled police officers to solve nuisance or crime problems. The problem-oriented philosophy became the foundation for the community-oriented approach to policing. Under the community-oriented policing concept, the police are recognizing that they need the support of the community in order to solve crime. With crime, especially crimes of violence on the rise in the latter part of the twentieth century, the fear of crime had also increased. The big hope that community-oriented policing offered was that crime could be prevented and reduced. If the police were successful in these areas, the fear of crime would decline. The major question that has not been answered is whether community-oriented policing will be successful in keeping crime under control. A wide approach to community oriented policing existed initially, but eventually, evaluation of community-oriented programs made it possible to select its most successful aspects. Both police administrators and line officers came to realize that community-oriented policing had to work if they were to obtain community support and cooperation. The police of the twentieth century became aware that they were successful in solving crimes only when the public cooperated by providing information that could lead to the arrest and conviction of law violators.

During the 1970s, research on policing increased substantially. These findings indicated that the police must make a serious effort to work with people whom they were to serve and protect. The police could not deal with the crime problem alone. The citizen also had a role in preventing and controlling crime. The research of the latter twentieth century was an eye opener for the police. The major research findings came to the following conclusions (Manning 1988:41–44):

1. Increasing the numbers of police does not necessarily reduce crime rates or raise the proportion of crimes solved; social conditions such as income, unemployment, population, and social heterogeneity are far more important predictors of variation in crime and clearance rates.

2. Randomized motorized patrolling neither reduces crime nor improves the chances of catching criminals.

3. The use of two-person cars neither reduces crime nor helps to catch criminals more effectively than does the use of one-person cars, and police are no more likely to be injured in one-person cars.

4. Although saturation patrolling does reduce crime, it does so at the cost of displacing it to other areas.

5. The legendary "good collar" is a rare event; even more rarely does a police patrol confront a crime in progress.

6. Response time doesn't matter.

7. Criminal investigations are not very effective in solving crime.

THE CRIME PROBLEM

From the mid-1960s to 1993, there was a substantial increase in the crime rate in the United States. During these decades, violent crimes, which include murder, rape, robbery, and aggravated assault, reached 2 million. The clearance rate for violent crimes hovered around 45 percent. At one point in the early 1990s the number of murders reached over 24,000, compared to 8,000 murders during the 1960s (a two-thirds increase in murders in a very short time span). With the increase in the number of murders, the police were less successful in solving them. The solvability rate was over 90 percent when there were 8,000 murders in our country. The solvability rate dropped to less than 70 percent when the number of murders was over 24,000. During this period the concept of serial murders evolved. A serial murderer is a person who kills a number of people over a period of time. An accurate count of serial murderers on the loose in U.S. society was unknown. This era also saw the evolution of the mass murderer, a person who kills a number of people at the same time, going into fast-food restaurants, shopping malls, and workplaces and killing whoever was in the area. The early 1990s observed the initiation of the recreational murderer as a person who kills simply for pleasure. Most of these murders were senseless, done for the sake of cruelty and without any feeling for the victim as a human being. Many such murderers were juveniles who appeared to have no sense of the value of a human life.

However, beginning in 1994 and continuing into the first decade of the twenty-first century, crime took a dramatic twist. It began to decline. For example, the Crime Index from 1994 to 2005 decreased 25 percent while the Crime Index for the nation decreased 2 percent in 2005 (NY Division of CJ Services 2006). A major factor for the decrease in the national crime rate is that crimes in the largest U.S. cities have decreased substantially. For example, New York City in 1994 recorded just three over 600 murders compared to 2,267 murders in 1990. In 1994, New York City had fewer murders than it had in 1964. However, New York City had 2,016 murders in 1994 compared with 540 in 2005. The trend has not abated. For instance, the 1999 crime data revealed that violent crimes fell by 10.4 percent from the previous year. This crime rate declined for most offenses except rape and sexual assault. Also, property crimes such as burglary, motor vehicle theft, and other types of thefts declined by 9 percent (Doming 2000:1A).

Although the second half of the 1990s saw a decrease in the crime rate, there are several negatives to the nation's crime rate that need to be addressed. There has been an increase in domestic violence, a growing acceptance of marijuana among young people, and drug use is still a serious problem for our nation. Minorities continue to be victimized and arrested at a rate disproportionate to their numbers. Teenagers have a greater chance of being victims of violence than do adults (Hansen 1998:81–82).

A variety of reasons are given for the reduction in crime over the last several years. Ronald Goldstock, chair of the American Bar Association's Criminal Justice Section, says: "The crime reductions we see in the report (ABA report on crime) appear to be due more to the innovative ways in which law enforcement officials now approach their jobs than to changes in demographics and other social conditions" (Hansen 1998:81). James Alan Fox, a criminal justice professor at Northeastern University in Boston, attributes the continuing decline in crime rates to "successes in many areas including better police tactics, increase in crime prevention programs, longer prison terms for convicted criminals, the shift in the drug market away from cocaine and the aging of the Baby Boom generation" (Dorning 2000:1A, 8A). However, the author of this chapter concurs with Alfred Blumstein, professor of criminology at Carnegie Mellon University in Pittsburgh, who believes that the trends of crime declining "can't continue forever, We've seen an indication that at least the leading edge is starting to flatten out" (Dorning 2000:8A). Generally crime rates are correlated to the nation's economy. When the economy is on an upswing and jobs are plentiful crime often decreases, and when the nation's economy is on a downswing and people are losing their jobs, crime usually increases. Since September 11, 2001, when international terrorists struck the World Trade Center and the Pentagon, the American economy has been in a downswing and we should pay careful attention to see if crime increases.

Whatever the cause of the violence, it has been accepted that the United States is a violent country. Crime scholars recognize that the police can only attempt to prevent crime or solve a crime after it occurs. Cooperation from informed citizens who are actively involved in crime prevention is required if the police hope to curb the rising crime rate. Using traditional police strategies, the police have been unable to control crime. The police would not have initiated community-oriented policing if the professional model of policing had been successful in curbing the crime rate. In 2005 there were about 1.4 million violent crimes; property crimes were estimated at 10.3 million (Uniform Crime Reports, Crime in the United States 2005). Property offenses include burglary, theft, and arson. With the increase in crime, the public's fear of crime, and the news media's onslaught of crime news, the police had their backs to the wall. Therefore, they adopted a policing philosophy with the argument that it offered a better strategy for preventing crime and reducing the public's fear of crime than did the professional police model.

Community Defined

What does the term *community* mean? The term is used loosely and often has a variety of meanings and perceptions. Peter Wilmot (1987:2) expounds that we may want to distinguish between "territorial community, defined by geography and meaning the people living in a specific area; the *interest community*, a set of people with something in common other than just territory (the black community, the Jewish community, the gay community); and the *attachment community*, where there is a kind of attachment to people or place that gives rise to a 'sense of community.'" He believes that the three types of community can overlap. For example, interest communities can be geographically dispersed. Also, an attachment and sense of community can join people into territorial or interest communities.

The community has functioned as a means of social control, and its importance to the community-oriented policing concept seems evident. The term community is often used interchangeably with *neighborhood*. The majority of Americans live in urban and suburban neighborhoods rather than in rural communities. In an industrialized civilization, communities or neighborhoods are drawn along socioeconomic lines, described as underclass or lower class, working class, middle class, and upper class. One's status in this socioeconomic structure is based on wealth, material possession, and the importance of one's position in society's structure.

The lower socioeconomic classes commit many of the predatory crimes that the rest of society considers intolerable. The police have always functioned in controlling the lower socioeconomic classes with the political and economic support of the middle and upper classes. With traditional policing strategies not succeeding in controlling predatory crimes, another strategy was needed. Community-oriented policing became the panacea for preventing and controlling crime. It was also offered as a means to diffuse the fear of crime.

Community-Oriented Policing Philosophy

Mollie Weatherise (1987:7) writes that "community policing is a conveniently elastic term which is often used loosely to accommodate virtually any policing activity of which its proponents approve." Weatherise claims that there exists no agreed definition of community policing, nor should there be one. Contrary to Weatherise, Robert Trojanowicz and Bonnie Bucqueroux (1990:5) have a basic definition for community policing:

> Community policing is a new philosophy of policing, based on the concept that police officers and private citizens working together in creative ways can help solve contemporary community problems related to crime, fear of crime, social and physical disorder, and neighborhood decay. The philosophy is predicated on the belief that achieving these goals requires that police departments develop a new relationship with the law-abiding people in the community, allowing them a greater voice in setting local police priorities and involving them in efforts to improve the overall quality of life in their neighborhoods. It shifts the focus of police work from handling random calls to solving community problems.

Community-oriented policing means a shift away from centralization and control of the line officer. The philosophy of community-oriented policing allows the line officer to be a decision maker and problem solver. The structure of police departments requires them to be more flexible and democratic. Under the concept of community-oriented policing, police work is not incident-driven any longer but instead, emphasizes community problem-solving. The goal will be to solve the problem in order to eliminate incidents of disturbances or annoyances to the community or neighborhood. Brown (1988) distinguishes community policing from traditional policing:

1. Community policing is oriented to problem solving and focuses on results. It encourages techniques such as problem identification, problem analysis, and problem resolution.

2. Community policing demands that police departments organize to incorporate citizen input in matters that affect the safety and quality of neighborhood life. Police–citizen partnerships and power sharing in crime control efforts are encouraged. Police are expected to be accountable to the community for their actions and results.

3. Decentralization is encouraged. Beats are drawn to coincide with natural neighborhood boundaries to encourage responsibilities for shared "turf." Beat officers are given permanent beat assignments and are encouraged to become actively involved in the affairs of the community and to initiate creative solutions to neighborhood problems. The patrol officer becomes the "manager" of their assigned beat.

4. Performance evaluations are based on problem-solving ability and success in involving citizens in crime-fighting efforts. The criterion for success becomes an absence of incidents such as criminal offenses, traffic accidents, and repeat calls for service.

Herman Goldstein (1993:4–6) claims that if policing is to be improved, the public's expectation of the police must change. Goldstein advocates realistic expectations of what the police can accomplish. By taking a realistic approach, the impossible job the police are asked to perform becomes possible. The police should concentrate on analyzing and responding to specific citizen problems that are brought to their attention. For community policing to be successful, the relationship between the community and the police has to improve. A partnership must develop.

POLICING IN THE EARLY TWENTY-FIRST CENTURY

American society exists in a changing world. The society in which we will live in the early twenty-first century will be different from what society has been in the late twentieth century. The age of information will have taken hold. We will be able to communicate visually and orally with anyone in the world instantaneously. Information about scientific, business, and political issues will be obtained in seconds. Sites for making steel and automobiles will be replaced by communities concerned about pollution. The U.S. economy will become a part of a global economy that became feasible with the fall of communism in Eastern Europe in 1989 and the consolidation of Western Europe's economy in 1992. Education will be a key component to the success of individuals and businesses. The workforce will be trained in high-tech equipment and people will be retrained continuously to keep up to date in new technological developments. More people will work from their homes than in an office or factory. A substantial portion of the population will be over 65 years of age. The baby boomers of post–World War II will have reached senior status. White males will be a minority in the workforce, being replaced by females and minority groups. The Hispanic population should approach 30 percent, while the Asian and black population will each have about 12 percent of the population. The United States will become a more culturally diverse society.

Futurist Gene Stephens (1992:22) believes that the justice process will be participatory—a mediation process where victim and defendant come to a satisfactory agreement. Stephens claims that police will possess tools that could invade individual privacy. A California study found six trends that can affect policing in California cities going into the twenty-first century (Schwab 1992:16–19):

1. There will be decreased resources.

2. The population will be wealthier, older, and more culturally diverse.

3. There will be a steady increase in the crime rate, and the diversity of crime will increase.

4. The perception of crime by the community will remain stable.

5. Community support should increase.

6. The public's demand for extra service will increase at no extra cost.

Community Influence

In the first decade of the twenty-first century, a large number of police departments claim that they have adopted the community-oriented policing philosophy. However, it is extremely difficult to determine if departments are actually committed to the community-policing concept or are just attempting to be politically correct. It does appear that many police departments are being influenced by the community-policing strategy and that the community-policing concept has had an influence on policing in the first decade of the twenty-first century. Community-oriented policing emphasizes listening rather than just talking to people. It takes seriously the concerns and input of citizens who live and work in the community or neighborhood. The police listen because they realize the following (Wycott 1988:105–106):

1. Citizens may legitimately have ideas about what they want and need from the police that may be different from what police believe they need.

2. Citizens have the information about the problems and people in their areas that police need to operate effectively.

3. Police and citizens each hold stereotypes about the other that, unless broken down by nonthreatening contacts, prevents either group from making effective use of the other.

With the police listening to citizens, it will become a common practice for the police in the twenty-first century to conduct periodic customer surveys. The police need regular feedback on how they are doing. This feedback can only be obtained from citizen clients whom the police serve. The police will survey victims, witnesses, and complainants on how the police are performing their job. Customer surveys will ask citizens to rate the police on such areas as concern, helpfulness, knowledge, quality of service, solving the problem, putting the citizen at ease, and professional conduct (Couper and Lobitz 1991:74). Based on customer service feedback, the police will make adjustments and improvements in their actions.

Citizen Police Academies

In the initial decade of the twenty-first century, the police recognized that they need the assistance of citizen volunteers if they are to keep crime under control. There has been an increase in direct citizen participation to keep crime and neighborhood disturbances under control. One commonly used avenue will be citizen police academies, which advance police interaction with citizens and can extend police accountability to the community. These training academies, which are usually offered once a week and taught by police officers, can provide citizens with realistic expectations of what the police can achieve in controlling and preventing crime. Citizens can learn how to prevent crime and how to control the fear of crime and disorders, and they can bring this information back to their communities, where they can put it to practical use. This concept may allow citizens in a neighborhood to police themselves.

Community Advisory Councils

A common practice in the initial decades in the twenty-first century will be the development of community advisory councils. These councils will meet on a regular basis and work with operational commanders and police department policy makers to decrease the crime rate, disorder, and the fear of crime. A partnership between the community advisory council and the police will focus on improving the quality of life for community citizens. The council will identify and prioritize problems within the community that a majority of residents want rectified. Once problems are identified, strategies will be devised to solve them. There will be an evaluation by the council to determine if the problems identified have been corrected or at least kept under control.

The council will have a variety of activities at its disposal. Under its bailiwick is the *neighborhood information network*, which provides information about crime in the area. The information network will be a direct source of crime information, providing accurate information in place of rumors, gossip, and accounts from the news media. The council would print a newsletter to inform residents of recent crime trends and provide crime prevention techniques to help citizens avoid becoming victims. The council will also have the responsibility to organize citizen patrols and to oversee the selection for this activity with the approval of the police department. Following the lead of the "broken windows" concept, which advocates that graffiti and rundown neighborhoods leave an impression of lack of concern and a crime infested community, the council working with the police will have graffiti and abandoned cars removed and will strive to clear the neighborhood of any appearance of disorganization. The goal is to establish a sense of community. The council will function as an advisory board to the police and work to provide solutions to community problems.

CIVILIAN OVERSIGHT

In the last half of the twentieth century there was an on-again off-again movement to have civilian review boards or, as it became known in the 1980s and into the 2000s, civilian oversight of police behavior. In the late twentieth century, as a result of police violence and police corruption, community residents demanded the opportunity to review police conduct. In the 1990s it became apparent that police were sometimes unable to clean their own houses. The Mollen Commission in New York City discovered that police officers were robbing drug dealers of their money and drugs and going into business for themselves. Police officers would not only sell drugs but would use illicit drugs such as cocaine while on duty. Officers intentionally abused citizens without any reason other than that someone had annoyed an officer. High-ranking administrators and supervisors looked the other way: They did not want a scandal or negative publicity. Police violence and corruption were not unique to New York; similar situations were found in urban, suburban, and rural communities. In Detroit, two police officers beat a suspect to death. Atlanta police officers were arrested for burglarizing adult entertainment clubs. Savannah, Georgia had a drug ring operated by a police officer. A New Orleans police officer murdered her partner during a restaurant robbery. Because of police scandals in the last decade of the twentieth century, community leaders were given the authority to oversee police conduct, directed by the community-oriented police concept, which can operate successfully only if there is a partnership between the community and the police. Under a closed system a partnership does not exist. When police organizations opened their operations to the public, a legitimate partnership was created. No longer was there a wall of silence among police officers. Police administrators and supervisors came to realize that it was in the best interest of the police department to open up their organization to the community. If they did not allow or cooperate with the community in civilian oversight of police behavior, the philosophy of community policing that they advocated would be fraudulent.

Civilian oversight consists only of civilians, who have the power to investigate and review allegations by members of the police department of police misconduct. The civilian oversight committee reviews any police activity involving unnecessary or excessive use of force, discourtesy, abuse of authority, and conduct or behavior. All accusations are investigated promptly and thoroughly, and upon completion of the investigation. The civilian oversight committee turns over its findings to a prosecutor for criminal prosecution or to the department for appropriate action. If the allegation is unfounded or uncorroborated, the officer, the department, and the accuser are notified.

The civilian oversight committee also has input on police promotions, hiring, and reassignments. This committee provides insight on department policies directly affecting police interaction with citizens. The committee has the authority to recommend specific training that may be lacking in a police department. For example, some officers may need sensitivity training if they are abrasive and rude when dealing with the community. The committee is a partner with the police, not an adversary. Members of the committee are recommended by the police department, community organizations such as the chamber of commerce, and elected political officials.

If the police are to be recognized as professionals, their activities have to be an open book. Their conduct and behavior should be above reproach. For community-oriented policing to be successful, the community and its citizens must trust and respect the police. How can the community be coproducers in crime prevention, eliminating neighborhood disorganization and controlling the fear of crime, if their only intention is to manipulate the community? There must be a sincere police–community partnership if community-oriented policing is to be successful. This means that in the twenty-first century the community will have a voice in policing.

Privatizing the Police

Because of slow economic growth in the early 1990s, some communities looked at alternative means for public safety. As a result of financial cutbacks and stagnant budgets, the police have forced the affluent, businesses, and others **citizens** who were concerned about their personal safety to play a larger role. The community-oriented philosophy of policing has been forced to include private security organizations. The conclusions drawn by the Hallcrest Report provide justification for the partnership of private policing agencies with public policing agencies. The Hallcrest report states: "Law enforcement resources have stagnated and in some cases are declining. This mandates greater cooperation with the private sector and its private security resources to jointly forge a partnership on an equal basis for crime prevention and reduction. Law enforcement can ill afford to continue isolation and, in some cases, ignore these important resources" (Cunningham and Taylor 1985:275).

Private police agencies can be involved in a variety of ways. They can function as alarm monitors and respond to intrusions when burglary and robbery alarms go off. The private police will respond in lieu of the public police. A volunteer police organization, under the supervision of the county sheriff or local police chief, can operate under a nonprofit, tax exempt private organization under state law. The organization has a board of directors with limited police powers. The volunteer police organization can free the police to perform proactive police work, for example, they can check vacant homes while residents are on vacation, or direct traffic.

Privatizing the police includes establishing guard forces for public housing, directing traffic, and providing security and crowd control for civil centers and publicly owned buildings. The guard force can be used for the management of parking enforcement. Regional shopping centers can use guard forces for public safety. Private police can perform patrol service. For example, San Francisco has licensed private persons provide patrol services to neighborhoods that want additional police protection. They go to the city's police academy to qualify as peace officers; they are armed, uniformed, and are given full police powers. The private patrol officers are expected to respond to calls in their neighborhood just as public police officers do. The key difference is that private police officers are entrepreneurs.

More private police will serve as switchboard operators in the twenty-first century than in the twentieth century. Public police will contract for this service as well as for records and property management, data processing, and so on. It will be more cost effective to contract with private police than for the public police to perform these functions.

The list of activities performed by private police involving the privatization of public policing services will be substantial during the twenty-first century. In the twenty-first century, U.S. citizens will decide that private policing agencies have an important role to play in crime prevention and control. The private police and the public police will be partners. The community-oriented policing philosophy will be extended to private police. Since the private police are citizens from the community, their role in private policing will increase the influence of the community in community policing.

Terrorism and Community Policing

Since September 11, 2001, the role of policing has taken on new responsibility. The incidents that lead to additional police responsibility include the following: two commercial airlines were hijacked by Arab extremists who piloted the airplanes into the twin towers of the World Trade Center in lower Manhattan of New York City; a third commercial airliner was crashed into the Pentagon in Washington, D.C.; a fourth hijacked commercial airliner crashed into an open field in Pennsylvania near Pittsburgh, this crash has been contributed to passengers who heard about the other incidents by cellular phones and overpowered the hijackers, causing the airliner to crash.

The following comment by Bernard B. Kerik, the former Police Commissioner of the New York City Police Department, reflects the way police agencies now deploy their personnel. "The way we deploy, perhaps the arms we carry, the precautions we take, we're doing any number of things which may not disappear until we feel the threat is passed" (Jones 2001:9). Acts of terrorism will appear to be a concern to the United States and law enforcement for years or perhaps decades to come. Kerik further states, "Officers now have training in subway evacuation and the handling of hazardous materials" (Jones 2001:10). Not only are police in our large metropolitan areas concerned about terrorism, police in mid-size and smaller communities are also concerned. Police have been given the responsibility to protect vulnerable buildings such as churches, mosques, hospitals, and government buildings. The police work with other agencies such as the fire department to deal with hazardous materials and air quality.

Through such organizations as Neighborhood Watch, community police officers can be able to train residents about suspicious acts that may be related to terrorism and what they can do to protect themselves from hazardous materials. Community-policing officers can provide residents in their areas training on how to prepare for and respond to potential terrorist acts. The role of community-policing officers in the first decade of the twenty-first century has expanded not only to working with residents to reduce and prevent crime but to preventing and preparing for possible terrorist attacks. Through the people in the community, community-policing officers can be the eyes and ears of their department.

CONCLUSIONS

In the last quarter of the twentieth century, police practitioners realized that the traditional reactive approach to crimes already committed had not worked and that the development of a new police strategy was imperative. This new philosophy has become known as community policing. A driving force behind community policing has been the desire by citizens who live in these neighborhoods to maintain their quality of life.

The philosophy of community-oriented policing allows the line officer to be a decision maker and problem solver. The structure of the police department requires that it be more flexible and democratic. Under the concept of community-oriented policing, police work is no longer incident driven but instead, emphasizes community-problem solving.

American society exists in a changing world. The society of the early twenty-first century is different from that of the late twentieth century. The age of information has taken hold. We are able to communicate visually and orally with anyone in the world instantaneously. The U.S. economy is strong and the leader of the global economy. The fall of communism in Eastern Europe in 1989 and the consolidation of the Western European economy in 1992 made this economy feasible. A substantial portion of the population will eventually be over 65 years of age. Expectations are that white males will become a minority in the workforce, replaced by women and minorities.

In the twenty-first century the community-oriented policing concept will become embedded in the strategies of policing. It will be a common practice for the police to conduct periodic customer surveys. The police will survey victims, witnesses, and complaints on how the police are performing their job. Citizen police academies will become common, with citizens being involved directly in crime prevention and control strategies.

A common practice in the twenty-first century will be the formation of community advisory councils. These councils will meet on a regular basis and work with operational commanders and police policy makers to decrease the crime rate, disorder, and the fear of crime. The council will have a variety of activities at its disposal. Because of police scandals in the last decade of twentieth century, community leaders have been given authority to oversee police conduct. They have been directed by the community-oriented policing concept, which can operate successfully only if a partnership exists between the community and the police.

Because of the anemic economy in the early 1990s and slow economic growth in this decade, some communities have looked at alternative means for public safety. Because of financial cutbacks and stagnant budgets, the police have forced the affluent, businesses, and others concerned about their personal safety to play a larger role. The community-oriented philosophy of policing has been forced to include private security organizations. Private police have functioned as alarm monitors, volunteer police, guard force, and switchboard operators. Even with an excellent economy in the late 1990s going into the first decade of the twenty-first century, the role of private security has not decreased. With a booming economy, Americans have more material possessions to protect.

Since September 11, 2001, because of terrorists acts committed in New York City, the Pentagon in Washington, D.C., and the hijacked commercial airliner crash in an open field in western Pennsylvania, the role of community-policing officers has expanded. In addition to working with residents to make their communities safer from crime the community-policing officer now has the added responsibility to make the community safer from terrorists.

REFERENCES

BROWN, L. (1988). *Community Policing: A Practical Guide for Police Officials.* Perspectives on Policing, No. 12. Washington, DC: U.S. Department of Justice, National Institute of Justice.

BROWN, E. G. (1990). To preserve the quality of life. *California Journal.*

COUPER, D. C., and S. H. LOBITZ (1991). *Quality Policing: The Madison Experience.* Washington, DC: Police Executive Research Forum.

CUNNINGHAM, W. C., and T. H. TAYLOR (1985). *Private Security and Police in America: The Hallcrest Report.* Portland, OR: Chancellor Press.

DORNING, M. (2000). Crime rates continue to fall. *Wichita Eagle* (August 28).

FEDERAL BUREAU OF INVESTIGATION (1999). *Crime in the United States, 1998.* Uniform Crime Reports. Washington, DC: U.S. Government Printing Office.

GOLDSTEIN, H. (1993). The new policing: Confronting complexity. Paper presented at the Conference on Community Policing, National Institute of Justice, U.S. Department of Justice, Washington, DC, August.

HANSEN, M. (1998). Taking a look at crime. *ABA Journal* 84 (February).

JONES, R. L. (2001). Police struggle to adjust fighting both crime and terrorism. *New York Times* (November 8).

MANNING, P. K. (1988). Community policing as a drama of control. In *Community Policing: Rhetoric or Reality*, ed. J. R. Greene and S. D. Mastrofski, 279. Westport, CT: Praeger.

NY DIVISION OF CJ SERVICES (2006). [http://criminal justice.state.ny.us/pioSept18]

SCHWAB, S. (1992). *Restructuring Small Police Agencies: A Transition Toward Customer Service.* Sacramento, CA: Peace Officer Standards and Training.

STEPHENS, G. (1992). Drugs and crime in the twenty-first century. *Futurist* (May-June).

TROJANOWICZ, R., and B. BUCQUEROUX (1990). *Community Policing: A Contemporary Perspective.* Cincinnati, OH: Anderson Publishing.

UNIFORM CRIME REPORTS, CRIME IN THE UNITED STATES (2005). [http://www.fbi.gov/ucr/05cius/]

WEATHERISE, M. (1987). Community policing now. In *Policing and the Community*, ed. P Wilmot, 7–20. London: Policy Studies Institute.

WILMOT, P. (ed.) (1987). *Policing and the Community.* London: Policy Studies Institute.

WYCOTT, M. A. (1988). The benefits of community policing: Evidence and conjecture. In *Community Policing: Rhetoric or Reality*, ed. J. R. Greene and S. D. Mastrofski, pp. 103–120. Westport, CT: Praeger.

Chapter 19

Contemporary Policewomen

A Working Typology

Mark Lanier, Ph.D., and Kelly Jockin, M.S.

ABSTRACT

This chapter examines the status of women in policing. Special emphasis is given to a female police typology, first presented in 1996. We also describe how policing will change in the beginning of this millennium with the expansion of private security, higher education requirements for police applicants, and changes in employment practices due to affirmative action policies and antidiscrimination legislation. We conclude with several policy recommendations critical to the continued success of women in policing.

INTRODUCTION

In this chapter we examine the role of women in policing in the twenty-first century. Nearly 50 years have passed since women first gained entry into police patrol in the United States by Title VII of the Civil Rights Act of 1964. Beginning in the mid-1960s and continuing through the 1990s, researchers examined the nature and function of police work itself (see Bittner 1970; Greene and Mastrofski 1988; Klockars 1985; Reiss 1971; Skogan and Hartnett 1997; Skolnick and Bayley 1986; Westley 1970; Wilson 1968, 1978). As this chapter demonstrates, placing policewomen on patrol contributed to advancing policing from the reactive, crime-fighter mentality of the first three quarters of the 1900s to the proactive, more service-oriented police advocated now (Miller 1999).

Women have only had a role in policing since the early 1900s (Hale 1992). Until the passage of Equal Employment Opportunity Act of 1972, policewomen occupied clerical positions, conducted activities concerning children (e.g., the juvenile bureau), and/or served as decoys in undercover investigations (House 1993). When women went on "regular" patrol in 1972, they came under scrutiny regarding whether or not they could successfully complete the activities associated with patrol work (Milton 1975).

The entry of policewomen coincided with research on the function of police that concluded that police work is actually more service-oriented than law enforcement. James Q. Wilson (1968) in *Varieties of Police Work* coined the terms for styles of police work as law enforcers (primarily arrest duties), order maintenance (keeping the peace functions), and community service activities. In the revised version of *Varieties of Police Work*, Wilson (1978:ix–x) discussed the consequences of research on policing since the mid-1960s:

> Ideas have consequences. Ten years ago, the police were popularly portrayed as "crime fighters" who "solved crimes" by investigation and "prevented crimes" by patrol. Police officers may privately have then known that this view was simplistic, if not false, but few pointed that out. Today, there are few big-city chiefs who use the old phrases. They speak instead of "order maintenance," "community service," "family crisis intervention," and "police–citizen cooperation" and they ask hard questions about the role of detectives, the best uses of patrol time, and the need for investigative priorities.

The publication of Wilson's second edition of *Varieties* (1978) occurred about the same time as proactive police officers were returning to foot patrol after years isolated from the community in patrol cars (i.e., the Newark and Flint foot patrol projects). In the late 1970s and early 1980s, patrol officers were often resistant to the return of foot patrol because they viewed it as an ineffective use of their time. These officers had become accustomed to the sanctuary of the patrol car, where they spent the majority of their shift isolated from the public they were assigned to patrol. Ironically, putting police officers in patrol cars was a consequence of the professionalization of policing of the early 1900s. The patrol car was used to increase the response time of the police.

An examination of Wilson's research (1968, 1978) that scrutinized the functions of policing, combined with Trojanowicz and Bucqueroux's (1990) description of community policing, and finally, Goldstein's (1990) analysis of problem-oriented policing depict police activities that policewomen historically conducted in American police departments of the early 1900s. Specifically, much of the work of the early policewomen was preventive by nature. These policewomen—many trained in social work—patrolled the streets looking for young girls and children in amusement parks, taverns, movie theaters, and at railway/bus stations and dance halls where all types of vice crimes were prevalent (Appier 1992; Odem and Schlossman 1991).

In our synopsis of the future of women in policing, we find that the crime prevention duties historically performed by policewomen will continue to be the ones that both female and male police officers will provide in the twenty-first century. Because of the public's concern with increasing juvenile delinquency and the increase in adolescent drug and alcohol abuse, police officers will continue to provide more services directly related to the prevention of adolescence drug use, and to process cases of juveniles involved in drug trafficking. Initially, police officers were trained as D.A.R.E. officers (drug abuse resistance specialists), to work with children at both the elementary and secondary school levels.

The major operational difference between the nineteenth- and early twentieth-century policewomen was that the pre-1972 policewomen were relegated to preventive duties concerning women and children (duties men did not want to do). The post-1972 policewomen performed the same patrol duties as policemen. However, in the twenty-first century, more women will enter police work due to the crime prevention and service aspects of community policing. Women will also be attracted to police work because of the opportunity to work with victims of crime. The research of the past 40 years supports that women as police are extremely effective (Brown 1994; Miller 1999) with communicating with victims of crime (Homant and Kennedy 1984; Kennedy and Homant 1983). Women are also effective at defusing volatile situations and making arrests (Grennan 1987).

DISCUSSION

Neither the numbers of women entering policing nor the numbers of women being promoted to management and supervisory roles have increased significantly. The reasons for this are difficult to explain to students, public officials, and, perhaps even police personnel. Why is it that over the past half century so few women have entered police work? Why have police departments not reached Peter Horne's (1979) prediction that 50 percent of sworn police officers would be women by the year 2000? Why is it impossible to implement the Independent Commission on the Los Angeles Police Department report's (1991) recommendation that the Los Angeles Police Department should have 50 percent of its sworn officers as women by the year 2000? Why is it we have the revealing statistics from the 1998 Uniform Crime Reports that just over 10 percent of total police agencies (U.S. Department of Justice 1998:296) are sworn policewomen? The U.S. Bureau of Labor Statistics (1998) reports that women as "police and detectives" have risen from 5.7 percent in 1983, to 10.4 percent in 1995, and to 11.8 percent in 1997. Why is it that very few women become police chiefs? The following comments attempt to provide answers to these fundamental questions.

First, more women should be interested in police work for several reasons. It is an occupation that does not require specific educational requirements; though more police departments now require a college degree. Police work, just as many other jobs that are blue-collar, male-dominated occupations (e.g., construction, electricians, and welders), offers more pay, fringe benefits, authority, and autonomy than jobs in female-dominated fields (Dubeck and Borman 1996). Also, higher pay and greater status are associated with men's jobs (Jacobs 1993:49; Williams 1989:132). Police work is a blue-collar occupation where "affirmative action policies and anti-discrimination legislation permits women's entry" (Williams 1989:142) to the workplace.

Also, it is important to indicate that the television and movie industries have played a role in shaping the public's perception of a policewoman's role in the traditionally male domain of patrol and investigation. The police officer's job is glamorized and often depicts policewomen right alongside of policemen fighting crime on a day-to-day basis.

In reality, women may not actually think of policing as a career option because of the shift work; may think of it as "dangerous work"; or, have been socialized to accept the more traditional occupations for women without a college education (e.g., secretarial or service). Police recruiters must address these issues in their recruitment strategies to attract women to police work (see Hale and Wyland 1993). In addition, successful police-women should be used as recruiters to attract more women to the field. Mentoring programs designed to facilitate the promotion of women to supervisory and managerial positions must be implemented to facilitate the advancement of women once they enter the police department (Sanders 1997).

Furthermore, police departments should take advantage of how their jobs are presented in the media. However, very little of the actual experiences of policewomen are depicted in television, movies, and videos (Hale 1998). The discrimination, sexual harassment, and restrictive policies that women experience in police work does not make box office sales and pay for production costs and advertisements. Television does impact youth. Research shows that the typical American child spends 27 hours a week watching television (see Stossel 1997). Consequently, our youth (and their successors will be) exposed to an image of policewomen in such television programs as *NYPD Blue, Crime Scene Investigation (CSI), Third Watch, Homicide, Law and Order,* and *The X-Files.* Many of our younger criminal justice and criminology students announce their career ambition as either "profiler," or FBI agent. Where do they see "profilers" and FBI agents? The steady information stream of crime investigations broadcast on local and national news and the weekly news programs keeps the viewing audience up to date on all the latest crime investigation techniques (DNA testing, and hair and fiber analysis). The television audience is introduced to expert "criminal profilers" associated with the Federal Bureau of Investigations (FBI) and Behavioral Sciences Unit (e.g., John Douglas, Robert Ressler, and Ann Burgess).

While television may portray female police officers as accepted by their peers and successful on the job, audiences should be cautioned that this is television and not reality (Hale 1998). Hollywood glorifies Kanter's (1977) concept of "tokenism" showcasing a woman in a highly visible nontraditional profession/occupation. For example, script writers may include scenes where the policewoman encounters some initial resentment/harassment from male officers, but eventually she overcomes their hostility and is accepted by the peer group. Furthermore, it is rare for a script to depict male officers acknowledging that a policewoman earned her promotion rather than receiving it because of affirmative action policies. However, Hollywood does not show on its weekly episodes the recurrent discrimination and harassment that policewomen or other professional women encounter from their peers when they enter nontraditional jobs of policing (*Law and Order* and *Homicide*), law (*L.A. Law* and *The Practice*), and medicine (*ER* and *Chicago Hope*). After all, the purpose of the series is to solve the crime, win the case, or save the patient, not to address personnel matters. Rarely does the television audience hear the complaints from the women's peers that they got these jobs because of affirmative action and quotas; these individuals are often referred to as "tokens" in the negative sense. The audience does not hear the stories that Connie Fletcher's (1995) policewomen disclosed about their experiences in the police academy, in the police locker room, or on the streets when they needed backup and it was not there. After all, our weekly episodes are for entertainment; Connie Fletcher's book is read by college students and policewomen.

Consequently, a caveat (i.e., "let the viewer beware") to television aficionados and movie buffs that real life policewomen's experiences are not always similar to those of the policewomen captured in the camera lens. In the everyday work world, the policewoman is a token, a representative of women in nontraditional police work. Therefore, as a token, if the policewoman succeeds, she is applauded; but, unlike the policeman, the policewoman must continue to prove herself incident after incident. As a token, if she fails, her failure symbolizes the failure of her gender, not her individual failure, or the particular situation itself. If a man fails, he fails; his failure is not symbolic of all men; it is his failure, his situation.

For example, Shannon Faulkner was the first female student admitted to the Citadel. As such, she was highly visible as the lone female cadet and was viewed as a failure when she withdrew after only days. Her failure was seen by many as a reflection on her gender, not the obstacles she encountered in a historically male-dominated organization. Her physical unpreparedness was used to explain her failure. There was little acknowledgment of her status as the only woman in the traditionally male organization, or recognition of the resentment and ostracism she may have experienced. The same scenario is true for women in policing or for women in any traditionally male profession/occupation.

IMPLICATIONS

Educators and policy makers should present information about the roles of women in the nontraditional field of policing, as well as law and corrections. It is important to illustrate that not just women in the field of criminal justice encounter these situations, but women in other traditionally male professions (business, construction, engineering, law, and medicine) and occupations (carpenters, electricians, and welders) have the same experience. It is also important to note that ethnic/racial minority males experience many of the same obstacles. This illustrates that it is both a gender and a racial issue.

To help facilitate societal discussion, it is useful to better understand women in policing. Part of that understanding can be enhanced through categorizing women who practice policing. A few caveats are in order however. Male officers can be categorized just as easily as female officers—however our focus here is on women. Second, no typology is discrete, universal, or stagnant. Some women may fit into two or more roles. Others may change their role with maturity and experience. Finally, this typology is not meant to be discriminatory or demeaning. It is based on years of empirical research, and while some may not view it as being politically correct, it is based on data. Unlike politicians and administrators, researchers are obligated to let the data speak regardless of popularity of personal beliefs.

TYPOLOGY OF WOMEN POLICE OFFICERS

Women have made substantial numerative advances in the field of law enforcement over the past 40 years, and the proportion of women has grown from virtually none to nearly 10 percent in the United States (Martin 1990). Now that female officers participate in all police activities it is important to understand that there is no "one" female police type, instead of viewing women in the previously conceived stereotypes describing them as "whore" (covertly masculine) or "dyke" (overtly masculine) by their degrading male counterparts (Fielding and Fielding 1992; Hale and Wyland 1993; Hunt 1984, 1990; Martin 1979, 1980, 1989, 1990; Sherman 1973, 1975). Several social scientists have noted that distinctions do exist between female law enforcement officers, however most distinctions never move beyond the realm of a bipolar distinction (with perhaps an overlapping combination category). These and other prior classification models have centered on overt behavioral characteristics and have neglected to account for the complexity of the causes of women joining or belonging to different groups. Lanier (1996) presents a typology of female officers based on their experiences, tensions, and resolutions founded on the contemporary practices of policing that take into account these complexities.

As mentioned already, in comparison with male officers, female officers currently share identical police training and patrol assignments and surprisingly exhibit similar psychological and occupational behaviors (Sherman 1973, 1975). Research has shown that female officers accomplish customary police tasks with equal ability and the same degree of competence as male officers (Bloch and Anderson 1974; Charles 1981; Sherman 1973). According to Hale and Wyland (1993:4), "it is no longer necessary to debate or discuss the effectiveness of women on patrol. It is time, however, to address the greater issue of how women can unconditionally be accepted by their peers and supervisors". Female officers may have required affirmative action to gain the positions in the pioneer stages of policing, but after proving their competence and abilities could they have secured their positions by their accomplishments? Female officers have even proven to perform certain functions better. For example, they tend to be more patient in dealing with domestic violence cases (Kennedy and Homant 1983) and receive far fewer citizen complaints (McDowell 1992). Despite these findings, women are still often perceived by other officers as being incompetent in comparison to male officers and police work is still perceived as a man's domain (Hale and Wyland 1993).

In addition to the stress created by the lack of acceptance, other tensions exist for women based on occupational expectations that are also created by men. For example, a female officer was given a particular assignment, purchasing drugs on the street level in an undercover operation, but she was asked to bring a male officer in the event a suspect might need to be run down or wrestled despite the athletic ability of the female officer. The denial of full participation coupled with role devaluation is a sign of the still-lurking means of controlling and sometimes devaluing of women. Considerable evidence indicates that the tensions faced by female officers are different and additional to those experienced by male officers. Lanier sought to provide an interpretive analysis of how female officers have adapted to these stressors by differentiating them into several categories and including the causal factors. In order to make the police organizational climate more receptive and potentially to increase the numbers of female police officers, it may prove to be useful to understand various types of female officers and the reasons for officers belonging to certain groups.[1]

Categorizations that have been previously presented describe female police officers in overly simplistic depictions and never moved beyond a bipolar distinction. Lanier presents the groups beyond one-dimensional categories and includes vertical and horizontal typologies. In the vertical plane, four distinguishing characteristics can be used to differentiate between officers, which includes

1. length of employment (13–16 years, 8–12 years, less than 7 years of experience)
2. motivation for entering police work (opportunity, security, lifestyle, and economic betterment)
3. education level (high school to graduate degree)
4. ambition (occupational survival, allowed to do the job free from unwarranted hassles, and progressing rank).

As mentioned earlier, the females were grouped into the three separate groups, categorized into the pioneers, settlers, and opportunists.

The pioneers comprised the first female officers who were included in regular patrol duties and participated in full-spectrum policing. The difficulties, role conflicts, expectations, and ambiguities facing pioneers were immense and often resulted in a "flight-or-fight" coping mechanism. Those women who chose "flight" often coped by resigning or accepting stereotypical positions (such as clerical positions or working in detective bureaus) and were often not well respected by other female or male officers. In contrast, few female pioneers chose to "fight" traditional male dominance and relied on their resourcefulness and determination.

The settlers were the second group of female officers (hired in the 1980s) who experienced many of the same stressors, but to a lesser extent. The additional benefits (including judicial support) and improvements were owed to a large extent to the sacrifices made by the pioneers. A dominant coping strategy used by this group was "resigned acceptance"

TABLE 19.1   Vertical Officer Classification

	Pioneers	Settlers	Opportunists
Length of employment	13–16 years	8–12 years	7 years or less
Motivation for joining	Opportunity, security	Lifestyle	Advancement
Education	HS, AS	HS, AS, BS	AS, BS, MS
Ambition	Survive	Do the job	Progress

*AS = Associate in Science.

such as avoiding conflicts, accepting and participating with joking, and relying on empathetic sergeants for "protection." The settlers approached police work with the outlook that they were hired to do a job and they attempted to fulfill that obligation, avoiding conflicts. They accepted harassment and isolation as an unfortunate part of the job.

The opportunists joined the police force most recently, and they appear to be largely unaware or unconcerned with the stresses and obstacles the pioneers and settlers were forced to endure. Opportunists are usually comprised of college-educated, upwardly mobile women who held high expectations of what police work can provide and were no longer content with simply surviving the profession. Rank, privilege, and status are aggressively sought despite male opposition and occasional gender-based prejudice.

In the horizontal classification, women often join or form cliques and can be categorized into four types. Two of the group classifications are a continuance of Brewer's (1991) typology: the Amazon and the Hippolytes. The Amazons adopted aggressive, masculine behavior to fit into the police culture and attempted to cope with the masculine occupational culture by "being one of the boys." Lanier found that these women were already engaged in behaviors that many erroneously attribute as being somehow "male" (e.g., contact athletics) and joined police work with little apprehension about being accepted into the culture. These officers were generally effective on the "streets" but sometimes lacked complete acceptance by other officers. The polar opposite of an Amazon was the Hippolytes. Hippolytes were women who "interactionally manage the question of gender identity by retaining as much of their femininity as the bureaucratic regimen allows" (Brewer 1991) and often spend more time than their female counterparts preparing their appearance.

The third categorical type of female officer played on was the current dominant societal conception of being female, proud to be both female and police officer. They espoused conventional conformist attitudes and priorities (family, home, etc.), cared about their appearance, and often sought marriage or were married. These officers tended to score high on promotional exams and at the gun range. Another group of officers could be described as seeking "group acceptance" by exploiting their femininity either in an effort to progress in their profession, acquire acceptance, or because they found this practice personally rewarding. Most male officers do not hold them in high esteem and they are perceived with negative reactions.

The final group discussed is differentiated by their sexual preference as either lesbian or bisexual. It was important to note that these officers could in no physical way be differentiated from other women. In the opinion of male officers, other female officers, and supervisors, bisexual and lesbian officers made very effective police officers. In general, these females were widely respected, liked, and very effective.

The ultimate objective should not be to lump all women into one group—bipolar distinctions or sophisticated categories—but rather to view each woman as a unique individual making diverse contributions. For the purposes of this research, understanding why women select or are prescribed to particular groups may assist with creating a more productive work environment. Theoretically, gender issues in policing may benefit from greater clarification founded on feminist perspectives. Many progressive departments are actively implementing proactive tactics (i.e., community policing) that may benefit from greater consideration of the unique contributions that female officers may make.

CONCLUSIONS

The functions of policewomen have evolved, expanded, and improved over the past nine decades since Alice Stebbins Wells became the first sworn policewoman with the power to arrest and carry a gun. Although women are enjoying increased acceptance as police officers, these improving conditions are largely due to the sacrifices made by the pioneers. The career aspirations of opportunists, as compared to the pioneers, reflect a fundamental change in the way this occupation is viewed. While increasing the number of female officers is a positive first step, it should also be stressed that changing organizational behavior is also crucial if females are to reach their full potential. This trend will continue as increasing numbers of women enter police work and reach management positions where they can develop and implement policy. We also anticipate increasing numbers of women entering the profession and having a lasting impact. With the acceptance of policewomen by their peers and supervisors, their token status will diminish, and they will no longer be considered an anomaly in policing. However, the majority of police departments will not reach the often cited goal of 50 percent, if any. The impact of gender socialization, work norms, family obligations and child-rearing desires will continue to limit some women.

Interestingly, rather than the role played by female police changing, the role of male officers is projected to change more. Community policing and proactive strategies dictate greater interaction with citizens, thus forcing successful male officers to learn interactional techniques from their female counterparts.

As a final thought, we would like to share the observation that one constant characteristic of policing is that it is constantly changing. Policing changes, as it should, to reflect changing social conditions and to rectify its own faults (corruption, deviance, excess, etc.). The continuous change will persist. We would like to suggest trends that will influence how and when the police will change.

In this century, policing will change in some fundamental ways. First, private security will greatly increase the number of people working in law enforcement and order maintenance. Many major American cities already have security officers in fast food restaurants, malls, convenience stores, and other locations. Presumably this trend will continue and escalate. Some private security officers now make more money than municipal police officers. If trends against increasing taxation continue, government budgets will not allow municipal salaries to compete with private industry. Will the best-and-brightest police applicants consequently be drawn to private security? How will this impact policing and female police?

Trends in criminal justice education will also affect the police force of the twenty-first century in the United States. Although there are no specific educational requirements for the police officer position (Career Information Center 1996:57), many local and state police departments are beginning to require at least 60 college credits, or a four-year degree in criminal justice. This requirement is primarily due to the large number of applications police departments receive whenever they advertise positions. Even in situations where only a high school degree is required, college graduates who flock to take the police examinations should score higher and perform at higher levels at the oral interview stage of the police selection process than their high school graduate counterparts. Optimistically, the entry of more college-educated police officers should be favorable for women entering patrol. These college graduates in criminal justice should have more favorable attitudes toward women in police because of their exposure to the research on the effectiveness of women as police officers.

Competition for police officer positions "will be keen," since the availability of positions depends on funding available to police departments (Career Information Center 1996:57). Unlike correctional officer positions that will be steadily increasing in the twenty-first century (Brindley et al. 1997:105), the total number of police officer positions available will "rise slowly . . . [with] openings to replace officers who retire or leave their jobs for other reasons" (Career Information Center 1996:57).

Second, America will continue to be a pluralistic society. The proportions of what we currently consider "minorities" will escalate. Currently, Caucasians are the "minority" in some California and Florida universities. This demographic shift will also impact policing. Other cultures have different views of the police. To provide two dichotomies, often for good reasons, the English generally hold police in high respect while Mexicans generally fear the local police. How will this effect policing? All this diversity will require a tolerant, interactive, and highly qualified police officer.

Third, medical advances, lifestyle changes, and improved nutrition will result in Americans living longer. As our society continues to "gray" into the next century, will the older members of society desire meaningful employment (such as policing)? Will an Equal Rights Amendment include letting the elderly become police officers, just as it did women? For example, the Aurora, Colorado police department hired two recruits in their fifties who were starting a second career after retiring from their first. Again, the ramifications may fundamentally change policing, perhaps for the better.

On November 3, 1997, the U.S. Supreme Court "let stand California's groundbreaking Proposition 209, a ban on race and gender preference in hiring and school admission. Affirmative action foes predicted other states now will follow California's lead" (Anonymous 1997:A6). Christine Williams (1989:142) specifies that affirmative action policies and anti-discrimination legislation are necessary for women to enter blue-collar occupations where they encounter "often explicit and organized resistance." Furthermore, she believes that "affirmative action policies and anti-discrimination legislation . . . allows [women] the possibility to transform these male-dominated organizations." This court action may hurt women in policing, or it may make them more accepted since their hiring and promotion will be based presumably solely on merit.

As we have described, policewomen have transformed—made a difference—in police work. And without affirmative action policies beginning with Title VII in 1972 and subsequent anti-discrimination legislation, women would probably have been denied entry to police patrol duties. What can we do to prevent all the advances women have made in policing from eroding? We have several recommendations to offer to ensure policewomen's continued success in the twenty-first century. First, organizations concerned with the advancement of women in policing must meld with similar organizations to form stronger coalitions to lobby for the continuation of affirmative action and anti-discrimination programs. These organizations include the National Association of

Women Law Enforcement Executives (NAWLEE), the International Association of Women Police (IAWP), the National Center for Women and Policing, the National Organization for Black Law Enforcement Officers (NOBLE), and the International Association of Chiefs of Police (IACP).

This solidarity presents a strong lobby advocating for the continuation of all current law enforcement recruitment, training, and advancement programs. The coalition must convince law enforcement agencies that the research on women in policing and the changes in the nature of police work itself support the need for women to remain and to continue advancement in police departments.

It is vital for educational institutions (high schools, community colleges, colleges, and universities) to implement programs that prepare young women for success in non-traditional occupations like policing. Programs should include sports programs that teach young women interpersonal skills necessary to be competitive in the work place (Marcus 1997:88). Junior police academies are another way that law enforcement agencies can work with secondary schools to educate and prepare students for future careers in law enforcement (National Association of Veteran Police Officers in association with New Century Productions and Sol Productions 1996).

Criminal justice programs in community colleges, colleges, and universities need to emphasize to students that diversity is essential if police departments are to be successful in performing their duties. The community the police serve is not only diverse in its needs, but diverse in population—it is not composed only of white males. Research supports that victims of crime benefit from the presence of women police officers.

An additional goal of higher education is to provide future police officers with the knowledge and skills to do their jobs well. Not only do students need courses in law, communication, and psychology, but also they must be able to analyze situations and write thorough reports. College classroom instruction must prepare students to perform well at both the written and oral interview stages of the police personnel selection process. When women students score higher on tests, they cannot be told that they got the job only because of affirmative action, or a quota system.

Our last recommendation is for individuals to become knowledgeable about political platforms and vote for those candidates who support equality. Finally, we must all work together to keep the momentum going for the advancement of women in policing. We do not want our achievements compared to the labors of Sisyphus.

ENDNOTE

1. These categories were taken from Fyfe et.al's (1997:409) chapter 12 on "Discipline." The authors point out that "discipline is a responsibility that permeates a police department, that is shared by everyone in it, and that results from several non-punitive processes that often are not included in lists of disciplinary activities. . . . Punishment fits at the end of this list and should come into play when none of these more positive disciplinary functions has produced the desired results." Women state troopers in Massachusetts expressed dissatisfaction with a new policy that permitted the state police physician (not the woman's doctor) to determine when a pregnant officer should be put on modified

duty. Modified duty specifies that officers "can't walk the beat, make traffic stops or even drive police vehicles" (Anonymous 1997b:A8). A content analysis of over 100 movies/videos produced since 1972 to the present concluded that by the end of the presentation, the policewoman (patrol, detective, or chief) is "kept in her place." The movie/video concludes with her as either injured, dead, or leaving police work to marry usually another police officer. The success of a woman police chief in "Fargo" (1996) is downplayed at the end with a bedroom scene where she is seen assuring her husband that his winning second place for his stamp design is valuable. At no time, does he compliment her on her success with solving the crime and apprehending the criminals.

REFERENCES

ANONYMOUS (1997a). *Court Ruling Could End Affirmative Action.* Carlisle, PA: Sentinel. November 4: A6.

ANONYMOUS (1997b). *State Troopers Unhappy with Pregnancy Policy.* Carlisle, PA: Sentinel. October 16: A8.

APPIER, J. (1992). Preventive justice: The campaign for women police, 1910–1940. *Women & Criminal Justice* 4(1): 3–36.

BITTNER, E. (1970). *The Functions of the Police in Modern Society: A Review of Background Factors, Current Practices, and Possible Role Models.* Chevy Chase, MD: National Institute of Mental Health.

BLOCH, P. B., and ANDERSON, D. (1974). *Policewomen on Patrol: Final Report.* Washington, DC: Police Foundation.

BREWER, J. D. (1991). Hercules, Hippolyte and the Amazons—or policewomen in the RUC. *British Journal of Sociology* 42: 231–247.

BRINDLEY, D., R. M. BENNEFIELD, N. Q. DANYLIW, K. HETTER, and M. LOFTUS (compilers). (1997). 20 hot job tracks. *U.S. News & World Report* 123(16): 95–106.

BROWN, M. C. (1994). The plight of female police: A survey of NW patrolmen. *The Police Chief* 61(9): 50–53.

CAREER INFORMATION CENTER (1996). *Public and Community Services,* 6th ed., Vol. 11. New York: Macmillan, Division of Simon and Schuster.

CHARLES, M. T. (1981). The performance and socialization of female recruits in the Michigan State Police Training Academy. *Journal of Police Science and Administration* 9: 209–223.

DUBECK, P. J., and K. BORMAN (eds.) (1996). *Women and Work: A Handbook.* New York: Garland Publishing, Inc.

FIELDING, N., and J. FIELDING (1992). A comparative minority: Female recruits to a British constabulary force. *Policing and Society* 2: 205–218.

FLETCHER, C. (1995). *Breaking and Entering: Women Cops Break the Code of Silence to Tell Their Stories from the Inside.* New York: Pocket Books.

FYFE, J. J., J. R. GREENE, W. F. WALSH, O. W. WILSON, and R. C. MCLAREN (1997). *Police Administration,* 5th ed. New York: McGraw-Hill.

GOLDSTEIN, H. (1990). *Problem-Oriented Policing.* New York: McGraw-Hill.

GREENE, J. R., and S. D. MASTROFSKI (eds.) (1988). *Community Policing: Rhetoric or Reality?* New York: Praeger.

GRENNAN, S. A. (1987). Findings on the role of officer gender in violent encounters with citizens. *Journal of Police Science and Administration* 15(1): 78–85.

HALE, D. C. (1992). Women in policing. In *What Works in Policing: Operations and Administration Examined,* ed. G. W. Cordner and D. C. Hale, pp. 125–142. Cincinnati, OH: Anderson Publishing Company.

HALE, D. C. (1998). Keeping women in their place: An analysis of policewomen in videos, 1972–1996. In *Popular Culture, Crime, and Justice,* ed. F. Y. Bailey and D. C. Hale, pp. 159–179. Belmont, CA: West/Wadsworth Publishing Company.

HALE, D. C., and S. M. WYLAND (1993). Dragons and dinosaurs: The plight of patrol women. *Police Forum* 3(2): 1–6.

HOMANT, R. J., and D. B. KENNEDY (1984). A content analysis of statements about policewomen's handling of domestic violence. *American Journal of Police* 3(2): 265–283.

HORNE, P. (1979). Policewomen: 2000 A.D. *The Police Journal* 52(1): 344–357.

HOUSE, C. H. (1993). The changing role of women in law enforcement. *The Police Chief* 60(10): 139–144.

HUNT, J. (1984). The development of rapport through the negotiation of gender is field work among police. *Human Organization* 43: 283–296.

HUNT, J. (1990). The logic of sexism among police. *Women & Criminal Justice* 1: 3–30.

INDEPENDENT COMMISSION ON THE LOS ANGELES POLICE DEPARTMENT (1991). *Report of the Independent Commission on the Los Angeles Police Department*. Los Angeles, CA: Independent Commission on the Los Angeles Police Department.

JACOBS, J. A. (1993). Men in female-dominated fields: Trends and turnover. In *Doing "Women's Work": Men in Nontraditional Occupations*, ed. C. L. Williams, pp. 49–63. Newbury Park, CA: Sage.

KANTER, R. M. (1977). *Men and Women of the Corporation*. New York: Basic Books.

KENNEDY, D. B., and R. J. HOMANT (1983). Attitudes of abused women toward male and female police officers. *Criminal Justice and Behavior* 10(4): 391–405.

KLOCKARS, C. B. (1985). *The Idea of Police*. Beverly Hills, CA: Sage.

LANIER, M. M. (1996). An evolutionary typology of women police officers. *Women & Criminal Justice* 8(2): 35–57.

MARCUS, M. B. (1997). If you let me play . . . a basketball or a hockey puck may shatter the glass ceiling. *U.S. News & World Report* 123(16): 88, 89.

MARTIN, S. E. (1979). Policewomen and policewomen: Occupational role dilemmas and choices of female officers. *Journal of Police Science and Administration* 7: 314–323.

MARTIN, S. E. (1980). *Breaking and Entering: Policewomen on Patrol*. Berkeley, CA: University of California Press.

MARTIN, S. E. (1989). Women in policing: The eighties and beyond. In *Police and Policing*, ed. D.J. Kenney, pp. 3–16. New York: Praeger.

MARTIN, S. E. (1990). *The Status of Women in Policing*. Washington, DC: Police Foundation.

MCDOWELL, J. (1992). Are women better cops? *Time* 139: 70–72.

MILLER, S. L. (1999). *Gender and Community Policing: Walking the Talk*. Boston: Northeastern University Press.

MILTON, C. H. (1975). Women in policing. In *Police and Law Enforcement 1973–1974*, ed. J. T. Curran and R. H. Ward, Vol. II, pp. 230–245. New York: AMS Press.

NATIONAL ASSOCIATION OF VETERAN POLICE OFFICERS IN ASSOCIATION WITH NEW CENTURY PRODUCTIONS AND SOL PRODUCTIONS (1996). *Future Cop*. NAVPO.

ODEM, M. E., and S. SCHLOSSMAN (1991). Guardians of virtue: The juvenile court and female delinquency in early 20th-century Los Angeles. *Crime and Delinquency* 37(2): 186–203.

REISS, A. J., JR. (1971). *The Police and the Public*. New Haven, CT: Yale University Press.

SANDERS, D. L. (1997). 21st-century issues for women in policing. *The Police Chief* 64(1): 6.

SHERMAN, L. J. (1973). A psychological view of women in policing. *Journal of Police Science and Administration* 1: 383–394.

SHERMAN, L. J. (1975). An evaluation of policewomen on patrol in a suburban police department. *Journal of Police Science and Administration* 2: 434–438.

SKOGAN, W. G., and S. M. HARTNETT (1997). *Community Policing, Chicago Style*. New York: Oxford University Press.

SKOLNICK, J. H., and D. H. BAYLEY (1986). *The New Blue Line: Police Innovation in Six American Cities*. New York: The Free Press.

STOSSEL, S. (1997). The man who counts the killings. *The Atlantic Monthly* 279(5): 86–105.

TROJANOWICZ, R., and B. BUCQUEROUX (1990). *Community Policing: A Contemporary*

Perspective. Cincinnati, OH: Anderson Publishing Company.

U.S. DEPARTMENT OF JUSTICE (1998). Federal Bureau of Investigation. Crime in the United States. Uniform Crime Reports.

WESTLEY, W. A. (1970). *Violence and the Police: A Sociological Study of Law, Custom, and Morality*. Cambridge, MA: MIT Press.

WILLIAMS, C. L. (1989). *Gender Differences at Work: Women and Men in Nontraditional Occupations*. Berkeley, CA: University of California Press.

WILSON, J. Q. (1968, 1978). *Varieties of Police Behavior: The Management of Law and Order in Eight Communities*. Cambridge, MA: Harvard University Press.

Chapter 20

Current and Future Practices and Strategies for Managing Police Corruption and Integrity

Vincent E. Henry and Charles V. Campisi

Since the beginning of the modern era of U.S. policing, corruption has proven to be among the most difficult, resilient, and enduring problems confronting police agencies as well as society as a whole. In terms of its etiology as well as in terms of the behavioral patterns and practices in which it becomes manifest, police corruption is a highly complex and multifaceted issue that often defies attempts at simple explanation. The same complexity also means that the police corruption typically defies simple attempts to find and implement effective solutions that will identify and interdict corrupt officers and prevent and deter future instances of corruption. Corruption remains one of the most puzzling and difficult sets of issues confronting police administrators, police reformers, and students of policing.

It seems that as long as there have been police, there have been corrupt police, and as the activities of corrupt police have come to public attention, there have also been innumerable corruption scandals of major or minor proportion. As these scandals play out in the media and in the courts, they often take a terrible toll on police agencies, resulting in tremendous embarrassment as well as great public concern and resentment—a resentment that is usually not merely directed toward the individual officers who engaged in corrupt activities but toward the agency and the institution of policing as a whole. Certainly not every instance of corruption results in scandal, but the scandals that do occur focus public attention on a range of police behaviors, and as they play out in the media, they may seem to magnify the quality and the extent of corruption that has actually taken place. Police play a complicated and difficult role in society, and in conjunction with the fact that many members of the public have a fairly superficial understanding of police work and relatively little understanding of the complexity of controlling corruption, extensive media attention can easily attract a host of fair or unfair criticisms. Scandals become a lightning rod for all sorts of public faultfinding and censure.

Scandals also do great damage to agencies in part because they diminish the tremendous faith most members of the public place in their police; the public has a legitimate right to expect that their police will obey the laws they are sworn to uphold, that they will not violate laws or standards of behavior they would enforce upon the public, and that they will generally act in accordance with the highest standards of personal and professional integrity. While some may argue that these public expectations of police behavior can be unreasonably high and that police officers are human beings who are no more or less fallible than the public in terms of their professional and private behavior, in a practical sense the argument is moot: The fact is that these are the public's expectations, just as it is a fact that any gross violation of these expectations will result in diminished respect and some degree of public hostility. Whether the corrupt acts are the overt symptoms of broader systemic failures and organizational dysfunctions or solely the behaviors of individual officers acting independently or in small groups to flout the law, they certainly serve to unfairly tarnish the reputations of honest police officers whose integrity should not be impugned.

When the corrupt activities that come to light are part of a broad pattern of behavior existing throughout the agency, as is often the case, public exasperation and resentment toward the agency may be entirely justified. Allegations or revelations of serious police criminality that are part of a broad pattern of behavior throughout the organization are perhaps especially disturbing since they typically indicate a significant breakdown in the agency's management capabilities over a significant period of time. There are some important differences between corrupt acts engaged in by individual officers and the kind of systemic or organized corruption that takes place throughout a police department; one of the most important differences is that organized corruption almost always requires either tolerance, indifference, neglect, or outright incompetence at the very highest levels of the agency.

The point here—and one of the main points of this chapter—is that despite its complexity, its durability, its resilience, its adaptability, and its long history, police corruption can be controlled by capable executives who vigorously and relentlessly bring their management skills to bear on the problem using a variety of highly focused tactics and strategies that have historically proven effective at reducing corruption and misconduct. Whether corruption can ever be entirely eliminated—whether a police agency can ever be absolutely free of criminal behavior or serious misconduct—is a difficult question that is akin to asking whether crime can ever be entirely eliminated in society. It would be foolish and counterintuitive, though, to assert that any medium-sized or large U.S. police agency is now or has ever been absolutely free of any and all corruption.

A more reasonable response to this question is that while some individual officers or small groups of officers may always feel the inclination to engage in criminal activities and while some officers may in fact act upon those inclinations, police departments can do a great deal to prevent and deter them from doing so. Vigorous and focused management can reduce opportunities for corruption, can deter corruption by using strategies and tactics that dramatically increase the probability that corrupt cops will be identified and prosecuted, and can implement policies and programs to ensure that corrupt activities are not tolerated or ignored at any level of the organization. If a police department's top executives are sufficiently serious about controlling corruption, if they create policies, procedures, and organizational systems designed to sustain and nurture an environment of intolerance for corruption, and if they can sustain their energies and attention across successive administrations, they can also prevent organized forms of corruption from emerging in the agency.

Corruption may well be a reality of contemporary policing, but it is also a problem that can be managed, controlled, and reduced. None of this is to say that even a minimal amount of corruption is ever acceptable or that police executives can rest on their laurels when corruption is significantly reduced. Like any other kind of crime, even one corrupt act is too many. Because corruption is essentially a problem that can be controlled through proper management, police executives and managers are culpable when they fail to prevent, detect, and deter corruption and when they fail to cultivate an organizational environment that will not tolerate any level of corruption. As in any other area of responsibility, managers must be held accountable for lapses and failures that permit corruption to flourish.

Over the past decade, many police agencies have achieved unprecedented reductions in traditional crime within their jurisdictions, to the extent that national crime rates have generally followed a downward trend. Some of the most dramatic crime reductions in the nation have taken place in New York City, where total crime (i.e., the seven major crime categories of murder, rape, robbery, burglary, grand larceny, felony assault, and auto theft) fell more than 64 percent between calendar years 1993 and 2002 (New York Police Department [NYPD] 2003a). Of these major crimes, murders, robberies, and burglaries each declined by almost 70 percent (69.6 percent, 68.4 percent, and 69.0 percent, respectively), the number of rapes fell slightly more than 37 percent (37.2 percent), felony assaults declined by almost half (49.6 percent), and the number of automobiles stolen in New York City fell an astounding 76 percent (76.4 percent). These astonishing crime declines in New York (and in many other cities) were achieved by applying a radically different management mind-set that maximizes police performance by establishing organizational transparency and an exceptionally high degree of accountability at every level of the agency. This mind-set, which is supported by technology and by the analysis of crime data and other management information, also involves a set of highly effective crime management policies, programs, and principles that are known collectively as the *Compstat paradigm* (Henry 2002a).

As we will explore further in this chapter, the methods, principles, and technology that made the Compstat management model so effective in reducing crime have also been adapted and applied to corruption control in the NYPD, and despite the intrinsic differences between traditional crime and police criminality, they have had similarly dramatic results. The application of the Compstat paradigm to the management of police integrity represents the cutting edge of corruption control policy and practice.

In this chapter, we will first review the historic context of U.S. police corruption, discussing some of the major theories and observations about corruption as revealed in various scandals. Our focus will be primarily on the rich history of corruption in the NYPD, where scandals have erupted at approximate 20-year intervals throughout the last century. Each of these scandals was followed by a public commission of inquiry that detailed the nature and extent of corruption in the agency and made recommendations for reforming it. As evidenced by the recurrence of corruption scandals, the reforms that the commissions recommended and the NYPD implemented were less than fully effective in preventing or deterring additional corruption. In particular, we will examine the two most recent scandals in the NYPD and the reports of the public commissions responsible for investigating them and making recommendations for reform, and we will explore the social, organizational, and cultural reasons those reforms were not fully effective. The goal of this historic review is to point out the fact that the patterns and behaviors of corruption evolve and change over time: Organizational strategies for reform may be somewhat effective in combating the type of corruption that exists when they are implemented, but unless they adapt to changing patterns and behaviors, they quickly become ineffective, and new forms and patterns of corruption arise.

We will then briefly review the major principles and practices of Compstat, showing how they have been adapted and applied to corruption control. Compstat is a highly adaptable management paradigm that permits managers to monitor crime with a high degree of precision and to implement highly focused crime reduction strategies and tactics that have proven effective in the past. Under the Compstat model, an array of specific strategies and tactics are adapted to address the particular crime problems and issues presented in a given situation. In this way, the NYPD has the capacity to both identify and carefully track new and emerging patterns of corruption, as well as to vigorously respond to them virtually as they emerge. The result of all this is that the policies, practices, and strategies the NYPD uses can evolve parallel to evolving corruption patterns. Finally, we will briefly examine some statistical data illustrating the overall effectiveness of the NYPD's new approach to corruption control.

To understand police corruption, we must first recognize that police work, by its nature, provides officers with ample professional opportunities they can exploit for personal gain and that the scope of police corruption can be exceptionally broad: It is easy to imagine how many specific types of behavior fall within the rubric of police corruption. We should point out that the public's concept of police corruption can be rather vague and that in general usage the term "police corruption" can encompass an extremely broad range of behaviors. We can see that this somewhat vague and amorphous notion of corruption can include traditional crimes, such as robbery, burglary, fraud, and sexual assault, that police can commit while on or off duty. Some of these crimes are typically committed while the officer is off duty—insurance fraud and the possession or use of narcotics, for example—and they may be entirely unrelated to the officer's official duties, but they are nevertheless subsumed by the vague term "police corruption" simply because the perpetrator has the legal status of police officer. Regardless of whether they are committed on or off duty and of whether they are related to official police duties or not, all of these behaviors clearly violate the criminal law. They may well be motivated by the same factors that motivate any criminal, but the fact that they are committed by police officers—especially police officers who use their office and their police powers to facilitate the crime—make them all the more heinous. They fall within the specialized scope of the agency's internal affairs function rather than its general investigative function because they have such great potential to damage the organization and because no police agency can maintain the public respect and cooperation it needs to fulfill its overall mission when its officers become criminals.

Brutality and the excessive use of force are frequently deemed forms of corruption. This is a complex issue, not only because brutality and the excessive use of force are typically motivated by factors and reasons other than the personal gain that underlies so much police criminality but because so many acts that fall into this category are subject to interpretation. Unlike most of the traditional crimes defined in the criminal law, there are few objective and bright-line distinctions between police use of "reasonable" and "excessive" force. The notion of "excessive force" depends not on the fact that force was used—police are legally entitled to use a reasonable degree of force to effect arrests and to overcome force used against them, for example—but on the *degree* and overall *reasonableness* of the force they use. In turn, the reasonableness of force depends on the particular situation in which it is used, and that can be determined only after considering a host of factors that are specific to the incident itself. While there are clearly some instances that demonstrate an excessive degree of force, the vast majority of allegations of excessive force fall into a gray area that requires extensive investigation and, ultimately, a subjective evaluation of reasonableness.

The term "police corruption" is also often applied by the public to various types of misconduct—more specifically, behavior that does not violate the criminal law, per se, but violates some administrative rule or regulation stipulated by the agency. These offenses run the gamut from serious abuses of overtime or violating off-duty employment guidelines to such minor offenses as wearing white socks in uniform. Here again, the vague and amorphous nature of the term serves as a kind of conceptual sponge that soaks up virtually any and all transgressions committed by police. We might even include in this category such behaviors as discourtesy to the public, disparaging or foul language, and the use of ethnic and racial slurs. We are certainly not implying that any of these behaviors by police should be tolerated or condoned or that the agency should not formally address them and discipline officers who engage in them. We are saying that there are important qualitative distinctions between minor misconduct (smoking or not wearing one's hat while in uniform, for example), rudeness and other social misbehavior (the use of derogatory language toward the public, for example), and outright crimes (bribery, robbery, and sexual assaults, for example) committed by police while on or off duty.

All of this highlights the need for a better and more workable operational definition of corruption—a definition we can use to focus more closely on the nature and scope of the issues involved. As Maurice Punch (1985:14) points out, there are numerous definitions of police corruption available, but few of them are satisfactory. Perhaps the best definition of corruption, and the one we chose to use here, is provided by John Kleinig (1996:166), who states that police officers are corrupt "when, in exercising or failing to exercise their authority, they act with the primary intention of furthering private or departmental/ divisional advantage." This definition encompasses the notion of so-called noble cause corruption, in which police are ostensibly motivated to abuse their authority in pursuit of some higher philosophical or practical goal rather than by their own self-interest.

COMPETING VIEWS OF POLICE CORRUPTION

As a general statement, we can say there are two competing theories or points of view used to explain police corruption. Individual (or "rotten apple") theories posit that, because of their inherent character traits, background, experiences, or some other motivating factor or combination of factors within the person, some individual officers will pursue and exploit the corrupt opportunities available to them. The "rotten apple" point of view—an explanation some police executives have used to avoid accountability by distancing themselves from their responsibility to prevent, detect, prosecute, and manage corruption—asserts that police officers' own greed (rather than that of the department) is the primary source of corrupt activities. The rotten apple position competes with the so-called rotten barrel theory by asserting that police are essentially led into corruption by their peers and by an organizational culture that tolerates or facilitates corruption. Both theories have been applied at various times to explain specific instances of corruption, but neither explanation is entirely satisfactory. A more reasonable point of view—and one that is informed by practical experience as well as the lessons of history—is that the complexities of corruption can be explained only in terms of the individual's response to the social, political, organizational, and legal environments that shape the police occupational culture and the police organization. The fact that these social, political, organizational, and legal environments are tremendously fluid and dynamic also explains how the patterns and practices of corruption continually evolve in response to them. We need only examine the successive waves of scandal and reform that have taken place in the NYPD over the past century to discern the evolutionary nature of corruption.

THE HISTORY OF CORRUPTION IN THE NYPD

The Lexow Commission—1894

New York's first major police corruption scandal resulted from allegations made by the Reverend Charles Parkhurst, a Presbyterian minister who in 1892 took on the police and the Tammany Hall political machine. Parkhurst's charges that the police were "a lying, perjured, rum-soaked lot" who conspired with crooked politicians to make the city "a very hotbed of knavery, debauchery, and bestiality" (Raab 1992) led to a grand jury investigation, but he could provide no evidence to support his charges of widespread police and political corruption (Lardner and Reppetto 2000:98–107; *New York Times* 1933).

Parkhurst gathered hard evidence and witness affidavits, resulting in another grand jury investigation and ultimately to a presentment charging police with collecting $7,000 in graft annually. A shake-up of the department led to the transfer of 35 police captains (Lardner and Reppetto 2000:98–107; *New York Times* 1933).

As a result of Parkhurst's campaign and the media attention it generated, the New York State Senate convened a special legislative investigation headed by Republican Senator Clarence Lexow. The Lexow Commission's report, issued in 1894, described "systemic corruption, the sale of police jobs, widespread police brutality, and police compliance in the fixing of elections for Tammany candidates" (Raab 1992). The Lexow report contributed to the election of a progressive Fusion Party administration in 1895, which reorganized the Police Department, incorporated a civil service system for appointments and promotions, and installed Theodore Roosevelt as one of the NYPD's police commissioners. The Lexow reforms apparently addressed the issue of the sale of police jobs since the civil service system eliminated the practice, but in the long term, it did little to resolve the problem of gambling and prostitution graft.

The Curran Committee—1913

The July 1912 murder of gambler Herman Rosenthal in Times Square precipitated the 1913 Curran Committee. Rosenthal, the victim of a shakedown by Lieutenant Charles Becker (who headed a gambling squad that reported directly to Police Commissioner Rhinelander Waldo), was scheduled to testify before a New York County grand jury probing Becker and his squad, and he was shot to death by four underworld assassins allegedly operating under Becker's orders. Becker was ultimately convicted and executed in the electric chair at Sing Sing Prison after several sensational trials and appeals, and New York City's Board of Aldermen quickly convened an inquiry into the Rosenthal incident as well as the larger picture of corruption in the agency.[1]

The inquiry concluded that Commissioner Waldo was incompetent because he failed to prevent a widespread system of blackmail and extortion and because he refused to heed repeated warnings against specific officers engaged in corrupt activities (Curran 1913:3). Among the specific charges against Waldo were that he repeatedly referred corruption complaints made by citizens for investigation by the very officers named in the complaints. The committee recommended his removal from office.

The Curran Report detailed police extortion in gambling and prostitution enforcement—gamblers and brothel keepers were compelled to make regular monthly payments in order to continue their operations—as well as the receipt of corrupt monies to "throw" cases in court. Corrupt activities were not limited to vice enforcement, though: Detectives often inspired the commission of various crimes in order to make arrests, and they frequently shared in the profits of those crimes or personally retained recovered stolen property. The Curran Report found that lax discipline and inefficient administrative procedures were rife in the agency, and it made a host of recommendations for organizational reform that had relatively few direct consequences in terms of immediate or lasting change. Becker and the four underworld figures who actually murdered Rosenthal were convicted and executed for the crime, and a handful of other officers were convicted of conspiracy and bribery charges, but Commissioner Waldo was not removed from office until 1914 when a new mayor appointed Arthur Woods, a protégé of Theodore

Roosevelt. Woods increased training and created squads to investigate police corruption (Chin 1997:ix, x).

The Seabury Investigation—1932

The 1932 Seabury investigation was a fairly unique inquiry insofar as it targeted and explored a fairly broad range of corrupt activities within New York City's criminal justice system; it focused not only on corruption involving lawyers, prosecutors, bail bondsmen, court clerks, magistrates, and cops but also on the patterns of corrupt collusion between these various actors. This wide-ranging and extensive investigation was unique insofar as it viewed police corruption as one facet of much larger systemic corruption within New York City's criminal justice system.

In 1931, Judge Samuel Seabury was appointed to investigate corruption and political patronage in New York City's Magistrates Courts. His far-ranging investigation revealed, though, that attorneys, bail bondsmen, and cops participated in various protection rackets, that case fixing was rampant, that clerks and judges could be bribed to secure dismissals, and that politicians often intervened in cases and determined their outcome.

The police, particularly members of the vice squad, were an integral part of the corruption and collusion within this system, conspiring with attorneys, prosecutors, bail bondsmen, magistrates, and court personnel to extort bribes. Vice squad officers also used complicit "stool pigeons" or paid informers who would "set up" potential victims for arrest on false charges. These schemes were quite lucrative: Seabury found that some vice squad officers amassed savings accounts totaling $500,000 in just a few years.

The NYPD responded with a shake-up of personnel and a few administrative reforms, transferring the entire vice squad, and officially prohibiting the use of stool pigeon informers. Commanding officers were also required to investigate and prepare written reports on every vice or public morals arrest that resulted in a dismissal of charges. The greatest contribution the Seabury investigation made to the study of corruption was its acknowledgment that systemic police corruption is often linked to corrupt activities in other spheres of government and other spheres of criminal justice.

The Brooklyn Grand Jury Investigation—1954

The 1954 Brooklyn Grand Jury Investigation, frequently referred to as the *Harry Gross scandal,* probed a lucrative and highly organized system of payoffs to protect gamblers from police enforcement. The inquiry, which focused primarily on the activities of bookmaker Harry Gross and the officers associated with him, illuminated the hierarchical nature of corrupt systems by implicating high-ranking officials in the scandal. The investigation found that Gross's Brooklyn gambling empire netted over $20 million annually and paid over $1 million annually to corrupt cops.

A series of indictments, trials, and appeals resulted from the inquiry. Mayor William O'Dwyer (a former police officer) resigned, as did the police commissioner and a number of high-ranking chiefs. The NYPD's entire plainclothes division of 366 men was transferred, about 110 officers retired or resigned, and 52 were charged administratively and terminated after department trial.

The Knapp Commission—1970

In 1970, allegations made to the *New York Times* by plainclothes Patrolman Frank Serpico, Sergeant David Durk, and a third, unnamed officer led to the formation of the Knapp Commission. Knapp's investigation was fairly unique insofar as there was no suggestion that political figures participated in the corruption. The Knapp Commission probed deeply to discover and describe how entrenched patterns of graft and bribery existed throughout the agency. The reform agenda it prescribed was championed and eventually taken over by the newly appointed reform Police Commissioner, Patrick V. Murphy, who capitalized on widespread public, media, and political support to sustain the agenda and to use it to bring about meaningful changes in the department and its organizational culture (Jasanoff and Stone 1977; Murphy and Plate 1977). Knapp's report (1972) concluded that corrupt "pads" existed in every plainclothes gambling enforcement squad in the city, and it found corruption in the narcotics enforcement, general crime investigation, and uniformed patrol functions as well. Knapp disclosed that a broad range of corrupt practices, including a system of internal payoffs, was prevalent in the department; within this organizational and cultural environment, officers found ways to exploit practically every avenue or opportunity for corruption (Henry 1990a).

The most salient features of corruption within the NYPD during the late 1960s and early 1970s were its sophistication, its highly organized nature, and the extent of formal and informal tolerance for it by the department's management. The NYPD's investigation of corruption complaints had been poorly resourced and generally reactive. The first full-fledged internal affairs unit was created in 1968, and prior to this, the responsibility for investigating corruption allegations was vaguely distributed among other entities within the agency. The NYPD's rhetoric about integrity was contradicted by its historically feeble efforts to investigate corruption allegations, and its policies and practices had little deterrent effect upon corrupt cops. As Kornblum (1976) notes, the public discovery of corruption historically resulted in the mass transfer of officers (but relatively few prosecutions) as well as rhetoric intended to reassure the public that a few rogue cops or rotten apples had been identified and dealt with severely by an agency that had no tolerance for corruption.

The Knapp/Murphy Reforms

The Knapp Commission's 1972 report highlighted the compelling need for a new management coalition dedicated to preventing corruption by changing the internal and external environments that shaped corrupt activities, recommending that the NYPD vigorously pursue five general mechanisms or strategies for asserting internal and external control and for achieving reform (Knapp 1972:17):

> First, corrupt activity must be curtailed by eliminating as many situations as possible which expose policemen to corruption, and by controlling exposure where corruption hazards are unavoidable.

> Second, temptations to engage in corrupt activity on the part of the police and the public must be reduced by subjecting both to significant risks of detection, apprehension, conviction and penalties.
> Third, incentives for meritorious police performance must be increased.
> Fourth, police attitudes toward corruption must continue to change.
> Fifth, a climate of reform must be supported by the public.

Reform Police Commissioner Patrick V. Murphy articulated and vigorously enforced a new policy of "command accountability" throughout the agency, threatening to remove any executive who failed to identify and correct corruption problems (Jasanoff and Stone 1977). This policy of strict accountability in all ranks and at all levels of the organization was probably the most important and enduring feature of Murphy's tenure, and it dramatically changed the NYPD's management practices. According to this policy, executives, managers, and supervisors were held strictly accountable for corruption taking place within their sphere of responsibility. Murphy pledged that commanders "who fail to act vigorously against corruption will be removed to make room for the advancement of those who will" (Murphy and Plate 1977:239).

Murphy's policy of strict accountability produced a 30 percent annual turnover in the executive corps—those members above the civil service rank of captain who could be promoted or demoted at the Commissioner's discretion—and in fact achieved this turnover rate over each year of his three-year tenure (Lardner and Reppetto 2002:271). They were replaced by a more loyal cadre of younger, more ambitious, and more capable administrators who interpreted the new policy of command accountability as their ticket to rapid promotion. Commanders began aggressively pursuing corruption and misconduct investigations, and for the first time in the department's history, commanders had both the responsibility and the capability to conduct proactive investigations of corruption and misconduct (Henry 1990a; Jasanoff and Stone 1977).

Murphy made accountability the cornerstone of his reforms, and an environment of pronounced intolerance for corruption and misconduct took hold as aggressive corruption fighters rose quickly through the management ranks. As actual corruption declined, however, the policy of command accountability and the more assertive management style it cultivated became generalized. Command accountability became a victim of its own success and ultimately undermined the agency's corruption control mechanisms as managers shifted their attention away from increasingly scarce corruption cases to minor misconduct and administrative violations. As Reuss-Ianni (1983) has pointed out, two separate and distinct occupational cultures evolved within the NYPD during this period—a street cop culture and a management cop culture—each possessed of vastly different values, belief systems, and animating principles. Ultimately, the agency became fragmented and highly divided, with a distinct antipathy and "us-versus-them" sentiment prevailing in both groups (Henry 2002).

By increasing the level and type of supervision and by reducing officers' exposure to many corruption hazards, Murphy imposed an array of new formal social controls on police behavior. New policies forbade patrol officers and precinct detectives from making gambling, narcotics, or prostitution arrests, for example, and those who persisted faced the threat of investigation and/or disciplinary sanction. Most officers got the message that enforcement activity in these areas by other than specialized narcotics enforcement personnel would lead to severe sanctions, and they effectively left these offenses alone. By dramatically limiting exposure to corruption hazards and by vigorously pursuing officers who violated these policies, a powerful and fairly lasting change took place: Officers quickly interpreted the hands-off policies to mean that certain types of criminal behavior were implicitly tolerated in the name of preventing corruption. By the early 1980s, the organizational sensibility was that a patrol officer put his or her career at great risk if he or she took summary police action in these enforcement areas (Henry 2002).

Murphy also redesigned the department's internal investigative function, strengthening the Internal Affairs Division (IAD) by dramatically increasing its staffing and resources. Field Internal Affairs Units (FIAU) were established in each bureau and patrol borough, giving commanders the operational means to conduct their own internal investigations. The new structure complemented the policy of command accountability by giving commanders the resources and personnel they needed to investigate and prevent the corruption for which they would ultimately be held accountable (NYPD 1992).

Within this bifurcated internal investigations structure, the responsibility to investigate corruption was shared—albeit unequally—between the central IAD and the decentralized FIAUs. All reports of corruption or serious misconduct were initially screened and evaluated by the central IAD staff, but IAD retained only those comparatively few cases that promised to involve a particularly long and/or particularly difficult investigation, that potentially involved high-ranking members of the department, or that involved especially particular areas of police work. The vast majority of cases—especially those concerning relatively minor offenses—were referred for investigation to the FIAU concerned. The Staff Supervisory Section within IAD was charged with the critical responsibility of providing technical advice and assistance to the FIAUs, but the 1994 Mollen Commission would later make it clear that this critical unit eventually deteriorated and failed to perform many of its mandated monitoring functions (NYPD 1992, 1994).

The Knapp/Murphy reforms had a powerful impact on the ethos of secrecy since the implementation of integrity tests, an aggressive "field associates" program,[2] and the new system of rewards and incentives undermined any implicit expectation of silence on the part of another officer (Henry 1990a). Officers were deterred from engaging in corrupt activities, particularly when those activities involved other officers who might be undercover IAD agents or otherwise inform on them one day. In conjunction with the overall policy of command accountability, these and other aggressive tactics created a functional divisiveness in the agency: Rank-and-file officers became suspicious of the supervisors they could no longer trust to ignore or participate in corrupt activities, and supervisors distrusted the subordinates who, if they engaged corruption, might compromise the supervisor's career. Finally, almost everyone distrusted the executives, who were feared and often vilified as "headhunters" who advanced their own careers at the expense of the subordinates they disciplined or exposed.

The Knapp/Murphy synergy and the specific strategies Murphy implemented were eventually successful in eliminating organized corruption within the NYPD (Jasanoff and Stone 1977), and in a relatively short time the highly organized and pervasive patterns and practices of corruption that existed prior to Knapp and prior to Murphy were virtually extinguished in the NYPD (Henry 2003b).

Although the Knapp/Murphy reforms virtually eliminated the type of organized corruption that flourished in the late 1960s and early 1970s and for many years brought individual acts of corruption to within manageable limits, the 1994 Mollen Commission made it clear that the reforms failed to prevent the emergence of new forms, patterns, and types of police corruption. As Mollen (NYPD 1994) and Henry (2003b) have noted, the strategies of the early 1970s were appropriate for the particular corruption dynamics existing at that time, but successive administrations left them virtually unaltered. The range of internal and external environments that shape corruption changed considerably in the two intervening decades, permitting new and substantially different forms of corruption to evolve, but the NYPD's anticorruption structures, policies, practices, and ideology remained static.

The Mollen Commission—July 7, 1994

In 1992, media revelations that a relatively small group of NYPD officers had been engaged in narcotics trafficking and other crimes and that the officers involved had been the subject of several unsuccessful investigations by NYPD internal investigative personnel led to the creation of the Mollen Commission. Like each of the previous commissions of inquiry, the Mollen Commission explored contemporary corruption trends and issued a host of recommendations. One of the most important findings associated with the Mollen Report (NYPD 1994) was the fact that the patterns and practices of corruption in the 1990s were radically different from those of the 1970s or any other era. The Mollen Commission did not find highly organized corruption involving vice enforcement and did not find that corruption was systemic or pervasive but that the deterioration of many internal mechanisms and policies allowed individual officers or small groups of officers to engage in criminal acts. Moreover, the commission found that these officers operated in secret and their activities were neither well known or condoned by the organization or by members of the police culture (Henry 1994, 2003b; NYPD 1994).

One of the most important outcomes of the scandal was the creation of an enhanced Internal Affairs Bureau to replace the faulty and feeble Internal Affairs Division. The new bureau was provided resources and personnel that had been lacking in the old IAD, and an extensive array of new and revised corruption control strategies and mechanisms were put in place. The NYPD also undertook a major internal study of its internal investigative function, reengineered that function, and disseminated the report throughout the agency in the form of a major strategy document outlining the scope of the problems as well as the solutions that would be implemented to correct them (NYPD 1996).

The corruption control strategies implemented in the early 1970s effectively rid the department of organized corruption, and while police criminality certainly did not completely cease within the agency, its prevalence and frequency declined quickly and precipitously. Buoyed by its apparent success, the NYPD's executive corps and management cadre gradually became complacent and turned their attention to more pressing matters. As the Mollen Report (1994) suggested, though, the decline in actual corruption, criminal activity, and serious misconduct caused managers to essentially lower their sights and pursue minor misconduct and administrative violations with the same zeal they had once pursued corruption. The continued competition among managers and executives placed great emphasis on maintaining high integrity-related statistics, and this gradually evolved into the pursuit of what became known as "white socks" complaints (Mollen 1994)—disciplinary infractions involving some of the most minor forms of noncriminal misconduct and administrative violations such as wearing white socks while in uniform.

Between the 1970s and 1990s, as public attention to police corruption issues began to subside as a function of the positive strides made toward eliminating it, a great many changes took place in the NYPD and its organizational culture. A more culturally diverse generation of officers entered the department, and although they received training and constant admonitions in the importance of integrity, the reality of corruption was something foreign to them: In an environment of high integrity and relatively high morale, the possibility of corruption seemed remote (Henry 1994, 2003b).

Two of the most critical issues in U.S. policing during this period were the increase in narcotics abuse in society and the rapid increase in narcotics-related crime. The NYPD responded to the drug problem by stepping up its enforcement efforts, and official proscriptions against patrol officers making drug arrests were eased. Department policy was equivocal, though: These arrests were still frowned upon, but because the agency could no longer afford to enforce the prohibition as strictly, it could not entirely shield its officers from the significantly increased corruption hazards of narcotics enforcement. The proliferation of drugs in society, and particularly the so-called crack epidemic of the mid-1980s, combined with the gradual erosion of the enforcement prohibition to radically alter the NYPD officer's task environment and increase his or her exposure to the corrupting influences of narcotics. Dombrink (1988:377) underscored the dimension of these temptations when he quoted a ranking police official from an unnamed agency: By the late 1980s, it was no longer "unusual for a police officer to stop a car in a routine traffic violation and find $20,000 in cash."

The NYPD's formal mechanisms and structures to detect and investigate corruption remained fairly static during this period (Henry 1994, 2003a; NYPD 1992, 1994). The basic structures of the IAD/FIAU system remained the same, as did the system's misplaced reliance on the effectiveness of the Staff Supervisory Unit. A 1992 report by Police Commissioner Raymond Kelly addressed the critical problems within the internal affairs function, identifying a deterioration of investigative practices within it (Henry 1994, 2003a; NYPD 1992).

In summary, the vigorous and effective anticorruption structures and policies implemented in the early 1970s deteriorated and, in time, became ineffective. While a multitude of factors contributed to this deterioration, two primary reasons were the agency's failure to maintain focused attention on corruption as a management issue and its failure to continually adapt, amend, and refocus its policies and structures in response to emerging organizational, political, and cultural trends (Henry 1994, 2003b).

Many of the problems associated with the internal investigative function were attributable to personnel issues since internal investigative units had great difficulty recruiting and retaining qualified investigators (NYPD 1992, 1994). Within the police occupational culture, internal investigative assignments typically involve some degree of stigma and as a result there is a general reluctance to volunteer for such assignments. There existed a prevailing sense of condescending antipathy toward IAD/FIAU personnel, and these perceptions were compounded by the aura of secrecy that surrounded the internal affairs function, by the fact that internal investigators tended to remain in those assignments for extended periods, and by the perception that inept and overburdened investigators frequently closed out allegations as "other misconduct noted" by issuing a complaint for some minor infraction (Henry 1994, 2003b).

In line with public demands for transparency and external oversight and to respond to increased public pressure for independent oversight, the City of New York also created an independent Commission to Combat Police Corruption in 1995, charging it with the responsibility to monitor and evaluate the NYPD's programs, activities, commitment, and overall efforts to control corruption. It does not directly investigate corruption complaints, but it has significant oversight into the agency's activities and regularly conducts analyses and issues reports concerning various aspects of corruption control.

A host of personnel changes were effected in the internal affairs function, including a new career path policy that created significant incentives for requesting an internal affairs assignment, and within a year virtually every member of the old IAD had been transferred and replaced by a new cadre of experienced investigators (Henry 1994, 2003b). The Internal Affairs Bureau also resumed using integrity tests and field associates as part of its overall proactive strategy. It had been a closely guarded secret that the IAD had effectively discontinued these programs in the 1980s and relied solely on the deterrent effect of the illusion that they were still being conducted. NYPD integrity tests are of two types. Targeted integrity tests may be conducted when an identified officer is the subject of a corruption allegation; random integrity tests are used to address statistically identified corruption trends and are not directed at a particular officer. In either case, the tests are sophisticated, creative, and realistic, and they do not focus on minor white socks misconduct (Henry 1994, 2003b).

Another essential reform was the so-called policy of inclusion articulated in 1994 by then-Commissioner William Bratton to enhance organizational transparency, to eliminate much of the secrecy that surrounded internal affairs activity, and to increase the level of mutual trust between commanders, field officers, and internal investigators. Internal Affairs Bureau personnel are now generally encouraged to advise commanding officers when a member of their unit is the subject of a corruption allegation and to enlist the commander's assistance in conducting the investigation. Commanders provide essential intelligence, background, and contextual information to assist the investigators, and they can be enlisted to carefully monitor the suspect officer's activities and behaviors. Most importantly, perhaps, the policy of inclusion communicates the essential notion that corruption control is the responsibility of every member of the organization (Henry 1994, 2003b; NYPD 1996).

The post-Mollen reforms eliminated the decentralized Field Internal Affairs Units in favor of a geographically based organizational model of investigative groups under the centralized Internal Affairs Bureau. The geographically based investigative groups are supplemented by a number of specialized groups including a police impersonators squad, a surveillance squad, and a squad devoted to investigating complaints of excessive force and brutality (Henry 1994, 2003b; NYPD 1996, 2000).

Another important innovation was the creation of the Corruption Prevention and Analysis Unit (CPAU) within the Internal Affairs Bureau to conduct various types of empirical and qualitative research into corruption within the agency. The CPAU uses a variety of qualitative and quantitative methods to identify emerging corruption patterns and trends and to identify measures that effectively deter corrupt activities. Using a systems analysis approach, corruption complaints and allegations are carefully tracked, monitored, and statistically analyzed to identify potential trends on a continuing basis. The unit quickly identifies trends and recommends appropriate responses and by monitoring the effectiveness of various investigative policies and practices, it fulfills a vital quality control function (Henry 1994, 2003b; NYPD 1996, 2000).

COMPSTAT AND CORRUPTION CONTROL

Perhaps the most important initiative to emerge from the reform process is the accountability system developed to ensure the quality of investigations. The system, modeled after the highly successful Compstat management system, ensures that cases are continually monitored and evaluated. A steering committee chaired by the chief of Internal Affairs Bureau and composed of senior IAB staff meets every two weeks to examine all investigations taking place within a particular geographic area. On a rotating basis, Investigative Group leaders and supervisors assigned to investigate the cases brief their commanders on developments, and statistical analyses prepared by the CPAU are disseminated and discussed. In this system, senior executives are directly involved in (and therefore accountable for) the quality of investigative processes.

As noted, the innovative and still-evolving Compstat management model has had tremendous success in reducing crime and improving the quality of life in jurisdictions where it has been employed, especially in New York City. Compstat was first developed in the NYPD in 1994, and despite the passage of time, its outstanding successes, and its general acceptance throughout U.S. police management circles as a viable and effective crime-fighting tool, it remains a much misunderstood process.

Compstat[3] has been portrayed as a high-pressure meeting between police executives and middle managers, an accountability mechanism, a computer program that predicts crime, and a system that enhances the flow of information throughout an agency. The fact is that Compstat involves all of these things and a great deal more. For our purposes, we need not provide an extensive description of Compstat or its history, but a brief overview of its principles and methods will suffice to illustrate how this dynamic process has been adapted for the control of corruption and serious misconduct.

The Compstat management model was developed and implemented in 1994, during the administration of Police Commissioner William Bratton. At that time, the NYPD was doing a rather poor job at controlling crime just as it was doing a poor job at controlling corruption. Bratton recognized that the department's executive corps needed to be reinvigorated and that middle managers would be the key to the agency's success in reducing crime.

At that time the agency was primarily driven from the top down: Most important decisions, including those regarding crime control, were made at the executive level. The problem was that an agency as large and complex as the NYPD called for a structure in which authority, discretion, and organizational power were devolved downward from the executive level to the ranks of middle management. Middle managers, especially precinct commanders, had much greater knowledge about complex crime and quality of life conditions within their jurisdictions than executives could hope to achieve, and they were therefore better situated to address those problems. Precinct commanders needed more direct control over the personnel and resources required to carry out enforcement operations and to rapidly and effectively address chronic crime conditions. Typically, by the time precinct commanders requested and received these resources from the executives controlling the resources, crime and quality of life problems had either escalated or changed patterns. Bratton also recognized that middle managers had to be held highly accountable for their use of the expanded authority, discretion, and organizational power that he would give them.

Prior to the advent of Compstat, the NYPD had no functional system in place to rapidly and accurately capture crime statistics or use them for strategic planning. By the time crime statistics were gathered, analyzed, and given back to commanders, they were often three to six months old. Because the data gave no indication of where crime was occurring today, they were of no strategic or tactical use. If crime data could be collected and analyzed in real-time or something close to it, though, and if that data could be rapidly linked to maps that depict the spatial distribution of crime by time and location, they would become tremendously important tools. Such data could essentially predict where and when crime would occur, and precinct commanders could marshal their resources to address it.

There was, in short, a compelling need in the NYPD to create an automated system that would capture and analyze crime intelligence and depict crime patterns in a timely and accurate way. Coupled with effective crime control strategies and tactics and the ability to rapidly deploy their personnel and resources, commanders could have a dramatic impact on crime and quality of life problems. Commanders could be sure their efforts were effective by relentlessly following up on these problems to make sure they were actually solved, not simply displaced (Henry 2002).

These concepts have been distilled into the four principles of crime control that the Compstat model supports:

- Timely and accurate intelligence
- Effective strategies and tactics
- Rapid deployment of personnel and resources
- Relentless follow up.

It was not enough to simply identify these principles and to ask middle managers to assume greater authority, discretion, and organizational power; formal structures and policies had to be implemented to make them a reality. These formal structures include the Compstat meetings. Twice each week, the commanders of all the precincts and operational units within a given geographic area of New York City gather at the NYPD's headquarters to give an accounting of themselves and their officers' activities.[4] The procedure is as follows (Henry 2003a):

> Each precinct commander takes his or her turn at the podium to present his or her activities and accomplishments and to be closely questioned by the police commissioner, several deputy commissioners, the chief of the department, the chief of detectives, the chief of patrol, and other top executives. Precinct commanders are accompanied by detective squad supervisors, narcotics and vice squad commanders, and ranking personnel from just about every operational and investigative unit within their geographic area of responsibility. Because of the intensity of the questioning, the quantity of statistical performance data, and the nature of the technology involved (including computerized pin mapping, comprehensive crime trend analyses, and other graphic presentations of data), Compstat meetings permit the agency's executives to have an unprecedented level of in-depth knowledge about the specific crime and quality-of-life problems occurring at specific locations in each of the NYPD's 76 precincts. With this wealth of highly specific knowledge, executives can ask commanders and managers probing questions about the particular activities and tactics they are using to address these problems at specific locations. Crime and quality-of-life trends and patterns can be more easily discerned through the discussions, and connections between seemingly disparate events and issues are more easily identified. Commanders are expected to have answers and to demonstrate results, and specialized squad commanders must show how they cooperate and coordinate their activities with other operational entities.

Because Compstat meetings are also attended by the commanders of support and ancillary units, the information discussed is widely disseminated throughout the agency. Their presence also permits commanders to immediately develop detailed plans and strategies and to better utilize the resources they control without having to cross bureaucratic lines or to schedule a series of meetings. Compstat meetings are about supporting and empowering commanders, sharing information and crime intelligence, communicating management's objectives, and ensuring accountability (Henry 2003a).

The basic processes briefly sketched out here have been adapted and applied by the NYPD's Internal Affairs Bureau (IAB) to manage corruption—to ensure oversight and accountability for specific corruption investigations, to monitor corruption conditions within the department, and to ensure that personnel and resources are used effectively. The process used by the Internal Affairs Bureau mimics the Compstat process insofar as it follows the same principles of crime control and relies on a meeting by a group known as the Steering Committee.

As described by the NYPD (2001), the Internal Affairs Bureau's

> Steering Committee sessions mirror the functions of weekly Compstat meetings. In each Steering Committee session, an investigative group briefs the IAB Executive Staff on selected cases and reviews investigative steps taken. Each meeting is also a problem solving session, and new tactics and investigative techniques are exchanged. As with Compstat, computerized maps of corruption complaints and command profiles aid in the identification of

clusters, patterns and trends. The Mayor's Commission to Combat Police Corruption observes and monitors selected sessions to assess the Department's anti-corruption efforts.

The Steering Committee meetings are supported by statistical data and corruption intelligence developed by the Corruption Prevention and Analysis Unit, and this timely and accurate intelligence makes it possible to track new and evolving patterns of corruption as well as to observe their spatial distribution. The data and maps may reveal, for example, that a slight statistical uptick in allegations of theft of property has taken place within a given precinct or geographic area of the city. This information, which has probably already been passed on to the IAB commander responsible for that area, is likely to be discussed at the Steering Committee meeting. The commander will likely be asked to comment on the uptick and to outline a strategic response to the intelligence information. Does he or she have additional information that would shed light on the situation? What is the status of current investigations into stolen property allegations? Do the allegations reveal that a pattern in which a particular type of property is alleged to be repeatedly stolen? Have any suspects been identified, and what progress has been made in the investigation?

If the commander has a suspect and believes that a targeted integrity test would be a valuable investigative step, the commander can immediately get approval and make arrangements for the test. The specifics of the proposed integrity test can be discussed and refined on the spot. Other commanders present at the meeting may offer the insights and experiences they have accumulated in similar cases, and the investigative techniques they offer can be a valuable tool.

An essential feature of the Steering Committee meetings and of the entire set of Compstat-based policies and programs that the Internal Affairs Bureau uses is the capacity to identify new and emerging corruption trends and patterns. These trends and patterns are not merely identified at the local level but on a citywide basis as well, and they are identified practically contemporaneous with their emergence. Current data can easily be compared to historic data, and new corruption control strategies and tactics can be developed and applied as the forms, patterns, and practices of corruption evolve in response to changes in the social, political, organizational, and cultural environments. Importantly, the process also allows executives in Internal Affairs Bureau to carefully monitor subtle changes in corruption conditions that take place over time throughout the department or in individual commands, and it allows them to assess the effectiveness of their corruption control policies and programs.

In addition to its other benefits, the application of Compstat-based management systems and processes allow executives and managers to probe potential or actual connections between emerging forms and patterns of corruption and other events or issues, and often to develop preventive strategies. Can a slight increase in complaints for off-duty domestic violence be attributed to subtle changes in the demographics of the agency? In what percentage of these new cases, as compared to last year's cases, is alcohol involved? As compared to the agency as a whole, do the officers involved in these incidents tend to be younger or older? Does the increase in domestic violence complaints indicate the need for additional or better recruit and/or in-service training? Are domestic violence complaints more frequent in the Bronx, say, than in Brooklyn? Why? Compstat-based management systems permit executives to examine all of these variables and many more.

As alluded to earlier, the history of corruption and reform in the NYPD highlights the absolute importance of sustaining executive attention to corruption problems and issues; we have seen how corruption can easily arise, especially in new forms, when top management turns its attention to other issues. The fact that Steering Committee meetings are attended by ranking members of the Internal Affairs Bureau executive staff as well as middle managers and investigative supervisors places a unique type of accountability on the executives. If they become lax in their efforts to fight corruption or permit their personnel to cut corners in investigations, those facts will be immediately apparent to their subordinates as well as to the members of the independent Commission to Combat Police Corruption in attendance. While the meetings are certainly not open to the public, everything that takes place at a Steering Committee meeting is a matter of record witnessed by other officers.

The final proof that the application of Compstat-based management principles to the control of corruption has effectively ended the recurring cycles of corruption and reform will be revealed only with time. These practices were first developed and put into place less than a decade ago, and additional time is required to fully assess their effectiveness. In the interim, though, corruption complaints have declined significantly within the NYPD in the past few years.

According to statistical data contained in the Internal Affairs Bureau's annual reports, which are another example of the NYPD's effort to demonstrate its ongoing commitment both to controlling corruption and to maintaining a transparent organization, corruption complaints against officers declined each year between 1995 and 2001. Although the NYPD experienced a slight increase in corruption complaints from 2001 to 2002, the increase must be understood in light of the impact of September 11 on the NYPD: The terrorist attacks on the World Trade Center significantly interrupted the department's normal operations for months as literally thousands of officers were detailed away from their usual commands to participate in rescue and recovery efforts. The NYPD believes that a correlation may exist between the moratorium on traditional police duties and the reduced number of allegations of corruption and serious misconduct reported in the later part of the year.

The reduction in corruption complaints is astounding: The total number of such complaints decreased by nearly half between 1994, when 2,258 cases were logged, and 2002, when 1,151 corruption cases were recorded. Indeed, with the exception of the anomalous 2001, the number of complaints fell each year between 1994 and 2002. These numbers are certainly impressive, but they are all the more significant when we account for fluctuations in the department's headcount and examine the number of complaints received per officer. In 1994, the corruption complaint per officer ratio stood at 1 for every 17 officers; by 1995 that ratio fell to 1 per 24 officers, and the ratio has continued to expand ever since. Based on 2002 data, the ratio currently stands at 1 corruption complaint for every 58 officers. By any measure, these data are impressive, and they illustrate the effectiveness of the NYPD's new strategic approach to controlling corruption.

CONCLUSION

Over the course of the last century, the NYPD endured no fewer than six major corruption scandals resulting in commissions of inquiry. As the reports published by those commissions reveal, the specific behaviors and patterns of corruption have changed dramatically over the years. Forms and patterns of corruption that were once prevalent are now extinct, and their extinction occurred as a result of organizational reforms as well as changes in the social, political, organizational, and cultural environments that shape policing. At the same time, changes in the social, political, organizational, and cultural environments opened up new opportunities for corrupt activity in other spheres, and when police officers exploited these opportunities, new behaviors and new patterns of corruption arose. As we have seen, police corruption is a highly resilient and durable phenomena that evolves in response to its environment.

Because corruption has evolutionary characteristics, the policies and practices that police agencies use to control it must also be capable of evolving. In the example of the Knapp Commission reforms, policies did not change substantially with time became ineffective in preventing the emergence of new forms of corruption and police criminality. The most successful crime control and management accountability model yet devised is the Compstat model, which is readily capable of evolving in response to environmental changes, and the NYPD has demonstrated how effective the model can be in reducing both traditional crime and police corruption. The NYPD's Internal Affairs Bureau adapted Compstat principles and techniques, applying them to the management of corruption, and has achieved a tremendous reduction in the number of corruption complaints as well as the ratio of complaints per officer. All measures indicate that significant declines in corruption have taken place in the NYPD since these principles were first introduced a decade ago.

It is likely that these Compstat-based strategies will continue to evolve and will continue to reduce corruption in the NYPD. Only through such continual evolution coupled with vigorous and sustained attention to corruption issues can significant inroads continue to be made against police corruption.

ENDNOTES

1. Becker was convicted of Rosenthal's murder and executed for the crime, and most subsequent histories and accounts of corruption in the New York Police Department assume his factual guilt. Logan (1970) and Klein (1927), however, each make a compelling case that while Becker was most certainly a grafter, he was probably not guilty of or complicit in Rosenthal's murder. A more likely scenario, according to Logan and Klein is that Becker was framed for the crime by Tammany Hall politicians and New York's ambitious District Attorney Charles Whitman. The tremendous media attention surrounding the case propelled Whitman's successful campaign for governor of New York.

2. Integrity tests involved a controlled situation in which officers were purposely placed in a potentially corruptive situation and carefully observed. In early tests, IAD personnel posing as civilians handed officers wallets containing cash and identification, claiming to have found them. Officers were monitored to determine whether they followed prescribed administrative procedures for recovered lost property (Montgomery 1973). More sophisticated integrity test scenarios were developed and implemented later. Field associates were officers assigned to ordinary police assignments who secretly reported information on corruption, misconduct, and other police activities to IAD

handlers. As I have described elsewhere (Henry 1990a), these controversial strategies were credited with changing the expectation of secrecy among cops, but they also alienated many honest officers who resented the treachery and basic lack of trust they perceived in these policies.

3. There has been much speculation about the derivation of the term *Compstat* in the police management literature. As Henry (2002) describes, the term was coined by accident when Sergeant John Yohe closed an early computer program he designed to analyze crime statistics and to generate a report that would be useful to precinct

commanders as well as police executives. Because his antiquated DOS-based computer would accept file names only up to eight characters, he saved the file as compstat for comparison statistics. Since no one had a formal name for the program or the management process it was designed to facilitate, the name stuck and was applied to the entire process and eventually the entire management model.

4. The NYPD's 76 precincts are divided into eight patrol boroughs for administrative purposes, and one patrol borough is represented at each meeting; every precinct commander can expect to attend a Compstat meeting at least once per month.

REFERENCES

CHIN, G. J. (ed.) (1997). *New York City Police Corruption Investigation Commissions*, Vol. I–VI. Buffalo, NY: W. S. Hein.

CURRAN COMMITTEE REPORT (1913). Report of the special committee of the Board of Alderman of the City of New York appointed August 5, 1912 to investigate the police department. In *New York City Police Corruption Investigation Commissions, 1894–1994*, ed. G. J. Chin, Vol. II. Buffalo, NY: W. S. Hein [1997].

DOMBRINK, J. (1988). The touchables: Vice and police corruption in the 1980s. In *Social Deviance: Readings in Theory and Research*, ed. H. N. Pontell, 373–398. Englewood Cliffs, NJ: Prentice Hall.

HELFAND INVESTIGATION REPORT (1995). Report ofspecial investigation by the District Attorney of Kings County, and the December 1949 grand jury. In *New York City Police Corruption Investigation Commissions, 1894–1994*, ed. G. J. Chin, Vol. IV. Buffalo, NY: W.S. Hein.

HENRY, V. E. (1990a). Lifting the "blue curtain": Some controversial strategies to control police corruption. *National Police Research Unit Review* 6: 48–56.

HENRY, V. E. (1990). *Patterns of Police Corruption: Comparing New York City and Queensland*. Griffith University, Centre for Australian Public Sector Management *Research Papers* Series.

HENRY, V. E. (1994). Police corruption: Tradition and evolution. In *Contemporary Policing:*

Un-Peeling Tradition, ed. K. Bryett and C. Lewis, 160–179. Sydney: Macmillan.

HENRY, V. E. (2002a). *The COMPSTAT Paradigm: Management Accountability in Policing, Business and the Public Sector*. Flushing, NY: Looseleaf Law.

HENRY, V. E. (2002b). *The Compstat Paradigm: Management Accountability in Policing, Security and the Private Sector*. Fresh Meadows, NY: Looseleaf Law.

HENRY, V. E. (2003a). Compstat: The emerging model of police management. In *Critical Issues in Crime and Justice*, ed. A. R. Roberts, 2nd ed. Thousand Oaks, CA: Sage.

HENRY, V. E. (2003b). Police corruption in a megalopolis: The case of New York City. In *The Uncertainty Series: Corruption, Police, Security and Democracy*, ed. M. Amir and S. Einstein. Huntsville, TX: Office of International Criminal Justice.

JASANOFF, S., and R. STONE (1977). *The Knapp Commission and Patrick Murphy (Parts A, B, Sequel)*. Harvard University, Kennedy School of Government *Case Study Program* series, C94-77-181.0; C94-77-182.0; C94-77-182.1.

KLEIN, H. H. (1927). *Sacrificed, The Story of Police Lieutenant Charles Becker*. New York: Henry H. Klein.

KLEINIG, J. (1996). *The Ethics of Policing*. Cambridge: Cambridge University Press.

KNAPP COMMISSION REPORT (1972). Report of the commission to investigate allegations of police corruption and the city's anti-corruption procedures. In *New York City Police Corruption Investigation Commissions, 1894–1994*, ed. G. J. Chin, Vol. V. Buffalo, NY: W. S. Hein [1997].

KORNBLUM, A. (1976). *The Moral Hazards: Police Strategies for Honesty and Ethical Behavior.* Lexington, MA: Lexington Books.

LARDNER, J., and T. REPPETTO (2000). *NYPD: A City and Its Police.* New York: Henry Holt.

LEXOW COMMITTEE REPORT (1895). Report of the special committee appointed to investigate the police department of the City of New York. In *New York City Police Corruption Investigation Commissions, 1894–1994*, ed. G. J. Chin, Vol. I. Buffalo, NY: W.S. Hein.

LOGAN, A. (1970). *Against the Evidence: The Becker–Rosenthal Affair.* New York: McCall.

MOLLEN COMMISSION REPORT (1994). Report of the New York City commission to investigate allegations of police corruption and the anti-corruption procedures of the police department. In *New York City Police Corruption Investigation Commissions, 1894–1994*, ed. G. J. Chin, Vol. VI. Buffalo, NY: W. S. Hein [1997].

MONTGOMERY, P. L. (1973). 15 policemen keep money "lost" in test. *New York Times* (November 17): 1.

MURPHY, P. V., and T. PLATE (1977). *Commissioner: A View from the Top of American Law Enforcement.* New York: Simon and Schuster.

NEW YORK POLICE DEPARTMENT (1992). *Police Commissioner's Report: An Investigation into the Conduct of the Dowd Investigation and An Assessment of the Department's Internal Investigation Capabilities.* New York: NYPD.

NEW YORK POLICE DEPARTMENT (1994). *Responses to the Mollen Commission Report.* New York: NYPD Office of Management Analysis and Planning.

NEW YORK POLICE DEPARTMENT (1996). *Internal Affairs Bureau Annual Report 1995.* New York: New York City Police Department, Internal Affairs Bureau.

NEW YORK POLICE DEPARTMENT (1998). *Internal Affairs Bureau Annual Report 1997.* New York:

New York City Police Department, Internal Affairs Bureau.

NEW YORK POLICE DEPARTMENT (1999). *Internal Affairs Bureau Annual Report 1998.* New York: New York City Police Department, Internal Affairs Bureau.

NEW YORK POLICE DEPARTMENT (2000). *Internal Affairs Bureau Annual Report 1999.* New York: New York City Police Department, Internal Affairs Bureau.

NEW YORK POLICE DEPARTMENT (2001). *Internal Affairs Bureau Annual Report 2000.* New York: New York City Police Department, Internal Affairs Bureau.

NEW YORK POLICE DEPARTMENT (2002). *Internal Affairs Bureau Annual Report 2001.* New York: New York City Police Department, Internal Affairs Bureau.

NEW YORK POLICE DEPARTMENT (2003a). *Internal Affairs Bureau Annual Report 2002.* New York: New York City Police Department, Internal Affairs Bureau.

NEW YORK POLICE DEPARTMENT (2003b). *Compstat Report Covering the Week of 7/21/2003 Through 07/27/2003.* New York: New York Police Department. Available on line [http://www.nyc.gov/html/nypd/pdf/chfdept/cscity.pdf]

NEW YORK TIMES (1933). Dr. Parkhurst dies of a fall in sleep; Reformer, 91, a somnambulist, plunges from porch roof of New Jersey home. *New York Times* (September 9): 13.

PUNCH, M. (1985). *Conduct Unbecoming.* New York: Tavistock (Metheun).

RAAB, S. (1992). In the past, police reorganization followed scandals. *New York Times* (May 17): 35.

REUSS-IANNI, E. (1983). *Two Cultures of Policing: Street Cops and Management Cops.* New Brunswick, NJ: Transaction.

SEABURY INVESTIGATION REPORT (1932). Official title: Final report of Samuel Seabury, referee, in the matter of the investigation of the Magistrates' Courts in the First Judicial Department and the Magistrates thereof, and of attorneys-at-law practicing in said courts. In *New York City Police Corruption Investigation Commissions, 1894–1994*, ed. G. J. Chin, Vol. III. Buffalo, NY: W. S. Hein.

PART V

Law

Chapter 21

The Bill of Rights in the
Twenty-First Century

Alexander B. Smith, (dec.), Harriet Pollack, and Matthew Muraskin

ABSTRACT

For approximately 40 years, the U.S. Supreme Court has interpreted the Fourth, Fifth, Sixth, and Eighth Amendments of the Bill of Rights in a manner protective of the rights of suspects, defendants, and prisoners, though as we moved into the twenty-first century the Court is no longer expansive on the issues and in many areas has actually chipped away on rights previously afforded. However, in recent years, the focus of the Court has shifted from restrictions on the police and the conduct of trials to concerns about sentencing and punishment. What the future holds depends largely on government policy in relation to drug use and trafficking and gun control, the chief elements of our crime problems, as well as changing personnel on the Court.

When the text of the Constitution emerged from the Constitutional Convention in 1787 and was presented to the states for ratification, it was not greeted with universal acclaim. The compromises struck by the Founding Fathers in relation to representation of large states versus small, the slave trade, and other controversial issues left many people unhappy. The biggest complaint, however, was that the proposed Constitution provided insufficient protection for individual rights, and indeed, that the new government-to-be might be as tyrannical as the old British monarchy. In many states it was only the promise that a bill of rights protecting individual liberties would be enacted immediately that enabled the Constitution to be ratified.

It is, in fact, true that while the Constitution itself set up the framework for a majoritarian representative government, it is the Bill of Rights, that is, the first ten amendments to the Constitution that protects individuals from the unwarranted intrusion of government into their daily lives. It is the Bill of Rights that guards personal integrity that gives us the right to be left alone.

The government is the only institution in society that has a legitimate right to exert physical force over us. Therefore, the right to be left alone means, above all, the right not to be arrested and punished for what we have said or done except under certain clearly specified conditions. It is not surprising, thus, that five of the first ten amendments concern how U.S. Supreme Court interpretations of those five amendments—the First, Fourth, Fifth, Sixth, and Eighth—have shaped the substance of the criminal law as well as the rules of criminal procedure, and second, those questions, currently unresolved, which have the potential for further changes in the system.

INTRODUCTION

For the latter part of the twentieth century the U.S. Supreme Court interpreted the Bill of Rights in terms of defendant's rights and limitations upon them. As we moved into this century, however, the focus of the Court has shifted from restrictions on the police and the conduct of trials to concerns about sentencing and punishment. What the future hold depends largely on governmental policy in relation to drug trafficking and gun control, which are the chief elements of our present crime problem. But, just as important, the composition of the Supreme Court itself will play a significant role in determining both the thrust and focus of the first ten amendments to the Constitution for at least the first few decades of this century.

When the text of the Constitution emerged from the Constitutional Convention in 1787 and was presented to the states for ratification, it was not greeted with universal acclaim. The compromises struck by the Founding Fathers in relation to representation of large states versus small, the slave trade, and other controversial issues left many people unhappy. The biggest complaint, however, was that the proposed Constitution provided insufficient protection for individual rights, and indeed, that the new government-to-be might be as tyrannical as the old British monarchy. In many states, it was only the promise that a bill of rights protecting individual liberties would be enacted immediately that enabled the Constitution to be ratified.

It is, in fact, true, that although the Constitution itself set up the framework for a majoritarian representative government, it is the Bill of Rights, that is, the first ten amendments to the Constitution, that protects individuals from the unwarranted intrusion of government into their daily lives. It is the Bill of Rights that guards personal integrity that gives us the right to be let alone.

The government is the only institution in society that has a legitimate right to exert physical force over us. Therefore, the right to be let alone means, above all, the right not to be arrested and punished for what we have said or done except under certain clearly specified conditions. It is not surprising, thus, that five of the first ten amendments concern the workings of the criminal justice system. It is our purpose in this chapter to discuss, first, how U.S. Supreme Court interpretations of those five amendments—the First,

Fourth, Fifth, Sixth, and Eighth—have shaped the substance of the criminal law as well as the rules of criminal procedure, and second, those questions, currently unresolved, which have the potential for further changes in the system.

THE STATE OF THE LAW AS OF THE END OF THE TWENTIETH CENTURY

First Amendment

> Congress shall make no law respecting an establishment of religion, or prohibiting the free exercise thereof; or abridging the freedom of speech, or of the press; or the right of people peaceably to assemble, and to petition the Government for a redress of grievances.

The First Amendment is not usually discussed in terms of its impact on the criminal justice system, yet in the context of the right not to be arrested or punished for speech-related activities, it is very important. Actually, with the exception of the short-lived Alien and Sedition Act of 1798, there was no federal regulation of speech until World War I in the Sedition and Espionage Acts. Although the states may have punished certain types of speech, the federal government did not, and although the road from the post–World War I period to the present traversed serious bumps in the form of Red scares and McCarthyism, at the present time we are living in an era of great freedom for both speech and religion. The U.S. Supreme Court has held virtually all speech to be constitutionally protected, except for speech that is pornographic or creates a danger of imminently inciting riot or rebellion. Speech, moreover, has been broadly defined as communication, meaning art, music, sculpture, drama, picketing, and street demonstrations. Some of these forms of communication obviously involve action as well as speech and can be restricted more than speech unmixed with action. Nevertheless, the Supreme Court generally has sided with the speaker, going so far as to indicate that in the case of a speaker with a hostile audience, the police, wherever possible, must restrain the audience and protect the speaker.

Although there continues to be discussion that "hate crime" legislation punishes thoughts and thereby runs afoul of the First Amendment, the Supreme Court has had no such problem with laws imposing sanctions because of the bias of the perpetrator toward a targeted group or person. In *Wisconsin v. Mitchell* (1993) a black man was convicted of leading a racial assault on a white teenager. Under the state's hate crime law, the sentence was doubled because of the racial motivation of the defendant. The defendant claimed that his First Amendment rights were violated in that his political beliefs enhanced the sentence. Wisconsin argued that it was the additional potential for violence that increased the term, not the perpetrator's political beliefs. The Court ruled that the state's interest in controlling violence outweighed any First Amendment claim.

Religion has been almost entirely free from regulation by the criminal law except for two relatively recent cases, one involving the use of peyote, a hallucinogenic drug, in religious rituals, and the other a form of animal sacrifice. In both cases, the U.S. Supreme Court upheld the state law that outlawed the forbidden practice.

Fourth Amendment

> The right of the people to be secure in their persons, houses, papers and effects, against unreasonable searches and seizures shall not be violated, and no Warrant shall issue but upon probable cause supported by Oath or affirmation, and particularly describing the place to be searched or the person or things to be seized.

The Fourth Amendment is the amendment that quintessentially restrains the police. It tells the police that they must have probable cause to arrest, that they must have a warrant to search, and that the warrant must specify where and what is to be seized. Given the complexity of the interactions between the public and the police, there is an enormous body of law dealing with the details of these restrictions on police action. The Court has said that probable cause is something more than mere suspicion and that the permissible thoroughness of the search must vary with the degree of certainty that the police officer has regarding the guilt of the suspect. *Terry v. Ohio* (1968) held that where a police officer merely suspects that someone is about to commit a felony, he may stop and frisk the person in a public place, but he may not conduct a full-scale search or arrest of such a person without additional information.

A police officer may also conduct a search without a warrant if given consent by a person authorized to give such consent (e.g., the owner of the premises the police wish to search). In the case of a valid arrest, the officer may also, without a warrant, search the premises immediately adjacent to the suspect. These procedural rules regarding arrests and searches are, for the most part, not new, but within the last 40 years or so, the Court has greatly expanded its impact on the police by ruling that evidence illegally seized (i.e., in violation of these rules) cannot be used in court to obtain a conviction. Evidence gained through leads obtained by illegal means is, moreover, to be considered fruit of the poisonous tree and cannot be used either.

This exclusionary rule led to a revolutionary change in police training and attitudes. It is generally agreed that, historically, American law enforcement, especially on the local level, was conducted without regard for constitutional niceties, until the decision in *Mapp v. Ohio* (1961), which removed most of the incentive and imposed penalties for illegal police activity. Since then, gradually, the police have become both better trained and more professional. The exclusionary rule, of course, was criticized severely by those who felt that the hands of law enforcement officials were being tied and criminals were being coddled. Crime did increase for some years after the *Mapp* decision; it has since decreased. Despite the firm belief of many police officials to the contrary, *Mapp* and the exclusionary rule seem to have had little impact on the rate of crime. Their chief effect has been on police training and culture. The exclusionary rule, moreover, has been modified by the Supreme Court to provide for good faith exceptions where the totality of the circumstances were such that the officer had reason to believe that he or she was acting legally (see *Illinois v. Gates* 1983; *New York v. Quarles* 1984; *Nix v. Williams* 1984; and *United States v. Leon* 1984).

The Court has also dealt with other intrusions on personal privacy, such as wiretapping, and after a long period of denying that wiretapping fell under the aegis of the Fourth Amendment, finally admitted that wiretapping was indeed a search that should be regulated by Fourth Amendment standards, *Berger v. New York* (1967). Subsequent to the

Berger decision, Congress enacted legislation regulating wiretapping, and although wiretapping still remains the dirty business that Justice Holmes called it, the situation is much better controlled.

In more recent times, the Court has dealt with more esoteric issues, such as the question of whether a person has a right to privacy in the garbage he has discarded. In *California v. Greenwood* (1988), a warrantless search of garbage revealed drug paraphernalia which the Court admitted into evidence, holding that Greenwood had no right to privacy in the garbage once it has been placed on the curb. Similarly, in *Oliver v. United States* (1984), marijuana growing in a secluded, fenced, open field marked "No Trespassing" was permitted into evidence on the ground that there was no right to privacy in an open field.

The Court has also addressed the problem of warrantless arrests. Such arrests are permitted when in hot pursuit of the suspect, but traditionally, had also been permitted when the suspect was thought to be hiding in private premises. The Court held that not only did the police require an arrest warrant to enter such premises but a search warrant as well, if there was no prior consent to their entry (see *Payton v. New York* 1980; *Steagald v. United States* 1981).

On the issue of consent, the Supreme Court has now held that the police may not normally search the common areas of a shared premise, even if one of the occupants agrees, where another is present and opposes the search (*Georgia v. Randolph* 2006). In the *Randoph* case, the police were not allowed to search the shared premises of the marital home on the wife's consent over the objection of the husband who was present.

In another area, the Supreme Court held that Fourth Amendment rights do not necessarily extend to parolees, for the Court in 2006 upheld a state statute allowing for the suspicionless arrest of a parolee in *Samson v. California.*

One of the most difficult areas for the Court has been deciding the constitutionality of various types of automobile searches and seizures, particularly in illegal drug cases. The multitudinous decisions in this area are truly bewildering and require a chapter of their own, but the clear tendency has been to allow the police more latitude in making such searches, both of the vehicle itself and of containers within the vehicle.

Fifth Amendment

No person shall be held to answer for a capital, or otherwise infamous crime, unless on a presentment or indictment of a Grand Jury, except in cases arising in the land or naval forces, or in the Militia, when in actual service in time of War or public danger; nor shall any person be subject for the same offense to be twice put in jeopardy of life or limb; nor shall be compelled in any criminal case to be a witness against himself, nor be deprived of life, liberty, without due process of law; nor shall private property be taken for public use, without just compensation.

Of all the guarantees mentioned in the Fifth Amendment, probably the most important in terms of impact on the criminal justice system is the protection against forced self-incrimination. In British law, from which we derive many of our legal traditions, suspects are warned that incriminatory statements that they made could be used against them, and that they had a right to remain silent under police questioning. In the United States, the Fifth

Amendment was thought to provide the same protection. However, until *Miranda v. Arizona* (1966), there was no specific penalty imposed on the police for ignoring this protection. *Miranda* for the first time required that the police give a specific set of warnings to suspects under arrest, informing them of their right to remain silent and their right to have a lawyer present during questioning by the police. Any statements obtained without regard for these protections would be inadmissible for the purpose of obtaining a conviction at a trial.

Like *Mapp*, *Miranda* was extremely unpopular not only with the police but with the public as well, who felt that voluntary admissions of guilt were being excluded on the basis of technicalities. Despite the furor, *Miranda* has never been overruled, although it has been modified in many respects. *Miranda* applies only to suspects who are in custody at the time of questioning, and custody has been defined very narrowly by the Court. Thus, people brought in by the police for questioning, unless they have been formally arrested, are not covered by *Miranda*, even though they may think that they are under arrest.

Eleven years after the decision, the Court refused to overturn *Miranda* even in a case that presented an excellent opportunity. In *Brewer v. Williams* (1977), the suspect, accused of kidnapping, raping, and killing a child, was being transported on Christmas Eve from one city to another. In the course of the ride, the sheriff, who had promised the suspect's counsel not to question him, made remarks designed to elicit a confession from Brewer, a known religious zealot. The Court refused to admit Brewer's confession, holding that the sheriff's statement, although not direct questioning, was designed improperly to pressure the suspect to confess. At the start of this century, when given another clear opportunity to overrule *Miranda*, the Supreme Court did not and held that the required warnings of the case were now part of our culture.

Another modification of *Miranda* was the *Quarles* decision where Quarles, while attempting to hold up a supermarket, was captured and handcuffed. While thus confined, the police, without giving him *Miranda* warnings, asked him where he had thrown his gun. Quarles told them, and the gun was admitted into evidence at the trial. The Court held the admission proper, holding that because of the imminent danger to public safety, the police had not had time to give *Miranda* warnings.

Another protection of the Fifth Amendment is the protection against double jeopardy which basically means that a person cannot be tried and punished twice for the same crime. However, since the United States is a federation of states rather than a unitary system, there is dual sovereignty exercised over every person. It is settled law that although a state may not try an accused person twice for the same crime, the federal government may institute a second prosecution for that crime regardless of the outcome of the first prosecution, and vice versa. Thus, when the local sheriff was acquitted of murder charges in the case of three civil rights workers in Mississippi, he was tried and convicted in federal court of violating the civil rights of the three men by murdering them.

Sixth Amendment

> In all criminal prosecutions, the accused shall enjoy the right to a speedy and public trial, by an impartial jury in the State and district wherein the crime shall have been committed, which district shall have been previously ascertained by law, and to be informed of the

nature and cause of the accusation; to be confronted with the witnesses against him; to have compulsory process for obtaining witnesses in his favor, and to have the Assistance of Counsel for his defense.

Closely related to the privilege against self-incrimination is the right to counsel at all times after arrest. At the pretrial stage, the purpose of the attorney is to see that the defendant's rights are not violated by torture or improper questioning. The purpose of the attorney at trial is to see that the defendant receives a fair trial with the opportunity to confront and cross-examine witnesses against him, present evidence in his own behalf, and have a judge and jury untainted by pretrial prejudicial publicity. *Escobedo v. Illinois* (1964), a forerunner of *Miranda*, involved a defendant who asked for, but was denied, the presence of his lawyer during police questioning. The Court held his confession inadmissible.

Similarly, in *Massiah v. United States* (1964), Massiah, an indicted defendant in a drug case, was induced by his indicted codefendant, who had turned informer, into making incriminating statements. The Court refused to admit Massiah's confession on the ground that after indictment, questioning of a defendant may not take place without the presence of his or her lawyer, and that use of an undercover informer constituted improper questioning.

Eighth Amendment

Excessive bail shall not be required, nor excessive fines imposed, nor cruel and unusual punishment inflicted.

The purpose of bail is to ensure the presence of a defendant at trial. If the crime, however, is egregious enough, there is a strong possibility that the defendant may run away and never come back. Therefore, very large amounts of bail, or indeed, the total denial of bail, have been imposed in certain kinds of cases.

The courts have always been conflicted over whether it is proper to use a money device to ensure the presence of the defendant at trial. On the one hand, the effect of money bail may be to keep poor people who pose little risk to the community in jail because they cannot make bail. On the other hand, releasing a defendant who can make bail may mean releasing a dangerous criminal. The riddle has not yet been resolved.

To alleviate the hardship of money bail on the poor, there have been many pilot projects that enable suspects with roots in the community and stable lifestyles to be released without bail. These projects have had a mixed record of success, depending on how well they have been administered, but well-run programs have managed to allow poor defendants their freedom pending trial and to ensure their return for adjudication. To address the second part of the bail riddle, some jurisdictions have enacted preventive detention laws that deny bail altogether to suspects thought to be too dangerous to be released. Such laws must be drawn narrowly and contain safeguards against long-term, unreasonable pretrial detention if they are to pass constitutional muster. In short, not much has changed since 1835, when a judge named Krantz was asked to set bail for a suspect who had attempted to assassinate President Jackson. He set bail at $1500 but complained that "if the ability of the prisoner alone were to be considered, $1500 is too much, but if the atrocity of the offense alone were to be considered, it was too small."

The cruel and unusual punishment clause of the Eighth Amendment was probably meant to prevent the infliction of barbarous methods of punishment, such as boiling in oil or drawing and quartering. However, in more recent years, the cruel and unusual punishment clause has been used to challenge the conditions under which prisoners have been incarcerated. In the earlier cases, the conditions brought to light were truly horrifying, as in *Holt v. Sarver* (1972), which dealt with the Arkansas prison system having used inmate trustees to perform the duties of prison guards. Trustees flogged inmates, used electric shock devices attached to their genitals, and applied burning cigarettes to their bodies. Many inmates were murdered and their bodies buried. In more recent cases, however, the abuses charged have been much less flagrant and relate to overcrowding, lack of medical care, poor food, and so on.

There have also been challenges to restrictions of prisoners' First Amendment rights, including the right to receive uncensored mail, to be interviewed by journalists, and the right to practice their religion and observe special holy days. In the last quarter of the twentieth century, as a result of suits brought by inmates under the Eighth Amendment, a large proportion of the state prison systems of the United States came under federal court orders to improve conditions under which inmates are held. Despite the Supreme Court's subsequent retreat to a more limited role in prison condition cases, as well as the Prison Litigation Reform Act of 1995, the twentieth century ended with the major inmate claims alleging restrictions of First Amendment rights being resolved in the prisoners' favor.

The cruel and unusual punishment clause has also been used to attack inequities in sentencing. Embedded in our legal traditions is the notion that there must be proportionality between a crime and its punishment. As far back as 1910, the U.S. Supreme Court held that a 15-year sentence at hard labor, chained at the ankle and wrist, was a disproportionate sentence for a wrongful entry in a cash book by a government employee (*Weems v. United States*). In more recent times, disproportionality in sentencing has been challenged in relation to mandatory sentencing laws for drug offenders, which have resulted in very harsh sentences for what are frequently low-level offenders.

The main challenges in sentencing, however, have come in relation to the death penalty. The death penalty was at first challenged on a per se basis, that is, that execution in and of itself was unconstitutional. The Court, in *Furman v. Georgia* (1972), denied that argument. Since then, however, the Court has attempted, by imposing rigorous procedural requirements, to eliminate the randomness of the death penalty, possible racial bias, and to limit the types of offenses for which the death penalty may be imposed. In capital cases, two trials are now required, one for the determination of guilt and one to decide whether the death penalty should be imposed.

From 1967 to 1977, the federal courts declared a moratorium on executions, pending resolution of legal challenges to their constitutionality. Since the moratorium ended, executions have taken place at an increasing pace, although fewer than before the moratorium, and mainly in the southern states. In the 1990s there was a quickening of executions, especially in Texas and Florida, but at the same time there was a slight drop in public support for the death penalty. This attitudinal change may be the result of concern over executing the innocent as the media carried several stories of persons on death row being exonerated. Indeed, as the century ended, Illinois imposed a moratorium on executions because a dozen inmates waiting to be put to death had their convictions overturned. In December 2002 as the then governor of Illinois' term came to an end he pardoned or commuted the sentences of all persons on death row because as he said the legislature had failed to enact necessary reforms.

Increased use of DNA evidence to exonerate persons found "guilty" of murder may spur further reforms in capital cases to ensure that those convicted are in fact guilty. Though an assistant attorney general in Missouri argued to that state's highest court that after all appeals were exhausted even a claim of innocence should not stop an execution. In order to effect closure and finality the courts should resist such claims and let the matter go to the executive for relief, if that be the case.

NEW ISSUES FOR THE TWENTY-FIRST CENTURY

First Amendment

As noted before, the First Amendment is usually not involved in a discussion of constitutional issues relating to criminal justice, especially since the climate for free speech is extraordinarily free at the present time, though the events of September 11 have generated antiterrorism statutes that will have an effect on First Amendment and other areas involving constitutional rights. Controversy, however, over "social" issues such as abortion and minority rights, has given rise to Supreme Court decisions that bear on the peacekeeping activities of the police. The most publicized of these was *Schenck v. Pro-Choice Network* (1997), concerning the right of groups opposed to abortion to hinder the operation of clinics where abortions were being performed, and to prevent or dissuade women seeking abortions from entering the clinics. In 1990, three doctors, four abortion clinics, and the Pro-Choice Network of Western New York filed a complaint in Federal Court in the Western District of New York against 50 individuals and three organizations, of which Operation Rescue was one. The defendants were accused of blockading clinics and conspiring to deprive women of abortion services by marching, kneeling, sitting, or lying in driveways, yelling, pushing, and shoving. The demonstrations were so large and violent that the police were overwhelmed. A temporary restraining order obtained from the Court by the plaintiffs was breached by Schenck on the ground that it violated his First Amendment rights. The Court affirmed its order, holding that it merely regulated the time, place, and manner of the demonstration, not the content. It concluded that in view of the defendant's tactics, a 15-foot buffer zone which demonstrators could not infringe was needed to protect persons wishing to enter the clinic. The Circuit Court of Appeals, en banc, affirmed the lower-court ruling. On appeal, the U.S. Supreme Court held unanimously that although a 15-foot buffer zone around a clinic was permissible, a 15-foot "bubble" around persons seeking to enter the clinic, no matter where they were located, was a burden on Schenck's free speech rights. It is not unreasonable to expect that the first few years of the twenty-first century will see additional cases before the Supreme

Court, further fine-tuning the rights of antiabortion demonstrators to protest in front of and around abortion sites.

Another free speech case, *Hurley and South Boston Allied War Veterans v. Irish-American Gay, Lesbian and Bisexual Group* (1995), involved the refusal of the sponsors of the annual St. Patrick's day parade in Boston to permit Irish homosexuals to march as an identified unit in the parade. The gays claimed that since the parade had received a permit from the city, and used the city streets, it should be open to all Irish persons in whatever unit they chose to march. The U.S. Supreme Court disagreed, holding that to force a private parade sponsor to include identified units of which they disapproved violated the sponsor's First Amendment right not to say something they didn't wish to say.

Limitations on bias crime legislation continue to come before the Supreme Court, but the discussion is about the Fifth and Sixth Amendments, not the First. In *Apprendi v. New Jersey* (2000), the Supreme Court held that enhancement of the defendant's sentence beyond the statutory maximum because his crime was racially motivated was improper because the Fifth Amendment due process clause and the notice and jury trial guarantees of the Sixth Amendment require that any factor other than a prior conviction that enhances the sentence must be submitted to the jury and determined, by them, beyond a reasonable doubt. However, in *People v. Rosen* (2001), the New York Court of Appeals held *Apprendi* did not require a jury trial where a sentence was being enhanced because of three prior felony convictions even though the trial court had to make the additional determination that the circumstances warranted the increased sentence.

Soon after the *Apprendi* decision federal prisoners began to challenge their terms of imprisonment as determined under the federal sentencing guidelines. This challenge was short lived as the lower federal courts quickly held that *Apprendi* did not apply to the sentence guidelines and that the decision is only implemented when a judge decided facts actually increase the sentence beyond the prescribed statutory maximum. See, *United States v. Sanchez* (2001). However, in *United States v. Booker* (2005) the Supreme Court, relying on *Apprendi* and its progeny, struck down the mandatory nature of the guidelines.

The First Amendment cases cited above are important and interesting, but as indicated, most of the criminal justice decisions of the U.S. Supreme Court involve the Fourth, Fifth, Sixth, and Eighth Amendments. Contrary to many people's expectations, since 1990, despite a change in the political climate of the country and of the membership of the Court, there have been no really substantial changes in the interpretations of those amendments though there is now a wait and see attitude on the impact of recent antiterror legislation. Rather, the Court has modified some of its earlier decisions in a more punitive direction. The *Mapp* and *Miranda* decisions, which imposed the exclusionary rule on illegally obtained evidence and confessions, were, in many ways, the high-water marks of constitutional change in our criminal justice system. They still stand, although in modified form. The tide of protection for defendants has been ebbing, but slowly and not dramatically. The newer interpretations are important not only to the litigants, but as a reflection of changes in our society.

One caveat needs to be addressed, however. Although it is true that the substance of Fourth, Fifth, Sixth, and Eighth Amendment jurisprudence has not changed markedly, the procedural rules for getting such cases to the U.S. Supreme Court have changed considerably, especially in relation to habeas corpus petitions. A habeas corpus petition is a device for bringing the custodian of an accused person or prisoner into court for the purpose of challenging the legality of the confinement. It is used, for example, to challenge the admissibility of evidence that might have been seized illegally, the admissibility of confessions that might have been involuntary, and most important, in death penalty cases, the constitutionality of an impending execution. The most significant use of habeas corpus has been to obtain federal oversight of state criminal procedure, since a writ of habeas corpus obtained in a federal court commands state officials to justify their actions. In legal terms, habeas corpus granted by a federal court for the purpose of examining a state court ruling results, in effect, in federal supervision of state practices. Understandably, state officials resent such suits, and the collateral relief process results in very long, complex, and expensive litigation, which congests both state and federal courts.

The U.S. Supreme Court has responded to this situation by limiting the granting of habeas corpus in certain kinds of situations. In 1976 in *Stone v. Powell*, the Court ruled that federal courts could not hear Fourth Amendment habeas corpus petitions from state prisoners, arguing that illegally seized evidence should have been excluded from their trials as long as each inmate had received a full and fair chance to make the argument in state court appeals. In addition to Court-imposed restrictions on Fourth Amendment habeas corpus appeals, Congress has enacted several statutes designed to restrict prison inmates from filing multiple habeas corpus appeals. Most of the challenges to these statutes have been rejected. *Felker v. Turpin* (1997) considered the question of whether severe restraints on the right to file habeas corpus petitions might not be construed as a total denial of the constitutional right to habeas corpus. Felker was convicted of murder and sentenced to death. He filed one unsuccessful habeas petition, followed by a second habeas petition. When the second petition was denied by a federal court of appeals, his attempt to appeal to the U.S. Supreme Court was forbidden by a 1996-congressional statute which denied appellants permission to appeal such a denial to the Supreme Court. The Supreme Court granted certiorari on the question of whether the statute amounted to an unconstitutional total denial of habeas corpus. A unanimous court held that the 1996 statute was constitutional and the Court could refuse to hear an appeal from the circuit court. Felker, however, could apply for habeas corpus in an original petition directly to the U.S. Supreme Court, thus preserving his constitutional right to habeas corpus.

One of the few decisions relating to habeas corpus favorable to defendants was *Lindh v. Murphy* (1997), which questioned the retroactivity of a 1966-congressional statute designed to make it harder for state prison inmates to file habeas corpus petitions in federal court. Lindh was convicted in Wisconsin of murder and attempted murder. He filed several applications for habeas corpus, but while his appeals were pending, Congress changed the rules regarding habeas corpus, so that Lindh's applications became invalid. He appealed to the U.S. Supreme Court, which held, in a five-to-four decision, that Congress did not intend for the law to be applied retroactively.

In another expansive decision the Supreme Court broadened the standard for the issuance of a certificate of appealability that is necessary for a prisoner to appeal the denial of his writ of habeas corpus petition in the federal district court. In *Miller-el v. Cockrell* (2003) the Supreme Court held that the certificate which can be issued by either the

District Court or a circuit Court of appeals should be granted where the appellant demonstrated a plausible claim and need not show that he was likely to succeed on the appeal.

Unless there is a dramatic change in the composition of the Supreme Court and/or legislative change vis-à-vis habeas corpus, both of which seem unlikely, the present limitations on habeas corpus will stand and may very well get more restrictive in the next decade especially as the government continues to balance individual rights with the security interests attendant to combating terrorism.

Fourth Amendment

Aside from habeas corpus restrictions, there have been very few changes in Fourth Amendment jurisprudence. In *Florida v. Bostick* (1991), a police officer who had no legal basis for suspecting a particular passenger, boarded a bus and at random asked for and received a passenger's consent to search his luggage after telling the passenger that he could refuse permission to search. The resulting search revealed contraband. The Supreme Court held that as long as the officer's request was not so coercive that the passenger was not free to refuse, the search was a legal consent search, even though the passenger, being on a bus, was not free to leave. Bostick expanded the meaning of "consent" in consensual searches, which are free from the requirements of probable cause or a warrant. However, in *Bond v. United States*, in 2000, the Supreme Court held that a traveler's personal luggage is clearly an "effect" protected by the Fourth Amendment, and merely exposing the luggage to the public does not cost a petitioner his or her reasonable expectation that his or her bag will not be physically manipulated.

Two other cases also involve motor vehicles. In *Ohio v. Robinette* (1996), a unanimous Supreme Court held that it would be unreasonable to require the police to inform a driver, before making a request to search a car, that he or she is free to refuse the request and go on his or her way. The police need not inform the driver of his or her right to leave. In another case, *Maryland v. Wilson* (1997), the police stopped a car for speeding and noticed that the front-seat passenger appeared to be very nervous. The officer ordered him to get out of the car, and when he did, a package of cocaine fell out. In *Pennsylvania v. Mimms* (1977), the Court had ruled that a police officer had the right to order the driver of a stopped vehicle out of the car. The question in Wilson, however, was whether a passenger could also be so ordered. The Court held seven to two that the passenger could be ordered out on the grounds that the safety of the policeman must prevail over the minimal intrusion on the passenger's privacy.

A more important case, perhaps, is *Richards v. Wisconsin* (1997), involving proper implementation of a search warrant. Police officers obtained a search warrant for Richard's hotel room, which specifically forbade them to enter the room without announcing their presence. Because this was a drug case and the police feared that Richards would destroy the evidence before admitting them, they broke down the door before knocking. Cocaine was found and Richard's motion to suppress the evidence as being illegally seized was denied by both the trial and appellate courts. On appeal to the U.S. Supreme Court, the question presented was whether in cases such as drug cases, where the evidence might be destroyed, the police have a right to enter without announcing themselves. A unanimous

Court held that although there is no blanket exception to the no-knock rule, where the police had reasonable suspicion that the evidence would be destroyed, the search was not illegal.

Fifth Amendment

The most notable development in Fifth Amendment jurisprudence was the refusal of the Court to extend the habeas corpus restrictions that it had applied to cases relating to illegally seized physical evidence to cases involving allegedly illegally obtained confessions. In *Withrow v. Williams* (1993), in a five-to-four decision, the Court refused to extend to confessions the limitation on habeas corpus that it had imposed on search and seizure cases in *Stone v. Powell* (1976). Withrow involved a defendant who claimed a violation of the *Miranda* rule and challenged the admissibility of his incriminating statements. To the surprise of most Court watchers, who expected the ban on habeas corpus in cases involving searches and seizures to be extended to cases involving incriminating statements, the Court granted his petition. The issue may not be entirely closed, however, because of the closeness of the vote and the fact that in another case, *Brecht v. Abrahamson* (1993), another five-to-four decision, the Court refused to permit habeas corpus petitions alleging constitutional errors committed by the state at trial unless the defendant could show that the error had a "substantial and injurious effect on the jury's verdict" and that he suffered from "actual prejudice from the error."

In 2004 in *Missouri v. Seibert,* the Supreme Court was faced with and struck down attempts by police to get around *Miranda* by holding that a confession must be suppressed because though it was obtained after *Miranda* warnings were given and waived the waiver was ineffective as it was preceded by impermissible questioning prior to the warnings.

In the same vein, comments by police officers to each other, made within the earshot of the defendant, for the purpose of evoking an incriminating statement have also been struck down as being the functional equivalent of interrogation (*Rhode Island v. Innes* 1980) As a result of *Innes*, the Courts now grapple with the question of whether the statements made by a police officer to a defendant were a simple statement of fact not designed to evoke an incriminating response. See *United States v. Lovell* (2004).

Double jeopardy is, however, a problem that continues to plague the courts, both because of our federal system, which gives separate jurisdictions to both the states and the federal government, and because the law recognizes both civil and criminal offenses, which carry separate punishments and which may result in a defendant being punished twice for an infraction relating to the same set of facts. In *United States v. Dixon* (1993), the Court upheld a second prosecution for a man who had beaten his wife after he had already been tried for violation of a court order of protection. The decision was five to four, and some recent events have reopened public discussion of the fairness of the dual sovereignty–dual jeopardy rules.

In Los Angeles, California, the acquittal in a state trial of four white policemen shown on television tape severely beating a black man in the course of an arrest aroused such public outrage that the federal government instituted a new trial. Although the acts were the same, the charge in federal court was violation of the victim's civil rights, and some of the previously acquitted defendants were convicted. The original state verdict, however, had led to severe rioting in Los Angeles, in the course of which a white truck driver was badly beaten by black rioters. The beating was filmed by a reporter. At the ensuing trial, only one defendant was convicted of a felony, which carried punishment far less than the original highest count in the indictment. There were some calls for a federal trial of the defendants, on the ground that the jury had been terrorized by the fear of a replay of the riots. There was no retrial of the black defendants, but the two cases provoked much discussion of when and whether a second trial by a different sovereign (i.e., the state or federal government) was appropriate.

In this new century, second trials, usually by the federal government, in cases where the state crime also makes out a federal civil rights violation, although not routine, are becoming more common. Indeed, prosecutors even get together before bringing charges to determine the appropriate jurisdiction within which to bring the case. These, of course, are political decisions since the prosecutors involved have broad discretion in deciding whether to bring charges at all.

Some double jeopardy cases involve, not prosecutions by different sovereigns, but multiple prosecutions by the same governmental unit. In *United States v. Usery* (1996), the question presented to the Court was whether civil forfeiture and criminal prosecution for the same illegal drug activity constituted double jeopardy. Usery's house was seized by the federal government in *in rem* proceedings after he had been found guilty of facilitating illegal drug transactions. After he had settled the *in rem* claims, he was indicted for and convicted of manufacturing marijuana, and sentenced to prison. The lower courts found for Usery, but on appeal, the U.S. Supreme Court ruled that the civil *in rem* proceeding was neither criminal nor punitive in nature and therefore the criminal conviction and punishment did not constitute double jeopardy. In *Hudson v. United States*, the U.S. Supreme Court agreed to review a 1996 decision of the 10th Circuit, which involved the question of whether a defendant was subjected to double jeopardy if he was criminally indicted for a banking violation after he had paid a fine for the same offense. Hudson had misapplied bank funds and had been convicted civilly and fined $46,000 when, in fact, the losses caused by his malfeasance were $900,000. The prosecution argued that since the fine was so small, it was only remedial, not punitive, and therefore a punitive criminal conviction would not constitute double jeopardy.

Even more unsettling was the denial of certiorari by the U.S. Supreme Court to a case involving the retrial for murder of a defendant who had previously been acquitted of the same offense. Harry Aleman was acquitted in a nonjury trial in Illinois of the murder of a union official (*Aleman v. Illinois* 1987). At the time, the prosecutor felt strongly that the case had been fixed by bribing the judge. Subsequently, a federal investigation begun in the 1980s of corruption in the Cook Country court system led to testimony by one Robert Cooley, a lawyer in Cook County, who had volunteered to be an undercover informer for the government, that the trial judge had been bribed. Illinois then retried and convicted Aleman on the original charge, reasoning that if the judge had been bribed, Aleman had never been in jeopardy. Aleman appealed his conviction on double jeopardy grounds ultimately to the U.S. Supreme Court which denied certiorari (*Aleman v. Illinois* 1997). Although denial of certiorari does not set a precedent, it is somewhat startling for the Court to have refused to hear a case that appears to have put in question all previous precedents on double jeopardy by retrial for the same offense after acquittal.

As we entered the twenty-first century, it appeared momentarily that the settled law of *Miranda v. Arizona* was about to be overturned. In the wake of the *Miranda* decision in 1966, Congress enacted section 3501 of title 18 of the U.S. Code, which in essence set forth that the admissibility of a statement should turn only on whether it was voluntary. The statute lay dormant until the Fourth Circuit Court of Appeals, making reference to the section cited above, reinstated a confession that had been excluded at the trial level because of a failure to give the accused the appropriate *Miranda* warnings. Writing for a seven-to-two majority, in *Dickerson v. United States* (2000), Chief Justice Rhenquist noted that the warnings of *Miranda* were now part of our culture and that *Miranda*, being a constitutional decision, could not be overturned by an act of Congress. The Court went on to state that *Miranda* and its progeny continue to govern the admissibility of statements made during custodial interrogation in both state and federal courts.

Sixth Amendment

Very few cases in recent years have come to the Court regarding the Sixth Amendment, and Sixth Amendment law seems to be fairly well settled. However, in 1996, the Court decided *Cooper v. Oklahoma*, in which Cooper challenged the right of Oklahoma to put the burden of proof on him to prove that he was incompetent to stand trial. Cooper had been accused of felony murder and was found to be incompetent to stand trial. He was committed to a state mental health facility for treatment and was released three months later when the doctors found him to be competent to stand trial. His behavior at the trial, however, was extremely bizarre, and he refused to cooperate with his counsel. Despite defense arguments that he was incompetent, he was convicted because the Court held that Cooper had not met the burden of proving his incompetency. In a unanimous decision, the U.S. Supreme Court reversed, holding that to place the burden of proof of incompetency on the defendant offended a principle of justice that was deeply rooted in the traditions and conscience of the American people.

Another fair trial case, accepted for review in 1997, was *United States v. Scheffer* (1997), where the Court agreed to consider the question of whether a defendant can be barred from presenting favorable polygraph evidence as part of his right to present his defense under the Sixth Amendment. Rule 707 of the Military Rules of Evidence bars polygraph evidence in court-martial proceedings. Does the rule apply to evidence for the accused as well as evidence against him?

Losing litigants, especially those convicted of crime, regularly complain that counsel was ineffective. Indeed, in many cases, evidentiary errors not preserved for review are turned into claims that counsel provided ineffective representation. As ineffective assistance of counsel is an issue of constitutional dimension a significant number of habeas petitions are grounded on that claim. Petitioners, however, were soon faced with the procedural problem of when and where to bring the claim in federal court with conflicting decisions abounding whether a federal defendant who failed to raise the claim on his direct appeal was precluded from raising same on a collateral attack of the conviction. In *Massaro v. United States* (2003) the Supreme Court resolved the issue by holding that whether or not the petitioner raised ineffective counsel as an issue on appeal he or she could bring the claim on a habeas petition.

In 2004 the Supreme Court broadened the scope of the confrontation clause of the Sixth Amendment by holding in *Crawford v. Washington* that out-of-court testimonial statements, such as those given to a police officer during questioning of a witness, are inadmissible because the defendant had no opportunity to cross-examine that person, regardless of how reliable the statement might be. The rule, however, applies only to statements sought to be used against the defendant. And, of course, Crawford is limited to testimonial statements which the Court did not explicitly define which sets the stage for continuing litigation of what is testimonial and what is not such as in *Davis v. Washington*, holding 911 emergency calls to the police are not.

Eighth Amendment

In over 200 years of existence, the U.S. Supreme Court paid almost no attention to the criminal justice system—until the 1960s. The post–World War II years have been a period when increasingly the Court has been concerned with individual rights rather than property rights, and part of that concern reflected itself in new interpretations of the Fourth, Fifth, Sixth, and Eighth Amendments. The Fourth Amendment dealing with police procedure was the first to receive attention, followed over the years by the Fifth Amendment, dealing with confessions and double jeopardy, and the Sixth Amendment, dealing with the right to counsel and fair trial. At the present time, however, it is the Eighth Amendment, dealing with sentencing that is at the top of the Court's agenda in the area of criminal justice.

The Eighth Amendment speaks of cruel and unusual punishment. The cases coming before the Court can be divided roughly into three categories: cases dealing with the death penalty, with unsatisfactory prison conditions, and with disproportionate sentencing in nondeath penalty cases. Most of the appeals from the death penalty come via a writ of habeas corpus asking the federal court to review certain procedural questions that the prisoner alleges violated his or her constitutional rights.

In *Herrera v. Collins* (1993), Herrera alleged that newly discovered evidence of his innocence had been discovered that entitled him to a new trial. The evidence consisted in part of affidavits tending to show that his now dead brother had committed the murders, evidence that was not available to him at the time of his original trial. Herrera's claim, however, was made 10 years after his original conviction, while under Texas law a new trial motion based on newly discovered evidence must be made within 30 days of the imposition of sentence. The U.S. Supreme Court denied Herrera's motion holding that the Texas limitation on the introduction of new evidence, even evidence purporting to show the defendant's innocence, was not a denial of fundamental fairness and did not violate Herrera's due process rights.

In another case, *McCleskey v. Zant* (1991), McCleskey claimed in his petition for habeas corpus that the evidence used to convict him had been obtained improperly from a prisoner in an adjoining cell and should have been excluded on the basis of the decision in *Massiah v. United States* (1964). In the Massiah case, the police had wired Massiah's codefendant, who had agreed to turn informer, and had him elicit damaging admissions after Massiah had been indicted and was without the presence of his attorney.

McCleskey's problem, however, was that although he might have prevailed on the merits of his Massiah claim, he had previously made several petitions for habeas corpus at both the state and federal levels, some of which did not include the Massiah claim, although 18 other claims had been made. The U.S. Supreme Court rejected his application for habeas corpus on the ground that he had abused the writ by filing multiple claims, some of which did not raise the Massiah issue. In both Herrera and McCleskey, three justices dissented, holding that in the case of the death sentence and its ultimate finality, technical procedural rules should not bar meritorious claims.

More recently, the attitude of the Court concerning technical procedural rules has, on the whole, become increasingly punitive. In *Lambrix v. Singletary* (1997), when Lambrix was convicted of first-degree murder in Florida, the jury was erroneously instructed on one of many aggravating factors. He was sentenced to death and appealed his sentence. While the appeal was pending, the Supreme Court decided *Espinosa v. Florida* (1992), which held that neither the judge nor the jury can consider invalid aggravating circumstances. Lambrix claimed that Espinosa should be applied retroactively to his sentence. In a five-to-four decision written by Justice Scalia, the Court held that Espinosa could not be applied retroactively because the Espinosa decision was a new rule, and the Court has a general policy against new rules being applied retroactively.

Another application of the "new rule" principal was *O'Dell v. Netherland* (1997). O'Dell was convicted of rape and murder in 1988, and sentenced to death. The jury was never informed that had it rejected the death sentence; O'Dell could have been sentenced to life imprisonment without the possibility of parole. Six years later, in 1994, in *Simmons v. South Carolina* (1994), the U.S. Supreme Court ruled that a capital defendant who is described as a future threat to society (as was O'Dell) has a due process right to have the jury know that he or she will never get out of prison if the jury spares his or her life. In 1997, O'Dell had not yet been executed. The question before the Court, thus, was whether the Simmons precedent should apply, invalidating O'Dell's death sentence. In a five-to-four decision, written by Justice Thomas, the Court held that new rules of constitutional law should not be available to state prison inmates who are seeking federal court review through petitions of habeas corpus. The Simmons holding was a new rule and therefore did not apply to O'Dell. The dissenters, Justices Stevens, Breyer, Souter, and Ginsberg, held that Simmons was not a new rule but a bedrock principle of a full and fair hearing.

Another death penalty case not involving the propriety of a request for a writ of habeas corpus was *Payne v. Tennessee* (1991). Payne was convicted of first-degree murder of a mother and her two-year-old daughter and assault on her three-year-old son. At the penalty phase of Payne's trial, the state called as a witness the victim's mother, who described the devastating effect on the family, and especially on the remaining child, of the crime. The constitutional question presented was whether a capital sentencing jury could, under the Eighth Amendment, consider victim impact evidence. Two previous precedents, *Booth v. Maryland* (1987) and *South Carolina v. Gathers* (1989), barred the admission of victim impact statements during the penalty phase of a capital trial, on the ground that the jury should consider only evidence relevant to the character of the offense and the character of the defendant. Impact statements that tend to differentiate victims on the basis of their different roles or value to society served no purpose but to inflame the jury. In Payne, the Court overruled the two previous precedents and held that the impact might properly be considered as an aggravating circumstance, related to the crime itself.

Another group of cases decided recently by the U.S. Supreme Court deals with prison conditions. In *Wilson v. Seiter* (1991), Wilson claimed that the overall prison conditions under which she was confined constituted cruel and unusual punishment. The Court rejected her claim, holding that it is incumbent on the petitioner both to specify the particulars of the allegedly unconstitutional conditions of confinement and to relate them to a policy of deliberate indifference on the part of prison officials.

On the other hand, in *Hudson v. McMillian* (1992), Hudson alleged that his Eighth Amendment rights were violated by the beating he received by state correctional officers. He was beaten while handcuffed and shackled following an argument with Officer McMillian, one of the prison guards. Hudson received minor bruises, facial swelling, loosened teeth, and a cracked dental plate. The supervisor on duty watched the beating and simply told the guards "not to have too much fun." At the federal court of appeals level, Hudson's claim was disallowed on the ground that inmates alleging excessive force in violation of the Eighth Amendment must prove significant injury, and since Hudson required no medical attention, his claim was dismissed. In a seven-to-two decision, the U.S. Supreme Court disagreed, holding that unnecessary and wanton infliction of pain violated the Constitution regardless of the extent of the injury.

In 1993, in *Helling v. McKinney*, McKinney brought suit against Nevada prison officials, claiming that his health was jeopardized by his cellmate, who was a heavy smoker, forcing him to breathe secondhand smoke whenever he was in his cell. The U.S. Supreme Court agreed that it was not necessary for McKinney to show that his confinement represented deliberate indifference on the part of the prison administration to his health needs, but that he was not entitled to a directed verdict, only to a hearing in which he could prove that the cigarette smoke was injurious to his health.

The remainder of the Eighth Amendment cases relate to disproportionate sentences—determining whether, as Gilbert and Sullivan said, "the punishment fits the crime." Many of these cases were triggered by the relatively recent implementation of federal sentencing guidelines, which punish drug possession very harshly and also allow for forfeiture of property thought to have been obtained through illegal drug activities. RICO (racketeer-influenced corrupt organizations), a federal law that provides for property seizure before conviction, is also giving rise to increasing litigation in this area.

In *Harmelin v. Michigan* (1991), the Court permitted imposition, under Michigan law, of a mandatory sentence of life imprisonment without parole for a nonviolent first offense: possession of more than 650 grams of cocaine. Harmelin contended that the mandatory nature of the sentence did not permit consideration of mitigating factors in his case. In a five-to-four decision, the Court held that although such a severe penalty might be unconstitutional for some crimes, Harmelin's sentence under Michigan law for having 2 pounds of cocaine in his possession was constitutional, even though under federal law he would have been sentenced to about 10 years. Two justices, Scalia and Rehnquist, went so far as to say that short of the death sentence, proportionality in sentencing was irrelevant in terms of the Eighth Amendment—that any prison sentence was constitutional.

Justices Kennedy, O'Connor, and Souter, however, said that although Harmelin's sentence was acceptable, the Eighth Amendment could invalidate grossly disproportionate sentences. White, Blackmun, Stevens, and Marshall dissented, holding that the sentence was disproportionate and unconstitutional. White noted that only one other state, Alabama, imposed a mandatory life sentence without parole for a first-time drug offender. Under Michigan law, Harmelin would have received a five-year sentence.

The Court revisited the excessive punishment question in *Kansas v. Hendricks* (1997). In 1994, Kansas enacted the Sexually Violent Predator Law, which allowed for the civil commitment of persons who, due to a mental abnormality or personality defect, are likely to engage in predatory acts of sexual violence. The act was invoked for the first time to commit Leroy Hendricks, an inmate who had a long history of sexually molesting children, and who had been scheduled for release from prison shortly after the act became law. Hendricks, who had been sentenced to 10 years in prison, challenged the law as violating the federal constitution due process, ex post facto, and double jeopardy clauses. The question before the Court was whether Hendricks could be confined in a state hospital for the mentally ill after he had completed his prison term even though he did not meet the standards for civil commitment under state law. Once again, Justice Thomas held in a five-to-four decision that Hendricks' continued confinement was not punishment but was a method the state had chosen to protect communities from violent sexual predators. The same dissenters as in O'Dell disagreed, holding that Hendricks' confinement was basically punitive because he was simply being restrained, not treated for his mental problems. The law could be constitutional if it were applied prospectively and if it provided treatment and not simply incarceration.

In Hendricks, Kansas sought to imprison an offender for longer than his original sentence. *Lynce v. Mathis* (1997), however, originated in Florida's attempt to shorten sentences as a means of clearing out overcrowded prisons. In 1983, because of overcrowding in its prisons, Florida enacted a law giving early release credit to inmates when the population of the prisons exceeded certain limits. In 1992, frightened by the number of violent criminals who were being released, Florida passed another law canceling credits for certain types of offenders. Lynce had been sentenced to 22 years in 1986 for attempted murder and was released in 1992 before enactment of the new law on the basis of the credit accumulated under the 1983 law. When the 1992 law went into effect, he was rearrested because his release credits had been canceled. He then went to federal court asking for a writ of habeas corpus on the ground that the application of the 1992 law was ex post facto and therefore, unconstitutional. On appeal, the U.S. Supreme Court held seven to two for Lynce.

Several 1993 cases were related to seizure of property from criminals and suspects, particularly in drug cases. In *United States v. a Parcel of Land* (1993), the Court, by a six-to-three vote, interpreted a federal drug forfeiture law to provide an exception for innocent owners. A woman was permitted to defend her house against forfeiture on the ground that she did not know that the money used to buy the house came from her boyfriend's drug dealing. In a second case, *Austin v. United States* (1993), the Court unanimously left to the lower courts the decision as to when a forfeiture violated the Eighth Amendment. Austin was the owner of a small body shop in South Dakota and lost his business and his mobile home, worth a total of $38,000, in addition to $4,000 in cash, when he sold 2 grams of cocaine to an undercover agent.

In a third case, *Alexander v. United States* (1993), the owner of a chain of adult bookstores and movie houses forfeited his businesses and almost $9 million in profits after he was convicted of racketeering by selling obscene material. Alexander had raised both an Eighth Amendment claim against excessive fines and a First Amendment claim relating to the destruction of books and other materials that were not obscene. His Eighth Amendment claim was unanimously upheld, but his First Amendment claim was narrowly rejected by a five-to-four vote. A remaining issue that the Court has undertaken to decide is the right to advance notice and hearing in forfeiture cases.

CRIMINAL JUSTICE ISSUES NOT RELATED TO THE BILL OF RIGHTS

An old issue that has surfaced for the Court in a new form is the question of how much control the federal government has over state and local enforcement of a federal law. Gun control brought the issue to a head. In 1968, Congress passed the Gun Control Act, which prohibited firearms dealers from selling handguns to certain categories of persons, such as minors or convicted felons. In 1993, Congress amended the act by enacting the Brady Bill, which required gun dealers to have prospective purchasers fill out certain forms to show that they are not in the prohibited classes. These forms were to be submitted to the chief law enforcement officer of the district, who was to ascertain whether the purchaser had a right to buy a gun. The sheriffs of two counties in Montana and Arizona challenged the constitutionality of the act, claiming that the federal government could not impose such duties on them. In *Printz v. United States* (1997), Justice Scalia, writing for the majority of the Court, agreed, holding that the federal government may not compel the states to enact or administer a federal regulatory program. In dissent, Justice Stevens wrote that the commerce power provided sufficient ground to support the regulations, besides which, the intent of the Founding Fathers, as expressed in the Federalist Papers, was to enhance the power of the new government to act directly upon local officials.

CONCLUSIONS

The function of the Bill of Rights in the Twenty-First Century, even as in the eighteenth century, will be to protect minorities, even minorities of one, against majorities. Criminal defendants are minorities, and the last 30 years, on the whole, have seen a generous interpretation of the Bill of Rights in their favor, a generosity which at the time of this writing appears to be waning somewhat with a spate of cases designed to test antiterrorism laws against established civil rights, but the body of the constitution exists to create and maintain a government for the benefit of the majority. The question then becomes, whose right shall prevail?

The post–World War II era has been a time of concern for minority rights, probably in reaction to the horrors resulting from the wholesale overriding of those rights in such countries as Germany and the Soviet Union. At the present time there seems to be no like-lihood that there will be a sweeping denial of basic human rights in the foreseeable future in the United States, but increasing crime and violence are straining the social fabric. The degree of success in dealing with those strains will determine the shape of the criminal justice system in the twenty-first century.

CASES

Aleman v. Illinois, 136 L.Ed.2d 868 (1997).

Alexander v. United States, 113 S.Ct. 2766 (1993).

Apprendi v. New Jersey, 540 U.S. 466 (2000).

Austin v. United States, 113 S.Ct. 2801 (1993).

Berger v. New York, 388 U.S. 41 (1967).

Bond v. United States, 529 U.S. 334 (2000).

Booth v. Maryland, 482 U.S. 496 (1987).

Brecht v. Abrahamson, 113 S.Ct. 1710 (1993).

Brewer v. Williams, 430 U.S. 387 (1977).

California v. Greenwood, 486 U.S. 35 (1988).

Cooper v. Oklahoma, 517 U.S. 348 (1996).

Crawford v. Washington, 541 U.S. 36 (2004).

Dickerson v. United States, 147 L.Ed.2d 405 (2000).

Escobedo v. Illinois, 378 U.S. 478 (1964).

Espinosa v. Florida, 505 U.S. 1079 (1992).

Felker v. Turpin, 518 U.S. 1051 (1997).

Florida v. Bostick, 111 S.Ct. 2382 (1991).

Furman v. Georgia, 408 U.S. 238 (1972).

Georgia v. Randolpoh, U.S. (2006).

Harmelin v. Michigan, 111 S.Ct. 2680 (1991).

Helling v. McKinney, 113 S.Ct. 2475 (1993).

Herrera v. Collins, 113 S.Ct. 853 (1993).

Holt v. Sarver, 309 Fed. Supp. 881 (1972); affirmed 501 F.2d 1291 (5th Cir. 1974).

Hudson v. McMillian, 503 U.S. 995 (1992).

Hudson v. United States, 92 F.3d 1026 (10th Cir. 1996), accepted for review by U.S. Supreme Court, April 14, 1997.

Hurley and South Boston Allied War Veterans v. Irish-American Gay, Lesbian and Bisexual Group, 132 L.Ed.2d 487; 515 U.S. (1995).

Illinois v. Gates, 462 U.S. 2113 (1983).

Kansas v. Hendricks, 138 L.Ed.2d 501; 521 U.S. (1997).

Lambrix v. Singletary, 520 U.S. 518 (1997).

Lindh v. Murphy, 138 L.Ed.2d 481 (1997).

Lynce v. Mathis, 137 L.Ed.2d 63; 519 U.S. 443 (1997).

Mapp v. Ohio, 367 U.S. 642 (1961).

Maryland v. Wilson, 519 U.S. 408 (1997).

Massaro v. United States, U.S. (2003).

Massiah v. United States, 377 U.S. 201 (1964).

McClesky v. Zant, 111 S.Ct. 2841 (1991).

Miller-el v. Cockrell, U.S. (2003).

Minnesota v. Dickerson, 113 S.Ct. 2130 (1993).

Miranda v. Arizona, 384 U.S. 436 (1966).

New York v. Quarles, 467 U.S. 649 (1984).

Nix v. Williams, 467 U.S. 431 (1984).

O'Dell v. Netherland, 138 L.Ed.2d 351 (1997).

Ohio v. Robinette, 519 U.S. 33 (1996).

Oliver v. United States, 466 U.S. 170 (1984).

Payne v. Tennessee, 111 S.Ct. 2597 (1991).

Payton v. New York, 445 U.S. 573 (1980).

Pennsylvania v. Mimms, 434 U.S. 573 (1977).

People v. Rosen, 96 N.Y.2d 329 (2001).

Printz v. United States, 521 U.S. 98 (1997).

Rhode Island v. Innes, 446 U.S. 291 (1980).

Richards v. Wisconsin, 520 U.S. 385 (1997)

Schenck v. Pro-Choice Network, 519 U.S. 357 (1997).

Simmons v. South Carolina, 512 U.S. 154 (1994).

South Carolina v. Gathers, 109 S.Ct. 2207 (1989).

Steagald v. United States, 451 U.S. 204 (1981).

Stone v. Powell, 428 U.S. 465 (1976).

Terry v. Ohio, 392 U.S. 1 (1968).

United States v. a Parcel of Land, 61 U.S.L.W. 4189 (1993).

United States v. Dixon, 113 S.Ct. 2849 (1993).

United States v. Leon, 468 U.S. 897 (1984).

United States v. Lovell, 317 F. Supp. 2nd 663 (W.D. Va. 2004).

United States v. Scheffer, 117 S.Ct. 1817 (1997).

United States v. Ursery, 518 U.S. 267 (1996).

Weems v. United States, 217 U.S. 349 (1910).

Wilson v. Seiter, 111 S.Ct. 2321 (1991).

Wisconsin v. Mitchell, 113 S.Ct. 2194 (1993).

Withrow v. Williams, 113 S.Ct. 1745 (1993).

Chapter 22

Trends in the Use of Capital Punishment

At the Dawn of the Twenty-First Century

David V. Baker

ABSTRACT

Early death penalty scholars identified trends in capital punishment suggestive of a movement away from its use in the United States including abolition of the penalty, reduction in capital offenses, permissive death sentences, reduction in the number of executions, selective enforcement of the death penalty, private executions, and swift and painless executions. This chapter explores the proposition that the trends in the use of capital punishment in the last half century are inaccurate predictors of the future of capital punishment in this country.

INTRODUCTION

Early death penalty scholars identified major trends suggestive of a movement away from the use of capital punishment in the United States.[1] These trends generally included an international and domestic movement toward the abolition of capital punishment, reduction in the number of capital offenses and subsequent executions, the use of permissive rather than mandatory death sentences, selective enforcement of capital punishment to marginalized groups, the exclusion of public executions, and the use of swift and painless execution methods. This chapter explores the proposition that the trends in the use of capital punishment in the last half century, while discerning, remain inaccurate predictors of a movement away from capital punishment in the new century in this country. In this regard, more recent scholarship has identified equally powerful trends in the use of capital punishment that predict greater use of the death penalty in the United States as we move quickly into the twenty-first century. This is particularly the case in the context of selective execution. It is not by happenstance that capital defendants are poor; that bigotry and intolerance accent prosecutorial selection of capital cases; that prosecutors use peremptory challenges to enhance the "whiteness" of capital juries; that prosecutorial wrongdoing is unrelenting in capital cases; that rampant prosecutorial and judicial homophobia accent capital cases involving gay and lesbian defendants; that prosecutors exploit the mental incapacities of capital defendants; that gross ineffectiveness pervades indigent capital defense; that prosecutorial lawlessness and false confessions often underscore wrongful convictions and the execution of innocent defendants of color; and that predominantly white and often racist juries pervade the capital punishment system.

THE UNITED STATES HAS FAILED TO JOIN THE INTERNATIONAL COMMUNITY AND ITS MOVEMENT TOWARD THE ABOLITION OF CAPITAL PUNISHMENT

An international movement against capital punishment represented a major trend away from the use of the death penalty among early death penalty scholars immediately following World War II since at the time several countries had abandoned the practice.[2] Accordingly, postwar surveys dispelled a then popular notion that countries revived death penalty statutes following periods of war. Postwar surveys showed that several European countries and at least one Latin American nation had abrogated the punishment in the 1940s.[3] The restoration of death penalty statutes witnessed in Italy, Austria, and Romania identified by early scholars were merely hold over fascist measures from World War II, and only Austria retained postwar statutes. England and France were the only European democracies that retained capital punishment for peacetime crimes. The surveys revealed that nations had abolished capital punishment more frequently in the immediate aftermath of World War II than in previous wartime periods.[4]

A worldwide movement continues today with all but a few of the world's industrialized nations prohibiting the death penalty. Despite continued use of the death penalty in the United States and a few other rogue countries, there is a strong international trend toward abolishing capital punishment. When Amnesty International convened its first global convention on capital punishment in Stockholm in 1977, only 16 countries had abrogated the use of the death penalty.[5] Since then, the United Nations Commission on Human Rights has passed a resolution every year appealing to death penalty countries to institute moratoriums. Presently, some 123 countries have banned capital punishment in law or practice.[6] Of these countries, 86 prohibit the death penalty for all crimes,[7] 11 forbid the penalty for ordinary crimes only,[8] and 26 disallow capital punishment in practice.[9] At least half of the countries prohibiting the death penalty for all crimes have implemented constitutional provisions against capital punishment, and five other countries impose constitutional limitations to its use.[10] Some 89 member states of the United Nations have adopted the resolution as of April 2005, an increase of five countries over 2004.[11]

Interestingly, all countries with English legal systems have abolished capital punishment except for the United States.[12] Most European and Latin American nations have banned capital punishment,[13] and every member of the European Union has outlawed capital punishment believing it to be a "throwback to the Middle Ages."[14] The South Korean Ministry of Justice recently announced that to protect human rights it is considering abolishing capital punishment and replacing the penalty with life imprisonment.[15] The Judicial Committee of the Privy Council abolished mandatory death sentencing for persons convicted of murder in the Bahamas because it violates the country's constitution, rendering the cases of current death row inmates ripe for review. The death penalty remains lawful in the Caribbean region but authorities have executed relatively few prisoners since 1973.[16] Philippine President Gloria Macapagal-Arroyo has spared the lives of some 1,230 death row prisoners by ordering the commutation of all death sentences to life in prison. Although the Philippines government abolished the death penalty in 1987, its Congress reimposed capital punishment in 1994. Since resuming executions in 1999, the Philippine government has executed seven defendants by lethal injection.[17] The Philippine Congress voted recently to repeal the death penalty and Amnesty International has called on President Arroyo to enact the legislation into law.[18] Although France outlawed the death penalty in 1981, the French National Assembly and Senate have voted overwhelmingly to pass an amendment officially inscribing a prohibition against capital punishment into its constitution. Former Justice Minister Robert Badinter told French lawmakers, "We are accomplishing the wish of Victor Hugo in 1848, the pure, simple, irreversible abolition of the death penalty."[19] As one expert concludes, "There is a global tide against the death penalty which has left us with just the hardened countries still using it."[20] Many commentators believe that several other countries would abide if the United States were to abolish the death penalty.[21]

With more countries than ever sponsoring the United Nations resolution, there has been an international reduction in executions. Despite the impressive record of the United Nations Commission on Human Rights and Amnesty International to end executions globally, however, about half of the world's nations retain capital punishment.[22] Most Middle Eastern and Asian countries have capital punishment, and retentionist countries account for 3,800 executions and 7,400 death sentences imposed annually.[23] Still, it is impractical for international observers to determine precisely how many prisoners nations execute annually because "many countries deliberately keep the true numbers of those executed secret, belying the supposed deterrent value of the death penalty."[24] In 2005, at least 22 countries executed 2,148 people,[25] and at least 53 countries sentenced 5,186 persons to death.[26] Amnesty International warns, however, that these are only minimum figures since the true figures are certainly higher—the total figure for those currently condemned to death and awaiting execution may be as high as 20,000 persons.[27]

China, Iran, Saudi Arabia, and the United States carry out the vast majority of executions internationally and together account for 94 percent of all executions worldwide. In 2005, China executed at least 1,700 people, Iran executed at least 94 people, Saudi Arabia executed 86 persons, and the United States executed 59 condemned prisoners. Amnesty International estimates from legal experts, local officials, and judges that China may have executed as many as 8,000 prisons, but official statistics on the death penalty are mostly unavailable because China considers capital punishment issues state secrets.[28] One researcher points out that China executes thousands of condemned criminals especially during periodic "Strike Hard" anticrime campaigns.[29] Others speculate that China may be executing as many as 10,000 persons a year, and still others argue the actual number of executions is 12,000 per year.[30] What's more, since at least the 1980s there has been mounting international concern that supplying China's lucrative organ transplant industry may be one reason for such excessive executions in that country.[31] One estimate is that executed prisoners in China unwittingly donate between 2,000 and 3,000 organs per year—4,500 in 1989. Organ transplants have risen sharply since the mid-1990s—from 18,500 between 1994 and 1999—to 60,000 from 2000 to 2005.[32] China earns approximately $100 million in annual organ sales.[33] The United States has also proposed using condemned prisoners as donors to curb its insurmountable need for organ transplants.[34]

Despite an international movement away from the use of capital punishment, one can gather from the discussion above that the United States is willing to join the international community and outlaw the death penalty. What's more, the United States is one of only two countries worldwide that has *not* ratified the International Covenant on the Rights of the Child.[35] International standards of human rights prohibit child executions, but U.S. authorities have executed more child offenders than any other country since 1990 and account for 70 percent of child executions worldwide since 1998.[36] Although the United States has recently banned the execution of persons convicted of capital offenses as juveniles, it still has some 2,225 youth offenders serving life sentences without parole.[37] The Democratic Republic of Congo, Iran, Nigeria, Pakistan, Saudi Arabia, and Yemen also execute child offenders. Iran, for instance, has executed 11 child offenders since 1990 and the executions of some 30 other child offenders are pending.[38] Reportedly, Iranian authorities recently sentenced to death two child offenders in violation of international human rights law, and in response, Amnesty International has requested that Iran end the use of the death penalty for child offenders.[39]

DOMESTIC ABOLITIONISTS HAVE FAILED TO MOVE THE UNITED STATES TOWARD OUTLAWING CAPITAL PUNISHMENT

Early researchers discerned a movement away from the use of capital punishment in the United States and rejected the notion that states were reviving the death penalty simply because some states had restored capital punishment after abrogation. In fact, most state legislatures were simply indecisive on abolition; while legislatures of abolitionist states were periodically restoring capital punishment, legislatures in retentionist states were abandoning the penalty.[40] Some states have long legislative histories of rejecting efforts to restore the death penalty. In 1846 Michigan became the first state to abolish the death penalty for all crimes except treason. Michigan abolished capital punishment because it had no extensive history of executing condemned inmates since officials had not conducted an execution since 1830, and because there were no established religious groups opposing the penalty as elsewhere in the country.[41] It is more likely that the people of Michigan became distrusting of justice officials after the hanging of Patrick Fitzpatrick in 1835 for rape-murder. The authorities later found Fitzpatrick innocent when his roommate confessed to the crime. Rhode Island and Wisconsin abolished the death penalty for all crimes in 1852 and 1853, respectively. Unitarians, Universalists, and Quakers led the abolition of the death penalty in Rhode Island, and Wisconsin eliminated capital punishment after the gruesome hanging execution of John McCaffary in May 1851 for the murder of his wife Bridget. Before some 3,000 spectators, McCaffary struggled for eight minutes suspended at the end of the rope, and a full eighteen minutes passed before a physician pronounced him dead.[42]

Over the next few decades, debate on capital punishment waned considerably when state legislatures became increasingly concerned with the tumultuous events surrounding the Civil War.[43] Maine abolished the death penalty in 1876, reinstated it in 1883, and abolished it again in 1887. Iowa abolished the death penalty in 1872 but reversed itself in 1878, and Colorado abrogated the death penalty in 1897 but restored it in 1901. Eleven states banned capital punishment between 1907 and 1918 even though five of these states eventually reinstated the punishment. Abolition obviously lost much of its appeal to state legislatures between the 1920s and the 1940s when jurisdictions executed some 4,300 prisoners over the period.[44] Recently, and after more than 150 years without capital punishment, Wisconsin's state legislature passed a resolution calling for an advisory referendum to restore the death penalty, but Michigan defeated a similar move to reintroduce the death penalty in 2004.[45]

Legislative reforms to capital punishment laws over the last several decades have proven more successful than total abrogation of the penalty.[46] Most changes to state death penalty statutes over the years have involved adding aggravating and mitigating factors, adding categories of victims, establishing procedural amendments, and altering execution methods.[47] States have generally revised their death penalty statutes to reflect the U.S. Supreme Court substantive law holdings in *Atkins v. Virginia* (prohibiting the execution of mentally retarded persons) and in *Roper v. Simmons* (barring the execution of juvenile offenders).[48] Even so, Alaska, Hawaii, Iowa, Maine, Massachusetts, Michigan, Minnesota, North Dakota, Rhode Island, Vermont, West Virginia, Wisconsin, and the District of Columbia have no death penalty laws, while the remaining 38 states, the federal government, and the U.S. military retain capital punishment.[49] Several state legislatures have proposed moratoriums on capital punishment only to have the bills defeated in judiciary committees.[50]

Some 4,000 groups across the United States have joined calls for moratoriums on capital punishment.[51] In one instance, a recent report has demanded a moratorium in Georgia on prosecuting capital cases and stopping executions because the state's death penalty statute fails to meet some 43 established standards for improving the fairness and accuracy of the punishment.[52] What's more, the report urged Georgia to correct for inadequate funding for defense counsel, the lack of representation for state habeas appeals, racial disparities in capital sentencing, and an inappropriate burden of proof for defendants with mental retardation. In 2004, the U.S. Conference of Catholic Bishops

(USCCB) called for an end to capital punishment in the United States noting that the death penalty "contributes to a cycle of violence in our society that must be broken." The statement, drafted by the USCCB Domestic Policy Committee, is the first comprehensive statement focused on the death penalty by the Catholic bishops of the United States in 25 years and is part of a wider "Catholic Campaign to End the Use of the Death Penalty." The program aims to improve victims' services, to educate Catholics and other citizens about the Church's teachings regarding the death penalty, and to advocate for an end to capital punishment in the United States. Several states and the federal government have implemented death penalty study commissions.[53]

One reason why execution moratoriums are gaining momentum among death penalty states is that public support for capital punishment is waning. A recent Gallup poll shows support for capital punishment is at its lowest level in 27 years with 64 percent supporting the death penalty.[54] A recent survey found that support for the death penalty among Catholics had dropped from 70 percent in the 1970s to fewer than 50 percent in 2005.[55] Still, in some states, namely California, death penalty proponents outnumber opponents 2 to 1. To many capital punishment supporters, the penalty is alive and well in the United States and there is little chance that the U.S. Supreme Court or Congress will strike down the punishment in the near future or even impose a national moratorium since most Americans support capital punishment.[56] As Richard Dieter, executive director of the Death Penalty Information Center, recently commented, "I don't think the country is about to get rid of the death penalty . . . but overall, the trend shows some rethinking and hesitance. . . . Because of flaws in the system and economics, everything is now being given a fresh look."[57]

THE UNITED STATES HAS FAILED TO HONOR ITS TREATY OBLIGATIONS CONCERNING FOREIGN NATIONALS AND THE DEATH PENALTY

Any discussion of an international or domestic movement away from the use of capital punishment must acknowledge the deliberate indifference of the United States to the 1963 Vienna Convention on Consular Relations and Optional Protocols. Pursuant to Article 36 of the treaty, local arresting authorities of all 165 signatories are required to notify without delay detained foreign nationals of their right to communicate with their respective consular representative. Ratified by the U.S. Senate in 1969, the provision assures that unfamiliar legal systems do not subject foreign nationals to trial and condemn them to death without the benefit of support from authorities of their native countries. The Optional Protocol to the treaty, proposed by the United States and ratified by the U.S. Senate, concedes jurisdiction over claims of foreign nationals denied consular rights to the International Court of Justice (ICJ) in The Hague—also known as *The World Court*. While U.S. authorities insist that foreign governments promptly advise the more than 6,000 Americans jailed in foreign countries of their right to contact their consular representative,[58] state and federal officials regularly ignore consulate rights to foreign nationals arrested in the United States.[59]

In the context of capital punishment, *foreign nationals* are noncitizens under a sentence of death in a state or federal jurisdiction. Presently, 16 states and the federal government house 119 foreign nationals representing 32 different nationalities on death row. Most of these foreign prisoners are Mexican nationals held in California, Texas, and Florida. Mexico recently sued the United States in the ICJ claiming that American authorities denied consular rights to 51 Mexican nationals. In *Mexico v. United States*,[60] the ICJ held that an arresting authority must notify foreign nationals of their consular rights when officials realize the person is a foreign national or they have grounds to believe the person is a foreign national.[61] Finding only one case in which authorities recognized consular rights, the ICJ ordered new hearings for the death row prisoners.[62] In response to the ICJ ruling, President George W. Bush directed U.S. Attorney General Alberto Gonzales to abide by the ICJ holding and review the cases in February 2005.[63] In an abrupt turnaround one month later, however, U.S. Secretary of State Condoleezza Rice conveyed to U.N. Secretary General Kofi Annan that the United States was immediately withdrawing from the optional protocol and refused to recognize ICJ authority over the cases. Some experts argue that President Bush's directive on the optional protocol had nothing to do with the death penalty. Rather the administration contrived the directive to contravene international law ostensibly over the Iraq War and "new revelations of torture and other criminal activity by the U.S. military."[64]

Nine justices of the Texas Court of Criminal Appeals rebuffed both President Bush's directive and that of the World Court in the case of Jose Ernesto Medellin, a Mexican national convicted of the rape and murder of two teenage girls in 1993. Per Presiding Justice Sharon Keller, "The president has made an admirable attempt to resolve a complicated issue involving the United States' international obligations, but the unprecedented, unnecessary and intrusive exercise of power over the Texas court system cannot be supported by foreign policy authority conferred on him by the United States Constitution."[65] Texas is now free to proceed with Medellin's execution despite violation of his consular rights. To international experts, the United States is playing a very dangerous game with the lives of Americans detained every year while traveling abroad.

> In some instances, the only thing standing between torture and/or the death of U.S. citizens being detained is the ability to ask for assistance from American consular officials. By denying that same basic human right to foreign visitors, the United States could be condemning its citizens to the same fate. Moreover, it gravely undermines U.S. credibility and sends the message that the United States is a nation that only honors its commitments to its allies if and when it is convenient.[66]

Since 1976, Louisiana, Florida, Texas, California, Arizona, Oklahoma, Virginia, and Nevada together have executed 23 foreign nationals without informing the defendants of their consulate rights. Roughly 27 percent of these executed prisoners were Mexican nationals despite repeated diplomatic and judicial efforts by Mexican officials to stop the executions.[67] Of the 160 death sentences imposed on foreign nationals in the United States (including executed defendants and persons whose cases courts reversed on appeal or released), researchers have identified only seven cases where U.S. authorities afforded foreign nationals compliance with the Vienna Convention.[68] In other cases, it was weeks, months, and in some cases years before detained foreign nationals learned of their consular rights. Even then, attorneys and other prisoners informed defendants of their consular rights rather than local arresting authorities as required by the treaty. Consequently, "consular officials were often unable to provide crucial assistance to their nationals when it would be most beneficial: at the arrest and pretrial stage of capital cases."[69] The refusal of Arizona officials to inform two German nationals, brothers Karl and Walter LaGrand, of their consular rights until just prior to their executions in February and March 1999—17 years after their arrests—illustrates the indifference of U.S. authorities to recognize the consular rights of foreign nationals.[70] Two years earlier, Texas executed Irineo Tristan Montoya (a Mexican national) knowing that arresting authorities had not informed Montoya of his consular rights. Equally ominous is that Texas authorities forced Montoya to sign an English written confession despite his inability to read and write the language.[71] Recently, a Virginia judge prohibited state prosecutors from seeking the death penalty against a Vietnamese man because arresting police officers violated his Vienna Convention rights by failing to inform the defendant that he could contact his embassy. In a related context, trial evidence brought forward in a noncapital case involving a Danish national denied consular rights by the New York Police Department revealed that officials afforded consular rights to only four of the more than 53,000 foreign nationals arrested in New York City in 1997.[72]

In November 2005, the U.S. Supreme Court granted certiorari in *Moises Sanchez-Llamas v. Oregon*[73] and *Bustillo v. Johnson*[74] to address the substantive and procedural rights of imprisoned foreign nationals. The Court granted certiorari to address whether Article 36 of the Vienna Convention grants rights that may be invoked by individuals in a judicial proceeding, whether suppression of evidence is a proper remedy for a violation of Article 36, and whether an Article 36 claim may be deemed forfeited under state procedural rules because a defendant failed to raise the claim at trial.[75] Although the cases involved noncapital defendants, the legal questions raised in the cases effect foreign nationals on death row.[76] Taking the cases together, the U.S. Supreme decided in June 2006 that the United States is *not* bound by Article 36 of the Vienna Convention because (1) government officials had withdrawn from the optional protocol and refused to recognize ICJ authority over foreign national cases, (2) that foreign nationals held in state prisons do not have a right to reopen their cases when state authorities violate inmates' rights under the Vienna Convention, and (3) that suppression of incriminating evidence is *not* an appropriate remedy under Article 35 even assuming the Convention creates judicially enforceable rights.

STATE AND FEDERAL GOVERNMENTS HAVE FAILED TO REDUCE THE NUMBER OF CAPITAL OFFENSES

Relying on national prisoner statistics, early researchers evidenced a trend toward reducing the number of capital offenses for crimes not involving murder, including armed robbery, kidnapping, burglary, espionage, and aggravated assault. Today, however, the U.S. Supreme Court restricts imposition of the death penalty to aggravated killings.[77] It is unlawful for death penalty jurisdictions, for instance, to execute rapists where no death results and executions for kidnapping are unconstitutional where victims are not murdered.[78] Still, death penalty jurisdictions insist on including crimes that do not involve killings in their capital statutes. Treason is a capital offense in California, Colorado, Georgia, and Louisiana, and aggravated kidnapping is a capital crime in Georgia, Idaho, Kentucky, and South Carolina. Death sentences are possible for aircraft hijacking in Georgia and Mississippi, aggravated rape of a child under 12 years old in Louisiana, sexual battery in Georgia and Mississippi, and narcotics conspiracy in Florida and New Jersey.[79] Recently, South Carolina's Senate approved a proposal to allow prosecutors to seek the death penalty for sex offenders convicted twice of raping a child younger than 11 years of age.[80] It is difficult to imagine, however, that under an "evolving standard of decency" the U.S. Supreme Court would find execution for any of these enumerated offenses constitutional absent a killing. As a result, while states may have abolished capital punishment for crimes not involving a victim's death, states have also moved comprehensively to expand their capital punishment statutes to include crimes that do not involve killings.

Congress too has expanded the *federal* death penalty over the last few decades. Congress enacted the Anti-Drug Abuse Act in 1988, calling for the death penalty in cases involving murder resulting from a drug-kingpin conspiracy.[81] The 1994 Violent Crime Control and Law Enforcement Act expanded the federal death penalty to 23 *new* offenses including espionage, killing foreign officials, wrecking trains, bank robbery, hostage taking, murder for hire, racketeering, genocide, and carjacking.[82] In 1996, law enforcement officials across the country pressured Congress and President Bill Clinton to expand the federal death penalty statute with the Antiterrorism and Effective Death Penalty Act (AEDPA).[83] The federal system provides for death penalty in cases of murder; treason; espionage; trafficking in large quantity of drugs; and attempting, authorizing, or advising the killing of any officer, juror, or witness in cases involving a continuing criminal enterprise, regardless of whether the killing actually takes place.[84] And since 1994, the federal government has dramatically increased its prosecution of capital defendants. There is no exact count of federal death penalty cases filed nationwide by U.S. Attorneys,[85] but the Federal Death Penalty Resource Counsel estimates that since 1988 federal prosecutors have sought the death penalty against 372 defendants.[86] Most of federal prosecutions involve cases pending appellate review, cases where courts have commuted death sentences to life imprisonment, cases where the government has withdrawn the death penalty, or cases where federal attorneys have discontinued the capital prosecution because of plea bargains before or at trial.

Not surprisingly, prisoners of color are more likely to face federal prosecution for capital offenses than white prisoners and are less likely to plea bargain capital sentences. Prisoners of color are 73 percent of the defendants against whom prosecutors seek the death penalty, and U.S. Attorneys accept plea agreements from 48 percent of white capital defendants, 25 percent of black defendants, and 28 percent from Latino defendants. One outcome of the racial disparity in federal plea agreements from defendants of color is that 75 percent of federal prisoners currently under active death sentence are prisoners of color.[87] The U.S. government has executed three condemned prisoners since its hanging of Victor Feuger in Iowa for murder kidnapping in 1963—federal authorities executed Juan Paul Garza and Timothy McVeigh in 2001 and Louis Jones in 2003. The U.S. military lists 15 separate capital offenses under its Uniform Code of Military Justice even though most are applicable only during wartime—such as desertion or disobeying a superior officer's orders.[88] The U.S. Army Corrections System recently revised its regulations and procedures for carrying out death sentences imposed by military courts—martial or military tribunals in its *Procedures for Military Executions*.[89] Race continues to be a conventional artifact of military executions.[90] Currently, there are six black prisoners, two white prisoners, and one Asian American prisoner on military death row.

One result of less public support for capital punishment may be that juries across the country are sentencing fewer murderers to death even though state prosecutors are seeking the death penalty with the same regularity.[91] Nationwide, death sentences dropped from 317 in 1996, to 125 in 2004, to 106 in 2005, while in the 1990s there were more than 300 death sentences per year. Lower death sentencing rates have lowered the death row population; over the past several years, the death row population in the United States has decreased from 3,652 inmates in 2000 to 3,350 inmates in 2007. Legal experts attribute lower death sentencing rates on growing public awareness of death row exonerations, lower murder rates, and a concern for the lack of substantive legal training for lawyers representing capital offenders.[92] Interestingly, Colorado, Kansas, Kentucky, Maryland, Missouri, Montana, Nebraska, New Jersey, New Mexico, South Dakota, and Washington are currently considering legislation that would repeal capital punishment laws or impose a moratorium. On the other hand, Georgia, Missouri, Texas, Utah, and Virginia are considering legislation that would expand state death penalty laws—Georgia's legislature wants to eliminate the unanimous jury requirement to imposing death sentences, Missouri would make the death penalty mandatory for the killing of a police officer, Texas and Utah legislation would execute repeat sex-offenders whose victims are children, and Virginia wants to include those who are accomplices to murder to the potential list of executed offenders.[93] While some capital punishment states are considering reforms in death penalty laws, states and the federal government are continuing a trend toward capital punishment.

The Racial Penalty Revisited

A consistent pattern of disproportionate execution of black men for rape led early researchers to conclude that rape is a *racial penalty*. Citing figures from the defense in the Martinsville Seven case involving the conviction and execution of seven black youths in 1950 for allegedly raping a white woman, Hartung charged that although state courts had convicted 809 white rapists since 1909, justice authorities did not execute any of these rapists for their crimes. In contrast, Virginia executed 59 black rapists between 1909 and 1949. Hartung claimed that in Louisiana, "Negroes are prosecuted on a charge of aggravated rape, which carries the death penalty. Whites are charged with simple rape, or carnal knowledge, which can carry a sentence as short as one year."[94] In *Coker v. Georgia*, however, the Court declared, "Although rape deserves serious punishment, the death penalty, which is unique in its severity and irrevocability, is an excessive penalty for the rapist who, as such and as opposed to the murderer, does not unjustifiably take human life."[95] Accordingly, the Court argued that the imposition of the death penalty for the rape of an adult woman where death does not result is excessive punishment and thus violates a defendant's Eighth Amendment protection against cruel and unusual punishment.

Although rape no longer qualifies a defendant for capital sentencing absent the death of the victim, a continuing trend in the United States is that black men still receive harsher penalties for rape than do white men. A recent study of rape cases in Indianapolis, for instance, revealed that when compared with other defendants blacks suspected of assaulting white women are more likely to have their cases filed as felonies, they are more likely to receive prison sentences if convicted, and they frequently receive longer sentences than do white men convicted of rape. Jurisdictions treat black men charged with raping black women far less severely.[96] Justice professionals view the rape of black women as less serious than the rape of white women although black women are 12 times more likely than are white women to suffer rape. Judicial bias toward black female rape victims explains why judicial officers afford less serious punishments to rapists of black women.[97]

Despite *Coker*, several states want to return to executing child rapists, including South Carolina, Oklahoma, Louisiana, Florida, and Montana that have enacted laws allowing for the execution of repeat child sex offenders.[98] Louisiana's revised capital punishment statute reads, for instance, "Whoever commits the crime of aggravated rape shall be punished by life imprisonment at hard labor without benefit of parole, probation, or suspension of sentence. However, if the victim was under the age of twelve years . . . the offender shall be punished by death or life imprisonment at hard labor without benefit of parole, probation, or suspension of sentence, in accordance with the determination of the jury."[99] In a consolidated Louisiana case, separate juries in distinct cases had convicted Anthony Wilson and Patrick Dewayne Bethley under the capital statute. Juries had convicted Wilson of the aggravated rape of a five-year-old girl; and Bethley of raping three young girls ages five, seven, and nine, one of whom was his daughter, in 1995 and 1996. Bethley knew that he was HIV positive at the time of the rapes. On appeal to the Louisiana Supreme Court, both defendants claimed that their death verdicts were unconstitutional because the imposition of the death penalty for a crime not resulting in a death is "cruel and unusual punishment" and unconstitutional pursuant to the Eight Amendment to the federal Constitution as dictated in *Coker*. The Louisiana Supreme Court upheld the convictions and capital sentences and concluded that "given the appalling nature of the crime, the severity of the harm inflicted upon the victim, and the harm imposed on society, the death penalty is not an excessive penalty for the crime of rape when the victim is a child under the age of twelve years old."[100] The U.S. Supreme Court denied certiorari to Bethley in June 1997. Legal scholars suggest that the Court will most likely review the case once the trial court issues a final judgment.[101] But how the Court will rule on child rapist capital statutes is highly debated.[102] Some are opposed to such legislation because they believe that it will have devastating and pernicious effects on women and children. As one scholar wrote, "The statutes will not achieve the goal of deterrence because they will decrease reporting, decrease convictions, and increase the incentives to murder those who are raped. Whatever retributive function may be served by executions will be similarly undermined as the death penalty will likely decrease the number of rapists caught and convicted. Thus, the best available evidence shows that these statutes are counterproductive to their stated aims."[103] Still, given the Court's conservative majority and open support for capital punishment, it is foreseeable that the Court could possibly overrule *Coker* and allow states to execute child rapists.

JURISDICTIONS HAVE NOT COMPLETELY ABANDONED MANDATORY DEATH SENTENCING

Mandatory death penalty statutes require the trier of fact (judge or jury) to sentence to death any defendant convicted of a capital offense, and permissive death penalty statutes allow for the trier of fact to use discretion in whether to sentence a capital defendant to death or life in prison. In practice, however, juries have effectively nullified mandatory death penalty laws in many jurisdictions with outright refusals to convict defendants even in the face of compelling evidence of guilt. Early researchers found that all states had mandatory death penalty statutes until 1809 when Maryland made capital punishment *optional* for treason, rape, and arson. But it was Tennessee in 1838 that became the first state to adopt a discretionary death penalty statute for murder, although Alabama adopted a similar statute soon afterward. States continued to fashion discretionary statutes throughout the Civil War period and into the twentieth century, and by 1963, only a few states mandated the death penalty for capital offenses. Rhode Island maintained the death penalty for a life-term prisoner convicted of murdering another inmate or prison guard; Massachusetts retained capital punishment for murder committed during forcible rape; and assassination of the U.S. president or a state governor warranted the death penalty in Ohio.[104]

Yet none of these discretionary statutes provided guided discretion to juries in choosing between the death penalty and life imprisonment for capital defendants. Beginning in the early 1970s, the U.S. Supreme Court began devising a rational structure of procedural safeguards ostensibly designed to curb jury discretion in capital sentencing. The Court developed these strategies in the landmark cases of *Furman v. Georgia*[105] and *Gregg v. Georgia*.[106] Earlier, in *McGautha v. California*[107] and *Crampton v. Ohio*,[108] capital defendants argued that the absolute and unguided discretion of capital juries in determining whether to impose the death penalty amounted to arbitrary and capricious sentencing. The issues before the Court in these earlier cases were (1) whether the absence of standards to guide the jury's discretion in determining whether to impose or withhold the death penalty violates due process and (2) whether Ohio's single-verdict procedure for determining guilt and punishment in capital cases is unconstitutional.[109] At the time, California and five other states had bifurcated capital trial systems where in one proceeding the jury heard evidence on the determination of guilt and at another proceeding the same jury determined the sentence. Ohio had no such system and the same jury decided both guilt and punishment in the same proceeding. A majority of the justices found that "the absence of standards to guide the jury's discretion on the punishment issue is constitutionally intolerable" and that Ohio's single-verdict procedure is also constitutional.[110] The Court argued that unfettered jury discretion in capital sentencing did not violate the constitution because it was impossible to guide jury discretion in capital cases.

The U.S. Supreme Court rejected this logic one year later in *Furman* when the defendant in the case argued that his death sentence should be set aside because the jury had such complete and unbridled discretion in imposing the death penalty that it violated his constitutional rights to the equal protection of the law and against cruel and unusual punishment.[111] The Court agreed and held that imposition of capital punishment as then administered contravened these constitutional protections because it was arbitrary and capricious in its application. The justices made it clear that death penalty jurisdictions were to devise procedural strategies to restrict unbridled discretion of juries in remanding prisoners to death. As a result, four years later in *Gregg v. Georgia* the Court affirmed the defendant's conviction and death sentence based on Georgia's revised death penalty statute providing for bifurcated trials, jury consideration of mitigating and aggravating circumstances concerning the defendant and the crime, and review of capital sentences by the state's Supreme Court. The U.S. Supreme Court affirmed these guidelines because Georgia intended them to prevent arbitrary and capricious imposition of the death penalty. The Court qualified its position in *Gregg* years later when it held the defendant's argument in *Blystone v. Pennsylvania* meritless that a state's death penalty statute is unconstitutional because it requires a jury to impose a death sentence if it finds at least one aggravating circumstance and no mitigating circumstances.[112]

Whether the Supreme Court's clarifications of permissive death penalty statutes indicate a movement away from capital punishment is doubtful. For one, the percentage of life sentences imposed by state courts for murder and non-negligent manslaughter has remained consistent over the last several years. In 2002, for instance, slightly more than 24 percent of the nearly 9,000 defendants convicted in state courts of murder or non-negligent manslaughter received life sentences and 1.7 percent received death sentences.[113] Ten years earlier, 25 percent of the 9,079 defendants convicted of murder or non-negligent manslaughter received life sentences and 1.6 percent received death sentences.[114] Thirty-three states and the federal government have executed 1,012 prisoners since 1976. This figure means that only five death penalty states have not conducted any executions over the period. Executions are concentrated in southern states where authorities have executed 826 prisoners since 1976, especially Texas and Virginia where officials have executed 453 prisoners. Far fewer executions occurred in jurisdictions geographically situated in the Midwest, West, and Northeast.

DEATH PENALTY JURISDICTIONS HAVE NOT SUBSTANTIALLY REDUCED THE NUMBER OF EXECUTIONS

Early death penalty researchers recognized a reduction in the annual number of executions that they believed demonstrated a movement away from the use of capital punishment in the United States.[115] Scholars attributed declines in executions to a lessening of the number of capital offenses and adoption of permissive provisions allowing juries to convict murder defendants on lesser-included offenses. Today, the proportion of death sentences to commitments for first-degree murder is very different from that observed by early researchers. The number of murders and non-negligent manslaughters has remained relatively consistent in the post-*Gregg* era while the number of persons sentenced to death and actually put to death has substantially increased.[116] The United States has witnessed the lowest level of new death sentences in the past 30 years with death sentences dropping nationwide from 317 in 1996 to 125 in 2005.[117] Yet slightly more than 2.2 percent of murders and non-negligent manslaughters resulted in death sentences in 1977 and increased nearly *tenfold* to 20.8 percent in 2004.[118] Thus, even though death penalty jurisdictions have reformed their capital statutes over the past several decades, authorities have actually increased the proportion of defendants sentenced to death for murder. Jurisdictions also increased the rate of execution as a proportion of death row inmates *tenfold* from 0.2 percent in 1977 to 2.0 percent in 2004. It is striking that jurisdictions have executed 14 percent of the 6,807 persons sentenced to death in the United States in the post-*Gregg* era.[119] One aspect of reducing the annual number of executions not considered by early scholars is the number of death sentences disposed of by means other than execution. Here, jurisdictions have disposed of roughly 4,200 capital cases since 1977 through indictment dismissals, judgment reversals, commutations, resentencings, new trials, and by death other than execution (i.e., natural causes). Whereas 4 percent of death row inmates have died from causes other than execution, 37 percent have received dispositions other than executions.[120] For example, California has executed 13 capital offenders since 1978 and some 49 other condemned inmates have died from natural causes, committed suicide, or died by some other means.[121] Research shows that most dispositions other than death from natural causes or execution in capital cases result mostly from wrongful convictions due to prosecutorial lawlessness and false confessions.[122]

Dissatisfied with the speed at which jurisdictions impose state killings, many congressional conservatives want to speed up executions. To do so, Pennsylvania Republican Senator Arlin Specter and Arizona Senator John Kyl introduced the "Streamlined Procedures Act of 2005" that would expedite executions by effectively limiting defendants' ability to seek federal habeas corpus review of their capital convictions.[123] Republican Representative Dan Lungren introduced a similar bill in the House. Critics maintain that the legislation will restrict federal courts from considering petitions from state prisoners claiming constitutional violations or from presenting evidence of innocence.[124] In response to Senator Specter's proposal, a national Conference of Chief Justices from state courts overwhelmingly passed a resolution suggesting that the U.S. Senate not support the legislation. Concerned that the legislation would challenge the constitutional rights of death row inmates, Pennsylvania's Chief Justice Ralph Cappy stated, "In a very delicate area where you are concerned with possible actual innocence in post-conviction hearings that gives us great pause."[125] What is more, the U.S. House of Representatives passed without debate an amendment to the Patriot Act Reauthorization Act to include a provision increasing the number of federal capital crimes, permitting judges to lower the number of jurors to less than 12 in federal capital cases, and allowing federal prosecutors to retry capital cases when at least one juror votes to resist imposing the death penalty.[126] An official with Human Rights Watch claims, "[t]hese provisions dramatically extend the reach of the federal death penalty and make it significantly easier for the prosecution to secure death, an inherently cruel penalty."[127]

Congress continues its debate on the Death Penalty Reform Act of 2006. The American Civil Liberties Union opposes passage of the reform act because it does nothing to address the continuing racial, economic, and geographic disparities in the fed-eral death penalty system; it would violate the Eighth Amendment because it subjects mentally retarded people to death, and it violates the Fifth Amendment against self-incrimination.[128] According to Jim Marcus, Executive Director of the Texas Defender Service, the only criminal cases ripe for federal review under the Streamlined Procedures Act "are those in which a defendant can show (1) that there are new facts in the case that were never brought to light through the due diligence of attorneys, (2) that those facts establish the defendant's innocence by clear and convincing evidence, and (3) that but for a constitutional violation, the defendant wouldn't have been convicted."[129] The bill would essentially shift the power of review to the chief prosecutor of the United States to determine "whether state courts behave fairly enough toward defendants appealing capi-tal convictions."[130]

Despite the fact that at least one convicted murderer a week is put to death in a state penitentiary, the death penalty remains a rare occurrence compared to the overall murder rate in the United States.[131] Currently, the execution rate is about one execution for every 700 committed murders and one execution for every 325 convictions for murder. There are regional differences in the imposition of capital punishment both between and within states, however.[132] A recent study shows that while jurisdictions sentence to death 2.5 percent of convicted murderers nationwide, Nevada sentences 6 percent of its con-victed murderers to death (higher than the national average) and Texas sentences 2 percent of its murderers to death sentence (lower than the national average). Texas executes 40 percent of its convicted murderers sentenced to death (four times higher than the national average), but California executes 1 percent of its convicted murderers (well below the national average).[133]

DEATH PENALTY JURISDICTIONS CONTINUE SELECTIVE ENFORCEMENT CAPITAL PUNISHMENT

One early death penalty scholar summarized the pattern of selective imposition of capital punishment in the United State this way: "The death penalty is in this country predomi-nantly and disproportionately imposed upon Negroes, the poor, and the less educated, and men."[134] This is an important observation because over the last several decades many criminal justice researchers have asserted that the U.S. criminal justice system is devoid of institutional race bias.[135] Interestingly, scholars make this assertion while largely ignoring one of the most comprehensive studies on the impact of crime and criminal jus-tice on persons of color in the United States.[136] Early research records reveal that the *race of the defendant* and the *race of the victim* were significant factors in jurisdictions impos-ing the death penalty.[137]

Racial discrimination resulting from jury discretion in capital sentencing underwent a series of constitutional challenges vis-à-vis *Gregg*. Yet, considerable post-*Gregg* research shows that the Supreme Court's holdings have had no diminishing effect on jury discretion in capital sentencing and that the discretionary guidelines established for juries have failed to reduce arbitrary and capricious sentencing.[138] A final challenge to race discrimination in capital sentencing came when Warren McCleskey claimed that Georgia administered its capital sentencing process in a racially discriminatory manner. McCleskey proffered the results of one of the most methodologically powerful studies of racial bias in capital sentencing to date. In it, Iowa University Professor David Baldus and his associates analyzed 2,484 murder and non-negligent manslaughter cases in Georgia between 1973 and 1979. Baldus had controlled for some 230 nonracial variables and found that none of the factors accounted for disparities in capital sentences among different defendant–victim racial categories. Baldus maintained that state jurisdictions were 4.3 times more likely to sentence convicted murders of whites than convicted murders of blacks to death, and these jurisdictions were 1.1 times more likely to sentence black defendants to death than other defendants.[139] Accordingly, McCleskey claimed that race had infected the administration of the death penalty in Georgia in two distinct ways: (1) that jurisdictions were more likely to sentence murderers of whites to death than were murderers of blacks and (2) that jurisdictions were more likely to sentence black murderers to death than white murderers. McCleskey alleged that Georgia's system of imposing the death penalty discriminated against him as a black man who killed a white man. The essence of the Court's holding in *McCleskey v Kemp 481 U.S. 297 (1987)* as that empirical studies showing that a discrepancy appears to correlate with race in imposing death sentences do not prove that race enters into any capital sentencing decisions or that race is a factor in the petitioner's case. The Court was concerned that a finding for the defendant would open other claims that defendants could extend to other types of penalties and to claims based on unexplained discrepancies correlating to membership in other minority groups and even to gender. In surmising the Courts decision in *McCleskey*, commentators have explained, "It is unimaginable that the U.S. Supreme Court, an institution vested with the responsibility to achieve equal justice under the law for all Americans, could issue an opinion that accepted the inevitability of racial bias in an area as serious and final as capital punishment. However, it is precisely this acceptance of bias and the tolerance of racial discrimination that has come to define America's criminal justice system."[140]

Post-*McCleskey* capital sentencing research reveals continued patterns of racial discrimination, however. The record shows that death penalty jurisdictions put black defendants to death at significantly higher rates than white defendants and that black defendants are particularly at risk of capital sentencing and actual execution when they victimize white persons. In effect, the U.S. Supreme Court has proven itself particularly impotent in its ability to eliminate systemic racism in capital punishment despite implementing procedural safeguards to eliminate racial discrimination in capital sentencing. To one scholar, "the procedural and substantive protections that have been erected by the Supreme Court in an effort to minimize arbitrariness in capital sentencing, if fully implemented, could yield rational, consistent and fair sentences in capital cases. The problem is that these procedures are rarely implemented."[141] Continued patterns of racial discrimination in capital sentencing result from prosecutorial abuse of legal strategies devised intentionally to deny fairness in prosecution and sentencing of black defendants. These procedural tactics include racist prosecutorial discretion in the selection of capital cases, racist prosecutorial abuse of peremptory challenges to unlawfully exclude persons of color from juries, prosecutorial lawlessness in trying capital cases, prosecutorial abuse in trying mentally retarded defendants, the ineffective assistance of racist defense counsel, and the racist prosecutorial homophobia in trying capital cases involving lesbian women.

Racist Prosecutorial Discretion

State and federal prosecutors possess unbridled discretion in filing criminal charges against persons accused of crime.[142] Arguably, courts impose formidable restrictions on the racist discretionary powers of police, sentencing judges, parole boards, and correctional officers, but they are unwilling to restrict racist prosecutorial discretion.[143] The charging discretion of prosecutors remains largely unregulated, unreviewable, and for the most part, there is no public accountability.[144] The U.S. Supreme Court has made it clear that "so long as the prosecutor has probable cause to believe that the accused committed an offense defined by statute, the decision whether or not to prosecute . . . generally rests entirely in his discretion."[145] Still, prosecutorial discretion in selecting capital cases is not absolute. As one judicial officer explains, "Prosecutors have an affirmative duty to make sure that racial and national origin bias, as well as gender bias and prejudice, do not enter into their charging decisions. In the course of the trial of the case, prosecutors must ensure that they do not *consciously* or *unconsciously* inject racial, national origin, or gender biases and prejudices into the trial."[146] Whereas the adversarial nature of criminal proceedings ostensibly offers impartiality in state and federal prosecutions, *fairness* in selective prosecution is illusive in capital cases because racial bias in selective prosecution remains pervasive.[147] Repeatedly, prosecutors breach ethical rules of professional conduct and deliberately deny indigent defendants of color well-defined constitutional protections.[148] To Barrown D. Lankster, an Alabama black district attorney, race matters in this country "because you have individuals who are making the decision to pursue the death penalty, and they bring their own biases to that."[149] A central finding of recent empirical studies on the impact of prosecutorial discretion in seeking the death penalty in homicide cases is that prosecutors' racist attitudes shape the administration of capital punishment in several states. Essentially, race and gender-based discrimination characterize prosecutors' unfettered discretion in selecting death penalty cases.[150]

One result of racist prosecutorial discretion in selecting capital cases is that 81 percent of all capital cases involve white victims, while nationally only half of all murder victims are white.[151] This means that most inmates on death row are there because they killed a white person and not a person of color. Execution data show similar disparities. Since 1976 death penalty officials have executed 14 white defendants for killing blacks but 211 black defendants for killing whites—revealing that authorities are more than *15 times* more likely to execute black defendants with white victims than white defendants with black victims.[152] Jurisdictions are three times as likely to execute Latino defendants with white victims as white defendants with Latino victims. An unpublished study has found that the *race of the offender* and the *race of the victim* are significant factors in prosecutors' decisions to seek the death penalty against Latinos in Fresno, California. When compared to Anglo offenders, state prosecutors are four times more likely to charge Latinos with special circumstances, and some fourteen times more likely to charge killers of Anglos with special circumstances than killers of Latinos. To one commentator, these finding suggests that California places a greater value on the lives of Anglos than on the lives of Latinos.[153] It is significant that only 35 cases exist historically in which jurisdictions executed white prisoners for killing blacks.[154] Some scholars have suggested reforming prosecutorial discretion with race impact studies by prosecutors,[155] and others have recommended jury nullification and the hiring of more black prosecutors.[156]

Selective prosecution of persons of color remains pervasive in death penalty cases because the U.S. Supreme Court has made it practically impossible for defendants of color to prove racial discrimination.[157] Simply put, the Supreme Court has flatly refused to impose restrictions on even the most blatantly racist prosecutorial conduct in capital cases. The Equal Protection Clause to the Fourteenth Amendment prohibits governments from treating people differently who are similarly situated. In the context of selective prosecution of capital cases, that is, state and federal prosecutors cannot base their prosecutorial decisions on unjustifiable standards such as race, religion, or other arbitrary classifications.[158] Government must afford equal protection of the law to all persons similarly situated and not impose arbitrary decision-making when prosecuting criminals. But proving selective prosecution is practically impossible because, as one scholar explains, "a defendant must show that administration of a law is directed so exclusively against a particular class of persons with a mind so unequal and oppressive that the system results in a practical denial of equal protection of the law."[159] Yet, not since *Yick Wo v. Hopkins* in 1886 has a state or federal court dismissed a criminal prosecution where prosecutors acted with racial animus.[160] The Court has made it clear in more recent cases that an equal protection claim will prevail only when a defendant can demonstrate that state and local governments do not prosecute similarly situated persons.[161]

Racist Prosecutorial Abuse of Peremptory Challenges

State and federal prosecutors use peremptory challenges as a procedural device to remove potential jurors during voir dire for unexplained reasons. Prosecutors must give a reason when challenging jurors for cause, but peremptory challenges require no justification and are "exercised without a reason stated, without impunity, and without being subject to the court's control."[162] It is the capricious nature of the peremptory challenge, however, that effectively obscures racial discrimination in jury selection by allowing prosecutors to discriminate intentionally against potential jurors of color.[163] In recent remarks, U.S. Supreme Court Justice John Paul Stevens called attention to the fairness of jury selection in capital cases, arguing, "Peremptory challenges are an unacceptable source of arbitrariness."[164] As one Colorado judge more concisely put it, the peremptory challenge is "the last best tool of Jim Crow."[165]

Despite a long history of the Court's holdings involving racist prosecutorial abuse of the peremptory challenge,[166] state attorneys continue to use peremptory challenges in capital cases to discriminate openly against blacks and Latinos in jury selection. Prosecutors are not only more likely than defense attorneys to direct peremptory challenges against blacks,[167] but they also prefer white jurors to black jurors in capital cases because they believe that white juries are more prone to convict black defendants.[168] Still, it is difficult to make the case of racial discrimination when prosecutors abuse peremptory challenges because courts allow "almost any conceivable justification for peremptory challenges, however arbitrary or irrational, while ignoring evidence that such challenges were exercised in a racially discriminatory manner."[169] In one case, the U.S. Supreme Court approved a prosecutor's " 'race-neutral reason' for striking a black from prospective jury service on the bases that the juror's long, unkempt hair, mustache and beard 'look suspicious to me.' "[170] The Court argued, "[w]hat it means by a legitimate reason is not a reason that makes sense, but a reason that does not deny equal protection."[171]

In another case, the Illinois Supreme Court let stand a prosecutor's exclusion of a black juror because the juror lived in a neighborhood that experienced gang activity.[172] The Missouri Court of Appeals rationalized that the state's prosecutor used peremptory challenges in a race-neutral manner against a black juror who lived in a high-crime neighborhood, was unemployed, and had a low educational attainment level.[173] An Alabama case illustrates the level of judicial tolerance of racist prosecutors in the justice system.[174] Judge McMillan of the Alabama Court of Criminal Appeals found that a prosecutor's race-neutral explanation for peremptory strikes of black venire persons rebutted a prima facie showing of discrimination even if the prosecutor excused a young black female because she was a homemaker. They may have trouble making the necessary judgments that have to be made and that is the knowledge of what life is like out on the street. A young black female student who would not have the necessary experience to be able to draw on to make a judgment in this case; an older retired black female who may be overly sympathetic based on the fact that she appeared to be a grandmotherly type; a young black male who had a beard and people with beards are somehow those who try to go against the grain. Additionally, an unemployed, middle-aged, black male may be somewhat irresponsible; and a middle-aged black female who appeared to be in the same age group as the defendants' parents or mothers would also have problems making the necessary judgments.[175]

Prosecutorial Lawlessness

Prosecutorial lawlessness in capital cases is the product of systemic racism in the justice system. Scholars have studied appellate court reviews of thousands of capital cases and found that courts overwhelmingly reverse capital sentences because of prosecutorial misconduct.[176] One study researched capital cases nationally and learned that nearly all death penalty jurisdictions in the United States have excessive error rates stemming mostly from severe forms of prosecutorial misconduct.[177] Some 30 percent of capital cases in an Ohio study involved severe ethical issues of prosecutorial misconduct.[178] Another study of wrongfully convicted capital defendants found that prosecutorial misconduct was one of the most significant factors leading to conviction in seven defendants' cases in Illinois. In one of the cases, Illinois executed Jesse Tafero who prosecutors convicted upon much of the same evidence that exonerated Sonia Jacobs, a white woman.[179] While these studies did not separately study the reversible error involved in female capital cases, Streib has calculated an error rate in female capital cases at 58 percent.[180]

A *Chicago Tribune* investigation found hundreds of homicide cases in which the prosecutors concealed or fabricated evidence.[181] A Texas study of cases involving serious prosecutorial misconduct revealed that state prosecutors have "used threats against defendants or their family members to coerce confessions."[182] In many cases, prosecutors knowingly tolerate police lawlessness such as planting evidence on unwary suspects to boost conviction rates.[183] Undoubtedly, prosecutorial misconduct weighs most heavily against black offenders since blacks are so overrepresented as capital defendants.[184] In Wanda Jean Allen's case, for example, the state's prosecutor withheld evidence at trial and later made false statements to the Parole and Pardon Board.[185] In fact, the prosecutor in Wanda's case engaged in seven separate instances of misconduct, including instances of biased behavior.[186] Other studies have focused on prosecutors' use of racist remarks while trying capital cases involving black defendants.[187] The literature reveals that courts are frustrated over the frequency in which prosecutorial misconduct occurs, yet courts are unwilling to overturn cases on grounds of racial bias and, in the alternative, assess the relative weight of the statements to other evidence or otherwise explain away the prosecutors' remarks.[188]

Efforts to deter prosecutorial misconduct have proven largely unsuccessful. The U.S. Supreme Court held in *Brady v. Maryland* that prosecutors are under a constitutional duty to disclose evidence favorable to the accused. But several studies attest to the ineffectiveness of *Brady*.[189] Authorities have not convicted any prosecutor of criminal conduct in all the documented cases of prosecutorial misconduct,[190] although there are some ongoing investigations.[191] In fact, Arizona is the only state that has even disbarred a prosecutor for wrongdoing. There, officials disbarred Pima County prosecutor Kenneth Peasley for intentionally presenting false evidence against three men in a triple-murder death penalty case.[192] Also, a problem with prosecutorial accountability for misconduct is that prosecutors enjoy absolute immunity from civil liability.[193] Often prosecutors who engage in official misconduct are elevated to the bar as judges.[194] Judge William J. Kunkle, for example, became a Cook County circuit judge even after he failed to investigate 148 claims of torture by Chicago police when he was a former official in the county state's attorney office.[195]

The law immunizes prosecutors who engage in misconduct from civil suits. In *Imbler v. Pachtman*, the U.S. Supreme Court. Pachtman obtained his release from a state prison through federal habeas corpus proceedings in which it was found that the prosecuting attorney in a California state court murder prosecution had knowingly used false testimony by suppressing evidence favorable to the defense. In the state prosecution Pachtman instituted an action against the prosecuting attorney and certain police officers in the United States District Court for the Central District of California, seeking to recover damages under Section 42 USCS 1983, which provides that any person who acts under color of state law to deprive another of a constitutional right shall be liable to the injured party in an action at law. Pachtman alleged that a conspiracy among the defendants to unlawfully charge and convict him had caused him loss of liberty and other injury, the gravamen of the complaint against the prosecuting attorney being that he had knowingly or negligently used false evidence and suppressed material evidence at the criminal trial. The District Court dismissed the complaint as to the prosecuting attorney, holding that as a public prosecutor, he was immune from civil liability for acts done as part of his official functions. The United States Court of Appeals for the Ninth Circuit affirmed.[196]

Prosecutorial Abuse and Mentally Retarded Defendants

Government figures reveal that more than half of the prison and jail population in the United States suffer from mental health problems. Estimates are that 56 percent of state prisoners, 45 percent of federal prisoners, and 64 percent of jail inmates have severe mental health problems.[197] The Treatment Advocacy Center reports that there are more than four times as many people with serious mental disorders in the nation's prisons and jails than in mental hospitals.[198] One commentator explained in a recent *New York Times* editorial that one reason for the ever-increasing number of mentally ill persons confined to the nation's prisons and jails is the trend away from institutionalizing mentally ill persons in mental hospitals and asylums. Harcourt notes that in the 1940s and 1950s, U.S. society largely institutionalized mentally ill persons in hospitals and other facilities, but today it primarily relies upon jails and prisons to house the mentally ill.[199] Interestingly, there are no definitive figures available on the proportion of death row inmates suffering from mental health problems. Some estimates put the figure at 70 percent of death row inmates suffering from schizophrenia and other severe mental illnesses,[200] yet estimates that are more conservative put the figure as low as 10 percent.[201] Regardless, a sizable proportion of death row inmates suffer from extreme mental deficiencies that experts argue should preclude their execution. Mental illnesses among the nation's death row population include conditions accented by impairment of an individual's normal cognitive, emotional, or behavioral functioning; such as the most common illnesses suffered by death row inmates—bipolar disorders, personality disorders, post-traumatic stress disorders, schizo-affective disorders, schizophrenia, depression, and suicidal tendencies.[202]

Since 1976, death penalty jurisdictions have executed more than one hundred capital offenders despite strong evidence of severe mental illness.[203] In the latest case, Texas executed mentally ill Troy Albert Kunkle in January 2005 for the August 1984 abduction, robbery, and shooting death of Steven Wayne Horton in Corpus Christi. At the time of Horton's murder, Kunkle was 18 years old with no criminal record. Still, Kunkle suffered serious deprivation and child abuse from parents who themselves suffered from mental illness. Kunkle's father subjected him to severe physical abuse. His mother recalled "a lot of times he'd slam Troy into a wall or onto the floor." She came home once and "there was a big hole in the wall. I found out later that Troy's father had slammed him so hard into the wall that he had smashed right through it." Other times, he "would get Troy into a chokehold. He choked Troy so hard sometimes that it looked like Troy couldn't even breathe." In post-conviction psychiatric evaluations, one expert concluded that Troy Kunkle suffered from schizophrenia and that most of Troy Kunkle's early adolescent behavior problems were "linked to his father's aggressive and psychotic behavior" toward him throughout his childhood. His mother lacked any nurturing skills toward Kunkle given the severity of her own mental illness. The jury heard none of this mitigating evidence.

The U.S. Supreme Court has *not* barred state and federal jurisdictions from executing mentally ill persons *unless* the mental illness renders the inmate legally insane.[204] The Court has qualified the constitutionality of executing mentally ill prisoners to the extent that it prohibits death penalty jurisdictions from executing anyone who does not understand why officials are putting them to death.[205] In his concurring opinion in *Ford v. Wainwright*, Justice Powell articulated the standard for determining whether a mentally ill inmate is eligible for execution, "The Eighth Amendment forbids the execution only of those who are [1] unaware of the punishment they are about to suffer and [2] why they are to suffer it."[206] Yet commentators explain, "Application of the death penalty to individuals suffering from serious mental illnesses does not comport with contemporary standards of decency and thus stands as cruel and unusual punishment." The reason for such criticism is that the Court in *Ford* left the determination of mental illness of capital defendants to individual jurisdictions. As a result, death penalty authorities in several states continue to execute mentally ill persons.

Virginia's execution of Morris Odell Mason in June 1985 illustrates Justice Powell's concern. Mason's execution constitutes a case in which a mentally ill defendant had absolutely no understanding of his impending execution or why he was undergoing an execution. Mason was mentally retarded with an IQ tested in the 62-to-66 range and was diagnosed as a paranoid schizophrenic at the age of eight. He spent most of his life institutionalized with a history of violence. At the age of 21 he began to hearing voices ordering him to "do things, break things, tear things, and destroy things." Despite his mental infliction, Mason knew what he was doing when he killed an elderly woman during an alcoholic rampage since a week before the killing he "had twice sought help from his parole officer for his uncontrollable drinking and drug abuse."[207] Yet, Mason had so little an understanding of his impending execution that he asked prison advisors what he should wear to his funeral. What's more, Mason told fellow inmates on his way to the death chamber, "When I get back, I'm gonna show him how I can play basketball as good as he can."[208]

Alabama's execution of David Kevin Hocker in September 2004 illustrates how death penalty jurisdictions in practice blatantly ignore the standard imposed in *Ford*. Despite the two-prong test for mental incapacity articulated by Justice Powell, Alabama executed Hocker after a jury had convicted him of the 1998 stabbing death of his employer while splurging on cocaine. Hocker had a long history of mental illness and was the victim of severe child abuse, a childhood his lawyer described as a "thoroughgoing regime of terror." Hocker's mental illness was so severe that while on death row he mutilated himself by cutting off his testicles. As one commentator aptly stated, "Alabama can take no pride in executing someone who is too unstable or too poor to protect themselves."[209]

Gendered-Racism and the Death Penalty

Gendered-racism is a pattern of selective imposition of capital punishment in the United States when jurisdictions execute black women more often than they execute white women. Early criminologists claimed that jurisdictions were more than *twice* as likely to execute black women as white women. This racial pattern of female executions continues. Jurisdictions have disproportionately executed black women; black women are 29 percent of female defendants sentenced to death in the United States since 1973.[210] As a result, black women constitute *twice* their proportionate representation in capital sentencing cases. Black women are 32 percent of the 52 females residing on death rows across the country—nearly three times their proportionate representation in the overall society.[211] Death penalty jurisdictions have executed 11 black women since 1976. Since Ohio's execution of Betty Butler in June 1954 for murder, however, authorities have executed two more black women—Oklahoma put Wanda Jean Allen to death by lethal injection for murder in 2001, and Texas executed Frances Elaine Newton by lethal injection in 2005.

One contemptible feature of gendered-racism in the criminal justice system is that white male prosecutors consistently marginalize black female lesbian defendants, using sexuality to malign and disparage them to juries. Scholars largely concede that the United States criminal justice system is a major location of homophobic-based oppression, and consequently, prosecutorial homophobia often becomes central to capital trials involving black lesbian defendants. Prosecutors use the transgression of feminine stereotypes to show the dangerousness of female capital defendants and that lesbian killers deserve the death penalty.[212] One result of prosecutors exploiting lesbianism to denigrate black women in capital cases is that lesbians disproportionately occupy death row. While more than half the women on death row are lesbian, a national study shows that only 0.32 percent of the total U.S. population is lesbian.[213] This means that lesbians are represented on death row more than 81 times their proportionate representation in overall society. One scholar explains that 40 percent of women accused of murder contend with prosecutorial assertions of lesbianism to purposefully masculate and dehumanize them.[214] Prosecutors resort to marginalizing prejudices and stereotypes to render female defendants more executable to jurors.[215] Disparaging black lesbian capital defendants is usually successful since lesbians rarely sit as jurors.[216] Interestingly jurors are more than three times as likely to think they could not be fair or impartial toward a lesbian defendant as toward other minority group defendants.[217]

Wanda Jean Allen was sentenced to death in 1988 for the murder of Gloria Jean Leathers age 29. Allen was the first black woman to be executed in the United States since 1954. She was also the sixth woman to be executed since the resumption of the death penalty in 1977. In the Wanda Jean Allen case, Allen's lesbianism overwhelmed the state's case primarily because her defense attorney failed to make the requisite objections against the state's introduction of such evidence at trial. Thus, the state's prosecutor freely yet erroneously asserted that Allen dominated her lover when in fact she and Leathers largely mistreated each other. The state's prosecutors won the trial court's rejection of defense motions outlining Leathers' violent nature.[218] The prosecution inaccurately, yet purposefully, portrayed Wanda as wearing "the pants in the family" and that she was the masculine one in the relationship. The state attorney solicited testimony from Allen's mother that Allen used the male spelling of her middle name. Wanda's sexuality played a prominent role in her trial and "evidences again that when a woman acts out from society's gender expectations, she faces harsher penalties."[219] Even Oklahoma's black churches rebuffed efforts for leniency for Allen from the state governor because she was a lesbian. As one commentator explained,

> Allen was convicted on the basis of a rash of stereotypes about lesbians which, combined with stereotypes about black people and poor people, played off juror biases to portray Allen

as an aggressive offender so dangerous to society that the only recourse was execution. One observer proposed that had Allen been a middle class, white heterosexual woman who killed her boyfriend, the jury would probably have been more sympathetic and Allen's sentence would have been considerably lighter.[220]

Poverty and Capital Punishment

Many early scholars of capital punishment recognized that jurisdictions imposed the penalty disproportionately on the poor and less educated. To Lawes, an "inherent defect" of capital sentencing was that the death penalty is "an unequal punishment in the way it is applied to the rich and the poor. The defendant of wealth and position never goes to the electric chair or to the gallows."[221] Some 71 percent of the 200 inmates committed to North Carolina state prison after conviction for capital crimes between 1910 and 1928 were "wholly illiterate." Most of the illiterate defendants were black. Yet, it was not until 1967 that any formal discussion on the issue of poverty in capital sentencing surfaces in the literature. Then, the President's Commission on Law Enforcement and Administration of Justice recognized discriminatory patterns in capital sentencing in the United States: "The death sentence is disproportionately imposed and carried out on the poor, the Negro, and the members of unpopular groups."[222] The U.S. Supreme Court recognized a few years later in *Furman* that "one searches our chronicles in vain for the execution of any member of the affluent strata of this society."[223] Recently, the Final Report of Pennsylvania Committee on Racial and Gender Bias in the Justice System identified in a report the inextricable link between racial bias in capital sentencing and issues of poverty: "Unless the poor, among whom minority communities are overrepresented, are provided adequate legal representation, including ample funds for experts and investigators, there cannot be a lasting solution to the issue of racial and ethnic bias in the capital justice system."[224]

Indeed, poor people of color disproportionately populate state and federal death rows because they are too poor to pay for their own legal defense. Following the U.S. Supreme Court's mandate in a series of cases beginning in the early 1930s that indigent defendants facing a loss of life or liberty require legal counsel, state and federal governments established various methods of delivering legal services to poor defendants. States employ public defenders, assigned counsel, and contract lawyers to provide indigent defendants with lawyers, while the federal government uses public defenders, community defender organizations, and panel attorneys.[225] Only Alabama does not provide indigent death row inmates seeking post-conviction relief with lawyers.[226] More so than indigent whites, poor defendants of color utilize the services of publicly financed lawyers than private attorneys.[227] Comparative rates of representation by public and private attorneys in state and federal courts show that 77 percent of blacks and 73 percent of Latinos in state prisons use public defenders or court-appointed counsel, compared to 69 percent of white inmates. In federal prisons, nearly 65 percent of black inmates and 56 percent of Latinos use court-appointed counsel or public defenders. Slightly more than 56 percent of white inmates in federal prisons use publicly financed attorneys. High rates of prison inmates using appointed counsel are other persons of color as well, mostly Asian

American/Pacific Islanders and American Indians; slightly more than 75 percent of state prisoners in this racial category and about 73 percent of others in federal prisons use court-appointed counsel.[228]

Critical levels of underfunding have left indigent defense programs across the country dreadfully inadequate to provide the legal representation required of disadvantaged defendants.[229] The United States spends $185 billion a year on police protection, corrections, and judicial and legal activities,[230] but authorities allocate only $3.3 billion to indigent defense services, less than 2 percent of criminal justice expenditures.[231] Of the allotted funds for indigent defense services, public defender agencies receive 73 percent, assigned counsel programs get 21 percent, and contract attorneys collect 6 percent.[232] One outcome of the acute discrepancies in public spending is that allocations to state and federal prosecutors are more than three times the figure for indigent defense services. What's more, police departments and state and federal crime labs provide much of the investigatory work to prosecutors, while indigent defense programs must finance investigations, laboratory work, and expert witnesses from their own budgets.[233]

The devastating consequences on the quality of legal representation in capital cases owing to the underfunding of indigent defense services are worse yet.[234] As Lanier and Acker put it, "There is no shortage of stories involving scandalous representation provided to indigent defendants on trial for their lives."[235] One commentator describes indigent capital defense in the United States as "scandalous, shameful, abysmal, pathetic, deplorable, and at best, exceedingly uneven."[236] U.S. Supreme Court Justice Ginsburg once noted, "I have yet to see a death case among the dozens coming to the Supreme Court on eve-of-execution stay applications in which the defendant was well represented at trial . . . People who are well represented at trial do not get the death penalty."[237] One commentator gives credence to this notion when arguing that a system where the right to counsel is based upon one's ability to pay "is little more than a parody of the constitutional guarantee of equal protection under the law."[238] Poverty remains an aggravating factor for capital defendants because poor defendants of color cannot afford private attorneys who often succeed in mitigating capital sentences to life imprisonment.[239] Poor capital defendants of color must most often rely on court-appointed lawyers or public defenders who do not always serve the best interests of their clients.[240] In one Georgia case, a court assigned 83-year-old James Venable to defend an indigent black man. Venable was a former Imperial Wizard of the Ku Klux Klan who had a notorious reputation of sleeping through trials.[241]

McClatchy Newspapers recently conducted a broad review of the trial transcripts and appeal records and conducted interviews with lawyers in 80 cases in which juries condemned capital defendants to death from 1997 through 2004 in Georgia, Mississippi, Alabama, and Virginia. The findings of the review are troubling:

- In 73 of the 80 cases, defense lawyers gave jurors little or no evidence to help them decide whether the accused should live or die. The lawyers routinely missed myriad issues of abuse and mental deficiency, abject poverty, and serious psychological problems.

- By failing to investigate their clients' histories, lawyers in these 73 cases fell far short of the 20-year-old professional standards set by the American Bar

> Association. Their performances also appear inconsistent with standards that the U.S. Supreme Court has mandated several times.
>
> • Appeals courts for the most part have ducked those Supreme Court directives about the importance of quality defense counsel. So far, only 2 of the 80 death sentences have been overturned for bad lawyering.
>
> • In 11 of the cases, the defendants already have been executed. Their cases moved through the appeals process without a single judge flagging lapses in the defense attorneys' performances.[242]

In the case Wallace Marvin Fugate III, for instance, poverty was a critical factor in his lethal injection execution in Georgia in August 2002 for the murder of his ex-wife. Fugate was poor and required court-appointed lawyers. Reprehensibly, Fugate's public lawyers were unfamiliar with even the most fundamentals of death penalty law, failed to engage in plea negotiations, refused the trial judge's offer of funds for investigators and experts, made no objections at trial, and presented no mitigating evidence. Fugate's trial lawyers filed only three motions with the court, none of which exceeded more than two pages and only one of which cited one case. Fugate's sentencing hearing lasted just 27 minutes.[243]

Poverty and an inability to afford reputable defense counsel also meant that Delma Banks, Jr., would spend 20 years attempting to correct the original trial record in his case while imprisoned. In 2003, the U.S. Supreme Court overturned the death sentence of Delma Banks (a black man) convicted of murdering Wayne Whitehead (a young white man) in Texas. The Supreme Court conceded that Banks' trial lawyer was grotesquely ineffective, that blatant prosecutorial misconduct and biased jury selection so prejudiced his case that the trial court denied Banks his constitutional right to a fair trial. Banks trial counsel failed to challenge the state's case at both the guilt and punishment phases of the trial with any meaningful pre-trial investigation or even to review the list of state witnesses or the autopsy report. Trial counsel did not even bother to cross-examine many of the state's witnesses. What's more, the state's prosecutor was able to chisel out an all-white jury by striking qualified black jurors that, according to Banks' appellate lawyer, was "consistent with a pattern and practice of the prosecution to exclude black jurors from felony jury service." Apparently, prosecutors in the county accepted more than 80 percent of white jurors but eliminated more than 90 percent of black jurors. The prosecution also suppressed evidence that state witnesses were paid informants and that prosecutors had promised them lesser sentences in unrelated crimes. To William Sessions, former FBI Director and U.S. District Judge, Banks' trial was so unashamedly distorted by biased jury selection, prosecutorial misconduct, perjury, and bad lawyering that the case "has broad implications for the nation's criminal justice system because it directly 'implicates the integrity of the death penalty in this country.' "[244]

In the case of Frances Elaine Newton the headlines at the time read "Texas Woman Faces Execution Despite Questions Regarding Her Guilt." In case, more than any other reason, Texas succeeded in executing Newton because her court-appointed trial lawyer was grossly incompetent. Newton had repeatedly requested that the trial court dismiss Ronald Mock. Several months after the trial judge had appointed Mock, Newton wrote a letter to the judge concerned that she had had only minimal contact with Mock and that he was not investigating her case. Without a hearing on the issue, the trial court summarily rejected Newton's plea. Her appellate attorneys, however, maintained that Mock failed to investigate claims that authorities found a second gun at the crime scene or accounts by Newton's relatives that a cellmate bragged about going to Newton's house the night of the killings to collect a drug debt "with orders to kill everybody present if the man did not have the money."[245] Mock never interviewed any witnesses involved in the case and failed to challenge the veracity of ballistics evidence processed by a county crime lab that had come under investigation for grievously mishandling forensic evidence.[246] Mock overlooked much about Newton's life that could have mitigated the crime to the jury—Newton was a young offender (she was 21 years old at the time of the crime), she became pregnant as a teenager, she had a philandering and drug-addicted husband, she was cooperative with the police investigation, she was churchgoing, and she was the daughter of a supermarket meat wrapper who had 11 children.[247] What's more, at least three jurors later argued that they would have not convicted Newton had they known all the evidence. Not surprisingly, Texas executed seven of Mock's previous death penalty clients because of his legal incompetence. Interestingly, Mock is an admitted alcoholic and has failed the state's certification examination required for appointment to capital murder cases.[248] "There is no doubt that Newton was prejudiced by Mock's ineffectiveness: no reasonable juror would have found her guilty beyond a reasonable doubt had she received competent counsel."[249]

A disturbing percentage of capital defense lawyers representing indigent defendants are subject to state disciplinary actions.[250] An investigation in Tennessee revealed that at least 39 disciplined attorneys convicted of bank fraud and perjury have represented capital defendants, including one lawyer who failed to order a blood test resulting in an innocent man lingering in a county jail for four years on a rape charge.[251] Texas officials discipline trial lawyers representing death row inmates at a rate *eight times* that of lawyers generally.[252] Virginia trial lawyers representing capital defendants are subjected to disciplinary proceedings at a rate *six times* that of other lawyers.[253] Attorneys who officials later disbarred or suspended represented 25 percent of Kentucky's death row inmates.[254] To one reporter, some of the state's worst lawyers in Washington represent people facing death sentences. According to Washington Supreme Court justices, appellate decisions, and state lawyer disciplinary records, "one-fifth of the 84 people who have faced execution in the past 20 years were represented by lawyers who had been, or were later, disbarred, suspended or arrested."[255] Studies in other states reveal similar results of incompetent death penalty lawyers.[256]

The Common Sense Foundation recently uncovered evidence that trial lawyers represented at least 37 people (mostly black) on death row in North Carolina who today could not meet the minimum standards of qualification established by the state's Indigent Defense Services Act. Worst still, at least 16 of the 43 defendants executed since 1977 "did not have lawyers with the minimum qualifications required of capital defense attorneys today."[257] North Carolina's bar has sanctioned more than 1 in 6 trial attorneys representing death row inmates for committing felonies, embezzling money, intentionally prejudicing clients, or failing to represent clients diligently.[258] In Illinois, a study by the *Chicano Tribune* found that in 285 death penalty cases, courts sentenced to death 33 defendants represented by trial lawyers with suspended licenses or disbarred from practicing law.[259] In Florida, one ranking jurist openly criticized the quality of private lawyers handling appeals for death row inmates. Florida Supreme Court Justice Cantero claims that attorneys have botched cases, muddled and omitted key arguments, and performed the worst lawyering he has ever seen.[260] According to one report, state authorities have reprimanded, placed on probation, suspended, or disbarred attorneys who have represented some 25 percent of 461 death row inmates in Texas.[261]

Scholars place much of the blame for the ineffective assistance of counsel in cases involving indigent defendants at the doorstep of the U.S. Supreme Court.[262] Interestingly, throughout its entire history the Supreme Court has found ineffective assistance of counsel in only three capital cases.[263] As one appellate lawyer points out, "Despite the parade of drunk, sleeping, unprepared, inexperienced, and otherwise inadequate attorneys that fill the pages of digests and regional reporters, the Court has . . . given no indication that it believes there to be a serious problem with the quality of capital representation."[264] The Court recognized in *Powell* that ineffective assistance of counsel violates an indigent defendant's constitutional rights.[265] Still, the Court did not define ineffective lawyering until 1984 in *Strickland v. Washington* when it affirmed a lower court's finding of ineffective assistance of counsel. There, confessed murderer David Leroy Washington's attorney failed to investigate the circumstances of the crime, Washington's life history, reputation, level of intelligence, and psychology.[266] The Supreme Court put forth that to support a claim of ineffective assistance of counsel a capital defendant must show that the defense lawyer's representation fell below acceptable standards of legal practice and that the lawyers incompetence prejudiced the outcome of the trial—meaning "that there is a reasonable probability that with better counsel, the outcome of his trial would have been different."[267] Then, in the summer of 2003 in *Wiggins v. Smith*, the Supreme Court expanded its view of ineffective assistance of counsel in capital cases to include defense lawyers' failure to investigate a defendant's social history and to do a proper penalty phase investigation. In 2005 in *Rompilla v. Beard*, the Supreme Court ruled further that the defense counsels' failure to investigate mitigating evidence amounted to ineffective assistance of counsel.[268] The Court found that in the *Rompilla* case the trial lawyers did not adequately investigate Rompilla's school records, history of alcohol dependence, juvenile and adult incarceration records, and a prior rape conviction. Scholars have also argued that ineffective assistance of counsel pervades capital cases involving mentally retarded defendants when trial lawyers fail to recognize and present evidence of the defendant's mental retardation.[269] In any event, the future does not look bright for poor defendants and capital defendants of color waging claims of ineffective assistance of counsel beyond *Strickland* and its progeny since newly appointed Justice Alito often dissented while on the Third Circuit Court of Appeals in cases involving ineffective assistance of counsel.[270] Noteworthy also is that Justice Alito frequently dissented on issues of racial bias in jury selection.[271]

THE MOVEMENT FROM PUBLIC TO PRIVATE EXECUTIONS HAS NOT HAD AN INTENDED DETERRENT EFFECT

To early scholars, one indication of a movement away from the use of capital punishment was the exclusion of the public from viewing executions. This was an important observation because the transfer of responsibility for the carrying out of executions from local (city and county) to state jurisdictions fundamentally changed how officials actually impose capital punishment in the United States. With the development of state prison systems, states began requiring that officials conduct executions exclusively under state authority and use execution facilities in state prisons.[272] The purpose of isolating executions in prison facilities was to avoid the public fanfare and carnival-like atmosphere that often characterized public executions in the past.[273] A major supposition of public executions was that they would deter capital offenses, but as one early death penalty expert noted, "it had become abundantly clear that public executions had completely failed in their avowed purpose."[274]

Deterrence remains a major controversy in death penalty research because, despite decades of social scientific research beginning with Ehrlich's work in the 1970s, there is still no definitive answer to capital punishment as a deterrent to murder.[275] In his testimony before the New York Assembly on the future of capital punishment in that state, Columbia Professor of Law and Public Health Jeffrey Fagan denounced deterrence research as so methodologically flawed that it reflects nothing more than "junk science."[276] Even so, there is some anecdotal thinking on capital punishment and deterrence. Southern jurisdictions, for instance, have conducted nearly 82 percent of executions since 1976 yet continue to have the highest homicide rates in the United States.[277] Homicide rates do not appear to decline in death penalty states any more than in non-death penalty states.[278] There is also evidence that the death penalty may actually increase murder rates. One study found that in California the annual increases in homicides were significantly higher in years in which authorities carried out executions than in years when no executions occurred.[279] A similar study in New York found that homicide rates increased during the month following an execution.[280] Researchers John Donnohue and Justin Wolfers do not find the positive effect of capital punishment to increasing murder rates that outlandish. In their most recent examination of statistical studies claiming to show a deterrent effect from the death penalty, they argue that estimates showing that executions save lives are not credible.[281] What's more, they argue that using the same data but analyzed without the severe methodological flaws would lead one to the opposite conclusion that executions actually *increase* murder rates. They show that "with the most minor tweaking of the [research] instruments, one can get estimates ranging from 429 lives saved per execution to 86 lives lost. These numbers are outside the bounds of credibility."[282] The authors conclude:

> The view that the death penalty deters is still the product of belief, not evidence. The reason for this is simple: over the past half century the U.S. has not experimented enough with capital punishment policy to permit strong conclusions. Even complex econometrics cannot sidestep this basic fact. The data are simply too noisy, and the conclusions from any study are too fragile. On balance, the evidence suggests that the death penalty may increase the

murder rate although it remains possible that the death penalty may decrease it. If capital punishment does decrease the murder rate, any decrease is likely small.[283]

JURISDICTIONS HAVE FAILED TO DEVELOP A SWIFT AND PAINLESS EXECUTION METHOD

Early capital punishment scholars confirmed that jurisdictions had replaced traditionally torturous and sadistic methods of execution with more swift and painless practices. The adoption of more humane execution methods was a discerning observation because the trend continues with lethal injection, now the preferred method of execution in 37 states, the federal system, and the U.S. military. Then again, 10 states allow inmates to select electrocution as an alternative execution method to lethal injection; Nebraska is the only state that requires electrocution. Five states provide for asphyxiation as an execution method, two states permit hanging, and still two other states allow for firing squad although these states offer lethal injection as an alternative method. Utah, for example, continued to use the firing squad to execute condemned killers for inmates who chose the method prior to its elimination as an option until March 2004 when Governor Olene Walker signed state legislation outlawing firing squad execution in that state.[284]

Today, lethal injection is the primary execution method used in every death penalty state except Nebraska, which requires electrocution. Invented by a medical examiner with no pharmacological experience, lethal injection protocol in most states involves a three-stage procedure in which in the executioner (usually a corrections officer and not a trained medical professional) injects a condemned inmate with lethal chemicals to bring about a painless death. The inmate first receives an injection of the anesthetic sodium thiopental that deadens pain, a second injection of pancuronium bromide that paralyzes muscles including the lungs and diaphragm, and a third injection containing potassium chloride that brings about cardiac arrest. Autopsies of executed prisoners reportedly reveal that the drug used to paralyze prisoners' muscles (pancuronium bromide) can effectively mask severe suffering. Critics of lethal injection argue that where an executioner administers an improper dose of the first injection (sodium thiopental) of the three-drug cocktail, the condemned inmate will suffer an excruciating death as breathing and heartbeat are stopped with the second (pancuronium bromide) and third injections (potassium chloride).[285] Strangely enough, while 30 states prohibit the use of neuromuscular blocking agents such as pancuronium bromide to euthanizing animals given its painful effects, 28 states use the drug to execute prisoners by lethal injection.[286] Human Rights Watch recently reported on more than a dozen executions where inmates suffered excruciating pain during lethal injections.[287] Autopsies of executed inmates in North and South Carolina revealed that eight executed prisoners had a 50 percent or greater chance that they were conscious throughout the executions, in one case, the likelihood increased to 90 percent, and in four cases there was a 100 percent certainty that the defendants were conscious during the execution.[288]

At least three states limit their lethal injection protocols to only two drugs. South Dakota, Oklahoma, and North Carolina have death penalty laws suggesting that authorities use only two drugs in their lethal injection protocols—"a lethal quantity of an ultra-short-acting barbiturate in combination with a chemical paralytic agent." South Dakota's Governor Rounds postponed Elijah Page's execution just four hours before he was due to be put to death because the state's two-drug lethal injection law failed to conform to the three-drug execution protocol mandated by the state's Department of Corrections. Officials had convicted Page in 2001 for the kidnapping, torture, and murder of Chester Allan Poage a year earlier. Page had given up his appeals and was volunteering to be executed when the governor granted the reprieve until July 2007. In the case of another death row defendant, Donald Moeller, attorneys have raised the issue in federal court in June 2006 whether South Dakota can even legally carry out the execution using the three-drug protocol.[289]

Judge Ellen Segal Huvelle of the U.S. District Court for the District of Columbia stayed indefinitely the federal executions of three codefendants challenging the constitutionality of lethal injection. Defense attorneys in the cases claimed that "while one of the drugs used supposedly will render the plaintiffs insensible to the pain of their deaths, it in fact can and will merely cast a chemical veil over this excruciating pain, leaving the plaintiffs conscious but trapped in a paralyzed body wracked with the pain of suffocation and heart attack."

On at least six separate occasions since January 2006, state judges issued stays of execution after death row inmates raised constitutional challenges to lethal injection as a painful method of execution.[290] In a case stemming from the pending execution of Michael Taylor, sentenced to death in 1989 for the murder of a 15-year-old girl in Kansas City, U.S. District Judge Fernando J. Gaitan, Jr., ordered Missouri to stop all executions until it changes its lethal-injection protocol and thereby not create "an unnecessary risk that an inmate could be subjected to 'unconstitutional pain and suffering when the lethal-injection drugs are administered.'"[291] Judge Gaitan was particularly dismayed that the physician who mixes the three-drug cocktail used in Missouri executions is dyslexic and has difficulty reading numbers. In fact, the physician admitted that he had administered only half the normal dosage of sodium thiopental in several recent executions. What's more, and by his own admission, patients have sued the doctor who presides over lethal injections in Missouri for malpractice more than 20 times. He was publicly reprimanded in 2003 by the state Board of Healing Arts for failing to disclose malpractice suits to a hospital where he treated patients.[292] Judge Gaitan's order has caused a political uproar in Missouri's legal community; apparently, state officials have recently informed the judge that the state cannot comply with his directive that the state change its lethal injection protocol because no anesthesiologist will participate in executions.

The American Society of Anesthesiologists (ASA) supports the American Medical Association's position that physicians should not participate whatsoever in putting condemned inmates to death.[293] The ASA sent letters to its 40,000 members urging them not to participate in an execution.[294] In response, two assistant attorney generals sent letters to 298 board-certified anesthesiologists in Missouri and Southern Illinois seeking their willingness to participate in execution. Still, no anesthesiologist has come forward.[295] Judge Gaitan claims that board-certified anesthesiologists should actively participate in lethal injection executions to the extent of mixing the drugs that are used in lethal injection or at the very least directly observe those individuals who are responsible for doing so. To Dr. Orin F. Guldry, President of the ASA, however, "the legal system has painted itself into this corner, and it is not our obligation to get it out."[296] Missouri state's attorneys have argued in the briefs that to enforce Judge Gaitan's order that using an anesthesiologist in executions "may effectively bar implementation of the death penalty in Missouri."[297] The irony of these developments is that physicians have a long history of participating in state and federal executions given requirements that only physicians can pronounce death. Moreover, physicians actively participate in lethal injection executions. As Human Rights Watch explains,

> In 1990, three physicians administered the first lethal injection execution in Illinois. For a number of years, anesthesiologists injected the drugs in Arizona's lethal injection executions, although that function is no longer undertaken by a doctor. During Texas's first lethal injection execution, Dr. Ralph Gray, the state prison medical director, was present, along with Dr. Bascom Bentley, a physician in private practice, to pronounce the prisoner's death. They watched as execution team members struggled to find intravenous access. Eventually, the team convinced Gray to examine the prisoner and point out the best injection site. Gray had also watched the warden mix the chemical agents. When the warden tried to push them through the syringe, he saw that because the warden had accidentally mixed all the chemical agents together, they had "precipitated into a clot of white sludge." When Gray went to pronounce the prisoner dead, he found the prisoner was still alive. Gray and Bentley suggested allowing more time for the drugs to circulate.[298]

At yearend 2006, there were at least 41 lethal injection executions challenged in federal courts nationwide, and 10 states have imposed temporary moratoriums or effectively put executions on hold and ordered reviews of their execution procedures.[299] While Illinois and New Jersey have placed formal moratoriums on executions, Arkansas, California, Delaware, Florida, Maryland, Missouri, Ohio, and South Dakota have stayed most executions unless defendants have waived appellate review of their capital sentences.[300] Recent hearings at a federal district court in Maryland revealed some very disturbing flaws in the state's lethal injection protocol. Testimony from Columbia University professor and anesthesiologist, Mark Heath, revealed that corrections officers chosen to carry out lethal injections in Maryland are unprepared and unqualified for the task. As Professor Heath put it, "The totality of all their knowledge is grossly inadequate." Testimony from a state trooper responsible for injecting the lethal chemicals into the intravenous lines, for instance, revealed that he had never read the state's operations manual for properly conducting lethal injections. One medical professional and execution team member testified that she would flatly refuse to "slice into an inmates limb to insert a catheter into a deeper vein if the team's nursing assistant could not start a standard IV."[301]

In California, U.S. District Judge Jeremy Fogel held hearings on lethal injection as an unconstitutional method of execution. During four days of testimony and thousands of pages of depositions in February and September 2006, the court learned that California's lethal injection process "is performed in a dark, cramped room by men and women who know little, if anything, about the deadly drugs they inject under extreme stress."[302] Trial testimony characterized lethal injection as a chaotic, haphazard method of execution that has very little medical oversight.[303] Judge Fogel ruled in December 2006, however, that the evidence is more than adequate to establish that California's application of lethal injection death penalty procedures violates the constitutional protection against cruel and unusual method.[304] The most serious problems noted in Judge Fogel's latest ruling included inconsistent and unreliable screening of execution team members; poorly trained staff; inconsistent and unreliable recordkeeping of drugs used in the process; improper mixing, preparation, and administration of drugs by the execution team; over-crowded conditions; and poorly designed facilities in which the execution team must work. Judge Fogel added that the state could resume lethal injection executions when it develops a procedure that the judge finds constitutionally acceptable. He noted that he was particularly troubled with the state's lack of professionalism. In response, the state's governor ordered his administration to fix the problems in California's lethal injection protocol to ensure its constitutionality.[305]

Following the execution of Angel Nieves Diaz in December 2006, Florida's governor halted executions in that state until a commission could investigate why the botched execution had gone so badly. Reportedly, the state took 34 minutes (three times longer than usual) and used a second dose of the fatal drugs to kill Diaz. One execution witness stated that the defendant appeared to be in pain and struggle for breath until executioners gave him a second dose of the fatal drugs. Apparently, the executioner had missed a vein and instead injected the drugs into soft tissue, which would take considerably longer to reach the vital organs. Dias was Puerto Rican convicted in 1979 for the killing of a bar manager. The state proceeded with the execution despite the fact that a key prosecution witness had recanted his trial testimony against Diaz.[306]

Racial disparity is evident in court decisions granting appeals based on the legality of lethal injection as an execution method, however. Forty-two death row inmates challenged the constitutionality of legal injection from January to July 2006. Of these challenges, U.S. District Courts of Appeal and the U.S. Supreme Court granted stays of execution to 12 defendants but denied similar challenges to 30 other defendants whose executions courts allowed to go forward. Of these executions, about 43 percent are white defendants and roughly 56 percent are defendants of color.[307] These figures suggest that courts excessively deny appeals from black and Latino appellants on the constitutionality of lethal injection. In any event, it remains troubling to the legal community why the courts are granting execution stays to some defendants and not to other defendants when these cases are raising the same issue—the legality of lethal injection as the means of execution.[308] As one jurist recently pointed out,

> We are currently operating under a system wherein condemned inmates are bringing nearly identical challenges to the lethal injection procedure. In some instances stays are granted, while in others they are not and the defendants are executed, with no principled distinction to justify such a result. This adds another arbitrary factor into the equation of death and thus far, there has been no logic behind the Supreme Court's decision as to who lives and who dies.[309]

On one narrow issue concerning lethal injection, however, the U.S. Supreme Court recently ruled that condemned inmates could challenge lethal injection as an execution method with a civil rights claim rather than a habeas corpus petition after exhausting regular appeals. The case *Hill v. McDonough* stemmed from Clarence Hill's (a black man) murder conviction for the 1982 killing of a white Pensacola police officer, Stephen Taylor, during a bank robbery.[310] The Supreme Court stopped Hill's execution after prison officials had already strapped him to a gurney and prepared him for execution. Writing for the Court, Justice Kennedy held that Hill and other death row inmates could file special appeals but they are not necessarily entitled to delays in their executions; the court appears not to grant execution stays for death row inmates that raise the claim at the last minute.[311] To some, the decision provides "further evidence of the U.S. Supreme Court's increasing discomfort with many aspects of the death penalty."[312] The Court remanded the case for disposition to the lower federal courts, but those courts refused to hear those challenges and denied Hill an evidentiary hearing on the merits of his lethal injection challenge claiming that he should have raised the issues earlier when the Florida replaced electrocution as a method of execution with lethal injection. Florida executed Clarence Hill in September 2006 by lethal injection. Still, the Court has not answered the underlying question imperative to resolving many recent cases; that is, whether the chemicals used in lethal injections are unconstitutional because they may cause excruciating pain.[313] As a result, the Supreme Court has failed to rule on the constitutionality of a specific method of execution, and consequently, the macabre practice surrounding lethal injection questions the notion that the U.S. death penalty system has substituted the gruesome and sadistic execution methods of decades past with more humane methods that are swift and painless.[314]

The trend continues, however, with lethal injection now the preferred method of execution in 37 states, the federal system, and the U.S. military. Then again, 10 states allow inmates to select electrocution as an alternative execution method to lethal injection; Nebraska is the only state that requires electrocution.[315]

CONCLUSION

Unfortunately, the research record reveals that the United States has not moved substantially away from the use of capital punishment. In this regard, the United States has yet to join much of the international community and abolish the death penalty even if it has stopped executing child offenders and the mentally retarded. Furthermore, the United States has failed to recognize its obligations under the 1963 Vienna Convention on Consular Relations and Optional Protocol and continues to deny foreign nationals consular rights while concomitantly requiring foreign governments to ensure the consular rights of detained Americans. While most state jurisdictions have reduced the number of capital offenses and prohibit executions for crimes where no death results, the federal government has substantively expanded its capital punishment statutes to authorizing executions in the absence of a killing. Although most jurisdictions have abandoned mandatory death sentences for permissive sentencing, many states still mandate capital punishment in direct violation of constitutional protections against equal protection of the law and cruel and unusual punishment. Nor have state death penalty jurisdictions actually reduced the number of executions over the last several decades because the number of persons sentenced to death and put to death has substantially increased over the period. Similarly, death penalty jurisdictions have come no further in eradicating selective enforcement in capital sentencing than that noted in a 1926 House of Representatives report.

> As it is now applied the death penalty is nothing but an arbitrary discrimination against an occasional victim. It cannot even be said that it is reserved as a weapon of retributive justice for the most atrocious criminals. For it is not necessarily the most guilty who suffer it. Almost any criminal with wealth or influence can escape it, but the poor and friendless convict, without means or power to fight his case from court to court or to exert pressure upon the pardoning executive, is the one singled out as a sacrifice to what is little more than tradition.[316]

Moreover, even though jurisdictions execute condemned inmates under private, antiseptic conditions involving few observers, considerable research shows that the death penalty has no more deterrent value today than it did when officials publicly executed condemned prisoners with spectacle and fanfare. And even with claims of modern painless execution methods, forensic evidence reveals that lethal injection involves the same pain and barbarism as the most heinous and sadistic forms of execution. Despite the righteous rhetoric of judges, prosecutors, and other judicial officers to the constitutional cannons of equity, fairness, and evenhandedness in criminal justice processes, the U.S. legal system remains in a pathetic state regarding its capital punishment scheme. Regrettably, the United States has yet to move away from the use of capital punishment over the last half century as predicted by early investigators. What is more, these trends dictate a future of refining the death penalty's imposition toward a virtually powerless group of capital defendants.

ENDNOTES

1. See, for instance, F. Hartung, "Trends in the Use of Capital Punishment," *Annals of the American Academy of Political and Social Sciences* 284 (1952): 8–19.

2. Ibid.

3. L. Deets, "Changes in Capital Punishment Policy Since 1939," *Journal of Criminal Law and Criminology* 38 (1948): 584–94; V. Templewood, *Shadows of the Gallows* (London: Victor Gallancz, 1951).

4. Hartung, "Trends in the Use of Capital Punishment."

5. Amnesty International, *Bahamas: Privy Council Abolished Mandatory Death Sentence* (2006), available at http://amnesty-news.c.topica.com/ maaezEdaboUeNbdUtUBb/; *Los Angeles Times,* "Number of Executions Declines Worldwide," A24.

6. Amnesty International, *Bahamas: Privy Council Abolished Mandatory Death Sentence* (2006), available at http://amnesty-news.c.topica.com/ maaezEdaboUeNbdUtUBb/; Amnesty International, *Death Penalty Developments in 2005* (2006), available at http://web.amnesty.org/web/ web.nsf/print/7F1DAA21CB800C90802571-550053E0DE.

7. Andorra, Angola, Armenia, Australia, Austria, Azerbaijan, Belgium, Bhutan, Bosnia-Herzegovina, Bulgaria, Cambodia, Canada, Cape Verde, Colombia, Costa Rica, Cote D'Ivoire, Croatia, Cyprus, Czech Republic, Denmark, Djibouti, Dominican Republic, Ecuador, Estonia, Finland, France, Georgia, Germany, Greece, Guinea-Bissau, Haiti, Honduras, Hungary, Iceland, Ireland, Italy, Kiribati, Liberia, Liechtenstein, Lithuania, Luxembourg,

Macedonia (former Yugoslav Republic), Malta, Marshall Islands, Mauritius, Mexico, Micronesia (Federated States), Moldova, Monaco, Mozambique, Namibia, Nepal, Netherlands, New Zealand, Nicaragua, Niue, Norway, Palau, Panama, Paraguay, Poland, Portugal, Romania, Samoa, San Marino, Sao Tome and Principe, Senegal, Serbia and Montenegro, Seychelles, Slovak Republic, Slovenia, Solomon Islands, South Africa, Spain, Sweden, Switzerland, Timor-Leste, Turkey, Turkmenistan, Tuvalu, Ukraine, United Kingdom, Uruguay, Vanuatu, Vatican City State, Venezuela.

8. Albania, Argentina, Bolivia, Brazil, Childe, Cook Islands, El Salvador, Fiji, Israel, Latvia, Peru.

9. Algeria, Bahrain, Benin, Brunei, Darussalam, Burkina Faso, Central African Republic, Congo (Republic), Gambia, Grenada, Kenya, Madagascar, Maldives, Mali, Mauritania, Morocco, Myanmar, Nauru, Niger, Papua New Guinea, Russian Federation, Sri Lanka, Suriname, Togo, Tonga, Tunisia.

10. Amnesty International, *Stop Child Executions: Ending the Death Penalty for Child Offenders* (2004), available at http://web.amnesty.org/library/Index/ENGACT500152004; Amnesty International, *Children and the Death Penalty: Executions Worldwide Since 1990* (2002), available at http://web.amnesty.org/library/Index/ENGACT500072002.

11. Amnesty International, *The Death Penalty*, available at http://web.amnesty.org/pages/deathpenalty-index-eng; See also Amnesty International; Amnesty International, *Globalizing the Fight Against the Death Penalty*, available at http://web.amnesty.org/pages/deathpenalty-010207-feature-eng.

12. F. Zimring, "Plenary Address: Symbol and Substance in the Massachusetts Commission Report," *Indiana Law Journal* 80 (2005): 113–29; F. Zimring, *The Contradictions of American Capital Punishment* (New York: Oxford University Press, 2003).

13. E. Mandary, *Capital Punishment: A Balanced Examination* (Sudbury, MA: Jones and Bartlett Publishers, 2005), 629.

14. F. Rohatyn, "Dead to the World," *The New York Times,* January 26, 2006, 23.

15. K. Rahn, Life Sentence Could Replace Death Penalty," *The Korea Times* , February 24, 2006,

available at http://search.hankooki.com/times/times_view.php?term=death+penalty++&path=hankooki3/times/lpage/200602/kt2006022117574010220.htm&medai=kt

16. Amnesty International, *Bahamas: Privy Council Abolished Mandatory Death Sentence* (March 9, 2006), available at http://web.amnesty.org/library/Index/ENGAMR14001_2006?open&of=ENG-BHS.

17. Death Penalty Information Center, *Philippine President Orders Commutations of All on Death Row*, available at http://www.deathpenaltyinfo.org/article.php?did=1752&scid=64.

18. Amnesty International, *Philippines: Abolition of the Death Penalty*, news release issued June 7, 2006, by the International Secretariat of Amnesty International, available at http://web.amnesty.org/ library/Index/ENGASA3500-42006?open&of=ENG-2AS.

19. K. Ossenova, "France Parliament Amends Constitution to Ban Death Penalty, Allow Impeachment," *Jurist Legal News and Research,* February 20, 2007; K. Ossenova, "France Inscribes Banning of Death Penalty in Constitution," *International Herald Tribune,* February 19, 2007, available at http://www.iht.com/articles/ap/2007/02/19/europe/EU-GEN-France-Constitutional-Changes.php.

20. "Number of Executions Declines Worldwide," *Los Angeles Times*, April 21, 2006, A24.

21. C. Anna, "Worldwide Wedge: Death Divide: Capital Punishment Faces a Fresh Round of Global Scrutiny," *The Atlanta Journal-Constitution*, August 28, 2005, 1E; See also Justice Scalia's angry response to Justice Souter's impassioned dissent in *State v. Marsh*, 2006, p. 7, note 3, concerning the European Union and capital punishment.

22. These countries include Afghanistan, Antigua and Barbuda, Bahamas, Bangladesh, Barbados, Belarus, Belize, Botswana, Burundi, Cameroon, Chad, China, Comoroa, Congo (Democratic Republic), Cuba, Dominica, Egypt, Equatorial Guinea, Eritrea, Ethiopia, Gabon, Ghana, Guatemala, Guinea, Guyana, India, Indonesia, Iran, Iraq, Jamaica, Japan, Jordan, Kazakhstan, North Korea, South Korea, Kuwait, Kyrgyzstan, Laos, Lebanon, Lesotho, Libya, Malawi, Malaysia, Mongolia, Nigeria, Oman, Pakistan, Palestinian Authority, Philippines, Qatar,

Rwanda, Saint Christopher and Nevis, Saint Lucia, Saint Vincent and Grenadines, Saudi Arabia, Sierra Leone, Singapore, Somalia, Sudan, Swaziland, Syria, Taiwan, Tajikistan, Tanzania, Thailand, Trinidad and Tobago, Uganda, United Arab Emirates, United States of America, Uzbekistan, Viet Nam, Yemen, Zambia, Zimbabwe.

23. Amnesty International, *Death Penalty News* (2005), available at http://web.amnesty.org/library/pdf/ACT530022005ENGLISH/$File/ACT5300205.pdf.

24. Amnesty International, *Worldwide Executions Double in 2001*, available at http://web.amnesty.org/library/Index/engACT_500052002?OpenDocument&of=THEMES\DEATH+PENALTY.

25. These countries include Bangladesh, Belarus, China, Indonesia, Iran, Iraq, Japan, Jordan, Korea (North), Kuwait, Libya, Mongolia, Pakistan, Palestinian Authority, Saudi Arabia, Singapore, Somalia, Taiwan, United States, Uzbekistan, Vietnam, and Yemen.

26. These countries include Afghanistan, Algeria, Bahamas, Bahrain, Bangladesh, Belize, Barbados, Burkina Faso, Burundi, China, Congo (Democratic Republic), Egypt, Ethiopia, Ghana, Guinea, India, Indonesia, Iran, Iraq, Jamaica, Japan, Jordan, Kazakstan, Korea (North), Korea (South), Kuwait, Laos, Lebanon, Libya, Malawi, Malaysia, Mali, Mongolia, Morocco, Nigeria, Oman, Pakistan, Philippines, Qatar, Saudi Arabia, Singapore, Somalia, Sri Lanka, Sudan, Syria, Taiwan, Tanzania, Trinidad and Tobago, United States, Uzbekistan, Vietnam, Yemen, and Zimbabwe.

27. Amnesty International, *Death Penalty New: May 2006* (May 1, 2006), available at http://web.amnesty.org/library/Index/ENGACT530022006?open&of=ENG-BHS.

28. Amnesty International, *Death Sentences and Executions in 2005*, available at http://web.amnesty.org/web/web.nsf/print/6463BC51D4FD6A0A80256D51005DE662.

29. S. Trevaskes, "Severe and Swift Justice in China," *British Journal of Criminology* 47 (2007): 23–41.

30. C. Anna, "Worldwide Wedge: Death Divide," 1E.

31. Human Rights Watch, *Organ Procurement and Judicial Execution in China,* August 1994,

available at http://www.hrw.org/reports/1994/china1/china_948.htm#_1_13.

32. D. Saunders, "Global Bazaar in Body Parts," *San Francisco Chronicle*, July 20, 2006 B9.

33. D. Burton, "Outraged at China's Sale of Organs," *Indianapolis Star*, June 29, 1998, A5.

34. L. Patton, "A Call for Common Sense: Organ Donation and the Executed Prisoner," *Virginia Journal of Social Policy and the Law* 3 (1996): 387–434; D. Perales, "Comment: Rethinking the Prohibition of Death Row Prisoners as Organ Donors: A Possible Lifeline to Those on Organ Donor Waiting Lists," *St. Mary's Law Journal* 34 (2003): 687–732; L. Palmer, Jr., "Capital Punishment: A Utilitarian Proposal for Recycling Transplantable Organs as Part of a Capital Felon's Death Sentence," *University of West Los Angeles Law Review* 29 (1998): 1–41; P. Coleman, "Brother, Can You Spare a Liver? Five Ways to Increase Organ Donation," *Valparaiso University Law Review* 31 (1996): 1–41; Indiana University Center for Bioethics, *Death Row Organ Donation Resources*, available at http://www.bioethics.iu.edu/deathrow_resources.html.

35. S. Bright, "Will the Death Penalty Remain Alive in the Twenty-First Century? International Norms, Discrimination, Arbitrariness and the Risk of Executing the Innocent," *Wisconsin Law Review* 2001 (2001): 1–27.

36. Juvenile and Criminal Justice, *Cruel and Unusual Punishment: The Juvenile Death Penalty*, September 2004, available at http://ccjr.policy.net/relatives/22640.pdf?PROACTIVE_ID=cececdcdcbcec7c7cac5cecfcfcfc5cecec6c8cccfc8c9c8c8c5cf; Amnesty International, *Children and the Death Penalty: Executions Worldwide Since 1990*, available at http://web.amnesty.org/library/Index/ENGACT500072002; See also *Roper v. Simmons*, 543 U.S. 177 (2005).

37. Human Rights Watch/Amnesty International, *The Rest of Their Lives: Life Without Parole for Child Offenders in the United States*, 2005, available at http://hrw.org/reports/2005/us1005/TheRestofTheirLives.pdf.

38. Amnesty International, *Stop Child Executions: Ending the Death Penalty for Child Offenders*, 2004, available at http://web.amnesty.org/library/Index/ENGACT500152004.

39. Amnesty International, *Iran: Amnesty International Calls for End to Death Penalty for Child Offenders*, 2006, available at http://web.amnesty.org/library/Index/ENGMDE1 30052006?open&of=ENG-IRN.

40. Hartung, "Trends in the Use of Capital Punishment."

41. P. Mackey, *Voices Against Death: American Opposition to Capital Punishment, 1787–1975* (New York: Burt Franklin, 1976), xvii–xviii.

42. C. Cropley, "The Case of John McCaffary," *Wisconsin Magazine of History* (Summer 1952): 281–87, available at http://freepages.genealogy.rootsweb.com/~sewis/cropley_p_281.htm.

43. R. Bohm, *DeathQuest II: An Introduction to the Theory and Practice of Capital Punishment in the United States* (Cincinnati, OH: Anderson, 2003); W. Bowers, *Legal Homicide: Death as Punishment in America, 1864–1982* (Boston: Northwestern University Press, 1984).

44. M. Espy and J. Smykla, *Executions in the United States, 1608–1987: The Espy File* [machine-readable data file]. Tuscaloosa, AL: John Smykla [producer], Ann Arbor, MI: Inter-University Consortium for Political and Social Research [distributor] 2004.

45. "Editorial: Wrong Then and Now," *Milwaukee Journal Sentinel* JSOnline, March 13, 2006, available at http://www.jsonline.com/story/index.aspx?id=407916.

46. "Honorable James J. Gilvary Symposium on Law, Religion, and Social Justice: Evolving Standards of Decency in 2003–Is the Death Penalty on Life Support?: The Death Penalty Experiment: The Facts Behind The Conclusions," *Dayton Law Review* 29 (2004): 223–63.

47. S. Banner, *The Death Penalty: An American History* (Cambridge, MA: Harvard University Press, 2002); W. Bowers, *Legal Homicide*.

48. *Atkins v. Virginia*, 536 U.S. 304 (2002); *Roper v. Simmons*, 543 U.S. 177 (2005). See also Abid Aslam, "Hundreds of Mentally Ill To Be Executed in America," *Common Dreams News Center*, February 2, 2006, available at http://www.commondreams.org/headlines06/0202-02.htm.

49. Death Penalty Information Center, *Facts About the Death Penalty*, available at http://www.deathpenaltyinfo.org/FactSheet.pdf.

50. Death Penalty Information Center, *News and Development–Recent Legislative Activity*, available at http://www.deathpenaltyinfo.org/newsanddev.php?scid=40.

51. J. Borenstein, "The Death Penalty: Conceptual and Empirical Issues," *Cardozo Public Law, Policy and Ethics* 2 (2004): 377–99; National Urban League, *The State of Black America 2005*, http://www.nul.org; "Over 4,000 Groups Join the Call for a Moratorium on Executions," *Equal Justice USA,* November 2005, http://www.quixote.org/ej.

52. American Bar Association, *Evaluating Fairness and Accuracy in State Death Penalty Systems: The Georgia Death Penalty Assessment Report. An Analysis of Georgia's Death Penalty Laws, Procedures, and Practices*, January 2006, http://www.abanet.org/moratorium/assessmentproject/georgia/finalreport.doc.

53. These states are Arizona, Connecticut, Delaware, Kansas, Maryland, North Carolina, Illinois, Indiana, Nebraska, Nevada, Pennsylvania, Tennessee, and Virginia. See Death Penalty Information Center, *State-by-State Information*, http://www.deathpenaltyinfo.org/state.

54. Gallup Poll, *Death Penalty Gets Less Support from Britons, Canadians than Americans,* February 20, 2006, http://www.deathpenaltyinfo.org/article.php?did=1693&scid=64.

55. United States Conference of Catholic Bishops, *A Culture of Life and the Penalty of Death: A Statement of the United States Conference of Catholic Bishops Calling for an End to the Use of the Death Penalty,* 2005, available at http://www.usccb.org/sdwp/national/penaltyofdeath.pdf. See also, Sara Catania, "Death Row Conversion," *Mother Jones*, December 2005, 60–67.

56. J. Ibbitson, "Digging a Grave for Capital Punishment? State Moratoriums Have Some in the U.S. Predicting the End is Near," *Common Dreams: News Center*, available at http://www.commondreams.org/cgi-bin/print.cgi?_file=/headlines02/0511-05.htm.

57. National Coalition to Abolish the Death Penalty, *Resistance to Death Penalty Growing*, April 8, 2007, available at http://www.democracyinaction.org/dia/organizations/ncap/news.jsp?key=3216.

58. G. Holland, "Justices Wade into International Death Penalty Debate," *Associated Press*, December 10, 2004.

59. A. Tranel, "Comment: The Ruling of the International Court of Justice in Avena and Other Mexican Nationals: Enforcing the Right to Consular Assistance in U.S. Jurisprudence," *American University International Law Review* 20 (2005): 403–64; L. Rothenberg, "International Law, U.S. Sovereignty, and the Death Penalty," *Georgetown Journal of International Law* 35 (2004): 547–95; M. Vandiver, "An Apology Does Not Assist the Accused," in *Sources: Notable Selections in Crime, Criminology, and Criminal Justice*, eds. D.V. Baker and R. P. Davin (Guilford, CT: McGraw-Hill/Dushkin, 2001), 342–59; J. Quigley, "Execution of Foreign Nationals in the United States: Pressure from Foreign Governments Against the Death Penalty," *ILSA Journal of International and Comparative Law* 4 (1998): 589–98.

60. *Mexico v. United States of America*, 2004 I.C.J. 128 (Mar. 31).

61. *International Law Update*, "In Death Penalty Case, Where Petitioner Is Appealing Denial of Habeas Corpus, Eleventh Circuit Denies Stay Where Petitioner Claims Vienna Convention Violations but Failed to Raise Issue on Direct Appeal," December 2005; R. Sloane, "Measures Necessary to Ensure: The ICJ's Provisional Measures Order in Avena and Other Mexican Nationals," *Leiden Journal of International Law* 17: 673; L. Young, "Setting Sail with the Charming Betsy: Enforcing the International Court of Justice's Avena Judgment in Federal Habeas Corpus Proceedings," *Minnesota Law Review* 89 (2005): 890–915; M. Steinmark, "The Case Concerning Avena and Other Mexican Nationals (*Mexico v. United States*): A Mexican Perspective on the Fight for Consular Rights," *Law and Business Review of the Americas* 10 (2004): 317.

62. Death Penalty Information Center, *Foreign Nationals and the Death Penalty in the United States–Consular Rights, Foreign Nationals and the Death Penalty*, http://www.deathpenaltyinfo .org/article.php?did=198&scid=31#backgroun; *Mexico v. United States of America*, 2004 I.C.J. 128 (Mar. 31); M. Donald, "Stuck in Habeas Hell: Bush Breathes New Life Into Texas Death-Row Inmate's Case," *Texas Lawyer* 21 (May 2, 2005): 1; D. Dow, *Executed on a Technicality: Lethal Injustice on America's Death Row* (Boston: Beacon Press, 2005).

63. Amnesty International, *USA: Another "Double Standard" on Consular Rights?* http://web .amnesty.org/library/Index/ENGAMR5105020 05?open&of=ENG-392.

64. K. Randall, "Bush Administration Repudiates World Court Jurisdiction in Death Penalty Cases," *World Socialist Web Site,* March 11, 2005, available at http://www.wsws.org/articles/ 2005/mar2005/icj-m11.shtml.

65. A. Liptak, "Texas Court Ruling Rebuffs Bush and World Court," *New York Times,* November 16, 2006, A29.

66. Amnesty International, *USA, Non-Compliance with Avena Decision Imperils US Citizens Traveling Abroad Consular Notification Is a Human Right and Must Be Protected*. Press Bulletin, 2005.

67. M. Fleishman, "Reciprocity Unmasked: The Role of the Mexican Government in Defense of Its Foreign Nationals in United States Death Penalty Cases," *Arizona Journal of International and Comparative Law* 20 (2003): 359–407; A. Macina, "Avena and Other Mexican Nationals: The Litmus for LaGrand and the Future of Consular Rights in the United States," *California Western International Law Journal* 34 (2003): 115–42; H. Schiffman, "Breard and Beyond: The Status of Consular Notification and Access Under the Vienna Convention," *Cardozo Journal of International and Comparative Law* 8 (2000): 27–60.

68. Death Penalty Information Center, *Foreign Nationals and the Death Penalty in the United States–Consular Rights, Foreign Nationals and the Death Penalty*, http://www .deathpenaltyinfo.org/article.php?did=198& scid=31#background.

69. Ibid.

70. S. Baker, "*Germany v. United States* in the International Court of Justice: An International Battle over the Interpretation of Article Thirty-six of the Vienna Convention on Consular Relations and Provisional Measures Orders," *Georgia Journal of International and Comparative Law* 30 (2002): 277–304; D. Lehman, "*The Federal Republic of Germany v. The United*

States of America: The Individual Right to Consular Access," *Law and Inequality Journal* 20 (2002): 313–40; C. O'Driscoll, "The Execution of Foreign Nationals in Arizona: Violations of the Vienna Convention on Consular Relations," *Arizona State Law Journal* 32 (2000): 323–43.

71. Amnesty International, *Abolish the Death Penalty: The Death Penalty Violates the Rights of Foreign Nationals*, http://www.amnestyusa .org/abolish/factsheets/foreign_nationals.html

72. Death Penalty Information Center, *Foreign Nationals and the Death Penalty in the United States–Consular Rights, Foreign Nationals and the Death Penalty*, http://www.deathpenaltyinfo .org/article.php?did=198&scid=31#backgroun; Anna, "Worldwide Wedge: Death Divide," 1E; *Sorensen v. City of New York*, 413 F.3d 292 (2005); "Dismissal of Danish Mother's Vienna Convention Rights Violation Claim Affirmed; Appeal Ineffective," *New York Law Journal,* July 19, 2005, http://www.law.com/jsp/nylj/ index.jsp.

73. *Moises Sanchez-Llamas v. Oregon*, 2006 U.S. LEXIS 5177 (2006).

74. *Bustillo v. Johnson*, 2006 U.S. LEXIS 5177 (2006).

75. *Moises Sanchez-Llamas v. Oregon*, 2006 U.S. LEXIS 5177 (2006), p. 20; David Savage, "U.S. Law Trumps World Treaty, High Court Says," *Los Angeles Times,* June 29, 2006, A23.

76. *Debevoise Represents Mexican National in the Supreme Court*, March 16, 2006, http://www .debevoise.com/vccr/

77. M. Foley, *Arbitrary and Capricious: The Supreme Court, the Constitution, and the Death Penalty* (Westport, CT: Praeger Press, 2003).

78. *Coker v. Georgia* (1977) and (*Eberheart v. Georgia*, 1977), respectively.

79. T. Bonczar and T. Snell, *Capital Punishment, 2004* (revised on February 1, 2006), available at http://www.ojp.usdoj.gov/bjs/pub/pdf/cp04.pdf.

80. S. Adcox, "S.C. Approves Seeking Death Penalty for Pedophiles," *ABCNews*, March 29, 2006, available at http://abcnews.go.com/US/wire Story?id=1779420.

81. S. Jordan, "Death for Drug Related Killings: Revival of the Federal Death Penalty," *Chicago-Kent Law Review* 67 (1991): 79–125; P. Robinson, "Judge Over Jury: Judicial Discretion in the Federal Death Penalty Under the Drug Kingpin Act. *Kansas Law Review* 45 (1997): 1491–526.

82. J. Cunningham, "Death in the Federal Courts: Expectations and Realities of the Federal Death Penalty Act of 1994," *University of Richmond Law Review* 32 (1998): 939–72; Comment, "Testing the Federal Death Penalty Act of 1994, 18 U.S.C. 3591–98 (1994): *United States v. Jones*, 132 F.3d 232 (5th Cir. 1998)," *Texas Tech Law Review* 29 (1998): 1043–109; E. Tolley and R. Hauser, "Federal Death Penalty Act of 1994," *The Champion* 19 (1995): 24–28.

83. S. Weinberg, *Punishing the Wrongfully Convicted: Federal Law Keeps Defendants Denied a Fair Trial—Including Those Who May Be Innocent—Behind Bars*, The Center for Public Integrity, June 26, 2003, available at http://www.publicintegrity.org/pm/default .aspx?act=sidebarsb&aid=35.

84. Death Penalty Information Center, *Federal Laws Providing for the Death Penalty*, available at http://www.deathpenaltyinfo.org/article.php?sci d=29&did=192.

85. Subcommittee on Federal Death Penalty Cases, Committee on Defender Services, Judicial Conference of the United States, *Federal Death Penalty Cases: Recommendations Concerning the Cost and Quality of Defense Representation*, May 1998, available at http://www.uscourts .gov/dpenalty/1COVER.htm.

86. Federal Death Penalty Research Counsel, available at http://www.capdefnet.org/fdprc/contents/ shared_files/docs/1_overview_of_fed_death_ process.asp.

87. U.S. Department of Justice, The Federal Death Penalty System: A Statistical Survey, 1988–2000, available at http://www.usdoj.gov/dag/ pubdoc/dpsurvey.html; U.S. Department of Justice, The Federal Death Penalty System: Supplemental Data, Analysis, and Revised Protocols for Capital Case Review, available at http://www.usdoj.gov/dag/pubdoc/deathpenalty-study.htm; Staff Report by the Subcommittee on Civil and Constitutional Rights, Committee on the Judiciary, One Hundred Third Congress, Second Session, *Racial Disparities in Federal Death Prosecutions 1988–1994*, available at http://www.deathpenaltyinfo.org/article.php?s cid=45&did=528#sxn4.

88. D. Sullivan, "A Matter of Life and Death: Examining the Military Death Penalty's Fairness," *The Federal Lawyer* 45 (June, 1998): 38; See also Major Mary M. Foreman, "Military Capital Litigation: Meeting the Heightened Standards of *United States v. Curtis*," *Military Law Review* 174 (2002): 1.

89. Department of the Army, *U.S. Army Corrections System: Procedures for Military Executions,* January 2006, available at http://www.fas.org/irp/doddir/army/r190_55.pdf.

90. Sullivan, "A Matter of Life and Death: Examining the Military Death Penalty's Fairness."

91. C. Cooper, "Support Strong for Death Penalty," *Riverside Press-Enterprise,* March 3, 2006, A3.

92. D. Conti, "More Juries Split Over Death Penalty Decisions," *Pittsburg Tribune-Review,* February 27, 2006.

93. E. Bazar, "Wider Death Penalty Sought," *USATODAY,* February 7, 2007, available at http://www.usatoday.com/news/nation/2007-02-06-death-penalty_x.htm.

94. Hartung, "Trends in the Use of Capital Punishment," 16.

95. *Coker v. Georgia,* 433 U.S. 584, 585 (1977).

96. G. LaFree, *Rape and Criminal Justice: The Social Construction of Sexual Assault* (Belmont, CA: Wadsworth Publishing Company, 1989); A. Taslitz, "Race and Two Concepts of the Emotions in Date Rape. *Wisconsin Women's Law Journal* 15 (2000): 3–76.

97. D. MacNamara and E. Sagarin, *Sex, Crime, and the Law* (New York: The Free Press, 1977); J. Wriggins, "Rape, Racism, and the Law," *Harvard Women's Law Journal* 6 (1981): 103.

98. J. Bailey, "Death Is Different, Even on the Bayou: The Disproportionality of Crime and Punishment in Louisiana's Capital Child Rape Statute," *Washington and Lee Law Review* 55 (1998): 1335–372; J. Broughton, "On Horror's Head Horrors Accumulate: A Reflective Common on Capital Child Rape Legislation," *Duquesne Law Review* 39 (2000): 1–42; J. Cordle, "*State v. Wilson*: Social Discontent, Retribution, and the Constitutionality of Capital Punishment for Raping a Child," *Capital University Law Review* 27 (1998): 135–62; E. Gray, "Death Penalty and Child Rape: An Eighth Amendment Analysis," *St. Louis University Law Journal* 42 (1998): 1443–469; A. Miller, "Constitutional Law: Can a Convicted Rapist Be Sentenced to Death for Raping a Child Under Twelve Years of Age?" *Washburn Law Journal* 37 (1997): 187–202; E. Moeller, "Devolving Standards of Decency: Using the Death Penalty to Punish Child Rapists," *Dickinson Law Review* 102 (1998): 621–48; B. Palmer, "Death as a Proportionate Penalty for the Rape of a Child: Considering One State's Current Law," *Georgia State University Law Review* 15 (1999): 843–78; H. Rizvi, "U.S. states widen scope of executions." *CommonDreams News Center,* August 29, 2006, available at http://www.commondreams.org/headlines06/0829-04.htm; D. Schaaf, "What If the Victim Is a Child? The Constitutionality of Louisiana's Challenge to *Coker v. Georgia, University of Illinois Law Review* 2000 (2000): 347–78; M. Silversten, "Sentencing *Coker v. Georgia* to Death: Capital Child Rape Statutes Provide the Supreme Court an Opportunity to Return Meaning to the Eighth Amendment," *Gonzaga Law Review* 37 (2002): 121–66; P. Zambrano, "The Death Penalty Is Cruel and Unusual Punishment for the Crime of Rape–Even the Rape of a Child," *Santa Clara Law Review* 39 (1999): 1267–293; A. Fleming, "Louisiana's Newest Capital Crime: The Death Penalty for Child Rape," *Journal of Criminal Law & Criminology* 89 (1999): 717–50; Y. Glazer, "Child Rapists Beware! The Death Penalty and Louisiana's Amended Aggravated Rape Statute," *American Journal of Criminal Law* 25 (1997): 79; M. Meister, "Murdering Innocence: The Constitutionality of Capital Child Rape Statutes," *Arizona Law Review* 45 (2003): 197; M. Mello, Executing Rapists: A Reluctant Essay on the Ethics of Legal Scholarship, *William and Mary Journal of Women and Law* 4 (1997): 129.

99. La. Rev. Stat. Ann. 14:42 (C) (West 1995), revised and codified in La. Rev. Stat. Ann. 14:42(D)(1), (2) (West Supp. 1999) with no relevant changes.

100. *Louisiana v. Anthony Wilson and Patrick Dewayne Bethley,* 685 So. 2d 1063 (1996).

101. A. Fleming, "Louisiana's Newest Capital Crime: The Death Penalty for Child Rape," *Journal of*

Criminal Law & Criminology 89 (1999): 717–50.

102. J. Bailey, "Death Is Different, Even on the Bayou: The Disproportionality of Crime and Punishment in Louisiana's Capital Child Rape Statute," *Washington and Lee Law Review* 55 (1998): 1335; M. Diamond, "Note, Assessing the Constitutionality of Capital Child Rape Statutes," *St. John's Law Review* 73 (1999): 1159; A. Fleming, "Louisiana's Newest Capital Crime: The Death Penalty for Child Rape," *Journal of Criminal Law & Criminology* 89 (1999): 717–50; P. Lormand, "Proportionate Sentencing for Rape of a Minor: The Death Penalty Dilemma," *Tulane Law Review* 73 (1999): 1014; L. Shirley, "*State v. Wilson*: The Louisiana Supreme Court Sanctions the Death Penalty for Child Rape," *Tulane Law Review* 72 (1998): 1913; P. Zambrano, "The Death Penalty Is Cruel and Unusual Punishment for the Crime of Rape–Even the Rape of a Child," *Santa Clara Law Review* 39 (1998): 1267.

103. C. Rayburn, "Better Dead than Raped?: The Patriarchial Rhetoric Driving Capital Rape Statutes," *St. John's Law Review* 78 (2004): 1119–165, at 1164.

104. J. Acker and C. Lanier, "Beyond Human Ability? The Rise and Fall of Death Penalty Legislation," in *America's Experiment with Capital Punishment: Reflections on the Past, Present, and Future of the Ultimate Penal Sanction*, eds. J. Acker, R. Bohm, and C. Lanier, 85–125 (Durham, NC: Carolina University Press, 2003), 91.

105. *Furman v. Georgia*, 408 U.S. 238 (1972).

106. *Gregg v. Georgia,* 428 U.S. 153 (1976).

107. *McGautha v. California*, 402 U.S. 1983 (1971).

108. *Crampton v. Ohio,* 402 U.S. 1983 (1971).

109. *McGautha v. California*, 402 U.S. 1983, 1983 (1971).

110. Ibid. 196).

111. *Furman*, p. 239)

112. *Woodson v. North Carolina,* 428 U.S. 280 (1976).

113. M. Durose and P. Langran, *Felony Sentences in State Courts, 2002*, Bureau of Justice Statistics, 2004, available at http://www.ojp.usdoj.gov/bjs/pub/pdf/fssc02.pdf.

114. P. Langan and H. Graziadei, *Felony Sentences in State Courts, 1992,* Bureau of Justice Statistics, 1995, available at http://www.ojp.usdoj.gov/bjs/pub/pdf/felsent.pdf.

115. Hartung, "Trends in the Use of Capital Punishment."

116. T. Bonczar and T. Snell, *Capital punishment, 2004* (revised on February 1, 2006), available at http://www.ojp.usdoj.gov/bjs/pub/pdf/cp04.pdf.

117. D. Fins, *Death Row USA: A Quarterly Report by the Criminal Justice Project of the NAACP Legal Defense and Educational Fund, Inc*, available at http://www.naacpldf.org/content/pdf/pubs/drusa/DRUSA_Winter_2007.pdf; D. Conti, "More Juries Split Over Death Penalty Decisions," *Pittsburg Tribune-Review,* February 27, 2006, available at http://www.puttsburgh-live.com/x/search/print_427959.html.

118. T. Bonczar and T. Snell, *Capital punishment, 2004* (revised on February 1, 2006), available at http://www.ojp.usdoj.gov/bjs/pub/pdf/cp04.pdf.

119. Ibid.

120. Ibid.

121. California Department of Corrections, *Summary of Condemned Inmates Who Have Died Since 1978* (2006), available at http://www.corr.ca.gov/ReportsResearch/docs/CIWHD.pdf.

122. J. Liebman, "The Overproduction of Death," *Columbia Law Review* 100 (2000): 2030–156; J. Liebman, J. Fagan, V. West, and J. Lloyd, "Capital Attrition, Error Rates in Capital Cases, 1973–1995," *Texas Law Review* 78 (2000): 1839–865; See also A. Gelman, J. Liebman, V. West, and A. Kiss, "A Broken System: The Persistent Patterns of Reversals of Death Sentences in the United States," *Journal of Empirical Legal Studies* 1 (2004): 209; Center for Public Integrity, *Harmful Error: Investigating America's Local Prosecutors,* 2006, available at http://www.publicintegrity.org/pm/default.aspx

123. *HoustonChronicle.com*, "Republicans Want to Speed Up Death Penalty," July 6, 2005, available at http://www.chron.com/cs/CDA/ssistory.mpl/nation/3254784.

124. H. Weinstein, "Top Jurists Pan Faster Death Penalty Appeals," *Los Angeles Times*, August 6, 2005, A14.

125. Ibid.

126. "The House's Abuse of Patriotism," *New York Times,* October 31, 2005, available at http://www.nytimes.com/2005/10/31/opinion/31mon1.html?ex=1131685200&en=c07697f77cdcd3f7&ei=5070; "Patriot Death Games," *Washington Post,* November 2, 2005, 20; Kate Randall, "Bush Administration Repudiates World Court Jurisdiction in Death Penalty Cases," *World Socialist Web Site,* March 11, 2005, available at http://www.wsws.org/articles/2005/mar2005/icj-m11.shtml.

127. Human Rights Watch, *House Amendment Tilts Playing Field for Death Penalty,* 2005, available at http://www.hrw.org/english/docs/2005/10/26/usdom11924.htm.

128. American Civil Liberties Union, *Letter to the House Judiciary Committee Regarding H.R. 5040, the Death Penalty Reform Act of 2006,* March 29, 2006, available at http://www.aclu.org/capital/general/24798leg20060329.html.

129. J. Smith, "All Aboard for the Death Penalty Express: Republican Aid to Kill Federal Criminal Appeals Law," *Austin Chronicle,* August 12, 2005, available at http://www.austinchronicle.com/gyrobase/Issue/story?oid=oid%3A284237.

130. Editorial, "Court Gutting in Congress," *The New York Times,* July 16, 2005, available at http://www.nytimes.com/2005/07/16/opinion/16edit4.html?ex=1157774400&en=9e34e82d46ea25d1&ei=5070.

131. National Coalition to Abolish the Death Penalty, *Resistance to Death Penalty Growing,* April 8, 2007, available at http://www.democracyinaction.org/dia/organizations/ncadp/news.jsp?key=3216.

132. A. Ditchfield, "Challenging the Intrastate Disparities in the Application of Capital Punishment Statutes," *Georgetown Law Journal* 95 (2007): 801–30.

133. J. Blume, T. Eisenberg, and M. Wells, "Explaining Death Row's Population and Racial Composition," *Journal of Empirical Legal Studies* 1 (2004): 165–207.

134. F. Hartung, "Trends in the Use of Capital Punishment," *Annals of the American Academy of Political and Social Sciences* 284 (1952): 8–19, 14.

135. M. DeLisia and R. Regoli, "Race, Conventional Crime, and Criminal Justice: The Declining Importance of Skin Color," in *Race, Crime, and Justice: A Reader,* eds. S. Gabbidon and H. Green (New York: Rutledge, 2005), 87–95; D. Georges-Abeyie, "The Myth of a Racist Criminal Justice System?" in *Racism, Empiricism, and Criminal Justice,* eds. B. MacLean and D. Milovanovic (Vancouver: Collective Press, 1990); P. Langan, "No Racism in the Justice System," *The Public Interest* 117 (1994): 48–52; D. Milovanovic and K. Russell, *Petit Apartheid in the U.S. Criminal Justice System: The Dark Figure of Racism* (Durham, NC: Carolina University Press, 2001); M. Thomas, *Anything but Race: The Social Science Retreat from Racism* (2000), available at http://www.rcgd.isr.umich.edu/prba/perspectives/winter2000/mthomas.pdf.

136. National Minority Advisory Council on Criminal Justice, *The Inequality of Justice: A Report on Crime and the Administration of Justice in the Minority Community,* xxxii, 1982.

137. For a review of this literature, see David V. Baker, "Purposeful Discrimination in Capital Sentencing," *Journal of Law and Social Challenges* 5, no. 1 (2003): 189–223.

138. Ibid.

139. D. Baldus, C. Pulaski, and G. Woodworth, "Comparative Review of Death Sentences: An Empirical Study of the Georgia Experience (Symposium on Current Death Penalty Issues)," *Journal of Criminal Law & Criminology* 74 (1983): 661–753.

140. B. Stevenson and R. Friedman, "Deliberate Indifference: Judicial Tolerance of Racial Bias in Criminal Justice," *Washington and Lee Law Review* 51 (1994): 509–27, 510).

141. D. Vick, "Poorhouse Justice: Underfunded Indigent Defense Services and Arbitrary Death Sentences," *Buffalo Law Review* 43 (1995): 329–460, 333.

142. R. Misner, "Recasting Prosecutorial Discretion," *Journal of Criminal Law and Criminology* 86 (1996): 717; P. S. Kare, "Why Have You Singled Me Out? The Use of Prosecutorial Discretion for Selective Prosecution," *Tulane Law Review* 67 (1993): 2293; G. Thomas, III, "Discretion and Criminal Law: The Good, the Bad, and the Mundane," *Pennsylvania State Law Review* 109 (2005): 1043; C. Lanier and J. Acker, "Capital Punishment, the Moratorium Movement, and

Empirical Questions: Looking Beyond Innocence, Race, and Bad Lawyering in Death Penalty Cases," *Psychology, Public Policy, and Law* 10 (2004): 577, 598; N. Lovre-Laughlin, "Lethal Decisions: Examining the Role of Prosecutorial Discretion in Capital Cases in South Dakota and the Federal Justice System," *South Dakota Law Review* 50 (2005): 550–74; A. Smith, "Can You Be a Good Person and a Good Prosecutor?" *Georgetown Journal of Legal Ethics* 14 (2001): 355–400.

143. D. Benson, "Capital Sentencing Evidence After *Penry* and *Payne*," *Thurgood Marshall Law Review* 17 (1991): 1–29.

144. A. Davis, "Prosecution and Race: The Power and Privilege of Discretion," *Fordham Law Review* 67 (1998): 13–67; M. Oberman, "Mothers Who Kill, 1870–1930," *Journal of Criminal Law and Criminology* 92 (2002): 707–37; "Developments in the Law: Race and the Criminal Process: IV. Race and the Prosecutor's Charging Decision," *Harvard Law Review* 101 (1988): 1520–557; G. Cole, "The Decision To Prosecute," *Law and Society Review* 4 (1970): 331–44.

145. *Bordenkircher v. Hayes*, 434 U.S. 357, 364 (1978).

146. A. Burnett, Sr., "Permeation of Race, National Origin and Gender Issues from Initial Law Enforcement Contact Through Sentencing: The Need For Sensitivity, Equalitarianism and Vigilance in the Criminal Justice System," *American Criminal Law Review* 31 (1994): 1153–173, 1167.

147. J. Vorenberg, "Decent Restraint of Prosecutorial Power," *Harvard Law Review* 94 (1981): 1521; R. Heller, "Selective Prosecution and the Federalization of Criminal Law: The Need for Meaningful Judicial Review of Prosecutorial Discretion," *University Pennsylvania Law Review* 145 (1997): 1309–358; C. Ramsey, "The Discretionary Power of 'Public' Prosecutors in Historical Perspective," *American Criminal Law Review* 39 (2002): 1309–393.

148. P. Butler, "Starr Is to Clinton as Regular Prosecutors Are to Blacks," *Boston College Law Review* 40 (1999): 705–16, 708–14; A. Davis, "Benign Neglect of Racism in the Criminal Justice System," *Michigan Law Review* 94 (1996): 1660–686, 1679; K. Nunn, "The Darden Dilemma Should African Americans Prosecute Crimes?," *Fordham Law Review* 68 (2000): 1473–508, 1492–497; J. McCarthy, "Implications of County Variance in New Jersey Capital Murder Cases: Arbitrary Decision-Making by County Prosecutors, *New York Law School Journal of Human Rights* 19 (2003): 969–96; Y. Sapir, "Neither Intent Nor Impact: A Critique of the Racially Based Selective Prosecution Jurisprudence and a Reform Proposal," *Harvard BlackLetter Law Journal* 19 (2003): 127–79; D. Greene, "Abusive Prosecutors: Gender, Race and Class Discretion and the Prosecution of Drug-Addicted Mothers," *Buffalo Law Review* 39 (1991): 737–802, 745; A. Poulin, "Prosecutorial Discretion and Selective Prosecution: Enforcing Protection After *United States v. Armstrong*," *American Criminal Law Review* 34 (1997): 1071–125, 1109–19; A. Levine, "Current Issue, A Dark State of Criminal Affairs: ADR Can Restore Justice to the Criminal Justice System," *Hamline Journal of Public Law and Policy* 24 (2003): 369–405; R. Pinto, "Note, The Public Interest and Private Financing of Criminal Prosecutions," *Washington University Law Quarterly* 77 (1999): 1343–368, 1353–54; M. Radelet and G. Pierce, "Race and Prosecutorial Discretion in Homicide Cases," *Law and Society Review* 19 (1985): 587, 615–19 (1985).

149. J. Phillips, "Execution of Justice," *Birmingham Post-Herald,* December 2001, available at http://www.postherald.com/justice.shtml

150. M. Songer and I. Unah, "The Effect of Race, Gender, and Location on Prosecutorial Decision to Seek the Death Penalty in South Carolina," *South Carolina Law Review* 58 (November 2006); S. Hindson, H. Potter, and M. Radelet, "Race, Gender, Region and Death Sentences in Colorado, 1980–1999," *University of Colorado Law Review* 77 (2006): 549–94; G. Pierce and M. Radelet, "The Impact of Legally Inappropriate Factors on Death Sentencing for California Homicides, 1990–1999," *Santa Clara Law Review* 46 (2005): 1–46.

151. U.S. General Accounting Office, *Death Penalty Sentencing: Research Indicates Pattern of Racial Disparities*, Washington, DC: Government

Printing Office, 1990; Death Penalty Information Center, *Race of Death Row Inmates Executed Since 1976* (2005), available at http://www.deathpenaltyinfo.org/article.php?scid=5&did=184.

152. D. Fins, *Death Row USA: A Quarterly Report by the Criminal Justice Project of the NAACP Legal Defense and Educational Fund, Inc*, available at http://www.naacpldf.org/content/pdf/pubs/drusa/DRUSA_Winter_2007.pdf.

153. These findings are from an unpublished study by Robert Berk, Director of the Center for the Study of the Environment and Society at the University of California at Los Angeles. See R. Garcia, "Latinos and Criminal Justice," *Chicano-Latino Law Review* 14 (1994): 6–19, 14, note 53.

154. Carter Center Symposium on the Death Penalty, *Georgia State University Law Review* 14 (1997): 329–445; See also Michael L. Radelet, "Executions of Whites for Crimes Against Blacks," *Sociological Quarterly* 30 (1989): 529–44.

155. A. Davis, "Prosecution and Race: The Power and Privilege of Discretion," *Fordham Law Review* 67 (1998): 13–67.

156. P. Butler, "Racially Based Jury Nullification: Black Power in the Criminal Justice System," *Yale Law Review* 105 (1995): 677–725; P. Scott, "Jury Nullification: An Historical Perspective on a Modern Debate," *West Virginia Law Review* 91 (1989): 389. See also A. Liepold, "Race-Based Jury Nullification: Rebuttal (Part A)," *John Marshall Law Review* 30 (1997): 923–27; R. Kennedy, *Race, Crime, and the Law* (New York: Pantheon Books, 1997); A. Scheflin, "Jury Nullification: The Right to Say No," *Southern California Law Review* 45 (1972): 168; R. Howard, "Change the System from Within: An Essay Calling for More African Americans to Consider Being Prosecutors," *Widener Law Symposium* 6 (1999): 139.

157. A. Davis, "Prosecution and Race: The Power and Privilege of Discretion," *Fordham Law Review* 67 (1998): 13–67.

158. *Oyler v. Boles*, 368 U.S. 448, 456 (1962).

159. J. Larson, "Supreme Court Review: Unequal Justice: The Supreme Court's Failure to Curtail Selective Prosecution for the Death Penalty," *Journal of Criminal Law and Criminology* 93 (2003): 1009–031, 1010.

160. 188 U.S. 356 (1996). See David Cole, *No Equal Justice: Race and Class in the American Criminal Justice System* (New York, NY: The New Press, 1999), 159.

161. *Oyler v. Boyles*, 368 U.S. 448 (1962); *Wayte v. United States* 470 U.S. 598 (1985); *United States v. Armstrong*, 517 U.S. 456 (1996); *United States v. Bass*, 266 F.3d 532 (2001).

162. A. Siebert, "*Batson v. Kentucky*: Application to Whites and the Effect on the Peremptory Challenge System," *Columbia Journal of Law and Social Problems* 32 (1999): 307–30, 308–12.

163. P. Griffin, "Jumping on the Ban Wagon: *Minetos v. City University of New York* and the Future of the Peremptory Challenge," *Minnesota Law Review* 81 (1997): 1237–270, 1267; R. Broderick, "Why the Peremptory Challenge Should be Abolished," *Temple Law Review* 65 (1992): 369–423, 416–423; R. Kennedy, "Racial Trends in the Administration of Criminal Justice," in *America Becoming: Racial Trends and Their Consequences, Volume II, National Research Council*, eds. N. Smelser, W. Wilson and F. Mitchell (Washington, D.C.: National Academy Press, 2001).

164. J. Stevens, Associated Justice, Supreme Court of the United States. Address to the American Bar Association Thurgood Marshall Awards Dinner Honoring Abner Mikva. Hyatt Regency Hotel, Chicago, Illinois (August 6, 2005), http://www.supremecourtus.gov/publicinfo/speeches/sp_08-06-05.html.

165. S. McGonigle, "Race Bias Pervades Jury Selection: Prosecutors Routinely Bar Blacks, Study Finds," *Dallas Morning News*, March 9, 2005, 1A.

166. *Strauder v. West Virginia*, 100 U.S. 303, 308 (1880); *Swain v. Alabama*, 380 U.S. 202 (1965); *Batson v. Kentucky*, 476 U.S. 79 (1986); *J.E.M. v. Alabama*, 511 U.S. 127 (1994); *Taylor v. Louisiana*, 419 U.S. 522 (1975); *Hernandez v. New York*, 500 U.S. 352 (1991); *Edmonson v. Leesville Concrete Company*, 500 U.S. 614 (1991); *Georgia v. McCollum*, 505 U.S. 42 (1992).

167. H. Fukurai, E. Butler, and R. Krooth, *Race and the Jury: Racial Disenfranchisement and the Search for Justice* (New York: Plenum Press, 1993).

168. D. Baldus, G. Woodworth, D. Zuckerman, N. Weiner, and B. Broffitt, "The Use of Peremptory Challenges in Capital Murder Trials: A Legal and Empirical Analysis," *University of Pennsylvania Journal of Constitutional Law* 3 (2001): 3–170; J. Brand, "The Supreme Court, Equal Protection and Jury Selection: Denying that Race Still Matters," *Wisconsin Law Review* 1994 (1994): 511–629; D. Colbert, "Challenging the Challenge: Thirteenth Amendment as a Prohibition Against Racial Use of Peremptory Challenge," *Cornell Law Review* 76 (1990): 1–128; B. Underwood, "Ending Race Discrimination in Jury Selection: Whose Right Is It Anyway?" *Columbia Law Review* 92 (1992): 725–74; S. Johnson, "Black Innocence and the White Jury," *Michigan Law Review*, 83 (1985): 1611–708; P. Griffin, "Jumping on the Ban Wagon: *Minetos v. City University of New York* and the Future of the Peremptory Challenge," *Minnesota Law Review* 81 (1997): 1237–270, at 1267; R. Broderick, "Why the Peremptory Challenge Should Be Abolished," *Temple Law Review* 65 (1992): 369–423, at 416–23. For a review of recent cases revealing methods used to limit black participation in juries, see A. Higginbotham, Jr., *Shades of Freedom: Racial Politics and Presumptions of the American Legal Process* (New York: Oxford University Press, 1996), 263–64, note 74.

169. C. Conrad, *Jury Nullification: The Evolution of a Doctrine* (Durham, NC: Carolina Academic Press, 1998), 190; See also J. Mintz, "Note, *Batson v. Kentucky*: A Half Step in the Right Direction (Racial Discrimination and Peremptory Challenges Under the Heavier Confines of Equal Protection)," *Cornell Law Review* 72 (1987): 1026–046; T. Coke, "Lady Justice May Be Blind, But Is She A Soul Sister? Race-Neutrality and the Ideal of Representative Juries," *New York University Law Review* 69 (1994): 327–86; D. Colbert, "Challenging the Challenge: The Thirteenth Amendment as a Prohibition Against the Racial Use of Peremptory Challenges, 76 (1990: 1; D. Savage, "Justices Weigh State's Jury Selection Law," *Los Angeles Times*, April 19, 2005 at A12.

170. *Purket v. Elem* 514 U.S. 765 (1995), p. 767.

171. Ibid., 769.

172. *People v. Easley*, 736 N.E.2d 975, 990 (Ill. 2000).

173. *Missouri v. Alexander*, 755 S.W.2d 397 (1988).

174. *Wallace v. Alabama*, 530 So.2d 849 (1987).

175. C. Ogletree, Jr., "Black Man's Burden: Race and the Death Penalty in America," *Oregon Law Review* 81 (2002): 15–38, at 26.

176. K. Williams, "The Deregulation of the Death Penalty," *Santa Clara Law Review* 40 (2000): 677–728; B. Scheck, P. Neufeld, and J. Dwyer, *Actual Innocence: Five Days to Execution and Other Dispatches from the Wrongly Convicted* (New York: Doubleday, 2000); J. Dwyer, P. Neufeld, and B. Scheck, *Actual Innocence: When Justice Goes Wrong and How To Make It Right* (New York: New American Library, 2003).

177. J. Liebman, J. Fagan, and V. West, *A Broken System: Error Rates in Capital Cases, 1973–1995* (2000), available at www.justice.policy .net/proactive/newsroom/release.vtml, reprinted in part in J. Liebman, J. Fagan, V. West, and J. Lloyd, "Capital Attrition, Error Rates in Capital Cases, 1973–1995," *Texas Law Review* 78 (2000): 1839–865; See also A. Gelman, J. Liebman, V. West, and A.Kiss, "A Broken System: The Persistent Patterns of Reversals of Death Sentences in the United States," *Journal of Empirical Legal Studies* 1 (2004): 209; Center for Public Integrity: Investigative Journalism in the Public Interest, *Harmful Error: Investigating America's Local Prosecutors* (2003), available at www.publicintegrity.org/pm/default.aspx.

178. E. Brewer, III, "Let's Play Jeopardy: Where the Question Comes After the Answer for Stopping Prosecutorial Misconduct in Death Penalty Cases," *Northern Kentucky Law Review* 28 (2001): 34–49.

179. R.Warden, Center on Wrongful Convictions, *Eyewitness Study, How Mistaken and Perjured Eyewitness Identification Testimony Put 46 Innocent Americans on Death Row* (2001), available at http://www.law.northwestern.edu/depts/ clinic/wrongful/Causes/eyewitnessstudy01 .htm

180. V. Streib, "Gendering the Death Penalty: Countering Sex Bias in a Masculine Sanctuary," *Ohio State University Law Review* 63 (2002): 433–72.

181. K. Armstrong and M. Possley, "Trial and Error: How Prosecutors Sacrifice Justice to Win"

(Series: Tribune Investigative Report. The Failure of the Death Penalty in Illinois. Parts 1-V), *Chicago Tribune* (January 10–14, 1999).

182. Texas Defender Service, *A State of Denial: Texas Justice and the Death Penalty* (2000), available at http://www.texasdefender.org/publications.htm; See also Steven Bright, "Discrimination, Death and Denial: The Tolerance of Racial Discrimination in Infliction of the Death Penalty," *Santa Clara Law Review* 35 (1995): 433–83; P. White, Errors and Ethnics: Dilemmas in Death, *Hoftra Law Review* 29 (2001): 1265.

183. C. Parenti, "Police Crime" (March 1996), available at http://zmag.org/ZMag/articles/mar96parenti.htm

184. M. Kroll, *Killing Justice: Government Misconduct and the Death Penalty* (1992), available at http://www.deathpenaltyinfo.org/article.php?scid=45&did=529.

185. M. Goodwin, "Gender, Race, and Mental Illness: The Case of Wanda Jean Allen," in *Critical Race Feminism: A Reader*, ed. A. Wing (New York: New York University Press, 2003), 228–37, 229.

186. M. Shortnacy, "Guilty and Gay, A Recipe for Execution in American Courtrooms: Sexual Orientation as a Tool for Prosecutorial Misconduct in Death Penalty Cases," *American University Law Review* 51 (2001): 309–65.

187. S. Johnson, "Racial Derogation in Prosecutors' Closing Arguments," in *Petite Apartheid in the U.S. Criminal Justice System: The Dark Figure of Racism*, D. Milovanoic and K. Russell (Durham, NC: Carolina Academic Press, 2000), 79–102.

188. E. Earle, "Banishing the Thirteenth Juror: An Approach to the Identification of Prosecutorial Racism," *Columbia Law Review* 92 (1992): 1212–242; A. Lyon, "Setting the Record Straight: A Proposal for Handling Prosecutorial Appeals to Racial, Ethnic or Gender Prejudice During Trial," *Michigan Journal of Race and Law* 6 (2001): 319–38.

189. *Brady v. Maryland*, 373 U.S. 83 (1963).

190. N. Gordon, "Misconduct and Punishment. State Disciplinary Authorities Investigate Prosecutors Accused of Misconduct," *Harmful Error: Investigating America's Local Prosecutors. The Center for Public Integrity* (2003), *at*

www.publicintegrity.org/pm/default.aspx?sID=sidebarsb&aID=39.

191. J. Neff, "State Bar Accuses 2 of Misconduct: Prosecutors Lied and Cheated in Capital Cases, Regulators Say," *Newsobserver.com* (2005), available at http://www.newsobserver.com/news/crime_safety/v-printer/story/2789640;9229197c.htm.

192. J. Toobin, "Killer Instincts: Did a Famous Prosecutor Put the Wrong Man on Death Row?," *The New Yorker*, January 17, 2005, 54.

193. S. Weinberg, "Shielding Misconduct: The Law Immunizes Prosecutors from Civil Suits," *Harmful Error: Investigating America's Local Prosecutors*, The Center for Public Integrity (2003), available at www.publicintegrity.org/pm/default.aspx?sID=sidebarsb&aID=36; See also Lee Romney, "Outside Prosecutors Feel Urban-Rural Rift," *Los Angeles Times*, April 19, 2005, B1, B10.

194. D. Brown, "Criminal Procedure Entitlements, Professionalism, and Lawyering Norms," *Ohio State Law Journal* 61 (2000): 801–65; See also D. Brown, "Rationing Criminal Defense Entitlements: An Argument from Institutional Design," *Columbia Law Review* 104 (2004): 801.

195. P. J. Huffstutter and J. Beckhm, "Chicago Police Used Torture, Inquiry Says," *Los Angeles Times*, July 20, 2006, A14. S. Gross, K. Jacoby, D. Matheson, N. Montgomery, and S. Patil, "Symposium: Innocence in Capital Sentencing: Article: Exonerations in the United States 1989 Through 2003," *Journal of Criminal Law and Criminology* 95 (2005): 523–55, at 544–45. S. Weinberg, "Anatomy of Misconduct," *Harmful Error: Investigating America's Local Prosecutors. The Center for Public Integrity* (2003), available at http://www.publicintegrity.org/pm/default.aspx?sid=sidebarsb&aid=33.

196. 500 F2d 1301.

197. D. James and L.. Glaze, *Mental Health Problems of Prison and Jail Inmates*, U.S. Department of Justice, Bureau of Justice Statistics (December 2006), available at http://www.ojp.usdoj.gov/bjs/pub/pdf/mhppji.pdf.

198. Treatment Advocacy Center, *Criminalization of Americans with Severe Mental Illnesses*, available at http://www.psychlaws.org/General Resources/Fact3.htm.

199. B. Harcourt, "The Mentally-Ill Behind Bars," *New York Times*, January 15, 2007, A15.

200. R. Jenkins, "Comment, Fit To Die: Drug-Induced Competency for the Purpose of Execution," *Southern Illinois University Law Journal* 20 (1995): 149–79; See also, N. Horton, "Restoration of Competency For Execution: Furiosus Solo Furore Punitur," *Southwestern Law Journal* 44 (1990): 1191–228.

201. G. Fields, "On Death Row, Fate or Mentally Ill Is Thorny Problem," *Wall Street Journal*, December 14, 2006, A1; See also R. Blumenthal, "A Growing Plea for Mercy for the Mentally Ill on Death Row," *New York Times*, November 23, 2006, A26.

202. American Civil Liberties Union, *Mental Illness and the Death Penalty in the United States* (January 2005), available at http://www.aclu.org/capital/mentalillness/10617pub20050131.html.

203. Amnesty International, *United States of America: The Execution of Mentally Ill Offenders* (January 2006), available at http://web.amnesty.org/library/Index/ENGAMR-510032006.

204. Death Penalty Information Center, *Mental Illness and the Death Penalty*, available at http://www.deathpenaltyinfo.org/article.php?did=782&scid=66. See also, *Ford v. Wainwright*, 477 U.S. 399 (1986).

205. K. Miller and M. Radelet, *Executing the Mentally Ill: The Criminal Justice System and the Case of Alvin Ford* (Woodland Hills, CA: Sage Publications, 1993); J. Blume and S. Johnson, "Killing the Non-Willings: *Atkins*, the Volitionally Incapacitated, and the Death Penalty," *South Carolina Law Review* 55 (2003): 93; See also M. Dolan, "Justices Rule on Death Penalty and Retardation," *Los Angeles Times*, April 13, 2007, B1, B8.

206. 477 U.S. 399, 422 (1986).

207. Human Rights Watch, *Beyond Reason: The Death Penalty and Offenders with Mental Retardation. VIII. Defendants with Mental Retardation: Their Stories* (March 2001), available at http://www.hrw.org/reports/2001/ustat/ustat0301-07.htm#P639_123209.

208. "Executing Mentally Impaired Prisoners is Unjust and Cruel," *Dallas Morning News*, November 22, 1998. S. DePanfilis, "Singleton v. Norris: Exploring the Insanity of Forcibly Medicating, then Eliminating the Insane," *Connecticut Public Interest Law Journal* 4 (2004): 68–121.

209. K. Randall, "More than a Quarter Million Mentally Ill in America's Jails and Prisons," *World Socialist Web Site* (1999), available at http://www.wsws.org/articles/1999/jul1999/pris-j15_prn.shtml; Human Rights Watch, *Ill-Equipped: U.S. Prisons and Offenders with Mental Illness* (2003), available at http://www.hrw.org/report/2003/usa1003.

210. V. Streib, "Death Penalty for Female Offenders," *University of Cincinnati Law Review* 58 (1990), 845–80.

211. D, Fins, *Death Row USA: A Quarterly Report by the Criminal Justice Project of the NAACP Legal Defense and Educational Fund, Inc*, available at http://www.naacpldf.org/content/pdf/pubs/drusa/DRUSA_Winter_2007.pdf.

212. R. Howard, "Change the System from Within: An Essay Calling for More African Americans to Consider Being Prosecutors. *Widener Law Symposium 6* (2000): 139.

213. D. Anderson, "Caged Women," *Girlfriends*, November/December, 1996, 24–27; V. Brownworth, "Dykes on Death Row," *The Advocate*, June 16, 1992, 62; See also R. Goldstein, "Queer on Death Row," *The Village Voice* (2001), available at http://www.villagevoice.com/news/0111,goldstein,23066,1.html; E. Laumann, *The Social Organization of Sex: Sexual Practices in the United States* (Chicago: University of Chicago Press, 1994); *Amicus Curiae* in support of petitioners. *Lawrence and Garner v. State of Texas*, No. 02-102 (March 26, 2003), p. 16.

214. S. Kohn, "Greasing the Wheel: How the Criminal Justice System Hurts Gay, Lesbian, Bisexual and Transgendered People and Why Hate Crime Laws Won't Save Them," *New York University Review of Law and Social Change* 27 (2001), 257–80; Victor Streib, "Death Penalty for Lesbians," *National Journal of Sexual Orientation* 1 (1994), 104–26.

215. M. Shortnacy, "Guilty and Gay, A Recipe for Execution in American Courtrooms: Sexual Orientation as a Tool for Prosecutorial Misconduct in Death Penalty Cases," *American University Law Review* 51 (2001): 309–65.

216. J. Mogul, "The Dykier, The Butcher, The Better: The State's Use of Homophobia and Sexism to Executed Women in the United States," *New York City Law Review* 8 (2005): 473–93.

217. W. Lester, "Jurors Say They Follow Beliefs, Not Instructions," *Chicago Sun Times*, October 24, 1998, A37.

218. American Civil Liberties Union, *The Forgotten Population: A Look at Death Row in the United States Through the Experience of Women* (2004), available at http://www.aclu.org/capital/women/10627pub20041129.html.

219. J. Kopec, "Avoiding a Death Sentence in the American Legal System: Get a Woman To Do It," *Capital Defense Journal* 15 (2003): 353–82, at 362.

220. S. Kohn, "Greasing the Wheel," 257–80, at 264.

221. Quoted in Frank E. Hartung, "Trends in the Use of Capital Punishment," *Annals of the American Academy of Political and Social Sciences* 284 (1952): 8–19.

222. President's Commission on Law Enforcement and Administration of Justice, *The Courts*, 1967, 28

223. *Furman v. Georgia*, 408 U.S. 238, 251–52.

224. *The Final Report of the Pennsylvania Supreme Court Committee on Racial and Gender Bias in the Justice System.* (2003), available at http://www.courts.state.pa.us/Index/supreme/BiasCmte/FinalReport.pdf.

225. Carol J. DeFrances, *State-Funded Indigent Defense Services, 1999* (September 2001), U.S. Department of Justice, Bureau of Justice Statistics, available at http://www.ojp.usdoj.gov/bjs/pub/pdf/sfids99.pdf; Carol J. DeFrances and Marika F. X. Litras, *Indigent Defense Services in Large Counties, 1999* (November 2000), U.S. Department of Justice, Bureau of Justice Statistics, available at http://www.ojp.usdoj.gov/bjs/pub/pdf/idslc99.pdf; Caroline Wolf Harlow, *Defense Counsel in Criminal Cases* (November 2000), U.S. Department of Justice, Bureau of Justice Statistics, available at http://www.ojp.usdoj.gov/bjs/pub/pdf/dccc.pdf; Steven K. Smith and Carol F. DeFrances, *Indigent Defense* (February 1996), U.S. Department of Justice, Bureau of Justice Statistics, available at http://www.ojp.usdoj.gov/bjs/pub/pdf/id.pdf.

226. A. Liptak, "In Alabama, Execution Without Representation," *New York Times*, March 26, 2007, A12.

227. T. MacCarthy, "Unanimous Resolution," *Champion* 20 (April 1999): 20–25.

228. C. Harlow, *Defense Counsel In Criminal Cases*, U.S. Department of Justice, Bureau of Justice Statistics (November 2000), available at http://www.ojp.usdoj.gov/bjs/pub/pdf/dccc.pdf

229. American Bar Association, *Gideon's Broken Promise: America's Continuing Quest for Equal Justice–A Report of the American Bar Association's Hearings on the Right to Counsel in Criminal Proceedings* (2004), available at http://www.abanet.org/legalservices/sclaid/defender/brokenpromise/fullreport.pdf.

230. K. Hughes, *Justice Expenditures and Employment in the United States* (April 2006), U.S. Department of Justice, Bureau of Justice Statistics, available at http://www.ojp.usdoj.gov/bjs/pub/pdf/jeeus03.pdf.

231. R. Spangenberg, M. Beeman, and J. Downing, *State and County Expenditures for Indigent Defense Services in Fiscal Year 2002*, September 2003, available at http://www.abanet.org/legalservices/downloads/sclaid/indigentdefense/indigentdefexpend2003.pdf. See also R. Uphoff, "Convicting the Innocent: Aberration or Systemic problem?" *Wisconsin Law Review* 2006 (2006): 739–841.

232. U.S. Department of Justice, Bureau of Justice Statistics, *Indigent Defense Statistics*, October 2001, available at http://www.ojp.usdoj.gov/bjs/id.htm.

233. *Gideon's Broken Promise* (2004); See also R. Klein, "The Emperor Has No Clothes: The Empty Promise of the Constitutional Right to Effective Assistance of Counsel," *Hastings Constitutional Law Quarterly* 13 (1986): 625.

234. R. Uphoff, "Convicting the Innocent," 739–841; D. Vick, "Poorhouse Justice," 329–460, 333.

235. C. Lanier and J. Acker, "Capital Punishment, the Moratorium Movement, and Empirical Questions: Looking Beyond Innocence, Race, and Bad Lawyering in Death Penalty Cases," *Psychology, Public Policy, and Law* 10 (2004): 577, 590.

236. S. Bright, "Death by Lottery–Procedural Bar of Constitutional Claims in Capital Cases Due to

Inadequate Representation of Indigent Defendants." *West Virginia Law Review* 92 (1990): 679, 685.

237. American Civil Liberties Union, *Inadequate Representation*, October 8, 2003, available at http://www.aclu.org/news/NewsPrint.cfm?ID=9313&c=62; See also Kenneth Williams, "Mid-Atlantic People of Color Legal Scholarship Conference: The Death Penalty: Can It be Fixed?" *Catholic University Law Review* 51 (2002): 1177, 1189.

238. J. Reiman, *The Rich Get Richer and the Poor Get Prison: Ideology, Class, and Criminal Justice* (Boston, MA: Allyn and Bacon, 2007), 209.

239. A. Wing, "Examining the Correlation Between Disability and Poverty: A Comment from a Critical Race Feminist Perspective–Helping the Joneses to Keep Up!," *Journal of Gender, Race and Justice* 8 (2005): 655–66; W. Lofquist, "Putting Them There, Keeping Them There, and Killing Them: An Analysis of State-Level Variations in Death Penalty Intensity," *Iowa Law Review* 87 (2002): 1505–557.

240. American Bar Association, *Gideon's Broken Promise: America's Continuing Quest for Equal Justice*, A Report of the American Bar Association's Hearings on the Right to Counsel in Criminal Proceedings (December 2004), available at http://www.abanet.org/legalservices/sclaid/defender/brokenpromise/fullreport.pdf. R. Dieter, *With Justice for Few: The Growing Crisis in Death Penalty Representation*, Death Penalty Information Center (October 1995), available at http://www.deathpenaltyinfo.org/article.php?scid=45&did=544#fnB21.

241. R. Sherrill, "Death Trip: The American Way of Execution," *The Nation,* January 8, 2001, available at http://www.thenation.com/doc/20010108/sherrill.

242. S. Henderson, "Indefensible? Lawyers in Key Death Penalty States Often Fall Short," *McClatchy Newspapers*, January 21, 2007, available at http://www.realcities.com/mld/krwashington/news/special_packages/death_penalty/16491868.htm. See also S. Henderson, "Nonstop to the Death House: Appeals Courts Often Overlook Lawyer's Errors," *McClatchy Newspapers*, January 21, 2007, available at http://www.realcities.com/mld/krwashington/news/special_packages/death_penalty/16491953.htm; S. Henderson, "Between Life and Death: A Group of Young Lawyers Is Some Prisoners' Only Hope," *McClatchy Newspapers*, January 21, 2007, available at http://www.realcities.com/mld/krwashington/news/special_packages/death_penalty/16491986.htm.

243. E. Kennedy, "The Promise of Equal Justice," *Champion*, January/February, 2003, 22; S. Bright, "Judging from State's Latest Execution, The Price of Life Is A 'Real' Lawyer," *Atlanta Journal Constitution* (2002), available at http://www.geocities.com/gfadp/fugate-op-ed-082302.html.

244. G. Kendall, "Prosecutorial Misconduct and Ineffective Counsel: The Case of Delma Banks, Jr.," Death Penalty Information Center, available at http://www.deathpenaltyinfo.org/article.php?scid=38&did=588; *New York Times*, Editorial, "Preventing a Miscarriage of Justice" (April 18, 2003), available at http://www.deathpenaltyinfo.org/article.php?scid=17&did=587; Press Release, "Supreme Court Says Texas Death Row Inmate Who Came Within Minutes of Execution Was Denied Right to a Fair Trial," Death Penalty Information Center (February 24, 2004), available at http://www.deathpenaltyinfo.org/PR-DPIC-20040224-Banks.pdf; *Banks v. Dretke*, Slip Opinion No. 02-8286 (October 2003).

245. Death Penalty Information Center, *Texas Woman Faces Execution Despite Questions Regarding Her Guilt* (2005), available at http://www.deathpenaltyinfo.org/article.php?did=1545&scid=64.

246. National Coalition to Abolish the Death Penalty, *Do Not Execute Francis Newton* (2005), available at http://www.demaction.org/dia/organizations/ncadp/campaign.jsp?campaign_KEY=1132.

247. *Newton v. Dretke*, 371 F.3d 250 (2004).

248. Texas Defender Service, *A State of Denial: Texas Justice and the Death Penalty* (2000), available at http://www.texasdefender.org/publications.htm.

249. D. Row and J. Taylor, *Ex parte Francis Elaine Newton*, Application for Postconviction Writ

of Habeas Corpus and Motion for Stay of Execution, In the 263rd Judicial District, Texas, and In the Court of Criminal Appeals of Texas (2005), 8.

250. American Civil Liberties, *The Forgotten Population: A Look at Death Row in the United States Through the Experience of Women* (December 2004), available at http://www.aclu.org/DeathPenalty/DeathPenalty.cfm?ID=17085&c=68

251. J. Shiffman, "Troubled Lawyers Still Allowed to Work Death Cases,' *The Tennessean,* January 25, 2001. See also D. Dow, *Executed on a Technicality: Lethal Injustice on America's Death Row* (Boston: Beacon Press, 2005), 83.

252. "Defense Called Lacking for Death Row Indigents," *Dallas Morning News*, September 10, 2000, 1A; See also Texas Defender Service, *A State of Denial: Texas Justice and the Death Penalty*, Chapter 6: The Right to Counsel in Texas: You Get What You Pay For (2000), available at http://www.texasdefender.org/publications.htm.

253. "Defense Called Lacking for Death Row Indigents," A.

254. Ibid.

255. L. Olsen, "Uncertain Justice," *The Seattle Post-Intelligencer*, August 6, 2001, A1.

256. For a comprehensive review of the literature on incompetent defense counsel in capital cases, see J. Liebman, "The Overproduction of Death," *Columbia Law Review* 100 (2000): 2030–156.

257. Commons Sense Foundation, The Plain Truth, *Death Row Injustice* (October 2006), http://www.common-sense.org/pdfs/DP%20IDS%20Study.pdf. See also L. Chandler, "Lawyers, Inadequate Defense Cited in a Third of Death Case Reversals," *The Charlotte Observer*, September 11, 2000, A1; "Uncertain Justice: The Death Penalty on Trial," Five Part Series. *The Charlotte Observer*, September 10–15, 2000. See also North Carolina Department of Corrections, *Offenders on Death Row*, available at http://www.doc.state.nc.us/DOP/deathpenalty/deathrow.htm.

258. F. Ferris, *Common Sense Says that People on Death Row Often Had the State's Worst Lawyers at Trial,* The Common Sense Foundation (last visited on May 6, 2005), available at http://www.commonsense.org/?fnoc=/common sense says/DPSpecialReport2002.

259. K. Armstrong and S. Mills, "Death Row Justice Derailed," *Chicago Tribune*, November 14, 1999, A1.

260. G. Therolf, "Death Penalty Defense Worst Lawyering I've Seen, Justice Says," *Tampa Tribune*, January 29, 2005, 7.

261. Human Rights Watch, *The Miscarriage of Justice: Mental Retardation and Capital Trials*, March 2001, available at http://www.hrw.org/reports/2001/ustat/ustat0301-03.htm#P554 101364.

262. D. Cole, *No Equal Justice: Race and Class in the American Criminal Justice System* (New York, NY: The New Press, 1999), 76–81.

263. D. Cole, "The Liberal Legacy of *Bush v. Gore*," *Georgetown Law Journal* 94 (2006): 1427–451, 1438.

264. I. Mickenberg, "Drunk, Sleeping, and Incompetent Lawyers: Is It Possible to Keep Innocent People Off Death Row?" *Dayton Law Review* 29 (2004): 319–27, 322.

265. 287 U.S. 45 (1932).

266. 466 U.S. 668 (1984).

267. I. Mickenberg, "Drunk, Sleeping, and Incompetent Lawyers," 319–27, 323.

268. 125 S. Ct. 2456 (2005).

269. A. Borromeo, "Mental Retardation and the Death Penalty," *Loyola Journal of Public Interest Law* 3 (2002): 175–200.

270. *United States v. Kauffman*, 109 F.3d 186, 191 (3d Cir. 1997) (Alito, J., dissenting)

271. *Riley v. Taylor*, 277 F.3d 261, 317 (3d Cir. 2001) (en banc) (Alito, J., dissenting).

272. W. Bowers, *Legal Homicide*.

273. M. Madow, "Forbidden Spectacle: Executions, the Public and the Press in Nineteenth Century New York," *Buffalo Law Review* 43 (1995): 461–562; L. Masur, *Rites of Execution: Capital Punishment and the Transformation of American Culture, 1771–1865* (New York: Oxford University Press, 1989); N. Teeters and J. Hedblom, *Hang by the Neck* (Springfield, IL: Thomas, 1967).

274. Frank E. Hartung, "Trends in the Use of Capital Punishment," *Annals of the American Academy of Political and Social Sciences* 284 (1952): 8–19, 17.

275. I. Ehrlich, "The Deterrent Effect of Capital Punishment: A Question of Life and Death," *American Economic Review* 64 (1975): 397–417.

276. J. Fagan, *Deterrence and the Death Penalty: A Critical Review of New Evidence*, Testimony to the New York State Assembly Standing Committee on Codes, Assembly Standing Committee on Judiciary and Assembly Standing Committee on Corrections (January 21, 2005), available at http://www.deathpenaltyinfo.org/FaganTestimony.pdf; See also R. Berk, *New Claims About Executions and General Deterrence: Déjà vu All Over Again?* (March 11, 2005), available at http://preprints.stat.ucla.edu/396/JELS.pap.pdf; J. Donohue and J. Wolfers, "Uses and Abuses of Empirical Evidence in the Death Penalty Debate," *Stanford Law Review* 58 (2005): 791–845; J. Fagan, *Deterrence and the Death Penalty: Risk, Uncertainty, and Public Policy Choices*, Testimony to the Subcommittee on the Constitution, Civil Rights and Property Rights Committee on the Judiciary, United States Senate (February 1, 2006), http://judiciary.senate.gov/testimony.cfm?id=1745&wit_id=4992; J. Fagan, "Death and Deterrence Redux: Science, Law and Causal Reasoning on Capital Punishment," *The Ohio State Journal of Criminal Law* 4 (2006): 255–321.

277. J. Fox and M. Zawitz, *Homicide Trends in the United States*, September 28, 2004, http://www.ojp.usdoj.gov/bjs/pub/pdf/htius.pdf

278. F. Fessenden, "Deadly Statistics: A Survey of Crime and Punishment," *New York Times*, September 22, 2000, 23.

279. M. Godfrey and V. Schiraldi, *How Have Homicide Rates Been Affected by California's Death Penalty*, April 1995, http://www.justice-policy.org/downloads/homicide_rates.pdf

280. W. Bowers and G. Pierce, "Arbitrariness and Discrimination Under Post-*Furman* Capital Statutes," *Crime and Delinquency* 26 (1980): 563–635; E. Thompson, "Effects of an Execution on Homicides in California," *Homicide Studies* 3 (1999): 129.

281. J. Donohue and J. Wolfers, "Uses and Abuses of Statistical Evidence in the Death Penalty Debate," *Stanford Law Review* 58 (2005): 791–845.

282. J. Donohue and J. Wolfers, "The Death Penalty: No Evidence for Deterrence," *The Economists' Voice*, 3 (April 2004): 1–6, http://www.bepress.com/ev/vol3/iss5/

283. Ibid., 5.

284. Death Penalty Information Center, *State-by-state information* (2006), available at http://www.deathpenaltyinfo.org/state.

285. K. Randall, "Last-Minute Reprieve for California Death Row Inmate," *World Wide Socialist Web Site*, February 23, 2006, http://www.wsws.org/articles/2006/feb2006/exec-f23_prn.shtml.

286. T. Alper, Lethal Incompetence, *The Champion*, September/October, 2006, 41–44.

287. Human Rights Watch, *So Long as They Die: Lethal Injection in the United States*, April 2006, http://hrw.org/reports/2006/us0406/us0406webwcover.pdf.

288. A. Liptak, "On Death Row, A Battle Over the Fatal Cocktail," *New York Times*, September 16, 2004, 16.

289. B. Harlan, "Lethal Injection Statutes in Use," *Rapid City Journal.com*, September 2, 2006, http://www.rapidcityjournal.com/articles/2006/09/02/news/local/news02.prt; Amnesty International, *USA (South Dakota): Further Information on Death Penalty/Legal Concern: Elijah Page*, August 29, 2006, http://www.amnestyusa.org/news/document.do?id=ENGAMR511392006

290. Death Penalty Information Center, *Three Men Facing Federal Execution Receive Stays*, http://www.deathpenaltyinfo.org/newsanddev.php?scid=29

291. H. Weinstein. "Anesthesiologists Advised to Avoid Executions." *Los Angeles Times*, July 2, 2006, p. A32; See also Ann Rubin, "Judge Says Lethal Injection Is Flawed; Some Politicians Pushing for Return to Gas Chamber," *KSDK NewsChannel 5*, http://www.ksdk.com/printfullstroy.aspx?storyid=102541.

292. K. Keys, *Capital Defense Weekly for Cases Decided from July 14 to July 21, 2006*, http://capitaldefenseweekly.com/index.html

293. The full text of the AMA's code of ethics concerning physician participation in lethal injections is available at http://www.ama-assn.org/ama/pub/category/8419.html.

294. H. Weinstein, "Missouri Says It Can't Find Execution Doctor," *Los Angeles Times*, July 16, 2006, A32.

295. Ibid.

296. H. Weinstein. "Anesthesiologists Advised to Avoid Executions." *Los Angeles Times*, July 2, 2006, A32.

297. H. Weinstein, "Missouri Says It Can't Find Execution Doctor," *Los Angeles Times*, July 16, 2006, A32; See also H. Weinstein, "Missouri Execution Ban Stands," *Los Angeles Times*, July 26, 2006, A14.

298. The American College of Physicians, Human Rights Watch, The National Coalition to Abolish the Death Penalty, and Physicians for Human Rights, *Breach of Trust: Physician Participation in Executions in the United States* (March 1994), http://www.hrw.org/reports/pdfs/g/general/general943.pdf.

299. Human Rights Watch, *Florida, California: Lethal Injection Under Attack*, December 16, 2006, available at http://www.hrw.org/english/docs/2006/12/15/usdom14889.htm.

300. Death Penalty Information Center, *The Death Penalty in 2006: Year End Report*, December 2006, available at http://www.deathpenalty-info.org/2006YearEnd.pdf.

301. Death Penalty Information Center, *Lethal Injection: Hearings in Maryland Reveal Serious Flaws in Procedures*, http://www.deathpenalty-info.org/article.php?did=1902&scid=64

302. Human Rights Watch, *Florida, California*; Sarah Tofte, *Worse than We Thought*, Human Rights Watch, available at http://hrw.org/english/docs/2006/10/13/usdom14388.htm.

303. M. Dolan and H. Weinstein, "The Chaos Behind California Executions: Trial Testimony Paints Lethal Injection Methods as Haphazard, With Little Medical Oversight," *Los Angeles Times*, October 2, 2006, A1.

304. *Morales v. Tilton*, No. C 06 219 & 926 JF RS, U.S. Dist. Ct. for N. Dist. of Calif., Dec. 15, 2006) (Memorandum).

305. H. Weinstein, "Governor Demands Changes in Lethal Injection Protocol," *Los Angeles Times*, December 19, 2006, A1; H. Weinstein, "Ruling Halts State Method of Execution," *Los Angeles Times*, December 16, 2006, A1.

306. C. Williams, "Florida Suspends Executions After Trouble Injecting Inmate," *Los Angeles Times*, December 16, 2006, A25; See also Amnesty International, *New Year's Resolution: End a Cruel and Outdated Punishment*, December 21, 2006, available at http://web.amnesty.org/library/Index/ENGAMR51205200 6?open&of=ENG-2M4.

307. Death Penalty Information Center, *Lethal Injections: Some Cases Stayed, Other Executions Proceed*, http://www .deathpenaltyinfo.org/article.php?did=1686&scid=64.

308. C. Lane, "Supreme Court Puzzles Some with Mixed Answers on Lethal Injection," *Washington Post*, February 10, 2006, A03.

309. *Alley v. Little*, 447 F.3d 976, Justice Boyce F. Martin, Jr., dissenting from denial of a rehearing en banc (May 16, 2006).

310. *Hill v. McDonough*, 2006 U.S. LEXIS 4674 (2006).

311. C. Lane, "Supreme Court Puzzles Some With Mixed Answers on Lethal Injection," A03.

312. K. O'Guinn, "Highest Court Grants Death Row Inmate One Last Appeal," *Civilrights.org*, July 21, 2006, http://www.civilrights.org.

313. D. Savage. "Justices' Heaviest Lifting Is Ahead," *Los Angeles Times*, May 30, 2006, A4; See also Jamie Fellner, *Human Rights Watch Urges Gov. Jeb Bush to Postpone the Execution of Clarence Hill* (September 18, 2006), Human Rights Watch, available at http://hrw.org/english/docs/2006/09/18/usdom14216.htm.

314. Human Rights Watch. *So Long As They Die*.

315. Death Penalty Information Center, *State-by-State Information*, http://www.deathpenaltyinfo.org/state; Deborah W. Denno, "When Legislatures Delegate Death: The Troubling Paradox Behind State Uses of Electrocution and Lethal Injection and What It Says About Us," *Ohio State Law Journal* 63 (2002): 63–128.

316. F. Hartung, "Trends in the Use of Capital Punishment," *Annals of the American Academy of Political and Social Sciences* 284 (1952): 8–19, 17.

Chapter 23

The U.S. Supreme Court and Capital Punishment

Past, Present, and Future

Kenneth C. Haas, Ph.D.

ABSTRACT

This chapter analyzes the U.S. Supreme Court's past, present, and future role in sanctioning, monitoring, and eventually ending capital punishment. The Supreme Court established the parameters of modern death-penalty law in 1976. Since then, the Court has gone through several phases. The Court proceeded cautiously and set clear limits on the applicability of capital punishment from 1976 to 1982. From 1983 to 2001, however, the Court took a more aggressive stance in favor of capital punishment, rejecting major constitutional challenges to the fairness of death-penalty laws and upholding the constitutionality of executing mentally retarded offenders, juvenile offenders, and offenders who neither killed nor intended to kill. From 2002 to 2005, the Court took a more critical perspective. It reversed the holdings that permitted executions of offenders who are mentally retarded and offenders under the age of 18, and it tightened the standards for appellate review of the competence of capital defense attorneys. During its 2005–2006 and 2006–2007 terms, the Court, though sharply divided on capital punishment issues, rejected the constitutional claims of death-row inmates in several important cases.

Although the Court is unlikely to make any fundamental changes in death-penalty law over the next decade, I predict that the Supreme Court will abolish capital punishment in the mid-twenty-first century. Opposition to capital punishment has intensified in the first decade of the new century. Legislation to abolish the death penalty has been introduced in a growing number of states and executions are on hold in a number of states. Most telling, the number of death sentences imposed annually in the United States has declined significantly since 2000. Over the next decade, at least 12 of the 38 states that presently authorize capital punishment will eliminate it, some as a result of legislation and some as a result of decisions by a state supreme court. This trend will accelerate and by 2030 another dozen states, perhaps more, will prohibit the death penalty. The Supreme Court will reject every challenge to the constitutionality of capital punishment for at least the next 20 years. Death sentences and executions, however, will become increasingly rare, and public support for the death penalty will decline significantly. By the year 2050, with only 10 to 15 states retaining capital punishment, the U.S. Supreme Court will hold that the death penalty, under all circumstances, violates the U.S. Constitution.

INTRODUCTION

On June 29, 1972, the U.S. Supreme Court, ruling in *Furman v. Georgia*, put a halt to all executions, thereby removing some 600 condemned prisoners from the nation's death rows (Marquart and Sorensen 1989:11–13). *Furman* held only that all *then-existing* state and federal death-penalty laws violated the Eighth Amendment's cruel and unusual punishment clause because of the arbitrary and discriminatory way in which these laws were applied (*Furman* at 239–374). The decision, nevertheless, was greeted with great optimism by opponents of capital punishment. Many abolitionists saw *Furman* as a decision that left little room to reconcile any death-penalty law with the Constitution, and it was predicted that the Court would soon bring an end to the American practice of capital punishment (Meltsner 1973:289–305).

Four years later, however, the Supreme Court refused to take the next step—declaring the death penalty in and of itself to be unconstitutional. In *Gregg v. Georgia* (1976) and its companion cases,[1] the Court upheld new death-penalty laws that require the jury (or in a few states, the judge) to conduct a separate penalty hearing in order to consider "aggravating" and "mitigating" factors concerning the capital offender's crime and character. Under most of these so-called "guided-discretion" laws, the jury is instructed to weigh all of the relevant factors and circumstances and to return with either a sentence of death or life imprisonment.

On the same day *Gregg* was decided, the Court struck down another type of death-penalty law that several states had enacted in the aftermath of *Furman*. In *Woodson v. North Carolina* (1976) and *Roberts v. Louisiana* (1976), a five-to-four majority found *mandatory* death-penalty laws to be violative of the Eighth Amendment because such laws would undermine the Court's new requirement that sentencing authorities must consider *all* relevant information concerning the nature of the offense and the character of the defendant (*Woodson* at 297–304). This, the majority declared, was now an indispensable part of the process of determining which defendants shall live and which shall die (*Woodson* at 303–305).

Today, more than three decades after *Gregg*, the legal landscape has changed in some respects. However, the constitutional framework established in 1976 remains substantially intact. The result is that while every other Western democracy has abolished capital punishment, the United States has a death-row population of over 3,300 men and women (Death Penalty Information Center [DPIC] 2007).

This chapter examines the Supreme Court's past, present, and future role in monitoring the death penalty. To the surprise of many, the Court recently limited executions based on the offender's age and mental capacity. The predominant trend, however, is typified by decisions that retreat from the *Gregg* promises of fairness and consistency, and limit capital defendants' rights of appeal. In the past few years, a growing number of states have demonstrated an unwillingness to take full advantage of the Court's pro-death-penalty decisions. The pace of executions has slowed and the annual number of death sentences imposed by judges and juries has lessened. Legislation to abolish capital punishment has been introduced in a number of states, and many pending executions are on hold as a result of legal challenges to lethal injection procedures. All things considered it is predicted that growing concerns about capital punishment will ultimately convince the American people—and the Supreme Court—that the time has come to abolish the death penalty. An increasing number of states will abolish capital punishment in the second, third, and fourth decades of the twenty-first century. Citing this movement away from capital punishment, the Court will conclude that the American people of the middle decades of the twenty-first century have reached a sufficient consensus against capital punishment to justify a Supreme Court holding that the Constitution prohibits capital punishment altogether. Capital punishment will be abolished by 2050.

THE POST-*GREGG* YEARS: 1976–1982

Gregg and *Woodson* established the framework for evaluating the constitutionality of all American death-penalty laws. *Gregg* made it clear that the death penalty per se is not forbidden by the Eighth Amendment. But many important questions concerning the constitutional status of capital punishment remained unanswered. Indeed, the 1976 decisions arguably added to the confusion by articulating two major goals that seemed to be quite contradictory. On the one hand, the sentencing authority is commanded by the *Gregg* majority to apply the death penalty even-handedly and without arbitrariness, thus suggesting that it is paramount to provide judges and juries with clear and objective standards that can be applied the same way in all cases. On the other hand, both *Woodson* and *Gregg* arguably stand for the proposition that the sentencing authority is obligated to place great emphasis upon the individual characteristics of each offender and the particular circumstances surrounding his or her crime. These two goals seem inherently incompatible. How can the sentencing authority be expected to give full consideration to the uniqueness of each individual defendant when its discretion has been sharply limited in order to promote fairness and consistency?

From 1976 to 1983, the Supreme Court proceeded carefully while attempting to clarify the constitutional boundaries of capital punishment. *Gregg* and *Woodson* had invalidated mandatory death-penalty laws, but had given states the green light to enact capital statutes that provide for a bifurcated trial and clear guidelines—aggravating and mitigating factors—for judges and juries to consider in deciding whether to sentence the offender to death. This suggested that guided-discretion statutes such as the one upheld in *Gregg* were generally constitutionally acceptable. But no two states had identical death-penalty laws, and many important questions remained to be addressed.

In the years immediately following *Gregg*, the Court seemed inclined to resolve the conflict between consistent sentencing and individualized sentencing in favor of the latter alternative. In 1977, for example, the Court reaffirmed its *Woodson* stance against manda-tory death-penalty laws. In *Roberts v. Louisiana*, a sharply divided Court struck down a Louisiana statute that made death the mandatory punishment for anyone convicted of the first-degree murder of a police officer engaged in the performance of his or her lawful duties. A five-justice majority made it clear that the fact that a murder victim was a police officer could be regarded as an aggravating circumstance (*Roberts* at 636). However, the majority held that the sentencing authority must always be permitted to consider such mitigating facts as the youth of the offender, the absence of any prior convictions, or the influence of extreme emotional disturbance (*Roberts* at 637). Because the Louisiana law did not allow the jury to consider these kinds of mitigating factors when the victim was a law-enforcement officer, it violated the Eighth Amendment (*Roberts* at 637–638).

A year later, the Court again indicated that promoting individualized sentencing was its foremost priority. In *Lockett v. Ohio* (1978), with Justices Rehnquist and White as the only dissenters, the Court invalidated the sentence of Sandra Lockett, a young black woman who had been condemned to die on the basis of her participation in a pawnshop robbery in which one of her confederates shot and killed the pawnshop owner while Lockett waited in the getaway car. The trial judge had found two statutory aggravating circumstances to exist but did not consider the full range of possible mitigating factors. This was because Ohio law stipulated that judges *must* impose a death sentence unless they found by a preponderance of the evidence that (1) the victim had induced or facili-tated the murder; (2) the offender was under duress, coercion, or strong provocation; or (3) the murder was primarily attributable to the offender's psychosis or mental deficiency. By so sharply limiting the number of mitigating circumstances that could be considered, the Ohio statute deprived Lockett of the opportunity to offer into evidence such mitigat-ing factors as her youth and her relatively minor role in the crime (*Lockett* at 589–594).

Reaffirming its commitment to promoting individualized sentencing in capital cases, the Court held that "in all but the rarest kind of capital case," the sentencer must not be precluded from considering any mitigating factors bearing on the defendant's character, prior record, or the circumstances of the offense (*Lockett* at 604). The Constitution may not require individualized sentencing in noncapital cases, wrote Chief Justice Burger, but preventing a judge or a jury from giving "independent mitigating weight" to all aspects of the defendant's character, record, and offense is incompatible with the Eighth Amendment (*Lockett* at 604–605). "The need for treating each defendant in a capital case with that degree of respect due the uniqueness of the individual is far more important in capital cases" (*Lockett* at 605). With these words, the chief justice established the primacy of individualized decision making in capital cases. Although *Lockett* did not explicitly renounce the objective of reducing arbitrariness and bias in cap-ital sentencing, it certainly signaled that this objective was now subordinate to the goal of promoting individualized capital sentencing. But as will be explained later, the tension between these two conflicting goals still exists and may yet work to the advantage of those who oppose the death penalty.

In the first few years after *Gregg*, the Court refused to extend death-penalty eligibility to crimes other than murder. Thus in *Coker v. Georgia*, decided in 1977, six justices agreed that death is an impermissible punishment for the rape of an adult woman. Writing on behalf of a plurality and joined by Justices Brennan and Marshall, both of whom concurred in the judgment on the basis of their belief that capital punishment is in all circumstances unconstitutional, Justice White took the position that rape, though a reprehensible crime deserving of severe punishment, simply does not compare to murder in terms of the harm done to the victim and to society (*Coker* at 597–598).

> The murderer kills; the rapist, if no more than that, does not. Life is over for the victim of the murderer; for the rape victim, life may not be nearly so happy as it was, but it is not over and normally is not beyond repair (*Coker* at 598).

Stressing that the Court must look to objective indicators as to whether contemporary society's "evolving standards of decency" (*Trop v. Dulles* at 101) are incompatible with executing rapists, Justice White found it particularly significant that only three of the 35 states that had enacted post-*Furman* death penalty laws had authorized the death penalty for the rape of an adult woman (*Coker* at 591–594). Thus, the judgments of state legislatures, though not unanimous, weighed heavily against death as an acceptable punishment for rape (*Coker* at 596). Moreover, the sentencing decisions actually made by juries in cases in which the prosecutor sought the death penalty for rape also pointed to a growing consensus that death is a disproportionate punishment for rape (*Coker* at 596–597). In Georgia, for example, juries had sentenced to death only six of 63 convicted rapists since 1973 (*Coker* at 596–597). The jury's rejection of capital punishment for rape in the vast majority of cases, like the legislative response to *Furman*, provided significant evidence that the American people were now in agreement "that death is indeed a disproportionate penalty for the crime of raping an adult woman" (*Coker* at 597).

Five years later, in *Enmund v. Florida* (1982), the Court stood by the principle arguably established by *Coker*—that the death penalty is unique in its severity and irrevocability, and therefore must be reserved only for those who take another human life or at least intend or attempt to take another human life. Indeed, Earl Enmund, the getaway driver for two robbers who shot and killed an elderly farm couple who resisted their hold-up attempt, was parked approximately 200 yards from the scene of the murders (*Enmund* at 784). He did not shoot the victims and there was no evidence that he had planned or even anticipated that lethal force would or might be used in the course of the robbery (*Enmund* at 788). A Florida judge nevertheless sentenced him to die, a decision upheld by the Florida Supreme Court (*Enmund* at 784–787).

With Justice White again writing on behalf of the majority, the Court, by the narrowest of margins, struck down Enmund's death sentence. Justice White began by stressing that "to the maximum possible extent," the Court's decisions as to whether a particular punishment is grossly disproportionate to a particular crime must be informed by objective criteria (*Enmund* at 788–789). Accordingly, he turned first to an analysis of legislative judgments on the appropriateness of executing a non-triggerman such as Earl Enmund (*Enmund* at 788–793). Pointing out that only eight of the 36 states that then had capital-punishment statutes allowed the death penalty to be imposed solely because the defendant somehow participated in a robbery in the course of which an accomplice committed a murder, Justice White found that the legislative consensus "weighs on the side of rejecting capital punishment for the crime at issue" (*Enmund* at 792–793). The sentencing behavior of juries provided even stronger evidence that contemporary American society rejects the death penalty for accomplice liability in felony murders (*Enmund* at 794). Of the 362 exe- cutions that had been carried out since 1954, only six were for merely participating in a felony in which a confederate had committed a murder (*Enmund* at 794–795). Moreover, only three of the 739 people who were under sentence of death as of late 1981 had been condemned to die without a finding that they did more than merely participate in an under- lying felony that had led to an unplanned murder (*Enmund* at 795). The final decision, however, must always be made by the Court, and the majority of the justices were in agree- ment with the judgments of legislators and jurors (*Enmund* at 797). The executions of offenders such as Earl Enmund would serve neither the goal of deterrence (since the threat of death is unlikely to deter when murder is not premeditated) nor the purpose of retribu- tion (since retribution requires penalties that are tailored to fit the offender's *personal* responsibility and moral guilt) (*Enmund* at 798–801). Such executions, therefore, accom- plish "nothing more than the purposeless and needless imposition of pain and suffering" and thus are prohibited by the Eighth Amendment (*Enmund* at 798). Accordingly, death is an impermissible punishment for "one who neither took life, attempted to take life, nor intended to take life" (*Enmund* at 787).

Decisions such as *Lockett*, *Coker*, and *Enmund* typify the Court's cautious approach to death-penalty issues in the 1976–1983 period. With few exceptions,[2] the Court insisted that the states follow strict procedural guidelines and make reasonable efforts to ensure fairness, reliability, and individualized consideration in the capital-sentencing process. Thus, the Court repeatedly reaffirmed the *Lockett* holding that the sentencer must con- sider all relevant mitigating circumstances proffered by the defense (*Bell v. Ohio* (1978); *Green v. Georgia* (1979); *Eddings v. Oklahoma* (1982)).

Between 1977 and 1983, there were other significant decisions in which the Court established new protections for capital defendants. For example, *Godfrey v. Georgia* (1980) established that the aggravating circumstances considered by capital juries must be defined clearly enough to avoid the arbitrary imposition of the death penalty. Also in 1980, the Court invalidated an Alabama law that prohibited the trial judge from instructing the jury as to its option to find a capital defendant guilty of a lesser included noncapital offense (*Beck v. Alabama*). And in 1981, the Court held that a jury's initial vote for life over death was an implied acquittal of death-penalty eligibility, thus precluding reimposi- tion of the death penalty after the defendant's reconviction for the same crime (*Bullington v. Missouri*). In these and in other cases that invalidated death sentences, the High Court seemed to be acutely aware that "death is a different kind of punishment from any other" (*Beck* at 637) and must always be accompanied by stringent safeguards designed to ensure fairness and consistency in capital sentencing.

THE POST-*GREGG* YEARS: 1983–2001

Beginning in 1983, the Court began to retreat from its cautious, "go-slow" approach to capital punishment. The insistence on strict procedural safeguards was replaced by an attitude that it was time to "get on with it" and stop interfering with the will of the people as reflected by the laws passed by state legislatures.[3] Such deference to the political branches of government had the effect of broadening the class of death-eligible defendants and weakening the special safeguards against unfairness and caprice. In *Zant v. Stephens* (1983), the majority stressed that the states had a legitimate interest in finding speedier ways to handle death-penalty cases and that "not every imperfection in the deliberative process is sufficient . . . to set aside a state court judgment" (*Zant* at 884–885).

For the rest of the twentieth century, most of the Court's death-penalty jurisprudence would prove to be disappointing and disadvantageous for capital defendants and their attorneys. This trend became evident in cases raising the issue of whether state death-penalty procedures give the defendant a full opportunity to make juries aware of all relevant mitigating evidence. The Court has not repudiated its position that the sentencing judge or jury must be permitted to consider any relevant mitigating circumstances when deciding whether or not to sentence a defendant to death (*Skipper v. South Carolina* 1986; *Hitchcock v. Dugger* 1987). However, the reach of these decisions has been circumscribed by decisions such as *Johnson v. Texas* (1993). In *Johnson*, the Court held that the judge's failure to explicitly instruct the jury to consider mitigating evidence about the defendant's age did not *prevent* the jury from considering the mitigating effect of the defendant's youth.

Similarly, in *Buchanan v. Angelone* (1998), the attorney for a capital defendant in Virginia requested instructions on the meaning of the concept of mitigation generally and on four statutorily defined mitigating factors that had been placed into evidence—the accused's (1) age; (2) lack of prior criminal activity; (3) extreme mental or emotional disturbance at the time of the offense; and (4) impaired ability to appreciate the criminality of his conduct or to conform his conduct to the requirements of law (*Buchanan* at 271–274). The judge refused to include these instructions, but told the jury to base its decision on "all the evidence" (*Buchanan* at 273–274). Writing for the majority, Chief Justice Rehnquist upheld the trial judge's refusal to instruct the jury on the concept of mitigation generally and on the four specific mitigating factors (*Buchanan* at 274–279). The jury instructions, according to the chief justice, were constitutional because by directing the jury to examine "all the evidence," the trial judge had done enough to ensure that jurors would consider mitigating evidence and would not think that they were precluded from considering mitigating evidence (*Buchanan* at 277).

Joined by Justices Stevens and Ginsburg, Justice Breyer issued a strongly worded dissenting opinion that accused the majority of ignoring the likelihood that "so serious a misinstruction" had the effect of misleading the jurors and preventing them from considering relevant mitigating evidence (*Buchanan* at 281–282). Justice Breyer added that by upholding the trial judge's inadequate instructions, the Supreme Court "breaks the promise . . . that the imposition of the punishment of death will 'reflect a reasoned moral response to the defendant's background, character, and crime'" (*Buchanan* at 285, quoting *California v. Brown* at 762).

In the 1980s, the Supreme Court also began to back away from its *Woodson–Roberts* stance against mandatory death-penalty statutes. However, in an important 1987 decision, the Court invalidated a mandatory death-penalty law because it did not allow jurors to consider any mitigating circumstances. In *Sumner v. Shuman*, the Court struck down a Nevada law that required the jury to impose the death penalty in all cases in which a prisoner is convicted of murder while serving a life sentence without the possibility of parole. Interestingly, Justice Blackmun, who had voted to uphold the mandatory death-penalty laws at issue in *Woodson* and *Roberts*, wrote the majority opinion in *Shuman*. He reasoned that even when an inmate serving a life-without-parole sentence commits a murder, there might be mitigating factors such as the defendant's age or mental condition, that weigh against a death sentence (*Shuman* at 81–82). To the argument that a mandatory death sentence is necessary in order to deter and provide retribution against life-termers, the majority responded that under a non-mandatory guided-discretion sentencing law, those who deserve to die are likely to receive the death penalty in most cases and those not condemned to die can still be punished in other ways, "such as through a transfer to a more restrictive . . . correctional facility or deprivation of privileges" (*Shuman* at 83–84). Since the state's legitimate interests in deterrence and retribution can be satisfied through the use of a guided-discretion statute, the Court would not depart from the position that mandatory death-penalty laws violate the Eighth Amendment (*Shuman* at 85).

Although *Shuman* remains in effect, the Court in 1990 embraced an element of mandatoriness in capital sentencing. In *Boyde v. California*, a five-justice majority held that the existence of a mandatory component in a guided-discretion death-penalty statute does not always violate constitutional strictures. Specifically, the *Boyde* Court upheld the constitutionality of a California law that requires the jury to impose the death penalty if it finds that the aggravating circumstances in the case outweigh any mitigating circumstances. Similarly, in *Blystone v. Pennsylvania* (1990), the Court approved a Pennsylvania law that requires a death sentence when the jury finds at least one statutory aggravating circumstance and no mitigating circumstances. Writing for the *Boyde* and *Blystone* majorities, Chief Justice Rehnquist distinguished *Woodson*, stressing that under the California and Pennsylvania statutes,

> Death is not automatically imposed upon conviction for certain types of murder. It is imposed only after a determination that the aggravating circumstances outweigh the mitigating circumstances present in the particular crime committed by the particular defendant, or that there are no such mitigating circumstances (*Blystone* at 305).[4]

In *Boyde* and *Blystone*, the Supreme Court merely "chipped away" at past precedents requiring strict scrutiny of death-penalty laws. For opponents of the death penalty, this was ominous enough in itself. But in other important cases in the 1980s and 1990s, the Court went much further, jettisoning prior holdings and retreating from the pursuit of fairness and consistency in death-penalty cases. To be sure, the Court continued to invalidate egregiously unconstitutional capital-sentencing provisions.[5] However, the predominant trend was clearly in the direction of expanding the reach of the death penalty and promoting expeditious executions.

Several 1983 decisions portended the Court's movement away from the strict regulation of capital sentencing procedures. For example, in *California v. Ramos*, the Court found nothing constitutionally deficient in a law that seemingly gives the jury the mistaken impression that the *only* way to keep the defendant off the street is to execute him. The law in question required judges to instruct the jury that the governor had the authority to reduce a life-without-parole sentence to a sentence that includes the possibility of parole. But it did not require the judge to call the jury's attention to the governor's power to commute a death sentence (*Ramos* at 994–998).

In two 1983 cases (*Barclay v. Florida*; *Zant v. Stephens*), the Court refused to invalidate death sentences even though a judge (*Barclay*) and a jury (*Zant*) had considered an illegitimate aggravating circumstance along with two or more legitimate aggravating circumstances. The majority's determination that a sentence of death could rest upon both valid and invalid aggravating circumstances provoked a strong dissent from Justice Blackmun, who wrote, "[t]he end does not justify the means even in what may be deemed to be a 'deserving capital punishment situation'" (*Barclay* at 991).

In a particularly controversial 1983 case dealing with Texas' death-penalty statute, the Court upheld the admissibility of testimony by state-hired psychiatrists who routinely predicted that capital defendants would commit future violent crimes. Under Texas law—then and now—jurors must vote as to whether a capital defendant is likely to commit such crimes in the future, and an affirmative vote renders the defendant death-eligible. Writing for the majority in *Barefoot v. Estelle*, Justice White acknowledged research studies showing that "expert" predictions about future dangerousness turn out to be incorrect 66 percent of the time (*Barefoot* at 898–903). He dismissed the importance of such studies, however, noting that psychiatrists are not wrong all of the time, "only most of the time" (*Barefoot* at 901). Since the defense has the opportunity to cross-examine the state's witnesses and can always call its own witnesses, the jurors will hear both sides of the debate over the defendant's dangerousness and can sort out the differences themselves (*Barefoot* at 898–899). Thus, the scientifically dubious expert testimony does not in and of itself render the sentencing hearing so unfair as to violate the Constitution (*Barefoot* at 905–906). The *Barefoot* majority also bestowed its approval on "expedited review procedures" to be followed by federal courts in order to speed death-penalty appeals toward a final resolution (*Barefoot* at 887–896). Ironically, as several legal commentators pointed out, the procedures approved in *Barefoot* give capital defendants *less time* to prepare their appeals than prisoners who do not face the death penalty (Mello 1988:547–548; Amsterdam 1987:889–890).

The Supreme Court continued to demonstrate its "tougher" attitude toward capital punishment in the 1984–1985 and 1985–1986 terms. For example, in *Wainwright v. Witt* (1985), the Court by a seven-to-two vote relaxed the longstanding standard that required judges to remove a prospective juror from both phases of a capital trial only when the juror made it "unmistakably clear" that he or she could never vote to impose death in the penalty phase of the trial. This standard, derived from a 1968 decision, *Witherspoon v. Illinois*, helped to make capital juries at least somewhat representative of the community at large—a community that typically includes some people who are potentially receptive to the defense attorney's arguments for life as well as the prosecutor's arguments for death. But the *Witt* holding replaced *Witherspoon* with a rule holding that a prospective juror could be eliminated merely on the ground that the judge believed that the juror's doubts about capital punishment would "substantially impair" his or her ability to impose a death sentence (*Witt* at 424–425).

One year later, Justice Rehnquist, the author of the *Witt* majority opinion, again wrote for the Court in *Lockhart v. McCree* (1986). Here the holding was that "death qualification"—the practice of removing from capital juries those who were reluctant to impose death in the penalty phase—does not violate the defendant's Sixth Amendment right to a fair trial in the guilt phase of the trial. The *McCree* decision contradicted the findings of numerous social-science studies showing that death-qualified juries were significantly more likely to impose the death penalty than were juries in noncapital cases (Ellsworth 1988). To opponents of capital punishment, the *Witt* and *McCree* holdings were seen as heralding a new era in which the scales of justice would be weighted against life and in favor of death.

In 1987, many of the worst fears of death-penalty opponents were realized. In a trilogy of five-to-four decisions, the Court rejected two important challenges to death-penalty laws and extended death-penalty eligibility to a new category of defendants—those who did not actually take another human life. First, in *California v. Brown*, Chief Justice Rehnquist authored a majority opinion upholding a death sentence imposed by a jury that had been instructed by the trial judge that it "must not be swayed by mere sentiment, conjecture, sympathy, passion, prejudice, public opinion or public feeling" (*Brown* at 540). The California Supreme Court had found that an instruction to disregard any sympathy factors raised by the defense violated the *Lockett* mandate that juries must be permitted to consider all relevant mitigating evidence before reaching a decision (*Brown* at 539–540). The chief justice, however, asserted that a reasonable juror would read the instruction as a whole rather than focus only on the admonition against being swayed by sympathy (*Brown* at 542–543). Therefore, he reasoned, the instruction did nothing more than advise jurors to ignore emotional responses that are not rooted in the aggravating and mitigating evidence, thereby minimizing the risk of arbitrary and capricious decisions (*Brown* at 543).

In dissent, Justice Brennan contended that the state Supreme Court was right in the first place: the anti-sympathy instruction would almost certainly lead jurors to believe that they could not consider the very kind of mitigating factors that the *Lockett* majority "[had] decreed *must* be considered by the sentencer" (*Brown* at 555). The result will be that juries will be confronted with confusing and contradictory instructions, a state of affairs that should not be tolerated when life itself is at stake (*Brown* at 560–561).

Several months after *Brown*, the Court rejected a major systemic challenge to the constitutionality of capital punishment. In *McCleskey v. Kemp* (1987), the Court was confronted with strong statistical evidence that post-*Gregg* capital-sentencing procedures were still saturated with arbitrariness and racial discrimination, and thus violated both the Eighth Amendment's cruel and unusual punishment clause and the Fourteenth Amendment's guarantee of equal protection under the law. A comprehensive study (known as the Baldus study)[6] of 2000 murder cases that occurred in Georgia during the 1970s revealed that defendants charged with killing white victims were 4.3 times as likely to receive a death sentence as those whose victims were black (*McCleskey* at 287).

Moreover, the death penalty had been imposed in 22 percent of the cases involving black defendants and white victims; 8 percent of the cases involving white defendants and white victims; 3 percent of the cases involving white defendants and black victims; and 1 percent of the cases involving black defendants and black victims (*McCleskey* at 286).

Did such overwhelming evidence of racial discrimination in capital sentencing establish a constitutional violation? Writing for the majority, Justice Powell answered this question in the negative. The majority assumed that the Baldus study was reliable, but held that to prevail under the equal protection clause, a capital defendant would have to meet the difficult burden of proving "that the decision makers in *his* case acted with discriminatory purpose" (*McCleskey* at 292). To the argument that the statistical evidence demonstrated that the death penalty in Georgia was arbitrarily applied in violation of the Eighth Amendment, Justice Powell responded:

> At most, the Baldus study indicates a discrepancy that appears to correlate with race. Apparent disparities in sentencing are an inevitable part of our criminal justice system . . . Where the discretion that is fundamental to our criminal process is involved, we decline to assume that what is unexplained is invidious. In light of the safeguards [Georgia has] designed to minimize racial bias in the process . . . we hold that the Baldus study does not demonstrate a constitutionally significant risk of racial bias affecting the Georgia capital sentencing process (*McCleskey* at 312–313).

In a dissenting opinion, Justice Brennan, joined by Justices Marshall, Stevens, and Blackmun, accused the majority of ignoring "precisely the type of risk of irrationality in sentencing that we have consistently condemned in our Eighth Amendment jurisprudence" (*McCleskey* at 320–321). He vehemently objected to Justice Powell's assertion that the risk of racial bias in Georgia's capital-sentencing system were not "constitutionally significant" (*McCleskey* at 325–328). Pointing out that the Baldus study showed that "blacks who kill whites are sentenced to death at nearly *22 times* the rate of blacks who kill blacks and more than *7 times* the rate of whites who kill blacks," Justice Brennan contended that "we should not be willing to take a person's life if the chance that his death sentence was irrationally imposed is more likely than not" (*McCleskey* at 327–328).

The *McCleskey* decision dealt a major blow to opponents of the death penalty, but some abolitionists were even more dismayed by the Court's 1987 holding in *Tison v. Arizona*. The *Tison* decision significantly modified the Court's aforementioned 1982 ruling in *Enmund v. Florida*, which had forbidden the execution of those who participate in a felony that leads to murder but who do not actually kill, attempt to kill, or intend to kill. In *Tison*, the justices considered the fate of Ricky and Raymond Tison, two young brothers who helped their father, Gary Tison, and his cellmate, Randy Greenawalt, escape from the Arizona State Prison in 1978. Several days later, the escape car lost a tire on a desert road, and the group decided to flag down a passing motorist and steal his car. After a Mazda occupied by John Lyons, his wife, his 2-year-old son, and his 15-year-old niece pulled over to offer help, Gary Tison and Randy Greenawalt took the family back to the escape car, held them there at gunpoint, and told the brothers to go back to the Mazda to get some water. When they did so, their father and his friend brutally shotgunned their four captives to death. Although Ricky and Raymond subsequently testified that they were surprised by the shooting, they nevertheless stayed with their father until they were captured several days later after a shootout with the police in which Randy Greenawalt was also captured and their father was killed (*Tison* at 139–141).

The Tison brothers and Randy Greenawalt were all convicted for the murder of the Lyons family and sentenced to death. Randy Greenawalt, one of the actual murderers, certainly was eligible for the death penalty. But could the Tison brothers be executed for murders that the state could not prove that they committed or even intended to commit? The *Enmund* holding would seem to answer this question in the negative, but the Supreme Court disagreed. Writing for the majority, Justice O'Connor asserted that there was nothing cruel and unusual about executing defendants who neither committed nor intended to commit murder (1) if they participated in a "major" way in the underlying felony that led to murder and (2) if they demonstrated a "reckless indifference to human life" while doing so (*Tison* at 158). As Justice O'Connor explained it, the defendant's role in the armed robbery and murders in *Enmund* was "minor"; the Tison brothers, on the other hand, participated fully in the escape, kidnapping, and robbery "and watched the killing after which [they] chose to aid those whom [they] had placed in the position to kill rather than their victims" (*Tison* at 152). Focusing on the question of whether or not the defendants intended to kill, she continued, did not take into account that "reckless disregard for human life may be every bit as shocking to the moral sense as an 'intent to kill' " (*Tison* at 157).

In a lengthy dissenting opinion joined by Justices Marshall, Stevens, and Blackmun, Justice Brennan accused the majority of creating "a new category of culpability" and blithely discarding a fundamental principle found in virtually all European and Commonwealth countries—that the death penalty—if it is ever to be used—must be reserved for those who either killed or intended to kill another human being (*Tison* at 170–171). The Court's holding, he concluded, was inconsistent with *Enmund*, violated basic standards of fairness and proportionality, and went well beyond the retributive principle of "an eye for an eye . . ." (*Tison* at 174–185).

After *Tison*, it seemed safe to predict that the Court was poised to expand further the category of death-eligible defendants. This is what the Court in fact did in two important 1989 decisions, both announced on June 26 of that year. First, in *Penry v. Lynaugh*, the Court held that executing a person who is mentally retarded does not constitute cruel and unusual punishment. Johnny Paul Penry, who was 22 at the time he committed murder, was diagnosed as "moderately" mentally retarded with an IQ ranging between 50 and 63. This meant that he had the mental capacity of an average 6-1/2-year-old child (*Penry* at 308). But according to Justice O'Connor's majority opinion, this was outweighed in importance by the fact that the State of Texas had found Penry to be competent to stand trial and to have "a reasonable degree of rational understanding . . . as well as factual understanding of the case against him" (*Penry* at 333). Justice O'Connor suggested that it might be cruel and unusual to execute "profoundly" or "severely" retarded people, but that the mental limitations of someone who was merely "moderately" retarded did not automatically preclude imposition of the death penalty (*Penry* at 333–340). Four dissenting justices failed to convince the majority that "[t]he impairment of a mentally retarded offender's reasoning abilities [and] control over impulsive behavior limit his or her culpability so that, whatever other punishment might be appropriate, the ultimate penalty of death is always . . . disproportionate to his or her blameworthiness and hence is unconstitutional" (*Penry* at 346).[7]

On the same day the holding in *Penry* was decided, the Court announced its decision in a case that raised the issue of whether the prohibition against cruel and unusual punishments precluded the execution of defendants who were 16 or 17 years old at the time of their offense. One year earlier, a closely divided Court held that 15-year-old offenders could not be executed unless and until more states enacted laws authorizing such executions (*Thompson v. Oklahoma* 1988). But in *Stanford v. Kentucky*, the Court found that it was sufficiently clear that there was no national consensus against imposing capital punishment on 16- and 17-year-old offenders. Writing for the majority, Justice Scalia noted that of the states that permit capital punishment, 15 declined to impose it on 16-year olds and 12 declined to impose it on 17-year olds (*Stanford* at 372). These numbers, according to Justice Scalia, did not establish enough of a national consensus to show that executing such young offenders was contrary to America's evolving standards of decency and thus violative of the Eighth Amendment (*Stanford* at 372–373). As Justice Brennan pointed out in dissent, the majority's holding would ensure that the United States would remain in a minority position in the world community, which "overwhelmingly disapproved" the imposition of the death penalty on juvenile offenders (*Stanford* at 389). Justice Scalia, however, characterized such international comparisons as irrelevant, emphasizing that only "*American* conceptions of decency are dispositive" (*Stanford* at 369, n. 1).

Justice Scalia also rejected another of Justice Brennan's arguments: that executing those who are too young, immature, and impulsive to take full responsibility for their actions fails to serve the penological goals of retribution and deterrence (*Stanford* at 377).[8] Justice Scalia asserted that arguments grounded in the claim that juveniles are less mature, more impulsive, and less likely to possess fully developed cognitive skills than adults must fail because they rest on social-science studies rather than the judgment of the American people (*Stanford* at 377–378). Social-science studies, according to Justice Scalia, are irrelevant because the Court has no business evaluating such studies in order to determine whether a particular punishment violates the Eighth Amendment (*Stanford* at 378). It is the citizenry of the United States, not judges, who must be persuaded that children are less blameworthy and are therefore ineligible for the death penalty (*Stanford* at 378). Accordingly, the Court in future death-penalty cases would ignore "ethioscientific" evidence and consider only "objective indicia"—the most important of which are the laws passed by Congress and the state legislatures (*Stanford* at 377–378). In the future, Justice Scalia warned, the Eighth Amendment would be taken literally. A challenged punishment would have to be *both* cruel and unusual, as determined by objective factors, to fail the Court's Eighth Amendment tests (*Stanford* at 369). In other words, a cruel punishment would withstand constitutional scrutiny if enough states still authorize it. Just how many states are enough will be determined by the Court on a case-by-case basis.

In the early 1990s, Justice Scalia's brand of jurisprudence—extraordinary deference to laws and procedures that broaden the application of the death penalty—was clearly in the ascendancy. For example, in *Payne v. Tennessee*, Chief Justice Rehnquist ended the 1990–1991 term by authoring a majority opinion that reversed the Court's previous holdings (*Booth v. Maryland* 1987; *South Carolina v. Gathers* 1989) prohibiting the use of so-called "victim-impact" statements in the penalty phase of capital trials. In *Payne*, a six-justice majority rejected the argument that permitting juries to base death-penalty decisions on such idiosyncratic factors as the victim's reputation and the persuasiveness of the victim's family in describing their loss would distract jurors from examining the character of the defendant and the nature of the crime (*Payne* at 811–844). This, according to the dissenting justices, posed a "constitutionally unacceptable risk" that juries would impose the death penalty in an arbitrary and discriminatory manner (*Payne* at 844–867).[9]

In 1993, the Court announced an especially important decision—*Herrera v. Collins*—on the scope of the right to seek meaningful appellate review of capital sentences. In *Herrera*, the Court considered the case of Leonel Torres Herrera, a Texas death-row inmate who sought federal habeas corpus relief on the ground that he was factually innocent of the murder for which he had been sentenced to die. Most habeas petitions focus on constitutional questions pertaining to the fairness of the defendant's arrest, pre-trial proceedings, or trial. Herrera's petition, however, asserted that even though the appellate courts had found his trial to be fair, he was nevertheless "actually innocent." He and his attorneys supported this claim with affidavits containing recently discovered evidence indicating that Herrera's now-dead brother was the actual perpetrator of the crime (*Herrera* at 396).

The case against Herrera was overwhelming and the new evidence was not credible. One can only wonder why the Court chose to review this case rather than one with stronger evidence of innocence. Nevertheless, Herrera's petition raised two very important questions: (1) Can a death-sentenced prisoner obtain federal habeas corpus relief solely on the ground of newly discovered evidence of factual innocence when he has no accompanying claim of a violation of his constitutional rights in the state criminal proceedings against him? (2) Would the execution of a factually innocent person violate the Eighth Amendment's prohibition of cruel and unusual punishments, the due process clause of the Fourteenth Amendment, or any other provision of the U.S. Constitution? To the dismay of death-penalty opponents, the majority opinion, authored by Chief Justice Rehnquist, answered both questions in a manner that would do nothing to help those who are wrongfully convicted and sentenced to die. With respect to the first question, Rehnquist stressed that federal habeas corpus review traditionally has been limited to questions of alleged constitutional violations (*Herrera* at 400–402). Accordingly, claims of factual innocence based on newly discovered evidence do not state a ground for relief when they are not accompanied by an underlying constitutional claim (*Herrera* at 400–402). This rule, Rehnquist added, "is grounded in the principle that federal habeas courts sit to ensure that individuals are not imprisoned in violation of the Constitution— not to correct errors of fact" (*Herrera* at 400).

In response to Herrera's assertion that the Eighth and Fourteenth Amendments prohibit the execution of a factually innocent person, Rehnquist conceded that such an argument "has an elemental appeal" (*Herrera* at 398). But this argument, according to the chief justice, was irrelevant in the context of Herrera's case. The proper judicial proceeding to determine "guilt" or "innocence" is the defendant's trial, and "once a defendant has been afforded a fair trial and convicted of the offense for which he was charged, the presumption of innocence disappears" (*Herrera* at 399). Since the state met its burden of proof at trial, Herrera comes before the Supreme Court not as one who is "innocent," but as one who has been convicted of murder (*Herrera* at 399–400). "The question before us, then, is not whether the Constitution prohibits the execution of an innocent person, but rather whether it entitles petitioner to review of his 'actual innocence' claim" (*Herrera* at 408, n. 6). The answer to this question, Rehnquist reiterated, was "no," since "a claim of 'actual innocence' is not itself a constitutional claim, but instead a gateway through which a habeas petitioner must pass to have his otherwise barred constitutional claim considered on the merits" (*Herrera* at 404). Thus, Rehnquist's majority opinion did not squarely answer the question of whether the Constitution prohibits the execution of an innocent person. Clearly, however, the *Herrera* opinion established a formidable catch-22 for death-row inmates who might want to raise the question in the future.

Joined by Justices Souter and Breyer, Justice Blackmun issued a dissenting opinion that disagreed with virtually every aspect of the majority opinion. First, Blackmun declared that it was "crystal clear" that execution of the innocent violates both the Eighth and Fourteenth Amendments (*Herrera* at 430–435). Second, he asserted that the majority should realize that even a prisoner who appears to have had "a constitutionally perfect" trial retains a strong and legitimate interest in overturning a wrongful conviction, particularly when he faces the death penalty (*Herrera* at 437–439). Justice Blackmun argued that claims of actual innocence, even when unaccompanied by a claim of constitutional error, should be reviewed by federal habeas courts in all cases where the petitioner can make a threshold showing that he is "probably innocent" (*Herrera* at 442–444). In a part of the dissenting opinion in which he spoke only for himself, Justice Blackmun castigated the majority for its "obvious eagerness to do away with any restriction on the States' power to execute whomever and however they please" (*Herrera* at 446). Permitting an innocent person to be executed, he added, "comes perilously close to simple murder" (*Herrera* at 446).

Five years later, another catch-22 became apparent in cases in which a condemned prisoner attempts to show that he is factually innocent. Chief Justice Rehnquist's majority opinion in *Herrera* had extolled the virtues of executive clemency as "the historical remedy for preventing miscarriages of justice where judicial process has been exhausted" (*Herrera* at 411–412). A death-sentenced inmate would not be permitted to bring a freestanding claim of actual innocence to the federal courts in a habeas petition. But, according to Rehnquist, this was appropriate and fair:

> Executive clemency has provided the "fail safe" in our criminal justice system. . . . It is an unalterable fact that our judicial system, like the human beings who administer it, is fallible. But history is replete with examples of wrongfully convicted persons who have been pardoned in the wake of after-discovered evidence establishing their innocence (*Herrera* at 415).

In dissent, Justice Blackmun countered that although clemency proceedings had saved the lives of some wrongfully convicted people, executive clemency, at best, was an ad hoc exercise of authority by elected officials that was highly fallible in itself and, in fact, had failed to save the lives of a number of factually innocent people (*Herrera* at 431, n. 1).

The stage was thus set for an important 1998 ruling on the question of whether death-sentenced prisoners were entitled to due process protection during clemency hearings. In

Ohio Adult Parole Authority v. Woodard, Eugene Woodard complained of the lack of procedural protection offered by the Ohio Adult Parole Authority, the state board that votes on clemency petitions and sends its recommendation to the governor. As the ultimate decision maker, the governor has the authority to take a broad range of actions including commuting a death sentence to a sentence of life imprisonment (*Woodard* at 275–277). Woodard contended that the Authority's procedures fell woefully short of fair standards. He complained, in particular, that he was given only 10 days notice of the date of his clemency hearing, that he was given only three days notice of his option of requesting an interview with a member of the Parole Authority, that his attorney was not permitted to be present for any such interview, that his attorney would be permitted to attend the clemency hearing only at the discretion of the Parole Authority, and that Woodard, himself, was not allowed to testify or to present documentary evidence at the clemency hearing (*Woodard* at 289–290).

Having praised clemency hearings as the "fail safe" of the criminal justice process, Chief Justice Rehnquist might have been expected to find these procedures to be inadequate, especially in that they gave the condemned man so little time to prepare his case, sabotaged his right to the assistance of counsel, and did not even permit him to testify or present new evidence during the clemency hearing. In *Woodard*, however, Chief Justice Rehnquist, joined by Justices Scalia, Thomas, and Kennedy, took an extraordinarily narrow view, asserting that clemency proceedings simply do not implicate due process (*Woodard* at 275–288). According to Rehnquist, clemency is *not* an integral part of Ohio's system of adjudicating guilt or innocence and it therefore follows that forcing clemency boards or governors to follow any due process standards "would be inconsistent with the heart of executive clemency, which is to grant clemency as a matter of grace. . . ." (*Woodard* at 280–281). Rehnquist concluded:

> Clemency proceedings are not part of the trial—or even of the adjudicatory process. They do not determine the guilt or innocence of the defendant, and are not primarily intended to enhance the reliability of the trial process. They are conducted by the Executive Branch, independent of direct appeal and collateral relief proceedings. . . . While traditionally available to capital defendants as a final and alternative avenue of relief, clemency has not traditionally been the business of courts (*Woodard* at 284).

The majority of the justices were unwilling to hold that no due process whatsoever is required in capital clemency proceedings. Justice O'Connor, in an opinion joined by Justices Souter, Ginsburg, and Breyer, contended that in capital cases, when life itself is at stake, clemency proceedings implicate due process (*Woodard* at 288–290). These four justices, however, declared that only *minimal* procedural safeguards apply to clemency hearings (*Woodard* at 289). As examples of procedures that might be found to violate due process, O'Connor cited two hypothetical cases—a case where a state denied a death-sentenced prisoner any access at all to its clemency process and a scheme in which a state official flips a coin in order to decide whether to grant clemency (*Woodard* at 289). Thus, eight justices found that Ohio's clemency procedures were constitutional and that Woodard's due process rights had not been violated. Only Justice Stevens, who pointed out that the Rehnquist opinion would permit clemency procedures to be infected by "the deliberate fabrication of false evidence" (*Woodard* at 290–291) and that the O'Connor opinion provided only "minimal, perhaps even barely discernible" procedural safeguards for condemned people (*Woodard* at 290), was willing to cast a dissenting vote. He would have remanded the case back to the lower Ohio courts for an assessment of what particular procedural safeguards are required in capital clemency proceedings (*Woodard* at 294).

The trend exemplified by *Herrera* and *Woodard* continued through the Court's 2000–2001 term with the announcement of a number of decisions that raised questions of fairness with respect to the administration of the death penalty. For example, in *Strickler v. Greene* (1999), the Court upheld a Virginia man's death sentence despite the prosecution's suppression of important exculpatory evidence that the defense might have used to discredit the state's key eyewitness. That witness had changed her story several times before her testimony at Tommy Strickler's trial for allegedly abducting a woman from a shopping mall and killing her. However, state prosecutors, contrary to state and federal law, never disclosed this to Strickler's defense attorneys. The Court acknowledged that discrediting the testimony "might have changed the outcome of the trial" and that there was a "reasonable possibility" that Strickler would have been spared (*Strickler* at 290). A "reasonable possibility," however was not good enough. Strickler, the Court concluded, needed to show a "reasonable *probability*" that his conviction or sentence would have been different had the prosecution not suppressed the evidence in question (*Strickler* at 291). Thus, although the question was "close," Strickler's death sentence was affirmed (*Strickler* at 296).

In *Weeks v. Angelone* (2000), the Court held that a judge presiding over a capital case was not obligated to clear up the jury's confusion over a crucial sentencing instruction. Writing for a five-justice majority, Chief Justice Rehnquist reasoned that the Constitution was not violated when the judge refused to explain, in response to the jury's query, that a death sentence was *not* mandatory if the jurors found that the state had proved one of two aggravating factors. Rehnquist conceded that there was a "slight possibility" that the jury mistakenly believed a death sentence to be mandatory when the judge responded to the jurors' question by simply telling them to reread his original instructions (*Weeks* at 236). The chief justice, nonetheless, said that "a jury is presumed to understand a judge's answer to its question . . . and to presume otherwise would require a reversal every time a jury inquires about a matter of constitutional significance, regardless of the judge's answer" (*Weeks* at 234). Writing for the four dissenting justices, Justice Stevens noted that the jurors spent several hours debating the meaning of the instruction that continued to confuse them and that when the jurors were polled, most of them were "in tears" (*Weeks* at 248). Stevens added that the judge's failure to answer the jury's question in a clear-cut way was constitutionally deficient and that it was a "virtual certainty" that the jury was confused (*Weeks* at 238).[10]

THE POST-*GREGG* YEARS: 2002–2005

From 2002 to 2005, the Supreme Court announced two major decisions reducing the categories of offenders eligible for capital punishment and several other decisions that demonstrated greater caution and concern about defendants' rights in capital cases. Nevertheless, many decisions in this time period tightened restrictions on death-penalty appeals and rejected capital defendants' constitutional claims. In 2003, for example, the Court held that limits on capital appeals that were included in the Antiterrorism and Effective Death Penalty Act of 1996 (AEDPA) apply even to capital appeals that were in a preliminary stage *before* the AEDPA was enacted (*Woodford v. Garceau*). Writing for a six-justice majority, Justice Thomas asserted that only substantive appeals that had been formally filed in a federal court before the passage of the AEDPA were exempt from the new appeals limits (*Woodford* at 205–210). Thus, death-sentenced inmates who had taken only such preliminary steps as seeking a motion for a stay of execution or requesting court appointment of an attorney had not truly initiated what could be called a "case" and would be bound by the AEDPA's new restrictions (*Woodford* at 207–209).

In another significant 2003 ruling, the Court undermined its 1981 ruling in *Bullington v. Missouri* that the Fifth Amendment's double jeopardy clause applies to capital-sentencing proceedings. In *Sattazahn v. Pennsylvania* (2003), the Court explained that in *Bullington*, the jury, by voting for life imprisonment over a death sentence, had, in effect, "acquitted" the defendant of the factors necessary to impose the death sentence (*Sattazahn* at 107–108). In Sattazahn's case, however, the trial judge, pursuant to Pennsylvania law, had imposed a life sentence after the jury deadlocked on whether to sentence the defendant to death (*Sattazahn* at 104–106). Writing for a five-justice majority, Justice Scalia contended that this was a "non-result" that was not the equivalent of an "acquittal" that would establish a legal entitlement to a life sentence (*Sattazahn* at 109–110).

However, the Court's greater willingness to rule in favor of capital defendants from 2002 until 2005 was unmistakable. For example, in *Miller-El v. Cockrell* (2003), the Court, with only Justice Thomas dissenting, ordered a federal appeals court to grant a habeas hearing to a death-row inmate who made a "substantial showing" that the selection of his jury had been infected by racial prejudice (*Cockrell* at 326). After the appellate court again denied the inmate's claim, the Supreme Court again took his case and reversed the ruling of the appellate court. Stressing that prosecutors had used peremptory challenges to remove 10 of 11 eligible black jury panelists from the trial jury and had offered "race-neutral" reasons for doing so that simply were not credible, the Court vacated the conviction and death sentence (*Miller-El v. Dretke* 2005).

It is also noteworthy that after years of routinely rejecting death-penalty appeals based on claims of ineffective assistance of trial counsel, the Supreme Court began to take such claims seriously. For example, in *Wiggins v. Smith* (2003), the Court reversed a federal appellate court's finding that a death-row inmate's lawyers had performed competently even though they failed to investigate and inform the sentencing jury of their client's severe childhood abuse. The seven-to-two majority held that it was clear from the trial record that the performance of the attorneys fell well below minimally acceptable standards and that there was a reasonable possibility that if the jury had been aware of the nature and extent of the mitigating evidence, it would have returned with a different sentence (*Wiggins* at 523–524). In light of all the circumstances, the majority concluded that trial counsel had rendered ineffective assistance of counsel, thereby violating the defendant's Sixth Amendment right to effective assistance of counsel (*Wiggins* at 534–535). Two years later, in *Rompilla v. Beard* (2005), the Court upheld an ineffective-assistance claim even though defense attorneys had interviewed their capital client, his family, and mental health experts in an effort to uncover mitigating evidence. A five-to-four majority nevertheless found that defense attorneys had been deficient because they failed to examine their client's prior conviction file—a readily available public document—and the file would have yielded significant mitigating evidence about the defendant's childhood, mental health, and alcoholism (*Rompilla* at 388–393).

Death-penalty laws in five states were changed as the result of the Supreme Court's decision in *Ring v. Arizona* (2002). In *Ring*, the Court held that the Sixth Amendment's guarantee of the right to a jury trial requires that a jury, not a judge, must make the factual findings (e.g., the finding that at least one aggravating factor exists) that subject a murder defendant to the death penalty (*Ring* at 604–609). By striking down Arizona's death-sentencing law, under which judges alone decided whether the crime included aggravating factors sufficient to warrant a possible death sentence, the *Ring* holding had the effect of invalidating similar laws in Colorado, Idaho, Montana, and Nebraska (Greenhouse 2002). *Ring* also raised questions that still have not been clearly resolved about the constitutionality of laws in four other states—Alabama, Delaware, Florida, and Indiana—in which the judge decides between life and death after considering the jury's recommendation. In *Schiro v. Summerlin* (2004), the Court made it clear that *Ring* applies only prospectively, not retroactively, to death-row inmates whose convictions and sentences were final at the time *Ring* was decided. As a result, over 100 prisoners who were sentenced to death by a judge were not entitled to a new sentencing hearing. However, many legal scholars believe—although there is some debate over the matter—that over the long run, juries will impose fewer death sentences than judges would have imposed in the states where judges no longer make the factual determinations that can lead to a death sentence (Liptak 2002).

Two recently decided cases resulted in major victories for opponents of capital punishment, and there is no doubt that these holdings will reduce the number of death sentences imposed in the United States. In *Atkins v. Virginia* (2002), the Supreme Court held that the Eighth Amendment prohibits the execution of mentally retarded offenders and in *Roper v. Simmons* (2005), the Court held that the Eighth Amendment prohibits the execution of 16- and 17-year-old offenders. In *Atkins*, the Court, by a six-to-three rate, overruled its decision in *Penry v. Lynaugh* (1989). As explained earlier, the *Penry* Court, in an opinion authored by Justice O'Connor, concluded that the Eighth Amendment did not prohibit the execution of mentally retarded offenders. The *Penry* majority stressed that as of 1989 only two states had passed laws exempting the mentally retarded from death sentences (*Penry* at 333–334).

However, by 2002, as Justice Stevens pointed out in his *Atkins* majority opinion (which was joined by Justice O'Connor as well as by Justices Breyer, Ginsburg, Kennedy, and Souter), the legislative landscape had changed (*Atkins* at 314). Between 1989 and 2002, 16 more states passed laws banning the execution of mentally retarded offenders (*Atkins* at 314–315). This brought the total number of states banning such executions to 30—the 12 states that ban all executions and 18 of the 38 states with capital-punishment laws (*Atkins* at 314–315). According to the majority, this was enough to establish a national consensus (*Atkins* at 316).

The *Atkins* dissenters (Chief Justice Rehnquist, Justice Scalia, and Justice Thomas) rebuked the majority for discerning a national consensus against executing mentally retarded offenders in the face of the fact that 20 states still had laws permitting such executions (*Atkins* at 321–322). But Justice Stevens claimed that "[i]t is not so much the number of these states that is significant, but the consistency of the direction of change" (*Atkins* at 315). He added that it is also significant that executions of mentally retarded offenders were rare in most states and that in the years after *Penry*, only five states—Alabama, Texas, Louisiana, South Carolina, and Virginia—executed any offenders known to be mentally retarded (*Atkins* at 316). "The practice, therefore, has become truly unusual and it is fair to say that a national consensus has developed against it" (*Atkins* at 316).

This new legislative consensus, Justice Stevens contended, was supported by an emerging social and professional consensus (*Atkins* at 316, n. 21). Public opinion polls indicated that the majority of Americans were against executing the mentally retarded (*Atkins* at 316, n. 21). Several respected professional and religious organizations, including the American Psychological Association and the U.S. Catholic Conference, were opposed to such executions (*Atkins* at 316, n. 21). The majority also took into account the fact that "within the world community, the imposition of the death penalty for crimes committed by mentally retarded offenders is overwhelmingly disapproved" (*Atkins* at 316, n. 21).

The *Atkins* majority also asserted that it was difficult to square the practice of executing the mentally retarded with the *Gregg*-approved goals of retribution and deterrence (*Atkins* at 318–319). The purpose of retribution—making sure that a criminal gets his "just deserts"—cannot be truly achieved by executing people who have a diminished ability to understand the consequences of their actions (*Atkins* at 319). Similarly, the goal of deterrence is not likely to be achieved by threatening to execute people who have impaired abilities to learn from experience and process information about the possibility of execution as a punishment for their conduct (*Atkins* at 319–320). Accordingly, the majority concluded that the execution of mentally retarded offenders is little more than the purposeless infliction of suffering and violates the Eighth Amendment's ban on cruel and unusual punishments (*Atkins* at 321).

The *Atkins* decision prompted some legal observers to predict that the Supreme Court would soon reverse its decision in *Stanford v. Kentucky* (1989) to permit executions of 16- and 17-year-old offenders (Haas 2004). The arguments for excluding juvenile offenders from death eligibility are very similar to the arguments that were offered by the *Atkins* majority. But the *Atkins* majority had pointedly noted that even though *Stanford* and *Penry* were decided on the same day in 1989, only two states had raised the minimum age for imposing the death penalty to 18, as compared to the 16 states that had enacted legislation ending the execution of mentally retarded offenders (*Atkins* at 316, n. 18). By 2005, however, three more states raised the threshold age for death eligibility to 18, and this was enough to convince the majority of the Court to reverse *Stanford*.

In *Roper v. Simmons* (2005), five of the six justices who constituted the *Atkins* majority held that the cruel and unusual punishment clause forbids execution for crimes committed by offenders under 18 years of age. Justice O'Connor joined the majority in *Atkins*, but she dissented in *Roper* for two major reasons. First, she argued that there had not been enough change in the legal landscape to justify overruling *Stanford* (*Roper* at 594–598). Second, she contended that whereas mentally retarded offenders as a class suffer from major, lifelong impairments that make death an excessive punishment, some 17-year-old murderers are mature enough, and competent enough, to deserve the death penalty (*Roper* at 598–603).

Writing for the majority, Justice Kennedy, joined by Justices Breyer, Ginsburg, Souter, and Stevens, countered both of O'Connor's arguments. He acknowledged that changes in state laws pertaining to the minimum age for imposing capital punishment had come more slowly than had changes relevant to the issue of executing mentally retarded criminals (*Roper* at 565–567). He asserted, however, that the contemporary evidence of a national consensus against executing juveniles was in many respects similar to the evidence relied upon in *Atkins* (*Roper* at 564–565). He also made the case that juveniles under the age of 18 were similar to mentally retarded adults in that they are more vulnerable to negative influences, less likely to be capable of controlling their immediate surroundings, and are in other ways substantially less blameworthy than most adult criminals (*Roper* at 567–571).

Justice Kennedy's comparison of the legislative landscapes applicable to both *Atkins* and *Roper* showed that one of the key indicia used in both cases was in fact identical. By 2002, when *Atkins* was decided, 18 of the 38 states that authorized capital punishment banned executions of the mentally retarded and by 2005, when *Roper* was decided, 18 of the 38 states authorizing capital punishment banned executions of offenders under the age of 18 (*Roper* at 564). Thus, *Roper* was analogous to *Atkins* in that "30 states prohibit the juvenile death penalty, comprising 12 that have rejected the death penalty altogether and 18 that maintain it but, by express provision or judicial intervention, exclude juveniles from its reach" (*Roper* at 564).

Justice Kennedy conceded that the pace of change had been much faster on the issue of executing mentally retarded offenders (from two death-penalty states banning such executions in 1989 to 18 in 2002) than it had been on the issue of executing juvenile offenders (from 13 death-penalty states banning such executions to 18 in 2005) (*Roper* at 565–567). The slower rate of abolition, according to Justice Kennedy, was not nearly as important as what was the most significant similarity in both cases—"the consistency of the direction of change" (*Roper* at 565–566). He added that it would make little sense to permit juvenile executions to continue simply because the wrongfulness of executing juveniles was widely recognized sooner than it was recognized for the mentally retarded (*Roper* at 566–567). Cinching the argument for Justice Kennedy was the rarity of executing juveniles even in the 20 states that still allowed it. "Since *Stanford*, six states have executed prisoners for crimes committed as juveniles [and in] the past 10 years, only three states have done so: Oklahoma, Texas and Virginia" (*Roper* at 564–565).

Justice Kennedy's majority opinion also relied heavily upon the kind of evidence that Justice Scalia's *Stanford* opinion characterized as irrelevant. Kennedy cited social-science studies indicating that juveniles are more likely to be immature, impetuous, and reckless than are adults (*Roper* at 569–570). Juveniles are also much more likely than adults to be influenced by antisocial peer pressure, to have an underdeveloped sense of responsibility, and to lack control of their emotions (*Roper* at 569–570). "In recognition of the comparative immaturity and irresponsibility of juveniles, almost every State prohibits those under 18 years of age from voting, serving on juries, or marrying without parental consent" (*Roper* at 569). This was enough to satisfy the majority that the two major penological justifications for the death penalty—retribution and deterrence—apply to juveniles with considerably less force than to adults (*Roper* at 571–573).

In *Atkins*, Justice Stevens' majority opinion cited the overwhelming disapproval of the practice of executing mentally retarded offenders among other nations, but did so in a brief footnote (*Atkins* at 316, n. 21). By contrast, Justice Kennedy devoted six full paragraphs of the *Roper* majority opinion to international law. It was appropriate for the Court to look to the laws of other nations and international organizations as instructive for interpreting the meaning of the Eighth Amendment, he explained, because "[t]he opinion of the world community, while not controlling our outcome, does provide respected and significant confirmation for our own conclusions" (*Roper* at 578). Justice Kennedy cited Article 37 of the United Nations Convention on the Rights of the Child as expressly prohibiting capital punishment for crimes committed by juveniles under the age of 18 and pointedly noted that every nation in the world had ratified it except for the United States and Somalia (*Roper* at 576). He found it especially compelling that since 1990 only seven nations other than the United States had executed juveniles—Iran, Pakistan, Saudi Arabia, Yemen, Nigeria, the Democratic Republic of Congo, and China—and all of these countries now have renounced the practice, leaving the United States as "the only country in the world that continues to give official sanction to the juvenile death penalty" (*Roper* at 575–576). Justice Kennedy concluded that the weight of international opinion was very much in line with the emergence of a national consensus in the United States against executing those who were under the age of 18 when their crimes were committed, and the time had come to join the rest of the world in abolishing juvenile executions (*Roper* at 577–579).

In addition to Justice O'Connor's dissenting opinion, Justice Scalia, joined by Chief Justice Rehnquist and Justice Thomas, wrote a scathing dissent that took issue with every argument proffered by the majority. Like the *Atkins* dissenters, he criticized the majority for finding a national consensus against imposing the death penalty on 17-year-old offenders despite the fact that 20 of the 38 states with death-penalty laws still authorized juvenile executions (*Roper* at 607–611). "Words have no meaning if the views of less than 50% of death penalty States can constitute a national consensus" (*Roper* at 609). The 12 states with no death penalty, Justice Scalia asserted, should not be part of the calculus for discerning a national consensus against juvenile executions because these states have not had to grapple with the specific issue of whether to exempt juveniles from the death penalty (*Roper* at 610–611). Including these states in the legislative analysis "is rather like including old-order Amishmen in a consumer-preference poll on the electric car" (*Roper* at 611). The truth of the matter, as Scalia saw it, was that the majority of states that authorize executions had considered arguments to abolish juvenile executions, but had decided that the best policy was to leave it to state officials—and ultimately to juries—to make the admittedly rare decision, based on the evidence accrued at a fair trial, that a particular 17-year-old, with full understanding of what he was doing, committed an especially heinous murder and deserved to die for it (*Roper* at 609–615). He sarcastically added that "[t]he attempt by the Court to turn its remarkable minority consensus into a faux majority by counting Amishmen is an act of nomological desperation" (*Roper* at 611).

Justice Scalia also chastised the majority for taking the views of "the so-called international community" into account when interpreting the U.S. Constitution (*Roper* at

622). He cautioned that the majority's notion that American law should be informed by, let alone conform to, the laws of other countries or international bodies should be repudiated, and he accused the majority of pointing to trends in international law only when doing so supported the personal views of the majority justices (Roper at 622–628). It was telling, he wrote, that no one in the *Roper* or *Atkins* majorities ever pointed out that the controversial American exclusionary rule, which prohibits the use of illegally seized evidence in criminal cases, has been rejected by every other nation in the world and even by the European Court of Human Rights (*Roper* at 624–625). It was even more noteworthy, he added, that none of the majority justices had ever taken the position that the Court's abortion jurisprudence, making the United States "one of only six countries that allow abortion on demand until the point of viability," should be informed by the international community (*Roper* at 625–626). "Because I do not believe that the meaning of the Eighth Amendment, any more than the meaning of other provisions of our Constitution, should be determined by the subjective views of five Members of this Court and like-minded foreigners, I dissent" (*Roper* at 608).

THE SUPREME COURT'S 2005–2006 AND 2006–2007 TERMS

The tone of the majority and dissenting opinions in *Atkins* and *Roper* revealed a Court that was bitterly divided on death-penalty questions. Both holdings reduced the reach of the death penalty and must be considered major victories for opponents of capital punishment. However, the death-penalty holdings of the Court's 2005–2006 and 2006–2007 terms indicate that similar victories are not likely over the next decade. As will be shown, the legal landscape of the American death penalty has changed in recent years. But the more important change is in the composition of the Supreme Court.

From 1994 to 2005, the composition of the Court did not change. In the area of capital-punishment law, this more often than not resulted in voting alignments in which Justices Breyer, Ginsburg, Souter, and Stevens found constitutional problems with death-penalty laws and in which Chief Justice Rehnquist, Justice Scalia, and Justice Thomas found no such problems. This often put Justice O'Connor or Justice Kennedy in the position of a so-called "swing justice" whose fifth vote could tilt the balance in favor of invalidating death-penalty laws and reversing death sentences. This pattern began to emerge with greater frequency from 2002 until 2005, most significantly in *Atkins* where O'Connor and Kennedy provided the fifth and sixth votes and in *Roper* where Kennedy provided the fifth vote.

Eleven years was an unusually long time for the same nine justices to serve on the Supreme Court, and the beginning of change came on July 1, 2005 when Justice O'Connor announced her intention to retire effective upon the confirmation of her successor. Soon thereafter, President Bush announced the appointment of Judge John Roberts of the U.S. Court of Appeals for the District of Columbia. However, on September 3, before the U.S. Senate could act on the Roberts nomination, Chief Justice Rehnquist passed away after several years of struggling with thyroid cancer and other health problems. This left two vacancies on the Court and the president quickly withdrew his nomination of Roberts to replace O'Connor as an associate justice and instead appointed him to succeed Rehnquist as chief justice. The Senate easily confirmed Roberts as the new chief justice on September 29, 2005. With her successor still to be determined, Justice O'Connor continued to serve well into the Court's 2005–2006 term. On October 31, 2005, President Bush nominated Judge Samuel Alito of the U.S. Court of Appeals for the Third Circuit to replace O'Connor. The Senate confirmed Alito on January 31, 2006, thereby allowing O'Connor to step down.

When the Supreme Court's 2006–2007 term ended on June 28, 2007, it was very clear that the two changes in the Court's composition had yielded a Court that was more ideologically conservative than its predecessor in every area of law including criminal law generally and capital-punishment law in particular (Greenhouse 2007; Lane 2007). It appears very likely that Chief Justice Roberts will mirror the thinking and voting of Chief Justice Rehnquist in capital cases. As a federal appeals judge, Roberts was regarded as moderate-to-conservative on most issues, but his ideological tendencies in criminal cases could not be reliably predicted because the District of Columbia Circuit handles few criminal cases. In press interviews, the new chief justice said that he hoped that he could help to achieve greater consensus among the justices in important areas of law and to reduce the number of five-to-four decisions, particularly the ones that produce acrimonious opinion writing. In the 2005–2006 term, the Court decided relatively few controversial cases in the criminal-law area and in other areas of law, and there was an increase in unanimous opinions and a decrease in five-to-four decisions (Schauer 2006).

It is noteworthy, however, that the two most significant death-penalty cases of the term were decided to the detriment of death-row petitioners by a five-to-four vote. In *Brown v. Sanders* (2006), Justice Scalia, joined by Justice O'Connor, serving her last month on the Court, as well as by Chief Justice Roberts and by Justices Thomas and Kennedy, authored the Court's most expansive decision yet on the issue of upholding death sentences procured, in part, on the basis of invalid aggravating circumstances. *Brown* held that a jury's consideration of two invalid aggravating factors will not make a death sentence unconstitutional if appellate courts determine that the facts supporting those factors also tend to support at least one valid aggravating factor (*Brown* at 892). Later in the term, Justice Thomas, joined by the newly appointed Justice Alito and by Justices Roberts, Scalia, and Kennedy, wrote the majority opinion in *Kansas v. Marsh* (2006), holding that a Kansas law that required the jury to return a death sentence when the jury found the aggravating and mitigating factors to be *equally* balanced did not violate the Eighth Amendment. Although this law clearly had a mandatory element, the majority reasoned that it was not a *Woodson*-type full-fledged mandatory punishment law because it satisfied the constitutional mandates of *Furman* and *Gregg* by giving the jury the discretion to consider and weigh the significance of relevant mitigating evidence (*Marsh* at 2525–2526). As in *Brown v. Sanders*, Justices Breyer, Ginsburg, Stevens, and Souter joined in dissent, with Justice Souter arguing that the constitutional provision against cruel and unusual punishment should be understood to disallow a "doubtful" death sentence when aggravating and mitigating factors are of equal weight, especially in light of recent years in which we have seen "repeated exonerations of convicts under death sentences, in numbers never imagined before the development of DNA tests" (*Marsh* at 2544).

The Court's 2006–2007 term saw a continuation of the pattern by which the most important death-penalty cases would be decided in favor of the state and against petitioning prisoners, with Justices Roberts, Alito, Scalia, Thomas, and Kennedy prevailing over Justices Breyer, Ginsburg, Stevens, and Souter. That Chief Justice Roberts has been consistently voting to uphold death-penalty laws may be somewhat surprising to some Court-watchers, but Justice Alito's consistently pro-capital-punishment positions so far have surprised no one. As a judge on the federal court of appeals for the third circuit, Alito earned a reputation as a reliably conservative voice and, as was widely reported, some attorneys jokingly referred to him as "Scalito." During his Senate confirmation hearings, Alito's supporters denied that Alito would be "Scalia's clone," and he was confirmed by a 58-to-42 vote.

It clearly simplistic to claim that Alito sees law and his role as a justice in the same way as Scalia or any other justice, past or present. But Alito overwhelmingly voted against criminal defendants as a federal judge, and his pro-capital-punishment votes proved critical during the 2006–2007 term. There is little doubt that he will vote to uphold death-penalty laws more consistently than did Justice O'Connor.

The Court's death-penalty jurisprudence in the 2006–2007 term suggests that there will be few, if any, *Atkins*- or *Roper*-like holdings over the next several years. Nine death-penalty holdings were announced and eight were decided by a vote of five to four. Justice Kennedy was the "swing" vote in each of these cases, joining Justices Breyer, Ginsburg, Stevens, and Souter in four decisions in favor of death-row litigants and joining Chief Justice Roberts and Justices Alito, Scalia, and Thomas in four decisions that rejected constitutional challenges to death-penalty laws or procedures. The latter decisions, however, involved especially critical questions about the fairness of trial and appellate death-penalty procedures, and the outcomes demonstrate a greater willingness than was seen in the 2002–2005 period to side with prosecutors and to overlook errors by defense attorneys in capital cases. The Court's 2006–2007 death-penalty jurisprudence also points to the pivotal role that justice Kennedy can be expected to play as well as to the difference that Justice Alito's presence on the Court will make in capital cases (and in many other areas of law) in the years to come.

The only case, strictly speaking, that was not decided by a five-to-four vote was *Roper v. Weaver* (2007). Even though a five-justice majority simply dismissed the case without deciding its merits, the dismissal triggered disagreement from Chief Justice Roberts and a stinging dissent by Justices Scalia, Thomas, and Alito. The question was whether a federal court of appeals had exceeded its authority under the Antiterrorism and Effective Death Penalty act of 1996 (AEDPA) when it reversed a death sentence on the ground that the prosecutor's closing argument was "unfairly inflammatory" (*Weaver* at 2022). After examining the procedural history of the case, Justices Breyer, Ginsburg, Stevens, Souter, and Kennedy joined in a brief per curiam opinion that took note of the fact that Weaver actually filed his petition for habeas corpus before the AEDPA took effect and it reached the court of appeals after AEDPA's effective date only because the trial court had erroneously dismissed it as premature (*Weaver* at 2023). Because two other capital cases filed in the same jurisdiction raising the same issue—unduly inflammatory closing statements by prosecutors—had been correctly dismissed as pre-AEDPA cases, the majority believed that it would be unfair to decide Weaver's case under the stringent standards of the AEDPA (*Weaver* at 2023–2034). A dismissal was necessary, the majority explained "to prevent these three virtually identically situated litigants from being treated in a needlessly disparate manner" (*Weaver* at 2024).

Chief Justice Roberts responded with a cryptic, one-sentence concurrence noting that while he was willing to go along with the dismissal, he did not agree with all of the reasons given by the majority (*Weaver* at 2024). By contrast, Justice Scalia, joined by Justices Thomas and Alito, characterized the majority's action as having "no justification," "quite wrong," "wasteful," and "particularly perverse" (*Weaver* at 2024–2026). The error made by the trial judge, he argued, "does not affect the *legal* conclusion that AEDPA applies to this case," and the result was that a "grossly erroneous" interpretation of the AEDPA that works to the disadvantage of prosecutors remains in effect (*Weaver* at 2027).

The four cases that resulted in fully decided victories for death-row inmates came from Texas and three were announced on the same day, April 25, 2007. *Abdul-Kabir v. Quarterman*, *Brewer v. Quarterman*, and *Smith v. Texas* dealt with an idiosyncratic aspect of Texas death-penalty law that is no longer in effect. As part of its decision in the aforementioned case of *Penry v. Lynaugh* (1989), the Supreme Court ruled that the jury instructions then used in Texas capital cases were constitutionally deficient because they could not ensure that jurors would give full consideration to a defendant's mitigating evidence. Jurors had been told to address only two questions—whether the murder was deliberate and whether the defendant was likely to commit future acts of violence—and if both answers were "yes," a death sentence was automatic. The Texas legislature in 1991 addressed the problem by instructing judges to tell jurors to take "all of the evidence into consideration," but in the intervening two-year period, many judges either took no corrective measures or measures that the Supreme Court eventually found to be inadequate (*Penry v. Johnson* 2001).

Abdul-Katir, Brewer, and Smith were tried and sentenced to death during this period and appealed their death sentences. However, the U.S. Court of Appeals for the Fifth Circuit refused to grant habeas corpus hearings to Abdul-Kabir or to Brewer on the ground that the law pertaining to proper jury instructions in Texas was muddled and confusing at the time of their trials and thus their death sentences were not obtained on the basis of "an unreasonable application of clearly established federal law" as required by the (AEDPA) (*Abdul-Kabir* at 1662–1664; *Brewer* at 1709–1711). Smith's appeals were rejected by the Texas Court of Criminal Appeals on the ground that there was little likelihood that the jury had failed to consider the mitigating evidence and thus the inadequate jury instructions amounted to a "harmless error" that was not subject to state postconviction review (*Smith* at 1694–1696).

The majority in all three cases held that the lower courts had misapplied the procedural rules invoked to uphold the death sentences. Justice Stevens wrote for the Court in *Abdul-Kabir* and in *Brewer*, and he rebuked the fifth circuit for "ignoring the fundamental principles established by our most recent precedents" (*Abdul-Kabir* at 1671) and for failing to "heed the warnings that have repeatedly issued from this Count" that the jury must be allowed to fully consider all relevant mitigating evidence "in its calculus of deciding whether a defendant is truly deserving of death" (*Brewer* at 1714). Justice Kennedy authored the majority opinion in *Smith v. Texas*, explaining that he agreed with the other majority justices that the Texas court had erred in finding that it was unlikely that Smith's jury had not considered the mitigating evidence and that the inadequate jury instructions could not be considered to be harmless (*Smith* at 1697–1699). The dissenting justices in the three Texas cases expressed strong disagreement with the majority's approach, with Chief Justice Roberts accusing the majority of taking an "utterly revisionist" view of the Court's mitigating-factors jurisprudence and giving the Court "far too much credit in claiming that our sharply divided, ebbing and flowing decisions in this area of law gave rise to 'clearly established' federal law" (*Brewer* at 1715).

The final 2006–2007 term decision to block an execution came in the case of *Panetti v. Quarterman* (2007), but the holding did not go nearly as far as opponents of capital punishment had hoped. The Court in *Ford v. Wainwright* (1986) held that the Eighth Amendment does not permit the execution of prisoners who are insane at the time of their pending execution. Such inmates cannot be executed unless and until their sanity is restored. However, the standard to be used in determining whether an inmate suffers from mental illness to a sufficient degree to warrant postponing his execution was left vague and was not laid out beyond Justice Powell's concurring opinion that "the Eighth Amendment forbids the execution only of those who are unaware of the punishment they are to suffer and why they are to suffer it" (*Ford* at 422).

Death-penalty foes hoped the *Panetti* case would lead to a clear and also to a broad definition of insanity that would forestall executions when there was evidence of substantial mental illness, even in cases where the inmate seems to comprehend the reality of his death sentence. But, writing for the majority, Justice Kennedy declined to define a new standard for determining a prisoner's competency to be executed. However, he did find that the Texas courts and the fifth circuit court employed an overly restrictive standard in determining that Scott Pannetti was sane enough to execute (*Panetti* at 671). Panetti had been found to be a schizophrenic by doctors both before and after his 1995 trial for killing his wife's parents (*Panetti* at 672). Court-ordered psychiatric evaluations disclosed that Panetti suffered from " a fragmented personality, delusions, and hallucinations," and evaluations done after his trial indicated that his condition had only worsened (*Penetti* at 671–672). Nevertheless, in response to Panetti's petition to postpone his scheduled execution, court-appointed experts in 2004 concluded that he "knows that he is to be executed, and that the execution will result in his death" (*Panetti* at 674). The Texas courts and the fifth circuit courts subsequently ruled that Panetti had a minimal understanding of the fact of his impending execution and the reason for it and that that was enough to go forward with the execution.

The *Panetti* majority rejected the standard used by the lower courts as too restrictive to satisfy the standard required by *Ford v. Wainwright* (*Panetti* at 684). Justice Kennedy conceded that *Ford* "did not set forth a precise standard for competency" (*Panetti* at 684). Nevertheless, he declared that the minimal standard employed by the fifth circuit— whether a prisoner is aware "that he [is] going to be executed and why he [is] going to be executed"—was too simplistic in that it did not allow decision makers to consider the evidence that Panetti "suffers from a severe, documented mental illness that is the source of gross delusions preventing him from comprehending the meaning and purpose of the punishment to which he has been sentenced" (*Panetti* at 686). "Gross delusions stemming from a severe mental disorder may put an awareness of a link between a crime and its punishment in a context so far removed from reality that the punishment can serve no proper purpose" (*Panetti* at 689).

Asserting that the records in Panetti's case were not informative enough to permit the majority to articulate a clear standard for determining competency for execution, Justice Kennedy remanded the case to the federal trial court "for further proceedings consistent with this opinion" (*Panetti* at 687–688). Justice Thomas wrote for the dissenting justices and argued that the majority had erred procedurally and that under the AEPPA and its own precedents, the Court should not have accepted Panetti's case for review (*Panetti* at 688–692). But having done so, according to Justice Thomas, the majority succeeded only in misconstruing *Ford* and producing "a half-baked holding that leaves the details of the insanity standard for the District Court to work out" (*Panetti* at 698).

The four cases in which the Court voted to uphold state laws and procedures that led to death sentences, like the four Texas cases, reveal a Court that is bitterly divided on death-penalty issues. They also indicate that in the cases that matter the most, Justice Kennedy is likely to join with the four justices who consistently vote to endorse death sentences. Indeed, in the first death-penalty case to be decided in the 2006–2007 term—*Ayers v. Belmontes* (2006)—Justice Kennedy delivered the majority opinion. In *Belmontes*, the Court considered whether California's death-sentencing scheme had misled a capital-sentencing jury into believing that they were not permitted to consider so-called forward-looking evidence introduced by the defendant. The Supreme Court has made it clear that mitigating evidence of a defendant's good behavior in prison and the likelihood that he will be nonviolent and make positive contributions if sentenced to life imprisonment must be considered by a capital jury (*Skipper v. South Carolina* 1986). California's death-penalty law, however, asks capital jurors to consider a set of general "special factors" rather than circumstances that are specifically labeled as "aggravating" or "mitigating," and this has led to concerns that the inherent vagueness of the special circumstances often befuddles jurors, leading them to ignore relevant mitigating evidence (*Boyde v. California* 1990). In *Belmonte*, the defense complained that none of the special circumstances made it clear to the jury that they were to take Belmontes' prior good prison behavior and his religious beliefs into account. Moreover, it was argued that one of the factors that the jury was asked to consider—"[a]ny other circumstance which extenuated the gravity of the crime even though it is not a legal excuse for the crime"—increased the likelihood that jurors would think that they could not consider the evidence showing that Belmontes would lead a constructive life if incarcerated rather than executed (*Belmontes* at 472–473). Justice Kennedy's majority opinion acknowledged that the future-prison-conduct evidence was central to the defense's case against a death sentence, but based on a review of the trial record, he concluded that it was "quite implausible" that the jurors would have thought that they were foreclosed from considering the mitigating evidence (*Belmontes* at 477). It was especially noteworthy, he argued, that the trial judge told the jury to consider "all of the evidence," and since this admonition presumably included the forward-looking evidence, there was no reason to reverse the death sentence (*Belmontes* at 478–480).

The four dissenting justices examined the trial record and reached a very different conclusion. Writing for the dissenters, Justice Stevens stressed that the prosecutor told the jurors that he doubted that they should consider the evidence of the defendant's religious experiences at all; that the trial judge's instructions, taken as a whole, would have led a reasonable juror to think that he could not consider the prison-conduct evidence under the "gravity of the crime" factor; and that during deliberations the jurors asked numerous questions about this evidence, none of which the judge answered in a way that would eliminate "their obvious confusion" (*Belmontes* at 484–487). "I simply cannot believe that the jurors took it upon themselves to consider testimony they were all but told they were forbidden from considering" (*Belmontes* at 492). At the very least, he concluded, the jurors were confused as to whether they could take the mitigating evidence into account, and this kind of confusion created enough risk of error to invalidate Belmontes' death sentence (*Belmontes* at 492).

In *Lawrence v. Florida* (2007), the Court tackled an important procedural question requiring the justices again to decide the extent to which the AEDPA circumscribes prisoners' ability to bring a federal habeas corpus petition challenging their convictions or sentences. The AEDPA established a one-year deadline for state prisoners to file a federal habeas petition for review of a state judgment, and the one-year period is tolled while the inmate's state postconviction appeals are "pending" (*Lawrence* at 1080). Lawrence filed a petition against his death sentence 113 days after the Florida Supreme Court ruled against his state appeal, but he claimed that he did so because he and his attorney believed that the tolling period did not begin until his petition for certiorari—his concurrent appeal to the U.S. Supreme Court—had been denied and that his petition for certiorari was still pending when he filed his federal habeas petition (*Lawrence* at 1082–1085).

Writing for the majority, Justice Thomas quoted the applicable provision of the AEDPA:

> The time during which a properly filed application for State post-conviction or other collateral relief with respect to the pertinent judgment or claim is pending shall not be counted toward any period of limitation under this subsection (*Lawrence* at 1082).

This language, according to Justice Thomas required a strict interpretation: "Read naturally, the text of the statute must mean that the statute of limitations is tolled only while the state courts review the application" (*Lawrence* at 1082–1083). The U.S. Supreme Court, he explained, is a federal court, not a state court, and thus does not participate in the state's postconviction procedures (*Lawrence* at 1083). The tolling period began when the Florida Supreme Court denied relief, and the fact that Lawrence's separate certiorari petition was still pending before a *federal* court was irrelevant (*Lawrence* at 1083). Therefore, the federal courts were barred from considering Lawrence's habeas petition (*Lawrence* at 1085–1086).

The dissenting justices were led by Justice Ginsburg, whose dissenting opinion criticized the majority's reading of the AEDPA as unsound and unwarranted (*Lawrence* at 1089–1090). Petitions to the U.S. Supreme Court for certiorari, she stressed, "do not exist in a vacuum" (*Lawrence* at 1086). They arise from suits filed in lower courts and "[w]hen we are asked to review a state court's denial of habeas relief, we consider an application for that relief—not an application for federal habeas relief" (*Lawrence* at 1086). She concluded that the majority's unduly narrow interpretation of the tolling provision was contrary to the intention of Congress and unfairly terminates the tolling process before the Supreme Court has the opportunity to consider the merits of a prisoner's claims (*Lawrence* at 1087–1088).

The two death-penalty holdings of the 2006–2007 term that offer the best evidence of the Court's retreat from its 2002–2005 direction—and its likely path for at least the next several years—are *Schriro v. Landrigan* (2007) and *Uttecht v. Brown* (2007). The *Landrigan* case arguably underscores the importance of Justice Alito's presence on the Court. His predecessor Justice O'Connor joined five-to-four majorities in the two aforementioned cases—*Wiggins v. Smith* (2003) and *Rompilla v. Beard* (2005)—in which the Court signaled its willingness to hold defense attorneys to a higher standard than in past cases when evaluating claims of ineffective assistance of counsel brought by death-row inmates. In *Landigran*, however, Justice Alito provided the fifth vote to deny an ineffective-assistance claim that raised issues similar to those in the *Wiggins* and *Rompilla* cases.[11]

The question was whether a federal district court had properly dismissed an Arizona death-row inmate's habeas petition as so weak as not even to deserve an evidentiary hearing (*Landrigan* at 1934–1935). Jeffrey Landrigan alleged that his attorney failed to do a reasonably adequate job of investigating mitigating evidence of his serious mental illness at the time of his crime and its origins in his turbulent childhood and the violent behavior and drug use of his biological father and other relatives who were not interviewed by the defense (*Landrigan* at 1937–1939). Justice Thomas' majority opinion acknowledged that Landrigan's biological father and other relatives were not interviewed, but he contended that this must be considered in the context of Landrigan's behavior at his trial (*Landrigan* at 1941–1943). He repeatedly interrupted his attorney, told him not to call his birth mother and ex-wife to testify on his behalf, and told the judge: "I think if you want to give me the death penalty, just bring it right on; I'm ready for it" (*Landrigan* at 1941–1943). After recounting these facts, Justice Thomas needed only two short paragraphs to conclude that the district court was correct to deny Landrigan a hearing because the new mitigating evidence Landrigan wanted to introduce was "weak" and "would not have changed the result" (*Landrigan* at 1943–1944).

In a vigorous dissenting opinion, Justice Stevens charged that the majority's decision rests on "a parsimonious appraisal of a capital defendant's constitutional right to have the sentencing decision reflect meaningful consideration of all relevant mitigating evidence, a begrudging appreciation of the need for a knowing and intelligent waiver of constitutionally protected trial rights, and a cramped reading of the record" (*Landrigan* at 1944–1945). That record, he asserted, showed that the defense lawyer's investigation of possible mitigating evidence clearly was constitutionally insufficient under the Court's recent precedents (*Landrigan* at 1945). Landrigan's bizarre behavior during his trial should not have been taken as a waiver of his rights and should have made the necessity of taking the appropriate steps to gather and present evidence of serious psychological problems all the more evident; instead, significant mitigating evidence that would have shed important light on Landrigan's criminal conduct was unknown at his sentencing

(*Landrigan* at 1944–1950). Accordingly, this was a case that, at the very least, warranted an evidentiary hearing (*Landrigan* at 1952–1954). Justice Stevens contended that the majority's decision "can only be explained by its increasingly familiar effort to guard the floodgates of litigation" (*Landrigan* at 1954). But, noting that it was already the case that district courts hold evidentiary hearings in only 1.17 percent of all federal habeas cases, he concluded that "[t]his figure makes it abundantly clear that doing justice does not always cause the heavens to fall" (*Landrigan* at 1954–1955).

The Court's final pro-capital-punishment ruling of the 2006–2007 term also reveals a Court polarized on death-penalty questions and a Court that tilts in favor of the state in the most significant cases. Tellingly, in *Uttecht v. Brown* (2007), Justice Kennedy delivered the majority opinion. *Uttecht* raised a particularly important question—whether a Washington State trial judge had improperly granted a prosecutor's motion to dismiss a potential capital juror who expressed some qualms about capital punishment, but who also said that he would be willing to impose it in an appropriate case. The standard for excusing a member of the jury panel was established in the previously discussed 1985 case of *Wainwright v. Witt*: "[W]hether the juror's views would prevent or substantially impair the performance of his duties as a juror in accordance with his instructions and his oath" (*Witt* at 424). In *Uttecht*, the excused juror during a lengthy voir dire told the judge that he supported capital punishment, but would not be as inclined to impose it unless the defendant otherwise might go free and kill again (*Uttecht* at 2226–2227). When asked whether he could vote for a death sentence when there was no chance of parole, the juror answered, "[I]f I was convinced that was the appropriate measure" (*Uttecht* at 2227). Because Washington, like most death-penalty states, offers life imprisonment without parole as the alternative to the death penalty, prosecutors argued that the juror's responses showed that he would automatically vote against the death penalty (*Uttecht* at 2227). The trial judge's decision to grant the request to dismiss the juror was reversed by the U.S. Court of Appeals for the Ninth Circuit, which found that the trial transcript unambiguously showed that the juror was not "substantially impaired" and overturned the death sentence that the trial jury imposed (*Uttecht* at 2227–2228).

Stressing that federal appellate courts owe substantial deference to a trial judge's ability to determine the qualifications of a potential juror, Justice Kennedy's majority opinion accused the court of appeals of misreading the trial record and failing to accord the proper deference to the trial judge (*Uttecht* at 2228–2231). Justice Kennedy pointed out that trial judges are present during the voir dire process and are in a much better position to assess a potential juror's demeanor and thinking than are appellate courts, which have to rely upon a written trial transcript that cannot capture all of the nuances and human elements of what happens in the courtroom (*Uttecht* at 2224). He added that the majority's review of the transcript showed that the court of appeals was simply wrong and that the transcript revealed "substantial impairment" on the part of the dismissed juror (*Uttecht* at 2228–2230). Accordingly, the decision to overturn the death penalty was reversed and the case was remanded for further proceedings (*Uttecht* at 2231).

As he had done in *Schriro v. Landrigan*, Justice Stevens wrote on behalf of the four dissenting justices and minced no words in denouncing the majority's holding. The majority, he asserted, had gone much too far in reversing the judgment of the federal court of appeals and had extended a "completely unwarranted" level of deference to state trial courts in capital cases (*Uttecht* at 2239). The court of appeals, he said, carefully reviewed the transcript, correctly noted that the potential juror repeatedly affirmed in response to the prosecutor's questions that he could impose the death penalty in any situation, and correctly applied the applicable Supreme Court precedents in deciding to reverse the death sentence (*Uttecht* at 2241–2242). "Under our precedents, a juror's statement that he would vote to impose a death sentence where there is a possibility that the defendant may reoffend, provided merely as an example of when that penalty might be appropriate, does not constitute a basis for striking a juror for cause" (*Uttecht* at 2241). The majority, he declared had redefined the meaning of "substantially impaired" and gotten it "horribly wrong" (*Uttecht* at 2243). A death sentence should not be upheld, he concluded, when trial judges disqualify potential jurors whose only failing is "to harbor some slight reservation in imposing the most severe of sanctions" (*Uttecht* at 2244).

THE SHORT-TERM AND LONG-TERM PROSPECTS FOR SUPREME COURT ABOLITION OF CAPITAL PUNISHMENT

Uttecht and most of the other major death-penalty decisions in 2006 and 2007 have strengthened the hands of prosecutors in capital cases and weakened the power of federal courts to grant relief to inmates who have a constitutional basis for challenging a death sentence. This trend is likely to continue for the next several years and probably for at least the next decade. As the Court is presently constituted, the dynamics of interaction among the justices appear to have influenced Justice Kennedy to cast his vote in favor of the state imposing capital punishment in the cases that are particularly contentious and matter the most. For the past two years, Justice Kennedy increasingly has been inclined to join the Roberts, Scalia, Thomas, Alito bloc in capital cases and other controversial cases, and he is not likely to author another majority opinion like *Roper v. Simmons* (2005).

It is imperative to note that the average age of Justice Kennedy and the four justices who consistently vote in favor of death-penalty laws is 61, with Chief Justice Roberts the youngest at 52. The average age of the four justices who consistently vote to reverse death sentences is 75, with Justice Stevens the oldest at 87. Thus, even if a Democrat is elected president in 2008 and even if Democrats continue to maintain a majority of the U.S. Senate and House of Representatives, the Court's demographics are likely to work against a major change in the ideological tendencies of the Court in capital cases and other areas of law.

Although the Court's present composition and decisional leanings probably will trump politics and policy arguments in the near future, it is clear that the political momentum over the past few years has swung against capital punishment. The most telling indicator is that the number of death sentences imposed by juries in the United States has declined to its lowest level in decades. From 1985 to 1999, the number of death sentences averaged about 300 a year. However, the total dropped to 232 in 2000 and then began to drop even more precipitously, to 162 in 2001, 167 in 2002, 153 in 2003, 138 in 2004, 128 in 2005, and 114 in 2006 (DPIC 2007). This dramatic decrease almost certainly reflects increased publicity and greater public—and juror—awareness of persistent problems with the death penalty (Lewis 2006). Cases in which death-row inmates have been exonerated on the basis of new evidence have been highly publicized in recent years. As of July 2, 2007, 124 inmates in 25 states have been released because of compelling evidence of innocence (DPIC 2007). Also, jurors are more likely than in the past to have concerns about racial discrimination in capital cases and defense attorneys in many states have become more skilled in making arguments for mitigation. Furthermore, some prosecutors have become well aware of the higher costs of prolonged death-penalty cases and appeals as compared to life imprisonment without parole (Lewis 2006).

Growing doubts about the death penalty also are reflected in a recent drop in the number of executions carried out each year in the United States. Executions were slow to resume after the *Gregg* decision clarified the legal status of capital punishment in 1976. From 1976 to 1990, the number of executions averaged slightly less than 10 per year. From 1991 to 2000, the average jumped to 54 per year, with highs of 98 in 1999 and 85 in 2000. Since then, however, a downward trend in executions has emerged, with 66 in 2001, 71 in 2002, 65 in 2003, 59 in 2004, 60 in 2005, and 53 in 2006, the lowest since 1996 when 45 executions took place (NAACP 2007).

Moreover, executions have been occurring with regularity only in southern states. As of January 1, 2007, 897 of the 1,057 post-*Gregg* executions (85 percent) had been carried out in 11 southern states. Texas alone accounted for 379 (36 percent) executions, followed by Virginia (98), Oklahoma (83), Missouri (66), Florida (65), North Carolina (43), Georgia (39), South Carolina (36), Alabama (35), Arkansas (27), and Louisiana (27) (NAACP 2007). With relatively few executions occurring in nonsouthern states, it is fair to say that capital punishment has been and continues to be largely a southern phenomenon; only two other states, Ohio (24) and Arizona (22), have executed more than 20 inmates since 1976 (NAACP 2007).

The recent decline in executions and their relative rarity in nonsouthern states reflect increasing ambivalence toward capital punishment on the part of the public and public officials. The decrease in executions has occurred even though the U.S. death-row population has not changed much over the past decade, averaging approximately 3,400 and standing at 3,350 as of January 1, 2007 (NAACP 2007). Even though one of the predominant trends of Supreme Court jurisprudence over the past 30 years has been support for prosecutors' efforts to expedite the capital-appeals process, the gap between the death-row population and the number of people executed can be largely attributed to the length of the appeals process (generally 7 to 15 years and sometimes longer) and the fact that many of these appeals ultimately are successful in overturning death sentences.

In June 2000, Columbia University issued a study of 4,578 death-sentence appeals that had been decided by federal and state appellate courts between 1973 and 1995. In 68 percent of these cases, a federal or state court reversed the conviction or death sentence. Misconduct by prosecutors who suppressed exculpatory or mitigating evidence accounted for 16 percent of the reversals. In 37 percent of the reversals, appeals courts ruled that defendants' attorneys were so incompetent that their performance substantially altered the trial outcome. Overall, 82 percent of the reversed convictions and sentences resulted in defendants receiving lesser sentences, and 7 percent of the defendants were found not guilty in retrials. The report concluded that the American capital punishment system "is collapsing under the weight of its own mistakes." The lead author, Columbia University law professor James Leibman commented that "[i]t's not just one case, it's not just one state. Error was found at epic levels across the country." (Davies 2000).

The Columbia University study is one of several noteworthy recent developments that have lifted the spirits of opponents of capital punishment. For example, in May 2000, the New Hampshire legislature became the first in the nation to vote to abolish capital punishment in the post-*Gregg* era. However, the bill was vetoed by Governor Jeanne Shaheen and the legislature could not muster the two-thirds majority required to override the veto (Ferdinand 2000). New Hampshire thus retains its capital punishment law, but arguably nothing has changed; the state has not executed anyone since 1939.

Also in 2000, Illinois became the first death-penalty state in the modern era to impose a formal moratorium on executions. Former Governor George Ryan imposed the moratorium because of concerns that the Illinois system of capital punishment was plagued by error and caprice. Since the state reinstated capital punishment in 1977, he pointed out, 12 prisoners had been put to death, but 13 death-row inmates had been cleared of murder charges, often only because journalists and students and professors at Northwestern University unearthed vital exculpatory evidence that state officials had either missed or ignored (Johnson 2000).

Governor Ryan also cited a recent series by the *Chicago Tribune* that examined nearly 300 Illinois cases in which a death sentence had been imposed. Of the cases that were appealed, over half were reversed for a new trial or sentencing hearing. In 30 cases death-row inmates were found to have been represented by lawyers who were disbarred or suspended from practice. In many other cases, false testimony by witnesses, misconduct by prosecutors, and improper rulings by judges resulted in convictions that had to be reversed. In announcing the moratorium, Governor Ryan stated: "Until I can be sure that everyone sentenced to death in Illinois is truly guilty, until I can be sure with moral certainty that no innocent man or woman is facing lethal injection, no one will meet that fate" (Johnson 2000).

In January 2003, shortly before leaving office, Governor Ryan emptied his state's death row as his final act of office. During the fall of 2002, Governor Ryan conducted clemency hearings for nearly every death-row inmate in Illinois. The hearings, replete with both the bloody details of gruesome crimes and shocking stories of erroneous convictions, created anguish for the families and friends of everyone involved. But in the end, Governor Ryan, declaring that "[o]ur capital system is haunted by error," pardoned four more inmates he said he believed to be innocent (bringing the total number of exonerated Illinois inmates to 17) and commuted the death sentences of 167 others to life in prison (Wilgoren 2003). Legislators have been considering legislation designed to lessen errors and restore credibility to the capital-sentencing system, but as of July 31, 2007, the moratorium remains in effect (DPIC 2007).

In 2002, the governor of Maryland, Paris Glendening, imposed a moratorium on executions in anticipation of a comprehensive study of the Maryland death-sentencing process conducted by Professor Raymond Paternoster and his team of University of Maryland criminologists. The study found that Maryland prosecutors were far more likely to seek the death penalty in cases where black defendants were accused of killing white victims and that geography—the particular county in which a case was prosecuted and the attitudes of prosecutors in that county—was a major factor affecting whether a defendant faced capital charges (Becker 2003). Nevertheless, in 2003, Glendening's successor Robert Ehrlich, rescinded the moratorium. However, in 2006, Maryland elected a governor, Martin O'Malley, who strongly opposes capital punishment and who in 2007 sought its repeal by the Maryland legislature. In March 2007, legislation to replace the death penalty with life without parole failed by a single vote in a senate committee. Meanwhile, Maryland's highest court has ordered a halt to all executions on the ground that the state's lethal-injection procedures have not been properly adopted. Governor O'Malley has refused to issue regulations that may allow executions to resume and in a July 2007 interview, he said that he would press the legislature to repeal the death penalty when it reconvenes in 2008 (Wagner and Rich 2007). Thus, Maryland now has a de facto moratorium on executions, and it is very possible that it will abolish capital punishment in the next few years.

Another state that seems close to abolishing the death penalty is New Jersey. Although there are nine prisoners under a death sentence in New Jersey, none of them is likely to be executed. In fact, the last execution in New Jersey occurred in 1963, well before *Furman* and *Gregg* changed the legal parameters of capital punishment. The state passed a new death-penalty law shortly after *Furman*, but the New Jersey Supreme Court has found numerous problems with the law and has imposed procedural rules under its interpretation of the state constitution that make it difficult for prosecutors to seek or to obtain death sentences or to prevail against appeals brought by death-row inmates. The court recently held that capital prosecutors must secure a grand jury indictment as to the facts of alleged aggravating circumstances before they can present these facts to a trial jury, and the court has been consistently sympathetic to claims of ineffective assistance of counsel (Smothers 2007a).

The New Jersey legislature placed a formal moratorium on executions in 2006 and appointed a special commission to study the pros and cons of death-penalty abolition. In January 2007, the commission, citing the risks of wrongful executions, the exorbitant costs of capital litigation, and the dearth of evidence showing that the death penalty deters murder any more effectively than does life imprisonment, overwhelmingly recommended the elimination of capital punishment. In May 2007, the state senate's judiciary committee approved legislation to replace capital punishment with life without parole and voted to release the measure to the full senate. The bill's backers believe that it is likely to win approval in 2007 or 2008, and Governor John Corzine, a long-time opponent of the death penalty, has said he would sign the bill (Smothers 2007b).

I predict that Maryland and New Jersey are going to be the first two of the 38 states with death-penalty laws to abolish capital punishments and that both states will do so before 2010. Legislative and judicial momentum against capital punishment also is on the upsurge in a number of other states. In 2004, the New York Court of Appeals, the state's highest court, declared the existing death-penalty law (which was passed in 1995 and under which no one has been executed) to be unconstitutional. Since then, the New York legislature has rejected every effort to pass a new law (DPIC 2007). New York may very well become the third state to formally renounce capital punishment, perhaps before the end of the present decade or several years thereafter.

In March 2007, a measure to repeal the death penalty in Nebraska came within one vote of moving to the second of three necessary stages. The vote was 25 to 24, and two months later, the Nebraska Supreme Court stayed an execution to consider whether electrocution is an unconstitutional method of execution (DPIC 2007). Nebraska is the only state that relies solely on the electric chair to impose the death penalty, and the court's action seems likely to heighten public and legislative concerns about capital punishment in Nebraska.

Altogether, at least 18 states currently are considering legislation that would either abolish capital punishment or impose a moratorium on it: Illinois, Maryland, New Jersey, New York, Arizona, Colorado, Connecticut, Kansas, Kentucky, Missouri, Montana, New Hampshire, New Mexico, Oregon, South Dakota, Tennessee, and Washington (DPIC 2007). It should also be noted that in 2007 at least five states—Georgia, Missouri, Texas, Utah, and Virginia—have also considered legislation that would have the effect of expanding capital punishment. Texas, in fact, recently became the sixth state—joining Oklahoma, South Carolina, Georgia, Montana, and Louisiana—that authorizes capital punishment for offenders convicted of the rape of a minor.[12] In Virginia, on the other hand, Governor Timothy Kaine, a strong foe of the death penalty, recently vetoed several death-penalty expansion bills (DPIC 2007).

The political movement against the death penalty also has gained ground over the past two years because of mounting concerns that lethal injection—originally touted as a humane method of execution—may actually inflict greater pain and suffering than did previous methods of execution. Quite a few lethal injections have been botched, many taking more than 30 minutes while the condemned inmate struggled to breathe or to speak. Members of execution teams have testified that lethal injections have been carried out in dark, cramped rooms by nonmedical personnel who often are unsure of the correct dosage of lethal chemicals necessary to ensure a quick death. Moreover, evidence has emerged that one of the chemicals used in most lethal-injection states, pancuronium bromide (also known as pavulon and long banned for use in euthanizing animals), causes excruciating pain while simultaneously paralyzing its victims, leaving them unable to move or to talk. Concerns about these and other problems have led 12 states and the federal government to issue temporary bans on lethal injections (Weil 2007). As of July 31, 2007, nine of these bans were still in effect (DPIC 2007), but most can be expected to be lifted when courts and public officials are satisfied that improvements have been made in lethal-injection protocols.

Although abolitionist movements are gaining strength in an increasing number of state capitols, the latest public opinion polls show that nearly two-thirds of Americans still support capital punishment. The highest level of support came in 1994 when a Gallup Poll found 80 percent of Americans to support the death penalty. In May 2006, a Gallup Poll showed the support level at 65 percent and a June 2007 poll conducted by the Pew Research Center found that 64 percent of U.S. adults favor retaining the death penalty for those convicted of murder (DPIC 2007). Although research shows that some of those who endorse capital punishment in the abstract would be willing to reconsider if they could be assured that murderers would be given a sentence of life without parole (Bowers 1993), the current polling figures present a formidable obstacle for abolitionists.

The best hope for an abolitionist future almost certainly lies in greater public knowledge concerning the death penalty. In *Furman v. Georgia*, Justice Marshall asserted that if the American people were given accurate information about capital punishment— its failure to deter crime any more effectively than life imprisonment,[13] its high costs relative to life imprisonment, and the many cases of wrongfully executed defendants—they would renounce the death penalty and replace it with lengthy prison sentences (*Furman* at 360–363). Studies lend support to what has become known as the "Marshall hypothesis." Interview and questionnaire studies have shown that support for the death penalty is indeed founded on misinformation about the effects of capital punishment and how it is used (Ellsworth and Ross 1983). Moreover, when representative samples of the American adult population are presented with pamphlets that provide factual, unbiased material on the realities of capital punishment, enough people change their minds to turn what had been minority opposition to the death penalty into a majority (Sarat and Vidmar 1976).

If anything will turn the current minority position on capital punishment into a majority position, it is the cumulative impact of the Supreme Court death-penalty decisions discussed earlier in this paper. For example, how will Americans react when the evidence becomes irrefutable that *McCleskey v. Kemp* (1987) was wrongly decided? If the evidence becomes irrefutable—and well known—that human beings simply are incapable of administering the death penalty without racial discrimination, the pendulum of public opinion may very well begin to swing back toward the prevailing attitude in 1966 when a Harris survey found 47 percent of the public opposed to capital punishment, 38 percent in favor of it, and 15 percent unsure (Haas and Inciardi 1988:11).

Tison v. Arizona (1987) also could eventually lead people to rethink their assumptions about the fairness of capital punishment. It is not at all certain that the killing of those who themselves never killed, intended to kill, nor attempted to kill will ultimately square with basic American notions of fairness and justice.[14] In the long run, Americans are not likely to reject the longstanding principle of "an eye for an eye" and replace it with a principle calling for "an eye for an eye and then some" (Haas 1994). This will be a hotly debated issue by the year 2010. And possibly by the year 2020, if not sooner, the answer may turn out to be "no."

There is, of course, another problem—made all the more likely by the Supreme Court's 1983–2007 decisions curtailing habeas corpus appeals by death-row inmates—that may prove pivotal in convincing the public that the death penalty can no longer be tolerated. Indeed, it was the chilling impact of this particular problem that helped lead to the abolition of capital punishment in England—the execution of defendants who are later discovered to be innocent (Christoph 1962). Legal scholars have already convincingly demonstrated that the erroneous conviction of people charged with capital crimes has long been—and continues to be—a major problem in the United States (Scheck, Neufeld, and Dwyer 2003). In the most thorough study to date, Michael Radelet, Hugo Bedau, and Constance Putnam (1992) carefully documented the cases of 416 innocent Americans convicted of capital crimes between 1900 and 1991. Although some two dozen of these people were executed—and although the problem of wrongful capital convictions appears to be growing—the magnitude of the problem has so far eluded the American public (Davies 2000).

But as a result of inherent human fallibility, the process of determining guilt in capital cases will always be plagued by such problems as mistaken eyewitness identification, perjured testimony, coerced confessions, laboratory errors, overzealous officials who conceal exculpatory evidence, and inattentive or confused jurors. The Supreme Court's recent efforts to expedite the capital-appeals process may help to reduce somewhat the crushing financial costs of the death penalty, but they will also deprive those who have been wrongfully convicted of a full and fair opportunity to prove their innocence. As more such cases occur and become highly publicized in the print and broadcast media, it stands to reason that a growing number of Americans will have second thoughts about the wisdom of imposing an irreversible punishment on criminal defendants.

My prediction, therefore, is that public support for capital punishment will continue to decline as we move into the second decade of the twenty-first century. By 2020, at least 10 more states will join Maryland and New Jersey in eliminating the death penalty. Some states will accomplish this through legislative action and some states will do it as the result of a decision by the state's highest court. This trend will accelerate and by 2030 another dozen states, perhaps more, will abolish capital punishment. Although the number of executions will decline in the 10 to 15 mostly southern states that will retain capital punishment, the problems of arbitrariness, discrimination, and error will become more obvious than ever before. Sometime in the mid-twenty-first century, with no more than 10 to 15 states retaining death-penalty statutes, the U.S. Supreme Court, citing the dwindling number of death-penalty laws—and executions—as convincing evidence of a new societal consensus against the death penalty, will declare capital punishment in all cases to be a violation of the cruel and unusual punishment clause of the Eighth Amendment.

CONCLUSION

If this scenario proves correct, the American public will have gone through the same transition as Justice Harry Blackmun. Justice Blackmun had joined not only in the *Gregg* majority but had supported the *mandatory* death-penalty laws under review in *Woodson v. North Carolina* (1976) and *Roberts v. Louisiana* (1977). But on February 23, 1994, after 24 years on the Supreme Court and shortly before announcing his retirement, Justice Blackmun repudiated capital punishment. In *Callins v. Collins*, he pointed to the central dilemma underlying all of the Supreme Court's post-*Gregg* jurisprudence. How can an appropriate balance be struck between the promise of consistency and equality in capital sentencing and the seemingly contradictory requirement of individualized sentencing in capital cases? Justice Blackmun's answer was that these two goals simply cannot be reconciled. "It seems that the decision whether a human being should live or die is so inherently subjective—rife with all of life's understandings, experiences, prejudices and passions—that it inevitably defies the rationality and consistency required by the Constitution" (*Callins* at 1134–1135). A quarter of a century of handling the hundreds of death-penalty cases that came to the nation's highest court, he wrote, had convinced him that human beings are not capable of devising procedural or substantive rules that can prevent the inevitable intrusion of arbitrariness and racial discrimination into the capital-sentencing process (*Callins* at 1135–1136).

Justice Blackmun also made it clear that his decision to renounce capital punishment was heavily influenced by what he called the Court's "obvious eagerness to do away with any restrictions on the States' power to execute whomever and however they please" (*Callins* at 1137). He singled out the Court's 1993 decision in *Herrera v. Collins* for especially strong criticism (*Callins* at 1137–1138). The *Herrera* majority, he asserted, had not only refused to afford Leonel Torres Herrera an evidentiary hearing "despite his colorable showing of actual innocence," but it had erected "nearly insurmountable barriers" to any capital defendant's ability to get a federal habeas corpus hearing on a claim of actual innocence (*Callins* at 1138). The result of *Herrera*, he predicted, will be an increasing number of innocent people who will never have a full and fair opportunity to challenge their conviction and death sentence (*Callins* at 1138). Under these circumstances, he declared, he would no longer "tinker with the machinery of death" (*Callins* at 1130). He was optimistic, however, that "this Court will eventually conclude that . . . the death penalty must be abandoned altogether" (*Callins* at 1138).

To be sure, Justice Blackmun's hope will not become a reality in the immediate future. The Supreme Court will not abolish capital punishment until well into the twenty-first century. The current Court includes no justices who have taken the position that the death penalty, in and of itself, is unconstitutional. The predominant trend since 1983 has been a strong tendency to value notions of finality and states' rights over concerns about unfair trial procedures and obstacles to federal appellate review of capital appeals.

Atkins, *Roper*, and other decisions in the 2002–2005 period showed the Court moving in the direction of abolition. But while the appointment of Chief Justice Roberts to replace Chief Justice Rehnquist in 2005 clearly has had—and will continue to have—virtually no effect on the decisional tendencies of the Court in death-penalty cases, the retirement of Justice O'Connor and her replacement by Justice Alito in early 2006 has had—and will continue to have—a major impact. Justice Kennedy now provides the pivotal vote in most death-penalty cases, and the major decisions of the 2005–2006 and 2006–2007 terms suggest that he will be inclined to support Justices Roberts, Scalia, Thomas, and Alito in upholding the current legal infrastructure of capital punishment.

The Court's composition makes it likely that this trend will continue for the next several years even as public and legislative support for the death penalty erodes. There is no realistic possibility that the Supreme Court will abolish the death penalty in the next 10 to 12 years. But there undoubtedly will be significant changes in the composition of the Court by 2020 and, of course, *many* more by 2050. By then, the American people and the majority of state governments, like Justice Blackmun, will repudiate capital punishment, and the Supreme Court will declare it in all cases to be unconstitutional.

ENDNOTES

1. See *Proffitt v. Florida* (1976) and *Jurek v. Texas* (1976).
2. See, for example, *Dobbert v. Florida* (1977) (holding that changes in Florida's capital punishment law between the time of the murder and the defendant's sentencing did not amount to an ex post facto violation) and *Estelle v. Smith* (excluding psychiatric testimony on *Miranda* grounds, but pointedly noting that psychiatric evidence as to a defendant's "future dangerousness" is generally admissible).

3. Arguably, the Court's emerging new attitude first became apparent in Justice Rehnquist's dissent from a denial of certiorari in *Coleman v. Balkcom* (1981). Urging his colleagues to take all necessary steps to expedite the administration of the death penalty, Justice Rehnquist referred to the slow pace of executions as a "mockery of our criminal justice system" (*Balkcom* at 958). Pointing to the lengthy appeals process in capital cases, Justice Rehnquist lamented that "[g]iven so many bites at the apple, the odds favor petitioner finding some court willing to vacate his death sentence because in its view his trial or sentence was not free from constitutional error" (*Balkcom* at 957).

4. *Boyde* and *Blystone* are problematic, among other reasons, because capital juries often are confused about mitigating evidence and how to give effect to it. See Barron (2002).

5. See, for example, *Ake v. Oklahoma* (1985) (overturning a death sentence on the ground that an indigent capital defendant was denied access to a psychiatric examination that was necessary to prepare an effective defense based on his mental condition); *Francis v. Franklin* (1985) (invalidating a conviction and death sentence on the ground that the instructions to the jury violated the Fourteenth Amendment requirement that the state must prove every element of a criminal offense beyond a reasonable doubt); *Caldwell v. Mississippi* (1985) (vacating a death sentence because the prosecutor, citing the inevitability of appellate review, urged the jury not to view itself as actually determining whether the defendant dies); *Maynard v. Cartwright* (1988) (reversing a death sentence because one of the statutory aggravating circumstances was unconstitutionally vague); *Mills v. Maryland* (1988) (vacating a death sentence imposed under a state law that led jurors to believe that they could not consider all relevant mitigating factors); *Lankford v. Idaho* (1991) (invalidating a death sentence in a case in which the prosecution announced that it would not seek the death penalty and the trial judge failed to provide adequate notice that death could still be imposed as the punishment); *Dawson v. Delaware* (1992) (reversing a death sentence imposed by a jury that had been told to consider the defendant's racist political views as an aggravating circumstance); and *Morgan v. Illinois* (1992) (invalidating a death sentence because the

defense was not permitted to challenge the eligibility of jurors who would *automatically* impose the death penalty after a conviction).

6. For a detailed analysis of the study, its implications, and its treatment by the courts, see Baldus, Woodworth, and Pulaski, Jr. (1990).

7. The *Penry* decision was greeted with an outpouring of criticism. See especially Reed (1993), Cohen (1991), and Dick-Hurwitz (1990). It struck many as paradoxical that in *Ford v. Wainwright* (1986), the Court held that the Eighth Amendment prohibits the execution of insane death-row inmates. The *Ford* case and its implications are examined by Miller and Radelet (1993).

8. In *Gregg v. Georgia* (1976:184–187), the Court cited retribution and deterrence as two legitimate penological rationales for the death penalty. Cryptically, the Court relegated a third justification—incapacitation—to a footnote stating only that "[a]nother purpose that has been discussed is the incapacitation of dangerous criminals and the consequent prevention of crimes that they may otherwise commit in the future" (*Gregg* at 183, n. 28). Many opponents of capital punishment will acknowledge that this rationale is not totally without merit. Studies consistently show that convicted murderers are less likely to commit murders in prison or after release than are inmates convicted of such lesser crimes as robbery, burglary, and aggravated assault (Sellin 1980:103–120). Never-theless, there are some death-row inmates who appear to be incorrigible, willing to kill guards or fellow inmates, and capable of escape. It thus can be argued that the death penalty is the only way to be 100 percent certain that a sociopath or a serial killer will never kill again. On the other hand, the noted attorney and abolitionist Anthony Amsterdam has responded to this argument by declaring that "[y]ou cannot tell me . . . that a society which is capable of putting a man on the moon is incapable of putting a man in prison, keeping him there, and keeping him from killing while he is there" (Amsterdam 1982:354).

9. The *Payne* decision provoked highly critical commentaries in law reviews. See, for example, Levy (1993), Casimir (1993), and Oberlander (1992).

10. An empirical study done after the *Weeks* holding showed that nearly half of a group of mock jurors who were read the same instructions as the

Weeks jury did not understand the instructions and thought that they were *required* to return the death sentence if they found at least one aggravating circumstance. See Garvey, Johnson, and Marcus, (2000).

11. It is also noteworthy in this regard that late in the 2006–2007 term the Court declined to review an ineffective-counsel claim brought by a Kentucky death-row inmate who was represented by a lawyer who did not know his name. See *Leonard v. Simpson*, 127 S. Ct. 2914 (2007).

12. The Louisiana Supreme Court recently upheld for the second time a law permitting the execution of the rapist of a child, even when no murder is committed. See *State v. Kennedy* (2007). It is likely that the U.S. Supreme Court will grant review sometime in the near future to determine whether such a law is unconstitutional in light of the holding in *Coker v. Georgia* (1977).

13. After over 70 years of research and dozens of published studies, most studies have found that the death penalty is no more effective than life imprisonment in deterring murder. Several studies done by economists have concluded that the death penalty deters murder more effectively than does life imprisonment, but these studies have been criticized as methodologically flawed. See generally Donahue and Wolfers (2005). Several studies indicate that executions may have a "brutalizing effect" that causes a small but discernible short-term *increase* in the murder rate. See generally Cochran, Chamlin, and Seth (1994) and Bowers (1988).

14. In fact, studies indicate that the majority of Americans soundly support the principle of proportional justice and reject the death penalty as a fair punishment for felony–murder accessories. See Finkel and Smith (1993) and Finkel and Duff (1991).

REFERENCES

AMSTERDAM, A. (1987). In favorem mortis. *Human Rights* 14: 889–890.

AMSTERDAM, A. G. (1982). Capital punishment. In *The Death Penalty in America*, ed. H. A. Bedau, 3rd. ed., pp. 346–358. New York: Oxford University Press.

BALDUS, D. C., G. WOODWORTH, and C. A. PULASKI, Jr. (1990). *Equal Justice and the Death Penalty: A Legal and Empirical Analysis*. Boston, MA: Northeastern University Press.

BARRON, D. (2002). I did not want to kill him but thought I had to: In light of *Penry II's* interpretation of *Blystone*, why the Constitution requires jury instructions on how to give effect to relevant mitigating evidence in capital cases. *Journal of Law and Policy* 11: 207–247.

BECKER, J. (2003, March 7). Death penalty moratorium in question. *Washington Post*, B4.

BOWERS, W. J. (1988). The effect of executions is brutalization, not deterrence. In *Challenging Capital Punishment: Legal and Social Science Approaches*, ed. K. C. Haas and J. A. Inciardi, pp. 49–89. Newbury Park, CA: Sage.

BOWERS, W. J. (1993). Capital punishment and contemporary values: People's misgivings and the Court's misperceptions. *Law and Society Review* 27: 157–175.

CASIMIR, G. (1993). *Payne v. Tennessee*: Overlooking capital sentencing jurisprudence and stare decisis. *New England Journal on Criminal and Civil Confinement* 19: 427–458.

CHRISTOPH, J. B. (1962). *Capital Punishment and British Politics: The British Movement to Abolish the Death Penalty 1945–57*. Chicago, IL: University of Chicago Press.

COCHRAN, J. K., M. B. CHAMLIN, and M. SETH (1994). Deterrence or brutalization? An impact assessment of Oklahoma's return to capital punishment. *Criminology* 32: 107–134.

COHEN, V. S. (1991). Exempting the mentally retarded from the death penalty: A comment on Florida's proposed legislation. *Florida State University Law Review* 19: 457–474.

DAVIES, F. (2000, June 12). Death-row cases often filled with error, study says. *Philadelphia Inquirer* A2.

DEATH PENALTY INFORMATION CENTER (2007). [Retrieved from http://www.deathpenaltyinfo.org]

DICK-HURWITZ, R. (1990). *Penry v. Lynaugh*: The Supreme Court deals a fatal blow to mentally retarded capital defendants. *University of Pittsburg Law Review* 51: 699–725.

DONAHUE, J. J., and J. WOLFERS (2005). The ethics and empirics of capital punishment: Uses and abuses of empirical evidence in the death penalty debate. *Stanford Law Review* 58: 791–844.

ELLSWORTH, P. C. (1988). Unpleasant facts: The Supreme Court's response to empirical research on capital punishment. In *Challenging Capital Punishment: Legal and Social Science Approaches*, ed. K. C. Haas and J. A. Inciardi, pp. 177–211. Thousand Oaks, CA: Sage.

ELLSWORTH, P. C., and L. ROSS (1983). Public opinion and capital punishment: A close examination of the views of abolitionists and retentionists. *Crime and Delinquency* 29: 116–169.

FERDINAND, P. (2000, May 18). A death penalty bellwether? *Washington Post*, A3.

FINKEL, N. J., and K. B. DUFF (1991). Felony–murder and community sentiment: Testing the Supreme Court's assertions. *Law and Human Behavior* 15: 405–429.

FINKEL, N. J., and S. F. SMITH (1993). Principals and accessories in capital felony–murder: The proportionality principle reigns supreme. *Law and Society Review* 27: 129–156.

GARVEY, S., S. JOHNSON, and P. MARCUS (2000). Correcting deadly confusion: Responding to jury inquiries in capital cases. *Cornell Law Review* 85: 627–655.

GEY, S. G. (1992). Justice Scalia's death penalty. *Florida State University Law Review* 20: 67–132.

GREENHOUSE, L. (2002, June 25). Justices say death penalty is up to juries, not judges. *New York Times*, A1.

GREENHOUSE, L. (2007, July 1). In steps big and small, Supreme Court moved right. *New York Times*, 1.

HAAS, K. C. (1994). The triumph of vengeance over retribution: The United States Supreme Court and the Death penalty. *Crime, Law and Social Change* 21: 127–154.

HAAS, K. C. (2004). A matter of years: The juvenile death penalty and the United States Supreme Court. In *Juvenile Justice Sourcebook: Past, Present, and Future*, ed. A. R. Roberts, pp. 309–335. New York: Oxford University Press.

HAAS, K. C., and J. A. INCIARDI (1988). Lingering doubts about a popular punishment. In *Challenging Capital Punishment: Legal and Social Science Approaches*, ed. K. C. Haas and J. A. Inciardi, pp. 11–28. Newbury Park, CA: Sage.

JOHNSON, D. (2000, February 1). Illinois, citing verdict errors, bars executions. *New York Times*, A1.

LANE, C. (2007, June 29), Narrow victories more Roberts court to the right. *Washington Post*, A4.

LEVY, J. H. (1993). Limiting victim impact evidence and argument after *Payne v. Tennessee*. *Stanford Law Review* 45: 1027–1060.

LEWIS, N. A. (2006, December 15). Death sentences decline and experts offer reasons. *New York Times*, A1.

LIPTAK, A. (2002, June 25). Fewer death sentences likely if juries make ultimate decision, experts say. *New York Times*, A19.

MARQUART, J. W., and J. R. SORENSON (1989). A national study of the *Furman*-commuted inmates: Assessing the threat to society from capital offenders. *Loyola of Los Angeles Law Review* 23: 5–28.

MELLO, M. (1988). Facing death alone: The postconviction attorney crisis on death row. *American University Law Review* 37: 513–607.

MELTSNER, M. (1973). *Cruel and Unusual: The Supreme Court and Capital Punishment*. New York: Random House.

MILLER, K. S., and M. L. RADELET (1993). *Executing the Mentally Ill: The Criminal Justice System and the Case of Alvin*. Newbury Park, CA: Sage.

NAACP LEGAL AND EDUCATIONAL DEFENSE FUND (2007, Winter). *Death Row U.S.A. Reporter*. New York: NAACP Legal and Educational Defense Fund.

OBERLANDER, M. I. (1992). The *Payne* of allowing victim impact statements at capital sentencing hearings. *Vanderbilt Law Review* 45: 1621–1662.

RADELET, M. L., H. A. BEDAU, and C. E. PUTNAM (1992). *In Spite of Innocence: Erroneous Convictions in Capital Cases*. Boston, MA: Northeastern University Press.

REED, E. F. (1993). *The Penry Penalty: Capital Punishment and Offenders with Mental Retardation*. Lanham, MA: University Press of America.

SARAT, A., and N. VIDMAR (1976). Public opinion, the death penalty, and the eighth amendment: Testing the Marshall hypothesis. *Wisconsin Law Review* 1976: 171–206.

SCHAUER, F. (2006). The Court's agenda—and the nation's. *Harvard Law Review* 120: 5–64.

SCHECK, B., P. NEUFELD, and J. DWYER (2003). *Actual Innocence*. New York: New American Library.

SELLIN, T. (1980). *The Penalty of Death*. Beverly Hills, CA: Sage.

SMOTHERS, R. (2007a, June 6). New Jersey Court voids death penalty conviction. *New York Times*, A19.

SMOTHERS, R. (2007b, May 11). Panel seeks end of New Jersey's death penalty. *New York Times*, A21.

WAGNER, J., and E. RICH (2007, July 8). Ire over O'Malley's inaction on executions. *Washington Post*, A1.

WEIL, E. (2007, February 11). The needle and the damage done. *New York Times*, 46–51.

WILGOREN, J. (2003, February 7). After sweeping clemency order, Ex-governor Ryan is a celebrity, but a solitary one. *New York Times*, A16.

CASES

Abdul-Kabir v. Quarterman, 127 S. Ct. 1654 (2007).

Ake v. Oklahoma, 470 U.S. 68 (1985).

Atkins v. Virginia, 122 S. Ct. 2242 (2003).

Ayers v. Belmontes, 127 S. Ct. 469 (2006).

Barclay v. Florida, 463 U.S. 939 (1983).

Barefoot v. Estelle, 463 U.S. 880 (1983).

Beck v. Alabama, 477 U.S. 625 (1980).

Bell v. Ohio, 438 U.S. 637 (1978).

Blystone v. Pennsylvania, 494 U.S. 299 (1990).

Booth v. Maryland, 482 U.S. 496 (1987).

Boyde v. California, 494 U.S. 370 (1990).

Brewer v. Quarterman, 127 S. Ct. 1706 (2007).

Brown v. Sanders, 126 S. Ct. 884 (2006).

Buchanan v. Angelone, 522 U.S. 269 (1998).

Bullington v. Missouri, 451 U.S. 430 (1981).

Caldwell v. Mississippi, 472 U.S. 320 (1985).

California v. Brown, 479 U.S. 538 (1987).

California v. Ramos, 463 U.S. 992 (1983).

Callins v. Collins, 510 U.S. 1141 (1994).

Coker v. Georgia, 433 U.S. 584 (1977).

Coleman v. Balkcom, 451 U.S. (1981).

Dawson v. Delaware, 503 U.S. 159 (1992).

Dobbert v. Florida, 432 U.S. 325 (1977).

Eddings v. Oklahoma, 455 U.S. 104 (1982).

Enmund v. Florida, 458 U.S. 782 (1982).

Estelle v. Smith, 451 U.S. 454 (1981).

Ford v. Wainwright, 477 U.S. 399 (1986).

Francis v. Franklin, 471 U.S. 307 (1985).

Furman v. Georgia, 408 U.S. 238 (1972).

Godfrey v. Georgia, 446 U.S. 420 (1980).

Green v. Georgia, 442 U.S. 95 (1979).

Gregg v. Georgia, 428 U.S. 153 (1976).

Herrera v. Collins, 506 U.S. 390 (1993).

Hitchcock v. Dugger, 481 U.S. 393 (1987).

Johnson v. Texas, 509 U.S. 350 (1993).

Jurek v. Texas, 428 U.S. 262 (1976).

Kansas v. Marsh, 126 S. Ct. 884 (2006).

Lankford v. Idaho, 500 U.S. 110 (1991).

Lawrence v. Florida, 127 S. Ct. 1079 (2007).

Leonard v. Simpson, 127 S. Ct. 2914 (2007).

Lockett v. Ohio, 438 U.S. 586 (1978).

Lockhart v. McCree, 476 U.S. 162 (1986).

Maynard v. Cartwright, 486 U.S. 356 (1988).

McCleskey v. Kemp, 481 U.S. 279 (1987).

Miller-El v. Dretke, 545 U.S. 231 (2005).

Miller-El v. Cockrell, 537 U.S. 322 (2003).

Mills v. Maryland, 486 U.S. 367 (1988).

Morgan v. Illinois, 504 U.S. 719 (1992).

Ohio Adult Parole Authority v. Woodard, 523 U.S. 272 (1998).

Panetti v. Quarterman, 168 L. Ed. 2d 662 (2007)

Payne v. Tennessee, 501 U.S. 808 (1991).

Penry v. Johnson, 502 U.S. 782 (2001).

Penry v. Lynaugh, 492 U.S. 302 (1989).

Proffitt v. Florida, 428 U.S. 242 (1976).

Pulley v. Harris, 465 U.S. 37 (1984).

Ring v. Arizona, 536 U.S. 584 (2002).

Roberts v. Louisiana, 428 U.S. 325 (1976).

Roberts v. Louisiana, 431 U.S. 633 (1977).

Rompilla v. Beard, 545 U.S. 374 (2005).

Roper v. Simmons, 543 U.S. 551 (2005).

Roper v. Weaver, 127 S. Ct. 2022 (2007)

Sattazahn v. Pennsylvania, 537 U.S. 101 (2003).

Schriro v. Landigan, 127 S. Ct. 1933 (2007).

Schriro v. Summerlin, 542 U.S. 348 (2004).

Skipper v. South Carolina, 476 U.S. 1 (1986).

Smith v. Texas, 127 S. Ct. 1686 (2007).

South Carolina v. Gathers, 490 U.S. 805 (1989).

Stanford v. Kentucky, 492 U.S. 361 (1989).

State v. Kennedy, No. 05-KA-1981 (Louisiana 2007).

Strickler v. Greene, 527 U.S. 263 (1999).

Sumner v. Shuman, 483 U.S. 66 (1987).

Thompson v. Oklahoma, 487 U.S. 815 (1988).

Tison v. Arizona, 481 U.S. 137 (1987).

Trop v. Dulles, 356 U.S. 86 (1958).

Uttecht v. Brown, 127 S. Ct. 2218 (2007)

Wainwright v. Witt, 469 U.S. 412 (1985).

Weeks v. Angelone, 528 U.S. 225 (2000).

Whitmore v. Arkansas, 495 U.S. 149 (1990).

Wiggins v. Smith, 539 U.S. 510 (2003).

Witherspoon v. Illinois, 391 U.S. 510 (1968).

Woodford v. Garceau, 538 U.S. 202 (2003).

Woodson v. North Carolina, 428 U.S. 280 (1976).

Zant v. Stephens, 462 U.S. 862 (1983).

Chapter 24

Bias-Motivated Offenses

A Review of Prosecutorial Investigation Reports

Silvina Ituarte

ABSTRACT

Bias-motivated offenses extend across a continuum of behaviors that range from harassment to murder, yet both researchers and practitioners concur that the majority of bias-motivated events involve lower-level offenses, which are often overlooked by the criminal justice system. As there is a relatively limited amount of scholarly literature regarding the prosecution of bias-motivated offenses, the researcher reviewed prosecutorial investigation reports in order to (1) examine how the process of categorizing bias-motivated events impacts the manner in which offenders are filtered through the criminal justice system and (2) illustrate the sentiments expressed in acts of bias taking place within one county in New Jersey through the use of narratives. The examination yielded 140 investigations with 28 confirmed bias-motivated cases. Of the confirmed bias-motivated violations, 14 were processed formally through the courts, while the other 14 were handled informally through mediation, a written apology, or other informal means after the victim chose not to file a formal complaint.

INTRODUCTION

Bias crimes,[1] commonly referred to by the media as "hate crimes," are defined as "offenses motivated by hatred against a victim based on his [or her] race, religion, sexual orientation, handicap, ethnicity, or national origin" (Bureau of Justice Assistance 1997:ix). In contrast, a bias-motivated *incident* consists of offenses such as name-calling that do not meet the criteria, or contain the elements necessary, to be regarded as a crime. While the Uniform Crime Report (UCR) provides insight into the number and types of bias-motivated crimes reported across the nation, it does not account for the jurisdictional differences in varying recording practices or the processes by which behaviors reported to law enforcement are distinguished, categorized, and labeled as bias-motivated. In order to better understand the official information gathered in the UCR, an examination of the processes by which behaviors are classified, labeled, and handled at the local level must be undertaken. This study examines how the process of categorizing bias crimes impacts the manner in which offenders are filtered through the criminal justice system, depicts narratives describing the sentiments expressed in acts of bias-motivated harassment, and raises questions regarding the appropriate interventions to more frequent types of bias-motivated offenses.

Bias-motivated offenses extend across a spectrum of behaviors that include acts of harassment or vandalism as well as aggravated assault or homicide. Although acts of name-calling and harassment have a profound impact on the victim, the targeted group, and the community as a whole, the terms "lower-level offense" or "serious offense" are used throughout this study to indicate the placement of the offense according to a crime-based continuum of behaviors. These terms are in no way intended to minimize the impact and seriousness of the offense on individuals and communities.

Bias Crime Definitions, Legislation, and Data Collection

Bias crimes were first nationally addressed when the 1990 Hate Crime Statistics Act was enacted requiring the U.S. Department of Justice to gather data on crimes committed due to the victim's race, national origin, religion, or sexual orientation. Documenting these crimes emerged as a priority in an effort to legitimize any further government response to the issue (Herek and Berrill 1992). The Federal Bureau of Investigation (FBI) was given the responsibility of creating and implementing the standards for assessing how law enforcement should determine whether an offense merits a bias classification. Statutes protecting individuals against hate-motivated violence were enacted, and they were closely scrutinized. The Act was much debated, and various legislators disagreed as to whom should be protected under the Act.

At the federal level, the Hate Crime Sentencing Enhancement Act of 1993 "order[ed] the United States Sentencing Commission to adopt guidelines increasing the penalty by a minimum of three offense levels for those crimes that a jury found beyond a

---

[1] Bias crimes, hate crimes, and bias-motivated crimes are all used synonymously.

reasonable doubt to be a hate crime" (Spillane 1994:237). The Violent Crime Control and Law Enforcement Act of 1994 reaffirmed the use of sentencing enhancements and expanded the definition of hate crimes to include "disability" as a protected group. Subsequently, the federal Violence Against Women Act of 1994 (VAWA) stated that "all persons within the United States shall have the right to be free from crimes of violence motivated by gender" (ADL 1997:8). Then, the Church Arsons Prevention Act was enacted by Congress in 1998, to "facilitate criminal prosecutions for attacks against houses of worship, increase penalties for these crimes, establish a loan guarantee and recovery fund for rebuilding, and authorize additional [federal] personnel" (ADL 1997:9) to investigate incidents.

At the state level, bias crimes represent a particularly difficult category of offenses for data collection since states have implemented various statutes that differ from one another. Ninety percent of the states possess bias crime legislation protecting victims according to the categories of race, ethnicity, and religion. Slightly less than half of the states include sexual orientation, gender, and disability or political affiliation in the list of protected groups. Indiana and South Carolina only offer specific protection against institutional vandalism, while Wyoming does not offer any legal or civil protections against acts of bias-motivated violence. Including the states without bias-motivated violence legislation, 86 percent have specific laws against institutional vandalism of sites such as religious houses of worship. Instead of, or in conjunction with criminal penalties, 62 percent of the states have created civil remedies with which victims may seek injunctions and restitution for harm suffered (ADL 2003).

In a 1999 study of the 50 states and the District of Columbia, the Southern Poverty Law Center concluded that although the number of bias-motivated crimes recorded by the FBI has consistently approximated 8,000 cases for almost 10 years, a more accurate measure would reveal approximately 50,000 crimes (Southern Poverty Law Center 2001). According to the Southern Poverty Law Center, "law enforcement jurisdictions in at least 10 States failed to report 1999 incidents that surely qualified as hate crimes" (Southern Poverty Law Center 2001:12).

Nationally, the largest proportions of bias-motivated crimes reported to the FBI for the years 1990 through 2004 include acts of intimidation, simple and aggravated assault, and vandalism (Uniform Crime Report 1991–2004). In analyzing both crimes against persons and crimes against property, the national distribution of reported offenses indicated that bias-motivated behaviors are not primarily intended for any sort of financial gain, but rather as a means of distressing the victim and the victim's group.

Intimidation could represent either verbal and written threats, or acts of harassment aimed at intimidating the victim and/or the victim's group. Although name-calling can be emotionally damaging for the victim, without an implied or implicit threat, name-calling is protected speech safeguarded by the First Amendment of the U.S. Constitution. One significant contribution of this study is the description using exact wording from examples of harassing letters and recorded phone messages. Without these descriptions one may underestimate the impact of lower-level acts of bias and find it difficult to appreciate the true nature of intimidation and harassment.

Identifying and Classifying Bias Crimes

Beyond the obstacles of determining what constitutes protected and unprotected speech, ascertaining what comprises a bias crime can be challenging. The criterion established by the FBI states that "hatred need not be the entire motivation for the offense" (Spillane 1994:235; United States Department of Justice 1990), yet officers often experience confusion in distinguishing bias from non-bias events (Nolan, McDevitt, and Cronin 2004). As stated by Jenness and Grattet in their (2005) analysis of law enforcement agencies in California, police agencies with clearly defined hate crime policies experience less confusion among officers and higher reporting rates of bias crimes. Although California consistently reports the highest number of bias-motivated offenses in the nation, Jenness and Grattet's examination revealed 161 law enforcement agencies that do not possess an established hate crime policy. Clearly, even within the same state, a local department's autonomy shapes how bias crimes are identified and recorded. "Law enforcement agencies can facilitate or impede the implementation of innovative crime control policies by enforcing—or not enforcing—law" (Jenness and Grattet 2005:338). Without the police taking the first steps to enforce the law, hate crime legislation is of little value.

In her book titled *Policing Hatred: Law Enforcement, Civil Rights, and Hate Crime*, Jeanine Bell (2002) examines the role of police officers' discretion on the determination of what constitutes a bias crime. Bell draws attention to the fact that police officers represent the street-level enforcers who have the power to use their discretion in a manner that defines what will, and will not, be classified as a hate crime. The author explains, "Since most bias-motivated incidents are first placed in other categories such as battery, assault, and vandalism, bias crime do not exist in practice until police say they do" (Bell 2002:12). Officers who are the first to respond to an incident "serve as gatekeepers with the discretion to discard incidents that prosecutors and judges will never see" (Bell 2002:9). Ground-level enforcers of the criminal law, including but not limited to, police and prosecutors "are powerful, not so much for their control over final outcomes but for their low-visibility power not to enforce the law" (Bell 2002:187). These criminal justice professionals have the authority to determine which cases will be disregarded, investigated, and prosecuted as well as which cases will be dismissed or classified as "junk" (Bell 2002:187).

Despite the fact that police are mandated by federal and state law, each individual law enforcement agency enforces and carries out the law using different protocols according to the varying values and perceptions of the department's leaders and the citizenry's priorities. "Each agency is autonomous in terms of how it orients to state statutes, develops policy to enforce the law, and indeed, actually enforces the law" (Jenness and Grattet 2005:342). Wilson and Ruback's (2003) examination of 2,075 bias-motivated incidents reported to the Pennsylvania Human Relations Commission revealed an overall majority of reports involved noncriminal behaviors and minor property offenses. Their findings also revealed how police responded to these offenses as they varied with the composition of the community. "Such autonomy grants the agency significant freedom to develop its own approach to crime control based upon its assessment of the nature of its specific community problems" (Jenness and Grattet 2005:342). In communities in which the citizenry is more concerned with other criminal behaviors, police may be more likely to overlook smaller acts of bias and may choose to report the crime without listing the bias motivation. "Hate crime statutes therefore present officers with more options because the decision not to charge an offender with a hate crime does not necessarily mean that the offender will escape punishment. Since bias-motivated incidents can be dealt with as 'ordinary' crimes without being labeled as hate crimes, officers are more vulnerable to community pressures not to identify crimes as bias-motivated" (Bell 2002:4). In several circumstances, police may be deterred from charging an incident as bias-motivated since media attention could lead to public unrest or negative labels of the community as prejudiced.

A critical component of identifying and recording bias crimes is the explicit procedures and training of the police officers who must enforce the abstract principles created by legislators into enforceable laws. Without the proper police protocol and training, chances are that "in the vast majority of possible bias crimes that are committed each year, a decision by police not to invoke the law determines to a great extent that the incident will not be pursued as a hate crime" (Bell 2002:2). In 2002, Nolan and Akiyama examined the survey responses of law enforcement professionals of all ranks and classified the law enforcement agencies as either "good-reporting" agencies or "non-reporting agencies" according to the agencies that did, and did not, collect hate crime data. In the comparison, it became evident that the good-reporting agencies had established internal protocols to train officers and prevent the misidentification of cases, aspired to stronger community-police ties, perceived hate crimes as a significant and worthwhile endeavor, and received greater support from their local governments and police administrators.

The discussion of police discretion within the context of organizational structure, community priorities, and police training create the foundation for undertaking an exploration of the next level of the criminal justice process—prosecution. Researchers have rarely focused on the processes by which bias-motivated behaviors are screened, labeled, and prosecuted. Since hate crime legislation is relatively new and involves numerous controversies ranging from issues of free speech to proving motivation, prosecutors have often avoided prosecuting using these statutes. As a result, in 1995, the American Prosecutors Research Institute of the National District Attorneys Association was awarded a grant by the National Institute of Justice to conduct a survey of prosecutor protocols in handling bias-motivated cases. The objective of the initiative was to develop a hate-crimes training guide for prosecutors. More recently, some of the Offices of the Attorney General, as exemplified by the state of California, have started publishing the hate crime prosecution dispositions in their yearly report of bias-motivated behaviors.

As with police officers who initially submit reports of possible bias-motivated offenses, prosecutors also have tremendous discretion in handling acts of bias. "In addition to the problems presented by the requirement that cases be motivated by bias, ADAs [have] a troublesome time in bias crime cases getting witnesses to come forward" (Bell 2002:162). Very little information is known about the prosecutorial screening process, the classification of offenses as possible bias crimes, and the overall prosecution of bias-motivated behaviors. This analysis of the labeling process, along with the narratives included in this study, assists in understanding the variety of lower-level offenses and raise questions regarding other bias-motivated acts that may remain unreported by victims.

Although there is a limited amount of scholarly literature regarding the prosecution of bias-motivated offenses, researchers and practitioners all recognize that the majority of bias-motivated events involve lower-level offenses such as name-calling and harassment. The narratives included within this study provide the best depiction of the variety of cases reported to bias crime units and most clearly portray the distinctions within these lower-level offenses.

The official records from the Prosecutor's Office in County Y, New Jersey were used in this study to provide insight into the processes that classify bias-motivated acts, delineate the distinctions between bias-motivated incidents and bias-motivated crimes as determined by prosecutors, and illustrate how bias-motivated incidents are handled both formally and informally within the criminal justice system.

METHODOLOGY

Research Site

Throughout the 1990s and the early part of the twenty-first century, California, New York, and New Jersey have been the three states to consistently report the highest number of recorded bias crimes (Uniform Crime Report). Although some research has been conducted in the areas of bias crimes in California, little research has examined acts of bias reported in the state of New Jersey.

New Jersey was chosen as the site of this inquiry as a result of the state's established hate crime policies, procedures, and trainings for law enforcement officers; reliable history of data collection; and regular monthly New Jersey Bias Crime Officers Association meetings. According to Jenness and Grattet (2005:339), "the existence of training procedures, special policies, and formal statements made by high-ranking law enforcement officials" are critical to the success of hate crime laws. New Jersey has complied with all these components. New Jersey state officials have been at the forefront of bias crime data collection and have implemented "training regarding the Attorney General's Bias Incident Investigation Standards . . . [into] the Basic Course for Police Officers since February 26, 1988".

Like many of the suggestions of Jenness and Grattet (2005), New Jersey has possessed an established hate crime policy for all law enforcement agencies since the early 1990s. The statewide procedures established and enforced by the New Jersey Attorney General's Office serve to "reduce officer discretion and to help officers prepare for situations they may confront (Brooks 2001 as quoted in Jenness and Grattet 2005:346). Police officers in each of New Jersey's 21 counties receive training regarding the Bias Incident Investigation Standards and are prepared to attach the additional one-page form that must accompany any police report in which a bias motivation is suspected. A designated investigator in the prosecutor's office examines all the incidents referred by police with a bias crime designation, and the Attorney General's Office of Bias Crime and Community Relations is "notified of all suspected or confirmed bias incidents as soon as possible, but in no event later than 24 hours after a law enforcement agency gains knowledge of such incidents" (Jenness and Garattet, 2005).

New Jersey officials continuously review the established policies as exemplified by the Bias Incident Investigation Standards, Policy and Procedures for New Jersey Law Enforcement issued in 1991 and revised in 1994, 1995, and 2000. According to the (Jenness and Garattet, 2005).

> For New Jersey law enforcement purposes, a bias incident is defined as any suspected or confirmed offenses or unlawful act which occurs to a person, private property, or public property on the basis of race, color, religion, gender (except matters involving a violation of N.J.S.A. 2C:14-2 or 2C:14-3), handicap, sexual orientation, or ethnicity. An offense is bias-based if the motive for the commission of the offense or unlawful act pertains to race, color, religion, gender, handicap, sexual orientation or ethnicity. For the purpose of this definition, the term "handicap" shall be construed consistently with N.J.S.A. 10:5-5(q) . . .

Procedures

The researcher initiated the study with a petition to the New Jersey Supreme Court requesting permission to view prosecutorial investigation reports. Simultaneously, letters were mailed to each of the 21 bias crime officers in the prosecutors' offices explaining the research. One-third of the officers responded to the requests. Upon speaking with the bias crime officers who responded to the letter, the varying quality of records maintained by the units and skepticism about the research became evident.

Two counties stood out as most organized, cooperative, and dedicated to working with the community to suppress bias crimes. For the purpose of preserving the anonymity of the victim's and offender's identity, the county of the Prosecutor's Office will be referred to as "County Y Prosecutor's Office." County X held yearly Hate Crimes Forums with key speakers, films, and activities to raise community awareness, yet cases referred by police that were not deemed bias-motivated by the bias crime officer were removed from the office files. Instead, County Y's files were maintained for every case that was referred to the Bias Crime Unit. Some of these cases in fact involved a bias motivation, while others were stated to lack any bias intention.

After receiving permission to thoroughly review the files from the New Jersey Supreme Court and the Administrative Offices of the Court, the researcher was granted permission by the County Y's Prosecutor's Bias Crimes/Gang Unit to examine the prosecutorial files. The researcher was introduced to the bias crime officer in charge of the Unit and arrangements were made to examine the records.

County Y encompasses nearly 500 square miles and is positioned within the New York Metropolitan area. In 2000, County Y had a population of over 600,000 largely made up of Caucasian (84 percent) inhabitants, with a small percentage of African American (8.1 percent) and Latino/a (6.2 percent) residents (United States Census 2000). According to the census data, the median income in County Y for 2000 was slightly over $60,000 while the national median average was $41,994.

Since only one person was assigned the investigation and follow-up of all bias crimes and gang incidents reported to the Unit, the cases were stored in file cabinets and only minimal information was computerized. Each file contained the bias crime information sheet submitted by local police departments as well as the lieutenant's interview transcripts and any additional materials. Each case file was examined and thorough notes with multiple quotes were taken. To maintain the confidentiality of anyone mentioned within the reports, the names of any participant, whether victim or offender, were removed immediately from any notes. The typed notes from these reports were analyzed in 2007 using NVivo7 (a research software) in order to (1) demonstrate how acts of bias are labeled and processed within the criminal justice system at one jurisdiction, (2) illustrate the process of distinguishing bias crimes from bias incidents, and (3) provide a context of the bias acts taking place within one jurisdiction in New Jersey.

DATA

In examining the reports[2] collected by County Y's Prosecutor's Office, four report groupings emerged: "bias-motivated," "no bias motivation," "closed pending further information," and "false claims." One of these four labels was designated at the end of each report by the Unit, and the researcher did not change any of these designations. The researcher did however divide the category of "no bias motivation" into the following three subsections: (1) cases involving other crimes without a bias motive, (2) cases involving constitutionally protected bias speech not rising to the level of an actual crime, and (3) cases involving no bias at all.

Of the 140 bias offense files investigated by the Bias Crime Unit, only 28 cases were confirmed to be bias-motivated, while the rest were categorized as "no bias motivation" (50), "closed pending further information" (61), and "false claims" (1). Twenty percent of the cases investigated were confirmed to be bias-motivated incidents, while forty-three percent lacked adequate information to determine the bias motivation or the identity of the suspect(s) (see Table 24.1). Of the reported incidents that were "no bias motivation," some incidents involved another crime such as trespassing without a bias intent; several involved no criminal act but prejudicial slurs; and others involved no criminal act and no bias motivation. If either the motivation or the suspect was unknown, the case was classified "closed pending further information."

Seventy-five percent of the 64 offenders in this study classified to have been involved in a bias act, acted alone, and twenty-five percent acted in groups of two or more offenders. Forty-three percent (61 incidents) of the cases reported to the Bias Crime Unit in County Y's Prosecutor's Office remained closed pending further information. Examples of cases closed pending further information included phone messages stating, "Are you ready for a hanging this weekend?" describing a nun as a "nigger-loving bull dyke," and finding a swastika engraved in the side of a Latino man's vehicle.

Twenty-two percent of these offenses (30 incidents) originated at or near the victim's residence, and eighteen percent (25 incidents) took place in public areas, such as

---

[2]The language recorded in the prosecutorial investigation reports was not altered in the data section. It is not the author's intention to offend the reader with the graphic and offensive language. It was this author's belief that the exact language recorded in the documents was critical in understanding the impact of the events described in the narratives.

TABLE 24.1 County Y's Bias Crime Case Processing

Type of Incidents	Bias Crimes		Not Bias Crime			Closed Pending Information	False Claim
	Formally Processed	Informally Processed	Crime No Bias	Bias No Crime	No Bias No Crime		
Graffiti/vandalism	6	0	1	0	3	43	0
E-mail/mail/written slur	2	0	0	3	0	6	0
Phone/harass/threat/verbal slur	2	12	10	25	3	9	1
Assault/robbery/robbery and assault	4	2	2	0	0	2	0
Break and enter/graffiti and trespass	0	0	2	0	0	1	0
Discrimination	0	0	0	0	1	0	0
Total	**14 (10%)**	**14 (10%)**	**15 (11%)**	**28 (20%)**	**7 (5%)**	**61 (43%)**	**1 (0.70%)**

parks, streets, and parking lots. Junior and senior high schools accounted for 34 percent (48 incidents) of the reported bias cases in which, for example, young students used markers, spray paint, or pencils to write "I hate all white trash," "KKK," "white power," and "dyke" on school walls, desks, and parking signs.

Of the 28 bias-motivated crimes investigated by the County Y's Prosecutor's Office, 14 confirmed bias-motivated cases were processed formally through the courts, while the other 14 were handled informally through mediation, a written apology, or other informal means after the victim chose not to file a formal complaint. The incidents processed formally by the County Y Courts include running over the victim's bicycle after yelling racial slurs and driving too close to the cyclist; leaving threatening anti-Semitic messages on the victim's answering machine stating the victim was a "shithead Jew left out of the oven"; repeatedly beating and robbing Latino victims; phoning a threat to rape a teacher and her daughters; and producing a publication of a differently abled young man in obscene and sexually explicit portrayals.

In multiple instances, the Prosecutor's Office received cases reported to police in which prejudiced comments were made but did not rise to the level of a crime. Such instances include a 10-year-old male stating he was "not going to let a white bread teacher teach him"; a woman placing a phone call to her cable company and referring to the customer service representative as a "nigger"; a 14-year-old male stating, "I'm going to roll this penny down the hall and start a Jewish parade"; and a customer referring to a Department of Motor Vehicles employee as a "stupid fucking spic asshole bitch."

On occasion, the reported offenses did not involve bias at all. For example, school officials reported a bias-motivated occurrence after having found the words, "New World Order (NWO)," on the boys' bathroom wall, yet investigators informed the principal that the NWO referred to the increasingly popular sport of professional wrestling and not to any form of hate organization. Another incident involved a male urinating on the side of the building without recognizing the meaning of his actions when he urinated on the walls of a Jewish Community Center.

Of those cases that were closed pending further information, 70 percent (43 cases) involved graffiti or vandalism left on personal, school, or other public property; 15 percent (nine cases) involved prejudiced phone messages left on answering machines, harassment, or threats; 10 percent (six cases) involved receiving hate mail, e-mail, or written slurs; 2 percent (one case) included a robbery and assault where the suspects could not be identified; 2 percent (one case) involved an assault with no identifiable suspect; and 2 percent (one case) included both graffiti and trespassing.

Offender and Victim Characteristics

Of the known offenders recorded in County Y, 82 percent were male and 18 percent were female. Eighty-three percent of the offenders were Caucasian, followed by the second largest group comprised of African Americans with nine percent. Of the 171 known offenders in County Y's sample, the age was known for only 43 offenders. Of the 43, 47 percent (20) were between the ages of 15 to 18, and 28 percent (12) ranged in age from 11 to 14 years old. Nine percent (4) of the offenders were under ten years of age and 34 (84 percent) were under 19 years old.

Racially motivated bias crimes accounted for 41 percent of victims and 58 incidents. Bias-motivated offenses against religion explained 20 percent of the victims of bias crimes, with ethnicity accounting for 11 percent of cases investigated in that year. Those most likely to have been victimized included various racial, ethnic, and religious groups, including Latino/a, Asian, Hindu, Indian, Christian, Jewish, Italian, interracial couples, immigrants, and Haitians.

Eight victims were targets of gender, sexual orientation, or disability bias, but ten additional individuals were victimized for a combination of categories, including gender and race, as well as sexual orientation and religion. These numbers only represent bias-motivated incidents targeting only one victim group and do not include those cases involving multiple biases.

When assessing the investigation reports, incidents not specifically stating a clear identifying demographic description of the victim were recorded as "unsure of victim group." Many of the incidents solely containing swastikas or the letters "KKK" spray painted on walls, etched on property, or drawn on surfaces without any other identifying factors were classified as "unsure," since the victim group could include members of various groups.

Multiple Offending

Of the 28 cases confirmed to be bias-motivated offenses, in two instances, the same defendants pled guilty to more than one reported incident of violence. Two separate pairs of juveniles who committed numerous bias acts accounted for 7 of the 28 bias crimes. In one set of bias-motivated acts, two 14-year-old white males pled guilty to placing graffiti on a Russian Orthodox Church and the mailboxes of two different residences and to etching derogatory words on the side of another victim's vehicle. The pastor of a Russian Orthodox Church complained of finding graffiti stating, "Fuck you," "Die Niggers," "Fuck God," "Satan Rules," and "Niggers" on the walls of the church, along with a swastika and a pentagram. The two 14-year-old juveniles were later apprehended and pled guilty to the charges of desecration of a venerated object, harassment, disorderly conduct, and damage to religious premises. The two were also involved in placing a swastika with a black magic marker on a woman's mailbox, as well as on the mailbox of an 82-year-old female victim. Their last reported incident involved a 46-year-old white male who found "homo," "fuck you," and "nigger" inscribed on his truck, along with satanic symbols and three large scratches on the right side of his vehicle.

Another 3 out of the 28 cases confirmed to be bias-motivated involved two 17-year-old white males who drove past a group of 18-year-old males yelling, "You should die, you Jewish bastards," and throwing an M-80 firecracker at them. They also drove past a 20-year-old male, who reported that the two teenagers yelled racial slurs and destroyed the bicycle of three children playing on a lawn, and also pointed a lighter at him in a threatening manner. The investigation reports documented that

> both juveniles later admitted to the above incident which they stated started over a motor vehicle incident that reportedly escalated to the point that both subjects on all sides exchanged remarks at each other. The accused also admitted to throwing an M-80 firecracker.

Furthermore, a 20-year-old victim also accused the two of driving past him shouting, "Fuck you" with an ignited lighter that they pointed in a threatening manner. A 37-year-old female victim who picked up children at a residence reported that

> three (3) unknown vehicles, two (2) small cars and a red Jeep Cherokee stopped at her location and yelled racial slurs at two boys and a girl who were standing on the lawn of the residence. The males exited the Jeep and picked up a bicycle throwing it on the lawn and leaving prior to the arrival of the police.

In these cases, the offenders pled guilty to having participated in several bias-motivated events.

Likewise, three 17-year-olds and one 16-year-old boy were accused of targeting Latinos for robberies. In a police interview with one of the juveniles who had a supporting role in the crimes, the boy made the following statements (the names of the defendants have been altered):

> Q: Why are the Mexicans being targeted by these guys?
>
> A: 'Cause they are easy targets and they don't speak English to go to the police.
>
> Q: What information do you have in regards to numerous assaults on Mexicans or people that appear to be Mexican or Hispanic prior to July of 1997, over the several months?
>
> A: What I know from word and from them bragging about it, . . . that they passed and beat up Mexicans. They always say they ran em for their money. From what I hear, me personally, I think there is more than five times . . . all of em were assaults, I've seen 3 of em. We saw a Mexican on a bike [and Fred] hung out the window and tried to hit the Mexican as he went by. Four blocks up the road, [Fred] said he had to stop to take a piss, so [Dave] stopped. [Fred] then walked down the street, several feet, waited by a tree, the next thing I seen was the Mexican taking off on his bike, jumped off his bike, and ran on foot. [Fred] didn't catch him, but then picked up his bike and slammed it into a telephone pole and bent the rims.

Neighborhood Bigotry

Several of the instances in which victims refused to file a complaint involved disputes between neighbors, or residents engaged in harassment through prejudiced slurs, desecrated signs on property, unleashed pets encouraged to attack, and erratic drivers threatening pedestrians. A 41-year-old African-American male asserted that he and his family had been victims of harassment by neighbors since 1995. The neighboring family had verbally abused African-American children, calling them "black niggers," "black motherfuckers," and numerous other offensive remarks. The police had been called many times before, and mediation was provided after the dog was released to run loose on African-American children. When other neighbors were interviewed, they remembered the dog being turned loose while the mother of the defendant was also calling out racial slurs. When interviewed by investigators, a neighbor stated that the teenage defendant "threatened two black females in 1995, by stating that he was going home to get his gun. When he returned, he [said he] was going to shoot them," but the girls had left. Since then, numerous slurs had been confirmed.

When the defendant was questioned in the presence of his parents and asked if he had used a BB gun to shoot at anyone's house (on his block), he smiled and stated, "It was just a prank." When questioned about a sign the family had placed on their property regarding the victim, they claimed, "No one saw it, so it was no big deal." In actuality, numerous neighbors expressed feeling offended but the victims ultimately chose not to file a complaint, but asked that the police intervene through requesting mediation. As a result, the case was not taken to the grand jury but instead handled informally.

In a similar case involving harassment by a neighbor, a white male stated that "for the past several days, he had been harassed by the accused who had made anti-Semitic remarks and had hung a derogatory flag in front of his home." The victim refused to sign the complaint but requested that the police speak with the accused. Other neighborhood disputes were handled informally as well. An accused white 32-year-old female referred to a group of children as "niggers" and directed other racial slurs toward them while at a pool. She later commented to them, "This was a nice neighborhood until you people moved in. . . . You people cause nothing but trouble and you should go back to Africa." At that same time, her 10-year-old son spit on one of the victims who was only 11 years old. The victim and his siblings "began walking out of the recreation complex with a friend by way of the access road when the accused exited the road with her vehicle and drove on the side of the road and just missed striking the victim." Since no other incidents had taken place, the victimized family also decided not to pursue the incident any further.

Thirty-five percent of the incidents investigated as bias-motivated occurred at schools, and were therefore handled informally through the schools. In one circumstance, the defendants phoned a 64-year-old white male three times within 15 minutes and threatened to break into his home and "beat his ass," while also making both sexual and anti-Semitic remarks. The police were able to trace the phone calls to a 15-year-old, who had left the message, "Jew, Jew, Jew, Go to hell," on the victim's answering machine. The local school took responsibility for disciplining the student, and no further action was taken by the prosecutor's office. In several instances, the school requested that the students attend a mandatory assembly dedicated to the topic of intolerance or choose to have the principal meet with the parents to discuss the matter.

Other bias-motivated actions committed by juveniles were processed formally through the criminal justice system. A 56-year-old African-American woman who was riding a bicycle on the street observed two young males and two young females in a vehicle laughing and referring to her as a "nigger and a bitch." After driving by her the first time, they drove back around, and the "vehicle came speeding in her direction so fast as to sideswipe [her] bike and [her]self." She fell off the bicycle and the vehicle turned around to run over it. Later, the driver was identified as an 18-year-old mechanic with an 11th-grade education who told interviewers:

Ah, I was driving . . . looking for a junkyard for parts for my truck. . . . I went down this street, . . . and ah there was this lady riding on a bike. . . . My truck backfired . . . and ah,

> I guess it startled the lady on the bike, . . . then I went down, I noticed that the junkyard was closed. . . .
>
>   I did not mean to cause any harm to this lady. I didn't mean to startle her by the backfire. Ah, I don't like hurting old ladies. I'm not racist. . . . I would help an old lady across the street if she was having trouble.

When asked if his friends had made racial remarks to the victim, he remarked, "Ah, I'm not positive. It was something racial, but I'm not positive exactly what he said."

    One of the other more serious formally processed bias crimes, targeting women as the victim group, was committed by a 14-year-old male, who left the following message on the answering machine of his previous seventh- and eighth-grade teacher and her daughters:

> Yo, . . . I hope your crotch hole's big enough for the size of my penis because I'm sure as hell sticking it in. Don't you forget this night. Call me back at _____ or else I'll be there before 7 to stab your ass and your whole family . . . and watch your house mischief night 'cause it could get bombed, bombed, BOMBED!

    The examination of numerous acts of graffiti and phone harassment without a recognized offender exemplify the challenge of identifying and processing bias-motivated acts. This analysis not only demonstrated the processes by which criminal justice officials distinguish, classify, and label offenses as "motivated by bias", but also compiled examples of the language and/or behaviors used by offenders to intimidate and harass victims.

DISCUSSION

Bias-motivated offenses stretch across a continuum of actions comprised of low-level acts of nuisance to serious acts of violence. While legislators, government officials, and court employees largely focus on the impact and handling of the severe end of the continuum, it is the more commonplace acts of bias that include varying forms of harassment and intimidation that have a profound impact on communities. Penalty enhancements have been implemented to address serious bias-motivated crimes involving murders, yet few alternatives have been employed to address what is often regarded as inconsequential acts of bias such as name-calling, harassment, and intimidation.

    This study confirmed the complexity of determining which offenses represented bias crimes, and which involved criminal behaviors without a bias motivation. Various files documented cases involving criminal acts such as assault, harassment, threatening behavior, and spitting on others, yet they did not constitute a bias crime. According to the Bias Crime Unit, during these criminal offenses, the offender may have used a prejudiced epithet to demean the victim further, but the offense did not constitute a bias crime since the actual crime was not motivated by hatred or bias.

    The investigative reports from County Y's Prosecutor's Office illustrated how incidents located in the lower and middle ranges of the continuum of bias-motivated behaviors were handled both formally and informally within the criminal justice system, while also delineating the distinctions between bias-motivated incidents and bias-motivated crimes. As a result of the numerous acts of graffiti, vandalism, and phone/mail harassment, apprehending the offenders was rather challenging and many cases had to be closed until further information leading to the identity of a suspect surfaced. Since these acts of harassment and destruction accounted for 127 out of 140 reported offenses, it is no wonder that so many cases were unsolved and "closed, pending" the discovery of further information.

The examination of the more common, yet less serious, acts of bias revealed that criminal justice agencies often handle low-level offenses informally outside the criminal justice system in collaboration with agencies such as schools or social service organizations. While County Y is very dedicated and devoted to the fight to suppress bias crimes, this raises issues about the numerous criminal justice agencies, including law enforcement and prosecutors, who do not have an established policy. What happens to these "low-level" acts of bias in counties with no official commitment toward addressing *all* bias crimes?

Unlike most previous research, the majority of offenders in this study found to have been involved in a bias act acted alone, and 25 percent acted in groups of two or more offenders. Although these findings may appear surprising, upon further analysis, one can recognize that 44 out of 57 incidents perpetrated by a single offender consisted of phone harassment, verbal slurs, threats, or harassment. Thirty-three out of the forty-four were verbal slurs that would typically not be considered crimes. Furthermore, bias-motivated acts perpetrated through the phone, e-mail, the postal service, or in written publications may also be recorded as being committed by a single offender, when in actuality, several offenders may have participated in the bias behavior.

Both national statistics and the findings of this study indicate the importance of paying attention to the behaviors situated at the less serious segment of the continuum of bias-motivated behaviors. In one of the narratives, the juveniles who robbed Latinos expressed the opportunistic nature of the attacks since the victims may be afraid of reporting their crimes to the police due to language barriers.

While the narratives of the bias-motivated offenses demonstrate the range and scope of bias acts within one county, it also demonstrates the number of victims who are reluctant to file formal charges in bias-motivated offenses. Several of the bias-motivated dilemmas between neighbors resulted in the victim requesting that prosecutors speak with the offender, but not file formal charges. It is possible that, for these victims, "not rocking the boat" remains the preferred manner of maintaining the delicate balance between safety and neighborly hospitality. It is possible that victims whose offender involves a neighbor may be afraid of the possibility of increased hostility if the criminal justice system formally sanctions their neighbor-aggressor. If this is the case, the justice system and social organizations need to collaborate to find alternatives that limit the victim's fear and intervene with the offender in a manner that promotes safety for everyone in the community.

The Los Angeles County District Attorney's Office and the Anti-Defamation League have been at the forefront of creating diversion programs specifically designed for youthful offenders involved in bias-motivated behaviors. The Juvenile Offenders

Learning Tolerance program sponsored by the Los Angeles County District Attorney's and the Anti-Defamation League's Diversion Program offer youthful offenders involved in acts of bias an opportunity to attend the program as part of their probation sentence (Steinberg, Brooks, and Remtulla 2003). Both programs seek to aid offenders in understanding the consequences of their actions, yet the influence of these programs is limited since they are only available in a handful of locations throughout the country. While it is unknown whether diversion programs have an effect on offenders of bias crimes, studies have shown that offenders whose prejudiced behaviors are not interrupted will continue to escalate their level of bias-motivated behaviors.

The greatest contribution of this review is the possibility of viewing bias-motivated incidents as opportunities for improving community safety by systematically addressing bias acts committed in the low-to-middle ranges of the continuum. A large number of the incidents reported to the Prosecutor's Office were committed by offenders engaged in multiple offenses. With the proper intervention with these repeat offenders and intervention in what may be deemed as acts of bias located within the low-to-mid range of the bias-motivated continuum, one may generate significant change in the fight against prejudice and intolerance.

CONCLUSION AND POLICY IMPLICATIONS

The number of bias-motivated offenses remains relatively low compared to other crimes, yet bias crimes and bias incidents have the ability to broadcast a threatening message to all members of the community. Despite the fact that police and prosecutors are mandated by federal and state law, each agency enforces and carries out the law using different protocols according to the varying values of its leaders and the citizenry's priorities. This study focused on the types of cases recorded by the County Y Prosecutor's Office and provided a compilation of descriptive narratives that reveal the nature of these incidents. Without the narrative of the events, the term *harassment* cannot quite convey the same image as the description of the actual words left on a phone answering machine. While the sample size of prosecutorial investigation reports remains relatively low, the focus of this study was intended to expose the types of offenses coming to the attention of criminal justice professionals, provide a description of the events, and elucidate the bias crime designation process at the prosecutorial level.

In looking at 140 cases investigated by the Bias Crime Unit, only 28 cases were confirmed to be bias-motivated, while the remaining files were categorized as "no bias motivation" (50), "closed pending further information" (61), or "false claims" (1). Of the 28 cases investigated by the County Y Prosecutor's Office confirmed to be bias-motivated offenses, in two instances, the same defendants pled guilty to having participated in several bias-motivated events. Two separate pairs of juveniles, who committed numerous bias acts, accounted for 7 of the 28 bias crimes. Of these confirmed bias-motivated cases, 14 were processed formally through the courts, while another 14 were handled informally through mediation, a written apology, or other informal means after the victim chose not to file a formal complaint.

The analysis of the data gathered in the study has clear implications for both policymakers and other officials. By including acts of bias deemed less serious, this study shows the ambiguities in classifying the lower-level offenses. Quite often, it is the actions of offenders involved in bias-based murders that impact policy more severely than the numerous less lethal acts that are often disregarded as too time-consuming for consideration. Although bias-motivated homicides are more rare than acts of assault and intimidation, studies have documented offenders convicted in more violent bias-motivated attacks admitting to involvement in numerous bias-motivated assaults for which they were not apprehended (Ituarte 2000).

Bias-motivated offenders often begin with small acts of bias and desist their participation in these acts through the mere maturation process. Yet, a small number continue to increase the intensity of their bias actions. Although researchers do not know why some offenders choose to engage in bias-motivated behaviors while others engage in others forms of criminal behavior, this researcher recommends a further examination into the creation of multi-agency collaborations coordinated to design appropriate prevention and intervention strategies at the early stages of apprehension in order to prevent more heinous bias-motivated offenses later on. This study is a first step toward recognizing the need for sanctions that specifically address the acts of lower-level bias-motivated offenders who account for the majority of the bias acts.

REFERENCES

ANTI-DEFAMATION LEAGUE (2003). *Hate Crime Laws.* New York, NY.

BELL, J. (2002). *Policing Hatred: Law Enforcement, Civil Rights, and Hate Crime.* New York, NY: New York University Press.

CRIMINAL JUSTICE STATISTICS CENTER (1997). *Hate Crimes.* Sacramento, CA: California Department of Justice, Division of Criminal Justice Information Services. Hate Crimes Statistical Reports: A Policymaker's Guide to Hate Crimes Monograph.

HEREK, G. M., and K. T. BERRILL (Eds.). (1992). *Hate Crimes: Confronting Violence Against Lesbians and Gays.* Newbury Park, CA: Sage.

ITUARTE, S. (2000). *Inside the Mind of Hate: Ethnographic Case Studies of Bias-Motivated Offenders.* Unpublished doctoral dissertation, Rutgers University.

JENNESS, V. Policing Hatred: Law Enforcement, Civil rights, and Crime. *American Journal of Sociology*: 1410–1413.

JENNESS, V., and R. GRATTET (2005). The Law-in-between: The effects of organizational perviousness on the policing of hate crime. *Social Problems* 52(3): 337–359.

NOLAN, J., and Y. AKIYAMA (2002). Assessing the climate for hate-crime reporting in law enforcement organizations: A force-field analysis. *Justice Professional* 15(2): 87–103.

NOLAN, J., J. McDEVITT, and S. CRONIN (2004). Learning to see hate crime: A framework for understanding and clarifying ambiguities in bias crime classifications. *Criminal Justice Studies* 17(1): 91–105.

SPILLANE, L. A. (1994). Hate crimes: A legal perspective. In *Multicultural Perspectives in Criminal Justice and Criminology,* ed. J. E. Hendrichs and B. Byers. Springfield, IL: Charles C. Thomas.

SOUTHERN POVERTY LAW CENTER (2001). *The Mathematics of Hate. Intelligence Reporter.* Montgomery, AL: Author.

STEINBERG, A., J. BROOKS, and T. REMTULLA (2003). Youth hate crimes: Identification, prevention, and intervention. *American Journal of Psychiatry* 160: 979–989.

UNITED STATES DEPARTMENT OF JUSTICE (1997 and 1998). *Hate Crimes Statistics 1997*. Washington, DC: Uniform Crime Report.

UNITED STATES DEPARTMENT OF JUSTICE (1997). *Hate Crimes Statistics 1996*. Washington, DC: Uniform Crime Report.

UNITED STATES DEPARTMENT OF JUSTICE (1990). *Hate Crime Data Collection Guidelines*. Washington, DC: Federal Bureau of Investigation.

WILSON, M., and B. RUBACK (2003, June). Hate crimes in Pennsylvania, 1984–99: Case characteristics and police responses. *Justice Quarterly* 20(2): 373–399.

Chapter 25

The Evolution of the Local Prosecutor from Case Processor to Community Problem-Solver

M. Elaine Nugent-Borakove and Gerard Rainville

INTRODUCTION

In recent years, much of the attention paid to prosecution in the research literature deals with the community prosecution movement, which is generally thought to represent a new way of thinking about case processing and maintaining public order through community involvement and the use of varied enforcement methods, including problem-solving techniques (Nugent, Fanflik, and Bromirski 2004). The common notion about community prosecution is that it is borne out of the successes with community policing (Coles and Kelling 1999).

This chapter explores developments in prosecution that suggest the community prosecution movement is not a mere adjunct of community policing. Rather, many of the seeds for community prosecution can be found as far back as the Colonial era. As our nation grew, decisions about the political placement of the prosecutor in the governmental structure, the resources and jurisdiction of prosecutors' offices, and the types of discretionary powers afforded the prosecutor also evolved. Over time, the American prosecutor increasingly became an elected official who managed increasingly larger offices of assistant prosecutors working to process increasingly large numbers of criminal cases. Though this evolution of the prosecutor's role led to a routinized and efficient production of sanctions, many recognized that it was not truly producing a brand of "justice" that benefited communities. Ultimately, modern prosecutors, now with the resources of large offices and recognized public authority, turned to the community to determine the nature of "justice" that best suited the populations they served. In regarding the community as the main patron of the services of prosecutors, the modern American prosecutor harkens back to earlier prosecutors who argued cases that were directly initiated by community members.

A detailed consideration of the history of American prosecution shows that the modern community prosecution movement should not be seen as a sudden departure from the traditional, routinized case-processing model, but rather a "coming full circle" in the evolution of prosecution. That is, prosecutors did not become aware of the community in recent times, rather they returned to the community, once again, to better define the justice needs of the populace.

The evolutionary path of the American prosecutor can be divided into three relatively distinct periods. Each period represents a differing prosecutorial model. Table 25.1 summarizes these time periods and some of the defining features of the different models.

The proposed thesis in the development of community prosecution is that the American prosecutor, in the period of the office's development, provided direct service to their patrons (i.e., the monarchy, crime victims, public order). In the traditional model, prosecutors grew increasingly removed from their earlier patrons as responsiveness was less critical than processing the growing number of cases endemic to a rapidly growing population. These cases were met almost entirely with criminal sanctions. In fact, two different but intertwined types of prosecution strategies seemed to emerge—one focused on swift investigation and prosecution of criminal matters and the other focused on due process (Packer 1968). Ultimately, however, the due process strategy was destined to fail (discussed later in this chapter) because the resources of the justice system cannot keep

TABLE 25.1   Three Models of Prosecution and Their Features

Prosecution Model	Time Period	Prosecutor Role	Methods	Patrons
Developmental	Colonial era to the Civil War	An appointed official or an attorney hired by victims	Patron/victim advocacy at trial	The monarchy; crime victims; increasingly, the states' interest in public safety
Traditional	Civil War to early 1970s	Generally an elected official	Case-processing sanctioning	Public safety interest of the state
Community Prosecution	Early 1970s to present	Remains an elected official	Case-processing, victim advocacy, community-based initiatives, law enforcement coordination	Public safety interest of the state; victims and those affected by disorder (those in at-risk communities)

pace with a continually increasing caseload, which in turn causes prosecutors to look to the public to help guide priorities (Packer 1970; Roach 1999). In the community prosecution model, various shortcomings of traditional prosecution (such as over-sanctioning) were realized and prosecutors turned to the community, their initial patrons, both to identify the justice needs prosecutors should serve and the alternative, often non-sanctioning, means of seeing justice done.

A HISTORY OF PROSECUTION AND KEY EVENTS[1]

A number of scholars have sought to uncover the origins of the American local prosecutor, who is unlike any other prosecutor in the world (see, e.g., Alstyne 1952; Jacoby 1980; Kress 1976; Wickersham Commission 1968). Virtually everyone who has explored local prosecution has a different opinion about the basis for the role and function of the Colonial prosecutor and how this prosecutor evolved from a relatively minor actor to become the gatekeeper for the criminal justice system with tremendous power over individuals' life and liberty. One thing is clear, however, the local prosecutor's role has slowly and steadily expanded over the past 300 years to become one of the most powerful, yet understudied figures in the American judicial system. Though there are bound to be gaps and guesswork in any history of American prosecution, it is useful to synthesize what is known (and generally accepted) about prosecution at various points in our history as well as the context that may have shaped different roles that prosecutors undertook in their evolution. Table 25.2 shows the timeline for the evolution of American prosecutors.

THE DEVELOPMENTAL PERIOD OF THE AMERICAN PROSECUTOR

A nation founded initially as 13 colonies, all of which sought to tailor their own individual forms of governance is bound to have differences in their approach to crime and justice. Thus, it is not surprising that the history of the prosecutor is quite varied across the colonies as shown in Table 25.2. However, there are several general readily discernible patterns in the development of the local prosecution function, particularly in terms of the structural and legal decisions that occurred in the prosecutor's early history. Structural changes and legal decisions affecting prosecution in the United States can be seen as an ongoing attempt to resolve two seemingly contradictory ideals—that of a rigorous, independent prosecution function and that of one in which the public plays an active role in guiding and controlling the output of law enforcement agencies (DiFederico 1998).

---

[1]It is important to note that in Colonial America, a system of federal prosecution was emerging concurrently with state and local prosecutorial functions. Although the developments that led to the modern day U.S. Department of Justice, U.S. Attorney General, and U.S. Attorney system are important in the overall history of prosecution, their function was largely to protect government interests and the prosecution of violations of federal law. As such, this chapter deals exclusively with the state and local prosecutorial function.

TABLE 25.2 Timeline of Significant Changes in State and Local Prosecution and Key Events Shaping Prosecution

Date	Event
1643	Officer appointed to the courts in Virginia to represent the King (role was largely advisory and was only directly involved with the violation involved royal interest)
1653	Presiding officer, or *schout*, used in some colonies (New York and New Jersey, for example) to present criminal charges against defendants (received complaints from citizens, took statements, and collected available evidence)—police/prosecutor function
1653	First case in which *schout* was recorded acting as the prosecutor in court
1662	William Pitkin appointed to serve as county attorney in Hartford, Connecticut
1665	English law provided for sheriff in former Dutch settlements and the *schout* had performed the functions of a sheriff, who apparently continued on as the prosecutor even under English rule
1674	English common law again established in Dutch colonies and *schout* disappeared formally but informally function remained in the sheriff's office
1676	Governor of Delaware directed sheriff to act as principal officer in the execution of laws, and who subsequently acted as a prosecutor in the Delaware courts
1676	Pennsylvania governor appointed attorney general for the colony who in turn appointed deputy attorneys general
1685	Provincial Council of Pennsylvania appointed prosecuting attorney for Philadelphia County
1687	Virginia attorney general appointed deputy attorneys general to outlying counties
1704	Connecticut assembly passed a law creating public prosecutors offices province-wide
1711	All Virginia deputies handling serious criminal matters; local men were nominated to serve as deputy attorney general
1732	Virginia counties began paying for deputies
1738	North Carolina passed law authorizing deputy attorneys general for every county
1704	Connecticut abandoned private prosecutors and named public prosecutors, included in this was the authority to investigate crimes and to prosecute offenses
1691–1721	Courts of original jurisdiction were being adopted in many colonies
1751	Virginia ordered all witnesses and accusers to confer with the deputy attorneys general, granting them the opportunity to review charges and make charging decisions

Date	Event
1789	Primary responsibility for prosecution was in the hands of local officials
1789	U.S. district attorneys provided for by the judiciary act appointing lawyers to each U.S. district
End of seventeenth century	System of public prosecution established
1798	Georgia allowed citizens to elect judges
1807–1846	Mississippi created separate attorney general and prosecuting attorneys' offices in which PA's were elected by district; followed by Alabama in 1819; Ohio, Indiana, Illinois, Rhode Island, New York, Pennsylvania, Delaware, Georgia
1812	Los Angeles's constitution established the office of the prosecuting attorney as separate and apart from the attorney general
1832	Mississippi was the first state to include a provision in its constitution for the popular election of prosecuting attorneys
1850	Prosecuting attorneys generally provided for in state constitutions
1883	*People v. Wabash, St. Louis and Pacific Railway,* Illinois Court of Appeals uphold the discretionary power of the prosecutor
End of nineteenth century	Plea bargaining was widely used in the disposition of cases
1912	New Mexico provided for prosecuting attorney by law
1912	Prosecutor was primary representative of the public in criminal law and the "process of consolidating prosecutorial power and discretion in the local prosecuting attorneys had been completed"
1920–1930	States began bypassing the grand jury process, allowing prosecutors to file criminal charges by information
1960s–1970s	Prosecutors began using mediation and arbitration to dispose of certain types of crimes
1980–1990s	First few prosecutors began assigning prosecutors to the community in what become known as community prosecution
1960s	Antiwar movements, civil rights protests, antigovernment demonstrations drew attention to the disconnects between the public and the criminal justice system (mostly focused on police)
1967	President Johnson's Commission on Law Enforcement and Administration of Justice shaped modern criminal justice policy to ensure lawful investigations and to improve relations with minority communities
1984	Victims of Crime Act was passed
1986	Anti-Drug Abuse Act was passed, increasing penalties for drug offenses and adding more drugs to the list of scheduled, illegal narcotics increasing caseloads across the country

It may be appropriate that little is known about the origin of prosecution in the American colonies. The proto-prosecutor would certainly have been a minor character in that prosecution functions were dependent on populations large enough to warrant a court system. The authority to create such court systems was a second prerequisite to a prosecution function. In the early Colonial period, no such system was in place owing to the British government claiming the sole right to establish courts and a sparse (there were only 2,499 colonists in 1620) and diffuse population in the colonies (Jacoby 1997a). As may be appropriate for small, independent, and totally homogenous colonies, the legal authorities were not differentiated from the community leaders.

The earliest courts were tribunals in which governors heard criminal cases introduced directly by victims. There was no trained bar and no advocacy function. As such, the treatment of legal questions in these tribunals were not bound by any one discernible legal or ethical principle but reflected the varied natures and purposes of colonies such as the ecclesiastical Plymouth colony and the business enterprise of Jamestown, Virginia. When colonies grew large enough to warrant a permanent court structure, advocacy systems that were slightly more advanced than the tribunals were established. However, there was some tension as to which parties these systems would serve and as such creating ambiguity about which official or combination of officials can be viewed as the precursor to the modern prosecutor.

Although the various colonies had differing arrangements for addressing prosecution, there were two historical officials who generally operated on a colony-wide level—the King's attorney and the attorney general. A series of other justice actors (some of whom evolved from the previous officials) were the precursors to the modern local prosecutor, including the Dutch *schout*, the deputy attorney general, the county attorney, and others.

Colony-wide Prosecutors—The King's Attorney

Though a dubious precursor to the American prosecutor, the King's attorney was among the earliest actors in the American justice system (on the prosecution side). As would be expected, attorneys for the Crown were mainly concerned with matters of law related to monarchical governance (which would exclude most domestic crime). Given this, colonist victims of crime were not served very aggressively by advocates loyal to monarchs.

Colony-wide Prosecutors—The Attorney General

Even at this early stage, the public played an active role in affecting the timbre of prosecution. Given the King's attorney's lack of service to colonists, an expansion in the attorney general's role (to focus more on criminal issues) and the development of local court organizations (and local court actors) was affected. Toward the latter part of the 1600s and in the early 1700s, several colonies created a system of colony-wide prosecution— the attorney general—to represent the interests of the colony in court. Although in many of the colonies the role of the attorney general was more advisory, and in some, more investigative, this period clearly represents the first formal recognition of a "prosecutor."

First "Local" Prosecutors—The Deputy Attorneys General

In most of the colonies, within a few years of the creation of the attorney general, the governing bodies and/or the attorney general himself, recognized a need for deputy attorneys general to be assigned to outlying counties in the colony. In the latter half of the 1600s, attorneys general commonly sent deputies to the outlying counties of the Delmarva colonies to handle criminal prosecutions. These deputies instantly became figures of local importance, meeting a local demand that was wholly neglected by England and that could not be addressed directly by the attorney general. In Virginia, local men were being nominated to serve as deputy attorneys general (1711) and in 1732, counties in Virginia began paying a salary to the deputy attorneys general (Jacoby 1980; Wickersham Commission 1968).

Local Prosecutors—The Dutch *Schout*

One early precursor to the local prosecutor was found in the former Dutch colonies of New York and New Jersey. Although English common law was adopted in these regions, this prosecutor with no apparent allegiance to the monarchy undertook a few of the criminal case-processing functions associated with modern prosecutors (as well as a few of the functions of sheriffs and investigators) as early as 1653. This character, the *schout*, undertook all of these functions for fees supplied by victims. This early private prosecutor had little discretion in case screening and charging decisions as victims' willingness to pay was regarded as a fair determinant of criminal caseloads. Nonetheless, it was in these colonies that the victim (and by proxy the public) set priorities for prosecution.

Local Prosecutors—The County Attorney

By the mid-1700s, prosecutors were operating at the county level and courts of original jurisdiction were being created. As local governments continued to seek control over legal matters that did not appear to interest the monarchy (i.e., crimes of local importance), county attorneys were established. The first county attorney, William Pitkin, was appointed in Hartford, Connecticut in 1662. In 1704, Connecticut became the first colony to pass a law creating public rather than private prosecutors and named public prosecutors adjuncts to all county courts. These local prosecutors remained in the council for the Queen (of England), but were also entrusted to prosecute criminals and suppress vice, functions that were not of particular concern to the monarchy. Public prosecution, since that time, is an American trademark (though for a compelling argument that private attorneys continued to serve as prosecutors, at least in Philadelphia, during this and later periods, see Steinberg 1984). By the end of the 1700s, public prosecution in the fledging nation was largely the responsibility of local government officials (Jacoby 1980).

Though the *schout*, the deputy attorney general, and the county attorney are all examples of early local prosecutors, there are no doubt other candidates who have been lost to posterity. With what is left of the record, a distinct template for the local prosecutor has been established. These prosecutors were increasingly appointed or nominated by local courts or governments and, with the exception of the privately paid *schouts*, were public agents who took action against crime and disorder based on public priorities. Thus, at the time of American independence, the American prosecutor already resembled the modern prosecutor by serving in a local capacity as a public advocate in criminal cases. Many of the strictures upon modern prosecutors were also in place, such as due-process rights and the prohibition of double jeopardy established in the Bill of Rights. In only one regard did the early prosecutor not resemble the modern one—they were not elected officials.

Increasingly prosecutors were elected officials during the highly democratizing Jacksonian era (1820–American Civil War). In the years immediately after the Revolution, public prosecutors exercised little personal initiative (and had few clear incentives to respond to local demands) as they were often subordinates to other, appointive public officials in a very limited democracy (Jacoby 1997b). The era shortly before and after the presidency of Andrew Jackson saw an expansion of local governments and a continued decentralization of authority. This populist movement commonly altered the mode of selection for public officials. In states that had been former colonies, the appointive status of many officials (notably the prosecutor) was often retained. However, as the country expanded westward, states entering the union commonly afforded for elective offices in their constitutions.

As the prosecutor was, in these times, a minor public official, few state constitutions bothered to make specific reference to the mode of selection for the office. It was not until the 1830s that state constitutions commonly specified the mode of selection for court officers. During this period, other social and demographic changes and the persistent spirit of the Progressive era all but foreclosed on the possibility of expanding the appointive status of public officials.

Inspired by the French tradition of public prosecutors (and French conceptions about the complete separation of branches of government), local prosecutors were considered to be officials in the executive branch of government rather than adjuncts to judges in the judiciary. Given this arrangement, prosecutors were not subject to judicial challenges for a failure to proceed in criminal cases. The great powers afforded to the prosecutor, as an executive agent, and the fact that many of the prosecutor's decisions were not subject to judicial review, seemingly demanded that prosecutors be subject to popular review. As such, by 1850, subsequent states entering the union provided for a publicly elected prosecutor in their constitutions or by law (Jacoby 1997c). In summary, the 1800s were marked with a period of state constitutional and legislative activity that solidified the position and function of the prosecutor as a local official and one who was generally elected to serve the people (Jacoby 1980).

The Traditional Period of the American Prosecutor

By the middle of the nineteenth century, many of the features of the modern local prosecuting attorney were fixed. The prosecuting attorney was an elected office holder with independence from judicial review. The salary of the prosecutor and his assistants, as well as the budget for the prosecutor's office, came from tax revenues (either locally and/or through grants from more centralized levels of government). Though the prosecutor of this era resembles the modern prosecutor in regard to a few key features, subsequent developments in legal markets account for a final transformation of the prosecutor. The prosecutor in 1850 had only a potential for the extensive powers now commonly associated with the prosecutor. The major developments that raised the prosecuting attorney from a minor actor to the official with "more control over life, liberty and reputation than any other person in America" (Jackson 1940) were yet to come.

The Industrial Revolution brought unprecedented population growth to cities. Opportunities in the city brought successive waves of immigrants to the United States. Both the volume of people living in urban areas as well as the heterogeneity of urban populations rendered informal solutions to deviant behavior impractical. Large bureaucracies became necessary to address increasing crime rates. A professional police force had been established in England in 1829, and this innovation was soon copied in the larger American cities. Though police in large cities like Boston and New York were largely corrupt benefactors of local political machines until the twentieth century (Sante 1993), they increasingly provided a greater volume of cases, some well-developed, to local prosecutors.

On the other end of the justice system, large penitentiaries were also built with an attendant professional correctional force. In a rapidly growing, multicultural America, appeals to community norms that could effectively guide public behavior in small, homogenous communities proved less tenable.

Additionally, the nature of many of the crimes associated with swelling growth in urban areas did not necessarily have identifiable victims. All of these developments led to a defining feature of the traditional prosecution model—as a public function. Public justice bureaucracies and diffuse victim bases spelled the last gasp of private prosecution markets (Steinberg 1984). The involvement of the private citizen was more direct in the administration of justice at earlier times. For one, a system of fees had commonly been used in cities to generate information from the public in certain serious criminal cases (McDonald 1979). Additionally, in cases handled by the Dutch *schout*, for instance, private citizens were not solely victims or witnesses, but also the complainants. With the professionalized police force as the new case initiators and the prosecutor arguing cases in the interest of the state (i.e., in criminal cases, the government served as the aggrieved party), the administration of justice was taken out of the hands of citizen/victims—to be largely taken up by growing public bureaucracies.

Prosecutors' offices expanded in an attempt to keep pace with the growth in urban populations. However, due process demands were very often at odds with increased case volumes. As such, the increased volume of crime (particularly low-level offenses) had to be met with some filtering function so that prosecutors could manage their caseloads expeditiously, yet retain a due process framework. Two prosecutorial practices developed (or were reaffirmed by case law) that enabled prosecutors to control the nature and volume of their caseloads—case-screening and plea bargains.

Case-screening

Prosecutors had the power to not prosecute (*nolle prosequi*) cases when they did not feel pursuit of such cases served the aims of justice. McDonald (1979) contends that this expanded power, on the part of prosecutors, encroached on the traditional case-initiation domain of police. It is equally likely that prosecutors, by establishing standards for accepting cases (such as a "trial-sufficiency" standard), refined police work by failing to reinforce police effort on weak (in terms of investigative effort or in regard to the offense's level of harm) cases (Mellon, Jacoby, and Brewer 1981). If we regard the prosecutor nobly in that regard, we may also suggest, cynically, that it may not be a historical coincidence that the demise of the private prosecution market, in which prosecutors took fees related to all criminal complaints, led to a desire to screen out a large portion of cases.

The factors that govern a prosecutor's decision to "screen out" a case may just as readily relate to evidentiary (Boland, Mahanna, and Sones 1992; Feeney, Dill, and Weir 1983; Forst, Lucianovic, and Cox 1977) or non-evidentiary considerations (Adams and Cutshall 1987; Spears and Spohn 1997). Whatever the case, the prosecutor's discretion in opting not to prosecute has been repeatedly affirmed by post–Civil War case law (*Milliken v. Stone* 1925; *People v. Wabash St. Louis and Pacific Railway* 1883) as not subject to judicial review. This power can certainly introduce accountability issues where citizens desire prosecutorial resources to be devoted to cases of local importance but prosecutors establish other prosecutorial priorities. The complexities of the question "Who should serve as the gatekeeper to the justice system?" led to initial uncertainties as to whether a single uniform standard could be developed in all localities. The Wickersham Commission (1968) failed to specify which party (police or prosecutor) to be entrusted with this power, weakly suggesting that the question required additional study. In 1967, the President's Commission of Law Enforcement and Administration of Justice endorsed the prosecutor as the party to bring criminal charges as well as condoning high rates of screened out cases (to better focus prosecutorial resources on worthy cases). Finally, in 1970, the American Bar Association (ABA) stated that the decision to initiate criminal proceedings needed to be entrusted to a professional, public official (American Bar Association 1993). Alluding to the elective status of the chief prosecutor as well as a general educational advantage of prosecutors over police, the ABA helped to solidify the prosecutor's domain over case initiation decisions.

Plea Bargaining

Once a complaint passes the screening stage and becomes a formal criminal case, the prosecutor enjoys a second arena of choice—whether to accept a plea or to take the case to trial. Prior to the Civil War, the plea bargain was not a generally available method of case disposition. By the end of the nineteenth century, plea bargains were the norm (Moley 1929). Again, the terms of the plea bargain (which are explicated by judges to defendants) are not commonly overturned. As such, prosecutors can process more cases by accepting pleas, potentially in exchange for significant concessions in the defendant's sanction (see Alschuler (1968) and Boland and Forst (1985) for divergent views on the extent of concessions). Compelling efficiency arguments exist for the plea bargain (most notably Easterbrook 1983; Landes 1971), while arguments against the plea bargain commonly appeal to moral intuition (Kipnis 1976; Palmer 1975). The merits of such policies are not addressed here. However, the transformation of the justice system from a jury-based to a plea-based system provides another characteristic of the traditional prosecutor—an actor who influences the entry of cases into the formal criminal justice system, as well as affecting the ultimate disposition of such cases. All of these choices are subjected to no external review—save that of the electorate.

The Community Prosecution Period of the American Prosecutor

By the early 1970s, the American prosecutor had reached the zenith of their traditional role. Their main focus was to maintain public safety through expeditious criminal case processing and sanctioning. Public accountability seemed assured, to prosecutors at least, by their elective status and operation in a professionalized, publicly funded justice system with an evolved legal framework. In spite of this, social changes led many communities and prosecutors to realize that "justice" as it was needed at that moment was not being produced through traditional prosecution means.

In a timely theoretical development, two models of prosecution were identified in the late 1960s that led to a rethinking of the roles of prosecutors (Packer 1968) among policy makers:

- The crime control model focused on the system's capacity to efficiently and effectively repress criminal conduct through enforcement, arrest, conviction, and punishment. The swift and expeditious pursuit of justice is paramount.

- The due process model, on the other hand, focuses on the structure and operations of law and the criminal prosecution. Under this model, the prosecutor is more concerned with procedural accuracy and the reliability of the investigative process.

Interestingly, despite its focus on enforcement and deterrence, the crime control model outlined by Packer provided an early recognition that the capacity of the judicial system was simply not sufficient to handle the volume of criminal cases. Moreover, for certain types of offenses like gambling, prostitution, public intoxication, and drug crimes, noncriminal sanctions might be better suited for dealing with the behaviors than criminal sanctions (Packer 1970; Roach 1999).

Whereas Packer's (1970) models focused on societal interests with regard to crime and the rights of persons accused of crimes, Roach's (1999) models were victim-centered. Driven by a greater understanding of victims and victimization revealed in research conducted in the 1970s and 1980s, the new models offered by Roach include "a punitive model of victims' rights which relies upon the criminal sanction and punishment, and a non-punitive model of victims' rights which stresses crime prevention and restorative justice" (p. 699). It is the latter of these models that provides additional insight into change that was occurring in the justice system at the time, and in particular with prosecutors, suggesting that crime prevention and intervention can help to control crime and that future attempts to respond to crime include the nonpunitive model (Roach 1999).

Though theory is useful for framing observations about changes in society, there is nothing comparable to sweeping societal changes when it comes to factors that affect our core institutions. In the latter half of the 1900s there were many changes in the legislative and social fabric of the country, some of which had direct bearing on changes in prosecution. Among the key events in the late twentieth century were the protests, civil rights movement, and antigovernment sentiment in the 1960s that led to calls for reform in the justice system. Later as drugs emerged in urban areas, passage of laws designed to increase penalties for drug use created huge backlogs in the justice system (Zimring and Hawkins 1988). At the same time, there was an increasing recognition that prosecutors specifically needed to pay more attention to victims and their restoration following a crime, which resulted in the passage of the Victims of Crime Act that was later enacted in nearly every state.

The events of the latter half of the twentieth century, along with the tremendous power afforded to prosecutors in the early formulation of the role, set the stage for another round of significant changes in prosecution. These changes were borne in part out of necessity to configure modern prosecution with modernist ideologies, but also a desire to truly have an impact on crimes that most immediately affect victims or victim classes (such as at-risk communities).

In the 1960s and 1970s, there was increasing recognition that prosecutors must play a role other than just the enforcer of state or local laws. One reason was that traditional prosecution methods simply were no longer effective. By the 1980s, there was increasing concern among prosecutors that despite all the public resources being spent on arrests and prosecutions, little seemed to be changing with regard to overall public safety. "The mounting press of arrest cases and workloads, the complex challenge of drugs in the communities, the impairment and collapse of important mediating institutions around them such as schools and families, the falling price of crime and the declining value of arrest, and the insolvency or bankruptcy of key social service and criminal justice agencies were causing fundamental shifts in prosecutors' operating styles and strategies to develop" (Tumin 1990:2).

Another reason is that the traditional sanction-based method was brutalizing communities. The incarceration binge beginning in the early 1980s caused many scholars to reconsider the ends of the American court and correctional systems (Mauer 1993; Sabol and Lynch 1997). The destabilizing effect on communities in which large percentages of community members were incarcerated for, generally, minor offenses did not appear consistent with the service-oriented, political offices of the prosecutor, judge, and chief of police (Hagan and Dinovitzer 1999). As criminal sanctions had been applied indiscriminately and without proportion to the harm of offenses, communities began to question the legitimacy of the criminal justice system (Akerlof and Yellen 1994). Whether or not police and prosecutors destabilized communities during the "get tough" years, without a doubt, these law enforcement bureaus were not particularly responsive to the needs of high-crime communities during this period (Tumin 1990).

With increasing caseloads and a recognition that not all forms of criminal offending should result in incapacitation, theorists and prosecutors got to work to explore alternatives to traditional criminal prosecution. Between 1986 and 1990, the Kennedy School of Government at Harvard University in its Executive Sessions on State and Local Prosecutors recognized the indications that change was again occurring in the nature and role of local prosecutors. From these sessions emerged several distinct, and as of that time, undocumented, prosecutorial strategies:

- Pure jurist or case processor, whose goal is efficient and equitable case processing;
- Sanction setter, whose goals are rehabilitation, retribution, and deterrence;
- Problem solver, whose goal is to prevent and control crime;

- Strategic investor, whose goal is to bolster the efficacy of prosecutors by adding capacities to respond to crime; and

- Institution builder, whose goal is to restore the social institutions that help to control crime (Tumin 1990).

What is revolutionary about these identified prosecution strategies is the inclusion of a "problem-solving" and "institution-restoring" role of prosecutors. Given that these roles were not fulfilled through traditional prosecution means, differing prosecutorial practices had to be devised. But where could prosecutors look to find a template for a new community-oriented approach to prosecution? It is popularly believed that prosecutors moved from the courtroom to the community after being inspired by the successes of the community-policing movement in the 1980s and 1990s. The emerging practices of what came to be known as community prosecution do seem, on their face, to extend from community policing, but many of these practices invariably predate community policing (in the twentieth century) or have antecedents in eras before the traditional prosecution period. These community-oriented prosecution practices are discussed below.

Mediation, Arbitration, and Victim Restoration

Faced with growing case backlogs, systems delays, and the costs of processing high volumes of minor criminal offenses, prosecutors and courts began looking at alternatives to traditional case processing for low-level offenses as early as the late 1960s. In particular, prosecutors began exploring mediation and arbitration, attempting to divert less-serious criminal matters and family disputes from criminal caseloads. Using administrative hearings to provide the opportunity for the "victim" to confront the "victimizer," the focus was on resolving the dispute in lieu of criminal charges thus preventing the cases from becoming criminal matters and resolving the problems at hand (McGillis 1997; Palmer 1975).

Law Enforcement Coordination and Vertical Prosecution

Specialized prosecutorial units or dedicated attorneys "partner" with law enforcement agencies in coordinated task forces (Jacoby and Gramckow 1994). As such, prosecutors, through active coordination with police, may address specific forms of crime of greatest concern to community members. Of note is that crimes that communities identify as endemic are not necessarily the ones that are addressed well in a traditional case-processing model. A targeted enforcement effort on methamphetamines, street-walkers, or car thefts will invariably channel more offenders who employ these modes than the traditional case-initiation dynamic will. With an increased focus on crimes that communities identify as problematic, greater law enforcement coordination will lessen the impact of these particular crimes on communities.

Once cases are initiated through task forces or other coordinated efforts, a second practice associated with community prosecution provides for a swifter and more certain deterrent–vertical prosecution. Vertical prosecution is the practice of assigning the same prosecutor to a case from initial charging through disposition. This practice necessitates witnesses relaying their testimony to only a single attorney, further reducing the costs associated with coordinating witnesses and seeking convictions (Forst 2000). The expertise of these specialized attorneys (and their inherent familiarity with a case at each juncture) expedites the processing of such cases—providing a ready deterrent for a crime that communities desire to see addressed.

This practice harkens back to the all-encompassing role of early prosecutors in serving as sheriff, investigator, and trial advocate for community-initiated criminal cases. In the modern context, this role is not supported by fees from victims to a private agent willing to handle the case (as had been the case with various proto-prosecutors and the *schout*), but to a public prosecutor with the authority and public resources to address the crime problems identified by communities and who attains some economy of scale in doing so. The diffuse roles of the prosecutor were noted by Wickersham, but appear to refer more to the prosecutor of old than to Wickersham's contemporaries—

> The prosecuting attorney has or undertakes to exercise four quite different functions, namely, the function of a criminal investigator, concurrently with the sheriff or police and the coroner; in substance the function of a magistrate in determining who shall be prosecuted and who brought to trial and who not; the function of a solicitor in preparing cases for trial; and that of an advocate in trying them and in arguing appeals. (Wickersham 1968:12)

Problem Solving

It is a truism that community prosecution requires increased interaction with community members (Stevens 1994; Weinstein 1998). When prosecutors increase their interaction with community members, they discover that many of the problems confronting communities are informal in nature, may be relatively easy to address, and often require strategies other than the use of traditional criminal sanctions. As such, prosecutors working in the community prosecution vein may help out with informal problems of local importance that require little legal action (Boland 1996, 1998a,b). If the timbre of prosecutorial effort in targeted communities is to be established by the communities themselves, local demands, and prosecutorial responses to them, may require a good deal of legal flexibility. Although many community prosecutors retain their case-processing, sanction-setting role for crimes that are best addressed by sanctions, for informal problems, their arsenal has to expand. In fact, the elements that distinguish community prosecution from "traditional" prosecution include the use of varied enforcement methods, including problem-solving techniques to address lower-level quality of life crimes, as well as community partnerships (Nugent, Fanflik, and Bromirski 2004).

In jurisdictions where community prosecution is practiced, citizens have greater access to prosecutors and may work to influence the development of overarching office policy and prosecution priorities (Boland 1996; Coles and Kelling 1999). Through this process, the strategies used by community-based prosecutors often turn from attaining criminal convictions to solving community problems and addressing quality of life concerns (Nugent, Fanflik, and Bromirski 2004; Weinstein 1998). These strategies reflect the "grassroots" tenets of community-based approaches, generally necessitating meeting with and attempting to understand and address the demands of the prosecutor's constituency

(Boland 1998a). Nonetheless, in this regard, community prosecution may represent a slight return to a period when citizens and victims had a more active role in the pursuit of justice. The focus on nuisance abatement, informal problems, and general sources of community disorder also harkens back to the post-revolutionary prosecutor who, unyoked from service to the Crown, assumed responsibilities for matters of greater concern to domestic communities. Nelson (1974) notes that to maintain general order, post-revolutionary prosecutors began to assume increased responsibilities for matters such as public order crimes, drunkenness, and other actions that did not involve identifiable victims, but rather a diffuse victim class.

DISCUSSION

In spite of views that community prosecution involved some sort of revolutionary shift in thinking, the prosaic truth is that no aspect of it was directly borrowed nor created of whole cloth. Community prosecution's focus on mediation, arbitration, and victim restoration predates the community policing movement. The law enforcement coordination and vertical prosecution practices of community prosecution do nothing so much as remind us that the precursor to the traditional prosecutor was a jack of all trades in the justice system—serving as sheriff, investigator, and trial advocate. Finally, community prosecution's focus on problem solving and lower-level offenses recalls the public order focus of pre-revolutionary prosecutors.

Taken as a whole, community prosecution returns the prosecutor full circle to an awareness that the public is the patron of justice services. It is on this latter point that community prosecution appears to be such a stunning development. In that community prosecutors seem to have rediscovered their populist roots after the high orthodoxy of their traditional case-processing period is somewhat miraculous. The evolution of the American prosecutor presents an actor who adapts to the times, sometimes with grace, sometimes without mercy. However, no matter how far societal forces cause prosecutors to stray from first principles, they eventually return to the realization that they do not serve some abstraction such as "the state's interests" or "crime control," rather they serve real people with real interests in their communities. These communities are more complex than were the early American colonies. This only necessitates new tools for serving the modern community, but the principle remains the same as when we were a fledgling nation.

Certainly it is clear that the arrival at community prosecution has been a long, dynamic process. As the nation and the public deal with new challenges—terrorism, global threats, technology crimes, and advances in scientific evidence, to name a few—will prosecutors again undergo transformation? Although community prosecution does not necessarily represent a paradigm shift, can it help meet the needs of an actively changing nation? Moreover, increasingly the federal government is taking an interest in crimes and disorder that have generally fallen under the purview of the local prosecutor. How will federalism impact the local prosecutorial function? As we move further into the twenty-first century, these questions and others will be important to the development of a continued and deeper understanding of local prosecution.

REFERENCES

ADAMS, K., and C. CUTSHALL (1987). Refusing to prosecute minor offenses: The relative influence of legal and extralegal factors. *Justice Quarterly* 4: 4.

AKERLOF, G., and J. YELLEN (1994). Gang behavior, law enforcement and community values. In *Values and public policy*, ed. H. Aaron, T. Mann, and T. Taylor, pp.173–209. Washington DC: Brookings Institute.

ALSCHULER, Al. (1968). The prosecutor's role in plea bargaining. *University of Chicago Law Review* 36: 50–112.

ALSTYNE, V. (1952). The district attorney: A historical puzzle. *Wisconsin Law Review*: 120–138.

AMERICAN BAR ASSOCIATION (1993). *Standards for Criminal Justice: Prosecution Function and Defense Function*. Chicago, IL: American Bar Association.

BOLAND, B. (1996). What is community prosecution? *National Institute of Justice Journal* 231: 35–40.

BOLAND, B. (1998a). Community prosecution: The Portland experiment. In *Community Justice*, ed. D. Karp. Lanham, MD: Rowman and Littlefield.

BOLAND, B. (1998b). Manhattan experiment: Community prosecution. In *Crime and Place: Plenary Papers of the 1997 Conference on Criminal Justice Research and Evaluation*, pp. 51–67). Washington, DC: Office of Justice Programs.

BOLAND, B., and B. FORST (1985). Prosecutors don't always aim to pleas. *Federal Probation* 49: 10–15.

BOLAND, B., P. MAHANNA, and R. SONES (1992). *The Prosecution of Felony Arrests, 1988*. Washington, DC: Bureau of Justice Statistics.

COLES, C., and G. KELLING (1999). Prevention through community prosecution. *The Public Interest* 136: 69–84.

DIFEDERICO, G. (1998). Prosecutorial independence and the democratic requirement of accountabilty in Italy. *British Journal of Criminology* 38 (3): 371–387.

EASTERBROOK, F. (1983). Criminal procedure as a market system. *Journal of Legal Studies* 12 (2): 289–332.

FEENEY, F., F. DILL, and A.WEIR (1983). *Arrests Without Conviction: How Often They Occur and Why*. Washington DC: US Government Printing Office.

FORST, B. (2000). Prosecutors discover the community. *Judicature* 84 (3): 135–141.

FORST, B., J. LUCIANOVIC, and S. COX (1977). *What Happens After Arrest?* Washington DC: Institute for Law and Social Research.

HAGAN, J., and R. DINOVITZER (1999). Collateral consequences of imprisonment for children, communities and prisoners. In *Crime and Justice: An Annual Review of Research*, pp. 26–54 Chicago: University of Chicago Press.

JACKSON, R. (1940). The federal prosecutor. *Journal of the American Judicature Society* 24: 18.

JACOBY, J. (1980). *The American Prosecutor: A Search for Identity*. Lexington, MA: Lexington Books.

JACOBY, J. (1997a, May). The American prosecutor in historical context. *The Prosecutor*: 33–38.

JACOBY, J. (1997b, October). The American prosecutor's discretionary power. *The Prosecutor*: 25–39.

JACOBY, J. (1997c, September). The American prosecutor: From appointive to elective status. *The Prosecutor*: 25–29.

JACOBY, J., and H. GRAMCKOW (1994). Prosecuting drug offenders. In *Drugs and the Criminal Justice System: Evaluating Public Policy Initiatives*, ed. D. L. MacKenzie and C. D. Uchida. Newbury Park, CA: Sage Publications.

KIPNIS, K. (1976). Criminal justice and the negotiated plea. *Ethics* 86: 46–56.

KRESS, J. (1976). Progress and prosecution. *Annals of the American Academy of Political and Social Sciences* 423: 99–116.

LANDES, W. (1971). An economic analysis of the courts. *Journal of Law and Economics* 14: 61–107.

MAUER, M. (1993). *Young Black Men and the Criminal Justice System: A Growing National Problem*. Washington, DC: The Sentencing Project.

McDONALD, W. (1979). The rosecutor's domain. In *The Prosecutor*, ed. W. McDonald, pp.15–51. London: Sage.

McGILLIS, D. (1997). Community mediation programs: Developments and challenges. In *Issues and Practices*. Washington DC: National Institute of Justice, NCJ: 165698.

MELLON, L., J. JACOBY, and M. BREWER (1981). The prosecutor constrained by his environment: A new look at discretionary justice in the United States. *Journal of Criminal Law and Criminology 72*: (1): 52–81.

MOLEY, R., (1929). The medieval colleagues of the prosecutor. In *Politics and Criminal Prosecution*, ed. R. Moley. New York: Minton, Balch & Company.

NELSON, W. (1974). Emerging notions of modern criminal law in the revolutionary era: An historic perspective. In *Criminal Justice in America*, ed. R. Quinney. Boston: Little Brown.

NUGENT, M. E., P. FANFLIK, and D. BROMIRSKI (2004). *The Changing Nature of Prosecution: Community Prosecution vs. Traditional Prosecution Approaches*. Alexandria, VA: American Prosecutors Research Institute.

PACKER, H. (1968). Two models of the criminal process. In *The Limits of the Criminal Sanction*, ed. H. Packer, pp. 149–173. UK: Stanford University Press.

PACKER, H. (1970, January). Law and order in the seventies. *New Republic* 162 (2): 12–13.

PALMER, J. (1975). Pre-arrest diversion. *Crime & Delinquency* 21 (2): 100.

ROACH, K. (1999). Four models of the criminal process. *Journal of Criminal Law & Criminology* 89 (2): 671.

SABOL, W., and J. LYNCH (1997). Did getting tough on crime pay? *Intellectual Capital* vol. 2, 39. Washington DC: Urban Institute Press.

SANTE, L. (1993). *Low life: Lures and Snares of Old New York*. New York: Farrar, Straus and Giroux.

SPEARS, J., and C. SPOHN (1997). The effect of evidence factors and victim characteristics on prosecutors' charging decisions in sexual assault cases. *Justice Quarterly* 14 (3): 501–524.

STEINBERG, A. (1984). From private prosecution to plea bargaining: Criminal prosecution, the district attorney, and American legal history. *Crime & Delinquency* 30 (4): 568–592.

STEVENS, N. (1994, March). Defining community prosecution. *The Prosecutor* 28: 13–14.

TUMIN, Z. (1990). *Summary of the proceedings: Findings and discoveries of the Harvard University executive session for state and local prosecutors at the John F. Kennedy School of Government (1986–90)*. Working Paper #90-02-05.

WEINSTEIN, S. (1998, April). Community prosecution: Community policing's legal partner. *The FBI Law Enforcement Bulletin* 67: 19–25.

WICKERSHAM COMMISSION (1968). Wickersham commission reports no. 4 report on prosecution. In *Publication No. 6 Patterson Smith Reprint Series in Criminology, Law Enforcement, and Social Problems. (Originally published by the USGPO, 1931)*. Montclair, NJ: Patterson Smith.

ZIMRING, F., and G. HAWKINS (1988). The new mathematics of imprisonment. *Crime & Delinquency* 34 (4): 425–436.

CASES

Milliken v. Stone, 7 F.2d 397, 399 (S.D.N.Y. 1925)

People v. Wabash, St Louis and Pacific Railway, 12 Ill. App. 263 (1883).

PART VI

Corrections

Chapter 26

Introduction and Overview of Correctional Counseling and Treatment

Albert R. Roberts, Ph.D., and Pia Biswas

Correctional counseling and rehabilitation, in the broadest sense, seeks to transform a convicted felon into a responsible and productive member of society. The focus in correctional counseling should be on changing behavior and helping offenders to enhance mental health and cognitive functioning as well as academic, vocational, and social skills. This chapter includes the summary findings of a nationwide survey on the state of the art of correctional counseling and treatment, staffing patterns, medical and mental health needs of offenders, and academic and vocational education programs. Twenty different state departments of corrections will be highlighted in terms of specific evidence-based assessment counseling and treatment programs.

This chapter is not designed to give definitive solutions to all problems and issues regarding correctional counseling of the offender; rather the goal is to formalize ideas, raise issues, and document best practices from which effective programs can be replicated. A foundation will be delineated so that program planners and administrators may be better able to meet the individual and special needs of the inmate population.

There is wide variation in corrections from state to state and there are differences within some states on whether or not offender counseling and treatment programs are offered on a very limited scale or on a daily and intensive level. Correctional administrators have a tremendous amount of discretionary power regarding the extent to which offenders are provided with opportunities for individual and group counseling, substance abuse treatment, academic education, or vocational training. The underlying basis of whether correctional administrators are punitive versus rehabilitation-oriented stems from their political beliefs and viewpoint of both inmates in general and specific types of offenders. We believe that through intensive counseling and treatment most offenders have the ability to change their antisocial and law-breaking patterns of behavior as long as they are motivated to change. We also firmly believe that if one treats an inmate like a wild animal and continually punish them, in all likelihood they will become more hardened and violent upon release. Therefore, the objective of this chapter is to put "corrections" back into policies and practices with offenders. This can be done when a full range of opportunities for individual and group treatment is provided to all inmates regardless of the offense they have committed.

TREATMENT STRATEGY

The availability of program and service choices should be maximized to the extent that each offender can participate in rehabilitation programs. The philosophy underlying this therapeutic approach is that each person possesses unique needs, abilities, and dispositions, and requires a flexible program. Instead of depersonalizing the offender through rigid regimentation of his or her time, attempts should be made to bolster self-confidence, individuality, and socialized identity. Most men and women have the potential to rationally and selectively plan their own destiny and come to grips with the problems of free choice in our complex industrialized society. The offender has failed in society; in order to motivate him or her for success after release, the correctional facility should resemble free society in some areas, such as providing several program options.

The offender's chances for success the second time around are diminished if conditions in prison are totally unlike those outside. "Success" in a traditional prison is dependent on the abnegation of responsibility for one's actions and passive acceptance of living conditions, food, medical services, etc. Success in the outside world, however, is not measured by those criteria but by independently meeting one's own needs, working for a living, earning a good wage, having self-confidence, and attaining prestige in the eyes of the community members. To attain success after release, the offender must be able to handle free choice wisely and make law-abiding decisions. He can benefit from intensive individual and group counseling or staff role models, but most importantly, he must be aware that to go straight and "make it" in free society depends on a willingness to work toward goals, make sacrifices, and be responsible for himself and his family. The rigid paternalistic correctional philosophy of "I know what is best for you" has failed time and time again. In a truly therapeutic correctional environment, each individual has continuous opportunities to make a number of program choices. By choosing to pursue a particular vocational area, for example, it is hoped that the inmate will learn to make rational decisions and transfer this ability to the community when he or she is released.

The organizational milieu in most correctional institutions is conflict-prone. The emphasis on security and punitive control measures exerted by custodial personnel all too often conflict with the therapeutic objectives of professionally trained treatment specialists. A treatment specialist provides supportive counseling and promotes initiative and positive self-direction among prison inmates.

Conflict arises because most correctional officers have little training in human relations and are threatened by the nonpunitive approach of treatment specialists. For example, the counselor may recommend that inmates become involved with vocational training in the sheet metal shop and may also order 20 pounds of clay for inmate hobby time. Although professional counselors recognize that clay modeling provides a healthy, nonviolent outlet for a prisoner's aggressive energies, and vocational training in a marketable skill contributes to rehabilitation goals, many guards are disdainful of such efforts, regarding them as permissive and a means of coddling the inmate. From the guard's frame of reference, the clay will only be modeled into a replica of a 38-revolver or made to resemble a man's head to be placed on a cot so as not to arouse suspicion while the inmate attempts to escape. The sheet metal shop is thought of as the place where shivs and shanks are made.

The diametrically opposed attitudes of the untrained guard and the treatment specialist undermine and inhibit the rehabilitation effort of the treatment team. The custodial orientation leads to the growth of an inmate code that requires loyalty to other inmates, opposition to the entire prison staff, and at most lip service to so-called treatment programs.

There are several different conceptions of the ideal characteristics of therapeutic milieu, but the most significant aspect is that, if the inmate is to achieve any self-respect, he must be treated as an individual worthy of the respect of others. When both professional and nonprofessional staff work together to provide a therapeutic atmosphere and when inmates have the opportunity to make decisions and choose program options, the necessary climate for a therapeutic milieu emerges. Early rehabilitation efforts overlooked the relationship between fostering positive attitudes and values and building the offender's initiative, self-direction, and responsibility.

If rehabilitation is to be a reality, the development of a therapeutic community is of paramount importance. In accordance with the psychotherapeutic ideals of Maxwell Jones, a therapeutic community allows the inmate to "act out" within acceptable limits and to become motivated to participate in the available rehabilitation programs. The major objective is to reverse the regimented authoritarian structure of traditional prisons by encouraging communication between all levels of staff and between staff and inmates.

Several therapeutic communities can be set up at each correctional facility so that inmates can begin to act responsibly for the welfare of their community. Although it is more difficult to initiate therapeutic communities in the highly regimented structure of most maximum-security institutions, they can be developed and operated effectively. In maximum-security prisons, each tier or cell block can be a therapeutic community; in minimum-security settings, the location of the community can be a dormitory. Within these physical confines, the inmates and staff make collective decisions based on democratic principles. Examples of some of the decisions that could be made include permitting inmates with minimum-security ratings to attend a funeral of a close family member in another state without a guard, allowing the better-educated inmates to tutor educationally disadvantaged adults in an inner-city basic education program, initiating a program to train inmates and guards to work as crisis counselors on a prison suicide prevention team, and suspending a correctional officer who takes it upon himself to harass the inmates by turning off the television 15 minutes before the suspenseful climax of the Wednesday night movie.

The primary goal of comprehensive therapeutic services is to help the offender build self-esteem, adjust to the correctional facility, learn to communicate more effectively with family and community members, and be able to confront and act upon alternatives available as he or she considers his or her future. In some cases, these goals can be accomplished through the individual's informal everyday contact with staff and through the group counseling sessions. In many other cases, individual methods of treatment will be more beneficial.

INTERNAL VERSUS EXTERNAL CONTROL

Individual and group counseling is encouraged for all committed offenders. Several techniques of counseling should be employed by the staff in fostering an offender's increased self-awareness of self-destructive patterns and appropriate alternative behaviors. Some of the available treatment approaches are behavioral diagnosis, cognitive-behavioral treatment, counseling with focus on internal–external locus of control, milieu therapy, family counseling, psychodrama, and guided group interaction.

Counselors and other correctional treatment specialists are concerned with determining why some inmates seem motivated to try to reach socially acceptable goals, while other inmates do not seem to try any task or expend any goal-oriented effort. Characteristics of inmates who do not manifest goal-oriented behavior are feelings of helplessness, alienation, and powerlessness. Offenders who are motivated to invest the necessary efforts to attain specific goals appear to be more capable of coping with the situations that affect their daily lives.

The degree to which an inmate feels he has control over his or her environment has a significant influence on his or her behavior. The control expectancy notion allows treatment specialists to observe offenders with regard to the degree to which they feel able to give direction to, or have control over, their own lives. The "internal–external locus of control" is derived from J. B. Rotter's social learning theory. Internal control refers to those individuals whose behavior reflects the feeling that they do have some control over their destiny. They feel that the outcomes of positive and/or negative events are consequences of their own actions. On the other hand, those individuals who perceive that control is outside themselves and that their destiny is in the hands of fate, chance, luck, or powerful others have an external locus of control.

The implications of studying the internal–external control orientation relate to the desire for identifying and changing the inmate's feelings of lack of control over his or her environment. If an inmate believes that his or her actions can positively affect his or her future, there is a greater chance that he or she will actively participate in a successful rehabilitation plan. In changing the low expectancies of inmates with an external orientation the goals are to increase their literacy rate and improve goal-oriented behavior.

Seeman's research findings indicated that inmates with an internal locus of control were more willing to correct their deficiencies through participation in rehabilitative programs. He presented three kinds of information to 85 inmates at Chillicothe Federal Prison to measure their expectations of controlling their own destiny. The three types of information related to the individual's awareness of and ability to learn about the following: successful achievement of parole, the immediate reformatory situation, and their long-range prospects for a criminal career. Seeman's study indicated that "internals" retained a significantly greater number of parole-related items than did "externals," but no significant difference was found in their ability to learn the other two kinds of information.

Achieving parole status is one of the most important goals of an inmate. Obtaining parole puts the offender in a better position to control his environment. Therefore, an internal inmate would be more likely to invest the effort necessary to learn the information relevant to obtaining a parole than would an external inmate. The internal is motivated to learn information related to achieving parole because he or she views this information as essential to achieving this goal. In contrast, the external, perceiving that obtaining parole is unrelated to his or her efforts, would see little purpose in learning such information.

Peters' research in a medium-security institution for adult felons in North Carolina provides further evidence of inmates' differing motivations for participating in occupational education programs. His results indicate that internals were more likely to participate in courses such as baking, small-engine repair, typing, and high school refresher courses than were externals.

Treatment specialists should receive training that will enable them to foster an increased sense of control in external inmates. Implementing the prison option system developed in this chapter can increase the inmate's cooperation and participation in treatment programs by allowing him or her to feel in control of some of the events and programs that most directly affect him or her.

The authors have emphasized the need to reduce the external's low expectancy of control, thereby encouraging self-direction and goal-oriented behavior. In contrast, the inmate with extremely high internal control can be just as maladjusted as the extremely external individual. The highly internal offender has been referred to as a sociopath, one who feels compelled to dominate his environment. Two counseling approaches may be recommended for the "sociopath": helping them accept and adjust the aspects of their environment that they cannot or should not control; helping them to channel their aggressive energies into constructive and socially acceptable pursuits.

Methods for helping externals to become more internally controlled are to reinforce internal statements, to replace an offender's external control statement with an internal question, and to assist the inmate in recognizing the consequences of their behavior. This may be accomplished by helping the inmate consider alternate behaviors that could have changed the outcome of events in the past and that can influence current and future events. The relationship between individual expectancies of control and inmate behavior has been shown. Treatment efforts geared toward reducing extreme expectancies of internal or external control may well result in the inmates' improved self-concept, participation in rehabilitation programs, and successful readjustment to community life.

GROUP THERAPY

Group treatment programs in which small groups of offenders meet with a leader are becoming increasingly popular in correctional settings. Pressure to adopt group methods of treatment may be an outgrowth of the following: it is less costly to hire a group therapist who can work with many inmates at once than it is to employ a counselor who can see inmates only on an individual basis; some prison administrators subscribe to the theory that group methods can be effective due to the widely accepted sociological theories of crime causation that imply that criminal behavior is learned through association with deviant peer groups. By this reasoning, an anticriminal peer group would be a viable means for unlearning or renouncing criminal behaviors.

For group treatment to be effective, the group leader should be aware of the need to overcome initial resistance and conning on the part of group members. There are two distinct classes of group treatment with offenders: group psychotherapy and group counseling. The role of the group leader/therapist varies accordingly. The primary methodological distinction between the two is that group psychotherapy focuses on a psychotherapeutic approach toward the individual group members, while group counseling focuses on changing behaviors and interaction of the members through group process.

There are various advantages to group therapy for offender rehabilitation. Oftentimes, individualized therapy is not as effective as group therapy because inmates endure an enormous amount of peer pressure to conform to certain types of behavior. Criminal behavior tends to thrive in a criminal subculture, where many people share certain views that promote and justify deviant behavior. It can be said that a vast majority of inmates were exposed to that subculture, which led to their deviant acts. Naturally, prisons are a haven for these views since most criminals carry their beliefs from the criminal subculture during the time of their incarceration. Therefore, creating a change in the views and attitudes through therapy of the group, as opposed to the individual, enhances the likelihood that the new views and attitudes will be adopted and sustained since they will now be part of the views of the subculture. If a few or many of the inmates begin to embrace what they learn during the counseling sessions, the attitude of the subculture as a whole will begin to change as well. Additionally, group therapy allows for the group specialist to reach out simultaneously to more individuals, whereas it may be more difficult to set up individual sessions for every single inmate; if sessions are set up for individuals, they probably will not be held as frequently as group sessions.

The primary goal of group therapy is to prepare inmates for life in the outside world by teaching them to become law-abiding citizens. A crucial part of attaining this goal is ensuring that the subculture within the prison shifts toward more socially acceptable behavior. Though there has not been any definitive reason to believe that group therapy in and of itself reduces the recidivism rate of offenders, it is believed that it does at least improve the interaction between offenders in prison. Staff members also reported that their communication with inmates undergoing group therapy improved and that those individuals seemed to get into less trouble on average than other inmates.

Individuals who were more extroverted and open to new ideas benefited the most from the group therapy sessions. Additionally, those who committed multiple offenses with others were influenced the most by the group therapy sessions. In sharp contrast, the introverts, or loners, tended to be less receptive to the group therapy and were more likely to recidivate upon release. Therefore, those who are most likely to be influenced by peers are more likely to benefit from group therapy methods. Voluntary participation in group therapy will lead extroverted individuals to emerge and self-select themselves for treatment. Staff members can also assist in the process to ensure that those who are likely to be helped by treatment are the ones being selected for group therapy.

The type of group therapy session leader does not seem to make much difference in terms of effectiveness of the treatment as long as they are able to conduct discussions and convey warmth and encouragement to the offenders. Other factors, such as the leader's specific type of training or background, do not seem to have as much of an impact on the level of effectiveness.

Group therapy should mainly focus on creating discussions, which are the most conducive to facilitating active participation from all of the group members. Once group members are engaged in discussion, they are more receptive to ideas that are being conveyed to them. Since group therapy essentially tries to persuade offenders to adopt new and more socially acceptable behavior, the best way to achieve this is by reinforcing positive behavior and discouraging any antisocial behavior.

Offenders should be seated in a circle to promote a roundtable type of discussion. There should be at least six individuals in the group to prevent anyone from feeling uncomfortable or defensive; however, there should not be too many members, which may cause some to feel intimidated by a large crowd. The topics discussed in therapy sessions will vary from one group to another. Inmates may wish to discuss problems or issues that they are presently dealing with or topics that they all share interest in. Incorporating psychodrama (see next section) also allows for self-expression and discussion. The inmates should always address the topic of life in the outside community after release.

If possible, group members should be selected according to the peer groups that naturally form in an institution. Since those who are most susceptible to treatment are the extroverts who are influenced by their peers, creating a group in which these individuals are among their peers facilitates learning socially acceptable behavior. By experiencing the treatment as a group, the individuals may feel as though they are beginning to conform to the new norms (after therapy) of the group. Thereafter, the whole group's views may begin to shift away from deviant behavior and may transition toward more law-abiding behavior. This, in turn, will help to prepare them for interaction and acceptance in the outside community.

PSYCHODRAMA

Psychodrama is a group therapeutic technique involving the dramatic enactment of events and issues that are important to the individual. The technique has been used mainly with people suffering from alcoholic, marital, psychotic, and neurotic problems. Psychodrama is, however, a valuable technique for prison inmates but has been used by only a few innovative correctional psychodramatists.

When psychodrama is used with offenders, the scenes that are acted out may be part of their past, present, or future lifestyle. Psychodrama offers the offender the opportunity to act out antisocial and illegal behaviors in a controlled setting. In addition to depicting an important issue, it provides for open discussion and candid feedback by other group members.

The word drama comes from a Greek word meaning "action" or "a thing done." J. L. Moreno, the renowned founder of this approach, defines psychodrama as "the science which explores the truth by dramatic methods." Ideally, a particular area, such as a platform, should be designated for psychodrama; the groups should know that they can step up whenever their emotions require dramatic expression.

Psychodrama can provide an inmate with an outlet for characterizing experiences that are of such intensity that words alone are insufficient. The unique population of a prison makes the reaction to psychodrama different from what it is on the outside. Inmates who hear through the grapevine about a new group therapy approach may well be cynical and skeptical that it will turn out to be a psychologist leading just another group meeting. But psychodrama is different; it allows inmates to vent pent-up hostility and frustration at the system and authority figures, at the fear of losing a girlfriend, boyfriend, or spouse, and finally over the anxiety of reintegration into an unknown society. Guided by a skilled therapist trained in psychological and dramatic techniques, a new and unique method of treatment is afforded the inmate.

This process is especially valuable in "future projections" in which the inmate, acting out a future situation, can get the feel for the actions, attitudes, and responses commensurate with a law-abiding person. Future situations that may pose a particular problem for offenders include applying for and maintaining a job, being reunited with family, participating in community life, and relating to parole and other correctional personnel.

In psychodrama, the pressure of the other group members makes distortion or conning difficult, which causes the inmate to more carefully assess his words and actions. Through psychodrama, offenders are able to reenact past behavior, project future actions, and reflect upon effective methods for coping with life's difficulties—without resorting to unlawful activities.

CHEMICAL DEPENDENCY AND ADDICTION TREATMENT

Convicted felons tend to be abusers of both alcohol and illegal drugs. In fact, a large percentage of state inmate populations are substance abusers. The percentage of the total state inmate population with drug addiction problems ranges from a low of 25 percent in North Carolina to a high of 80–85 percent in Kentucky, Maryland, Montana, and New Hampshire. In the types of chemical dependency programs that range from 6- to 12-month therapeutic communities and 12-step programs that meet 7 days per week. Some states like South Carolina have Addiction Treatment Units where a therapeutic community model is maintained 24 hours a day, with 3–4 intensive groups per day. Other states like Wisconsin have residential treatment programs specializing in substance abuse treatment, aftercare and transitional programs, and treatment for dually diagnosed inmates.

Other states like Maryland have modified therapeutic communities with an emphasis on cognitive-behavior counseling.

The three different types of programs for chemical dependency are residential, intensive outpatient, and outpatient. The residential program provides an entire housing unit for inmates participating in the substance abuse program. During this program various disciplines are visited, which include acupuncture, mental health, therapeutic communities, and cognitive behavioral approaches. The program is six months long and offers two group sessions per week as well as one individual session every two weeks. The intensive outpatient program is offered to inmates who do not reside in the unit but receive rigorous treatment. The program runs for approximately six months and targets cognitive behavioral rehabilitation. Finally, the outpatient program is offered as an aftercare program, which consists of weekly group meetings after the completion of the other two programs mentioned above. This type of treatment is provided to the inmate indefinitely or until the time of release.

PSYCHOLOGICAL SERVICES

Psychological services provide inmates with the opportunity to discuss any issues that they may be concerned with in protected group environment. The individual will then receive feedback from the psychologist, as well as from other members of the group. The objective is to enhance the offenders' problem-solving skills. There is no prerequisite in receiving psychological services; however, preference is given to those inmates who are monitored clinically. Additionally, there is a finite time frame for the sessions; inmates may receive them as needed on an indefinite basis.

ANGER MANAGEMENT

Anger management group therapy is provided for inmates to help them determine what causes anger and discover methods by which anger can be controlled. Elements include relapse prevention, stress reduction, conflict resolution, and training in assertive and rational behavior. By teaching offenders about anger as well as other negative emotions, negative and aggressive behavior can be prevented. Learning how to control anger will allow inmates to improve their self-expression and their relationships with others. The average duration for the anger management therapy course ranges from eight to twenty weeks, with an average of twelve weeks. Classes are held once a week for approximately 90 minutes on average.

COGNITIVE INTERVENTIONS

The Cognitive Interventions Program is presented in a group format and strives to help participants understand themselves better and to train them to better control their lives. The underlying theory of the program is how an individual thinks determines how they will act, so if we can modify their thought process, the corresponding actions will be sure to follow. By showing offenders how to control their thoughts, they are able to control more aspects of their lives. The duration of this program ranges from 12 to 36 weeks, with an average of 15 weeks. On average, groups meet approximately twice per week for two hours; however, this varies slightly from one location to another.

NATIONAL SURVEY FINDINGS

When reviewing the national survey findings, we were struck by the low priority given to treatment staff—social workers, psychologists, or counselors by many of the state correctional systems. In sharp contrast, many states have a low ratio of guards per inmate, possibly due to an administrative priority of custody and punishment or to the strong unions, which advocate for custodial officers. More specifically, two southern states stand out as deficient when it comes to employing full-time clinical staff. Mississippi's Department of Corrections (DOC) has 23 counselors and one psychologist treating 23,996 inmates, a ratio of one clinician per every 1,000 inmates. There is a dramatic difference when examining the ratio of inmates per guard, 1:13 with a total of 1,843 guards.

On a more positive note, several states stand out for their demonstrated commitment to offender counseling and rehabilitation. New Hampshire and Wisconsin seem to be innovative and progressive with a ratio of one clinician for every 35.5 inmates incarcerated in New Hampshire and one clinician for every 64 inmates incarcerated in Wisconsin. At the same time, these two rehabilitation-oriented states are still concerned for public safety and hold inmates accountable for their behavior; thereby, having a ratio of one guard for every four inmates in New Hampshire and one guard for every 6.1 inmates in Wisconsin. The state of Washington has an even more impressive record than both New Hampshire and Wisconsin with a ratio of one clinician for every 34.4 inmates and one guard for every 5.4 inmates, holding the best ratios of the states that were examined.

EXEMPLARS OF SEX OFFENDER TREATMENT PROGRAMS

Examining the Wisconsin DOC sex offender treatment program in more detail conveys the high level of commitment the state has toward the rehabilitation of offenders. Wisconsin offers a selection of different offender programs, which include educational-based programs, psychotherapeutic interventions, as well as customized therapy groups that cater to the needs and risk level of the offenders. Participants undergo an evaluation and are provided with the treatment that best suits their individual needs. All three programs manage the offender's risk of recidivism through supervision and polygraph exams. Involvement in at least one of the programs is mandatory under the offender's supervision rules. Failure on the behalf of the offender to comply can possibly lead to increased sanctions.

A plethora of different factors are considered before placing an offender into a program. Some of these include the length of the offender's sentence, parole eligibility, mandatory release dates, the offender's willingness to participate in treatment, the accessibility of programs that best cater to the offender's needs, the amount of security risk the offender poses, and other program needs of the offender. Once these factors are considered, the offender is placed into one of the sex offender treatment programs.

The programs include Education Awareness Sex Offender Program, Pretreatment/ Deniers, Sex Offender Treatment, Sex Offender Treatment (SOT) Program, Beacon Residential Program, as well as programs for juvenile offenders.

The Education Awareness Sex Offender Treatment Program is an entry-level program designed to prepare offenders for a more comprehensive treatment program. In this program, offenders receive approximately 25 hours of programming in 1.2 to 2.5 hour increments for groups ranging from 12 to 25 offenders. The staff generally consists of two people who are either psychologists or licensed social workers. The waiting list for the program varies from 12 to 24 months.

The Deniers Program is a mandatory program for all sex offenders. The offenders in this group represent a wide range of resistance to programming, from vehement denial to reducing the significance of the offense. The program's goal is to encourage offenders to participate in the treatment programs in a nonthreatening manner by informing the offenders that they will ultimately require treatment to reduce the risk of recidivism. This program is offered for three to four months and meets once a week for two hours. Groups of 10 to 12 offenders are supervised by one or two staff members, a psychologist, or a social worker. Average waiting lists for these programs are relatively short, ranging from three to four months.

The SOT Program provides therapeutic interventions and is voluntarily attended by the offender. A majority of the treatment groups consist of a heterogeneous mix of offenders who show a less compulsive and repetitive pattern of sexual deviancy. Offenders who require special attention are placed in targeted offender groups such as SOT Female Offenders, SOT Spanish-speaking, SOT Lighthouse for the lower functioning, SOT Special Management Unit for the cognitively challenged and/or emotionally disturbed, SOT Child Victim, and SOT Adult Victim. The general group program runs from 6 to 12 months and meets once or twice a week for 1.5 to 2 hours for groups of 6 to 12 offenders. The staff consists of either two psychologists or one psychologist facilitator in conjunction with one treatment specialist, crisis intervention worker, or social worker.

The SOT Programs vary a bit from other programs mentioned above, as they are long-term residential programs. This program is offered to offenders who display predictable patterns of compulsive and repetitive acts of sexual deviancy. The course of the program is 152 weeks and is provided to groups of 12 offenders. The staff consists of one psychologist supervisor, one unit manager, one psychological services associate, two psychologists, two social workers, and one treatment sergeant. The average waiting list varies for this program, depending on the offender.

The Beacon Residential Program is a new three-phase residential program that is an alternative to the traditional sex offender program. The programs attempts to change the offender's impulsive behavior by gaining an understanding of the offender's past to create a relapse-prevention plan and to change any dynamic risk factors. The length of the program is approximately 104 weeks with groups of 8 to 10 offenders. The staff includes approximately five people, including at least one psychologist and four social workers. The average wait for this program is approximately 96 months but is less for those who have an SOT Program need.

There are also special programs for juvenile offenders, which consist of a comprehensive four-phase treatment plan. The four-phase program addresses offense description, sex history, social history, and relapse prevention. Youths must satisfactorily complete one phase of treatment to move up to the next. The length of the program ranges from 1 to 1.5 years and is offered to groups of 8 to 10 offenders. The staff consists of psychologists, social workers, and youth counselors. The average waiting lists ranges from no wait to 6 weeks, depending on the location.

COMMUNITY AFTERCARE

Although various types of drug abuse treatment in prison are extremely beneficial to offenders, community aftercare is an essential step in reducing relapse and recidivism. Community aftercare essentially provides individuals with treatment after release into the community to assist in their rehabilitation. The most effective aftercare mimics the type of treatment offered during incarceration. Whether offered during supervision or after supervision has ended, aftercare helps to maintain discipline of the offenders.

Intensive drug treatment programs focus on cognitive and behavioral treatment, group therapy, health and wellness, role playing, as well as techniques to boost self-esteem. Many programs hire ex-addicts to serve as examples for the groups, some even train the group. Treatment programs during incarceration can last anywhere from six to twelve months, however, aftercare does not have a definitive time frame. Some programs screen inmates to see which individuals would be best suited for particular programs, while others take any inmate.

Each drug treatment program varies in its approach. The Key-Crest program for example, is an intervention program that is broken into three phases. The first phase is therapeutic community for inmates in prison. The second phase entails releasing inmates into a community work release center where they have jobs but still reside in a facility and continue to receive treatment from phase one. The last phase releases individuals into the community under some form of supervision. The results of the program show that residential treatment in conjunction with aftercare, significantly reduce recidivism rates.

Oftentimes, intervention after release is more effective than treatment during incarceration. According to the New Vision residential treatment program, individuals who participated in aftercare, in addition to treatment during incarceration, had a recidivism rate of 7 percent for new convictions, whereas individuals who did not participate in aftercare had a recidivism rate of 16 percent. The study examined individuals within six months of release. Additionally, a study conducted by Wexler also confirms that those who received community aftercare were considered lower risk offenders than those who did not receive aftercare. Therefore, the effectiveness of treatment during incarceration can be increased with post-release community aftercare.

PRISONER RE-ENTRY PROGRAMS

Approximately 650,000 prisoners are released from federal and state prisons into communities throughout the nation each year. According to the 2006 National Governors Association (NGA) Center for Best Practices report, about 67 percent (435,500) are rearrested and 50 percent (325,000) are re-incarcerated within 3 years of release. In past decades many of these ex-offenders have not been prepared to obtain realistic and marketable job skills, steady employment, substance abuse and mental health services, and/or subsidized and transitional housing upon release. Because of the dearth of prison vocational training and counseling programs, and prisoner re-entry programs available during the 1980s and 1990s, many released offenders commit new offenses and/or violate parole policies within 3 years of release.

A promising major federal initiative began in 2001. The Serious and Violent Offender Re-entry Initiative was developed by the Federal Office of Justice Programs of the U.S. Department of Justice and the National Institute of Corrections. Cosponsors of this large project also include the U.S. Department of Labor and the U.S. Department of Housing and Urban Development (HUD). This major national project provides funding to develop federal, state, and local community-based transition and re-entry programs for juvenile and adult ex-offenders. The overridding goal of prisoner re-entry programs is to help ex-offenders seek, find, and maintain employment as well as the full range of housing and social services.

In recent years, this federally funded program has received increased funding. In 2002, $100 million was given to 68 programs in 49 states to support prisoner re-entry programs. In 2005, President Bush proposed and then supported a $300 million 4-year expansion of the federal prisoner re-entry program.

There are many examples of comprehensive prisoner re-entry programs. For example, the National Governors Association's Center for Best Practices is currently operating seven prisoner re-entry academies in six states—Georgia, Idaho, Massachusetts, Michigan, Rhode Island, and Virginia. On the local level, Exodus Transitional Community Program in East Harlem, New York, seems to be highly effective in preventing recidivism. It served 213 ex-offenders in 2002, and just 6 were returned to prison. Exodus served 290 ex-offenders in 2003, and only 3 of the men were returned to prison. The City of Memphis, Tennessee developed the Second Chance re-entry program over three years ago and has served over 1500 ex-offenders–only 4 ex-offenders were returned to prison.

During the 1960s, new prisoner re-entry programs were referred to as Federal Prerelease Guidance Centers, reintegrative programs (e.g., work-release and study-release centers), in-prison social education programs, and job information and placement labs at the federal and state level. Unfortunately, many of these programs lost funding and staff during the punitive era of the 1980s and 1990s. However, the re-emergence of comprehensive prisoner re-entry programs in recent years is extremely promising if the goal is to sharply reduce recidivism while rehabilitating and resocializing offenders.

Chapter 27

A Significant Challenge for Communities and Families in the Twenty-First Century

The Reintegration Process for Prisoners Coming Home

Dale J. Brooker, Ph.D.

ABSTRACT

The criminal justice system will see an ever growing number of prisoners released from imprisonment in the early twenty-first century—more than have ever been released in past centuries. According to a nationwide analysis of reentry trends in the United States conducted by the Bureau of Justice Statistics (2003), at least 95 percent of all state prisoners will be released from prison at some point; nearly 80 percent will be released to parole supervision. Problems arise as to what can be done with these individuals when they are released: where will they go, and what exactly are they returning to? The complexities associated with the reentry and reintegration process will be explored to better understand how this phenomenon impacts community life, family life, and the implications for the criminal justice system.

INTRODUCTION

Despite the fact that from 1990 to 2000 there was a decline in prisoner release rates, the number of those released has continued to grow. The Bureau of Justice Statistics (2003) estimates that close to 600,000 people were released from prison in 2001 and that a significant portion of these individuals were out on parole. Furthermore, according to the most recent data, the adult parole population reached a total of 784,408 on December 31, 2005, and grew 1.6 percent, or slightly more than the average annual increase of 1.4 percent since 1995 (Glaze and Bonczar 2006). These statistics suggest that a challenge lies ahead for the stakeholders in the reentry process, namely, correctional personnel (especially parole officers), the community, and families. Furthermore, this information provides a starting point for a discussion on a complex societal transition that has many trajectories that run deep into the criminal justice system as well as a number of other social institutions that are impacted.

Not just the criminal justice system has full ownership in this phenomenon. The community into which prisoners are released and the family members of those released are also significant (if not, the most important) stakeholders in the process of reintegration. This particular challenge is interesting in that it has been readily defined as "reentry" for sometime in the United States. The United Kingdom uses the term "resettlement" and there has been some call (see Maruna 2006) to reframe the discussion in terms of restorative reintegration, which will be discussed later in the chapter in more detail. The key element at play is that no matter how one frames the paradigm, the challenges still exist. Some of these challenges are (1) How does society and the system respond to those returning home from prison? (2) How do families cope with those coming home? and (3) How is the community coping with and adjusting to the influx? The chapter also explores these challenges to give the reader a deeper understanding of this serious emerging issue in the field of criminal justice.

The "Reintegration" and "Reentry" Process in Perspective

Part of any challenge is determining its meaning, and examining its underlying assumptions. The fact is the word *reentry* is used by contemporary criminal justice professionals to describe a process that can have many different manifestations. Generally speaking, reentry refers to the process persons who were incarcerated go through as they move forward on their various life trajectories. But what does reentry really and truly mean to those people who study it, and how does this impact the way in which they view this particular social process? This question prompts exploration into the paradigms that attempt to frame and organize thought and theory around a key criminal justice outcome. This in turn leads to the discussion regarding how reentry or reintegration is supposed to work. Moreover, what does successful reentry into society actually mean? Does it mean one must be fully reintegrated? Or is reintegration a multifaceted goal, while reentry is a complex and systemic process? Much of the reentry discourse seems centered on surveillance and the need to control the movement of offenders through official mechanisms (parole) and processes (reentry) without considering the larger and more complex idea of reintegration. Within the last decade some significant strides have been made in addressing the need to focus on reintegration. Travis (2005:129) refers to the reentry perspective as a motion picture that,

> reflects the fact that our imprisonment policies not only send people to prison, but also create ripple effects that undermine our society's efforts to promote safety, child and family welfare, strong labor markets, safe and affordable housing, healthy individuals, civic participation, and vibrant neighborhoods.

This motion picture analogy pinpoints the limitation of this paradigm of thought in that it fails to address the real social issues that need a significant amount of attention if any hope is to emerge. Returning home after prison must be seen as much more than a process in and of itself; there must be some ownership in the process for policy makers, community leaders, families, and the individuals themselves. This cannot happen if there is a lack of specificity about the key steps to fully integrating people released from prison back into a community. This chapter explores the various issues surrounding reintegration and also discusses the ways in which current policy impacts the process.

The concept of restorative justice and reintegration (see Bazemore and Erbe 2004), while still in its early stages, warrants discussion as it directly relates to the framework surrounding the reentry process and the reintegration that tends to be more focused on goals and outcomes. From a restorative justice mode of thought, the informal social control mechanisms in society are crucial in the reintegration of a previously incarcerated person. These informal social control mechanisms that emanate from families in particular can in turn be relied upon instead of the official formal social control mechanisms within the criminal justice system. Along with informal social control there is a serious need for social support in some form so individuals returning home will have the opportunity to desist from crime and, at the same time, repair the harm they have caused to the victims and their community. The harm may also be within the family and this too must be addressed so that reconciliation can take place and harmony can be restored. The restorative justice framework can provide some guidance in the reintegration discussion and is integrated throughout the following sections.

The Reintegration Process and the Family

This discussion highlights the family as a significant part of the reintegration process and focuses specifically on the social support that can be gained from strong family bonds. Family bonds have a good deal of history prior to and during incarceration and may be disorganized upon release. It is in the family where those who are released from prison can find a significant amount of support, not only emotionally, but many times financially as well. Irwin's classic work, *The Felon* (1970) examined the family as a "buffering agent." He noted that the family provides the parolee with a place to live, it can be a source of employment for those returning and can also provide just some of the bare necessities like clothes, transportation, and toiletries upon release. However, in his study Irwin found that a few of the parolees had difficulty adjusting to the family situation. According to Irwin (1970:129),

> The absence or presence of conflict within the family, conflict between the parolee and his family, the compatibility of the parolee's and the family's commitments, the total character of the family's and parolee's past history together will have an important bearing on the solution of problems.

These difficult times are foreseeable in many instances and can present a significant challenge to the successful reintegration of a person. Nelson, Deess, and Allen (1999) examined post-incarceration experiences in New York. Their study examined people at the moment of release from incarceration to see where people were going, how much money they had, and what their expectations were. The study also followed 49 adults released from New York State prisons and city jails for 30 days, interviewing them on seven separate occasions. The main focus was on the challenges that the returning prisoners faced during the one-month period. The study noted a number of hurdles encountered by the returning prisoners: finding a job, finding housing, and getting access to needed health care. A major finding of this study was that most returning prisoners who found a job within the first month following their release were either rehired by a former employer or had help from family and friends. Relatively few found new jobs on their own because they lacked the skills necessary to conduct an effective job search or could not find employers willing to hire ex-offenders. Strong family support was seen as an important indicator of successful reintegration among the offenders studied. Those returning prisoners who indicated they had strong support from family and friends reported lower levels of drug use, greater success in finding a job, and less continued criminal activity. Most of the people in the study lived with family members upon release and noted some level of support. If this is the case, perhaps a more concentrated approach to promoting family bonds during incarceration would be prudent.

However, there are a number of significant barriers to maintaining family bonds (and in the long run, informal social control mechanisms). First, is the issue of distance. Many prisoners may be in a facility that is too far away for their family members to visit on a regular basis. In a large state like Texas, for example, prisoners could be held a few hundred miles away from their home, and families may not have the financial resources to afford a trip. Second, prison visitation rules and procedures may make it difficult for family members to physically see their loved ones. Third, many families may not have the time to actually make a visit to show support, so they must rely on other methods of communication such as phone calls (usually collect calls made by the prisoners, which can be costly) and letters.

Shapiro and Schwartz (2001) further discussed at length the importance of family support in the reentry process. Specifically, the authors examined a program in New York City that offers a model for strengthening the relationships between offenders and their families and partnering with community supervision agencies to improve compliance. A number of relevant issues were brought out. The idea that each family has strengths on which prisoners being released can rely is crucial to a deeper understanding of how familial support operates after incarceration. One could hypothesize that those without any family to return to could very well be much worse off than those who do have family on the outside waiting to greet them upon return.

Hairston (1988) specifically examined the issue of family ties and provided a conceptual base for studies that focus on this phenomenon. The author noted that a number of studies (Adams and Fischer 1976; Burnstein 1977; Holt and Miller 1972; Howser and McDonald 1982; Leclair 1978) dealing with family ties of those incarcerated and recidivism seem to come to the same conclusion: maintaining community and family ties during incarceration is positively associated with success upon release. Hairston (1998) reviewed two frameworks, social support and primary relationships, and noted that conceptually, prisoner–family relationships are useful because they are primary relationships that can establish a solid reliable base and provide opportunities for prisoners just released from prison. Without such a base, an individual may begin to move away from socially proscribed norms once again and enter into an anomic state in which they quickly return to the lifestyle and the decision-making processes that resulted in their incarceration in the first place.

The family is also seen as a social support network that provides concrete resources like food, money, and shelter for people who were incarcerated. The lack of social support is also discussed. For example, when a family denies aid to an inmate the results can be problematic because the inmate then has no group to identify with and loses all roles that they may have once played as a member of that family unit. Hairston (1988) did not note that the social support network has a deep history and needs to be examined more carefully to fully understand the family support phenomenon as it relates to individuals being released from incarceration.

Beyond the issue of family support is the challenge of reintegrating back into a family and regaining an identity and a role. Those who commit a crime and are incarcerated face the fact that they will be separated from their family members for an extended period and in this time their role as wife/husband, mother/father, daughter/son, aunt/uncle, and cousin will be diminished. Families are disrupted which can result in long-term problems for the family's structure, the family's financial status, and the development of children within the family. Once prisoners are released, these problems are not remedied easily, but require long-term reconciliation measures that are crucial to the reintegration process. Braman (2004) highlighted the dilemmas faced by families when a loved one is incarcerated, and found that there are significant challenges for families who not only have to deal with the absence of an incarcerated family member, but what happens when the family member returns. These dilemmas are not always resolved when the person is released; incarceration is associated with other issues, especially for children. As noted by Braman (2004), many children of the incarcerated men who were interviewed were leading lives that included drug use and other criminal activities.

The Reintegration Process and the Community

The major staging area for reentry and a major stakeholder in the reintegration process is the community. As Braithwaite (1989:8) notes, "crime is best controlled when members of the community are the primary controllers through active participation in shaming offenders, and, having shamed them, through concerted participation in ways of reintegrating the offender back into the community of law abiding citizens." The problem though lies in the assumption that the community is willing to participate in the reintegration process. Furthermore, communities are already plagued with the inability to keep up with the changing shift in the economy, the levels of poverty, and the battery of public health issues. Many communities across the United States are in the midst of also dealing with an influx of individuals who have served time in prison. In response to the release of sex offenders there has been an uproar about where they are placed and how they are to be watched and controlled by the criminal justice system. New sex offender registry laws are becoming more and more restrictive and proponents are beginning to translate this concern into a fear of all former prison inmates. This is crucial because reintegration can be brought to a slow and grinding halt if the community has a significant unwillingness to be a positive and constructive part of the process. The community must continually weigh the safety of the citizenry and the protection of those victimized with the idea of having an open mind toward reintegration. Given that some data indicate that more than 60 percent of those released from prison will be rearrested within three years (Langan and Levin 2002), community members have little hope in reintegration. Public sentiment follows the logic that community residents would feel much safer and the quality of life would be better if previously incarcerated persons were taken out of their neighborhood (see Clear, Rose, and Ryder 2001). This in turn can impact the ability of former prisoners returning home to make any type of social bond with others that could act as the support mechanism crucial for reintegration.

While the focal points for many studies on reentry are immediate social control mechanisms such as family and employment, it is necessary to examine the community and its ability to create opportunity for those who were previously incarcerated. As Hagan and Coleman (2001:362) noted, "there is little doubt about the decline in social capital available to persons returning to communities from prison." Building on Bourdieu (1980), Coleman (1990), and Putnam's (2000) concept of social capital, this research explored the inability of recently released inmates to build solid social networks at the individual and community level. Such networks could prove useful in the reintegration process. Putnam (1995:67) defined social capital as "the features of social organization such as networks, norms and social trust that facilitate coordination for mutual benefit." Many of these social networks are established and maintained at one's place of employment. Another mechanism of social capital is the family, one that is sometimes the only source available to recently released inmates. However, as Braman (2004) pointed out, families oftentimes have difficulty in maintaining social networks even with extended family members because of the stigma associated with having someone in the family who is incarcerated or was previously incarcerated. Pro-social networks could prove useful to those returning to society. As Putnam (1995:66) commented, at the community level the "quality of social life and the performance of social institutions are indeed powerfully influenced by norms and networks of civic engagement." Civically engaged communities are better at providing sturdy norms and social trust among members than those neighborhoods/communities that are not civically engaged. Social capital is scarce in poor, minority communities where large numbers of recently released inmates currently live and have few services or community programs available to revive the capital to the area.

Putnam (2000) further explored the concept of social capital to identify ways in which people in the United States have slowly disengaged from civil involvement so much so that the trust of others in communities has diminished. Three key elements make up the concept of Putnam's notion of social capital in this work: (1) reciprocity, (2) trust or trustworthiness, and (3) honesty. In terms of reciprocity, Putnam (2000) pointed out that people interact with others hoping that their deeds will be reciprocated, thus increasing the number of interactions among neighbors and community members. These interactions also open up and expand social networks to allow for opportunities for future social capital building. In terms of trust, "people who trust others are well-rounded, good citizens and those more engaged in community life and both more trusting and more trustworthy" (Putnam 2000:137). What is crucial to understand in this context of trust is the old adage of giving people the benefit of the doubt. Putnam (2000) suggested that communities with a great deal of social capital will be likely to provide members with this type of trust. Those communities with decaying trust will become more cautious when it comes to trusting people. Lastly, honesty is formed from personal experiences and based on a general community norm. Putnam (2000:317) pointed out, "inner cities are too often marked by a vicious circle, in which low levels of trust and cohesion lead to higher levels of crime, which lead to even lower levels of trust and cohesion." This proves problematic to establishing a solid foundation of norms for the community to rely upon.

Clear, Rose, and Ryder (2001) explored the spatial impact of incarceration and the problems associated with remaining and returning offenders to communities that suffer from high rates of incarceration. This research utilized focus groups of community members and ex-offenders from two high-incarceration neighborhoods to identify the effects of incarceration on the neighborhoods. The focus group of ex-offenders reported on the pressure they felt returning to society from a variety of sources: the criminal justice system, society in general, neighbors, and family members. The decaying trust mentioned previously is highlighted by Clear, Rose, and Ryder (2001:342) who found that the neighbors of ex-offenders were oftentimes, "cautious, suspicious and frequently fearful." The study also revealed four domains that describe the impact of incarceration on the community: (1) stigma, (2) financial impacts, (3) identity issues, and (4) maintenance of interpersonal relationships.

Clear, Rose, and Ryder (2001) noted that in terms of stigma, focus group participants commented that there was a sense of distrust on the part of people in the community toward those who are recently released from incarceration. This, in turn, limited the ability of ex-offenders to establish social networks (outside the family) to rely upon for support. From the community standpoint, the research indicated that people in these areas feel stigmatized by having so many ex-offenders living in their area. This research also explored the perceived financial impact on the community. The authors noted that not only do families lose a breadwinner when a member is incarcerated, but when the ex-offender returns home and does obtain a job, their employers lose when the ex-offender fails as an employee. Identity issues were also explored. From the community's perspective, these areas are seen as "problem places." From the ex-offender's perspective, Clear, Rose, and Ryder (2001:342) remarked, "the ability of a person to thrive socially is partly a result of that person's sense of identity and an identity associated with the cycle of incarceration is a different foundation on which to build life choices." This is closely associated with the last domain of interpersonal relationships.

There are other challenges that the community faces along with those returning from prison. Three areas are prominent in the literature on reentry/reintegration: the economy (jobs), housing, and health care. Communities where those who were formerly incarcerated reside are oftentimes those where joblessness is more prevalent. This compounded with the fact that many parolees must find a job as a condition of their parole makes the reintegration process all that more difficult. The stark and often very bleak reality for many returning offenders is that there is a stigma attached to being previously incarcerated.

Visher, La Vigne, and Farrell (2003) examined the prisoner reentry phenomenon in the state of Maryland. That research indicated a number of needs of returning prisoners as they begin the process of reintegration. One major finding was that over two-thirds of those studied who were returning to society had previous records, and this could serve as a barrier to employment, housing, and eligibility for food stamps and other forms of welfare, and can limit opportunities for civic participation. The research also explored the conditions of the communities the offenders faced after their release. Over 59 percent of the released inmates returned to the Baltimore City area. In their examination, Visher, La Vigne, and Farrell (2003) noted that many people returning from prison are at a great social and economic disadvantage because of the poor conditions of Baltimore City. They noted the difficulty that many recently released inmates faced in trying to get to services available to ex-prisoners. The researchers also examined the limited programming resources available to prisoners while they were incarcerated. They found that there are fewer opportunities for prisoners to take advantage of what could assist them outside.

As Irwin (1970:120) noted, "the initial and probably the biggest obstacle in this problem area is obtaining employment." Many offenders preparing to be released may very well understand what lies ahead of them in terms of acquiring a job, and some may very well have the skills to acquire employment upon release. However, the reality is that prior to incarceration a number of inmates may have been involved in acquiring money through illegal activities. A report by Visher, La Vigne, and Farrell (2003:2) from The Urban Institute noted that of the 400 prisoners studied who were released, "almost two-thirds (61 percent) of respondents worked for money prior to incarceration, 60 percent reported that at least some of their income came from illegal activity, including 29 percent who indicated that all or most of their income was illegal." While many may have had jobs prior to incarceration, there are a number of prisoners who did not; while incarcerated, the jobs that prisoners hold may be far from what they were doing on the outside. Crucial to reentering society is how prepared inmates are to find a job when released and their beliefs or perceptions about getting a job to support themselves.

Compounding the employment issue is the lack of education many prisoners enter with, receive while incarcerated, and have upon release. The Bureau of Justice Statistics Special Report on Education and Correctional Populations (Harlow 2003) indicated that 68 percent of state prison inmates did not receive a high school diploma. Only 26 percent of state prison inmates said that they had completed the General Educational Development (GED) while serving time in a correctional facility. Frustrations over not being educated or not having any sort of skill upon release could very well affect the prisoners' perception of their preparedness to face the world upon release.

PARTNERSHIPS: TOWARD A SUCCESSFUL REINTEGRATION PROCESS

While there is a good deal of pressure for the community to be part of the reintegration and reentry process, much more emphasis seems to be placed on the formal social controls at work in our society, namely the police and corrections. Byrne and Hummer (2004) examine the role of the police in Reentry Partnership Initiatives and how this can apply to the complexities of offender reentry. This cooperative effort attempts to combine the resources of both law enforcement and corrections to focus on a strategy for problem solving. The police are seen as instrumental in the month just prior to release and in the long-term reentry process. In the structured reentry phase (just prior to release and the first month out), the police may be consulted by community boards in order to examine the offender's status and provide input regarding the conditions of release. As noted by Byrne and Hummer (2004:68), "it is remarkable that these programs have emerged and appear to be successful in terms of their implementation." What is even more interesting is that there seems to be some sense of ownership by the police in the overall reentry process and outcomes associated with it.

Beyond police partnerships, correctional agencies have started to recognize their role in the reentry process. Many of these partnerships have failed to emerge, and when they have, there is a bit of skepticism on the part of community members. A new report from the Urban Institute examines the Maryland Reentry Partnership Initiative that coordinates a number of stakeholders (Maryland Department of Corrections, Probation and Parole, the Parole Commission, the Mayor's Office and the Baltimore Police Department, nonprofit groups, and community-based organizations) to bring services (housing, substance abuse treatment, mental health counseling, education, vocational training) to prisoners who are retuning to select Baltimore neighborhoods (Roman, J. et al. 2007). The overall goal was to enhance public safety by reducing recidivism, increase offender accountability and community reparation, and increase community and correctional capacity to assess needs and match resources in the community. The results showed some signs of success in terms of lessening the probability of committing new crimes. This partnership highlights the possibilities that exist for reentry programs and successful reintegration outcomes that can help communities that may be overwhelmed with social problems. It also promotes an effective way of combining efforts and focusing on a series of specific criminal justice outcomes (reducing crime rates, victimization, etc.) with success for the offender (reducing drug use, finding proper housing, addressing mental health issues, getting an education, and gaining employment).

RESPONDING TO REINTEGRATION: A FAITH-BASED APPROACH

One approach to dealing with reintegration and reentry has been through the use of various faith-based programs that attempt to provide support for those previously incarcerated. A recent study by C. G. Roman, et al. (2007) examined one such program in Nevada. The three-month program is designed around a halfway house residential setting, and is geared toward attempting to reduce recidivism by providing a series of support mechanisms that focus on treatment, life skills, and employment within a spiritual environment (no religion has to be identified by the individual). The study noted that about 33 percent of the clients who entered the program did not successfully complete it. While the study finds no conclusive evidence that faith-based programming is successful in reducing future recidivism rates, it does shed light on the use of such a program in the reintegration process. It highlights the fact that there is a movement toward using such a program and the need for further research in the area.

THE FUTURE OF REINTEGRATION AND REENTRY

While reintegration is seemingly a difficult task on its surface, there are many underlying processes that must take place in order for communities and families to effectively cope with this transition. The community is bound to serve as a landing and staging area for those recently released offenders and there is a need for groups within the community to emerge and serve as liaisons. This of course can be very problematic as there remains an unwillingness on the part of community members. Citizens oftentimes see crime control and reintegration as being outside their hands and see no purpose in taking ownership in any of it, leaving it up to the criminal justice professionals and policy makers to decide what is best. This mode of thought may need to be shifted if any progress is to be made in reducing the amount of recidivism. However, it is not just the potential for future crime that is of importance, it is also the health of the community, the stability of the family, and the reintroduction of the disenfranchised that is at stake.

A great deal is yet to be done on how communities are adjusting and reacting to those who are reentering society after incarceration. Furthermore, while some research has been done on various existing reentry programs, there is nothing conclusive as of yet that suggests one particular method as the most effective at reintegrating someone back into a community. Problematic in this endeavor is the fact that much research is mainly focused on assessing only one particular dependent variable: re-offending.

The reentry phenomenon is not only complex in its conceptualization, but it also creates a great number of avenues to explore in terms of future research. Especially when dealing with familial support issues, it would be useful for future researchers to explore the family situation prior to the person's incarceration in depth. Braman (2004) has examined this to some extent with his anthropological work, but even more should be done to create a stronger understanding. Future studies must make efforts to gain insight into the families' communication process with their incarcerated loved ones and ascertain why they do or do not communicate, as well as qualitatively explore what they are saying to one another. Also a future study should probe the issues of women who are dealing with the reentry process.

Lastly and more importantly, it has been suggested that reentry be placed into the paradigm of reintegration if successful processes are to be put into place. Success for the individual is likely to entail stronger bonds with their family and the community, the greater possibility of employment, and the increase in social capital as well as the resistance of harmful behaviors. Success for the community is a safer and healthier environment that can focus on other issues and empower members to take on a series of challenges once only seen as being in the criminal justice system realm. As Bazemore and Erbe (2004:28) remark, "the traditional literature of parole and aftercare remains devoid of broader policy visions and of theory that places the offender in the context of community and gives specific consideration to the role of neigbourhood organizations, local socializing institutions or citizen supporters in the reintegration process." This highlights the need for continued efforts on the part of scholars, researchers, policy makers, and community organizations to effectively explore the complexities of reintegration of former prisoners.

REFERENCES

ADAMS, D., and J. FISCHER (1976). The effects of prison residence community contacts on recidivism rates. *Journal of Behavioral Technology Methods and Therapy* 22: 21–27.

BAZEMORE, G., and C. ERBE (2004). Reintegration and restorative justice: Towards a theory and practice of informal social control and support. In *After Crime and Punishment: Pathways to Offender Reintegration*, ed. S. Muruna and R. Immarigeon, pp. 27–56. Devon, UK: Willan Publishing.

BOURDIEU, P. (1980). Le capital social (social capital). *Actes de la Recherche en Sciences Sociales* 31: 2–3.

BRAITHWAITE, J. (1989). *Crime, Shame and Reintegration*. New York, NY: Cambridge University Press.

BRAMAN, D. (2004). *Doing Time on the Outside: Incarceration and Family Life in Urban America*. Ann Arbor: University of Michigan Press.

BUREAU of JUSTICE STATISTICS (2003). *Reentry Trends in the United States*. Washington, DC: U.S. Department of Justice.

BURNSTEIN, J. (1977). *Conjugal Visits in Prison*. Lexington, MA: Lexington Books.

BYRNE, J. M. and D. HUMMER (2004). Examining the role of the police in reentry partnership initiatives. *Federal Probation* 68(2): 62–69.

CLEAR, T. R., D. ROSE, and J. RYDER (2001). Incarceration and the community: The problem of removing and returning offenders. *Crime and Delinquency* 47(3): 335–351.

COLEMAN, J. S. (1990). *Foundations of Social Theory*. Cambridge, MA: Harvard University Press.

GLAZE, L. E., and T. P. BONCZAR (2006). *Probation and Parole in the United States, 2005*. NCJ 215091. Washington, DC: U.S. Department of Justice.

HAGAN, J., and J. P. COLEMAN (2001). Returning captives of the American war on drugs: Issues of community and family reentry. *Crime and Delinquency* 47(3): 352–367.

HAIRSTON, C. F. (1988). Family ties during imprisonment: Do they influence future criminal activity? *Federal Probation* 52(1): 48–52.

HARLOW, C. W. (2003). *Education and Correctional Populations*. Washington, DC: Bureau of Justice Statistics, U.S. Department of Justice.

HOLT, N., and D. MILLER (1972). *Explorations in inmate–family relationships*. Anaheim: California Department of Corrections.

HOWSER, J. F., and D. MACDONALD (1982). Maintaining family ties. *Corrections Today* 44(4): 96–98.

IRWIN, J. (1970). *The Felon*. Berkley: University of California Press.

LANGAN, P. A., and D. LEVIN (2002). *Recidivism of prisoners released in 1994*. NCJ 193427. Washington, DC: U.S. Department of Justice.

LECLAIR, D. P. (1978). Home furlough program effects on rates of recidivism. *Criminal Justice and Behavior* 5(3): 249–259.

MARUNA, S. (2006). Who owns resettlement: Towards restorative re-integration. *British Journal of Community Justice* 4(3): 23–33.

NELSON, M., P. DEESS, and C. ALLEN (1999). *The First Month Out: Post-Incarceration Experiences in New York City*. New York: The Vera Institute of Justice.

PUTNAM, R. D. (1995). *Bowling Alone: The Collapse and Revival of American Community*. New York: Simon & Schuster.

ROMAN, C. G, A. WOLFF, V. CORREA, and J. BUCK (2007). Assessing intermediate outcomes of a faith-based residential prisoner reentry program. *Research on Social Work Practice* 17(2): 199–215.

ROMAN, J., L. BROOKS, E. LAGERSON, A. CHAFLIN, and O. B. TERESHCHENKO (2007). *Impact and Cost-Benefit Analysis of the Maryland Reentry Partnership Initiative*. Washington, DC: The Urban Institute Press.

SHAPIRO, C., and M. SCHWARTZ (2001). Coming home: Building on family connections. *Corrections Management Quarterly* 5(3): 52–61.

TRAVIS, J. (2005). *But They All Come Back: Facing the Challenges of Prisoner Reentry*. Washington, DC: The Urban Institute Press.

VISHER, C., N. LA VIGNE, and J. FARRELL (2003). *Illinois prisoners' reflections on returning home*. Washington, DC: The Urban Institute.

Chapter 28

Prisoner Reentry

Moving Beyond the Identification of Inmate Needs Upon Release

Martha Henderson and Dena Hanley

ABSTRACT

A great deal of emphasis has been placed on prisoner reentry in recent years. Researchers have devoted much attention toward identifying the social, emotional, and economic barriers that inmates face upon release from correctional institutions. Thus, numerous studies show the impact of release from incarceration on family, education, employment, substance abuse, housing, and mental illness. Consequently, correctional officials are well versed on the issues that need to be addressed and have taken bold steps in allocating funds and other resources to support the implementation of reentry programming for offenders both behind prison walls and within communities. Every state now has some form of reentry programming designed to address the needs of offenders. Unfortunately, little attention has focused on *how* to effectively implement reentry programming within correctional contexts. Thus, what constitutes reentry programming within one state or agency may not constitute reentry programming within another. A comprehensive strategy for implementing reentry programming, which does more than simply recognize needs of offenders, should be incorporated into the release process, and a discussion by agencies concerning their organizational capacity to implement reentry programming is needed.

The chapter explores the past, present, and future of prisoner reentry in the United States. Included a description of the driving forces behind the movement, an overview of the literature on the reentry needs of offenders released back into the community, and a discussion of current practices. The chapter concludes with a discussion of future directions for the reentry movement.

WHAT IS PRISONER REENTRY?

Any discussion of the future of prisoner reentry should begin with a precise definition of the concept. Unfortunately, differing definitions for prisoner reentry exist, which can be classified into two divisions (see Hanley and Allen 2006 for complete discussion). First and foremost, reentry refers to inmates who reenter society after a period of incarceration. Included in this definition is an understanding that reentry is inevitable for the majority of inmates[1] (Travis and Visher 2005:3) and that reentry represents a transient state that exists for a limited time (Blumstein and Beck 2005:50). Second, prisoner reentry refers to the criminal justice process of releasing inmates from prison (Petersilia 2005a). This process includes all activities that criminal justice agencies, community-based agencies, faith-based organizations, and other stakeholders engage in to prepare inmates for return to society and to aid former inmates in their efforts to reestablish community connections. Thus, prisoner reentry is not a new concept. What has changed is our willingness to consciously invest in the process of reentry and to make changes in activities and programming provided to returning offenders in order to increase public safety. In short, many of the activities that have traditionally been part of corrections are now classified under one umbrella term: reentry.

DRIVING FORCES OF THE MOVEMENT

Prisoner reentry has emerged, during the past seven years, as a dominate theme in corrections at local, state, and national levels. In 2000, Attorney General Janet Reno was one of the first national level officials to publically recognize prisoner reentry as a significant issue, stating that reentry is "one of the most pressing problems we face as a nation" (Reno 2000). The driving forces underlying the initial attention toward prisoner reentry were related to five factors: (1) increases in the number of offenders entering, being released, and ultimately returning to prison; (2) recognition of the escalating costs associated with incarceration; (3) studies revealing that most of the offenders return to a small number of communities; (4) greater recognition of the impact of barriers related to prisoner reentry within institutional and community contexts; and (5) increased availability of federal dollars to fund reentry initiatives.

---

[1]The U.S. Department of Justice reports that at least 95 percent of all state prisoners will be released from prison at some point (http://www.ojp.usdoj.gov/bjs/reentry/releases.htm).

Growth in Offender Populations

At the time that U.S. Attorney General Janet Reno testified before Congress about the growing dangers of failing to address prisoner reentry, the United States was releasing more than 650,000 individuals to the community and more than half of state prisoners were returned to prison or jail (Hughes, Wilson, and Beck 2001). The U.S. Department of Justice estimated that approximately two out of three people released from prison in the United States would, at minimum, be rearrested within three years of release (Langan and Levin 2002). At the same time that the Hughes, Wilson, and Beck (2001) report was released, researchers Lynch and Sabol (2001) revealed to local, state, and national leaders that there would be a 350 percent increase in the numbers of people released from prison across a 20-year time span and that they continued expectations of rising rates.

Correctional statistics continue to reveal an unprecedented number of offenders returning to the community after a period of incarceration. At the end of 2005, federal and state adult correctional facilities housed in excess of 1.5 million people (Harrison and Beck 2006). At the same time, more than half a million inmates were released on parole with nearly two-thirds of these released offenders expected to be rearrested for a felony or serious misdemeanor within three years of release (Glaze and Bonczar 2006). The release figures show no sign of abating anytime soon as annual incarceration rates continue to increase the number of offenders released back into the community escalates as well. According to Public Safety, Public Spending Forecasting America's Prison Population 2007–2011 "imprisonment levels are expected to keep rising in all but four states, reaching a national rate of 562 per 100,000, or one of every 178 Americans. If you put them all together in one place, the incarcerated population in just five years will outnumber the residents of Atlanta, Baltimore and Denver combined" (2007:ii). Consequently, the nation must prepare for 95 percent of those offenders to be released at some point in the future, which translates into astronomical numbers of formerly incarcerated individuals living in the community.

Costs Associated with Incarceration and Recidivism

The costs associated with the incarceration and supervision of large numbers of inmates are staggering. As indicated in Figure 28.1, state correctional budgets have increased over the last 20 years. At the beginning of the reentry movement, correctional authorities were spending $38.2 billon to sustain state level correctional systems (Stephan 2001). At the present time, federal and state correctional agencies spend more than $62 billion per year on adult and juvenile corrections (Bureau of Justice Statistics 2005). (Bureau of Justice Statistics, *Key Facts at a Glance: Direct Expenditures by Criminal Justice Function, 1982–2004* available at http://www.ojp.usdoj.gov/bjs/glance/tables/exptyptab.htm and Public Safety Performance Section). Recent projections suggest that agencies will need an additional $27.5 billion over the next five years to accommodate the correctional agency needs (http://www.pewpublicsafety.org/pdfs/PCT_CorrectionsReport_3-1.pdf). The financial demands of incarcerating these

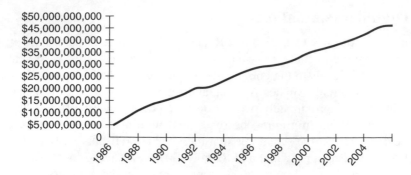

FIGURE 28.1   State Correctional Spending
Source: Graph taken from the Public Safety Performance Section
on State Correctional Spending. Available at http://www
.pewpublicsafety.org/statistics/corrections spending.aspx.

individuals place incredible burdens on state budgets, requiring decisions to be made regarding what other areas (e.g., education, health, and family support) should be reduced to support corrections.

Released Inmates Return to a Small Number of Communities

Many national and state level reports revealed that released offenders were primarily returning to a small number of communities, often characterized by significant social and economic deficits. The limitations of these communities exacerbate the difficulties associated with large numbers of offenders returning to the community. According to an Urban Institute report, two-thirds of released prisoners return to major metropolitan areas in the United States (Lynch and Sabol 2001). In New Jersey, for example, one-third of released offenders return to two counties in the state, Essex and Camden (Travis et al. 2003:4). In Maryland, over half of released prisoners return to Baltimore City and were concentrated in 6 of 55 communities—Southwest Baltimore, Greater Rosemont, Sandtown-Winchester/Harlem Park, Greenmount East, Clifton-Berea, and Southern Park Heights (La Vigne et al. 2003a:3). Returning inmates in Ohio were concentrated in the city of Cleveland with 28 percent of those returning to the city residing in five neighborhoods—Hough, Central, Glenville, Mount Pleasant, and Union Mills (La Vigne et al. 2003b). These areas are considered socioeconomically disadvantaged, providing few employment opportunities for law-abiding citizens, much less for those returning from prison. Many other states exhibit similar trends (e.g., the Urban Institute Reports for Illinois and Texas). The end result is that states have high concentrations of offenders returning to communities that are more economically and socially disadvantaged than other communities, making them ill equipped to deal effectively with the reentry needs of returning offenders (Clear, Waring, and Scully 2005; Lynch and Sabol 2001; Petersilia 2003; Travis 2005).

Recognition of Barriers to Reentry and Collateral Consequences

Starting in the early 2000s, there was a surge in the number of criminal justice policy makers and scholars highlighting that an emphasis on prisoner reentry was essential for the reduction of recidivism (Lynch and Sabol 2001; Petersilia 2003; Travis, Solomon, and Waul 2001; Travis and Visher 2005). Four scholars dominated the early literature on prisoner reentry and are still shaping reentry policy today. One of the most influential policy makers spearheading the movement was Jeremy Travis. In the wake of U.S. Attorney General Janet Reno's testimony before Congress, the National Institute of Justice (NIJ), under the direction of Jeremy Travis, was given the task of developing a research agenda around prisoner reentry issues. Travis published numerous monographs on the issues facing returning offenders while at NIJ and continued those efforts after taking a position with the Urban Institute.[2] His book, *But They All Come Back* (2005) is widely considered essential reading for those interested in corrections.

At the same time that Travis was beginning to publish initial studies on prisoner reentry, Lynch and Sabol (2001) released their groundbreaking report *Prisoner Reentry in Perspective* identifying the relationship between the growth in numbers of offenders released, community issues, and return to prison. They coined the term "churning," which is often used in many reentry publications. Churning refers to the process of an offender being released from prison into the community, returning to prison for a new crime or technical violation, being released for a subsequent time, and returning to prison again (Lynch and Sabol 2001).

Further attention to prisoner reentry was provided by Joan Petersilia in her 2003 book *When Prisoners Come Home*. She placed "churning" within community contexts and suggested that reentry was a public safety issue. The book associated the large numbers of inmates returning to distressed communities with negative social patterns of behavior, economic inequalities, increased victimization, and the failure of the criminal justice system. As a consequence, criminal justice stakeholders and the public were forced to face the consequences of releasing large numbers of offenders into communities unprepared and without corresponding social supports. More importantly, the book presented the first comprehensive guide for preparing inmates for release, reducing recidivism, and restoring released offenders to full citizenship. Petersilia's book called for states and the nation to determine the reentry needs of offenders and to create a standardized process for addressing those needs.

Identified Reentry Needs

Early reentry scholars indicated that an overwhelming number of released inmates entered prison with significant deficits that would continue to plague them upon reentry back into the community (Lynch and Sabol 2001; Petersilia 2003; Travis and Waul 2004). Table 28.1 provides a basic description of the reentry needs of offenders upon admittance

---

[2]Travis still impacts reentry publications at the Urban Institute today. The Urban Institute alone currently provides access to over 465 publications dealing with reentry related topics (http://www.urban.org/justice/index.cfm).

TABLE 28.1   Review of Inmates Reentry Needs During Incarceration and
Restricted Review of the Literature Showing How Addressing or
Failing to Address the Needs Impacts Public Safety[3]

Offender Needs During Arrest	Inmate Deficit	Literature Support
Education/ vocational	• More than half (50.8%) are without a high school diploma (Hughes, Wilson, and Beck 2001)	• Earning a skill while incarcerated increases the likelihood of obtaining employment after release (Lynch and Sabol 2001) • Participation in educational or vocational programs in prisons reduces recidivism (Burke and Vivian 2001; Nuttall, Hollman, and Staley 2003; Wilson, Gallagher, and MacKenzie 2000)
Employment	• 31% of inmates participate in a vocational/training program (GAO 2001)	• Employment upon release reduces recidivism (Piehl 2003; Travis and Visher 2005; Uggen 1999)
Substance abuse	• More than 80% have a history of substance abuse (Hughes, Wilson, and Beck 2001)	• Participation in substance abuse treatment during incarceration reduces recidivism and future drug use (Harrison 2001; Harrell and Roman 2001)
Mental health	• More than 14% inmates were considered mentally ill (Hughes, Wilson, and Beck 2001) • Serious mental illness rates are two to four times higher among prisoners than among the general population (Hammett, Roberts, and Kennedy 2002)	• Mentally ill offenders recidivate at higher rates (Feder 1992) • Participation in mental health programs reduces recidivism (Lurigio 2001, 2002; Lurigio, Fallen, and Dincin 2000)
Homelessness	• Close to 12% homeless at time of arrest (Hughes, Wilson, and Beck 2001)	• Homeless individuals are more likely to be rearrested and incarcerated (Snow, Baker, and Anderson 1989)

---

[3]The list of items and literature reviewed in Table 28.1 is not intended to be exhaustive. The table is designed to introduce students to some of the commonly accepted offender needs upon release.

and release from prison. Moreover, inmates are often not provided with necessary services to address deficits during their incarceration. The lack of services in prison is due to the overwhelming demand for rehabilitative services within institutions, the inability of correctional agencies to staff treatment programs, decreases in state and federal support for funding correctional programs, and lack of political will to implement rehabilitative programming (Petersilia 2000; Travis 2002). The failure to address the reentry needs of offenders puts the public at risk and ultimately leads to increased "churning."

Increased Availability of Federal Funding

Between 2001 and 2004, federal and state governments had allocated millions of dollars in their attempt to address the reentry needs of offenders (Petersilia 2004). The most visible example of funding provided to states by the federal government were monies allocated for the Serious Violent Reentry Initiative provided by the U.S. Department of Justice.[4] The state and federal governments still contribute considerable funds to prisoner reentry. This interest was most recently demonstrated by President Bush in his 2004 State of the Union Address. President George W. Bush stated, "We know from long experience that if [former prisoners] can't find work, or a home, or help, they are much more likely to commit more crimes and return to prison. . . . America is the land of the second chance, and when the gates of prison open, the path ahead should lead to a better life." President Bush proposed that the federal government provide close to $300 million dollars to help faith-based and community organizations develop programs to aid returning inmates. Further evidence of the push for new prisoner reentry initiatives can be found through Congressional efforts to pass The Second Chance Act (H.R. 1704) over the last three years.

CURRENT STATUS OF REENTRY PROGRAMMING

In the wake of such tremendous pressures to develop reentry programming for offenders, all 50 states had implemented some form of reentry initiative funded in part by federal and state government allocations by 2004 (Petersilia 2005). Often the federal government has provided the initial funds to pilot reentry programming and offered blueprints through the NIJa or the National Institute of Corrections for agencies to follow. These blueprints are purposely broad in order to accommodate differences in the needs of jurisdictions attempting to implement reentry. The lack of specificity allows for differing implementation strategies and emphases, creating problems for agencies hoping to replicate or evaluate programs. Henderson and Hanley (2006) characterize the consequences of the vague mandates given to agencies implementing reentry programming in the following manner:

> Throughout the country, agencies have engaged in the implementation of reentry programming without a solid idea of whether or not reentry works or even how to define the concept of reentry. In less than five years, all of the correctional jurisdictions in the United States are

---

[4]Information on the total amounts of funding and types of programs developed under the Serious Violent Offender Initiative can be found at http://www.svori-evaluation.org/index.cfm?fuseaction=dsp_site_information.

operating differently with regard to the release of offenders back to the community.[5] Consequently, there is a mercurial nature to reentry; what constitutes reentry programming in one area is not considered a reentry program elsewhere. In some state agencies, helping offenders' complete necessary paperwork for obtaining social services in the community constitutes reentry programming; elsewhere such work is only considered a part of a reentry program, if a correctional agent directly links the offender to a person within the social service agency itself. It is not only the inconsistency but the lack of clarity that has led to the fall of many correctional initiatives (Nelson and Trone 2000; Reentry Policy Council 2005b). Reentry may not be an exception to the unsuccessful attempts experienced by its policy predecessors.

ISSUES SURROUNDING THE IMPLEMENTATION OF REENTRY

The implementation of reentry programming across the country has been hampered by three major obstacles. First, many agencies rushed to develop reentry programming without first considering how the program fits within the larger criminal justice system in their jurisdiction and without coordinating with community-based agencies and treatment providers to deliver services. Harrell et al. (2003:6) report that successful partnerships with community agencies require two factors: (1) the development of detailed strategic plans that specify needed changes to policy for each agency, set deadlines and assign responsibility for tasks, and (2) the preparation of written memorandums of understanding on the purpose and role of each agency in implementation. Without such plans and understanding on the part of all stakeholders, state departments of corrections would be unable to provide seamless transition back into the community. All parties must be working toward the same goals and objectives in order for reentry efforts to be successful. For example, the state of Ohio developed a reentry program designed to connect seriously mentally ill offenders released from prison with mental health and disability services in the community. Recent evaluations of the Ohio program reveal that the Department of Corrections has been unable to coordinate effectively with the community agencies to ensure service continuity (Visher et al. 2005). Released offenders were not receiving adequate medication supplies upon release nor being connected with local mental health service providers. Similarly, less than 10 percent of inmates in Illinois reported referrals to community mental or physical health services in the community upon release (Solomon et al. 2006).

Second, agencies failed to adequately consider whether the organization has the capacity to implement reentry programming. Organizational capacity has been defined as formal agencies' or organizations' "commitment, knowledge, skills, and resources necessary to identify and address problems and affect change" (Elliott et al. 2003:273). Therefore, organizational capacity refers to the ability of the agency to understand its

---

[5]See, for example, the wide variation in reentry programming available from the National Governors Association (http://www.nga.org/cda/files/REENTRYNATIONAL.pdf), as part of the Serious Violent Offender Reentry Initiative (http://www.svori-evaluation.org/index.cfm?fuseaction=dsp_site_information), and Nelson and Trone (2000).

current operations and how these operations need to be modified in order to meet the goals and objectives. For correctional agencies, particularly those embarking on reentry initiatives, identifying current operational problems and addressing these problems prior to introducing changes is imperative for success. Without a clear understanding of current operations (and issues of those operations), agencies will compound ineffective correctional activities, with no positive end result.

Several recent research reports detail how the failure to assess organizational capacity for reentry hinders implementation and outcomes. For example, the evaluation of the Breaking the Cycle Report (Harrell et al. 2003) suggests that the failure of the Tacoma site to reduce drug use was in part due to the failure of the program to consider whether it had enough staff to deliver treatment (e.g., the demand for treatment outweighed the supply) and a failure to consider that program implementation would be affected by the type of drug user involved in the program.[6] The Tacoma program was comprised of a greater number of participants with methamphetamine problems, who, according to the authors of the report, are more difficult to treat than users of other drugs. The influence of line staff (those in direct, daily contact with clients and/or offenders) can be instrumental to the success or failure of new initiatives (Cameron and Wren 1999; Flores et al. 2005; Moon and Swaffin-Smith 1998; Perry-Wooten and Crane 2003). One example of line staff having a detrimental effect on the success of a program is the evaluation of Project Greenlight.[7] This evaluation reported that participants in the Project Greenlight program did not fare as well as the control group. The evaluators suggested that these outcomes may result from an inability of case managers to effectively deliver the program (Brown and Campbell 2005).

Third, agencies have historically failed to plan how they would fund programs once federal and state grant funding sources were depleted. Reentry initiatives could learn from the experiences of correctional predecessors. For example, Intensive Supervision Programs (ISPs) were a fad of the mid-1980s. Many programs (including those in Texas, Virginia, California, and Wisconsin) had difficulties successfully implementing the ISP model, as required by the initial federal grant. For example, the initial model required a ratio of three supervision officers to a caseload of 25 offenders (Petersilia 1989; Petersilia and Turner 1993). However, this ratio was difficult to maintain, particularly once federal monies were no longer available. The lack of continual funding had a significant impact on the programs, which could have affected the outcomes of many of the evaluations. ISPs were often found to be ineffective (GAO 1990; Latessa et al. 1998; Tuner and Petersilia 1991). Similarly, Project Greenlight, originally designed to run for three years, was suspended after one year when funding was no longer available (Brown and Campbell 2005). Reentry programs should be wary of this type of limitation on federal funds and plan for their future.

---

[6]In the two other Breaking the Cycle sites (Birmingham and Jacksonville) where cocaine use was on the part of participants was high, illicit drug use decreased after participation in the program.

[7]Project Greenlight was a prison-based reentry program conducted by the Vera Institute of Justice at the Queensboro Correctional Facility in Queens, New York, from February 2002 to February 2003.

THE NEXT STEPS FOR THE MOVEMENT

The focus on implementation is crucial for any correctional program to be effective. History demonstrates that a failure to consider implementation of initiatives can prove detrimental. ISPs and Project Greenlight are just two examples of how seemingly successful pilot programs have failed in replication efforts.

For reentry programs and initiatives to be effective, planning must be more comprehensive and deliberate. Planners must begin to assess the current organizational capacity and then design programs that will be most beneficial for the *individual* jurisdiction. In the assessment of organizational capacity, programs must determine the status of the following:

1. *Administrative guidance and vision*—how the leadership of the organization has defined the mission and vision of the organization, the quality of the leadership itself, as well as the communication strategies of the administration.

2. *Internal and external communication*—the extent to which the people (internal and external to the program) agree on the mission and vision of the organization; how the organization communicates results; and cooperative agreements with other agencies and organizations.

3. *Consumer capital*—the degree to which the program "fits" within the local criminal justice system (e.g., does the program offer beneficial resources for the community?); the appropriateness of the population the program serves; and the satisfaction of that population that participates in the program.

4. *Information capital*—the types of data collected by the program (e.g., do these data correspond to the mission, vision, and values of the organization?); the quality of information technology used by the organization; and how the program uses these data to inform progress toward achieving the mission, vision, and values.

5. *Human resource capital*—the program's investment in its staff; how well the program demonstrates this investment; as well as staff satisfaction and commitment.

6. *Adherence to evidence-based practice*—the program's identification of appropriate evidence-based practice and the use of this research literature in daily practices.

7. *Results and outcomes*—the ability of the program to analyze and produce research relating to successful outcomes; the extent to which the organization shares this information with internal and external stakeholders; and the use of this information to improve practice.

CONCLUSION

Historically, the field of corrections, both in academic literature and practitioner fields, has rushed to implement some of the latest fads without considering individual jurisdictional differences in implementing new programs and initiatives. Further complicating this lack of individuality during implementation is the failure to consider the impact that these changes will have on the operations of the agency or organization. Without a comprehensive understanding of the organization's current practices and operations, any attempt to institute change will be unsuccessful. Administrators must realize that change will require an investment of time and resources. Without that investment, correctional agencies are doomed to the legacy of unsuccessful efforts that have plagued the field so many times before.

REFERENCES

BLUMSTEIN, A., and A. J. BECK (2005). Reentry as a transient state between liberty and recommitment. In *Prisoner Reentry and Crime in America*, ed. J. Travis and C. Visher, pp. 50–79. New York: Cambridge University Press.

BROWN, B., and R. CAMPBELL (2005). *Smoothing the Path from Prison to Home. A Round Table Discussion of Lessons Learned from Project Greenlight*. [Retrieved March 20, 2007, from http://www.vera.org/project/project1_3.asp?id=3&project_id=46&sub_id=38]

BUREAU OF JUSTICE STATISTICS (2005). *Key Facts at a Glance: Direct Expenditures by Criminal Justice Function, 1982–2004*. Retrieved April, 07, 2007 from http://www.ojp.usdoj.gov/bjs/glance/tables/exptyptab.htm and Public Safety Performance Section.

BURKE, L. O., and J. E. VIVIAN (2001). The effect of college programming on recidivism rates at the Hampden County House of Correction: A 5-year study. *Journal of Correctional Education* 52(4): 160–162.

CAMERON, G., and A. M. WREN (1999). Reconstructing organizational culture: A process using multiple perspectives. *Public Health Nursing* 16(2): 96–101.

CLEAR, T., E. WARING, and K. SCULLY (2005). Communities and reentry: Concentrated reentry cycling. In *Prisoner Reentry and Crime in America*, ed. J. Travis and C. Visher, New York: Cambridge University Press.

ELLIOTT, S. J., J. O'LOUGHLIN, K. ROBINSON, J. EYLES, R. CAMERON, D. HARVEY, K. RAINE, and D. GELSKEY (2003). Conceptualizing dissemination research and activity: The case of the Canadian heart health initiative. *Health Education & Behavior* 30(3): 267–282.

FEDER, L. (1992). A comparison of the community adjustment of mentally ill offenders with those from the general population: An 18-month follow-up. *Law and Human Behavior* 15: 477–493.

FLORES, A., A. L. RUSSELL, E. LATESSA, and L. TRAVIS (2005). Evidence of professionalism or quakery: Measuring practioner awareness of risk/need factors effective treatment strategies. *Federal Probation* 69(2): 9–14.

GENERAL ACCOUNTING OFFICE (2001). *Prison Releases: Trends and Information on Reintegration Programs*. (GAO-01-483). [Retrieved March 15, 2007, from http://www.gao.gov/new.items/d01483.pdf]

GLAZE, L., and T. P. BONCZAR (2006). *Probation and Parole in the United States, 2005*. Bureau of Justice Statistics. Report No. NCJ 215091. [Retrieved March 15, 2007, from http://www.ojp.usdoj.gov/bjs/abstract/ppus05.htm]

HAMMETT, T. M., C. ROBERTS, and S. KENNEDY (2002). Health-related issues in prisoner reentry. *Crime & Delinquency* 47(3): 390–409.

HANLEY, D., and M. K. ALLEN (2006). *Reentry: Fighting Crime Through Public Safety and Cost Effectiveness*. Report submitted to Ohio Community Corrections Association.

HARRELL, A., and J. ROMAN (2001). Reducing drug use and crime among offenders: The impact of graduated sanctions. *Journal of Drug Issues* 31(1): 207–232.

HARRELL, A., O. MITCHELL, J. C. MERRILL, and D. B. MARLOWE (2003). *Evaluation of Breaking the Cycle*. Washington, DC: The Urban Institute.

HARRISON, L. D. (2001). The revolving prison door for drug-involved offenders. *Crime & Delinquency* 47(3): 462–485.

HARRISON, P. M., and A. J. BECK (2006). Prisoners in 2005. Bureau of Justice Statistics. Report No. NCJ 215092. [Retrieved March 17, 2007, from http://www.ojp.usdoj.gov/bjs/abstract/p05.htm]

HENDERSON, M. L., and D. HANLEY (2006). Planning for quality: A strategy for reentry initiatives. *Western Criminology Review* 7(2). [Retrieved March 13, 2007, from http://wcr.sonoma.edu/v07n2/62-henderson/henderson.pdf]

HUGHES, T. A., D. J. WILSON, and A. J. BECK (2001). *Trends in State Parole, 1990–2000*. Bureau of Justice Statistics. Report No. NCJ 184735. [Retrieved March 22, 2007, from http://www.ojp.usdoj.gov/bjs/pub/pdf/tsp00.pdf]

LANGAN, P., and D. LEVIN (2002). *Recidivism of Prisoners Released in 1994*. Bureau of Justice Statistics Special Report. Washington, DC: U.S. Department of Justice, Bureau of Justice Statistics.

LATESSA, E., L. TRAVIS, B. FULTON, and A. STICHMAN (1998). *Evaluating the Prototypical ISP*. Report submitted to the National Institute of Justice (95-IJ-CX-0032).

LA VIGNE, N. G., V. KACHNOWSKI, J. TRAVIS, R. NASER, and C. VISHER (2003a). *A Portrait of Prisoner Reentry in Maryland*. Washington, DC: The Urban Institute.

LA VIGNE, N. G., G. L. THOMSON, C. VISHER, V. KACHNOWSKI, and J. TRAVIS (2003b). *A Portrait of Prisoner Reentry in Ohio*. Washington, DC: The Urban Institute.

LURIGIO, A. J. (2001). Effective services for parolees with mental illness. *Crime & Delinquency* 47: 446–461.

LURIGIO, A. J. (2002). Coerced drug treatment for offenders: Does it work? *GLATTC Research Update* 4: 1–2.

LURIGIO, A. J., J. FALLON, and J. DINCIN (2000). Helping the mentally ill in jails adjust to community life: A description of a post-release ACT program and its clients. *International Journal of Offender Therapy and Comparative Criminology* 44: 450–466.

LYNCH, J. P., and J. SABOL (2001). *Prisoner Reentry in Perspective*. Washington, DC: The Urban Institute.

MOON, C., and C. SWAFFIN-SMITH (1998). Total quality management and new patterns of work: Is there life beyond empowerment. *Total Quality Management* 9(2): 301–310.

NELSON, M., and J. TRONE, (2000). The Role of Prerelease for Prisoner Reentry. (Mellow, J. and Dickinson, J. (eds.) *Federal Probation* 70(1).

NUTTALL, J., L. HOLLMAN, and E. M. STALEY (2003). The effect of earning a GED on recidivism rates. *Journal of Correctional Education*.

PERRY-WOOTEN, L., and P. CRANE (2003). Nurses as implementers of organizational culture. *Nursing Economics Journal* 21: 275–279.

PETERSILIA, J. (1989). Implementing randomized experiments: Lessons from BJA's intensive supervision project. *Evaluation Review* 13(5): 435–458.

PETERSILIA, J. (2000). Challenges of prison reentry and parole in California. *California Policy Research Center Brief Series* http://www.ucop.edu/cprc/parole.html]

PETERSILIA, J. (2003). *When Prisoners Come Home: Parole and Prisoner Reentry*. New York: Oxford University Press.

PETERSILIA, J. (2004). What works in prisoner reentry? Reviewing and questioning the evidence. *Federal Probation* 68(2). [Retrieved March 15, 2007, from http://www.uscourts.gov/fedprob/September_2004/whatworks.html]

PETERSILIA, J. (2005a). *Hard Time: Ex-offenders Returning Home After Prison*. http://www.seweb.uci.edu/users/joan/Images/hard_time.pdf]

PETERSILIA, J. (2005b). From cell to society: Who is returning home? In *Prisoner Reentry and Public Safety in America*, ed. J. Travis and C. Visher, pp. 15–49. New York: Cambridge University Press.

PETERSILIA, J., and S. TURNER (1993). Intensive probation and parole. In *Crime and Justice: A Review of the Research*, ed. M. Tonry, pp. 281–335. Chicago, IL: University of Chicago Press.

PIEHL, A. (2003). *Crime, Work and Reentry*. Paper prepared for the Reentry Roundtable, The

Employment Dimensions of Prisoner Reentry: Understanding the Nexus between Prisoner Reentry and Work, New York, May 19–20.

PRESIDENT GEORGE W. BUSH (2004). *State of the Union Address*. [Retrieved March 15, 2007, from http://www.whitehouse.gov/news/releases/2004/01/print/20040120-7.html]

REENTRY POLICY COUNCIL (2005a). *Report of the Reentry Policy Council*. [Retrieved March 11, 2007, from http://www.reentrypolicy.org/report/order-report.php]

REENTRY POLICY COUNCIL (2005b). *Ensuring Timely Access to Medicaid and SSI/SSDI for People with Mental Illness Released from Prison*. [Retrieved February 13, 2008 from http://www.reentrypolicy.org/document/Summary_4statesfinal.pdf]

RENO, J. (2000). *Remarks at John Jay College of Criminal Justice on the Reentry Court Initiative*. [Retrieved March 20, 2007, from http://www.usdoj.gov/archive/ag/speeches/2000/doc2.htm]

SERIOUS VIOLENT OFFENDER REENTRY INITIATIVE 2007). *Site Information*. [Retrieved March 15, 2007, from http://www.svori-evaluation.org/index.cfm?fuseaction=dsp_site_information] U.S. Dept. of Justice – Office of Justice Programs

SOLOMON, A. L., C. VISHER, N. G. LA VIGNE, and J. OSBORNE (2006). *Understanding the Challenges of Prisoner Reentry: Research Findings from the Urban Institute's Prisoner Reentry Portfolio*. [Retrieved March 20, 2007, from http://www.urban.org/url.cfm?ID=411289]

SNOW, D., L. ANDERSON, and S. GONZALEZ-BAKER (1989).Criminality and homeless men: An empirical assessment. *Social Problems* 36 (1989): 532–549.

STEPHAN, J. (2001). *State Prison Expenditures, 2001*. Bureau of Justice Statistics. Special Report. Washington, DC: U.S. Department of Justice, Bureau of Justice Statistics.

THE SECOND CHANCE ACT OF 2005, H.R. 1704, 109d Cong. (2005).

TRAVIS, J. (2005). *But They All Come Back: Facing the Challenges of Prisoner Reentry*. Washington, DC: Urban Institute Press.

TRAVIS, J., and C. VISHER (2005). *Prisoner Reentry and Crime in America*. New York: Cambridge University Press.

TRAVIS, J., and M. WAUL (2004). *Prisoners Once Removed: The Impact of Incarceration and Reentry on Children, Families, and Communities*. Washington, DC: Urban Institute Press.

TRAVIS, J. (2002). Facing the challenges of prisoner reentry. Urban Institute.

TRAVIS, J., A. S. SOLOMON, and M. WAUL (2001). *From Prison to Home: The Dimensions and Consequences of Prisoner Reentry*. Washington, DC: New Press.

TRAVIS, J., S. KEEGAN, E. CADORA, A. SOLOMON, and C. SWARTZ (2003). *A Portrait of Prisoner Reentry in New Jersey*. Washington, DC: The Urban Institute.

TURNER, S., and J. PETERSILIA (1991). *Focusing on High-Risk Parolees: An Experiment to Reduce Commitments to the Texas Department of Corrections. Working Draft: NIJ (WD-5376-1_NIJ)*.

UGGEN, C. (1999). Ex-offenders and the conformist alternative: A job quality model of work and crime. *Social Problems* 46(1): 127–151.

U.S. GENERAL ACCOUNTING OFFICE (GAO) (1990). *Intensive Sanctions: Their Impacts on Prison Crowding, Costs and Recidivism Are Still Unclear. Report to the Chairman, Subcommittee on Crime and Criminal Justice*. Committee on the Judiciary, House of Representatives. PEMD-90-21.

VISHER, C. A., N. L. NASER, D. BAER, and J. JANNETTA (2005). *In Need of Help: Experiences of Seriously Mentally Ill Prisoners Returning to Cincinnati*. Washington, DC: The Urban Institute.

WILSON, D. B., C. A. GALLAGHER, and D. L. MACKENZIE (2000). A meta-analysis of corrections-based education, vocation, and work programs for adult offenders. *Journal of Research in Crime and Delinquency* 37(4): 347–368.

Chapter 29

The Current Status of Inmates Living with HIV/AIDS

Mark M. Lanier, Ph.D., and Roberto Hugh Potter, Ph.D.

ABSTRACT

This chapter reviews the obstacles and challenges facing HIV-positive offenders and then outlines the latest research and policy programs. Demographic, epidemiological, and social determinants are discussed. Over the past few years tremendous strides have been realized regarding providing incarcerated HIV-positive populations health care. However, a glaring deficiency remains with postrelease treatment. We conclude with policy suggestions.

INTRODUCTION

Institutionalized individuals are one of society's most ostracized groups. Much like leper colonies of the eighteenth century, today's correctional facilities segregate the disempowered, the poor, drug users, and the violent from the rest of society. Also like leper colonies, inhabitants of contemporary institutions face serious medical threats, including acquired immunodeficiency virus (AIDS), hepatitis, human immunodeficiency virus (HIV), and tuberculosis. Unlike leper colonies, however, most of the inhabitants of modern penal colonies will one day reenter society—some infected with serious, contagious diseases, and many unarmed with knowledge about the disease and prevention.

542

In addition to physical separation, the stigma associated with institutionalization further isolates the incarcerated from mainstream society. Victims of HIV and AIDS also face considerable stigma and social isolation even when not incarcerated. Since the early 1990s, society has shown a marked interest in exploring the lives of those living with HIV/AIDS. Made-for-television movies such as *Our Sons* (1991) and more recently, *Angels in America* (2003) and big budget films like *Philadelphia* (1993) and *RENT* (2005) have chronicled the lives of those living with AIDS and exemplify how the disease can affect anyone, from white-collar lawyers to transsexual street performers. Most of these media portrayals have shown white, working professionals and their illness. However, most sufferers do not have the resources available to working, upper-class white Americans. More victims per capita are poor and are people of color. In our society, women and people of color have a history of being marginalized and disempowered by sexism and racism. When any individual is simultaneously a member of each of these groups, the psychological and physical pressures are immense. Persons who belong to these high-risk groups (drug users, economically disadvantaged, and people of color) are concentrated in correctional institutions.

Medical researchers have the formidable task of identifying a vaccine that prevents the spread of HIV and treatments that improve the longevity and quality of life for those already infected. Social scientists have the task of developing theory that can be used to guide policy initiatives that slow the spread of HIV. Recently medical breakthroughs have started to increase the length of life for AIDS patients, but a cure or vaccine remains an enigma. Social scientists have also had mixed results: AIDS cases are decreasing among certain high-risk groups but are rapidly increasing among heterosexual women and people of color (indicating gender- and ethnic-specific theoretical guides are needed). However, AIDS and HIV continue to spread through all societal groups. If current trends continue, the number of incarcerated Americans will increase, victims of HIV/AIDS will multiply, and the burdens faced by correctional systems will intensify. In short, the cost in physical, emotional, and fiscal terms will escalate as we progress through the twenty-first century unless effective theoretically driven and culturally appropriate policies are implemented now.

The following discussion focuses on incarcerated populations. This population was selected for several reasons. First, high-risk groups are concentrated in correctional facilities, affording correctional administrators an ideal opportunity to positively influence the at-risk behaviors of this captive group (Lanier and McCarthy 1989). Second, persons, especially women, who are under correctional supervision, have been seriously neglected by researchers and in the AIDS literature (Altice et al. 1998).

This chapter describes the current problems facing these individuals and provides a theoretical model, which, if used to shape correctional policy, could help reduce the occurrence of HIV in the twenty-first century and decrease the stigma suffered by those already infected. The policy suggestions would make humane treatment more normative for those incarcerated—and for those returning to mainstream society. Despite the focus on incarcerated persons, the treatment information, theoretical model, and policy suggestions presented here are applicable with any at-risk group.

LIVING WITH HIV AND AIDS

As of 2005, the Centers for Disease Control and Prevention (CDC 2005) reported that 244,868 persons (14 or older) were living with HIV (non-AIDS) in the United States and affiliated territories. Another 946,578 were living with full-blown AIDS. During 2005, 35,107 new cases of HIV were reported. Of those, 35,107, or 30 percent were female and 70 percent were male. Also in 2005, 41,900 new cases of AIDS were reported, with 74 percent of the cases being male and 26 percent female.

Among women currently living with HIV where mode of transmission was known, African-American women accounted for the largest "racial" category (approximately 67 percent), white women the next most frequent (approximately 22 percent), and Hispanic women (approximately 10 percent) comprise the majority of the remaining cases. For these women, where method of transmission was known, heterosexual sex was the most common method of HIV acquisition (46 percent), followed by intravenous drug use (17 percent), and heterosexual sex with an intravenous drug user (9 percent). However, nearly half (49 percent) were unable to identify a mode of transmission.

Among women living with AIDS, approximately 57 percent of cases were among African-American women, approximately 22 percent among White women, and approximately 18 percent among Hispanic women. In this group, heterosexual sex was again the leading known method of transmission (44 percent), followed by injection intravenous drug use (36 percent). For both HIV- and AIDS-infected women, sex with an HIV-infected man was the most likely mode of transmission within the heterosexual sex category. For HIV- (non-AIDS) women, sex with an HIV-infected man was more than twice as common as sex with an injecting drug user male. However, among the women with AIDS, sex with an injecting drug user was almost as common as sex with a known HIV-infected man (CDC 2005).

Men accounted for close to 73 percent of persons living with HIV and 70 percent of individuals living with AIDS. HIV-infected men were primarily African American (46 percent), with white men not far behind (43 percent), and Hispanic men accounting for the largest part of the remaining HIV (non-AIDS) cases. Among those with AIDS, African-American men accounted for nearly 47 percent of known cases, white men for 35 percent, and Hispanic men for close to 18 percent of the total cases. Men who have sex with men (MSM) represent the largest single proportion of known transmission causes for both HIV- and AIDS-affected males (49 percent and 54 percent, respectively). Intravenous drug use was the next most common known transmission route for men with HIV (13 percent) and AIDS (21 percent), followed by both intravenous drug use and MSM behavior for AIDS- and HIV-affected men (8 percent and 5 percent, respectively). Again, heterosexual sex with an intravenous drug user was a substantial transmission route among men who were infected through heterosexual sex (CDC 2005).

Of course, the percentages of known HIV/AIDS cases present a different view of the problem than the proportional picture. African Americans represent only around 13 percent of the total U.S. population, so the impact of HIV/AIDS on the African-American community is grossly disproportionate for that community. Hispanic/Latinos are only slightly overrepresented, and whites are underrepresented in population terms when it comes to the impact of HIV/AIDS. These disparities in health status are also mirrored in over-representation of African Americans and Hispanics in the corrections systems around the United States.

LIVING IN PRISON AND JAIL

At the end of 2004, the Bureau of Justice Statistics (BJS) reported there were 1,446,269 individuals in American state or federal prisons. At the mid-year jail census, there were an additional 747,529 individuals in local jails. These combined numbers account for well over 2 million individuals. The Bureau of Justice Statistics (Beck, Karberg, and Harrison 2002:12) census of prison and jail inmates on June 30, 2001, reveals that minority status individuals comprised 64 percent of all male inmates; those figures remained unchanged by year-end 2001 (Harrison and Beck 2002). African-American males comprised the largest single group (45 percent of total, or 803,400) of incarcerated individuals (in jails, African Americans accounted for 40.6 percent of the population). Hispanic males comprised 16 percent ($n = 283,000$) of jail inmates and the total incarcerated Hispanic population was 14.7 percent. Whites are 38 percent ($n = 684,800$) in jails and accounted for 43 percent of the total. These proportions are unchanged from the previous year (Beck and Karberg 2001:9) and have remained relatively unchanged over time. BJS estimated that 12 percent of males ($n = 601,800$) in their twenties and early thirties in the African-American community were in jail or prison during 2001. Even in older age groups, the percentage of African-American males incarcerated was up to 3.4 times higher than among Whites of the same age group. The percentage (3.4 percent) of Hispanic males age 25–29 (3.4 percent) incarcerated was substantially lower than that for African Americans, but still higher than the percentage for whites (1.9 percent).

Women have been the fastest growing segment of the prison population. According to the BJS, in mid-2004 there were 123 female inmates per 100,000 women in the United States. BJS also reports that African-American women make up 43 percent of the incarcerated population, white women 42 percent, and Hispanic women 1 percent. The rates of incarceration also show a pattern similar to that found among males. African-American women are three times more likely to be incarcerated than Hispanic women, and five and one-half times more likely than white women to be incarcerated. This discrepancy held across all age categories.

The BJS (Beck, Karberg, and Harrison 2002:12) report shows great variation in the incarceration rates for African Americans and Hispanics across the nation. While overall incarceration rates are highest in southern states, Wisconsin had the highest incarceration rates for blacks, followed by Iowa. New Hampshire had the highest rate for Hispanics, followed by Pennsylvania and Connecticut. Northeastern states had the highest overall differences in rates between white and black imprisonment, as well as for whites and Hispanics (other than North Dakota).

BJS reported that between 1995 and 2001 the total incarcerated population grew an average 4 percent annually. Local jail, state and federal prison populations grew at average annual rates of 3.7 percent, 3.4 percent, and 8.8 percent respectively, over that time period. The good news was that the rate of growth in local jail populations has slowed, with the 1.6 percent increase from 2000 to 2001 being the smallest increase in 10 years. Similarly, state prison populations have slowed, with the 0.3 percent increase between 2000 and 2001 being the lowest increase in 28 years. Unfortunately, federal prison admissions have risen substantially over the same time period. No matter at which level of correctional facilities one looks, African Americans are overrepresented relative to their proportion of the population of the United States.

Most of the men and women who are incarcerated in correctional facilities are parents and many have used "*serious*" drugs (Center on Addiction and Substance Abuse 1998). More than three-quarters of all women in prisons in 1991 had children, and two-thirds had children under the age of 18 (Women in Prison 1994). Also, in 1991, 36.5 percent used cocaine or crack, and 14.8 percent had used heroin (BJS 1994:622). Thus, many incarcerated mothers are at risk for HIV infection.

As the data suggest, it is not difficult to draw a connection between the disproportionate burden of HIV/AIDS on communities of color and the disproportionate rates of incarceration among members of those same communities. These disparities hold for almost every category of infectious and chronic diseases that enter correctional facilities. By and large the people incarcerated in U.S. jails and prisons come from communities of color and/or economic disadvantage. The high-risk behaviors associated with substance use/ dependency, other criminal behaviors, sex work or trading, and life on the streets place these groups at high probability of acquiring HIV/AIDS, Hepatitis B and C, and other sexually transmitted diseases (STDs). In the next section we develop the conditions that require coordination of health efforts in jails and prisons and communities based on these risks.

AIDS IN CORRECTIONAL FACILITIES

Recognition that HIV/AIDS was a problem in correctional populations began to emerge in the mid-1980s, and by the early 1990s was the object of both applied programs and academic research (Hammett 1988; Lanier and McCarthy 1989; Lurigio 1989). Since the late 1980s AIDS was the second leading cause of deaths among state prisoners nationally (Maruschak 2002) and was identified as the leading cause of death in some correctional systems (Acquired Immunodeficiency Syndrome 1986; Florida 1989). For example, the BJS wrote "In 2002 the overall rate of confirmed AIDS in the prison population (0.48%) was nearly 3.5 times the rate in the U.S. general population (0.14%)." The picture looked bleak, indeed. More recently, there were an estimated annual 37,241 new HIV infections in the United States between 2001 and 2005. This represented a decline between 2001 and 2004, with an upturn in 2005 (possibly due to new emphasis on testing and infection identification). The epidemic remained disproportionately in minorities especially among African Americans and males. Male-to-male sexual activity continued to account for the greatest transmission route, followed by high-risk heterosexual contact and injection drug use (CDC 2006a).

With the increasing introduction of combination therapies (discussed later) as "standard of care" in prisons in the mid-1990s, the HIV picture in prisons began to change.

From 1995 to 1997 the number and percent of prison inmates identified as HIV positive declined, only to rise in 1998 and drop through 1999 and 2000. In 1995 there were 24,256 HIV-positive inmates (2.3 percent of total) in prisons; by 2000 there were 25,088 HIV-positive inmates (2.0 percent of total). Thus, while the number of known HIV-positive inmates increased slightly over the six-year period, the proportion of all inmates known to be HIV positive actually declined. This is because the growth in known HIV-positive inmates was slower than the overall prison population growth (3 percent versus 16 percent). Yet, the rate of confirmed AIDS cases among prisoners remained about four times higher than in the U.S. general population over that time period (Maruschak 2002).

Between 2001 and 2004 the percentage of state and federal prisoners known to be living with HIV ranged from 1.9 percent (2001–2003) to 1.8 percent (2004). The absolute number of state and federal prisoners has also continued to decrease to a low of 23,046, as compared to 24,256 in 1995. Thus, the decrease is both in terms of a continued expansion of the prison population and an actual decrease in the number of prisoners with the disease.

Unfortunately, the number of confirmed AIDS cases among state and federal prisoners rose in 2004. The rate of confirmed AIDS cases was around three times higher than among the general public, down from five times greater only a few years earlier. Some good news in this bleak scenario is that the confirmed death rate from HIV/AIDS-related conditions dropped more than 84 percent between 1995 and the end of 2004. However, the percentage of deaths attributed to AIDS-related conditions was about 1.5 times higher among prisoners than the general public in 2004 (age 15–54; Maruschak 2002, 2006a).

There are some distressing continuities even in this apparently positive news regarding HIV/AIDS in corrections. Early in the epidemic, it was reported in Massachusetts that around 5 percent of the 735 females who elected to have an AIDS antibody test in 1993 were HIV positive—compared to just 2 percent of the male inmates (Hammett et al. 1995:16). In 1994, the HIV seroprevalence rate for state inmates ranged from 0.2 percent to 20.1 percent for women (HIV in Prison 1996:6). The rate for women surpassed that of male inmates whose HIV rate ranging from 0.1 to 12.0 percent (HIV in Prison 1996:6). By the end of 2004, women still had higher rates of HIV (2.6 percent of total) than did men (1.8 percent of total) among prisoners (Maruschak 2006a). Women continue to have disproportionately higher rates of HIV among prison populations, though the percentages have declined since the late 1990s.

The most recent jail-based data on HIV among inmates (Maruschak 2006b) indicates that an average 1.3 percent of jailed individuals knew themselves to be HIV positive (i.e., self-reported). Women again show a higher percentage than men (2.0 percent and 1.2 percent, respectively). Older individuals, especially those in the 45 and older category, reported higher rates of HIV than those in the below 35 groups.

The "Known" Caveat

Throughout this discussion the reader may have noticed the stress on "known HIV positives" in correctional populations. Knowledge about an individual's HIV status is generally gained through one of three primary methods. Some inmates will self-disclose their

HIV-positive status to medical staff or it will be recognized by medical staff based on medications being taken by the individual. Another route of discovery comes through results of voluntary counseling and testing programs offered to inmates in jails and prisons. Finally, in 2004, 18 state prison systems and the Federal Bureau of Prison (BOP) offered or conducted mandatory HIV testing upon entry to prison, and three states and BOP conducted exit testing; all prison systems will test inmates upon request or if there are indications of HIV-related symptoms. Some states target high-risk groups, such as injecting drug users and/or sex criminals upon entry. Although only about 25 percent of all prison inmates are mandated to be or routinely offered testing on admission, data from a nationally representative sample in 2004 show that 84.5 percent of state and 86.8 percent of federal prisoners had received an HIV test at least once in their lives, and 69 and 77.4 percent, respectively, had been HIV-tested since admission (Maruschak 2006a).

A related method of estimating HIV prevalence in a correctional system involves the utilization of "blinded seroprevalence" studies. Blood drawn from inmates for other purposes is also tested for the presence of the HIV antibody (and other diseases). The blood specimens are not identifiable, so there is no way to link them back to a particular inmate. While this gives an idea of the proportion of the inmate population living with HIV infection, it does not allow follow-up for counseling and treatment. It may help to inform administrators about the need for HIV transmission prevention efforts needed for their population, however. Both New York and the BOP employ this method.

The key for our discussion here is that there is no standard approach to determining an inmate's HIV status across all prison jurisdictions, much less the more than 3,000 county jails in the United States. There is no standard methodology utilized to estimate the prevalence of HIV/AIDS across these jails and prisons, either. All discussions of HIV-infected correctional inmates must be couched in these terms. Our knowledge is no doubt an undercount, especially among jail inmates. We turn to a brief implication of this caveat next.

Returning to the Community

The majority of the HIV/AIDS infections encountered among prison (and especially jail) inmates are imported into prisons (CDC 2006b; Krebs and Simmons 2002; May and Williams 2002), they do not originate from the deprivations of prison life. Hammett, Harmon, and Rhodes (2002; see also, National Commission on Correctional Health Care 2002) examined the burden of selected infectious diseases in inmates being released from jails and prisons. These researchers sought to compare the incidence of certain diseases in the inmate population and then compare them with the incidence of these diseases in the general public. They developed estimates of the prevalence of certain infectious diseases among inmates and then applied these estimates to the numbers of persons released from correctional facilities in 1997.

Hammett, Harmon, and Rhodes (2002) estimated that between 112,000 and 157,000 people with HIV were released from correctional facilities (mostly jails) in 1997. They further estimate this represents between 20 and 26 percent of all people living with HIV in the United States in 1997. Over the course of the year, 39,200 persons with AIDS were released from correctional facilities; this represents almost 16 percent of all persons living with AIDS in the country. Thus, of all persons living with HIV/AIDS in the United States in 1997, Hammett, Harmon, and Rhodes (2002) suggest that 20–26 percent passed through a correctional facility.

The cycling of HIV-positive persons from community to incarceration to community (free world to prison to free world and so forth) presents a number of issues for treatment of HIV and prevention that will be discussed later in this chapter. For now, we want to emphasize that HIV is a problem that begins primarily in the community (free world) and that poses special challenges to both the correctional system and to the communities to which the incarcerated persons will return.

One of the persistent rumors in the HIV and corrections world is that the alleged explosion in HIV among African-American women is being driven by African-American men becoming HIV-infected while imprisoned, often as a result of being raped in prison. There has been a flurry of stories ranging from African-American–centered media to *The New York Times* and editorials in *The Washington Post*, alleging this transmission route; all without any credible evidence to support them. Looking at the CDC surveillance information presented earlier, it is also evident that there has been no radical change in the number of African-American women becoming HIV-infected in the community. The question becomes why these rumors of rampant HIV transmission within prisons are so prevalent?

One answer is that there has been relatively little direct examination of HIV transmission within correctional settings. Krebs' work (Krebs 2006; Krebs and Simmons 2002) is among the few studies that looked at cases of sero-conversion among those continuously imprisoned over a long period of time. Researchers from the CDC utilized a case-control approach to studying 88 inmates who had sero-converted from negative on intake to positive at some point in their imprisonment over a multiyear period and a matched control group. Only a few other studies have addressed sero-conversion in any methodical manner, and most of those covered only a short time period (see Krebs 2006). In the end, we do not know the exact percentage of individuals who sero-convert for any reason while incarcerated or as a result of their incarceration experiences. Most estimates are quite low (i.e., around one half of one percent of "known" cases); but others decline to estimate given the unknown factors. Without universal testing on entry and exit, this figure will remain unknown and rife for speculation and further stigmatization of prisoners, both those who are living with HIV and those who are not.

What happens to former prisoners living with HIV once they return to the community is also largely a matter of speculation. While HIV-infected inmates are the only category of medically affected individuals who have automatic access to postrelease medical services through Ryan White. Ryan White was a young child who died of AIDS—he was at one time the national poster child funds, we have relatively little research that follows these individuals for any significant period of time. In the previous edition of this chapter, we discussed a federal research initiative that sought to answer some of these questions. Unfortunately, the follow-up of released individuals proved quite difficult, and the results of an overall evaluation and of multiple local evaluations was less comprehensive than anticipated.

It was learned that it is possible to link returning jail and prison inmates to services for those living with HIV, as well as those whose prior behavioral history put them at high risk of acquiring HIV. Retaining those former inmates in an evaluation of those services past a relatively short time frame proved more difficult. The open questions for future research include whether a continuity of care program requires continuity of provider or whether it can be a segmented approach; whether certain types of services form the basis of adequate care upon which other services may be built; whether a general approach or a client-centered approach is necessary; and whether or not retention in HIV support services has any effect on the likelihood of subsequent criminal behavior and/or incarceration.

About the only other well-researched HIV continuity of care services operates in Connecticut. This is also the only study to document medical evidence of the improvement of HIV-infected inmates during their prison stay and their medical condition at re-incarceration within only a few months of release. Generally, a marked increase in the health of the HIV-infected prisoners was noted from initial prison entry until release. Although the authors do not specify any information about the continuity of care or other services received by that substantial proportion of inmates who returned to the custody of the Connecticut prison system, they do measure the significantly poorer health condition in which they return. Many of those who returned to the prison system were in worse shape than on their initial entry into the prison HIV program in terms of all HIV markers.

Given the general risk behaviors in which incarcerated individuals tend to engage in the free world and to which they return at reentry (Margolis et al. 2006), more prevention programs for prisoners who are released are needed. The Project Start group tested two forms of prevention education on volunteers from prisons in four states with a prospective case control research design. One group received an in-prison prevention education experience only, while the second group received the in-prison experience and an in-community booster session. After about six months in the community, the "booster" group showed significantly fewer risk behaviors than the in-prison prevention-only group. This suggests that HIV risk behavior reduction programs that begin inside can have community-protective effects, so long as there is at least some postrelease support for those behaviors back in the community.

In the end, we do not know much about what happens to people living with HIV as a result of their incarceration experiences. There is a clear need for rigorous evaluation of theoretically driven, evidence-based HIV prevention programs that operate inside prison walls and back in the community. These evaluations will need to be paired with better surveillance/monitoring of the HIV status of individuals entering and leaving components of the corrections process. While we know only a little about those inside, we know almost nothing about the HIV status, risk factors, and/or treatment for those living with the disease while in the community or forms of community control. The latter may be the next great research area to lead to earlier diagnosis of HIV-infected individuals and linking them to early, effective medical and psychosocial services.

Unique Problems

Incarcerated men, women, and prison officials face many problems related to HIV. For those infected, the sophistication and availability of medical care is still suspect in some systems. For administrators, the medical expenses associated with caring for HIV inmates are high. One article suggested that on average an American who is diagnosed with HIV/AIDS could expect to pay nearly $600,000 in medical care. This is up 40 percent from the late 1990s (Associated Press 2006). There is a drastic difference in budget allocations when comparing prison systems. For example, New Jersey prison authorities report that the average cost associated with caring for an infected inmate (from diagnosis to death) was $67,000, and that the average length of hospitalization was 102 days (Prisons confront dilemma 1986). One source found that correctional budgets have been overwhelmed by the cost of new treatments, which have sent the annual expense of treating an HIV-infected patient from about $2,000 to as much as $13,000 (Purdy 1997). Over a decade ago, the state of Florida was spending over $6.7 million a year for the care of inmates with HIV (Program developed for AIDS 1994).

Medical

Biological factors give women a disproportionately high probability of contracting HIV and consequently AIDS compared to men with similar risk behaviors. Women who are most likely to become infected come from socially and economically deprived groups. Therefore, they may also receive inferior medical treatment. Thus, greater risk coupled with insufficient medical care places women at increased risk of premature death due to AIDS.

There are also indications that, as a group, incarcerated women have more health problems than male prisoners (Waring and Smith 1990:5). Concerns with gynecological care are also unique to female populations.

According to the findings of several studies, gender-specific diseases also have implications that are more serious for women who are HIV positive. One study found that among women suffering from cervical cancer, those who were HIV positive had a median of 10 months until death compared to a median of 23 months for women who were HIV negative. It has also been shown that gynecological infections develop much more rapidly in women who are HIV positive (Minkoff and DeHovitz 1991). For example, pelvic inflammatory disease (PID) progresses more rapidly in women who are HIV positive (Hoegsberg, Abulafia, and Sedlis 1990; Safrin et al. 1990). HIV-positive women also appear to have a large number of infections with vaginal candidiasis (Rhoads et al. 1987). The Centers for Disease Control (CDC) reported that for HIV-infected women, "the prevalence of cervical dysplasia on Papanicolaou (Pap) smear for HIV positive women was eight to eleven times greater than the prevalence of dysplasia for women residing in the respective communities" (Risk for Cervical Disease 1991:23). Finally, it has also been suggested that, "seropositive women with herpes infection might shed virus more frequently than women not infected with HIV and thereby pose an increased risk of HIV transmission to sexual partners" (Minkoff and DeHovitz 1991:2254).

Compounding Medical Problems

There are also factors that increase both the threat and severity of HIV infection in correctional facilities. Related diseases are also increasing in correctional health systems.

Tuberculosis   Tuberculosis (TB) remains a real threat in closed secure environments such as correctional facilities. According to the editors of the *Journal of the American Medical Association*,

> The recent emergence of multi-drug-resistant TB (tuberculosis) as an important opportunistic infection of HIV infected people underscores the need for secondary HIV-prevention services in correctional facilities. Persons in correctional institutions are at increased risk for TB because of high prevalence of HIV infection and latent TB, overcrowding, poor ventilation, and the frequent transfer of inmates within and between institutions. (1993:23)

TB, after being controlled for over 40 years, is once again posing a health threat (on a positive note, the rates of infection dropped significantly in 2005). A particularly dangerous strain, resistant to standard antituberculosis drugs (isoniazid, rifampin, and streptomycin), has been identified in 16 different states. The recent outbreaks of TB primarily involve HIV-positive individuals. However, since TB is spread through airborne droplets others are also at-risk. Close, prolonged contact (such as is found in correctional facilities) increases risk of infection. In one case, it was reported that more than 50 health care workers were infected from a single patient, though none have yet developed TB (Altman 1992). However, TB, like HIV, can remain dormant for years. Healthy individuals can harbor the TB bacillus for years without ever being ill. Because of these reasons, and due to the concentrations of high-risk individuals found in correctional facilities, some medical experts are arguing for centering detection and treatment efforts among the incarcerated (DiFerdinando in Altman 1992).

Contraceptive Devices   Among all the reported cases of AIDS among women, 80 percent occurred in women in the childbearing years (age 15–44). Of these, 20 percent are between the ages of 20 and 29 and many were probably infected while teenagers (HIV/AIDS Surveillance Report 1999). Thus, safe contraceptive devices are a relevant concern for women.

Women who are HIV positive cannot take it for granted that the uses of common contraceptive methods are safe for either the women or their sexual partners. First, Minkoff and DeHovitz stated that, "[t]here are several reasons to be cautious about the use of intrauterine devices . . . they may render the woman more infectious . . . The woman herself might be rendered more susceptible to ascending infections and hence PID" (1991:2255). Second, oral contraceptives have also generated theoretical debate as to whether or not they alter the natural course of HIV disease among women (Grossman 1984; Minkoff and DeHovitz 1991). Finally, research is lacking on the effect of microbicides.

Psychological Stress

Compared to other infected groups, people who are infected with HIV or AIDS face increased psychological pressures. Men, being the more commonly affected by HIV/AIDS, face many social and emotional stresses while dealing with the virus. They are often ostracized by family and friends. If they are in a relationship, they can become not only an emotional but also a financial burden as their partner can be left caring for them. When incarcerated, these men must deal with sporadic or irregular medication schedules, discrimination by fellow inmates or officials, and the possibility of spreading the disease, all while dealing with their continual failing health. Many economically disadvantaged women are the primary and often sole caretakers for their dependent children; others are thus financially and emotionally dependent on them. When these women have HIV/AIDS, they also have the concern of caring for others while often being ill themselves. Incarceration forces a separation and additional stress for the woman who must now rely on others or the state to care for their dependents.

Social Stigmata   As we have noted several times, groups that are most highly represented among those HIV infected already belong to highly stigmatized groups—women of color and intravenous drug users (Richardson 1988). According to the 2000 Census, over 143,505,720 women lived in the United States, only 18,193,005 of those women were African American (Census 2000). In accordance with the CDC, of the 127,150 women living with HIV/AIDS, nearly 64 percent were African American, 19 percent were white, and 15 percent were Hispanic (CDC 2005). According to Wiener, "[h]istorically, these women have been tangled in a web of poverty, illness, and oppression; by the dictates of racism and poverty, they are disempowered, disenfranchised, and alienated from traditional sources of help and support" (1991). Young and McHale added that, "HIV infection makes visible and explicit the hidden and implicit links between conceptions of disease and criminality. Both are seen as (symbolically or literally) life-threatening. The HIV positive prisoner is a deadly icon of a psycho-social malaise" (1992:90). Others have also articulated how societal sexism, racism, and classism have effected public perceptions of HIV and women (Anastos and Marte 1989; Marte and Anastos 1990). McKenzie (1989) argued that HIV-positive women's legal rights have also been neglected.

Self-Efficacy   Most theoretical models addressing risk reduction practices have included self-efficacy as a central component. Several factors (drug and alcohol use, poverty, cultural norms, gender roles, and sexuality issues) have been identified as decreasing women's self-efficacy (Wermuth et al. 1991:132). Also according to Wermuth et al.,

> [w]hen individuals believe they can exercise control over actions and situations that might pose a risk for HIV infection, they are more likely to exercise that control (Bandura 1994). However, the extent to which this holds true for individuals with less actual control over their material and relational world's remains to be learned. For example, it has been pointed out that women are at greatest risk for AIDS. (1991:133–134)

Of all women in our society, those who are incarcerated probably have the *least* control over their lives. Thus, the thesis that lack of control results in decreased self-efficacy would be more consequential for incarcerated women.

Finally, women who are HIV positive may also not enjoy the widespread and organized support that gay men have. When current or past incarceration is also present, stigma may intensify and with current practices, support may decrease.

In summary, gender influences the social and biological treatment and consequences of people with HIV/AIDS (Minkoff and DeHovitz 1991). So far, an overview of the demographics, behaviors, and problems facing incarcerated women has been presented. In the next section, a review of treatment options is presented. Theoretical guides may prove useful for slowing the spread of HIV among women. These theories and policy recommendations conclude this chapter.

HIV/AIDS MEDICAL TREATMENT

On a positive note, medical advances have greatly increased the longevity of AIDS patients. This trend should continue. A complete cure or preventive vaccine remains elusive, however. The latest treatment regimes are presented in this section.

Most of the HIV treatment regiments include two components. The first involves the use of prophylactic drugs to prevent and treat opportunistic infections. The second component is the use of antiviral drugs to reduce replication of the virus (Linsk 1997). Most of the recent increases in life span have been due to advances in prophylactic drugs (Linsk 1997:70). For example, substantial progress has been made in developing and testing drugs to prevent the many otherwise fatal opportunistic infections caused by bacteria, fungi, protozoa, or other viruses in people with HIV-weakened immune systems (Cooper 1996:160). The most vivid examples are a variety of treatments that prevent pneumocystis carinii pneumonia (PCP). These treatments range from a simple dose of a sulfa drug to complex management using aerosolized pentamidine (Linsk 1997:70).

The most successful treatment innovation to combat HIV and AIDS is the "cocktail" approach (AMNews 1997). Previously people with AIDS had only one drug option: zidovudine or, AZT. There are at least 9 separate drug combinations that can work in more than 100 different combinations (Leland 1996:64). The first clinical trials of these combination drugs (reverse transcriptase inhibitors) were shown to have benefits including prolonged survival and fewer "AIDS defining events" when given to asymptomatic individuals with relatively early stage disease, compared to AZT alone (Fauci 1996). AZT in combination with other reverse transcriptase drugs, such as didanosine (ddI) and zalcitabine (ddC), has been found to be greatly superior to AZT treatment alone (Cooper 1996:160).

Following these medical breakthroughs came improvements in the capability of protease inhibitors to block virus replication (Fauci 1996:276). The use of this new class of drugs in combination with the first generation reverse transcriptase inhibitors holds great promise for improved control of HIV and AIDS (Fauci 1996:276). The greatest gains have been made by using different combinations of drugs that attack HIV at different stages of its replication process (Markowitz 1996). Reverse transcriptase inhibitors disrupt the HIV enzyme soon after HIV infects a cell—much earlier than when protease inhibitors are involved (Markowitz 1996:2). Consequently, survival and delay of AIDS progression are significantly improved among those patients receiving combination therapy (Study confirms 1997). Combination therapy with ritonavir (a protease inhibitor) plus two reverse transcriptase inhibitors (such as AZT and ddC) is significantly more effective than reverse transcriptase inhibitors alone (Study confirms 1997:1; Voelker

1996:436). With these types of treatments, AIDS-related illnesses (including opportunistic infections and cancers) and deaths have decreased (Study confirms 1997:2).

Advances in combination therapy and the introduction of protease inhibitors have permitted sustained suppression of plasma viral load to undetectable levels in patients in various clinical trials (St. Louis, Wasserheit, and Gayle 1997). These findings make plausible the possibility of substantially improving the survival and quality of life of HIV-infected persons through chemotherapy (St. Louis, Wasserheit, and Gayle 1997:10). Consequently, medical personnel are starting to consider HIV a chronic, manageable disease rather than a death sentence (Leland 1996:64). This means not only fewer deaths but also more people living with HIV and AIDS.

Because of these advances, many people with HIV are living longer and have more productive lives than 10 years ago; however, the vast majority still eventually succumb to the disease (Cooper 1996:160). Consequently, rather than quickly succumbing to illnesses such as PCP patients instead suffer from what is commonly referred to as "wasting syndrome" (which is severe weight loss, chronic diarrhea, and fever) or from the more difficult-to-treat opportunistic infections, such as mycobacterium avium complex (MAC) or cytomegalovirus (CMV) (Cooper 1996:160).

To date, these drugs have been largely tested only on white males. Thus, little information is available regarding possible gender or ethnic differences in the efficacy, or toxicity, of antiviral medication (Kloser 1997; Leland 1996). Differences between the response of women and men to some treatments may be attributed to differences in size, body fat, and hormonal environments (Kelly 1995). Additionally women of childbearing age must be monitored carefully for pregnancy so that appropriate management can take place early in the pregnancy (Kloser 1997:180).

If racial and ethnicity differences in the efficacy of AIDS-related drugs are found, questions can be anticipated that ask if the differences truly derive from race or ethnicity, or if they derive from differences in standard of living and access to health care experienced by different racial/ethnic groups (Kelly 1995:52). For example, African American and Latino patients generally have more advanced HIV disease when they begin taking medication (Kelly 1995). In this situation, the use of antiviral medication has often been less effective.

It has been estimated that 90 percent of the world's population of HIV patients cannot access the more effective, and expensive, treatments (Voelker 1996:435). Thus for many, the new drugs and treatment modalities remain illusive (Leland 1996). What does this mean for HIV-positive inmates and correctional administrators?

HIV/AIDS Treatment in Prison

Prison environments are not the ideal location for AIDS patients (Leland 1996:67) though correctional settings provide an improvement over the *health* environment in which some HIV-positive offenders would otherwise reside (Braithwaite, Hammett, and Mayberry 1996). Prisoners with AIDS become sick at twice the speed of those on the outside (Hope and Hayes 1995:12). In addition, among prison populations there is a greater likelihood that a person's HIV status is unknown, and it is this group of patients (those unknowing) that are most likely to come in too late for effective treatment (AM News 1997). Moreover, efforts to treat HIV and AIDS within prisons have been severely hampered by uneven medical care and a short supply of the promising new treatments described here (Purdy 1997). For example, while the drugs AZT (zidovudine) and bactrim (for PCP prophylaxis) have been available in most correctional systems, other treatments widely used among nonprisoners with HIV, such as pentamidine, ddI, ddC, and combinations therapies are much less available (Stein and Headley 1996:4). Some prison systems are following old treatment protocols that do not take advantage of the new drugs, especially protease inhibitors (Purdy 1997:1). More importantly, resistance to AZT is almost certain to develop when given the monotherapy (one drug at a time) commonly used in prison settings (Markowitz 1996:4). Despite these obstacles, correctional settings provide much needed data and give inmates access to medication and counseling that they otherwise would not receive (Braithwaite, Hammett, and Mayberry 1996).

The quality of treatment also varies from prison to prison and from state to state, often depending on whether court actions have forced improved medical care (Purdy 1997:28). Courts have mandated that prisons must meet community standards (Braithwaite, Hammett, and Mayberry 1996). Some prison systems (currently very few) continue to put HIV-positive prisoners in isolation or special units, depriving them of limited programs and recreational opportunities available to other inmates (Berkman 1995:1618). Maruschak (2002) reports that nearly one-third of all "confirmed AIDS" cases were held in 25 prisons across the country. Further, nearly one-quarter of all HIV-positive inmates were housed in medical treatment facilities, and 51 percent of the residents in these facilities had confirmed AIDS.

Many correctional systems do not permit prisoners to participate in clinical studies, denying them the potential benefits of promising new treatment approaches (Stein and Headley 1996:3). In addition, now that treating HIV and AIDS is becoming as complex as treating cancer, with drugs and dosages carefully calibrated to each patient's medical condition, specialist are required. Unfortunately, many infected inmates are being treated by primary-care doctors and see a specialist only occasionally, if at all (Purdy 1997:1). AIDS care should be delivered by the best medical care providers possible, not those lacking specialization (Voelker 1996:438). Dr. Altice of Yale Medical School, who treats inmates in Connecticut's prisons, stated that,

> Prison doctors around the country are not trained specialists. We used to say that AIDS treatment is primary care. This is no longer true. We would no more have the average primary care provider deliver chemotherapy to cancer patients, than we would have the same people provide complex HIV treatment. (Cited in Purdy 1997:28)

An additional concern is the fact that the recent combination therapies require incredibly demanding regimens (Leland 1996:69). Some drugs have to be taken with food, others on an empty stomach (Leland 1996:69). Most correctional systems are crowded and must operate on a strict timeline making this type of specialized care difficult, and often impossible.

Finally, the organization of healthcare systems within prisons operates according to a "sick-call model." In other words, they respond to discrete and immediate health problems (e.g., injuries and specific illnesses) (Smith and Dailard 1994). Systems designed in such a way lack the flexibility that HIV-positive individuals require.

Just to provide one illustration, consider that since inmates are not trusted with the responsibility of controlling their own medication, prisoners who require medication on a regular basis must follow a rigorous procedure. AIDS patients who are incarcerated will require this medical attention several times a day. Concerns have also been raised because inmates going to the medical dispensary numerous times daily to receive medication poses a security risk (Purdy 1997:28). Consequently, correctional medical staff may have difficulty accepting or understanding the need for the large number of pills required or the frequency with which they must be administered (Kelly 1995:67). As a result, prisoners often miss doses of medication (Smith and Dailard 1994:82), thus aggravating adherence to the treatment regime.

When patients divert from the required medical regimen, they risk cultivating a strain of the virus that is resistant to one or more of the drugs (Leland 1996:69). These drug-resistant viruses threaten the general and prison public health as well as that of the HIV-infected patient. This growing concern is illustrated by the increasing spread of multidrug-resistant tuberculosis (Linsk 1997:70). Therefore, adherence to drug regimens is critically important (Purdy 1997:28) despite the difficulty imposed on correctional administrators.

Making sure inmates get uniform care is a problem not only when they are released, but also when they move from one prison to another. A prisoner's medical records may fail to follow him or her as he or she moves through the prison system, and prison health care providers rarely coordinate treatments with community-based physicians once a prisoner is released (Smith and Dailard 1994:82). Continuity of care is critically important to prisoners with HIV, but the concerns and realities presented here make it difficult to provide consistent treatment (Smith and Dailard 1994:82).

As we progress through the twenty-first century, treatment of HIV and AIDS patients will improve. Lives of those infected will increase in length and quality. At the same time, the complexity of treatment and the expenses associated with these treatments will severally test even the best-funded correctional systems (Solomon et al. 1989). Systems experiencing financial burdens will be hard pressed to provide effective treatment. To date, the medical community is still uncertain about the ethnic and gender effects of the newest treatment protocols. This situation will soon be remedied. However, should differences be found, the complexities facing correctional administrators will geometrically increase. In addition to considering medical care, prevention should be of paramount concern since HIV-positive people living longer could lead to increased infections. The next section reviews promising theoretical models that may meet prevention needs.

THEORETICAL MODELS

Lacking a cure or preventive vaccine, retardation of further spread of HIV among women in correctional facilities is urgent. However, the most commonly used theoretical models have difficulty encompassing the needs and experiences of women of color—those most likely to be found in correctional facilities. Commonly used theories (Feldman and

Johnson 1986) to develop AIDS interventions are the AIDS Risk Reduction Model (ARRM) (Catania, Kegeles, and Coates 1990), Social Cognitive Theory (Bandura 1994), and models founded on the Health Belief Model (Becker 1974; Maiman and Becker 1974; Rosenstock 1974; Rosenstock, Strecher, and Becker 1988). Unfortunately, several problems are evident with these models (Lanier and Gates 1996; Wingood and DiClemente 1997) that result in their unsuitability for use with those most likely to be incarcerated. These models fail to consider the contextual issues of rationality, psychosocial issues, class, gender, or ethnicity (Cochran and Mays 1993; Lanier and Gates 1996).

Each of the theoretical models is based on the concept of rationality. Concerning the ARRM, Lanier and Gates noted,

> . . . the ARRM is based on assumptions concerning the rationality of human behavior. . . . Concerning possibly hedonistic adolescents, such a cost/benefit analysis may have little relevance. This may be especially true when faced with the prospect of immediate sexual and/or drug-induced gratification, opposed to the remote possibility of contracting a disease that may not manifest symptoms for several years. (1996: 40)

These theories also focus on decision making as being individualistic. Gasch et al. (1991) noted that African-American women are more likely to focus on family and community norms when making decisions. Another psychosexual variable focuses on the concept of power and control. Findings show that women in heterosexual relationships are more psychologically, economically, and socially dependent on the male (Kelley and Thibaut 1978; Wingood and DiClemente 1997). Thus, the male yields power over the female and this presumably impacts sexual negotiations (e.g., using condoms) (Wingood, Hunter, and DiClemente 1993). Indeed, research has found males to refuse using condoms against their female partners' wishes (Wingood and DiClemente 1997).

The models also fail to consider the effect of socioeconomic factors. Income differentially impacts women of color because they are less likely to finish high school and more likely to have extremely low household incomes (Diaz et al. 1994). In fact, when the rates of HIV/AIDS are adjusted for socioeconomic factors, analyses reveal that the incidence is higher in areas having lower income as compared to those areas with higher incomes (Fife and Mode 1992; Morse et al. 1991). Among women who acquired AIDS through heterosexual contact, over 80 percent of the African-American women have incomes under $10,000 compared to under half of the white women (McKinnon and Humes 1999). Wingood and DiClemente (1997) added that taking precautions against HIV/AIDS might be complicated by the immediate concern of caring for their families.

Finally, each of the theoretical models also fails to consider the influence of gender and ethnicity. Models that fail to account for these variables are problematic. For one thing, "gender blind models" assume "static" sex roles and may neglect social processes that could influence risk reduction strategies (Wingood and DiClemente 1995). What is needed are gender and culturally sensitive theoretical models.

One promising theoretical guide is the Theory of Gender and Power (Connell 1987). Most epidemiological research defines "gender" based on biological sex rather than "gender differences" that are not just biological but also result from "prevailing socially defined societal norms that dictate appropriate sexual conduct" (Wingood and

DiClemente 1997). The Theory of Gender and Power moves beyond this rudimentary classification by addressing social norms that influence sexual behavior; further, it considers power differentials in relationships—though only in a male/female classification. Incarcerated women are also in a subordinate position due to their incarceration.

The Theory of Gender and Power considers the division of labor, the structure of power, and the structure of cathexis. This theory is particularly useful for explaining why economically disadvantaged, minority women (those found most often in prison) are more likely to have HIV (Wingood and DiClemente 1997). First, the sexual division of labor—the preponderance of unpaid work associated with housework and childcare, coupled with inequalities in education and wages—explain why socioeconomic factors influence African-American womens' greater vulnerability to HIV. The women, and their children, are economically dependent on the better-paid male partner. Second, power differentials between the genders contribute to greater exposure since the "stronger" partner holds authority and coercive power. Wingood and DiClemente (1997) illustrated this by describing sexual politics that limit (and more commonly deny) accessibility of condoms in schools, lack of efforts devoted to development of a device to protect women from HIV, and norms supporting male control over condom use. Finally, the structure of cathexis characterizes the erotic and affective influences in sexual relationships. It provides an explanation for why many women are passive in demanding safe sex since they are more focused on securing basic living accessories for themselves and family from the more economically secure male—who may not desire to practice safe sex. This also explains how the sex-ratio found in the African-American community favors the male, since there are fewer available males (due to premature death, incarceration, etc.) that further weaken the women's "bargaining" position.

The Theory of Gender and Power is useful for explaining why economically disadvantaged, racial, and ethnic minority women face greater risk, but it is less useful for providing methods of behavior change. It can provide a basis for HIV prevention policies directed at incarcerated women (discussed next) that also include models for behavior change.

POLICY RECOMMENDATIONS

Incarcerated persons face a myriad of social, economic, psychological, and medical problems. Infection and the threat of infection with HIV and AIDS create additional stress. Obviously sane, humane, and realistic care of people infected with HIV is necessary. However, it is also critical that effective preventive programs are implemented and evaluated (Gaiter and Doll 1998; Hammett, Gaiter, and Crawford 1998). Due to the vast diversity found among incarcerated people, no single strategy can be considered effective. A combination of case management, individual counseling, group sessions, role playing, and constant reinforcement while incarcerated needs to be supplemented with postrelease treatment. This constellation of strategies may prove effective while under correctional supervision. The eclectic approach suggested here should be based on a theoretical model that incorporates power and gender (such as the Theory of Gender and Power).

Case Management

A comprehensive strategy would take a case management approach toward prevention and treatment. Each person would be assigned to a treatment or educational program based on his or her unique past experiences and practices. For example, commercial sex workers could be grouped with similar people for individual counseling and group sessions. Experts who are sensitive to each person's history and (perceived) degree of rationality should devise the specific program. Social Justice for Women has suggested that an interdisciplinary group comprised of clinicians, psychologists, Department of Corrections employees, parole workers, and others be used to collaborate on "medical management, psychosocial services, family counseling, discharge planning, . . . (and) early consideration for parole" (Waring and Smith 1990). Such a team-centered approach would be more likely to comprehensively and congruently address the sometimes-overlapping problems facing these individuals.

Counseling

Both group and individual sessions should be used for educational purposes. Group sessions have shown some value (Valdiserri et al. 1987), and peer-led sessions have great potential. Incarcerated men and women who are seen as positive role models by the other inmates should be recruited and enticed to lead the group sessions. Peer-led sessions may be more effective with inmates since they may resist the educational efforts of correctional officials (Lanier, Pack, and DiClemente 1999). Groups should be formed based on the experiences of each inmate. For example, bankers or bikers should be grouped together so that they can relate and share common past risky experiences and jointly develop resistance devices unique to their culture. In part, this grouping based on prior experiences will help identify and perhaps improve existing social networks.

Role-playing should be a major component (e.g., teaching female commercial sex workers how to demand that customers and sexual partners use condoms). The group leaders and those who develop the program should base it on proven theoretical models. It must be stressed that such programs should be rigorously evaluated by outside, neutral observers.

Health Services

Health services for incarcerated women show great potential. For example, some men and women who are incarcerated may not have been able to take advantage of comprehensive health services (dental, gynecological, etc.) prior to incarceration. (One goal of health educators within the correctional setting should be to make inmates aware of community services that are available upon their release.) Correctional institutions should conduct mandatory HIV screening at intake (commonly done in many correctional systems) and at six-month intervals for the first 18 months of incarceration (a less frequent practice).

All facilities should also have HIV treatment facilities where the latest drug therapy is provided on a timely basis. It is not improbable that many of those incarcerated would also volunteer to participate with testing new HIV and AIDS drugs prior to FDA approval (see Young and McHale 1992 for further discussion of this).

Postrelease Services

Virtually all incarcerated persons are eventually released back into the community. Being cognizant of their rights after parole, they should be strongly encouraged to continue participation in counseling sessions, drug therapy, and whatever AIDS/HIV prevention and/or treatment program that was devised for them while under correctional supervision. Many incarcerated individuals could also be monitored with alternative means of control such as community corrections.

Alternative Sanctions (Community Corrections)

Since most people are not incarcerated for violent offenses (BJS 2005a) perhaps it would be more humane and cost effective for people who develop symptomatic AIDS to be supervised in community corrections. Community corrections offer several benefits. For one thing, community health care services are available. Young and McHale noted that,

> . . . A considerable difference does exist in both choice and standard of care in relation to prisoners with HIV . . . A HIV positive patient has a far wider choice of care outside prison . . . he [sic] may seek psychotherapeutic care and counseling to bring him to terms with the fact that he has AIDS or is HIV positive. If he has the means, he may also obtain care from 'alternative' medical practitioners . . . (1992:97)

Courts have also recognized this fact. At least one prisoner with AIDS was ordered released from a federal prison because he could not receive adequate medical care (Young and McHale 1992). More support groups also exist in the community. Despite the potential negative influences, family and friends should be available to assist the woman physically, financially, and emotionally.

There are four additional factors that should be considered. First, community corrections should be increasingly used due to humanitarian reasons. For one thing, the mortality rate is higher among incarcerated individuals.

Second, from a managerial perspective, community corrections solve many potential problems. One issue facing correctional administrators is whether or not to segregate HIV-infected individuals, only a few systems still do so (Braithwaite, Hammett, and Mayberry 1996). Inmate violence against those infected is another related problem. In addition, detention personnel have been found to be uncomfortable supervising HIV-positive offenders (Lurigio 1989). Community corrections eliminates each of these administrative concerns for inmates who do not pose a threat of violence to community members, and, again, most people are incarcerated for nonviolent offenses.

Third, monetary concerns should be considered. Prisons are designed to be punitive institutions. They are not hospitals. Thus, care for critically ill inmates' demands replicates services that are already available through the health care sector. Many institutions cannot afford expensive drugs needed to fight AIDS [such as azdothymidine (AZT) and cocktail combinations]. The National Institute of Justice has found that many inmates who are eligible for AZT and who need it are not receiving it while incarcerated (Young and McHale 1992).

Finally, community corrections are preferable for reasons related to the spread of disease. TB and other infectious diseases are becoming an increasing problem in close custody correctional institutions. "The circumstances and conditions in custody, including overcrowding and lack of privacy, may foster high risk behaviors such as unprotected anal sex, drug injecting, tattooing; and self-injury with consequent blood-spillage" (Dolan, Donoghoe, and Stimson 1990). It is also much more likely for inmates, who would otherwise be heterosexual; to engage in homosexual activity (often called "prison homosexuality") while incarcerated. Since condoms are often not provided to inmates, this behavior is even more risky. Incarcerated HIV and AIDS patients thus pose additional problems for other inmates and staff (see McCarthy and McCarthy 1997 for additional information on community corrections).

SUMMARY AND CONCLUSION

Administrators of correctional facilities are going to face increasing problems related to HIV and AIDS. More women than men will develop AIDS since women are more likely to be infected than to infect men (European Study on Heterosexual Transmission of HIV 1992; Padia, et al. 1991). Between 1980 and 1994, the number of incarcerated women increased 386 percent (Seeking Justice 1995). As of today, women make up nearly 7 percent of the prison population. If current incarceration trends continue, women will be incarcerated at even greater rate in the future. As more incarcerated women with HIV develop symptomatic AIDS, correctional health care costs will rise dramatically. The current climate of tax reduction is likely to persist, forcing consideration of community-based corrections for economic reasons. The expense and complexity with the recent treatment modalities also favor a community-based approach for HIV-positive inmates. Elimination of duplicated government services (specifically, public health care and correctional health care) will further add to the impetus for increasing the use of community sanctions. Current mandatory sentencing requirements and increased sentence lengths for drug offenders mean that more at-risk women will remain under correctional supervision for longer periods of time (Lanier and Miller 1995). From a medical viewpoint, these resultant overcrowded conditions are not conducive to effective treatment or prevention for those uninfected—further supporting community-based options for HIV-positive women. The burdens on correctional officers, inmates, medical staff, and society will geometrically increase during the twenty-first century unless effective policies are implemented. Correctional administrators must therefore seriously and rigorously engage in HIV educational and treatment programs. Community corrections should be one increasingly used option. Federal and state initiatives are seeking comprehensive efforts to link incarcerated HIV-positive inmates with community care providers in an effort to improve health and decrease the spread of HIV. On another positive note, correctional administrators are in an excellent position to reach one high-risk group and thus help slow the spread of HIV among the general population.

REFERENCES

ACQUIRED IMMUNODEFICIENCY SYNDROME (1986) A Demographic profile of New York State mortalities 1982–1985. Albany, NY: New York State Commission of Corrections.

AIDS ASSOCIATED WITH INJECTING-DRUG USE UNITED STATES (1995). *Morbidity and Mortality Weekly Report (MMWR)*, 45, 19, 392–398. Atlanta, GA: Centers for Disease Control.

AIDS IN WOMEN—UNITED STATES (1991). *Morbidity and Mortality Weekly Report (MMWR)*, 265, 1, 23–24. Atlanta, GA: Centers for Disease Control.

ALTMAN, L. K. (1992). Deadly strain of Tuberculosis is spreading fast, U.S. finds. *Themes of the Times: Sociology. New York Times*. New York: Prentice Hall.

ALTICE, F. L., F. MOSTASHIRI, P. A. SELWYN, P. J. CHECKO, R. SIGHN, S. TANGUAY, and E. A. BLANCHETTE (1998). Predictors of HIV infection among newly sentenced male prisoners. *Journal of Acquired Immune Deficiency Syndrome Human Retroviral* 18: 444–453.

ANASTOS, K., and C. MARTE (1989). Women—the missing persons in the AIDS epidemic. *Health/PAC Bulletin* 19 (4): 6–13.

BANDURA, A. (1994). Social cognitive theory and exercise of control over HIV infection. In *Preventing AIDS: Theories and Methods of Behavioral Intentions,* ed. DiClemente and Peterson, 25–54. New York: Plenum Press.

BECK, A. J., J. C. KARBERG, and P. M. HARRISON (2002). Prison and Jail Inmates at Midyear 2001. Washington, DC: Bureau of Justice Statistics Bulletin. April. (NCJ 191702).

BECK, A. J., and J. C. KARBERG (2001). Prison and Jail Inmates at Midyear 2000. Washington, DC: Bureau of Justice Statistics Bulletin. April. (NCJ 185989).

BECKER, M. (1974). The health belief model and personal health behavior. *Health Education Monographs* 2: 220–243.

BERKMAN, A. (1995). Prison health: The breaking point. *American Journal of Public Health* 85 (12): 1616–1618.

BRAITHWAITE, R., T. HAMMETT, and R. MAYBERRY (1996). *Prisons and AIDS: A Public Health Challenge*. San Francisco, CA: Jossey-Bass.

BUREAU OF JUSTICE STATISTICS (1994). *Sourcebook of Criminal Justice Statistics—1991*. Washington, DC: U.S. Department of Justice.

BUREAU OF JUSTICE STATISTICS (2005a). *Jail Statistics*. [Retrieved April 5, 2007, from http://www.ojp.usdoj.gov/bjs/jails.htm]

BUREAU OF JUSTICE STATISTICS (2005b). *Prison Statistics*. [Retrieved April 5, 2007, from http://www.ojp.usdoj.gov/bjs/prisons.htm]

CATANIA, J., S. KEGELES, and T. COATES (1990). Toward and understanding of risk behavior: An AIDS risk-reduction model, *Health Education Quarterly* 17: 53–92.

CENTER ON ADDICTION AND SUBSTANCE ABUSE (1998). *Behind Bars: Substance Abuse and America's Prison Population*. New York: CASA.

CENTERS FOR DISEASE CONTROL AND PREVENTION (2001). *HIV/AIDS Surveillance Report*. 12 (2). Atlanta, GA: Centers for Disease Control and Prevention.

CENTERS FOR DISEASE CONTROL AND PREVENTION (2005). *HIV/AIDS Surveillance Report, 2005*. Vol. 17. Atlanta, GA: U.S. Department of Health and Human Services, Centers for Disease Control and Prevention. [Retrieved April 1, 2004, from http://www.cdc.gov/hiv/topics/surveillance/resources/reports/]

CENTERS FOR DISEASE CONTROL AND PREVENTION (2006b). "HIV Transmission Among Male Inmates in a State Prison System—Georgia, 1992–2005. *Morbidity and Mortality Weekly Report* 55(15): 421–426. [Retrieved April 1, 2004, from http://www.cdc.gov/mmwr/preview/mmwrhtml/mm5515a1.htm]

CENTERS FOR DISEASE CONTROL AND PREVENTION (2006c). *HIV/AIDS Surveillance Report, 2005*. Vol. 17. Atlanta, GA: U.S. Department of Health and Human Services, Centers for Disease Control and Prevention.

CENTERS FOR DISEASE CONTROL AND PREVENTION (2005). "HIV/AIDS among Women." [Retrieved April 7, 2004, from http://www.cdc.gov/hiv/topics/women/resources/factsheets/women.htm]

CHBOSKY, S. (Screenplay), and COLUMBUS, C. (Director). (2005), *RENT* [Motion Picture]. Sony Pictures.

CLEARY, P., T. ROGERS, E. SINGER, J. AVORN, N. VAN DEVANTER, S. PERRY, and JOHANNA PINDYCK (1986). Health education about AIDS among Seropositive blood donors. *Health Education Quarterly* 13: 317–329.

COMPARISON OF FEMALE TO MALE AND MALE TO FEMALE TRANSMISSION OF HIV IN 563 STABLE COUPLES. (1992). *European Study Group on Heterosexual Transmission of HIV. BMJ* 304: 809–813.

CONNELL, R. W. (1987). *Gender and Power: Society, the Person and Sexual Politics.* Stanford, CA: Stanford University Press.

COOPER, E. C. (1996). Treatment of HIV disease: Problems, progress, and potential. In *AIDS in the World II*, ed. Jonathan M. Mann and Daniel J. M. Tarantola, 159–164. New York: Oxford.

DIAZ, T., S. Y. CHU, J. W., BUEHLER et al. (1994). Sociodemographic differences among people with AIDS: Results from a multistate surveillance project. *American Journal of Preventive Medicine* 10: 217–222.

DOLAN, K., M. DONOGHOE, and G. STIMSON (1990). Drug injecting and syringe sharing in custody and in the community: An exploratory survey of HIV risk behavior. *The Howard Journal* 29 (3): 177–186.

FAUCI, A. (1996). Much accomplished, much to do. *Journal of the American Medical Association (JAMA)* 276: 155–156.

FELDMAN, D. A., and T. M. JOHNSON (1986). *The Social Dimensions of AIDS: Method and Theory.* New York: Praeger Press.

FIFE, D., and C. MODE (1992). AIDS incidence and income. *Journal of Acquired Immunodeficiency Syndrome* 5: 1105–1110.

FLORIDA: AIDS primary cause of death in prison. (1989). *CDC Weekly* 2: 7.

GAITER, J., and L. DOLL (1998). Improving HIV/AIDS prevention in prisons is good public health policy (editorial). *American Journal of Public Health* 86: 1201–1203.

GASCH, H., D. M. POULSON, R. E. FULLILOVE, and M. T. FULLILOVE (1991). Shaping AIDS education and prevention programs for African Americans amidst community decline. *Journal of Negro Education* 60 (1): 85–96.

GROSSMAN, Z. (1984). Recognition of self and regulation of specificity at the level of cell populations. *Immunological Reviews* 79: 119–138.

HAMMETT, T. (1988). *AIDS in Correctional Facilities: Issues and Options.* (Bureau of Justice Statistics Report). Washington, DC: National Institute of Justice.

HAMMETT, T., R. WIDOM, J. EPSTEIN, M. GROSS, S. SITRE, and TAMMY ENOS (1995). *1994 Update: HIV/AIDS and STDs in Correctional Facilities.* Washington, DC: US Department of Justice.

HAMMETT, T., J. GAITER, and C. CRAWFORD (1998). Reaching seriously at-risk populations: Health interventions in criminal correctional facilities. *Health Education and Behavior* 25: 99–120.

HAMMETT, T., M. PATRICIA HARMON, and W. RHODES (2002). The burden of infectious disease among inmates of and releasees from US correctional facilities 1997. *American Journal of Public Health* 92(11): 1789–1794.

HANLEY, W. (Writer). (1991, May 19). *Our Sons* [Television broadcast].

HARRISON, P. M., and A. J. BECK. (2002). *Prisoners in 2001.* Washington, DC: Bureau of Justice Statistics Bulletin. April. (NCJ 195189).

HIV IN PRISON–1994. (1996). March. Washington, DC: U.S. Department of Justice.

HIV PREVENTION IN U.S. CORRECTIONAL SYSTEM 1991. (1992). *Journal of the American Medical Association* 268: 1, 23.

HIV/AIDS SURVEILLANCE REPORT, 11, 2 (1999). December. Atlanta, GA: Centers for Disease Control.

HOEGSBERG, B., O. ABULAFIA, and A. SEDIS (1990). Sexually transmitted diseases and human immunodeficiency virus infection among women with pelvic inflammatory disease. *The American Journal of Obstetrics and Gynecology* 163: 1135–1139.

HOPE, T., and P. HAYES (1995). A clear pattern of neglect: Prisons and the HIV crisis. Gay *Community News* 20 (4): 12–15.

KELLEY, H. H., and J. W. TRIBAUT (1978). *Interpersonal Relations: A Theory of Interdependence.* New York, NY: John Wiley & Sons.

KELLY, E. (1995). Expanding prisoners' access to AIDS-related clinical trials: An ethical and clinical imperative. *Prison Journal* 75 (1): 48–69.

KLOSER, P. (1997). Primary care of Women with HIV disease. In *The Medical Management of AIDS in Women*, ed. D. COTTON and D. HEATHER Watts, 177–191. New York: John Wiley & Sons.

KREBS, C. P. (2006). "Inmate factors associated with HIV transmission in prison." *Criminology and Public Policy* 5(1):113–136.

KREBS, C. P., and M. SIMMONS (2002). Intraprison HIV transmission: An assessment of whether it occurs, how it occurs, and who is at risk. *AIDS Education and Prevention* 14(Supplement B) October: 53–64.

KUSHNER, T. (Writer). (2003, Dec. 7). *Angels in America* [Television broadcast]. HBO.

LANIER, M. M., R. P. PACK, and R. DiCLEMENTE (1999). Changes in incarcerated adolescents HIV knowledge and selected behaviors from 1988 to 1996. *Journal of Adolescent Health* 25 (3): 182–186.

LANIER, M., and S. GATES (1996). An empirical assessment of the AIDS Risk Reduction Model (ARRM) employing ordered probit analyses. *Journal of Criminal Justice* 24 (6): 537–547.

LANIER, M., and B. R. McCARTHY (1989). AIDS awareness and the impact of AIDS education in juvenile corrections. *Criminal Justice and Behavior* 16 (4): 395–411, December.

LANIER, M., and C. MILLER (1995). Attitudes and practices of Federal probation officers toward pre-plea/trial investigative report policy. *Crime and Delinquency* 41 (3): 364–377.

LELAND, J. (1996). The end of AIDS? The plague continues, especially for the uninsured, but new drugs offer hope for living. *Newsweek* 128 (23): 64–71.

LINSK, N. L. (1997). Of magic bullets and social justice: emerging challenges of recent advances in AIDS treatment. *Health and Social Work* 22 (1): 70–75.

LURIGIO, A. (1989). Practitioner's views on AIDS in probation and detention. *Federal Probation* 53 (4): 16–24.

MAIMAN, L., and M. BECKER (1974). The health belief model: Origins and correlates in psycho-logical theory. *Health Education Monographs* 2 (4): 337–353.

MARGOLIS, A. D., R. J. MacGOWAN, O. GRINSTEAD, J. SOSMAN, I. KASHIF, T. P. FLANIGAN, and THE PROJECT START GROUP (2006). Unprotected sex with multiple partners: Implications for HIV prevention among young men with a history of incarceration. *Sexually Transmitted Diseases* 33(3): 175–180.

MARKOWITZ, M. (1996). Booklet. Protease inhibitors. AEGIS: International Association of Physicians in AIDS Care. Policy prescription for HIV. 1997. April 28. *American Medical News (AMNews)*

MARTE, C., and K. ANASTOS (1990). Women—the missing persons in the AIDS epidemic: Part II. *Health/PAC Bulletin* 20(1): 11–18.

MARUSCHAK, L. M. (2002). *HIV in Prisons, 2000.* Washington, DC: Bureau of Justice Statistics (NCJ 196023).

MARUSCHAK, L. M. (2006a). *HIV in Prisons, 2004.* Washington, DC: Bureau of Justice Statistics. NCJ 213897.

MARUSCHAK, L. M. (2006a). *Medical Problems of Jail Inmates.* Washington, DC: Bureau of Justice Statistics. NCJ 210696.

MAY, J. P., and E. L. WILLIAMS, Jr. (2002). Acceptability of condom availability in a U.S. jail. *AIDS Education and Prevention* 14(Supplement B), October: 85–91.

McCARTHY, B. R., and B. J. McCARTHY (1997). *Community-Based Corrections,* 3rd ed. Pacific Grove, CA: Brooks Cole.

McKINNON, J., and K. HUMES 2000. The Black Population in the United States: March 1999. U.S. Census Bureau. Current Population Reports, Series P20–530. U.S. Government Printing Office.Washington, DC.

McKENZIE, N. (1989). The changing face of the AIDS epidemic. *Health/PAC Bulletin* 19 (4): 3–5.

MINKOFF, H. L., and J. A. DeHOVITZ (1991). Care of the woman infected with the human immun-odeficiency virus. *The Journal of the American Medical Association* 266: 2253–2258.

MORSE, D. L., L. LESSNER, M. G. MEDVESKY, D. M. GLEBATIS, and L. F. NOVICK (1991). Geographic distribution of newborn HIV seroprevalence in relation to four sociodemographic variables. *American Journal of Public Health* 81: 25–29.

MSNBC/ASSOCIATED PRESS (2006, Nov. 10). *HIV patients will spend $600K For Lifetime Care.* Associated Press. [Retrieved April 6, 2007, from http://www.msnbc.msn.com/id/15655257/]

NATIONAL COMMISSION ON CORRECTIONAL HEALTH CARE (2002). "Leadership Conference on Civil Rights" Washington, D.C.

NYSWANER, R. (Writer), and J. DEMME (Director). (1993), *Philadelphia* [Motion Picture]. Columbia TriStar.

PADIA, N. S., S. C. SHIBOSH, and N. P. JEWELL (1991). Female-to-male transmission of HIV. *The Journal of the American Medical Association* 226: 1664–1667.

PRISONS CONFRONT DILEMMA OF INMATES WITH AIDS (1986). *Journal of the American Medical Association* 255 (8): 2399–2404.

PROGRAM DEVELOPED FOR AIDS INFECTED INMATES (1994). January. *States Legislatures* 20 (1): 7–8.

PURDY, M. (1997). As AIDS increases behind bars, costs dim promise of new drugs. *New York Times* 146, A 1.

RHOADS, J. L., C. WRIGHT, R. R. REDFIELD, and D. S. BURKE (1987). Chronic vaginal candidiasis in women with human immunodeficiency virus infection. *Journal of the American Medical Association (JAMA).*

RICHARDSON, D. (1988). *Women and AIDS.* New York: Methuen.

RISK FOR CERVICAL DISEASE IN HIV-INFECTED WOMEN—NEW YORK CITY. (1991). *Morbidity and Mortality Weekly Report (MMWR)* 265 (1): 23–24. Atlanta, GA: Centers for Disease Control.

ROSENSTOCK, I. (1974). The health belief model and preventive health behavior. *Health Education Monographs* 2 (4): 355–386

ROSENSTOCK, I., V. STRECHER, and M. BECKER (1988). Social learning theory and the health belief model. *Health Education Quarterly* 15 (2): 175–183.

SAFRIN, S., B. J. DATTEL, L. HAUER, and R. L. SWEET (1990). Seroprevalence and epidemiologic correlates of human immunodeficiency virus infection in women with acute pelvic inflammatory disease. *The American Journal of Obstetrics and Gynecology* 75: 666–670.

SEEKING JUSTICE: CRIME AND PUNISHMENT IN AMERICA (1995). New York, NY: The Edna McConnell Foundation.

SMITH, B., and C. DAILARD (1994). Female prisoners and AIDS: On the margins of public health and social justice. *AIDS & Public Policy Journal* 9 (2): 78–85.

SOLOMON, D., A. HOGAN, R. BOUKNIGHT, and C. SOLOMON (1989). Analysis of Michigan Medicaid costs to treat HIV infection. *Public Health Reports* 105 (5): 416–424.

SPRINGER, S. A., E. PESANTI, J. HODGES, T. MACURE, G. DOROS, and F. L. ALTICE (2004). Effectiveness of antiretroviral therapy among infected prisoners: Reincarceration and the lack of sustained benefit after release to the community. *Clinical Infectious Diseases* (38):1754–1760.

STEIN, G. L., and L. D. HEADLEY (1996). Forum on prisoners' access to clinical trials: Summary of recommendations. *AIDS & Public Policy Journal* 11 (1) 3–20.

STUDY CONFIRMS THAT COMBINATION TREATMENT USING A PROTEASE INHIBITOR CAN DELAY HIV PROGRESSIONDISEASE PROGRESSION AND DEATH. (1997). NIAID NEWS. Wahington DC: U.S. Department of Health and Human Services.

UNITED STATES CENSUS BUREAU, (2005). In *Detailed Tables.* (sect. Race). [Retrieved April 6, 2007, from http://factfinder.census.gov/servlet/DT Table? bm=y&-geo id=01000US&ds name= ACS 2005 EST G00 &redoLog=false& mt name=ACS 2005 EST G2000 B02001]

Update: AIDS among women-United States, 1994 (1995). *Morbidity and Mortality Weekly Reports (MMWR)* 44 (5): 81–84. Atlanta, GA: Centers for Disease Control.

VALDISERRI, R., D. LYTER, L. KINGSLEY, L. LEVITON, J. SCHOFIELD, J. HUGGINS, M. HO, and C. RINALDO (1987). The effect of group education on improving attitudes about AIDS risk reduction. *New York State Journal of Medicine* 87 (5): 272–278.

VOELKER, R. (1996). Can researchers use new drugs to push HIV envelope to extinction? *The Journal of the American Medical Association (JAMA)* 276 (6): 435–438.

VLAHOV, D., T. F. BREWER, and K. G.CASTRO (1991). Prevalence of antibody to HIV-1 among entrants to U. S. correctional facilities. *Journal of the American Medical Association (JAMA)* 265: 1129–1132.

WERMUTH, L. A., R. L. ROBBINS, K. H. CHOI, and R. EVERSLEY (1991). Reaching and counseling women sexual partners. In *Preventing AIDS in Drug Users and Their Sexual Partners,* ed. J. L. Sorensen, L. A. Wermuth, D. R. Gibson, K. H. Choi, J. R. Guydish, and S. L. Batki, 130–149. New York: Guilford Press.

WIENER, L. S. (1991). Women and human immunodeficiency virus: A historical and personal psychosocial perspective. *Social Work* 36 (5): 375–378.

WINGOOD, G., and R. DICLEMENTE (1995). Understanding the role of gender relations in HIV prevention research. *Journal of Public Health* 85: 4.

WINGOOD, G., and R. DICLEMENTE (1997). Prevention of human immunodeficiency virus infection among African-American women: Sex, gender and power and Women's risk for HIV. In *Cross-cultural perspectives on HIV/ AIDS education*, ed. D. C. Umeh. Trenton, NJ: African World Press.

WINGOOD, G., D. HUNTER-GRAMBLE, and R. J. DICLEMENTE (1993). A pilot study of sexual communication and negotiation among young African American women: Implications for HIV prevention. *Journal of Black Psychology* 19 (2): 190–203.

WOMEN IN PRISON (1994). March. Annapolis Junction, MD: Bureau of Justice Statistics Clearinghouse.

WOMEN IN THE UNITED STATES (1995). August. Washington, DC: Bureau of the Census.

Chapter 30

Counting Children of Incarcerated Parents

A Methodological Critique of Past and Present Literature

Bahiyyah M. Muhammad

ABSTRACT

Children of incarcerated parents are a hidden population. To date there is no reliable way to directly calculate children who have an incarcerated parent. Therefore, the numbers of children whose parents are incarcerated have only been estimated by data collected in large-scale studies of their parents. This chapter uses existing literature on counting "hidden populations" to provide insight on counting children of incarcerated parents. This is accomplished by examining methodological strategies and identifying special issues faced by children of incarcerated parents. This chapter also provides direction for future studies.

INTRODUCTION

As early as 1978, McGowan and Blumenthal state, "we can only estimate the actual number of children of prisoners because they have been overlooked statistically, as well as, in every other way" (p. 5). Today, this statement still holds truth (Bernstein 2005). The numbers of children affected by parental incarceration continue to rise and be overlooked (Seymour 1998). Alarmingly, the rate of parental incarceration has gone up sharply in the last decade. In 1991, there were 452,500 parents in state and federal prisons, with

936,500 minor children. By 2000, the number of parents in prisons nearly doubled, and the number of children affected rose to 1,531,500 (Mumola 2000). These numbers are proof that this population of children is growing rapidly. If the U.S. incarceration trends continue to grow as they have (Gilliard and Beck 1998), the number of children affected by parental incarceration have greater odds of increasing, rather than decreasing. If this population continues to be overlooked, the continual growth of the use of imprisonment will pose major problems for the future of the United States (Bernstein 2005; Henriques 1982).

Nationally, 54.7 percent of men and 65.3 percent of women in state prison reported having a minor child (Harrison and Beck 2003). Fathers in state prison had an average of 2.04 minor children, while mothers in state prison had an average of 2.38 minor children (Harrison and Beck 2004). The estimated count of children who have a parent incarcerated in any given state equals the sum of the number of incarcerated parents multiplied by the average number of children per prisoner for each sex (Johnston 1995a; Mumola 2005). This methodology uses national estimates to calculate state estimates, leading to the assumption that all states have the same percentages of incarcerated parents. It also assumes that the national average of reported children per prisoner, by gender, is the same in every state in this country and remains relatively stable over time.

Currently, national estimates are the most concrete information we have to identify this population. It is important to note that these estimates will not identify the number of children in a given state who have an incarcerated parent (Mumola 2005). Rather they *only* provide *information* on the numbers of children who have a parent incarcerated in a given state. A parent's incarceration in a particular state does not guarantee that their children live in that same state. In fact, female inmates are more likely to report living with their children prior to incarceration than their male counterparts (Hairston 1990; Johnston 1995a; Mumola 2000; U.S. Department of Justice 1993). It may be the case that children of female inmates reside in the same state as their incarcerated parent, but this is not known for sure. This is one of the reasons these children remain hidden within the population.

Children of incarcerated parents often go unrecognized in the criminal justice arena (Bernstein 2005; Henriques 1982; Johnston 1995a; McGowan and Blumenthal 1978). Although the Bureau of Justice Statistics (BJS) has provided national estimates of the number of children affected by parental incarceration, the scope of the problem remains uncertain. No federal, state, city, or county agency has the responsibility of keeping track of this population (Johnston 1995a; Mumola 2005; Seymour 2001). On the contrary, accurate counts of parents to these children are kept by each state's Department of Correction. As a result, extensive information on prisoners has become accessible to the public via the Internet (Department of Correction 2005). Because records are not kept on children of these prisoners, sampling problems arise for those researchers interested in expanding their knowledge of this hidden population (Friedman and Esselstyn 1965; Gabel and Shindledecker 1991; Johnston 1995a; Virginia Department of Criminal Justice Services 1994). It is known from estimates that there are millions of minor children affected by parental incarceration. What remains unknown are descriptive and geographical residency data that have the potential to bring this population of children out into the open.

HIDDEN POPULATIONS

Referring to children who have an incarcerated parent as a "hidden population" is not a new phenomenon (Rosenkrantz and Joshua 1982; Weissman and LaRule 2001). A hidden population is a group of individuals for whom the size and boundaries are unknown, and for whom no sampling frame exists (Tyldum and Brunovskis 2005). Children of incarcerated parents are not the only hidden population in this world. In fact, hidden populations can be found all around the world (Beata 2000; Griffiths et al. 1993; Luan et al. 2005;). Research into hidden populations is not new (Rosenkrantz and Joshua 1982). Researchers have employed a wide range of techniques to conduct research on populations for which there is no easily accessible sampling frame (Cordray and Pion 1990; Griffiths et al. 1993; Sifaneck and Neaigus 2001). It is informative to analyze existing methodologies used to count hidden populations because it will provide insight on what has been done to sample other hard-to-reach populations.

Studies on hidden populations raise unique methodological questions and concerns, that may be absent in research involving known populations (Faugier and Sargeant 1997). Studying hidden populations is a good starting point for gaining knowledge to make an invisible population visible. This chapter analyzes existing literature on hidden populations to provide approaches that can be used to count children of incarcerated parents. This is accomplished by examining the methodological strategies used to count several hidden populations, such as the homeless, homosexuals, drug users, and prostitutes. Findings provide lessons learned about defining the target population, methodological choices, the importance of geographical location of the target population, and the emergence of subgroups embedded within the population at large. This chapter identifies special issues that are paramount to the difficulties with counting children of incarcerated parents. These problems include the use of indirect population measures and punishment for disclosure, secrecy, stigmatization, and children as research subjects, including issues of age and consent. In conclusion, the author provides directions for future studies on counting children of incarcerated parents. This is not to criticize what has or has not been done, rather to use prior research on hidden populations to identify methodological strategies that have been successful.

EXISTING METHODOLOGIES

Homeless Populations

Most studies that have counted homeless populations included an ethnographic component (Beata 2000; Burt and Cohen 1989; Cordray and Pion 1990). Ethnographic techniques can be used to determine the characteristics of a population. Such techniques can help in developing both conceptual and operational definitions for a study. Any estimate of the numbers of homeless persons involves several definitional issues, including (1) the underlying definition of "homelessness" and (2) methodological choices (Cordray and Pion 1990). Definitions have the strength to guide the research process, including the methodological strategies chosen to estimate the size of a population. Definitional issues pertaining to counting homeless individuals include who has been counted and who could be counted (Morrison 1989) because this population tends to move around a lot, so double counting could easily occur. It is impossible to make meaningful decisions about whom to count as homeless and how to derive that estimate without a firm grasp of the concept one intends to measure (Cordray and Pion 1990). Conceptual definitions can guide decisions to include or exclude an individual by limiting or expanding the target population to be counted.

Conceptual Definitions

A study done by the Urban Institute on homeless individuals in the United States (Burt and Cohen 1989) exemplifies the strength of definitions in guiding who *could* and *should* be counted. In this study, definitions of homeless individuals included those: (a) not having a home or permanent place to live, (b) residing in a shelter or hotel/motel paid for by voucher or other instrument, (c) staying in an indoor or outdoor space that was not intended for habitation, and (d) staying with a relative or friend "with whom they did not have a regular arrangement to stay for five or more days a week" (Burt and Cohen 1989). The definitional approach chosen by the Urban Institute reflects a broad view of who is considered homeless. By employing a broad definition of homelessness, researchers were able to expand the numbers of individuals counted for inclusion in this population (Morrison 1989). Expansive definitions also require the development of multiple sampling frames, for example, shelters, parks, train stations, and soup kitchens (Cordray 1991).

Operational Definitions

Operational definitions identify the specific procedures used to carry out methodological strategies in a study. These definitions implement specific rules for identifying *who* should be counted. The rules pertain to individual characteristics (e.g., age) and settings where homeless persons are to be found (e.g., in shelters, in institutions, or on the streets) (Cordray and Pion 1990). A study counting homeless persons in soup kitchens and meal programs found a subset of the population present in these locations not to be homeless (Burt and Cohen 1989). This exemplifies why it is important to identify precise definitions of who should be counted.

Methodological Choices

Methodological choices identify how a researcher will go about collecting data on a population. Researchers used different methods to measure homelessness (Beata 2000; Burt and Cohen 1989; Cordray and Pion 1990). The major problem faced while counting this population is its transient and ever-changing nature. This is why so many different methodologies are used to estimate the size of this population. For example, some researchers count persons in shelters or public/private places not designed for human habitation. Others count such persons during a specific time frame (e.g., one night) or a specified time period (e.g., 12 A.M. through 4 A.M. or Friday to Sunday) (Cordray and Pion 1990). Counting people who are homeless on a given day or during a given week has been termed *point-in-time counts,* and counting homelessness over a period of time is known as *period prevalence counts* (National Coalition for the Homeless 2002). Choosing between point-in-time counts and period-prevalence counts has significant implications for understanding the magnitude and dynamics of homelessness. It is important to note that point-in-time studies will only provide a "snapshot" of a particular situation (National Coalition for the Homeless 2002). Counting populations through the use of time-sampling procedures does not assure that everyone will be counted. Link (1995), for example, found that the most common places to find homeless individuals are in places that researchers cannot easily find. For example, homeless people were found to be staying in vehicles, tents, boxes, or caves.

Homosexual Populations

A study of men who have sex with men used specific requirements in deciding place selection. The researchers chose several places where men in the sample were thought to have frequently visited. Each place was required to have a large capacity with plenty of customers (Luan et al. 2005). Frequent visitation was their prerequisite for deciding on places to conduct their study. The multiplier method, used by Luan et al. (2005), used information from two sources to identify homosexual populations: the institution or service that the target population is in contact with and the population at risk itself. The greatest limitation in using two data sources is clearly and consistently defining the differences between the two. To get rid of this limitation all definitions and time frames should be consistent among the two data sources chosen. In addition, the researcher must provide clear definitions of the population, clearly identify the reference time, and identify the institution or service of concentration (Luan et al. 2005). The major problem faced with counting homosexual populations is the secrecy of those involved with this chosen lifestyle. Membership in this population is often kept secret due to hate, scorn, and fear of disclosure. As a result, homosexuals may do whatever they can to hide their connection to this population (Benoit et al. 2005). In an attempt to reveal this population, researchers have conducted documentary reviews (Benoit et al. 2005) and gathered primary interview data (Benoit et al. 2005; Bloor et al. 1991; Luan et al. 2005). Similar, to researchers studying homeless populations, multiple methods were adopted to obtain information.

Drug Users

Similar to the previous two hidden populations, drug users were also sampled through the use of multi-methodologies (Bloor et al. 1991; Duncan, White, and Nicholson 2003; Griffiths et al. 1993; Sifaneck and Neaigus 2001). Populations of non-injecting heroin users were found to be far less visible than their injecting counterparts. Most often the presence of marks is the main physical identifier of this population. In this study, researchers integrated qualitative techniques with quantifiable, structured survey methodologies. These authors conclude that ethnographic methods should be integrated with epidemiologic survey research and are necessary for conducting research among noninstitutionalized hidden populations (Sifaneck and Neaigus 2001).

Every population is made up of subpopulations. Sifaneck and Neaigus (2001) identified two subpopulations within the drug-using population. These subgroups included injecting and non-injecting users. Ethnographic methods were used to develop knowledge about these populations. The use of ethnographic methods (participant-observations) also provided access into the unknown environment of drug users, specifically non-injecting drug users (Sifaneck and Neaigus 2001). There are major differences between non-injecting and injecting users; the most obvious is physical appearance. The subgroup of non-injecting drug users tends to use drugs in the privacy of their homes, while injecting drug users can be found on the streets trying to find ways to support their addiction (Sifaneck and Neaigus 2001). This is the exact case for drug-injecting and non-injecting female street prostitutes (Bloor et al. 1991), which is also a subgroup of the population of drug users.

To identify those populations that fall under the umbrella of a larger population, a researcher must have some knowledge about the population at hand. It is not always the case that ethnographic studies have to be conducted to gain knowledge (Duncan, White, and Nicholson 2003). Research methodologies used to study drug-using populations were enhanced by integrating qualitative techniques with quantifiable, structured survey methodologies (Griffiths et al. 1993). In the studies described thus far, researchers have gone to the target population to study them. An alternative strategy is to have the target population come to the researcher (Griffiths et al. 1993). Target populations can be encouraged to come to a specified site to participate in the study; this is usually accomplished by paying the participant (Goldstein et al. 1990).

Prostitutes

Research on sexual matters poses unique methodological problems. These problems were addressed through the use of community–academic research on this hidden population. The difficulty of achieving a representative sample is one of the many reasons academic researchers have started to team up with community partner organizations whose local knowledge of and access to members of the hidden population are indispensable (Benoit et al. 2005). Local knowledge of a population can help in identifying a population. This method can be very helpful in conducting studies that have an ethnographic component. Community members will be able to shed light on successful strategies that allow researchers direct access to the target population. Community collaboration has its advantages as well as disadvantages.

Some advantages include funding of proposals to be supported by research findings; community relationships remain beyond the completion of research, nonacademic organizations provide a viewpoint different from the researcher. On the other hand, disadvantages include community organizations' negative views of academics (i.e., ivory tower), and skepticism and mistrust from the community may be projected toward the researcher (Benoit et al. 2005). Working with any organization—community or academic based—has its advantages and challenges. Persistent efforts must come from both parties in order for collaboration to be successful. The goal of collaboration is to work to address the needs of the population of interest.

LESSONS LEARNED FROM HIDDEN POPULATIONS

The best way to find out how to do something is to research it. To find out what methods are used to study hidden populations, the author analyzed numerous hard-to-reach populations. This approach is very helpful in providing lessons learned that will help to guide future studies on other hidden populations, such as children of incarcerated parents. Studying hidden populations allows researchers the opportunity to become aware of the unique challenges faced by these populations. Research on a hidden population is complicated by problems of definitions and methodology (National Coalition for the Homeless 2002). This does not mean that studies on hidden populations cannot be successful. Rather, definitions of key concepts play a major role in the methodological decisions that are made. Therefore, researchers should have a clear understanding about the population of interest, so that definitions can be as straightforward as possible.

Definitions

It is very important to have a clear understanding of what you are studying before you begin. Generally, the accepted practice in social science research is to state the conceptual definition of the phenomenon to be investigated (Cordray and Pion 1990). Definitions have a direct effect on who gets counted and where. Commonsense approaches or the use of formal definitions can be used to identify the population to be counted (Cordray and Pion 1990). Prior to constructing project definitions, brainstorming with a community organization that works with the population of interest can be helpful to operationalize definitions (Benoit et al. 2005). Defining the problem guides methodological decisions. Definitions are translated into operational procedures and methodological choices (Cordray and Pion 1990). The bottom line is that definitions are very important. Thought should go into defining the population, operationalizing key terms, and deciding on methodological strategies.

Methodological Choices

Analysis of methodological approaches used to conduct studies on hidden populations reveals the use of numerous study designs. Studies discussed in this chapter used numerous multimethod approaches (Beata 2000; Benoit et al. 2005; Burt, and Cohen 1989; Cordray and Pion 1990; Sifaneck and Neaigus 2001). It was found to be helpful to incorporate some aspect of community involvement into the study. Community members can offer the direct benefit of local knowledge of and access to members of the hidden population (Benoit et al. 2005). The indirect benefit of community collaboration lies in funding. Community organizations have the ability to demonstrate the worth of a research project through service-related data collection and favorable program evaluation (Benoit et al. 2005). Supportive research is critical to sustainability.

Methodological approaches are the focal point of this chapter. Analysis of past and current research on hidden populations shows these populations not to be limited by the use of a specific method. Similar to studies on visible populations, hidden population studies employ the use of multimethods. All hidden populations addressed in this chapter used some form of ethnographic method.

Ethnographic Components

Ethnographic studies assume the researcher understands where to find the target population. Ethnographic methods provide detail and context of social interactions among human groups. In order to develop knowledge about these populations the researcher must gain access to these environments. Ethnographers learn about populations through the use of structured questionnaires and interviewing. This method helps in providing access to hidden populations and provides invaluable knowledge to enhance survey research (Sifaneck and Neaigus 2001). Gaining access to a population is not always easy. Working with the community can help build relationships between the target population and researcher (Griffiths et al. 1993). A better understanding of hidden populations was found through learning the views of members associated with a specified population.

Subgroups

Ethnographic studies allow for the identification of subpopulations. Large populations are made up of smaller subgroups (Duncan, White, and Nicholson, 2003; Sifaneck and Neaigus 2001). Unique features characterize each subpopulation and the population of interest may be studied in two different locations. This must be considered when deciding on methodological approaches for a research design. The inclusion of subgroups within the setting of a larger population allows more individuals to be identified. It is important to be aware that hard-to-reach populations can be embedded within hidden populations.

Geographical Location

Geographical location is needed in order for a researcher to conduct any kind of study, especially an ethnographic design. All hidden populations discussed here were accessed through particular locations in which the population was thought to be in frequent contact with. Researchers went to the target population (Luan et al. 2005), or solicited population members to come to a specified location to participate in the study (Goldstein et al. 1990). It is very important that the researcher is able to locate the target population. The importance of geographical location is not limited to hidden populations. Research has yet to clearly identify locations where children of incarcerated parents can be found. Information regarding these children is limited to extrapolated data collected in large-scale studies of their parents (Johnston 1995a). Such information provides no insight into geographical location of the children. This poses major concerns with this hidden population.

SPECIAL ISSUES OF COUNTING CHILDREN
OF INCARCERATED PARENTS

Researchers conducting studies on this hidden population of children should be made aware of the special issues faced by the individuals who work to keep them even more invisible than they already are. All hidden populations researchers were found to have special problems in counting Benoit et al. 2005; Cordray and Pion 1990; Luan et al. 2005; Sifaneck and Neaigus 2001). Researchers of children of incarcerated parents also face methodological problems. The researchers of these children face some unique problems, such as children as research subjects (i.e., age, consent of parent, and assent of child) (Glass and Speyer-Ofenberg 1996; Meaux and Bell 2001), indirect population measures (Johnston 1995a; Mumola 2000), and unawareness of parental status. Other problems for researchers of populations of children are stigmatization, secrecy, and punishment for disclosure also present in hidden populations. Next we discuss (1) the issues of indirect population measures, such as information on children derived from parents and caregivers and (2) the issues faced by direct examination of children, specifically addressing concerns dealing with age and consent.

INDIRECT POPULATION MEASURES

All hidden population studies discussed here start with the primary population. There were studies in the past that primarily examined children of incarcerated parents (Henriques 1982) Sack 1977; Stanton 1980), but there are very few recent studies of this kind (Bernstein 2005; Hungerford 1993; Johnston 1992, 1993a,b). Children, by virtue of their age, are not free to give their own consent and are vulnerable to coercion and undue influence (Rutgers University IRB 2005). Therefore, most studies conducted on this population have been collected from incarcerated parents and/or their caretakers (Bloom and Steinhart 1993; Dalley 1997; Fritsch and Burkhead 1982; Johnston 1991; McGowan and Blumenthal 1978; Morris 1965; Sack, Seidler, and Thomas 1976; Zalba 1964). Incarcerated parents are easily accessible to researchers because of the nature of their situation. Even though some researchers have been successful in obtaining information on this population (Mumola 2000), it is unknown how much of this information is actually true. Incarcerated parents face special problems that may keep them from disclosing truthful information about their children.

Parents

Incarcerated Mothers: Punishment for Disclosure

Incarcerated parents are not rewarded in any way for disclosing information on children. Prisoners fear losing their children through termination of parental rights; as a result, they may remain silent on the topic or give dishonest answers to questions about their children. Two major reasons that parents might not want to provide information on their children are fear of losing parental rights through the Adoption and Safe Families Act

(ASFA) and issues concerning debt owed from child-support fines. Parents who are incarcerated are vulnerable to having their parental rights terminated. This is especially true for imprisoned mothers who are likely to have been the sole caretakers for their children before their imprisonment (Barry 1985; BJS 1994; Mumola 2000; Pollock-Byrne 1990). Parents who do not have the resources or relatives who are willing to care for their children during their imprisonment must turn to the foster care system for child placement (Dalley 1997).

The Adoption and Safe Families Act (ASFA) was implemented in 1997 to provide young children in foster care with permanent living arrangements (Beckerman 1998; Genty 2001; Johnson and Waldfogel 2002; Seymour 2001). This act imposes a requirement that states must file a petition to terminate parental rights when a child has been in state care for 15 of the previous 22 months. Given the increases in sentence lengths and amount of time served, this requirement is particularly consequential for incarcerated parents (Genty 2001). Incarcerated parents can prevent permanent termination of custody by having their child placed with a relative who can provide care.

Child support issues also pose problems for incarcerated parents especially upon their release back into society (Cammett 2005). Parents may deny having minor children to avoid paying child support. Parents who paid child support prior to their incarceration are required to pay child support upon their release from prison. For many prisoners, child support debt continues to accumulate during their sentence (Cammett 2005). Prisoners may view this as a punishment for disclosing information about their children. Having to pay support while in prison does not give parents an incentive to disclose truthful and precise information about their children. In fact, this may have the opposite effect.

Incarcerated Fathers: Unaware of Parental Status

Male inmates may not be aware that they are parents due to a number of reasons, including not being made aware of their status as father or their female partner may not know who the father is. Men must be told that they are parents. Women know they are a parent because they bear the children themselves. Incarcerated fathers who don't think they have children, for whatever reason, will not report being a parent. Fathers who are aware of their status as a parent may be in denial about the situation or may deny their parental status to avoid paying child support during their sentence. Unawareness or denial of parental status leads to undercounting of children of incarcerated parents.

Caregivers

Secrecy   Children who keep information about their parents' incarceration and their feelings concealed from others are engaging in secrecy (Hagen and Myers 2003). Family deception and secrecy contribute to the difficulty in the identification of children of incarcerated parents. Secrecy poses a big threat to identification of this population. This threat poses a double hurdle for researchers. Secrecy makes this already invisible population silent. Children are often told by their caregivers not to reveal any information about their parent's incarceration (Chaney, Linkenhoker, and Horne 1977; Sack, Seidler, and Thomas 1976), but to keep such information a secret. Kampfner (1995) refers to this as "conspiracy of silence" (p. 92), "or forced silence" Johnston (1995b). Caregivers may feel that they can deny the reality by acting as though it never happened. Forced silence limits the support that children can receive from others, through their fear of disclosure of the situation (Kampfner 1995).

Children may also be deceived about their parent's incarceration (Gabel 1992). Caretakers often try to protect children by avoiding the truth about the whereabouts of the incarcerated parent. Children may be told that their parents are away at school, working far away, in the military, or in the hospital (Adalist-Estrin 2005). This is not done to purposely hurt these children, but to alleviate some of the stress they may encounter knowing that their parent is incarcerated (Johnston 1995b). Parents may also request that the caregiver not tell the child about their situation.

Stigmatization   The stigma of parental incarceration makes identifying this group of children difficult. The social stigma attached to incarceration encourages both children and families to conceal the problem. People are less likely to disclose a problem that has a stigma attached (Hagen and Myers 2003). Stigmatization is a problem faced by caregivers rather than incarcerated parents and their children (Johnston 1995b).

CHILDREN AS RESEARCH SUBJECTS

Children by virtue of their age are considered to be a vulnerable population. Children of incarcerated parents, are very different from other hard-to-reach populations, who lack access to agency help. Access to this population is granted through consent of the child's parent or legal guardian, as well as consent of the caregiver. Obtaining parental consent can pose yet another problem that is significant to this population. More studies that directly access children of incarcerated parents need to be conducted to give the field the perspective of the child. When conducting studies on this population, researchers should understand the age and consent barriers faced by this population. Most discussion on the issues faced with children as research subjects has been done in the medical and psychological fields (Broome 1999; Broome and Stieglitz 1992; Conrad and Horner 1997; Lederer and Grodin 1994; National Institutes of Health 1998). Age and consent has not been addressed through research in counting children of incarcerated parents. In order for studies on this population to be expanded, researchers must be made aware of the special issues that children face as research subjects.

Age and Consent

People less than 18 years of age are considered children. Children are not able to give informed consent (National Institutes of Health 1998), so the law requires that researchers obtain consent from parents or legal guardians on behalf of minor children. Parents must sign an informed consent that allows the researcher permission to approach the child to solicit his or her participation in the research study (Broome and Stieglitz 1992; Conrad and Horner 1997). Researchers must seek assent (a child's agreement to the conditions of participation) from minor children after obtaining parental consent and before enrolling the children in the research study (Broome and Stieglitz 1992). (Conrad and Horner 1997; National Institutes of Health 1998). Parental consent does not guarantee that the child will agree to participate in the study. Children, similar to their adult counterparts, must voluntarily agree to participate in the study.

CONCLUSIONS AND FUTURE RECOMMENDATIONS

Hidden populations have three characteristics: no sampling frame is available; their members are, stigmatized within the larger society; and their members avoid being identified as belonging (Tyldum and Brunovskis 2005). Children of incarcerated parents satisfy all three characteristics; therefore, they continue to be a hidden population. All of the hidden population studies addressed in this chapter were done through direct examination of the research population. Researchers counting children of incarcerated parents are faced with special issues regarding a difficult population to access through direct measures. Direct examinations of the children pose problems but have been accomplished (Bernstein 2005; Henriques 1982; Hungerford 1993; Johnston 1992, 1993a,b; Sack 1977; Stanton 1980). What remain unaccomplished are direct counts of this population.

To date, estimates on this population have provided known information (Mumola 2000) and national estimates are the most concrete information. These estimates provide point-in-time counts, which provide a snapshot of the magnitude of the problem (National Coalition for the Homeless 2002). Unfortunately, snapshots provide limited information on this population of children (Johnston 1992). It is known that this population is everywhere (Mumola 2005), and it continues to grow (Mumola 2000; Seymour 1998). What remain unknown are hard counts of this population and geographical residency data that are vital to the visibility of this hidden population. Once this population is made visible researchers will have a sampling frame and begin to conduct more studies that directly examine the children. Research on children of the incarcerated suggests that systematically determining the scope of the problem is an important first step in understanding the impact on children. A better measuring of the scope of the problem will contribute to a better understanding of the substantive nature of this growing problem.

A close examination of research on hidden populations reveals there are many problems in trying to conduct research on hard-to-reach populations. Researchers collecting information on homeless populations were confronted with definitional issues (Burt, and Cohen 1989) and found that broad definitions should be employed when dealing with hidden populations. Studies indicate that adopting a multimethod approach to data collection, including some sort of ethnographic component to the study, can be very helpful. In the studies on the homeless, homosexuals, drug users, and prostitutes, for example, researchers had an idea of where to go to find these populations. They also knew when to go to particular locations. For example, to find prostitutes, researchers typically went out late at night or early in the morning.

In order to find someone you must know where to look. This will be very difficult to achieve when dealing with children of incarcerated parents because researchers are not exactly sure where they are. Drawing on research on hidden populations, this chapter identifies a range of issues that are faced by hidden populations, especially the special issues of counting children of incarcerated parents. The key recommendations include

Use Broad Definitions to Define Children of Incarcerated Parents

- *Provide definitions of who will be counted.* Definitions pertaining to this population of children should be broad. This allows for more individuals to be included in this population—inclusion of children who have parents in jails, prisons, and juvenile detention centers.

- *Identify reference time and specify reasons for this decision.* In reports of studies make sure to identify when, where, and how the study was conducted. This will allow other researchers to implement similar studies. In order for this population to be identified, numerous studies must be conducted. Identification of research procedures allow for others to test the reliability of the study.

- *Identify the institution or service that was chosen.* The greatest limitation in using two data sources is clearly and consistently defining the differences between the two. Make sure to provide clear definitions of the institution or service of population.

Methodological Choices Should Include the Use of Multiple Methods

- *Secondary data analysis.* It might be helpful to use information that has already been collected about this population of children. This information may be derived from child welfare agencies, prisoner records, jail intake forms, or parole records. The use of secondary data will allow for a random sample to be drawn.

- *Ethnographic component.* Even though geographical location of this population is not known, one can speculate about places where this population of children can be found. For example, children of incarcerated parents might be found visiting the prison. A researcher can conduct participant-observations at prisons on visiting days. This will allow for a researcher to see how many children are present, and how often they come to the prison. Of course, you cannot assume that the children at the prison are children of prisoners, unless you ask them.

- *In-depth child interviews.* Direct examination of children of incarcerated parents is needed in order to obtain the child's perspective of the situation. Studies on children should always include the children.

Use of Direct Population Measures and Identification of Subgroups

- *Children with parents in prison.* Children with parents in prison can be interviewed. Interviews should address concerns that have shown gaps in the current literature on this population. For example, children could be asked questions about stigmatization, number of placements since their parent's incarceration, and feelings about placement. There have been no studies on incarcerated children who have children, who are a subpopulation of children of incarcerated parents.

- *Children with parents in jail.* Children with parents in jail should be asked similar questions to those children who have parents in prison. Research on children of incarcerated parents should not be limited to parents who are only in prison. Unique differences in the child's perceptions may be found.

- *Children with both parents incarcerated.* Studies need to address the concerns of children who are affected by parental incarceration of both parents. There have been no studies that have addressed this issue. Include survey questions that ask children about both parents, rather than one.

Deciding on Place Selection

- *Institution or service with which children of incarcerated parents are in contact.* Place selection is very important when studying members of hidden populations. Don't be afraid to use two data sets to conduct your studies. This will help to identify the best places to count this population.

- *Large capacity with plenty of children of incarcerated parents.* Do you want to start by sampling a population that has a lot of children? Programs that work to address the needs of these children would also have data on the children. For example, Mentoring Children of Prisoner Programs.

Community Collaboration

- *Work with organizations in the community that work with children of the incarcerated.* Community organizations with local knowledge on children of incarcerated parents can help researchers to design their study, define key concepts, and provide access to this hidden population. Working within the community will have its advantages and disadvantages.

Studies on Incarcerated Parents and Caregivers

- *Use others when children cannot be directly examined.* When children cannot be directly examined, parents or caregivers should be examined. Information given should disclose ways to count their children. This will help to identify the best procedures for counting this population, from the view of those who care for the children.

- *Unawareness of parental status and disclosure issues.* These issues are directly related to ways in which undercounts may be produced. Questions concerning who prisoners claim to be their children are important. It could be that some inmates identify their girlfriend's children as their children. This will help to identify if nonbiological children are claimed by inmates, and under what circumstances. Disclosure issues should focus on incarcerated parents and caregivers to their children.

- *Information on geographical locations of children.* This chapter provides a methodological critique on counting children of incarcerated parents. Geographical location is needed in order to count, study, and access the needs of these children. All future studies on children of incarcerated parents in this century should include information on geographical residency data.

ACKNOWLEDGMENT

The author expresses sincere thanks and gratitude to Dr. Johnna Christian and Dr. Bonita Veysey for their assistance with this work.

REFERENCES

ADALIST-ESTRIN, A. (2005). *Conversations: Questions Children Ask*. Children of Prisoners Library: Family Connection Network.

BARRY, E. (1985). Reunification difficult for incarcerated parents and their children. *Youth Law News* July–August: 14–16.

BEATA, D. (2000). *Estimating the Size of Homeless Population in Budapest, Hungary*. The Research Support Scheme of the Open Society Support Foundation. Czech Republic: Research Support Team.

BECKERMAN, A. (1998). Charting a course: Meeting the challenge of permanency planning for children with incarcerated mothers. *Child Welfare* 77: 513–530.

BENOIT, C., M. JANSSON, A. MILLAR, and R. PHILLIPS (2005). Community academic research on hard to reach populations: Benefits and challenges. *Qualitative Health Research* 15(2): 263–282.

BERNSTEIN, N. (2005). *All Alone in the World: Children of the Incarcerated*. New York: The New Press.

BLOOM, B., and D. STEINHART (1993). *Why Punish the Children? A Reappraisal of the Children of Incarcerated Mothers in America*. San Francisco, CA: National Council on Crime and Delinquency.

BLOOR, M., A. LEYLAND, M. BARNARD, and N. MCKEGANEY (1991). Estimating hidden populations: A new method of calculating the prevalence of drug-injecting and non-injecting female street prostitutes. *British Journal of Addiction* 86(1): 1477–1483.

BROOM, M. E. (1999). *Consent (assent) for research with pediatric patients*. Seminars in Oncology Nursing, 15(2): 96–103.

BROOM, M. E., and K. A. STIEGLITZ (1992). *The consent process and children*. Research in Nursing and Health, 15(2): 147–152.

BUREAU OF JUSTICE STATISTICS (1994). *Special Report on Women in Prison*. Washington, DC: U.S. Department of Justice.

BURT, M. R., and B. S. COHEN (1989). *American's Homeless: Numbers, Characteristics, and Programs that Serve Them*. Washington, DC: The Urban Institute.

CAMMETT, A. (2005). *Making Work Pay: Promoting Employment and Better Child Support Outcomes for Low-Income and Incarcerated Parents*. New Jersey Institute for Social Justice.

CHANEY, R., D. LINKENHOKER, and A. HORNE (1977). The counselor and children of imprisoned parents. *Elementary School Guidance Counselor* 11: 177–183.

CONRAD, B., and S. HORNER (1997). Issues in pediatric research: Safeguarding the children. *Journal of the Society of Pediatric Nurses* 2(4): 163–171.

CORDRAY, D. S. (1991). Counting the homeless: What counts? In *Conference Proceedings for Enumerating Homeless Persons: Methods and Data Needs*, ed. C. Taeuber, pp. 91–101. Washington, DC: Bureau of the Census.

CORDRAY, D. S., and G. M. PION (1990). What's behind the numbers? Definitional issues in counting the homeless. *Housing Policy Debate* 2: 587–616.

DALLEY, L. P. (1997). Montana's imprisoned mothers and their children: A case study on separation, reunification and legal issues. *Dissertation Abstracts International* (University Microfilms No. 9735666).

DUNCAN, D., J. B. WHITE, and T. NICHOLSON (2003). Using Internet-based surveys to reach hidden populations: Case of nonabusive illicit drug users. *American Journal of Health Behavior* 27(3): 208–218.

FAUGIER, J., and M. SARGEANT (1997). Sampling hard to reach populations. *Journal of Advanced Nursing* 26: 790–797.

FRIEDMAN, S., and T. C. ESSELSTYN (1965). The adjustment of children to parental absence due to imprisonment. *Family Relations* 30: 83–88.

FRITSCH, T. A., and J. D. BURKHEAD (1982). Behavioral reactions of children to parental absence due to imprisonment. *Family Relations* 30: 83–88.

GABEL, S. (1992). Behavioral problems in sons of incarcerated or otherwise absent fathers: The issue of separation. *Family Process* 31: 303–314.

GABEL, S., and R. SHINDLEDECKER (1991). Incarceration in parents of day hospital youth: The issue of separation. *Family Process* 31: 303–314.

GENTY, P. M. (2001). Permanency planning in the context of parental incarceration: Legal issues and recommendations. In *Children with Parents in Prison: Child Welfare Policy, Program, and Practice Issue*, ed. C. Seymour and C. F. Hairston. New Brunswick, NJ: Transaction Publishers.

GILLIARD, D. K., and A. J. BECK (1998). *Bureau of Justice Statistics Bulletin: Prison and Jail Inmates at Midyear 1997*. Washington, DC: U.S. Department of Justice, Bureau of Justice Statistics.

GLASS, K. C., and M. SPEYER-OFENBERG (1996). Incompetent persons as research subjects and the ethics of minimal risk. *Cambridge Quarterly of Healthcare Ethics* 5(1): 362–372.

GOLDSTEIN, P., B. SPUNT, T. MILLER, and P. BELLUCCI (1990). Ethnographic field stations. In *The Collection and Interpretation of Data from Hidden Populations*, ed. E. Lambert, Rockville, MA: NIDA Research Monograph 98.

GRIFFITHS, P., M. GOSSOP, B. POWIS, and J. STRANG (1993). Reaching hidden populations of drug users by privileged access interviews: Methodological and practical issues. *Addiction* 88: 1617–1626.

HAGEN, K. A., and B. J. MYERS (2003). The effects of secrecy and social support on behavioral problems in children of incarcerated women. *Journal of Child and Family Studies* 12(2): 229–242.

HAIRSTON, C. F. (1990). Mothers in jail: Parent–child separation and jail visitation. *Affilia* 6(2).

HARRISON, P. M., and A. J. BECK (2003). *Prisoners in 2002*. Washington, DC: U.S. Department of Justice, Office of Justice Programs, Bureau of Justice Statistics Bulletin. Report No. NCJ 200248.

HARRISON, P. M., and A. J. BECK (2004). *Prisoners in 2003*. Washington, DC: U.S. Department of Justice, Office of Justice Programs, Bureau of Justice Statistics Bulletin. Report No. NCJ 205335.

HENRIQUES, Z. W. (1982). *Imprisoned Mothers and Their Children: A Descriptive and Analytical Study*. Washington, DC: University Press of America.

HUNGERFORD, G. P. (1993). The children of inmate mothers: An exploratory study of children, caretakers and inmate mothers in Ohio. *Dissertation Abstracts International* (University Microfilms No. 9401279).

JOHNSON, E. I., and J. WALDFOGEL (2002). Parental incarceration: Recent trends and implications for child welfare. *Social Services Review* 32: 460–479.

JOHNSTON, D. (1991). *Jailed Mothers*. Pasadena, CA: Pacific Oaks Center for Children of Incarcerated Parents.

JOHNSTON, D. (1992). *Children of Offenders*. Pasadena, CA: Pacific Oaks Center for Children of Incarcerated Parents.

JOHNSTON, D. (1993a). *Children of the Therapeutic Intervention Project*. Pasadena, CA: Pacific Oaks Center for Children of Incarcerated Parents.

JOHNSTON, D. (1993b). *Intergenerational Incarceration*. Pasadena, CA: Pacific Oaks Center for Children of Incarcerated Parents.

JOHNSTON, D. (1995a). The care and placement of prisoners' children. In *Children of Incarcerated Parents*, ed. K. Gabel and D. Johnston, pp. 103–123. New York: Lexington Books.

JOHNSTON, D. (1995b). Effects of parental incarceration. In *Children of Incarcerated Parents*, ed. K. Gabel and D. Johnston, pp. 59–88. New York: Lexington Books.

KAMPFNER-JOSE, C. (1995). Post-traumatic stress reactions in children of imprisoned mothers. In *Children of Incarcerated Parents*, ed. K. Gabel and D. Johnston, pp. 89–100. New York: Lexington Books.

LEDERER, S. E., and M. A. GRODIN (1994). Historical overview: Pediatric experimentation. In *Children as Research Subjects*, ed. M. A. Grodin and L. H. Glantz, New York: Oxford University Press.

LINK, B. (1995). Life-time and five-year prevalence of homelessness in the United States: New evidence on an old debate. *American Journal of Orthopsychiatry* 65(3): 347–354.

LUAN, R., G. ZENG, D. ZHANG, L. LUO, P. YUAN, B. LIANG, and Y. LI (2005). A study on methods of estimating the population size of men who have sex with men in southwest china. *European Journal of Epidemiology* 20: 581–585.

MCGOWAN, B. G., and K. L. BLUMENTHAL (1978). *Why Punish the Children? A Study of Women Prisoners*. Hackensack, NJ: National Council on Crime and Delinquency.

MEAUX, J. B., and P. L. BELL (2001). Balancing recruitment and protection: Children as research subjects. *Issues in Comprehensive Pediatric Nursing* 24: 241–251.

MORRIS, P. (1965). *Prisoners and Their Families*. New York: Hart.

MORRISON, J. (1989). Correlations between definitions of the homeless mentally ill population. *Hospital and Community Psychiatry* 40: 952–954.

MUMOLA, C. (2000). *Incarcerated Parents and Their Children*. Washington, DC: U.S. Department of Justice, Office of Justice Programs, Bureau of Justice Statistics. Report No. NCJ 182335.

MUMOLA, C. (2005). *Estimating the Count of Children Affected by Parental Incarceration*. Washington, DC: U.S. Department of Justice, Office of Justice programs, Bureau of Justice Statistics.

NATIONAL COALITION FOR THE HOMELESS (2002). *How Many People Experience Homelessness?* Washington, DC: National Coalition for the Homeless.

NATIONAL INSTITUTES OF HEALTH (1998). *NIH Policy and Guidelines on the Inclusion of Children as Participants in Research Involving Human Subjects*. Washington, DC: Department of Health and Human Services.

POLLOCK-BYRNE, J. M. (1990). *Women, Prison, and Crime*. Pacific Grove, CA: Brooks/Cole.

ROSENKRANTZ, L., and V. JOSHUA (1982). Children of incarcerated parents: A hidden population. *Children Today* January–February: 2–6.

SACK, W. H. (1977). Children of imprisoned fathers. *Psychiatry* 40: 163–174.

SACK, W. H., T. SEIDLER, and S. THOMAS (1976). Children of imprisoned parents: A psychosocial exploration. *American Journal of Orthopsychiatry* 46: 618–628.

SEYMOUR, C. (1998). Children with parents in prison: Child welfare policy, program and practice issue. *Child Welfare Journal of Practice and Program* 9(1): 1–13.

SEYMOUR, C. (2001). Children with parents in prison: Child welfare policy, program, and practice issues. In *Children with Parents in Prison: Child Welfare Policy, Program and Practice Issues*, ed. C. Seymour and C. F. Hairston, pp. 1–25. New Brunswick, NJ: Transaction Publishers.

SIFANECK, S. J., and A. NEAIGUS (2001). The ethnographic accessing, sampling and screening of hidden populations: Heroin sniffers in New York City. *Addiction Research & Theory* 9(6): 519–543.

STANTON, A. (1980). *When Mothers Go To Jail*. Lexington, MA: Lexington Books.

TYLDUM, G., and A. BRUNOVSKIS (2005). Describing the unobserved: Methodological challenges in empirical studies on human trafficking. *International Migration* 43: 17–34.

U.S. DEPARTMENT OF JUSTICE (1993). *Survey of State Prisoners*. Washington, DC: U.S. Bureau of Justice Statistics. Report No. NCJ 136949.

VIRGINIA DEPARTMENT OF CRIMINAL JUSTICE SERVICES (1994). *Report on the Department of Criminal Justice Services on Developing a Methodology for Counting Children of Incarcerated Parents.* Richmond, VA: Senate Document No. 16.

WEISSMAN, M., and C. M. LaRULE (2001). Earning trust from youths with none to spare.

In *Children with Parents in Prison: Child Welfare Policy, Program, and Practice Issues*, ed. C. Seymour and C. F. Hairston, pp. 111–125. New Brunswick, NJ: Transaction Publishers.

ZALBA, S. (1964). *Women Prisoners and Their Families.* Sacramento, CA: Department of Social Welfare and Department of Corrections.

PART VII

Terrorism

Chapter 31

Public Safety and Private Sector Responses to Terrorism and Weapons of Mass Destruction

Vincent E. Henry and Douglas H. King

July Fourth was a beautiful day in Veterans Memorial Park, and Central City Police Officers Pedro (Pete) Bernal and Dennis O'Loughlin were happy to be assigned to the Park Car. The thousand-acre park was full of people strolling, cycling, and rollerblading; a band was playing at the gazebo; and families spread their picnic blankets on the lawns and barbecued at the small beach at the edge of MacArthur Lake. "It doesn't get much better than this," Officer Bernal said to his partner as they cruised slowly past the playground filled with laughing children, "and it sure beats answering jobs all day in Sector Charlie. It's too bad every day can't be as nice and relaxed as today. A day like today makes you glad to be alive. Good country, America."

"It sure is. What should we do for lunch?" O'Loughlin replied, savoring the aromas of various ethnic foods emanating from all the push carts in the park. "It's almost one o'clock and I'm starving." After some discussion, they settled on a Cuban sandwich for Dennis and two hot dogs with mustard, relish, onions, and sauerkraut for Pedro. The call came just as they were getting back in their cruiser.

"Park Car One on the air?"

"Park Car One. Go ahead, Central."

"Park One, we have multiple aided calls in the vicinity of the gazebo on the Great Lawn. Callers state several people are having seizures. An ambulance is on the way. Please check and advise."

Dennis and Pete looked at each other. Both were experienced and well-trained cops, and the implications of the call were readily apparent to them. Just this week the precinct's Intelligence Liaison Officer, Lieutenant Kennedy, had briefed the outgoing roll call to be especially on guard for potential terrorist events during the holiday weekend. Based on information received at the weekly regional Terrorstat meeting, Kennedy related that credible but unspecified threats—"intelligence chatter" had been received by the Federal Bureau Investigation (FBI) and passed on to local agencies. Although the information was not specific, and although the nation and the city remained at Threat Condition Yellow, officers should be especially attentive when responding to unusual events.

"Ten-four, Central. Please try the callback numbers and determine the number of victims and if there are any other symptoms. Have the ambulance stand by at the south entrance to the park and have Park Two stand by near the Boathouse until we check and advise."

Dennis and Pete regretfully put aside their food, started up their cruiser, and headed slowly toward the Great Lawn. They had been partners for almost 10 years and were experienced enough to know that they should not rush into a situation like this, but instead respond carefully and gather as much information as possible on their way to the scene. A great many things had changed in police work during 10 years, not the least of which was the strategic and tactical approach they now took to calls that might involve a possible terrorist act. The terrorist attacks on the World Trade Center and the Pentagon seven years ago required cops across the nation to adopt a new and very different orientation to the way they worked, and the possibility that even the most mundane and seemingly ordinary call for service might have some terrorist connection was always in the back of their minds. So far, Central City had escaped the realities of terrorism, but Bernal and O'Loughlin and their entire department were well prepared and well trained to handle terrorist incidents.

Despite the warmth of the day, they rolled up the cruiser's windows and turned off the air conditioner—if the situation turned out the way they hoped it wouldn't, at least they would be partially protected from airborne contaminants drawn in through the ventilation system. Pete rummaged in the gear bags on the cruiser's back seat, pulling out two pair of binoculars, a small radiation detector, and a copy of the department's field guide to hazardous materials and weapons of mass destruction.

On the way to the scene, they carefully watched the holiday crowds for anything unusual or out of the ordinary. No one they passed appeared to be ill, and no one seemed to be in a particular hurry to leave the area. Dennis stopped the cruiser at the edge of the woods surrounding the Great Lawn, about a quarter mile from the gazebo.

Pete scanned the area with the binoculars, first looking at the commotion near the gazebo and then scanning the trees at the edge of the lawn. Dennis also scanned the scene with his binoculars. The band had stopped playing and highly excited people were milling around, trampling the picnic blankets, and turning over barbecue grills. Some civilians lay prone or rolled on the ground as others tired to administer aid, while others gathered their children and tried to flee the chaotic scene. Some fell to the ground as they ran, and others fell to their knees to vomit. Dennis and Pete could hear frenzied shouting and several civilians, spotting the cruiser, ran toward the cops.

"No birds. I don't see any birds in the trees. And there's a mist or cloud hanging over the area. It could be barbecue smoke, but I don't know. There's a dog having some kind of seizure, too. What have you got?" Dennis said to his partner.

"Rats. Look at the rats crossing the road. The rats are running away. The wind is blowing toward the west, spreading the cloud. Move the car up the hill to the east road-way, but don't get any closer to the gazebo. I think I see dead pigeons at the verge of the woods. I get nothing on the radiation detector for now, but we may be too far away."

The first civilian—a highly distraught man with a flushed face, streaming tears, and vomit on his shirt—reached the cruiser and shouted frantically at the cops to help. Pete and Dennis both knew that time, distance, and shielding were the keys to their self-preservation, just as they both knew that they would become a liability if they became contaminated or affected by whatever substance was making these people sick. Time, distance, and shielding were the keys to their survival as well as the survival of the victims. Pete used the loudspeaker to order the man to back off from the police car: The civilian could potentially be a vector to spread whatever chemical or biological agent was afflicting the crowd, and the two cops would be of no help to anyone if they became affected by it. They'd later say that one of the hardest things about the situation was avoiding the urge to rush in to immediately render aid—it is, after all, the natural tendency of cops and rescue workers to run toward trouble in order to help—but the very fact that they lived to say it was evidence that they acted wisely and according to the way they'd been trained.

Pete communicated with the man using the loudspeaker, learning more about what had gone on near the gazebo as the first victims fell ill and taking notes about the symptoms. He learned there was a faint odor, like the smell of newly cut grass, at the time the first people fell ill.

Dennis picked up the radio and spoke calmly.

"Park Car One to Central. Be advised we have a likely mass chemical or biological event on the Great Lawn. Numerous civilians down. There is a crowd of several hundred people, and we'll be moving them away from the scene to the east side of the park near the Boathouse. Notify the Emergency Response Unit. Notify Midtown Hospital, Saint Mary's, and all the other hospitals to expect casualties. Notify the Patrol Supervisor that we'll set up a temporary emergency headquarters in the Parks Department office north of the Lawn pending his arrival. Notify the Chief and the Fire Department. Have all available PD units respond to seal the park exits and perimeter, and have a unit respond to the Broadway bus station to prevent further contamination from people leaving the park. Have the ambulances respond to the Boathouse area to set up an aid station. Central, caution the responding units not to approach the gazebo or the Great Lawn itself until we have further information about the contaminant and its effects. Also caution the responding units to be aware of secondary devices or events. Here are the symptoms, Central. . . ."

INTRODUCTION

The threat of terrorist events involving weapons of mass destruction (WMD) is real, and the futuristic scenario just described is not at all far-fetched.

The September 11, 2001, terrorist attacks on the World Trade Center and the Pentagon changed the United States forever, ushering in a host of new and unprecedented realities for the American people; for the intelligence and national security communities; for medical personnel; for private security entities; and perhaps especially for the police, fire, and emergency medical personnel. In particular, police, fire, and emergency medical service personnel—the agencies and individuals most likely to be the first responders to possible terrorist attacks—now face compelling demands to adopt new strategies and tactics, to undertake new training, and to view their roles and their work in an entirely different way. As first responders, they are our first line of defense in case of terrorist attack, but the enormity and complexity of the challenges they face make it abundantly clear that they alone cannot bear the responsibility for ensuring our safety. Although first responders play an absolutely critical role in homeland security and domestic preparedness, and although a great deal of attention and resources have been already focused on them in order to counter the terrorist threat, much more needs to be done. Perhaps most importantly, the realistic potential that American people, towns, and cities may again come under attack from terrorists demands that significant systemic changes occur throughout the range of public agencies and private entities charged with the responsibility for ensuring public safety. We must develop and implement a broader, more coordinated, more cohesive, and more focused approach to terrorism and to WMD, and that approach must involve new relationships between and among all of these public agencies and private entities.

The actions necessary to bring about all these changes are extensive, and they lie well beyond the scope of this chapter to fully describe or explore. This chapter will, however, focus more narrowly on the issue of WMD in the hands of terrorist groups, on the danger they pose to the American people and our nation as a whole, on the current lapses and gaps in our approach to the WMD threat, and on the steps necessary to create a more viable system to counter the threat. The importance of adequate preparation for future terrorist acts involving WMD is illuminated by the virtual consensus among knowledgeable experts that these future acts are a practical inevitability. It is not a matter of whether such incidents will occur, but when they will occur (Lynch 2002; Shenon and Stout 2002).

In the first part of this chapter, we define WMD in general and provide an overview of specific types of WMDs as a way of understanding the nature of the threat they pose. We then examine, in a general way, the type of response protocols police, fire, emergency medical service, and other agencies currently have in place, and we highlight some of the problems and issues that tend to hinder their overall effectiveness. Finally, we explore some of the possible solutions for these problems and issues and set forth a rudimentary design or plan for achieving better, more effective, and more efficient interactions between public agencies and private entities—to achieve the kind of integrated system that will (1) help ensure public safety through the timely and accurate analysis of terrorist intelligence, (2) develop effective tactical and strategic responses to different types of events, (3) rapidly deploy necessary personnel and resources, and (4) relentlessly follow up on terrorist intelligence to interdict future attacks and apprehend and prosecute terrorists.

WEAPONS OF MASS DESTRUCTION: AN OVERVIEW

Weapons of mass destruction (WMD) are devices, biological organisms, or chemical substances that, when successfully detonated or dispersed, are readily capable of causing massive casualties. WMDs have been defined in various ways. The Department of Defense (Henneberry 2001), for example, defines WMDs as "weapons that are capable of a high order of destruction and/or of being used in such a manner as to destroy large numbers of people." The definition goes on to note that these can include nuclear, chemical, biological, and radiological weapons. For legal purposes, Title 18 of the US Code (18 USC 113B) includes various types of firearms and other weapons in its definition of WMDs, as well as "any weapon designed or intended to cause death or serious bodily injury through the release, dissemination, or impact of toxic or poisonous chemicals, or their precursors; any weapon involving a disease organism; or any weapon that is designed to release radiation or radioactivity at a level dangerous to human life."

The Federal Emergency Management Agency (FEMA 2002) defines WMDs as "any weapon that is designed or intended to cause death or serious bodily injury through the release, dissemination, or impact of toxic or poisonous chemicals; disease organisms; radiation or radioactivity; or explosion or fire." The FEMA definition also points out that WMDs are distinguished from other types of terrorist tools because they may not be immediately obvious, because it may be difficult to determine when and where they have been released, and because of the danger they pose to first responders and medical personnel. Although a great deal of research has been done on battlefield exposure to WMDs, scientists have a more limited understanding of how they can affect civilian populations.

Examples of WMD include nuclear devices (ranging from nuclear bombs to smaller and more easily constructed "dirty bombs" that spread deadly radiation in a relatively small area), biological devices (such as anthrax, smallpox, and other deadly toxins), and chemical agents (such as nerve agents and gaseous poisons). These three categories of weapons are often referred to collectively as nuclear, biological, and chemical (NBC) weapons. While we will be primarily concerned with these three categories of substances and devices for the purposes of this chapter, we should recognize that the airliners used in the September 11 terrorist attacks on the Pentagon and the World Trade Center clearly conform to the FEMA definition provided earlier. The hijacked airliners used in the attack were essentially flying bombs—they were high-powered explosive devices loaded with highly flammable fuel that caused a tremendous number of casualties, though they were not immediately obvious as weapons, and they posed an exceptionally high degree of danger to first responders and medical personnel.

Biological and Chemical Agents in Warfare and Terrorism

Chemical and biological agents have been used in warfare between nations for many years, and they have been extremely effective weapons in terms of causing casualties and death as well as in spreading fear and panic among an enemy's soldiers. More recently, they have become the weapons of choice for terrorists and extremist groups for essentially

592 Chapter 31   Public Safety and Private Sector Responses to Terrorism WMDs

the same reasons, as well as the fact that they are rather easily manufactured and deployed. The first modern wartime use of chemical weapons of war occurred during World War I, when German forces used chlorine gas against Allied forces in April 1915 during the Second Battle of Ypres. British forces retaliated in September of that year, firing artillery shells containing chlorine gas against the German forces at Loos. Although they were certainly not known as WMD at that time, WMDs in the form of poison gas were generally successful on the battlefield. They were not, however, perfect weapons: although French and Algerian troops fled in a panic when they confronted chlorine gas at Ypres, shifting winds during the British action at Loos also caused numerous casualties among British forces (Duffy 2002). The fact that the spread and the effect of poison gases and some biological agents can be so easily affected by the wind and by environmental factors makes them particularly unpredictable and especially dangerous to first responders, rescue personnel, and civilians in densely populated urban areas.

The development of use of poison gases continued throughout World War I. Phosgene gas was used by both sides in the conflict, and it was seen as an improved weapon because it caused less choking and coughing than chlorine gas and was therefore more likely to be inhaled. Phosgene also had a delayed effect in which soldiers might suddenly die up to 48 hours after their exposure. Mustard gas, an almost odorless chemical, was developed by Germany and first used against Russian troops at Riga in 1917. The strategic advantages of mustard gas (also known as Yperite) included inflicting painful blisters, the fact that it was more difficult to protect against than chlorine or phosgene, and the fact that it could remain potent in the soil for weeks, making it dangerous to recapture trenches infected with the gas (Duffy 2002).

The use of chlorine, phosgene, and mustard gas continued throughout World War I and inflicted a terrible casualty rate. According to one estimate, there were almost 1,240,000 casualties from poison gas during World War I, including more than 90,000 deaths. Russia alone suffered nearly 420,000 gas casualties (Duffy 2002).

The horrible potential of poison gases to bring about massive numbers of casualties and deaths had been recognized long before their use on World War I battlefields, but their actual use by combatants on both sides, along with a recognition of their terrible consequences, led to the passage in 1928 of the Geneva Convention's Protocol for the Prohibition of the Use in War of Asphyxiating Gas, and of Bacteriological Methods of Warfare. This convention, which more specifically outlawed the use of poison gas and the practice of bacteriological warfare, was not ratified by the United States until 1974.

In the decades following World War I, development of poison gases as well as some use on the battlefield continued. During the 1920s, British forces used chemical weapons against Kurdish rebels in Iraq, in the 1930s Italy used mustard gas during its conquest of Ethiopia, and in the early 1930s Japan used chemical weapons during its invasion of China. The first nerve agent, Tabun, was developed in Germany in 1938.

In the United States, the first known attempt by a terrorist or extremist group to use biological agents on the civilian population occurred in 1972, when members of a right wing group known as the Order of the Rising Sun were found to possess more than 30 kilograms of typhoid bacteria. The group intended to spread typhoid through the water supply systems of several major Midwestern cities (Sachs 2003:3).

Another bioterrorism event occurred in the United States in 1984, when members of a religious cult known as Rajneeshee infected an estimated 751 people in Oregon with salmonella bacteria. The bacteria were easily grown from cultures purchased from a medical supply company, and cult members disseminated the bacteria by spraying them on restaurant salad bars. The cult's goal was to influence the results of an upcoming local election by making a large number of voters too sick to vote on election day (McDade and Franz 1988; Sachs 2003: 4–5). Investigators considered the possibility of bioterrorism when the outbreak occurred, but the possibility was deemed unlikely and the source of the contamination became apparent only when the FBI investigated the cult for other criminal violations. This incident highlighted how difficult it can be to distinguish a bioterrorist attack from a naturally occurring infectious disease outbreak (McDade and Franz 1988).

Although the individual or individuals responsible have yet to be identified, the series of anthrax attacks that took place across America in 2001 certainly have all the hallmarks of a terrorist attack, and the attacks certainly spread alarm and fear throughout the population. In these incidents, anthrax spores were distributed—perhaps at random—through the U.S. Postal Service to individuals, corporations, and political figures, and at least 10 cases of anthrax infection were documented by health officials (Jernigan et al. 2001; Traeger et al. 2002).

Iraqi dictator Saddam Hussein used both chemical weapons (nerve agents) and biological weapons (anthrax) on Iranian forces during the 1980–1988 war between Iran and Iraq, and he used cyanide against Iraqi Kurds in 1987 and 1988. In 1995, members of the Aum Shinrikyo (Supreme Truth) cult dispersed deadly sarin gas on the Tokyo subway system, killing a dozen people and injuring more than 5,500 others.

Aum Shinrikyo's 1995 Tokyo subway attack, which represents the first known use of poison gas or other WMD by terrorists, had a tremendous impact on Japan and on Japanese society because it spread such fear and alarm among the public. The Japanese people, like the rest of the world community, were not well prepared for the possibility that a fairly small religious cult would carry out such an attack, nor were they prepared for the possibility that a fairly small religious cult *could* carry out this type of attack. The fact that such a small group could marshal the resources necessary to kill and injure large numbers of people and spread panic across an entire nation had repercussions throughout the world since it also demonstrated just how easy it would be for terrorists or extremist groups to manufacture and disseminate deadly WMDs.

Aum Shinrikyo was a doomsday cult centered around leader Shoko Asahara's apocalyptic philosophy and his twisted notion that only the true believers belonging to the cult would be saved once the world ended. Asahara's goal in undertaking the attack was to hasten the end of the world. Asahara's cult, which accumulated immense wealth from its members, recruited young scientists as cult members and put them to work producing biological and chemical weapons. It also began to stockpile hundreds of tons of deadly chemicals and acquired a helicopter to help distribute the gas over densely populated Japanese cities (Kristof 1995; Lifton 1999).

Sarin, an exceptionally toxic nerve agent that is several hundred times more toxic than cyanide, was first developed by Nazi scientists in the 1930s. Sarin, which is also known as GB, is a fairly complex chemical compound that can take either liquid or gaseous forms.

Although its manufacture requires a fairly high level of skill, training, and knowledge of chemistry, it is made from widely used chemicals that are readily available to the public.

Once cult members manufactured a quantity of sarin, it was a rather simple to disseminate: Liquid sarin was sealed in paint cans and other containers that cult members carried into subway stations in shopping bags. They simply put down the bags, casually punctured the containers with the tips of their umbrellas, and walked away while the liquid evaporated into a gas and spread through the area. Experts concur that the 1995 subway attack was simply a test—a dry run in anticipation of and preparation for a much larger and much more deadly attack. Experts also concur that many more lives would have been lost and many more would have been injured if Aum Shinrikyo had been able to manufacture a purer form of Sarin or distribute it more effectively (Kristoff 1995; Lifton 1999).

Perhaps one of the most frightening aspects of Aum Shinrikyo's attack on the subway system was the relative ease with which the group obtained the necessary precursor chemicals and manufactured large quantities of deadly sarin. There are many other biological and chemical agents that are relatively easy to obtain, manufacture, and disseminate, making them very attractive to terrorist organizations. Depending upon the particular chemical or biological agent involved, a relatively small and easily transportable amount of the substance can easily spread throughout an area and contaminate or infect people coming in contact with it. Especially when toxic biological substances with a prolonged incubation period (as some bacteria and viruses have) are involved, signs of illness may not be immediately apparent. Individuals infected with the toxic substance may act as a "vector," spreading the substance to others with whom they have contact. Since it might be days or weeks before the first infected individuals become ill, they can spread the infection to literally hundreds or thousands of other people, many of whom will in turn become vectors spreading the disease.

A chemical event is likely to immediately produce dozens of victims, and first responders who lack adequate personal protection equipment may also become victims. All exposed victims must be decontaminated before leaving the scene, since hospital emergency rooms will not accept the victims of a biological or chemical incident until they have been properly decontaminated.

Chemical agents can enter the body in various ways. Some agents are disseminated as aerosols or gases and enter the body through the respiratory tract, while others are disseminated in a liquid form and enter the body through contact with the skin. Because the eyes and mucous membranes are particularly sensitive to many toxic agents, irritated eyes and nasal passages often indicate exposure. While other chemical agents can be ingested via contaminated food or liquid, inhalation and skin contact are the primary hazard for victims and emergency responders.

There are three basic categories of chemical agents: nerve agents, blister or vesicant agents, and choking agents.

Nerve Agents

Nerve agents, which include the substances tabun (GA), soman (GD), sarin (GB), and methylphosphonothioic acid (VX), are an especially toxic class of chemical weapons that act upon the body by interrupting the central nervous system to prevent the transmission of nerve impulses, resulting in the twitches and spasms that are the characteristic symptoms of exposure to this type of WMD.

Symptoms of exposure to nerve agents typically include dilation of pupils (pin-point pupils), runny nose and lacrimation (tearing of eyes), salivation (drooling), difficulty breathing, muscle twitches and spasms, involuntary defecation or urination, nausea, and vomiting.

Depending upon their purity, nerve agents generally take the form of colorless liquids, although some may have a slight yellowish tinge if impurities are present. Tabun and sarin may have a slightly fruity odor, soman may have a slight odor of camphor, and VX smells like sulfur. Nerve agents evaporate fairly quickly and can be absorbed into the body either through inhalation or absorption through the skin. Nerve agents vary a bit in terms of their toxicity and the amount of exposure necessary to bring on symptoms or cause death, but all are exceptionally deadly at exceptionally low dosages. Exposure to a fatal dose of a nerve agent, if untreated, will typically cause death in a matter of minutes. The typical treatment for nerve agents is an injection of atropine.

Blister or Vesicant Agents

Blister or vesicant agents act by producing burns or blisters on the skin or any other body part they come in contact with, and they can be fatal. They act quickly upon the eyes, lungs, skin, and mucous membranes, inflicting severe damage upon the lungs and respiratory tract when inhaled and resulting in vomiting and diarrhea when ingested.

Blister agents include mustard gas (also known as Yperite or sulfur mustard), nitrogen mustard (HN), Lewisite (L), and phosgene oxime (CX). Mustard gas and Lewisite are particularly dangerous because they produce severe injuries for which there is no known antidote or therapy; a single drop of liquid mustard on the skin can cause serious damage and itching in only a few minutes, and exposure to even a slight amount of mustard in its gaseous state can cause painful blistering, tearing and, eventually, severe lesions of the eyes. Depending upon weather conditions as well as the extent and duration of exposure, the effects of mustard gas can also be delayed for a period of up to a day. Several hours after the exposure, respiratory effects become apparent in the form of severe burning pain in the throat, trachea, and lungs. Although most mustard gas victims survive, severe pulmonary edema or swelling of the lungs may result in death. The only effective form of protection against mustard gas is the use of a full-body protective suit (Level A protection) and the use of a gas mask or respirator.

Lewisite, which is typically colorless and odorless in its liquid state but may emit the faint scent of geraniums, causes symptoms that are generally similar to mustard gas but also include a drop in blood pressure and decreased body temperature. Inhalation of Lewisite in high concentrations can lead to death in a few minutes, and the antidote (Dimercaprol) for skin blistering must be applied before the actual blistering begins.

Phosgene oxime can be a white powder or, when mixed with water or other solvents, a liquid. Contact with phosgene oxime is extremely painful, and it quickly irritates the skin, the respiratory system, and the eyes, leading to lesions of the eye, blindness, and respiratory edema. Contact with the skin immediately produces an area of white surrounded by reddened skin and swelling. Because phosgene oxime is heavier than air, it can remain in low-lying areas for quite some time, so it poses a particular danger for rescue workers. Phosgene oxime has a sharp and penetrating odor.

Choking Agents

These agents enter the body via the respiratory tract and often cause severe pulmonary edema. Because these agents are most effectively deployed as gases, they are typically stored and transported in bottles or cylinders prior to being disseminated into the air. As their name implies, choking agents quickly attack and cause severe damage to the lungs and respiratory system, and they can cause pulmonary edema and death. Choking agents include phosgene (CG), diphosgene (DP), and chlorine (CL) in liquid or gaseous form. Note that phosgene and phosgene oxime are chemically different substances that have different properties and different symptoms. Symptoms include severe coughing, choking, nausea, lacrimation, difficulty breathing, and vomiting. The initial symptoms may subside for a period of up to a day, but the symptoms typically return when pulmonary edema takes place and individuals exposed to choking agents may go into shock as their blood pressure and heart rate drop precipitously.

BIOLOGICAL AGENTS

Biological agents share some common characteristics with chemical agents, but some important differences can help distinguish this class of WMDs from chemical agents. One of the most important differences is that chemical agents typically produce symptoms relatively quickly, while biological agents may not produce symptoms for periods of up to several weeks. As a result, there may be no early warning signs, and first responders to biological events may not easily or immediately recognize that a biological WMD has been released. In contrast to the three classes of chemical agents, with few exceptions biological agents do not produce immediate symptoms on the skin or in the respiratory system. Because many biological agents are often living organisms—bacteria or viruses—they cannot be detected by any of our senses, and the scientific devices used to detect and/or identify them are complex and difficult to use. Detection generally occurs only after a person has been infected and an incubation period has elapsed.

Biological agents, which include anthrax, tularemia, cholera, plague, botulism, and smallpox, can be disseminated through a population in several ways. Although some biotoxins (such as anthrax) may be spread through contact with the skin (either through direct contact with the skin or through cuts and lacerations), in terms of WMDs and the terrorist's goal of causing widespread casualties, the most effective means of dissemination are to aerosolize the biological agent into a fine mist of powder that is inhaled or to contaminate food or water that members of the public will ingest.

There are three classes of biological agents: bacteria, viruses, and toxins. Bacteria and viruses are living organisms, so they require a host organism in order to survive and reproduce. After entering the body (usually through inhalation or ingestion), the organism establishes itself within the host and begins to reproduce and produce poisonous toxins. In some cases they produce severe and often fatal illnesses.

The difficulties involved in detecting and diagnosing biological WMD attacks can be especially pronounced when the biological agents create a slowly developing community health crisis or epidemic. Because they often involve a prolonged incubation period before symptoms become apparent, biological WMD are difficult to trace back to their source and may not be easily recognized as part of a terrorist act (for example, recall the difficulties involved in detecting and diagnosing cases of anthrax infection across the nation in the fall of 2001). While a more focused direct attack, such as the rapid release of a large quantity of fast-acting biological toxin in an office building or mass transportation center, would probably be recognized and dealt with more quickly, both forms of attack can have a potent psychological impact on the public. Beyond the deaths and illnesses that may occur, WMD suit the needs and objectives of terrorists because they can generate substantial fear and public alarm.

TERRORISM AND THE USE OF NUCLEAR MATERIAL

While the likelihood remains small that a terrorist organization could obtain or manufacture a high-grade nuclear device capable of destroying a large area, much less transport it to the United States and detonate it, there is a much greater potential for terrorists to construct an improvised nuclear device (IND) or "dirty bomb." Such an improvized weapon would nevertheless have a devastating physical and psychological impact by spreading radioactive contamination throughout a densely populated urban area.

A dirty bomb is essentially a conventional explosive device surrounded by radioactive materials that, upon detonation, spreads radioactive material within a relatively small fallout zone. Depending upon the size of the device and the type and amount of radioactive material involved, the immediate area surrounding the detonation might be uninhabitable for a long time, and those directly exposed to the radioactive fallout are likely to suffer radiation sickness. Exposed victims might also eventually develop cancer, leukemia, or other diseases related to radiation exposure.

The possibility that improvised nuclear devices or dirty bombs might be detonated in urban areas is particularly alarming, since the materials required for such devices can be obtained fairly easily, because large amounts of radioactive material are not required for an effective device, and because radiation cannot be detected through human senses. A seemingly "ordinary" small explosion in or near a large crowd of people could spread nuclear contaminants through the crowd, with no immediately apparent symptoms. The low-grade nuclear materials required to construct such a device are used, transported, and stored in various locations including hospitals and medical facilities, research laboratories, and industrial manufacturing facilities across the nation. While these materials are more carefully guarded today than they have been in the past, it is probably not beyond the capacity of a determined terrorist organization to obtain them.

FIRST RESPONDER SAFETY—TIME, DISTANCE, AND SHIELDING

Generally speaking, the police and emergency workers who might be called upon to respond initially to a nuclear, biological, or chemical event are not adequately trained to deal effectively with such events. This is not to say that most police and emergency workers lack *any* training in this area but rather that they lack the highly specific training and special expertise required to recognize and deal with many of the unique threats posed by such events. At present, many also lack the special tools, gear, and protective equipment that may be called for in these events. Patrol officers, firefighters, and emergency medical service personnel who initially respond to an event involving WMD should not be expected to undertake the specific duties and responsibilities that are better performed by well-equipped and more highly trained specialists. Their primary role should be to recognize the threat, to minimize additional exposure to chemical or biological agents, to ensure the safety of victims, to safeguard the scene, and to report their findings to those competent to deal with these issues. Another primary responsibility is to minimize their own contact with the chemical or biological agent and to provide as much information as possible to ensure the safety and the effectiveness of other responding units. Police and emergency workers who rush into the scene are likely to become contaminated themselves and may become victims. First responders who rush in to a WMD event not only risk death or serious injury from secondary devices that may have been placed at or near the scene precisely to disable rescuers but also become a significant liability to other victims as well as to other responders. The first responder who rushes in and becomes a victim may contribute to and exacerbate the overall problem, consuming time and resources other rescuers will need to deal with the problem.

As Gordon M. Sachs (2003:vii–viii) points out, responders must make some tough choices and difficult decisions:

> The first instinct for emergency responders at any incident is always to rush in and save as many people as possible; however, in a terrorist-related incident there are many factors to consider. Can the victims be saved? Will responders become targets? Was an agent of some type released? If it was, will responders have the means to detect it? Will their gear provide adequate protection? These are but a few of the questions that we must become accustomed to asking when responding to terrorist-related incidents. There is no reason to allow civilians to suffer needlessly; neither can there be any reason to send responders haphazardly into unknown and dangerous environments.

There are four types or levels of protective gear used by emergency workers during WMD events. *Level A* protection is a chemical-resistant suit that entirely encapsulates the emergency worker, and it includes a self-contained breathing apparatus (SCBA) or an independent air supply so the wearer is not exposed to fumes, biological agents, or other toxic substances that may be present in the environment. This level of protection provides maximum respiratory and skin protection and is typically used when the situation involves a high potential for liquid splashes, vapor hazards, or when the chemical agent is unidentified. Generally speaking, this level of protection is used by workers who enter the "hot zone," or the area closest to the WMD's point of dispersal.

Level B protection is a chemical-resistant suit and gloves that do not entirely encapsulate the rescue worker, but does include SCBA or an independent air supply. This type of gear provides a high level of respiratory protection but less protection against liquids and gases that may affect the skin or be absorbed through the skin. This type of gear provides the minimum amount of protection one should use in the hot zone and is not recommended for prolonged exposure or use in the hot zone.

Level C protection is provided by hooded chemical-resistant clothing and gloves and is equipped with an air-purifying respirator or gas mask. It is generally utilized when there is minimal or no hazard posed by the potential for liquid splashes or direct contact.

Level D protection is the type of protection most police, fire, and emergency medical workers typically have available to them: their uniforms and clothing. This type of protective gear provides minimal protection from chemical, biological, or nuclear hazards, and should not be worn within or near a hot zone.

Perhaps the most important tools available to ensure the safety of first responders, though, have nothing to do with equipment or gear. They are the concepts of *time, distance,* and *shielding,* and when properly applied and used, they can be the key to the first responder's self-preservation. In terms of *time,* emergency responders should keep the time they spend in the vicinity of the incident to an absolute minimum. Minimizing the time spent in proximity to a nuclear, biological, or chemical substance generally reduces one's chance of illness or injury because it minimizes one's exposure to the toxic substance. If emergency workers absolutely need to approach the scene to rescue someone or to inspect it more closely, they should not remain there a moment longer than is necessary. They should also be aware that if they do approach the scene, they may inadvertently become a vector to spread the substance, and they should take appropriate steps to decontaminate themselves as quickly as possible. First responders who come in proximity to the scene should promptly notify their supervisors and medical personnel to ensure a proper decontamination, and until decontamination occurs, they should avoid contact with others.

Similarly, emergency workers should maintain a safe and appropriate *distance* from the hazard, and they should try to move uphill from the source if possible. In terms of distance, emergency responders must also bear in mind that many substances can be spread by wind currents, and they should consider the direction of the wind in determining a safe distance and position. We should note that there are different recommended distances for safety depending upon the type and quantity of the substance involved. There are various charts and tables available to first responders to help them determine an interval of safety between themselves and a particular type and source of toxic substance, and police, fire and, emergency workers should prepare themselves for the possibility of a WMD attack by obtaining these tables and consulting them before approaching the scene. An excellent source—and one that every emergency responder should obtain and carry in his or her gear bag—is the *North American Emergency Response Guide.* This guidebook was developed jointly by the U.S. Department of Transportation (DOT), Transport Canada (TC), and the Secretariat of Communications and Transportation of Mexico (SCT) for use by emergency services personnel who may arrive first at the scene of a transportation incident involving a hazardous material. The guide permits responders to quickly identify the type of substance involved in the incident and to protect both themselves and the public during the initial response phase.

First responders should also bear in mind that these charts and tables provide general guidelines, and that qualified experts who arrive at the scene are likely to evaluate the situation and adjust the distances of the "hot," "warm," and "cold" zones. In establishing these initial zones, first responders should remain flexible and, if necessary, should err on the side of safety to extend the distance. In terms of distance, they should also bear in mind that secondary devices or booby traps designed to injure and disable rescuers may be in the area, and they should proceed cautiously. The secondary device(s) might be as powerful or perhaps more powerful than the primary device.

Shielding refers to any object that can be used to protect the first responder from a specific hazard and can include buildings, vehicles, and any personal protective equipment that may be available. The type of shielding responders should use will be determined by a number of factors, including weather, the physical environment, the geography, and the topography of the area. Buildings in urban areas may, for example, provide shielding (as well as a better vantage point) that is not available in a rural area, where a hill or elevation may serve much the same functions. Simply rolling up the windows of a police car, turning off the air conditioner, and putting on gloves can provide some degree of safety and protection to police officers approaching the scene of a potentially toxic event, and even if an officer's department does not furnish personal protective gear (as it should), it may be advisable to purchase an inexpensive and lightweight Tyvek jumpsuit for one's gear bag.

The most critical concerns for first responders must be their own safety and protection, and they must avoid the compelling urge to rush into a situation to render help. It can be very difficult for a dedicated police officer, firefighter, or emergency medical worker not to rush in and not to render aid to someone in need, but training and commonsense must prevail. As noted, the rescuer who becomes a victim exacerbates and complicates the situation, which other responders must confront.

THE PRIVATE SECTOR'S ROLE

The problems associated with preventing, deterring, responding to, and investigating terrorist attacks involving WMDs are enormously difficult and complex, and they require solutions that are equally complex. We must recognize that the threat posed by a terroristic WMD attack involves much more than simply developing effective first response capabilities and that an actual attack will have resounding impact and repercussions throughout the local (and possibly the national) economy, the health care system, the corporate and business communities, public utilities, and government operations at every level. We must also recognize that depending upon the type, the quality, and the extent of a WMD attack, literally hundreds of public agencies and private sector entities may be called upon to participate in initial response, in rescue and recovery, and in ongoing rebuilding efforts. We need look no further than the World Trade Center attacks in New York to realize that literally hundreds of organizations become involved in the overall recovery effort. While police, fire, and emergency medical personnel handled most of the first-responder duties in the first minutes and hours following the attack, they were very quickly joined at the scene by personnel from a host of other organizations.

These organizations included the American Red Cross and other relief organizations; the telephone, gas, and electric utilities operating in New York City; federal law enforcement agencies (the FBI, BATF, Secret Service, and U.S. Customs, to name a few); law enforcement from other states and jurisdictions (the New York state police, the New Jersey state police, and practically every local municipality in the region immediately dispatched officers to the scene); the FEMA; every branch of the U.S. military; the national guard; and a raft of others. Personnel from all of these organizations quickly converged on the scene, and while they were willing and to a large extent able to help, the lack of central direction and focus created enormous confusion and duplication of efforts. Without for a moment reducing the commitment and bravery displayed by these individuals, the area that became known as Ground Zero quickly degenerated to a state of near chaos as everyone tried to pitch in and help. The state of near chaos resulted in part because of the nature of the event itself, but also because the City of New York lacked adequate plans for an event of this magnitude.

Immediately after the attack, hospital emergency rooms within a hundred-mile radius of New York City were mobilized and put on alert. Medical personnel were called in to hospitals and medical facilities, and medical personnel in private practices showed up to volunteer at hospitals. Private ambulance services were mobilized for the transport of casualties, and buses from the city's Transit Authority were commandeered to bring police and other rescuers to the scene. Corporate facilities, office buildings, and college campuses went into a high security mode, often deploying their security personnel to evacuate and lock down their facilities. The city's transportation infrastructure—public transportation, subways and buses, bridges and tunnels, roads and highways—quickly became overwhelmed by the effort to evacuate tens of thousands of people from Lower Manhattan.

Communications systems were overwhelmed. Most cell phone service throughout Lower Manhattan ended when the towers fell and cellular repeaters were destroyed, and a main switching station for the city's hard-wire telephone system flooded and interrupted most service in the area. As noted, there was little or no interoperability between the police and fire radio communication systems to begin with, and the loss of radio repeaters made radio communications even more difficult.

In the days following the attack, help poured in from across the nation in the form of personnel, equipment, food, and medical supplies, and a complex logistical system of depots and distribution points had to be established and implemented. The work went on 24 hours a day for months, and workers required food, medical attention, and places to rest and recuperate between shifts. Heavy construction equipment, including some of the world's largest cranes, were rushed to New York to aid in the removal of debris, and thousands of construction workers from dozens of states were deployed to make the area safe. The rescue and recovery phase of operations continued for several weeks in the futile hope that additional survivors would be located, and fires burned at the World Trade Center site for 99 days. Given the fires and the smoke they produced, public health officials set up monitoring equipment to test air quality throughout the Lower Manhattan area. As bodies and body parts were recovered, they were removed to a medical examiner's facility for DNA testing in hope of identifying the dead and bringing closure to surviving family and friends. Canine rescue teams were brought in to aid in the search for victims, and the animals required extensive and specialized veterinary care. Psychiatrists, psychologists, and mental health workers arrived to provide crisis intervention and therapy for those traumatized by the event, and a special center for family and friends of victims was established to help them deal with their loss and with the legal, financial, and personal consequences.

Even before the rescue and recovery phase ended, the process of removing millions of tons of debris via truck and barge to a site on Staten Island commenced. The debris would be sifted by hand by NYPD detectives and other law enforcement officers to locate body parts as well as any personal effects or crime scene evidence that might be recovered, and all recovered items had to be logged, vouchered, and forwarded to the morgue or to temporary storage facilities. Complicating the entire operation was the fact that the World Trade Center site became the world's largest and most difficult crime scene; all the precautions ordinarily undertaken to discover and preserve evidence were put in place. Providing security for the site was a monumental effort.

The list of actions and activities that took place in the aftermath of this horrific and devastating attack goes on and on, and without belaboring the point further, it should suffice to say that this was the largest and most complicated enterprise ever undertaken as the result of a terroristic WMD attack. Tens of thousands of individuals, hundreds of public agencies, and dozens of private sector entities played a role in the initial response, in the rescue and recovery or in the removal operations phases.

The recovery efforts involved in this monumental undertaking were all the more remarkable for the fact that there were practically no formal recovery plans in place prior to the event and that the plans that did exist were developed with practically no input from the many private sector entities and organizations that were ultimately involved. Readers can well imagine how much more efficient and effective operations might have been if coordinated policies, procedures, plans, and protocols had existed, and if these plans accounted for the role of the private sector. To explore or even list the organizational lessons to be learned from this undertaking is well beyond the scope of this chapter, but even this brief recitation of some of the problems involved should highlight the compelling need for flexible and adaptable planning for future WMD events and terrorist acts. This planning process must rely upon and incorporate these lessons, just as it must involve representatives from each of the agencies and entities that might be called upon to participate.

POLICIES AND PROCEDURES, PROTOCOLS AND PLANS

One of the most critical considerations in preparing for potential WMD incidents is whether the public safety agencies and private sector entities that are likely to be called upon to respond to such an event have developed and implemented comprehensive and realistic policies, procedures, and operational protocols to deal with terrorist incidents.

The importance of developing effective policies, procedures, and operational protocols can scarcely be overstated: First responders cannot realistically hope to function with full effectiveness at the scene of a disaster, and agencies cannot realistically expect to maximize their effectiveness and the saving of lives unless all actors and agencies involved have a coordinated response plan in place. By their very nature, disasters and terrorist incidents tend to be exceptionally chaotic, confused, and disordered events—especially during their initial stages. Without a plan or protocol in place, they can degenerate even further, putting lives and safety at unnecessary risk as rescue workers sort out their respective roles, organize themselves, and generally figure out what to do to begin addressing the myriad problems involved in these types of events. When emergency responders (as well as the supervisors, experts, and managers who will respond later) are fully aware of these policies, procedures, and protocols, they can begin the task of saving lives much more quickly.

As illustrated by the vignette that began this chapter, first responders who have been well trained to recognize and analyze various types of events and who are equipped and prepared to respond safely and effectively are the first line of defense against terrorist acts involving WMD. The actions they take will have a tremendous impact on the overall success of the rescue and rebuilding efforts. Without diminishing the importance of their role in any way, though, we must recognize that the process of preparing for terrorist, WMD, and other mass casualty events begins long before the first responders arrive at the scene. To ensure a safe, effective, and seamless response that does not unnecessarily endanger lives, all public agencies and private entities that may be called upon to have a role in resolving the crisis must be involved in the process of planning for the event. All must be involved in the development of coordinated policies and procedures to ensure there are no conflicts and no duplication of efforts once the event takes place, and all must be aware not only of their own roles and responsibilities but also of the roles and responsibilities of other parties.

The process of planning for such events is an amazingly complex undertaking that is often further complicated by a host of organizational and jurisdictional issues, as well as the difficulty in developing flexible plans that can be adapted to meet the particular circumstances of a given incident. Agencies charged with the responsibility for law enforcement, fire, and emergency medical care generally have a primary role in developing coherent and effective response protocols, but because the realities of a given incident may require that a host of other public agencies and private entities become involved; those agencies and entities must also be involved in the planning process. More specifically, there is a compelling need for members of the medical and health care communities, the corporate community, and the private security industry to be involved in planning for WMD events. The private security industry, in particular, plays an essential role in preventing terrorism when it operates effectively to make so-called "soft targets" more resistant to attack. Terrorists, like other criminals of opportunity, are to some extent deterred when high security arrangements make it difficult to penetrate a potential target. We must not ignore the fact that a critical part of planning must involve activities to prevent or interdict terrorist acts, and because effective private security entities play a critical role in this regard, they must be enlisted to assist police and public safety agencies.

The same need for additional training that applies to local law enforcement also applies to the private security industry.

Typically, the problem is not that an agency has no response plan in place—particularly in the aftermath of the September 11 terrorist attacks, most public safety agencies have developed some sort of response plan—but that agencies often develop their procedures and protocols in isolation. These agency response plans may well account for available personnel and resources, they may consider the logistical needs involved in various kinds of events, and they may fit well with the overall mission and function of the agency. Protocols that are developed in isolation, though, often do not account for potential conflicts with the procedures adopted and followed by other agencies. They may not, in other words, mesh well with the activities and abilities of other agencies, and therefore cannot achieve an effective and integrated multiagency response.

A case in point is the response of the police and fire departments in New York City during the September 11 terrorist events and their aftermath. Historically, there has been a kind of competition between the elite NYPD Emergency Services Unit and the FDNY Rescue Units, and under ordinary circumstances a bit of competition can be a good thing. Both units are composed of specialized personnel who perform essentially similar rescue functions, and it is inevitable that they would compete for recognition and status. In a fairly substantial number of well-documented cases, though, this sense of competition—which extended beyond competition between members of those units as to who does the best job to include competition between the agencies themselves for budgets and equipment—has resulted in outright conflict when both units responded to the same incidents.

Aside from the informal competition between personnel from different agencies, there can also be conflict and competition at the highest levels of the agency, even when the agencies serve the same municipality, and these turf wars and the politics that go with them jeopardize public safety because they preclude the development of effective, efficient, and integrated response protocols. Again, one need look no further than the NYPD and FDNY: As this chapter is written, more than six years after the September 11 terrorist attacks, the two agencies were still trying to iron out conflicts and establish a single, unified, and predesignated command and control structure (Gardiner 2003; Haberman 2003; Rashbaum 2002). Indeed, a set of studies commissioned by both agencies and conducted by the McKinsey and Company management consulting firm as a follow-up to the September 11 attacks revealed a host of organizational difficulties and shortcomings that reduced the effectiveness of their respective responses to the incident. Prominent among these shortcomings were insufficient training of personnel in necessary skills and areas of knowledge, inadequate equipment, poor inter- and intra-agency communication, and a lack of interoperability between the agencies' radio systems. The police and fire departments set up separate command centers, for example, which were unable to communicate with each other (FDNY 2002; NYPD 2002).

The point of this is certainly not to disparage the reputations of two fine agencies or to diminish the remarkable heroism displayed by their personnel, but to frankly acknowledge a persistent political and organizational reality that can and does occur in other municipalities across the nation and that can and does continue to pose a significant threat to public safety. The conflict and lack of communication between these two agencies is not unusual, but it is indicative of an even larger and more significant set of issues that affect national security and homeland defense. The problem, stated succinctly, is that far too often the federal, state, and local agencies responsible for ensuring public safety and reducing the threat of terrorism do not share information or resources and have not established structures that would permit them to do so. The FBI, for example, which plays a critical role in gathering and disseminating intelligence for homeland defense, has been criticized for failing to cooperate or share information with state and local law enforcement agencies (MacDonald 2001; Oates 2001; Van Natta and Johnston 2002).

The fact that there are few structures and channels currently in place for law enforcement agencies to share intelligence information can be attributed to a number of causes. First, we must bear in mind that the U.S. system of law enforcement is highly decentralized, stratified, and complex: There are approximately 17,784 separate and relatively autonomous state and local law enforcement agencies and nearly 70 federal law enforcement agencies in the United States, and these employ more than 700,000 sworn officers (Hickman and Reaves 2001; Reaves and Hart 2001; Reeves and Hickman 2002). These agencies range in size from single-officer departments to an agency with nearly 40,000 sworn members, and they run the gamut in terms of their mandates, the size and complexity of the jurisdictions they cover, and the training and experience of their officers. The upshot is that, in the absence of a national network for sharing crime intelligence, the complexity of the system and the organizational barriers that exist between and among all these agencies effectively preclude the efficient sharing of information. To date there has been no coherent and cohesive formal system developed to share information and intelligence between and among these agencies, and the prospect of quickly establishing such a communication network is daunting.

Terrorism prevention and interdiction efforts begin with gathering, analyzing, and disseminating intelligence information. We typically conceive of the intelligence function as residing within the federal sphere and such federal agencies as the Central Intelligence Agency (CIA), the National Security Agency (NSA), the Defense Intelligence Agency (DIA), the FBI, and a host of other semiclandestine agencies. In the aftermath of the September 11 attacks, these agencies have been criticized for failing to develop, analyze, and share intelligence. The failure to share intelligence information has been prevalent not only between and among these competing agencies, but also with state and local law enforcement (Oates 2001). Federal intelligence and law enforcement agencies are only part of the terrorism prevention and interdiction equation, however: Especially in an age of community policing, state and local law enforcement officers often have extensive relationships and sources within communities where terrorists or terrorist sympathizers may reside. These relationships and sources cannot be fully exploited, nor can local officers recognize the potential intelligence value of information they encounter unless they are to some extent brought into the intelligence-gathering loop. With rare exception, though, there are few established structures or channels that allow for information to pass between local agencies or, as importantly, across local, state, and federal jurisdictional lines. As a result, an essential resource with tremendous potential is being wasted. It is also important to point out that state and local law enforcement agencies and officers could conceivably possess essential bits of information that might help federal intelligence agencies "connect the dots" and identify terrorist activities but they simply do not recognize the value of the information because they have not been briefed on the larger intelligence picture.

It is indeed unfortunate that such an information-sharing network has not been developed, since these 700,000 sworn law enforcement officers observe innumerable events and activities as they interact with literally millions of Americans each day. Every interaction and every observation is potentially a source of basic crime intelligence. Most law enforcement officers informally gather, analyze, and disseminate crime intelligence on a daily basis: they interact with the community; obtain information; analyze that information in some rudimentary way; and in many cases, they pass that information on to other officers or agencies in order to prevent, deter, or solve traditional crimes. When it comes to traditional crimes, police officers generally know what to look for—they know what kind of information to gather and how to act on it. Fighting traditional crime is their business, they know how criminals operate and are therefore attuned to criminal methods, and they are regularly alerted by their agencies and by the community to emerging crime patterns and crime conditions. The same cannot be said when it comes to terrorism, however. In sharp contrast to their expertise in fighting traditional crime, most American police officers probably lack the training, expertise, and informational context to recognize behaviors and activities that may be indicative of terrorist activities (Henry 2003a).

At the same time, we must bear in mind that the same complexity and decentralization that makes it difficult for law enforcement agencies to share information and intelligence is an essential safeguard for American principles of liberty; there are legitimate practical and policy concerns with creating a law enforcement network that, improperly used, could deprive individuals of their civil rights. The authors do not suggest that local law enforcement agencies unilaterally engage in overt or covert surveillance, or that they proactively investigate "suspicious" persons or organizations. The process of gathering, analyzing, and disseminating intelligence is a complicated business requiring particular skills, resources, and special expertise that are, generally speaking, beyond the current capabilities of most local law enforcement agencies. To preserve the proper delicate balance between the pursuit of public safety and the protection of civil liberties, intelligence activities must also be subject to a superceding layer of administrative and judicial supervision. In short, the complexity of the intelligence process, the level of skills and expertise it involves, the resources it consumes, justifiable concerns for civil liberties, and the current absence of structures and channels for sharing information all militate against local law enforcement agencies unilaterally engaging in extensive intelligence operations.

The point here is that the American law enforcement community has a great deal of unexploited potential for gathering raw terrorist intelligence that might prove valuable to other agencies at the local, state, and federal levels. If existing organizational and structural barriers that restrict the flow of information between agencies and across jurisdictional layers were erased or diminished; if the turf wars and petty conflicts that emerge between agencies were minimized; if formalized liaison and a communications infrastructure designed to maximize the flow of information were established; and if a formal process for gathering, collating, analyzing, and disseminating information were created, the threat of terrorism would be greatly reduced and public safety would be greatly enhanced. If a system or process designed to meet these goals were created in municipalities across the nation, and if each of the public safety agencies and private sector entities involved in preventing, deterring, responding to, and investigating terrorism within that municipality used the process to meet, to discuss, and to remain current on terrorism issues and terrorism threats, the enhancements to public safety would be tremendous. The same process could be used to develop integrated policies, procedures, and protocols that would help ensure the most effective response to terrorist actions involving WMDs, just as it could be used to plan, carry out, and critique multiagency training exercises.

Fortunately, a viable model for such a system exists, and that model has been used very effectively by police agencies across the nation to maximize the effectiveness of their resources and reduce crime. The organizational management model or system known as Compstat has revolutionized U.S. law enforcement and achieved drastic reductions in crime since it was first developed in the NYPD in 1994, and its principles have been applied to managing a host of other law enforcement functions (Henry 2002). An essentially similar model, called "network-centric warfare" and based in part on Compstat concepts and practices, is used by the U.S. military to prosecute wars (Cebrowski and Garstka 1988).

Heather MacDonald (2001) was the first to suggest that the adaptation of Compstat principles could make a tremendous difference in reducing the threat of terrorism, although the theme was subsequently taken up by others (Henry 2002a, 2003b). After outlining many of the intrinsic difficulties in collecting and sharing information across agency lines, MacDonald (2001) notes that major cities have Joint Terrorist Task Forces (JTTF) that operate under the leadership of the FBI but include state and local law enforcement officers.

Insofar as the JTTFs are comprised of agents from several federal agencies as well as local and state law enforcement personnel, they would seem to be an integral part of an effective intelligence system, especially because local law enforcement officials might have better sources of information in the communities that could harbor terrorists. As MacDonald (2001) points out, though, the FBI's demand that intelligence cannot be disseminated to law enforcement officials who lack a proper security clearance often means that the same local detectives who collect and provide intelligence to the FBI are often precluded from sharing the same information with their own agencies. One of the dilatory tactics federal law enforcement agencies have employed to limit the transmission of intelligence information to local law enforcement executives, in fact, is to delay their required security clearances. It is an ironic reality that local law enforcement officers can be legally forbidden from sharing information with their own chief until the chief receives an FBI security clearance—a process that can take months or years. MacDonald (2001) cites this and a variety of additional sources and evidence to make a compelling case that turf wars and federal law enforcement's penchant for secrecy have severely hampered terrorist investigations.

To address these problems, she argues for the creation of an intelligence system similar in form, format, and structure to the NYPD's Compstat system. While the scope of this chapter does not permit a full explication of the Compstat management system, the Compstat process helps facilitate accountability and eliminate turf wars by bringing the commanders of various units together and requiring them to share information with commanders of other units and with the agency's top executives. The Compstat process is based on four key principles of crime reduction, but these principles apply equally well to other law enforcement functions as well. The four keys to effective crime control are timely and accurate intelligence, effective tactics and strategies, rapid deployment of personnel and resources, and relentless follow-up to ensure that crime and other problems have been eliminated. Compstat involves regular meetings at which department executives question precinct commanders intensely about the number, type, and distribution of crimes within their precincts as well as about the strategies the commanders are employing to reduce crime. In that respect, Compstat system facilitates communication and the flow of critical crime intelligence up and down the organizational pyramid. Commanders are held highly accountable for their activities and the activities of their personnel, as well as for the tactics and strategies they implement to reduce crime and the results they achieve. Importantly, Compstat ensures that commanders of units throughout the agency are aware of what takes place in other units. The meetings also permit executives to identify those commanders who are team players and those who are not (Henry 2002a). In the fourteen years since it was developed and implemented in 1994, Compstat has been responsible for a more than 65 percent reduction in crime in New York City.

MacDonald (2001) suggests that biweekly "Fedstat" meetings should be convened in major U.S. cities, to be chaired by the FBI special agent in charge with all other relevant law enforcement agency heads attending. The purpose of these meetings would be twofold: to ensure that every agency involved in terrorism response is aggressively pursuing its obligations and that intelligence is being shared between, among, and within the agencies. Security concerns would be addressed by requiring agency heads to obtain FBI security clearances—a highly subjective process that could, at the FBI's discretion, be easily expedited. Through liaison between Fedstat systems in various cities, intelligence information developed in one area could easily be passed along to affected agencies in other cities or regions, and local agencies could request specific items of intelligence information from other cities.

It has also been suggested that local law enforcement agencies in regions without JTTFs could organize their own regularly scheduled intelligence sharing meetings along Compstat lines, and that other law enforcement and public safety agencies within a region could participate (Henry 2003b). The specific structures and constellations of the participating agencies is less important than the fact that some sort of intelligence network (what we might call "Terrorstat") is required, and that Compstat provides an effective and easily implemented existing model to create that network. An important function of these meetings, beyond sharing intelligence and refining tactical and response plans in light of emerging threats, would be to identify training needs within the agencies as well as the public sector. A practical example of this kind of training is the program developed by the NYPD to train landlords to recognize terrorist activities and behavior patterns with regard to the rental of apartments and housing (Fries 2002).

To address some of these critical lapses—the paucity of coordinated procedures and response protocols, the absence of a system dedicated to the ongoing sharing of information, and the lack of awareness of other agencies' resources and capabilities—a separate structure devoted to the design, implementation, and testing of coordinated procedures and protocols would also be established. Within this structure, meetings would include representatives from federal, state, and local law enforcement agencies operating in the region; fire and emergency medical service agencies; the medical health care community; private security entities; public utilities; and all other organizations that might be involved in responding to a terrorist event. Security concerns would be less pressing in these meetings since their primary focus would be to bring all parties together to ensure mutuality of purpose and coordination of activities. Similarly, the responsibilities for leadership could be rotated among the chief executives of the public safety agencies involved, or a single agency could be designated to chair the meetings on a permanent basis. Once again, liaison to other regions could be established to facilitate the flow of information.

CONCLUSION

The new realities of terrorism and WMD presented in our contemporary world demand a new set of policies, practices, and relationships among and between a host of entities and institutions charged with the responsibility to ensure public safety and effective homeland defense. As illustrated by the experiences and lessons of the September 11 attacks on the World Trade Center and the Pentagon, police, fire, and emergency medical services face unprecedented challenges in the future, and similar challenges confront virtually every institution in the United States.

In this chapter, we have outlined some of the issues, problems, and threats posed by the specter of terrorism and terrorists' use of WMD, and we have indicated some of the potential solutions that may help prevent inevitable future attacks as well as to respond to and recover from attacks we are unable to prevent. Most importantly, we identified the compelling need for highly coordinated response and recovery planning that integrates resources, skills, personnel, and capabilities of a range of public sector agencies and private sector organizations. No plan can pretend to be perfect—there are simply too many unforeseen issues and exigencies that arise in specific events—and the planning must therefore be flexible enough to adapt as necessary. This involves nothing less than a new mind-set that accepts, accounts for, and takes up the challenges posed by the realities of our world.

Recent history reveals the extent and dimension of the threat posed by WMD, their availability to terrorists and extremist groups, and the massive casualties they can inflict on public safety personnel and members of the public. These threats are not likely to subside, and, in fact, may increase. There is a pressing need for more and better training for the first responders to such events so they can recognize events involving WMDs, and so they can operate safely in order to minimize deaths, injuries, and damage. Similarly, there is a pressing need for more and better equipment to help first responders achieve their goals, but here again we see the need for emergency workers to have a new mind-set of safety and preparedness that infiltrates all their duties and activities. Beyond the essential role played by first responders, the issues of better training, better equipment, and better coordination apply as well to the broad array of secondary responders and institutions that will be called upon once the immediate crisis has passed.

In light of the terrorist threat posed by WMD, institutions must find the means to achieve greater coordination of efforts and resources across organizational boundaries, and we must strengthen our nation's law enforcement function to make better use of intelligence that can help prevent, deter, and investigate terrorist acts. We must also achieve these goals without sacrificing the freedoms and liberties that have sustained our nation and that define its greatness. One way to achieve these goals is through the implementation of intelligence systems and planning mechanisms based on the Compstat model.

In some respects this chapter has raised more issues and more questions than it has answered, but the reality of our contemporary world is one of uncertainty. The effectiveness of the solutions developed to resolve these problems, issues, and questions and to restore a valid sense of safety and security among members of the public will depend in large measure upon the commitment demonstrated by the police, fire, and emergency medical service agencies who are our first line of defense in public safety and homeland security.

REFERENCES

CEBROWSKI, A. K., and J. J. GARSTKA (1998). Network-centric warfare: Its origin and future," *U.S. Naval Institute Proceedings*: 28–35

DUFFY, M. (2002). Weapons of war: Poison gas. [http://www.firstworldwar.com/weaponry/gas.htm]

FEDERAL EMERGENCY MANAGEMENT AGENCY (2002). *Managing the Emergency Consequences of Terrorist Incidents: Interim Planning Guide for State and Local Governments.* Washington, DC: Federal Emergency Management Agency. [Retrieved February 16 from www.gao.gov/htext/do3260.html]

FIRE DEPARTMENT OF THE CITY OF NEW YORK (2002). *Increasing FDNY's Preparedness (Report Prepared by McKinsey & Company Based on Information Provided by the Fire Department of the City of New York).* New York: Fire Department of the City of New York.

FRIES, J. (2002). City landlords get a primer for spotting terrorist tenants. *New York Times*: B1.

GARDINER, S. (2003, June 27). Finest fight bravest over man stuck in chimney: Chimney-caught burglar sets off firefighter, cops battle. *Newsday*: 5.

HABERMAN, M. (2003). Bravest, finest map crisis plan. *New York Daily News* (July 13): 3.

HENDERSON, D. A. (1998). Bioterrorism as a public health threat. *Emerging Infectious Diseases* 4 (1). [Retrieved from http://www.cdc.gov/ncidod/eid/vol4no3/hendrsn.htm]

HENNEBERRY, O. (2001). Bioterrorism information resources. Paper presented at the New Jersey Hospital Association's Conference, *Thinking the Unthinkable—Biochemical Terrorism and Disasters: Information Resources for Medical Librarians.* Princeton, NJ. [Retrieved February 16 from www.niha.com/ep/pdf/bio-cdchandout.pdf]

HENRY, V. E. (2002a). *The Compstat Paradigm: Management Accountability in Policing, Security and the Private Sector.* Fresh Meadows, NY: Looseleaf Law.

HENRY, V. E. (2002b). The need for a coordinated and strategic local police approach to terrorism: A practitioner's perspective. *Police Practice and Research: An International Journal* 3 (4): 319–338.

HENRY, V. E. (2003a). Compstat: The emerging model of police management. In *Critical Issues in Crime and Justice,* 2d ed., ed. Albert R. Roberts. Thousand Oaks, CA: Sage.

HENRY, V. E. (2003b). The Compstat management model and other emerging policing strategies for homeland security. In *Homeland Security for Police Administration: Recruitment, Retention, and Organizational Strategies,* ed. Joseph Pascarella. Upper Saddle River, NJ: Prentice-Hall.

HICKMAN, M. H., and B. A. REAVES (2001). *Local Police Departments, 1999.* Washington, DC: Bureau of Justice Statistics. NCJ #186478.

INTERNATIONAL CITY/COUNTY MANAGEMENT ASSOCIATION (2001). Managing the threat of terrorism. *ICMA IQ Report* 33(12).

JERNIGAN, J. A., D. S. STEPHENS, D. A. ASHFORD, C. OMENACA, M. S. TOPIEL, M. GALBRAITH, M. TAPPER, T. L. FISK, S. ZAKI, T. POPOVIC, R. F. MEYER, C. P. QUINN, S. A. HARPER, S. K. FRIDKIN, J. J. SEJVAR, C. W. SHEPARD, M. McCONNELL, J. GUARNER, W. SHIEH, J. M. MALECKI, J. L. GERBERDING, J. M. HUGHES, B. A. PERKINS, and MEMBERS OF THE ANTHRAX BIOTERRORISM INVESTIGATION TEAM (2001). Bioterrorism-related inhalational anthrax: The first 10 cases reported in the United States. *Emerging Infectious Diseases* 7 (6). [Retrieved from http://www.cdc.gov/ncidod/eid/vol7no6/jernigan.html]

KRISTOF, N. D. (1995). Police find more chemicals tied to sect. *New York Times* (March 25).

LIFTON, R. J. (1999). *Destroying the World to Save It: Aum Shinrikyo, Apocalyptic Violence, and the New Global Terrorism.* New York, Henry Holt.

LYNCH, C. (2002). U.N. monitors warn of Afghan missiles; Panel says Taliban, Al Qaeda. *Washington Post* (January 24).

MACDONALD, H. (2001). Keeping New York safe from terrorists. *City Journal* 11(4): 58–68.

McDADE, J. E., and D. FRANZ (1988). Bioterrorism as a public health threat. *Emerging Infectious Diseases,* 4 (3). [http://www.cdc.gov/ncidod/eid/vol4no3/mcdade.htm]

NEW YORK POLICE DEPARTMENT (2002). *Improving NYPD Emergency Preparedness and Response (Report Prepared by McKinsey & Company Based on Information Provided by the New York Police Department).* New York: New York Police Department.

OATES, D. J. (2001). The FBI can't do it alone. *New York Times* (November 5): A. 31.

RASHBAUM, W. K. (2002) Commissioners seek closer ties for fire dept. and the police. *New York Times* (May 24): B1.

REAVES, B. A., and MATTHEW J. HICKMAN (2002). *Census of State and Local Law Enforcement Agencies, 2000.* Washington, DC: National Institute of Justice, Bureau of Justice Statistics Bulletin. NCJ #194066.

REAVES, B. A., and T. C. HART (2001). *Federal Law Enforcement Officers, 2000.* Washington, DC: National Institute of Justice, Bureau of Justice Statistics Bulletin. NCJ #187231.

SACHS, G. M. (2003). *Terrorism Emergency Response: A Handbook for Responders.* Upper Saddle River, NJ: Prentice-Hall.

SHENON, P., and D. STOUT (2002). Rumsfeld says terrorists will use weapons of mass destruction. *New York Times* (May 21): A1.

TRAEGER, M. S., S. T. WIERSMA, N. E. ROSENSTEIN, J. M. MALECKI, C. W. SHEPARD, P. L. RAGHUNATHAN, S. P. PILLAI, T. POPOVIC, C. P. QUINN, R. F. MEYER, S. R. ZAKI, S. KUMAR, S. M. BRUCE, J. J. SEJVAR, P. M. DULL, B. C. TIERNEY, J. D. JONES, B. A. PERKINS, and FLORIDA INVESTIGATION TEAM (2002). First case of bioterrorism-related inhalational anthrax in the United States, Palm Beach, Florida, 2001. *Emerging Infectious Diseases* 8 (10). [http://www.cdc.gov/ncidod/EID/vol8no10/02-0354.htm]

U.S. ARMY MEDICAL RESEARCH INSTITUTE OF CHEMICAL DEFENSE (2000). *Medical Management of Chemical Casualties Handbook,* 3d ed. Aberdeen Proving Ground, MD: U.S. Army Medical Research Institute of Chemical Defense. [http://www.gmha.org/bioterrorism/usamricd/Yellow_Book_2000.pdf]

VAN NATTA, D., and D. JOHNSTON (2002). Wary of risk, slow to adapt, F.B.I. stumbles in terror war. *New York Times* (June 2): A1.

WHITE, J. R. (2002). *Terrorism: An Introduction: 2002 Update,* 4th ed. Belmont, CA: Wadsworth.

Chapter 32

Looking Back

Self-Interest and U.S. Terrorism Policy

M. A. DuPont Morales and Jibey A. Asthappan

INTRODUCTION

As terrorism transitioned into a civil war in the Middle East, the veracity of Bush's premise that the United States should have a "humble foreign policy" (Allison 2004:182) is in question. What can foreign policy makers, in a collective process, learn from the individual acts of serialists? While deterrence is a goal in the control of violence, the entrenchment of violence within social groups as legitimate political action prompts a return to the study of the individual rather than solely the group. A terrorist frames his self-interest as indistinguishable from community or state goals. How does such bias absolve a group from collateral damage—the killing of noncombatants for the greater good? Bentham's (1789) utilitarian premise of the greatest good for the greatest number of people is significantly challenged when both falter due to war and intergroup violence. This chapter balances the politics of a terrorist's self-interest with a serialist's compulsion for violent notoriety. This chapter suggests that violent serial predation and terrorism have common factors—factors that need exploration for policy.

THE INDIVIDUAL

Nonfiction literature and social scientific research views terrorism as an aspect of civilization that cannot be eradicated but only sustained at varying levels of influence either through military response or co-option (Kegley and Kegley 2002, Carr 2003, Hoffman 2006, Gregory and Pred 2006). While historians and international experts look at terrorism in terms of the dogma of "leaders," we believe that looking at the brutalization of the individuals by their own promotes added comprehension.

Macias (2002) writes,

> A wider perspective alerts us to the fact of human violence, whether we call it terrorism or not, is constantly around us. Examples include domestic violence and child abuse, criminal and civil acts of violence, "road rage," the social and psychological conditions created by material poverty, and institutional structures that favor some while compromising the right and opportunities of others. (p. 281)

Pre-terrorists learn about powerlessness at an early age from those in their immediate environment. There is reciprocity between violence in the home, the community, religious institutions, and the geographical region.

Athens (1992, 1997) and Athens and Ulmer (2002) provide a model for comprehending the formation of violence by defining the physical and mental subjugation of the individual by his primary group. Here we note the impact of the immediate family environment combined with the permissiveness of the closer community that tolerates violence against and by an individual. Athens refers to "the subjugators" as those who use violence to promote compliance. It is compliance that can stop the victim's physical and threatened continued victimization (1997:8). As the compliance is internalized, Athens' model follows the new terrorist recruit as he or she participates in the violent subjugation of someone within his or her immediate relationships—the repugnance is not enough to intervene to stop the violence, as the recruit is relieved not to be the recipient. Lastly, the new recruit is encouraged by the original subjugator to engage in violence as a public demonstration of defiance and refusal to be controlled or persecuted by others (Roy 2000:398). The emotional and objective processing of the recruit's brutal and violent experiences sets the tone for their "future relationships with other human beings" including their community, their region, and their political environment (Rhodes 1999:126).

TRANSITIONING TO THE COMRADE

Absent outside intervention and the instinct to survive impending threats moves one's political and personal philosophies toward engagement without emotional entanglement in "preemptive strikes" against the larger community. It is individual self-interest— self-interest as defined by the collective group. Zealous camaraderie develops as the terrorist's political and personal identity merges with fellow assailants against the same enemy. The emotionality is so diluted that even suicide, while tragic and often a religious violation, is a political statement in countries where terror is the environment. Horowitz (1980:18) wrote, "We have a concept of suicide, but essentially as a private and individual event: not as social and collectivized." Thus, the pre-terrorist becomes a terrorist by engaging in and practicing brutal and homicidal acts with comrades against victims who mirror him in ethnicity, culture, and marginalization. Initiating violence against someone for any myriad of reasons is synonymous with predatory and serialistic acts of violence.

The literature surrounding multicide (multiple homicide) reflects the development of a personality through profiling and then places that personality within a narrative that can be used in an investigation. Canter (2000) studies the mapping of murder as a means of comprehending how far an assailant might travel to engage in predation. Canter writes,

> If we can find out how to interpret the wake left behind by a criminal when he plunges through a community, we can understand those special qualities of his transactions that will lead us to him. The direction and distance he travels is one important indicator of his personal silhouette. (p. 101)

As the serialist determines a site for his or her criminality, absent is empathy for the individuals or the community that will be victimized by his or her brutality. Likewise, the terrorist plots a path of homicidal acts by selecting victims, sites, and economies that will feel devastation from the acts. Even if such devastation is temporary, the satisfaction comes from the fulfillment of the attack and the immersing of the target in horror. There are ironies.

In the serialist, the benefit is the satisfaction of following an internal personal script that culminates in multicide. If the terrorist engages in dangerous and selfless acts of violence, where is the policy that will terminate the need for the violence? What is the political script of the terrorist? How does the political script of "compliance or death" morph into a constitution of rights without strong moderates who negotiate with words rather than deaths?

Forensic experts (psychiatrists, psychologists, and chemists) using deduction and induction attempt prediction about target selection in an effort to apprehend the assailant. Routinely it appears that a quirk leads to the arrest of the predator. The Report of the Future of Terrorism Task Force (2007), created by the Homeland Security Advisory Council, found that predicting terrorism is likewise impossible (Homeland Security Advisory Council 2007). One reason may be that the political manifest of the terrorist is solely the eradication of the enemy. The only feasible prediction is that the violence will continue at varying levels of intensity.

As for the serialist, predicting apprehension often results in failure and frustration. Amid the impossibilities attributed to terrorism, we wondered if Game Theory might be employed to predict aspects of terrorism. This mathematically based theory quantifies the environment and entities or persons involved in any given situation much like profiling multicide. Players of the game then attempt to maximize their results using strategies and the rules. This theory allows decision makers to use a formal modeling approach (Davis 1970). In the case of terrorism the game would encompass political power and influence rather than an individual aberrant fantasy or self-aggrandizement of that fantasy as in the serialist.

The "players" would include those who participate in the strategy of terrorism (Davis 1970). The United States and terrorist groups such as Hezbollah would be considered obvious players. When Game Theory is applied, defining optimal strategies may become evident. Other players' best strategies become clearer and anticipating potential threats becomes possible (Davis 1970). Furthermore as in multicide, it is the number of individuals slaughtered and the randomness of the event that increase the terror.

Unfortunately, the two basic principles of Game Theory do not readily apply to terrorism because as the number of players increases so do the possible strategies open to each player (Davis 1970). In the case of terrorism, there are many players and the complexity is great. Thus, it is the unknown individual, the inner political ideologies of an individual, or the masking of lethality that challenges Game Theory. Here we see similarities to the serialist, who when captured has a number of "acquaintances" who label them as "quiet, a hard worker, or a great family man." One mask is to avoid apprehension and the other mask is to engage in violent domination.

Likewise, the act of terrorism can be inherently deceptive as the "rules" of the game are always subject to change. Furthermore, the competitive strategy must have an ultimate outcome that is deemed a successful conclusion—the win (Davis 1970). In Washington and globally, a unique definition remains illusive as there is no precise roster indicating all the players in any terrorism game and what comprises a "win" as the terrorists' politics and ideology consistently reframe purpose.

POLICY AND TERROR

Policy that addressed terror is complicated; therefore, political ideology and "blanket" security within foreign policies should be implemented with caution. Attempts to quantify the complexity may assist policy analysts sifting through the possible outcomes. Policy analysts cannot foretell terrorist events, but extrapolating from current information (general intelligence) can limit the potential for a surprise terrorist strategy, attack, or cascading impacts.

Even for the known state and group terrorists, grasping all motivations and possible terrorist events is extremely challenging. Actors who do not have a strong influence on the outcome of the scenarios may act irrationally or seek out others who will join their perspective. Thus, what may have been originally seen as irrational by one group of terrorists may gain a significant number of followers and take on power but not necessarily rationality. This is, of course, in respect to those powerful players who are rationally. Therefore, terrorist states and groups cannot be expected to act *consistently* rational. This may mean a willingness to accrue considerable loss of life for the cause or refuse reform by more powerful players.

THE IRAQ EXAMPLE

Based on intelligence, the United States charged Iraq with manufacturing and stockpiling weapons of mass destruction (WMD) in 2002. Iraq could have allowed inspectors to search for these weapons and therefore would have been found innocent of the allegations; yet doing so would have *possibly* left the country strategically disadvantaged (Lebovic 2007). Turmoil in the Middle East may have left Iraq a defenseless target, it might have initiated relief from neighboring countries, or it might have allowed Iraq to formulate policies to let others know what would happen if it were invaded. Iraq chose to deny inspectors access and employ surreptitious operations as their best hope, although a U.S. perspective would have contradicted such an assumption (Lebovic 2007). Ultimately, Game Theory cannot be applied to terrorism precisely. Assumption of the theory may not be met without applying a complexity that defeats the purpose of the theory.

While Game Theory has matured in application and sophistication, predicting crime is far different from predicting terrorism. There is often a unique environment for the serial killer that reflects comfort zones, geographical spans of operation, and a series of ritualistic behaviors that Canter (2000:33) calls "looking for more detail about the criminal's action." DeFronzo et al. (2007) moved beyond the scientific issues within multicide by including cultural and structural variables. Their conclusions point to the relationship of living in urban areas, percentage of divorced population, and percentage of one-person households as contributing to the making of the serialist as well as providing a pool of victims (p. 11). Here Athens' subjugation process is an aspect of the society and community in which these potential assailants are reared and mature. An answer might be to provide more social assistance and intervention in the complex environments of the potential serialist and the victims they find vulnerable. Given what is known about intervention into social ills, this appears to be unpredictable in consistency and resources. Family, community, and acquaintances leave the potential assailants to their own devices to survive marginalization. The same can be seen in countries where terrorism survives.

POWER, TERRORISM, AND COMMUNITY

The family and the values of those family members often define the pathway to violence for a pre-terrorist. In the terrorist community there is urban danger in the form of bombings, single-parent families as a result of terrorism, and family members left to their own resources for survival. There is often a gatekeeper who will encourage a new recruit and if both come from the same family, the same fractured community, and have the same cultural beliefs, depravity in the guise of survival becomes tolerable. This particular network is often homogeneous in family composition, religion, economic resources, political environment, and victimization. Here, victimization is a basis for an affective disorder in that repeatedly surviving violence promotes a standard of engagement and tolerance. These victims may carry low political viability or be members of institutions sanctioned for victimization.

The pre-terrorist learns that he or she is powerless to alleviate the plight of the aged, the very young, the infirmed, or the maimed. However, their frailties of these individuals prove useful when terrorists can place them in the wake of retaliation from victims of prior attacks. Consider the number of times schools, hospitals, or religious institutions have been used by terrorists as a guise or shield from attack and as a political backlash from attacking such targets. Consistent with this is the organized inattention to the plight of these victims by some state and international groups. After all, it is often the same groups that are the cause of the trauma as well as the providers of relief from the trauma. The numerous depictions of the carnage and the increasing odds that those killed will be acquaintances and family create a pretext for participation. It is the helplessness to control the violence of an outsider that often lures the pre-terrorist to a terrorist group. The new affiliate peripherally moves through the heinous termination of lives while internally dismantling the fragile foundation of what remains of a belief in punishment and retribution.

The new recruit is no longer punishing specific individuals for what they might have done but seeks to punish scores of individuals for what they are thought to have allowed to be done. This is the second manner in which brutalization and the act of violence is tolerated. If collateral damage is heinous, it may be acceptable to preemptively strike against those who are charged with doing nothing to stop the violence and the violent. It is this brutalization that causes the new recruit to simultaneously act within and outside the context of his or her previous life. The previous life is diminished as new violent experiences are examined, rehearsed, and perfected by the predator who is now a terrorist. Power is finally achieved.

The study of predators, be they serialists or terrorists, can add to the discussion of terrorism. Cantor (2000:16) refers to the expert as having "increased sensitivity to salient aspects of the situation and . . . implicit knowledge of known patterns of action" and adds that the "criminal who becomes an expert develops analogous cognitive skills." Likewise, there is a developmental aspect to the maturation of the terrorist, and finding points of intervention within that maturation process provides opportunity for change. This change can be in individual ideology, the thwarting of developing leaders, or through policy changes that diminish the need for terrorism.

Here is the qualitative aspect of the context of terrorism that produces nuances that often become collapsed into one category rather than teased out for deterrence. It is the social complexities of the individual that leads toward a comprehension of the terrorist group. Which persons or what level of participants can be taken from the terrorist group, causing the remaining members to seek other priorities and resources to address their individual and community political violence? What emotional and environmental factors play into a terrorist's return as a viable and peaceful member of a family and community? Cultivating self-interest through social moderation offers a terrorist the possibility to return to a political balance outside the acts of violence and carnage.

In light of the horrific events inflicted by terrorists, a balance can be difficult to find. Political pressures urge governments and individuals to make rash choices that carry societal and individual costs. One may assume this is true of terrorism in general and, in particular, the war in the Middle East that is simultaneously termed the war on terror. It may be said that a significant driving power of current U.S. policy is the self-interest of politicians, but inherent in the policy are the fears of the American society. Yet today's society is different from that of late 2001.

Over the past four years the American public has become weary of the war against terrorism and the enormous costs in lives associated with it. Americans too look for a means of promoting social change not only in the Middle East but also in the minds of those who see war as the only answer to terrorism. Ironically, both the terrorist and those who fight terrorism become enamored with their specific approach to combat the violence. Even when former comrades propose a less violent strategy, the rigidity remains and both sides are lost in their impotence. Rather than seeking a collective and collaborative process, one where due process and a just process promotes social change; resources are wasted defending a unique and entrenched approach. Does the prior choice of escalating war and violence need to be followed through, or are there opportunities to de-escalate the violence while seeking international assistance and collaboration? Here is evidence that seeking a de-escalation of violence can promote self-interest but how is the message communicated?

ISOLATION AND TERRORISM

Can a war on terrorism be termed as half accomplished, sustained, managed or won? The events that transpire between Palestine and Israel are evidence that an incomplete conflict may result in a strengthened terrorist party, such as Hammas. Despite that further negotiations continue, experts foresee the 200-year-old tactics of carnage to continue. Is it permissible to encapsulate that war while extracting global participation? Can the rest of us live with an area geographically defined by latitude and longitude as "The War Zone?" Current U.S. policy is designed to identify, capture, and destroy terrorist cells. Terrorism experts find these tasks arduous, as prediction has not been successful in other types of multicide unless the predator takes his or her own life. U.S. politicians, however, seem optimistic that the killing of a terrorist leader can decrease terrorism. But, if the lead terrorist dies, how can those who participated in the violence give up terrorism as a prerequisite for re-assimilation into their community? How can negotiations be framed when terrorists refrain from writing policy, participating in global modernity, and follow a treatise with one imperative—death to the opposition?

CURRENT POLICY TRENDS

Instincts to envision the future control of terrorism policy are plagued by one undeniable fact; security and personal freedom are opposing needs (Congressional Research Service 2003). Americans expect terrorists to be dissuaded from attacking innocent civilians through security measures that prevent planning and implementing an event. Simultaneously, aspects of the military, the government, and society want to punish terrorists. This is an important distinction. Americans want the terrorist permanently stopped and their planning prevented, which is the tension between general security, individual rights, and due process. Lastly, too many Americans want retaliation. These constraints overshadow all policy in this field and cannot be ignored (Congressional Research Service 2003).

Perl (2003:7–12) lists six methods used by the United States to curb state or group terrorism: diplomacy or constructive engagement, economic sanctions and inducements, covert actions or rewards for information programs, extradition/law enforcement cooperation, military force, and international conventions.

Diplomacy includes organizations such as the United Nations (U.N.) or the North American Treaty Organization (NATO) to impose measures upon nations that employ terrorist tactics or sponsor groups that do so. The use of such international organizations can prove to be the least aggressive and, therefore, is often used as the first measure against a threat (Congressional Research Service 2003).

Constructive engagement can entail various means to dissuade the support of a terrorist state or group. Methods such as international legislation can prohibit states from forming alliances with groups suspected of terrorist behaviors. Terrorist groups rely on the media to disseminate their message, but if that message were to be clouded, the United States might undermine the group's purpose. Furthermore, an international and collective use of the media can also prove fruitful (Congressional Research Service 2003). Domestically, the media's report of civic attitudes toward terrorism and the positive feelings related to feelings of community and nationalism appeared to diminish over time (Schmierbach, Boyle, and McLeod 2005:336–337).

Economic sanctions have been used and will continue to be used to deny terrorist states or groups the funds needed to act. Economic manipulations may urge those who support terrorist groups to discontinue doing so. On September 23, 2001, President Bush enacted Executive Order 13224, which froze 27 accounts suspected of supporting Osama bin Laden. By November 2002, an estimated $121 million were frozen to deny terrorist groups of funds. Individual states may also reprimand with economic sanctions to discourage the support of terrorist groups (Congressional Research Service 2003). The use of such tactics can be categorized as those that restrict trading, "technology transfer, foreign assistance, export credits and guarantees, foreign exchange and capitalistic transactions, and economic access" (Perl 2003:9). These forms of economic sanctions may range from the denial of trade to withholding financial aid. Although the United States can impose such sanctions, international cooperation can further stress the economy of the punished state (Congressional Research Service 2003).

Economic inducements attempt to solve terrorism through loss in recruitment. This tactic, which stems from the popular belief that those who join a terrorist group are unskilled and are predominantly of low socioeconomic status, seeks to improve economic conditions. Education and assistance programs may improve the lives of would be terrorists and change their opinion regarding American motives (Congressional Research Service 2003). One may say that the use of economic inducements stems from programs designed to prompt change during America's struggle with its own criminals in the 1960s. Policies at the time were implemented from a positivist criminological perspective, which suggests social programs to help those who cannot reach goals or stature using societal means such as education (Cullen and Agnew 1999). Additionally, Cloward and Olin (1960) proposed that deviant behavior might be due to a struggle to gain economic success (Cullen and Agnew 1999). Likewise, terrorists may use their violence to achieve the types of successes they perceive in U.S. citizens in terms of power and control. Cohen (1955), unlike Cloward and Ohlin (1960) did not relegate sources of deviant behavior to finances alone. Instead, Cohen found that a struggle for status was also a motivating factor (Cullen and Agnew 1999). This too may be applied to terrorism since such groups attempt to gain a *voice* through their religious or political struggle. Although Cohen (1955) and Cloward and Ohlin (1960) primarily applied their theories to gangs, their application to terrorism may be beneficial. Therefore, U.S.-led economic inducements seem to be policy throwbacks from over half a century ago that have proven less than effective.

Following the policies of crime control and confidential informants, terrorist groups may be infiltrated by teams designed for covert action. The use of these teams in conjunction with reliable intelligence can fragment a terrorist group. Covert actions are comprised, in large part, of non-aggressive behaviors. Effort is placed on gaining knowledge of the working strengths and weaknesses of a group and, if needed, assisting a country with their operations. Assistance may be in the form of arms or intelligence, but credit for assistance is kept clandestine. Indeed, the most glamorized actions are those of covert operations that have been necessary at times. Operations entail the interception of unlawful deliveries or preemptively striking a terrorist group before an event can take place. On the other hand, assassinations are prohibited, as directed by Executive Order 12333 (Congressional Research Service 2003). In addition, failed covert actions can be counterproductive as was the case with The Bay of Pigs. Resentment continues to be harbored by Cubans for the unsuccessful CIA operation.

"Rewards for information" programs attempt to find suspects by financially compensating informants or those who hunt terrorists. This method can support unethical practices that cannot be monitored; yet the outcome can be beneficial. In the case of Mir Amel Kansi and Ramzi Yousef the rewards for information program proved fruitful, yet the $25 million reward for Osama bin Laden has not proved to be alluring enough (Congressional Research Service 2003).

Similar tactics have been used to fight organized crime, gang-related activities, and the hydra known as the drug trade. Rewards for information, rewards for information leading to convictions, and plea bargains have tainted the criminal justice system in the United States because of criminals who have their criminality forgiven, and sometimes with financial bonuses.

Law enforcement cooperation is useful in combating groups that cross jurisdictions. However, jurisdictional jealousies routinely allow serialists to go undiscovered, gangs to infiltrate new areas, and resources to be inefficiently dispersed. Yet, some have found that within the United States, even with governmental support of shared intelligence, law enforcement bodies have been withholding information concerning criminal activity, intelligence, and even terrorism (Congressional Research Service 2003).

One beneficial tool in prosecuting terrorists is extradition. Negotiations between governments to extradite terrorists can not only allow prosecution of a terrorist event but can also lead to valuable information on other suspected terrorists. However, the Inter-American Convention on Forced Disappearance of Persons (1994) states,

> The Member States of the Organization of American States are disturbed by the persistence of the forced disappearance of persons:
> Considering that the forced disappearance of persons violates numerous non-derogable and essential human rights enshrined in the American Convention on Human Rights, in the American Declaration of the Rights and Duties of Man, and in the Universal Declaration of Human Rights. (Multilateral Treaties, Preamble:1)

The simultaneous practice of forced disappearance and forced extradition and protocol extradition by the United States poses increased political dilemmas. Foreign policy encouraging extradition has enhanced intelligence, but "forced" actions and America's use of the death penalty as punishment have made some countries hesitant (Congressional Research Service 2003). Again, America's self-interest in the need for the death penalty and aggressive captures places others at risk and our efforts in jeopardy.

MILITARY FORCE

Military force, through technology and might may hamper the plans of a terrorist state or group. U.S. dominance in this arena can force smaller countries to cower under American pressure (Congressional Research Service 2003). Yet mistakes can undermine a mission. Civilians who are casualties of attacks by a superpower can be seen as victims of an oppressive force. This effect can strengthen terrorist organizations and ideology, therefore generating higher recruitment rates (Congressional Research Service 2003). The final tool used by the United States to curb terrorism is the use of international conventions. Organizations such as the Convention for the Marketing of Plastic Explosives and Anti-Terrorism Financing Convention serve to construct a community that resists acts of terrorism. The encouragement of extradition and prosecution of acts of terrorism make these conventions valuable.

Using the aforementioned methods, Figure 32.1 attempts to capture the majority of initiatives.

As depicted in the figure, nine conventional methods of terrorism policy are most prevalent in the current U.S. administration. The distance from the source represents the willingness of our government to use such tactics. Diplomacy or constructive engagement and international conventions carry the least resistance, yet such methods may reap the fewest rewards within a targeted amount of time. Covert actions and military force face the greatest amount of resistance due to high risk and financial burden, but

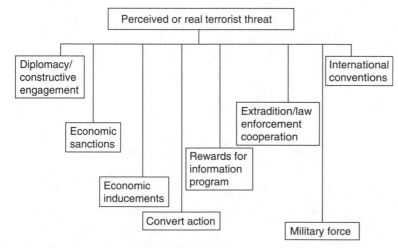

FIGURE 32.1   Model of Current U.S. Terrorism Policy

can prove the most productive. A moderate government would seek those sanctions that lie in between.

Pillar (2001) suggests that a variety of approaches, as illustrated in Figure 32.1, are essential to a successful counterterrorism program. Previously, speculation on how terrorists are made and their complex maturation made typologies difficult to agree on. A portion of the terrorist population, although very small, will still maintain the ideology that formed the terrorist group. This ideology could have religious or political overtones fueled by extremist beliefs (Pillar 2001).

Therefore, policy directed toward discouraging terrorist beliefs is difficult to initiate (Pillar 2001). Because terrorism policy cannot be the only or most important policy concern, funds must be shared among many interests. There will be associates, sanctuaries, and financial supporters that will remain on the fringes of the ideology but disavow previous knowledge of the violence.

EXPERT RECOMMENDATIONS

Stern (1999) finds that to prevent terrorist attacks much of our routine lives must change. The cost of needed security will come at the price of some privacy and civil rights, an aspect Americans must struggle with. Her model reflects a number of changed policies and that a balanced effort to address more is important for deterrence (see Figure 32.2).

Comparatively, Pillar's (2001) policy recommendations attempt to attack the problem realistically. Terrorism has been used as a tool for hundreds of years with varying success and its use will continue into the future as a means to prompt change. Pillar seeks recommendations that take this into account while understanding a war against terrorism

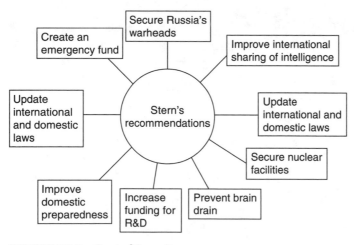

FIGURE 32.2   Cost of Security

will be long and arduous. Victories will occur, but their benefit will produce little change (Pillar 2001). Pillar's recommendations are as follows:

- Change foreign policy to account for counterterrorism perspectives. This task would include amending long-held policies, and doing so would be a difficult process.
- Identify all terrorist threats to the United States. Doing so will prevent the country from being vulnerable to attack from a terrorist organization that was not considered. Pillar suggests that the infrastructures of terrorist organizations, logistical operations, and financial resources be destroyed.
- Use a variety of methods to combat terrorism. This also can be useful to disallow an over-reliance on only a few.
- Laws need to have the flexibility to lead to peaceful efforts to alleviate threats. Pillar states that such a tactic can be more feasible that have terminated their terrorist pursuits are rewarded.
- Give assistance to countries that do not have the resources of the United States, so that standards of security are met. Since terrorism is a global problem, efforts should be global. Allocation of funds not only benefits the state that receives the funds, but also the global community.
- Encourage alliances between countries in a counterterrorism efforts (Pillar 2001).

MERGING CRIMINALITY AND TERRORISM: THREE MODELS

Congress, military strategists, and law enforcement work to hamper terrorism but with goals limited by their perspective of apprehension and punishment. Federal policy portrays terrorist threats as a constant force: if policy fails to defend all points of weakness, an attack will occur. The proposed model views terrorism as a general and consistent disregard for a civil society. It is believed that terrorists seek a constructed society through violence much as criminals derive their commitment to violence from abusive marginalization or socialization.

A terror event satisfies the planners since it disturbs those who live without crisis of existence looming at all times. These beliefs may result from religiosity. Unlike conventional rational thought, righteous thoughts based on religion don't require the believer to find fault in reasoning based on a partnership with an omnipotent being. The thought process described sets the foreground for a model that includes three variables. The first is *personality traits*, which are a reverberation from past and present irrational beliefs. In addition, the intensity of the personality fluctuates. Personal experiences can cause variances and for the most part are unpredictable. The second variable is *timing*, which involves the ability of an event to occur and fluctuate by season or religious holidays. The third variable is the *tension of social fabric*, which considers the terrorist's social setting and the urgency of the group to relieve stress caused by another nation. Such stressors

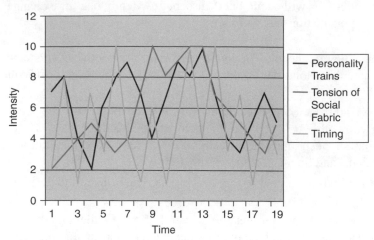

FIGURE 32.3   Tension: Variables Demonstrating Possible
Terrorist Attack

could be real or perceived and propagated by the terrorists groups themselves, for example, Hezbollah's influence over the Gaza strip. In some cases, U.S. occupation can drive this urgency, while in other terrorist groups it may delay it. Unfortunately this variable is also difficult to predict but may be tested by assessing the frustration of those within that society. Attempts to address criminality also carry negative results as increased police patrol may increase fear of crime and is often associated with significant criminality. These three variables are shown in Figure 32.3.

As Figure 32.3 depicts, the three variables can fluctuate independently, yet when a majority of factors are concentrated in high levels of intensity, the result could be a terrorist event.

Military Planners

Current strategies to combat terrorism entail the capture or death of terrorist leaders; yet, this does little to dissuade terrorism since a leader can be easily replaced. Consider the plight of living organisms, which can live independently and can destroy other cells or particles. One may illustrate the actions of terrorist cells by comparing them to living organisms. As with terrorist groups, if an organism dies, those around it become stronger as they assimilate the remaining resources. Eventually, the finality of the resources is reached, terrorist cells fight among themselves, and destruction becomes evident. Therefore, military posture according to this model would seek operations that attempt to divide cells and stress the resources. Focusing missions on middle management, supply chains, financial sources, and propaganda depicting diminishing numbers may accomplish this.

National and Local Law Enforcement

Law enforcement comprises the greatest number of responders to an incident. This next experimental model attempts to predict such events. Each of the following properties symbolizes a characteristic needed to plan a successful terrorist event. If each of the following has a likelihood of occurring, then the likelihood of a terrorist event is equally as high:

Target-person(s) or item of great importance Person(s) of importance allow for events of high value; this potentially allows for monetary value, explosives, biological, chemical, or nuclear materials. Additionally, the size of the population gathered may, in and of itself, be the target.

Unsecured environment This refers to an event or facility that may be of interest as a target. An event in honor of a person of distinction or a nuclear power facility may be targets that should be protected. A word of caution, assess a target accurately, distributing resources to secure areas having little threat is unwise but may garner goodwill.

Lack of redundant security Security is obviously needed to restrict possible terrorists from completing a task; yet setting redundant security can ensure that security is tight.

Planned event without confidentiality During events that include high-yield targets or transportation of biological or explosive substances, confidentiality is vital. Release of information including times and routes should be held for immediacy and distributed to a limited few.

High terrorist sophistication Suspected terrorists who may attempt an attack should be assessed for sophistication. Currently, insurgents have little knowledge of complex devices, but as time passes insurgents and terrorists are learning more complex device design as well as simpler but more lethal tactics.

Ease in acquiring explosives, biological/chemical agents, and nuclear materials Ironically the least lethal of the potential materials is generally the most difficult to manufacture and transport. Sensitive explosives are easy to make, but difficult to handle and transport, and insensitive explosives are difficult to manufacture. Chemical and biological agents are generally easy to create, but biological agents have the added difficulty of sustaining the organisms. Nuclear materials (weapons grade) material requires enriching (an expensive process) and can be used as a part of a weapon. A more practical method of nuclear materials use is dissemination of non-enriched types.

Intelligence of terrorist threat It would be an understatement to say that intelligence is vital to prevent a terrorist attack. But intelligence does not only occur from wiretaps and aerial photography. Each person in law enforcement or security can add to the intelligence that is available. All team members should understand the importance of sharing information that could be vital, regardless of how insignificant that information may seem. Formal and informal methods to muster information should be implemented.

NEW THREATS

After hurricane Katrina a new threat was evident. Areas that are prone to environmental catastrophes have the potential for a greater loss of life and are therefore at a higher risk of attack. Terrorists can plant devices that cause minor damage, but due to environmental conditions, the effect can be devastating. In addition, an environmental cascading effect can cause damage beyond the event alone. An example of this is the influx of respiratory problems in New York City years after September 11. The effects of the terrorist act linger and its cost increases.

An interesting potential threat is the use of a human to disseminate radioactive waves. This strategy would involve injecting or having a transporter ingest radioactive material. The transporter would then spend time with others in a public setting. Due to the high levels of radiation needed to cause others to be effected, it is likely the transporter would not live more than a few hours but the fallout would be severe to those around him or her as well as to the first responders.

The case of extreme drug-resistant tuberculosis reflects the very real threat of a human vector that will meet all of the security measures at an airport but leave the potential for death and compromised health in its wake.

CONCLUSION

Current policy needs sophistication and resources to address terrorism rather than relying solely on stopping threats by entering into war. Personal and political self-interest do not promote remediation or collaboration. The current administration has allotted tremendous resources and infrastructure to terrorism, but has the plan only one model? Experts in the field have suggested other means of solving the problem. It may be a culmination of collaboration and interdisciplinary collegiality may provide the greatest benefit. Applying aspects of multicide and what we know of associated behaviors encourages academics and victimologists to share what they know about predation, stalking, and the ideology of killing.

The federal government, military, and law enforcement could model new threats and alternative policies in an atmosphere that views terrorism as an evolutionary hydra. Keeping abreast of the possibilities of a terrorist attack may not seem fruitful, but applying critical thinking to counterterrorism policy prepares and brings awareness to participating bodies. Violent crime and terrorism offer a juncture where those who have worked with violence can find common ground for intervention. Neither will be stopped but different acts may be modulated. Moderation in the approach is a first step.

REFERENCES

ATHENS, L. (1992). *The Creation of Dangerous Violent Criminals.* Champaign, IL: University of Illinois Press.

ATHENS, L. (1997). *Violent Criminals and Actors Revisited.* Champaign, IL: University of Illinois Press.

ATHENS, L., and J. ULMER (eds.). (2002). *Violent Acts and Violentization.* Amsterdam: Elsevier.

ALLISON, G. (2004). *Nuclear Terrorism: The Ultimate Preventable Catastrophe.* New York: Owl Books.

BENTHAM, J. (1789). *Introduction to the Principles of Morals,* rev.ed. UK: University College of London.

CANTER, D. (2000). *Criminal Shadows.* UK: Harper-Collins.

CARR, C. (2003). *The Lessons of Terror.* New York: Random House.

CULLEN, F. T., and R. AGNEW (1999). *Criminological Theory Past to Present.* Los Angeles, CA: Roxbury Publishing Company.

DAVIS, M. D. (1970). *Game Theory: A Nontechnical Introduction.* New York: Basic Books.

GREGORY, D., and A. PRED (2006). *Violent Geographies.* UK: Taylor & Francis.

HOFFMAN, B. (2006). *Inside Terrorism.* New York: Columbia University.

HOMELAND SECURITY ADVISORY COUNCIL (2007). *Report of the future of terrorism task force.* [Retrieved on May 19, 2007, from http://www.dhs.gov/xlibrary/assets/hsac-future-terrorism-010107.pdf]

HOROWITZ, I. (1980). *Taking Lives.* NJ: Transaction Books.

INTER-AMERICAN CONVENTION ON FORCED DIS-APPEARANCE OF PERSONS (1994). [Retrieved on May 22, 2007, from http://www.oas.org/juridico/English/Treaties/a-60.html]

KEGLEY, C. W. Jr., and C. W. KEGLEY (2002). *The New Global Terrorism.* Prentice-Hall.

MACIAS, J. (2002). The tragedy of terrorism: Perspectives, reflection, and action in the aftermath. *Anthropology and Education Quarterly* 133 (3): 280–283.

PERL, R. (2003). *Terrorism, the Future, and U.S. Foreign Policy (Order Code IB95112).* Washington, DC: Congressional Research Service.

PILLAR, P. R. (2001). *Terrorism and U.S. Foreign Policy.* Washington DC: Brookings Institution Press.

RHODES, R. (2000). *Why They Kill.* New York: Knoph.

SCHMIERBACH, M., M. BOYLE, and D. MCLEOD (2005). Civic attachment in the aftermath of September 11. *Mass Communication & Society* 8 (4): 323–346.

STERN, J. (1999). *The Ultimate Terrorist.* UK: Harvard University Press.

Chapter 33

Profiling and Detention in the War on Terror

Human Rights Predicaments for the Criminal Justice Apparatus

Michael Welch

INTRODUCTION

The war on terror, particularly in the wake of the events of September 11, 2001, has assumed a new resonance not only in the United States but also in nations around the globe. Ironically though, many democratic governments are adopting antiterrorism legislation that has traditionally been associated with repressive states, including the criminalization of peaceful activities, clampdown on asylum seekers, and detention without trial (Amnesty International 2003; Jilani 2002; Schuster 2003). While realizing the importance of maintaining national security, critics argue that such tactics violate civil liberties and human rights. Compounding those problems is evidence of profiling whereby members of certain ethnic and religious groups are stereotyped as possible terrorists (Cole and Dempsey 2002; Welch 2002a,b, 2003a,b).

One of the more tragic incidents involving profiling is the case of Muhammad Rafiq Butt, who was found dead in the Hudson County Correctional Center in New Jersey. Butt, a native of Pakistan, had been arrested for being in the country illegally, one of hundreds who had been picked up on the basis of tips from an anxious public. An autopsy revealed that Butt, 55, whose one-year stay in the United States seems to have been hapless from the very start, had coronary disease and died of a heart attack. His death forced the Immigration and Naturalization Service (INS) to do something it had not had to do during the 33 days it had him in custody: talk about him publicly and explain the circumstances behind his arrest, detention, and death.

> It was revealed that he had been picked up after a tip to the Federal Bureau of Investigation from the pastor of a church near his home in South Ozone Park, Queens. His sole crime was overstaying his visitor visa. It took the F.B.I. a day to determine that it had no interest in him for its investigation into terrorism. He chose to appear at his deportation hearing without a lawyer, even though he spoke virtually no English and had little education. From jail, he made no calls to his relatives or to the Pakistani Consulate in New York. (Sengupta 2001a:EV1–2, 2001b)

As we shall see, such profiling has propelled several controversial measures in the war on terror. This chapter focuses specifically on two of those tactics: the special registration program and detention, both of which have been further compounded by government secrecy.[1] While maintaining a human rights perspective, the discussion explores issues of race/ ethnicity. It concludes by drawing parallels between the war on drugs and the fight against terrorism while calling into question the effectiveness of current law enforcement tactics.

PROFILING IN THE WAR ON TERROR

In response to the attacks of September 11, 2001, the Federal Bureau of Investigation (FBI) and the INS immediately embarked on a sweeping process that involved questioning thousands of persons who might have information about terrorist activity (Welch 2004a,b). While the search for information was frequently haphazard and random, Middle Eastern males (and those who appeared to be Middle Eastern) became the profiled in the course of the investigation. In its report, *Presumption of Guilt: Human Rights Abuses of Post-September 11th Detainees* (2002), Human Rights Watch discovered a growing use of profiling on the basis of nationality, religion, and gender. Being a male Muslim noncitizen from certain countries became a basis for suspicious behavior. The cases suggest that where Muslim men from certain countries were involved, law enforcement agents presumed some sort of a connection with or knowledge of terrorism until investigations could subsequently prove otherwise. The questioning led to the arrest and detention of as many as 1,200 noncitizens, although the precise number is unknown because of the Justice Department's unwillingness to divulge such information. Of those arrested, 752 were charged not with terrorism-related crimes but with immigration violations (e.g., overstaying a visa). Human Rights Watch (2002:12) reports the following:

> Using nationality, religion, and gender as a proxy for suspicion is not only unfair to the millions of law-abiding Muslim immigrants from Middle Eastern and South Asian countries, it may also be an ineffective law enforcement technique. The U.S. government has not charged a single one of the thousand-plus individuals detained after September 11 for crime related to terrorism. Such targeting has also antagonized the very immigrant and religious communities whose cooperation with law enforcement agencies could produce important leads for the investigation.

It should also be noted that a series of cases in which there is more substantive evidence of links to acts of terror clearly demonstrate that a national-origin terrorist profile is flawed. Most notably, Zacarias Moussaoui, the so-called "twentieth" hijacker, is a French citizen. The "shoe bomber" Richard Reid is a British citizen. José Padilla (aka Abdullah Al Muhajir) "the dirty bomber," is a U.S. citizen of Puerto Rican descent.

SPECIAL REGISTRATION PROGRAM

Despite objections from civil liberties and human rights organizations, the Department of Justice expanded its use of profiling in the war on terror by introducing a special registration program in December 2002. The program, intended to produce vital information about terrorist activity, required all nonimmigrant male visitors who are over the age of 16 and who entered the United States before September 30, 2002 to register. Specifically, special registration applied to those males from countries that, according to the U.S. government, have links to terrorism, including 12 North African and Middle Eastern countries plus North Korea. It affected more than 82,000 students, tourists, businessmen, and relatives. Those who attended special registration were required to complete a personal information form and then were fingerprinted, photographed, and interviewed by the FBI. Justice Department spokesman Jorge Martinez believes that this information is necessary intelligence for the war against terrorism. "These people are considered a high risk," he said. "The goal of the system is to know who is coming in and out, and that they are in fact doing what they said they would do" (Gourevitch 2003:EV2).

In the first few months of special registration, the Justice Department failed to discover any links to terrorism, raising questions of its effectiveness. Initially, about 1,000 people were detained but only 15 were charged with a criminal violation and none was charged with a terrorism-related crime. Most of those detained were in violation of immigration laws, most commonly overstaying their visas in hope of finding a job and eventually adjusting their status to legal resident. From its start, the program was confusing for registrants and the INS, suggesting that the initiative was poorly planned. The Justice Department neglected to issue a press release or post information on its website until 10 days before the first deadline explaining why many foreign nationals had not known they had to register and were subsequently arrested for showing up late. In another mishap, an Arabic rendering of the rules was embarrassingly mistranslated to identify individuals *under* the age of 16 rather than *over* the age of 16 (Gourevitch 2003:EV3).

Many immigration officials and immigration lawyers are perplexed over the precise meaning of the law. The special registration program states that "foreign citizens and nationals" must register; but the language of the requirements does not clearly define the difference between a "citizen" and a "national," or even what a "national" is. The only available guidance is a phrase from a 50-year-old statute that defines a "national" as "a person owing permanent allegiance to a state" other than the United States. Even Justice Department spokesman Jorge Martinez did not know how to define "national"

(Gourevitch 2003:EV3). Due to the confusion, several foreign nationals not covered by the program (e.g., from Canada, Liberia, and Norway) showed up to register. Immigration officials did not know how to interpret the procedures, so they arrested them. Similarly, two Canadian citizens who were born in Iran but had emigrated when they were children were detained for several days. They were in the United States on work visas for the high-tech industry and had appeared at an INS office uncertain whether they were required to register. The special registration program also created problems for the INS, an agency already strained by other operations in the war on terror. INS employees complained that they received very little special training; moreover, they frequently had to work overtime to process the thousands of registrants. The Arlington (Virginia) INS office became so inundated with registrants that it had to send many to the Dulles International Airport office for processing (Gourevitch 2003).

One of the most controversial incidents occurred in Los Angeles where more than 400 foreign nationals who appeared for registration were handcuffed and detained. Soheila Jonoubi, a Los Angeles–based attorney representing several of the men, said that the detainees spent the next several days (and in some cases weeks) in custody. Many of them were strip searched, verbally accosted, deprived of food and water, bedding, and adequate clothing, and denied information as to why they were being detained. The Justice Department reported that the men were detained because their visas had expired; after completing background checks, all but 20 were released. Still, many of those detained held legal immigration status and were waiting to receive work permits that had been delayed by the INS because of the backlog in processing the high volume of applications (Talvi 2003a,b).

Whereas the registration of more than 82,000 failed to uncover any major links to terrorism, the Justice Department has moved forward with plans to deport as many as 13,000 Arab and Muslim men whose legal immigration status had expired. Many of the men had hoped for leniency because they had cooperated fully with the program. Detentions coupled with deportations have sent shock waves through immigrant communities across the nation, producing unprecedented levels of fear. Many Middle Eastern men and their families (many of whom are U.S. citizens) have fled the country, particularly to Canada where they intend to apply for political asylum (Cardwell 2003; Elliot 2003).

Those developments bring to light the significance of human rights in the realm of immigration, criminal justice, and the war on terror. Still, government officials stationed in the Department of Homeland Security (DHS) and the Bureau of Immigration and Customs Enforcement (BICE, the so-called newly reorganized INS) point to the need for national security. Jim Chaparro, acting director for interior enforcement at the DHS, emphasizes: "We need to focus our enforcement on the biggest threats. If a loophole can be exploited by an immigrant, it can also be exploited by a terrorist" (Swarns 2003a:A9). Still, civil liberties and human rights groups denounce the government for using the immigration system as a weapon in the war on terror. Similarly, they complain about selective enforcement since the government focuses on immigrants from Arab and Muslim nations while ignoring similar violations by those from Mexico and Central America.

The overall logic of implementing the special registration program as a tactic in the war on terror raises serious doubts among criminologists and legal scholars. Why would a terrorist risk detection and detention by appearing before the special registration program, especially since the exhaustive procedure involves fingerprinting, photographing, and interrogation by FBI agents? "And if intelligence officials are right that Al Qaeda sleepers generally lead quiet, unremarkable lives in conformity with legal requirements, the INS would have no way of knowing even if an Al Qaeda member *were* to walk in" (Cole 2003b:5). Moreover, experts point out that deportation is among the worse antiterrorism maneuvers. According to David Cole, professor of law at Georgetown University, "The last thing you want to do with a real terrorist is send him abroad . . . What we want to do is charge him and lock him up. Which, of course, would also spare the innocent thousands caught in the middle" (Gourevitch 2003:EV5; see Cole and Dempsey 2002; Welch 2003a).

Even government agencies have weighed in on the debate over the utility of the special registration program. The General Accounting Office (2003) issued a report that left many questions unanswered as to the value of the project. That study included interviews with officers, many of whom expressed doubts over the usefulness of registration in the campaign against terrorism. Still, the Justice Department defended the special registration program. "To date, the program has not been a complete waste of effort," replied Jorge Martinez, who points out that it has led to the arrest of "a wife beater, narcotics dealer and very serious violent offenders" (Gourevitch 2003:EV6), to which critic Alex Gourevitch countered, "But that isn't exactly the same as catching terrorists. And if what we really want is to catch wife beaters, narcotics dealers and violent offenders, the Justice Department should simply require everyone in America to show up and register" (2003:EV6; see Swarns 2003b).

Again, issues of profiling and human rights figure prominently in the war on terror, producing an array of contradictions that undermine efforts to detect terrorist activity.

> The racist component to these directives is hard to overlook. The escalation of selective registration, detention and deportation of immigrants has taken the form of a large, very poorly guided fishing expedition. One of the great ironies of this kind of social control is that it erodes the cooperation of these immigrant communities. When a government embarks on a fishing expedition like this one, they're admitting that they don't have a lot of clues to begin with. (Welch quoted in Talvi 2003a:3)

Civil liberties organizations, such as the American Civil Liberties Union (ACLU) and the Center for Constitutional Rights, caution against the government's claim that in order to fight effectively the war on terror, people must surrender some of their freedoms. That reasoning marks a false paradigm insofar as national security is not predicated on diminishing civil liberties. Mass detention produced by the special registration program is dysfunctional and ineffective. Former executive director of the ACLU, Ira Glasser, reminds us: "No one can be made safe by arresting the wrong people. In focusing on them [wrong targets], the government certainly violated their civil rights but, more important to most Americans, abandoned public safety as well" (2003:WK12).

In a major development in June 2003, President George W. Bush announced guidelines barring federal agents from relying on race or ethnicity in their investigation. One exception to that policy, however, is terrorism, allowing agents to use race and ethnicity aimed at identifying terrorist threats. Officials in the immigration service will continue to require visitors from Middle Eastern nations to undergo registration and special scrutiny. Civil rights groups swiftly denounced the policy since it perpetuates stereotyping and provides authorities with legal justification to single out Arabs, Muslims, and others who may fall under suspicion. The initiative also falls short of what Bush claimed to do about racial profiling. In a February 2001 national address, he declared that racial profiling was "wrong, and we will end it in America" (quoted in Lichtblau 2003a:A1). Ibrahim Hooper of the Council on American-Islamic Relations also complained about the policy, especially in light of a recent government report criticizing the Justice Department for rounding up and detaining hundreds of Middle Eastern men following the September 11 attacks (to be discussed in a later section) (Lichtblau 2003a:A1).

MISUSE OF DETENTION

In addition to problems posed by profiling as embodied in its special registration program, the government continues to face similar charges of human rights violations, particularly in the realm of detention. Shortly after the Justice Department began its post-September 11 sweeps and roundups, allegations surfaced involving arbitrary detention, abuse of detainees, and a host of other procedural infractions. Civil liberties and human rights organizations issued stern warnings to the government that, despite the unique circumstances caused by the attacks on the Pentagon and the World Trade Center, such abuses would not be tolerated. Several groups released reports documenting serious violations of civil liberties and human rights (American Civil Liberties Union 2001; Amnesty International 2003; Lawyers Committee for Human Rights 2003). The chief complaint among civil liberties and immigration attorneys is that the government, in waging its war on terror, misuses immigration law to circumvent its obligations under the criminal justice system. Moreover, the Department of Justice has established new immigration policies and procedures that undermine previously existing safeguards against arbitrary detention by the INS. Those violations are cataloged into three key areas: denial of access to counsel, arbitrary detention, and harsh conditions of detention (Human Rights Watch 2002). As we shall see, each of those problems was exacerbated by the government's reliance on secrecy whereby the Department of Justice refused to divulge information concerning the persons being detained.

Denial of Access to Counsel

In line with the U.S. Constitution as well as international human rights law, all persons, citizen or noncitizen, have the right to be represented by legal counsel after being deprived of liberty for alleged criminal or immigration law violations. Human Rights Watch (2002) discovered that "special interest" detainees (those the government suspected of being involved in terrorism-related activity) were questioned in custody as part of a criminal investigation, even though they were subsequently charged with immigration violations. Many of those detainees were interrogated by FBI and INS agents concerning criminal matters as well as the individual's immigration status. Immigration attorneys complain the FBI relies on administrative proceedings under the immigration law as a proxy to detain and interrogate terrorism suspects without affording them the rights and protections that the U.S. criminal system provides. Among those safeguards is the right to have a lawyer present during custodial interrogations, including free legal counsel if necessary (Cole and Dempsey 2002).

Abusive Interrogations

The right to have an attorney present during custodial interrogations serves to prevent coercive interrogations. As the war on terror escalated in the aftermath of the September 11 attacks, detainees were not only denied access to attorneys but also were subjected to abusive treatment in violation. Both the U.S. Constitution and *Principle 21* of the *United Nations Body of Principle for the Protection of All Persons Under Any Form of Detention or Imprisonment* specifically prohibit abusive interrogations since such mistreatment impairs a person's judgment and capacity to make decisions. Similarly, abusive interrogations produce false confessions.

Consider the case of Abdallah Higazy, a 30-year-old Egyptian graduate student with a valid visa, who was detained as a material witness on December 17, 2001. A pilot's radio had allegedly been found in the New York City hotel room where he had stayed on September 11. Higazy was placed in solitary confinement at the Metropolitan Correctional Center (MCC) in Manhattan. Eager to establish his innocence, Higazy volunteered to take a polygraph examination. He then was subjected to a grueling five-hour interrogation during which he was not given a break, food, or drink. Due to some unusual restrictions concocted by the Justice Department, Higazy's attorney was forced to remain outside the interrogation room, unable to advise his client. Higazy reported that from the beginning of the interrogation, the agents threatened him and his family. Yielding to intense emotional and physical fatigue as a result of the abusive interrogation, Higazy eventually said that the radio belonged to him. The Justice Department charged Higazy with lying to the FBI but three days later, an American pilot went to the hotel to claim it. Charges against Higazy were dropped, and after one month in solitary confinement, he was released from the MCC onto the streets of New York City wearing a prison uniform and given $3 for subway fare. Months later, Ronald Ferry, the former hotel security guard who found the pilot's radio, admitted that he had fabricated the story accusing Higazy. Ferry was sentenced to six months of weekends in prison for lying to the FBI. He admitted that he knew that the device was not in a safe belonging to Higazy. Ferry, who is a former police officer, said that he lied during a "time of patriotism, and I'm very, very sorry." The judge said that his conduct was "wrongly motivated by prejudicial stereotypes, misguided patriotism or false heroism" (Human Rights Watch 2002:39; see Fritsch 2002; Weiser 2002).

Arbitrary Detention

Civil libertics organizations remind us that physical liberty is a fundamental human right affirmed in international law and in the U.S. Constitution contained in the due process clauses of the Fifth and Fourteenth Amendments. Correspondingly, arbitrary detention violates that right. "An individual who is arbitrarily detained is rendered defenseless by the coercive power of the state. While arbitrary detention is a hallmark of repressive regimes, democratic governments are not immune to the temptations of violating the right to liberty" (Amnesty International 2003; Human Rights Watch 2002:46). Regrettably, many detainees swept up during the early phase of the post-September 11 investigation were subjected to arbitrary detention and were held for lengthy periods of time. Such violations were not merely inadvertent due to the confusion surrounding the events of September 11. Rather arbitrary detention became a systematic tool in the Justice Department's campaign against terror under which new procedural rules had been created. Those rules provided greater power to the government and undermined previously existing protections for detainees. As noted earlier, the new rules enabled the government to use immigration detention as a form of preventative detention for criminal procedures even though it lacked evidence that detainees were flight risks or presented a danger to the community (Lawyers Committee for Human Rights 2003).

Harsh Conditions of Detention

According to the *International Covenant on Civil and Political Rights* (ICCPR; Article 10), "all persons deprived of their liberty shall be treated with humanity and with respect for their inherent dignity of the human person." Correspondingly, the ICCPR forbids cruel, inhuman, or degrading treatment or punishment. In the aftermath of September 11, human rights advocates complained that INS detainees were subjected to abuse and inadequate conditions of confinement even though they were not accused of criminal conduct, much less convicted of it. Simply put, from the early stages of the investigation on, those detainees were treated as if they were convicted terrorists, locked down in solitary confinement where they were rarely allowed to leave their cells for weeks and sometimes months. Additionally, they were subjected to extraordinarily strict security measures that prevented them from communicating with their family and attorneys. Even worse, some were victims of verbal and physical abuse, refused adequate medical attention, and housed with suspected or convicted criminals (Human Rights Watch 2002; Welch 2000, 2002a,b).

Physical and Verbal Abuse

With emotions running high after the attacks on the Pentagon and the World Trade Center, detainees feared reprisals from corrections officers and prisoners who might target them with violent behavior that can best be described as scapegoating (Welch 2003a,b). In some instances, those fears were realized. Human rights advocates report numerous incidents in which detainees were subject to physical and verbal abuse by staff and inmates (Amnesty International 2003; Human Rights Watch 2002, 2003). In one particular case, Osama Awadallah, a lawful permanent resident of the United States and a citizen of Jordan, was held as a material witness for 83 days during which he experienced a series of humiliating and physically abusive incidents. While he was at the San Bernardino County (California) jail, corrections officers forced Awadallah to strip naked before a female officer. At one point, an officer twisted his arm, forcing him to bow, and pushed his face to the floor. After he was transferred to a federal facility in Oklahoma City, a corrections officer hurled shoes at Awadallah's head and face, cursed at him, and issued insulting remarks about his religion.

Later, Awadallah was shackled in leg irons and flown to New York City. While in transit, U.S. marshals threatened to "get" his brother and cursed the Arabs. At the Metropolitan Correctional Center, he was confined to a room so cold that his body turned blue. Physical abuse continued as one corrections officer caused his hand to bleed by pushing him into a door and a wall while he was handcuffed. The same guard also kicked his leg shackles and pulled him by the hair to force him to face an American flag. In another incident, marshals kicked him and threatened to kill him. After being detained for 83 days, Awadallah was released on bond. A government investigation corroborated the physical mistreatment. His attorney has filed a complaint on his behalf (Human Rights Watch 2002; see Amnesty International 2003).

GOVERNMENT SECRECY

Contributing to the problems of profiling and the misuse of detention, the government has maintained a policy of secrecy (Dow 2001). Months following the investigation on the attacks of the World Trade Center and the Pentagon, Attorney General John Ashcroft repeatedly denied access to basic information about many of those in detention, including their names and current location. Such secrecy has been denounced by human rights and civil liberties advocates as well as by news organizations and even some political leaders who have complained that the Attorney General has failed to explain adequately the need for those drastic measures. Kate Martin, director of the Center for National Security Studies, said: "The rounding up of hundreds of people secretly, secretly arresting them and putting them in jail where their families don't know where they are and not telling the public is unprecedented and extraordinary in this country" (Donohue 2001:EV1). Martin added: "This is frighteningly close to the practice of 'disappearing' people in Latin America" where secret detentions were carried out by totalitarian regimes (Williams 2001:11). An attorney for three men held in detention in San Diego likened their detention to the sweeps for communists and sympathizers during the Red Scare of the 1920s; he complained that he was not even told where his clients were being held and was not permitted to contact them (Fox 2001). Harvey Grossman of the ACLU added: "There's been nothing as massive as this since the day after Pearl Harbor, when they rounded up 700 Japanese immigrants and held them incommunicado and without charges for a protracted period" (*Chicago Tribune* 2001:EV2).

Reports that detainees have been subjected to solitary confinement without being criminally charged as well as being denied access to telephones and attorneys raise questions about whether detainees are being deprived of due process. Moreover, those deprivations clearly contradict the assurances by the Department of Justice that everyone arrested since September 11 has access to counsel. Key members of Congress have begun to challenge the sweeps of aliens in search of terrorists. Seven Democrats, most notably a coauthor of Ashcroft's antiterror legislation—Senate Judiciary Committee Chairman Patrick Leahy from Vermont—and the only senator to vote against it—Russ Feingold from Wisconsin—requested from the attorney general detailed information on the more than 1,200 people detained since the terror attacks. Specifically, the lawmakers asked for the identity of all those detained, the charges against them, the basis for holding those cleared of connection to terrorism, and a list of all government requests to seal legal proceedings along with the rationale for doing so. The lawmakers stated that while the officials "should aggressively investigate and prevent further attacks," they stressed the Justice Department's "responsibility to release sufficient information . . . to allow Congress and the American people to decide whether the department has acted appropriately and consistent with the Constitution" (Cohen 2001:EV1).

Similarly, human rights groups have admonished the Justice Department for operating a war on terror behind a thick wall of secrecy, a tactic that "reflects a stunning disregard for the democratic principles of public transparency and accountability" (Human Rights Watch 2002:5; Lawyers Committee for Human Rights 2003; Welch 2002a, 2003a, 2004a). The government puts forth an effort to shield itself from public scrutiny by concealing information that is crucial to determining the extent to which its investigations have been conducted in accordance with the law. Civil liberties advocates also take strong exception to the government's attempt to silence criticism of its antiterrorist efforts, most notably with Attorney General Ashcroft's infamous statement (2003) to Congress:

> To those who scare peace-loving people with phantoms of lost liberty, my message is this: your tactics only aid terrorists, for they erode our national unity and diminish our resolve. They give ammunition to America's enemies, and pause to America's friends. They encourage people of goodwill to remain silent in the face of evil.

Legal experts strongly urge the government to amend its tactics in the war on terror so that its actions may be subject to public scrutiny, thus averting civil rights violations. Three areas of accountability are recommended. First, the Justice Department must release information about those it detains, including their names and locations. Secret detentions such as those used by the Justice Department in its antiterrorism campaign violate the *Declaration on the Protection of All Persons from Enforced Disappearances*, 1992 a nonbinding resolution by the United Nations General Assembly. Second, independent monitoring groups must be granted unrestricted access to detention facilities to ensure that detainees are treated in a fair and humane manner. "Such scrutiny is particularly important when dealing with foreigners who for reasons of language, lack of political clout, difficulty retaining counsel, and unfamiliarity with the U.S. justice system may be more vulnerable to violations of these rights" (Human Rights Watch 2003:23). Third, immigration proceedings must no longer be conducted in secrecy. Open hearings have been the practice at the INS for nearly 50 years, a tradition that is consistent with U.S. constitutional law.

In a major blow to civil rights initiatives aimed at striking down the government's use of secret detention, a federal appeals court, in 2003, ruled two-to-one that the Justice Department was within its rights when it refused to release the names of the more than 700 people rounded up in the aftermath of the September 11 attacks. The case stemmed from a campaign by civil liberties groups asserting that the Freedom of Information Act required the Justice Department to disclose the names of those detained on immigration charges. Moreover, such secrecy invites abuse since law enforcement officials are stripped of their accountability. The ruling will likely be appealed, setting the stage for another confrontation over secrecy and the war on terror (Lewis 2003).

THE 2003 INSPECTOR GENERAL'S REPORT

As discussed throughout the chapter, much of the criticism over the government's handling of the war on terror has been delivered by human rights and civil liberties organizations relying on their own investigations. In June 2003, that body of knowledge was greatly expanded by the government itself, particularly in a report released by Glenn A. Fine, the Inspector General at the Department of Justice. Civil liberties and human rights advocates hailed the report especially since it confirmed their complaints that the Justice Department's approach to the war on terror was plagued with serious problems. The report concluded that the government's round up of hundreds of illegal immigrants in the aftermath of September 11 was a mistake since it forced many people with no connection to terrorism to languish behind bars in unduly harsh conditions. The inspector general found that even some of the lawyers in the Justice Department had expressed concerns about the legality of its tactics only to be overridden by senior administrators. Suggesting that the Justice Department had cast too wide a net in the fight against terrorism, the report was critical of FBI officials, particularly in New York City, who made little attempt to distinguish between immigrants who had possible ties to terrorism and those swept up by chance in the investigation. Shanaz Mohammed, 39, who was held in Brooklyn for eight months on an immigration violation before being deported to Trinidad in 2002, responded to the report: "It feels good to have someone saying that we shouldn't have had to go through all that we did. I think America overreacted a great deal by singling out Arab-named men like myself. We were all looked at as terrorists. We were abused" (Lichtblau 2003b:A1).

Since the Justice Department has maintained a policy of secrecy concerning arrests and detentions, the report was hailed for its openness, offering to the public the most detailed portrait to date of who was held, the delays many faced in being charged or gaining access to a lawyer, and the abuse that some faced in jail. William F. Schulz, executive director of Amnesty International USA, said that the Inspector General's Office "should be applauded for releasing a report that isn't just a whitewash of the government's actions" (Lichtblau 2003b:A18). Figures cited in the report show that a total of 762 illegal immigrants were detained in the weeks and months after the attacks on the Pentagon and the World Trade Center. Most of the 762 immigrants have now been deported, and none has been charged as terrorists. The report validated complaints that the 84 detainees housed at the Metropolitan Detention Center in Brooklyn faced a pattern of physical and verbal abuse from some corrections officers and were subjected to unduly harsh detention policies, including a highly restrictive, 23-hour lockdown. Detainees also were hand-cuffed and placed in leg irons and heavy chains any time they moved outside their cells. Compounding their isolation, detainees were limited to a single phone call per week, and due to a communication blackout, families of some inmates in the Brooklyn facility were told their relatives were not housed there. The report faulted the Justice Department for not processing suspects more rapidly, a procedure that would have determined who should remain in detention while releasing others. In sum, the findings "confirm our long-held view that civil liberties and the rights of immigrants were trampled in the after-math of 9/11," said Anthony D. Romero, executive director of the ACLU (Lichtblau 2003b:A18; see Liptak 2003a; *New York Times* 2003b).

Despite strong evidence of civil rights violations contained in the report, Justice Department officials defended themselves saying that they believed they had acted within the law in pursuing terrorist suspects. Barbara Comstock, a spokeswoman for the depart-ment announced: "We make no apologies for finding every legal way possible to protect the American public from further terrorist attacks" (Lichtblau 2003b:A1). Despite their disagreements with some of the report's conclusions, Justice Department officials said that they have already adopted some of the 21 recommendations made by the inspector general, including one to develop clearer criteria for processing such detainees. Other areas of improvement encompass procedures that would ensure a timely clearance process, better training of staff on the treatment of detainees, and better oversight of the conditions of confinement.

CONCLUSION

As this chapter demonstrates, ethnicity and human rights are important considerations in antiterrorism campaigns, particularly in light of questionable profiling and detention practices. The war on terror, even in its early stages, is strikingly similar to another major criminal justice movement, namely the war on drugs. Both strategies are intricately linked to race/ethnicity and produce an array of civil liberties violations compounded by unnecessary incarceration (Talvi 2003b; Welch 1999, 2004b,c). Equally important is evi-dence that raises serious concerns over effectiveness. While the war on drugs has suc-ceeded in locking up unprecedented numbers of poor people who are disproportionately black or Latino, it has failed to reduce consumption of illegal and legal drugs (Husak 2002; Welch, Bryan, and Wolff 1999; Welch, Wolff, and Bryan 1998). Similar doubts suggest that the current campaign against terrorism also is capturing small fries rather than big fish.

Professor David Burnham, director of the Transactional Records Access Clearinghouse at Syracuse University, released a report showing that the war on terror and its reliance on ethnic profiling have produced small-scale success (TRAC 2003). That study found that a large proportion of so-called terrorist prosecutions involve minor charges (e.g., document fraud, identification theft, threats, and immigration violations) resulting in jail sentences of only a few months. In the year after the September 11 attacks, prosecution of crimes connected with terrorism increased tenfold to 1,208 cases from 115 the previous year, but the sentences dropped significantly, from a median of nearly two years in 2001 to just two months in 2002. Senator Patrick Leahy weighed in on the matter, saying: "It raises questions about whether too many resources are being tied up on minor cases that have nothing to do with terrorism" (Lichtblau 2003c:A16).

Contributing to growing skepticism, the General Accounting Office (2003) found that federal prosecutors inflated their success in terrorism-related convictions in 2002 by wrongly classifying almost half of them. Overall, 132 of the 288 convictions reported as international or domestic terrorism (or terrorism-related hoaxes) were determined by investigators to have been wrongly classified (see *New York Times* 2003b). Similar problems have been discovered in New Jersey where prosecutors report handling 62 "international terrorism" indictments in 2002. However, all but two involved Middle Eastern students accused of hiring imposters to take standardized English exams for them. Nearly all of the accused students have been released on bail pending trial while nine of them already have been convicted, fined between $250 and $1,000, and deported (*Associated Press* 2003).

As has been the experience with the war on drugs, the government's fight against terrorism promises to be a long-term commitment, demanding vast resources and funding. Still, with the lessons of a failed drug control policy in clear view, it is crucial that the government curb its tendency of blaming racial and ethnic minorities for problems associated with terrorism (see Marable 2003; Robin 2003). As Anthony D. Romero of the ACLU observes, "The war on terror has quickly turned into a war on immigrants" (Liptak 2003b:A18). Moreover, citizens ought not accept the false paradigm that diminished civil liberties is the price to pay for public safety (see Ratner 2003). Indeed, rather than weakening national security, protection of civil liberties is symbolic of a vibrant democratic government. As Supreme Court Justice Louis D. Brandeis wrote in 1927, the framers of the U.S. Constitution knew that "fear breeds repression; that repression breeds hate; [and] that hate menaces stable government" (*Whitney v. California* 1927; see Human Rights Watch 2002, 2003; Lawyers Committee for Human Rights 2003).

ENDNOTE

1. The scope of this chapter remains on the misuse of detention within the domestic war on terror. Therefore, the breadth of the topic will not include the current controversy over the detention of the estimated 600 "enemy combatants" in Guantanamo Bay and the U.S. government's unwillingness to comply with the Geneva Convention for the protection of prisoners of war (Cole 2003a).

REFERENCES

AMERICAN CIVIL LIBERTIES UNION (2001). *Know Your Rights: What To Do If You're Stopped by the Police, the FBI, the INS, or the Customs Service.* [http://www.aclu.org]

AMNESTY INTERNATIONAL (2003). *Annual Report.* New York: Amnesty International.

ASHCROFT, J. (2003). *Testimony of Attorney General John Ashcroft Before a Hearing of the Senate Judiciary Committee on "DOJ Oversight: Preserving Our Freedoms While Defending Against Terrorism"* (December 6). Washington, DC: U.S. Government Printing.

ASSOCIATED PRESS (2003). "Terrorism" cases in New Jersey relate mostly to test cheating (March 3): 1.

CARDWELL, D. (2003). Muslims face deportation, but say U.S. is their home. *New York Times* (June 13): A22.

CHICAGO TRIBUNE (2001). Concerns rise of civil rights being ignored. *Chicago Tribune* (October 17): EV1–3.

COHEN, L. P. (2001). Denied access to attorneys: Some INS detainees are jailed without charges. *Wall Street Journal* (November 1): EV1–3.

COLE, D. (2003a). Guantanamo Gulag. *The Nation* (June 8): 5.

COLE, D. (2003b). Blind sweeps return. *The Nation* (January 13/20): 5.

COLE, D., and J. X. DEMPSEY (2002). *Terrorism and the Constitution: Sacrificing Civil Liberties in the Name of National Security.* New York: The New Press.

DONOHUE, B. (2001). Rights groups prodding feds for information on detainees. *Star-Ledger* (NJ) (October 30): EV1–2.

DOW, M. (2001). We know what INS is hiding. *Miami Herald* (November 11): EV1–3.

ELLIOT, A. (2003). In Brooklyn, 9/11 damage continues. *New York Times* (June 7): A9.

FOX, B. (2001). Attacks probed in closed courts. *Associated Press* (October 4): EV1–3.

FRITSCH, J. (2002). Grateful Egyptian is freed as U.S. terror case fizzles. *New York Times* (January 13).

GENERAL ACCOUNTING OFFICE (2003). *Better Management Oversight and Internal Controls Needed to Ensure Accuracy of Terrorism-Related Statistics.* Washington, DC: General Accounting Office.

GLASSER, I. (2003). Arrests after 9/11: Are we safer? *New York Times* (June 8): WK12.

GOUREVITCH, A. (2003). Detention disorder: Ashcroft's clumsy round-up of foreigners lurches forward. *The American Prospect* (January): EV1–7.

HUMAN RIGHTS WATCH (2002). *Presumption of Guilt: Human Rights Abuses of Post-September 11th Detainees.* New York: Human Rights Watch.

HUMAN RIGHTS WATCH (2003). *World Report 2003: Events of 2002.* New York: Human Rights Watch.

HUSAK, D. (2002). *Legalize This! The Case for Decriminalization of Drugs.* New York: Verso.

JILANI, H. (2002). Antiterrorism strategies and protecting human rights. *Amnesty Now* 27(2): 1, 15–17.

LAWYERS COMMITTEE FOR HUMAN RIGHTS (2003). *Imbalance of Powers: How Changes to U.S. Law & Policy Since 9/11 Erode Human Rights and Civil Liberties.* New York: Lawyers Committee for Human Rights.

LEWIS, N. (2003). Secrecy is backed on 9/11 detainees: Appeals Court, 2-1, says U.S. can withhold their names. *New York Times* (June 19): A1, A16.

LICHTBLAU, E. (2003a). Bush issues racial profiling ban but exempts security inquiries: Use of race and ethnicity in "narrow" instances. *New York Times* (June 19): A1, A16.

LICHTBLAU, E. (2003b). U.S. report faults the roundup of illegal immigrants after 9/11: Many with no ties to terror languished in jail. *New York Times* (June 3): A1, A18.

LICHTBLAU, E. (2003c). Terror cases rise, but most are small-scale, study says. *New York Times* (February 14): A16.

LIPTAK, A. (2003a). The pursuit of immigrants in America after Sept. 11. *New York Times* (June 8): 14WK.

LIPTAK, A. (2003b). For jailed immigrants, a presumption of guilt. *New York Times* (June 3): A18.

MARABLE, M. (2003). 9/11: Racism in a time of terror. In *Implicating Empire: Globalization and Resistance in the 21st Century World Order*, ed. S. Aronowitz and H. Gautney, pp. 3–14. New York: Basic Books.

NEW YORK TIMES (2003b). Report finds U.S. misstated terror verdicts. *New York Times* (February 22): A10.

RATNER, M. (2003). Making us less free: War on terrorism or war on liberty? In *Implicating Empire: Globalization and Resistance in the 21st Century World Order,* ed. S. Aronowitz and H. Gautney, pp. 31–46. New York: Basic Books.

ROBIN, C. (2003). Fear, American style: Civil liberty after 9/11. In *Implicating Empire: Globalization and Resistance in the 21st Century World Order,* ed. S. Aronowitz and H. Gautney, pp. 47–64. New York: Basic Books.

SCHUSTER, L. (2003). *The Use and Abuse of Political Asylum in Britain and Germany.* London: Frank Cass.

SENGUPTA, S. (2001a). Ill-fated path to America jail and death. *New York Times* (November 5): EV1–4.

SENGUPTA, S. (2001b). Arabs and Muslims steer through an unsettling scrutiny. *New York Times* (September 13): EV1–3.

SWARNS, R. L. (2003a). More than 13,000 may face deportation. *New York Times* (June 7): A9.

SWARNS, R. L. (2003b). Report raises questions on success of immigration interviews. *New York Times* (May 10): A13.

TALVI, S. (2003a). Round up: INS "special registration" ends in mass arrests. *In These Times* (February 17): 3.

TALVI, S. (2003b). *It Takes a Nation of Detention Facilities to Hold Us Back: Moral Panic and the Disaster Mentality of Immigration Policy.* (January 15): EV1–8. http://www.lipmagazine.org] TRAC (Transactional Records Access Clearinghouse) (2003). *Criminal Enforcement Against Terrorists and Spies in the Year After the 9/11 Attacks.* Syracuse, NY: Syracuse University.

WEISER, B. (2002). Judge considers an inquiry on radio case confession. *New York Times* (June 29).

WELCH, M. (1999). *Punishment in America: Social Control and the Ironies of Imprisonment.* Thousand Oaks, CA: Sage.

WELCH, M. (2000). The role of the immigration and naturalization service in the prison industrial complex. *Social Justice: A Journal of Crime, Conflict & World Order* 27(3): 73–88.

WELCH, M. (2002a). *Detained: Immigration Laws and the Expanding I.N.S. Jail Complex.* philadelphia, PA: Temple University Press.

WELCH, M. (2002b). Detention in I.N.S. Jails: Bureaucracy, brutality, and a booming business. In *Turnstile Justice: Issues in American Corrections,* 2nd ed., R. L. Gido and T. Alleman. Englewood Cliffs, NJ: Prentice Hall.

WELCH, M. (2003a). The trampling of human rights in the war on terror: Implications to the sociology of denial. *Critical Criminology: An International Journal* 12(2): 1–20.

WELCH, M. (2003b). Ironies of social control and the criminalization of immigrants. *Crime, Law & Social Change: An International Journal.* 73–80

WELCH, M. (2004a). Immigrant clampdown: How the INS jail complex produces human rights violations. In *Race, Gender and Punishment: Theorizing Differences,* ed. M. Bosworth and S. R. Bush-Baskette. Boston, MA: Northeastern University Press.

WELCH, M. (2004b). Immigration and naturalization detention centers. *Encyclopedia of Prisons,* ed. M. Bosworth. Thousand Oaks, CA: Sage.

WELCH, M. (2004c). *Corrections: A Critical Approach,* 2nd ed. New York: McGraw-Hill.

WELCH, M., N. BRYAN, and R. WOLFF (1999). Just war theory and drug control policy: Militarization, morality, and the war on drugs. *Contemporary Justice Review* 2(1): 49–76.

WELCH, M., R. WOLFF, and N. BRYAN (1998). Decontextualizing the war on drugs: A content analysis of NIJ publications and their neglect of race and class. *Justice Quarterly* 15(4): 719–742.

WILLIAMS, P. J. (2001). By any means necessary. *The Nation* (November 26): 11.

CASE

Whitney v. California, 247 U.S. 357 (1927).

*EV refers to electronic version.

PART VIII

Gender, Diversity, and the Law

Chapter 34

Women

Second-Class Citizens?

Roslyn Muraskin

ABSTRACT

The twenty-first century is here. The past several hundred years have seen women struggling for equality—struggling to help make changes occur. Today, we still advocate change. Change in the criminal justice system is part of the change needed. What is equality? No society exists that can actually boast about its principles of equality. According to Catherine MacKinnon "the second class-status of women as a group is widely documented to be socially and legally institutionalized, cumulatively and systematically shaping access to life chances on the basis of sex" (2001:2). Using the words of Richard Rorty, philosopher, a woman "is not yet the name of the way of being human" (MacKinnon 2001:3).

Women are being arrested at higher rates than ever before, although males are still the predominant groups in correctional facilities. Women are also the victims of crimes more than ever before. Witness the cases of domestic violence, the cases of rape, and women who find themselves being sexually harassed (see Chapter 35 "The Response of the U.S. Supreme Court to Sexual Harassment" by Martin O'Connor). The contention is that the continuum of violence against women includes sexual harassment as well as domestic violence. As women gain more equality, they become harassed by employers in a manner that is akin to criminal violence. During this new century a strategy must be developed to combat all violence against women. The argument is made that while the public has slowly recognized the dynamics of rape and domestic violence, cases of sexual harassment need to be taken seriously and dealt with seriously.

INTRODUCTION

Historically, women have been discriminated against by law. Women have, in fact, sometimes been victimized by policies designed to protect them. During the last decades, women have been especially strong in arguing for equality. The history of women's struggles has taught us that litigation is simply a catalyst for change. A change in attitude is still needed, discrimination still exists, and women continue to struggle. When Abigail Adams wrote to her husband John, who helped write the Constitution of the United States, she told him to "remember the ladies." The ladies still wish to be remembered. Controversy still abounds.

Women's issues still infuse every aspect of social and political thought. As early as 1913, Rebecca West stated that she had never been able to find out precisely what feminism is, but added that people called her a feminist whenever she expressed sentiments to differentiate her from a doormat. Women's basic human rights are inextricably linked to their treatment by and with their participation in today's political world. Due to the fact that the lives of women are reflections of what they do, what they say, and how they treat each other, women as participating members of the human race are ultimately responsible for human affairs.

What, then, is the agenda for change in the criminal law in the twenty-first century? There is no way to guarantee both men and women equal protection of the laws unless we commit to eliminating all gender discrimination. Over the years the criminal justice system has slowly come to grips with an understanding of women and justice. In the twenty-first century, more and more cases are being heard and will be heard in the courts, where legal procedures and precedents have been established to ensure that complainants will receive a fairer hearing than envisioned previously. Courts need to allow time for discovery of evidence as well as the opportunity to hear expert testimony in cases of sexual violence.

The data continue to show that women are involved in the criminal justice system in greater numbers than before. Crimes such as rape, domestic violence, and sexual harassment are all part of the continuum of violence against women. Rape is not a crime of sex; it is a crime of power. It is "an act of violence, an assault like any other, not an expression of socially organized sexuality" (MacKinnon 1979:218). The fact that rape is acted out in sex does not mean that it is an act of male sexuality. Rape is simply an act of violence. Think of the social construction of battering. "Take a moment and think about the image that comes to mind when you hear words such as *domestic violence, spouse abuse, wife battering*, and *women battering.* Close your eyes and think about an assault between two adults who are in an intimate relationship. Visualize the events leading up to the assault and the event itself. Who is the perpetrator? Who is the victim? What is the context surrounding the assault?" (Eigenberg 2001:15). Sexual abuse has never been seen as "an act of sex inequality but as a crime or a tort. Neither criminal law nor tort law has taken the social context of sex inequality systematically into account in defining and adjudicating as sexual assaults" (MacKinnon 2001:766).

The reason that sexual abuse has happened is that historically it was not defined nor treated as a crime. The rules that pertain to cases of sexual abuse such as rape were defined prior to women even winning the right to vote or being allowed to serve on juries.

"A sex equality analysis of sexual subordination would seek to understand the place of sexual assault in the status of the sexes, and the role of gender status in sexual assault and its treatment by law" (MacKinnon 2001:767). The acts of rape and domestic violence have drawn parallels with that of sexual harassment. If sex or sexual advances are unwanted, if they are imposed on a woman who is in no position to refuse, why is this act any different from rape or domestic violence? Some consider sexual harassment a lesser crime, and that in and of itself is questionable, but it is, nevertheless, an act of violence against women. Both women and men spend the better part of their day at work. Sexual harassment is sexual discrimination, and attention must be paid to these acts. In recent years, there has been a current of public discussion about the cases of women accused and sometimes convicted of assaulting and killing partners who abuse them. The actual volume of these cases is relatively small, but the attention given the cases illuminates the larger problem for which they have come to stand: the common disparity of power between men and women in familial relationships. What about working relationships? We need to understand whether sexual assault is truly based on sex alone.

Looking at the crime of rape, in the words of Susan Brownmiller (1975):

The rapist performs a myrmidon function for all men
by keeping all women in a thrall of anxiety and fear.
Rape is to women as lynching was to blacks: the ultimate
physical threat by which all men keep all women in a state
of psychological intimidation

Can any woman imagine what it must be like to be a victim of a rape? In the words of Sue Lees, *Carnal Knowledge: Rape on Trial* (1996),

Imagine for one moment what it is like, from a woman's perspective, to give evidence
    against a man who
has raped you. The case does not come up for a year. You are then obliged
to relive the whole life-threatening experience, face to face
with the man who assaulted you, the mere sight of whom brings
back the horror of the attack. You avoid looking at him. You
face ranks of barristers in wigs, the judge up high, police
everywhere, all in the awe-inspiring surroundings of the
crown court. You have no legal representative of your own,
and you are not allowed to meet the prosecuting counsel.
You must describe in intimate detail every part of your body that was assaulted in words
    which would be embarrassing
To use with friends, let alone in a public setting. The paradox
Is that the very use of such language is sufficient to render
A woman "unrespectable". Except in pornography, the kinds
of detail described in rape cases would never be voiced. It
is hardly surprising that so many women find court a nightmare

This could very well be why crimes of rape are rarely reported in the United States, let alone prosecuted.

If a sexual crime is a crime of power, these acts constitute the subordination of women to men. This continues the powerlessness in the criminal law of women as a gender. "If sexuality is set apart from gender, it will be a law unto itself" (MacKinnon 1979:221). There still exists the reasoning that men rape to establish power and that women are raped because they are still considered the property of men.

According to Katharine K. Baker, *Once a Rapist? Motivational Evidence and Relevance in Rape Law* (1997:606–608),

> *The U.S. soldiers left the 11th Brigade patch [in My Lai]*
> *in order to impugn the honor of North Vietnamese men.*
> *The U.S. soldiers could have gotten their sex without leaving*
> *manifest evidence that they had done so. They could have*
> *just killed the women in the same way they destroyed the*
> *villages' animals, property, and elderly men. By making*
> *the fact of their rapes public, the soldiers added further*
> *insult to the enemy. This view explains why rapes during*
> *war time often take place in public or are committed in*
> *front of civilian witnesses, and it explains why rape and*
> *war have gone hand in hand since there has been war. . . .*

HISTORY

When this country was founded, it was founded on the two principles that (1) "all men are created equal" and (2) "governments derive their powers from the consent of the governed." Women were not included in either concept. The Constitution of the United States did not include women as citizens or as persons with legal rights. Women were not considered persons under the Fourteenth Amendment to the Constitution, which guaranteed that no state shall deny to "any person within its jurisdiction the equal protection of the laws." Remember the words of Justice Miller in the case of *Bradwell v. Illinois:* "The paramount destiny of women is to fulfill the noble and benign offices of wife and mother. This is the law of the Creator. And the rules of civil society must be adopted to the general constitution of things, and cannot be based upon exceptional cases" (Muraskin 2007:6). Therefore, in the face of the law, women had no rights—women did not exist on a legal footing with men.

The women's movement was the most integrated and populist force in this country. More than 80 years later, after women won the right to vote, a right granted to women *after* the slaves were freed, women still wait for the promise of the Declaration of Independence of equality before and under the law.

The English common law of the "rule of thumb" allowed a husband to beat his wife with a whip or stick no wider than his thumb. The husband's prerogative was incorporated into the law of the United States. The sad fact is that several states had laws on the books that essentially allowed a man to beat his wife with no interference from the courts. Blackstone referred to this action as the "power of correction." For too many decades women have been victims of sexual assault. Each act of "sexual assault is recognized as one of the most traumatic and debilitating crimes for adults . . ." (Roberts 1993:362). The victimization of women has been most prevalent and problematic for the criminal justice system. As pointed out by Susan Faludi (1991): "Women's advances and retreats are generally described in military terms: battles won, battles lost, points and territory gained and surrendered. In times when feminism is at a low ebb, women assume the reactive role—privately and most often covertly struggling to assert themselves against the dominant cultural tide. But when feminism becomes the tide, the opposition doesn't simply go along with the reversal, it digs in its heels, brandishes its fists, builds walls and dams."

"Under the federal constitution and most state constitutions, women have not yet been raised to the status of constitutional protections enjoyed by males" (Thomas 1991:95). Gender-neutral language does not solve the problem either. All such language does is to allow employers to hide prevalent discrimination.

Women represent half of the national population. They deserve the same rights as men. When rape victims speak out, rape becomes a crime that demonstrates the victim no longer has the facility to control her own personal being. The rape victim's ego defense is diminished. This act, the act of rape, even more so than any other criminal act, deprives the victims and their acquaintances of the protective mantle of privacy—converting their private agony in finding themselves discussing what happened to them in private into what is termed a public forum. In rape cases, there was a time when required corroboration denigrated the testimony of women who claimed to have been sexually violated was in and of itself indefensible (Muraskin 2007:181). The aura of dishonesty was raised—because what woman would allow herself to be a victim of a rape? Historically, rape laws, similar to many other laws that direct their attention to women as victims, have been based on the premise that women are basically liars. After all remember the words of Justice Matthew Hale:

> A charge such as that made against the defendant in this case is one which is easily made and once made, difficult to defend against, even if the person accused is innocent. Therefore, the law requires that you examine the testimony of the female person named in the information with caution. (Muraskin 2007:182)

The quandary faced by thousands of women who are victims of rape is whether or not to report the rape in the first place. Oftentimes, the answer is not to report because the feeling is that "she asked for it." A pattern has evolved—both the lack of support from the community and the low priority given rape cases by the police and prosecutors—that appears to alienate the victims. Unfortunately, those victims who do persevere to the trial stage historically have found themselves put on trial as the defense attorney has grilled them about their prior sexual history, citing its relevance to the case. Under the rape shield laws, a victim of a rape cannot be questioned about her prior sexual history unless it has relevance to the defense's case.

> Rape is an unbelievably vicious and personal form of attack. Many a female victim fears her assailant will return (and some do). Many a victim is reluctant to return home or to return to her normal home life upon being raped. Rape legislation has had a long-standing and sordid history as sexist legislation designed not to protect women, but rather to protect men's social and property interests in female chastity. (Muraskin 2007:183–184)

Unfortunatelyfor many victims rape has become an instrument of forced exile (Russell-Brown 2002:35).

Historically, the criminal justice system has been inadequate in responding to the problems of domestic violence. Law enforcement throughout this country has mandatory arrest policies. Like crimes of rape, crimes of domestic violence have been cloaked in secrecy. "Both legal and social institutions reinforced the 'hands-off approach' that characterized early responses to woman battering. . . . since the 1970s, efforts initiated by the battered women's movement have successfully propelled the issue of intimate violence into the national spotlight" (see Dobash and Dobash 1979; Muraskin 2007:239).

Similar to cases of rape and all cases of violence against women, responding to disputes of domestic violence has brought on deep feelings of frustration both from those involved in law enforcement and from the women seeking protection. Year after year, "battered women faced police officers who routinely supported offenders' positions and challenged the credibility of victims—often trivializing their fears and even blaming them for their own victimization" (Miller and Peterson 2007:239). As the momentum has grown toward mandatory arrest policies, we find that both the psychological benefits to these victims are great—"Arrest demonstrates an official willingness to assert that battering will not be tolerated"—and the factor of mandatory arrests also provides the police with the necessary training and guidance needed in dealing with cases of violence against women (240).

> One potential problem with mandatory arrest policies is that they almost certainly produce unanticipated and negative consequences for women. But due to limited opportunities, resources, and alternatives, men who abuse women from minority or lower socioeconomic groups may be disproportionately arrested in jurisdictions favoring pro-arrest policies, creating additional problems for these battered women (Miller and Peterson, 2007:246).

In establishing policies for women and violence, we understand that the policies of law enforcement cannot subsist in a vacuum. There are alternative programs that deal with such problems. "It has been suggested that a collaboration of legal sanctions and social services, such as court-mandated counseling, generally tend to complement one another, and correct power imbalances between victims and offenders with a minimum of coercion. Prosecutor's offices have introduced pretrial mediation programs as an alternative to formal criminal processing. The idea behind mediation is to informally educate both the victim and the offender about more effective methods for resolving conflict and to inform both parties about their legal rights" (Miller and Peterson 2007:249).

THE NEED FOR A NATIONAL COMMITMENT TO END VIOLENCE AGAINST WOMEN

Addressing violence against women requires a national commitment and a national remedy. Toward this end, in the early 1990s Congress began assembling a mountain of data about gender violence. A summary of this data was included in the dissenting opinion of Supreme Court Justice David Souter in *United States v. Morrison* (2000:1761–1763):

- Three out of four American women will be victims of violent crimes sometime during their lives.

- Violence is the leading cause of injuries to women ages 15 to 44.

- As many as 50 percent of homeless women and children are fleeing domestic violence.

- Since 1974, the assault rate against women has outstripped the rate for men by at least twice for some age groups and far more for others.

- Battering is the largest cause of injury to women in the United States.

- An estimated 4 million women in the United States seek medical assistance each year for injuries sustained from their husbands or other partners.

- Between 2,000 and 4,000 women die every year from domestic abuse.

- Arrest rates may be as low as 1 for every 100 domestic assaults.

- Partial estimates show that violent crime against women costs this country at least $3 billion a year.

- Estimates suggest that the United States spends $5 to $10 billion per year on health care, criminal justice, and other social costs of domestic violence.

- The incidence of rape rose four times as fast as the total national crime rate over the past 10 years.

- According to one study, close to one-half million females now in high school will be raped before they graduate.

- 125,000 college women can expect to be raped during this or any year.

- Three-fourths of women never go to the movies alone after dark because of the fear of rape, and nearly 50 percent do not use public transit alone after dark for the same reasons.

- Forty-one percent of judges surveyed in a Colorado study believed that juries give sexual assault victims less credibility than other victims of crime.

- Less than 1 percent of rape victims have collected damages.

- An individual who commits rape has only 4 chances in 100 of being arrested, prosecuted, and found guilty of any offense.

- Almost one-fourth of convicted rapists never go to prison and another one-fourth received sentences in local jails, where the average sentence is 11 months.

- Almost 50 percent of rape victims lose their jobs or are forced to quit because of the crime's severity.
- The attorneys general from 38 states urged Congress to enact a civil rights remedy, permitting rape victims to sue their attackers because "the current system of dealing with violence is inadequate.

Based on these extensive data that were collected over four years, Congress has found that "crimes of violence motivated by gender have a substantial adverse effect on interstate commerce, by deterring potential victims from traveling interstate, from engaging in employment in interstate business . . . [and being] . . . involved in . . . [other] . . . interstate commerce" (H.R. Conf. Rep., No. 103–711 1994:385).

Because of its findings, Congress deemed it necessary to supplement the inadequate State remedies in combating gender violence by creating and passing the Violence Against Women Act (VAWA) in 1994. This Act attacked violence against women in several ways. First, it provided substantial sums of money to States for education, rape crisis hotlines, training criminal justice personnel, victim services, and special units in police and prosecutors' offices to deal with crimes against women. The Act specifically provided incentives for the enforcement of statutory rape laws, the payment of the cost of testing for sexually transmitted diseases for victims of crime, and studies of campus sexual assaults, and the battered women's syndrome. As a condition of receiving federal monies states would have to demonstrate greater efforts toward arresting and prosecuting domestic violence offenders. Several states changed and strengthened their domestic violence laws and moved from policies of arrest avoidance in domestic cases to mandatory arrest policies.

Second, criminal provisions of the VAWA provide that it is a federal offense to cross state lines with the intent of contacting a domestic partner when the contact leads to an act of violence. In addition, the Act also makes orders of protection enforceable from one state to another.

Third, the civil rights component of the Act permitted a victim of gender violence to sue his or her attacker and seek compensatory and punitive damages for a crime of violence motivated in part by gender animus. Victims of gender violence were thus empowered to bring lawsuits against their attackers even if the prosecutors were unwilling or unable to pursue a criminal action.

Finally, the Act was an important vehicle to raise the consciousness level of the nation to the problem of violence against women. The VAWA was not the millennium, but an important first step by our national government in its commitment to combat gender violence.

Shortly after the VAWA became law, it encountered a significant constitutional challenge. In the Fall of 1994, a young woman named Christy Brzonkala enrolled in college at Virginia Polytechnic Institute. Early in her freshman year, Christy alleged that she was gang raped by two other students named Crawford and Morrison who were also varsity football players. Subsequently, Christy reported the attack and became severely emotionally disturbed and depressed. She sought assistance from a University psychiatrist, was prescribed anti-depressant medication, stopped attending classes and eventually withdrew from the University. Neither man was ever charged with a crime.

The victim filed a complaint against Morrison and Crawford pursuant to University procedures. Virginia Tech held a hearing and Crawford produced an alibi witness who said that he left the room before any sexual activity occurred. Morrison admitted having sexual contact with Christy even though she had told him twice, "no." After a hearing, Morrison was suspended for two semesters. There was insufficient evidence to punish Crawford.

Subsequently, a University official set aside Morrison's punishment as being "excessive when compared to other cases. . . ." The victim then became the first to file a lawsuit against her attacker and Virginia Tech under the newly created VAWA. Although the case began as a victim suing her alleged rapists, by the time the case reached the United States Supreme Court, some called the case a clash between feminism and federalism (American Spectator 1999/2000:60–61).

Unfortunately, under the concept of federalism (sharing of power between the state and federal government) the U.S. Supreme Court, by a narrow margin (five to four), ruled that Congress did not have the constitutional authority to create this federal civil remedy. Chief Justice Rehnquist writing for the majority said: "[I]f the allegations—[of rape by the football players] . . . are true, no civilized system of justice could fail to provide her a remedy for the conduct of respondent Morrison. But under our federal system that remedy must be provided by the Commonwealth of Virginia, and not by the United States." Four justices disagreed. They contended that "Congress has the power to legislate with regard to activity that in the aggregate has a substantial effect on interstate commerce." The impact of the *Morrison* decision is that civil remedies designed to assist women who have been victims of violence will be balkanized. Women will have to seek legislative approval in communities throughout the United States so that they are authorized to bring lawsuits against their attackers for gender violence. In response to the *Morrison* decision, the city of New York became one of the first U.S. communities to create such a remedy for victims of gender violence.

The VAWA has been an important national vehicle in addressing the issue of violence against women. It is unfortunate that this important federal civil remedy relied on by the victim in *Morrison* has been ruled unconstitutional. Nevertheless, the other provisions of the act are still intact and billions of federal dollars will still flow to states over the next few years to support various provisions of the act. Violence against women still requires an urgent national response.

SUMMARY

Sexual equality has been affirmed, but it is rarely practiced; sexual equality is more hypothetical than real. The law has seen and treated women the way that men have viewed and treated women. Like the crime of rape, cases of domestic violence and sexual harassment are not issues of lust; but issues of power. In voluntary sexual relationships, everyone should exercise freedom of choice in deciding whether to establish a close, intimate relationship. Such freedom of choice is absent in cases where women are victims of violence. Rape, incest, battering, as well as sexual harassment may be understood as an extreme acting out of qualities that are regarded as supermasculine: aggression, power, dominance, and force. Men who harass are not pathological but rather people who exhibit behaviors that have been characteristic of the masculine gender role. Most cases in which women are the victims of violence start at the subtle end of the continuum and escalate over time. Each year, women experience the unfortunate consequences of being violated, yet cultural mythologies consistently blame the victim for sexual abuse and act to keep women in their place.

Women who speak as victims of violence use words such as *humiliating, intimidating, frightening, financially damaging, embarrassing, nerve-wracking, awful*, and *frustrating*. These are not words used to describe a situation that one enjoys.

Historically, the rape of women was considered to be an infringement of the property rights of men. All cases of violence have been viewed in the same light. The message in the twenty-first century is the recognition that changes are needed. We can no longer blame the messenger. We need to understand the message. There is no question that "women's hidden occupational hazard"—being victimized as a woman—is nothing less than sexual victimization. The existence of cases of rape and domestic violence demonstrate that they must be understood as part of the continuum of violence against women. In a typical case of violence, the female accuser becomes the accused and the victim is twice victimized. This holds true in all cases where women are victims because of their sex because of the use of power over women. Underlying these dynamics is the profound distrust of a woman's word and a serious power differential between the accused and the accuser.

What actions are being taken? As noted in this chapter, more and more cases are coming to light. Now there is the understanding that conduct that many men consider unobjectionable may very well offend women and be prosecuted.

AGENDA FOR CHANGE

Litigation is occurring. Although we do not have a federal equal rights amendment, there are states that recognize its potential worth. As an example, the use of male terms to indicate both sexes is slowly being examined. There are those who choose to use gender-neutral terms such as *reasonable person*. Words are meant to have definitive meaning. "Words are workhorses of law" (Thomas 1991:116). Sexual harassment as noted in Chapter 35 is a major barrier to women's professional and personal development and a traumatic force that disrupts and damages their personal lives. For ethnic-minority women who have been victimized, economic vulnerability is paramount. Women feel powerless, not in control, afraid, and not flattered by any act of violence. As stated previously, women's basic human rights are inextricably linked to their treatment by and with their participation in today's political world.

The courts need to continue to look at the totality of circumstances. One action without evidence of extreme emotional distress cannot be construed to be an act of violence regardless of the political atmosphere. Calling an act an act of violence simply because a person makes an accusation will not create the change that is needed.

What, then, is the agenda for change in this century? Elected officials, public policy makers, religious institutions, educational institutions, the criminal justice system, the media, and business and labor organizations need to do more. For justice to be gained, everyone must be concerned with the long arduous fight for freedom and equality for everyone. Gloria Steinem noted that cultural myths die hard, especially if they are used to empower one part of the population. We must do whatever is necessary to fight oppression and alleviate repressive conditions wherever they exist. The struggle of women continues under the law. There is no way to allow both sexes automatically to enjoy equal protection of the laws unless we are committed to eliminating all sexual discrimination. The criminal justice system over the years has slowly come to grips with the need to understand both women and justice. Recent Supreme Court cases have regarded violence against women; these have become "a mathematically precise test," calling for an examination of all the circumstances of a case. In this new century more cases will be heard, and legal procedures and precedents will be established to ensure that complainants will receive a fairer hearing than before. By presenting the agenda of all women who represent half of the world's population there is a need to meet the challenge.

If we were to go back to 1979 and review the tenets of the *Convention on the Elimination of All Forms of Discrimination Against Women* (UN Document/A/REs/34/180), we find the following:

> *Recalling* that discrimination against women violates the principles of equality of rights and respect for human dignity
>> is an obstacle to the participation of women, on equal terms with men, in the political, social, economic and cultural
>> life of their countries, hampers the growth of the prosperity of society and the family and makes more difficult the
>> full development of the potentialities of women in the service of their countries and of humanity

It was agreed that the term "discrimination against women" shall mean any distinction, exclusion, or restriction made on the basis of sex that has the effect or purpose of impairing or nullifying the recognition, enjoyment, or exercise of men and women of human rights and fundamental freedoms in the political, economic, social, cultural civil, or any other field (MacKinnon 2003:49)

> Women deserve the same rights and opportunities afforded men. There has existed/does exist/will exist the rhetoric of gender equality (yesterday, today, and tomorrow), but it has yet to match the reality of women's experiences. The question remains: Are men ready? The twenty-first century is here; are we all ready to meet the challenges necessary for much needed change? In the words of Abigail Adams, "Remember the ladies."

REFERENCES

BAKER, K. K. "Once a Rapist? Motivational Evidence and Relevancy in Rape Law." 110 Harv. L. Rev. 563 (1997)

110 CONGRESSIONAL RECORD, February 8, 1964, 2577 [Retrieved February 18, 2008 from http://www.jofreeman.com/lawandpolicy/titlevii.htm]

BROWNMILLER, S. (1975). *Against Our Will: Men, Women, and Rape.* New York: Simon and Schuster.

DOBASH, R. E., and R. DOBASH. (1979). Violence against wives. New York: Free Press

EIGENBERG, H. M. (2001). *Woman Battering in the United States: Till Death Do Us Part.* Prospect Heights, IL: Waveland Press.

FALUDI, S. (1991). *Backlash: The Undeclared War Against Women.* New York: Crown Publishers.

LEES, S. (1996). Carnal knowledge: Rape on trial. Hamish Hamilton: Great Britain.

MACKINNON, C. A. (1979). *Sexual Harassment of Working Women.* New Haven, CT: Yale University Press.

MACKINNON, C. A. (2001). *Sex Equality: Rape Law.* New York: Foundation Press.

MACKINNON C. A. (2003). *Sex Equality: Sexual Harassment.* New York: Foundation Press.

MILLER, S., and E. S. L. PETERSON (2007). The impact of law enforcement policies on victims of intimate partner violence. In *It's a Crime: Women and Justice*, ed. R. Muraskin, 4th ed. Upper Saddle River, NJ: Prentice Hall.

MURASKIN, R. (2007). "Sexual Harassment and the Law: Violence Against Women" in *It's a Crime: Women and Justice.* 4th ed. Upper Saddle River, NJ: Prentice-Hall.

THOMAS, C. S. (1991). *Sex Discrimination.* St. Paul, MN: West.

CASES

Bradwell v. Illinois, 83 U.S. 130 (1872).

United Nations Document. (1994). "Human Rights Conference" Rep. No. 103-711 1994-385.

United States v. Morrison, 120 S. Ct. 1740 (2000).

Chapter 35

The Response of the U.S. Supreme Court to Sexual Harassment

Martin L. O'Connor

Sexual harassment is a significant problem in our society, and our court system is struggling with a vast array of legal issues pertaining to harassment. Although legal claims for workplace sexual harassment have their genesis in statutes created by Congress and the guidelines of the Equal Employment Opportunity Commission (EEOC), the law for sexual harassment has for the most part been created by the courts. The term *sexual harassment* was not even coined until 1975 (Belknap and Erez 1997:143), and some 11 years later the U.S. Supreme Court decided its first sexual harassment case. The following pages attempt to sketch the significant response of the U.S. Supreme Court to sexual harassment.

Sexual harassment legal claims have their genesis in the Civil Rights Act of 1964. In this law, Title VII provides that it is an unlawful employment practice for an employer:

> (1) to fail or refuse to hire an individual, or otherwise discriminate against any individual with respect to his compensation, terms, conditions, or privileges of employment, because of such individual's race, color, religion, sex, or national origin. (42 U.S.C. section 2000e-2(a) (1988)

This Civil Rights law was not originally designed to address sex discrimination. Actually, the word *sex* was added to the legislation at the last minute on the floor of the House of Representatives by opponents of the measure in an attempt to prevent its passage (110 Cong. Rec. 2577–84, 1964). Hence, there is little legislative history to guide the courts as to the meaning of *sex* discrimination unlike the significant legislative history that exists regarding the law pertaining to race discrimination. Therefore, the earliest cases that were reviewed by the courts alleging sexual harassment as a form of sex discrimination were unsuccessful, and the courts simply held that there was no such legal claim as sexual harassment (*Tomkins v. Public Service Electric & Gas Co.*, 1976; *Miller v. Bank of America*, 1976; *Corne v. Bausch and Lomb, Inc.*, 1975; *Barnes v. Train*, 1974). Following these cases Catherine MacKinnon published a compelling article arguing that the courts should consider sexual harassment as a form of sex discrimination and an actionable legal claim (MacKinnon 1979). In 1980, the EEOC, the government agency created to enforce Title VII, issued guidelines defining sexual harassment and establishing parameters for unacceptable behavior in the workplace. The EEOC determined that harassment on the basis of sex is a violation of section 703 of Title VII and defined sexual harassment as:

Unwelcome sexual advances, requests for sexual favors, and other verbal or physical conduct of a sexual nature when:

1. submission to such conduct is made either explicitly or implicitly a term or condition of an individual's employment;

2. submission to or rejection of such conduct by an individual is used as the basis for employment decisions affecting such individual; or

3. such conduct has the purpose or effect of unreasonably interfering with an individual's work performance or creating an intimidating, hostile, or offensive working environment (EEOC Guidelines on Discrimination Because of Sex, 29 C.F.R. Sec. 1604.11 (a) 1981).

These guidelines clearly recognized two forms of sexual harassment. The first form is quid pro quo, which literally means "something for something." Therefore, quid pro quo sexual harassment involves an employer using his or her authority to extort sexual favors. Because supervisors have sufficient power to extort sexual favors and subordinates do not, only supervisors are capable of quid pro quo sexual harassment. Of course, employer liability may also exist when supervisors base employment decisions upon an employee's refusal to submit. The second type and the most frequent form of sexual harassment is "hostile environment." In a typical hostile environment case, a victim suffers a number of sex-related inquiries, jokes, slurs, propositions, touching, or other forms of abuse. For this behavior to violate Title VII it must be so severe or pervasive that it alters the conditions of the victim's employment and creates a hostile or abusive work environment. Supervisors and fellow employees can engage in hostile environment sexual harassment.

Some of the following cases will demonstrate how some employees, both male and female, have endured extraordinary, shocking, and pervasive hostile work environments. A number of studies of sexual harassment in the workplace indicate it is a serious problem. For example, 53 percent of working women report having encountered behavior they describe as sexual harassment (Gutek 1985). In 1995, the results of a survey of 1.7 million civilian employees in the executive branch of the federal government revealed that in the last two years 44 percent of the women and 19 percent of the men experienced some unwanted sexual attention. In addition, 37 percent of the female respondents said that they had experienced unwanted sexual teasing, jokes, remarks, and questions (U.S. Merit System Production Board 1995). After the EEOC guidelines regarding sexual harassment were created all federal courts began to recognize sexual harassment as a bona fide legal claim. Eventually, a bank teller named Mechelle Vinson became the first plaintiff to find her sexual harassment claim on the docket of the U.S. Supreme Court.

MERITOR SAVINGS BANK V. VINSON (1986)

In 1974 Mechelle Vinson was hired as a teller trainee at the Meritor Savings Bank in Washington, D.C. She was quickly promoted to teller, head teller, and by 1978 assistant branch manager. In September 1978, Mechelle notified her supervisor that she was taking sick leave for an indefinite period. Two months later she was fired for using excessive sick leave. Shortly thereafter, Mechelle filed a lawsuit against her former supervisor, Sydney Taylor, and the bank, alleging that she had been subjected to sexual harassment by Taylor in violation of Title VII. Mechelle testified that during her probationary period, her supervisor, Taylor, treated her in a fatherly way and made no sexual advances. However, shortly there-after he invited her to dinner, made sexual advances, and suggested they go to a motel. At first, Mechelle said she refused the advances, but because she feared losing her job she eventually agreed to engage in sexual intercourse. She testified that she engaged in sexual intercourse with Taylor about 40 or 50 times and that he raped her on a few occasions. In addition, she testified that Taylor fondled her during working hours, exposed himself to her, and even entered the women's restroom while she was there alone. Although Mechelle was afraid of Taylor she never filed a complaint pursuant to the bank procedures and the actions of Taylor stopped when she started going steady with her boyfriend in 1977.

Taylor denied all of the allegations and the district court found for Taylor and the bank deciding that no sexual harassment occurred. The district court concluded that Mechelle's promotions were obtained by merit alone, that she had not been required to grant Taylor any sexual favors, and that any sex that may have occurred between them was voluntary. In holding that the bank was not liable, the court noted the bank's express policy against discrimination and stated that neither Mechelle nor any other employee had ever lodged a complaint of sexual harassment against Taylor and the bank could not be liable because it had no notice of the supervisor's actions. The U.S. Court of Appeals for the District of Columbia reversed, concluding that Mechelle stated a claim for sexual harassment under Title VII based upon a "hostile environment" and an employer is strictly liable for discriminatory acts by a supervisor. The U.S. Supreme Court decided to hear the case and affirmed the decision of the Court of Appeals but differed significantly regarding the issue of employer liability. The Court, citing EEOC guidelines, ruled that Title VII does cover both quid pro quo and hostile environment sexual harassment. The Court said that Title VII provides an employee with the right "to work in an environment free from discriminatory intimidation, ridicule and insult."

Meritor is a very important case because for the first time the U.S. Supreme Court recognized that sexual harassment is a form of discrimination covered by Title VII. The Court said that the Court of Appeals erred when it concluded that employers are always liable for a supervisor's sexual harassment. The Court did not issue a definitive ruling regarding employer liability and suggested that the lower courts should consider agency principles to determine employer liability. Agency law has been criticized because many judges and lawyers do not have a grasp of these principles and agency law is "not a simple set of basic principles that find easy application in many contexts" (Phillips 1991:1271). Hence, the lower courts were left with the task of forging a coherent analysis of when a supervisor is acting as an agent of the employer.

A troubling aspect of the Court's decision in *Meritor* is Chief Justice Rehnquist's suggestion that a plaintiff's speech and dress is "obviously relevant" to the issue of whether the defendant's conduct was welcome. The problem with this approach is that it focuses upon the behavior of the plaintiff and not the defendant, which is reminiscent of defense tactics in rape cases before rape shield laws were created to protect victims. However, since *Meritor* was decided Rule 412 of the Federal Rules of Evidence dealing with rape shield laws has been amended to apply to civil as well as criminal cases involving sexual misconduct or harassment. Evidentiary rules require the court to balance the probative value of the evidence against its potential prejudice. It would seem that speech and dress in most sexual harassment cases would be of little relevance, highly prejudicial, and therefore inadmissible. Finally, the Court did not decide whether a victim of sexual harassment must suffer "psychologically" as some lower courts held.

HARRIS V. FORKLIFT SYSTEMS, INC. (1993)

As the courts of our nation began to consider the law of sexual harassment some courts concluded that before a victim of sexual harassment could prevail the victim had to demonstrate psychological damage to his or her well-being. In the *Harris* case the U.S. Supreme Court directly confronted this issue.

Theresa Harris worked for an equipment rental company for two years in the mid-1980s. Her immediate supervisor was Charles Hardy, who was also the company president. Hardy often insulted Theresa because of her gender and frequently made her the target of sexual innuendos. Hardy told Theresa on several occasions, in the presence of other employees, "You're a woman, what do you know?" and "We need a man as a rental manager." In addition Hardy referred to Theresa as a "dumb ass woman" and again in front of others suggested that Theresa should go with him "to the Holiday Inn to negotiate a raise." Hardy occasionally asked Theresa and other women to get coins from his pants pockets. Theresa complained to Hardy about his conduct. He expressed surprise that Theresa was offended and claimed he was joking and apologized. He promised that he would stop his offensive behavior and, based upon these assurances, Theresa stayed on the job. However, one month later Hardy began anew. Theresa was arranging a deal with one of the company's customers when Hardy said in front of other employees, "What did you do, promise the guy . . . some [sex] Saturday night?" Shortly thereafter, Theresa quit her job and brought a sexual harassment lawsuit against Hardy based upon the theory of hostile environment.

The district court found Hardy to be a "vulgar man" but concluded that Hardy's conduct did not constitute a hostile environment under Title VII because Theresa failed to prove that she suffered serious damage to her psychological well-being. The court of appeals affirmed and Theresa found her case in the U.S. Supreme Court. One month after oral argument, Justice O'Connor, writing for a unanimous Court, reversed the lower courts and held that a victim of sexual harassment does not have to demonstrate "psychological injury" to recover under a claim for sexual harassment. The Court said that for a plaintiff to state a sexual harassment claim the "sexually objectionable environment must be both objectively and subjectively offensive . . . to a reasonable person." The objective standard appears to limit sexual harassment claims by protecting the employer from very sensitive employees. The subjective test provides for the perceptions of the harassment victim. The Harris Court also adopted the "reasonable person" standard that had been adopted by several courts of appeals. So harassment issues will be decided regarding what a reasonable person in the victim's position would have believed regarding the harassment activity. Some feminist groups have argued for the "reasonable woman" standard and have expressed concern with the reasonable person approach because research studies suggest that women view harassing activities very differently than men.

On remand, Forklift was ordered to institute a sexual harassment policy, and Theresa Harris was awarded $151,435 plus interest, costs, and attorney fees. Forklift appealed this award, but withdrew the appeal when the case was settled for an undisclosed sum. In *Harris* the Court said that there is no "mathematically precise test" to tell when an environment is hostile or abusive. The Court also said that one must look at the "frequency of the discriminatory conduct; its severity; whether it is physically threatening or humiliating, or a mere offensive utterance; and whether it unreasonably interferes with an employee's work performance." In his concurring opinion, Justice Scalia expressed concern that some of the words and phrases in the Court's decision are so vague that "as a practical matter [the Court's decision] lets virtually unguided juries decide whether sex related conduct engaged in by an employer is egregious enough to warrant damages." However, Justice Scalia noted, "be that as it may, I know of no alternative."

CLINTON V. JONES (1997)

Can the president of the United States be sued for sexual harassment while in office? Should a sexual harassment allegation against the president wait until he leaves office so he can concentrate on the affairs of state?

In 1994 Paula Jones, an Arkansas state employee, filed a sexual harassment lawsuit against the President of the United States William Jefferson Clinton. Paula alleged that when President Clinton was the governor of Arkansas, he had an Arkansas State police officer summon Paula to Clinton's hotel room in Little Rock. Paula alleged that shortly after she entered the hotel room Clinton exposed himself and made "abhorrent" sexual advances to her and her rejection of those advances led to punishment by her supervisors in her state job. President Clinton denied the allegations and filed a motion to dismiss the charges on presidential immunity and other grounds. The district court denied the dismissal on immunity grounds but ordered any trial stayed until the Clinton presidency ended. Both sides appealed and the U.S. Supreme Court held that the district court ". . . abused its discretion . . . in deferring trial until the president leaves office."

The Federal District Court " . . . has jurisdiction to decide this . . . [sexual harassment] . . . case . . . [and] . . . like every other citizen who properly invokes that jurisdiction [Paula Jones] has a right to an orderly disposition of her claim." Hence, the U.S. Supreme Court held that a sexual harassment case against a sitting president of the United States should not be delayed and must go forward.

ONCALE V. SUNDOWNER OFFSHORE SERVICES, INC. (1998)

Some 19 years after Catherine MacKinnon wrote her compelling article proposing that sexual harassment should be a legal claim, the U.S. Supreme Court decided to review no fewer than four sexual harassment cases during the 1998 term of the Court. *Oncale*, the first of these cases raised some interesting issues. Can men sexually harass other men? Must a person be sexually harassed by a member of the opposite sex to state a legal claim?

During 1991, Joseph Oncale was working for Sundowner Offshore Services on an oil platform in the Gulf of Mexico. Joe was employed as a roustabout on an eight-man crew. On several occasions, Joe was forcibly subjected by some crew members to humiliating actions and physically assaulted in a sexual manner, and one crew member threatened to rape him. Joe's complaints to supervisors produced no remedial action, and the company's safety compliance clerk told Joe that the crew members picked on him too, and then he called Joe a name "suggesting homosexuality." Eventually Joe quit his job and listed "sexual harassment and verbal abuse" as the reason for leaving. Joe filed a Title VII lawsuit alleging that he had been discriminated against because of his sex. The district court dismissed the suit and the court of appeals affirmed holding that there was no legal cause of action for same sex sexual harassment.

The U.S. Supreme Court unanimously reversed and ruled that discrimination in the form of same-sex sexual harassment is actionable under Title VII. The Court noted that there was nothing in the statutory language of Title VII to preclude a claim of same-sex sexual harassment. Hence, one does not have to be of the opposite sex to engage in sexually harassing conduct. In fact sexual desire does not have to be the motivation for sexual harassment. In regard to harassing conduct the Court said:

> [T]he objective severity of harassment should be judged from the perspective of a reasonable person in the plaintiff's position, considering all of the circumstances . . . In same sex [as in all] harassment cases, that inquiry requires careful consideration of the social context in which the particular behavior occurs and is experienced by its target . . . The real social impact of workplace behavior often depends on a constellation of surrounding circumstances, expectations and relationships which are not fully captured by a simple recitation of the words used or the physical acts performed. Common sense, and an appropriate sensitivity to the social context, will enable courts and juries to distinguish between simple roughhousing among members of the same sex, and conduct which a reasonable person in the plaintiff's position would find severely hostile or abusive.

The Court found that these standards are necessary so that courts and juries do not mistake "male on male horseplay or intersexual flirtation for discriminatory conditions of employment." The evaluation of whether there is a hostile work environment should be made by a reasonable person in the plaintiff's position, giving careful consideration to the social context in which the behavior occurs. The Court noted that in a football player's working environment, the coach may "smack" a player on the buttocks as he heads off the field, but this same behavior "experienced by the coach's secretary back at the office" may be quite different.

Since *Oncale* was decided one federal judge has written that in borderline cases of sexual harassment juries, not federal judges, may be more appropriate to decide factual issues.

> Whatever the early life of a Federal Judge, he or she lives in a narrow segment of the enormously broad American socioeconomic spectrum, generally lacking the current real life experiences required in interpreting subtle sexual dynamics of the workplace based upon nuances, subtle perceptions, and implicit communications . . . a jury made up of a cross-section of our heterogeneous communities provides the appropriate institution for deciding whether borderline situations should be characterized as sexual harassment and retaliation . . . " (Jack B. Weinstein, Federal District Judge sitting in the Second Circuit Court of Appeals in *Gallagher v. Delaney*, p. 342, 1998)

This is an interesting statement commenting on the experience of members of the federal judiciary. If this view is adopted by the federal courts, there may be fewer cases dismissed, more jury trials, protracted litigation, and greater pressure on employers to settle sexual harassment claims.

FARAGHER V. CITY OF BOCA RATON 542 U.S. 17 (1998)

If an employee does not complain about sexual harassment until two years after quitting the job, can an employer still be liable for the harassment? When is an employer liable for sexual harassment that occurs in the workplace? The *Faragher* case clearly shows the kinds of behaviors that employees are sometimes subjected to and the possibility of employer liability for failing to enact reasonable policies and procedures in an attempt to rid the workplace of sexually harassing behavior. In sexual harassment cases it is not uncommon for employers who are sued for sexually harassing behavior to produce a sexual harassment policy from a file drawer in its main office and allege that they cannot be liable because their company policy prohibits sexual harassment. This is the see-no-evil defense to sexual harassment; some employers have attempted to use the mere presence of a policy as a shield from liability. This case examines this issue.

Beth Ann Faragher worked part-time during the summer in 1990 as a lifeguard for the Parks Department of the City of Boca Raton, Florida. The city employed about 40 lifeguards, 6 of whom were women. Bill Terry, David Silverman, and Robert Gordon were Beth Ann's immediate supervisors. Terry had authority to hire new lifeguards, supervise all aspects of a lifeguard's work, deliver oral reprimands, and make a record of such discipline. After five years of part-time work Beth Ann resigned, and two years after her resignation she brought a sexual harassment lawsuit against Terry and Silverman and the City of Boca Raton. Beth Ann asserted that her supervisors discriminated against her by creating a "sexually hostile atmosphere" in her work environment. Beth stated that she and other female lifeguards were repeatedly subjected to uninvited and offensive touching and lewd remarks, and women were spoken of in offensive terms. Specifically, Beth alleged that Terry once said, that he "would never promote a woman to the rank of Lieutenant," and Silverman said, "Date me or clean the toilets for a year." During a five-year period Beth alleged that "Terry repeatedly touched the bodies of female employees . . . would put his arm around [Beth] with his hands on her buttocks . . . [and] . . . once commented disparagingly about [Beth's] shape." During an interview with a woman he hired as a lifeguard, Terry said that "female lifeguards have sex with their male counterparts . . . [will you] . . . do the same." Beth said that "Silverman behaved in similar ways and once "tackled [Beth] and commented that but for a physical characteristic he found unattractive, he would readily have sexual relations with her, and another time, he pantomimed oral sex."

Beth did not complain to higher management about Terry and Silverman, although she spoke to the other supervisor Gordon. Beth said she did not regard her conversations with Gordon as formal complaints. Other female lifeguards had similar complaints, and Gordon responded to one of the female lifeguards, "[T]he city just doesn't care . . . " Two months before Beth resigned another female lifeguard wrote a letter to the city's personnel director complaining that Terry and Silverman had sexually harassed her and other female lifeguards. The city investigated the complaint and found that Terry and Silverman had behaved improperly, reprimanded them, and required them to choose between a suspension without pay and forfeiture of annual leave.

In the *Faragher* lawsuit the district court found that Terry and Silverman indeed discriminated against Beth. Even though the city of Boca Raton had a sexual harassment policy the court said that the city was liable for the harassment because the harassment was so pervasive that the city "had knowledge or constructive knowledge" and that as supervisors Terry and Silverman were acting as agents of the city when they engaged in their harassing behavior. On appeal the Eleventh Circuit affirmed the finding of harassment by Terry and Silverman toward Beth, but reversed the judgment against the city because the court decided that Terry and Silverman were not working within the scope of their employment when the harassing behavior occurred and the city had no knowledge of the harassment.

The U.S. Supreme Court decided to take the case to clarify when an employer is liable for sexually harassing behavior. The Court reversed the judgment of the court of appeals that excused the city of liability and in an extraordinary exercise of its power sent the case back to the district court with a directive that a judgment be entered in Beth Ann's favor because the city was liable for the harassment encountered by Beth. The Court concluded that although the city had a sexual harassment policy it failed to disseminate its sexual harassment policy to beach employees and lifeguards. In addition, the city made no attempt to keep track of the conduct of its beach supervisors, and the city's sexual harassment policy did not include any provision that the harassing supervisors could be bypassed in registering complaints. Obviously, if the harasser is the supervisor, the employee must have a method or avenue of bypassing the harasser to report the harassment to the employer. The Court ruled as a matter of law that the city of Boca Raton could not be found to have exercised reasonable care in preventing the supervisor's misconduct. Hence, the Court put an end to the typical employer defense "I have an anti-harassment policy and I did not see any evil." The Court's decision makes it clear that possession of incomplete anti-harassment policy in a book in the main office will not shield an employer from liability. The employer's anti-harassment policy must be comprehensive, and disseminated to all employees. The employees must be trained in the policy and the employer must carefully monitor the work environment, adopt a zero tolerance policy regarding sexual harassment, and take swift action to enforce the policy when harassment occurs.

BURLINGTON INDUSTRIES V. ELLERTH (1998)

Suppose a female employee is subjected to certain comments about her breasts and threats of retaliation from a mid-level manager about her dress and whether she is "loose enough." Can these unfulfilled threats constitute sexual harassment?

Kimberly Ellerth was a salesperson at Burlington Industries; she quit her job after 15 months because of sexual harassment by one of her supervisors. Ted Slowik was a mid-level manager who had the power to hire and fire employees. In the summer of 1993 while on a business trip with other employees, Ted invited Kimberly Ellerth to the hotel lounge. Ted was not Kim's immediate supervisor, but Kim felt compelled to accept because Ted was a boss. At this time Ted made comments about Kim's breasts, and when Kimberly gave no encouragement to the remarks Ted told her to "loosen up" and warned, "[y]ou know, Kim, I could make your life very hard or very easy at Burlington." Several months later when Kim was being considered for promotion, during the promotion interview Ted expressed reservations because Kim was "not loose enough." The comment was followed by his reaching over and rubbing her knee. Kim did receive the promotion, but when Ted called Kim to announce it, he told her "you're going to be out there with men who work in factories, and they certainly like women with pretty butts/legs." During other telephone calls, Ted asked Kim what she was wearing and once said, "Are you wearing shorter skirts yet, Kim, because it would make your job a whole heck of a lot easier." Kim rejected all of Ted's suggestions even though there were veiled threats of job retaliation if she did not comply. No job retaliation occurred. A short time later Kim's immediate supervisor cautioned her about returning telephone calls to customers in a prompt fashion. In response, Kim quit. She did not inform anyone in the company about Ted's comments though Burlington had a sexual harassment policy in place and the company urged the employees to report sexual harassment. Kim brought a sexual harassment lawsuit against Ted and Burlington Industries. The district court dismissed the suit and the court of appeals reversed the decision with no fewer than 8 separate opinions of the 12 judges on the appellate court regarding when an employer is liable for sexual harassment. The various opinions had no consensus or controlling rationale so the U.S. Supreme Court, in order to "bring order to a chaotic field of practice," accepted the case to clarify the law regarding employer liability for sexual harassment.

The Court concluded that unfulfilled threats can constitute sexual harassment and an employee does not have to suffer a tangible employment action before a sexual harassment claim is actionable. Because this case involves unfulfilled threats it should be categorized as a hostile work environment claim and we accept the district court's finding that the conduct was severe and pervasive. In regard to employer liability, the Court in *Faragher/Ellerth* delineated two categories of sexual harassment claims: "(1) those alleging a tangible employment action (official act, e.g., no promotion, a dismissal, reassignment, etc.) for which employers may be held strictly liable and (2) those alleging no tangible employment action, in which case the employers may assert an affirmative defense." The defense comprises two necessary elements: (a) the employer exercised reasonable care to prevent and correct promptly any sexually harassing behavior and (b) the employee unreasonably failed to take advantage of any preventive corrective opportunities provided by the employer. Thus the *Faragher/Ellerth* cases clearly mandate that employers become very proactive in the work environment if they want to lessen their exposure to liability for sexual harassment. A comprehensive anti-harassment policy promulgated to all employees is critical. It is also vital that the policy be effective and that it not be a policy in name only. The employer must continually and effectively monitor the work environment. If an employer does not take these steps to train its employees and attempt to rid the work environment of harassment and adopt a zero tolerance policy toward harassment, the employer will have significant exposure to liability for sexual harassment that takes place in its work place.

PENNSYLVANIA STATE POLICE V. SUDERS (2004)

Suppose an employee is subjected to sexual harassment that is so severe and intolerable that the employee simply resigns to avoid further harassment. Can such an employee file a claim in court under Title VII even if the employee does not formally complain to the employer before resigning? In labor law the concept of *constructive discharge* has existed for many years. Constructive discharge means an employee feels compelled to quit a job because the working conditions have become intolerable. In the following case, the U.S. Supreme Court was called upon to decide if the concept of constructive discharge also applies to sexual harassment cases.

Nancy Drew Suders, the mother of three children, was hired as a police communications operator for the Pennsylvania State Police Department. Almost immediately she was subjected to continual outrageous sexual harassment by several male supervisors. Some of the allegations reported by Nancy were as follows: The police sergeant who was the barracks commander would talk about having sex with animals every time Nancy entered his office. He also suggested that fathers should teach their daughters how to perform oral sex. The sergeant would also sit down near Nancy wearing spandex shorts and spread his legs apart. Another supervisor frequently grabbed his crouch and yelled, "Suck it." This supervisor made this gesture as many as five to ten times each night. When Nancy said she "didn't think he should be doing this," the supervisor responded by jumping on a chair and again grabbing his crouch with the accompanying vulgarity.

Nancy told the police department equal opportunity officer that she might need help but the official did not follow up on the conversation. In addition, Nancy had taken several computer skills exams to comply with her job requirement. Her supervisors repeatedly told her that she failed the exam, but she believed that the supervisors had never forwarded the tests for grading and their reports of her failures were false. Nancy came upon the exams in the women's locker room and regarded the tests as her property so she took them from the locker room. Two months later Nancy again contacted the police equal opportunity officer to complain about the continuing sexual harassment, and she told the official she was afraid in her work environment. The equal employment opportunity officer told Nancy to file a complaint but did not tell Nancy how to obtain the necessary form. Two days later Nancy's supervisors arrested and handcuffed her for the theft of the computer exams. She was taken to an office and given Miranda warnings. Nancy told the supervisors that she was resigning and the handcuffs were removed and the barracks commander let her leave and never filed larceny charges against her. Nancy sued the Pennsylvania State Police and alleged that she had been subjected to severe sexual harassment and constructively discharged in violation of Title VII. Although the district court recognized that a jury could conclude that Nancy had been subjected to a sexually hostile environment, the court dismissed Nancy's complaint and found that the police department was not liable for the supervisor's conduct. The court found that Nancy's claim of a hostile work environment causing her to resign (constructive discharge) was untenable as a matter of law because Nancy did not avail herself of the police department's procedures for reporting harassment. The Court of Appeals for the Third Circuit disagreed with the district court on several aspects, particularly the issue of constructive discharge, and concluded that Nancy had presented evidence that a jury could conclude was sexual harassment and the case should go to trial. The appeals court ruled that a constructive discharge, if proved, constitutes a tangible employment action that renders an employer strictly liable and precludes an employer's recourse to the *Ellerth/Faragher* affirmative defense. The police department appealed to the U.S. Supreme Court.

The U.S. Supreme Court (8-1) decided that an employer may be liable for an employee's constructive discharge. The plaintiff must simply demonstrate that the abusive working environment became so intolerable that resignation qualified as a fitting response.

BURLINGTON NORTHERN & SANTA FE RAILWAY CO. V. WHITE (2006)

A concern of many employees who consider filing sexual harassment claims is the distinct possibility that a supervisor or manager may retaliate in some way against them. Fear of retaliation may operate to induce an employee to quietly accept some level of harassment. Thus, the following case is an important development in Title VII law regarding what constitutes retaliation.

Sheila White was the only woman working in the maintenance department of the Burlington railroad Tennessee yard. Sheila was hired as a "track laborer," a job that involves removing and replacing track components, cutting brush, and clearing litter and cargo spillage. However, shortly after being hired Sheila was assigned to operate a forklift because of her previous experience with this equipment. A few months later Sheila complained to railroad officials that her male supervisor repeatedly told her that women should not be working in the maintenance department and he made insulting and inappropriate remarks to her in front of male colleagues. After investigation of Sheila's complaint, Burlington suspended the supervisor for 10 days and ordered him to attend sexual harassment training.

At the same time Sheila was told of the supervisor's suspension, Sheila was reassigned from forklift duty to standard track laborer tasks. She was told that the reassignment reflected coworker complaints that a "more senior man should have the less arduous and cleaner job of forklift operator." Sheila then filed a complaint with the EEOC alleging that her reassignment amounted to unlawful retaliation because she had complained about sexual harassment. A few days later Sheila and another supervisor disagreed regarding which truck should transport Sheila from one location to another. Sheila was suspended without pay for being insubordinate. Without pay for more than a month, Sheila said, "That was the worst Christmas I had out of my life. No income, no money, and that made all of us feel bad . . . I got very depressed." In fact Sheila had to seek medical treatment for her emotional distress. The railroad's internal grievance procedure cleared her of the insubordination charge and she was awarded 37 days back pay by her employer for the time she was suspended.

Sheila then filed a Title VII claim against the railroad in federal court alleging that her reassignment to track duties and her 37-day suspension amounted to unlawful retaliation because she filed sexual harassment charges against her supervisor. After a trial, a jury agreed with Sheila and awarded her $43,500 compensatory damages and $3,250 in medical expenses. The railroad appealed.

The question that arose from this case was how to interpret Title VII law pertaining to retaliation. Does retaliation occur only when an employee is unlawfully discharged, denied a promotion, or denied compensation? The railroad management took the position that reassignment to a less desirable position was not retaliation and the reassignment was to the duties she was hired to perform. The U.S. Supreme Court decided to hear the case and unanimously disagreed with the railroad's position about what constitutes retaliation. The Supreme Court noted that the purpose of the anti-retaliation provisions of Title VII is to ensure that employees are free from coercion against reporting unlawful practices. The Court said that when an employee reports sexually harassing behavior the employee cannot be immunized from petty slights or minor annoyances that often take place in the workplace. They noted to constitute retaliation "material adversity" is necessary as opposed to a trivial harm. Applying this standard to Sheila White, the U.S. Supreme Court concluded that there was sufficient evidentiary basis to support the jury's verdict that reassignment from forklift duty and the 37-day suspension without pay amounted to unlawful retaliation. The Court said that Sheila and her family had to live 37 days without income. She did not know whether or when she would return to work. A month without a paycheck is a serious hardship. Hence the anti-retaliation provisions of Title VII cover a reasonable employee or applicant who is subjected to materially adverse conduct. The Court noted that the real social impact of workplace behavior depends ". . . on a constellation of surrounding circumstances, expectations, and relationships. . . ."

For example, the Court stated that a change in work schedule for some may not be important but a change in schedule to a young mother with school-age children may matter enormously. A supervisor's refusal to invite an employee to lunch is normally trivial and a petty slight. Yet, the Court clearly stated that a supervisor "excluding an employee from a weekly training lunch that contributes significantly to the employee's professional advancement might well deter a reasonable employee from complaining about discrimination." Therefore, when an employee files a sexual harassment claim, employer actions that are materially adverse to a reasonable employee or applicant can constitute retaliation.

GEBSER V. LAGO VISTA INDEPENDENT SCHOOL DISTRICT (1998)

Sexual harassment has raised its ugly head in schools and the persons engaging in harassing behaviors have been fellow students and in some cases teachers. The next two cases demonstrate that classrooms and school environments must also be monitored to prevent and control sexual harassment.

Alida Star Gebser was an eighth-grade student at the Lago Vista middle school in Texas. She joined a school book-discussion group led by teacher Frank Waldrop. It appears that Waldrop often made sexually suggestive comments to the students. When Alida entered high school and was assigned to classes taught by Waldrop, he began to direct more of his sexually suggestive remarks to Alida. He subsequently initiated sexual contact with Alida and kissed and fondled her. Alida and Waldrop engaged in sexual intercourse on numerous occasions and had sexual intercourse during class time but not on school grounds. Alida did not report this relationship to school officials. More than a year after the relationship began, parents began to complain to the school principal about Waldrop's comments in class. At a meeting between the parents, the principal, and the teacher, Waldrop indicated that he did not believe that he made offensive remarks but apologized to the parents and said it would never happen again. The principal did not report the parents' complaints to the school superintendent. Several months later, the police discovered Waldrop and Alida engaging in sexual intercourse and Waldrop was arrested. The school district terminated Waldrop's employment, and the state of Texas revoked his teaching license. The school district had not promulgated or distributed a grievance procedure for lodging sexual harassment complaints, nor had it issued a formal anti-harassment policy. Alida and her mother filed a lawsuit against the school district for alleging sexual harassment and failure of the school district to protect Alida from Waldrop under Title IX of the Education Act. The school district claimed it could not be liable because it did not know of the conduct of Waldrop. The district court dismissed the case, and Alida and her mother appealed to the U.S. Supreme Court.

The U.S. Supreme Court in a 5-4 decision decided that the school district was not liable for the sexual harassment of the teacher. The majority reasoned that Title IX does not create a private right of action and a school district is not liable "unless an official who at a minimum has authority to address the alleged discrimination and to institute corrective measures has actual knowledge of the discrimination . . . and fails to adequately respond." Unlike Title VII cases, the Court found that school districts cannot be held liable for the acts of their employees pursuant to common law agency principles. In *Gebser*, four justices (Stevens, Souter, Ginsburg, and Breyer) vigorously dissented. The dissenting justices stated that when Congress creates a statute such as Title IX, there is a presumption that "Congress intends to authorize all appropriate remedies," which would include the right of a child and parent to bring a discrimination lawsuit against a school district for the sexual misconduct of its teachers. The dissenters further noted that "as long as school boards can insulate themselves from knowledge about this sort of conduct, they can claim immunity from damages." It is clear that *Gebser* provides no encouragement to school districts to promulgate comprehensive sexual harassment policies and root out discrimination. In fact this decision may result in some school districts further insulating themselves from knowledge of sexual harassment so that they can avoid vicarious liability for their harassing employees.

AURELIA DAVIS V. MONROE COUNTY BOARD OF EDUCATION ET AL. (1999)

In *Gebser*, the harasser was a teacher, but the all too common harasser in schools is a fellow student, and school surveys have demonstrated that many students have experienced sexually harassing actions from other students.

LaShonda Davis was a fifth-grade student in an elementary school operated by the Monroe County Board of Education in Georgia. For several months LaShonda was sexually harassed by another fifth-grade student. The harassing student attempted to touch LaShonda's breasts and genital area and made vulgar statements such as "I want to get in bed with you" and "I want to feel your boobs." The harassing student engaged in this behavior repeatedly and each time Lashonda reported the conduct to the classroom teacher and her mother. The classroom teacher informed Lashonda's mother that the school principal had been informed of the harassing conduct. No disciplinary action was taken against the harassing student and the harassing conduct continued. The harassing student frequently rubbed his body against LaShonda. LaShonda's previously high grades dropped as she became unable to concentrate on her studies. Her parents discovered that LaShonda was so depressed about the harassing conduct that she had written a suicide note. When LaShonda's parents asked the school principal what action the school intended to take against the harassing student, the principal allegedly stated, "I guess I'll have to threaten him a little bit harder." At the time of the harassment, the County Board of Education had not instructed its personnel on how to respond to peer sexual harassment and had not established a policy dealing with the issue. The harassment finally stopped when criminal charges were brought against the harassing student, and he pleaded guilty to sexual battery against LaShonda.

LaShonda's mother Aurelia Davis brought a lawsuit against the school board on behalf of her daughter alleging that the board failed to take corrective action to eliminate the sexually hostile environment confronting Lashonda. The district court dismissed the lawsuit on the ground that student on student sexual harassment provides no ground for a private lawsuit by a parent against a school board. The court of appeals affirmed. The U.S. Supreme Court in a 5-4 decision reversed and held that Title IX does create a private right of action against a school board when there is deliberate indifference to sexual harassment to which the school board has knowledge and the harassment is so severe and pervasive as to deprive the victim of access to educational opportunities and benefits. The Court noted that the school board can only be liable for its misconduct and the parents were not attempting to hold the board liable for the actions of a fifth grader. However, the Court determined that the board may be liable for its "decision to remain idle in the face of known student-on-student harassment in its schools."

Four dissenting justices (Kennedy, Chief Justice Rehnquist, Scalia, and Thomas) were concerned that there would be a significant increase in lawsuits against school districts by simply alleging a decline in school grades and almost "every child at some point has trouble in school because he or she is being teased by his or her peers . . . An overweight child may skip gym classes because other children tease her about her size, a student may refuse to wear glasses to avoid taunts of 'four eyes,' or a child may refuse to go to school because a bully calls him scaredy-cat." In response, the majority argued that the dissent is misreading its decision and that school districts are not facing sweeping liability. Rather, the majority stated that in a school setting "students often engage in insults, banter, teasing, shoving, pushing, and gender specific conduct that is upsetting to students subjected to it." However, the majority noted that damages are not available for simple acts of teasing and name-calling among school children. Liability can occur only where the behavior is so severe, pervasive, and objectively offensive that it denies its victims the equal access to education that Title IX is designed to protect.

CONCLUSION

Sexual harassment law was not intentionally created by Congress. The law had its origins in the Civil Rights Act of 1964, which was designed to address racial discrimination. Opponents of the bill inserted the word *sex* in the bill to help prevent its passage. The bill became law and subsequently Catherine MacKinnon proposed that sexual harassment become an actionable legal claim. The EEOC created such a claim in its regulations and the U.S. Supreme Court since *Meritor* has repeatedly endorsed and developed the legal concepts associated with the law of sexual harassment. Almost every plaintiff (Vinson, Harris, Jones, Faragher, Ellerth, Oncale, Suters, and White) has received favorable rulings by the U.S. Supreme Court. The Supreme Court has been so responsive to plaintiffs in workplace sexual harassment cases that some business interests have complained that "antibias laws are creating a more hostile environment for employers" (*Forbes* 1998:154) and that the Court is "exaggerating the benefits of anti-harassment policies and willfully refusing to acknowledge their costs" (*New Republic* 1998:8). The Supreme Court decisions in *Meritor* and its progeny have been indispensable to the advancement of workplace sexual harassment protection. However, policing employee sexual relationships is a difficult task, and sometimes the line between voluntary and involuntary is not easy to ascertain. No one can expect a workplace that is forever free of envy, jealousy, personal grudges, sexual banter, and horseplay. There is no litmus test that can tell us precisely when innocuous banter becomes sexual harassment. The commonsense social context and the "reasonable person" standard adopted in *Harris* may be well suited for sexual harassment claims because they embrace feminine as well as masculine perspectives.

The issue of sexual harassment is no longer on the back burner. It is a major public policy issue, in part because of the decisions of the U.S. Supreme Court. The courts have provided much guidance regarding the elements of sexual harassment claims. There is no doubt that strong anti-harassment policies can assist in controlling harassment in the workplace and in schools. In addition, there is also truth in the old adage that "money talks" and employers are now concerned about employer liability.

Finally, no matter what substantive or procedural changes are made in the law to benefit victims of discrimination, if sexual harassment is to be significantly reduced or eliminated, gender power balances in our society must be changed, and the values underlying the law of sexual harassment (equal treatment, nondiscrimination, and fair play) must be internalized by all who function in our workplaces.

REFERENCES

CONGRESSIONAL RECORD, February 8, 1964, 2577 [www.jofreeman.com/lawandpoliy/titlevii.htm]

BROWNMILLER, S. *Against our will: Men, women and rape.* NY: Simon and Schuster 1975.

EIGENBERG, H. M. (2001). *Women battering in the United States: Till death do us part.* Prospect Heights, Il: Waveland Press.

FALUDI, S. (1991). *Backlash: The undeclared war against women.* New Haven, CT: Yale University Press.

MACKINNON, C. A. (1979). *Sex Equality: Rape Law.* New York: Foundation Press.

MACKINNON, C. A. (2003). *Sex equality: Sexual harassment.* New York Foundation Press.

MURASKIN, R. (2000). *It's a crime: Women and justice,* 2d ed. Upper Saddle River, NJ: Prentice Hall.

ROBERTS, A. R. (1993). Women: Victims of sexual assault and violence. In *It's a Crime: Women and Justice,* ed. R. Muraskin and T. R. Alleman. Upper Saddle River, N.J.: Prentice Hall.

THOMAS, C. S. (1991). *Sex Discrimination.* St. Paul, MN: West.

CASES

Aurelia Davis v. Monroe County Board of Education et al., 526 U.S. 629 (1999).

Bradwell v. Illinois, 83 U.S. 130 (1872).

Burlington Industries v. Ellerth, 524 U.S. 742 (1998).

Clinton v. Jones, 520 U.S. 682 (1997).

Faragher v. City of Boca Raton, 542 U.S. 775 (1998).

Gebser v. Lago Vista Independent School District, 524 U.S. 274 (1998).

Harris v. Forklift Systems, Inc., 510 U.S. 17 (1993).

Meritor Savings Bank, FSB v. Vinson, 477 U.S. 57, 106 S. Ct. 2399, 91 L.Ed.2d 49 (1986).

Oncale v. Sundowner Offshore Services, Inc., 523 U.S. 75 (1998).

United States v. Morrison, 529 U.S. 598 (2000).

Chapter 36

The Administration of Justice Based on Gender and Race

Etta F. Morgan

THE ADMINISTRATION OF JUSTICE BASED ON GENDER AND RACE

The administration of laws by our criminal justice system has come under scrutiny for various reasons. It has been suggested that the influence of extralegal factors is more important in determining the outcome of a case than the law itself. Gender and race have been identified as perhaps the most consistent extralegal factors that influence criminal justice personnel and juries concerning offensive behaviors. In this chapter, the author reviews the literature that examines the influence of race and gender on decisions within the criminal justice system from initial contact with law enforcement to sentencing in the twenty-first century.

A THEORETICAL BEGINNING

Laws of American society, whether civil or criminal, represent the acceptable boundaries of behaviors established by various social contracts inherent in our society. In the past, American society was represented by stability and long-term relationships, unlike the temporary, unstable relationships of today (Rubin 1996). As a result of this shift in relationships and social changes, there is some disorder. According to Rubin (1996):

> the images of disorder . . . reflect two very different things . . . the disorder that grows out of a society in transition. . . . [or] a society that has institutionalized continual change. (Institutionalization refers to the process of making something permanent, either by law or because people take it for granted. (p. 4)

The creation of laws denoting acceptable boundaries of behavior also establishes and maintains both an economic as well as a social hierarchy within society. Economically, this means that only certain individuals or organizations are able to participate in the exchange relationship for the production and distribution of goods and services (Rubin 1996). In a country like the United States, which perpetuates an Anglo-Saxon, patriarchal society, most meaningful economic opportunities have been blocked for women and minorities. According to strain theorists (Durkheim 1965; Merton 1957; and Messner and Rosenfeld 2001), blocked opportunities, both socially and financially, cause crime and deviant behaviors, thereby placing society in an anomic state. When society is in an anomic state, its social controls are not functional. Therefore, the exchange relationship in society is no longer a legitimate enterprise of goods and services but becomes one with an illegal component because the population's desires and goals are uncontrollable. As a means of regaining control, the criminal justice system uses extralegal factors to control those members of society who have deviated from their respective places in the social and economic hierarchy.

Merton (1957) suggests that a society that places enormous emphasis on material success, although the institutionalized means of achieving this success is not equally obtainable for all members of the population, creates strain within society. Merton (1957) identifies five modes of adaptation in response to the strain in society. Some of these modes, namely innovation, retreatism, and rebellion, have been labeled as deviant behaviors. One could assume that these modes of adaptation have been labeled as deviant behaviors because the individual rejects the institutionalized means of achieving cultural goals. However, we should note that the retreatist and rebellionist modes of adaptation also reject the cultural goals. The goals and means conflict in society directly affects society's ability to maintain social control over its members.

Messner and Rosenfeld (2001) state that individuals are in pursuit of the American Dream. They define the American Dream as "a broad cultural ethos that entails a commitment to the goals of material success to be pursued by everyone in society, under conditions of open competition" (p. 5). Crime has to be examined within the social organization of the United States in order to provide a complete view of how each feature impacts criminal behavior. In their explanation of crime in society, Messner and Rosenfeld (2001) state, "at the cultural level, the dominant ethos of the American Dream stimulates criminal motivation and at the same time promotes a weak normative environment (anomie). At the institutional level, the dominance of the economy in the institutional balance of power fosters weak social control" (pp. 76–77). The ideology of the American Dream only pressures individuals to achieve monetary success, but it does not encourage that legitimate means be used to achieve this success. Thus, the focus remains economic gain, not the means. Members of society are constantly encouraged to pursue the American Dream but the avenues available to achieve this dream are not the same for all members of society.

Some members of society have been hindered from achieving the American Dream because of their race or gender. Specifically, the American Dream is based on a class system and as a result it helps to maintain the class hierarchy by denying members of certain racial and gender groups the opportunity to fully participate in the accumulation of wealth by socially acceptable means. The class hierarchy in the United States devalues blacks and women. However, the structure of the class hierarchy does have an inherent value system that determines the degree of devaluation of certain members of society. The devaluation of persons based on the class system can be characterized as follows: (a) white men are valued more than all other persons, (b) white women are valued more than black women and men, and (c) black women are valued more than black men. This devaluation continues throughout the socialization process of our children and into the workplace.

Previously, girls and boys were socialized differently in preparation for various occupational roles. In terms of educational training, boys were most often encouraged to take math and science courses while girls were directed toward courses more closely related to their prescribed gender roles. As a result, women were most often hired in occupations that earned much less than men (Doyle and Paludi 1991). As society continues to change economically, so does the path that leads to the American Dream from "education, hard work, luck, and motivation" (Rubin 1996:8) to anything goes. Ironically, Merton (1968) suggested that the American Dream creates and destroys American society.

THE PATHWAY TO CIVIL RIGHTS AND AFFIRMATIVE ACTION

American society has always functioned according to the ideology of a preferential system. Privilege and opportunity for success in America has been determined by one's race, class, and gender. Although the passage of the Thirteenth Amendment and the Civil Rights Act of 1866 gave blacks the same rights as whites, it has never really come to fruition. Instead, southern states responded with state legislation, which became known as Black Codes, in an attempt to "keep blacks in their places." Congress then responded by enacting the Fourteenth (providing the foundation for civil rights and affirmative action legislation) and Fifteenth (prohibiting discrimination based on race, not other factors) Amendments in hopes of curtailing the differential treatment of blacks and to ensure that blacks (males) had the right to vote.

Women did not receive voting rights along with black men; instead black and white women together continued to fight for the right to vote for many years. According to Aptheker (1982), the relationship that developed between Cady Stanton, Frederick Douglas, and Susan B. Anthony during the struggle to abolish slavery "was an alliance unable to survive the post Civil War crucible of racism, male supremacy, and class collaboration" (p. 42). When members of the Equal Rights Association supported the passage of the Fifteenth Amendment, Stanton and Anthony resigned from the organization and focused on the National Woman Suffrage Association "with little or no further interest in the cause of Afro-American freedom" (Aptheker 1982:49). Under the leadership of Susan B. Anthony, the National American Woman Suffrage Association embraced a racist and classist position on the importance of gaining the right to vote for white women (Davis 2001). Anthony suggested that the white woman's ability to vote represented a power to be contended with which could have a profound impact politically (Davis 2001). Therefore, she actively campaigned for the right of white women to vote. It was not until the passage of the Nineteenth Amendment that black and white women were given the right to vote. Still, those persons opposed to black women having the right to vote instituted various measures to keep them from exercising that right (Aptheker 1982). It was not until the Voting Rights Act of 1965 that blacks (men and women) began to register and vote in record numbers. Voting was not the only area in which blacks and minorities experienced differential treatment. The lack of an equal and quality education for black children was the basis for legal challenges to the previous educational system.

In 1787 and 1847 black parents filed a petition requesting the desegregation of Boston's public schools. The petition filed in 1787 failed, but the 1847 petition was argued before the Massachusetts Supreme Court in 1849. By 1855, Boston's public schools were desegregated (Aptheker 1982). It should be noted that the Massachusetts decision was the precedent used for the decision in *Brown v. Board of Education* (1954). The Supreme Court of the United States ruled in *Brown* that the segregation of public schools was unconstitutional and in violation of the Fourteenth Amendment, however, many states believed that the *Brown* ruling was another example for federal interference and chose instead to ignore the decision and as a result many school districts came under federal court orders to desegregate or face the penalties. A few years later (1957), the Civil Rights Commission was established as "an independent, bipartisan, fact-finding commission" (Jordan 1985:21) that would investigate any allegations of civil rights violations. Another area in which blacks encountered discrimination was in employment.

According to Fair (1997):

> there were white jobs and black jobs. . . . In those days, merit was not the basis for employment. . . . No matter how well educated or accomplished a black worker was, he or she could not obtain a job explicitly reserved for whites, mostly men. (p. 116)

In the past, jobs were first filled with white males, and, if any positions were left in which a black was permitted to work, then he or she was given the job. Although President Roosevelt issued an executive order requiring the elimination of discrimination based on race, creed, color, or national origin for purposes of employment, future administrations ignored it. It was not until the Kennedy administration that overt discrimination was outlawed in 1964 by Titles II, VI, and VII of the Civil Rights Act. It was also during this administration that women were afforded protection against discrimination and the Equal Employment Opportunity Commission was established.

Another accomplishment of the 1960s was the passage of the Voting Rights Act of 1965, which was enacted to insure that all persons would have the right to vote. "Although the voting protections of the Fifteenth Amendment and Section 2 of the Voting Rights Act are permanent, Section 5 remains in effect through 2007" (U.S. Department of Justice Civil Rights Division Voting Section 2003). Section 5 insures that jurisdictions do not change voting procedures that would allow discriminatory practices based on race, color, or language. All proposed voting procedural changes must receive preclearance from the U.S. Attorney General or the U.S. District Court for the District of Columbia (U.S. Department of Justice Civil Rights Division Voting Section 2003). Also, under the Johnson administration, federal affirmative action law became compulsory. With all the good faith doctrines in place that specifically prohibited acts of discrimination based on race, gender, creed, color, or national origin, in both the public and private sectors in education, employment, housing, and etc., some gains were made in an attempt to replace the inequalities of the past with positive changes in all spheres of society. For example, women and blacks were employed in occupations previously closed to them. They were able to earn higher wages than ever before and be in positions of authority, including high-level management positions (Fair 1997). Educational opportunities that had been unavailable for various reasons were obtainable as a result of affirmative action programs. Also, persons were able to purchase or lease homes in *any* area of a city as a result of affirmative action programs. But programs created to provide equal access and opportunity, such as affirmative action, were challenged in the courts.

In *Regents of the University of California v. Bakke* (1978), the plaintiff claimed that he had been denied admission to Davis Medical School because their special admissions program reserved 16 of 100 seats for various minorities and therefore had created a case of reverse discrimination. The Supreme Court ruled that Bakke should be admitted to Davis and that any programs that specifically establish quotas were unconstitutional. The Court's ruling suggested that race could be considered along with other factors in determining admission, but it should not carry more weight than any other factor. This case opened the door for several other cases involving "reverse discrimination."

Another important case involving affirmative action was *United Steelworkers of America v. Weber* (1979). In this case the company and the employees' union worked together to formulate an acceptable affirmative action plan. An employee who was not selected for the training program that had been instituted as a part of the affirmative action plan felt that he had been discriminated against. However, the Supreme Court ruled that companies and employees' union were permitted to devise an affirmative action plan because "its purposes mirrored those of Title VII . . . [and] the plan was only a temporary measure" (Fair 1997:130).

Without the protections of affirmative action, the Alabama Department of Public Safety would not have promoted any black employees (*United States v. Paradise* 1987) even though they had been so ordered by the courts. The Supreme Court in *Grutter v. Bollinger* (2003) reviewed an affirmative action case against the University of Michigan. At issue was the University's admission policy that awards points based on race for undergraduate admissions and uses race and ethnicity as law school admission factors. The Court ruled, "The Law School's narrowly tailored use of race in admissions decisions to further a compelling interest in obtaining the educational benefits that flow from a diverse student body is not prohibited by the Equal Protection Clause, Title VI, or §1981. Pp. 9–32" (*Grutter v. Bollinger* 2003:306). These are not the only cases that have challenged affirmative action programs, but they do represent some of the issues raised as a result of affirmative action programs.

Affirmative action is an integral part of the progress of blacks and minorities in this country. Without its programs, some opportunities would have never been available to blacks and minorities. According to Fair (1997), "affirmative action was not established as a subsistence program for the poor. . . . affirmative action was an antidiscrimination policy" (p. 158). The attack on affirmative action began with the institution of the

Philadelphia Plan (Fair 1997) and has continued. Affirmative action has not eliminated racial or gender discrimination nor has all of its effects been positive, but the overall impact of affirmative action cannot be dismissed as insignificant. The ideology of inclusiveness, equality, and opportunity encompassed in affirmative action creates a better society for all people and discrimination, regardless to where it occurs, in court, on the job, or at school, indirectly affects all persons in society in a negative way.

THE ADMINISTRATION OF LAW

In a collection of essays on law, crime, and sexuality, Smart (1995) explores two very powerful arguments (1) that law is gendered and (2) the law itself is used as a gendering strategy. A further examination of these arguments will perhaps assist us in understanding the treatment of women in the criminal justice system. The idea that the law is gendered is based upon three specific phases (a) "law is sexist"; (b) "law is male"; and (c) "law is gendered" (Smart 1995:187). What do we really mean when we say that the law is sexist? First, there have always been dual standards for men and women in our society. These standards and laws established by our society have placed men in a more advantageous position while causing women to be disadvantaged in areas such as material resources and opportunities (Smart 1995). Additionally, lawmakers for the most part have chosen to ignore the harm caused to women as a direct result of laws that have been advantageous for men (Smart 1995). For example, most prostitution laws focus on female prostitutes not males, who are the main customers "but courts have been almost as reluctant to find an equal protection violation in statutes that criminalize only female prostitution as they have been in male-only statutory rape laws (Bartlett and Rhode 2006:716)." In most instances, the person who profits from prostitution is male, yet, seldom, is he prosecuted for pimping (Bartlett and Rhode 2006).

Instead, women are considered the problem regardless of the circumstances because they are continually viewed as irrational and incompetent, but the problem is not with women. According to Smart (1995), "[the] law suffers from a problem of perception which can be put right such that all legal subjects are treated equally (p. 188)." It is therefore necessary to change the perception of women from that of mother, sister, and homemaker to whatever roles they so desire, especially since role expectations are so much a part of our thought processes, actions, and reactions. If these roles are no longer gender specific, then perhaps we can start eradicating differential treatment of men and women.

The fact that sexual difference is embedded in our structure and as such influences not only our language, but also the meanings associated with that language suggest that the law itself must be structured to eliminate sexual difference in its meaning. Language is power, if it is the accepted language. For example, this country has fought to remain monolingual instead of embracing a bilingual society. Nowhere is it more evident than in our schools that we do not want a truly bilingual society. Persons who do not identify English as their first language are viewed differently in this society. Soto (1997:1) notes, "the voices of the bilingual parents, community leaders, and bilingual educators . . . rang out loudly but were disregarded and silenced by 'more powerful elements' . . . it was evident that current educational structures . . . have encouraged the disenfranchisement of the less valued and less powerful." We must remember that the same educational structure determines our perceptions and beliefs about the members of our society. That same structure also determines the meaning we associate with our language. It is through language usage that social control is dictated.

Because law is directly related to politics and most of our politicians are men, our laws reflect the beliefs of the male majority when laws are written; therefore, women are judged based on male criteria. In the present state, the laws of this country must be changed to reflect ideals that represent universal values that are gender neutral and truly objective—based on people standards, not male standards. In the past, laws referred to the idea of the "reasonable man" suggesting that only men could be reasonable and thereby excluded women as logical beings. In order to deconstruct law as gendered, Smart (1995:191) suggests "that . . . we begin to analyze law as a process of producing fixed gender identities rather than simply as the application of law to previously gendered subjects." Finally, the argument of law as a gendering strategy suggests that over time, laws have excluded and included women from various positions in society. Smart (1995:195) notes "that nineteenth-century law brought a more tightly defined range of gendered subject positions into place. We can also see how law and discipline 'encouraged' women to assume these identities or subjectivities."

Laws, in any society, define behaviors that are deemed unacceptable based on the morals and values of the community at large. They also determine who will be punished (Price and Sokoloff 1995). In societies that are not very complex, informal rather than formal methods are used as means of social control. Both society and individuals are presumably protected by laws. These laws may prescribe punishments, direct or restrain certain actions, and access financial penalties (Reid 2007). Price and Sokoloff (1995:14) state "the law protects what those in power value most." Laws are created and passed by legislative bodies composed mainly of rich white men and persons who share their interests (Price and Sokoloff 1995). Laws are the mechanism by which the dominate class ensures that its interests will be protected (Quinney 1975). However, challenges to specific laws are not uncommon (Price and Sokoloff 1995).

Historically, women have been considered the property of their fathers or husbands without full acknowledgment of them as individuals with rights granted by the Constitution (Price and Sokoloff 1995). Several cases have come before the Supreme Court concerning the rights of women. In the landmark case of *Reed v. Reed* (1971), the Supreme Court ruled that women were indeed persons and should be treated as such under the U.S. Constitution. The Court stated that the Fourteenth Amendment clause:

> does not deny to States the power to treat different classes of persons in different ways. . . . [it] does, however, deny to States power to legislate that different treatment be accorded to persons placed by a statute into different classes on the basis of criteria wholly unrelated to the objective of that statute. A classification "must be reasonable, not arbitrary, and must rest upon ground of difference having a fair and substantial relation to the object of the legislation." . . . (*Reed v. Reed*, 404 U.S. 75, 76 (1971))

According to the justices, preference based on sex that is used merely to reduce the number of court hearings that could arise because two or more persons are equally entitled is in direct violation of the Fourteenth Amendment clause forbidding arbitrariness, nor can sex be used as a preventive measure against intrafamily controversies (*Reed v. Reed*, 1971). Based on this ruling, the Court recognized women as individuals with the right to individualized treatment, but it did not identify sex in relation to the suspect-classification argument under the Fourteenth Amendment.

It was not until *Frontiero v. Richardson*[1] (1973) that the Court ruled that sex was a suspect-classification which "must be subjected to strict judicial scrutiny" (677). This case involved differential treatment of men and women in the military in regard to their respective spouses being classified as dependents. The ruling by the Court also stated that the current statute was in violation of the Due Process Clause of the Fifth Amendment. Justice Powell suggested that the Court should not rule on sex as a suspect-classification because the Equal Rights Amendment (ERA) had been approved by Congress and it would eliminate the need for such a classification (*Frontiero v. Richardson*, 1973). Unfortunately, the states did not ratify the ERA. It is difficult to imagine the extent to which sex discrimination would have evolved if indeed *Frontiero* became law.

Women were still seeking equal rights during the Ford and Carter administrations. Regardless the Court had ruled in *Craig v. Boren* (429 US 190, 197 (1976)), that "classification by gender must serve important governmental objectives and must be substantially related to achievement of those objectives." The Craig case did not have a true impact on constitutional law; instead, it most notably suggested that there were changes in alliances among the justices. These cases represent only small legal gains by women.

According to Hoff (1994):

> some of the most disturbing gender-biased decisions the Supreme Court has reached in the last seventeen years have involved pregnancy cases. . . . other recent decisions are either discouraging or disquieting for the cause of complete female equality, especially where redistributive economic issues are at stake. (p. 251)

Knowing that many households are now headed by women has not moved Congress or the Supreme Court to properly address the comparable worth issue. Instead, they avoid the comparable worth issue as though it was a plague. Women must decide "whether they prefer equal treatment as unequal individuals (when judged by male standards) or special treatment as a protected (and thus implicitly) inferior group" (Hoff 1994:274). The legal system has not always treated women and girls fairly, and this could be due in part to the perceptions men (who are the majority in the legal system) have of females (Price and Sokoloff 1995). A prime example is the difficulty associated with the passage of the Anti-Violence/Domestic Violence Act presented to Congress during the 2000 session. The bill

---

[1]Though sex was ruled to be a suspect classification, the decision was made by a plurality vote of the Justices (4-4) meaning that the decision *was not* to become law. Each case from then on has been decided on its own merits.

almost did not pass because of several insignificant items that were attached to the bill that had nothing to do with stopping violence against women. It is unfortunate that in the twenty-first century, women are still being treated as less than equal. This unequal treatment extends from civil law to criminal law. Roberts (1994:1) states, "the criminal law most directly mandates socially acceptable behavior. Criminal law also helps to shape the way in which we perceive women's proper role." Women who do not adhere to prescribed gender roles and commit criminal offenses are viewed differently by our criminal justice system. This issue will be discussed more fully in the following section on female criminality.

FEMALE CRIMINALITY

Female criminals are not as prevalent as male criminals and previously have not been considered a social problem (Belknap 2007). Women are also likely to commit fewer and less serious violent crimes than men (Belknap 2007; Mann 1984a; Pollock 2002; Simon and Landis 2005). Yet, we have been led to believe that female crime has reached outlandish proportions and far exceeds male crime. The basis for this information has been the Uniform Crime Reports (UCR) complied by the Federal Bureau Investigation from data supplied by law enforcement agencies.

According to Steffensmeier (1995), these data (UCR) are problematic in assessing female crime patterns. Steffensmeier (1995) suggests the following: (a) the changes in arrest rates may be related more to "public attitudes and police practices . . . than actual behaviors, (b) because of the broadness of categories they include "dissimilar events and . . . a range of seriousness," and (c) the definition of serious crime as used by the UCR tends to lead one to believe that serious female crime has risen dramatically, when in fact, women have been arrested more for the crime of larceny, "especially for shoplifting" than any other Type I offense (consisting of the more serious offenses committed) (p. 92). Previous research (Mann 1984a; Naffine 1987; Simon and Landis 2005; Steffensmeier 1980) has revealed that overall female crime rates have remained fairly stable in most areas. The notable changes are in the areas of "less serious property offenses and possibly drugs" (Belknap 2007:84).

In order to better assess the rate of female crime, Steffensmeier (1995) completed a 30-year study of arrest statistics. Although the study examined trends in individual offenses, of particular importance here is the trend by type of crime based on male/female arrests. The types of crimes chosen to develop trends for male/female arrests were "violent, masculine, index ("serious"), and minor property" (Steffensmeier 1995:94). He found that female participation in masculine crimes increased slightly, which led to more arrests, but this was not the case for violent crimes. Steffensmeier (1995) again attributes the increase in arrests for index crimes as a result of an increase in the number of women committing larcenies. Women have also had an increase in arrest rates for minor property crimes (Belknap 2007; Steffensmeier 1995). Simpson (1991) suggests that violent behavior varies among females and it is difficult to separate the individual influence of race, class, and gender because they are so intermingled.

EXTRA LEGAL FACTORS

Gender

Having examined briefly female criminality, we now turn our attention to the processing of female criminal cases by the criminal justice system. It has been suggested
(Chesney-Lind 1982; Farnworth and Teske 1995; Frazier, Bock, and Henretta 1983;
Harvey et al. 1992; Spohn and Spears 1997; Steffensmeier 1980) that women receive
differential treatment during the processing of criminal cases. The differential treatment may be negative or positive. For example, Steffensmeier (1980) suggested that
the likelihood of future offending and the perceived danger to the community influenced the preferential treatment of women in the criminal justice process and as a
result increased their chances of receiving probation instead of prison. Yet, Chesney-
Lind (1982) discovered that female juveniles have always received negative differential treatment. She noted that the females were processed into the juvenile justice
system as a result of status offenses and received institutionalization more often than
male juveniles.

Frazier, Bock, and Henretta (1983) examined the effect of probation officers in
determining gender differences in sentencing severity. In their study, they collected data
from presentence investigation reports with various information concerning the offender
as well as recommendations from the probation officers regarding sentences. According
to Frazier, Bock, and Henretta (1983), "there is a strong relationship between gender of
offender and final criminal court disposition. . . . probation officers' recommendations
have major effects and . . . being female greatly increases the likelihood of receiving a
non-incarceration sentence recommendation "(pp. 315–316). Harvey et al. (1992) in an
international comparison of gender differences in criminal justice found that women
were processed out of the criminal justice system more often than men. Their study also
revealed that men who were processed through the criminal justice system were convicted and imprisoned at a higher rate than women worldwide. Harvey, et al. (1992:217)
note "that criminal justice worldwide operates differentially by gender (but not necessarily in a discriminatory way)."

In another study, Farnworth and Teske (1995) found some evidence of gender disparity in relation to charge reductions if there was no prior criminal history. The absence
of prior offending was noted to increase the possibility of probation for females. Based
on the selective chivalry thesis, Farnworth and Teske (1995:40) discovered "that white
females were twice as likely as minority females to have assault charges changed to non-
assault at sentencing." There was also supportive evidence which suggested that the use
of discretionary powers influenced informal rather than formal decisions (Farnworth and
Teske 1995).

More recently, Spohn and Spears' (1997) study of the dispositions of violent felonies
for both men and women revealed that more men (71.4 percent) than women (65.0 percent) were prosecuted, but their conviction rates were very similar and major differences
appeared in sentencing. For example, males were incarcerated 77.4 percent of the time
versus 48.2 percent for females. Overall females normally served "428 fewer days in

prison" than males (p. 42). This study also found that charge reduction or total dismissal of charges was more likely for females than males. Spohn and Spears (1997) state:

> Females were more likely than males to have injured their victims. . . . Female defendants were much less likely than male defendants to have a prior felony conviction. Females were charged with and convicted of less serious crimes and were less likely . . . to be charged with or convicted of more than one offense . . . less likely than males to have used a gun to commit the crime or to have victimized a stranger. . . . females were more likely to have private attorneys and to be released prior to trial. (p. 42)

Based on their findings, Spohn and Spears (1997) suggest that violent female offenders are looked upon differently by judges for various reasons such as (1) females may be perceived as less dangerous to the community; (2) females may have acted as an accomplice instead of being the primary perpetrator; (3) the risk of recidivism is lower for females; and (4) there is better chance of rehabilitating female offenders. Spohn and Spears (1997) also found an interaction between race and gender that will be discussed in the next section.

Race

In many instances we are led to believe that any race other than minorities is pure, but Headley (2006) noted that centuries of interbreeding have eliminated most "pure" races. He further stated that:

> human genes occur in every imaginable combination. . . . [and] many people fit into more than one racial category or none at all. . . . Our highly race-conscious society attributes greater meaning and significance to skin color than the objective realities could possibly justify. (Headley 2006:23–24)

Race is a topic that many people feel uncomfortable discussing, but it touches every segment of society in numerous ways. Perhaps, we tend not to discuss race because if we do we are forced to acknowledge that American society is flawed and these flaws include "historic inequalities and longstanding cultural stereotypes" (West 1994:6). The racial injustices encountered by minority groups indirectly affect society as a whole.

Higginbotham (1998) noted that the American system of injustice has been constructed and reconstructed since the founding of America. Perhaps one of the most important facts about minorities still has not been fully realized, that is minorities have human rights. According to Higginbotham (1998), several factors have contributed to the injustices experienced by blacks. For example, during slavery "many legal decisions" (p. 253) were influenced by "the economics of slavery" (p. 253). Slave masters were to have total control over the slaves and "total submission" was expected of blacks. Another factor in the development of the American legal process was "whether or not blacks were inherently inferior to whites" (Higginbotham 1998:255). These and other factors have resulted in adverse legislation, adjudication, and racial deprivation of minorities in this country (Higginbotham 1998). "The legal process has never been devoid of values, preferences, or policy positions. . . . The legal process has always acted as an expression of social control" (Higginbotham 1998:257).

The main objective of legislation and criminal court processing is controlling blacks and minorities. The race card becomes very evident in the processing of criminal cases. Some researchers (Mann 1989, 1995; Spohn and Spears 1997) have found a relationship between race and gender. Mann (1989, 1995) studied the treatment of minorities from arrest to incarceration and found that arrest rates for black women exceed other ethnic groups, which could be due in part to law enforcement biases based on racial stereotyping. In other instances, black women received higher bails, were not adequately represented in court, received longer sentences, and served more time in prison. According to Mann (1989:95) "minority women offenders [are] doubly discriminated against because of their gender and race/ethnicity status." Spohn and Spears (1997) also noted that incarceration rates were influenced by the gender of the defendant. Specifically, they found that:

> Even after taking other legal predictors of sentence severity into account, the incarceration rate for black males is 17.9 percentage points higher than the rate for white females, 14 percentage points higher than the rate for black females, and 5.6 percentage points higher than the rate for white males. (Spohn and Spears 1997:50–51)

The disparities in sentencing are also evident as they relate to the death penalty.

Foley (1987) discovered that in capital cases "there was a highly significant relationship between the race of the offender and the race of the victim. . . . with persons adjudicated guilty of an offense against a white victim more likely to be convicted of a serious offense than persons adjudicated guilty of murder of a black victim" (pp. 460–461). Foley's findings of capital sentencing in the post-*Gregg* decision are the same as Bowers and Pierce (1980), Paternoster (1983), and Radalet (1981). Based on their research, Aguirre and Baker (1991) concluded that "blacks have been subjected to systematic racial discrimination throughout most of the United States and throughout the entire history of the imposition of capital punishment in this country" (p. 40).

The imposition of the death penalty is not just racially biased, but it is also gender biased. Currently (as of March 31, 2007), there are 3,350 males including 1 juvenile and 59 females serving time under the sentence of death. Since capital punishment was reinstated in 1976, there have been 1,057 executions (NAACP Legal Defense and Educational Fund, Inc. 2007). Of these executions, there have been 11 women. Oklahoma and Texas lead the nation in the execution of women with three each, while Florida has executed two. Alabama, Arkansas, and North Carolina each have executed one woman (Streib 2007). For some, this may come as a surprise, but, historically, it is not. During the period 1632–2002, there were 566 confirmed executions of women and, according to Streib (2003), "female executions constitute about 2.8 percent (566/20,000) of all American executions." Recent data suggest that women (as a gender) received slightly more than 2 percent of the total death sentences imposed in the past 33 years (Streib 2007). However, being sentenced to death does not always mean an execution is forthcoming. The reversal rate of women sentenced to death is approximately 98 percent (Streib 1990). Previously, society was willing to sentence women to death, but society was not willing to execute them; in recent years, there has been an increase in female executions, and this trend may continue (Streib 2003).

THE FUTURE

We are currently in a regressive phase of affirmative action. The gains in educational and employment opportunities experienced by blacks and minorities will soon be overshadowed by a consistent reduction in growth in these areas. Attitudes and behaviors that were controlled because of affirmative action will no longer be suppressed because there will no longer be consequences for exhibiting those attitudes and behaviors. Pipes and Lynch (1996:30) asserted that there may be a "lowering [of] legal standards against sex-based discrimination." Although this issue was raised in response to California Civil Rights Initiative's Bona Fide Qualifications clause, it should be a national concern because states tend to pass the same or similar legislation. Based on the attitudes of the current political forces in control of Congress, the recent elimination of affirmative action, and the overall racial climate in this country, the discriminatory practices in the administration of justice will only increase.

One might wonder how the elimination of affirmative action will impact the administration of justice for women. The elimination of affirmative action will send a strong message to women indicating that their place is in the home not in the workplace. The paternalistic forces of our society have begun reducing opportunities for women in the workplace since there are no longer any safeguards to insure that equally qualified women be given the same consideration as men. In the future, fewer women will be entering the workplace in professions previously considered male professions. Instead, those men in positions of power will revert back to the traditional standards of networking with only the "old boys" who have some type of direct connection to the company, a relative, or a friend. Women who have achieved some power will find their authority being undermined or challenged by the male associates in the company who are in positions of power or are being groomed for advancement, while they will remain stagnant until they either retire or are forced to leave because of unbearable conditions. The camaraderie between men will continue to increase since important "information, resources and support" are gained from these interactions while women are excluded (Shukla and Tripathi 1994:1280). Lyness and Thompson (1997) suggest that women have not risen above the glass ceiling but have instead discovered a second and higher ceiling, which would imply that with the elimination of affirmative action, the workplace atmosphere will become one of intolerance and discrimination.

The elimination of affirmative action will eventually impact sexual harassment legislation. In time, the paternalistic forces will suggest that women who desire to work in a male-dominated profession expect to be treated "like one of the boys," which means there is no need to watch one's language or gestures. In other words, all behaviors are acceptable to the "boys." Most of the paternalistic males will consider women who remain in occupations more closely related to their prescribed gender roles as conforming to the norm and as women who are trying to help their mates rather than being too independent. In these occupations there will not be a lack of respect for women, again because these women are conforming. The woman who is viewed as independent, intelligent, and aggressive will continue to be considered a threat to some men, especially those who believe in stereotypical gender roles.

The impact of affirmative action will also be noted in race relations in this country. America has already regressed in terms of race relations. Instead of becoming closer as one nation, we have again become a nation divided by color. Since blacks have never really assimilated into American society, it was not difficult to dissimulate from mainstream society. Blacks have been the only group of people to come to this country and not be truly accepted as members of this country, but instead as a people here on a temporary journey. American society not yet brought closure to the racial incidents of the 1960s, and already the problems of the 1990s are on the rise. Incidents of the 1990s such as police brutality, the hanging of a black youth in Virginia, the burning of black churches, the destructive painting and burning of homes owned by blacks in predominately white neighborhoods, racial slurs directed at interracial couples and their children, and the list goes on, are all indicators that we have not progressed to the point where we are able to live in harmony as a diverse population. Instead, many persons of various ethnic backgrounds live in a constant state of fear. The land of opportunity is sometimes the land of a daily nightmare. Yet there are those who say we do not need affirmative action. Affirmative action was in some instances the only mechanism to introduce persons of different ethnic backgrounds to each other. As a result, persons were able to move beyond the stereotypes they once held about a particular group of people. Interaction helps people understand each other. The criminal justice system will not be immune from the impact of race relations in this country.

Race again will become more prevalent in the administration of justice. The current regressive state of the criminal justice system represents a shift from the rehabilitative model of treating offenders to one of increased incarceration due in part to society's low level of tolerance for any type of offender. Those persons most affected during increased periods of protecting society from the criminal elements are blacks, the poor, and the legally underrepresented. These persons are usually more visible to law enforcement and are, therefore, more likely to be arrested and processed into the criminal justice system.

Although there are mandatory sentences and supposedly safeguards to insure that the laws are applied in a nondiscriminatory fashion, we will see an increase in the arrest, conviction, and incarceration rate of blacks and other minorities because prosecutors will revert to scare tactics to encourage cooperation and admission of guilt. The uneducated and underrepresented black or minority offender will once again be railroaded to prison. The administration of justice will also affect women. Women who come before the criminal justice system will be treated more harshly because they will be considered disreputable and lacking morals and values. They will be viewed as women who have ventured away from their prescribed gender roles and are therefore in need of guidance. Of course, this guidance can only be achieved by incarceration and as a result we will have an increase in the incarceration rate of women, regardless of the offense.

Prison overcrowding will reach enormous proportions because of this new attitude toward blacks and minorities along with the lack of tolerance on the part of those in power to devise alternative methods to deal with minor offender problems. The overall mentality will be to eliminate those who they deem to be offensive. For a period of time those in power will try to break the spirits of the oppressed groups in an attempt to regain total control of all persons in society.

We must remember that affirmative action was only a temporary "fix" for a problem that has existed since the beginning of this country (Citrin 1996). Unfortunately, some members of the citizenry were misinformed and led to believe that affirmative action was a permanent solution to this age-old problem. Affirmative action was only the beginning of the termination of rights and equality in this country. We will find during each session of Congress some right previously granted will be legislated away unless we as a society begin to voice our concerns. Rights we take for granted are only rights until new legislation is introduced to remove them. Although it may take several years for us to realize the full true impact of this legislation, we are already beginning to see the ripple effects. The educational system, the brain center of any society, has already been affected. For example, new guidelines for admission in some universities and colleges will eliminate specific groups from educational opportunities beyond high school. There are those who are asking for unitary status so they may resegregate their school districts and not be required by the courts to provide an equal and quality education to all members of a metropolis. Without education, we create a population of illiterates who will become society's problem, supported by taxpayers in some form of social service or in the criminal justice system. Those in power who desire to control the members of society are better able to do so with an illiterate populous. We are slowly moving toward becoming a mechanical society as identified by Durkheim in his text *The Division of Labor in Society* (1964).

CONCLUSION

Study after study continues to find evidence that our criminal justice system is plagued with discriminatory practices. In the past, we were led to believe that the removal of discretionary powers by legislators for particular offenses would solve the problems associated with discriminatory practices, but it has not. In order to solve any specific problem, we must first make changes in the program as a whole. The problems of the criminal justice system are merely extensions of society's problems. As a society, we must be willing to examine and correct "the way racism has influenced the law" (Washington 1994:22) as well as gender if we are to establish a fair and efficient system of justice from arrest to incarceration. In the words of Cornell West (1994):

> In these downbeat times, we need as much hope and courage as we do vision and analysis; we must accent the best of each other even as we point out the vicious effects of our racial divide and the pernicious consequences of our maldistribution of wealth and power. (p. 159)

REFERENCES

AGUIRRE, JR., A., and D. BAKER (1991). *Race, Racism, and the Death Penalty in the United States*. Berren Springs, MI: Vande Vere.

AGUIRRE, A., and D. V. BAKER (1993). Racial prejudice and the death penalty: A research note. *Social Justice* 20: 150–155.

APTHEKER, B. (1982). *Woman's Legacy: Essays on Race, Sex, and Class in American History*. Amherst: The University of Massachusetts Press.

BARTLETT, K., and D. RHODE (2006). *Gender and Law: Theory, Doctrine, Commentary*. Boston: Little, Brown & Company.

BELKNAP, J. (2007). *The Invisible Woman: Gender, Crime and Justice*, 3rd ed. Belmont, CA: Wadsworth.

BOWERS, W., and G. PIERCE (1980). The pervasiveness of arbitrariness and discrimination under Post-Furman capital statutes. *Crime and Delinquency* 26 (4): 563–635.

CHESNEY-LIND, M. (1982). Guilty by reason of sex: Young women and the juvenile justice system. In *The Criminal Justice System and Women, ed.* B. Price and N. Sokoloff, pp. 77–105. New York: Clark Boardman.

CITRIN, J. (1996). Affirmative action in the people's court. *The Public Interest* 22: 39–48.

DALY, K. (1996). *Gender, Crime and Punishment.* New Haven: Yale University Press.

DAVIS, A. (2001). *Women, Race & Class.* New York: The Women's Press, LTD.

DOYLE, J., and M. PALUDI (1991). *Sex and Gender: The Human Experience.* Dubuque, IA: Wm C. Brown.

DURKHEIM, E. (1964). The *Division of Labor in Society.* New York: The Free Press.

DURKHEIM, E. (1965). The *Rules of the Sociological Method.* New York: Free Press.

FAIR, B. (1997). *Notes of a Racial Caste Baby: Color Blindness and the End of Affirmative Action.* New York: New York University Press.

FARNWORTH, M., and R. TESKE, JR. (1995). Gender differences in felony court processing: Three hypotheses of disparity. *Women and Criminal Justice* 6(2): 23–44.

FOLEY, L. (1987). Florida after the Furman decision: The effect of extralegal factors on the processing of capital offense cases. *Behavioral Sciences & the Law* 5(4): 457–465.

FRAZIER, C., E. BOCK, and J. HENRETTA (1983). The role of probation officers in determining gender differences in sentencing severity. *The Sociological Quarterly* 24: 305–318.

HARVEY, L., R. BURNHAM, K., KENDALL, and K. PEASE (1992). Gender differences in criminal justice: An international comparison. *British Journal of Criminology* 32(2): 208–217.

HEADLEY, J. (2006). *Race, Ethnicity, Gender and Class: The Sociology of Group Conflict and Change*, 4th ed. Thousand Oaks, CA: Pine Forge.

HEIDENSOHN, F. (1996). *Women & Crime*, 2nd ed. Washington Squares, NY: New York University Press.

HIGGINBOTHAM, JR., A. (1998). Race and the American legal process. In *Race, Class & Gender: An Integrated Study*, P. Rothenberg, pp. 250–258. NY: St. Martin's Press, Inc.

HOFF, J. (1994). *Law, Gender & Injustice: A Legal History of U.S. Women.* New York: New York University Press.

JORDAN, B. (1985). Still two nations-One black, one white? *Human Rights 13*(1): 21.

LYNESS, K. and D. THOMPSON (1997). Above the glass ceiling? A comparison of matched samples of female and male executives. *Journal of Applied Psychology 82*(3): 359–375.

MANN, C. (1984a). *Female Crime and Delinquency.* Tuscaloosa, AL: University of Alabama Press.

MANN, C. (1989). Minority and female: A criminal justice double bind. *Social Justice 16*(4): 95–114.

MANN, C. (1995). Women of color and the criminal justice system. In *The Criminal Justice System and Women: Offenders, Victims, and Workers, ed.* B. Price and N. Sokoloff, 2nd ed., pp. 118–135. New York: Clark Boardman.

MERLO, A., and J. POLLOCK (2006). *Women, Law, & Social Control,* 2nd *ed.* Boston: Allyn and Bacon.

MERTON, R. (1957). *Social Theory and Social Structure.* Glencoe, IL: Free Press.

MERTON, R. (1968). *Social Theory and Social Structure.* New York: Free Press.

MESSNER, S., and R. ROSENFELD (2001). *Crime and the American Dream*, 3rd ed. Belmont, CA: Wadsworth.

NAFFINE, N. (1987). Female Crime: The Construction of Women in Criminology. Sydney, Australia: Allen & Unwin.

PATERNOSTER, R. (1983). Race of victim and location of crime: The decision to seek the death penalty in South Carolina. *The Journal of Criminal Law & Criminology 74*(3): 754–785.

PIPES, S., and M. LYNCH (1996). Smart women, foolish quotas. *Policy Review 78*:30–32.

POLLOCK, J. (2002). Women, *Prison & Crime*, 2nd ed. Belmont, CA: Brooks/Cole.

PRICE, B., and N. SOKOLOFF (1995). The criminal law and women. In *The Criminal Justice System and Women: Offenders, Victims, and Workers, ed.* B. Price and N. Sokoloff, pp. 11–29. New York: McGraw- Hill.

QUINNEY, R. (1975). *Class, State and Crime: On the Theory and Practice of Criminal Justice.* New York: Longman.

RADALET, M. (1981). Racial characteristics and the imposition of the death penalty. *American Sociological Review 46*(6): 918–927.

REID, S. (2007). *Criminal Law*, 7th ed. New York: Oxford University Press.

ROBERTS, D. (1994). The meaning of gender equality in criminal law. *The Journal of Criminal Law & Criminology 85*(1): 1–14.

RUBIN, B. (1996). *Shifts in the Social Contract: Understanding Change in American Society.* Thousand Oaks, CA: Pine Forge.

SHUKLA, A., and A. TRIPATHI (1994). Influence of gender and hierarchical position on interpersonal relations at work. *Psychological Reports 74*(3): 1280–1282.

SIMON, R. (1993). *Rabbis, Lawyers, Immigrants, Thieves: Exploring Women's Roles.* Westport, CT: Praeger.

SIMPSON, S. (1991). Caste, class, and violent crime: Exploring differences in female offending. *Criminology 29*(1): 115–135.

SMART, C. (1995). *Law, Crime and Sexuality: Essays in Feminism.* London: Sage.

SOTO, L. (1997). *Language, Culture, and Power: Bilingual Families and the Struggle for Quality Education.* Albany, NY: State University of New York.

SPOHN, C., and J. SPEARS (1997). Gender and case processing decisions: A comparison of case outcomes for male and female defendants charged with violent felonies. *Women & Criminal Justice 8*(3): 29–59.

STEFFENSMEIER, D. (1980). Assessing the impact of the women's movement on sex-based differences in the handling of adult criminal defendants. *Crime and Delinquency 26*: 344–357.

STEFFENSMEIER, D. (1995). Trends in female crime: It's still a man's world. In *The Criminal Justice System and Women: Offenders, Victims, and Workers, ed.* B. Price and N. Sokoloff, pp. 89–104. New York: McGraw- Hill.

STREIB, V. (1988). American *Executions of Female Offenders: A Preliminary Inventory of Names, Dates, and Other Information*, 3rd ed. Cleveland: Author.

STREIB, V. (1990). Death penalty for female offenders. *University of Cincinnati Law review 58*(3): 845–880.

STREIB, V. (2003). Death penalty for female offenders January 1, 1973 through June 30, 2003 Cleveland: Author. [Retrieved August 8, 2007, from www.deathpenaltyinfo.org/FemDeat Dec2007

STREIB, V. (2007). Death penalty for female offenders January 1, 1973 through March 31, 2007 Cleveland: Author. [Retrieved April 9, 2007, from www.deathpenaltyinfo.org/ FemDeathMar2007.pdf]

U.S. DEPARTMENT OF JUSTICE CIVIL RIGHTS DIVISION VOTING SECTION (2003). About Section 5 of the Voting Rights Act. [Retrieved May 3, 2003, from www.usdoj.gov/crt/voting/sec_5/about.htm]

WASHINGTON, L. (1994). *Black Judges on Justice: Perspectives from the Bench.* New York: The New Press.

WEST, C. (1994). *Race Matters*. NY: Vintage Books.

CASES

Brown v. Board of Education, 347 U.S. 483 (1954).

Craig v. Boren, 429 US 190, 197 (1976).

Frontiero v. Richardson, 411 U.S. 677 (1973).

Gregg v. Georgia, 428 U.S. 153 (1976).

Grutter v. Bollinger, 539 U.S. 306 (2003).

Reed v. Reed, 404 U.S. 71, 92 S.Ct. 251, 30 L. Ed. 2nd, 255 (1971).

Regents of the University of California v. Allan Bakke, 438 U.S. 265 (1978).

United States v. Paradise, 480 U.S. 149 (1987).

United Steelworkers of America v. Weber, 443 U.S. 193 (1979).

Chapter 37

Transgender Prisoners and Gender Identity Discrimination

Janice Joseph

The low social status of prisoners implies that they experience discrimination within the prison system. However, this discrimination is amplified by a prisoner's race, sexual orientation, or gender identity. The limited information on transgender prisoners indicates that they are disproportionately disadvantaged in the prison system. They are objectified, dehumanized, and rendered invisible in prison because of the discriminatory practices and rules used against them. This chapter examines various forms of discrimination that transgender prisoners experience behind prison walls because of their gender identity as transgender people. One type of discrimination relates to access to appropriate housing placement resulting in the marginalization of many transgender prisoners. Another major problem is the indifference of correctional officers toward the victimization of transgender prisoners. Finally, a major issue relates to access to health care and treatment, with many transgender prisoners being denied treatment and adequate medical care.

WHAT IS TRANSGENDERISM?

Transgender is an umbrella term that describes those who live outside of normative sex and gender relations. These are people who identify with a specific gender identity that society believes is not congruent with their external genitalia. This term was first coined by Dr. Virginia Prince, who used the term to refer to biological men who were satisfied with their male genitalia, but who wanted to be seen and to live as women. A transgender person usually experiences a conflict between his or her physical sex and his or her gender identity as a man or a woman. They have an innate sense of gender conflicts with their anatomical sex, and sometimes undergo surgery to eliminate this conflict—as well as those who may plan no surgery or other treatments, but feel that their biological sex does not reflect their true self. It is assumed that they are suffering from "gender dysphoria" or "gender identity disorder," a condition in which a person has been assigned one gender but identifies as belonging to another gender (Currah and Shannon 2000).

There are different groups of transgender people within the transgender community. One group consists of transsexuals who prefer to change their bodies to match their emotional and psychological identity and are either "postoperative" or "preoperative" transsexuals. Postoperative transsexuals are those who have undergone sex reassignment surgery, while preoperative transsexuals are those people who are moving toward the genital surgery by undergoing hormonal treatment and cosmetic surgery. Transgender people "in transformation" include men and women who have undergone hormonal treatments and/or cosmetic surgery to modify their bodies but do not plan to undergo sex reassignment surgery. Inter-sexed people are those who share the physical characteristics of both sexes. Often their genitalia appear to be that of the opposite sex, while they internally have the reproductive organs of their actual sex. Untreated transgender people do not undergo genital surgery or any other medical procedure to further their gender transformation. This group includes transvestites, crossdressers, drag queens, and drag kings, who regularly or irregularly present themselves as another gender (Currah and Shannon 2000; Green and Brinkin 1994; Lombardi et al. 1998).

GENDER IDENTITY AND DISCRIMINATION

Gender Identity

Gender identity refers to a person's internal and deeply felt sense of being either male or female. It is a form of self-identification as a person of a particular gender. A person may identify himself or herself as a member of a particular gender by his or her style of dress, medical intervention, or by other means, including a change of name. Medical intervention may include hormone therapy, counseling, and sex reassignment surgery (Currah and Minter 2000).

Discrimination

Discrimination is the act of treating someone unfairly because of a personal characteristic. Discrimination against a transgender person because of gender identity involves the discriminator treating the transgender person less favorably than other people in the same circumstances or in circumstances that are not materially different. A transgender person is discriminated against when another person requires the transgender person to comply with a requirement or condition that is considered to have a disadvantageous effect on him or her. Discrimination against transgender people is based on transphobia, which refers to various kinds of aversions toward transgenderism or transgender people.

Discrimination against transgender people includes harassment, which is an act that offends, insults, humiliates, or intimidates a transgender person. It also includes assault, murder, or failure by others to acknowledge that he or she wishes to be known as a member of a specific gender and has made this preference clear. It also includes refusal to provide access to goods and services such as employment, housing, education, or health care on the basis that a person's dress or appearance suggests he or she is a transgender person. Indirect discrimination is manifested in the refusal to take steps to ensure that transgender people are treated in the same way as nontransgender people.

Rights of Transgender People

While few states have laws against discrimination based on sexual orientation—only 17 states and the District of Columbia recognize sexual orientation as a protected class, and even fewer protect the rights of people whose gender identity is not the same as their biological identity. Currently, California, Minnesota, Rhode Island, and New Mexico are the only states that explicitly include the term gender identity in their antidiscrimination laws. Many states have modeled their disability laws after the Americans with Disabilities Act (ADA), so in those states, the transgender community is also exempt from coverage. Several states, such as California, Colorado, Connecticut, Iowa, Illinois, Maine, Minnesota, Oregon, Rhode Island, Vermont, Washington, and the District of Columbia, have policies prohibiting both sexual orientation and gender identity discrimination in employment. Some state courts, commissions, or agencies have interpreted the existing state law to include some protection against transgender individuals in Connecticut, Florida, Hawaii, Massachusetts, New Jersey, and New York (Romesburg 2005).

About 70 U.S. cities have enacted city ordinances that protect transgender people, while other jurisdictions have added gender identity to their local nondiscrimination ordinances. Those include Chicago and Cook County, Illinois; Pittsburgh, Philadelphia and Allentown, Pennsylvania; Dallas, Texas; Denver, Colorado; Ypsilanti, Michigan; Baltimore, Maryland; and Portland, Oregon. In 2001, San Francisco became the first U.S. city to grant its employees health coverage for medical needs related to being transgender (Minnesota Department of Human Rights Online Newsletter 2006).

Federal law currently provides only limited protection to transgender people. Although Title VII of the Civil Rights Act of 1964 prohibits sex discrimination in the workplace, most federal courts have held that Congress did not intend this to include gender identity or sexual orientation. In addition, no federal coverage is provided by the ADA. When enacting the ADA, Congress specifically exempted the transgender community from coverage (Minnesota Department of Human Rights Online Newsletter 2006). In 2005, the U.S. House of Representatives passed to the Senate a transgender-inclusive federal hate crimes law, Employment Non-Discrimination Act (ENDA), that prohibits discrimination against employees on the basis of sexual orientation or gender identity. The bill provides employment protections similar to those of the Civil Rights Act of 1964, but is specifically directed to gay, lesbian, bisexual, and transgender employees (Romesburg 2005).

Despite these protections, transgender people face several problems. They are often underemployed or unemployed, especially since they may lose their jobs during or after their gender transitions. Access to restroom facilities in the workplace can also be a problem as well as their attire. They often lose their jobs over issues unrelated to their job performance. Discrimination in housing and places of public accommodation is also a large problem for transgender people. They can be evicted while transitioning, or landlords are often reluctant to rent apartments to a transgender person. The results can lead to homelessness, and the additional problem of discrimination in sex-segregated homeless shelters (Moulton and Seaton 2005).

Transgender people also face discrimination in obtaining health care. Most transgender people, especially transsexuals, undergo hormone therapy and/or sex-reassignment surgery but due to discrimination, both in health insurance and in access to basic care, it is difficult for many transgender people to get appropriate treatment. They are often excluded from health insurance policies because coverage is usually explicitly excluded for treatment related to transsexualism, even though the claim would be paid if the exact same treatment or procedure were utilized for some other medical reason. For example, insurance policies will pay for testosterone therapy if a nontransgender man has a low level of the hormone, but a transsexual man who uses the same hormone as part of his medically supervised gender transition will not be covered. Transgender people also face hate violence and the crimes against them are often under-investigated and under-prosecuted by local, state, and federal law enforcement officials (Moulton and Seaton 2005).

EXTENT AND NATURE OF INCARCERATION OF TRANSGENDER PEOPLE

Because housing and employment discrimination leave many transgender people with few income-generating options, some turn to sex work or other criminalized activities. Transgender people may also be the target of harassment and selective prosecution by law enforcement. As a result, the transgender community tends to be overrepresented in the criminal justice system (Moulton and Seaton 2005). They therefore face higher rates of incarceration than the general population, often for nonviolent theft, drug offenses, and sex work.

Information on the number of transgender persons incarcerated in the United States is scarce. There are few statistics on the number of transsexuals in the United States, let alone the number that are incarcerated. The reasons for the scarcity are that many transsexuals are self-defined, without medical or psychiatric diagnoses, and there are different types of transsexuals as described earlier.

It is estimated that in California, there are probably 200 transgender inmates throughout the state penal system—and at least another thousand people who are gender variant, which includes particularly masculine women or effeminate men (Woodward 2006). A San Francisco Department of Public Health survey conducted in 1997 found that almost two-thirds of male to female respondents had been incarcerated. More than 30 percent had spent some time behind bars during the preceding 12 months (Woodward 2006). In fact, transgender and gender-variant people, as a population, are incarcerated at even higher rates than African-American men. Dr. Lori Kohler, founder of California's only health clinic for transgender prisoners located at the California Medical Facility (CMF) in Vacaville, has been working with transgender prisoners in California since 1994. When the clinic was established in 1999, it was estimated that Kohler would be serving a total population of 10 to 15 patients. Six years later, she had served 3,000 unduplicated patients, and there are about 60 transgender prisoners at CMF at any given time (Alpert 2005).

The majority of transgender prisoners are likely to be male to female (MTF) rather than female to male (FTM) (Woodward 2006). There are several major reasons for this pattern: the criminalization of prostitution and drug addiction related to sex work, and the stereotyping of all transgender women as sex workers. Since transgender women often have difficulties finding and keeping employment, in order to survive they often turn to sex work, drug dealing, or other illegal forms of money-making activities (survival crimes), which greatly increase their risk of arrest. In addition, since police tend to stereotype female transgender persons as sex workers, they are also at risk for police arrest even if they are not sex workers. Moreover, the use of illegal drugs by these women brings them to the attention of law enforcement officers. Therefore, the combination of sex work and drug use inevitably leads to the incarceration of a disproportionate number of transgender women (Alpert 2005).

Because of employment discrimination, arrests, sentencing practices, and low-socioeconomic status, transgender women of color are the majority of transgender prisoners. The dominant health issue among transgender prisoners is HIV/AIDS. According to Dr. Lori Kohler, between 60 and 80 percent (of transfeminine prisoners) at any given time are HIV-infected. Many may also be infected with Hepatitis C (Alpert 2005). The majority of transgender prisoners are transsexuals.

GENDER IDENTITY DISCRIMINATION IN PRISON

A transgender prisoner is often more marginalized than one living in free society. He or she faces double marginalization of being a transgender person and a prisoner. Once imprisoned, transgender people face various forms of discrimination, including inappropriate housing placement, higher rates of assault and sexual assault, and limited access to health services. Policies and procedures vary significantly by state, county, federal, and military prisons.

Housing Placement

One of the biggest problems transgender people face upon incarceration is the segregation of prison facilities by gender. It is left to individual prison officials to decide with which sex a transgender inmate should be housed. A primary concern that prison administrations must take into account when determining housing placement is whether a transgender prisoner has undergone sex reassignment surgery prior to incarceration.

There are two bases for housing placement of transgender inmates in prison: genitalia-based placement and gender identity-based placement. Genitalia-based placement is the process by which transgender prisoners are classified according to their birth sex, regardless of how long they may have lived as a member of the other gender, and regardless of how much medical treatment they may have undergone. Prison administrations using the genitalia-based placement consider only the anatomical sex of the transgender individual even if the inmate identifies himself or herself with the opposite gender (Mann 2006). The argument in favor of genitalia-based placement is that as long as the inmate possesses internal and external sex organs corresponding with a specific sex, especially in the case of preoperative transsexuals, then he or she will be housed in accordance with that sex (Joslin 2006).

Using identity-based placement, prison administration places transgender inmates in facilities based on their gender identity. This practice considers the psychological as well as the physical aspect of transgenderism, does not force individuals to lose their sense of identity, and it promotes gender equality. Although identity-based placement is perhaps the ideal, the common practice in most of the prison systems in the United States is to house prisoners based on their birth sex (Mann 2006). Consequently, prison authorities generally place transgender prisoners, regardless of the extent of their nongenital transformation, in housing units based on their genitalia. An inmate with a penis is considered male; one with a vagina is considered female. Postoperative transgender people have had their genitalia surgically modified to resemble those of their desired gender, so the practice of relying solely on genitalia for placement does not generally pose a problem for them. However, preoperative male to female transgender prisoners are at a significant risk for physical injury, sexual harassment, sexual battery, rape, and death because they are usually placed within a highly aggressive segment of the population (male inmates) (Mann 2006; Peek 2004). This type of classification, therefore, places not only the transgender inmate at substantial risk of harm but also the prison administration at risk of civil liability.

One mechanism that is sometimes used by prison officials to protect transgender women who are at risk of violence due to being housed in male prisons is to separate them from other prisoners. This is referred to as "administrative segregation," or "protective custody" during which the transgender inmate is segregated, generally in a single cell in 24-hour-a-day custody in security housing units (SHUs) designed for the prison's most violent and dangerous inmates (Alpert 2005).

Another option prison authorities use to "protect" transgender inmates has been to create special wards, "transgender-only wards," or "segregated pods" for vulnerable inmates. These have been modeled on the gay wards in California and Hawaii. In these prison systems, prisoners who request such housing and prisoners deemed to require the protection are placed in the gay ward (Israel 2002). These approaches to housing placement of transgender prisoners have led to accommodation that is either unsafe or overly isolating for transgender prisoners.

Issue of Punitive Punishment

A major discriminatory issue with this housing placement is the use of segregation. The purpose of segregation is to monitor closely a prisoner who is a threat to the security of the institution, other inmates, himself, or the prison staff. By using this classification for transgender prisoners, the message is that a person's gender identity itself is threatening to the institution and that a transgender person must be separated from other prisoners.

Segregation is designed to be used for only short periods of time, and should not be used for long periods of confinement. Segregated transgender prisoners, however, often serve their entire sentence in segregation. This means that the segregated transgender prisoner will be subjected to less than equal treatment within the prison system and will be exposed to a far more restrictive daily regime than other nonviolent prisoners (Edney 2004). Segregation, therefore, basically limits a transgender prisoner's constitutional rights and may make such confinement more punitive, resulting in a disproportionate sentence.

When transgender prisoners are placed in segregation they have only minimal interaction with other prisoners. As a result, transgender prisoners who are segregated in SHUs usually do not have access to rehabilitative programs available to inmates within the general population. Moreover placing transgender inmates in "administrative segregation" does not always guarantee safety and may have dehumanizing and negative psychological consequences (Edney 2004). Furthermore, administrative segregation and special wards do not protect transgender prisoners from abuse at the hands of guards and may even lead to increased exposure to violence (Alpert 2005). Segregation, therefore, is clearly punitive and a form of discrimination. In fact, prisons could be liable under the Eighth and Fourteenth Amendments if prisoners are subjected to indefinite administrative and protective segregation on the basis of their transgender status. The housing classification used in many prisons, therefore, certainly plays a role in the discrimination of transgender prisoners because it often imposes tremendous restrictions on transgender prisoners under the guise of safety.

VICTIMIZATION OF TRANSGENDER PRISONERS

The misassignment of transgender prisoners to inappropriate housing units can result in victimization of transgender inmates. Transgender prisoners often find themselves forced into the victim role in prison. They also face sexual assault, harassment, and abuse above and beyond that of the traditional male and female prison population.

Sexual Violence and Sexual Coercion

When housed with male prisoners, male to female transgender prisoners often become the targets of frequent sexual assault or rape. The sexual violence can be perpetrated by a lone fellow prisoner; a group of fellow prisoners; deputies, guards, or officers; or an inmate assisted by a deputy, guard, or officer. When the victims report their victimization to the officers, they are often called liars or are accused of enticing the perpetrator. To make matters worse, when sexual assault is reported, the victim and the perpetrator may get the same treatment; both can be placed in Administrative Segregation (Ad Seg). Consequently, these victims remain silent for fear of being revictimized by the administration (Woodward 2006).

Transgender women are also subjected to coercive sex in the prison system. The coercion often comes from fellow prisoners, deputies, guards, and officers. It is often exchanged for protection or special privileges and is too often viewed by officials as consensual (Peek 2004).

Harassment, Humiliating, and Demeaning Behaviors

One of the most common issues for transgender prisoners seems to be simple harassment; they are most commonly subjected to verbal harassment. The harassment can include ridicule, objectification, overt sexual propositions, and aggressive flirting. They are also subjected to taunts and catcalls. One of the most consistent complaints from transgender prisoners is that they are referred to by pronouns associated with their birth-identified gender instead of pronouns that respect their gender identity. These prisoners are also referred to as "that" or "it" or "whatever he is." Male to female transgender prisoners are sometimes referred to as "he" or "faggot," despite their feminine bodies. Some guards routinely demean and ridicule these prisoners over the PA system. In general, prison officials and other prisoners regard these trans- and gender-variant prisoners as deviant (Alpert 2005). These practices serve no legitimate administrative or security purpose and can rob a transgender prisoner, especially a woman, of any sense of security (Woodward 2006).

Transgender inmates are sometimes subjected to unnecessary strip searches and forced nudity by deputies, guards, officers, or medical personnel. These searches are not always related to visits or contraband. Instead, they seem to come randomly and occasionally involve two or more people doing the search (Alpert 2005; Daley 2005).

Issue of Deliberate Indifference

While in prison, transgender prisoners are to be protected by prison officials from violence at the hands of other prisoners. Prison officials who display a "deliberate indifference" to this duty violate the Eighth Amendment prohibition of cruel and unusual punishment. The U.S. Supreme Court adopted a narrow definition of "deliberate indifference" in the case *Farmer v. Brennan* (1994) that involved a male-to-female transsexual who was badly beaten and raped by her male cellmate in a maximum security prison. In this case, the Court argued that a prison official violates an inmate's Eighth Amendment right only when the official is subjectively aware of the risk of harm toward an inmate and purposefully ignores that risk—thus establishing a high burden of proof for the abused inmate. In other words, a prison official could be liable for violence inflicted on a prisoner only when the risks are obvious enough that the official "should have known" the prisoner was in danger. According to the Court in *Farmer v. Brennan*, correctional staff must have actual knowledge of the risk and fail to take reasonable measures to protect the inmate from harm. Furthermore, under the ruling, officials can use four main defenses to indicate that they are not liable for the victimization of transgender prisoners. First, prison officials could claim that they had no knowledge of the facts underlying the risk of harm, or that they knew of the facts but believed the risk was insignificant. Second, they may assert that they responded reasonably to the risk, even if the harm was not averted. Third, they may claim qualified immunity; however, the Ninth Circuit has stated that under *Farmer*, the shield that immunity provides is limited to those officials who are either unaware of the risk or who take reasonable measures to counter it. Furthermore, immunity is not available when the guards themselves are responsible for the abuse. Fourth, in the case of injunctive relief, prison officials may argue that the claim is moot, because at some point during the litigation, they took remedial steps to halt the abuse.

The requirement that the plaintiff must prove to the Court that the officials had knowledge of a substantial risk to his or her safety places a great burden on transgender victims in prison. Consequently, the Court ruling in *Farmer v. Brennan* has made it difficult for transgender prison victims to prove "deliberate indifference" as is illustrated in the following case:

> In Texas, Keith Roderick Johnson alleged that he was forced into sexual slavery by a prison gang and that corrections officers ignored his requests for protective housing. Prisoners who saw Johnson forced into sexual acts testified that they heard his screams for help while being raped and saw staff look the other way. Two witnesses, who were former members of the Gangster Disciples, testified that Johnson was owned by their gang and was considered its property. If Johnson resisted the gang's control he would be severely beaten or killed, they said. One prisoner testified that gang leaders told him to prostitute Johnson for money or commissary. He rented Johnson out for $3–$7 a sex act. Another witness told the jury he overheard the prison's Assistant Warden tell Johnson, who had approached officials in the hall for help, "Get your gay snitching ass out of my face before I put you in close custody where you will really get fucked." This witness also testified that a ranking officer standing with the Warden then said to Johnson, "That's what you get for being gay." There was, however, no physical evidence of rape, because Johnson did not seek medical care for the assaults. As a result, a Texas jury found the prison officials not liable. (Hatcher-Peralta 2006:para 7–10)

Johnson went through numerous official channels to persuade prison officials to grant him protection but it was not until the American Civil Liberties Union became involved that Johnson was moved to another prison and the assaults stopped (Hatcher-Peralta 2006). It is clear that discrimination on the part of correctional officials ranges from simply looking the other way to actively participating in attacks on transgender prisoners. Consequently, transgender prisoners who are victimized may not get justice in the court because they may not be able to prove "deliberate indifference" on the part of the officials.

LACK OF ADEQUATE CARE

Another significant problem faced by transsexual prisoners involves access to medical treatment. A serious concern for transgender prisoners is their physical and mental health care. For transgender offenders who were undergoing hormonal therapy or sex reassignment at the time of arrest, the continuation of hormone treatment is important to their physical health. However, access to hormonal therapy or sex reassignment surgery can be temporarily or permanently suspended while incarcerated.

Hormone Therapy

Hormone therapy (HT), also called hormone replacement therapy (HRT), for transgender people involves taking estrogen and testosterone. Hormones are produced by the endocrine system, which is made up of glands that release chemical hormones into the bloodstream. Among other functions, hormones control sex characteristics, like breast development, facial hair, and reproductive systems. Both men and women produce these hormones, but biologically, women produce more estrogen while men produce more testosterone.

Hormone therapy is a "medically necessary" treatment for transgender people. In most jurisdictions, however, the law does not require prisons to provide hormones to transgender prisoners. Since prisons are not required to begin hormone therapy if a prisoner shows symptoms of gender identity disorder while incarcerated, most prisons do not provide hormones, and some go to great lengths to avoid providing any treatment to transgender prisoners. A few states do allow inmates to continue hormone treatments if they are already on hormones when they begin their sentences. However, state prisons and federal prisons provide hormones for transgender prisoners only at the same level they received before incarceration (Joslin 2006).

Even if the prison does provide hormones, some transgender prisoners have difficulty documenting their use of hormones prior to incarceration so they are unable to receive hormones while incarcerated. Because of the many health care hurdles facing transgender people, it is often difficult for many transgender inmates to document that they had a regular, (or any) approved health care provider who provided them with hormone therapy before incarceration. This is because many transsexual persons cannot afford legitimate treatment for their gender identity disorder while in the community and are often forced to seek dangerous black market hormones and even surgical procedures. Consequently, their inability to secure legitimate treatment outside of prison affects their ability to produce the documentation needed to secure treatment while incarcerated (Israel 2001). More importantly, however, there is no guarantee that these prisoners will be provided with the appropriate levels of hormones. Furthermore, many prisons also do not provide hormones to seropositive HIV-infected transgender prisoners because of the potential aggravation of HIV-related conditions, so HIV-infected transgender prisoners will be denied hormones in most states.

Sex Reassignment Surgery

Sex reassignment surgery is the final phase of gender transformation. No prison system currently allows inmates to undergo sexual reassignment surgery and courts have consistently held that prisons are not required to perform surgery on transgender prisoners to further the transformation process. Opponents to sex reassignment surgery for transgender prisoners argue that sex reassignment surgery is too expensive for prisons to provide such treatment (Mann 2006).

The consequences of denial of proper treatment can be devastating for transgender prisoners. Transgender prisoners, who do not receive adequate hormones or no hormones at all while incarceration, often experience several physical and psychological effects. They may experience periods of vomiting, depression, and suicidal tendencies. The lack of hormones can also reverse many of the feminine/masculine characteristics that the transgender prisoner had attained during the years of gender transformation. Other possible effects include, but are not limited to, the return of facial hair growth and male pattern baldness, the recession of surface fat, and a markedly changed gender appearance. Some inmates who are refused the sex reassignment surgery may resort to self-castration (Rosenblum 2000).

Unequal Treatment

The issue of whether a transsexual person is entitled to hormone therapy while in prison has been litigated extensively. The litigations have been based on the constitutional principle that it is a violation of the Eighth Amendment prohibition on cruel and unusual punishment for prison officials to deny "serious medical needs." Until the last several years, in almost every case, courts have ruled in favor of prison officials. More recently, however, transgender prisoners have had more success. For example, in *De'Lonta v. Angelone* (2003), the Fourth Circuit held that a transsexual prisoner had presented facts sufficient to establish that treatment is necessary and that the denial of treatment which caused her to mutilate herself constituted deliberate indifference to her medical needs. The court also held that the prison's refusal to provide her with hormone treatment was based solely on a policy rather than on a medical judgment concerning the prisoner's specific circumstances. In *Kosilek v. Maloney* (2002), a federal district court held that the plaintiff's gender identity disorder constituted a serious medical need and directed prison officials to provide adequate treatment. Similarly, in *Wolfe v. Horn* (2001), the court ruled that abrupt termination of prescribed hormonal treatment by a prison official with no understanding of the plaintiff's condition, and failure to treat her severe withdrawal symptoms or after-effects, could constitute a violation of the transgender constitutional rights. However, not all recent litigation has been successful. In 2003, for example, the Kansas Legislature's Special Committee on Claims Against the State ruled against Christopher Sorrels, who argued that the Department of Corrections has shown deliberate indifference to his serious medical needs by refusing to provide hormone therapy (Hanna 2003).

Transgender inmates in several states have sued prison officials for denying them sex reassignment surgery but to date none of them has succeeded in persuading a judge to order a sex-change operation. These inmates argue that treatment for their condition is a "medical necessity" and denying it would violate the Eighth Amendment's prohibition against cruel and unusual punishment. In Colorado, for example, inmate Christopher "Kitty" Grey, who is serving 16 years to life for molesting an 8-year-old girl, sued the state to provide him with a gender specialist he hopes will determine that he needs a sex-change operation. Colorado officials say that providing a sex-change operation for Grey or any of the other two dozen transgender inmates in the state's prisons would create security concerns (Associated Press 2006).

Since 1993, Michelle Kosilek, who was convicted of murder, has been fighting with prison officials in Massachusetts to complete her transformation into a woman. In 2002, she successfully petitioned the court to allow hormone treatment to facilitate female sex characteristics. She recently requested the state Department of Correction to pay for a sex-change operation. After two lawsuits and two trials, the decision now rests with a federal court judge (Burke 2006). There has been no ruling as yet on the case[1] although there have been hundreds of hours of testimony from witnesses, including 10 medical specialists who were paid tens of thousands of dollars. The judge himself even hired an expert to help him make sense of it all. It is estimated that the Correction Department and its outside health care provider have spent more than $52,000 on experts to testify about an operation that would cost about $20,000. This case is being watched closely across the country by advocates for other inmates who want to undergo a sex change. The Massachusetts Correction Department is vigorously fighting Kosilek's request for surgery, saying it would create a security nightmare and make Kosilek a target for sexual assault. Advocates, however, argue that in some cases—such as that of Kosilek, who has twice attempted suicide—sex-change surgery is as much a medical necessity as treatment (CNN 2007).

Over the objections of the Department of Corrections, the Wisconsin legislature passed the *Inmate Sex Change Prevention Act*, (2005) that prevents prison doctors from deciding the best course of treatment for transgender people by denying them access to any type of hormone therapy or sex reassignment surgery while in state custody. This law was introduced after Wisconsin inmate Scott Konitzer filed a lawsuit seeking a sex-change operation. Legislators supporting the law claimed that it was necessary to reduce expenses (ACLU 2006). Five inmates have sued after this law was passed, and the case is expected to go to trial in October, 2007 (CNN 2007). Wisconsin is perhaps the only state in the country to have enacted a law denying transgender people access to medical care while in state custody.

Unlike the prisons in the United States, Canadian prisons do provide sex reassignment surgery for transgender prisoners. In 2003, the Federal Court of Canada upheld a Canadian Human Rights Commission ruling in the case of Synthia Kavanagh, who requested sex reassignment surgery while serving a life sentence for a 1989 second-degree murder conviction. The Human Rights Commission said that it was discriminatory for prisons to have a blanket ban on sex-change operations. On appeal, the Federal Court of Canada agreed with the Human Rights Commission stating that since sex reassignment surgery is an essential service for a particular inmate, it should be paid for by Correctional Services Canada, as would any other essential medical service. The judge also stated that providing sexual reassignment surgery should be no different for Canadian prisoners, especially since sex-change surgery is covered by health care in most provinces when a patient has been diagnosed with gender identity dysphoria. The court also agreed with the Human Rights tribunal that candidates for sex changes would need

---

[1]What is accepted is that prison officials must provide adequate treatment as recommended by a Doctor experienced in treating gender identity disorders.

medical assessment from one of five medical specialists. The Canadian Correctional Service has also been ordered to house transgender prisoners in the facility of their new gender after the surgery has taken place (Tibbetts 2003).

The documentary *Cruel and Unusual Punishment* (2006, 66 minutes) examined the experiences of five transgender females in male prisons across the United States. It is a vivid portrayal of the lives of these transgender women in men's prisons and highlights the issues discussed in this chapter. The women were Yolanda, a 21-year youth, who was incarcerated in New Jersey; Ophelia, who was 46 years old at the time of the documentary and in a correctional facility in Virginia, having been sentenced to 67 years for bank robbery with an unloaded gun; Anna, who was serving time in a Florida prison; Ashley, who was imprisoned in Arkansas; and Linda, who was imprisoned in Wyoming.

These five transgender women lived as women on the outside but were nevertheless placed in male prisons where they endured humiliation, degradation, and violence. They candidly described how they were strip searched, ridiculed, and raped by multiple inmates while incarcerated. During their time in prison, Ophelia mutilated her genitals because she was denied hormones; Anna was refused treatment and placed in solitary confinement which caused her to attempt suicide; and Linda castrated herself after she was refused sex reassignment surgery. In all cases, they received very little sympathy from prison staff.

The documentary is riveting and compelling and it presents the voices of a silent minority by providing a glimpse into how women in general are treated in the prison system. It also raises thought-provoking questions about wanton violence against these women, the denial of medical care such as hormone therapy and surgery, and the constitutional rights of prisoners.

RECOMMENDATIONS

It is quite evident that there is a great deal of discrimination against transgender prisoners. They are marginalized in the prison system and are treated differently from the nontransgender prisoners. The following are some recommendations that prisons can implement to avoid violating the rights of transgender prisoners.

- In order to ensure their safety, transgender prisoners should be held in accommodation appropriate to their preferred gender identity. In some cases the best interests of the prisoner may be better served by segregation from nontransgender inmates. However, segregation in prisons should avoid further marginalizing transgender people or rendering them at further risk of torture or ill-treatment.

- Because prisons have a great deal of autonomy on how to deal with individual transgender cases, there have been gross inequalities in the treatment of transgender prisoners. There should, therefore, be protocols on the treatment of transgender prisoners that focus on housing, searches, name usage, medical treatment, and access to nonmedical services. These protocols will help prison officials prevent discrimination against transgender inmates by following procedures that are both respectful of the needs of transgender prisoners and more "transgender-friendly."

- The prison medical staff should be trained on the evaluation and counseling process used to determine whether hormones are appropriate therapy for transgender prisoners. Daley (2005) suggested that prison health care professionals and staff receive a minimum of eight hours of transgender cultural competency and health care training.

- It is clear from the available information on transgender prisoners that there is little or no understanding of transsexualism among staff. Deputies, correctional officers, and all correctional personnel should, therefore, be trained in understanding the transgender culture, its diversity, and medical issues that face transgender people. The training should also provide information on how to protect transgender prisoners from abuse, how to address them respectfully, and how to conduct strip searches that are not dehumanizing. It is important to have prison officials who are well informed about transgenderism.

- There should be an outside agency designated to mediate disputes between transgender prisoners and prison officials if these disputes cannot be resolved within the prison walls.

- There needs to be a code of practice or rigorously applied guidelines that are both consistent and available across the prison system, and freely given to every prisoner who self-diagnoses.

In general, these recommendations, if followed, will provide a framework for a better relationship between transgender prisoners and prison officials. Implementation of these recommendations will provide improved, progressive, and appropriate prison conditions for transgender inmates. At the same time, improved conditions for transgender prisoners would decrease the number of litigations filed against institutions.

CONCLUSION

A few years ago, the issue of transgender persons in prison was nonexistence. However, over the years, the number of transgender people incarcerated in the prisons in the United States has increased tremendously. The limited data indicate that they disproportionately come in conflict with the law, therefore the number of transgender prisoners is likely to continue to increase. Prisons, therefore, will have to be more inclusive if they want to avoid civil litigations filed against them by transgender prisoners. The challenge for states, therefore, is to make major reforms to their prison systems so they are more accommodating to the diverse prison population, including transgender prisoners, that fall under their jurisdiction. Prison officials need to recognize the difficulties that transgender prisoners face when they enter the prison system and should establish formal policies to address the needs of this special group of prisoners.

REFERENCES

ACLU (2006). Prisoners can keep receiving sex hormones. [Retrieved June 1, 2007, from http://stoptheaclu.com/archives/2006/02/03/prisoners-can-keep-receiving-sex-hormones/]

ASSOCIATED PRESS (2006, August 25). Inmates push prisons to pay for sex-change surgery. [Retrieved April 15, 2007, from http://www.sptimes.com/2006/08/25/Worldandnation/Inmates_push_prisons_.shtml]

ALPERT, E. (2006, November 21). Best of identify 2005. IN THE FRAY Magazine. [Retrieved June 10, 2007, from http://www.inthefray.com/html/article.php?sid=138]

BURKE, M. K. (2006, Sept. 15). Murderer wants state-funded sex change. [Retrieved May 23, 2007, from http://abcnews.go.com/US/Legal Center/story?id=2440310&page=1]

CNN (2007, June 26). Convicted killer's bid for sex change draws big costs. [Retrieved June 30, 2007, from http://www.cnn.com/2007/LAW/06/26/sex.change.inmate.ap/index.html]

CURRAH, P., and S. MINTER (2000, June 19). *Transgender Equality: A Handbook for Activists and Policymakers.* Washington, DC: The Policy Institute of the National Gay & Lesbian Task Force.

DALEY, C. (2005, August 15). *Advocating for our communities.* [Retrieved June 25, 2007, from www.transgenderlawcenter.org/pdf/prisonrape.pdf]

EDNEY, R. (2004). To keep me safe from harm? transgender prisoners and the experience of imprisonment. *Deakin Law Review:* 17. [Retrieved February 19, 2008, from http://www.austlii.edu.au/au/journals/DeakinLRev/2004/17.html]

GREEN, J., and L. BRINKIN (1994). *Investigation into Discrimination Against Transgendered People.* San Francisco, CA: Human Rights Commission.

HANNA, J. (2003, December 18). Transsexual inmate seeks $500,000 from state. *Associated Press.* [Retrieved June 12, 2007, from http://www.cjonline.com/stories/121703/bre_inmate.shtml]

HATCHER-PERALTA, A. (2006, January 25). Rikers Island seeks to balance liberty and safety concerns for gay inmates. *American Constitution Society for Law and Policy.* [Retrieved June 22, 2007, from http://www.acsblog.org/equal-protection-and-due-process-rikers-island-seeks-to-balance-liberty-and-safety-concerns-for-gay-inmates.html]

ISRAEL, G. (2002, Spring). Transsexual Inmate Treatment Issues. *Transgender Tapestry* (97). [Retrieved May 15, 2007, from http://www.firelily.com/gender/gianna/inmates.html]

JOSLIN, C. (2006). Fact Sheet: Rights of Transgender Prisoners. National Center for Lesbian Rights. [Retrieved April 20, 2007, from http://www.nclrights.org/publications/tgprisoners.htm#1#]

LOMBARDI, E., L. EMILIA, R. A. WILCHINS, D. PRIESING, and D. MALOUF (2001). Gender violence: Transgender experiences with violence and discrimination. *Journal of Homosexuality* 42: 89–101.

MANN, R. (2006). The treatment of transgender prisoners, not just an American problem—A comparative analysis of American, Australian, and Canadian prison policies concerning the treatment of transgender prisoners and a "Universal" recommendation to improve treatment. *Law & Sexuality: A Review of Lesbian, Gay, Bisexual, and Transgender Legal Issues* 15 (91): 1–34. [Retrieved June 11, 2007, from http://www.wcl.american.edu/nic/documents/10.TransgenderPrisoners.pdf?rd=1]

MINNESOTA DEPARTMENT OF HUMAN RIGHTS ONLINE NEWSLETTER (2006). When gender and gender identity are not the same. [Retrieved June 1, 2007, from http://www.humanrights.state.mn.us/rsonline12/genderidentity.html]

MOULTON, B., and L. SEATON (2005). *Transgender Americans: A Handbook for Understanding Human Rights Campaign.* Washington, DC: Human Rights Foundation.

PEEK, C. (2004). Breaking out of the prison hierarchy: transgender prisoners, rape, and the Eighth Amendment. *Santa Clara Law Review*

44: 1211. [Retrieved June 23, 2007, from http://www.spr.org/pdf/Breaking%20out%20of%20the%20Prison%20Hierarchy.pdf]

ROMESBURG, D. (2005). Transgender rights. *Advocate* 951: 1-6.

ROSENBLUM, R. (2000) "Trapped" in Sing Sing: Transgendered prisoners caught in the gender binarism, *Michigan Journal of Gender & Law* 6 (499): 510–511.

THE EMPLOYMENT NON-DISCRIMINATION ACT (ENDA), *H.R. 2015*

TIBBETTS, J. (2003, February 7). CSC loses appeal in transsexual Human Rights Case. [Retrieved May 13, 2007, from http://www.prisonjustice.ca/starkravenarticles/trans_CHRC_article_0706.html]

WOODWARD, T. (2006, March 21). Life in hell: In California prisons, an unconventional gender identity can be like an added sentence. *San Francisco Bay Guardian.* [Retrieved February 19, 2008, http://womenandprison.org/violence/woodward.html]

DVD DOCUMENTARY

Cruel & Unusual Punishment
Directors Janet Baus, Dan Hunt and Reid Williams

Produced By Reid Productions LLC Running Time 66min/High-Definition Video

CASES

De'Lonta v. Angelone, 330 F.3d 630 (4th Cir. 2003).
Farmer v. Brennan (92-7247), 511 U.S. 825 (1994).

Kosilek v Maloney 221 F. Supp. Ed 156
Wolfe v. Horn, 130 F. Supp. 2d 648 (D. PA. 2001).

PART IX

Conclusion

Summing Up

The Twenty-First Century to Date

Roslyn Muraskin

Despite the rhetoric of our officials, much needs to be done in this century regarding our justice system. Over time we have attempted to put technological changes in place without necessarily considering the rights of individuals. We also need to understand the impact that these changes will have on our system. If we lack a comprehensive understanding of current practices and operations in criminal justice, any attempt to instill changes will be unsuccessful. With change comes understanding and investment in the use of the latest resources.

Today we live in a more complicated world than ever before. We face threats of violence never foreseen or believed. We have discovered that personal and political self-interests do not promote remediation or collaboration. As we remain aware of the possibility of further terrorist attacks on our nation, we need to keep abreast of those individuals who enjoy committing crimes against our people and our property.

To predict the future is to gaze into a crystal ball and say this is what we will be and where we are. Such a prediction is almost impossible. We can plan, and plan we must and plan we are, but we must always stand prepared and be prepared. As we have witnessed so far in this very short period of time in the twenty-first century, individual events can have an overwhelming effect on all our lives and personal freedoms.

We understand that we have sophisticated technology in place that is ready to use. As each day passes we become increasingly aware of more and more technology that is ready to be employed. As crime rates are dropping the numbers in our correctional facilities are growing. This problem needs to be addressed. Do we continue to punish people by "locking them up and throwing away the key" or are there alternatives to incarceration available?

Prediction is a risky business, but based on demographics, we can probably predict within reason that a larger population of defendants will be incarcerated than previously suggested. The use of advanced technology becomes of great importance. If we add up the number of felons in each state we have correctional facilities with larger populations than those of some states. Rather than being limited to a single approach regarding juvenile justice, as an example we look to an approach that eliminates problems of juvenile delinquency and related problems, such as gangs. We need leaders in criminal justice who are proactive rather than simply being reactive. With globalization, we see that domestic problems are transformed into transnational problems. Officials in the United States and abroad must integrate their domestic and foreign efforts at eradicating gangs and their criminal activities. Visible alternatives that address the deteriorating social and economic conditions in the United States are needed now and for the future.

The administration of justice appears at the outset to be an easy task to accomplish, yet there have been problems, which include prosecutorial misconduct, ineffective assistance of counsel, judicial overrides, mis-identifications, improper police investigations, overuse of plea bargains, and perjured testimony.

The problems within the criminal justice system are extensions of society's problems. There has to be a time when the necessary changes are made to ensure a system that provides fairness and continuity. In the worst of times and in the best of times, we need to have the vision to change, and change we must. Our dilemma is can we preserve the rights of both victims and defendants to maintain the protection of our most basic freedoms and liberties?

Are current television shows that focus primarily on criminal justice issues fair in their representation of what is depicted? Research suggests that the news media affect policy. The media appear to play a decisive role in the social construction of reality. If the media alters reality and affects how the audience views the criminal justice system, then we have inherited a serious problem. It appears that the portrayal of crime by the mass media is assumed to report the truth, but in truth, it distorts the kind of crime that exists and the crimes being committed. A person cannot pick up a newspaper, watch or hear the news, or go to the movies without seeing violence. Is this the wave of the future that we continually hear about others being murdered, maimed, robbed, raped, attacked, or abused? Or is there a way of depicting the criminal justice system as capable of protecting its citizenry?

What about the problems of drug abuse, which haunt us today? The funds spent on drug interdiction, law enforcement, the courts, and incarceration should allow us to make significant progress in making treatment available to those who need it. Courts dispense justice. The crime challenges facing us in the twenty-first century are more serious than they were in previous centuries. The law arena has had to adjust to the changes in this "new world" of globalization whereby we see a reduction of the rights of our citizens to a certain extent.

How do we protect against identity theft—a large problem in the twenty-first century? The use of fingerprints and biometric data has been suggested, but information that has been public for many years cannot now be made private and protected by the simple passing of legislation. How do we convince the public of the possibility of identity theft, and how do we protect against it?

The nonwhite minority seems to be at risk when it comes to the criminal justice system. The ratio of minorities to whites incarcerated is larger than in the general population.

This has to be stopped, but how is a different question. The crisis of justice administration in the United States is the factor of restricted access of nonwhites to the opportunities afforded to the majority. The demand for a fair criminal justice system remains, but not all those who commit horrendous crimes are from the lower echelons of society. We need to wake up and be awakened.

The events of September 11, 2001 are always in the back of our minds; for many of us that day that will continue to live in infamy. We know how vulnerable we are to a further attack. In four quick actions, the September 11 terrorists attacked some of the core symbols of U.S. society. The challenge we face is being prepared for all future attacks, if and when they come.

The police have come to realize that reactive policing does not work, they need to be proactive. We need on balance to maintain the peace and order in our communities. Cooperation between all law enforcement officials can help to make our neighborhoods safe from both hoodlums and terrorists.

This text also suggests that community prosecution goes hand in hand with community policing. Over time the prosecutor has become an elected official who oversees large offices with assistant prosecutors. With the community as the main patron of prosecutorial services, the American prosecutor harkens back to earlier prosecutors who argued cases initiated directly by members of the community. Changes in the system of prosecution are predicted for the twenty-first century. As we as a nation and public deal with the challenges presented to us—terrorism, global threats, technological crimes, advances in scientific evidence—prosecutors will need to transform. As the federal government takes more interest in crimes and disorders that have previously fallen under the purview of the local prosecutor, we may see changes in the way the prosecutor handles cases as well.

Research on punishment is in full-fledged renaissance of late. A transnational "reinvention of the prison with a focus on incapacitation and punishment" has arguably positioned the United States as the global archetype for contemporary imprisonment and its practices, industries, and rhetoric of justification. The trend is toward spending more on security and less on social welfare, especially since September 11th. The study of punishment is more important than ever before.

When we consider capital punishment in our country, we see that early death penalty scholars have identified trends in capital punishment that suggests a movement away from its use. Trends in the use of capital punishment in the last half century are inaccurate predictors of the future. An international movement against capital punishment represents a major trend away from the use of the death penalty; all countries with English legal systems with the exception of the United States have abolished capital punishment. Though jurisdictions execute condemned inmates under private and antiseptic conditions thereby attempting to counter the cruel and unusual punishment argument, nevertheless research indicates that the death penalty has no deterrent value whatsoever. Despite the righteous rhetoric of judges, prosecutors, and other judicial officers to the constitutional cannons of equity, fairness, and evenhandedness in criminal justice processes, the U.S. legal system remains in a pathetic state regarding its capital punishment scheme.

The issues of gender and race will continue to plague us until we fully comprehend the meaning of equity and fairness. Elected officials, policy makers, educational institutions, the criminal justice system itself, the media and businesses, as well as labor organizations need to accomplish more. Cultural myths die hard. There is no way to allow both genders and all minorities to enjoy the equal protection of the laws unless and until Americans are committed to the elimination of all discrimination. The rhetoric of both gender and racial equality has existed for centuries, but has yet to match everyday life experience. An agenda for change must come to fruition. We must do whatever is essential to fight oppression and alleviate repressive conditions in this century.

Criminal justice in this country will continue to face a number of problems: global acts of terrorism; new types of criminals; questions of citizens' rights versus acts of privacy; issues of security, and problems we have not yet anticipated. We need to elevate and discipline ourselves accordingly. The twenty-first century has ushered in the kind of violence no one ever anticipated or deemed probable, and we need to plan and act accordingly. We cannot afford to wait for another terrorist act. Every time a crime of magnitude occurs, the residents continue to be enraged. But rage does nothing, except infuriate others.

It would be great to believe we have all the answers, though the rhetoric alone will not change the system; new policies and plans of action are needed to renew today's vision for tomorrow. We need a vision for change.

Index